OXFORD PAPERBACK REFERENCE

The Concise Oxford Dictionary of

Art and Artists

Ian Chilvers is a freelance writer and editor. He is author of *A Dictionary of Twentieth-Century Art*, editor of *The Oxford Dictionary of Art*, and co-editor of *The Concise Oxford Companion to Classical Literature*.

Oxford Paperback Reference

The most authoritative and up-to-date reference books for both students and the general reader.

ABC of Music
Accounting
Allusions
Animal Behaviour
Archaeology
Architecture and Landscape Architecture
Art and Artists
Art Terms
Arthurian Legend and Literature*
Astronomy
Battles*
Better Wordpower
Bible
Biology
British History
British Place-Names
Buddhism
Business and Management
Card Games
Catchphrases
Celtic Mythology
Chemistry
Christian Art
Christian Church
Chronology of English Literature
Chronology of Modern Words*
Classical Literature
Classical Myth and Religion
Classical World*
Computing
Contemporary World History
Countries of the World
Dance
Dynasties of the World
Earth Sciences
Ecology
Economics
Encyclopedia
Engineering*
English Etymology
English Folklore
English Grammar
English Language
English Literature
English Surnames
Euphemisms
Everyday Grammar
Finance and Banking
First Names
Food and Drink
Food and Nutrition
Foreign Words and Phrases
Geography
Humorous Quotations
Idioms
Internet

Islam
Kings and Queens of Britain
Language Toolkit
Law
Law Enforcement*
Linguistics
Literary Terms
Local and Family History
London Place-Names
Mathematics
Medical
Medicinal Drugs
Modern Design
Modern Quotations
Modern Slang
Music
Musical Terms
Musical Works
Nicknames
Nursing
Ologies and Isms
Philosophy
Phrase and Fable
Physics
Plant Sciences
Plays*
Pocket Fowler's Modern English Usage
Political Quotations
Politics
Popes
Proverbs
Psychology
Quotations
Quotations by Subject
Reverse Dictionary
Rhymes*
Rhyming Slang
Saints
Science
Shakespeare
Ships and the Sea*
Slang
Sociology
Space Exploration
Statistics
Superstitions
Synonyms and Antonyms
Weather
Weights, Measures, and Units
Word Histories
World History
World Mythology
World Place-Names
World Religions
Zoology

*forthcoming

The Concise
Oxford Dictionary of

Art and Artists

THIRD EDITION

Edited by IAN CHILVERS

OXFORD
UNIVERSITY PRESS

OXFORD
UNIVERSITY PRESS

Great Clarendon Street, Oxford OX2 6DP

Oxford University Press is a department of the University of Oxford.
It furthers the University's objective of excellence in research,
scholarship, and education by publishing worldwide in

Oxford New York

Auckland Cape Town Dar es Salaam Hong Kong Karachi
Kuala Lumpur Madrid Melbourne Mexico City Nairobi
New Delhi Shanghai Taipei Toronto

With offices in

Argentina Austria Brazil Chile Czech Republic France Greece
Guatemala Hungary Italy Japan Poland Portugal Singapore
South Korea Switzerland Thailand Turkey Ukraine Vietnam

Oxford is a registered trade mark of Oxford University Press
in the UK and in certain other countries

Published in the United States
by Oxford University Press Inc., New York

First edition 1990
Second edition 1996
Third edition 2003

British Library Cataloguing in Publication Data
Data available

Library of Congress Cataloging in Publication Data
Data available

Typeset by SPI Publisher Services, Pondicherry, India
Printed by Clays Ltd, St Ives plc

ISBN-13: 978-0-19-860477-8
ISBN-10: 0-19-860477-7

5

Preface

This book is a revised and abridged version of *The Oxford Dictionary of Art*, which was first published in 1988. Although it is shorter in overall extent than the parent work, most of the entries it contains are unchanged or amended only slightly; the reduction in length has been achieved not by trying to condense each entry by an average amount, but by recasting the longer, discursive articles (such as those on printmaking techniques) in much pithier form and by dropping certain marginal entries. The time span of the book is from the 5th century BC (the Classical age of Greek art) to the present day; an arbitrary cut-off point has been adopted for contemporary art, in that no artist born after 1965 is included. As well as biographies of artists, the book has entries on techniques, groups, styles, movements, writers, patrons, dealers, collectors, museums, and galleries. Also included are the celebrated antique statues (such as the *Apollo Belvedere*, the *Belvedere Torso*, and the *Laocoön*) that were so influential on European art from the Renaissance onwards, and one or two (such as the *Venus de Milo*) whose fame is more recent. Architecture is excluded, although there are entries on individuals who were active chiefly as architects but who made significant contributions to other fields of the visual arts (Bramante and Brunelleschi, for example). Oriental art, too, is omitted, although there is an entry on Ukiyo-e, as the subject of Japanese prints occurs so frequently in the discussion of late 19th-century French painting.

The length of an entry can usually be taken as an indication of the significance of the subject, but with many qualifications, some artists' lives being much more easily summarized than others. Those who travelled a great deal, or had fingers in many pies, or who for one reason or another led especially interesting lives are likely to have longer entries than equally accomplished artists who stayed at home and devoted themselves to one speciality. It is of course tempting to write more about one's own favourites, but I hope that this kind of personal bias has intruded only rarely.

There is no system of alphabetizing artists' names that will satisfy logic but not offend against usage. Thus, one says 'van Dyck' or 'van Gogh', rather than 'Dyck' or 'Gogh', but they are almost invariably indexed under D and G (as they are here) rather than V. The following general rules may be taken as guidelines to alphabetical positioning, but in cases of doubt the reader is advised to try alternative headings before deciding that a particular artist is not included. Prefixes such as 'de', 'van', and 'von' are generally ignored, but an exception is 'La' or 'Le' (thus La Tour, Georges de). There are certain names where usage goes against this principle—thus Willem de Kooning and Peter De Wint are found under D. Italian Old Masters whose names include 'da', 'del', or 'di' are usually found under their first name (Leonardo da Vinci, rather than Vinci, Leonardo da), but again usage occasionally dictates otherwise: thus Andrea del Verrocchio is found under Verrocchio, not Andrea. Names beginning with Mc or St are ordered as though they were spelled Mac and Saint respectively. Artists from the same family are usually covered in one composite entry, except where it seemed more reasonable to treat major and distinct personalities separately. In line with the practice of the National Gallery in London and the Witt Library at the Courtauld Institute of Art, artists from the Low Countries are called Netherlandish up to about 1600; they are then distinguished as either Dutch or Flemish; and after about 1830 'Flemish' becomes 'Belgian'.

Artists' names are given in the form most commonly used in English; so various elements of full names have sometimes been dropped, and nick-names or pseudonyms are used as the heading where these are better known than the artist's real name. Thus Delacroix's Christian name is given as Eugène rather than Ferdinand-Victor-Eugène; Velázquez is called Diego Velázquez rather than Diego Rodríguez de Silva y Velázquez; and Giovanni Francesco Barbieri appears under his nickname Guercino.

Names of galleries are also sometimes given in slightly shortened form: thus the Museum Boymans–van Beuningen in Rotterdam is generally re-ferred to as 'Boymans Mus'. Both Tate Britain and Tate Modern are usually cited as 'Tate, London'. In most instances it will be obvious from the context which of the two galleries is meant (a Turner will be in Tate Britain, a Matisse in Tate Modern). With modern British works, however, the situ-ation is different: such works are displayed in both Tate Britain and Tate Modern, and they are liable to be transferred between the two institutions, so it is not usually possible to specify one location or the other as the permanent home—hence the use of the umbrella title. When a gallery is mentioned more than once within the same entry, the town in which it is located is generally omitted after the first mention. Locations are not given for prints unless they are known to be exceptionally rare.

Cross-references from one article to another are indicated by an asterisk (*) within the main part of the text or by the use of small capitals when the formula 'see so-and-so' is used. Names of all people who have their own entries are automatically asterisked on their first mention in another entry, but cross-references are used more selectively for styles, terms, etc., and given only when further elucidation under that heading might be helpful.

Dr Johnson defined a lexicographer as 'a writer of dictionaries, a harmless drudge'. I can vouch for the drudgery, but there is also much satisfaction involved in compiling a book such as this, and I would like to thank the various people who have helped to make the task often such an enjoyable one. My chief indebtedness is to Dr Dennis Farr, who as consultant editor read all the copy for *The Oxford Dictionary of Art*, making numerous correc-tions and a great many suggestions for improvements to both content and style, and later commented wisely and wittily on the modifications that transformed it into the first edition of the present book.

At the Oxford University Press, I am grateful to everyone who has worked on successive editions of the book—for their enthusiasm and encourage-ment no less than for their skills: Rowena Anketell, Pam Coote, Joanna Harris, Pat Lawrence, Hilary McGlynn, Betty Palmer, Angus Phillips, Thomas Webster, and Nicholas Wilson. In a more general sense, I would like to say what a comfort it is to anyone involved in the field of reference books to be able to draw on the resources and tradition of the OUP. I have been able to use the various members of the family of Oxford English Dictionaries to help with definitions, and I have taken much information from *The Dictionary of National Biography* and the various *Oxford Companions* outside the field of art. Margaret Drabble's edition of *The Oxford Companion to English Literature*, for example, contains many excellent entries (by Helen Langdon) on artists and their relationship to literature, and I have also made frequent use of the *Oxford Companions* to *French Literature* and *German Literature*, and of *The Oxford Classical Dictionary* and *The Oxford Dictionary of the Christian Church*. The *Oxford Companions* to *Film*, *Music*, and the *Theatre* have likewise proved helpful when their fields overlapped with mine, and, less obviously, I have also benefited from *The Oxford Companion to Chess* (for some information concerning a Lucas van Leyden painting and for the delightful anecdote in the Duchamp entry).

On a more personal note, I would like to thank my sister, Doreen Chilvers, for undertaking the tedious task of pasting up the slips from *The Oxford Dictionary of Art* that formed the raw material for the first edition of this book; my niece, Kendra Hall, for expert advice on government publications; my nephew, Gavin Chilvers, for checking some facts and figures; and my cousin Harry Allsop for help with computer problems and other technical matters. Many friends and former colleagues have given me advice, information, or encouragement, and several have read and commented on entries in fields in which they have specialist knowledge. Among them I would like to thank, first, Dr Claudia Stumpf, and then in alphabetical order: Jonathan Alden, Dr Tim Ayers, Rachel Bean, Alison Bolus, Ashley Brown, Caroline Bugler, Rachel Bulbulian, Caroline Christian, Sue Churchill, Emma Clifton, Alison Cole, Célestine Dars, Erica Davies, Nic Dean, Celia de la Hey, Lorraine Dickey, Lavinia Down, Dr Tom Faulkner, Roz Fishel, Vanessa Fletcher, John Gaisford, John Glaves-Smith, Amy Glossop, Bina Goldman, Suzie Green, Julia Hanson, Juliet Hardwicke, Flavia Howard, James Hughes, Dr Michael Jacobs, Jessica Johnson, Heather Jones, Caroline Juler, Frances Kelly, Blaise Keogh, Vanessa Lacey, Frank Landamore, Robin Loerch, Cathy Lowne, Calista Lucy, Lorrie Mack, Margaret Mauger, Sir Felix Moore, Anna Morter, Jenny Mulherin, Nigel O'Gorman, George Otigbah, Alice Peebles, David Pinder, Maggie Ramsay, Clare Randall, Benedict Read, John Roberts, Guy Robson, Carolyn Rogers, Penelope Byrde Ruddock, Antonia Spowers, Pauline Stride, Ruth Taylor, Jack Tresidder, Nicholas Turner, Dr Malcolm Warner, Christine Webb, Jude Welton, Dr Peter Willis, and Iain Zaczek. I am also particularly grateful to Valerie Levitt, whose wonderful Newcastle Bookshop has supplied me with many publications that I could not otherwise have obtained. Finally, for inspiration from afar, thanks to Deborah Lambert and Victoria Kirkham.

IAN CHILVERS
Jesmond, Newcastle upon Tyne
May 2002

Abbreviations

AG	Art Gallery
Alte Pin.	Alte Pinakothek
ARA	Associate of the Royal Academy
Bib. Nat.	Bibliothèque Nationale
BL	British Library
BM	British Museum
Coll.	Collection(s)
DNB	*Dictionary of National Biography*
Gal.	Gallery, Galerie, Galleria
Gal. Naz.	Galleria Nazionale
Inst.	Institute
KH Mus.	Kunsthistorisches Museum
Lib.	Library
Met. Mus.	Metropolitan Museum
MFA	Museum of Fine Arts
MoMA	Museum of Modern Art
Mus.	Museum(s), Musée(s), Museo
Mus. B.-A.	Musée des Beaux-Arts, Museo de Bellas Artes
Mus. Naz.	Museo Nazionale
Nat. Mus.	National Museum
Neue Pin.	Neue Pinakothek
NG	National Gallery, Nationalgalerie, Nasjonalgalleriet
NPG	National Portrait Gallery
NT	National Trust
OED	*Oxford English Dictionary*
PRA	President of the Royal Academy
priv. coll.	private collection
RA	Royal Academy, Royal Academician
Univ.	University
V&A	Victoria and Albert Museum

AAA. *See* ALLIED ARTISTS' ASSOCIATION and AMERICAN ABSTRACT ARTISTS.

Aachen, Hans von (1552–1615). German painter, born in Cologne (in spite of his name, which derives from his father's birthplace). He had an international career, working principally in Italy (*c*.1574–87) and Prague, where he was appointed court painter by the emperor Rudolf II (*see* HABSBURG) in 1592. In 1596 he settled permanently in the city (although he made several visits to Germany), and after Rudolf's death in 1612 he worked for his successor, the emperor Matthias. His paintings, featuring elegant, elongated figures, are—like those of his colleague Bartholomeus *Spranger—leading examples of the sophisticated *Mannerist art then in vogue at the courts of northern Europe, and he was particularly good with playfully erotic nudes (*The Triumph of Truth*, 1598, Alte Pin., Munich). Engravings after his work gave his style wide influence and he ranks as one of the most important German artists of his time.

Aaltonen, Wäinö (1894–1966). Finnish sculptor, whose work was regarded as an embodiment of his country's national spirit, particularly of the patriotic ardour that flourished in the years following the declaration of independence from Russia (1917). He made his name as a sculptor of war memorials, and his most characteristic works are tributes to national heroes such as the monument to the runner Paavo Nurmi (1925, the best-known cast is outside the athletics stadium in Helsinki) and the bust of the composer Sibelius (1928, various casts exist). Aaltonen worked in bronze, stone, and other materials, including glass (he also painted and made collages). His style was heroic and essentially naturalistic, although sometimes touched with *Cubist stylizations.

Abate, Niccolò dell' (*c*.1510–71). Italian *Mannerist painter, active for much of his career in France. He was born in Modena, and spent his early career there and in the neighbourhood, mainly as a decorator of secular buildings (little of this work survives intact). From 1547 to 1552 he lived in Bologna, his work of this period including decorations in the Palazzo Poggi (now part of the university). The subjects include landscapes and musical parties, with elegantly dressed, elongated figures influenced particularly by *Parmigianino. In 1552 Niccolò moved to France, where he remained for the rest of his life. For much of this time he worked at *Fontainebleau, initially under *Primaticcio. Most of his work in the palace itself has been lost, and he is now remembered more for his landscapes with figures from mythological stories (*Landscape with the Death of Eurydice*, NG, London). In these he was a precursor of *Claude and *Poussin in the long-lived tradition of French classical landscape. Niccolò also painted portraits in both Italy and France.

Abbey, Edwin Austin (1852–1911). American painter, etcher, and book illustrator, highly successful in England (where he settled in 1878) as well as in his native country. He specialized in historical scenes and had several large and prestigious commissions, most notably a set of murals representing the quest for the Holy Grail (completed 1902) in Boston Public Library (his friend *Sargent also painted murals there) and the official painting commemorating Edward VII's coronation in 1902 (Buckingham Palace, London). Such paintings now seem rather overblown and ponderous, and his reputation rests mainly on his lively book illustrations. He was particularly prolific for *Harper's Weekly*, his association with the magazine lasting from 1870 until his death. Although he always remained an American citizen, Abbey was devoted to cricket and had a private ground at his house at Fairford in Gloucestershire.

Abbott, Lemuel Francis (*c*.1760–1802). English portrait painter. All his pictures are of male sitters; his clientele included many naval officers and he is best known for his portrayals of Lord Nelson, of whom he did several portraits with slight variations (1797–8). In 1798 Abbot was declared insane, and some of his unfinished works were completed by other hands.

Abildgaard, Nicolai Abraham (1743–1809). Danish *Neoclassical painter, mainly of historical, literary, and mythological subjects. He studied at the Copenhagen Academy and then from 1772 to 1777 in Rome, where his friendship with *Fuseli helped to introduce *Romantic elements to his style. On his return to Denmark his work became more classical, as is best seen in his cycles of paintings illustrating the Roman writers Terence and Apuleius (1802–4 and 1808–9 respectively, Statens Mus., Copenhagen). He became one of the leading figures in Danish art and had great influence as director of the Copenhagen Academy (1789–91 and 1801–9), where his pupils included *Runge and *Thorvaldsen. Abildgaard occasionally worked as an architect, sculptor, and designer, and he also wrote on art. His most ambitious work, a huge decorative scheme (1778–91) at Christiansborg Palace, Copenhagen, was largely destroyed by fire in 1794.

Abramtsevo Colony. A name applied to a circle of Russian artists associated with the country estate of the patron Savva Mamontov (1841–1918) at Abramtsevo, about 60 km (40 miles) north of Moscow. Mamontov, who earned a fortune from railway building, bought the estate in 1870, and from then until about the end of the century he often played host to distinguished artists, some of whom stayed for several months at a time during the summer, enjoying the attractive surroundings as well as the stimulating company. One of them, Viktor *Vasnetsov, said of Mamontov: 'There was in him a sort of electric current that ignited other people's energies. God gave him a special talent for stimulating the creativity of others.' Among the other visitors were *Repin, *Serov, and *Vrubel. Serov's celebrated *Girl with Peaches* (1887, Tretyakov Gal., Moscow), a portrait of Mamontov's 12-year-old daughter Vera, was painted at Abramtsevo. The estate is now a national museum.

abstract art. Art that does not depict recognizable scenes or objects, but instead is made up of forms and colours that exist for their own expressive sake. Much decorative art can thus be described as abstract, but in normal usage the term refers to modern painting and sculpture that abandon the traditional European conception of art as the imitation of nature. Abstract art in this sense was born and achieved its distinctive identity in the decade 1910–20 and is now regarded as the most characteristic form of 20th-century art. It has developed into many different movements and 'isms', but two or three basic tendencies are recognizable. In *Cubism and Abstract Art* (1936), Alfred H. *Barr, 'at the risk of grave oversimplification', divided abstraction into two main currents: the first (represented by *Malevich) he described as 'intellectual, structural, architectonic, geometrical, rectilinear and classical in its austerity and dependence upon logic and calculation'; the second (exemplified by *Kandinsky) he described as 'intuitional and emotional rather than intellectual; organic or *biomorphic rather than geometrical in its forms; curvilinear rather than rectilinear, decorative rather than structural, and romantic rather than classical in its exaltation of the mystical, the spontaneous and the irrational'. Looking at the subject in a slightly different way (and from a later viewpoint than Barr's), it is possible to see three main strands in abstract art: (*a*) the reduction of natural appearances to radically simplified forms, exemplified in the sculpture of *Brancusi (one meaning of the verb 'abstract' is to summarize or concentrate); (*b*) the construction of works of art from non-representational basic forms (often simple geometric shapes), as in Ben *Nicholson's reliefs; (*c*) spontaneous, 'free' expression, as in the *Action Painting of Jackson *Pollock. Many exponents of such art dislike the word 'abstract' (*Arp, for example, hated it, insisting on the word *'Concrete'), but the alternatives they prefer, although perhaps more precise, are usually cumbersome, notably non-figurative, non-representational, and *Non-Objective.

The basic aesthetic premiss of abstract art—that formal qualities can be thought of as existing independently of subject matter—existed long before the 20th century. Ultimately the idea can be traced back to Plato, who in his dialogue *Philebus* (c.350 BC) puts the following words into Socrates' mouth: 'I do not mean by beauty of form such beauty as that of animals and pictures . . . but understand me to mean straight lines and circles, and the plane or solid figures which are formed out of them by turning-lathes and rulers and measures of angles; for these I affirm to be not only relatively beautiful, like other things, but eternally and absolutely beautiful.' More explicitly, in his Tenth *Discourse* (1780) to the students of the *Royal Academy, Sir Joshua *Reynolds advised that 'we are sure from experience that the beauty of form alone, without the assistance of any other quality, makes of itself a great work, and justly claims our esteem and admiration'; and in discussing the *Belvedere Torso* he referred to 'the perfection of this science of abstract form'. In the 19th century several notable writers followed this line (Maurice *Denis, for example) and many of the leading painters of the 1890s—notably the *Symbolists—stressed the expressive properties of colour, line, and shape rather than their representative function. This process was taken further by the major avant-garde movements of the first decade of the 20th century—especially *Cubism, *Expressionism, and *Fauvism. By 1910, then, the time was ripe for abstract art, and it developed more or less simultaneously in various countries. Kandinsky is often cited as the first person to paint an abstract picture, but no artist can in fact be singled out for the distinction. (A work by Kandinsky known as 'First Abstract Watercolour' (Pompidou Centre, Paris) is signed and dated 1910, but some scholars believe that it is later and was inscribed by Kandinsky several years after its execution. This kind of problem arises not only with Kandinsky: several early abstract artists were keen to stress the primacy of their ideas and were not above backdating works.) Among the other artists who produced abstract paintings at about the same early date as Kandinsky were the American Arthur *Dove and the Swiss Augusto Giacometti, cousin of Alberto *Giacometti.

The individual pioneers were soon followed by abstract groups and movements—among the first were *Orphism and *Synchromism in France. There was a particularly rich crop in Russia, with *Constructivism, *Rayonism, and *Suprematism all launched by 1915. With some artists, abstraction represented merely a brief phase in their careers (among them the British artists Vanessa *Bell, Duncan *Grant, and Wyndham *Lewis), but with others it

was a vocation or even a mission. The almost religious fervour with which some of the Russian artists pursued their ideals was matched by the members of the De *Stijl group in Holland, founded in 1917. To such artists, abstraction was not simply a matter of style, but a question of finding a visual idiom capable of expressing their most deeply felt ideas. *Mondrian, for example, believed that his art of clarity and balance would lead to a society in which life would be governed by a universal visual harmony. In the period between the two world wars, the severely geometrical style of De Stijl and the technologically orientated Constructivism were the most influential currents in abstraction (they came together in the *Bauhaus). Paris was the main centre of abstract art at this time, partly because it attracted so many refugee artists from Germany and Russia, where abstract art was banned in the 1930s under Hitler and Stalin. There was also a strong abstract element in *Surrealism, which was born in Paris. The first exhibition devoted solely to abstract art was held there by the *Cercle et Carré group in 1930, and its successor, the *Abstraction-Création association, founded in 1931, brought together a large number of abstract artists of various types and provided a focus for their activities. However, in general figurative art was dominant in the interwar period and abstract art won little public acceptance. It was very much a minority taste in Britain and the USA, for example, in spite of such outstanding individual contributions as the sculptures of *Hepworth and *Calder and the efforts of groups such as *Unit One (founded in 1933) and *American Abstract Artists (founded in 1936).

The second heroic period of abstract art came after the Second World War, when the enormous success of *Abstract Expressionism in the USA and its European equivalent *Art Informel made abstraction for a time virtually the dominant orthodoxy in Western art. Abstract art no longer seemed to need philosophical justification of the kind given by Kandinsky and Mondrian (although several of the Abstract Expressionists were equally high-minded in approach); however, abstraction was sometimes invested with a moral dimension as an embodiment of Western freedom of thought, as opposed to the totalitarianism that had banned avant-garde art in Nazi Germany and Soviet Russia (*see* DEGENERATE ART and SOCIALIST REALISM). In this respect it is significant that many of the Abstract Expressionists were influenced by European Surrealists who had fled to New York during the Second World War to escape the fear of such repression. Thus, in the USA particularly, support for abstract art could be regarded almost as a form of patriotism. Abstract Expressionism represented a great watershed in art and many later developments were either evolutions from it or reactions against it. These included a revival of figuration, in the form particularly of *Pop art, but also new styles of abstraction, notably *Post-Painterly Abstraction, *Op art, and *Minimal art, all of which flourished in the 1960s.

Abstract Expressionism. The dominant movement in American painting in the late 1940s and 1950s, characterized by a desire to convey powerful emotions through the sensuous qualities of paint, often on canvases of huge size. It was the first major development in American art to achieve international status and influence, and it is often reckoned the most significant art movement anywhere since the Second World War. The energy and excitement it brought to the American art scene helped New York to replace Paris as the world capital of contemporary art, and to many Americans the heyday of the movement has already acquired a kind of legendary status as a golden age.

The phrase 'Abstract Expressionism' had originally been used in 1919 to describe certain paintings by *Kandinsky, but in the context of modern American painting it was first used by the *New Yorker* art critic Robert Coates in 1945; by the end of the decade it had become part of the standard critical vocabulary. The painters embraced by the term worked mainly in New York and there were various ties of friendship and loose groupings among them, but they shared a similarity of outlook rather than of style—an outlook characterized by a spirit of revolt against tradition and a desire for spontaneous freedom of expression. The stylistic roots of Abstract Expressionism are complex, but despite its name it owed more to *Surrealism—with its stress on *automatism and intuition—than to *Expres-

sionism; a direct source of inspiration came from the European Surrealists who took refuge in the USA during the Second World War. The most famous Abstract Expressionist is Jackson *Pollock, whose explosive *Action Painting best sums up the movement, but the work of other leading exponents was sometimes neither abstract (the leering *Women* of *de Kooning) nor expressionist (the serene visions of *Rothko). Even allowing for these wide differences, however, there are certain qualities that are basic to most Abstract Expressionist painting: the preference for working on a huge scale; the emphasis placed on surface qualities, so that the flatness of the canvas is stressed; the adoption of an *all-over type of treatment, in which the whole area of the picture is regarded as equally important; the glorification of the act of painting itself; the conviction that abstract painting could convey significant meaning and should not be viewed in *formalist terms alone; and a belief in the absolute individuality of the artist (for which reason most of the Abstract Expressionists disliked being labelled with an 'ism', preferring *New York School as a group designation).

Alongside de Kooning, Pollock, and Rothko, the painters who are considered central to Abstract Expressionism include *Gorky, *Gottlieb, *Guston, *Kline, *Motherwell, *Newman, and *Still. Most of them struggled for recognition early in their careers, but during the 1950s the movement became an enormous critical and financial success. It had passed its peak by 1960, but several of the major figures continued productively after this and a younger generation of painters carried on the Abstract Expressionist torch. Sculptors as well as painters were influenced by the movement, the leading figures including Ibram Lassaw (1913–), Seymour Lipton (1903–86), and Theodore Roszak (1907–81). By 1960, also, reaction against the emotionalism of Abstract Expressionism was under way, in the shape principally of *Pop art and *Post-Painterly Abstraction. Indeed, much of the subsequent history of American art can be written in terms of developments from or responses to the movement, and Robert *Hughes considers that its success has 'encouraged a phony grandiloquence, a confusion of pretentious size with scale, that has plagued American painting ever since'.

Abstraction-Création. An association of abstract painters and sculptors formed in Paris in February 1931, a successor to the short-lived *Cercle et Carré. It was open to artists of all nationalities and its organization was loose, so that at one time its numbers rose to as many as 400 (among the members were *Arp, *Kandinsky, and *Mondrian, as well as several artists who were never permanently resident in Paris, notably Barbara *Hepworth and Ben *Nicholson). The association was extremely catholic in its outlook and embraced many kinds of non-figurative art, although the emphasis was increasingly on geometrical abstraction. It operated by arranging group exhibitions and by publishing an illustrated annual called *Abstraction-Création: Art non-figuratif*, which appeared from 1932 to 1936; after this its activities declined.

académie. A French term for a private art school, several of which flourished in Paris in the late 19th and early 20th centuries. The term *atelier libre* has also been used to refer to such establishments. Entry to the official École des *Beaux-Arts was difficult (almost impossible for foreigners, who from 1884 had to take a vicious examination in French) and teaching there was conservative, so private art schools, with their more liberal regimes, were often frequented by progressive young artists. Four of them are particularly well known. The **Académie Carrière** was opened in 1890 by Eugène Carrière (1849–1906), a painter of portraits, religious pictures, and—his speciality—scenes of motherhood. His style was misty, monochromatic, and vaguely *Symbolist. *Rodin was a great admirer of his work. There was no regular teaching at the school, though Carrière visited it once a week. It was here that *Matisse met *Derain, thus helping to form the nucleus of the future *Fauves. The **Académie Julian** was founded in 1873 by Rodolphe Julian (1839–1907), whose work as a painter is now forgotten. The school had no entrance requirements, was open from 8 a.m. to nightfall, and was soon the most popular establishment of its type. Julian opened several branches throughout Paris, one of them for women artists, and by the 1880s the student population was about 600. Although the Académie Julian became famous for the unruly behaviour of its students, it

was regarded as a stepping stone to the École des Beaux-Arts (Julian had been astute in engaging teachers from the École as visiting professors). Among the French artists who studied there were *Bonnard, *Denis, Matisse, and *Vuillard. The list of distinguished foreign students is very long. The **Académie Ranson** was founded in 1908 by Paul Ranson (1864–1909), who had studied at the Académie Julian. After Ranson's early death, his wife took over as director, and his friends Denis and *Sérusier were among the teachers. Among later teachers the most important was Roger *Bissière, whose style of expressive abstraction influenced many young painters in the 1930s; his pupils included *Manessier. The **Académie Suisse** was founded in about 1850 by a former artists' model called Suisse 'in an old and sordid building where a well-known dentist pulled teeth at one franc apiece...artists could for a small fee work from the living model without any examinations or tuition' (John *Rewald, *The History of Impressionism*). *Courbet, *Manet, and several of the *Impressionists drew at the Académie Suisse, and it was there in 1861 that Camille *Pissarro first noticed the 'strange Provençal' Paul *Cézanne, whose life drawings were ridiculed by his fellow students.

Académie Royale de Peinture et de Sculpture, Paris. *See* ACADEMY.

academy. An association of artists, scholars, etc. that aims to maintain professional standards and to promote the affairs of its members. Although the name was applied to various informal gatherings of artists from *c*.1500, the first formal art academy was not set up until 1563, when the Accademia del Disegno was founded in Florence. It was the brainchild of Giorgio *Vasari, whose aim was to emancipate artists from control by the guilds, and to confirm the rise in social standing they had achieved during the previous hundred years. *Michelangelo, who more than anyone else embodied this change of status, was made one of the two honorary heads; the other was Duke Cosimo I de' *Medici. The next important step was taken in Rome, where the Accademia di S. Luca was founded in 1593, with Federico *Zuccaro as its first president. More stress was laid on practical instruction than at Florence, but the Academy was unsuccessful in its war against the guilds until it received support from Pope Urban VIII (Maffeo *Barberini, reigned 1623–44), who recognized it as 'an authority superior to the crafts guilds'. Thereafter it grew in wealth and prestige. There were few other permanent academies in Italy before the 18th century, but the word was frequently used of private institutions where artists met to draw from life. The most famous example of this kind was organized by the *Carracci in Bologna in the 1580s.

Several institutions of the Carracci type were set up in northern Europe (the 'academy' founded in Haarlem in about 1600 by *Cornelis van Haarlem, Hendrick *Goltzius, and Karel van *Mander was probably some kind of life drawing class). However, the first official art academy outside Italy was not established until 1648. In that year a group of French painters, moved by the same reasons of prestige as had earlier inspired the Italians, successfully petitioned Louis XIV to found the Académie Royale de Peinture et de Sculpture. Here too the guilds put up powerful opposition, and the Académie's supremacy was not assured until Louis's chief minister, Jean-Baptiste Colbert, was elected vice-protector in 1661 and saw that he could use it as an instrument of state—for imposing official standards and principles of taste that would help to create a national artistic identity and a style appropriate for glorifying the king. *Le Brun was appointed director of the Académie in 1663 and he and Colbert ensured that it assumed a virtual monopoly of teaching and over the exhibiting of works of art. Implicit in the Académie's theories and teaching was the assumption that everything to do with art can be brought within the scope of rational understanding and reduced to logical precepts that can be studied and taught.

After the middle of the 17th century, art academies were founded in Germany, Spain, and other countries and by the end of the 18th century well over a hundred were flourishing throughout Europe. Among these was the *Royal Academy in London, founded in 1768. Everywhere the academies became champions of *Neoclassicism in opposition to the surviving styles of *Baroque and *Rococo. There was some opposition to these bodies from the start, and towards the end of the 18th century French Revolutionary sentiment was espe-

cially bitter about the exclusive privileges enjoyed by members of the Académie; many artists, with J.-L. *David in the lead, demanded its dissolution. This step was taken in 1793, but the École des *Beaux-Arts, which took over its teaching role, embodied much the same principles.

The principal threat to academies came not from political developments, however, but from the *Romantic notion of the artist as a genius who produces his masterpieces by the light of inspiration that cannot be taught or subjected to rule. Virtually all the most creative artists of the later 19th century stood outside the academies and sought alternative channels for exhibiting their works, although *Manet for example, always craved traditional success at the *Salon. Academies still retained prestige in conservative circles, but they were condemned out of hand by the adventurous, and in 1898, in his book *Modern Painting*, the novelist and critic George Moore (1852–1933) wrote, 'that nearly all artists dislike and despise the Royal Academy is a matter of common knowledge'. In the face of competition from rival teaching institutions and artists' groups (such as the *Slade School and the *New English Art Club in England and the *Sezessionen in Germany and Austria) academies tended to become more liberal, but by the middle of the 20th century they were increasingly marginalized. The word 'academic' now almost always carries a pejorative meaning, and is associated with mediocrity and lack of originality.

academy board. A type of cardboard sheet used as a *support for painting, especially in oils. It is made of sheets of paper sized and pressed together, treated with a *ground, and sometimes embossed with an imitation canvas grain. Academy board was introduced in about 1850 and because of its relative cheapness was popular in art schools and with amateur painters, although it was also used by professional artists for sketches and studies. It has now largely been superseded by *canvas board.

academy figure. A careful painting or drawing (usually about half life-size) from the nude human figure made as an exercise, typically in an art school or academy. The figure is usually depicted in a heroic pose, and there is a tradition of suitable postures that goes back to the *Carracci.

Acconci, Vito. *See* BODY ART.

Achilles Painter. Greek vase painter, active in Athens in the mid-5th century BC, named after a *red-figure amphora decorated with a figure of Achilles (Vatican Mus.). He was a contemporary of *Phidias and his paintings have some of the nobility associated with the great sculptor's work. His compositions are usually limited to one or two figures depicted in a serene and graceful way.

Ackermann, Rudolph. *See* ROWLANDSON.

acrylic. A modern synthetic paint, made with a resin derived from acrylic acid, that combines some of the properties of oils and watercolour. It was the first new painting medium in centuries and has become a serious rival to oil paint. Acrylics are a refined version of paints developed for industrial use and can be applied to almost any surface with a variety of tools (brush, *airbrush, knife, sponge, and so on) to create effects ranging from thin washes to rich impasto and with a matt or gloss finish. Most acrylic paints are water-based, although some are oil-compatible, using turpentine as a thinner. Thinly applied paint dries in a matter of minutes, thickly applied paint in hours—much quicker than oils. Acrylic paint first became available to artists in the 1940s in the USA and certain American painters discovered that it offered them advantages over oils. Colour Stain painters (*see* COLOUR FIELD PAINTING) such as Helen *Frankenthaler and Morris *Louis, for example, found that they could thin the paint so that it flowed over the canvas yet still retained its full brilliance of colour. David *Hockney took up acrylic during his first visit to Los Angeles in 1963; he had earlier tried and rejected the medium, but American-manufactured acrylic was at this time far superior to that available in Britain, and he felt that the flat, bold colours helped him to capture the strong Californian light. Hockney used acrylic almost exclusively for his paintings until 1972, when he returned to oils because he now regarded their slow-drying properties as an advantage: 'you can work for days and keep altering it as well; you can scrape it off if you don't like it. Once acrylic is down you can't get it off.' In spite of these differences in properties, the finished appearance of an acrylic painting is sometimes more or less indistinguishable from an oil, and some artists have often combined the two techniques in the same painting. In addition to being versatile, acrylics are less susceptible to heat and damp than traditional media, but in the 1990s some doubts began to be expressed about their permanence.

Action Painting. A type of dynamic, impulsive abstract painting in which the artist applies paint with energetic *gestural movements—sometimes by dribbling or splashing—and with no preconceived idea of what the picture will look like. Sometimes the term is used loosely as a synonym for *Abstract Expressionism, but this is misleading, as Action Painting represents only one aspect of that movement. The term was coined by Harold *Rosenberg in an article entitled 'The American Action Painters' in *Art News* in December 1952. Rosenberg regarded Action Painting as a means of giving free expression to the artist's instinctive creative forces and he regarded the act of painting itself as more significant than the finished work. Although the term soon became established, many critics were unconvinced by Rosenberg's idea of the canvas being 'not a picture but an event': Mary McCarthy, for example, wrote that 'you cannot hang an event on a wall, only a picture'. Rosenberg's article did not mention individual painters and was unillustrated, but the artist who is associated above all with Action Painting is Jackson *Pollock, who vividly described how he felt when working on a canvas laid on the floor: 'I feel nearer, more a part of the painting, since this way I can walk around it, work from the four sides and literally be *in* the painting ... When I am *in* my painting, I am not aware of what I'm doing. It is only after a sort of "get acquainted" period that I see what I have been about. I have no fears about making changes, destroying the image, etc., because the painting has a life of its own. I try to let it come through.' In the work of lesser artists, Action Painting could easily degenerate into messy self-indulgence, and it generated a good deal of outrage and mockery, especially after the British painter William Green (1934–2001) took to riding a bicycle over the canvas, a feat imitated by the comedian Tony Hancock in the film *The Rebel* (1961).

Adam, François-Gaspard (1710–61); **Lambert-Sigisbert** (1700–59); and **Nicolas-Sébastien** (1705–78). French sculptors from Nancy, brothers. All three spent several years in Rome after training with their father **Jacob-Sigisbert** (1670–1747), and on their return adapted the Roman *Baroque style to French *Rococo taste. Lambert-Sigisbert was the most distinguished member of the family. His masterpiece is the Neptune Fountain (1735–40) at Versailles, a work showing the influence of *Bernini in its exuberant movement. Nicolas-Sébastien often collaborated with Lambert-Sigisbert, notably on the Neptune Fountain; his most important independent work is the monument of Queen Catharina Opalinska (1749) in the church of Notre-Dame de Bon Secours in Nancy. François-Gaspard was the least accomplished of the brothers; his best works are probably his garden statues for Frederick the Great of Prussia at Sanssouci, Potsdam. Better known than any of the three brothers is their nephew *Clodion.

Aelst, Willem van (1625–c.1683). Dutch painter of lavish flower pieces and still lifes, born in Delft, where he was a pupil of his uncle **Evert van Aelst** (1602–57), by whom no works are known. From 1645 to 1649 Willem worked in France and from 1649 to 1656 in Florence, where he was court painter to Ferdinando II de' *Medici, Grand Duke of Tuscany. In 1657 he settled in Amsterdam, where his pupils included Rachel *Ruysch.

aerial perspective. Term describing the means of producing a feeling of distance in a painting by imitating the effect of atmosphere whereby objects look paler and bluer the further away they are from the viewer. Dust and large moisture particles in the atmosphere cause some scattering of light as it passes through it, the amount of scattering depending on the wavelength (hence colour) of the light. Short wavelength (blue) light is scattered most and long wavelength (red) is scattered least. This is the reason why the sky is blue and why distant dark objects appear to lie behind a veil of blue. The term 'aerial perspective' (*prospettiva aerea*) was invented by *Leonardo, but the device was used by

Roman painters, for example at Pompeii. In the work of Italian painters of Leonardo's time, backgrounds sometimes look artificially blue, and in general aerial perspective has been more subtly exploited in northern Europe, where the atmosphere tends to be hazier. No one used it more beautifully than *Turner, in some of whose late works it is virtually the subject of the painting.

Aertsen, Pieter (1508/9–75). Netherlandish painter. He was born and died in Amsterdam but spent most of his career in Antwerp. A pioneer of still life and *genre painting, he is best known for scenes that at first glance look like pure examples of these types, but which in fact incorporate a religious scene (*Butcher's Stall with the Flight into Egypt*, 1551, Univ. of Uppsala). Aertsen had two painter sons, **Pieter the Younger** (1540–1603) and **Aert** (1550–1612), and he also taught his nephew Joachim *Bueckelaer.

Aestheticism. A term applied to exaggerated expression of the doctrine that art is self-sufficient and need serve no ulterior purpose, whether moral, political, or religious. Both the doctrine and its exaggeration are succinctly expressed in the phrase 'art for art's sake', which in England became the catchword of the 'Aesthetic Movement' in the late 19th century. Central figures of the movement include *Whistler and Oscar Wilde, both of them notorious dandies, and the movement was often satirized for its tendency towards preciousness and affectation, most notably in Gilbert and Sullivan's *Patience* (see GROSVENOR GALLERY). Nevertheless, the movement helped to focus attention on the formal qualities of works of art, and so contributed to the critical outlook of writers such as *Berenson and *Fry.

aesthetics. The branch of philosophy dealing with questions of beauty and taste. The term, which derives from a Greek word meaning 'to perceive', was coined by the German philosopher Alexander Gottlieb Baumgarten (1714–62), the author of a two-volume Latin treatise called *Aesthetica* (1750–8). It is usually used in connection with the arts, but it can also embrace beauty in nature.

Agam, Yaacov (Jacob Gipstein) (1928–). Israeli sculptor and experimental artist, active mainly in Paris, where he settled in 1951. In 1955 he participated, with *Bury, *Calder, *Tinguely, and other artists, in the exhibition 'Le Mouvement' at the Denise René Gallery, the exhibition that put *Kinetic art on the map, and from this time he established a reputation as one of the most inventive figures working with the kinds of abstract art that lay stress on movement and spectator participation. Agam often uses light and sound effects in conjunction with his sculptures, and sometimes the components of his works can be rearranged by the spectator. He has had several major public commissions in France, among them the design of a square in the Défense quarter of Paris (1973).

Agasse, Jacques-Laurent (1767–1849). Swiss-born animal painter who settled permanently in England in 1800 and became one of the principal successors to *Stubbs. He studied veterinary science in Paris as well as painting (with J.-L. *David) and his work is distinguished by anatomical accuracy as well as grace of line. Although Agasse was initially successful in England (George IV was among his patrons), he died poor and virtually forgotten (his decline was perhaps connected with his difficult temperament). The Musée d'Art et d'Histoire in his native Geneva has the best collection of his work.

Agostino di Duccio (c.1418–c.1481). Florentine sculptor and architect. He was an artist of distinction and originality—the only 15th-century sculptor born in Florence who owed little to *Donatello or *Ghiberti. His fresh and lively style was linear and graceful, with attractive swirling draperies. Agostino led a peripatetic life, working in various places in north Italy. He is first recorded as a sculptor in 1442, in Modena, and nothing is known of his training or career before this. In 1446 he fled from Florence to Venice after being accused of stealing silver from a church, and from 1449 to 1456 he worked in Rimini on his masterpiece—the sculptural decoration of the Tempio Malatestiano (see MALATESTA). His other major surviving work is the series of reliefs, partly in *terracotta, on the façade of the Oratory of S. Bernadino at Perugia, on which he worked 1457–61, as architect as well as sculptor. Agostino also executed several delightful reliefs of the Virgin and Child. In 1464 he began a large marble

sculpture for Florence Cathedral but abandoned the work; the block was later used by *Michelangelo for his *David*.

airbrush. An instrument for spraying paint or varnish by means of compressed air. It looks rather like an outsize fountain pen and is operated in a similar fashion, the pressure of the forefinger on a lever regulating the air supply. It can be controlled so as to give large areas of flat colour, delicate gradations of tone, or a fine mist. The device was invented by Charles Burdick, an American watercolour painter, who patented it in England in 1893. He adopted the tradename Aerograph, which for many years was used as a general term for airbrushes (like Biro for ballpoints); *Man Ray called paintings he did with an airbrush 'aerographs'. In the early 20th century airbrushes were mainly used for photographic retouching, and their principal use is now in commercial art. However, they are also used by painters such as *Hard-Edge Abstractionists and *Superrealists, who require a very smooth, impersonal finish.

Aken, Joseph van. *See* DRAPERY PAINTER.

alabaster. A term applied to two types of soft, translucent stone that are similar in appearance but different in composition. The first, known variously as calcite alabaster, Egyptian alabaster, or onyx marble, is a form of calcium carbonate. It was much used by the ancient Egyptians, particularly for small items, including vases and boxes, but also for larger objects such as sarcophagi. Subsequently it has been used in various types of carving (generally small-scale), sometimes to exploit beautiful colours streaking the stone (caused by the presence of iron or other minerals). The second type, sometimes distinguished as gypsum alabaster or true alabaster, is a form of gypsum (calcium sulphate). It was extensively used in sculpture in the later Middle Ages. In addition to being easily cut and polished, it has the advantage that it can be painted and gilded without any priming. Its most notable use was in small altarpieces, which from about 1350 to 1550 were made in great numbers in England, many of them for export—they were sent mainly to France but also as far afield as Iceland and Russia. The best collection of such altarpieces is in the Victoria and Albert Museum, London, and other fine examples are in the Castle Museum at Nottingham, a town that was famed for its 'alabastermen' (the industry was mainly based in the Midlands, the chief quarries being in Derbyshire and Staffordshire). The production of religious images was cut off abruptly by the Reformation, but alabaster continued to be used for tomb sculpture until the 18th century. Some modern sculptors, for example Henry *Moore, have used alabaster for small-scale sculptures.

Albani, Cardinal Alessandro (1692–1779). Italian churchman, collector, and art patron, a dominant figure in the art world of Rome for half a century. He came from a distinguished family that included several cardinals and also Pope Clement XI (his uncle), but he led a worldly life and was notorious for his lucrative dealings in the art market, not hesitating to have *antique sculptures heavily restored if it made them sell better. His own superb collection (much of which is now in the Glyptothek at Munich) was housed in a sumptuous villa he had built in Rome; the decoration included *Mengs's famous ceiling painting *Parnassus* (1761), one of the key works of *Neoclassicism. *Winckelmann was Albani's friend and protégé.

Albani (or **Albano**), **Francesco** (1578–1660). Bolognese painter. After a period in the studio of Denys *Calvaert and subsequently in the *Carracci academy, he moved to Rome in about 1601 and for the next fifteen years worked mainly on fresco decorations, initially as an assistant to Annibale Carracci and Guido *Reni, then winning important commissions of his own. By 1617 he had returned to Bologna, where he became one of the leading painters of the day and a notable teacher, his pupils including *Cignani, *Mola, and *Sacchi. His later works were mainly altarpieces for local churches and small pictures (sometimes on copper) of allegorical or mythological subjects with prominent landscape backgrounds—very much in the *ideal landscape tradition of Annibale Carracci and *Domenichino. These charmingly lighthearted works were highly popular with collectors in the 18th century.

Albers, Josef (1888–1976). German-born painter, designer, writer, and teacher, who became an American citizen in 1939. He studied (1920–3) and taught (1923–33) at the *Bauhaus, where his activities embraced stained glass, typography, and furniture design. When the Bauhaus closed in 1933 he emigrated to the USA. He was one of the first of the Bauhaus teachers to move there and one of the most energetic in propagating its ideas. From 1933 to 1949 he taught at *Black Mountain College, and from 1950 to 1959 he was head of the Department of Design at Yale University (the art gallery there has an outstanding collection of his work); he lectured at many other places and won numerous academic awards. From 1949 until his death he worked on a long series of paintings called *Homage to the Square* and it is for these uncompromisingly abstract pictures that he is best known; they consist of three or four squares of carefully planned size set inside one another, painted in flat, usually fairly subdued colours. He favoured the square so much because he believed that of all geometrically regular shapes it best distanced a work of art from nature, emphasizing its man-made quality. The colours in which they were painted often demonstrated the tendency of colours placed in proximity to expand or contract, advance or recede, in relation to each other. Albers's research in this area appeared in *Interaction of Color* (1963), the most important of his numerous publications. His rational approach and disciplined technique were influential on geometrical abstract painters such as *Op artists. Albers' wife, **Anni Albers** (1899–1994), whom he met when she was a student at the Bauhaus, was a weaver; her rectilinear designs have something of the severe economy of her husband's paintings.

Alberti, Leon Battista (1404–72). Italian architect, sculptor, painter, and writer, the most important art theorist of the *Renaissance. Born in Genoa, the illegitimate son of an exiled Florentine banker, he was educated in Padua and at Bologna University, and was an outstanding Latinist (at the age of 20 he wrote a Latin comedy that was acclaimed as a rediscovered Roman work). For most of his career he was based in Rome (he held a secretarial post in the papal court from 1432 to 1464), but he travelled extensively and had close contacts with the most advanced Florentine artists of the day, particularly *Brunelleschi. His first artistic treatise was written in Latin as *De pictura* in 1435 and translated into Italian the following year (as *Della pittura*) with a dedication to Brunelleschi (*Donatello, *Ghiberti, Luca della *Robbia, and *Masaccio are mentioned alongside him). Alberti wrote on a wide variety of other topics, complementing *De pictura* with a lengthy treatise on architecture (*De re aedificatoria*) and a much shorter one on sculpture (*De statua*). *De re aedificatoria* was probably written in the late 1440s and was presumably finished by 1452, when it was presented to Pope Nicholas V; it became the first printed book on architecture in 1485. *De statua* is generally dated to the 1460s. In these works Alberti turned away from the medieval outlook in which art was considered a symbolic expression of theological truths. Instead he emphasized the rational basis of the arts, and the necessity for the artist to have a thorough grounding in such 'sciences' as history, poetry, and mathematics (*De pictura* contains the first written exposition of the principles of perspective).

At about the time he was writing *De re aedificatoria* Alberti began to work as an architectural designer, his first certain work in this field (*c.*1450) being the exterior remodelling of the church of S. Francesco in Rimini (now known as the Tempio Malatestiano; *see* MALATESTA). His other buildings include the churches of S. Andrea and S. Sebastiano in Mantua, and in Florence the façades of S. Maria Novella and the Palazzo Rucellai—all of them ranking among the outstanding architectural works of the early Renaissance. Alberti also practised as a painter and sculptor, but little trace survives of his work in these fields. No paintings by him are extant, but two bronze self-portrait plaques are attributed to him (Louvre, Paris, and NG, Washington); judging by his apparent age, these are usually assigned to the mid-1430s, so they may well antedate (and perhaps influenced) *Pisanello's first portrait medals.

Albertinelli, Mariotto (1474–1515). Florentine painter, trained by Cosimo *Rosselli, in whose studio he met Fra *Bartolommeo. The two worked in partnership in the 1490s and again in 1509–13. Evidently the arrangement ended because Albertinelli temporarily abandoned painting to become an innkeeper, saying (according to *Vasari) that he was fed up with criticism and wanted a 'less difficult and more cheerful craft'. Vasari also comments that he was 'a restless man, a follower of Venus, and a good liver'. His paintings are elegant but rather insipid.

Albright, Ivan Le Lorraine (1897–1983). American painter, the son of **Adam Emory Albright** (1862–1957), a painter who had studied under *Eakins. During the First World War Albright served in France as a medical draughtsman and worked with a meticulous detail and clinical precision that anticipated the paintings of his later career, which show a morbid obsession with death and corruption: sagging, almost putrescent flesh (which he described as 'corrugated mush'), decrepit, decaying objects, and lurid lighting are typical of his work. Often it evokes a feeling of melancholy for a beauty that is past. He came from a wealthy family and his financial independence allowed him to work slowly, producing a small number of elaborate, highly finished paintings. For most of his life he lived in or near Chicago, and the city's Art Institute has the best collection of his works. It includes the painting Albright did for the Hollywood film (1943) of Oscar Wilde's *The Picture of Dorian Gray*, showing the loathsomely corrupted title figure; Albright's identical twin brother, **Malvin Marr Albright** (1897–1983), did the portrait of the young and beautiful Dorian for this film.

Aldegrever, Heinrich (1502–*c.*1555). German printmaker and painter. He worked mainly in Soest and was one of the leading artists in Westphalia in his day. His numerous prints, which include religious subjects, portraits, and ornamental designs, show the all-pervading influence of *Dürer (he even signed his work with an AG monogram shaped much like Dürer's AD). These prints are mainly line engravings, but Aldegrever also made a few etchings. Little is known of his activity as a painter.

Alechinsky, Pierre (1927–). Belgian painter, printmaker, draughtsman, and film-maker, active mainly in France. In 1947 he became a member of *Jeune Peinture Belge and in 1949 joined the *Cobra group. He left Cobra in 1951 and settled in

Paris, where he studied under S. W. *Hayter. In 1955 he visited the Far East and produced a prize-winning film *Calligraphie japonaise*. Subsequently he has travelled widely in Europe, the USA, and Mexico. His paintings are in a style of vigorous, even violent, expressive abstraction. They retain residual figurative motifs and their sense of turbulent fantasy shows a strong debt to his countryman *Ensor. Alechinsky is regarded as one of the leading Belgian artists of the 20th century and has an international reputation.

Alexander VII, Pope. *See* CHIGI.

Algardi, Alessandro (1598–1654). Italian sculptor, born in Bologna, where he had his initial training in the *Carracci academy. He settled in Rome in 1625 and became, apart from *Bernini, the leading sculptor in the city. During the pontificate of Innocent X (1644–55) Bernini was out of favour and Algardi replaced him at the papal court. His three most prestigious commissions were the tomb of Leo XI (1634–44) and the huge relief of *Pope Leo Driving Attila from Rome* (1646–53), both in St Peter's, Rome, and the free-standing group of *The Decapitation of St Paul* (1641–7) in S. Paolo, Bologna. He was a prolific sculptor of portrait busts, and these are his works that are now generally most admired—indeed he ranks as one of the greatest portrait sculptors of all time. His style was more sober and classical than Bernini's (although portraits have occasionally been disputed between them), reflecting his Bolognese upbringing, his work as a restorer of *antique statuary, and his friendship with artists such as *Domenichino, *Duquesnoy, *Poussin, and *Sacchi. In his early career Algardi worked mainly in stucco and terracotta (Bologna lacked local stone), but he became a highly sensitive carver in marble. He was also an accomplished draughtsman (he made designs for engravers) and in addition worked as an architect, although his activity in this field is unclear. He ran a busy studio and copies and casts of his work continued to be made long after his death.

Algarotti, Francesco (1712–64). The foremost Italian art critic of his day, also a collector and patron. He travelled widely and his friendship with some of the leading men of Europe—notably the French philosopher

Voltaire and Frederick the Great of Prussia—played a part in spreading the culture of his native Venice. His writings proclaimed a watered-down version of the *Neoclassicism that was then gaining ground in Europe (though not yet in Venice). For some years he influenced the practice of his friends Giambattista *Tiepolo ('restraining his wilder fantasies' as he claimed) and *Canaletto (encouraging his architectural *capriccios), as well as *Piazzetta and other Venetian painters. His many publications include *Saggio sopra la pittura* (1762), translated into English as *An Essay on Painting* (1764).

Alken. Family of British sporting artists of Danish origin. The family tradition was begun by **Samuel Alken, Sen.** (1750–1815), who engraved hunting and sporting landscapes in the manner of *Stubbs. Four of his sons became artists, including **Samuel, Jun.** (1784–*c*.1825), and most notably **Henry** (1785–1851), who was one of the most prolific sporting painters and illustrators of his time. His sprightly style was already archaic in his day, but he excelled at representing the life and movement of the hunting field and produced a huge output of coloured prints (some of them produced under the pseudonym 'Ben Tally-Ho'), which continue to be popular with collectors. He had four sons, among them **Samuel Henry Gordon Alken** (1810–94), generally known as Henry Alken, Jun., with whose work his own is often confused.

Allan, David (1744–96). Scottish portrait and *genre painter. From about 1767 to 1777 he lived in Rome, where he studied with Gavin *Hamilton and won a prize for *history painting at the Accademia di S. Luca. In 1777 he moved to London, then in 1780 settled in Edinburgh as a painter of portraits and *conversation pieces. When abroad he had made studies of French and Italian peasants and he painted scenes of Scottish life in a similar vein, which earned him the misleading title of 'the Scottish *Hogarth'. Such works influenced *Wilkie.

Allan, Sir William (1782–1850). Scottish historical painter, active mainly in his native Edinburgh. From 1805 to 1814 he travelled extensively in Russia, and this gave him a taste for exotic subject matter involving Circassians, Cossacks, Tartars, and Turks (he collected arms and armour and other artefacts to use as props and sometimes wore Circassian costume himself). These pictures did not sell well, but in the 1820s he successfully took up Scottish subjects, including scenes from the novels of Sir Walter Scott, who was Allan's enthusiastic supporter. With his friend *Wilkie, Allan did much to establish the vogue for historical *genre painting in Scotland. He also painted portraits.

alla prima. Method of painting, primarily in oils, in which the finished surface is achieved in a single application of paint rather than through the traditional method of building up successive layers. *Alla prima* is Italian for 'at first'; synonymous terms are 'direct painting', 'wet on wet', and the French *au premier coup* (at first stroke). Direct painting was practised from the 17th century (for example by *Hals), but it was not until the middle of the 19th century that it became the chief method in oil painting. Its growing popularity was connected with the availability of commercial paints of a buttery consistency, as well as with *Romantic ideas about spontaneity of expression.

Allegri, Antonio and **Lorenzo.** *See* COR-REGGIO.

Allied Artists' Association (AAA). A society of British artists formed in London in 1908 by the critic Frank Rutter (1876–1937) and artists in *Sickert's circle for the purpose of organizing annual exhibitions of progressive painters in the jury-free manner of the French *Salon des Indépendants. It held annual exhibitions at the Albert Hall from 1908 (more than 3,000 works were shown at the first show) and then smaller shows at the Grafton Galleries between 1916 and 1920. *Brancusi (1913), *Kandinsky (1909), and *Zadkine (1913) received the first British showing of their works at these exhibitions. The *Camden Town Group, founded in 1911, was made up largely of members of the Allied Artists' Association.

Allori, Alessandro (1535–1607). Florentine painter, the pupil and adopted son of *Bronzino. From 1554 to 1560 he was in Rome, where he added the influence of *Michelangelo's *Last Judgement* to that of his master's courtly *Mannerism. His varied output included altarpieces, portraits, and tapestry designs. *The Pearl Fishers* (1570–1, Studiolo of Francesco I, Palazzo Vecchio, Florence) is generally considered his masterpiece; playful and full of artifice, it combines nude figures obviously drawn from Michelangelo with Bronzino's sveltness and enamelled colouring. He was one of the last notable Italian exponents of Mannerism, painting in a style that was becoming outmoded by the time of his death. His son **Cristofano** (1577–1621) was one of the leading Florentine painters of his period, and his style was more naturalistic and *Baroque than that of his father. He produced various types of work, but he is remembered primarily for one picture, *Judith with the Head of Holofernes* (c.1615, Pitti, Florence, and other versions), which in the 18th and 19th centuries was one of the most famous paintings in Italy. Allori led a notoriously dissipated life (interspersed with bouts of pious asceticism) and here his femme fatale mistress is portrayed as Judith and he has depicted his own features in Holofernes' severed head. The Ashmolean Museum in Oxford possesses portraits by both Alessandro and Cristofano Allori.

all-over painting. A type of painting in which the whole surface of the canvas is treated in a relatively uniform manner and traditional ideas of composition—of the picture having a top, bottom, or centre—are abandoned. The term was first used in the 1950s with reference to the 'drip' paintings of Jackson *Pollock, and it has since been applied to other pictures in which the overall treatment of the canvas is relatively uniform, whether relying on texture or on 'scribbled' material, as with Cy *Twombly, or on colour, as with the *Colour Field Painters.

Alloway, Lawrence (1926–90). British art critic and curator, active for much of his career in the USA. In the 1950s he worked at the *Institute of Contemporary Arts, London (he was deputy director, 1957–9), and he was prominent in the *Independent Group, the cradle of British *Pop art (Alloway himself coined this term). He was also a strong supporter of American *Abstract Expressionism, and in 1961 he emigrated to the USA, settling in New York, where he became a curator at the *Guggenheim Museum and art critic for

The Nation. His books include *American Pop Art* (1974) and *Topics in American Art since 1945* (1975). He was married to the British-born painter Sylvia Sleigh (1916-) (*see* FEMINIST ART), who settled with him in the USA.

Allston, Washington (1779–1843). American painter and writer, considered the most important artistic personality of the first generation of *Romanticism in the USA. Samuel Taylor Coleridge, whose portrait Allston painted (1814, NPG, London), considered him 'a man of... high and rare genius... whether I contemplate him in the character of a Poet, a Painter, or a Philosophic Analyst'. Allston spent most of his working life in or near Boston apart from two lengthy visits to Europe: during the first, 1801–8, he studied under Benjamin *West in London and visited Paris and Rome; the second stay in Europe was from 1811 to 1818. Up to *c*.1818 his Romanticism was expressed in the grandiose and dramatic (*The Rising of a Thunderstorm at Sea*, 1804, MFA, Boston). In his later period he was a forerunner of the subjective and visionary trend in American landscape painting, which relied more upon mood and reverie than upon observation or drama, as in his famous *Moonlight Landscape* (1819, MFA, Boston). Through his example, this type of landscape painting became indigenous to the USA. Allston's writing included poetry, a Gothic novel entitled *Monaldi* (1841), and the posthumously published *Lectures on Art* (1850), the first art treatise by an American.

Alma-Tadema, Sir Lawrence (1836–1912). Dutch painter who settled in London in 1870 and became a British citizen in 1873. He specialized in historical genre scenes, beginning with medieval subjects, but then—following a visit to Pompeii in 1863—turning to the ancient world. His paintings evoke a Hollywood vision of ancient Greece and Rome (and sometimes Egypt), with their sensuous depiction of beautiful women, exotic costumes, and marbled settings—*Punch* called him a 'marbellous artist'. Such works were enormously successful and Alma-Tadema had a sumptuous lifestyle in his house in St John's Wood (previously owned by *Tissot), which he remodelled as a Roman villa. He was knighted in 1899 and received the Order of Merit in 1905. His success encouraged several imitators, including his wife **Laura** (1852–1909), his daughter (by a previous wife) **Anna** (1865–1943), and painters such as John William Godward (1861–1922) and Edwin Long (1829–91). However, Alma-Tadema's work went completely out of favour after his death, and his reputation did not revive until the 1970s. Now he once again pleases a large public: visitor surveys at the Getty Museum, Los Angeles, have revealed that his *Spring* (1894) is the most popular work in the collection.

altarpiece. A picture, sculpture, screen, decorated wall, or combination of any of these, standing on or behind an altar in a Christian church. Altarpieces vary enormously in size and conception, from tiny portable pictures to huge structures embracing the arts of architecture, sculpture, and painting. In theory, a useful distinction can be made between two broad types: the reredos, which rises from ground level behind the altar; and the retable, which stands either on the back of the altar itself or on a pedestal behind it. In practice, however, the words are not usually used with any precision; 'retable' is often used more or less as a synonym for altarpiece and in particular is commonly applied to the type of enormous structure—sometimes filling the entire east wall of a church—that became popular in Spain and Portugal and their American colonies in the *Baroque period.

Altdorfer, Albrecht (*c*.1480–1538). German painter, printmaker, draughtsman, and architect, active in Regensburg, of which town he was a citizen from 1505 onwards. Nothing is recorded of his training, but his early work was influenced by *Cranach and he was also familiar with *Dürer's woodcuts and engravings. Mingled with these German elements was a knowledge of the art of *Mantegna, perhaps through the mediation of Michael *Pacher. Yet in spite of these varied influences Altdorfer's style always remained personal. Most of his paintings are religious works, but he was one of the first artists to show an interest in landscape as an independent genre. In works such as *Christ Taking Leave of His Mother* (1520?, NG, London) he achieved a wonderful unity of mood between action and landscape, and two pure landscape paintings (without any figures) by him are known (NG, London, and Alte Pin., Munich) (*see also*

DANUBE SCHOOL). His patrons included the emperor Maximilian I (*see* HABSBURG) and also Louis X, Duke of Bavaria, for whom he painted the celebrated *Battle of Issus* (1529, Alte Pin., Munich), which formed part of a large series of famous battle pieces from classical antiquity. With its dazzling light effects, teeming figures, and brilliant colours, it is one of the finest examples of Altdorfer's rich imaginative powers. In addition to his paintings, he produced engravings, etchings, and woodcuts, and he was an outstanding draughtsman. From 1526 until his death he also worked as town architect of Regensburg. No architectural work by him survives, but his interest in architecture and his skill in handling intricate problems of perspective are demonstrated in several of his paintings, including *Susannah and the Elders* (1526, Alte Pin., Munich).

Altichiero (active 1370s and 1380s). Italian painter. He probably came from Zevio near Verona and is sometimes considered to be the founder of the Veronese School, although the only surviving example of his work in that town is a fresco in S. Anastasia. Most of his surviving work is in Padua, where he had a hand in fresco cycles in the Basilica of St Anthony (1372–9) and in the Oratory of St George (1377–84), in the latter of which he collaborated with an artist called Avanzo, who is otherwise unknown and whose contribution to the work is uncertain. A document of 1393 implies that he had died by then. The solidity and solemnity of Altichiero's figures clearly reveal his debt to *Giotto's frescos in the Arena Chapel of Padua. But his pageant-like scenes with their elaborate architectural views express the taste of the late 14th century for *Gothic intricacy, while his naturalism in the study of plants and animals formed the point of departure for a new style that is reflected in *Pisanello.

Alvarez Cubero, José (1768–1827). The leading Spanish sculptor of the *Neoclassical period. He spent much of his career in Rome (1805–25), where he was a friend and disciple of *Canova, and he is sometimes called 'the Spanish Canova'. His work included classical subjects and portraits, but his best-known piece is the marble *Defence of Saragossa* (1823) on the façade of the *Prado, Madrid, celebrating Spanish heroism during the Peninsular War.

Amberger, Christoph (*c*.1505–61/2). German painter (mainly of portraits) and designer. He worked in Augsburg, which had many cultural and economic ties with Italy (he met *Titian when he visited the city in 1548), and his style emulates the grandeur and richness of the Venetian School, paying as much attention to dress and jewellery as to characterization (*Charles V*, *c*.1532, Gemäldegalerie, Berlin). His rare figure compositions (*Virgin and Child between Sts Ulrich and Afra*, 1554, Augsburg Cathedral) are less distinguished. Amberger also designed coins, façade paintings, and statuary.

American Abstract Artists (AAA). An association of American abstract painters and sculptors formed in New York in 1936 with the aim of promoting their work and fostering public understanding of it. The association held annual exhibitions (the first in 1937) and disseminated the principles of abstract art by lectures, publications, etc. The first president was Balcomb Greene (1904–90) and among the early members were Josef *Albers, Willem *de Kooning, Jackson *Pollock, and David *Smith. In 1940 members picketed the *Museum of Modern Art, demanding that it should show American art, but by the mid-1940s abstract art had achieved recognition and the activities of the association dwindled. In the 1950s, however, it revived and had more than 200 members.

American Academy of the Fine Arts. *See* NATIONAL ACADEMY OF DESIGN.

American Scene Painting. A broad term applied to the work of various painters who in the 1920s and 1930s depicted aspects of American life and landscape in a naturalistic, descriptive style. The term does not signify an organized movement, but rather an aspect of a general tendency for American artists to move away from abstraction and the avant-garde in the period between the two world wars. Part of this tendency was a patriotic repudiation of European, specifically French, influence. *Burchfield and *Hopper are among the best known exponents of American Scene Painting, and the *Regionalists, who were more self-consciously nationalistic, are also embraced by the term.

Amigoni, Jacopo (*c*.1685–1752). Italian *Rococo decorative painter and portraitist.

His early life is obscure, but he was probably born and trained in Venice. From about 1715 he had an international career, working in Bavaria, England, France, and finally Spain, where he died. His English sojourn lasted from 1729 to 1739 (with a break for a visit to Paris in 1736), his finest surviving work from this period being a series of four paintings on the story of Jupiter and Io at Moor Park (now Moor Park Golf Club) in Hertfordshire. He was the last of the Venetian decorators to come to England in the wake of *Pellegrini and the *Ricci, as the demand for large-scale decorative painting was fairly short-lived. Amigoni, however, earned a good living with his portraits and is said to have persuaded *Canaletto to try his fortune in England.

Amman, Jost (1539–91). Swiss printmaker and draughtsman, born in Zurich and active mainly in Nuremberg, Germany, where he is documented from 1561. He was perhaps the most prolific book illustrator of his day and one of his pupils boasted that he produced more drawings in four years than could be carted away in a hay-wagon (in spite of this huge productivity, he was constantly in financial trouble). His woodcuts and engravings are more important as documents of contemporary life than for their artistic value and in particular there is a wealth of material on 16th-century crafts in his *Eygentliche Beschreibung aller Stände auff Erden* (Frankfurt, 1568; an expanded Latin edition was published in the same year, with 132 woodcuts in place of the 114 in the German original). The title translates as 'Exact Description of All Ranks on Earth' and the book is popularly known as the *Ständebuch* (Book of Trades).

Ammanati, Bartolommeo (1511–92). Florentine *Mannerist architect and sculptor. His best-known works in Florence are the Ponte S. Trinità (1567–70, destroyed during the Second World War, but rebuilt) and his additions to the *Pitti Palace (1558–70), including the rusticated courtyard. In sculpture he was strongly influenced by *Michelangelo and by the suaver style of Jacopo *Sansovino (on whose Library in Venice he worked); his chief work in this field is the rather ponderous fountain (1560–75) in the Piazza della Signoria, Florence, with its marble *Neptune* and bronze *Nymphs*. Ammanati beat several sculptors, including *Cel-

lini and *Giambologna, in a competition for this commission, but the work was not well received. In old age, influenced by Counter-Reformation piety, he wrote a recantation of his secular works (denouncing nude figures as lustful) and he is said to have destroyed some. He was married to Laura Battiferri, a poet who was the subject of a memorable portrait by *Bronzino.

anamorphosis. A picture (or a part of one) executed in such a way that the image appears distorted or unintelligible until it is seen from an unusual angle or by means of a special lens or mirror, when it appears in lifelike aspect. Anamorphosis is first mentioned in the notes of *Leonardo da Vinci, and perhaps the most famous example of its use is in *Holbein's *The Ambassadors* (1533, NG, London), which features a distorted skull, probably a symbol of the brevity of life. Generally, however, the purpose of anamorphosis was to mystify or amuse, and it rarely occurs in major works such as this.

Ancients. Group of English *Romantic artists inspired by William *Blake and active for about a decade in the late 1820s and early 1830s. Their name (evidently first used in 1827, shortly before Blake's death) expressed their admiration for the more spiritual art of the past in preference to that of their own day. At most there were about nine members, of whom the best known was Samuel *Palmer; others included Edward *Calvert and George *Richmond, with John *Linnell on the fringes. They sometimes worked at Shoreham in Kent, where Palmer had a house from 1826 to 1835, and they also held meetings in London (at Blake's house in the early days). Usually they worked on a small scale, concentrating on biblical and pastoral subjects in an idyllic or visionary vein.

Anderson, Laurie. *See* PERFORMANCE ART.

Andre, Carl (1935–). American sculptor, a leading exponent of *Minimal art. Typically he produces his works by placing identical ready-made commercial units such as bricks, cement blocks, metal plates, etc. (occasionally 'natural products' like logs or bales of hay) in simple geometrical arrangements without adhesives or joints; the works are dismantled when not on exhibition. His most characteristic products abjure height and are arranged as horizontal configurations on the ground ('more like roads than buildings', in his own words); some are even intended to be walked over. In Britain Andre is best known for the sensational publicity accompanying the 'Tate bricks' incident in 1976. His *Equivalent VIII* (1966) (consisting of 120 bricks arranged two deep in a rectangle) was vandalized and there was an outcry about the alleged waste of public money on its purchase by the Tate Gallery. In 1985 Andre again made headlines when he was charged with murdering his wife (who died after falling from a window); he was acquitted at his trial.

Andrea da Firenze (Andrea Bonaiuti) (d. 1378?). Florentine painter, first documented in 1346. He is remembered mainly for his frescos (1366–8) in the chapter house (now known as the Spanish Chapel) of S. Maria Novella, Florence. This is a church of the Dominican Order, and the frescos—which form the most impressive Florentine cycle of the time—are concerned with the power of the Church in general and the importance of the Dominicans in particular. The best-known scene in the scheme, covering an entire wall of the chapel, is *The Triumph of the Church*, which features a pack of dogs protecting the sheep of the Christian flock (*domini canes*—'dogs of the Lord'—a pun on Dominicans), and also a view of Florence Cathedral showing it imaginatively completed, with a dome similar to the one eventually begun by *Brunelleschi in 1420 (Andrea was among the artists who had been consulted over the construction of the building). Andrea's dignified style is similar to that of *Orcagna.

Andrea del Castagno (Andrea di Bartolo di Bargilla) (c.1418–57). One of the most powerful Florentine painters in the generation after *Masaccio. He is named after his birthplace, Castagno, a village north-east of Florence. Nothing is known of his training, and the first recorded episode in his career dates from 1440, when he painted frescos at the Palazzo del Podestà depicting rebels against Cosimo de' *Medici who were sentenced to be hanged by the heels, earning him the sobriquet Andreino degli Impiccati (of the hanged men). These have been destroyed, and Andrea's earliest known surviving works are frescos in the church of S. Zaccaria in Venice (1442). By 1444 he was

back in Florence, designing a stained-glass window for the cathedral, and soon after he began his greatest work, a series of frescos on Christ's Passion for the monastery of S. Apollonia (now a Castagno museum), dominated by one of the most celebrated of all portrayals of the Last Supper (1447). In their emotional vigour and sinewy realism these paintings have been regarded as the pictorial equivalent of the sculpture of *Donatello, but they also have something of Masaccio's monumentality. Andrea's other noteworthy works in Florence include a frescoed equestrian portrait in the cathedral (*Niccolò da Tolentino*, 1455–6)—a pendant to *Uccello's earlier *Sir John Hawkwood*—and two extraordinarily intense altar frescos for SS. Annunziata (c.1455): *St Julian Receiving Absolution from Christ* and *The Trinity Appearing to Sts Jerome, Paula, and Eustochium*. *Vasari wrote that Castagno murdered his friend *Domenico Veneziano, and it was not until the 19th century that it was discovered that Castagno had died young of the plague and that Domenico had in fact outlived him. The story, however, makes it easy to believe that the intensity of his work reflected a fierce temperament.

Andrea del Sarto (1486–1530). Florentine painter. The epithet 'del sarto' (of the tailor) is derived from his father's profession; his real name was Andrea d'Agnolo di Francesco Lanfranchi. According to *Vasari, he was first apprenticed as a goldsmith and then taught by *Piero di Cosimo; another early source says he studied under Raffaellino del Garbo (d. c.1527). However, his poised and graceful style was more obviously influenced by Fra *Bartolommeo and *Raphael, and following the departures of *Leonardo, Raphael, and *Michelangelo (all of whom had left Florence by 1508) he became established with Bartolommeo as the leading painter of the city. Apart from a visit to Fontainebleau in 1518–19 to work for Francis I, Andrea was based in Florence all his life, although he probably visited Rome soon after his return from France, and made short visits elsewhere. He excelled as a fresco decorator (there are outstanding examples in Florence in SS. Annunziata and the Chiostro dello Scalzo), and he also painted superb altarpieces (*Madonna of the Harpies*, 1517, Uffizi, Florence) and portraits (*A Young Man*, c.1517, NG,

London). His posthumous image was largely made and marred by *Vasari, who described Andrea's works as 'faultless' but represented him as a weakling completely under the thumb of his wicked wife. In Robert Browning's poem on the painter (1855) and in a psychoanalytic essay by Freud's disciple Ernest Jones (1913) attempts are made to link a supposed lack of vigour in his mellifluous art with these traits of character. This approach, however, is hardly just and a good deal of Vasari's account of Andrea's private life has been shown to be factually inaccurate (the scandalmongering is mainly in the 1550 edition of his book and was suppressed in the 1568 edition). Andrea has suffered from being judged against such giants as Michelangelo and Raphael, but he nevertheless ranks as one of the greatest masters of his time. In grandeur and gracefulness he approaches Raphael, and he had a feeling for colour and atmosphere that was unrivalled among Florentine painters of his period. He also numbers among the finest draughtsmen of the Renaissance (the best collection of his drawings is in the Uffizi). Certain features of his art foreshadow the *Mannerist experiments of his great pupils *Pontormo and *Rosso Fiorentino. The many other artists who trained in his busy workshop included *Salviati and Vasari.

Andrews, Michael (1928–95). British painter. He studied at the *Slade School under *Coldstream, 1949–53. A slow, fastidious worker, he concentrated on ambitious figure compositions, subtly handled and often with an underlying emotional tension. He shunned publicity and was little known to the public until an *Arts Council exhibition of his work in 1980, after which he achieved a considerable reputation, although some critics found his work rather plodding. In the mid-1980s he had a change of direction with a series of huge, brilliantly coloured landscapes featuring Ayers Rock in Australia. *See also* SCHOOL OF LONDON.

Angelico, Fra (Guido di Piero) (*c.*1395–1455). Florentine painter, a Dominican friar. His nickname means 'the angelic brother', and in popular tradition he has been seen as 'not an artist properly so-called but an inspired saint' (*Ruskin); however, he was in fact a highly professional painter, who was in touch with the most advanced developments in contemporary Florentine art, and in later life he travelled extensively for prestigious commissions. He is first recorded as a painter in 1417 and by 1423 he had become a member of the Dominican Order at S. Domenico, Fiesole, near Florence, where he took the name Fra Giovanni. He probably began his career as a manuscript *illuminator, and his early paintings are strongly influenced by *International Gothic. But even in the most lavishly decorative of them all—the *Annunciation* (*c.*1432) in the Diocesan Museum in Cortona—*Masaccio's influence is evident in the insistent perspective of the architecture. For most of his career Angelico was based in Fiesole (he became prior there in 1450), but his most famous works were painted at S. Marco in Florence (now an Angelico museum), a Sylvestrine monastery that was taken over by his Order in 1436. He and his assistants painted about fifty frescos there (*c.*1438–45)—works that are at once the expression of and a guide to the spiritual life of the community. Many of the frescos are in the friars' cells and were intended as aids to devotion; with their immaculate colouring, their economy in drawing and composition, and their freedom from the accidents of time and place, they attain a sense of blissful serenity. In the last decade of his life Angelico also worked in Orvieto and Perugia, and most importantly in Rome, where he frescoed the private chapel of Pope Nicholas V in the Vatican with scenes from the lives of Sts Stephen and Lawrence (1447–50). These differ considerably from the S. Marco frescos, with new emphasis on the story and on circumstantial detail, bringing Angelico more clearly into the mainstream of 15th-century Italian fresco painting. Angelico died in Rome and was buried in the church of S. Maria sopra Minerva, where his tombstone still exists. He painted numerous altarpieces as well as frescos, several outstanding examples being in the S. Marco museum, including a *Madonna and Saints* (*c.*1438–40) commissioned by Piero de' *Medici for the high altar of S. Marco, Florence. His assistants included Benozzo *Gozzoli and he had considerable influence on Italian painting, notably on *Domenico Veneziano and *Piero della Francesca. *Vasari, who referred to Fra Giovanni as 'a simple and most holy man', popularized the use of the name Angelico for him, but he says it is the name by which he was always known, and it was certainly used as early as 1469. The painter has long been called 'Beato Angelico' (the Blessed Angelico), but his beatification was not made official by the Vatican until 1984.

Angry Penguins. An Australian avant-garde quarterly journal (1940–6) devoted to art and literature, published first in Adelaide and then from 1943 in Melbourne; the title comes from a line in a poem by its founder, the writer Max Harris (1921–96). It encouraged and provided a focus for a group of young painters who worked in an *Expressionist vein and attempted to create an authentic Australian art free from European influences; among them were Arthur *Boyd and Sidney *Nolan. They were opposed by a group of *Social Realist painters, among them Noel Counihan (1913–86), and the debate between the two factions in the pages of *Angry Penguins* helped to make Melbourne a lively artistic centre in the early 1940s. In 1944 the journal was the victim of a celebrated hoax when it devoted an issue to the poems of the non-existent 'Ern Malley', whose works were concocted from arbitrarily selected quotations put together by two fairly traditional poets who thought the journal was pretentious and wanted to test the critical judgement of the editors. It never really recovered from the bad publicity this caused.

Anguier, François (c.1604–69) and **Michel** (c.1613–86). French sculptors, brothers, who stood somewhat apart from the mainstream, which in the middle of the 17th century was dominated by the classical style of *Sarrazin. They are said to have gone to Rome in about 1641 and joined the studio of *Algardi. On their return to France (François by 1649, Michel in 1651), the brothers collaborated on the tomb of Henry de Montmorency in the chapel of the Lycée at Moulins (1649–52), which reveals the new Roman influence they introduced to France. Later the two brothers worked mainly apart, Michel having the more interesting career. His work includes the decoration of the interior of the church of the Val-de-Grâce, Paris (1662–7), and the Nativity group in St Roch, Paris (1665).

Anguissola, Sofonisba (c.1535–1625). Italian painter, mainly of portraits, one of six painter sisters from Cremona, where she studied with Bernardino Campi (1522–91). She was the first woman artist to achieve international renown, and in 1559 she was invited to Spain to work at the court of Philip II (*see* HABSBURG), remaining there for more than a decade before settling in Sicily. In 1624, when she was about 90, she was visited in Palermo by van *Dyck, who drew a portrait of her (BM, London). Her self-portraits (of which about a dozen survive) and portraits of her family are considered her finest works; they are somewhat stiff, but can have great charm.

Angus, Rita (1908–70). New Zealand painter, mainly of portraits and landscapes. She was considered one of the leading figures in New Zealand art, particularly in the 1940s. Working in both oils and watercolours, she painted in a forthright, brightly coloured style that won her a reputation as a pioneer of modernism in her country. She also painted under her married name, Rita Cook.

animaliers. *See* BARYE.

Annigoni, Pietro (1910–88). Italian painter (and occasional sculptor), the only artist of his time to become internationally famous as a society and state portraitist. The turning point in his career was a commission from the Worshipful Company of Fishmongers to paint a portrait of Queen Elizabeth II (1954–5, Fishmongers' Hall, London); it was reproduced endlessly, notably on the postage stamps and banknotes of various countries, and the jacket blurb of Annigoni's autobiography (*An Artist's Life*, 1977) claims that it made him 'the most famous artist in the world—not excluding even 'Picasso'. Subsequently he painted many other celebrity sitters, including several other members of the British royal family, Presidents Kennedy and Johnson, and Pope John XXIII. In style and technique he based himself on the masters of the Italian *Renaissance, placing great stress on draughtsmanship and often working in *tempera. Characteristically his work was smoothly finished, melodramatic in lighting, and often rather melancholy in mood. Annigoni also painted religious works (including frescos in Italian churches) and ambitious allegorical scenes, and he regarded these as more important than his portraits. Critics often dismissed his work as portentously inflated and tasteless, but it claimed public attention in a remarkable way: more than 200,000 people saw his second portrait of the Queen (NPG, London) during the fortnight when it was first exhibited in 1970.

Anquetin, Louis (1861–1932). French painter, designer, and writer. Early in his career he moved in circles that included some of the outstanding avant-garde painters of the day, including *Bernard, van *Gogh, and *Toulouse-Lautrec (all four had been pupils of *Cormon). With Bernard, he was one of the pioneers of *Cloisonnism, but after about 1890 his work was much more traditional, and he became interested in research into the techniques of the Old Masters, notably *Rubens, on whom he wrote a book (1924). He was a prolific draughtsman and made tapestry cartoons for the Beauvais and Gobelins factories.

Anrep, Boris (1883–1969). Russian-born mosaicist and painter, active mainly in England. He organized the Russian section of Roger *Fry's second *Post-Impressionist exhibition in 1912 and after the First World War, in which he served in the Russian army, he settled in London, although he lived for a time in Paris after his wife left him for Fry in 1926. Anrep was deeply interested in Byzantine art and came to specialize in mosaic pavements, the best-known examples being in Tate Britain, representing William Blake's *Proverbs* (1923), and the National Gallery—four floors on and around the main staircase, executed between 1926 and 1952. The subjects are 'The Awakening of the Muses', 'The Modern Virtues', 'The Labours of Life', and 'The Pleasures of Life'; portraits of many well-known contemporaries are incorporated in them, for example the philosopher Bertrand Russell representing Lucidity and the film actress Greta Garbo as Melpomene, the Muse of Tragedy. They were paid for by Samuel *Courtauld and other benefactors.

Anshutz, Thomas. *See* HENRI.

Antal, Frederick (1887–1954). Hungarian-born art historian who settled in England in 1933 and became a British citizen in 1946. He was deeply interested in historical methodology, and is regarded as the leading exponent of the Marxist interpretation of art history. His views are most fully expressed in *Florentine Painting and its Social Background* (1948), in which he argues that developments in style and subject matter were directly influenced by social and political changes. The book was widely admired, but it was also attacked as being over-rigid in the way it linked artistic phenomena with social and economic causes. Antal's other books include the posthumously published *Hogarth and his Place in European Art* (1962), in which he applied his methods more subtly and flexibly, revealing his fascination with *Hogarth as an expression of English middle-class morality and culture. A collection of his articles, *Classicism and Romanticism, with Other Studies in Art History* (1966), includes 'Remarks on the Method of Art History', which is a statement of his own credo. Antal never held a regular teaching post in England (he occasionally lectured at the *Courtauld Institute), but he was an influential figure. Ernst *Gombrich described him as 'by far the most learned and sophisticated' of the Marxist art historians of his time. 'He was very doctrinaire in his political views, but he had a good eye.'

Antelami, Benedetto (active late 12th century). Italian *Romanesque sculptor, the most notable figure in the history of Italian sculpture before Nicola *Pisano. His name first appears on a *relief of the *Descent from the Cross* (1178) in Parma Cathedral. The major works associated with him are the three carved portals of the adjacent Baptistery, one of which is signed and dated 1196; it has been suggested that he may have overseen the whole structure as architect as well as sculptor. On stylistic grounds he or his workshop have been credited with other work in north Italy. His sculptures have a gravity and dramatic expressiveness hitherto unknown in the region.

Anthonisz., Cornelis (*c*.1505–53). Netherlandish printmaker, painter, and cartographer. He was active mainly in his native Amsterdam and in 1544 published a large bird's-eye view of the city in woodcut. He worked as a cartographer in the service of the emperor Charles V (*see* HABSBURG) and also painted portraits, most notably *The Civic Guard* (1533, Historical Mus., Amsterdam), an early example of a type of group portrait for which *Hals later became renowned.

Antico (Pier Jacopo Alari Bonacolsi) (c.1460–1528). Italian sculptor, goldsmith, and medallist. His nickname derived from his classically inspired bronze statuettes, many of which were versions of famous antique statues such as the *Apollo Belvedere* (he also restored ancient sculpture). He visited Rome in the 1490s, but worked mainly in and around Mantua, particularly for members of the *Gonzaga family and Isabella d'*Este.

Antinous. A representation in sculpture of the beautiful youth of this name who was a favourite of the emperor Hadrian. After Antinous was drowned while accompanying Hadrian up the Nile in AD 130 his name became surrounded by romantic legend, and the grief-stricken emperor commemorated him in lavish fashion. He founded a city called Antinoöpolis in Egypt, erected temples in his memory, and had him honoured in festivals. Antinous was frequently represented in sculpture, sometimes as Apollo or Dionysus, and several examples survive; typically he is shown with curly hair and a sad-sweet expression, although the identification is not always certain, and the title 'Antinous' has sometimes been given loosely to similar figures of beautiful and graceful youths. Particularly famous were the *Belvedere Antinous* (Vatican Mus.), which was regarded as one of the standards of male beauty (for *Bernini's views on it, *see* ANTIQUE), and a relief excavated at Hadrian's Villa at Tivoli in 1735. It was one of the greatest treasures of Cardinal *Albani and was regarded by his librarian *Winckelmann as one of the peaks of ancient art; it is still in Albani's villa in Rome, now renamed the Villa Torlonia.

Antipodeans (or **Antipodean Group**). The name adopted by a group of Australian painters (Arthur *Boyd was the best known) who held an exhibition in Melbourne in 1959; the catalogue contained a manifesto of their aims and ideas, attacking abstraction and championing figurative art.

antique, the. The physical remains of the Greek and Roman world, or more particularly the remains of antique sculpture, which have been for later artists an inspiration, a challenge, and a canon of perfection. Such remains have never been totally forgotten or disregarded. Stone from ruined Roman buildings was often reused, and memories of classical ornament or drapery forms recur throughout the Middle Ages. However, it was not until the Italian *Renaissance that the recovery and revival of the classical past became a deliberate ideal. *Ghiberti's writings, for example, testify to his admiration for antique statues and *cameos, and much of *Donatello's sculpture would be unthinkable without a close study of the antique (most obviously, the *Marcus Aurelius* is the work against which he measured himself in his *Gattamelata*). Lorenzo de' *Medici and Pope Julius II (Giuliano della *Rovere) were among the pioneer collectors of ancient art, and *Vasari attributed the attainment of perfection by the generation of *Leonardo, *Michelangelo, and *Raphael in no small measure to the discovery of such famous marbles as the *Apollo Belvedere* and the *Laocoön*, although it was mainly the next generation, particularly visitors from northern Europe (*Heemskerck for example), who systematically drew after the antique. Towards the middle of the 16th century the role of the antique in the curriculum of artists became firmly established. In *De' veri precetti della pittura* (1587), the painter and writer Giovanni Battista Armenini (c.1525–1609) already gives a list of 'canonic' antiques, including the famous *Belvedere Torso*, and such works were carried by means of engravings, casts, and copies into every artist's studio. The philosophical justification for this dependence on antique models was given in *Bellori's famous oration *Idea* (1664), where he claimed that ancient statuary embodied a revelation of an absolute beauty that had been discovered once and for all (*see* IDEAL). To the followers of the academic doctrine, each of the great antiques, to which now were added the *Farnese Hercules*, the *Borghese Warrior*, the *Medici Venus*, and the *Barberini Faun*, represented a type of physique that could serve as a permanent standard for the artist. Nor was antique influence confined to those artists whose work was most obviously classical (such as *Poussin). *Bernini, for example, when he addressed the *Academy in Paris in 1666, said, 'In my early youth I drew a great deal from classical figures, and when I was in difficulties with my first statue I turned to the *Antinous* as to the oracle.' Reverence for the antique was given a new lease of life when the *Neoclassical movement reacted against the frivolities of *Rococo fashions. In opposition to earlier ideas, *Winckelmann preached the belief that classical artists had deliberately avoided representing extreme passions, and he regarded the antique less as a source of expressive formulas than as a model of noble restraint. The authority of the antique declined with the onset of *Romanticism, with its stress on self-expression, but its influence has continued. Making drawings from casts of antique sculpture remained a part of most official art training into the 20th century, and *Picasso, for example, often used classical art as a source of inspiration; in particular, his 'Neoclassical' paintings of the 1920s owed much to visits to the Archaeological Museum in Naples.

Antolínez, José (1635–75). Spanish painter, active in his native Madrid. Like *Murillo in Seville, he had a penchant for paintings of the Immaculate Conception (an example, c.1670, is in the Ashmolean Museum, Oxford), and his colourful, sweet style has much in common with Murillo's. His temperament was anything but sweet, however, for he was renowned for his arrogance and vanity; according to *Palomino, he died of a fever after overexerting himself and suffering wounds in a fencing bout. Apart from religious works, his output included a few portraits and genre scenes, notably the *Picture Dealer* (c.1670, Alte Pin., Munich), an intriguing glimpse into the studio of a poor artist.

Antonello da Messina (c.1430–79). Italian painter, born and mainly active at Messina in Sicily, the most famous artist to come from the island. He was one of the major pioneers of *oil painting in Italy. According to *Vasari he learnt the technique from Jan van *Eyck, but there is no evidence that he ever visited northern Europe and he was in any case still probably a boy when Jan died in 1441. It is more likely that he acquired his knowledge of northern techniques in Naples, then artistically dominated by the Netherlands. He made at least two extensive visits to the Italian mainland, and in 1475–6 he was in Venice, where he painted a large altarpiece for the church of S. Cassiano, of which only three fragments remain (KH Mus., Vienna). Vasari says that Antonello brought the 'secret' of oil painting to Venice,

and while this is an exaggeration, his altarpiece and other works he painted there did have 'a far-reaching influence ... during the decade or two succeeding his visit' (Johannes *Wilde, *Venetian Art from Bellini to Titian*, 1974). He showed how the medium could be used to create previously unknown atmospheric and colouristic effects, and Giovanni *Bellini, most notably, was greatly impressed by the lucidity and spaciousness of his work. Antonello's bust portraits—in three-quarter view, of Netherlandish type—also enjoyed a notable vogue in Venice; their expressions were more lively than in the portraits by *Memlinc then being imported and, like Antonello's religious works, they show a remarkable ability to combine northern particularity of detail with the Italian tradition of grandeur and clarity of form. Good examples of Antonello's portraits are in the National Gallery, London (this one is often considered a self-portrait), and in the Louvre, Paris.

An Túr Gloine. See PURSER.

Anuszkiewicz, Richard. See OP ART.

Apelles. Greek painter active in the 4th century BC, born at Colophon in Asia Minor. Apelles was reckoned in antiquity to be the greatest of Greek painters, renowned particularly for his gracefulness, but none of his work survives. He was court painter to Philip II of Macedon and his son Alexander the Great, and one of the many anecdotes concerning the artist tells how Alexander gave him his mistress Pancaspe after the artist had fallen in love with her while painting her in the nude. The names of about 30 of his works are recorded by ancient sources. Among them were portraits of Alexander the Great (particularly famous was one for the temple of Artemis at Ephesus), *Aphrodite Anadyomene* (Venus rising from the sea) made for the temple of Asclepius at Cos, brought to Rome by Augustus, and set up in the temple of Caesar, and *Calumny*. Descriptions of his work by classical authors were well known during the *Renaissance and inspired several major artists to attempt to emulate them. *Botticelli made a painting and *Mantegna a drawing of *Calumny* (Uffizi, Florence, and BM, London, respectively), and *Titian painted an *Aphrodite Anadyomene* (NG, Edinburgh).

Aphrodite of Cnidus. Statue by *Praxiteles, made for the city of Cnidus in Asia Minor. It is now lost, but it was his most famous work in antiquity (*Pliny thought it was the finest statue in the world), and was the ancestress of the modern female nude—the first life-size statue showing the goddess completely naked. Several Roman copies survive (for example in the Vatican); they show Aphrodite (Venus) in a gently twisted pose, with the right hand casually masking the pudenda and the left hand dropping her robe over an urn. The statue was placed in an open shrine so it could be seen from all four sides, each view being equally admired. According to some ancient sources, Praxiteles' mistress, the celebrated courtesan Phryne, was his model for the statue.

Apollinaire, Guillaume (1880–1918). French poet and art critic. Apollinaire was 'the most influential art critic writing in France during the decade before the outbreak of war in 1914 . . . a cardinal figure in creating the artistic climate of Paris early in this century—a climate in which anything and everything was thought possible' (John *Golding, *Visions of the Modern*, 1994). He earned his living mainly with journalism and was one of the prototypes of the modern critic, his writing containing much that is superficial and gossipy. His importance stems not so much from the quality of his writing as from his brilliance as a propagandist on behalf of those artists he most admired. In particular he championed *Picasso (his first substantial articles, in 1905, were on him) and later the *Cubists in general (including the *Orphists, whose name he coined). Among the other artists whose reputations he either established or consolidated were *Chagall, de *Chirico, *Derain, *Matisse, and Henri *Rousseau. He was also influential on *Dada (his friend Marcel *Duchamp's interest in visual punning was partly inspired by Apollinaire's love of jest and linguistic acrobatics) and on *Surrealism (he coined the term in 1917 and his suggestion that artists should explore 'interior universes' stimulated André *Breton, who dedicated the first Surrealist manifesto to his memory). Apollinaire was wounded in the head serving in the French army in 1916; weakened by this, he died of influenza two years later.

Apollo Belvedere. Marble statue (Vatican Mus.) of the Greek god Apollo, discovered towards the end of the 15th century and long regarded as one of the supreme masterpieces of world art and the absolute standard for male beauty (it is named after the Belvedere Court in the Vatican, in which it was once displayed). The statue is a copy from the Roman period of a *Classical or *Hellenistic Greek bronze, and *Leochares has been proposed as the sculptor of the lost original. It was often copied or adapted, for example by *Bernini in his *Apollo and Daphne* and by *Reynolds, who painted his *Commodore Keppel* in the posture of the statue but in 18th-century dress. *Winckelmann's rapturous description of the *Apollo Belvedere* enshrined it as one of the models of *Neoclassicism, but from the later 19th century its reputation declined and it now seems cold and academic to many critics. Whereas to Winckelmann it appeared 'the highest ideal of art among all the works of antiquity', to Kenneth *Clark it seemed that 'in no other famous work of art are idea and execution more distressingly divorced.'

Apollonio di Giovanni. *See* CASSONE.

Appel, Karel (1921–). Dutch abstract painter, sculptor, printmaker, ceramicist, designer, and writer, regarded as the most powerful of the post-war generation of Dutch artists. In 1948 he was a founder of the *Cobra group. He moved to Paris in 1950 and by the end of the decade he had gained an international reputation, having travelled widely and won several prestigious prizes. His most characteristic paintings are in an extremely uninhibited and agitated *Expressionist vein, with strident colours and violent brushwork applied with very thick *impasto. The images usually look purely abstract at first glance, but they often retain suggestions of human masks or of animal or fantasy figures, sometimes fraught with terror as well as a childlike naivety: Herbert *Read wrote that in looking at his pictures one has the impression 'of a spiritual tornado that has left these images of its passage'. Such works were influential on *Neo-Expressionism. Appel has also made sculpture, prints, and ceramics, and he has done a wide range of design work, including the scenery for a ballet, *Can We Dance a Landscape*, for which he also wrote the plot; it was performed at the Paris Opéra in 1987.

Appiani, Andrea (1754–1817). Italian painter. He was the leading Italian painter of the *Neoclassical period, but more on account of the lack of native competition than because of the quality of his work, which is graceful and impeccably finished but often rather bland. Most of his career was spent in his native Milan; his work there includes the fresco decoration of the church of S. Maria presso S. Celso (1792–8). This is sometimes described as his masterpiece, but his portraits have generally appealed more to modern taste than his decorative work.

applied art. Term describing the design or decoration of functional objects so as to make them aesthetically pleasing. It is used in distinction to *fine art, although there is often no clear dividing line between the two areas.

Apt, Ulrich the Elder (d. 1532). German painter, the best-known member of a family of artists. He worked in Augsburg, painting altarpieces, portraits, and in 1516 a series of wall paintings (destroyed) in the town hall in collaboration with his pupil Jörg *Breu the Elder.

aquarelle. The French word for *watercolour; it is sometimes used in English to distinguish 'true' watercolour painting—in transparent washes—from *gouache, which is opaque.

aquatint. A printmaking method related to *etching but producing finely granulated tonal areas rather than lines. The term applies also to a print made by this method. There are several variants of the technique, but in essence the process is as follows. A metal plate is sprinkled with acid-resistant resin, which is fused to the plate by heating, and when the plate is immersed in an acid bath the acid bites between the tiny particles of resin and produces an evenly granulated surface. The design is created by drawing on the plate with acid-resistant varnish, and great variety of tone can be obtained by immersing in acid and varnishing in turn (the longer the acid bites, the darker the tone). Aquatint was invented in the mid-17th century, but it initially made almost no impact. The technique lay

dormant until it was revived in France around the middle of the 18th century, and in the late 18th and early 19th centuries it became highly popular in England for reproducing watercolours (colour could be added by hand or by using several plates with different coloured inks). It has also been used as an original creative medium (sometimes in conjunction with other graphic techniques) by many distinguished artists, including *Goya, *Degas, Camille *Pissarro, *Rouault, and *Picasso.

Archaic art. Term applied to Greek art in the period before the *Classical period, from about 650 BC until about 480 BC (the date of the Persian sack of Athens). The Archaic period is marked by the development of the life-size stone statue (the *kouros and *kore) and by the change from *black-figure vase painting to *red-figure.

Archipenko, Alexander (1887–1964). Russian-born sculptor who became an American citizen in 1928. In 1908 he moved from Moscow to Paris, where he was introduced to *Cubism by *Léger and became one of the outstanding sculptors of the movement. In works such as the bronze *Walking Woman* (1912, Denver Art Mus.), he analysed the human figure into geometrical forms and opened parts of it up with concavities and a central hole to create a contrast of solid and void, issuing in a new idiom in modern sculpture. At about the same time he began making sculptures that were assembled from pieces of commonplace materials, paralleling the work of *Picasso. Archipenko quickly built up a reputation in France and elsewhere (especially Germany), and although his career was interrupted by the First World War, he vigorously relaunched it afterwards, and by the time of his first one-man show in the USA (given by the *Société Anonyme in 1921) he was undoubtedly the best known and most influential of all Cubist sculptors. In 1921–3 he lived in Berlin, then settled in the USA. He taught in various places, but principally in New York, where he ran his own school of sculpture from 1939 until his death. The work he produced in America did not compare in quality or historical importance with that of his European period, but he continued to be imaginative and technically resourceful. In 1924, for example, he invented the *Archipentura* (a kind of *Kinetic painting), and after the Second World War he experimented with 'light' sculptures, making structures of plastic lit from within. His work was influential in both Europe and America, notably in the revival of *polychromy, in the use of new materials, and in pointing the way from a sculpture of solid form towards one of space and light.

Arcimboldo, Giuseppe (c.1527–93). Milanese painter, famous for his allegorical or symbolical compositions in which he arranged objects such as fruits and vegetables into the form of the human face. He began his career as a designer of stained-glass windows for Milan Cathedral, but from 1562 to 1587 he worked successively for the emperors Ferdinand I, Maximilian II, and Rudolf II (see HABSBURG), first in Vienna and then in Prague. A typical work is *Rudolf II as Vertumnus* (c.1590, Skoklosters Castle, Sweden), showing the emperor as the Roman god of orchards, his head composed of fruit, flowers, and so on. Arcimboldo returned to Milan in 1587. His paintings, though much imitated, were generally regarded merely as curiosities until the *Surrealists revived interest in 'visual punning'.

Arman (Armand Fernandez) (1928–). French-born artist who became an American citizen in 1972. In 1957, with his friend Yves *Klein, he decided to be known by his first name only, and the form 'Arman' was adopted in 1958 as a result of a printer's error on the cover of a catalogue. He moved to New York in 1963. Arman is best known for his assemblages of junk material, ranging from modest collections of household debris (*Accumulation of Sliced Teapots*, 1964, Walker Art Center, Minneapolis) to towers of crushed automobiles encased in concrete.

armature. A framework or skeleton round which a figure of clay, plaster, or similar material can be modelled. The term is also applied to the iron framework of *stained-glass windows.

Armenini, Giovanni Battista. *See* ANTIQUE.

Armitage, Kenneth (1916–2002). British sculptor. In 1952 he had his first one-man show in London and in the same year his work was exhibited in the Venice *Biennale; thereafter he rapidly developed an international reputation. His pre-war work consisted mainly of carvings (most of which he later destroyed), but soon after the war he began to work in bronze, which remained a favourite material for what he described as 'the fluid, unifying and sensual quality it can give'. Bronze was also much more suitable than carving for the spindly-legged, slab-bodied shapes that were characteristic of his figures at this time; he depicted them singly or in groups, in everyday attitudes, with a sense of affection and often humour: 'I find most satisfying work which derives from careful study and preparation but which is fashioned in an attitude of pleasure and playfulness.' *People in the Wind* (1951, Tate, London, and other casts) is a well-known example from this phase of his career and one of the first works in which he achieved a distinctively individual style. From the mid-1950s his figures became more impersonal in character and often larger in scale, and from the late 1960s he became more experimental in technique, combining sculpture and drawing in figures of wood, plaster, and paper. In the 1970s he returned to bronze and began to explore non-human subject matter. He also worked in fibreglass.

Armory Show. An art exhibition (officially entitled the International Exhibition of Modern Art) held in New York, 17 February–15 March 1913, at the Armory of the National Guard's Sixty-Ninth Regiment, Lexington Avenue, Manhattan. It was a daring presentation of new and still controversial art on a mammoth scale (about 1,300 works by about 300 artists) and is regarded as the most important exhibition ever held in the country and one of the milestones in 20th-century American culture. The initiative for it came from a group of artists, several of them from the circle of Robert *Henri, who in 1911 formed an organization called the Association of American Painters and Sculptors to find exhibition space for young artists. The breadth of vision with which the show was conceived was primarily due to the Association's president, Arthur B. *Davies, whose enthusiasm for presenting a comprehensive picture of current European movements largely overshadowed the original idea of an exhibition of American art. In effect, the Armory Show was two exhibitions in one. The American portion presented a cross-section of contemporary art from the USA, heavily weighted in favour of younger and more radical artists. The foreign section, which was the core of the exhibition and became the main centre of controversy, traced the evolution of modern art, showing work by *Goya, *Delacroix, *Courbet, and the *Impressionists and *Post-Impressionists, as well as leading contemporary artists including *Kandinsky, *Matisse, and *Picasso. French artists were best represented, and there was comparatively little German art. From New York a reduced version of the exhibition went to Chicago (Art Institute) and Boston (Copley Hall). More than a quarter of a million visitors paid to see it, and its impact was enormous on a public that generally knew little of Post-Impressionism, let alone *Fauvism, *Cubism, or abstract art (the Metropolitan Museum, New York, bought a *Cézanne at the Show and this was the first picture by the artist to enter an American public collection). Though there was a good deal of ridicule and indignation (directed particularly at Marcel *Duchamp's *Nude Descending a Staircase*), there were also many favourable reviews and the show stirred up public interest in art and created a climate more favourable to experimentation. It had a profound effect on many American artists, for example Stuart *Davis, who regarded it as the turning point of his career, and several important patrons and collectors made their first tentative purchases of modern art at the show, among them Katherine *Dreier. It has therefore become a commonplace to speak of the Armory Show as the real beginning of an interest in progressive art in the USA.

Armstrong, Elizabeth. *See* NEWLYN SCHOOL.

Arnold, Ann and **Graham.** *See* BLAKE, SIR PETER.

Arnolfo di Cambio (d. 1302?). Italian sculptor and architect. He is first mentioned in 1265 as Nicola *Pisano's assistant on the pulpit for Siena Cathedral. In 1277 he is documented in Rome, where he seems to have spent most of the 1280s and 1290s, before settling in Florence in his final years. In Rome he worked in the service of Charles I of Naples and Sicily (Charles of Anjou): his portrait of Charles (c.1280, Capitoline Mus., Rome) was one of the earliest portrait statues since the ancient world. The famous bronze statue of St Peter (c.1290) in St Peter's, Rome, has also been attributed to him. His most important surviving sculpture, however, is the tomb of Cardinal de Braye (d. 1282), in S. Domenico at Orvieto, which set the type of wall tomb for more than a century. As an architect, Arnolfo had a great reputation in his day and began the building of Florence Cathedral. No other buildings are documented as being by him, but several other important Florentine buildings, including S. Croce and the Palazzo Vecchio, have been attributed to him, notably by *Vasari. If they really are to be credited to Arnolfo, he must rank as one of the greatest architects of the Middle Ages, as well as a distinguished sculptor.

Arp, Jean (or **Hans**) (1886–1966). French sculptor, painter, and poet who was prominently involved with several major avant-garde groups and movements in the first half of the 20th century. He was born in Strasbourg, then under German rule, and spoke French and German with equal ease (he wrote poetry in both languages). In 1912 he met Robert and Sonia *Delaunay in Paris and *Kandinsky in Munich, where he participated in the second *Blaue Reiter exhibition. In 1915 he moved to Zurich, where he was one of the founders of the *Dada movement and met his future wife Sophie *Taeuber (they married in 1922), with whom he collaborated in experiments with cut-out paper compositions and *collages. During the war years in Zurich he also made his first abstract polychrome relief carvings in wood (*Dada Relief*, 1916, Kunsthaus, Basle). In 1919–20 he lived in Cologne, where he continued his Dada activities in collaboration with his friend Max *Ernst. From 1920 Arp worked mainly in Paris and in 1928 he settled at nearby Meudon. At this time he was involved in the *Surrealist movement, his work including experiments with chance arrangements. He joined *Cercle et Carré; in 1930 and he was a founder member of *Abstraction-Création in 1931. Also in 1931 he took up sculpture in the round (previously he had made only reliefs) and began to produce what are now his most familiar and distinctive works—

sensuous abstract pieces (usually in bronze or marble) that convey a suggestion of organic forms without reproducing actual plant or animal shapes (*Growth*, 1938, Guggenheim Mus., New York). In 1941 Arp fled to Grasse on the French Riviera, then in 1942 to Switzerland. After the war he returned to Meudon. In his post-war work he did not seriously add to his earlier achievements, but he won many honours and prestigious public commissions; in 1954, for example, he was awarded the International Sculpture Prize at the Venice *Biennale, and in 1958 he made a relief for the Unesco building in Paris.

Arpino, Cavaliere d'. *See* CESARI, GIUSEPPE.

arriccio (or *arricciato*). In *fresco painting, a layer of fairly coarse plaster applied to the wall before the *intonaco* (the smoother top layer of plaster that forms the painting surface).

Art Autre. A term coined by the French critic Michel Tapié (1909–87) in his book *Un art autre* (1952) to describe a type of art that he regarded as appropriate to the turbulent mood in France in the post-war period—an art that worked through 'paroxysm, magic, total ecstasy'. The term is a vague one and is sometimes used synonymously with *Art Informel (also coined by Tapié). However, Art Autre can be seen as a broader term, for it embraces figurative art (for example that of *Dubuffet) as well as abstract art. In using the phrase 'art autre' (other art) Tapié claimed that post-war art showed a complete break with the past. In addition to Dubuffet, he cited *Mathieu, *Matta, and *Wols as leading representatives of Art Autre.

Art Brut (Fr.: 'Raw Art'). Term coined by Jean *Dubuffet for art produced by people outside the established art world—solitaries, the maladjusted, patients in psychiatric hospitals, prisoners, and fringe-dwellers of all kinds. In English, the term 'Outsider art' (the title of a book by Roger Cardinal, 1972) is sometimes used to cover this type of work. Dubuffet claimed that such art— 'springing from pure invention and in no way based, as cultural art constantly is, on chameleon- or parrot-like processes'—is evidence of a power of originality that all people possess but which in most has been stifled by educational training and social constraints. He began to make a collection of Art Brut in 1945, and in 1972 he presented it, by then numbering more than 5,000 items, to the city of Lausanne, where it was opened to the public at the Château de Beaulieu in 1976. Although nearly half the collection was produced by patients, usually schizophrenics, in psychiatric hospitals, Dubuffet repudiated the concept of psychiatric art, claiming that 'there is no art of the insane any more than there is an art of dyspeptics or an art of people with knee complaints'. He also distinguished Art Brut from *naive art on the more dubious ground that naive painters remain within the cultural mainstream, hoping for public recognition, whereas Art Brut artists create their works for their own use as a kind of private theatre.

Art Deco. The most fashionable style of design and interior decoration in the 1920s and 1930s in Europe and the USA, characterized by sleek geometrical or stylized forms and bright, sometimes garish colours. The style takes its name from the Exposition Internationale des Arts Décoratifs et Industriels Modernes, held in Paris in 1925. Initially it was a luxury style, with costly materials such as ivory, jade, and lacquer much in evidence, but partly because of the effects of the Depression it also found expression in materials that could be easily and economically mass produced. Art Deco may have owed something to several of the major art movements of the early 20th century—the geometry of *Cubism (it has been described as 'Cubism tamed'), the bold colours of *Fauvism, and the machine forms of *Constructivism and *Futurism. Similarly, although the term is not often applied to painting or sculpture, the Art Deco style is clearly reflected in the streamlined forms of certain artists of the period, for example the painter Tamara de *Lempicka and the sculptor Paul *Manship. There was a revival of interest in Art Deco during the 1960s (it was then that the name was coined) and its bold, bright forms have a kinship with *Pop art.

Arte Povera (or **Art Povera**) (It.: 'poor' or 'impoverished art'). Term coined by the Italian art critic Germano Celant (1940–) to describe a type of work, related to *Conceptual and *Minimal art, in which the materials used—such as soil, twigs, and newspaper—are deliberately chosen for their 'worthlessness'. The term has been used in a bewilderingly diffuse way. It has been applied to *happenings, *installations, and *Land art, for example, and to the work of many non-Italian artists, including Carl *Andre, Joseph *Beuys, Walter *De Maria, Richard *Long, and Robert *Morris. Celant organized several exhibitions on the theme, and in 1969 edited a book entitled *Arte Povera* (it was translated into English the same year as *Art Povera: Conceptual, Actual or Impossible Art?*). He hoped that the use of meagre materials and the avoidance of the traditional idea of art as a collectable 'product' would undermine the art world's commercialism. However, dealers have shown that even this kind of art can be commercially exploited.

Arthois, Jacques d' (1613–86). Flemish landscape painter, active in Brussels. He specialized in wooded landscapes, with figures that were often added by other artists, notably *Teniers the Younger. Few dated works exist, the development of his style is not easily followed, and the work of his brother, **Nicolas** (b. 1617), and his son, **Jean-Baptiste** (b. 1638), is sometimes indistinguishable from his. D'Arthois was the outstanding landscape painter of his time in Brussels and earned a good living from his work, but he led an extravagant life (he was briefly imprisoned for debt in 1658) and died in poverty. Paintings from his busy studio were often used to decorate churches; examples are in Brussels Cathedral.

Art Informel. Term coined by the French critic Michel Tapié to describe a type of spontaneous abstract painting popular among European artists in the 1940s and 1950s, roughly equivalent to *Abstract Expressionism in the USA. Tapié popularized the term in his book *Un art autre* (1952), and these two terms—*Art Autre and Art Informel—are sometimes used more or less synonymously. They are rarely used with any precision, but some critics regard Art Informel as a narrower term, representing only one aspect of the broader trend of Art Autre (which includes figurative as well as abstract work). In English the term 'Informalism' is sometimes used as an equivalent to Art Informel, but the word 'informel' (which Tapié himself devised) might be translated as 'without form' rather than 'informal'. *See also* TACHISME.

Art Nouveau. Decorative style flourishing in most of western Europe and in the USA from about 1890 to the First World War. As the name suggests, it was a deliberate attempt to create a new style in reaction against the imitation of historical forms that had been such a prominent feature of 19th-century architecture and design. Its most characteristic theme was the use of sinuous asymmetrical lines based on plant forms: flower, leaf, and tendril motifs are common features, as are female figures with abundant flowing hair. At their most typical these motifs are found in the decorative and applied arts, such as interior design, metalwork, glassware, and jewellery, but Art Nouveau also had a major vogue in illustration and poster design and its influence can be seen to varying degrees in much of the painting and sculpture of the period—in a fairly pure form in the work of Alfred *Gilbert and Jan *Toorop, for example, and in certain aspects of such diverse artists as Munch (his penchant for undulating lines) and Matisse (the flat arabesque forms of the trees in some of the landscapes of his *Fauve period).

The style takes its name from a shop called La Maison de l'Art Nouveau opened in Paris in 1895 by the German-born art dealer Siegfried Bing (1838–1905), a leading propagandist for modern design. Paris was one of its most important centres, but its origins were diverse (Celtic and Japanese art have been cited as influences) and its roots were less on the Continent than in England, where the *Arts and Crafts movement had established a tradition of vitality in the applied arts. In France, indeed, Art Nouveau is sometimes known by the name 'Modern Style', reflecting these English origins. In Germany the style was called Jugendstil (from the Munich journal *Die Jugend*, founded in 1896); in Austria, Sezessionstil (after the Vienna *Sezession); in Spain, Modernista; and in Italy, Stile Liberty (after the London store that played so large a part in disseminating its designs). The style was truly international, its archetypal exponents ranging from *Mucha, a Czech whose most characteristic work was done in Paris, to *Tiffany in New York, and to the Spanish architect Antoní Gaudí

(1852–1926) in Barcelona, the centre of a distinctive regional version of the style characterized by exaggerated bulbous forms. This cosmopolitanism was encouraged by the great international exhibitions that flourished during this period, and the style perhaps reached its apogee at the Paris 'Exposition Universelle' of 1900. It nowhere survived the outbreak of the First World War to any extent, but with its stress on the expressive qualities of form, line, and colour, it played a significant part in shaping modern aesthetic attitudes.

Arts and Crafts movement. A social and aesthetic movement of the late 19th and early 20th centuries that championed good design and craftsmanship at a time of increasing mechanization and mass production. The movement, which was concerned mainly with architecture and the decorative arts, originated in Britain and chiefly flourished there, but it also had a significant impact in several Continental countries and in the USA. It was a very broad, loosely structured movement, embracing numerous strands of thought and practice: for the most serious-minded adherents, it involved fundamental issues about human society, but for others it was little more than a decorative fad. There was no particular style associated with the movement (influences came from many different sources), but there was an emphasis on 'honesty'—on producing products that showed clearly what they were made of and how they worked. This advocacy of simplicity and integrity often involved emphasizing plain materials and surfaces—an approach that has had a lasting influence on modern design.

The movement's name derives from the Arts and Crafts Exhibition Society, founded in 1888, but its origins go back to the 1850s, particularly to the ideas of John *Ruskin, who was the most eloquent and influential of the writers who deplored the aesthetic as well as the social effects of industrialization. He hated the type of highly decorated, machine-made products that dominated the Great Exhibition (1851) and believed that the beauty of medieval art sprang from pride in individual craftsmanship. His ideas greatly influenced William *Morris, who wrote that art was 'man's expression of his joy in labour' and believed that good

design could help create a better society. Through the decorative arts firm he established in 1861, Morris set about the re-creation of hand industry in a machine age, producing textiles, printed books, wallpaper, furniture, and so forth. Aesthetically his work was a triumph, and his firm was a commercial success, but his ideal of producing art for the masses failed for the simple reason that only rich people could afford his products. Nevertheless, his ideas had great influence on craftsmen, teachers, and propagandists, and in the 1880s various organizations were founded to promote Arts and Crafts ideas, including the Art Workers' Guild (1884), which aimed to increase understanding and collaboration between different branches of the visual arts. Walter *Crane was one of the leading figures of the Guild. The movement had passed its peak in Britain by the time of the First World War, but its ideas continued to be influential, for example on Eric *Gill. Outside Britain, the movement had a particularly strong impact in Austria, notably on the *Wiener Werkstätte.

Arts Council. An organization established in 1945 and incorporated by Royal Charter in 1946 'to preserve and improve standards of performance in the various arts'. It was a successor to the Council for the Encouragement of Music and the Arts (CEMA), a wartime organization that had operated from 1940 to 1945. Originally it was called the Arts Council of Great Britain, with separate committees for Scotland and Wales, but in 1994 the Scottish and Welsh Arts Councils became autonomous bodies and the main organization was renamed the Arts Council of England. There is also an Arts Council of Northern Ireland (likewise a successor to CEMA), and the Republic of Ireland has its own Arts Council, founded in 1951. In the visual arts, the main activity of the Arts Council consists of the organization of exhibitions, many of which are accompanied by scholarly catalogues. It has two galleries in London for such exhibitions: the Hayward Gallery, part of the South Bank arts complex alongside the Thames—a large, rather grim concrete building opened in 1968; and the much smaller and prettier Serpentine Gallery in Kensington Gardens, which was originally an Edwardian tea-house and was opened as a gallery in 1970.

Many exhibitions travel to other venues in Britain. The Arts Council inherited from CEMA the policy of purchasing works by living artists and it has built up a large collection of 20th-century British art; this, however, does not have a permanent home. It also makes grants directly to artists and galleries. It is the one of the most important sources of art patronage in Britain, but it is frequently attacked for alleged shortcomings, including too much bureaucracy and too little vision.

Art Students League of New York. An art school established in 1875 when that of the *National Academy of Design temporarily closed. Unlike the Academy School (which reopened in 1877), the Art Students League had no entrance requirements and no set course. Its more progressive methods soon attracted many students—by the turn of the century the enrolment stood at nearly a thousand and it was established as the most important art school in the country. The teachers have included *Benton, *Chase, *Eakins, *Henri, *Saint-Gaudens, and *Sloan; and the students have included many of the most illustrious figures in 20th-century American art.

Arundel, Thomas Howard, 2nd Earl of (1585–1646). English diplomat, collector, and patron. Apart from Charles I, he was the greatest English collector of his time. His knowledge of art was based partly on extensive travels in Europe, his most important journey being made with Inigo *Jones in 1613–14. His agents sought out antiquities from all over Europe and even the Levant. He also patronized living artists, notably *Rubens and van *Dyck (both of whom painted him), and he brought *Hollar to England in 1636. Among the Old Masters, he was particularly interested in *Holbein, whose *Christina, Duchess of Milan* (1538, NG, London) he owned. Arundel became bankrupt in 1639, leading to the break-up of his collections; they are now widely dispersed, but much of his classical sculpture is in the *Ashmolean Museum, Oxford.

Asam, Cosmas Damian (1686–1739) and **Egid Quirin** (1692–1750). German architects and decorators, brothers. They had their first training from their father, the painter **Hans Georg Asam** (1649–1711). After his death, Cosmas Damian spent three years studying in Rome (1711–14); it is generally assumed that Egid Quirin accompanied him, although there is no documentary evidence for this. Cosmas Damian was a fresco painter; Egid Quirin also painted, but he was primarily a sculptor and *stuccoist. Both brothers also worked as architects. They did much of their work as a team, specializing in the interior decoration of churches—uniting architecture, painting, and sculpture in a sumptuous display and developing the dramatic effects of light and illusionism pioneered by Italian *Baroque artists such as *Bernini and Andrea *Pozzo. The best known of their churches is that of St John Nepomuk, Munich (1733–46). The brothers themselves paid for the building (which was attached to Egid Quirin's house), and it is often referred to simply as the 'Asamkirche'. It is a small building but creates an overpowering feeling of religious fervour. Apart from their native Bavaria, they worked in other parts of Germany and also in Austria, Switzerland, Bohemia, and Silesia.

Ashcan School. A term (first used in print in 1934) applied to a loose group of American painters active in New York from about 1908 until the First World War, in reference to the everyday urban subject matter they favoured. The painters embraced by the term were inspired largely by Robert *Henri (one of whose dictums was that 'Art cannot be separated from life'), and the four central figures—*Glackens, *Luks, *Shinn, and *Sloan—had been members of The *Eight, a short-lived group founded by Henri in 1908. (The two terms are often confused, but 'The Eight' has a precise meaning, whereas 'Ashcan School' is a broader and vaguer notion; there is overlap between them, but some of the members of The Eight did not paint Ashcan-type subjects.) Before settling in New York, the four central Ashcan artists had all been artist-reporters on the *Philadelphia Press* and so had been used to making rapid sketches of scenes of everyday life. In style and technique, however, they are now seen to have differed less from contemporary academic painting than they themselves believed. Although they often painted slum life and outcasts, they were interested more in the picturesque aspects of these subjects than in the social issues they raised. *Bellows and

*Hopper are among the other artists associated with the group.

Ashmolean Museum, Oxford. The most important of the museums belonging to the University of Oxford. It is named after the antiquary Elias Ashmole (1617–92), who in 1675 offered his collection to the university as a gesture of 'filial respect'. The collection had been largely formed by John Tradescant the Elder (c.1570–1638) and his son John the Younger (1608–62), gardeners and travellers. They assembled a remarkable 'closet of rarities' (a collection of curiosities rather than works of art), which John the Younger gave to his friend Ashmole in 1659. Ashmole stipulated that a building should be erected to house the collection, and this was constructed in 1679–83, probably to the design of Thomas Wood, a local mason and sculptor. When it opened in 1683 it was the first public museum in Britain. Various other collections were accumulated by the university (some presented by former students like Ashmole) and a much larger museum was eventually created to house them. An impressive *Neoclassical building, designed by C. R. Cockerell, it opened in 1845, and at this time was known as the University Galleries. An extension was opened in 1894. The institution was renamed the Ashmolean Museum in 1899 and in 1908 was formally titled the Ashmolean Museum of Art and Archaeology; the original building is now known as the 'Old Ashmolean Building' and houses the Museum of the History of Science. Little of the Tradescant–Ashmole collection remains in the Ashmolean, having been distributed to other institutions (the famous stuffed dodo that was an inspiration to Lewis Carroll in *Alice in Wonderland* is now in the University Museum, opened in 1860, which is devoted to natural history). The Ashmolean has four departments—Western Art, Eastern Art, Antiquities, and Coins—and has great riches in all of them. Among the antiquities are marbles from the collection formed by Thomas *Arundel in the 17th century, and the Old Master drawings include a superlative representation of *Michelangelo and *Raphael from the collection of Sir Thomas *Lawrence.

Aspertini, Amico (c.1475–1552). Italian *Mannerist painter, sculptor, and draughtsman, the best-known member of a family of artists from Bologna. *Vasari describes him

as having an eccentric personality and this comes out in his paintings, which are often bizarre in expression: *The Holy Family with Saints* (St Nicolas aux Champs, Paris) is described by S. J. Freedberg (*Painting in Italy: 1500–1600*, 1971) as 'suggesting to the spectator the image of what he would expect from a demented Michelangelo'. Aspertini spent several years in Rome and two sketchbooks of Roman remains by him (BM, London) are important sources about contemporary knowledge of the *antique.

Asselyn, Jan (c.1615–52). Dutch painter, active mainly in Amsterdam. He spent several years in Italy in the late 1630s and early 1640s and came to specialize in real and imaginary scenes of the Roman Campagna, his glowing light effects owing much to *Claude. His most famous painting, however, is not a landscape, but *The Threatened Swan* (c.1650, Rijksmuseum, Amsterdam), an unusual work—showing a bird defending its nest against a dog—that is said to be an allegory of Dutch nationalism (inscriptions added by an unknown hand identify one of the swan's eggs as 'Holland' and the dog as 'the enemy of the state'). Because of a crippled hand Asselyn was nicknamed 'Crabbetje' (Little Crab). His friend *Rembrandt made an etched portrait of him (c.1647) in which he hid the deformed hand through the position of the arm.

assemblage. Term coined by Jean *Dubuffet in 1953 to describe a type of work made from fragments of natural or preformed materials, such as household debris. Some critics maintain that the term should apply only to three-dimensional found material and not to *collage, but it is not usually employed with precision and has been used to embrace *photomontage at one extreme and room *environments at the other. It gained wide currency with an exhibition called 'The Art of Assemblage' held at the Museum of Modern Art, New York, in 1961. The exhibits included *ready-mades by Marcel *Duchamp, boxed constructions by Joseph *Cornell, 'sacking' pictures by *Burri, compressed automobile bodies by *César, tableaux by *Kienholz, collages by a wide range of artists, sculptures by *Nevelson and *Tinguely, and much else besides.

Ast, Balthasar van der (c.1594–1657). Dutch still-life painter, the brother-in-law of Ambrosius *Bosschaert the Elder, with whom he trained in Middelburg. He worked in Utrecht (where he influenced the early work of Jan Davidsz. de *Heem) before settling in Delft in 1632. His touch was less exquisite than Bosschaert's, but his range was wider, his paintings often including fruit and shells as well as flowers.

atelier. French term for an artist's workshop or studio. The term *ateliers libres* was sometimes applied to the private *académies that became centres for avant-garde art in 19th-century Paris.

atlas (pl. atlantes). A sculpted male figure functioning as a column or other supporting feature in architecture, particularly popular in the *Baroque period. In Greek mythology, Atlas was the giant who held up the sky, and atlantes are often depicted so as to suggest the strain of carrying a huge weight on the shoulders. The female equivalent—the *caryatid—is, in contrast, usually shown standing serenely upright.

atmospheric perspective. An alternative term for *aerial perspective.

Audran, Claude III (1658–1734). The best-known member of a family of French painters and decorators. He was one of the leading decorative painters of the time, his output including such things as painted panelling and harpsichord cases, but most of his work has been destroyed or obscured by later additions. A great number of drawings survive, however (mainly in the Nationalmuseum, Stockholm), and these show him to have been a significant figure in the creation of the *Rococo style. In 1704 he was appointed curator at the Luxembourg Palace, Paris, where *Rubens's *Marie de Médicis* cycle was then housed, and he introduced his assistant *Watteau to this masterpiece by an artist who was to have an enormous influence on his work.

Audubon, John James (1785–1851). American painter-naturalist. Born at Haiti, the illegitimate son of a chambermaid and a French sea captain, he was brought up in France and received instruction in drawing from J.-L. *David. He moved to the USA in 1803 to avoid conscription in Napoleon's army and lived as a naturalist, hunter, and taxidermist, also earning some money as a portraitist and drawing master. His com-

bined interests in art and ornithology grew into a plan to make a complete pictorial record of all the bird species of North America. Unable to find a publisher in America, Audubon spent three years in England (1826–9) and found an engraver and publisher in the London firm of Robert Havell and Son. His *The Birds of America, from Original Drawings, with 435 Plates Showing 1,065 Figures* appeared in four volumes of hand-tinted aquatints (1827–38) and now ranks among the most famous and prized books of the world. It was followed by *The Viviparous Quadrupeds of America* (1845–8), which was completed by his son **John Woodhouse Audubon** (1812–62) after the master's sight failed in 1846. His other son, **Victor Gifford Audubon** (1809–60), also assisted his father. Many of Audubon's original drawings are in the New-York Historical Society. *See also* BEWICK.

Auerbach, Frank (1931–). German-born painter who moved to England in 1939 as a refugee from Nazism and became a British citizen in 1947. He studied under David *Bomberg, whom he found an inspiring teacher. His work (characteristically nudes and townscapes) is in the *Expressionist vein of Bomberg's late paintings and is remarkable for its use of extreme *impasto, so thick that the paint at times seems modelled rather than brushed. He has a reputation as one of the leading British painters of his time, although some critics find his pictures muddy and overworked.

Ault, George. *See* PRECISIONISM.

Auto-Destructive art. A term applied to works deliberately intended to self-destruct. Works of art that are inherently short-lived are not unique to the 20th century—witness the butter sculptures of Tibet, the sand paintings of some North American Indian tribes, and the snowman made by the young *Michelangelo for Piero de' *Medici. However, the idea of using self-destruction as the point of a work did not emerge until the late 1950s. The most committed exponent of the genre has been the German-born Gustav Metzger (1926–), who originated the term and wrote several manifestos on the subject, the first in 1959, when he was living in England. From 1960 he gave public demonstrations in which he 'painted' with acid, spraying it on nylon cloth, creating rapidly changing patterns until the nylon was destroyed. Such displays have been interpreted as expressions of fatalism at the impermanence of all things and as protests against consumerism. Metzger himself maintained that he was protesting against arms expenditure. He also believed that Auto-Destructive art could provide an acceptable channel for human aggression. Among those said to have been influenced by his ideas is the rock musician Pete Townshend, whose stage act with his group the Who used to include smashing guitars. Apart from Metzger, the artist most associated with Auto-Destructive art is Jean *Tinguely, whose approach was very different, stressing fancifulness and humour.

automatism. Method of producing paintings or drawings (or writing or other work) in which the artist suppresses conscious control over the movements of the hand, allowing the unconscious mind to take over. There are various precedents for this kind of work, most notably the 'blot drawings' of Alexander *Cozens, who stimulated his imagination by using accidental blots on the paper to suggest landscape forms. Cozens remarks that *Leonardo da Vinci had proposed a similar method and quotes him as saying: 'If you look upon an old wall covered with dirt, or the odd appearance of some streaked stones, you may discover several things like landscapes, battles, clouds, uncommon attitudes, humorous faces, draperies, &c. Out of this confused mass of objects, the mind will be furnished with abundance of designs and subjects perfectly new.' Slightly before Leonardo, Leon Battista *Alberti (in his treatise *De statua*, c.1460) gives an imaginative account of the origins of sculpture, describing ancient peoples observing 'in tree trunks, clumps of earth, or other objects of this sort, certain outlines which through some slight changes could be made to resemble a natural shape'. Alberti's version of events may be not far from the truth, for scholars of prehistoric art have found examples of such spontaneous discovery of representational images in chance natural formations of cave walls. However, automatism in its fully developed form did not appear until the 20th century. The *Dadaists made some use of the idea, but they were more interested in chance effects than in automa-

tism as such, and it was the *Surrealists who first made automatism an important part of their creative outlook; whereas the Dadaists used the idea dispassionately, to the Surrealists exploration of the unconscious through such methods was deeply personal. They devised various means to facilitate automatism (*see* FROTTAGE, for example) and some of them regarded the use of dream imagery (as in the work of *Dalí) as a kind of psychological—as opposed to mechanical—automatism. The Surrealist interest in automatism had a strong influence on the *Abstract Expressionists, some of whom took their ideas further. With Surrealists, once an image had been formed by automatic or chance means, it was often exploited deliberately with fully conscious purpose, but with *Action Painters such as Jackson *Pollock, automatism in principal permeated the whole creative process.

Other types of automatism are those in which the artist works under the influence of drugs or by alleged occult means. The offbeat British painter Austin Spare (1886–1956) claimed to be able to conjure up horrific survivals of man's pre-human ancestry from deep within his mind, but more usually the artist is said to work under the inspiration of a beneficent spirit guide (a notion not necessarily to be taken lightly, as no less an artist than William *Blake claimed to have direct inspiration from his dead brother). Unlike Blake, most psychic artists of this kind have no particular artistic gifts or inclinations in their 'normal' life.

Automatistes, Les. A radical group of seven Canadian abstract painters active in Montreal from 1946 to 1951. The oldest of them, mainly responsible for the formation of the group, was Paul-Émile *Borduas, and the other outstanding member was Jean-Paul *Riopelle. Members of the group were influenced by the *Surrealists, from whom they took over their techniques of *automatism. Their initial show, in 1946, was the first exhibition by a group of abstract painters to be held in Canada. In 1948 they caused outrage by publishing *Refus global* ('Total Refusal'), an anarchistic manifesto attacking various aspects of Canadian life and culture, including the Church.

avant-garde. A term originally used to describe the foremost part of an army advancing into battle (also called the vanguard) and now applied to any group, particularly of artists, that considers itself innovative and ahead of the majority; as an adjective, the word is applied to work characteristic of such groups. In its original sense the term is first recorded in English in the late 15th century (in Malory's *Morte d'Arthur*). During the 19th century, it was associated particularly with radical political thought, but from the early 20th century it was used more neutrally to denote cultural innovators of any persuasion; the earliest quotation in the *Oxford English Dictionary* to illustrate this sense ('the pioneers or innovators in any art in a particular period') dates from 1910.

Avanzo. *See* ALTICHIERO.

Avercamp, Hendrick (1585–1634). Dutch painter and draughtsman, active in Kampen, the most famous exponent of the winter landscape, which he established as a distinct category in Dutch art. He was deaf and dumb and known as 'de Stomme van Kampen' (the mute of Kampen). His paintings are colourful and lively, with carefully observed skaters, tobogganers, golfers, and pedestrians. Such works enjoyed great popularity and Avercamp also sold his drawings, many of which are tinted with watercolour, as finished pictures (an outstanding collection is at Windsor Castle). His nephew and pupil **Barent Avercamp** (1612–79) carried on his style in an accomplished manner.

Avery, Milton (1885–1965). American painter, active mainly in New York. Avery was an independent figure: at a time when most of his leading contemporaries were working in fairly sober, naturalistic styles (*see* AMERICAN SCENE PAINTING), he followed the example of *Matisse in using flat areas of colour within flowing outlines. He was the main and practically only channel through which this subtle colouristic tradition was sustained in America until a new interest was taken in it during the 1940s by younger artists such as *Rothko (his close friend) and *Gottlieb. Rothko in particular acknowledged the debt that he and other abstract painters owed to the 'sheer loveliness' of Avery's work, in which he had 'invented sonorities never seen nor heard before'. Although Avery himself never abandoned representation (his favourite subjects included landscapes and beach scenes), some of his later works are so broadly conceived and ethereally painted that they can at first glance be mistaken for abstracts (*Spring Orchard*, 1959, Nat. Mus. of American Art, Washington).

Avignon, School of. Tradition of painting associated with the city of Avignon in southern France, originating during the period when the papal court was transferred there because of anarchic conditions in Rome (1309–77). The presence of this great source of patronage drew many artists to the city, including illustrious Italian masters, among them Simone *Martini and possibly *Giotto. The centre of artistic activities was the Palace of the Popes, begun in the 1330s, which has several frescos dating from around 1350. After the departure of the popes, Avignon became the centre of a school of painting that amalgamated Italian with Netherlandish influences, notably in the work of Enguerrand *Quarton and Nicolas *Froment. The famous *Avignon Pietà* (*c.*1460, Louvre, Paris), is now generally attributed to Quarton, but many works that were at one time attributed to the School of Avignon have since been reassigned and it is no longer a clearly defined stylistic entity.

Aycock, Alice. *See* LAND ART.

Ayrton, Michael (1921–75). British painter, sculptor, stage designer, book illustrator, writer on art, and broadcaster. His career was often marred by ill health, but he travelled widely and had a long and varied list of works to his credit. He was an erudite, inventive, and highly individual artist, much of whose work revolved around his obsession with the myth of Daedalus and Icarus, which he treated as analogous to his own artistic endeavours. The most extreme expression of his obsession is the enormous maze of brick and stone (1968) he built for an American millionaire at Arkville in New York State, imitating the labyrinth Daedalus built for King Minos of Crete at Knossos. He wrote several books, including *The Testament of Daedalus* (1962), and illustrated many others. From 1944 to 1946 he was art critic of the *Spectator* (succeeding John *Piper), in which position he was a leading spokesman for *Neo-Romanticism, and at about the same time he became a regular radio broadcaster on art (he also appeared often in the BBC's *Round Britain Quiz*).

B

Baburen, Dirck van (*c*.1595?–1624). Dutch figure painter, mainly of religious scenes. After training in Utrecht with *Moreelse, he went (*c*.1612) to Rome, where his style became strongly influenced by *Caravaggio. He returned to the Netherlands in about 1621 and although he died only a few years after this, he played a leading role, with *Honthorst and *Terbrugghen, in establishing Utrecht as a stronghold of the Caravaggesque style. His best-known work is *The Procuress* (1622, MFA, Boston). This picture is seen in the background of two paintings by *Vermeer, whose mother-in-law evidently owned it.

Baciccio, Il. *See* GAULLI.

Backer, Jacob (1608–51). Dutch portrait and history painter, active mainly in Amsterdam, where he had a prosperous career. The tradition (stemming from *Houbraken) that he was a pupil of *Rembrandt is now doubted, but his work was certainly strongly influenced by him; indeed, attributions have sometimes been disputed between them (*see* BOL). His best-known painting is the beautiful *Portrait of a Boy in Grey* (1634, Mauritshuis, The Hague). His nephew, **Adriaen Backer** (1630/2–84), also had a successful career as a portraitist in Amsterdam.

Bacon, Francis (1909–92). British painter, born in Dublin of English parents. He left home in 1925 at the age of 16 and moved to London, where he worked for a time as an interior decorator. In the late 1920s he lived in Berlin and then Paris (where he was powerfully affected by an exhibition of *Picasso's work), then returned to London in 1929. He had no formal training as a painter. In the 1930s he began exhibiting in London commercial galleries, but he destroyed much of his early work and dropped out of sight until 1945, when his *Three Studies for Figures at the Base of a Crucifixion* (Tate, London), painted in the previous year, was exhibited at the Lefevre Gallery, London, and made him overnight the most controversial painter in the country. John Russell (*Francis Bacon*, 1971) writes that visitors to the exhibition were shocked by 'images so unrelievedly awful that the mind shut snap at the sight of them. Their anatomy was half-human, half-animal, and they were confined in a low-ceilinged, windowless and oddly proportioned space. They could bite, probe, and suck, and they had very long eel-like necks, but their functioning in other respects was mysterious. Ears and mouths they had, but two at least were sightless. One was unpleasantly bandaged.' Bacon's imagery later became more naturalistic, but at same time the emotional impact of his work was increased by a change in technique, as he moved away from fairly impersonal brushwork to develop a highly distinctive handling of paint, by means of which he smudged and twisted faces and bodies into ill-defined jumbled protuberances suggestive of formless, slug-like creatures from some nightmare fantasy: 'I would like my pictures to look as if a human being had passed between them, like a snail, leaving a trail of the human presence and memory trace of past events as the snail leaves its slime.' Characteristically his paintings show single figures in isolation or despair, set in a bleak, sometimes cage-like space, and at times accompanied by hunks of raw meat: 'we are all meat, we are potential carcasses'. Often his work was based on his own everyday world (he did numerous self-portraits), but he also used imagery from photographs and film-stills as a starting point. In particular he based a series of paintings (begun in 1951) on *Velázquez's celebrated portrait of Pope Innocent X, but in place of the implacable expression of the original, he sometimes gave the pope a screaming face derived from a still from Sergei Eisenstein's film *The Battleship Potemkin*.

Bacon's work was so novel and unsettling that for many years 'Critics and public vacillated uneasily between the opinions that he was a flashy sensationalist and that he was the most significant painter whom Britain had produced for several generations' (John *Rothenstein, *Francis Bacon*, 1967). In 1962, however, a retrospective exhibition of 90 of his paintings was held at the Tate Gallery, London, subsequently touring to several venues on the Continent, and this event firmly established him as a major figure. Thereafter his international reputation grew rapidly, and in the catalogue of a second major retrospective exhibition at the Tate, in 1985, the director of the Gallery, Alan Bowness, wrote that Bacon was 'surely the greatest living painter; no artist in our century has presented the human predicament with such insight and feeling'. Many critics at the time concurred in this judgement, although others found his despairing vision—his view of life as a 'game without reason'—hard to take. Alongside his reputation as a painter he built up a sulphurous personal legend on account of his promiscuous homosexuality, hard drinking, and heavy gambling.

Bacon, John the Elder (1740–99). English sculptor. His style was essentially *Neoclassical, but he had none of the intellectual interest in the *antique that characterized contemporaries such as *Banks and *Flaxman (unlike them, Bacon never visited Italy). He began his career as a modeller in a porcelain factory and this experience left a permanent mark on him, as his work, even in marble, tends to be soft in feeling, often with much pretty detail. His prolific output consisted mainly of church monuments, but also included numerous statues and portrait busts. In addition he worked as chief designer to the *Coade artificial stone company from 1771. His career was helped by the favouritism of George III, of whom he produced a portrait in 1774 (Windsor Castle and other versions), and one of his most conspicuous works is *George III and the River Thames* (1780–6) in the courtyard of Somerset House, London (this is unusual in being in bronze at a time when English sculptors favoured marble almost exclusively for monumental work). The king helped him to gain the commission for his largest work, the monument to William Pitt, Earl of Chatham (1779–83), in Westminster Abbey. His finest work is the much smaller and more intimate monument to Thomas Guy (1779) in Guy's Hospital, showing the founder of the hospital succouring a sick man. Bacon ran a large workshop, whose efficiency was aided by an improved *pointing machine he devised. The practice was carried on by his son **John the Younger** (1777–1859).

Bacon, Sir Nathaniel (1585–1627). The first English amateur painter of note, a high-born country gentleman, nephew of the Lord Chancellor Francis Bacon. Fewer than a dozen paintings by him are known; with the exception of a miniature landscape on copper in the manner of *Bril, which has been claimed as the earliest British landscape (Ashmolean Mus., Oxford), they are either portraits (mainly of members of his family) or kitchen still lifes (*Cookmaid with Still Life of Vegetables and Fruit*, c.1625, Tate, London). His ambitious full-length self-portrait (Gorhambury, Hertfordshire, c.1620), displays a more coherent realization of space, greater subtlety of colouring, and sharper characterization than had hitherto been achieved in English portraiture and shows he was the equal of *Mytens or Cornelius *Johnson, the most renowned portraitists in England before the arrival of van *Dyck.

Badile, Antonio. *See* VERONESE.

'Bad Painting'. *See* NEO-EXPRESSIONISM.

Baglione, Giovanni (c.1566–1643). Italian painter and writer, born and mainly active in Rome. He is of little account as a painter and is remembered mainly as the author of *Le vite de' pittori, scultori, ed architetti . . .*, published in 1642. This collection of biographies is one of the fundamental sources of information for the period covered (1572–1642); it deals mainly with Italian artists but also discusses foreigners working in Rome, such as *Bril and *Rubens. In 1603 Baglione sued *Caravaggio and three other painters for circulating coarse satirical poems about him. His hatred of Caravaggio comes out in the biography devoted to him in his *Vite*, so it is ironic that his best pictures are his most Caravaggesque.

Baily, Edward Hodges (1788–1867). English sculptor, born in Bristol, the son of a carver of ships' figureheads. He studied with *Flaxman, becoming his favourite pupil, and at the *Royal Academy. His output included a good deal of public sculpture; his two most conspicuous works are also his most inaccessible—the statues at the top of Nelson's Column in Trafalgar Square (1843) and the almost equally tall Grey's Monument in Newcastle upon Tyne (1837). He also produced numerous portrait busts, including many of fellow artists (examples are in the NPG, London), as well as church monuments and ideal figures, notably *Eve at the Fountain* (1822, City AG, Bristol), which was one of the most acclaimed British sculptures of the 19th century. Although he had a busy and successful career, he was extravagant and died bankrupt.

Bakhuizen, Ludolf (1631–1708). Dutch painter, mainly of marine subjects, active in Amsterdam. After the van de *Veldes moved to England in 1672/3, Bakhuizen became the most successful marine painter in Holland, his clients including distinguished collectors from other countries, notably Peter the Great of Russia, who visited his studio. He captured the drama and movement of ships, but seldom achieved the poetic effects of either van de Velde the Younger or Jan van de *Cappelle. His grandson, **Ludolf Bakhuizen the Younger** (1717–82), imitated his work.

Bakst, Léon (1866–1924). Russian painter, graphic artist, and stage designer, active for much of his career in Paris. He was a founder member of the *World of Art group in 1898. Originally he made his reputation as a portraitist, but from about 1902 he turned increasingly to stage design and is now remembered above all for his costumes and sets for *Diaghilev's Ballets Russes, his work playing a major part in the tremendous impact the company made in the West. The Diaghilev ballets for which he made designs include some of the most celebrated works in the history of dance, notably *The Firebird* (1910, music by Stravinsky), *L'Après-Midi d'un faune* (1912, music by Debussy), and *Daphnis and Chloe* (1912, music by Ravel). Bakst's work revolutionized stage design. His costumes and sets are remarkable for their sheer uninhibited splendour, combining Oriental fairy-tale magnificence with the gaudy colours of Russian peasant art (he believed that colour could have a significant emotional effect on spectators).

baldachin (or **baldacchino**). A canopy over an altar or other hallowed object; it may be portable for use in processions or fixed (either supported on columns or suspended from the ceiling). The most famous baldacchino is *Bernini's huge bronze structure (1624–33) in St Peter's, Rome.

This type, with twisted columns and fringed canopy, became popular in *Baroque churches. *See also* CIBORIUM.

Baldinucci, Filippo (1625–96). Florentine writer, collector, and amateur artist. His *Notizie de' professori del disegno* (6 vols., 1681–1728) contains lives of artists from *Cimabue to his own time and is particularly valuable for the information it gives about 16th-century Florentine artists and Baldinucci's contemporaries. He was an innovator as an art historian in making use of every kind of document. Apart from the *Notizie*, his most important work is his biography of *Bernini (1682), the primary source for the artist's life. He also wrote a history of engraving (1686), which contains one of the earliest accounts of *Rembrandt's life.

Baldovinetti, Alesso (1425–99). Florentine painter, mosaicist, and worker in stained glass. Nothing is recorded of his training, but his graceful and refined style shows strong influence from *Domenico Veneziano, who may well have been his master. Baldovinetti's finest works include a damaged but still enchanting fresco of the *Nativity* (1460–2) in the forecourt of SS. Annunziata, Florence; a *Madonna and Child* (c.1460) in the Louvre, Paris; an *Annunciation* (c.1460) in the Uffizi, Florence; and *Portrait of a Lady in Yellow* (c.1465) in the National Gallery, London. They show his remarkable sensitivity to light and landscape and his engaging blend of naivety and sophistication. In his *History of Italian Renaissance Art* (1970), Frederick Hartt writes that Baldovinetti was 'the finest painter in Florence' in the 1460s, and considers him 'a very gifted master who somehow never quite seemed to fulfil his great initial promise'.

Baldung (or **Baldung Grien**), **Hans** (1484/5–1545). German painter, printmaker, and designer. The nickname 'Grien' (green) perhaps referred to his liking for the colour. He probably trained with *Dürer in Nuremberg, but his brilliant colour, expressive use of distortion, and taste for the gruesome (he was fascinated by witchcraft) bring him closer in spirit to his other great German contemporary, *Grünewald. His output was varied and extensive, including religious works, allegories and mythologies, portraits, designs for stained glass and tapestries, and a large body of graphic work, particularly book illustrations. He was active mainly in Strasbourg, but from 1512 to 1517 he lived in Freiburg-im-Breisgau, where he worked on his masterpiece, the high altar for Freiburg Cathedral (unusually for an artist of the time, he came from a scholarly family and his brother was a professor at Freiburg University). The centre panel of the altarpiece (which is still in situ) is a radiant *Coronation of the Virgin*. Baldung's most characteristic paintings, however, are in a different vein—erotic allegories such as *Death and the Maiden*, a subject he treated several times. Eroticism is also often strongly present in his prints (mainly woodcuts), the best known of which is *The Bewitched Stable Boy* (1544), which has been interpreted as an allegory of lust.

Balen, Hendrick van (*c*.1575–1632). Flemish *Mannerist painter, active mainly in his native Antwerp (he spent virtually all his life there apart from a sojourn in Italy in the 1590s). His speciality was mythological scenes painted in the highly finished manner of Jan *Brueghel, one of the numerous artists with whom he collaborated. Van Balen was a popular teacher, his most important pupil being van *Dyck. He also had three painter sons.

Balestra, Antonio. *See* CIGNAROLI.

Balla, Giacomo (1871–1958). Italian painter and sculptor, active mainly in Rome, one of the leading *Futurist artists. From a visit to Paris in 1900–1 Balla brought back to Italy a feeling for *divisionism and for colour and light that he passed on to *Boccioni and *Severini. His early works included landscapes and portraits, but after the turn of the century he became increasingly interested in portraying aspects of modern industrialized life. In 1910 he joined the Futurists and soon became preoccupied with their characteristic aim of portraying movement. Unlike the other Futurists, however, Balla was not interested in machines and violence and his paintings tend towards the lyrical and the witty, as in the delightful *Dynamism of a Dog on a Leash* (1912, Albright-Knox AG, Buffalo), in which the multiple impressions of the dog's legs and tail convey movement in a manner that later became a cartoon convention. In 1913–16 he went beyond the principles of the Futurist manifestos, painting pictures that approach pure abstraction, showing only the most residual

resemblance to the observations in reality that inspired them (*Abstract Speed—the Car Has Passed*, 1913, Tate, London). Following the First World War, Balla stayed true to the ideals of Futurism after his colleagues had abandoned them, but in the 1930s he turned to a more conventional style. By the end of his long life he was much admired as the last survivor of a brilliant phase of modern Italian art.

Balthus (Balthazar Klossowski de Rola) (1908–2001). French painter (and occasional stage designer), born in Paris of cultured Polish parents, both of whom painted. He had no formal training but was encouraged by the family friends *Derain (of whom Balthus painted a memorable portrait (1936, MoMA, New York)) and *Bonnard. His work was dominated by erotic imagery, his favourite theme being the adolescent girl awakening to sexual consciousness; characteristically these girls are shown languidly sprawled or kneeling awkwardly over books in claustrophobic interiors that have a suggestion of *Surrealist oddness (*The Living Room*, 1941–3, Minneapolis Inst. of Arts). From 1961 to 1977 he was director of the French Academy in Rome, but otherwise he spent most of his life living in seclusion in France or Switzerland. He worked slowly and his output was small, but his highly distinctive images made him internationally famous, indeed something of a cult figure. His work was generally warmly received by critics as well as the public (although some have accused him of having a Lolita complex) and he is widely regarded as one of the 20th century's leading upholders of the great tradition of figure painting.

bambocciate. *See* LAER.

Bandinelli, Baccio (1493–1560). Florentine sculptor, painter, and draughtsman. He was a favourite of the *Medici family, but he is remembered more for his belligerent character and the antipathy of his contemporaries than for the quality of his work. His most famous and conspicuous sculpture is *Hercules and Cacus* (1527–34, Piazza della Signoria, Florence), a pendant to *Michelangelo's *David*. The commission had originally been intended for Michelangelo himself, and Bandinelli's ponderous figure, which he had boasted would surpass *David*, was ridiculed by *Cellini and others. Bandinelli had a habit of failing to fulfil his commissions and Cellini's accusations of incompetence had much justification. In return, Bandinelli attempted to sabotage Cellini's career, as he also did with another rival, *Ammanati. Bandinelli was at his best as a draughtsman. His paintings include a pompous self-portrait in the Isabella Stewart Gardner Museum, Boston.

Banks, Thomas (1735–1805). English sculptor. He was one of the most serious-minded of British *Neoclassical artists, aiming at noble treatment of elevated subjects. Like-minded contemporaries greatly admired him (*Reynolds called him 'the first British sculptor who has produced works of classic grace' and *Flaxman ranked him alongside *Canova), but he had limited opportunities to produce works in the *antique vein, and he was less successful in worldly terms than his contemporaries John *Bacon and Joseph *Nollekens, who were more in tune with the demands of the market. Banks trained as a mason and ornamental carver, and also studied in the evenings in Peter *Scheemakers's studio. In 1772 he was awarded a *Royal Academy scholarship to Rome, where he remained until 1779. During this period he met *Fuseli, who became a life-long friend. Back in England, he had little initial success, and in 1781–2 he visited Russia, hoping for major commissions from Catherine the Great. However, his stay was brief, partly because he disliked the climate. After his return to England, he at last began to prosper, but mainly with church monuments, rather than with classical subjects such as *Thetis Dipping the Infant Achilles in the River Styx* (c.1788, V&A, London); he also produced a few portrait busts. His most famous work is the monument to Penelope Boothby (1793, Ashbourne church, Derbyshire), in which the 6-year-old child is shown sleeping rather than dead; several people, including Queen Charlotte, are said to have been moved to tears when it was shown at the Royal Academy before installation. His larger monuments, however, tend to be somewhat ponderous.

Barbari, Jacopo de' (active c.1497, d. 1516?). Venetian painter and printmaker. His early career is obscure and he is first documented in 1500 in connection with his huge (nearly 3 m (10 ft) wide) woodcut view of Venice, which had taken three years to complete. Most of his known career was spent in Germany and the Netherlands, where he worked for several royal patrons. His delicate engravings, many of mythological figures, helped to spread the Italian conception of the nude in northern Europe. As a painter he is best known for his *Dead Bird* (1504, Alte Pin., Munich), an early example of an independent still life.

Barberini. Italian family who achieved prominence with the election of **Maffeo** (1568–1644) as Pope Urban VIII in 1623 and ranked among the chief art patrons in 17th-century Rome. Urban's favourite artist was *Bernini, from whom he commissioned two great works in St Peter's—the statue of St Longinus and the *baldacchino over the High Altar. Some of the enormous quantity of bronze required for the baldacchino was taken from ancient metal stripped from the Pantheon, giving rise to the adage 'Quod non fecerunt barbari, fecerunt Barberini' (What the barbarians failed to do, the Barberini did). Urban used most of the metal to cast cannon for the Castel Sant' Angelo, saying it was more important to defend the pope than to keep rain out of the Pantheon. Apart from Urban, the most important member of the family was his nephew Cardinal **Francesco Barberini** (1597–1679), who was *Poussin's first important patron in Rome. The Barberini also employed Pietro da *Cortona, *Romanelli, Andrea *Sacchi, and others in the decoration of the family palace and of St Peter's. The Palazzo Barberini, in the design of which Bernini and two other outstanding contemporary architects—Carlo Maderno and Francesco Borromini—all played parts, now houses part of the Galleria Nazionale.

Barberini Faun (*Sleeping Satyr*). *Hellenistic marble statue of a satyr sprawled in drunken sleep (Glyptothek, Munich). It is first recorded in the possession of Cardinal Franceso *Barberini in 1628, and during the 17th and particularly the 18th century it was generally regarded as one of the greatest works of antiquity. The figure is still admired (unlike most of the formerly celebrated antique statues) and is considered by some authorities to be an original work of around 200 BC, although others believe it to be merely a good copy. It has been several times restored, sometimes with substantial changes to its posture.

Barbizon School. An informal group of French landscape painters, active from the 1830s to about 1870, who took their name from a small village on the outskirts of the Forest of Fontainebleau, where they worked and where some of them eventually settled. The central figure of the group was Théodore *Rousseau; the other members included Charles-François *Daubigny, Narcisse *Diaz de la Peña, Jules Dupré (1811–89), and Constant *Troyon. They were united in their opposition to the conventions of the classical tradition stemming from *Claude and *Poussin and by their interest in landscape painting for its own sake, a fairly new development in French art. Their inspiration came partly from England, particularly *Constable, and partly from the 17th-century Dutch painters whom Constable so admired. They advocated painting direct from nature, but unlike the *Impressionists, they usually painted only studies in the open air; their finished pictures were almost always done in the studio. *Corot, who was one of the first artists to work in the forest, is often associated with the group, but his work has a poetic and literary quality that sets him somewhat apart. *Millet is also often linked with the School, as he settled in Barbizon in 1849 and during his last period painted pure landscapes. Most of the Barbizon painters initially struggled for recognition, but they generally achieved success during the 1850s. The peak of their popularity came (posthumously for most of them) in the 1880s and 1890s.

Bargello. Museum in Florence housing an unrivalled collection of Italian *Renaissance sculpture. It is located in one of the city's best-preserved medieval buildings, the Palazzo del Podestà, begun in 1255; initially it was the residence of the chief magistrate of the city and then of the head of government (*podestà*). In 1574 it was converted into a prison and assigned to the head of the police (*bargello*), and in 1857–65 it was restored and remodelled as a museum. The collection contains works by virtually all the leading Italian Renaissance sculptors (including the celebrated bronze statues of David by *Donatello and *Verrocchio) and also has an extensive collection of applied arts, including armour, enamels, medals, and tapestries.

Barker, Thomas (1769–1847). British painter and lithographer, mainly of landscapes and *genre scenes. He was born in Pontypool but is known as 'Barker of Bath' from his main place of work. His work was strongly influenced by the landscapes and *fancy pictures of *Gainsborough (the most famous artist to work in Bath), and he made his name mainly as a painter of rustic scenes. He was successful for most of his career, but his popularity declined and he died in poverty. His brother **Benjamin Barker** (1776–1838) and his son **Thomas Jones Barker** (1815–82) were also painters, mainly of landscapes and military scenes respectively.

Barlach, Ernst (1870–1938). German sculptor, printmaker, and writer, a major figure of *Expressionism. Until he reached his thirties Barlach was as much a ceramicist as a sculptor, working in a fairly derivative *Art Nouveau style, but a turning point in his career came in 1906, when he visited Russia. The vast empty landscape and the sturdy Russian peasants made a great impact on him; these hardworking people, with their simple faith, symbolized for him 'the human condition in its nakedness between Heaven and Earth' and helped inspire him to create a massively powerful figure style. He was influenced also by medieval German carving, with which he recognized both a spiritual and a technical affinity — he preferred to carve in heavy, close-grained woods, but even when his figures were modelled in clay and cast in bronze they retain the broad planes and sharp edges typical of woodcarving. In 1910 Barlach settled at Güstrow, a small town near Rostock, where he spent the rest of his life. By this time he had created his mature style, which changed little thereafter. His most characteristic works are massive, block-like, heavily robed single figures or pairs of figures symbolizing some aspect of the human condition (*The Solitary One*, 1911 Kunsthalle, Hamburg). He also produced several monuments commemorating the First World War and he was a prolific maker of lithographs and woodcuts, particularly of illustrations to his own plays, of which he published seven; they are sombre works, typically showing the individual wrestling with the ties of the material world in search of God, but they sometimes have a grotesque humour not seen in his sculpture.

After the First World War Barlach was much honoured, but when the Nazis came to power in 1933 he was declared a *degenerate artist and his war memorials at Güstrow, Kiel, and Magdeburg were dismantled. The memorial in Güstrow Cathedral was restored after the Second World War and a copy made for the Antoniterkirche in Cologne; it takes the form of a hovering bronze angel and is considered by many to be Barlach's most deeply spiritual work. His studio in Güstrow is now a museum of his work and there also museums dedicated to him in Hamburg and Ratzeburg.

Barlow, Francis (1626?–1704). English painter, etcher, and draughtsman, mainly of animal subjects, known as 'the father of British sporting painting'. He painted numerous large canvases for decorative schemes (examples are at Ham House in London and Clandon Park in Surrey) and was also a prolific book illustrator, his etchings for an edition of Aesop's *Fables* published in 1666 being particularly well known. His work is vividly observed, with an almost naive charm.

Barna da Siena (active *c*.1350). Sienese painter. The source material on him is vague and confusing, and although he has been described as the leading Sienese painter of his period, some scholars think that he is a fictitious character and prefer to assign the works attributed to him to other hands. In his *Commentarii*, *Ghiberti said that Barna worked in the Collegiata at S. Gimignano, and the fresco series on the Life of Christ there is the core around which attempts have been made to reconstruct his oeuvre (among the works that have been given to him is *Christ Carrying the Cross* in the Frick Collection, New York). As with Simone *Martini (traditionally Barna's master), drawing plays a dominant part in this oeuvre, but whereas Simone's line is a graceful arabesque, Barna's is direct and thrusting, his figures having a more dramatic vigour than any in previous Sienese painting. According to *Vasari, Barna died in a fall from scaffolding.

Barnard, George Grey. *See* METROPOLITAN MUSEUM OF ART.

Barnes, Dr Albert C. (1872–1951). American drug manufacturer and art collector. He made a fortune with the antiseptic Argyrol, which he created in 1901 (its success is said to have depended largely on its being adopted as the standard anti-venereal treatment of the French army), and by 1913 he was devoting his life to collecting. His greatest interest was in modern French painting, but he also bought Old Masters and primitive art. In 1922 he established the Barnes Foundation at Merion, Pennsylvania, to house his collection and to provide education in art appreciation, and in 1931 he commissioned *Matisse to paint a mural decoration for the building. When the mural turned out to be unusable because of an error in the measurements he had been given, Matisse did a new version; the abortive scheme, *The Dance I* (1931–2), is in the Musée d'Art Moderne de la Ville de Paris, and the second scheme, *The Dance II* (1932–3), is in situ in the Barnes Foundation. Barnes has been described as 'perhaps the greatest single American art collector of the twentieth century' (Joseph Alsop, *The Rare Art Traditions*, 1982), but he was a highly unattractive character: John *Rewald (who was among the distinguished art historians refused admission to the Foundation) refers to his 'dreadful, crude, and unspeakably stupid manners', and Kenneth *Clark wrote that 'His stories of how he had extracted Cézannes and Renoirs from penniless widows made one's blood run cold.' (His redeeming feature was his outspoken promotion of racial equality.) The museum Barnes created was closed to the public during his lifetime, but after his death legal moves were made to try to force the trustees to open it or lose its tax-exempt status. An agreement was reached in 1960 allowing restricted public entry, but it retained its reputation as a virtually inaccessible treasure house. In his will Barnes had stipulated that his pictures should remain exactly as he left them, but in 1991 a court ruled that this directive could be overruled to raise funds for the upkeep of the building, and in 1993–4 a selection of paintings went on tour to Paris, Tokyo, and several American cities.

Barocci (or **Baroccio**), **Federico** (1535?–1612). Italian painter and draughtsman, generally considered the greatest and most individual artist of his time in central Italy. Barocci was born in Urbino and apart from two visits to Rome early in his career (1556, 1560–3), he was based there all his life. During the second visit he is said to have abandoned his frescos in the Casino of

Pius IV in the Vatican gardens because he thought that rivals were trying to poison him, and for the rest of his life he suffered from debilitating stomach pains (possibly the result of ulcers rather than poison). Whether the cause of his illness was physical or psychosomatic, he certainly had an acutely sensitive temperament that comes out in his work, in which he combined the influence of *Correggio and *Raphael (also a native of Urbino) in a refined and highly personal manner. His colour harmonies are sharp but subtle, and although his paintings often convey a feeling of intimate tenderness, his handling has great vigour. Apart from a few portraits, such as that of his chief patron Francesco Maria II della *Rovere, Duke of Urbino (c.1572, Uffizi, Florence), he concentrated almost exclusively on religious subjects; he was the leading painter of altarpieces in Italy in the second half of the 16th century and he also produced numerous smaller devotional pictures (*Madonna and Child with St Joseph and the Infant Baptist*, c.1575, NG, London). Despite the fact that he worked away from the main centres of art, his work was widely sought after, his patrons including the emperor Rudolf II (*see* HABSBURG), for whom he painted his only known classical subject (*The Flight of Aeneas from Troy*, 1586–9, Borghese Gal., Rome). And although his illness limited the hours he could work, he had a long and productive career; he was especially prolific as a draughtsman (more than 2,000 sheets of drawings by him survive) and he was one of the first artists to make extensive use of *pastels (he also made a handful of etchings). Certain features of his work are thoroughly in the *Mannerist tradition (his rather indefinite treatment of space, for example, and his delight in fluttering draperies), but in his directness and freshness he looked forward to the *Baroque. *Bellori, the pre-eminent biographer of the Baroque age, considered him the finest Italian painter of his period and lamented that he had 'languished in Urbino'.

Baroque. A term used in the literature of the arts with both historical and critical meanings and as both an adjective and a noun. The term has a long, complex, and controversial history. Until the late 19th century it was used mainly as a synonym

for 'absurd' or 'grotesque' (it possibly derives from a Portuguese word for a misshapen pearl), but in English it is now current with three principal meanings. Primarily, it designates the dominant style of European art between *Mannerism and *Rococo. This style originated in Rome and is associated with the Catholic Counter-Reformation, its salient characteristics—fervent rhetoric and dynamic movement—being well suited to expressing the self-confidence and proselytizing spirit of the reinvigorated Catholic Church. It is by no means exclusively associated with religious art, however, and aspects of the Baroque can be seen even in works that have nothing to do with emotional display—for example in the dynamic lines of certain Dutch still-life paintings. Secondly, it is used as a general label for the period when this style flourished, broadly speaking, the 17th century and in certain areas much of the 18th century. Hence such phrases as 'the age of Baroque', 'Baroque politics', 'Baroque science', and so on. Thirdly, the term 'Baroque' (often written without the initial capital) is applied to art of any time or place that shows the qualities of vigorous movement and emotional intensity associated with Baroque art in its primary meaning. Much *Hellenistic sculpture could therefore be described as 'baroque'. The older meaning of the word, as a synonym for 'capricious', 'overwrought', or 'florid', still has some currency, but not in serious criticism.

*Caravaggio and Annibale *Carracci are the two great figures who stand at the head of the Baroque tradition, bringing a new solidity and weightiness to Italian painting, which in the late 16th century had generally been artificial and often convoluted in style. In doing so they looked back to some extent to the dignified and harmonious art of the High *Renaissance, but Annibale's work has an exuberance that is completely his own, and Caravaggio created figures with an unprecedented sense of sheer physical presence. From the Mannerist style the Baroque inherited movement and intense emotion, and from the Renaissance style solidity and grandeur, fusing the two influences into a new and dynamic whole. The supreme genius of Baroque art was Gianlorenzo *Bernini, an artist of boundless energy, total spiritual conviction, and the utmost virtuosity, whose work dominates the period sometimes called the 'High Baroque' (*c*.1625–75). Slightly later, Andrea *Pozzo marks the culmination in Italy of the Baroque tendency towards overwhelmingly grandiose display.

In the 17th century Rome was the artistic capital of Europe, and the Baroque style soon spread outwards from it, undergoing modification in each of the countries to which it migrated, as it encountered different tastes and outlooks and merged with local traditions. In some areas it became more extravagant (notably in the fervent religious atmosphere of Spain and Latin America) and in others it was toned down to suit more conservative tastes. In Catholic Flanders it had one of its finest flowerings in the work of *Rubens, but in neighbouring Holland, a predominantly Protestant country, the Baroque made comparatively slight inroads; nor did it ever take firm root in England. In France the Baroque found its greatest expression in the service of the monarchy rather than the Church. Louis XIV realized the importance of the arts as a propaganda medium in promoting the idea of his regal glory, and his palace at Versailles —with its grandiose combination of architecture, sculpture, painting, decoration, and (not least) the art of the gardener— represents one of the supreme examples of the Baroque fusion of the arts to create an overwhelmingly impressive whole. (The German term *Gesamtkunstwerk* ('total work of art') has been applied to this ideal.) In France, as in other countries, the Baroque style merged imperceptibly with the Rococo style that followed it.

Barr, Alfred H., Jr. (1902–81). American art historian and museum administrator who played an enormously influential role in establishing an intellectual framework for the study and appreciation of modern art: his obituary in the *International Herald Tribune* described him as 'possibly the most innovative and influential museum man of the 20th century'. For most of his career Barr worked at the *Museum of Modern Art in New York, of which he became director when it was founded in 1929 (he resigned this post in 1943 so he could devote more time to writing, but he continued as director of research, and retired in 1967 with the title of director of museum collections). Barr was chiefly responsible for

building the museum's collections and establishing its reputation. He widened the traditional concept of the art museum to embrace visual arts as a whole, including architecture, industrial design, and motion pictures, and he did much to create the modern idea of an art exhibition, through such means as special lighting, expository wall captions, and scholarly, fully illustrated catalogues (he organized more than a hundred exhibitions at the museum, including such famous shows as 'Cubism and Abstract Art' and 'Fantastic Art, Dada, Surrealism', both in 1936). He wrote numerous books and catalogues himself, setting impressive standards of scholarship but presenting his findings in an accessible style; his monographs on *Picasso (1946) and *Matisse (1951) are still considered standard works. In spite of the praise he received for his work, Barr was a controversial figure. He was attacked by sectarians within the world of modern art as well as by conservatives, and some critics thought that the museum he created had too powerful an influence in shaping—rather than reflecting—the course of modern art.

Barret, George (1732?–84). Irish landscape painter in oils and watercolour, born and trained in Dublin. In 1763 he moved to London, where he quickly made a reputation and became a foundation member of the *Royal Academy in 1768. Although he sometimes imitated the classical manner of his rival Richard *Wilson (who described Barret's foliage as 'spinach and eggs'), he was primarily a painter of topographical views. His most famous work in his day was a panorama of the Lake District painted in *distemper on the walls of a room at Norbury Park in Surrey (*c*.1780; still in situ). Many other pictures by him are still in stately home collections. In spite of his success with aristocratic clients, Barrett had an improvident and quarrelsome nature and became bankrupt. He had three painter sons, **George Jun., James,** and **Joseph,** and his daughter **Mary** was a *miniaturist.

Barry, James (1741–1806). Irish painter, active mainly in England. In 1763, in Dublin, he met Edmund Burke, an Irish-born statesman and writer (*see* SUBLIME), who encouraged him to move to London and financed a lengthy Continental visit (1766–71), which he spent mainly in Rome. There

Barry was overwhelmed by the work of the great masters of the *Renaissance, underlining his ambition to paint elevated subjects with moral messages. In a British art world dominated by portraiture there was little patronage for this type of picture, but Barry pursued his independent path with fervour—he was the only British artist of his time who adhered consistently to *Reynolds's precepts for *history painting in the *Grand Manner. His most famous work, a scheme of six large decorative paintings entitled *The Progress of Human Culture* (1777–83), for the Great Room of the Society of Arts, London, is the most grandiose achievement of this kind by any artist of the British School, but its weak draughtsmanship and flabby rhetoric show that his ambitions far outstripped his talent. Barry's portraits have appealed more to modern taste. They include several self-portraits, in which he suggests the truculent nature that caused friction with his fellow *Royal Academicians. He was appointed professor of painting at the Academy in 1782, but he was expelled in 1799 for making slanderous attacks on his colleagues (he had something of a persecution complex). He died in poverty, but he was sufficiently esteemed to be buried in St Paul's Cathedral, and some British artists of the following generation regarded him as a kind of anti-establishment hero.

Barry, Robert. *See* CONCEPTUAL ART.

Bartlett, Jennifer. *See* NEW IMAGE PAINTING.

Bartolommeo, Fra (Baccio della Porta) (1472–1517). Florentine painter, a leading figure of the *High Renaissance. He trained under Cosimo *Rosselli and in about 1494 set up a joint workshop with Mariotto *Albertinelli, who had been his fellow pupil. Little survives of his early work, and he is said to have destroyed his profane pictures and drawings under the influence of Girolamo Savonarola's fiery preaching against worldliness. He was greatly distressed by Savonarola's execution in 1498, and in 1500 he gave up painting and became a novice at the Dominican convent at Prato. The following year he took his vows, assumed the name Fra Bartolommeo, and moved to the convent of S. Marco in Florence (famous for its Fra *Angelico paintings). In 1504 the prior of S. Marco authorized him to resume

painting, and the rest of his life was devoted to religious art. After 1508 (by which time *Leonardo, *Michelangelo, and *Raphael had all left Florence), he was the leading painter in the city, although he was rivalled by *Andrea del Sarto in the second decade of the century.

Bartolommeo's style was strongly influenced by Leonardo, and his work has much in common with Raphael's. His most characteristic subjects are the Madonna and Child with Saints and the Holy Family; the figures are noble, calm, and remote from the everyday world, dressed in timeless draperies and sometimes placed in non-specific settings, with a complete absence of the kind of anecdotal details beloved of the *quattrocento. In 1508 he visited Venice and his work became richer, warmer, and more atmospheric in style under the influence of Giovanni *Bellini; his *Mystic Marriage of St Catherine* (1512, Accademia, Florence) has the kind of majestic architectural setting used by Bellini in several of his major altarpieces and such Bellinesque motifs as music-making angels seated at the foot of the Virgin's throne. In 1514 he visited Rome, and some of his later work has a tendency towards empty rhetoric, as he struggled to come to terms with Michelangelo's Sistine Ceiling. A very different side to his art is seen in his drawings, which are often remarkably fresh and spontaneous, particularly his landscapes. With Leonardo, he was one of the first artists to produce drawings of pure landscape, and they seem to have been made for his own pleasure.

Bartolozzi, Francesco (1728–1815). Italian engraver, active mainly in England, where he settled in 1764 with the position of official engraver to George III. In 1768 he was a founder member of the *Royal Academy (admitted as a painter; engravers were orginally not eligible). He engraved the works of many leading contemporary painters, such as *Copley and *Reynolds, but he was also celebrated for prints after the Old Masters. Much of his work was in the *stipple engraving technique. His output was enormous and he had many assistants and pupils. In 1802 he moved to Lisbon to become director of the Academy.

Barye, Antoine-Louis (1796–1875). French sculptor, painter, and printmaker, born and active in Paris. Barye was the most famous animal sculptor of the 19th century and was largely responsible for making the small animal bronze a recognized genre; artists specializing in this kind of work became known as *animaliers*. He trained as a goldsmith (his father's profession) and also studied sculpture and painting (*Gros was briefly his teacher). His knowledge of animals came partly from observing them in the Jardin des Plantes, Paris, and partly from extensive reading. In 1831 he had his first notable success at the *Salon with *Tiger Devouring a Gavial* (Louvre, Paris, and other casts) and this launched his career; only two years later he was made a member of the Legion of Honour. Much of his work is in a similar *Romantic vein, stressing the drama and savagery of nature. Barye also created large-scale sculptures, including a stone pediment relief of *Napoleon Crowned by History and the Arts* (1857) on the Sully Pavilion of the *Louvre and a bronze equestrian statue of Napoleon (1860–5) at Ajaccio, the emperor's birthplace in Corsica.

Baschenis, Evaristo (1617–77). Italian painter, the outstanding member of a dynasty of artists. Although he was an ordained priest, almost all his pictures depict arrangements of musical instruments—beautifully poised and polished works that led Rudolf *Wittkower to describe him as 'probably Italy's greatest still-life painter'. His inclination for his favourite subject may have been influenced by the contemporary fame of the Amati family of violin-makers of Cremona, which is near to Baschenis's native town of Bergamo. The Accademia Carrara there has the best collection of his paintings.

Baselitz, Georg (1938–). German painter and sculptor. He is regarded as one of the leading exponents of *Neo-Expressionism and his work has often been the subject of controversy, particularly since, in 1969, he began painting the images in his pictures upside down. Since 1980 he has also made sculptures; in these the figures are the normal way up.

Basire, James. *See* BLAKE, WILLIAM.

Basquiat, Jean-Michel. *See* GRAFFITI ART.

Bassa, Ferrer (active 1324–48). Spanish painter and *illuminator who worked for the Aragon court in Barcelona. He is con-

sidered the founder of the Catalan School, but the only certain surviving work by his hand is a series of murals (in oil rather than fresco) in the chapel of S. Miguel at the convent of Pedralbes near Barcelona, executed in 1345–6 and strongly Italianate in style.

Bassano, Jacopo (Jacopo da Ponte) (*c.*1515–92). Italian painter, the most celebrated member of a family of artists who took their name from the small town of Bassano, about 65 km (40 miles) north-west of Venice. Jacopo is regarded as a member of the Venetian School and among his contemporaries is ranked inferior only to the great triumvirate of *Titian, *Tintoretto, and *Veronese. However, apart from a period in the 1530s when he worked with *Bonifazio Veronese, he was not resident in Venice itself; he lived almost all his life in his native town, where he was easily the leading artist of the day, producing a large and varied output of pictures. His father, **Francesco the Elder** (*c.*1475–1539), was a village painter and Jacopo always retained something of the peasant artist, even though the influence of, for example, the fashionable etchings of *Parmigianino is evident in his work. Most of his pictures are on religious subjects, but he often treated biblical themes in the manner of rustic *genre scenes, using genuine country types and portraying animals with real interest. In this way he helped to develop the taste for paintings in which the genre or still-life element assumes greater importance than the ostensible religious subject. From around 1560 his work showed a concern with novel effects of light, taking on something of the iridescent colouring of Tintoretto.

Bassano had four painter sons who continued his style and sometimes collaborated with him—**Francesco the Younger** (1549–92), **Gerolamo** (1566–1621), **Giovanni Battista** (1553–1613), and **Leandro** (1557–1622). Francesco and Leandro both acquired some distinction and popularity working in Venice—indeed Leandro was knighted by the Doge in 1595 or 1596 (thereafter he sometimes added *Eques* to his signature). Francesco was mentally unstable and died after throwing himself from a window. Leandro's death in 1622 brought the artistic dynasty to an end. The work of the family is well represented in the Museo Civico at Bassano.

Bastien-Lepage, Jules (1848–84). French painter. He grew up on a farm and is best known for sentimental scenes of rural life such as *The Haymakers* (1877, Mus. d'Orsay, Paris). Émile Zola described Bastien-Lepage's work as 'Impressionism corrected, sweetened and adapted to the taste of the crowd', and he was highly influential in spreading a taste for *plein-air painting, not only in France, but also in Britain (*Clausen and *La Thangue were among his admirers), in other European countries, in the USA, and even—via Tom *Roberts—in Australia. He was also much admired as a portraitist. His early death was caused by cancer.

Batoni, Pompeo (1708–87). Italian painter and draughtsman, born in Lucca, the son of a distinguished goldsmith, and active in Rome, where he settled in 1727. He has been described as 'Italy's last Old Master' and he was certainly the last great Italian personality to dominate painting in Rome. Initially he made his name with exquisite drawings of ancient statuary (which were much prized by antiquarians), then as a history painter, mainly of religious subjects. However, by the 1750s he was devoting most of his time to portraits and it is for these that he is principally famous. After *Mengs left Rome for Madrid in 1761, Batoni's pre-eminence in this field was unchallenged, and he was particularly favoured by foreign visitors making the *Grand Tour, whom he often portrayed in an *antique setting; one of his most celebrated works shows the sitter in spectacular Highland dress against a backdrop of the Colosseum (*Colonel William Gordon*, 1766, Fyvie Castle, Aberdeenshire, NT). Batoni's characterization is not profound, but it is usually vivid (he had a reputation for creating a good likeness), and he presented his sitters with dignity and elan. His polished and learned style shows his admiration for the classical tradition of *Raphael, *Reni, and *Maratta, but his work also has a *Rococo grace and delicacy of touch. Batoni earned a fortune from his work and his large house was a social, intellectual, and artistic centre, frequented by many distinguished visitors to Rome. At the time of his death he was probably the most famous artist in Europe, but his reputation went into eclipse in the 19th century and did not seriously revive until the later 20th century.

Battistello. *See* CARACCIOLO.

Bauchant, André (1873–1958). French *naive painter. He was a market gardener until 1914 and did not begin painting until 1919, when he was demobilized after war service (in the army he had shown a talent for drawing and had been trained as a mapmaker). In 1921 his work was shown at the *Salon d'Automne, and he soon became one of the best-known painters of his type. He was promoted by Wilhelm *Uhde, and his admirers and patrons included *Diaghilev, *Le Corbusier, *Lipchitz, and *Ozenfant. Bauchant's favourite subjects were history and mythology, for which he found inspiration in old illustrated books (*Greek Dance in a Landscape*, 1937, Tate, London). His style was meticulously detailed.

Baudelaire, Charles (1821–67). French poet and critic. As well as being a major poet, Baudelaire was one of the liveliest art critics of his day, passionate and partisan in his views. He thought that there are no universal aesthetic standards, but a different type of beauty for different peoples and cultures. Moreover, the individuality of the artist is essential to the creation of beauty and if it is suppressed or regimented, art becomes banal: 'the beautiful is always bizarre' was a favourite maxim. His favourite contemporary artist was *Delacroix, whom he extolled for his imagination, intelligence, and technical skills. However, he singled out the relatively minor artist Constantin *Guys as the representative *par excellence* of contemporary society, and wrote a long appreciation of his work entitled 'Le Peintre de la vie moderne', published as a series of articles in *Le Figaro* in 1863. The other artists with whom Baudelaire was involved include *Courbet (he is one of the people depicted in *The Painter's Studio* (1854–5, Mus. d'Orsay, Paris)), *Manet (he likewise appears in *Music in the Tuileries Gardens* (1863, NG, London)), and *Rops, whose career he helped to launch. His writings later had great influence on the *Symbolists.

Baugin, Lubin (*c*.1610–63). French painter, active in Paris. He specialized in religious works and has earned the nickname 'Le Petit Guide' (Little Guido) because he was strongly influenced by Guido *Reni. This suggests that he visited Italy, but there is no documentary evidence. A small group of strikingly austere still lifes, signed simply 'Baugin' (examples are in the Louvre), has also been attributed to him; however, there is little in common between these pictures and the religious works and some scholars think they are by an otherwise unrecorded namesake.

Bauhaus. A school of art and design founded by Walter *Gropius in Weimar in 1919 and closed by the Nazis in 1933 after moving successively to Dessau (1925) and Berlin (1932); although it had such a short life it was the most famous art school of the 20th century, playing key roles in establishing the relationship between design and industrial techniques and in breaking down the hierarchy that had previously divided 'fine' from 'applied' arts. The Bauhaus was created when Gropius was appointed head of two art schools in Weimar in 1919 and united them in one; they were the Kunstgewerbeschule (Arts and Crafts School) and the Hochschule für Bildende Kunst (Institute of Fine Arts). He gave his new school the name Staatliches Bauhaus in Weimar (Weimar State 'Building House'), coining himself the word 'Bauhaus' (an inversion of *Hausbau*: 'house construction'). His prospectus formulated three main aims for the school: first, to unite the arts so that painters, sculptors, and craftsmen could in future embark on co-operative projects, combining all their skills harmoniously; secondly, to raise the status of the crafts to that enjoyed by the fine arts; and thirdly, to establish 'constant contact with the leaders of the crafts and industries of the country' (an important factor if the school were to survive in a country that was in economic chaos after the war).

All students had to take a six-month 'preliminary course' (*Vorkurs*) in which they studied the principles of form and colour, became familiar with various materials, and were encouraged to develop their creativity. After that they moved on to workshop training in the field of their choice. Gropius brought together a remarkable collection of teachers at the Bauhaus. The first head of the preliminary course was Johannes *Itten, and when he left in 1923 he was succeeded by László *Moholy-Nagy, who replaced Itten's rather metaphysical approach with an austerely rational one.

The other teachers included some illustrious painters, most notably *Kandinsky and *Klee. Several students went on to become teachers at the school, notably Josef *Albers. In 1924 right-wingers gained power in the provincial elections and cut funding to the Bauhaus, which consequently moved to Dessau the following year; it was housed in a group of new buildings designed by Gropius. The school had been involved in architectural commissions from the beginning, but it was only in 1927 that an architectural department was established, with the Swiss architect Hannes Meyer (1889–1954) as its first professor. When Gropius resigned in 1928 to devote himself to his own practice he named Meyer as his successor. It was an unpopular choice with the staff, as Meyer was a Marxist and instituted a sociological approach that changed the whole tone of the school, with politics occupying an important place in the curriculum. In 1930 Meyer was forced to resign and was replaced by Ludwig Mies van der Rohe (1886–1969), one of the greatest architects of the 20th century. Mies tried to rid the Bauhaus of its political associations and thereby make it a less easy target for its right-wing opponents, but in 1932 the Dessau parliament closed the school. In an attempt to keep it alive Mies rented a disused factory in Berlin and reopened the Bauhaus there as a private enterprise, but it was closed by the Nazis in April 1933, soon after Hitler assumed power. In its last few years the Bauhaus was dominated by architecture, but it produced a great range of goods, with many of them (furniture, textiles, and electric light fittings in particular) being adopted for large-scale manufacture. They were highly varied in appearance, but the style that is generally thought typical of the Bauhaus was severe, geometric, and undecorated. The Bauhaus published a journal (*Bauhaus*, 1926–31) and a series of books, and its ideas were spread also by the emigration of many of its teachers before and during the Second World War. It has had an enormous influence on art education in the Western world and on visual creativity in general: 'The look of the modern environment is unthinkable without it. It left an indelible mark on activities as varied as photography and newspaper design...[and] achieved a language of design liberated from the historicism of the previous hundred years' (Frank Whitford, *Bauhaus*, 1984). After the Second World War Dessau became part of East Germany and the Bauhaus buildings were left derelict. In 1976 the school was faithfully restored for the 50th anniversary of its opening in Dessau, and after the reunification of Germany in 1990 it was reopened as a design institution.

Baumeister, Willi (1889–1955). German abstract painter. Unlike most significant German painters of his time, he stood apart from *Expressionism and is regarded as the most 'European' in spirit of his contemporaries. Between 1911 and 1914 he had several stays in Paris (sometimes in company with his close friend Oskar *Schlemmer) and his early work was influenced by *Cubism. After military service in the First World War, he began to develop a personal style in a series (1919–23) of *Mauerbilder* (wall paintings), so called because he added sand, putty, etc., to his pigments to give a textured effect. In the mid-1920s his work became more figurative, in a manner recalling *Léger and the *Purists (he met Léger, *Le Corbusier, and *Ozenfant when he revisited Paris in 1924), and his work received considerable acclaim in France. In 1928 he was appointed professor of typography at the Städel School in Frankfurt, but in 1933 he was dismissed by the Nazis, who declared his work *degenerate. From then until the end of the Second World War he worked in obscurity in Stuttgart. During this time his painting became freer, with suggestions of primitive imagery, creating a kind of abstract *Surrealism. His interest in imagery from the subconscious was described in his book *Das Unbekannte in der Kunst* (The Unknown in Art), written in 1943–4 and published in 1947. After the war Baumeister became a hero to a younger generation of German abstract artists. From 1946 until his death he was a professor at the Stuttgart Academy.

Baxter, George (1804–67). English engraver and printer. In 1835 he patented a method of making colour prints—the first commercially viable alternative to the hand-coloured print. The basic design, usually in *aquatint, was printed from a steel plate, and the colours were superimposed from up to twenty wooden blocks. Around the middle of the century 'Baxter prints' enjoyed a great vogue, making coloured reproductions of paintings widely available. Baxter licensed other firms to employ the process and did not himself profit greatly from the invention; in fact he became bankrupt in 1865. By this time his process was being superseded by colour *lithography.

Bayes, Gilbert. *See* NEW SCULPTURE.

Bayes, Walter (brother of Gilbert Bayes). *See* CAMDEN TOWN GROUP.

Bayeu, Francisco (1734–95). Spanish painter. He had an eminently successful career, becoming court painter to Charles IV and director of the Academy of San Fernando, but he is now remembered mainly because he was the brother-in-law of *Goya, who spent some time in Bayeu's studio in the 1760s and later painted a memorable portrait of him (1795, Prado, Madrid). Bayeu painted portraits and also did much decorative work, particularly making *cartoons for the royal tapestry factory, where he succeeded *Mengs as director in 1777.

Bazille, Frédéric (1841–70). French painter, one of the early *Impressionist group. In 1862 he became a student at *Gleyre's studio in Paris and there met *Monet, *Renoir, and *Sisley, with whom he painted out of doors at Fontainebleau and in Normandy. He was primarily a figure painter rather than a landscapist, but he sometimes set his compositions in the open air, as in his best-known work, the large *Family Reunion* (1867–8, Mus. d'Orsay, Paris). Bazille was killed in action during the Franco-Prussian War, cutting short a promising career. He came from a wealthy family and had given generous financial support to Monet and Renoir.

Baziotes, William (1912–63). American painter, one of the minor masters of *Abstract Expressionism. From 1936 to 1941 he worked for the *Federal Art Project, and during the Second World War he became interested in *Surrealism and experimented with various types of *automatism. In the early 1950s he developed his characteristic style, which was not fully abstract but used strange *biomorphic shapes, akin to those of *Miró, suggesting animal or plant forms in an underwater setting (*Mammoth*, 1957, Tate, London). He said, 'It is the mysterious that I love in painting. It is the stillness and the silence. I want my pictures to take effect very slowly, to obsess and to haunt.'

Beale, Mary (née Cradock) (1633–99). English portrait painter, active in London, where she moved in intellectual circles. She was the daughter of a clergyman and many of her portraits are of churchmen. They are mostly bland derivations from *Lely, but she was in considerable demand at the peak of her career, in the 1670s. Much of our knowledge of her work comes from notebooks kept by her husband recording sitters, payments, and other information; they provide a fascinating insight into contemporary artistic practice. A son, **Charles** (1660–1714?), was mainly a *miniaturist.

Beardsley, Aubrey (1872–98). English illustrator and writer. Beardsley had a talent for drawing from childhood and had almost no formal training in art (he attended evening classes at Westminster School of Art for a few months). However, he read voraciously and studied the art of the past and present, and his work drew on a variety of influences, including the sinuous line of *Burne-Jones (who encouraged him) and the strong patterns of Japanese prints (*see* UKIYO-E). In spite of these influences, his style is highly distinctive in the way he contrasts subtle use of line with bold masses of black and in his blending of grotesque humour with a sense of morbid depravity. He made a name for himself with illustrations for an edition of Malory's *Morte d'Arthur* (1893–4), and in 1894 he became notorious with the publication of his illustrations to the English version of Oscar Wilde's *Salome* and the appearance of the first issue of *The Yellow Book*, a quarterly periodical of which he was art editor. The decadent nature of his work horrified many contemporaries and the scandal of Wilde's arrest for homosexual offences in 1895 led to his dismissal from *The Yellow Book* (even though he disliked Wilde and his own personal life was blameless). In 1896 he worked for another short-lived periodical, *The Savoy*, which published extracts from his main work a writer, the unfinished erotic novel *Under the Hill* (an unexpurgated edition, with his own pornographic illustrations, was privately published in 1907 under the title *The Story of Venus and Tannhauser*). Although he was only 25 when he died of tuberculosis, his output was large. He became one of the best-known artists of his day (he was satirized in Punch as 'Aubrey Weirdsley') and he ranks as a major figure of *Aestheticism and of *Art Nouveau.

Beaumont, Sir George (1753–1827). English collector, connoisseur, and amateur painter, the friend of numerous artists and men of letters; his best-known painting, *Peele Castle in a Storm* (1806, priv. coll.), moved Wordsworth to write a poem. Beaumont was a key figure in the creation of the *National Gallery; in 1823 he offered his small but choice collection of pictures to the nation on condition that a suitable building were provided for them, and this encouraged the government to buy the Angerstein collection (the nucleus of the gallery) the following year. Beaumont's favourite painting among those he presented was *Claude's *Hagar and the Angel* (1646), which he frequently took with him when he travelled and which had a great impact on his friend *Constable. Constable's famous painting *The Cenotaph* (*c*.1833, NG, London) shows the memorial to Sir Joshua *Reynolds that Beaumont had erected in the grounds of his house at Coleorton, Leicestershire.

Beauneveu, André (d. *c*.1403). Franco-Netherlandish artist, primarily a sculptor but also active as an *illuminator and a designer of stained glass. He was born in Valenciennes and is first documented in about 1360. By 1364 he was in Paris working on a series of royal tombs commissioned by King Charles V for the abbey of Saint-Denis, near Paris. Most of the work was carried out by assistants, but the sensitively characterized effigy of Charles himself is regarded as entirely Beauneveu's work; it is the first French royal effigy to show the subject alive. For unknown reasons Beauneveu left Charles's employment in 1366. He possibly spent some years in England before moving to the Netherlands. In 1372 he was in Tournai and in 1374–7 he worked for Louis de Male, Count of Flanders, in Courtrai. From this period dates a handsome alabaster statue of St Catherine (church of Our Lady, Courtrai). In 1386 he entered the service of Jean, Duc de Berry (brother of Charles V), and evidently remained in his employment for the rest of his life, working mainly in Bourges. His only documented works as an illuminator date from this period—24 *grisaille miniatures of Prophets and Apostles in Jean's *Psalter* (*c*.1390,

Bib. Nat., Paris). Beauneveu was one of the leading artists of his day and his style, in both sculpture and painting, heralds the general northern European trend towards naturalism in the 15th century.

Beaux, Cecilia (1855–1942). American painter, active mainly in her native Philadelphia and in New York. Her training included a period in Paris, where she studied at the *Académie Julian. She was a highly successful and much-honoured society portraitist, working in a dashing and fluid style similar to that of *Sargent. Her sitters included celebrities such as Henry James and Theodore Roosevelt. She wrote an autobiography, *Background with Figures*, published in 1930.

Beaux-Arts, École des. Paris, The chief of the official art schools of France. Its origins go back to 1648, the foundation date of the Académie Royale de Peinture et de Sculpture (see ACADEMY), but it was not established as a separate institution until the Académie was dissolved in 1793, during the administrative reforms of the French Revolution. It moved to its present site, in the rue Bonaparte, in 1816. The École des Beaux-Arts controlled the path to traditional success with its awards and state commissions, notably the prestigious *Prix de Rome, and teaching remained conservative until after the Second World War. Entry was difficult—among the artists who failed were *Rodin and *Vuillard—and students often preferred the private *académies. Many progressive artists, however, obtained a sound technical grounding there—*Degas, *Manet, *Matisse, *Monet, and *Renoir all attended classes. The École, which is housed in a complex of early 19th-century buildings, has a large and varied collection of works of art. Many of them are primarily of historical interest (including a vast number of copies and portraits of teachers), but the collection of drawings is of high quality.

Beccafumi, Domenico (c.1484–1551). Sienese painter, sculptor, and printmaker. He is now generally considered the outstanding Sienese *Mannerist artist, although *Sodoma was more highly esteemed by his contemporaries. According to *Vasari, he visited Rome early in his career, and he was certainly aware of the work of *Michelangelo and *Raphael, as well as of contemporary Florentine art, combining the new ideas of the High *Renaissance with the bright and decorative colouring of Sienese tradition. His work is noteworthy for its sense of fantasy and striking effects of light, as in the *Birth of the Virgin* (c.1543), one of several outstanding examples of his work in the Pinacoteca, Siena. Late in his career he turned to sculpture, producing a series of eight bronze angels (1547–51) for Siena Cathedral. He also worked as an illuminator and occasionally made engravings and woodcuts.

Becerra, Gaspar (c.1520–68). Spanish *Mannerist painter and sculptor. He spent much of his early career in Italy and he was one of *Vasari's assistants in his decoration of the Cancelleria Palace, Rome (1546). In about 1557 he returned to Spain and in 1558 he began the main altarpiece of Astorga Cathedral, his most important work as a sculptor. In 1562 he was appointed court painter to Philip II (see HABSBURG), for whom his work included a ceiling fresco of *Perseus and the Golden Fleece* (1562–7) in the palace of El Pardo, near Madrid. His up-to-date knowledge of Italian art gave him a high contemporary reputation.

Beckford, William (1760–1844). English collector, writer, and eccentric. A pampered millionaire from boyhood (at the age of 5 he had piano lessons from the 8-year-old Mozart), he became a legendary figure in his own lifetime. One of his cousins referred to him as 'a second Lucifer' (a reference to both his youthful beauty and his depravity), and in 1784 he left England after a homosexual scandal involving a 13-year-old boy. For the next decade he travelled widely on the Continent and after his return to England he lived in eccentric seclusion at Fonthill in Wiltshire, where the architect James Wyatt built for him Fonthill Abbey (1796–1807, now mainly destroyed), a huge mansion dressed in ecclesiastical garb. He formed an excellent library and a vast collection of objects of every kind, both natural and artificial; it drew from William *Hazlitt the wry comment that 'the only proof of taste he has shown in this collection is his getting rid of it', but it included some outstanding paintings (twenty of them are now in the National Gallery, London). In 1826, when his fortunes had declined, Beckford built Lansdown Tower, Bath, a lesser but still highly impressive classical folly that is now a museum devoted to him. Beckford's most famous literary work is the fantastic oriental tale *Vathek*, written in French, but published first in English in 1786, a successor to *Walpole's The Castle of Otranto* in the vogue for the Gothic novel. The nightmarish visions of Beckford's book were inspired partly, as he himself said, by *Piranesi's engravings.

Beckmann, Max (1884–1950). German painter and graphic artist, one of the most powerful and individual of *Expressionist artists. Early in his career Beckmann painted in a conservative, more or less *Impressionist, idiom, with which he made a good living, but his experiences as a medical orderly in the First World War completely changed his outlook and his style. Although he rarely depicted scenes from the war itself, his work became full of horrifying imagery, and his forms were expressively distorted in a manner that reflected the influence of German *Gothic art. The combination of brutal realism and social criticism in his work led him to be classified for a time with the artists of the *Neue Sachlichkeit, but Beckmann differed from such artists as *Dix and *Grosz in his concern for allegory and symbolism and in his highly personal blend of the real and the visionary. His paintings were intended as depictions of lust, sadism, cruelty, etc., rather than illustrations of specific instances of those qualities at work, and he ceased to regard painting as a purely aesthetic matter, and thought of it as an ethical necessity. In 1933 Beckmann was dismissed by the Nazis from his professorship at the Städelsches Kunstinstitut in Frankfurt; the previous year he began *Departure* (MoMA, New York), the first of a series of nine great *triptychs painted between then and his death in which he expressed his philosophy of life and society, and his horror at man's cruelty. He moved to the Netherlands in 1937 (the year in which his work was included in the infamous Nazi exhibition of *degenerate art), settling in Amsterdam until 1947. The last three years of his life were spent in the USA, where he taught in Washington and New York. Beckmann's philosophical outlook, which he expressed in *My Theory of Painting* (a lecture delivered in London in 1937 and published in 1941), is somewhat incoherent, but his work forms one of the most potent artistic commentaries on the disorientation of the modern world. Apart from his allegorical figure compositions, Beckmann is best known for his portraits, particularly his self-portraits, in which he charted his spiritual experiences. He was also a prolific draughtsman and printmaker (mainly of etchings and drypoints).

Beechey, Sir William (1753–1839). English portrait painter. Beechey's careful, somewhat insipid style changed little throughout his successful career. He was appointed portrait painter to Queen Charlotte in 1793 and was knighted in 1798 in recognition of his most ambitious painting, the huge *Review of the Horse Guard with King George III and the Prince of Wales* (formerly Royal Coll.; destroyed in the fire at Windsor Castle, 1992).

Beert, Osias (*c*.1580–1623). Flemish painter of still life and flower pieces. Beert became a master in the Antwerp painters' guild in 1602 and also carried on business as a cork merchant. He is specially noted for his paintings of oysters, which show a masterly feeling for colour and texture.

'Beggarstaff, J. & W.' ('Beggarstaff Brothers'). Pseudonym used by the brothers-in-law William *Nicholson and James *Pryde for their poster designs. 'They joined forces in 1894, and for the next five years they produced a series of posters which by their bold simplicity and clarity of design revolutionized certain aspects of poster art throughout Europe...they presented the image in its starkest form: the background is stripped bare of unnecessary detail and the fullest use is made of the silhouette... Despite the brilliant originality of their work, or perhaps because of it, they received relatively few commissions and several of their designs never reached the hoardings' (Dennis Farr, *English Art: 1870–1940*, 1978). Nicholson explained their choice of the name 'Beggarstaff' thus: 'Pryde and I came across it one day in an old stable, on a sack of fodder. It is a good, hearty, old English name, and it appealed to us, so we adopted it immediately.' They signed their work 'J. & W. Beggarstaff'; in due course some people started referring to the 'Beggarstaff Brothers', but the artists themselves did not care for this version.

Beham, Sebald (1500–50) and **Barthel** (1502–40). German printmakers, brothers.

They were expelled from their native city of Nuremberg in 1525 for their extreme Protestant views. Although they were allowed to return later that year, Barthel soon left to work for Duke William IV of Bavaria in Munich and Sebald settled in Frankfurt in about 1531. Both brothers produced a great number of prints (engravings, etchings, and woodcuts), including illustrations to the Bible, mythology, and history, strongly influenced by *Dürer. They also painted, and several impressive portraits by Barthel survive.

Bell, Clive (1881–1964). British writer on art. In 1910 he met Roger *Fry and quickly became his chief apostle in helping to spread an appreciation of *Post-Impressionism in Britain. Bell helped with the organization of Fry's first Post-Impressionist exhibition (1910), and he chose the British section of the second one (1912), including work by his wife Vanessa *Bell, Fry himself, and Duncan *Grant among *Bloomsbury Group artists, with Spencer *Gore and Wyndham *Lewis representing the more radical wing. His aesthetic ideas, expressed most fully in his book *Art* (1914), were much concerned with the theory of 'significant form'. He invented this term to denote 'the quality that distinguishes works of art from all other classes of objects'—a quality never found in nature but common to all works of art and existing independently of representational or symbolic content. The book is not now taken seriously as philosophy, and it contains some absurd statements ('The bulk of those who flourished between the high Renaissance and the contemporary movement may be divided into two classes, virtuosi and dunces'); however, it is written with fervour, and his ideas were influential in spreading an attitude that placed emphasis on the formal qualities of a work of art (see FORMALISM).

Quentin Bell (1910–96), son of Clive and Vanessa Bell, was a painter, sculptor, potter, and author, probably best known for his writings on art, mainly on the Victorian period and the Bloomsbury Group. Between 1962 and 1975 he was a professor successively at the universities of Leeds, Hull, and Sussex. Quentin's son, **Julian Bell** (1952–), is a painter and writer on art.

Bell, Graham (1910–43). British painter and art critic, born in South Africa. He moved to England in 1931 and became a pupil of Duncan *Grant. In the early 1930s he painted abstracts, but from 1934 to 1937 he abandoned painting for journalism, writing art criticism in a socialist vein. When he returned to painting it was in the soberly naturalistic style associated with the *Euston Road School. His work included portraits, landscapes, interiors, and still lifes. He was killed on an RAF training flight in the Second World War. In 1947 Kenneth *Clark wrote of Bell: 'his critical intelligence was extremely acute . . . I think he would have become a very good painter. There is an air of largeness and essential truth in his best work which only needs filling out and enriching in order to become great.'

Bell, Vanessa (1879–1961). British painter and designer. She married Clive *Bell in 1907 and like him and her sister, Virginia Woolf, was a central figure of the *Bloomsbury Group. Her early work, up to about 1910, and her paintings produced after the First World War are tasteful and fairly conventional, in the tradition of the *New English Art Club, but in the intervening years she was briefly in the vanguard of progressive ideas in British art. At this time, stimulated by the *Post-Impressionist exhibitions of Roger *Fry (with whom she had an affair), she worked with bright colours and bold designs and by 1914 was painting completely abstract pictures. Her designs for Fry's *Omega Workshops included a folding screen (1913–14, V&A, London) clearly showing the influence of *Matisse. From 1916—while remaining on good terms with her husband—she lived with Duncan *Grant. Both of them painted vigorously into old age, even though their work went out of fashion after the Second World War. They spent a good deal of time in London and travelling abroad, but they lived mainly at Charleston Farmhouse, at Firle, Sussex, and did much painted decoration in the house; it has been restored as a Bloomsbury memorial and is open to the public (the couple are buried together nearby in Firle churchyard).

Bella, Stefano della (1610–64). Italian etcher and draughtsman. He was one of the greatest and most prolific printmakers of his day, producing more than a thousand etchings (as well as a huge number of drawings). Most of his career was spent in his native Florence, where his patrons included the *Medici family, but he also worked in Rome (1633–9) and in Paris (1639–50). His output was highly varied, including military scenes, landscapes, animal subjects, and designs for masques. Early in his career he was strongly influenced by *Callot, but later his style became more naturalistic, reflecting his admiration for *Rembrandt's prints (he visited the Netherlands in 1647).

Bellange, Jacques (d. 1616). French painter, etcher, draughtsman, and designer, active in Nancy, where he worked for the Dukes of Lorraine from 1602. Much of his time was taken up with ephemeral decorative work and only a few surviving paintings are attributed to him, including the *Lamentation* (Hermitage, St Petersburg) and the *Stigmatization of St Francis* (Mus. Historique, Nancy). His reputation now rests mainly on his etchings, which are among the finest of their time and represent the final flowering of the *Mannerist tradition. They are mainly on religious subjects, with very elegant, elongated figures—highly artificial in style yet expressing an intense mystical feeling. He also produced a few prints on *genre subjects, which are more naturalistic in style, notably the *Blind Hurdy-Gurdy Player*.

Bellano, Bartolommeo. *See* RICCIO.

Bellany, John (1942–). Scottish painter, working in a vigorous—at times rather tormented—*Expressionist style. He was born and brought up in the fishing village of Port Seton, near Edinburgh, and the imagery of his work is often derived from the sea, although it is transformed into a kind of personal mythology. His most characteristic pictures are large allegorical compositions involving hybrid human and animal forms, painted with explosive brushwork and suggesting some vague menace. In addition to such works, Bellany has painted many portraits, including a well-known one of the cricketer Ian Botham (1985, NPG, London). In the late 1980s he became seriously ill and he had a liver transplant in 1988; after his recovery his work became more optimistic in spirit. This is expressed in the coloured etchings he began to produce in the early 1990s as well as his paintings.

Bellechose, Henri (d. 1440/4). Netherlandish painter who in 1415 succeeded *Malouel as court painter to John the Fearless, Duke of Burgundy, in Dijon. Only one documented work by him survives, the *Martyrdom of St Denis* (*c*.1416, Louvre, Paris). The traditional view (based on some rather vague documentary evidence) is that this work was begun by Malouel and completed by Bellechose, but scholarly opinion now inclines to attribute it to Bellechose alone.

Bellini. Family of Venetian painters who played a dominant role in the art of their city for three-quarters of a century. **Jacopo** (*c*.1400–70/1) was the father of Gentile and Giovanni and the father-in-law of *Mantegna. He was a pupil of *Gentile da Fabriano, with whom he probably worked in Florence in the early 1420s (although the documentation is equivocal). From the 1430s he carried out a number of prestigious commissions in north Italy, including a fresco of the *Crucifixion* in Verona Cathedral (1436) and (after defeating *Pisanello in competition) a portrait of Leonello d'*Este in Ferrara. However, all these works have perished, and his surviving pictures are mainly fairly simple and traditional representations of the Madonna and Child, of which only one is dated (1448, Brera, Milan). Attractive though they are, they do little to suggest why he achieved such high esteem in his day, and a better indication of his quality and originality as an artist can be gained from his drawings. Two large, bound volumes of these survive (BM, London, and Louvre, Paris); together they contain almost 300 drawings, mainly finished compositions, some of them very elaborate. They show that he was keenly alert to new ideas, and many of them are remarkable for bold perspective effects, conveying an exhilarating sense of space. The volumes were inherited by Jacopo's sons, who used them as quarries for ideas.

Gentile (*c*.1430/5–1507) is generally thought to have been the elder son, although the evidence for this (and for his birthdate) is inconclusive. He presumably trained with his father, and is known to have collaborated with him around 1460. By 1465 he was working independently, and for the next 40 years he was one of the leading painters in Venice. As with his father, however, most of the major works on which his reputation was based have perished. They included a good deal of decorative work in the Doges' Palace, Venice, and erotic scenes painted for the harem of Sultan Mehmet II, when Gentile worked at his court in Constantinople in 1479–81; his portrait of Mehmet, however, survives (albeit much restored) in the National Gallery, London. The most famous of his extant works are probably the *Procession of the Relic of the True Cross* (1496) and the *Miracle at Ponte di Lorenzo* (1500), two huge canvases crowded with anecdotal detail of contemporary Venetian life. Both are in the Accademia, Venice.

Giovanni (*c*.1430/5–1516) was far and away the most important member of the family—one of the greatest and most influential artists of the *Renaissance. During his long and prolific career he transformed Venice from a city that was provincial in terms of its painting into a centre rivalling Florence and Rome in significance. He not only brought Venetian painting a prominence it had never known before, but also gave it a distinctive character, expressing himself through colour, light, and atmosphere in a way that contrasted with the traditional Florentine preoccupation with line, and he was a direct inspiration to the numerous Venetian painters of the following generation who trained in his studio. His importance in Venetian art is indeed so great that Kenneth *Clark considered that 'No other school of painting is to the same extent the creation of one man.' In spite of his fame, his career is in general poorly documented. He seems to have lived a life of uneventful devotion to his art, rarely if ever leaving the Veneto, and there are only scraps of biographical information about him. Few of his paintings bear a date or can be convincingly dated on external evidence. Therefore his development can usually be followed only in broad outline rather than precise detail, as—over a period of more than half a century—he moved from a sharp, linear manner with roots in the Middle Ages to a style of mellow breadth and classical dignity.

Giovanni was presumably trained by his father Jacopo, but the major influence in his formative years was that of his brother-in-law, Mantegna. This—and Bellini's own originality—are made clear by a comparison of their celebrated pictures of the *Agony in the Garden*, both painted about 1460–5 and both now in the National Gallery, London.

The compositions are closely related, both deriving from one of Jacopo's drawings, but there is great difference in treatment, particularly of the landscape: Mantegna's is sharp, precise, and analytical, Bellini's is lyrical and atmospheric. Another important influence on him was *Antonello da Messina, who was in Venice in 1475–6; Bellini admired not only his mastery of the new technique of *oil painting (of which he too became a consummate exponent), but also his lucid handling of space and form. To the end of his long life he continued to absorb new ideas: from the year before his death dates the dreamy *Woman with a Mirror* (KH Mus., Vienna), which is strongly influenced by *Giorgione, who was young enough to be his grandson. But despite his borrowings, Bellini always remained distinctly himself, for he had an extraordinary ability to assimilate ideas and blend them into a harmonious synthesis: as the Bellini specialist Jennifer Fletcher put it, 'Some artists invented more but none perfected so much.' His genius remained undiminished by advancing years, and it is easy to credit the remark made by *Dürer on his visit to Venice in 1505–7 that although Bellini was 'very old' he was still 'the best painter'. (Dürer's account of his meeting with Bellini gives a rare—and very favourable—glimpse of his personality: whereas other Venetian artists were hostile to the German visitor and jealous of his skills, the great man treated him with courtesy and respect.)

Bellini painted excellent portraits, of which the *Doge Leonardo Loredan* (*c*.1501, NG, London) is the best-known example, and a few mythologies and allegories, notably *The Feast of the Gods* (1514, NG, Washington; altered after his death by *Titian). Like his brother Gentile, he also painted several scenes from Venetian history (destroyed) in the Doges' Palace. However, he was above all a religious painter. His most characteristic subject was the Madonna and Child, and only *Raphael has rivalled him in the beauty and variety of his treatment of the theme, ranging from the wistful melancholy of *The Madonna of the Meadow* (*c*.1510, NG, London), one of the loveliest examples of his ability to bring together figures and landscape in perfect harmony, to the monumentality of the San Zaccaria Altarpiece (1505, S. Zaccaria, Venice), perhaps the grandest of all *sacre conversazioni*. Another favourite subject was the Dead Christ, which was particularly suited to the combination of gravity and tenderness at which he excelled. He rarely attempted subjects with a strong narrative element, as he was much more interested in atmosphere than action. This concern with the evocation of mood was one of his most important legacies to his pupils. From about 1490 almost all the painters who became eminent in Venice during the next generation (including Giorgione, *Sebastiano del Piombo, and Titian) are either known to or believed to have trained in his workshop. Bellini also had some influence in Florence, via Fra *Bartolommeo, who visited Venice in 1508.

Bellmer, Hans (1902–75). Polish-French graphic artist, painter, sculptor, photographer, and writer, all of whose work is explicitly erotic. In 1933 he constructed an articulated plaster figure of a young girl, inspired partly by an infatuation with his 15-year-old cousin Ursula. He photographed his creation in various attitudes and states of dismemberment (sometimes partly clothed) and published a collection of the photographs as *Die Puppe* ('The Doll') in Karlsruhe in 1934; a French edition, *La Poupée*, was published in Paris in 1936. Bellmer sent samples of the photographs to André *Breton in Paris, and the *Surrealists were highly excited by these striking images of 'vice and enchantment'. In 1938, in danger of arrest by the Nazis, Bellmer fled from Berlin to Paris to join the Surrealists. He was interned at the beginning of the war (with Max *Ernst), then lived in the south of France, 1942–6, before returning to Paris, where he began a long series of drawings and etchings that developed the violent eroticism of his dolls. Bellmer also produced paintings and sculpture in a similar vein. His work includes some of the acknowledged masterpieces of erotic art, but it was not well known until a large retrospective in 1971–2 at the Centre National d'Art Contemporain, Paris.

Bellori, Giovanni Pietro (1613–96). Italian biographer, art theorist, antiquarian, and collector. His most important work—a basic source for the history of 17th-century art—is *Le vite de' pittori, scultori et architetti moderni* (1672), in the preparation of which he was helped by his friend *Poussin. In contrast to former biographers, he concentrated on artists selected for their importance, limiting himself to only twelve subjects. The preface to the work (originally delivered as a lecture at the Accademia di S. Luca, Rome, in 1664) became the classic statement of the concept of *ideal art. It had a decisive influence on French academic theory and later became the theoretical basis of the *Neoclassicism preached by *Winckelmann.

Bellotto, Bernardo (1721–80). Italian painter, draughtsman, and etcher, nephew, pupil, and assistant of *Canaletto in Venice. He became a member of the Venetian painters' guild in 1738 and in the 1740s he travelled widely in Italy, painting views of Florence, Rome, and other cities. In 1747 he left Italy for good, spending the rest of his life working successfully at various European courts, notably Dresden (1747–58 and 1761–6) and Warsaw (where he lived from 1767 until his death). He called himself Canaletto, and this caused confusion (perhaps deliberate) between his work and his uncle's, particularly in views of Venice. Bellotto's early work is indeed sometimes difficult to tell apart from his uncle's, but his mature style is more individual, distinguished by an almost Dutch interest in massed clouds, cast shadows, and rich foliage. His colouring is also generally more sombre than Canaletto's, much of his work being characterized by a steely grey. The best collections of his work are in Dresden (Gemäldegalerie) and Warsaw (Nat. Mus.). In the rebuilding of Warsaw after the Second World War his pictures were used as guides, even in the reconstruction of architectural ornament.

Bellows, George Wesley (1882–1925). American painter and lithographer, a leading pupil and follower of Robert *Henri. An outstanding athlete in his youth and noted for his hearty, outgoing character, Bellows is best known for his boxing scenes. The most famous of them is *A Stag at Sharkey's* (1907, Cleveland Mus. of Art), remarkable for its vivid sense of movement and energetic, sketchy brushwork (a 'stag' was a boxing match held in a private club). Such works rapidly won him a reputation, and in 1909—aged 27—he became the youngest person ever elected an associate member of the *National Academy of Design. He took a highly active part in the art life of his day and was one of the organizers of the *Armory Show in 1913. After this, his work tended to become less concerned with movement, placing more emphasis on formal balance. He was a man of strong social conscience, and his work included scenes of the urban poor—of which the most famous is the crowded tenement scene *Cliff Dwellers* (1913, Los Angeles County Mus. of Art)—and a series of paintings and lithographs about First World War atrocities. He did not take up lithography until 1916, but in the nine remaining years of his life he produced almost 200 prints, and he is accorded a high place among modern American printmakers. In the last five years of his life Bellows turned to landscapes and portraits and was considered one of the finest American portraitists of his day. His early death was caused by a ruptured appendix. *See also* ASHCAN SCHOOL.

Belvedere Torso. A marble fragment showing the torso and upper legs of a powerful male figure seated on a rock, now in the Vatican Museums and named after the Belvedere Court in the Vatican in which it was once displayed. It is signed by a Greek sculptor, 'Apollonius, son of Nestor, Athenian', about whom nothing is known, and there is scholarly debate as to whether it is an original *Hellenistic work or a Roman copy. (It is sometimes alleged that the signature of Apollonius occurs also on the famous and stylistically similar bronze figure of a seated boxer in the Terme Museum in Rome, but most authorities now consider that this is a mirage.) The date of the discovery of the torso is uncertain, but it is first mentioned in the 1430s. It had become well known by 1500 and its majestic portrayal of heroic muscularity had a profound influence on *Michelangelo among other *Renaissance artists. From then until the 19th century it was widely regarded as one of the greatest works of art in the world, rivalled in status probably only by the *Apollo Belvedere and the *Laocoön among ancient sculptures, although its fame was generally more academic than popular. It was often referred to simply as 'the Torso'. Unusually, the figure has always been left unrestored, but various artists have attempted to reconstruct the statue, notably *Flaxman, who made of it a group as *Hercules and Hebe* (1792, University College

London, on loan to V&A). Although Hercules has been the most popular suggestion for the identity of the figure, there have been several others, including Ajax and Polyphemus. Between 1798 and 1815 the *Belvedere Torso* was in Paris, one of the many antique statues taken there by Napoleon.

Bening (or **Benig**). The name of two Netherlandish book *illuminators, father and son. **Sanders** (sometimes called Alexander) (d. 1519) worked in Ghent and Bruges. No documented works by him are known, but it has been suggested that he should be identified with the *Master of Mary of Burgundy, which would give him an artistic status appropriate to the contemporary reputation he enjoyed. **Simon** (c.1483–1561) worked in Bruges and was the most famous illuminator of his time, representing the final sparks of the tradition as the manuscript was supplanted by the printed book. There is a self-portrait *miniature (1558) by him in the Victoria and Albert Museum, London, and various documented manuscripts by him survive. His daughter, **Levina Teerlinc** (d. 1576), was also a miniaturist. She settled in London in about 1545 and worked for Henry VIII, Mary I, and Elizabeth I.

Benois, Alexandre (1870–1960). Russian painter, stage designer, art historian, and critic, a leader and spokesman of the *World of Art group. He was a close friend and collaborator of *Diaghilev, in Russia and later in Paris, and he is best known for his stage designs for the Ballets Russes (notably for Stravinsky's *Petrushka*, 1911), in which he harmonized the tradition of Russian folk art with French *Rococo elements. Following a difference of opinion with Diaghilev he worked at Stanislavsky's Moscow Arts Theatre, 1912–14. After the Revolution he was appointed curator of paintings at the *Hermitage in Leningrad. He held this post from 1918 to 1925, then settled permanently in Paris. His writings include several volumes of memoirs and books on art, including ones translated into English as *The Russian School of Painting* (1916), *Reminiscences of the Russian Ballet* (1941), and *Memoirs* (1960). Benois's son, **Nikolai** (1901–88), was a stage designer at La Scala, Milan; his niece, **Nadia Benois** (1896–1975), settled in London in 1920 and worked as a ballet designer. The actor and writer Sir Peter Ustinov was her son.

Benson, Ambrosius (d. 1550). Netherlandish painter of religious works and portraits. He was born in Italy (he was originally called Ambrogio Benzone), but from 1518 he worked in Bruges, where he continued the tradition of Gerard *David, to whom he worked as assistant for a time. Many of his pictures were done for the export trade to Italy and Spain, and he evidently had a flourishing business. There is a slightly southern flavour to his compositions and for a long time many of them were thought to be by an anonymous Spanish painter known as the Master of Segovia. His comparatively rare portraits are generally more individualized than his religious works.

Benton, Thomas Hart (1889–1975). American painter, the great-nephew of a famous American statesman of the same name. In 1908–11 he lived in Paris, where he studied at the *Académie Julian and became a friend of the *Synchromist Stanton *Macdonald-Wright. After his return to the USA he settled in New York and painted in the Synchromist manner for some years, but having failed to win success working in an avant-garde style, he abandoned modernism around 1920 and gained fame as one of the leading exponents of *Regionalism. His style became richly coloured and vigorous, with restlessly energetic rhythms and rather flat, sometimes almost cartoonish figures. His work included several murals, notably scenes of American life (1930–1) at the New School for Social Research in New York. In 1935 he left New York to become director of the City Art Institute and School of Design in Kansas City, Missouri, and he lived in that city for the rest of his life. When Regionalism declined in popularity in the 1940s Benton turned more to depicting scenes from American history, and some of his later work introduced American types into representations of Greek myths or biblical stories. Benton wrote two autobiographies, *An Artist in America* (1937) and *An American in Art* (1969). A passage from the second shows how completely he turned his back on the modernism he had espoused in his youth: 'Modern art became, especially in its American derivations, a simple smearing and pouring of material, good for nothing but to release neurotic tensions. Here finally it became like a bowel movement or a vomiting spell.' In view of these words, it is ironic that Benton was influential on Jackson *Pollock, whom he taught at the *Art Students League of New York in the early 1930s.

Bentvueghels. *See* SCHILDERSBENT.

Berchem, Nicolaes (1620–83). Dutch painter, active mainly in his native Haarlem (but also in Amsterdam, where he died). Berchem was the son of the still-life painter Pieter *Claesz., and it is not known why he adopted a different surname. Claesz. was his first teacher, but although Berchem tried his hand at most subjects, no still lifes by him are known. His speciality was the Italianate pastoral landscape, and among his contemporaries only Jan *Both rivalled his fame in this field. There is no documentary evidence that he visited Italy, but he was probably there at least once (the early 1650s is thought to be the likeliest time). His career was highly successful and he had numerous pupils and followers; later he exerted a strong influence on 18th-century English and French landscape painters, *Gainsborough and *Watteau being among the artists who particularly admired his work. His large output is well represented in British galleries. About 700 paintings by him survive, as well as more than 300 drawings and about 50 etchings.

Berckheyde, Gerrit (1638–98). Dutch painter of town views and architectural scenes, active in Haarlem (his native city), Amsterdam, and The Hague. His representations of these cities have documentary accuracy, but they are never dry, achieving a poetic harmony by a subtle use of light and shade (three of his pictures of Haarlem, including a church interior, are in the National Gallery, London). The work of Gerrit's elder brother, **Job** (1630–93), is often very similar, although he also painted other subjects, including *genre and biblical scenes.

Berenson, Bernard (1865–1959). American art historian, critic, and collector. He was born in Lithuania and educated in Boston and at Harvard University (his family emigrated to the USA when he was 10), but he spent most of his long life in Italy, first visiting the country in 1888 and settling there permanently in 1899. He built up a formidable reputation as an authority on Italian *Renaissance painting and was associated with several prominent dealers and collectors, notably Lord *Duveen and Isabella Stewart *Gardner, advising them on purchases. The fortune he earned in the picture trade has caused his impartiality to be questioned, and many of his attributions have been downgraded, but his lists of the work of Renaissance painters formed a basis for further work for many years. His most enduring work of scholarship is *The Drawings of the Florentine Painters* (1903; 2nd edn. 1938; 3rd edn.—in Italian—1961). He amassed a huge library of books and photographs and an impressive art collection at his villa, I Tatti, at Settignano, near Florence, which he left to Harvard University. In 1961 it opened as the Harvard University Center for Italian Renaissance Studies. Dapper and polylingual, Berenson often played host to visiting art historians and intellectuals at I Tatti and was a renowned conversationalist, diarist, and bon viveur. *See also* TACTILE VALUES.

Berger, John. *See* KITCHEN SINK SCHOOL.

Berlinghieri. Family of Italian painters active in Lucca during the 13th century. **Berlinghiero Berlinghieri** (d. *c*.1235) was the founder of the family and had three painter sons, **Barone, Bonaventura** (d. *c*.1274), and **Marco.** A painted *Crucifix* (Mus. Naz. di Villa Guinigi, Lucca) signed 'Berlingeri' without Christian name is generally attributed to Berlinghiero, and several other works have been given to him on the basis of it. Bonaventura, evidently the most talented of his sons, is known chiefly for his signed and dated altarpiece of *St Francis and Scenes from his Life* (1235) in the church of S. Francesco at Pescia. It is one of the earliest pictorial representations of Franciscan ideas, produced only nine years after the saint's death. There are no other signed or documented works by Bonaventura, but several have been attributed to him on stylistic evidence.

Berman, Eugene (1899–1972). Russian-born painter and stage designer who became an American citizen in 1937. In 1918 he fled the Russian Revolution and settled in Paris. There he became friendly with Pavel *Tchelitchew (another Russian émigré) and a group of painters who became known as *'Neo-Romantics', painting dreamlike scenes with mournful, drooping figures. In 1935 he emigrated to New York, where he worked mainly as a designer for ballet and opera, in which field he was considered one of the outstanding artists of his day.

Bermejo, Bartolomé (active 1468–95). Spanish painter, evidently from Cordova, but active in northern Spain—in Aragon and then from 1486 in Barcelona. His name was originally Bartolomé de Cárdenas; his nickname 'Bermejo' (Spanish for 'red') presumably indicates that he had red hair or a ruddy complexion. He was one of the first Spanish painters to work in *oils and it has been suggested that he learned the technique in the Netherlands. His most celebrated work is the powerfully emotional *Pietà* in Barcelona Cathedral, signed and dated 1490. It is one of the acknowledged masterpieces of the period and Bermejo is 'generally recognised as the greatest painter active in Spain in the Middle Ages' (Eric Young, *Bartolomé Bermejo*, 1975).

Bernard, Émile (1868–1941). French painter and writer. In 1884–6 he studied in the studio of *Cormon, where he became a friend of *Toulouse-Lautrec and also of Louis *Anquetin, with whom he developed *Cloisonnism in 1887–8. Between 1888 and 1891 he worked closely with *Gauguin at *Pont-Aven; he had a stimulating effect on his great colleague and together they created *Synthetism. Thereafter, however, Bernard's work as a painter greatly declined in importance, and he became of interest chiefly for his activities as a writer, playing a significant role as a sponsor of *Post-Impressionism. In 1890 he helped to organize the first retrospective exhibition of van Gogh's work (soon after his death), he published much journalism and criticism on *Cézanne, *Redon, and other artists, and his correspondence with some of the leading painters of the time has been a rich quarry for art historians.

Bernini, Gianlorenzo (1598–1680). Italian sculptor, architect, painter, and designer, the supreme artist of the Italian *Baroque. His father, **Pietro** (1562–1629), was a *Mannerist sculptor of some distinction, active in Naples and then from *c*.1605 in Rome, and Gianlorenzo owed to him not only his early training in the handling of marble but also his introduction to the powerful patrons, the *Borghese and the

*Barberini, who fostered his early career. For Cardinal Scipione Borghese he executed a remarkable series of life-size marble sculptures: *Aeneas, Anchises, and Ascanius* (1618–19), the *Rape of Proserpine* (1621–2), *David* (1623), and *Apollo and Daphne* (1622–5), all in the Borghese Gallery in Rome. In their dramatic vigour and movement these works made a complete break with the Mannerist tradition, and they showed unprecedented virtuosity in making cold stone seem as supple as living flesh (his biographer *Baldinucci commented that 'his chisel was applied in such a way that one could believe it had been cutting wax instead of marble'). After the election of Maffeo Barberini as Pope Urban VIII (1623) Bernini became the principal artist in the papal court and in Rome. According to Baldinucci, Maffeo had 'scarcely ascended the sacred throne' when he summoned Bernini and told him: 'It is your great fortune to see Cardinal Maffeo Barberini Pope, but our fortune is far greater in that Cavalier Bernini lives during our pontificate.' In 1629 he was appointed architect to St Peter's, for which his work included the great bronze *baldacchino over the high altar (1624–33), the huge marble statue of St Longinus (1629–38), which stands in a niche in one of the piers of the crossing, and Urban's tomb (1628–47), which is in bronze and white and coloured marbles. However, after Urban's death in 1644 Bernini fell under a cloud. This was partly because of one of his rare failures (a bell-tower he added to the façade of St Peter's was demolished in 1646 because of structural problems), but as much because of the different artistic tastes of the new pope, Innocent X, who favoured Bernini's rival, *Algardi.

During Innocent's papacy (1644–55) Bernini worked mainly for private patrons. The Cornaro Chapel, with the celebrated marble group of the *Ecstasy of St Teresa*, in S. Maria della Vittoria dates from this period (1645–52). Although it is a comparatively small work, it is the supreme example of Bernini's aims and achievement in the fusion of sculpture, architecture, and painting into a decorative and emotional whole. Bernini never lost his position as architect to St Peter's, however, and he did do some work for Innocent X, including the Fountain of the Four Rivers (1648–51) in the Piazza Navona. This is the most famous and spectacular of

Bernini's fountains, and with these, his buildings, and his outdoor statuary he has had a greater effect on the face of Rome than any other artist. After Innocent's death in 1655 and the accession of Alexander VII (Fabio *Chigi), he was restored to full favour and was almost immediately given two major commissions at St Peter's: the decoration of the *Cathedra Petri* (Throne of St Peter), and the building of the vast colonnade round the piazza in front of the church. The *Cathedra Petri* (1657–66), a setting for the wooden chair believed to have been used by St Peter, provides an appropriately spectacular sight to conclude the vista at the east end of the church. Four immense bronze figures of Doctors of the Church support the chair, also encased in bronze, and gilt angels and cherubs float above on stucco clouds; they surround a window bearing an image of the Dove of the Holy Spirit, from which a burst of light seems to emanate. The enclosure of the piazza in front of St Peter's is his greatest achievement as an architect—a design of the utmost dignity and grandeur, expressing the overwhelming authority of the Church. Bernini himself compared the sweeping colonnades to motherly arms that reach out to 'embrace Catholics to reinforce their belief'.

In 1665–6 Bernini visited Paris with the aim of designing the east front of the *Louvre, but his plans were abandoned in favour of a French design, and the trip—which he had made unwillingly—was not a success (the 'invitation' from Louis XIV was in effect a command—one of a series of humiliations that he inflicted on Pope Alexander VII and a sign that the balance of artistic power was beginning to shift from Italy to France). After his return to Rome Bernini continued to be extremely active into his old age. His late religious works are intensely spiritual, reflecting his own ardent faith (*The Blessed Lodovica Albertoni*, 1671–4, S. Francesco a Ripa, Rome). As an architect his late work included both secular and religious buildings, notably the façade (begun 1664) of the Palazzo Chigi, which had great influence on Baroque palace design throughout Europe, and S. Andrea al Quirinale (1658–70), a fairly small church but one of his most sophisticated designs in its use of rich architectural and sculptural decoration to create an appropriate setting for the mysteries of the

Catholic faith. In addition to large works of sculpture and architecture, Bernini executed many portrait busts, among the finest of which are those of his mistress Costanza Buonarelli (c.1635), in the Bargello, Florence, and Louis XIV (1665) at Versailles. He was also a brilliant wit, a *caricaturist, and —for his private pleasure—a painter of such high quality that his rare surviving works (which include several self-portraits) have sometimes been attributed to *Velázquez; his portrait of *Poussin (c.1627, York AG) was long considered to be a self-portrait by the French artist. Bernini also had a passionate interest in the theatre. There are few material remains of his activity in this field, but the diarist John Evelyn saw a remarkable demonstration of his versatility when visiting Rome in 1644: 'Bernini... gave a public opera wherein he painted the scenes, cut the statues, invented the engines [stage machinery], composed the music, writ the comedy, and built the theatre.'

Bernini's work was a dominant influence on sculpture in Italy (and to a certain degree in other Catholic countries) until well into the 18th century, but thereafter his reputation plummeted. To the *Neoclassical taste of the later 18th century, his approach to sculpture was anathema, to *Ruskin in the 19th century it seemed 'impossible for false taste and base feeling to sink lower', and to the devotees of the idea of *truth to materials in the 20th century he appeared, in the words of his most distinguished apologist, Rudolf *Wittkower, as 'the Antichrist personified'. It was only in the second half of the 20th century that he came to enjoy a reputation, comparable with his status in his lifetime, as the greatest sculptor since *Michelangelo and one of the giants of Baroque architecture.

Bernward of Hildesheim (c.960–1022). German ecclesiastic and art patron. He was abbot of the Benedictine monastery at Hildesheim in Saxony from 993 until his death, and for the church of St Michael there (begun 1001) he commissioned the famous bronze doors (c.1008–15) and a great bronze column (c.1018–20), probably intended to support the paschal candle. They are important not only for being among the outstanding European works of their period, but also for marking the revival of the *cire-perdue technique of casting, which had virtually disappeared since the time of Charlemagne. A contemporary biographer records that Bernward himself practised metalwork and manuscript *illumination, but no work can be attributed to him. He was canonized in 1192 and is a patron saint of goldsmiths.

Berruguete. Spanish artists, father and son, who are respectively associated with the beginnings of the *Renaissance and *Mannerist styles in their country. **Pedro** (d. c.1504) is said to have been court painter to Ferdinand and Isabella. He may be identifiable with the 'Pietro Spagnuolo' employed in 1477 with *Joos van Wassenhove on the decoration of the palace library at Urbino, but it is not until the 1480s that there is any firm documentation on his career. He did a good deal of work in fresco in Toledo Cathedral, but little of this survives. Most of his surviving paintings are altarpieces (several examples are in the Prado, Madrid); they are essentially in the Netherlandish idiom that prevailed in Spain at this time, but they show Renaissance influence in their spatial clarity and use of classical architectural details. **Alonso** (c.1488–1561), sculptor and painter, was the son and probably pupil of Pedro. Between about 1504 and 1517, he was in Italy, where his work included the completion of Filippino *Lippi's *Coronation of the Virgin* (Louvre, Paris). By 1517 Berruguete was back in Spain (in Valladolid), and in the following year he was appointed court painter to Charles I (Emperor Charles V; *see* HABSBURG). However, his career flourished mainly as a sculptor, chiefly in Toledo, where he spent most of his time between 1539 and his death. Among his finest works is a set of wooden choir stalls with carvings of biblical figures in Toledo Cathedral (1539–43). The expressive *contrapposto and emotional intensity characteristic of his style reflected the influence of *Michelangelo (who refers to Berruguete in his letters) and of the *Laocoön*, which he had studied in Rome. He is generally considered the greatest Spanish sculptor of the 16th century, his work having something of the spirit of El *Greco, who succeeded him as the outstanding artist in Toledo.

Bertin, Jean-Victor. *See* COROT.

Bertoldo di Giovanni (c.1430–91). Florentine sculptor. He was a fairly minor talent, but he is remembered for three things. First, he was the pupil and assistant of *Donatello and briefly the teacher or mentor of *Michelangelo, thus forming a link between the greatest Italian sculptors of the 15th and 16th centuries. Secondly (and relatedly), he was the 'guide and chief' (*Vasari) of the informal art *academy that Lorenzo the Magnificent maintained in the *Medici garden near S. Marco (it was there that he knew Michelangelo). Thirdly, he developed a new type of sculpture—the small-scale bronze, intended, like the *cabinet picture, for the private collector. Bertoldo was responsible for the completion of two pulpits in S. Lorenzo left unfinished by Donatello at his death. His own most noteworthy work is a bronze *relief of a battle scene (c.1480, Bargello, Florence), which inspired one of Michelangelo's first works, the *Battle of the Lapiths and Centaurs* (c.1491, Casa Buonarroti, Florence). Bertoldo was also one of the leading portrait medallists of his time.

bestiary. A type of medieval book in which accounts of real and imaginary creatures (and also plants and minerals) were used to point moral lessons. The first known illustrated examples date from the early 12th century and in the late 12th and early 13th centuries the bestiary was one of the most popular types of *illuminated manuscript. It declined in popularity after the mid-13th century, but many of the exotic and fanciful creatures it had helped to make familiar, such as the unicorn, continued to be prevalent in medieval art, for example in the decoration of initials in manuscripts and later on *misericords.

Beuckelaer, Joachim. *See* BEUCKELAER.

Beuys, Joseph (1921–86). German sculptor, draughtsman, teacher, and *Performance artist, one of the most influential figures in avant-garde art in Europe in the 1970s and 1980s. Like Yves *Klein, he was a leading light in shifting emphasis from what an artist makes to his personality, actions, and opinions, and he succeeded in creating a kind of personal mythology. (As a Luftwaffe pilot he was shot down in the Crimea in 1943 and according to his own account, which has been doubted, he was looked after by nomadic Tartars who kept him warm with fat and felt—materials that came to figure prominently in his work. The hat that he habitually wore hid the head injuries he received in the crash.) After the war he studied at the Düsseldorf Academy, 1946–51, and he became professor of sculpture there in 1961. He worked in various media, but is perhaps best known for his performances, of which the most famous was probably *How to Explain Pictures to a Dead Hare* (1965). In this he walked around an exhibition in the Schmela Gallery in Düsseldorf, his face covered in honey and gold leaf, carrying in his arms a dead hare, to which he gave an explanation of various pictures. He described the performance as 'A complex tableau about the problems of language, and about the problems of thought, of human consciousness and of the consciousness of animals.' In 1962 Beuys became a member of *Fluxus, an international group of artists, opposed to tradition and professionalism in the arts, and he was also active in politics, aligning himself with the West German ecology party, the Greens. His 'presumptuous political dilettantism' led to conflict with authority and in 1972 he was dismissed from his professorship. The protests that followed included a strike by his students, and a settlement was eventually reached whereby he kept his title and studio but his teaching contract was ended. He devoted a good deal of his later career to public speaking and debate, and in 1982 he had a meeting with the Dalai Lama in Paris. By the end of his life he was an international celebrity and was regarded by his admirers as a kind of art guru. To many people, however, his work is pretentious or incomprehensible.

Bevan, Robert (1865–1925). British painter and lithographer. During the 1890s he travelled a good deal and he met *Gauguin at Pont-Aven in 1894. In 1900 he settled in London, where he became a member of *Sickert's circle (he was a founding member of the *Camden Town Group in 1911 and of the *London Group in 1913). His work was much influenced by Gauguin's bold colour and flat patterning, and in his last years his style became increasingly simplified and schematic. He is best known for paintings featuring horses. His wife, the Polish-born Stanislava de Karlowska (1880–1952), whom he married in 1897, was also a painter. He made several visits to Poland with her.

Bewick, Thomas (1753–1828). English engraver, active for most of his life in Newcastle upon Tyne. Bewick ran a busy workshop in which most of the day-to-day jobs involved copper engraving, but for his own projects he preferred *wood engraving, and he was the first artist to show the full potential of this technique. He had a great love of the countryside, and his finest works are natural history illustrations, particularly those to his celebrated books *A General History of Quadrupeds* (1790) and *A History of British Birds* (2 vols., 1797 and 1804), for which he wrote most of the texts himself. The animals and birds are characterized with great skill, but Bewick is as much admired for his tailpieces—little (sometimes tiny) vignettes with which he concluded his account of each animal or bird. These miniature scenes give a wonderfully shrewd and sensitive picture of rural life, bringing out its bleakness and cruelty as well as its beauty and humour. Bewick himself punningly called these scenes 'Tale-pieces', for they were 'seldom without an endeavour to illustrate some truth or point some moral'. The success of his books helped to make wood engraving the dominant medium for book illustration for most of the 19th century and his work was carried on by several followers in Newcastle, notably his son **Robert** (1788–1849). Bewick wrote an autobiography, which was posthumously published (edited by his daughter) in 1862; a more authoritative text, based on the original manuscript (BL, London), appeared in 1975. A year before his death Bewick was visited by *Audubon, another great artist-naturalist, who left a touching account of his meeting with this 'perfect old Englishman', who was 'kind and attentive' and still—at the age of 74—'active and prompt in his labours', using 'delicate and beautiful tools ... all made by himself'.

Beyeren, Abraham van (1620/1–90). Dutch painter, little regarded in his day but now considered one of the greatest of still-life painters. He initially specialized in fish subjects, but in the 1650s he began to devote himself to sumptuous banquet tables laden with silver and gold vessels, Venetian glassware, fine fruit, and expensive table coverings of damask, satin, and velvet. Works of this kind, in which he was rivalled only by *Kalf, gave him even greater opportunity than his fish pieces to demonstrate his ability to show the play of light on varied surfaces and organize forms and colours into an opulent composition. He was born in The Hague and worked there and in various other towns before settling in Overschie in 1678. In addition to still lifes he painted seascapes.

Bibiena (or **Galli-Bibiena**). Family of Italian architects, *quadraturisti*, and stage designers based in Bologna, members of which practised from the 1680s until the 1780s throughout Europe, from Lisbon to St Petersburg. The founder of the dynasty was **Giovanni Maria Galli** (1625–65), who adopted the name of his birthplace, Bibiena, a small town in Tuscany. Other members of the family included **Alessandro** (1687–1769), **Antonio** (1700–74), **Carlo** (1728–87), **Ferdinando** (1657–1743), **Francesco** (1659–1739), and **Giuseppe** (1696–1757). Their work included fantastically elaborate stage-settings for operas, balls, and various kinds of festivities, mainly produced in the service of the *Habsburg family in Vienna and of various German princelings. They also built several theatres in Italy and elsewhere, but most of these have been destroyed or much altered. The most illustrious and prolific member of the family was Ferdinando, who produced several books on architecture and scenography.

Biedermeier. Term applied to an intimate, unassuming style characteristic of much German and Austrian art and interior decoration in the period roughly between the end of the Napoleonic Wars (1815) and the Year of Revolutions (1848). The name derives from an invented character, an unintentionally comic poet called Gottlieb Biedermaier [sic], who in the 1850s was a 'contributor' to the Munich journal *Fliegende Blätter* (Flying Leaves); *bieder* means plain or solid and *Maier* is a common surname, like Smith or Jones in English, so the character was meant to exemplify conventional bourgeois values. When it was applied to the visual arts, the term was originally used pejoratively, implying sentimentality and parochial dullness, but later it came to suggest more positive values, including comfort, good craftsmanship, and unostentatious charm. Biedermeier painting is concerned with the everyday world, in subjects such as portraiture and still life, contrasting with the grand gestures of *Neoclassicism and *Romanticism.*Spitzweg and*Waldmüller are among the painters who best exemplify the style. The term is sometimes extended to cover the work of artists in other countries, for example *Købke in Denmark.

Biennale (or **Bienale**). An art exhibition held every two years, particularly a large and prestigious exhibition of international scope. The first to be founded and still the most famous is the Venice Biennale, instituted in 1895 as the 'International Exhibition of Art of the City of Venice', and claiming to represent 'the most noble activities of the modern spirit without distinction of country'. At this first Biennale, artists from sixteen different countries were represented, and the committee included such famous personalities as *Burne-Jones, *Israëls, *Liebermann, *Moreau, and *Puvis de Chavannes. The exhibition soon acquired worldwide prestige, and after it resumed in 1948 following the Second World War it became the leading showplace for the established international avant-garde. Other exhibitions founded on the Venice model include the São Paulo Bienale, first held in 1951, and the Paris Biennale, first held in 1959.

Bierstadt, Albert (1830–1902). German-born American painter, active mainly in New York. He made several trips to the Far West and was the leading figure of the *Rocky Mountain School, specializing in grandiose pictures of awesome mountain scenery. His paintings—often huge in size —were immensely popular in his lifetime, but his on-the-spot sketches are now generally found much more appealing.

Bigaud, Wilson. *See* NAIVE ART.

Bigot, Trophime (1579–1650). French *Caravaggesque painter, active in Rome (c.1620–34) and then in the Aix-en-Provence area. His career is obscure (it was once surmised that there were two painters of the same name, one older than the other), but he has been identified as the author of a number of paintings, mainly intimate candlelit scenes, some of which were previously grouped under the name of 'the Candlelight Master'. He sometimes painted unusual subjects (*Doctor Examining a Sample of Urine*, Ashmolean Mus., Oxford).

Bill, Max (1908–94). Swiss painter, sculptor, architect, designer, teacher, and writer. From 1927 to 1929 he studied at the *Bauhaus, then returned to Switzerland, where he lived mainly in Zurich. He regarded himself primarily as an architect, but he was active in a variety of fields, his ultimate aim being to establish a unity among the individual branches of the visual arts—he once defined art as the 'sum of all functions in harmonious unity'. However, he has probably become best known for his sculptures, which characteristically employ smooth, elegant, spiralling abstract forms in stone or polished metal. He took the term *'Concrete art' from van *Doesburg to describe his work in this vein and popularized the term in Switzerland in place of 'abstract'. In 1941 he visited Argentina and Brazil, introducing the concept of Concrete art there, and he was a vigorous publicist of his ideas (he wrote several books and numerous articles, in English as well as German, and he organized exhibitions of abstract art). His sculptures have been considered precursors of *Minimal art, but in fact they represent a subtle blending of mathematics and intuition, and some Minimalists, including Donald *Judd and Robert *Morris, have denied his influence. As an architect, Bill's work included his own house in Zurich (1932–3) and the much-praised Hochschule für Gestaltung (College of Design) in Ulm (1951–5), where, working on a limited budget, he created an austerely elegant complex of buildings delicately placed in a romantic setting. He was co-founder of the school and head of the departments of architecture and produce design from 1951 to 1957.

Bingham, George Caleb (1811–79). American painter. He worked mainly in Missouri (where he held several political posts), painting the life of the frontier people. Except for a short period studying at the Pennsylvania Academy of Fine Arts, he was self-taught. His finest canvases, particularly the celebrated *Fur Traders Descending the Missouri* (1845, Met. Mus., New York), distil visual poetry from the commonplace, but after a trip to Düsseldorf (a major art centre that attracted several American painters) in 1856–8 his work lost much of its racy freshness and charm, tending to become self-conscious and sentimental.

biomorphic. A term applied to forms in abstract art that derive from or suggest organic (rather than geometric) shapes, as, for example, in the sculpture of Henry *Moore.

Bird, Francis (1667–1731). English sculptor. He trained in Flanders and later visited Rome at least once. This Continental background meant that he could work in a *Baroque idiom more convincingly than most of his English contemporaries, as is seen in his best-known work, the *Conversion of St Paul* (1706) in the west pediment of St Paul's Cathedral, London. Bird did other carving at St Paul's, but most of his output consisted of tomb sculpture. His work is uneven, but he ranks as the most significant figure in English sculpture between *Gibbons (for whom he worked for a time) and *Rysbrack.

Birolli, Renato (1905–59). Italian painter whose outspoken political views and advanced and energetic artistic outlook gave him a prominent place in his country's avant-garde. His early work was *Expressionist, influenced by *Ensor and van *Gogh, and a visit to Paris in 1936 introduced him to the work of the *Fauves. In 1938 he was one of the founders of the anti-Fascist *Corrente organization; he published articles in many journals and was persecuted and imprisoned for his political activities. After the Second World War he was strongly influenced by *Picasso and gradually moved towards abstraction, his work eventually coming within the orbit of *Art Informel. In 1947 he joined the *Fronte Nuovo delle Arti. From 1948 his work was shown at the Venice *Biennale on several occasions and was much exhibited elsewhere in Italy.

Bissière, Roger (1888–1964). French painter, sculptor, teacher, and writer on art. He was slow to mature as an artist and did not exhibit his work until 1920, first at the *Salon d'Automne, then at the *Salon des Indépendants. At this time he was influenced by *Cubism, which he attempted to 'humanize'. From 1925 to 1938 he taught at the *Académie Ranson, where he was a popular and influential figure among his students, who included *Manessier. However, his own work remained little known at this time. In 1938 he retired to his home in Lot-et-Garonne and the following year he contracted an eye ailment that left him unable to paint. He started painting again in 1945 and an operation in 1948 partially restored his sight. Thereafter he worked with renewed vigour and from the early 1950s he belatedly achieved an international reputation. His mature paintings are rich and glowing tapestry-like compositions. Representational elements were gradually submerged in scintillating patterns of colour, but Bissière said that they were always based on natural appearances and refused to accept the term 'abstract' for his work. In addition to paintings, from 1957 he made designs for stained glass, notably for Metz Cathedral (1960–1). Despite his success, he continued living quietly in Lot for the rest of his life.

bistre. A transparent brown *pigment derived from the soot of burned wood. The colour varies depending on the type of wood. It is often used as a *wash for pen-and-ink drawings and watercolours. *Claude and *Rembrandt were among the artists who most memorably exploited its potentialities. *See also* SEPIA.

bitumen (asphaltum). A resinous substance soluble in oils that can be used to produce a brown paint. At the time of use this gives a rich glowing quality, but it later becomes almost black and increasingly opaque. It never completely hardens and eventually develops a pronounced and often disfiguring *craquelure. It was most popular in the 18th century, and its damaging effects can be seen in works by *Reynolds and other British painters of the period.

black-figure vase painting. Technique of vase painting, originating in Corinth in the 7th century BC, in which figures were painted in black silhouette on the light red clay background. Details were added by incising through the black pigment or sometimes by overpainting in red or white. The technique had its finest flowering around the mid-6th century BC, notably in the work of *Execias; it then began to give way to *red-figure painting, although black-figure vases continued to be produced for another two centuries.

Black Mountain College. American art educational establishment at Black Mountain, North Carolina, founded by a group of progressive academics in 1933 and closed after long-standing financial problems in 1957. It was run by the teaching staff, with no outside control, and was kept deliberately small (with an average of about 50 students a year) to reduce administration; a variety of arts were taught and interaction between them was encouraged. Mary Emma Harris describes the college as 'a unique combination of liberal arts school, summer camp, farm school, pioneer village, refugee centre and religious retreat' and writes that it was 'a catalyst for the emergence of the American avant-garde after the Second World War' (catalogue of the exhibition 'American Art in the 20th Century', RA, London, 1993). In the visual arts, the teacher most associated with Black Mountain College was Josef *Albers, who arrived there with his wife Anni (who taught weaving) soon after it opened and stayed until 1949. Other illustrious figures who taught at Black Mountain include Robert *Motherwell and the composer John Cage (1912–92), whose ideas on chance and indeterminacy in the arts were widely influential. In 1952 he organized there a partly programmed performance (involving paintings and readings) that was later designated the first *happening. Famous former students of the college include John *Chamberlain, Kenneth *Noland, and Robert *Rauschenberg.

Blake, Sir Peter (1932–). British painter, printmaker, sculptor, and designer, a leading exponent of *Pop art. His use of imagery from comics, pin-up magazines, consumer goods, and advertisements captures the flavour of the times in a manner that now evokes nostalgia for the 'swinging sixties', as was made clear during his enormously popular retrospective exhibition at the Tate Gallery, London, in 1983 (his most famous work is the cover design for the Beatles LP *Sergeant Pepper's Lonely Hearts Club Band*, 1967). The combination of sophistication and naivety typical of Blake's style is seen particularly clearly in his work as a member of the Brotherhood of Ruralists, a group of seven painters based in the West Country, of which Blake (then living near Bath) was one of the founders in 1975. The members had several group exhibitions, took working holidays together, and shared a commission to design covers for the New Arden edition of Shakespeare's work, but they had common ideals rather than a

common style, taking as their inspiration 'the spirit of the countryside'. A series of winsome fairy paintings are characteristic of this facet of Blake's work, and many critics found the work of the group as a whole insufferably twee—one newspaper review of a 1981 Ruralists exhibition was headed 'Tinkerbell lives'. The Brotherhood last exhibited as a group at Blake's retrospective at the Tate in 1983. The other members were: Ann Arnold (1936–) and her husband Graham Arnold (1932–); the American-born Jann Haworth (1942–), who was married to Blake, 1963–81; David Inshaw (1943–); Annie Ovenden (1945–) and her husband Graham Ovenden (1943–).

Blake, William (1757–1827). English printmaker, painter, poet, and mystical philosopher, one of the most remarkable figures of the *Romantic period and one of the supreme individualists in the history of art. He was equally gifted in poetry and the visual arts, and in both fields he worked in a highly original, deeply personal idiom that expressed his unconventional views and fiercely independent personality. His unorthodoxy was bound up with his hatred of materialism and rationalism, which he thought fettered the mind and spirit and led to misery and oppression. He was deeply religious and often depicted Christian subjects in his paintings and prints, but he used private as well as traditional imagery in them, and he came to regard art, imagination and religion as indivisible. In matters of technique he was comparably original, developing new methods of printing to publish his poetry and pictures together. He had a few loyal patrons and admirers, but for most of his life he struggled to earn a living, being ignored or dismissed as eccentric (or mad) by the world at large. It was not until long after his death that he was widely recognized as one of the great men of his age.

Blake's parents were Nonconformists in religion, and his own individuality was evident from childhood (he first claimed to see angels when he was 10). From 1772 to 1779 he was apprenticed to the engraver James Basire (1730–1802), for whom his work included making drawings in Westminster Abbey for illustrations in antiquarian books. This helped to give him an enduring love of medieval art. After his apprenticeship ended he enrolled as a student at the *Royal Academy, but he was unhappy there (he particularly disliked *Reynolds) and soon left to set up as a commercial engraver, mainly producing book illustrations from other artists' drawings. His own first book, *Poetical Sketches*, appeared in 1783, partly sponsored by *Flaxman, one of his closest friends (his other friends included *Fuseli, who, like Blake, was one of the few painters in Britain to excel at imaginative subjects at a time when the country's art was dominated by portraiture and landscape). *Poetical Sketches* was conventionally produced, but all Blake's other books were done by his own method of 'illuminated printing', in which he combined illustrations and handwritten text on the same plate, making of them a decorative unity. The technique he used was a form of *relief etching; he experimented for a while with applying colours to the plate, but settled on hand colouring the pages with ink and watercolour, with the result that each copy of his books (which were produced in very small editions) differed in varying degrees from the others. Blake claimed that he was helped to solve the technical problems of creating his books by the spirit of his beloved younger brother, Robert, who died of consumption in 1787, aged 19. In the practical business of hand-tinting and binding the pages he was assisted by his devoted wife Catherine. Apart from some experimental booklets, Blake's first publication using his new method was *Songs of Innocence* (1789). In 1794 he added *Songs of Experience*, never issuing this separately, but always bound with the first volume to make *Songs of Innocence and Experience*. The two parts were intended to show the 'two contrary states of the human soul': *Songs of Innocence* are meditations on childhood, whereas *Songs of Experience* (which include the celebrated 'Tyger, Tyger') deal with the corruption of innocence by adult life.

Blake used several other techniques in his work. He avoided oils, which he thought encouraged blurring of forms, as clarity of line was essential to him (he saw his visions—whether of angels or his dead brother—so intently that they seemed part of the real world). For paintings he sometimes used tempera (confusingly he called the medium 'fresco'), which he associated with the predominantly linear style of the early *Renaissance, and in printing he produced some outstanding wood engravings. In 1795 he began a series of *monotypes that are usually referred to as the 'Large Colour Prints'. Twelve are now known; the subjects derive from the Bible, Milton, and Shakespeare, as well as from Blake's own writings, and the overall theme (if there is one) is uncertain. They have no accompanying text and in them Blake emerges for the first time as a great visual artist independent of Blake the writer (*Elohim Creating Adam*, 1795, Tate, London). None of these 'colour printed drawings' (as Blake called them) is known in more than three impressions, and the technique perhaps appealed to him more for its textural qualities than as a means of reproducing his work.

In about 1795 Blake was introduced to Thomas Butts, a civil servant who became his main patron for many years, paying him what was virtually a regular wage. Through Flaxman, Blake also met the poet and biographer William Hayley, who employed him from 1800 to 1803 at his home at Felpham, on the Sussex coast—the only time Blake lived outside London. However, the work provided by Hayley (such as decorating his library) was ill-suited to Blake's temperament. In 1809–10 he mounted the only exhibition of his work held in his lifetime. Few people came to see it and the only review described Blake as 'an unfortunate lunatic'. In 1818 he met his second great patron, John *Linnell, and largely thanks to him, his final decade was comparatively free of financial worries and one of the happiest and most productive periods of his life. His work for Linnell included a series of watercolour illustrations to Dante's *Divine Comedy*, begun in 1824 and left unfinished at his death. These include some of his finest work, in which he reached new heights in radiant use of colour and in the rendering of visionary experience.

Linnell introduced Blake to a circle of idealistic young painters—the *Ancients—who admired him and his work and brought to his old age a degree of protective sympathy he had never known before. One of them, George *Richmond, said that he 'died like a saint…singing of the things he saw in heaven'. In the next generation his memory was kept alive by a few admirers (including *Rossetti—another painter-poet with mystical leanings), but when the first substantial biography of him appeared in 1863—Alexander Gilchrist's *Life of William Blake*—it was subtitled 'Pictor Ignotus' (the unknown painter). The centenary of his death in 1927 stimulated a major revival of interest, and thereafter his reputation grew rapidly. His vast output now supports an academic industry of its own.

Blanchard, Jacques (1600–38). French painter, active mainly in his native Paris. From 1624 to 1628 he was in Italy and his style reflects both the polished classicism of contemporary Bolognese painting and the sensuous richness of the Venetian School. His contemporary reputation rested largely on decorative work, but little of this survives and he is now known chiefly as a painter of small, sensitive pictures of religious and mythological subjects (*Charity*, 1637, Courtauld Gall., London).

Blanche, Jacques-Émile (1861–1942). French painter. The son of Émile Blanche, a noted pathologist, he grew up in a cultured home and became a well-known figure in artistic and society circles—he was a friend of *Degas, *Renoir, *Whistler, the writers Henry James and Marcel Proust, and many other celebrities. His best-known works are stylish portraits of people from this milieu; the finest collection is in the Musée des Beaux-Arts at Rouen, and there are several examples in London (Tate). Blanche lived mainly at Offranville, near the Channel port of Dieppe (the local church has decorative painting by him), and he was a frequent visitor to Britain, painting numerous views of London (the Tate has an example). He wrote several books of criticism and reminiscence.

Blaue Reiter, Der (The Blue Rider). A loose association of artists formed in Munich in 1911 as a splinter group from the *Neue Künstlervereinigung. The name was also used in the title of the *Almanac* (a collection of essays and illustrations) published in 1912 by *Kandinsky and *Marc, two of the central figures of the group; the cover of the *Almanac* featured a drawing by Kandinsky of a blue horseman (blue was the favourite colour of Marc, who regarded it as particularly spiritual, and the horse was his most cherished subject; Kandinsky, too, often painted horses with riders, evoking ideas of medieval knights or warrior saints). Although the members of the group (who in-

cluded *Klee and *Macke) differed widely in their artistic outlooks, they were linked by a desire to express spiritual values in their work. They held two exhibitions (1911 and 1912) that brought the work of Der Blaue Reiter to several major cities of Germany, and the association had international affiliations; *Braque, *Derain, *Goncharova, *Larionov, and *Picasso were among those whose works were shown in the second exhibition. With the outbreak of the First World War the group disintegrated, but its short life is considered to mark the high point of German *Expressionism.

Blaue Vier, Die (The Blue Four). A group of four painters—Feininger, *Jawlensky, *Kandinsky, and *Klee—formed in 1924 at the instigation of the German art dealer Galka Scheyer (1889–1945) with the aim of promoting their work abroad (where there was a better market for art than in economically depressed Germany). Exhibitions were held in the USA and Mexico (as well as Germany) between 1925 and 1934. The venture was a moderate financial success and an important factor in spreading the reputation of the four artists (who had all been associated with Der *Blaue Reiter— hence the choice of name). Scheyer settled in the USA and became an American citizen. Her own collection of paintings by the Blaue Vier is now in the Norton Simon Museum, Pasadena, California.

Bles, Herri met de (active first half of 16th century). Netherlandish painter of landscapes with figures. He is an enigmatic artist, presumed to be one and the same as the Herri de Patinir who became a member of the Antwerp painters' guild in 1535. As van *Mander informs us, 'Herri met de Bles' is simply a nickname meaning 'Herri with the white forelock', and it is generally assumed that he was a relation of Joachim *Patinir, who certainly had a decisive influence on his work. No signed or documented work by Herri exists, but a small group of distinctive paintings has been ascribed to him, characterized by panoramic landscapes dominating the figure groups in the manner of Patinir. His work was popular with Italian collectors, who called him 'Civetta' (little owl) because he often included an owl in his pictures.

Bleyl, Fritz. *See* BRÜCKE.

block book. A type of illustrated book in which the words and image on each page are printed from a single *woodcut block, as distinct from books that use movable type for the words. Block books were made in China probably as early as the 6th century AD, but in Europe the earliest known examples seem to date from around 1450, that is, at very much the same time that Gutenburg introduced printing from movable metal type. (At one time they were thought to pre-date movable type, but it is now thought more likely that they were introduced very slightly after it.) As the entire text had to be cut letter by letter on wood blocks, the process was extremely laborious and suitable only for short books in continuous popular demand, usually popular religious texts. Very few block books were executed after 1480 and their place in the history of printing is as sterile descendants of the woodcut rather than as ancestors of printing from movable type.

Bloemaert, Abraham (1566–1651). Dutch historical and landscape painter and engraver, the son of a sculptor and architect, **Cornelis I Bloemaert** (c.1540–93). Most of his life was spent in Utrecht, where for many years he was the leading painter and an outstanding teacher. *Both, *Honthorst, *Terbrugghen, and virtually all the Utrecht painters of the period who attained any kind of distinction trained with him. Bloemaert was a good learner as well as a good teacher and rapidly assimilated the new ideas his pupils brought back from Italy. For a time he became a *Caravaggesque painter and late in his career adopted some aspects of the *classicism of the *Carracci. Although his landscape paintings are firmly in the *Mannerist tradition, his landscape drawings are naturalistic and his most original works. Many of his drawings were etched and published by his son **Frederick** (c.1616–90) in an instructional book for the use of art students (it first appeared c.1650 and continued to be reprinted into the 19th century). Bloemaert had three other painter sons, who like Frederick were his pupils: **Hendrick** (c.1601–72), **Cornelis II** (c.1603–c.1684), and **Adriaen** (c.1609–66).

Blondeel, Lancelot (1498–1561). Netherlandish painter, active mainly in Bruges, where he became a member of the painters' guild in 1519. He was highly versatile and also worked as a printmaker, architect, civil engineer, cartographer, and designer of sculpture, tapestries, and pageant decorations. In his day he was well known and highly regarded (he is mentioned by *Vasari) and in 1550 he and Jan van *Scorel were given the prestigious commission to restore the van *Eycks' celebrated Ghent Altarpiece. The *triptych of the *Martyrdom of Sts Cosmas and Damian* (1523, St Jacques, Bruges), is typical of his work as a painter in its profusion of Italianate ornament. By the 16th century Bruges had declined greatly in importance as a trading centre as its port silted up, and Blondeel represents one of the last sparks of its great artistic tradition.

Bloomsbury Group. A loose association of writers, artists, and intellectuals that was a distinctive force in British cultural life during the early decades of the 20th century. Leading members of the group included the writers E. M. Forster, Lytton Strachey, and Virginia Woolf, and the economist John Maynard *Keynes; among the artists and critics were Clive *Bell, Vanessa *Bell, Dora Carrington (1893–1932), Roger *Fry, Duncan *Grant, and Henry *Lamb. The group takes its name from the Bloomsbury district of London, where members often met at the houses of Clive and Vanessa Bell, or of Vanessa's sister, Virginia Woolf, and it stemmed from student friendships formed at Cambridge University; most of the 'Bloomsberries' had been at either King's College or Trinity College and many had been 'Apostles'—members of an exclusive, semi-secret intellectual club. However, the Bloomsbury Group had no formal membership and no common social or aesthetic ideology. The members were united mainly by their belief in the importance of the arts and—in revolt against the restrictions of Victorian society—by their frankness and tolerance in sexual matters (several of them were homosexual or bisexual and their love lives were often complexly intertwined).

In the visual arts, the Bloomsbury Group made its most significant impact in the 1910s, after it had been joined by Roger Fry (he had lived in New York from 1906 to 1910). Fry was highly influential in promoting an awareness of modern art—through his writing and lecturing, through his two

*Post-Impressionist exhibitions (1910 and 1912), and through his founding of the *Omega Workshops (1913). It was at this time, too, that Vanessa Bell and Duncan Grant were at their most adventurous, both of them producing pure abstracts by 1914. However, the richly coloured figurative style in which the couple worked in the period between the two world wars is considered the 'typical' Bloomsbury style. By the early 1930s the Bloomsbury Group had ceased to exist in its original form. After the Second World War, its ideas fell out of fashion and its members were attacked as dilettantish and elitist. However, from the late 1960s there has been a great revival of interest in all aspects of the group.

blot drawing. A technique devised by Alexander *Cozens, whereby an accidental mark or 'blot' on the paper is used as the starting point for an imaginative landscape composition. A similar suggestion had been made much earlier by *Leonardo da Vinci and somewhat similar techniques were later used by the *Surrealists for stimulating unconscious imagery (*see* AUTOMATISM).

Blue Rider. *See* BLAUE REITER.

Blunt, Anthony (1907–83). British art historian and spy. He was director of the *Courtauld Institute of Art from 1947 to 1974, Surveyor of the King's (later Queen's) Pictures from 1945 to 1972, and one of the leading figures in establishing art history as an academic discipline in Britain. His career was loaded with honours, but in 1979 he suffered disgrace (including being stripped of his knighthood) when it was sensationally revealed that he had spied for the Soviet Union during his service at the War Office in the Second World War. He wrote on a wide variety of subjects, but is best known for his contributions to the study of French and Italian art and architecture in the 16th and 17th centuries, above all for his numerous books and articles on *Poussin. His books include *Artistic Theory in Italy 1450–1600* (1940), *Art and Architecture in France 1500–1700* (1953 and subsequent edns.), *The Art of William *Blake* (1959), and *Guide to Baroque Rome* (1982). His brother **Wilfrid** (1901–87) was drawing master at Eton, 1938–59, curator of the *Watts Gallery at Compton 1959–85, and the author of numerous books on art and other subjects,

notably *The Art of Botanical Illustration* (1950) and '*England's Michelangelo*' (1975), a biography of Watts.

Boccioni, Umberto (1882–1916). Italian *Futurist painter, sculptor (the only major one in the movement), and art theorist. He signed the two Futurist manifestos of painting (both 1910), wrote the one on sculpture (1912), and became the most energetic member of the group. Advocating a complete break with the art of the past, Boccioni was centrally concerned with the two main preoccupations of the Futurists—the production of emotionally expressive works and the representation of time and movement. In his early Futurist works he often showed an interest in social themes, particularly big city life, but later (especially after a visit to Paris in 1912, when he was influenced by *Cubism) he tended to use his paintings more as vehicles for his theories than as comments on life around him. Eventually this tendency led him close to abstraction, in pictures such as *Dynamism of a Human Body* (1913, Gall. d'Arte Moderna, Milan). In common with the other Futurists, Boccioni believed that physical objects have a kind of personality and emotional life of their own, revealed by 'lines of force' with which the object reacts to its environment. This notion is perhaps best shown in his most famous piece of sculpture, *Unique Forms of Continuity in Space* (1913, casts in Tate, London; MoMA, New York; and elsewhere), which vividly expresses bodily movement. His ideas about sculpture were extremely forward-looking. He advocated the use of materials such as glass and electric lights and the introduction of electric motors to create movement. However, he died in an accident whilst serving in the Italian army before most of his ideas could be put into practice.

Böcklin, Arnold (1827–1901). Swiss painter. With *Hodler he ranks as the most important Swiss painter of the 19th century, and in the 1880s and 1890s he was the most influential artist of the German-speaking world, even though from 1850 he had spent most of his time in Italy. He established his reputation with *Pan in the Reeds* (1857, Neue Pin., Munich), the beginning of his preoccupation with the world of nymphs and satyrs, naiads, and tritons, the results of which are sometimes slightly absurd. Later his style became more sombre and charged with mystical feeling, bringing him into the orbit of *Symbolism, as in his best-known picture, *The Island of the Dead*, of which he painted five versions between 1880 and 1886 (an example of 1880 is in the Met. Mus., New York). This haunting work, which inspired a symphonic poem by Rachmaninov (1909), shows a rocky mausoleum-island approached by a boat carrying spectral figures; such morbid imagery appealed to the *Surrealists. A curious aspect of Böcklin's career is that like *Leonardo—whom he disliked—he spent much of his time experimenting with flying machines.

Bode, Wilhelm von (1845–1929). German art historian. His career was centred in Berlin; he became director of the Gemäldegalerie there in 1890 and from 1905 until his retirement in 1920 was director general of all the royal museums of Prussia. Under his administration the Gemäldegalerie became one of the world's outstanding collections. Apart from being a noted scholar, he was one of the pioneers of modern museum organization and display, combining pictures, sculptures, and frames in harmonious arrangements and achieving a balance between creating an up-to-date setting for works of art and reconstructing their historical milieu. His numerous publications were mainly on Italian *Renaissance sculpture and 17th-century Dutch painting (particularly *Rembrandt).

bodegón. Spanish term that was originally used to describe a low-class tavern and by the 1590s was applied to pictures featuring scenes of humble life in which food or drink plays a part. Some *bodegones* actually depict tavern interiors, but others are set in kitchens or unspecific surroundings. *Velázquez painted several *bodegones* early in his career, and these are the most famous examples of the type. *Bodegones* usually have a prominent still-life element, and in modern Spanish the term is used as a synonym for still life.

Body art. A type of art in which the artist uses his or her own body as the medium: it is closely related to *Conceptual art and *Performance art, and flourished mainly at the same time that these forms of expression were at their peak—the late 1960s and

1970s (there was something of a revival in the 1990s). Sometimes works of Body art are carried out in private and communicated by means of photographs or films; sometimes the execution of the 'piece' is public. The performance may be pre-choreographed or extemporaneous. Spectator participation is not usually invited. Body art is often playful in spirit, but several leading exponents have been concerned with self-inflicted pain or ritualistic acts of endurance. For example, in 'Seedbed' (1972) the American Body artist Vito Acconci (1940–) spent several hours daily masturbating under a gallery-wide ramp while the sounds of his activity were relayed via loudspeakers to visitors overhead. The philosophy behind such works is obscure.

body colour. Paint that is opaque rather than transparent. The term usually refers to opaque *watercolour, which is also known as *gouache.

Boilly, Louis-Léopold (1761–1845). French painter and printmaker. Boilly painted portraits, domestic and *genre scenes, and also *scènes galantes* that brought him into disrepute at the time of the Revolution. Generally he worked on a small scale, with a smooth and meticulous technique. He was extremely prolific, claiming to have produced 5,000 portraits. In the 1820s he took up *lithography and used this technique to popularize his scenes from contemporary life.

Bol, Ferdinand (1616–80). Dutch painter and etcher, active mainly in Amsterdam. He was a pupil of *Rembrandt in the mid-1630s and in his early work imitated his master's style so well as to create occasional difficulty in distinguishing between them. The portrait of Elizabeth Bas in the Rijksmuseum, Amsterdam, is the best-known instance; it was acknowledged as a Rembrandt until 1911, when it was attributed to Bol by *Bredius, and although this opinion is still widely accepted, there has been renewed support for Rembrandt as the author (as well as some for Jacob *Backer). As Bol's career prospered, both as a portraitist and a painter of historical subjects, his style moved away from that of Rembrandt, becoming blander and more elegant in the manner of van der *Helst. In 1669 he married a wealthy widow and seems to have stopped painting. *Kneller was Bol's most distinguished pupil.

Boldini, Giovanni (1842–1931). Italian painter, one of the most renowned society portraitists of his day. He was at his best with portraits of glamorous women: *Sickert referred to his 'wriggle-and-chiffon' style. His vivacious brushwork and gift for making his sitters look graceful and poised recall the work of his even more successful contemporary, John Singer *Sargent, and like Sargent he had an international career: he worked mainly in Paris, where he settled in 1871, but he travelled widely. Together with another flamboyant portraitist, Antonio Mancini (1852–1930), he was probably the best-known Italian artist at the turn of the century. Apart from portraits, his work includes some excellent street scenes of Paris. There is a Boldini museum in his native Ferrara. As with Sargent, his work went out of favour after his death, being considered merely glossy and superficial. *See also* MACCHIAIOLI.

Bolotowsky, Ilya (1907–81). Russian-born painter who settled in New York in 1923 and became an American citizen in 1929. In 1933 he was deeply impressed by some paintings by *Mondrian and he became one of America's most committed exponents of geometrical abstraction: 'In my paintings I avoid all associations. I try for perfect harmony, using neutral elements. I want things absolutely pure and simple.' He was a founding member of *American Abstract Artists in 1936 and his mural for the Williamsburgh Housing Project, New York, of that year was one of the first abstract murals to be commissioned. Bolotowsky was also a playwright and an experimental film-maker.

Boltraffio, Giovanni Antonio (c.1467–1516). Italian painter, the pupil and assistant of *Leonardo and the most talented of his followers in Milan. He painted religious subjects and portraits (an example of each is in the National Gallery, London). His style is more prosaic than his master's, but his best work is of high quality: the beautiful female portrait known as *La Belle Ferronnière* (Louvre, Paris) is attributed to Boltraffio by some authorities and to Leonardo by others.

Bomberg, David (1890–1957). British painter. He gave up an apprenticeship as a lithographer to devote himself to painting, studying under *Sickert and at the *Slade School. Whilst still a student he showed an advanced understanding of avant-garde Continental painting, particularly *Cubism and *Futurism (he visited Paris in 1913), and he exhibited with the *Vorticists (although he turned down Wyndham *Lewis's invitation to become a formal member of the group). His best-known work of this time is probably *In the Hold* (1913–14, Tate, London), a dazzlingly coloured abstraction of fragmented geometric forms. Although he received critical praise for this and other pictures, he had difficulty selling them and tended to work in isolation. From the 1920s he travelled widely, and at this time began moving away from abstraction to a heavily worked, somewhat *Expressionist figurative style, painting mainly portraits and landscapes. Much of his later career was devoted to teaching, and he had a strong influence on pupils such as *Auerbach and *Kossoff. At the time of his death he was little appreciated, but his reputation has since soared; a major exhibition was devoted to him at the Tate Gallery in 1988.

Bombois, Camille (1883–1970). French *naive painter. He was the son of a boatman and spent his childhood on canal barges until he became a farmhand at the age of 12. Later he was a road labourer and a wrestler in travelling circuses. From 1907 he lived in Paris, where after working as a porter on the Métro, a navvy, and a docker, he took a night job in a printing establishment so that he could paint during the day. In 1922 he came to the attention of Wilhelm *Uhde and other critics. With their encouragement he was able to devote all his time to painting and he became one of the best-known naive painters of his day, exhibiting his work widely. He painted various subjects but is best known for his circus pictures; they have great strength and vigour and sometimes an unconscious *Surrealist air. For example in *Carnival Athlete* (c.1930, Pompidou Centre, Paris) some of the bowler-hatted figures are similar to those seen in *Magritte's paintings.

Bon, Bartolommeo. *See* BUON.

Bone, Sir Muirhead (1876–1953). British draughtsman, printmaker (drypoint was his favourite medium), and occasional painter, mainly of architectural subjects. He studied architecture and painting in his native Glasgow, then settled in London in 1901 and became a member of the *New English Art Club. In 1916 he was the first person to be appointed an *Official War Artist and he played an important part in the founding of the Imperial War Museum in 1920; he was an Official War Artist again in the Second World War. His son **Stephen** (1904–58) was a painter and art critic.

Bonheur, Rosa (1822–99). French animal painter. She was trained by her father, **Raymond Bonheur** (d. 1849), and was precociously gifted, first exhibiting at the Paris *Salon in 1841, when she was 19. In 1853 she scored an enormous hit there with *The Horse Fair* (1853, Met. Mus., New York; reduced replica in NG, London), and it repeated its success when it went on tour in Britain and the USA. She became well known not only for her work but also as a colourful and formidable character, outspoken in her feminine independence (she made drawings at such places as horse auctions and obtained police permission to wear men's clothes to avoid undue attention). In 1865 she was the first women artist to become a member of the Legion of Honour. Her home at the Château de By, near Fontainebleau, is now a museum devoted to her.

Bonifazio Veronese (Bonifazio de' Pitati) (1487–1553). Italian painter. He was born in Verona, but all his recorded activity was in Venice, where he based his style on *Giorgione, *Titian, and *Palma Vecchio. There are few signed, dated, or documented works by him, but he appears to have run a busy studio whose output was varied in kind and variable in quality. Consequently he has become one of those artists whose names tend to be used as dustbins for dumping difficult attributions. Jacopo *Bassano was briefly his assistant, and *Schiavone and *Tintoretto were possibly his pupils.

Bonington, Richard Parkes (1802–28). English painter, active mainly in France (his family settled in Calais for business reasons when he was 15). In 1818 he moved to Paris, where he studied with *Gros and became a friend of *Delacroix. Their *Romanticism is reflected in his fondness for historical 'costume' pictures, but it

was as a landscapist that he established his reputation, particularly with works he exhibited at the 'English' *Salon of 1824, at which his own paintings (which won him a gold medal) and those of *Constable were the star attractions. Bonington travelled a good deal in France in search of subjects. He also spent time with Delacroix in England in 1825, and in 1826 he visited Italy, producing some of his finest work in Venice. He was overloaded with work and his delicate health suffered; he died of consumption in London a month before his 26th birthday. Although his career was so brief, he was highly influential, the freshness and spontaneity of his fluid style in both oil and watercolours attracting many imitators. Delacroix wrote of him: 'Other artists were perhaps more powerful or more accurate than Bonington, but no one in the modern school, perhaps no earlier artist, possessed the lightness of execution which makes his works, in a certain sense, diamonds, by which the eye is enticed and charmed independently of the subject or of imitative appeal.' Most of his work is on a small scale and the qualities Delacroix admired are particularly evident in his *pochades* (oil sketches done rapidly on the spot as records of transitory effects in nature); with Constable and *Turner he was instrumental in establishing a fashion for such sketches. The best collection of Bonington's work is in the Wallace Collection, London, and he is also well represented in the City Museum and Art Gallery at Nottingham, his home town.

Bonnard, Pierre (1867–1947). French painter, lithographer, and designer. His father, an official in the War Ministry, insisted that he study law, but from 1888 he also attended classes at the École des *Beaux-Arts and at the *Académie Julian, where he met several young artists (including his lifelong friend *Vuillard), who formed the *Nabis. After doing military service, 1889–90, he abandoned law and became a full-time artist; his first one-man exhibition was at *Durand-Ruel's gallery in 1896. At this time, as well as painting, he was producing posters and coloured lithographs, and designing for the stage; he worked on the original production of Alfred Jarry's *Ubu-Roi* (1896), considered the first work of the Theatre of the Absurd. He prospered steadily in his career and his life was quiet and uneventful (although he travelled a good deal before the First World War). Like Vuillard, he is best known for peaceful domestic scenes to which the term *Intimiste is applied. Bonnard generally painted on a larger scale than Vuillard, however, and with greater richness and splendour of colour. His favourite model was his wife, and some of his most characteristic pictures are those in which he depicted her in the bath (she had an obsession with personal cleanliness and spent much of her time in the bathroom). His other subjects included flowers and landscapes. He also did numerous self-portraits. The late ones show his desolation after the death of his wife in 1940, but in general his work radiates a sense of warmth and well-being. This quality and his lively broken brushwork make him one of the most distinguished upholders of the *Impressionist tradition.

Bonnat, Léon (1833–1922). French painter and collector. Bonnat's early works were mainly religious paintings in a *tenebrist style influenced by 17th-century Spanish painting (he lived in Madrid, 1846–53), but from about 1870 he turned increasingly to portraiture. His portraits are usually as glum as his religious paintings, but their almost photographic realism won them an appreciative audience and the fortune he earned painting them enabled him to form a superb art collection, particularly of Old Master drawings. He donated it to Bayonne, his native city, where it forms the nucleus of the Musée Bonnat, one of France's finest provincial galleries. His studio and personal effects can be seen in the nearby Musée Basque. Bonnat was a renowned teacher, his many pupils including *Braque and *Toulouse-Lautrec .

Bontemps, Pierre (c.1510–c.1570). French sculptor, first documented in 1536 as an assistant to *Primaticcio at *Fontainebleau. By 1550 he was in Paris, working on two important monuments for the royal burial church at Saint-Denis—the reclining effigies and bas-*reliefs for the tomb of Francis I, designed by the great architect Philibert Delorme, and the monument for the heart of Francis I. Only one other work is documented as being by him—the tomb of Charles de Maigny (1557) in the Louvre—but other works of the period are confidently

attributed to him on stylistic evidence, and he seems to have been the foremost French tomb sculptor of the mid-16th century. His style was elegant and decorative.

Book of Hours. A medieval prayer book used by laymen for private devotion, containing prayers or meditations appropriate to certain hours of the day, days of the week, months, or seasons. This type of book originated around 1300 and replaced the *psalter as the most popular prayer book for secular use; a great many examples survive (outnumbering all other types of *illuminated manuscript) and from the late 15th century there were also printed versions illustrated by *woodcuts. Most Books of Hours are small and easily portable, but more luxurious examples were made for major patrons; the most famous example is the *Très Riches Heures du duc de Berry* (Musée Condé, Chantilly), illuminated by the *Limbourg brothers for Jean, Duc de Berry.

Bordone, Paris (1500–71). Italian painter. Bordone was from Treviso, but he spent most of his life in Venice, where he is first recorded as a painter in 1518. *Vasari says he was a pupil of *Titian but that he soon left because he found his teaching disagreeable (Titian is then said to have stolen Bordone's first commission). Whatever the truth of these stories, Bordone's work was certainly strongly influenced by Titian and also by *Giorgione, 'for that master's style pleased him exceedingly' (Vasari). His most characteristic subjects included Holy Families in landscape settings, half-length figures of female beauties, and reclining nudes, but his most famous work, the *Presentation of the Ring of St Mark to the Doge* (c.1535, Accademia, Venice), is in a very different vein—a large, ceremonial composition that is remarkable for its spatial complexity. Bordone had a varied and successful career in Venice and is also said to have worked in France and Augsburg. However, in his later years his style, once warm and sensuous, became increasingly mechanical.

Borduas, Paul-Émile (1905–60). Canadian painter, active mainly in Montreal but also in Paris and New York. He trained as a church decorator under Ozias *Leduc, then studied in Paris. In the early 1940s, under *Surrealist influence, he started to experiment with *automatism and he was the driving force behind the radical abstract group Les *Automatistes. His later paintings have an *all-over surface animation recalling the work of *Pollock, although the only American influence Borduas acknowledged was that of Franz *Kline. In 1953-5 he lived in New York, then spent his final years in Paris, where he died of a heart attack. He ranks with *Riopelle as one of the outstanding Canadian abstract painters of the post-war years.

Borghese Gallery, Rome. Italian state museum housed in the Villa Borghese. The villa was built (1613-15) for Cardinal Scipione Borghese (1576-1633) as a rural retreat (it was then on the outskirts of Rome) and a place to house his magnificent art collection. The nephew of Pope Paul V (Camillo Borghese, 1552-1621), Scipione held numerous lucrative church positions and he used his huge income to indulge his love of fine living, which included a genuine passion for art. He was *Bernini's first important patron, and the Gallery has an unrivalled representation of the sculptor's early work, including two busts of Scipione. It also boasts more *Caravaggios than any other collection (Scipione was an early admirer). Scipione was ruthless in using his power and influence to acquire coveted works, most notably with *Raphael's *Entombment*, one of the most famous pictures in the collection; with the connivance of his uncle, he had it illegally removed from the chapel in Perugia for which it had been painted and replaced it with a copy. Other members of the family added to the collection after Scipione's death, notably Prince Marcantonio Borghese IV (1730-1800), who had much of the interior of the building remodelled in a Neoclassical style appropriate to the ancient sculpture displayed there. However, because of financial difficulties, Marcantonio's son, Prince Camillo Borghese (1775-1832), sold part of the collection to his brother-in-law Napoleon Bonaparte in 1807, including the *Borghese Warrior*. In 1891 paintings, sculptures, and antiquities from other Borghese properties were installed in the villa, and in 1902 the building and its contents were bought by the Italian government.

Borghese Warrior (*Borghese Gladiator*). Marble statue (Louvre, Paris) of a nude warrior in a vigorous attitude of combat (his sword and shield are missing, but he is evidently lunging at an opponent on horseback in a type of pose that has been described as a 'heroic diagonal'). It was discovered in 1611 at Nettuno (near Anzio), had entered the *Borghese collection by 1613, and was bought by Napoleon (brother-in-law of Prince Camillo Borghese) in 1807. The statue is signed by 'Agasias, son of Dositheos, Ephesian' and is generally considered to be a copy of a *Hellenistic work influenced by *Lysippus. It became famous soon after its discovery and for two centuries it was one of the most admired and copied of antique statues, praised particularly for its anatomical mastery: *Bernini's *David* (made for the statue's then owner, Cardinal Scipione Borghese) is an early instance of a derivation from it and a more curious adaptation is found in *Copley's *Brook Watson and the Shark*, in which the figure of Watson—horizontal in the water—is based, in reverse, on the *Warrior*. It is now much less admired as a work of art, Martin Robertson (*A History of Greek Art*, 1975) describing it as 'harsh and unappealing'.

Borglum, Gutzon (1867-1941). American sculptor of Scandinavian descent. He specialized in extremely large works and is best known for the 'carving' (he used dynamite and pneumatic drills) of a huge cliff at Mount Rushmore in the Black Hills of South Dakota with colossal portrait busts of Presidents Washington, Jefferson, Lincoln, and Theodore Roosevelt. The project, begun in 1927, was sponsored by the US Government and cost more than $1,000,000. Washington's head was completed in 1930, Jefferson's in 1936, Lincoln's in 1937, and Roosevelt's in 1939; the final details were added in 1941, after Borglum's death, by his son Lincoln. **Solon Hannibal Borglum** (1868-1922), Gutzon's brother, was also a sculptor, mainly of Wild West subjects.

Borofsky, Jonathan. *See* NEW IMAGE PAINTING.

Borrassà, Luis (active 1383; d. 1424/5). Spanish painter, active in Barcelona and its neighbourhood. About a dozen of his documented works survive, for example the altarpiece for the convent of S. Clara, Vich (1412-15, Vich Mus.), and about twenty more are attributed to him on stylistic evidence, making him the most prolific Catalan painter of his day. His work shows French and Sienese influences and is representative of the *International Gothic style.

Bosboom, Johannes (1817–91). Dutch painter, a member of the *Hague School. He specialized in paintings of church interiors and was much inspired by the work of Emanuel de *Witte—in many of his pictures the figures even wear 17th-century costumes.

Bosch, Hieronymus (c.1450–1516). Netherlandish painter, active for all his known career in 's Hertogenbosch (Bois-le-Duc in French), where he is first documented in 1474. His real name was Jerome van Aken (perhaps indicating family origins in Aachen, Germany), but on the few pictures that he signed he used the name by which he has become famous: 'Hieronymus' (or 'Jheronimus' as he spelt it) is the Latin form of Jerome, and 'Bosch' is a shortened version of the name of his town. Although it was fairly remote from the major art centres of the Netherlands, it was one of the most prosperous towns in the Duchy of Brabant, with a vigorous cultural and intellectual life. Bosch, who came from a long line of artists, was the leading painter of the day there, although he was married to a wealthy woman and probably had no need to paint for a living. He was a prominent member of a local religious organization, the Brotherhood of our Lady, but because his most characteristic paintings seem so bizarre to modern eyes, his work has inspired theories that he was involved in heresy, witchcraft, or various esoteric practices. However, all the contemporary evidence indicates that he held the orthodox religious views of his time and was a respected member of his community. It was evidently not until after his death that it was first suggested he had embodied unorthodox beliefs in his work, and it was not until the 20th century that speculation (sometimes wild speculation) about his character and motivation began in earnest. There is much about his art that is obscure and perplexing, but modern research has helped to show how his work is a reflection of the cultural traditions of his time rather than the expression of eccentric private concerns.

About 40 surviving paintings are generally regarded as autograph works by Bosch, but none is dated and it has proved difficult to construct a satisfactory chronology. More than half of these pictures are on traditional Christian subjects, and others deal with general moral themes, often by illustrating human greed and folly in a folkloric way. Almost all his pictures have some grotesque element, but only a few are dominated by the kind of weird and disturbing imagery from which his name is now inseparable—nightmare visions of monstrous creatures illuminated by the flames of Hell, showing the horrible consequences of sin (*The Garden of Earthly Delights*, c.1500, Prado, Madrid). These works have an extraordinarily vivid imaginative power and the subjects are heavily embroidered with subsidiary narratives and symbols, but the basic themes are sometimes quite simple and much of the imagery can be explained in terms of the popular culture of Bosch's age, notably proverbs and devotional literature. In purely visual terms, the monsters he painted have analogies in the strange creatures often seen in the margins of medieval manuscripts and in the gargoyles of *Gothic architecture—the cathedral at 's Hertogenbosch has some fine examples. This connection with popular culture underlines the fact that Bosch worked in a town that was fairly remote from the mainstream of Early Netherlandish painting stemming from Jan van *Eyck. He stands apart in technique, too, for his brushwork is vigorous and varied, rather than smooth and precise in the manner typical of the time. (His individuality also comes out in his work as a draughtsman: he was one of the first artists to make drawings as independent works.)

By the time of his death, Bosch's reputation had spread far from his own town: in Spain, Queen Isabella (d. 1504) owned three of his pictures, and in Venice, Cardinal Domenico Grimani (d. 1523) owned five. Through the medium of engravings his work reached a wide audience and he was influential in the Netherlands throughout the 16th century, although most of the artists who imitated him did so very superficially, turning his deeply serious diabolic imagery into 'an infernal amusement park, a Disneyland of the afterlife' (Walter S. Gibson, *Bosch*, 1973). Joachim *Patinir, in his eerie landscapes, and *Bruegel, with his vivid sense of the grotesque, were among the few who had artistic personalities strong enough to extend Bosch's vision rather than simply pastiche it, and it was in Spain rather than the Netherlands that he found his spiritual home. Philip II (see HABS-BURG) was the greatest of all collectors of his work and kept a favourite example (*Tabletop of the Seven Deadly Sins*, Prado) in his bedroom at the *Escorial. Writing about the treasures of the Escorial in 1605, a Spanish monk, José de Sigüenza, dismissed the idea that Bosch's work was 'tainted with heresy'. Far from being absurd, as some people maintained, he thought that his paintings were like 'books of great wisdom and artistic value. If there are any absurdities here, they are ours, not his... they are a painted satire on the sins and ravings of mankind'; other artists depicted 'people as they appear outwardly', but only Bosch had the audacity 'to paint them as they are on the inside'. In Spain, 'El Bosco' continued to be respected long after he had been forgotten elsewhere. It was not until the late 19th century that a major revival of interest in him began, and his strange and often apocalyptic imagery has appealed greatly to modern taste, not least to the *Surrealists, who regarded him as a forerunner.

Boschini, Marco. See VELÁZQUEZ.

Boshier, Derek (1937–). British painter, sculptor, designer, and experimental artist. He was one of the *Royal College of Art students who put British *Pop art on the map at the *Young Contemporaries exhibition of 1961. His work at this time was much concerned with the manipulative forces of advertising, treating human figures as if they were mass-produced goods. However, his involvement in Pop art was short-lived, and from 1966 he worked in sculpture, photography, film, and *Conceptual art, before returning to painting in 1979. Throughout the 1980s he taught painting at the University of Texas. Although his career has been fairly low key compared with those of some of his Pop art colleagues from the early 1960s, many critics think that Boshier's work has stood the test of time at least as well as theirs.

Bosschaert, Ambrosius (1573–1621). Flemish flower and still-life painter, active mainly in the Netherlands (he is recorded in Middelburg from 1593 to 1613 and afterwards worked mainly in Utrecht). Although he spent the major part of his life in the Netherlands, Bosschaert's style was basically Flemish—similar to that of Jan *Brueghel, with whom he ranks in quality and in historical status as one of the pioneers of flower painting as an independent genre. He specialized in formally arranged bouquets, showing a rich variety of flowers from different seasons (they were painted from separate studies made at various times of year). His *Vase of Flowers* (c.1620, Mauritshuis, The Hague), one of the most reproduced of all flower pieces, is characteristic of his polished brushwork and beauty of colour. Bosschaert may fairly be said to have initiated the Dutch tradition of flower painting and his style was continued by his three sons, **Ambrosius the Younger** (1609–45), **Abraham** (c.1613–43), and **Johannes** (c.1610–after 1628), and also by his brother-in-law, Balthasar van der *Ast.

Bosse, Abraham (1604–76). French printmaker and writer on art. His large output (more than 1,500 prints in etching and engraving) provides a rich source of documentation on 17th-century French life and manners. Many of his prints are *genre scenes, and even his religious works are in modern dress, often in elaborately descriptive interiors. However, his work is impressive artistically as well as valuable historically, for it shows a classical dignity of composition, sometimes coupled with sensitive handling of light. Bosse taught perspective at the Académie Royale (see ACADEMY) from its foundation in 1648 until 1661, when he was expelled for quarrelling with his colleagues over his opposition to *Le Brun's dogmatic theories. He wrote several treatises on art, notably *Traité des manières de graver* (1645). This was the first instruction manual for printmakers and went through many editions and translations, including one into English by *Faithorne (1662).

Botero, Fernando (1932–). Colombian painter and sculptor. His early paintings were influenced by various styles, including *Abstract Expressionism, but in the late 1950s he evolved a highly distinctive manner in which figures look like grossly inflated dolls; some of his paintings are sardonic comments on modern life, others are parodies of the Old Masters. Since the early 1970s he has lived mainly in New York and he has acquired an international reputation accompanied by huge prices for his work in the saleroom. He has made sculpture in a similar vein to his paintings, including several public monuments in bronze, notably *Broadgate Venus* (1990, Exchange Square, London).

Both, Jan (*c*.1618–52). Dutch painter, draughtsman, and etcher, with Nicolaes *Berchem the most celebrated of the Italianate landscape painters. He was born in Utrecht, and probably studied there with *Bloemaert before going to Italy, where he stayed for about four years, *c*.1637–41. Both's output was large (in spite of his short life), but few of the more than 300 paintings attributed to him can be convincingly dated to his Italian sojourn. Nevertheless, the main influence on his work was *Claude, whom he knew in Rome. His landscapes are typically peopled by peasants driving cattle or travellers gazing on Roman ruins in the light of the evening sun. Such contemporary scenes were an innovation, for the earlier Dutch painters of the Italian countryside had populated it with biblical or mythological figures. They express the yearning of northerners for the light and idyllic life of the south, and proved immensely popular with collectors, not least in England, helping to shape ideas about Italy for two centuries. Jan's brother **Andries** (*c*.1612–41) moved to Italy a few years before him. They lived together in Rome, 1639–41, and are said to have collaborated, but Andries is best known for paintings and drawings of lively peasant scenes that have little in common with Jan's idyllic landscapes. He was drowned in an accident in Venice.

Botticelli, Sandro (Alessandro Filipepi) (*c*.1445–1510). Florentine painter, neglected for centuries but now one of the best-loved artists of the *Renaissance. The name 'Botticelli' ('little barrel') was originally given to an older brother, presumably because he was portly, but it was adopted as the family surname. According to *Vasari, Sandro was first apprenticed to a goldsmith and then trained under Filippo *Lippi. Lippi's sweetness and grace certainly had a strong influence on him, but Botticelli was more refined, particularly in his draughtsmanship, in which he achieved an extraordinary combination of delicacy and flowing vitality: Bernard *Berenson described him as 'the greatest artist of linear design that Europe

has ever had'. Almost all Botticelli's life was spent in Florence, his only significant journey from the city being in 1481–2, when he worked on the decoration of the Sistine Chapel in the Vatican, alongside *Ghirlandaio, *Perugino, and other artists. The fact that he was called to Rome for such a prestigious commission shows that he must have had a considerable reputation by this time, and during the 1480s he seems to have been the most sought-after painter in Florence. His clients included the civic authorities, major churches, and members of distinguished families, particularly the *Medici, and in about 1485, when Ludovico *Sforza, Duke of Milan, asked his agent in Florence for information about leading artists there, Botticelli was described as 'A most excellent painter, both on panel and on wall. His works have a virile air and are done with the best judgement and perfect proportion.' He ran a busy workshop (Filippino *Lippi was his most important pupil) and some of his paintings (particularly those on the theme of the Virgin and Child) exist in several versions or copies, attesting to the vogue they enjoyed. In the 1490s, however, Botticelli's fortunes declined, and after *Leonardo's return to the city in 1500 his linear style must have looked archaic. In his final years he had financial problems and Vasari describes him as 'old and useless, unable to stand upright and moving about with the aid of crutches'. At his death he was a relic of a bygone age.

By the standards of his time, Botticelli's output was large and varied. The bulk of his work was devoted to religious subjects, but he also painted portraits and allegorical, literary, and mythological themes. In addition—and highly unusually—he made drawings as independent works. His most remarkable drawings are a series of illustrations for a deluxe manuscript edition of Dante's *Divine Comedy* (*c*.1490), commissioned by Lorenzo di Pierfrancesco de' Medici. The project was never finished and the 92 surviving drawings (which are in various states of completion) are now divided between the Kupferstichkabinett, Berlin, and the Vatican Library. It was perhaps for the same patron that Botticelli painted his two most celebrated pictures, *Primavera* (*c*.1480) and the *Birth of Venus* (*c*.1485), both now in the Uffizi, Florence. In Vasari's day they hung together in the Medici villa at

Castello, near Florence, and they are mentioned by him in the same sentence, since when they have always been closely linked. However, they were not necessarily painted as a pair (*Primavera* is slightly bigger than the *Birth of Venus* and is painted on panel, whilst its companion is on canvas). Botticelli was the first painter since antiquity to treat such mythological themes on a large scale and with the seriousness usually reserved for religious subjects. Vasari described the subject of *Primavera* as 'Venus as a symbol of spring [It., *primavera*] being adorned with flowers by the Graces'. Various other mythological figures are present, and a huge amount of scholarly effort has gone into trying to elucidate the symbolic meaning of the picture and of the *Birth of Venus*. While the debate about iconographical interpretation continues, the pictures are universally acknowledged as two of the most beautiful works of the Renaissance, and they are now so famous that they are virtually symbols of the age.

Like other artists (Fra *Bartolommeo for example), Botticelli seems to have been disturbed by the turbulent political climate of Florence in the 1490s. Vasari says that he became a follower of the fiery preacher Savonarola, 'which led him to abandon painting'. The second part of this statement is definitely incorrect and the evidence for the first part is inconclusive, but it is certainly true that some of Botticelli's later paintings are more obviously 'serious'—solemn, intense, sometimes ecstatic—than his early works. The most telling example is the *Mystic Nativity* (1500, NG, London); it is the only work he signed or dated and it bears a cryptic inscription in Greek suggesting that he expected the second coming of Christ. It is remarkably personal in style, disregarding all the advances in naturalism that Florentine painters had made during the 15th century; he has even used the medieval device of making the Virgin and Child bigger in scale than the other figures. Botticelli's spirituality was one of the characteristics that appealed to the Victorians, who rediscovered him after a long period of obscurity. When Walter *Pater published an essay on him in 1870 he described him as 'a comparatively unknown artist', but by the end of the century he had become something of a cult figure—a major influence on *Art Nouveau and on the wan,

elongated maidens of *Burne-Jones and his followers.

Botticini, Francesco (Francesco di Giovanni) (*c*.1446–98). Florentine painter. His style is based almost entirely on elements drawn from his more illustrious contemporaries—Sandro *Botticelli, Domenico *Ghirlandaio, Filippino *Lippi, Andrea del *Verrocchio. He painted one remarkable work, however, the *Assumption of the Virgin* (*c*.1474, NG, London), which has the distinction of being the only picture from the *quattrocento known to have been painted to illustrate a heresy. The *donor, Matteo Palmieri, who held various government positions in Florence, believed that human souls are the angels who stayed neutral when Satan rebelled against God.

Bouchardon, Edme (1698–1762). French sculptor whose work marks the beginning of the *Neoclassical reaction against the *Rococo style. He won the *Prix de Rome in 1722 and was in Italy from 1723 to 1732. His best-known work of this period is a marble bust of the antiquarian Philippe Stosch (1727, Skulpturengalerie, Berlin) that is very consciously in the *antique manner. Although his style later softened somewhat, notably in the famous *Cupid Making a Bow from Hercules' Club* (*c*.1750, Louvre, Paris), it remained too severe for court taste. Bouchardon had many supporters, however, and his contemporary reputation stood high—indeed he was generally regarded as the greatest French sculptor of his time (modern taste has inclined more towards artists with greater warmth, such as *Falconet and *Pigalle). His most important work was an equestrian statue of Louis XV, commissioned by the City of Paris in 1749. It was cast in 1758 but not erected until 1763, a year after Bouchardon's death. It stood in the Place Louis XV (later the Place de la Concorde) and was destroyed during the Revolution. Several small copies exist, as well as engravings, showing that it was based on the famous *Marcus Aurelius*. Bouchardon's father, **Jean-Baptiste** (1667–1742), and his brother, **Jacques-Philippe** (1711–53), were also sculptors.

Boucher, François (1703–70). French *Rococo painter, draughtsman, etcher, and designer, whose work best represents the frivolity and elegant superficiality of French court life at the middle of the 18th century. His father was a minor painter, who probably gave him his first training, and he briefly studied under François *Lemoyne before winning the *Prix de Rome in 1723. There were insufficient funds to pay for his scholarship and for the next few years he earned his living mainly as a printmaker, his work including etchings after drawings by *Watteau. In 1728 he went to Rome at his own expense and returned to Paris in 1731. Thereafter he was soon launched on a varied, prolific, and enormously successful career, punctuated by a stream of honours. In 1735 he received his first royal commission (for decorations at Versailles) and many others followed. At about the same time he took up tapestry design for the Beauvais factory, and he was a dominant figure in this field, becoming director of the *Gobelins factory in 1755. In 1765 he was appointed both director of the Académie Royale (*see* ACADEMY) and first painter to the king. He was also the favourite artist of Louis XV's most famous mistress, Mme de Pompadour, to whom he gave lessons and whose portrait he painted several times (Wallace Coll., London; NG, Edinburgh).

Boucher was immensely productive and highly versatile. He claimed that his output amounted to more than 1,000 paintings and 10,000 drawings, and his work was everywhere in fashionable society, for it ranged from colossal schemes of decoration for royal chateaux to designs for fans and slippers; it was reproduced in porcelain figures from the Sèvres and Vincennes factories and could be seen in his stage designs for the Paris Opéra. He painted many different kinds of pictures, including delightfully artificial landscapes (*Landscape with Watermill*, 1743, Bowes Mus., Barnard Castle). In his most characteristic paintings he turned the traditional mythological themes into wittily indecorous *scènes galantes*, and he painted female flesh with a delightfully healthy sensuality, as in the celebrated *Reclining Girl* (1751, Alte Pin., Munich), which probably represents Louis XV's mistress Louisa O'Murphy. Towards the end of his career, as French taste changed in the direction of *Neoclassicism, Boucher was attacked, notably by *Diderot, for his stereotyped colouring and artificiality; he relied on his own repertory of motifs instead of painting from the life and objected to nature on the

grounds that it was 'too green and badly lit'. Certainly his work often shows the effects of superficiality and overproduction, but at its best it has irresistible charm and great brilliance of execution, qualities he passed on to his most important pupil, *Fragonard.

Boucicaut Master (active early 15th century). Franco-Flemish manuscript *illuminator, active in Paris, named after a *Book of Hours (Musée Jacquemart-André, Paris) done for Jean II le Meingre Boucicaut (1365–1421), Marshal of France. This manuscript, which probably dates from about 1410, is a magnificent example of the *International Gothic style, but in its accomplished handling of space and *aerial perspective and its delightful *genre detail it heralds the achievements of the 15th-century Netherlandish School. Many other manuscripts have been attributed to the workshop of the Boucicaut Master, who has been tentatively identified with Jacques Coene, an artist with a high contemporary reputation but by whom no documented works are known.

Boudin, Eugène (1824–98). French painter. The son of a sailor, he began his career working in a stationery and picture-framing business in the port of Le Havre. His clients there included several well-known artists, notably *Millet, who encouraged him to paint. Although he studied intermittently in Paris, he spent virtually all his life on the Normandy coast and his paintings are mainly small-scale beach scenes and seascapes, notable for their luminous skies. Many of them were painted out of doors, and it was he who introduced the young *Monet to this practice. He is regarded as a link between the painters of the generation of Corot and the *Impressionists, and he took part in the first Impressionist exhibition of 1874. Boudin was highly prolific; there is a museum devoted to him in Honfleur, his native town, and a large collection of his work in the Musée des Beaux-Arts, Le Havre.

Bouguereau, William (1825–1905). French painter. In 1850 he won the *Prix de Rome, and after his return to France in 1854 he became an immensely successful and influential exponent of academic art, upholding traditional values and contriving to exclude avant-garde work from the

*Salon—*Cézanne once expressed regret at being excluded from the 'Salon de Monsieur Bouguereau'. He painted portraits of photographic verisimilitude, slick and sentimental religious works, and coyly erotic nudes. His reputation sank after his death and for many years his work was regarded as irredeemably empty and vulgar. However, he has recently achieved something of a rehabilitation, his work becoming the subject of serious study and fetching huge prices in the saleroom.

Bourdelle, Émile-Antoine (1861–1929). French sculptor, born at Montauban, the son of a cabinetmaker, from whom he received his first experience of carving. In 1876 he began to study at the École des Beaux-Arts, Toulouse, from where he won a scholarship to the École des *Beaux-Arts, Paris, in 1884. However, he soon left the school and worked for a while with Jules *Dalou before becoming *Rodin's chief assistant from 1893 to 1908. Bourdelle's work has been somewhat overshadowed by his association with Rodin (whom he revered), but he was already an accomplished artist when he started working for him and developed an independent style. His energetic, rippling surfaces owe much to Rodin, but his flat rhythmic simplifications of form, recalling *Romanesque art, are more personal. He was particularly interested in the relationship of sculpture to architecture, and his reliefs for the Théâtre des Champs-Élysées (1912) are among his finest works. Bourdelle had many other prestigious public commissions and also achieved great distinction as a teacher. From about 1910 he was generally regarded as the outstanding sculptor in France apart from Rodin himself. He was also a talented painter and draughtsman. His house and studio in Paris have been converted into the Musée Bourdelle, opened in 1961 to mark the centenary of his birth.

Bourdichon, Jean (c.1457–1521). French painter and manuscript illuminator, *Fouquet's successor as the leading French painter of the time. He was active in Tours, where he worked for several royal patrons, including Charles VIII, Louis XII, and Anne of Brittany, who married both these kings in turn. For Anne, Bourdichon produced his most celebrated work—the Hours of Anne of Brittany (completed 1508, Bib. Nat., Paris),

one of the loveliest of all *Books of Hours. It contains numerous exquisite borders of plants and insects, together with 49 full-page miniatures (originally there were probably two more)—mainly scenes from the New Testament and lives of the saints, but also including a portrait of Anne at prayer. Some of the religious scenes show such strong Italianate influence that it seems almost certain Bourdichon had visited Italy. Bourdichon is recorded as having painted works on a larger scale, but apart from a *triptych of the Madonna and Child with Saints in the Museo di Capodimonte, Naples, all his other known works are manuscript illuminations. He effectively ends the great French tradition in this art.

Bourdon, Sébastien (1616–71). French painter. From about 1634 to 1637 he lived in Rome, where he worked for a picture dealer and developed a talent for imitating the work of other artists—*Claude, *Dughet, van *Laer—sometimes probably with intent to deceive. He continued in this vein when he returned to France and his oeuvre is still ill-defined (contemporaries praised his work and admired his versatility but also criticized him for failing to find an individual style). From 1652 to 1654 he was court painter to Queen Christina of Sweden, of whom he did several portraits, and after his return to France he worked mainly as a portraitist. It was in this field that he produced his most distinctive works, using soft tonalities and skilful play with cascading draperies to create a languorous, romantic effect.

Bourgeois, Louise (1911–). French-American sculptor, born in Paris, where part of her training was with *Léger. She married the American art historian Robert Goldwater (1907–73) in 1938 and settled in New York. Bourgeois started as a painter and engraver and turned to sculpture only in the late 1940s. She first achieved recognition in the 1950s for her wood constructions painted uniformly black or white, which preceded the similar works of Louise *Nevelson. Subsequently Bourgeois has worked in various materials, including stone, metal, and latex, and she has built up a reputation as one of the leading contemporary American sculptors. Although her work is abstract, it is often suggestive of the human figure, sometimes with sexual overtones.

She has continued to be active into old age and in 1993 she represented the USA at the Venice *Biennale.

Boursse, Esaias (1631–72). Dutch painter, active mainly in his native Amsterdam. He joined the Dutch East India Company in 1661 and made two voyages to the Indies, on the second of which he died at sea. His few surviving paintings include some exquisite interior scenes that invite comparison with *Vermeer because of their tranquil beauty and subtle colour harmonies (*Interior with Woman Cooking*, 1656, Wallace Coll., London).

Bouts, Dieric (or **Dirk**) (d. 1475). Netherlandish painter, born probably in Haarlem and active mainly in Louvain, where he is first recorded in 1457 and was city painter from 1468. His major commissions there were the *Last Supper* altarpiece for the church of St Peter (1464–7, still in situ) and two panels (out of a projected set of four, left incomplete at Bouts's death) on the *Justice of Emperor Otto* for the town hall (1470–5, Mus. Royaux, Brussels). Apart from these, there are no documented works, but his style is highly distinctive—characterized most obviously by stiff, solemn, exaggeratedly slender and graceful figures—and a convincing oeuvre has been built up for him. Most of his pictures are of religious subjects, but there are also a few portraits, including *Portrait of a Man* (1462, NG, London). This is his earliest dated work and perhaps the first Netherlandish portrait to include a landscape viewed through a window—an arrangement that had become common by the end of the century. Bouts often includes exquisite landscape backgrounds in his religious works, the setting helping to create the mood of the picture: there is little action, but deep poetic feeling. Sources for his work have been sought in the mysterious Albert van *Ouwater (who likewise seems to have had Haarlem connections), Rogier van der *Weyden (in spite of the great difference in emotional temperature), and Petrus *Christus, but the individuality of Bouts's work transcends any models. His style was continued by his two sons, **Dieric the Younger** (c.1448–90/1) and **Aelbrecht** (c.1455–1549), and was widely influential, in Germany as well as the Netherlands. Particularly popular were small devotional images of the *Mater Dolorosa* and *Christ Crowned with Thorns* (a pair of pictures showing these two subjects, catalogued as 'Workshop of Bouts', is in the National Gallery, London).

Bowes, John (1811–85). English collector. The illegitimate son of the 10th Earl of Strathmore, he married Joséphine Benoîte Coffin-Chevallier (1825–74), a French actress and amateur painter, in 1852, and they devoted much of their wealth and energy to collecting. In 1869, they began to build an enormous museum at Barnard Castle in County Durham (near to the Strathmores' home at Streatlam) and it was opened to the public in 1892 (by which time the founders were dead). The building was designed by a French architect, Jules Pellechet, and Nikolaus *Pevsner describes it as 'big, bold, and incongruous, looking exactly like the town hall of a major provincial town in France . . . gloriously inappropriate for the town to which it belongs'. The museum is particularly rich in French paintings and applied art of the 18th century (it has been called 'the *Wallace Collection of the North') and it also has the best representation of Spanish painting in Britain outside London.

Boyd, Arthur (1920–99). Australian painter, printmaker, sculptor, designer, and ceramicist, the best-known member of a dynasty of artists. His father was a sculptor and potter, his mother a painter, but he was largely self-taught as an artist. After holding his first one-man show at the age of 17, his artistic career was interrupted by the Second World War. In the 1950s he became well known in Australia, particularly for his large ceramic totem pole at the entrance to the Olympic Pool, Melbourne (for the 1956 Olympic Games) and for his series (twenty pictures) *Love, Marriage and Death of a Half-Caste* (1957–9) concerned with the life and death of an aboriginal stockman and his half-caste bride. They are done in a style combining elements of *Expressionism and *Surrealism. Boyd moved to England in 1959 and soon established a reputation, which he subsequently consolidated, becoming probably the best-known Australian artist of his generation apart from Sidney *Nolan (his brother-in-law). He returned to Australia in 1971 but continued to spend a good deal of time in England and also in Italy.

Boydell, John (1720–1804). English engraver and print publisher. He made a fortune in the 1740s by publishing views of England and Wales, which he engraved from his own drawings. Later he published the work of other engravers and by developing a large foreign trade he spread the fame of English artists and engravers on the Continent. In 1790 he was Lord Mayor of London. His most ambitious undertaking was his celebrated Shakespeare Gallery: from 1786 he commissioned major artists (including *Fuseli, *Reynolds, and *Romney) to produce oil paintings (162 in all) illustrating Shakespeare's plays, and in 1789 he opened a purpose-built gallery in Pall Mall to exhibit them. Some of the engravings after them were published as illustrations to a nine-volume edition of Shakespeare in 1802 and others appeared separately in larger format in 1803. Boydell hoped by this venture to encourage the rise of a 'great national school of *history painting', and he intended to leave the collection to the nation, but he had heavy losses during the French wars and it was sold by lottery in 1805 shortly after his death. Boydell's nephew, **Josiah Boydell** (1752–1817), was a painter and engraver, his uncle's partner and successor in his engraving business.

Boys, Thomas Shotter (1803–74). English watercolour painter and lithographer. From 1825 to 1837 he was based mainly in France, where he was a friend of *Bonington, whose watercolours have sometimes been confused with those of Boys. He specialized in Continental urban scenes and in 1839 he published *Picturesque Architecture in Paris, Ghent, Antwerp, Rouen, etc.*, a work that marked the transition from hand-tinted lithography to *chromolithography. In 1842 he published *Original Views of London as It Is*, the plates of which constitute a fine topographical record of Regency London. In spite of the high quality of his work, Boys's career went into decline in the later 1840s (partly because of ill health) and he was often reduced to doing hackwork.

bozzetto. A small rough model, usually in wax or clay, made in preparation for a larger sculpture in more durable material. By extension, the term (a diminutive of the Italian *bozzo*, 'rough stone') is sometimes also applied to an oil sketch. In this second sense, the word is not always clearly differentiated from *modello*, but it is useful to reserve the latter word for a somewhat more elaborate type of preliminary design, especially one intended to be shown to a patron.

Bramante, Donato (Donato di Angelo) (c.1444–1514). Italian architect and painter. Bramante was the creator and greatest exponent of the High *Renaissance style in architecture, but most of his early career, which is ill-documented, seems to have been devoted to painting. He probably trained in Urbino and the first record of him dates from 1477, when he is said to have worked on fresco decorations at the Palazzo del Podestà in Bergamo. In about 1480 he settled in Milan, and in 1481 he produced his earliest surviving dated work, the design of an engraving of an elaborate architectural fantasy (the British Museum, London, possesses one of only two known impressions). At about the same time he began his first building, S. Maria presso S. Satiro, Milan, in which his knowledge of *perspective was used to create an illusion of recession in the choir, which is in reality only a few inches deep. Various fresco fragments are attributed to him (mainly in the Brera, Milan), but the best evidence of his skill as a painter is the only panel painting that is generally accepted as his (on the testimony of *Lomazzo)—a sombre and poignant *Christ at the Column* (c.1490, Brera), which shows some influence from his friend *Leonardo. In 1499 Bramante left Milan and settled in Rome, where in 1506 he began the rebuilding of St Peter's for Julius II (Giuliano della *Rovere). There is no evidence of any activity as a painter in Rome, but *Vasari says that Bramante designed the majestic architectural setting of *Raphael's fresco *The School of Athens* in the Vatican Stanze. Certainly Raphael paid tribute to Bramante by introducing his portrait into this painting as the mathematician Euclid. Bramante had an enormous influence as an architect, and his interest in perspective and *trompe-l'œil left a mark on Milanese painting, notably in the work of his follower *Bramantino.

Bramantino (Bartolomeo Suardi) (c.1460–1530). Milanese painter and architect, a follower of *Bramante, from whom he takes his nickname (meaning 'little Bramante'). He was appointed court painter and archi-

tect to Duke Francesco II *Sforza in 1525.
His style as a painter is complex and eclectic, drawing on *Piero della Francesca and
*Leonardo as well as Bramante; at its best it
has a certain stolid dignity. Perhaps his most
individual characteristic is his use of sombre
classical architectural backgrounds, as in
the *Adoration of the Magi* (c.1500, NG,
London).

Bramer, Leonaert (1596–1674). Dutch
*genre and history painter, active mainly
in his native Delft. He travelled widely in
Italy and France, 1614–28, and drew on a
variety of influences for his most characteristic paintings—small nocturnal scenes
with vivid effects of light. Works such as
the *Scene of Sorcery* (Mus. B.-A., Bordeaux)
have earned him the reputation of 'an interesting independent who cannot be pigeon-
holed' (Seymour Slive, *Dutch Painting: 1600–
1800*, 1995). Bramer was also one of the few
Dutch artists to paint frescos in Holland, but
none of his work in the medium has survived. In 1653, when *Vermeer's future
mother-in-law was trying to prevent him
from marrying her daughter, Bramer came
to the young man's defence. Because of this,
it has been plausibly suggested that he,
rather than Carel *Fabritius, was Vermeer's
teacher.

Bramley, Frank. *See* NEWLYN SCHOOL.

Brancusi, Constantin (1876–1957). Romanian sculptor, active for almost all his
career in Paris (he became a French citizen
the year before his death), one of the most
revered and influential of 20th-century
artists. He settled in Paris in 1904 (according
to his own romanticized account he had
walked from Romania) and spent several
years of poverty and hardship there. In
1906 he was introduced to *Rodin, whose
offer to take him on as assistant Brancusi
refused with the famous comment that 'No
other trees can grow in the shadow of an
oak.' His work of this time was in fact influenced by Rodin's surface animation, but
from 1907 Brancusi began creating a distinctive style, based on his feeling that
'what is real is not the external form but
the essence of things'. From this time his
work (in both stone and bronze) consisted
largely of variations on a small number of
themes (heads, birds, a couple embracing—
The Kiss) in which he simplified shapes and

smoothed surfaces into immaculately pure
forms that sometimes approach complete
abstraction. He was particularly fond of
ovoid shapes—their egg-like character
suggesting generation and birth and symbolizing his own creative gifts. (His woodcarvings, on the other hand, are rougher—
closer to the Romanian folk-art tradition
and to African sculpture.) His name was established abroad after five of his sculptures
were shown at the *Armory Show, New
York, in 1913, and during the 1920s he
became newsworthy when he was involved
in two celebrated art scandals. In 1920 his
Princess X was removed by police from the
*Salon des Indépendants because it had
been denounced as indecent (there is a
clear resemblance to a phallus); and in
1926 he had a dispute with the US Customs
authorities. They attempted to tax his *Bird in
Space* (one of his most abstract works) as raw
metal, rather than treat it as sculpture,
which was duty-free. Brancusi was forced
to pay up to get the work released for exhibition, but he successfully sued the Customs
Office, winning the court decision in 1928.
By this time he had a growing international
reputation and during the 1930s he travelled widely, notably to India in 1937–8 to
discuss designs for a Temple of Meditation
(never built) for the Maharajah of Indore.
Later in 1938 his largest work was inaugurated—a complex of sculpture (including the
enormous *Endless Column*, nearly 30 m
(100 ft) high) for the public park at Tirgu
Jiu near his birthplace. By the time of his
death he was widely regarded as the
greatest sculptor of the 20th century.

Brancusi's originality in reducing natural
forms to their ultimate—almost abstract—
simplicity had profound effects on the
course of 20th-century sculpture. He introduced *Modigliani to sculpture, *Archipenko and *Epstein owed much to him,
and *Gaudier-Brzeska was his professed admirer. Later, Carl *Andre claimed to have
been inspired by *Endless Column*, converting
its repeated modules into his horizontal arrangements of identical units. More generally, Henry *Moore wrote of Brancusi:
'Since the Gothic, European sculpture had
become overgrown with moss, weeds—all
sorts of surface excrescences which completely concealed shape. It has been Brancusi's special mission to get rid of this
undergrowth and to make us once more

shape-conscious.' On his death Brancusi bequeathed to the French Government his studio and its contents, which included versions of most of his best works (they often exist in multiple replicas in different materials). The studio has now been reconstructed at the *Pompidou Centre in Paris. There is another outstanding Brancusi collection in the Philadelphia Museum of Art.

Brangwyn, Sir Frank (1867–1956). British painter, printmaker, draughtsman, and designer, born at Bruges of Welsh parentage. In 1882–4 Brangwyn served an apprenticeship with William *Morris, and like his master he was active in a variety of fields. He was an *Official War Artist in the First World War, for example, he was one of the finest draughtsmen of the day and a skilful etcher and lithographer, and he made designs for a great range of objects (furniture, textiles, ceramics, glassware, jewellery, and so on); however, he became best known for his murals. His most famous undertaking in this field was a series of eighteen panels on the theme of the British empire, commissioned by the House of Lords. They were begun in 1926 and rejected—amid great controversy—in 1930, being considered too flamboyant for their setting. Offers for the panels came from all over the world, and in 1934 they were installed in the Guildhall in Swansea. Brangwyn's work at its most characteristic was floridly coloured, crowded with detail and incident, and rather *Rubensian, although it became somewhat flatter, lighter, and more stylized later in his career. During his lifetime he was one of the most famous of British artists (probably *the* most famous worldwide); there is a museum devoted to him in Bruges and another almost entirely given over to his work in Orange. His reputation crumbled after his death, his work tending to be dismissed as facile and sentimental, but there has recently been a modest revival of interest in him.

Braque, Georges (1882–1963). French painter, graphic artist, and designer. Initially he followed his father's trade of house painter, but in 1902–4 he took lessons at various art schools in Paris, including briefly the École des *Beaux-Arts. Through his friendship with his fellow students *Dufy and Friesz, he was drawn into the circle of the *Fauves, and in 1905–7 he

painted in their brightly coloured, impulsive manner. In 1907, however, two key events completely changed the direction of his work: first, he was immensely impressed by the *Cézanne memorial exhibition at the *Salon d'Automne; and secondly, he met *Picasso, in whose studio he saw *Les Demoiselles d'Avignon*. Although he was initially disconcerted by it, he soon began experimenting with the dislocation and fragmentation of form it had introduced, and the two men worked in close association until the outbreak of the First World War, jointly creating *Cubism. At times it is difficult to tell their work apart, but John *Golding (*Braque*, 1966) senses some fundamental differences of outlook: 'Picasso's approach was predominantly linear and sculptural; it was he who formulated the concept of "simultaneous vision"—that is to say, the concept of combining different viewpoints of a subject into a single, coherent image. Braque's approach was more painterly, more poetic; significantly, of all the major Cubist painters, only he retained an interest in the evocative properties of light. And he was the technician who through patient research was able to solve so many of the pictorial problems which arose in the creation of this supremely complex and sophisticated style.'

In 1914 Braque enlisted in the French army and was twice decorated for bravery before being seriously wounded in the head in 1915 and demobilized in 1916. After the war his work diverged sharply from that of Picasso. Whereas Picasso went on experimenting restlessly, Braque's painting became a series of sophisticated variations on the heritage of his pre-war years. His style became much less angular, tending towards graceful curves. He used subtle muted colours and sometimes mixed sand with his paint to produce a textured effect. Still life and interiors remained his favourite subjects, and many critics regard his *Studio* series, begun in 1947, as the summit of his achievement. From the 1930s his reputation had become international, and in his later years he accumulated an impressive list of prizes and honours, including the main prize for painting at the 1948 Venice *Biennale. The final accolade was a state funeral—an occasion that seemed at odds with his life of unassuming dedication to his art. In addition to the type of paintings for which he is best known, Braque also did much book illustration, designed stage sets and costumes, and carried out some decorative work, notably the ceiling of the Etruscan Gallery in the Louvre, 1952–3.

Bratby, John (1928–92). British painter and writer. Bratby was a versatile artist: he painted portraits, still lifes, figure compositions, landscapes, and flower pieces, and also designed film sets. He is probably best known for the scenes of drab domestic life he painted in the 1950s, when he was a member of the *Kitchen Sink School. Later his work became lighter and more exuberant. His talent for self-promotion helped to make him one of the best-known British artists of his generation. Among his publications are the novel *Breakdown* (1960) and a book on Stanley *Spencer (1970).

Bray, Jan de (c.1627–97). Dutch painter, principally of portraits. He worked in his native Haarlem and his vigorously characterized work shows the lasting influence of *Hals in the city, although de Bray's handling is much smoother, in the manner of van der *Helst. Jan's father, **Salomon** (1597–1664), was an architect and painter of biblical and allegorical scenes. He wrote a book, *Architectura Moderna* (1631), describing the buildings of Hendrick de *Keyser.

Bredius, Abraham (1855–1946). Dutch art historian and collector. Bredius excelled at archival research and published a large amount of new documentation relating to 17th-century Dutch artists. His best-known work is his complete illustrated catalogue of *Rembrandt's paintings, originally published in German in 1935 and then in an English edition in 1937; a second English edition, revised by Horst Gerson, Bredius's collaborator on the original edition, appeared in 1969. It is still a standard work (although the illustrations are of poor quality) and the Bredius numbering system is widely used in Rembrandt scholarship. Bredius made a choice collection of Dutch paintings; he presented or bequeathed many to the *Rijksmuseum in Amsterdam and the *Mauritshuis in The Hague (of which he was director from 1889 to 1909) and others are in the Bredius Museum in The Hague. His reputation as a connoisseur was blighted because he was taken in by the work of the *Vermeer forger Han van

Meegeren (1880–1947); however, Bredius was very old at the time (1937) and almost all his contemporaries were similarly deceived.

Breenbergh, Bartholomeus (1598–1657). Dutch painter, etcher, and draughtsman, with *Poelenburgh the leading pioneer of the taste for Italianate landscapes in the Netherlands. Breenbergh spent about ten years in Italy (c.1619–c.1629) and thereafter lived in Amsterdam. His work as a painter is very similar to Poelenburgh's, featuring biblical and mythological characters set in well-balanced views of the Roman Campagna, often complete with classical ruins. His drawings are fresher and bolder, and have often passed under the name of *Claude, as is the case with two examples in Christ Church, Oxford. Late in his career Breenbergh painted a few portraits.

Breitner, George Hendrik (1857–1923). Dutch painter and photographer. He was born in Rotterdam and studied in The Hague. Early in his career he was a friend of van *Gogh, whom he encouraged. His most characteristic works of this time were military scenes, particularly of cavalry manoeuvres, but a visit to Paris in 1884 introduced him to *Impressionism and he became the leading Dutch exponent of the style. In 1886 he settled in Amsterdam and he is best known for scenes of its busy harbour, its architecture, and its bustling street life. The unposed 'snapshot' compositions of many of these paintings reflect his interest in photography (he seems to have taken his camera with him everywhere). After 1910 he virtually gave up painting because of ill health.

Breker, Arno. See DESPIAU.

Breton, André (1896–1966). French poet, essayist, critic, and editor, the founder of the *Surrealist movement and its chief theorist and promoter. In 1924 he marked the official launch of the movement by publishing his *Manifeste du surréalisme* (dedicated to the memory of his friend *Apollinaire), and in 1925 he helped organize the first Surrealist exhibition, at the Galerie Pierre, Paris. He wrote numerous other books and articles on Surrealism and was also the driving force behind two of the major periodicals of the movement—*La Révolution surréaliste* (1924–9) and *Le Surréalisme au service* *de la révolution* (1930–3). In 1941–6 he lived in New York, where he was one of a group of expatriate Surrealists who had an important influence on the genesis of *Abstract Expressionism. After his return to Paris he continued to be regarded as the 'Pope of Surrealism', even though the movement was now long past its prime, and his death in 1966 was reckoned by many as marking its end.

Brett, John (1831–1902). English painter, mainly of coastal scenes and landscapes. He was influenced by the *Pre-Raphaelites and *Ruskin (whose work he read avidly), and a handful of his early paintings such as *The Stonebreaker* (1857–8, Walker AG, Liverpool) are tours de force of minute and brilliant detail. His later work, however, tended to become laboured and he died virtually forgotten.

Breu, Jörg the Elder (*c*.1475–1537). German painter and designer of woodcuts, a pupil of Ulrich *Apt the Elder. Breu was one of the leading painters of his time in his native Augsburg, but his most important works there—a series of frescos in the town hall—are no longer extant. His patrons included the emperor Maximilian I (*see* HABSBURG) and Duke William IV of Bavaria, for whom he painted the *Battle of Zama* (1529, Alte Pin., Munich) in the same series as *Altdorfer's celebrated *Battle of Issus*. His style was complex, sharing something of Altdorfer's passion and love of landscape, and showing strong influence from *Dürer and from a journey he is thought to have made to Italy in about 1514. His son, **Jörg the Younger** (*c*.1510–47), was his pupil and assistant. In his independent work he was a prolific illustrator of manuscripts.

Bril, Paul (*c*.1554–1626). Flemish landscape painter, active mainly in Rome, where he is first documented in 1582. Early in his career he specialized in large decorative pictures, including frescos, but he turned increasingly to small easel paintings and it is on these that his fame now rests. He lived long enough to assimilate some of the qualities of *Elsheimer's and Annibale *Carracci's landscapes and his work forms a transition between the fantastic, highly detailed 16th-century Flemish *Mannerist style and the more idealized, atmospheric Italian landscapes of the 17th century. He also made views of Rome for the tourist trade, and marine pictures. His conception of both these types of subject influenced Agostino *Tassi, *Claude's teacher, and Claude himself. Paul's brother, **Matthew** or **Mattheus** (1550–83), also worked successfully in Rome, and their work is hard to differentiate.

British Museum, London. The national museum of archaeology and antiquities, which formerly also housed the national library of manuscripts and printed books. It was established by Act of Parliament in 1753 when the government purchased the private collection of the physician and naturalist Sir Hans Sloane (1660–1753), consisting of 'books, manuscripts, prints, drawings, pictures, medals, coins, seals, *cameos and natural curiosities'. Initially the museum was housed in Montagu House, a large 17th-century mansion in Bloomsbury, and for nearly 50 years it was necessary to make formal application for admission. With the acquisition of Sir William Hamilton's collection of classical vases and antiquities (1772), a plethora of Egyptian antiquities (including the Rosetta Stone donated by George III) at the turn of the century, the *Elgin Marbles (1816), the magnificent library of George III (1823), and many other bequests and purchases, the Museum became established as one of the world's greatest treasure houses. Montagu House was now too small for its purpose and it was demolished in the course of construction of the present huge structure (1823–47), one of the masterpieces of Greek Revival architecture. The architect was Sir Robert Smirke and the great circular Reading Room at the centre of the building, designed by Smirke's brother Sydney, was completed in 1857. There have subsequently been various other additions to the building. Originally the Museum's collections embraced natural history, and one of its greatest attractions was a stuffed giraffe in the entrance hall, but the holdings in this area were transferred to the Natural History Museum in South Kensington, which opened in 1881. The Department of Prints and Drawings was originally part of the Library, but it led a separate existence from 1808 onwards. It began with over 2,000 drawings from the Sloane collections, which included an album of *Dürer's drawings. Among the most important acquisitions since was the Richard Payne *Knight bequest (1824) of over 1,000 drawings, including 273 by *Claude. It is now one of the largest and most comprehensive collections in the world, containing more than two million items. The British Museum Library (as it was formerly known) was reconstituted by Act of Parliament as part of the British Library in 1973, and has been transferred to a new building, near St Pancras Station, opened in 1997.

Briulov, Karl. *See* BRYULOV.

Brock, Sir Thomas (1847–1922). British sculptor, one of the most successful specialists in monuments and public statues at the turn of the century. His most famous work is the huge Queen Victoria Memorial (unveiled 1911), in stone, marble, and gilt bronze, outside Buckingham Palace, London, and also well known is his equestrian statue of the Black Prince (1903) in Leeds.

Brockhurst, Gerald Leslie (1890–1978). British-born painter and etcher who became an American citizen in 1949. Precociously gifted, an excellent draughtsman, and a fine craftsman, Brockhurst won several prizes at the *Royal Academy Schools and went on to have a highly successful career as a society portraitist, first in Britain and then in the USA, where he settled in 1939, working in New York and New Jersey. He is best known for his portraits of glamorous women, painted in an eye-catching, dramatically lit, formally posed style similar to that later associated with *Annigoni. As an etcher Brockhurst is remembered particularly for *Adolescence* (1932), a powerful study of a naked girl on the verge of womanhood staring broodingly into a mirror—one of the masterpieces of 20th-century printmaking.

Broederlam, Melchior (d. *c*.1411). Netherlandish painter. For much of his career he was court painter to Philip the Bold, Duke of Burgundy, and he also worked for his native city of Ypres. Documents show that he was a busy and versatile artist, but his only surviving works are two wings from an altarpiece painted for the Chartreuse de Champmol, Dijon (*see* SLUTER): the *Annunciation and Visitation* and the *Presentation and Flight into Egypt* (1394–9, Mus. B.-A., Dijon). They are among the first and finest examples of *International Gothic, combining lavish decora-

tive display with realistic touches that look forward to the later development of the Netherlandish School. The figure of St Joseph in the *Flight into Egypt*, for example, is represented as an authentic peasant.

bronze. An alloy of copper (usually about 90 per cent) and tin, often also containing small amounts of other metals such as lead or zinc. Since antiquity it has been the metal most commonly used in cast sculpture, because of its strength, durability, and the fact that it is easily workable—both hot and cold—by a variety of processes. It is easier to cast than copper because it has a lower melting point, and its great tensile strength gives it an advantage over *marble sculpture, in which it is much more difficult to create unsupported parts (such as protruding limbs). The colour of bronze is affected by the proportion of tin or other metals present, varying from silverish to a rich, coppery red, and its surface beauty can be enhanced when it acquires a *patina. *See also* CIRE PERDUE.

Bronzino, Agnolo (Agnolo di Cosimo) (1503–72). Florentine *Mannerist painter, the pupil of *Pontormo, who virtually adopted him as a son and introduced his portrait as a child into his painting *Joseph in Egypt* (*c*.1518, NG, London). The origin of Bronzino's nickname (literally 'bronze-coloured') is uncertain, but possibly derived from his having a dark complexion. He was deeply attached to Pontormo and his style was heavily indebted to his master (in paintings of *c*.1530 it is sometimes difficult to distinguish the hand of one from the other). However, Bronzino lacked the emotional intensity that was such a characteristic of Pontormo's work, his colouring and brushwork were typically harder, and he excelled as a portraitist rather than a religious painter. In 1539 he first worked for Duke Cosimo I de' *Medici and he spent most of the rest of his career in his service, becoming the leading painter in Florence and creating an unforgettable array of images of his patron's family and courtiers —immaculately polished works that convey the splendour and formality of the sophisticated world in which they lived. Bronzino was also a poet, and his most personal portraits are perhaps those of other literary figures (*Laura Battiferri*, *c*.1560, Palazzo Vecchio, Florence). With few exceptions he was less successful as a religious painter, tending towards empty, elegant posturing, as in the *Martyrdom of S. Lorenzo* (1569, S. Lorenzo, Florence), in which almost every one of the extraordinarily contorted poses can be traced back to *Michelangelo, whom Bronzino idolized, or to *Raphael. It is the type of work that got Mannerism a bad name and has been described as a 'fusion of ballet and Turkish bath'. Late in life, Bronzino (like *Ammanati) seems to have had a crisis of conscience about the use of naked figures in religious works, thinking that they tended to inspire lewd thoughts rather than holy ones, and his skill with the nude was certainly better deployed in the celebrated *Allegory with Venus and Cupid* (c.1545, NG, London), which conveys a feeling of icy eroticism under the pretext of a moralizing allegory (one of the subsidiary figures has recently been interpreted as symbolizing the effects of syphilis). His other major works include the design of a series of tapestries on the story of Joseph (1545–55) for the Palazzo Vecchio. He was a much-respected figure who took a prominent part in the activities of the Accademia del Disegno (*see* ACADEMY), of which he was a founder member in 1563. His pupils included Alessandro *Allori, who—in a curious mirroring of his own early career—was also his adopted son.

Brooking, Charles (c.1723–59). English marine painter. Little is known of his short career, but he was the finest British marine painter of his day, equally adept at calm or rough seas. In his early years he was evidently employed in some capacity at Deptford dockyard and he had an intimate knowledge of the ships he painted.

Brotherhood of Ruralists. *See* BLAKE, SIR PETER.

Brouwer, Adriaen (c.1605–38). Flemish painter who spent a great part of his short working life at Haarlem in Holland. He moved there in about 1625 and according to *Houbraken was a pupil of Frans *Hals. In about 1631 he left Holland for Antwerp and evidently spent the rest of his career there. He perhaps died from the plague that swept the city in 1638. Brouwer was an important link between the Dutch and Flemish schools and played a major role in popularizing low-life *genre scenes in both countries in

which he worked. Early sources depict him as a colourful bohemian character (he was imprisoned in 1633, perhaps for debt) and his most typical works represent peasants brawling and drinking. Although the subject matter is humorously coarse, his technique is delicate and sparkling. The virtuosity of brushwork and economy of expression are perhaps even more evident in his landscapes, which are among the finest of his period. *Rembrandt and *Rubens were among the admirers and collectors of Brouwer's paintings (Rubens at one time owned seventeen), and Adriaen van *Ostade and David *Teniers the Younger were among his many followers.

Brown, Ford Madox (1821–93). English painter. He was born in Calais, the son of a retired ship's purser, and spent his early life on the Continent; his training included a period with *Wappers in Antwerp. In 1840–3 he lived in Paris, then settled in London in 1844; he visited Rome in 1845–6 and was impressed by the work of the *Nazarenes. In 1848 he met *Rossetti and through him became part of the *Pre-Raphaelite circle; he was never a formal member of the Brotherhood, but he shared their beliefs that art should be true to nature and morally edifying. His *Chaucer at the Court of Edward III* (1851, AG of New South Wales, Sydney) contains portraits of several of the Brotherhood, and his best-known picture, *The Last of England* (1852–5, City AG, Birmingham), was inspired by the departure of *Woolner, the Pre-Raphaelite sculptor, for Australia. Brown's other famous anthology piece, *Work* (1856–63, Manchester AG), shows his dedicated craftsmanship and brilliant colouring, but is somewhat swamped by its social idealism (it is a crowded street scene presenting a cross-section of contemporary society engaged in various activities, emphasizing the moral value of labour). In 1865 Brown organized a one-man exhibition in London, in which *Work* was the centrepiece; the catalogue contains his highly detailed commentary on the picture. By organizing such an exhibition he showed his independence of the *Royal Academy, which he avoided after he thought some of his pictures had been badly hung there. He had a prickly temperament and sometimes had difficulty selling his work. In 1878, however, he was given a major commission for a cycle of paintings in Manchester Town Hall on the history of the city. This occupied him until his death and he was based in Manchester from 1881 to 1887. Apart from paintings, his work included the design of stained glass and furniture for William *Morris's decorative arts company, of which he was a founder member in 1861.

Brown, Frederick. *See* SLADE.

Brücke, Die (The Bridge). Group of German *Expressionist artists founded in Dresden in 1905 and disbanded in Berlin in 1913. The founders were four architecture students at the Dresden Technical School: Fritz Bleyl (1880–1966), Erich *Heckel, Ernst Ludwig *Kirchner, and Karl *Schmidt-Rottluff (Bleyl dropped out in 1906 and other artists joined from time to time, including Max *Pechstein in 1906, Emil *Nolde temporarily in 1906–7, and Otto Müller (1874–1930) in 1911). The name was chosen by Schmidt-Rottluff and indicated the members' faith in the art of the future, towards which their own work was to serve as a bridge. Their aims were vague, but in essence they were in revolt against passionless middle-class conventions and wished to create a radically new style of painting that would be in tune with modern life. Their subjects were mainly landscapes and figure compositions (a favourite theme being nudes in the open air); these were treated in an emotional style characterized by strong (and often unnaturalistic) colour and simplified, energetic, angular forms. Although there is some kinship of spirit with *Fauvism (founded in the same year), notably in the bold colour and sense of spontaneity, the work of the Brücke artists was markedly different in feeling and technique: in place of exuberance there was restlessness and anxiety, and in place of French sophistication there was the crude vigour of artists who had had almost no professional training as painters. They were influenced not only by late medieval German art, which is often extremely intense emotionally, but also by *primitive art, of which the Museum of Ethnology in Dresden had a substantial collection. By 1911 all the members of Die Brücke had moved to Berlin, where there was a more vigorous cultural scene. They were now beginning to achieve national recognition (they promoted their work in more than twenty exhibitions),

but they were also losing their group identity as their individual styles emerged more clearly. The personal rifts that had been present from the beginning became more intense and led to the dissolution of the group in 1913, but by this time it had given a powerful impetus to Expressionism in Germany.

Bruegel (or **Brueghel**), **Pieter** (*c*.1525–69). Netherlandish painter, draughtsman, and printmaker, the greatest artist of his time in northern Europe. There is little documentary evidence concerning his career, but van *Mander's laudatory biography, published in 1604, is a useful source of information, even though it misleadingly projects an image of Bruegel as above all else a comic painter. Far from being the yokel of popular tradition—'Peasant' Bruegel—he seems to have been a man of some culture: his work includes memorable scenes of village life, but he spent his career in major cities rather than the countryside, he had distinguished patrons, and he was a friend of the eminent geographer Abraham Ortelius (who described him as 'the most perfect painter of his century'). It is not known where Bruegel was born and there is no documentation on his life until 1550/1, when he is recorded in Malines, working on an altarpiece that is now lost. In 1551/2 he became a master in the painters' guild in Antwerp, where according to van Mander he had been the pupil of Pieter *Coecke van Aelst (who died in 1550); there is no stylistic affinity between their work, but Bruegel later married Coecke's daughter, so it is likely that he had links with her father. Soon after becoming a master, Bruegel made a lengthy visit to Italy, travelling as far south as Sicily. In Rome he met the miniaturist Giulio *Clovio, who bought several of his paintings. By 1555 he was back in Antwerp, designing engravings for the print publisher Jerome *Cock, who was his main source of employment for the next few years. The experience of crossing the Alps affected Bruegel much more than the example of any art he had seen in Italy, as was acknowledged by van Mander, who wrote that he 'swallowed all the mountains and rocks and spat them out again, after his return, on to his canvases and panels'. His work for Cock included a series of prints now known as the *Twelve Large Landscapes* (c.1555–8), featuring wonderfully spacious mountain views. (Most of the drawings of Alpine scenery associated with Bruegel's visit to Italy—as well as many other drawings traditionally given to him—have recently been reattributed to Jacob and Roelandt *Savery, who perhaps made some of them as deliberate forgeries.) Bruegel's work for Cock also included figure compositions of various subjects, including parables like 'Big Fish Eat Little Fish'. The engraving after Bruegel's drawing of this subject (published in 1557), bears the inscription 'Hieronymus Bos Inventor', an attempt by Cock to cash in on the continued popularity of *Bosch, whose moralistic outlook and sense of the grotesque influenced Bruegel considerably (he was indeed referred to in his lifetime as 'a second Bosch').

In 1563 Bruegel moved to Brussels and married there in that year. The move coincided with a change of direction in his career, for although he still made designs for engravings, he now worked primarily as a painter, and in the remaining six years of his short life he produced his best-known works. His patrons included Cardinal Granvelle, chief counsellor to Margaret of Parma (half-sister of Philip II (see HABSBURG) and his regent in the Netherlands), and the wealthy banker Niclaes Jonghelinck, who in 1565 commissioned the series of *The Months*, of which five survive today. Three of these (including the celebrated *Hunters in the Snow*) are in the remarkable collection of fourteen pictures by Bruegel in the Kunsthistorisches Museum, Vienna, which comprises nearly one-third of his surviving output as a painter; the other two are in the Metropolitan Museum, New York, and the National Gallery, Prague. His style changed during this final period: he abandoned the crowded panoramas of his earlier years, making his figures bigger and bolder, as is seen most notably in his novel treatment of proverbs, a genre that had previously been of minor account (*The Blind Leading the Blind*, 1568, Mus. di Capodimonte, Naples). Bruegel enjoyed a considerable reputation in his lifetime (he is mentioned by *Vasari and slightly later by *Lomazzo), and—through his original works and the many prints after them—he had an enormous influence on later Flemish painting, particularly landscape and *genre. It was not until the 20th century, however, that he was recognized

also as a profound religious painter and an artist whose human sympathy and understanding have hardly been excelled. His two painter sons were infants when he died and so they had no training from him (they were reputedly taught by their grandmother—the widow of Pieter Coecke—Mayken Verhulst). Both sons spelled their surname 'Brueghel', retaining the letter 'h' that their father had dropped in about 1559.

Brueghel, Jan (1568–1625). Flemish painter and draughtsman, younger son of Pieter *Bruegel. From 1590 to 1596 he worked in Italy, then settled in Antwerp, where he spent the rest of his highly successful career. His specialities were still lifes, especially flower paintings, and landscapes, but he worked in an entirely different spirit from his father, depicting brilliantly coloured, lush woodland scenes, often with mythological figures, in the manner of *Coninxloo and *Bril. His exquisite flower paintings were rated the finest of the day, and his virtuoso skill at depicting delicate textures earned him the nickname 'Velvet' Brueghel. Often he collaborated with other artists (notably his close friend *Rubens), painting backgrounds, animals, or flowers for them. He had considerable influence, notably on his pupil Daniel *Seghers, his sons **Jan II** (1601–78) and **Ambrosius** (1617–75), and his grandson Jan van *Kessel. Further descendants and imitators carried his style into the 18th century.

Brueghel, Pieter the Younger (1564/5–1637/8). Flemish painter, elder son of Pieter *Bruegel. He spent his career in Antwerp, where he became a master in the painters' guild in 1584/5. He is best known for his copies and variants of his father's peasant scenes, which sold well and are often of high quality, in contrast to the work of lesser copyists such as his son **Pieter Brueghel III** (1589–c.1640). His other speciality was scenes of fires, which earned him the nickname 'Hell' Brueghel. Frans *Snyders was his most notable pupil.

Brunelleschi, Filippo (1377–1446). Florentine architect and sculptor. Brunelleschi was one of the most famous of all architects—a Florentine hero on account of the celebrated dome (1420–36) he built for the city's cathedral—and one of the group of artists, including *Alberti, *Donatello, and

*Masaccio, who created the *Renaissance style. He trained as a goldsmith and was one of the artists defeated by another great goldsmith/sculptor, Lorenzo *Ghiberti, in the competition (1401–2) for the new doors for the Florence Baptistery; their competition panels are in the Bargello. The disappointment of losing is said to have caused Brunelleschi to give up sculpture and turn to architecture, but he seems to have taken up architecture fairly gradually and one important sculptural work of later date is attributed to him—a painted wooden *Crucifix* in S. Maria Novella (*c*.1412). Although he was not a painter, Brunelleschi was a pioneer of *perspective: in about 1413 he is said to have produced two demonstration pictures (representing buildings in Florence), in which he used a single vanishing point to represent pictorial depth in a completely consistent way.

Brunswick Monogrammist. *See* MASTER OF THE BRUNSWICK MONOGRAM.

brush. A painting or drawing implement consisting of flexible fibres set in a handle. Prehistoric artists used materials such as feathers and leaves to apply paint and the Egyptians used an implement consisting simply of a reed with the end macerated to separate the fibres, but animal hairs have been used since the ancient Greeks and are still the most important materials. For watercolour painting the 'sable' brush (made from the fur of the Siberian mink) is the best type; the 'camel-hair' brush (usually made from squirrel hair) is cheaper, but lacks springiness and durability. For oil painting a stiffer type of brush is needed; the best quality ones are made of white hog bristles. Synthetic fibres have been used since the 1960s; polyester has proved superior to nylon and has sometimes been blended with animal hairs to combine toughness with resilience. *See also* PENCIL.

Brygos Painter. Greek *red-figure vase-painter, active in Athens (*c*.500–*c*.475 BC), named after a potter called Brygos, several of whose signed works he decorated (it is possible that the potter and the painter are the same person). He is perhaps best known for a cup in the Louvre depicting the Sack of Troy. Showing consummate mastery of composition and movement, it is regarded as one of the masterpieces of Greek painting and is sometimes referred to simply as 'the Brygos cup'. More than 200 other vases have been attributed to the artist.

Bryulov, Karl (1799–1852). Russian painter. He spent much of his life in Italy (1822–34 and 1849–52), where he painted his chief work, *The Last Day of Pompeii* (1830–3, Russian Mus., St Petersburg), inspired by a performance of the opera of that name by Giovanni Pacini. An enormous (6 m (20 ft) wide) melodramatic composition, it brought him European fame (he was the first Russian artist to win such a reputation) and inspired Edward Bulwer-Lytton's novel *The Last Days of Pompeii* (1834).

Bueckelaer, Joachim (*c*.1535–*c*.1574). Netherlandish painter of large still lifes—market and kitchen pieces—active in Antwerp. Bueckelaer was the nephew and pupil of Pieter *Aertsen, and he followed his uncle's preference for scenes in which a religious subject is relegated to the background by the still life or *genre content (*Christ in the House of Mary and Martha*, 1565, Mus. Royaux, Brussels). He seems to have been the first painter to depict fish stalls.

Buffalmacco (Buonamico di Martino) (active first half of 14th century). Italian painter, a tantalizingly enigmatic figure. Various early sources, not only *Ghiberti and *Vasari, but also the authors Boccaccio and Sacchetti, attest to his celebrity as an artist—evidently one of the leading painters of the post-*Giotto generation—and also as a practical joker (hence his nickname, which might be translated as 'jester'). Their cumulative testimony is impressive, but no works can be securely attributed to him and there has been a tendency to regard him as a figure more of legend than of history. In the 1970s, however, he was proposed as the painter of the famous frescos of the *Triumph of Death* in the Campo Santo, Pisa (*see* TRAINI), an attribution that if correct would give him a stature commensurate with his literary reputation. Another school of thought has it that Buffalmacco may be identified with another obscure personality, the *Master of St Cecilia.

Buffet, Bernard (1928–99). French painter, etcher, lithographer, designer, and occasional sculptor. A precocious artist, he had developed a distinctive style and won considerable critical acclaim by the age of

20. His work, which includes religious scenes, landscapes, still lifes, and portraits, is instantly recognizable, characterized by elongated, spiky forms with dark outlines, sombre colours, and an overall mood of loneliness and despair. It seemed to express the existential alienation and spiritual solitude of the post-war generation, and Buffet enjoyed enormous success in the 1950s. Later, as he found himself overwhelmed by commissions, his work became more decorative, losing much of its original impact. His final years were marred by Parkinson's disease and he committed suicide.

Buon (or **Bon**), **Bartolommeo** (c.1400–c.1467). Venetian sculptor and architect. With his father **Giovanni** (c.1360–c.1443), he ran the most successful Venetian sculpture workshop of the period. Major works of the shop include the decoration of the Cà d'Oro (1422–34), and the Porta della Carta (1438–42) of the Doges' Palace. They epitomize the survival of the *Gothic style in Venice into the mid-*quattrocento.

Burchfield, Charles (1893–1967). American painter, mainly in watercolour. In 1921 he settled permanently in Buffalo, where he worked as head designer in a wallpaper factory until he was able to devote himself full-time to art in 1929. Burchfield's work divides into three clear phases. Up to about 1918 he painted scenes of nature that have an obsessive, macabre quality, often based on childhood memories and fantasies. In his second phase—during the 1920s and 1930s —he was one of the leading *American Scene Painters, portraying the bleakness of small-town life and the grandeur and power of nature. In the early 1940s, however, he became disenchanted with realism and changed his style again, reviving the subjective spirit of his youthful work but in a more monumental vein, as he turned to a highly personal interpretation of the beauty and mystery of nature (*The Sphinx and the Milky Way*, 1946, Munson-Williams-Proctor Inst., Utica). In the 1950s Burchfield taught at several institutions including the Buffalo Fine Arts Academy and the University of Buffalo. The Charles E. Burchfield Foundation, Buffalo, possesses his papers and a collection of his paintings.

Burckhardt, Jacob (1818–97). Swiss historian, professor at the universities of Zurich (1855–8) and Basle (1858–93). Much of his work was devoted to the history of art and culture and he is best known for his book *Die Kultur der Renaissance in Italien* (The Civilization of the Renaissance in Italy), published in 1860. In this survey of the arts, philosophy, politics, etc., of the period he propounds the view that it was at this time that man, previously conscious of himself 'only as a member of a race, people, party, family or corporation', became aware of himself as 'a spiritual individual'. This romanticized view has been highly influential but also much attacked. Burckhardt's other books include *Cicerone* (1855), a guidebook to Italian art that was a popular handbook for German tourists for many years, and *Erinnerungen aus Rubens* (Recollections of Rubens), published posthumously in 1898. *Wölfflin, his former student, succeeded him at Basle University.

Bürger, W. *See* THORÉ.

Burgkmair, Hans the Elder (1473–1531). German painter and designer of woodcuts, the leading artist of his day in his native Augsburg. He was the son of a painter, **Thoman Burgkmair** (c.1445–1523), who was probably his first teacher, and in about 1488–90 he studied with *Schongauer in Colmar. After his return to Augsburg he was soon busy producing illustrations for publishers and he kept up this work throughout his career, in addition to his output as a painter. Most of his paintings are on religious subjects, but he was also a good portraitist. In 1507 he is documented in Italy, and he probably made another visit or visits before this, for his work shows strong *Renaissance influence, in the breadth and dignity of his figures, his warmth of colour, and his use of classical motifs. Indeed, he occupied a place in Augsburg comparable to that of *Dürer in Nuremberg in introducing the new style. Like Dürer, he worked a good deal for Maximilian I (*see* HABSBURG); his *chiaroscuro woodcut of the emperor (1508) is one of the first examples of this type of print. His other patrons included Duke William IV of Bavaria, for whom he painted the *Battle of Cannae* (1529, Alte Pin., Munich), part of the same series as *Altdorfer's celebrated *Battle of Issus*. Burgkmair was married to the sister of Hans *Holbein the Elder. Their son, **Hans Burgkmair the**

Younger (c.1500–59), was a painter and engraver, also active in Augsburg.

burin (or **graver**). The engraver's principal tool, consisting of a short steel rod mounted in a rounded wooden handle. Usually the rod is lozenge-shaped in section, cut obliquely at the end to provide a point. The handle is pushed by the palm of the hand while the fingers guide the point.

Burliuk, David (1882–1967) and **Vladimir** (1886–1917). Russian painters, brothers, leading members of the avant-garde in the period leading up to the First World War. Some of their early work was in a vein of exaggerated primitivism close to that of *Goncharova and *Larionov, and they were among the first exponents of *Futurism in Russia, c.1911. They were friendly with *Kandinsky, and through him participated in the second *Neue Künstlervereinigung exhibition in Munich in 1910 and in the *Blaue Reiter exhibition there in 1911. Vladimir, who was considered by Kandinsky to be the more talented of the two, was killed in action in the First World War. David settled in New York in 1922 and became an American citizen in 1930. He edited an art magazine, *Color Rhyme*, and ran an art gallery. There was another painter brother, **Nikolai** (1890–1920), and two painter sisters, **Lyudmila** and **Nadezhda**.

Burman, Thomas. *See* BUSHNELL.

Burne-Jones, Sir Edward (1833–98). English painter, illustrator, and designer, a key figure in the second phase of *Pre-Raphaelitism. In 1853 he began studying at Oxford University, intending to train for the priesthood, but his interest was turned to art first by William *Morris, his fellow student, and then by *Rossetti, who remained the decisive influence on him. He left Oxford without taking a degree in 1856 and settled in London. Rossetti gave him a few informal lessons and he attended life drawing classes for a while, but essentially he was self-taught; his taste was more classical than Rossetti's and his elongated forms owed much to the example of *Botticelli. He favoured medieval and mythical subjects and hated such modernists as the *Impressionists, describing their subjects as 'landscape and whores'. His own ideas on painting are summed up as follows: 'I

mean by a picture a beautiful romantic dream, of something that never was, never will be—in a light better than any that ever shone—in a land no-one can define or remember, only desire—and the forms divinely beautiful.' He had a fairly low-key career until 1877, when he became famous overnight with the showing of eight large paintings at the opening exhibition of the *Grosvenor Gallery. Thereafter he acquired huge fame and prestige, not only in Britain, but also on the Continent; he had considerable influence on the French *Symbolists and the ethereally beautiful women who people his paintings, like the more sensuous types of Rossetti, had many imitators at the end of the century. Although he was lauded for his poetic qualities by many critics, some thought his pictures 'morbid' and 'unmanly'. His paintings tend to be flat and frieze-like in composition, with richly textured surfaces, and his feeling for pattern was put to good use in his work as a designer; he was a founder member of William Morris's decorative arts company in 1861 and designed some outstanding stained glass and tapestries for it, as well as making illustrations for *Kelmscott Press books. Burne-Jones's reputation crumbled after his death and did not seriously revive until the 1960s. The best collection of his work is in the City Art Gallery at Birmingham, his birthplace.

burr. A term applied in printmaking to the tiny upturned edge of the incision made in the metal plate by the cutting tool (in *line engraving or *drypoint) and also to the overall sandpaper-like roughening of the plate created by the rocker in *mezzotint. In line engraving, where maximum sharpness is required, the burr is removed, but in drypoint it is allowed to remain because the soft, velvety quality it gives to the printed line is considered one of the attractions of the medium. In mezzotint it is the foundation of the process. With both drypoints and mezzotints, only a limited number of impressions can be taken before the burr wears down.

Burra, Edward (1905–76). English painter, draughtsman, and stage designer, one of the most delightfully eccentric figures in British art. He was ravaged by ill health continuously from childhood and lived almost all his life in the genteel Sussex seaside town of

Rye (he called it an 'overblown gifte shoppe'), but he travelled indomitably and had a tremendous zest for life. His career, in fact, represents a revolt against his respectable middle-class background, for he was fascinated by low-life and seedy subjects, which he experienced at first hand in places such as the streets of Harlem in New York and the dockside cafés of Marseilles. By his mid-twenties he had formed a distinctive style, depicting squalid subjects with a keen sense of the grotesque and a delight in colourful detail. Usually he worked in watercolour, but on a larger scale than is generally associated with this medium and using layer upon layer of pigment so that— in reproduction at any rate—his pictures appear to have the physical substance of oil paintings. Burra's work has been compared with that of George *Grosz, whom he admired, but whereas Grosz bitterly castigated evil and ugliness, Burra concentrated on the picturesque aspects of his subjects, which he depicted with warmth and humour. Particularly well known are his Harlem scenes of 1933–4, with their flamboyant streetwise dudes and other shady characters. Burra's style changed little, but around the mid-1930s his imagery underwent a radical change and he became fascinated with the bizarre and fantastic (*Dancing Skeletons*, 1934, Tate, London). Many of his recurrent images—such as the birdman—and his manner of juxtaposing incongruous objects have a *Surrealist air, and although he generally kept aloof from groups, he exhibited with the English Surrealists (he was also a member of *Unit One, organized by his friend Paul *Nash). The Spanish Civil War and the Second World War evoked a sense of tragedy in Burra that found expression in occasional religious pictures and during the 1950s and 1960s his interest turned from people to landscape. By this time he had achieved critical and financial success, but he reacted with sardonic humour towards his growing fame.

Burrell, Sir William (1861–1958). Scottish art collector. He made an immense fortune from the family shipping business, from which he more or less retired in 1916 to devote himself to collecting, which had been his passion since boyhood (he is said to have once annoyed his father by spending his pocket money on a picture rather than a cricket bat). His interests were extremely diverse, but his collection became particularly strong in medieval art and in 19th-century French painting. Burrell eventually amassed 8,000 objects, which he presented to the City of Glasgow in 1944, followed by the sum of £450,000 to build a new museum to house them. Because he was worried about air pollution, he stipulated that the museum should be located several miles outside the city centre, and it was not until 1967, when Pollok Country Park was presented to the city, that a suitable site was available. The museum opened there in 1983 in an impressive new building by the British architect Barry Gasson; externally it is mainly of glass and steel, but inside stone predominates and fragments of medieval buildings collected by Burrell are sensitively incorporated into the structure. In the period since Burrell's death, most of his collection had been in storage, giving it something of a legendary reputation as a hidden treasure trove, and after the museum's keenly awaited opening it soon became one of the most popular artistic attractions in Britain. Burrell also gave paintings to the Museum and Art Gallery at Berwick-upon-Tweed; in his later years he lived nearby at Hutton Castle (three rooms from the castle have been reconstructed within the Burrell Collection, complete with their furniture and fittings).

Burri, Alberto (1915–95). Italian painter, *collagist, and designer. In 1943 he was captured whilst serving as a doctor with the Italian army in north Africa and he began to paint in 1944 as a prisoner of war in Hereford, Texas, using whatever materials were to hand, including sacking. After the war he settled in Rome and abandoned medicine for art. In 1948 his work became abstract, and in 1949 he began incorporating sacking in his pictures as collage elements; often he splashed red paint on the cloth in a way that suggested bloodsoaked bandages (*Sacking with Red*, 1954, Tate, London). From the late 1950s he also began to use more substantial materials in his pictures; they included objects such as pieces of charred wood or rusty metal that again reflected his experience of the carnage of war, even though the pictures are elegantly constructed. Burri was a fairly reclusive character, but he won international fame for his work; he was one of the first artists to exploit the evocative force of waste materials, looking forward to *Junk art in America and *Arte Povera in Italy. He also designed stage decor for La Scala in Milan and other theatres.

Bury, Pol (1922–). Belgian artist, best known as one of the leading exponents of *Kinetic sculpture. Originally he was a painter; from 1947 he exhibited with the *Jeune Peinture Belge group and was also active in the *Cobra group. In 1953, however, he abandoned painting for Kinetic sculpture. His early works could be rotated at will, inviting spectator participation, but from about 1957 he began to incorporate electric motors. The movement was usually very slow and the impression made was humorous and poetic, in contrast to the violent effects of *Tinguely. Bury's work also includes films and stage designs. Since 1961 he has lived mainly in Paris.

Bush, Jack Hamilton (1909–77). One of Canada's leading abstract painters, active mainly in his native Toronto. Initially he worked in the tradition of the *Group of Seven, but in the early 1950s, inspired by Jock *Macdonald and by *Borduas's paintings, he began to experiment with *automatism. In 1952 he made the first of what became regular visits to New York. The influence of these brought him, by the mid-1950s, to a type of *Abstract Expressionism. His later works, however, explore the unaffectedly direct use of colour in a more personal way, as in his most famous painting, *Dazzle Red* (1965, AG of Ontario), in which the colour is placed in joyous, broadly brushed bands. Bush worked as a commercial designer for most of his career and did not devote his whole time to painting until 1968, but by the end of his life he had an international reputation.

Bushnell, John (1636–1701). English sculptor. He fled to the Continent when he was an apprentice, after his master, Thomas Burman (1618–74), forced him to marry a servant he had himself seduced. In Italy Bushnell assimilated much of the *Baroque style (he probably saw *Bernini's work in Rome) and helped to produce a monument to Alvise Mocenigo (1663–4) in S. Lazzaro del Mendicanti, Venice. On his return to Eng-

land, c.1670, he received important commissions including a statue of Sir Thomas Gresham for the Royal Exchange (now in the Old Bailey), and would have received more but for his difficult and unstable temperament (he died bankrupt and insane). Bushnell's work is extremely uneven, but he is an important figure, for he showed untravelled Englishmen for the first time something of the possibilities of Baroque sculpture.

Butler, Elizabeth (Lady Butler, née Thompson) (1846–1933). British painter who concentrated almost exclusively on military scenes. During her heyday in the 1870s she was one of the most popular and talked-about artists in Britain. Her work appealed to popular patriotic sentiment, but she was also admired by critics such as *Ruskin, who said she had forced him to admit he had been wrong in believing that 'no woman could paint'. Lady Butler said, 'I never painted for the glory of war, but to portray its pathos and heroism', and although her pictures often have a glossy, Hollywood quality, they are sincerely felt, and she has been praised for trying to show the experience of the common soldier rather than concentrating—as was then usual—on the heroic deeds of officers. Her best-known painting is probably *Scotland for Ever!* (1881, City AG, Leeds), showing the charge of the Royal Scots Greys at the Battle of Waterloo. She continued working almost to the end of her life and her final paintings were of First World War subjects.

Butler, Reg (1913–81). British sculptor. He trained as an architect and did not take up sculpture full-time until 1950. In 1953 he suddenly came to prominence on being awarded first prize (£4,500) in an international competition for a 'Monument to The Unknown Political Prisoner' (defeating *Calder, *Gabo, and *Hepworth among other established artists). The competition, financed by an anonymous American sponsor and organized by the *Institute of Contemporary Arts, was intended to promote interest in contemporary sculpture and 'to commemorate all those unknown men and women who in our times have been deprived of their lives or their liberty in the cause of human freedom'. Butler's design was characterized by harsh, spindly forms, suggesting in his own words, 'an iron cage, a transmuted gallows or guillotine on an out-crop of rock'. The monument was never built, but the competition established Butler's name and he won a high reputation among British sculptors of his generation. He had learned iron-forging when he had worked as a blacksmith during the Second World War (he was a conscientious objector) and his early sculpture is remarkable for the way in which he used his feeling for the material to create sensuous textures. His later work, which was more traditional (and to many critics much less memorable), included some bronze figures of nude girls, realistically painted and with real hair, looking as if they had strayed from the pages of 'girlie' magazines. Butler was an articulate writer and radio broadcaster and he vigorously argued the case for modern sculpture. Five lectures he delivered to students at the *Slade School in 1961 were published in book form the following year as *Creative Development*. He was a widely read man, who numbered leading intellectuals among his friends, and his liberal sympathies were shown by his donation of works to such causes as the campaign against capital punishment.

Buys, Cornelis. *See* MASTER OF ALKMAAR.

Buytewech, Willem (1591/2–1624). Dutch painter and etcher, nicknamed 'Geestige Willem' (Witty, or Inventive, William). He was active in his native Rotterdam and in Haarlem, where he is said to have been friendly with Frans *Hals. Although his surviving output as a painter is tiny (about ten pictures), he is one of the most interesting artists during the first years of the great period of Dutch painting. His pictures of dandies, fashionable ladies, topers, and lusty wenches are among the most spirited Dutch *genre scenes, and instituted the category known as the 'Merry Company' (*Merry Company*, Boymans Mus., Rotterdam). His etchings are more numerous, and include genre scenes, fashion plates, and views of the Dutch countryside. He had an important influence on painting in Haarlem. His posthumously born son **Willem the Younger** (1625–70) was also a painter. An example of his very rare work—a landscape—is in the National Gallery, London.

Byzantine art. Art produced in or under the influence of the Eastern Roman (Byzan-tine) empire; the empire was founded in AD 330 by Constantine (the first Christian emperor of Rome) and ended in 1453 when the capital Constantinople (originally named Byzantium) was captured by the Turks and under the name of Istanbul became the capital of the Ottoman empire. The split between the Western and Eastern empires had become permanent in 395, when each adopted a separate ruler, and after the Western empire was overrun by barbarians in the 5th century the Byzantine empire became the great upholder of Christianity and of the cultural traditions of Greece and Rome. Byzantine territories varied greatly in extent; at one time they covered almost the entire Mediterranean basin, but from the 7th century many provinces were lost, first to the Arabs and later to the Turks. However, Byzantine art extended beyond the political or geographical boundaries of the empire, penetrating, for example, into the Slav countries, and in certain areas—where the Eastern Orthodox Church flourished—its tradition continued long after the collapse of the empire.

Byzantine art was, above all, a religious art. It was serious, other-worldly, and conservative; the Byzantine artist did not aspire to freedom of individual interpretation but was the voice of orthodox dogma. The choice of subjects and the attitudes and expressions of figures were determined according to traditional schemes charged with theological meaning. In the domes of churches, for example, Christ was usually shown as ruler of the universe (the Greek term is Pantocrater, meaning 'all-powerful'). Although Byzantine artists produced panel paintings, frescos, manuscript illuminations, ivories, enamels, textiles, jewellery, and metalwork of high quality, Byzantine art is seen at its finest and most typical in the mosaic decoration of churches. Mosaics were applied to all available surfaces of the interior, the luminous shimmering of the colours and the remote, implacably staring figures creating—in the finest works—a truly awe-inspiring effect, raising the art to unprecedented levels of grandeur and expressive power. Figures are flat and arranged frontally, occupying a spiritual dimension rather than a realistic space. Also typical of Byzantine art is the *icon, which usually represented the head of Christ, the Virgin and Child, or a particular saint, although there are also much more complex figure groups of subjects such as the Crucifixion. Icons tended to become cult images, and the view that this was idolatrous led to the various outbursts of iconoclasm ('image-breaking'), particularly in the 8th and 9th centuries, when many figurative works were destroyed and artists had to revert to ornamental forms or symbols such as the cross. The austere conventions of Byzantine art spread to Italy, where they were eventually challenged by the less ritualistic, more naturalistic ideals of artists such as *Giotto and *Duccio.

C

Cabanel, Alexandre (1823–89). French painter. The winner of the *Prix de Rome in 1845, he ranked with *Bouguereau as one of the most successful and influential academic painters of the period and one of the sternest opponents of the *Impressionists. *The Birth of Venus* (1862, Mus. d'Orsay, Paris) is his best-known work and typical of the slick and titillating (but supposedly chaste) nudes at which he excelled. It was the hit of the official *Salon of 1863, the year of the *Salon des Refusés, and was bought by the emperor Napoleon III, who gave Cabanel several prestigious commissions. His reputation quickly faded after his death.

cabinet painting. Term applied to fairly small *easel paintings, especially ones intended for a domestic setting. The term has no precise limits in terms of dimensions, but is often applied, for example, to 17th-century Dutch *genre paintings, which were usually painted to fit into unpretentious bourgeois interiors.

Cadell, F. C. B. *See* SCOTTISH COLOURISTS.

Cadmus, Paul (1904–99). American painter and draughtsman. He painted with an extremely meticulous technique, usually in egg *tempera, and often used the poses and compositional techniques of the Old Masters. However, his subjects were taken from modern American life, on which he commented pungently and satirically. This sometimes led to scandal, as with the work that established his reputation, *The Fleet's In!* (1934, Naval Historical Center, Washington), portraying sailors on shore leave; it was described by the Secretary of the Navy as 'a most disgraceful, sordid, disreputable, drunken brawl, wherein apparently a number of enlisted men are consorting with a party of streetwalkers and denizens of the red-light district'. Because Cadmus worked very slowly his output as a painter was small, but he was a comparatively prolific draughtsman: 'drawings are more saleable than paintings', he wrote; 'they're less expensive.'

Cage, John. *See* BLACK MOUNTAIN COLLEGE.

Caillebotte, Gustave (1848–94). French painter and collector. He came from a very wealthy family (he was rich enough to build and race yachts as a hobby) and for many years after his death he was remembered primarily for the financial help he gave the *Impressionists, by purchasing their paintings and sometimes by direct gifts of money. Since the 1960s, however, his own work as a painter has been reassessed and he is now regarded as an artist of considerable, although uneven, achievement. He exhibited at five of the eight Impressionist exhibitions, concentrating on scenes from everyday life. The most striking feature of his work is his liking for unusual viewpoints and bold perspective effects, as in *Paris, A Rainy Day* (1877, Art Inst. of Chicago), which has become a much-reproduced favourite. On his death Caillebotte bequeathed his collection of 67 pictures to the State. Against the opposition of various academic artists representing the taste of the École des *Beaux-Arts and the official *Salon (*Gérôme called the works offered 'filth'), 38 of the pictures were accepted after much wrangling and formed the nucleus of the Impressionist collection of the Luxembourg Museum. They are now in the *Musée d'Orsay, Paris.

Calder, Alexander (1898–1976). American sculptor and painter, famous as the inventor of the *mobile and thereby as one of the pioneers of *Kinetic art. His grandfather, **Alexander Milne Calder** (1846–1923), and his father, **Alexander Stirling Calder** (1870–1945), were sculptors and his mother was a painter, but he began to take an interest in art only in 1922, after studying mechanical engineering. From 1923 to 1926 he studied at the *Art Students League of New York, where his teachers included George *Luks and John *Sloan. Calder and his fellow students made a game of rapidly sketching people on the streets and in the subway and Calder was noted for his skill in conveying a sense of movement by a single unbroken line. From this he went on to produce wire sculptures that were essentially line drawings in space; the earliest, made on a visit to Paris in 1926, were amusing, toylike figures of animals, but he also made much larger works in this manner. His first exhibition of such works was in New York in 1928. From now on he divided his time between the USA and France and he knew many leading avant-garde artists in Paris, notably *Miró, who became his lifelong friend. In 1931 he joined the *Abstraction-Création association and in the same year produced his first non-figurative moving construction. Marcel *Duchamp baptized these constructions 'mobiles' and *Arp suggested 'stabiles' as a name for the non-moving constructions. Calder's first mobiles were moved by hand or by motor-power, but in 1934 he began to make the unpowered mobiles for which he is most widely known. Constructed usually from pieces of shaped and painted tin suspended on thin wires or cords, these were light enough to respond to the faintest air currents. They were described by Calder as 'four-dimensional drawings', and in a letter to Duchamp written in 1932 he spoke of his desire to make 'moving Mondrians'. Calder was greatly impressed by a visit to *Mondrian in 1930, and no doubt envisaged himself as bringing movement to Mondrian-type geometrical abstracts. However, the personalities of the two men were very different: Calder's delight in the comic and fantastic, which can often be seen even in his largest works, was at the opposite pole to the messianic seriousness of Mondrian. Nevertheless, for all his humour, Calder made a major contribution to the development of abstract and kinetic art: he was 'the first sculptor, European or American, to explore so intently the implications of motion . . . the first to allow process and chance to alter the forms of his pieces. No other American had yet contributed so fundamentally to the progress of modern art' (Matthew Baigell, *A Concise History of American Painting and Sculpture*, 1984). After winning first prize for sculpture at the 1952 Venice *Biennale Calder received numerous public commissions. Some of his late works are very large: the motorized hanging mobile *Red, Black, and Blue* (1967) at Dallas Airport, for example, is 14 m (45 ft) wide. He also worked in a variety of other fields, painting *gouaches and designing, for example, rugs and tapestries.

Callcott, Sir Augustus Wall (1779–1844). English painter. He studied with the portraitist John *Hoppner, but he soon changed course and went on to have a highly successful career as a landscape painter, patronized by numerous distinguished clients who preferred his work to that of his more innovative contemporaries *Constable and *Turner. His style, influenced by *Claude and 17th-century Dutch painters, was similar to that of Turner (who was a friend), but his work is rather pedestrian in comparison: *Ruskin commented that he 'painted everything tolerably, nothing excellently'. In 1827 he married the writer Maria Graham (1785–1842), the author of numerous books on topography and painting, and their home in London became a leading cultural salon. He was knighted in 1837 and the year before his death was appointed Surveyor of the Queen's Pictures.

Callot, Jacques (1592–1635). French etcher and draughtsman. He was born and died in Nancy (at this time capital of the independent Duchy of Lorraine), but his early career was spent in Italy, *c.*1611–21, initially in Rome but principally in Florence. His main patron there was Grand Duke Cosimo II de' *Medici; it was his premature death in 1621 that led Callot to return to Nancy. Cosimo was a great lover of festivities, and Callot's work for him included scenes of fêtes and ceremonies, some of them large plates featuring scores of figures. Among his numerous other subjects were beggars and characters from the commedia dell'arte. He combined the sense of fantasy and the sophisticated exaggerations of late *Mannerism with witty and acute observation of real life to create a highly distinctive style. In some respects he comes close to *Bellange, also active in Nancy, but Callot was more realistic. After his return to Lorraine he concentrated on religious subjects and his output became more serious in tone. His most famous work is the series of eighteen etchings entitled *Les Misères et les malheurs de la guerre*, published in 1633, which harrowingly depict the atrocities of the Thirty Years War (in the year in which they were published Lorraine was invaded by France). They were admired by *Goya and influenced his treatment of barbarity in his *Disasters of War* prints. Callot's output was prodigious; more than a thousand etchings and more than a thousand drawings by him are extant. He was one of the greatest of all etchers and one of the first major creative artists to work exclusively in the *graphic arts.

Calraet, Abraham. *See* CUYP.

Calvaert, Denys (Dionisio Fiammingo) (*c.*1540–1619). Flemish painter active in Italy. After training in his native Antwerp he settled permanently in Bologna in about 1560. His work is in an undistinguished *Mannerist style, but he played an important role as a teacher. In about 1575 he established an *academy, at which he taught more than 100 pupils, among them some of the most distinguished artists of the Bolognese School—Francesco *Albani, *Domenichino, and *Reni. The more celebrated academy of the *Carracci was probably inspired by Calvaert's.

Calvert, Edward (1799–1883). English painter and wood engraver. The son of a soldier, he spent five years in the navy, before moving to London in 1824 and studying at the *Royal Academy. He was introduced to *Blake and became one of his group of followers known as the *Ancients. Even before this, however, he had created an outstanding work that was very much in Blake's spirit—*A Primitive City* (1822, BM, London), a tiny watercolour full of poetic ardour. Calvert continued in this vein for about a decade, but after producing his masterpiece in wood engraving, *The Chamber Idyll* (1831), he created no more work of comparable quality. From this time he became something of a recluse and painted mainly for his own pleasure (he was wealthy and had no need to sell his work). Many of his later pictures were inspired by his love of ancient Greece.

***camaieu*.** A painting executed in several shades of a single colour; such a painting in greyish tones is known as a *grisaille.

Cambiaso, Luca (1527–85). Genoese painter and draughtsman. He was the outstanding Genoese painter of the 16th century, indeed the only one who was of more than local significance. Much of his large output consisted of fresco decorations in churches and palaces in and near Genoa, and he also produced numerous altarpieces

and devotional pictures. Some of his finest devotional works are austere night scenes and they have been claimed as sources for Georges de *La Tour, even though it is not clear how La Tour could have known them. Cambiaso visited Rome at least twice and *Michelangelo was a powerful influence on the massiveness of his figures, although in softness of modelling they have more in common with *Correggio. He was an almost compulsively busy draughtsman as well as a prolific painter; in some of his drawings the figures are constructed with simplified cubic shapes, giving them a remarkably modern look. In 1583 he accepted an invitation from Philip II of Spain (*see* HABSBURG) to join the team of artists at the *Escorial. The work he accomplished there in the remaining two years of his life was carried out very hastily and includes an enormous and extremely dull ceiling fresco of the *Holy Trinity in Glory* in the basilica. He was succeeded at the Escorial by Federico *Zuccaro and then Pellegrino *Tibaldi.

Camden Town Group. Group of British painters formed in 1911 who took their name from the drab working-class area of London (as it was then) made popular as a subject by *Sickert, who lived in the borough for several years. In addition to being the prime inspiration of the group, Sickert suggested the name. The group lasted only two years, but its name is also used in a broader sense to characterize a distinctive strain in British painting from about 1905 to 1920, and as Wendy Baron, the group's leading historian, has written, 'If we define Camden Town painting as the objective record of aspects of urban life in a basically Impressionist-derived handling, and recognize it as a distinct movement in British art, then we must accept that the heyday of Camden Town painting was over by the time the Camden Town Group was born.' Many of Sickert's disciples showed their work at the exhibitions of the *Allied Artists' Association, founded in 1908, and several of them also did so at the *New English Art Club, but for some of them these institutions were not progressive enough, which led to the decision to form the Camden Town Group in 1911. Women were excluded and it was decided to limit the membership to sixteen, who were originally: Walter Bayes (1869–1956), Robert *Bevan, Malcolm Drummond

(1880–1945), Harold *Gilman, Charles *Ginner, Spencer *Gore (president), J. D. *Innes, Augustus *John, Henry *Lamb, Wyndham *Lewis, Maxwell Gordon Lightfoot (1886–1911), J. B. Manson (1879–1945), who was secretary, Lucien *Pissarro, William Ratcliffe (1870–1955), Sickert himself, and John Doman Turner (c.1873–1938), an amateur painter who had been a pupil of Gore. Lightfoot soon resigned (and committed suicide a few months later); he was replaced by Duncan *Grant.

These artists varied considerably in their aims and styles. Their subjects included not only street scenes in Camden Town, but also landscapes, portraits, and still lifes. Several of them painted with a technique that can loosely be described as *Impressionist, with broad, broken touches, but particularly after Roger *Fry's *Post-Impressionist exhibitions of 1910 and 1912, the use of bold, flat areas of colour became characteristic of others, notably Bevan, Gilman, Ginner, and Gore. These four best represent a distinctive Camden Town 'style', one that was much imitated by painters of the urban scene up to the Second World War and beyond. The Camden Town Group held three exhibitions at the Carfax Gallery, London, in 1911–12. They were financially disastrous, and as the gallery then declined to put on more exhibitions, they merged with a number of smaller groups to form the *London Group in November 1913. The new body organized a collective exhibition in Brighton at the end of 1913; although it was advertised under the name of the Camden Town Group, it may be regarded rather as the first exhibition of the London Group.

cameo. Small-scale sculpture in which the design stands in *relief above the surface. It is the opposite of *intaglio. Often, the term refers specifically to a portrait cut in a gemstone; this form was highly popular among the Greeks and Romans for jewellery and it was revived during the *Renaissance. Commonly a banded or multicoloured stone, such as agate, was used, in such a way as to exploit the different layers of colour—with one colour for the background and another for the carving, for example.

camera lucida (Lat.: 'light chamber'). An apparatus used as an aid in drawing and copying, patented in 1807 by William Hyde Wollaston (1766–1828), a well-known man of science. It received its misleading name—for it is not a 'chamber' at all—because it performed the same function as the *camera obscura, but in full daylight. It consists essentially of a prism mounted on a metal arm above a drawing board. The draughtsman sets the prism between his eye and the paper in such a way that he can see an image of the object he wishes to draw apparently lying on the paper and can trace its outline. Various refinements were added to the basic format, including a lens to aid focusing. David *Hockney, who is fascinated by the history of artists' techniques, began experimenting with a camera lucida in 1999, using it to draw portraits.

camera obscura (Lat.: 'dark chamber'). An apparatus that projects the image of an object or scene on to a sheet of paper or other surface so that the outlines can be traced. It consists of a shuttered box or space with a small hole or lens in one side through which light from a brightly lit scene enters and forms an inverted image on a screen placed opposite the opening. The optical principle is essentially that of the photographic camera. For greater convenience a mirror is usually installed, which reflects the image the right way up on to a suitably placed drawing surface. The principle was known as early as Aristotle, but the first account of its use for drawing was published in 1558, in *Magia naturalis*, a scientific book by Giambattista della Porta, an Italian physician. Various 17th-century painters are known or thought to have used a camera obscura in their work, and by the 18th century it had become a craze. Both amateurs and professionals—among them *Canaletto—used it for topographical painting, and there are accounts of an apparatus, somewhat like a sedan chair, inside which an artist could sit and draw, at the same time actuating bellows with his feet to improve the ventilation. More modest versions were easily portable and even pocketable.

Campagnola, Giulio (c.1482–c.1518). Italian artist, active mainly as an engraver. He was born in Padua, the son of a humanist scholar, and is said to have been skilled in ancient languages and in music. After working at the *Gonzaga court in Mantua and the *Este court in Ferrara, by 1507 he had moved to Venice. It is with this city that he is chiefly associated, his engravings of idyllic landscape subjects playing a major role in spreading the style of *Giorgione and *Titian. His many copies after *Dürer likewise disseminated knowledge of this artist in Italy. Giulio's pupil and adopted son, **Domenico** (c.1500–64), was also a printmaker, but his preferred medium was woodcut rather than engraving. In addition he sold his drawings (mainly landscapes) as finished compositions, sometimes passing them off as the work of Titian. In about 1520 he settled in Padua and became one of the city's leading painters, as well as continuing his activities as printmaker and draughtsman.

Campaña, Pedro de. *See* KEMPENEER.

Campbell, Steven. *See* GLASGOW SCHOOL OF ART.

Campen, Jacob van (1595–1657). Dutch architect and painter. He was the greatest Dutch architect of the 17th century and occupied a role in his country similar to that of his contemporary Inigo *Jones in England by introducing a fully mature classical style: the contemporary diplomat Constantijn Huygens described him as the man 'who vanquished Gothic folly with Roman stateliness and drove old heresy forth before an older truth'. His most important building is Amsterdam town hall (begun 1648, later renamed the royal palace), a triumphant symbol of the city during its greatest period. The building was richly decorated: Artus I *Quellin led a team of sculptors, and *Rembrandt was among those who provided paintings, although his *Conspiracy of Julius Civilis* (1661–2, Nationalmuseum, Stockholm) was removed soon after installation and replaced with a picture by his pupil Juriaen Ovens (1623–78). Van Campen's other buildings include the beautiful *Mauritshuis in The Hague (begun 1633), designed as a royal palace and now a celebrated picture gallery. As a painter he concentrated on historical and decorative work and was one of the team, including *Jordaens and *Lievens, who worked on the decoration of the Huis ten Bosch, the royal villa on the outskirts of The Hague.

Campin, Robert. *See* MASTER OF FLÉMALLE.

Canaday, John. *See* DERAIN.

Canadian Group of Painters (CGP). A group of Canadian painters formed in Toronto in 1933 and disbanded in 1969. The CGP regarded itself as a successor to the *Group of Seven, whose last exhibition had been in 1931, and it aimed 'to encourage and foster the growth of art in Canada which has a national character'. Although landscape continued to be the dominant subject among the members of the group (who included some of the leading Canadian painters of the time), it recognized 'the right of Canadian artists to find beauty and character in all things' and encouraged 'more modern ideas of technique and subject'.

Canaletto (Giovanni Antonio Canal) (1697–1768). Venetian painter, etcher, and draughtsman, the most famous viewpainter of the 18th century. He began his career assisting his father, a theatrical scene painter; their work included sets for Vivaldi operas in Venice and Alessandro Scarlatti operas in Rome, which they visited in 1719–20. Whilst he was in Rome Canaletto made drawings of ancient monuments and famous modern buildings, and after his return to Venice he abandoned theatrical work for topographical painting (*see* VEDUTA). His early paintings of Venice include some intimate views of unremarkable pieces of townscape, treated with great freshness of observation and liveliness of touch (*The Stonemason's Yard*, c.1727, NG, London). However, he soon began to specialize in much grander views showing the public face of the city, including festivities on the canals. His colouring became stronger and brighter and his handling smoother and more precise. He worked from drawings made on the spot and also made use of a *camera obscura, but although his pictures give the feeling of being extremely accurate records, he in fact often made departures from topographical correctness in the interests of creating a better composition—changing the proportions of a building or shifting its position and so on. He also produced imaginary views (*see* CAPRICCIO). His work appealed greatly to wealthy visitors to Venice and his best customers were British aristocrats making the *Grand Tour, for whom he sometimes produced series of views in uniform size. Canaletto's dealings with his British clients were mainly done through an agent, Joseph Smith (c.1674–1770), who moved to Venice in about 1700 to work as a banker and stayed for the rest of his life. In addition to working as an art dealer (with an efficient organization for shipping Canaletto's pictures to England), he was a publisher, and in 1744 he was appointed British consul in Venice—he is sometimes known as 'Consul Smith' and also as the 'Merchant of Venice'. He had a superb art collection of his own, most of which he sold to George III in 1762, thus accounting for the fact that the British royal collection has the world's best representation of Canaletto's work.

Canaletto's business was badly hit by the War of the Austrian Succession (1740–8), which severely curtailed Continental travel and therefore cut him off from his main patrons. In the early 1740s he concentrated on drawings and etchings, and in 1746 he moved to England, evidently at the suggestion of Jacopo *Amigoni. He was based in England for the next decade (although during this time he made two visits to Venice). Initially he was very successful, painting views of London and of various country houses. However, some of the work he produced in England was mechanical (even though he never lost his gift for handsome composition), and rumours were put about, probably by rivals, that he was not in fact the famous Canaletto but an impostor. In about 1756 he returned permanently to Venice. He continued active for the remainder of his life, but he never recovered his former popularity, and by the time of his death he seems to have been far from prosperous. His work was highly influential in Italy and elsewhere: his nephew Bernardo *Bellotto took his style to central Europe and his followers in England included William *Marlow and Samuel *Scott.

Candlelight Master. *See* BIGOT.

Cano, Alonso (1601–67). Spanish sculptor, painter, architect, and draughtsman, sometimes called 'the Spanish *Michelangelo' because of the diversity of his talents. He spent most of his career successively in Seville, Madrid, and Granada (his native city), but he also worked in Valencia and Malaga. Some of his movements were dictated by his eventful personal life, for more than once he left a city hastily or under a cloud after brushes with the law. In 1636 he was imprisoned for debt; in 1637 he wounded a colleague in a duel; and in 1644 he was accused of murdering his wife but was released after torture (by royal command, his right arm and hand were not harmed). In spite of his stormy temperament, his work tends to be serene and often sweet. From 1614 to 1638 Cano lived in Seville, where he studied painting with *Pacheco (his fellow student *Velázquez became a lifelong friend) and probably also spent some time in the workshop of the sculptor *Montañés (early in his career he worked more as a sculptor than a painter). In 1638 he moved to Madrid to become painter to the Count-Duke Olivares and was employed by Philip IV (*see* HABSBURG) to restore pictures in the royal collection. Thus he became acquainted with the work of the 16th-century Venetian masters, whose influence is evident in his later paintings; they are much softer in technique than his earlier pictures, which are strongly lit in the manner of *Zurbarán. From 1652 he worked mainly in Granada, where he designed the façade of the cathedral (1667), one of the boldest and most original works of Spanish *Baroque architecture. He was ordained a priest in 1658, as this was necessary for him to further his career at the cathedral. It houses several of his works in painting and sculpture, including a *polychrome wooden statue of the *Immaculate Conception* (1655) that is sometimes considered his masterpiece.

Canova, Antonio (1757–1822). Italian sculptor. He was the most successful and the most influential sculptor of the *Neoclassical movement, outdoing even *Thorvaldsen and *Flaxman in international fame and prestige and being celebrated in prose and verse by some of the leading writers of the day. Born in Possagno, near Treviso, the son of a stonemason, he was apprenticed as a boy to a local sculptor, with whom he moved to Venice in about 1770. His early work is lively and naturalistic (*Daedalus and Icarus*, 1779, Mus. Correr, Venice), but after he settled in Rome in 1781 his style became graver and thoroughly imbued with *antique influence. *Theseus and the Minotaur* (1781–3, V&A, London) was his first major work in Rome, and he soon followed this with the prestigious commission for the tomb of Pope Clement XIV in SS. Apostoli (1783–7). After this Canova never looked back. He ran a large studio and worked for a galaxy of European notables, including Napoleon (who tried unsuccessfully to get him to settle in Paris), the Duke of Wellington, and Catherine the Great of Russia; his portrait of Napoleon's sister (*Pauline Borghese as Venus*, 1805–7, Borghese Gal., Rome) is one of his most celebrated works, a marble equivalent to J.-L. *David's *Madame Récamier*. Canova worked much for the papal court and after the Napoleonic Wars he became Pope Pius VII's representative in recovering works of art looted by the French. He visited Paris in this role in 1815 and later in the same year he went to London to see the *Elgin Marbles. On both occasions he was fêted as a celebrity. In 1816 he was created Marchese d'Ischia by the pope and soon afterwards retired to Possagno, where he built a church, known as the Temple of Canova, in which he was buried. Nearby is the house in which he was born; a sculpture gallery was added in the 1830s and this contains a large collection of his work, including examples of the paintings he occasionally produced. Canova was immensely influential and was renowned for his generosity to young sculptors. He went out of favour in the later 19th century, when—in the wake of *Romanticism—his sculptures seemed cold and static, but his reputation greatly revived in the 20th century. His work, in fact, was always much more individual than that of many of his Neoclassical contemporaries and he placed great importance on the personal handling of his material.

canvas. A woven cloth used as a *support for painting. The best-quality canvas is made of linen; other materials used are cotton, hemp, and jute. It is now so familiar a material that the word 'canvas' has become almost a synonym for an *oil painting, but it was not until around 1500 that it began to rival the wooden *panel as the standard support for movable paintings. Canvas had the advantages over panel of being cheaper, easier to produce, and more portable (it can be rolled for transport), as well as providing an attractive surface 'tooth' that encouraged the textural possibilities of oil paint. The transition to canvas took place first in Italy, with panels remaining popular in northern Europe well into the 17th century. Canvas is not suitable for painting on until it has been coated with a *ground, which isolates the

fabric from the paint; otherwise it will absorb too much paint, only very rough effects will be obtainable, and parts of the fabric may be rotted by the *pigments. It must also be made taut on a *stretcher or by some other means.

canvas board. Sheet of cardboard or pasteboard covered with sized and primed cloth, usually cotton. It was first made commercially in the 1870s and is now chiefly used by amateurs as a cheap substitute for canvas. *See also* ACADEMY BOARD.

Čapek, Josef (1887–1945). Czech painter, graphic artist, stage designer, and writer. Like *Filla and *Gutfreund, he was one of the earliest artists outside France to work in a *Cubist idiom, and with them he was one of the founders of the Group of Plastic Artists, which was established in Prague in 1911 with the object of combining Cubism and German *Expressionism into a new national style. Later the Expressionist current in his work prevailed, revealing his deep concern with fundamental moral and social questions (*Bad Conscience*, 1926, Moravian Gal., Brno). His humanist outlook was shared by his more famous younger brother, the writer Karel Čapek, several of whose books he illustrated. Both of them fervently opposed the threat from Nazi Germany in the 1930s; Karel died the year before the outbreak of the Second World War, but Josef lived to see its full horrors and died in Belsen concentration camp. His work as a writer included poetry, a novel, and plays written in collaboration with Karel, most notably *The Insect Play* (1920), a comic fantasy satirizing greed and selfishness.

Cappelle, Jan van de (*c.*1625–79). Dutch marine and landscape painter. He was a wealthy Amsterdam dyer who painted in his spare time, but there is nothing of the Sunday painter in his work. Typically his paintings show handsome vessels on calm rivers or seas; they have a grandeur of composition, a limpid quality of light, and an exquisite sense of tonality that place them among the finest marine paintings of any time or place. Cappelle also painted winter landscapes and beach scenes. His work is fairly rare; the best collection is in the National Gallery in London. He used his wealth to make a remarkable art collection. An inventory of it drawn up after his death lists some 200 paintings and more than 7,000 drawings, including 500 by *Rembrandt. It also mentions portraits of Cappelle by Rembrandt and *Hals; he is the only person known to have been portrayed by both these great contemporaries, but neither portrait has been certainly identified.

capriccio (It.: 'caprice'). Term that can be applied to any fantasy subject, but is most commonly used of a type of townscape popular in the 18th century in which real buildings are combined with imaginary ones or are shown with their locations rearranged. *Canaletto and *Guardi often painted pictures of this type, and there is a painting by William *Marlow in Tate Britain, London, showing St Paul's Cathedral overlooking a Venetian canal. *Goya's *Los Caprichos* are etchings of fantastic subjects of a completely different kind.

Caracciolo, Giovanni Battista (also known as Battistello) (1578–1635). Neapolitan painter. He was one of the greatest of *Caravaggio's followers, and his powerful work was an important factor in making Naples a stronghold of the Caravaggesque style. The decisive impact that Caravaggio made on him can be seen from his *Liberation of St Peter* (c.1615), painted for the same church (the Chiesa del Monte della Misericordia, still in situ) as the master's *Seven Acts of Mercy*. It shows how Caracciolo, unlike so many of the *Caravaggisti, looked beyond the obvious trademarks of Caravaggio's work, aspiring to its depth of feeling as well as its mastery of dramatic light and shade. In 1614 he visited Rome and his later work is more classical in style, influenced perhaps by the *Carracci. Unusually for a Caravaggesque artist, he was an accomplished fresco painter, and his finest late works are decorations in the Certosa di S. Martino in Naples, finished in 1631.

Caravaggio, Michelangelo Merisi da (1571–1610). The most powerful, original, and influential Italian painter of the 17th century. Although his career was short (he was only 38 when he died) and his output was fairly small (there are about 60 surviving pictures by him), he had an immense impact on his contemporaries, creating a bold and naturalistic style that broke decisively with the prevailing vapid *Manner-

ism and inspired a host of imitators. He was perhaps born in Milan, but he grew up in Caravaggio, near Bergamo, and takes his name from the town. From 1584 to about 1588 he served an apprenticeship in Milan under the undistinguished Simone Peterzano (c.1540–c.1596) and by about 1592 he had moved to Rome, the main centre of his activity. His career there is not firmly documented until 1599 and in his early years he is said to have endured hardship, taking on whatever hackwork he could to scrape a living. He progressed to assisting reputable artists, notably Giuseppe *Cesari, then to independent work, and in the mid-1590s a dealer sold some of his pictures to Cardinal Francesco del Monte, who became his first important patron (Caravaggio was a paid retainer in his household for about three years). Del Monte was a sophisticated and many-sided man who enjoyed various pleasures, including music and, so it said, parties at which boys dressed up as girls. Caravaggio's earliest surviving works are mainly pictures involving fleshy, effeminate young men, and they presumably reflect his own sexual tastes (he seems to have been bisexual but predominantly homosexual) as well as those of his patron. These pictures are fairly small in size and very intimate in feeling, with a startling sense of physical presence: the strongly lit, sharply detailed figures are brought up close to the front of the picture space and typically gaze at the spectator with a look of blatant erotic invitation (*Bacchus*, c.1597, Uffizi, Florence). Caravaggio kept this sense of immediacy and closeness throughout his career, his figures usually standing out against a plain background with little sense of depth, but in the late 1590s he abandoned clear lighting in favour of the murky *chiaroscuro that is one of the most distinctive features of his mature paintings; *Bellori describes his early work as 'sweet, clean and without those shadows that he later used'.

It was probably through del Monte that Caravaggio gained his first public commission—two large canvases of the *Calling of St Matthew* and the *Martyrdom of St Matthew* for the side walls of the Contarelli Chapel in S. Luigi dei Francesi; they were painted in 1599–1600 and are his first documented works. An altarpiece of *St Matthew and the Angel* was added in 1602 and by this time Caravaggio had already completed a second major public commission—two paintings for the Cerasi Chapel in S. Maria del Popolo: the *Crucifixion of St Peter* and the *Conversion of St Paul* (1600–1). All these pictures, and particularly the last two, were immensely original in their dramatic use of light and shade, their economy and force of design, and their down-to-earth realism—the familiar stories being seen in a completely new way and played out by solid, substantial, flesh-and-blood people rather than the traditional idealized figures. They established Caravaggio as the most exciting painter in Rome and changed the direction of his career: from now on he devoted himself mainly to large, deeply serious religious pictures for public settings, rather than intimate works for the rarefied taste of connoisseurs. From the beginning of his public career, his work was controversial, as many contemporaries found his realism inappropriate or abhorrent in a religious context. Several of his major works were refused on such grounds of decorum or theological incorrectness and were replaced with more conventional pictures by Caravaggio himself or other painters. Among the rejected paintings was the *Death of the Virgin* (1605–6, Louvre, Paris), which shows the Virgin as a thoroughly believable corpse rather than in the traditional way as a woman who appeared to be merely sleeping before being received into heaven. It was turned down by the church of S. Maria della Scala and replaced with a picture by *Saraceni. *Baglione writes that Caravaggio's picture was removed because he 'so disrespectfully made the Madonna swollen up and with bare legs', and another early account says that her figure was based on the body of a drowned prostitute fished out of the River Tiber. However, the controversial painting was soon bought by Vincenzo *Gonzaga, Duke of Mantua (on the recommendation of *Rubens), and Caravaggio's other rejected pictures were likewise quickly acquired by discerning collectors.

Whilst Caravaggio was becoming the most famous painter in Rome on account of such works, he was also achieving notoriety for his violent and loutish way of life. In the years 1600–5 he built up a lengthy criminal record for various cases of assault and insulting behaviour, then in 1606 he killed a man in a fight over a wager on a tennis match. He fled Rome, fearing he would be charged with murder, and spent the remaining four years of his life as a fugitive from justice, his travels taking him to Naples (1606–7), Malta (1607–8), Sicily (1608–9), and back to Naples again (1609–10). Wherever he went he gained important commissions and had a major influence on local artists. During these years his work became more austere and poignant, as in the *Beheading of St John the Baptist* (1608, Valletta Cathedral, Malta), his largest painting and a work of the utmost tragic power. His life continued to be fraught with danger: in 1608 he was imprisoned on Malta but escaped, and in 1609 he was badly wounded in the face in Naples. He died of fever on the way to Rome, where he thought a pardon was imminent. He had no pupils, but a legion of followers (the *Caravaggisti), and his work, together with that of the *Carracci, inaugurated a new era in Italian painting (*see* BAROQUE).

Caravaggio continued to be a famous name throughout the 17th century, but he was regarded by many as an 'evil genius' (in the words of Vicente *Carducho, writing in 1633), whose influence on other artists was pernicious. In 1672 Bellori wrote 'There is no doubt Caravaggio advanced the art of painting, because he came upon the scene when realism was not much in fashion and when figures were made according to convention and satisfied more the taste for gracefulness than for truth'; however, Bellori also thought he had 'debased the majesty of art', and that because of him 'everyone did as he pleased, and soon the value of the beautiful was discounted'. Interest in Caravaggio declined in the 18th century (he is not mentioned in *Reynolds's *Discourses*), but revived in the mid-19th century. By this time his rejection of ideal beauty could be seen to have the advantage of truth, although there were still those, like *Ruskin, who saw in him 'perpetual seeking for and feeding upon horror and ugliness, and filthiness of sin'. Serious historical research on him began in the early years of the 20th century, since when he has attracted an enormous amount of critical commentary and speculation, so much so that Ellis *Waterhouse has written that 'the innocent reader of art-historical literature could be forgiven for supposing that his place in the history of civilization lies somewhere in importance between Aristotle and Lenin'.

Caravaggisti. Term applied to painters who imitated the style of *Caravaggio in the early 17th century. Caravaggio's revolutionary approach to painting, particularly his dramatic use of *chiaroscuro, had extraordinary influence in Rome in the first decade of the 17th century, not only on Italian painters, but also on artists from other countries who flocked to what was then the artistic capital of Europe. His fame was already spreading outside Italy by 1604, when Karel van *Mander, in Haarlem, wrote of 'Michelangelo da Caravaggio, who is doing extraordinary things in Rome', and in 1642 *Bellori commented: 'The painters then in Rome were greatly impressed by his novelty and the younger ones especially gathered around him and praised him as the only true imitator of nature. Looking upon his works as miracles, they outdid each other in following his method.' The most prominent of the Italian Caravaggisti included Orazio *Gentileschi, one of the few followers to have close personal contact with the master, and Bartolommeo *Manfredi, who popularized gaming and drinking scenes, subjects that Caravaggio himself had rarely painted. In Naples, where Caravaggio worked intermittently between 1606 and 1610, *Caracciolo, Artemisia *Gentileschi, and *Ribera, a Spaniard by birth, ensured that the style took firm root. In Rome, Caravaggism went out of favour in the 1620s, but it persisted elsewhere in Italy, and in other parts of Europe, particularly in Sicily (which Caravaggio visited), Utrecht, and Lorraine, lingering into the 1650s in all three places. *Baburen, *Honthorst, and *Terbrugghen were the three most important artists in making Utrecht the Dutch centre of Caravaggism, and in Lorraine Georges de *La Tour created perhaps the most personal and poetic interpretation of the style. Few major painters worked in a Caravaggesque style throughout their careers; some, such as Guido *Reni, had a brief flirtation with it, while others, such as Honthorst (who became a court portraitist), had a complete change of direction. Echoes of the Caravaggesque style can be found in the work of some of the giants of 17th-century art: *Rembrandt, *Rubens, and *Velázquez.

cardboard. A thin but stiff board usually made from paper pulp or sheets of paper, sometimes used as an inexpensive *support for paintings. Millboard is a term applied to a relatively stout type. *Etty (for his nude studies) and *Toulouse-Lautrec are among the artists who have made extensive use of these materials. *See also* ACADEMY BOARD.

Carducho, Bartolomé (*c.*1560–1608) and **Vicente** (*c.*1576–1638). Spanish painters, brothers, of Florentine birth (they were originally called Bartolommeo and Vincenzo Carducci). They settled permanently in Spain in 1585 when Bartolomé accompanied Federico *Zuccaro to carry out work at the *Escorial (Vicente was a child at the time). Bartolomé became a court painter in 1598 and worked on royal commissions in Madrid, Segovia, and Valladolid. He painted in fresco as well as oils, and was influential in introducing Italian ideas to Spain. Vicente was appointed a court painter in Madrid in 1609, but he is now remembered mainly for his book *Diálogos de la pintura* (1633). In this he defended the heroic Italian tradition (championing *Michelangelo in particular), and excoriated the naturalism of *Caravaggio. This has been interpreted as a veiled attack on *Velázquez, whose success overshadowed Carducho.

caricature. A form of art, usually portraiture, in which characteristic features of the subject represented are distorted or exaggerated for comic effect or to make critical comment. The term is sometimes used more broadly to denote other forms of pictorial burlesque or ludicrous representation, such as the *grotesque heads of *Leonardo. The invention of caricature in the more limited sense is usually credited to Annibale *Carracci, who possibly also coined the word *caricatura*. He defended this type of art as a counterpart to idealization (*see* IDEAL): just as the serious artist penetrates to the idea behind appearances, so the caricaturist also brings out the essence of his victim, the way he should look if Nature wholly had her way. Few of Annibale's caricatures survive, but his pioneering role is well attested by early sources: *Bellori, for example, wrote that 'He was not only adroit in making witticisms and jests with words but also with the jocularities of drawings, many of them done by pen. Thus originated the delightful burlesque portraits or caricatures, as those drawings are sometimes called, of figures altered according to their natural defects, making us laugh by their ridiculous likeness.' Many other leading 17th-century artists were brilliant caricaturists (notably *Bernini), but the first artist to earn a substantial part of his living by caricature was probably Pier Leone Ghezzi (1674–1755). Political caricature as we know it today emerged in the late 18th century in Britain, notably in the work of *Gillray. It has remained a field in which British artists have excelled, but the greatest of all political caricaturists was a Frenchman, *Daumier. Many leading artists of the 19th and 20th centuries have shown a gift for caricature, but mainly as a sideline.

Carlevaris, Luca (1664–1730). Italian painter, born in Udine and active mainly in Venice. He is regarded as the father of 18th-century Venetian view painting (*see* VEDUTA), for although he was not (as is sometimes asserted) the first to specialize in the genre, he approached it with a new seriousness, his interest in mathematics being reflected in his rigorous perspective settings. His paintings and his set of 104 etched views of Venice, published in 1703, are the foundation on which *Canaletto and *Guardi built. A collection of oil sketches from nature in the Victoria and Albert Museum, London, shows his lively powers of observation.

Carline, Hilda. *See* SPENCER.

Carmichael, Franklin. *See* GROUP OF SEVEN.

Caro, Sir Anthony (1924–). British sculptor, one of the most influential figures in post-war British art. After training as an engineer at Cambridge University and serving in the navy in the Second World War, he studied sculpture in London, then from 1951 to 1953 worked as part-time assistant to Henry *Moore. His early works were figures modelled in clay, but a radical change of direction came after he visited the USA and met David *Smith in 1959. In the following year he began making abstract metal sculpture, using standard industrial parts such as steel plates and lengths of aluminium tubing together with pieces of scrap, which he welded and bolted together and then generally painted a single rich colour. The colour helped to unify the various shapes and textures and often set the mood for the piece, as with the bright and optimistic red of *Early One Morning* (1962,

Tate, London). This, like many of Caro's sculptures, is large in scale and open and extended in composition (he describes it as 'dancing along'); it rests directly on the ground, and Caro has been one of the leading figures in challenging the 'pedestal' tradition. He taught part-time at St Martin's School of Art in London 1953–79, and he had a major influence on several of the young sculptors who trained under him, initiating a new school of British abstract sculpture (*see* NEW GENERATION). In the 1970s his work became much more massive and rougher in texture, sometimes incorporating huge chunks of metal. In the 1980s he returned to more traditional materials and techniques and began making figurative (or semi-abstract) works in bronze, including (in the early 1990s) a series inspired by the Trojan War. His reputation is high in the USA as well as Britain, but he is not without detractors: the critic Peter Fuller described the work with which he became famous as 'nothing if not of its time: it reflected the superficial, synthetic, urban, commercial American values which dominated the 1960s'.

Carolingian art. The art and architecture of the reign of Charlemagne (800–814), the first Holy Roman emperor, and of his successors until about 900. Charlemagne's reign was noteworthy for reforms in many fields; his guiding principle was a renewal of the values of the Roman empire, and this was felt in the arts no less than in administrative, judicial, and religious matters. His capital was at Aachen (Aix-la-Chapelle), which became the centre of a cultural revival following a bleak period for the arts in the Franco-German lands that formed the heart of his vast empire. Charlemagne recognized the value of the arts for the education of his subjects and was himself the principal initiator of the cultural revival. Little survives of Carolingian mural paintings or mosaics, but several manuscripts contemporary with Charlemagne are known, showing a classical, naturalistic figure style, but also at times a vivid expressiveness. There was no large-scale sculpture, but Carolingian ivory sculpture and metalwork (on book covers, for example) often reached a high level. Carolingian art had great influence on *Ottonian and *Romanesque art.

Carolus-Duran (pseudonym of Charles-Émile-Auguste Durand)(1838–1917). French painter. His early works included peasant scenes influenced by *Courbet's *Realism, but from about 1870 he concentrated on portraits (particularly of women), becoming a great fashionable success with his slick style. *Sargent was the most important of his many pupils and was influenced by his rich, fluid brushwork. In 1905–10 Carolus-Duran was director of the French Academy in Rome.

Caron, Antoine (1521–99). French *Mannerist painter. He is one of the few French painters of his time with a distinctive artistic personality, and his work reflects the refined but unstable atmosphere of the Valois court during the Wars of Religion (1560–98). He worked at *Fontainebleau under *Primaticcio in the 1540s and later became court painter to Catherine de *Médicis, wife of Henry II of France. His few surviving works include historical and allegorical subjects in the manner of court ceremonies, scenes of magic and prediction, and massacres, as in *Massacres under the Triumvirate* (1566, Louvre, Paris), his only signed and dated painting. His style is characterized most obviously by extremely elongated, precious-looking figures set in open spaces that seem too large for them. He had a penchant for gaudy colours and bizarre architectural forms. Some of the works attributed to him may be by other hands, however, for French painting of his period is such an obscure area that Caron's name is liable to be attached to anything similar to his known œuvre.

Carpaccio, Vittore (c.1460–1525/6). Venetian painter. His life is poorly documented, and it is not known with whom he trained, but it is generally agreed that the chief influence on his work was Gentile *Bellini. This is especially evident in the first of the two great cycles of paintings that are his chief claim to fame—the scenes from the life of St Ursula, executed in the 1490s for the Scuola di S. Orsola and now in the Accademia, Venice. Carpaccio's salient characteristics—his taste for anecdote, and his eye for the crowded detail of the Venetian scene—found their happiest expression in these paintings, one of which, the *Miracle of the Cross*, looks forward to the 18th-century compositions of *Canaletto and *Guardi.

His other great cycle, mainly on the lives of St George and St Jerome, painted for the Scuola di S. Giorgio degli Schiavone, Venice, in 1502–7 (still in the Scuola), combines fantasy with wittily observed detail. After these two major commissions, however, Carpaccio's work declined in quality, although he still remained busy and continued to attract important patrons. In his later work he did an increasing number of altarpieces, a type of work for which he had little flair. On the other hand he was an excellent portraitist, as is seen particularly in his deservedly famous *Two Courtesans* (c.1510, Correr Mus., Venice), probably a fragment of a larger work. It was a favourite work of *Ruskin, who contributed to the great popularity Carpaccio enjoyed in the 19th century. His fame has perhaps declined somewhat since, but he is still rated as second only to Giovanni Bellini as the outstanding Venetian painter of his generation.

Carpeaux, Jean-Baptiste (1827–75). The outstanding French sculptor of his period (also a painter, draughtsman, and etcher). He studied for ten years at the École des *Beaux-Arts (where *Rude was his main teacher), before eventually winning the *Prix de Rome in 1854. His major work in Rome was *Count Ugolino and His Sons* (1860, Mus. d'Orsay, Paris, and other versions), a tragic scene from Dante. It made his reputation (although conservatives disliked it) and after his return to Paris in 1862 he won favour at Napoleon III's court, receiving many commissions for portrait busts. He also had several larger commissions, of which the most famous is *La Danse* (1866–9), a high-relief group for the façade of the Paris Opéra (the original is now in the Mus. d'Orsay). This uninhibitedly dynamic and sensuous work caused a sensation, was denounced as immoral, and had ink thrown over it. Partially because of such attacks on his work, Carpeaux suffered from a persecution complex in his final years before his early death from cancer. He was a pivotal figure in French sculpture, for his exuberance of feeling and vivacious modelling made a decisive break with the *Neoclassical tradition and presaged the work of *Rodin.

Carr, Emily (1871–1945). Canadian painter of *Expressionist landscapes. She felt the urge to paint from an early age, but her artistic development was slow and halting, interrupted by ill health and the need to undertake other work to earn a living. Her training was mainly in San Francisco, 1889–95, England, 1899–1904, and Paris, 1910–11. During her stay in France she probably studied briefly with the New Zealand painter Frances *Hodgkins, but the main influence on her at this time was the work of the *Fauves. After her return to Canada she painted the landscape of her native British Columbia with passionate feeling for the power of nature, executing much of her work out of doors. Discouraged by years of neglect, she had almost ceased to paint when in 1927 she was overwhelmed when she first saw the work of the *Group of Seven in Toronto. Thereafter she worked with renewed energy and deepened spirituality, overcoming her earlier disregard to attain the status of a national heroine. She wrote several autobiographical books.

Carrà, Carlo (1881–1966). Italian painter and writer on art, a prominent figure in both *Futurism and *Metaphysical Painting. He joined the Futurists in 1909, and visits to Paris in 1911 and 1912 introduced *Cubist influence into his work. In his best-known painting, *The Funeral of the Anarchist Galli* (1911, MoMA, New York), for example, he combined the dynamism typical of Futurism with a sense of Cubist structural severity. In 1915 he met Giorgio de *Chirico and turned to Metaphysical Painting, producing about twenty works with de Chirico's paraphernalia of posturing mannequins, half-open doors, mysteriously significant interiors, etc., though generally without his typically sinister feeling. In 1919 Carrà published a book entitled *Pittura metafisica*, but in the same year he broke with de Chirico and abandoned the style. In the 1920s and 1930s he supported the classical ideals of the *Novecento Italiano, championing the return to traditional values in the journal *Valori plastici* and also in the Milan newspaper *L'Ambrosiano*, of which he was art critic from 1921 to 1938. From 1941 to 1952 he was professor of painting at the Brera Academy. In his work after the Second World War his style became somewhat looser, with freer brushwork.

Carracci. Family of Bolognese painters, the brothers **Agostino** (1557–1602) and **Annibale** (1560–1609) and their cousin **Ludovico** (1555–1619). They were major figures in the transition from *Mannerism to *Baroque and were largely responsible for establishing Bologna (previously something of an artistic backwater) as the centre of the most distinctive tradition in 17th-century Italian painting. In reaction against the artificiality of Mannerism, they revived the solidity and grandeur of the High *Renaissance, to which they added a vigour and warmth reflecting their admiration for Venetian painting. They often worked together early in their careers, and it is not easy to distinguish their individual shares in, for example, the cycle of frescos on the *History of the Founding of Rome* in the Palazzo Magnani, Bologna (c.1589–90). In the early 1580s they opened a private *academy in Ludovico's studio, and it soon became a centre for progressive art. It is uncertain how it operated in its early days, but by about 1590 it had become a teaching institution. Originally it was called the Accademia dei Desiderosi ('Desiderosi' meaning 'desirous of fame and learning'), but it later changed its name to Accademia degli Incamminati (Academy of the Progressives). In their teaching the Carracci stressed drawing from life, and vigorous draughtsmanship became a quality particularly associated with artists of the Bolognese School, notably *Domenichino and *Reni, two of the leading members of the following generation who trained at the academy. All three Carracci were themselves outstanding draughtsmen, and *Malvasia writes that even when eating they had 'bread in one hand and a pencil or charcoal in the other'. Their naturalistic outlook was in tune with the reforming ideals of the Counter-Reformation Church; in 1582 the Bishop of Bologna, Gabriele Paleotti, published a treatise on religious art in which he spoke out against 'obscure and ambiguous paintings' and praised the kind of artist who 'knows how to explain his ideas clearly ... and to render them intelligible and plain to see'.

By the mid-1590s Annibale had emerged as the greatest artist of the family. His early work included landscapes, portraits, and *genre pictures, but his reputation was mainly based on a succession of large altarpieces for churches in Bologna and other cities in north Italy, in which he showed a growing mastery of composition and expression. In 1594 he was called to Rome by Cardinal Odoardo *Farnese to discuss decorations for his family palace, and after returning to Bologna to finish various commissions he had in hand, he settled in Rome in 1595 and embarked on the work in the Palazzo Farnese from which his fame is inseparable. He first decorated a small room called the Camerino (the cardinal's private study) with mythological scenes, mainly involving Hercules, then in 1597 began his masterpiece—the decoration of the Farnese Gallery. The gallery is one of the most imposing rooms in the palace and at this time was used to display choice pieces from the celebrated family collection of ancient sculpture. Annibale's paintings complemented these sculptures by evoking the world of classical antiquity, the overall theme of his frescos being the loves of the Gods, or, as *Bellori described it, 'human love governed by celestial love'. The ceiling was completed in 1600 or 1601, and the decoration of the walls, which is of much less importance, was done over the next two or three years, mainly by assistants, including Domenichino, who was part of a flow of Bolognese artists who followed Annibale to Rome and capitalized on his success. His contemporaries regarded the Farnese Ceiling as the successor to the great Vatican frescos of *Michelangelo and *Raphael, and throughout the 17th and 18th centuries it ranked almost as high in critical esteem. There are obvious similarities with Michelangelo's Sistine Ceiling, notably in the majesty of the nude figures, but Annibale's ceiling is entirely different in spirit, conveying a wonderful feeling of movement and exuberance. It was enormously influential, not only as a pattern book of heroic figure design, but also as a model of technical procedure: Annibale made hundreds of drawings for the ceiling, and until the age of *Romanticism such elaborate preparatory work became accepted as a fundamental part of composing any really large and ambitious work. In this sense, Annibale exercised a more profound influence than his great contemporary *Caravaggio, for the latter never worked in fresco, which was still regarded as the greatest test of a painter's mettle and the most suitable vehicle for painting in the *Grand Manner.

Although his work in the Farnese Palace occupied most of his time, Annibale carried out other important commissions in Rome and made momentous contributions in other branches of painting. Most tellingly, he was the inventor of *ideal landscape, in which *Claude and *Poussin were his greatest followers; the *Flight into Egypt* (c.1604, Gal. Doria Pamphili Rome) is Annibale's masterpiece in this genre. His altarpieces and devotional pictures are amongst the finest of the time and have an important place in the tradition of history painting: Poussin was influenced by the force, economy, and precision of composition and gesture seen in paintings such as 'Domine, Quo Vadis?' (c.1602, NG, London), in which Annibale was at his most severely classical, whereas other artists, for example *Rubens, responded to the muscular energy of his work. In his final years Annibale was overcome by a debilitating illness and after 1606 he virtually abandoned painting (according to Belloriane he sank into depression after being meagrely rewarded by Cardinal Farnese for his work in the Palazzo Farnese, but his sickness probably had physical as well as mental causes). When he died he was buried according to his wishes near Raphael in the Pantheon. It is a measure of his achievement that artists as important and diverse as *Bernini (who referred to Annibale's 'great big brain'), Poussin, and Rubens found so much to admire and praise in his work. They were aware mainly of the public face of his art, but it also had a less formal side that comes out in his *caricatures (he is generally credited with inventing the form) and in his early *genre paintings, which are remarkable for their lively observation and handling (*The Butcher's Shop*, c.1582, Christ Church, Oxford).

Agostino was Annibale's principal assistant in the Farnese Gallery from 1597 until 1599, when they quarrelled and Agostino moved to Parma. Although they had originally been so close artistically, the brothers were very different in character: Agostino was socially ambitious and inclined to put on airs, whereas Annibale was, in Bellori's words, 'amiable and modest'. In Parma, Agostino began his own 'Farnese Ceiling', decorating a vault in the Palazzo del Giardino with mythological scenes for Duke Ranuccio Farnese, but it was unfinished at his death. Among his paintings the most famous is probably the *Last Communion of St Jerome* (c.1592, Pinacoteca Nazionale, Bologna), which inspired Domenichino's celebrated picture of the same subject.

However, his contemporary reputation was based mainly on his engravings, of which he produced more than 200. They include original compositions as well as reproductions of the paintings of other artists (notably several by *Tintoretto).

Ludovico left Bologna only for brief periods (although he received many invitations from distinguished patrons to work elsewhere), and after his cousins had gone to Rome, he directed the Carracci academy by himself, regarding teaching as a central part of his life. Early in his career he painted some portraits, but most of his paintings are on religious subjects. His work is uneven in quality, but at his best he was an artist of power and originality. He was less classical in style than his cousins—often emotional or even mystical in feeling. In his later years, the suave style of Guido Reni made Ludovico's work look old-fashioned, but he continued on his own path, sometimes producing pictures of an almost *Expressionist force (*Christ Crucified above Figures in Limbo*, 1614, S. Francesca Romana, Ferrara).

The Carracci fell from grace in the later 19th century along with all the other Bolognese painters, who were one of *Ruskin's pet hates and whom he considered (1847) had 'no single virtue, no colour, no drawing, no character, no history, no thought'. They were saddled with the label *'eclectic' and thought to be ponderous and lacking in originality. Their full rehabilitation did not come until the second half of the 20th century (the great Carracci exhibition held in Bologna in 1956 was a notable landmark), but Annibale has now regained his place as one of the giants of Italian painting.

In addition to the three celebrated Carracci, three other members of the family became artists: **Paolo** (1568–1625), who was Ludovico's younger brother; **Francesco** (1595–1622), the nephew of Agostino and Annibale; and **Antonio** (c.1583–1618), Agostino's illegitimate son. Paolo and Francesco were undistinguished, but Antonio had a considerable reputation in his day. However, after his early death he was virtually forgotten, and it is only recently that his work has been rediscovered. He mainly painted religious works, in a graceful style influenced by Reni.

Carreño de Miranda, Juan (1614–85). Spanish painter, active mainly in Madrid. Initially he concentrated on religious works, but after he was appointed one of the royal painters in 1669 he worked mainly as a portraitist. Except for his friend *Velázquez, he was the outstanding court portraitist of 17th-century Spain; he was of noble birth and his paintings have an aristocratic dignity and something of Velázquez's sensitivity and taste, especially in his portrayals of the sickly Charles II (*see* HABSBURG). His religious paintings (which include several frescos, notably in Toledo Cathedral) are, however, more extravagantly *Baroque.

Carriera, Rosalba (1675–1757). Venetian *pastel portraitist, the sister-in-law of *Pellegrini. She had a European reputation and made triumphant visits to Paris (1720–1) and Vienna (1730). Her success helped to popularize pastel: Maurice-Quentin de *La Tour, for example, was converted to the medium through his admiration for her. It is now hard to appreciate why her work, which is highly accomplished but generally rather insipid, should have aroused such enthusiasm. After becoming blind in 1746, she had her sight temporarily restored by an operation, but lost it permanently in 1749 and retired into a state of melancholy dejection.

Carrière, Eugène. *See* ACADÉMIE.

Carrington, Dora. *See* BLOOMSBURY GROUP.

Carrington, Leonora. *See* ERNST.

Carstens, Asmus Jakob (1754–98). Danish-born German draughtsman and painter who spent the key years of his career in Rome. Apart from some initial training at the Copenhagen Academy he was largely self-taught. In 1783 he set out for Rome, but got only as far as Mantua before lack of funds obliged him to return north. After eking out a living in Germany for several years, in 1788 he became a teacher at the Berlin Academy, and in 1792 he was given a grant by the Prussian government to go to Rome, where he spent the rest of his life. He had a very high-minded concept of art, in tune with his inflated idea of his own genius, and he concentrated on heroic figure compositions (mainly drawings and tempera pictures, for he virtually abandoned oils after settling in Rome). In its austerity and insistence on the primacy of draughtsmanship, his style was essentially *Neoclassical, but it is often touched with a strong current of *Romanticism (the Romantic strain in his temperament was also expressed in his view of himself as a rebel against authority). His serious outlook was influential on northern artists of the next generation in Rome, notably *Thorvaldsen and the *Nazarenes.

cartoon. A full-size drawing made for the purpose of transferring a design to a painting or tapestry or other (usually large) work. Cartoons were an essential part of the process of making stained glass, and it was perhaps from this art that painters borrowed the idea; they were certainly employed in painting by the late 14th century and by the middle of the 15th century they were used extensively by, for example, *Piero della Francesca. The design was transferred either by pressing heavily along the outlines with a pointed metal implement called a stylus or by rubbing powdered charcoal through a series of pinpricks—a process called *pouncing. In 1843 designs submitted in a competition for frescos in the Houses of Parliament in London were parodied in the magazine *Punch*. From this the word has acquired its most common meaning today—a humorous drawing or parody.

caryatid. A carved female figure, usually clad in long robes, serving as a column. They were first used in Greek architecture and the most famous caryatids are on the Erechtheum at Athens (c.421–406 BC). The male equivalent of the caryatid is the *atlas; the term *canephorae* is applied to caryatids supporting baskets on their heads.

Casanova, Giovanni Battista. See LOUTHERBOURG.

casein. A substance with strong adhesive powers made from the curd of milk, formerly used in art as a binding material for certain types of paints (particularly for wall painting) and *grounds and as a glue for joining parts of a wooden *panel together.

Cassatt, Mary (1844–1926). American painter and printmaker active mainly in France. She settled in Paris in 1874 (following earlier studies there) and became friendly particularly with *Degas. He invited her to exhibit with the *Impressionists and she took part in four of their eight group shows (1879, 1880, 1881, 1886). Cassatt specialized in everyday life scenes, her favourite theme being a mother with her child or children. In the 1880s her work was thoroughly Impressionist in style, but from about 1890 her forms became more solid and firmly outlined. She was an outstanding pastellist and printmaker, her finest prints being in colour and in a combination of techniques (aquatint, drypoint, etching). Their bold flattened forms and unconventional viewpoints were influenced by an exhibition of Japanese prints she saw in Paris in 1890. Cassatt's eyesight began to fail when she was in her fifties and she had virtually stopped working by 1914. She came from a wealthy family and had an important influence on American taste by urging her rich friends to buy Impressionist works.

cassone. Italian term for a large, decorated chest, especially one that contained a bride's dowry or was given as a wedding present. They were popular from the 14th to the 16th century, and cassoni with painted fronts were particularly fashionable in 15th-century Florence. These paintings usually represented episodes from the Bible or classical history or mythology that pointed a lesson or contained a happy augury for the newly-weds. Often the cassoni were made as pairs, bearing the coats of arms respectively of the bride and groom, as with a pair, dated 1472, in the Courtauld Gallery, London (this pair is particularly noteworthy in retaining the original backboards—*spalliere). Cassone paintings are rarely of high quality, although some major artists such as *Domenico Veneziano, *Uccello, and *Botticelli seem to have done them once in a while. The chief documented exponent was Apollonio di Giovanni (1415–65). Often panels have been detached from cassoni and are now displayed as independent paintings. Any *Renaissance picture of appropriate subject, size, and proportions (roughly three or four times longer than it is high) is likely to be described as a cassone panel, although similar pictures were used in other furnishings (for example on beds).

Castelli, Leo (1907–99). Italian-born American art dealer. He settled in New

York in the late 1940s and originally sold modern European works, acquired mainly through contacts he had established during the 1930s when he had been a dealer in Paris. However, finding this market dominated by more established dealers, he turned to American art, and in 1958 he first showed work by Jasper *Johns and Robert *Rauschenberg, the two artists with whom he is most closely identified. In the catalogue of the exhibition 'American Art in the 20th Century' (Royal Academy, London, 1993), Castelli is described as 'perhaps the most influential art dealer of the twentieth century... The reputations of most of the major artists of the 1960s were made under his guidance. He established the careers of Cy *Twombly, Frank *Stella, and Roy *Lichtenstein, before enhancing the standing of Andy *Warhol... With his first exhibition of Claes *Oldenburg in 1974, Castelli completed his group of *Pop celebrities ... In the early years he helped to change the American gallery system by introducing a European-type retainer (monthly wages advanced against royalties from future sales), enabling his artists to concentrate exclusively on their art.'

Castiglione, Giovanni Benedetto (called Il Grechetto) (1609–64). Italian painter, printmaker, and draughtsman, active in his native Genoa and also in Rome, Naples, and Mantua (where he ended his career working at the *Gonzaga court). He was versatile and prolific, and was unusual among Italian artists of his period in being particularly responsive to foreign influence: Rudolf *Wittkower writes that he 'ran through almost the whole gamut of stylistic possibilities in the course of his astonishing career'. In painting, his fluid manner owed something to *Rubens, van *Dyck, and Bernardo *Strozzi, all of whom worked in Genoa, whilst his etchings are indebted to *Rembrandt. His paintings are mainly on religious subjects, but they are often most notable for their superb treatment of animals and still-life details. Some of his other works have a sense of fantasy recalling Salvator *Rosa, notably the etching *The Genius of Castiglione* (1648). In addition to being one of the finest Italian etchers and draughtsmen of his period, he is credited with inventing the *monotype. He had a high reputation in his day and his

work continued to be influential in the 18th century, notably on *Fragonard and Giambattista *Tiepolo. His brother **Salvatore** (1620–76) was a minor artist and a diplomat for the Gonzaga court, and his son **Giovanni Francesco** (1641–1710) was a painter—a skilful imitator of his father's work.

Catena, Vincenzo (c.1470/80–1531). Venetian painter of religious subjects and portraits. Catena was a man of good birth and independent means who moved in humanist circles and may have been the link between these circles and *Giorgione. He is first mentioned in 1506 in an inscription on the back of Giorgione's portrait *Laura* (KH Mus., Vienna), according to which they had entered into some kind of partnership. Nothing else is known of this arrangement. The main influence on his style was Giovanni *Bellini. His early paintings can be awkward and stiff, but from c.1510 his work matured under the influence of the late Bellini, *Cima da Conegliano, and *Titian into a style that was derivative but handsome, with pleasing handling of diffused light and warm colours. There are several paintings by or attributed to Catena in the National Gallery, London.

Catlin, George (1796–1872). American painter and writer, renowned for his portrayal of American Indian life. He practised law before becoming an artist in the early 1820s (initially as a portraitist in Philadelphia) and was completely self-taught. In 1830 he began a series of visits to various Indian tribes and from 1837 to 1845 he exhibited the resulting paintings as the 'Gallery of Indians' in the USA and Europe. He was better received in England and France than in his native country (*Baudelaire wrote about him enthusiastically), but the venture was not a commercial success and he became bankrupt in 1852. In addition to his paintings, he published various illustrated books on Indian life. Most of his work is in the Smithsonian Institution in Washington.

Cavallini, Pietro (active c.1270–c.1330). Italian painter and mosaic designer, active mainly in Rome, where he must have been the leading artist of his day. His two major surviving works (both dating from the 1290s) are mosaics of the *Life of the Virgin*

(S. Maria in Trastevere, Rome) and a fragmentary fresco cycle, the most important part of which is a *Last Judgement* (S. Cecilia in Trastevere, Rome). In 1308 Cavallini was invited to Naples by the reigning king, Charles II of Anjou, and various frescos in S. Maria Donnaregina have been attributed to him. His final work (*c*.1325–30) was probably a mosaic on the façade of S. Paolo fuori le Mura, Rome; this was destroyed by fire in 1823, but something of its appearance (as of other lost works) is known from copies. According to his son, a scribe at the papal court, Cavallini lived to be 100, but little else is recorded about him. Although he is an obscure figure, he occupies an important place in the history of Italian painting. He softened the rigidity of *Byzantine art, and his majestic figures have a real sense of weight and three-dimensionality. His achievements were built on by his great contemporary *Giotto, whose *Last Judgement* in the Arena Chapel at Padua features Apostles enthroned exactly as in Cavallini's fresco of the subject.

Cavallino, Bernardo (1616–56?). Neapolitan painter. He was the most individual and sensitive Neapolitan painter of his time, but his career is somewhat obscure. About 80 paintings by him are extant, but only one is dated, *St Cecilia in Ecstasy* (1645, Palazzo Vecchio, Florence; a *modello* is in the Museo di Capodimonte, Naples). Most of his pictures are small-scale religious works, peopled by exquisitely elegant and refined figures who evoke a feeling of tender melancholy. Their fragile sensitivity is in complete contrast to the earthy vigour of much Neapolitan painting of his period. Cavallino trained under Massimo *Stanzione, but his style has more in common with that of van *Dyck, whose work was fairly well known in Naples. He is presumed to have died in the plague that devastated Naples in 1656.

Cazes, Pierre-Jacques. *See* CHARDIN.

Celant, Germano. *See* ARTE POVERA.

Cellini, Benvenuto (1500–71). Florentine sculptor, goldsmith, medallist, and writer—the author of one of the most celebrated of all autobiographies. This racy book has been famous since the 18th century (it was first published in 1728) for its vivid picture of a *Renaissance craftsman proud of his skill and independence, boastful of his feats in art, love, and war, quarrelsome, superstitious, and devoted to the great tradition embodied in *Michelangelo. It has given him a wider reputation than could have come from his artistic work alone; but to modern eyes he also appears as one of the most important *Mannerist sculptors, and his statue *Perseus* is one of the glories of Florentine art. He spent most of his life in Florence, but he worked in several other places, his movements sometimes being influenced by his violent and vain temperament; he made enemies wherever he went, was several times imprisoned, and in 1534 killed a rival goldsmith in Rome (he was pardoned by Pope Paul III (Alessandro *Farnese)).

Cellini trained as a goldsmith and in his early career (which was spent mainly in Rome) he worked predominantly in precious metals; little survives from this phase of his life apart from some medals. Between 1540 and 1545 he worked in France in the service of Francis I (*see* FONTAINEBLEAU, SCHOOL OF), for whom he created a famous salt cellar of gold enriched with enamel (1540–3, KH Mus., Vienna), the most important piece of goldsmiths' work that has survived from the Italian Renaissance and the only one that is securely documented as Cellini's. He also made for the king a bronze *relief, the *Nymph of Fontainebleau* (*c*.1543, Louvre, Paris), which was his first large-scale sculpture. The remainder of Cellini's life was spent in Florence, and it was only in this period that he took up large-scale sculpture in the round with his celebrated bronze *Perseus* (1545–54, Loggia dei Lanzi, Florence), made for Cosimo I de' *Medici. He also made two bronze portrait busts, *Cosimo I* (1545–8, Bargello, Florence) and *Bindo Altoviti* (*c*.1550, Gardner Mus., Boston), and several marble sculptures, including a *Crucifix* (*c*.1555–62, Escorial, near Madrid). The somewhat dry, niggly quality of these sculptures shows that the exquisite precision of handling of his goldsmith's work did not always transfer easily to a larger scale. The triumphant completion of the *Perseus* in 1554 marked the summit of Cellini's career. In 1557 he was sentenced to four years' imprisonment for sodomy, and it was whilst under house arrest that he wrote his autobiography. Apart from the *Crucifix* (which he intended for his own tomb), his only substantial works after this were treatises on goldsmithing and sculpture, which he published in 1568.

Cennini, Cennino (c.1370–c.1440). Florentine painter and writer. None of his paintings has survived, but he is remembered as the author of *Il libro dell'arte* (translated by Daniel V. Thompson as *The Craftsman's Handbook*, 1933), written in about 1400, the most important source concerning artistic practice in the late Middle Ages. Cennini states in the book that he was a pupil of *Agnolo Gaddi, who learnt from his father Taddeo *Gaddi, who in turn was a pupil of *Giotto, so his detailed descriptions of *tempera and *fresco painting no doubt reflect, even if at several removes, the technical procedures of the founder of the great tradition of Florentine painting.

Cercle et Carré (Circle and Square). A discussion and exhibition society for abstract artists formed in Paris in 1929 by the critic Michel *Seuphor and the painter Joaquín *Torres-García. They published a journal of the same name, of which three numbers appeared in 1929–30. The association held only one exhibition, at Galerie 23 in April 1930, but this has the distinction of being the first group exhibition ever devoted solely to abstract art; 46 artists showed work, including *Mondrian and *Vantongerloo but also such non-geometricians as *Kandinsky and *Schwitters. In 1931 Cercle et Carré was superseded by the larger and longer-lived *Abstraction-Création association, but it had a sequel in Uruguay: in 1935 Torres-Garcia formed an Asociación de Arte Constructivo in Montevideo and edited a journal *Círculo y Cuadrado*, of which seven numbers appeared between 1936 and 1938.

Cerquozzi, Michelangelo (1602–60). Italian painter, known as 'Michelangelo of the Battles' because of his predilection for scenes of combat. He spent all his career in his native Rome, where he had considerable contact with northern painters; his friendship with the Dutchman Pieter van *Laer led to his becoming the leading Italian exponent of *bambocciate* (small pictures of low-life and peasant scenes).

César (César Baldaccini) (1921–98). French sculptor and experimental artist. His work was highly varied, but he became best known for his ingenious use of scrap material. In the mid-1950s he began to make sculptures from material that he found in refuse dumps—scrap iron, springs, tin cans, etc.—building these up with wire into strange winged or insect-like creatures. These had closer affinities, however, with the insect-creatures of Germaine *Richier than with the California school of *Junk sculpture. In 1960 he began making works consisting of car bodies crushed with a hydraulic press into dense packages (he called sculptures in this genre *Compressions*) and it is on these that his international reputation is mainly based (*The Yellow Buick*, 1961, MoMA, New York). In 1965 he began working with plastics, and in 1967, as a counterpart to his *Compressions*, he began making *Expansions*, using plastics that expand rapidly and quickly solidify; sometimes he made such works in public as a kind of *happening.

Cesari, Giuseppe (also known as Cavaliere d'Arpino) (1568?–1640). Italian *Mannerist painter, active mainly in Rome. He had an enormous reputation in the first two decades of the 17th century, when he gained some of the most prestigious commissions of the day, most notably the designing of the mosaics for the dome of St Peter's (1603–12). Although some of his early work is vigorous and colourful, his output is generally repetitious and vacuous, untouched by the innovations of *Caravaggio (who was briefly his assistant) or the *Carracci. He was primarily a fresco painter, but he also did numerous *cabinet pictures of religious or mythological scenes in a finicky Flemish manner. Cesari's alternative name, Cavaliere d'Arpino (Knight of Arpino), refers to the title he was awarded by Pope Clement VIII and to his place of birth, between Rome and Naples.

Cézanne, Paul (1839–1906). French painter, with *Gauguin and van *Gogh the greatest of the *Post-Impressionists and a key influence on the development of 20th-century art. He was born in Aix-en-Provence, the son of a prosperous hat manufacturer who was also part-owner of a local bank. In 1861 he abandoned the study of law, and his father reluctantly gave him permission (and a modest allowance) to train as an artist in Paris. He studied at the *Académie Suisse, where he met Camille

*Pissarro, but after a few months he went back to Aix discouraged (he was a touchy character who hid his insecurities by posing as a provincial boor, once refusing to shake hands with the elegant *Manet because he claimed he had not washed for days and did not wish to dirty the great man). The following year he resumed his studies in Paris and in 1863 he exhibited at the *Salon des Refusés (his attempts to get his work accepted for the official *Salon regularly ended in failure). At this time Cézanne's work consisted mainly of portraits and imaginative figure subjects, with occasional still lifes. The portraits—mostly of members of his family (including self-portraits)—are sombre, using thick, slab-like paint, often applied with a palette knife. The imaginative subjects are very different, their subjects typically being erotic or violent and the handling of paint impetuous (*The Murder*, c.1868, Walker AG, Liverpool). They show Cézanne's admiration for *Delacroix (of whose pictures he made several copies), but they have none of Delacroix's sophistication. Compared with Delacroix's work, indeed, they look brutally crude, and even with the benefit of hindsight it is hard to see the seeds of Cézanne's future greatness in them. In 1869 he met Hortense Fiquet, a model and seamstress, who became his mistress and bore him a son, Paul, in 1872. Cézanne initially managed to keep them a secret from his family in Aix—he was terrified of his domineering father—but the truth was discovered in 1878 and he eventually married Hortense in 1886, shortly before the death of his father (who had at last become reconciled to the relationship).

After the birth of his son, Cézanne could no longer afford to live in Paris, so he moved to Pontoise, about 30 km (20 miles) to the north-west, joining his friend Pissarro, who had recently settled there. The following year, 1873, he moved to nearby Auvers-sur-Oise, then in 1874 returned to Paris. Although this rural interlude was fairly brief, it was highly important in Cézanne's development, for under Pissarro's influence he took up landscape painting seriously, and the close study of nature this involved led him to move away from the imaginative subjects of his youth and concentrate instead on the real world around him. In line with this change of subject, he abandoned the gloomy tonality of his early work and discovered the joys of light and colour, as his style came under the influence of *Impressionism (*House of the Hanged Man*, 1873, Mus. d'Orsay, Paris). He exhibited at the first (1874) and third (1877) Impressionist exhibitions (his work was critically savaged on both occasions), but he always stood somewhat apart from the group and never wholly adopted their aims and techniques. He was interested in structural analysis rather than in surface effects, and his objective was to combine the formal grandeur of the Old Masters with the naturalism and colour of the best contemporary painting. His aims were summed up in two celebrated remarks: that it was his ambition 'to do *Poussin again, from Nature', and that he wanted to make of Impressionism 'something solid and enduring, like the art of the museums'.

After the death of his father in 1886, Cézanne inherited the family estate (the Jas de Bouffan, which features in many of his paintings), and lived mainly in Aix (he often visited Paris, but otherwise travelled little, only once going abroad in his whole life, to Switzerland in 1890). He was now free of financial worries for the first time in his career and able to concentrate entirely on his art; in the remaining twenty years of his life he did little else but paint—pursuing his ideals with extraordinary patience and self-discipline. He devoted himself principally to certain favourite themes—portraits of his wife, still lifes, and above all the landscape of Provence, particularly the Mont Ste Victoire, which came to have something of the same emotional significance for him that Mount Fuji has for Japanese artists. His painstaking analysis of nature differed fundamentally from Monet's exercises in painting repeated views of subjects such as Haystacks or Poplars. Monet's ideal was to finish a landscape painting in only one session of work so that it captured the feeling of a particular moment, whereas Cézanne returned to the same place again and again to create a deeply pondered image that presented his accumulated vision of the subject; his pictures rarely give any obvious indication of the time of day or even the season represented. He worked slowly and intuitively, creating a sense of depth and solidity not through conventional draughtsmanship and perspective, but through extremely delicate variations of tone, and he distorted natural appearances—subtly tilting and stretching forms—to achieve the pictorial balance that was his central concern. In his final years he created works of luminous beauty and classical dignity that are a world away from the wild, impulsive pictures of his youth. The culminating paintings of his career include three large pictures of *Bathers* (female nudes in a landscape setting) that are among his most majestic creations; one of them, in the Philadelphia Museum of Art, was perhaps entirely painted in 1906, the year of his death.

Cézanne had worked in comparative obscurity until he was given a one-man show in Paris by Ambroise *Vollard in 1895. It made little impact on the public but excited many younger artists, and because Cézanne himself was rarely seen he began to acquire a legendary reputation. By the end of the century he was revered as the 'Sage' by many of the avant-garde and in 1904 the *Salon d'Automne devoted a special exhibition to him. A memorial exhibition of his work at the same venue in 1907 was a major factor in the genesis of *Cubism, and his subsequent influence has been profound, varied, and enduring, earning him the title 'the father of modern art': the belief that the picture surface has an integrity of its own irrespective of what it represents—a characteristic of so much modern painting—stems largely from him. It is not only the quality of his work that has proved an inspiration, but also the example he set of complete devotion to art: Henri *Matisse bought a picture by Cézanne in 1899 and in 1936 wrote that 'It has sustained me spiritually in the critical moments of my career as an artist; from it I have drawn my faith and perseverance.'

Cézanne often worked on pictures over a long period—he is said to have had over 100 sittings for a portrait of Ambroise Vollard (1899, Petit Palais, Paris) before abandoning it with the comment that he was not displeased with the shirt front. In spite of this laborious slowness, he left a substantial body of work (drawings and watercolours as well as oils). There are examples in many major museums, with particularly fine collections in, for example, the Courtauld Gallery, London; the Musée d'Orsay, Paris; and the Barnes Foundation, Merion,

Pennsylvania. His studio in Aix is now a Cézanne museum, reconstructed as it was at the time of his death and displaying personal mementoes such as his hat and clay pipe.

Chadwick, Lynn (1914–2003). British sculptor. Initially he concentrated on *mobiles, often derived from insect forms (*Dragonfly*, 1951, Tate, London), and these were followed by ponderous, bristling, rough-finished metal structures supported on thin legs. In 1956 he won the International Sculpture Prize at the Venice *Biennale and subsequently consolidated his reputation as one of the leading British sculptors of his generation. His work is generally based on the human figure (often in couples), but is sometimes so strongly schematized that it comes close to abstraction. In the early 1960s, influenced by *Minimal art, it became more block-like, but in the later 1960s he returned to figuration, typically contrasting highly polished faceted surfaces with rougher areas. In the 1970s his style became less aggressive, and in the 1980s he began experimenting with sheet steel as a material.

Chagall, Marc (1887–1985). Russian-born painter and designer, active mainly in France. In 1910–14 he lived in Paris, where he was a member of an avant-garde circle including *Apollinaire, *Delaunay, *Léger, *Modigliani, and *Soutine. After going to Berlin in 1914 for his first one-man show (at the *Sturm Gallery) he visited Russia and had to remain because of the outbreak of war. Following the Revolution in 1917 he was appointed Fine Arts Commissar for his home province of Vitebsk, where he founded and directed an art academy. *Malevich was among the other teachers there, and after disagreements with him Chagall left in 1920 and moved to Moscow, where he made designs for the newly founded Jewish Theatre. He returned to Paris in 1923 at the invitation of Ambroise *Vollard, who commissioned much work from him, including illustrations for Gogol's *Dead Souls*, La Fontaine's *Fables*, and the Bible (these were not published until 1948, 1952, and 1956 respectively). In 1937 he became a French citizen, but he was stripped of his new nationality under the anti-Jewish laws passed after the German invasion. He escaped to Spain in 1941 and from there moved to the USA, where he lived for the next seven years. In 1948 he returned to Paris, and from 1949 he lived on the Riviera, near Nice, working to the end of his very long life—the last survivor of the generation of artists who had revolutionized painting in the years leading up to the First World War.

Chagall was prolific as a painter and also as a book illustrator and designer of stained glass (in which he did some of his most impressive late work) and of sets and costumes for the theatre and ballet. His work was dominated by two rich sources of imagery: memories of the Jewish life and folklore of his early years in Russia; and the Bible (he was born into a deeply religious family). He derived some of his spatial dislocations and prismatic colour effects from *Cubism and *Orphism, but he created a highly distinctive style, remarkable for its sense of fairy-tale fantasy. Because the scenes he depicted made no rational sense, André *Breton claimed him as one of the precursors of *Surrealism (and it was during the heyday of Surrealism—the 1930s—that his reputation became international), but Chagall himself stated in his autobiography *Ma vie* (1931) that however fantastic and imaginative his pictures appeared, he painted only direct reminiscences of his early years. Rather than exploring the unconscious mind, he was interested in great timeless themes, such as birth, love, marriage, and death, which he interpreted in his own warm and whimsical way. There is a museum devoted to Chagall's religious art in Nice. The work there does not always show him at his best, for he could be sentimental and overblown, but his finest paintings have won him an enduring reputation as one of the greatest masters of the *École de Paris.

chalk. Drawing material made from various soft stones or earths (or latterly from synthetic equivalents). There are three main types of natural chalk: black chalk (made from stones such as carbonaceous shale); red chalk, also called sanguine (made from red ochre or other red earths); and white chalk (made from various limestones). Chalk drawings are known from prehistoric times, but the medium really came into its own in the late 15th century, especially in the hands of *Leonardo, who

made many drawings in red and black chalk. Some artists, notably *Watteau, used black, red, and white chalks in the same drawing. Synthetic, or 'fabricated', chalks are made from powdered pigments mixed with a binding medium, then rolled or pressed into sticks and dried. They were in use by the 17th century, but were not common until the 18th century. Fabricated chalks are not always clearly distinguished from crayons and *pastels, and there is much ambiguity in the historical literature of the subject. However, crayons, as the term is now generally understood, are sticks of colour made with an oily or waxy binding substance, and pastels are sticks of powdered pigment bound with gum, producing a softer, more powdery effect than chalk.

Chamberlain, John (1927–). American sculptor. His early sculpture, influenced by that of David *Smith, was made largely from metal pipes, but in 1957 he began to incorporate scrap metal parts from cars in his work and from 1959 he concentrated on sculpture made entirely from crushed automobile parts welded together. Usually he retains the original colours, and the expressive energy of his work, with its twisted planes and crumpled surfaces, has been compared to that *Action Painting. Many of his compositions are intended for wall hanging rather than to stand on the ground. An example is *Dolores James* (1962, Guggenheim Mus., New York). Although he has continued with work of this type, which has been widely acclaimed, Chamberlain has also experimented with other types of sculpture and other media. In 1966, for example, he started using urethane foam, as in *Koko-Nor II* (1967, Tate, London). He has also done abstract paintings and made experimental films.

Champaigne, Philippe de (1602–74). Flemish-born painter who settled in Paris in 1621 and became a French citizen in 1629. His training in his native Brussels was mainly as a landscape painter, but almost all his work consists of religious pictures or portraits (his few landscapes serve as settings for religious subjects). As a religious painter he ranks high among his French contemporaries, and as a portraitist he stands head and shoulders above them. He worked for several distinguished patrons, including Louis XIII, the Queen Mother (Marie de *Médicis), and Cardinal Richelieu. Two of his best portraits of Richelieu (late 1630s) are in the National Gallery, London: a commanding full-length and a triple view of the head intended to be used by a sculptor as the model for a bust. They bring the personality of the cardinal vividly to life and show how Champaigne moderated the *Baroque idiom of *Rubens towards a classical dignity in line with French taste in the middle of the 17th century. He was a friend of *Poussin, and Anthony *Blunt has written that 'His portraits and his later religious works are as true a reflection of the rationalism of French thought as the classical compositions of Poussin in the 1640s.' His style became even more severe after he came under the influence of the Jansenists—a Catholic sect of great austerity—in the early 1640s. Some of his finest work was done for the Jansenist convent at Port-Royal, where his daughter was a nun: he commemorated her miraculous recovery from paralysis in his most celebrated work, the *Ex-Voto de 1662 (Louvre, Paris), of which Blunt writes that 'In its restraint and simplicity this painting is as typical of the Jansenist approach to a miracle as *Bernini's "St Theresa" is of the Jesuit.' His masterpiece in portraiture might well have been his self-portrait of 1668, which is lost, but is known through a copy by his nephew and pupil **Jean-Baptiste de Champaigne** (1631–81) in the Louvre and a superb engraving (1676) by *Edelinck.

Chantrey, Sir Francis (1781–1841). English sculptor. Initially he tried to establish himself as a portrait painter, but after about 1805 he painted only occasionally (a self-portrait, c.1810, is in Tate Britain, London). He made his reputation with a bust of the Revd John Horne-Took (Fitzwilliam Mus., Cambridge), exhibited at the *Royal Academy in 1811, and he succeeded *Nollekens as the most successful portrait sculptor in England. His enormous practice also included church monuments and statues; the monument to the Robinson children (1817) in Lichfield Cathedral and the bronze equestrian statue of George IV (1828) in Trafalgar Square are his best-known works in these fields. Although he had studied intermittently at the Royal Academy, Chantrey was essentially self-taught and his work

often has an impressive directness, unburdened by academic theory: 'I hate allegory; it is a clumsy way of telling a story.' He became extremely wealthy, and besides being very generous during his life he left the bulk of his fortune of £150,000 to the Royal Academy, the interest to be used for the purchase of 'works of Fine Art of the highest merit executed within the shores of Great Britain'. These are now housed in Tate Britain.

Chapman, Dinos and **Jake.** See YOUNG BRITISH ARTISTS.

charcoal. Charred twigs or sticks used for drawing. Its use dates back to Roman times and possibly much earlier. An essential characteristic of charcoal is that it is easily rubbed off the drawing surface unless a *fixative is used, so it has been much favoured for preparatory work, either for sketches or *cartoons or for outlining on wall or panel a design that could be gone over with a more permanent medium. The soft-edged effect it produces has been notably exploited by 16th-century Venetian painters, *Baroque artists, and the *Impressionists. *Pencils and *chalks have now taken its place to some extent, but it remains well suited to large-scale work and broad, energetic draughtsmanship; outstanding modern exponents include *Barlach and *Kollwitz.

Chardin, Jean-Siméon (1699–1779). French painter of still life and *genre, in which fields he was one of the greatest masters of all time. (His forenames have traditionally been given as Jean-Baptiste-Siméon, but the 'Baptiste' seems to have been a scribe's error, and Jean-Siméon is now the accepted form.) He was the contemporary of *Boucher and he briefly taught *Fragonard, but his work is a contrast to theirs in every way, representing the naturalistic strain—influenced by 17th-century Dutch painting—that ran through 18th-century French art alongside the more fashionable *Rococo style. Almost all his pictures are modest in size and simple in subject, depicting objects and scenes from everyday middle-class life, and they create their magic through an extraordinarily subtle mastery of composition and colour, tone and texture (he was a notoriously slow and fastidious worker). He studied under two history painters, Pierre-Jacques Cazes (1676–1754) and Noël-Nicolas *Coypel, but he gained little from them and seems to have been more or less self-taught in his specialities. In 1728 he was received into the Académie Royale as a 'painter skilled in animals and fruits'. It was customary for new members to give an example of their work to the Académie and Chardin presented two pictures—*The Rayfish* (c.1725) and *The Buffet* (1728), both now in the Louvre, Paris. *The Rayfish* is, by Chardin's standards, an unusually flamboyant work: the gutted fish has a strangely human-like 'face' twisted in a macabre grimace, and its raw flesh is depicted with virtuoso skill. For the rest of his life Chardin was a dedicated member of the Académie; he punctiliously attended its meetings and for almost twenty years he served as treasurer (1755–74), a position to which he was well suited, as he had an exemplary reputation for honesty and integrity. He reached his peak of esteem in the 1750s, when Louis XV granted him an annual allowance (1752) and gave him lodgings in the Louvre. In spite of royal favour, he led a life of uneventful dedication to his art; apart from short visits to Versailles or Fontainebleau, he is never known to have left Paris.

Chardin's career can be broadly divided into three phases, plus an epilogue. In the first phase, up to about 1733, he painted mainly still lifes, generally featuring dead game or kitchen utensils; in such works he goes far beyond matter-of-fact realism and through his simplicity and directness of vision achieves a sense of deep seriousness, in spite of the humble objects he portrayed. For about the next fifteen years he concentrated on genre scenes; they usually contain only one or two figures, and like his still lifes are completely without sentimentality or affectation (*The Young Governess*, c.1735, NG, London, and other versions; he often produced replicas or variants of favourite designs). In the late 1740s he returned again to still life as his main subject, often depicting more elaborate and costly objects than he had in his early career (*The Attributes of the Arts*, 1766, versions in Hermitage, St Petersburg, and Minneapolis Inst. of Arts). Finally, in the 1770s he abandoned oils (evidently because the lead in certain colours aggravated an eye complaint) and took up pastel portraiture. Although he had rarely

painted portraits before and had no previous experience of pastel, he immediately showed that he was a match for any of the great contemporary specialists in the field. He exhibited pastels at each of the *Salons from 1771 to 1779, the year of his death; they included several self-portraits and pictures of children and fellow artists. In spite of acclaim for these unexpected products of his old age, by this time Chardin was regarded—with the growing taste for *Neoclassicism—as something of an ancient relic, and after his death he was quickly forgotten. His reputation revived in the mid-19th century, when his integrity and directness impressed the exponents of *Realism. Subsequently, the formal strength and masterly technique of his paintings have appealed enormously to modern taste, and he is now one of the best-loved artists of the 18th century and perhaps the most revered of all exponents of still life.

Charles II, King of Spain. *See* HABSBURG.

Charles V, Emperor. *See* HABSBURG.

Charonton, Enguerrand. *See* QUARTON.

Chase, William Merritt (1849–1916). American painter. He was a versatile and prolific artist, but is remembered chiefly as the most important art teacher of his generation in the USA. His principal posts were in New York—at the *Art Students League, 1878–94, and at his own Chase School, 1896–1908—but he also taught in Chicago, Philadelphia, and elsewhere. From 1891 to 1902 he ran the Shinnecock Summer School on Long Island, the first important school of open-air painting in America, and he also pioneered study trips abroad (he visited Europe regularly throughout his career). A flamboyant and popular man, he was active in virtually every art organization in New York and he did a great deal to promote the art of his colleagues and countrymen. Apart from teaching, he made his living mainly through portraiture, but he was often in financial difficulties. His other subjects included still lifes, interiors, and landscapes. He took great joy in the process of painting, and the vigorous brushwork and fresh colour that characterizes much of the best American painting of the early 20th century owes much to his example. His students included Charles *Demuth, Marsden *Hartley, Edward *Hopper, Georgia

*O'Keeffe, and Charles *Sheeler. *See also* TEN, THE.

Chassériau, Théodore (1819–56). French painter and printmaker. He was the most gifted pupil of *Ingres, with whom he began to study when he was 11, but in the 1840s he came under the influence of *Delacroix and attempted, with considerable success, to combine Ingres's *classical linear grace with Delacroix's *Romantic colour. His chief work was the decoration of the Cour des Comptes in the Palais d'Orsay, Paris, with allegorical scenes of Peace and War (1844–8), but these were almost completely destroyed by fire in 1871. There are other examples of his decorative work, however, in various churches in Paris. Chassériau was also an outstanding portraitist and painted nudes and North African scenes (he visited Algeria in 1846). As a printmaker he is best known for a series of fifteen etchings illustrating Shakespeare's *Othello* (1844).

Cheere, Sir Henry (1703–81). English sculptor, possibly of French descent. In about 1729 he went into partnership with Henry *Scheemakers (they jointly signed several small monuments) and after Scheemakers left England in about 1733 Cheere extended the practice, his output including much work for Oxford University. His art is markedly *Rococo in feeling, and in his charming smaller monuments he often used coloured marbles (*Dean Wilcocks*, *c.*1756, Westminster Abbey, London). He was well thought of by his fellow artists and furthered the career of *Roubiliac by gaining him his first important commission in England—the statue of Handel for Vauxhall Gardens (1738, now V&A, London). Cheere was also prominent in public affairs and devoted efforts to an abortive scheme to found an academy of arts a decade before the *Royal Academy came into being. His brother **John** (1709–87) was also a sculptor —a prolific supplier of lead garden figures and other modestly priced works.

Chéron, Louis. *See* ST MARTIN'S LANE ACADEMY.

Chia, Sandro. *See* NEO-EXPRESSIONISM.

chiaroscuro (It.: 'bright–dark'). Term describing the effects of light and shade in a work of art, particularly when they are strongly contrasting. *Leonardo was the great pioneer of bold chiaroscuro, but the term is most usually associated with 17th-century artists, particularly the *Caravaggisti and *Rembrandt.

chiaroscuro woodcut. A type of *woodcut in which tonal effects are created by printing successively on to the same sheet from different blocks of varying tone. Two or more tones of a single colour are used, or of two closely related colours, one of which is darker than the other. The technique was invented in about 1508, one of the first examples being Hans *Burgkmair's *The Emperor Maximilian on Horseback* of that year; other notable German exponents were *Cranach, *Baldung, and *Altdorfer. In Italy, where the medium was used more extensively, *Ugo da Carpi made many prints after designs by *Raphael and by *Parmigianino, who was a prolific designer for the process.

Chicago, Judy. *See* FEMINIST ART.

Chigi, Agostino (1466–1520). Italian banker and merchant, one of the greatest patrons of the *Renaissance. The immensely wealthy Chigi was the leading financier in Europe (his family bank had branches throughout Italy and others in places as far apart as London and Cairo) and he also had various industrial and trading interests. He was born in Siena (and he favoured Sienese artists, including *Peruzzi and *Sodoma), but he spent most of his life in Rome. His two most important commissions were a villa in the suburbs of the city (now called the Villa Farnesina, as it was later owned by the *Farnese family) and a burial chapel in the church of S. Maria del Popolo. The villa was designed by Peruzzi and begun in about 1506; it is the most sophisticated residence of its time, with painted decoration by *Raphael and *Sebastiano del Piombo, as well as Sodoma and Peruzzi himself. The lavish chapel was designed by Raphael and begun in 1512. It was unfinished when he (and Chigi) died in 1520 and was not completed until the 1650s by *Bernini, working for **Fabio Chigi** (1599–1667), a descendant of Agostino who became Pope Alexander VII in 1655. In 1664 his nephew, Cardinal **Flavio Chigi** (1631–93), commissioned Bernini to design the façade of the Palazzo Chigi (now Palazzo Chigi-Odescalchi).

Chinnery, George (1774–1852). English painter, active for almost all his career in the Eastern world. After leaving London in 1802 he worked in India until 1825 and then for the rest of his life in Macao, from which he made visits to Canton and Hong Kong. He made his living principally as a portraitist, but his reputation now rests mainly on the pictures of Indian and Oriental life and scenery that he made for his own pleasure.

chinoiserie. The imitation or evocation of Chinese styles in Western art and architecture. The term is applied particularly to art of the 18th century, when pseudo-Chinese designs in a whimsical or fantastic vein were an aspect of the prevailing light-hearted *Rococo style. By the middle of the 18th century the enthusiasm for things Chinese affected virtually all the decorative arts, and there was also a vogue for Chinese-style buildings in garden architecture. The taste for chinoiserie faded during the dominance of the *Neoclassical style in the second half of the century, but there was something of a revival in the early 19th century.

Chirico, Giorgio de (1888–1978). Italian painter, sculptor, designer, and writer, the originator of *Metaphysical Painting. He was born in Greece, and trained in Athens, Florence, and Munich, where he was influenced by the *Symbolist work of Böcklin and *Klinger, with their juxtaposition of the commonplace and the fantastic. In 1909 he moved to Italy (dividing his time between Florence, Milan, and Turin) and there painted his first 'enigmatic' pictures, which convey an atmosphere of strangeness and uneasiness through their empty spaces, illogical shadows, and unexpected perspectives. From 1911 to 1915 he lived in Paris, becoming friendly with many members of the avant-garde, including *Apollinaire (who championed his work) and *Picasso. During this period he developed a more deliberate theory of 'metaphysical insight' into a reality behind ordinary things by neutralizing the things themselves of all their usual associations and setting them in new and mysterious relationships. To help empty the objects in his paintings of their natural emotional significance he depicted tailors' dummies and statues in place of human beings (from 1914). In 1915 he was conscripted into the Italian army and sent to Ferrara. There he suffered a nervous breakdown, and in 1917

met *Carrà in the military hospital and converted him to his views, launching Metaphysical Painting as a movement. It was short lived, virtually ending when de Chirico and Carrà quarrelled in 1919, but it was highly influential on *Surrealism, and it was during the later 1920s, when Surrealism was becoming the most talked-about artistic phenomenon of the day, that de Chirico's international reputation was established. However, it was his early work that the Surrealists admired and they attacked him for adopting a more traditional style in the 1920s, when his output included some distinctive pictures featuring horses on unreal seashores with broken classical columns. In the 1920s and 1930s he spent much of his time in Paris (and in 1935–7 he lived in the USA) before settling permanently in Rome in 1944. By this time his paintings had become repetitive and obsessed with technical refinement. His other work included a number of small sculptures and set and costume designs for opera and ballet; his writings include a Surrealistic novel, *Hebdomeros* (1929), and two volumes of autobiography (1945 and 1960) translated into English as *The Memoirs of Giorgio de Chirico* (1971).

Chodowiecki, Daniel Nikolaus (1726–1801). German painter, illustrator, and printmaker of Polish ancestry. He was born in Danzig (now Gdańsk) and spent his career in Berlin, where he settled in 1743. Largely self-taught, he began with miniatures and progressed to oil paintings and etchings. From the late 1760s he concentrated on book illustrations and became the most prolific and famous German artist of his time in this field, with a huge and varied output. His illustrations of literary works include many attractive scenes of contemporary bourgeois life, and it is for these that he is chiefly remembered. In 1797 he became director of the Berlin Academy.

Christie's. The popular name for the firm of Christie, Manson & Woods, the oldest fine art auctioneers in the world (*Sotheby's was founded earlier, but originally sold only books). It was founded by James Christie (1730–1803), who gave up a commission in the navy to become an auctioneer and held his first sale on 5 December 1766 in rooms in Pall Mall, in the same premises in which the exhibitions of the *Royal Academy were held until 1779. He was a friend of *Gainsborough and *Reynolds, and Christie's developed a tradition of holding the studio sales of prominent artists. The firm acquired its present name in 1859, when James Christie's grandsons took new partners. Its headquarters are still in London and there are branches and offices in many cities throughout the world.

Christo (Christo Javacheff) (1935–). Bulgarian-born sculptor and experimental artist who settled in New York in 1964 and became an American citizen in 1973. After brief periods in Prague, Vienna (where he studied sculpture with *Wotruba), and Geneva, he moved to Paris, where he lived from 1958 to 1964. Initially he earned his living there as a portrait painter, but soon after his arrival he invented *empaquetage* (packaging), a form of expression he has made his own and for which he has become world-famous. It consists of wrapping objects in materials such as canvas or semi-transparent plastic and dubbing the result art. He began with small objects such as paint tins from his studio (in this he had been anticipated by *Man Ray), but they increased in size through trees and motor cars to buildings and sections of landscape. He spends a great deal of time and effort negotiating permission to carry out such work and in planning the operations, which can involve teams of professional rock-climbers as well as construction workers. He finances such massive enterprises through the sale of his smaller works. The buildings that he has succeeded in wrapping include the Pont Neuf in Paris (1985, after nine years of negotiations), and the Reichstag in Berlin (1995). Among the landscape projects he has carried out is *Running Fence* (1976), something like a fabric equivalent of the Great Wall of China, undulating through 39 km (24 miles) of Sonoma and Marin Counties, California. Christo says of his work: 'You can say it's about displacement. Basically even today I am a displaced person, and that is why I make art that does not last ... Unlike steel, or stone, or wood, the fabric catches the physicality of the wind, the sun. They are refreshing. And then they are quickly gone.' Christo's wife, **Jeanne-Claude** (née de Guillebon) (1935–), collaborates with him.

Christus, Petrus (d. 1475/6). Netherlandish painter, active in Bruges. He is first documented there in 1444 and was the leading artist in the city in the generation after Jan van *Eyck, who died in 1441. Traditionally he has been regarded as Jan's pupil (and it has been suggested that he completed works the master left unfinished at his death), but it is now thought likely that he received his training elsewhere before arriving in Bruges. Nevertheless, he was strongly influenced by Jan and helped to spread his style. Christus's work is plainer and more summary, however, and his figures tend to be rather doll-like. The influence of Rogier van der *Weyden is also evident in some of Christus's work: his *Lamentation* (c.1450, Mus. Royaux, Brussels), for example, is clearly based on Rogier's celebrated *Descent from the Cross* (c.1440, Prado, Madrid), but the figures have completely lost their dramatic impact. Christus's most personal works are his portraits, notably *Edward Grimston* (1446, Earl of Verulam coll., on loan to NG, London), in which he abandons the dark backgrounds of Jan and Rogier and places his sitter in a clearly defined interior. His interest in representing space also comes out in some of his religious works, notably the *Virgin and Child in a Chamber* (c.1450–60, Nelson–Atkins Mus., Kansas City, Missouri), which has a particularly complex and attractive setting.

chromolithography. The process of making coloured prints by *lithography, using a separate stone or plate for each colour. The term is usually applied to reproductive prints rather than to original works.

chryselephantine. Term describing statues incorporating gold (Gk., *khrusos*) and ivory (Gk., *elephantinos*), the gold typically being used for draperies and the ivory for flesh. The technique was used on a small scale in ancient Egypt, Mesopotamia, and Crete, and in colossal statues by the Greeks from the 6th century BC, the gold and ivory being carried on a wooden framework. Because of the cost, the technique was used only in the most important religious images, the most famous examples being the enormous statues of Athena and Zeus that *Phidias made respectively for the Parthenon in Athens and the Temple of Zeus at Olympia.

Church, Frederic Edwin (1826–1900). American landscape painter. Church was a pupil and friend of Thomas *Cole and continued the *Hudson River School's interest in depicting spectacular natural scenery; his *Niagara* (1857, Corcoran Gal., Washington) established him as the most famous painter in the USA. However, Church looked beyond his native country for subjects, travelling widely and painting, for example, the tropical forests of South America, icebergs, and exploding volcanoes, often on a huge scale. His work was immensely popular in his day, and after a period of neglect is returning to favour again. His house, Olana, on the Hudson River, is now a museum.

Churrigueresque. Term applied to an extravagant style of architecture and ornament popular in Spain (and also Latin America) in the 18th century and sometimes used more loosely to refer to the *Rococo period as a whole in Spanish architecture. It is named after the Churriguera family of architects and sculptors, who were active mainly in Seville. The most important member of the family was José Benito de Churriguera (1665–1725), whose work is well represented by the main altarpiece (1693–1700) of the church of S. Esteban in Salamanca, an important early example of the style, full of lavishly decorated barley-sugar columns. In spite of its richness, it still retains a sense of architectural solidity, and is restrained compared with later manifestations of the style, in which surface ornament runs riot to such a degree that the underlying structure is hidden. To *Neoclassical taste the Churrigueresque style represented the last word in decadence and it died out completely in the last quarter of the 18th century.

Cibber, Caius Gabriel (1630–1700). English sculptor of Danish birth. He arrived in England shortly before the Restoration in 1660, probably via Amsterdam, and worked for John Stone, son of Nicholas *Stone. When Stone died in 1667, Cibber set up on his own. His first important work was the large *relief of *Charles II Succouring the City of London* (1674) on the base of the Monument erected in memory of the Great Fire of 1666. Other works in London included the dramatic figures of *Raving* and *Melancholy Madness* (c.1675) for the gate of old Bedlam Hospital (now in the Bethlem Royal Hospital Mus., Beckenham). Much of his later career was taken up with decorative sculpture,

notably for Sir Christopher Wren at Hampton Court and St Paul's Cathedral. With the exception of the figures of *Raving* and *Melancholy Madness*, which are powerful and original pieces, and the dignified tomb of Thomas Sackville at Withyham, Sussex (1677), Cibber's work is usually competent but uninspired; it is of interest, however, in reflecting *Baroque influence (still unusual in England at this time) from Italy (where Cibber is said to have studied early in his career) and also from the Netherlands. He was the father of Colley Cibber, the actor-manager and dramatist.

ciborium. A term applied to (a) a liturgical vessel, often chalice-shaped, used for holding the consecrated Host; and (b) an altar canopy supported on columns, popular particularly in Italy in the *Romanesque and *Gothic periods. In the second sense the word is not easily distinguished from *baldachin.

Cignani, Carlo (1628–1719). Bolognese painter. He was a pupil of Francesco *Albani, but his style was more influenced by *Domenichino and Guido *Reni, and he became the main force in upholding the tradition of Bolognese classicism into the 18th century; his sweetness and grace also show his admiration for *Correggio. He was a slow-working perfectionist, but he employed numerous assistants in his decorative commissions. Most of his work was religious, but he also painted mythological subjects and several self-portraits. He had an international reputation and was so highly regarded by his fellow artists in Bologna that when the Accademia Clementina, the city's first municipal art academy, was founded in 1709, he was appointed director for life.

Cignaroli, Giambettino (1706–70). Italian historical, religious, and decorative painter, active mainly in and around Verona. Cignaroli was the leading artist of his period there, working in an elegantly classical style. He was also a writer: in 1749 he published a history of painting in Verona, and in 1762 a biography of his teacher Antonio Balestra (1666–1740), who had likewise upheld the classical tradition.

Cigoli, Il (Ludovico Cardi) (1559–1613). The outstanding Florentine painter of his generation, whose work represents the complex stylistic cross-currents in the period of transition from *Mannerism to *Baroque. He was a pupil of Alessandro *Allori, from whom he inherited the tradition of late Mannerism, but his sensuous colour and brushwork reveals the influence of *Barocci, *Correggio, and Venetian painting. From 1604 he spent most of his time in Rome, and his dramatic handling of light shows the impact of *Caravaggio (*Ecce Homo*, 1606, Pitti, Florence). Cigoli also worked as an architect; he had scholarly inclinations and was a friend of Galileo.

Cimabue (Cenni di Peppi) (*c*.1240–1302?). Florentine painter. His nickname means 'Ox-head' or 'De-horner of oxen', perhaps indicating that he had an abrasive temperament. He was a contemporary of Dante, who in *The Divine Comedy* (*Purg*. xi. 94–6) describes him as an artist who was 'believed to hold the field in painting' only to be eclipsed by *Giotto's fame. This passage, meant to illustrate the brevity of earthly glory, has ironically become the basis for Cimabue's reputation, for, embroidering on it, later writers made him into the discoverer and teacher of Giotto and regarded him as the first in the long line of great Italian painters, the pioneer of the movement from *Byzantine stylization towards *Renaissance realism. *Vasari, for example, places Cimabue's biography at the very beginning of his *Lives* and says that he gave 'the first light to the art of painting'. There is little solid evidence against which to test this estimate, only one surviving work being securely documented as Cimabue's, a *St John* forming part of a larger mosaic in Pisa Cathedral (1301–2). However, tradition has tended to attribute to him many works of outstanding quality from the end of the 13th century, such as the *S. Trinità Madonna* (Uffizi, Florence), a cycle of frescos in the Upper Church of S. Francesco in Assisi, and a majestic *Crucifix* in S. Croce, Florence (badly damaged in the Florence flood of 1966). If these highly plausible attributions are correct, Cimabue was indeed the leading master of the generation before Giotto. The movement towards greater naturalism, however, may owe more to contemporary Roman artists (*Cavallini, *Torriti) than to him; he is documented in Rome in 1272 and could have known their work.

Cima da Conegliano, Giovanni Battista (*c*.1460–1517/18). Italian painter,

named after the town of his birth (Conegliano), and active mainly in nearby Venice, where he was one of the leading artists from about 1490 to 1510. His major works are almost all altarpieces, and he also produced numerous smaller pictures for private devotion, usually of the Virgin and Child. Nothing is known of his training, but his handsome and reflective style, which changed very little in the course of his career, was strongly influenced by Giovanni *Bellini, not least in his use of beautiful landscape settings. He has indeed been called 'the poor man's Bellini', although because of his calm and weighty figures he was also known in the 18th century (rather incongruously) as 'the Venetian Masaccio'. In addition to his religious pictures he painted a few mythological works. Nine of his paintings are in the National Gallery, London.

cinquecento (It.: '16th century'). *See* QUAT-TROCENTO.

Cione, Andrea, Nardo, and **Jacopo di.** *See* ORCAGNA.

Cipriani, Giovanni Battista (1727–85). Florentine decorative painter and designer, active mainly in England. In 1755 he was brought to London by the architect Sir William Chambers and the sculptor Joseph *Wilton, who had met him in Rome. He was employed in the decoration of many public buildings and private houses and in some cases designed such architectural details as plasterwork, woodwork, and stonecarving. Good examples of his paintings are at Somerset House (where he worked for Chambers) and in the Philadelphia Museum of Art (a series originally executed for Lansdowne House, London). He was also active as a teacher at the *Royal Academy (he was a foundation member in 1768 and designed its diploma), and his numerous decorative designs (many engraved by *Bartolozzi, his friend since student days) had wide influence. Cipriani's work is accomplished rather than inspired, but he was, in the words of Sir Ellis *Waterhouse, 'one of the great backroom figures of the *Neoclassic style in England'.

Circle. A collective manifesto of *Constructivism edited by the architect Leslie Martin (1908–2000), the painter Ben *Nicholson, and the sculptor Naum *Gabo, published in London in 1937. Subtitled *International Survey of Constructive Art*, it is nearly 300 pages long, with numerous illustrations, and was originally intended as an annual. The volume contains an editorial by Gabo entitled 'The Constructive Idea in Art', *Mondrian's essay 'Plastic Art and Pure Plastic Art', and a short statement by *Moholy-Nagy on 'Light Painting'. There are also essays or statements by, among others, *Hepworth (who took much of the responsibility for the layout and production), *Le Corbusier, Henry *Moore, and Herbert *Read. The artists illustrated included (in addition to those already mentioned), *Malevich, *Lissitzky, Antoine *Pevsner, and many others whose work did not conform with the theoretical concept of Constructivism, including *Braque, *Brancusi, *Giacometti, and *Picasso. *Circle* was reprinted in 1971.

cire perdue (Fr.: 'lost wax'). A method of making cast metal sculpture. In essence the technique involves producing a model of the sculpture consisting of a thin layer of wax over a heat-resistant core of clay or plaster; the wax is then covered with another heat-resistant layer, and when the wax is melted and drained off, molten metal is poured into the cavity that the 'lost wax' has created. The technique, developed independently in every continent except Australasia, was used by the Egyptians, Greeks, and Romans and is still the main means of casting used for traditional bronze sculpture. Casting sculptures of any size is an industrial process requiring great expertise, and there is a celebrated account in *Cellini's autobiography of the difficulties he encountered (and heroically overcame) with his statue of Perseus.

Claesz., Pieter (*c*.1597–1660). Dutch still-life painter, born in Germany and active in Haarlem, where he had settled by 1617. He and Willem Claesz. *Heda, who also worked in Haarlem, were the most important exponents of the *ontbijt* or breakfast piece. They painted with subdued, virtually monochromatic palettes, the subtle handling of light and texture being the prime means of expression. Claesz. generally chose objects of a more homely kind than Heda, although his later work became more colourful and decorative. The two men founded a distinguished tradition of still-life painting in

Haarlem, but Claesz.'s son, Nicolaes *Berchem, became famous as a landscape painter.

Clark, Kenneth (Lord Clark of Saltwood) (1903–83). British art historian, administrator, patron, and collector, born into a wealthy family whose fortune had been made in thread-manufacturing: 'My parents belonged to a section of society known as "the idle rich", and although, in that golden age, many people were richer, there can have been few who were idler.' After working as assistant to *Berenson in Florence, he was keeper of fine art at the *Ashmolean Museum in Oxford (1931–3), then director of the *National Gallery, London (1934–45), and at the same time Surveyor of the King's Pictures (1934–44). Clark also served on numerous boards and committees and was chairman of the *Arts Council (1953–60) and of the Independent Television Authority (1954–7). He published more than twenty books, his forte being appreciation and interpretation rather than exact scholarship, although his monographs on *Leonardo da Vinci (1939) and *Piero della Francesca (1951), both of which have been issued in revised editions, still remain standard works. His other books include *The Gothic Revival* (1928), *Landscape into Art* (1949), and *The Nude* (1956). He regarded *The Nude* as 'without question my best book, full of ideas and information, simplifying its complex subject without deformation, and in places eloquent'. A polished television performer as well as an elegant and stimulating writer, he did a great deal to popularize art history, most notably with his television series *Civilisation* (1969, also published then as a book), which was shown in over sixty countries. The part he played as a patron and collector (he inherited substantial wealth from his parents) is less well known, but was of considerable importance. He bought the work of Henry *Moore, *Pasmore, *Piper, and *Sutherland in the 1920s and 1930s when they were little known and helped to establish their reputations (he also made a regular allowance—in strict secrecy—to several artists), and during the Second World War he had a major influence as chairman of the War Artists' Advisory Committee (*see* OFFICIAL WAR ART). His two volumes of autobiography—*Another Part of the Wood* (1974) and

The Other Half (1977)—are highly entertaining, if not always accurate in detail, but some of the potboilers that appeared in his old age would have been better left unpublished.

Clarke, Harry (1889–1931). Irish artist, chiefly famous as one of the 20th-century's greatest designers of stained glass, but also a mural painter, textile designer, and book illustrator. He was born in Dublin, the son of a church decorator, and had his main training at the Dublin Metropolitan School of Art, 1910–13. Scholarships then enabled him to study medieval glass in France. He took over the family business on his father's death in 1921 and had a large output in spite of his short life (he died from tuberculosis). The Harry Clarke Stained Glass Studios Ltd continued in business until 1973. Clarke's glass was sumptuous and often rather bizarre in style—in the spirit of French *Symbolist painters. As an illustrator he had a taste for the macabre and is particularly remembered for his black-and-white drawings for an edition of Edgar Allan Poe's *Tales of Mystery and Imagination* (1923). His wife **Margaret Clarke** (née Crilley) (1888–1961), whom he married in 1914, was a painter. After Harry's death she became director of the stained-glass studios.

classicism. Term that, with the related words 'classic' and 'classical', is used in various (and often confusing) ways in the history and criticism of the arts. In its broadest sense, classicism denotes the opposite of *Romanticism, characterizing art in which adherence to recognized aesthetic ideals takes precedence over individuality of expression. The word often implies direct inspiration from *antique art, but this is not a necessary part of the concept, and according to context the word might be intended to convey little more than the idea of clarity of expression, or alternatively of conservatism. In the context of Greek art, the term 'Classical' (with a capital C) has a more precise meaning, referring to the period between the *Archaic and *Hellenistic periods, when Greek culture is thought to have attained its highest peaks. The term 'classic' is used to refer to the best or most representative example of its kind in any field or period. This is what *Wölfflin meant when he gave the title *Classic Art* to his book on the Italian High *Renaissance.

Thus, in this sense, it would be legitimate, if wilfully confusing, to refer to *Delacroix as the classic Romantic artist. The three terms 'classic', 'classical', and 'classicism' are, then, often not used with discrimination or exactness, the conflation of historical term and value judgement reflecting the idea (dominant for centuries) that the art of the Greeks and Romans set a standard for all future achievement. To clear up (or perhaps add to) the confusion, the rather ungainly words 'classicistic' and 'classicizing' have also entered the lists—they convey the idea of dependence on ancient models but without any sense of qualitative judgement.

Claude (Claude Gellée) (1604/5?–82). French painter, draughtsman, and occasional etcher, active for almost all his career in Rome; he is often called Le Lorrain (in France), or Claude Lorrain(e) (in the English-speaking world), after his place of birth, but he is usually referred to simply as Claude, a familiarity reflecting his enormous fame as the most celebrated of all exponents of *ideal landscape. At an early age (probably shortly before 1620) he moved to Rome, where he is said to have initially worked as a pastry cook (a favourite trade of Lorrainers). He then entered the household of Agostino *Tassi, progressing from domestic servant to studio assistant, and he also spent two years studying in Naples with the obscure German-born landscapist Goffredo Wals (*c*.1595–*c*.1640); he was deeply impressed by the beauty of the Gulf of Naples, memories of which recur in his paintings throughout his career. The chronology of this early period of Claude's life is vague, and it is not certain whether his association with Tassi began before or after his time with Wals; he is first firmly documented in Rome in 1623. In 1625 he returned to Lorraine, and collaborated with the court painter Claude Deruet (1588–1660) on church frescos (destroyed) in Nancy, but by 1627 he was back in Rome, where except for local journeys he remained for the rest of his life. His earliest surviving dated painting is of 1629 (*Pastoral Landscape*, Philadelphia Mus. of Art), although one or two undated pictures may precede it. In 1633 he became a member of the Accademia di S. Luca, and by this time he was already establishing himself as one of the leading landscape painters in Rome. Indeed his work soon attracted imitators, and according to his biographer *Baldinucci, it was to guard against forgeries that he began keeping a record of his paintings in his *Liber Veritatis* (Book of Truth). Claude began this album of drawings (which is now in the British Museum) in about 1635; it contains 195 sheets detailing virtually every picture he painted from that time until the end of his life. Each sheet has a drawn copy of the painting on the front and information about the patron on the back, and because of this, Claude's output is exceptionally well documented. By the end of the 1630s his clients included Pope Urban VIII (Maffeo *Barberini) and Philip IV of Spain (*see* HABSBURG), and he was unrivalled as the foremost landscape painter in Italy. He charged high prices for his work, but he was a dedicated craftsman who worked at his own pace, so he generally produced only a few pictures a year and he became moderately prosperous rather than wealthy. He lived very modestly, holding various minor offices in the Accademia di S. Luca but taking no part in public affairs; his friend *Sandrart describes him as a 'good-hearted and pious' man who 'searched for no other pleasure beside his profession'. The effects of age and illness (he suffered from gout or arthritis) caused his output to decrease (the *Liber Veritatis* indicates that he completed only one picture in 1671, for example), but the quality of his work did not decline at all; indeed he produced some of his greatest paintings in the final decade of his life.

At the beginning of his career Claude belonged essentially to the northern European tradition of landscape painting, exemplified by *Bril and *Elsheimer, as well as by his teacher Wals, with its emphasis on lively, picturesque charm. Soon, however, Claude blended this with the Italian tradition of classical or ideal landscape that had been initiated by Annibale *Carracci; he retained the northern sense of richness and variety, but his compositions became much grander (although not so austere as those of Annibale or *Poussin). His early pictures are usually fairly modest in size and several of them are on copper (a material that Bril, Elsheimer, and Wals often used), but as he matured and prospered, he tended to work on a larger scale—appropriate for the palatial homes of his distin-

guished patrons. Similarly, the figures in his early works tend to be anonymous and dressed in contemporary costume, but from about 1640 they are usually taken from religious or mythological stories (although unlike his friend Poussin he never tried to recreate these stories accurately). To the northern and Italian traditions Claude added something entirely his own—an extraordinary sensitivity to light that does so much to unify his pictures and create their particular moods. This sensitivity was based on loving observation of nature: Sandrart records that he would sometimes spend all day in the countryside around Rome watching the effects of light, and he made hundreds of drawings—works of great breadth and freedom—recording his impressions (many of them are in the British Museum). During the 1640s and 1650s, when Claude's work reached a peak of classical balance, the mood of his paintings was typically one of serenity, with the cool light of morning or the warm glow of evening suggesting harmony and contentment; in his grand views of seaports—a type of picture that he made his own—he often specifically shows sunrise or sunset (*Seaport with the Embarkation of the Queen of Sheba*, 1648, NG, London). In his later years, his style became more deeply personal: his compositions are more open and less solidly constructed, forms (whether of the human figure, trees, or architecture) are strangely elongated and ethereal, colours have a magical silvery quality, and the mood is often solemn and mysterious. All these characteristics are seen in his last painting, done in the year of his death, the dreamlike *Ascanius and the Stag* (1682, Ashmolean Mus., Oxford).

Until well into the 19th century Claude's reputation as the greatest of all landscape painters was virtually unassailable. He was particularly revered in England, where the aristocracy not only collected his work avidly but even tried to make the parkland of their country estates resemble his pictures, with artfully placed clumps of trees, classical 'temples', and so on. He had a great impact on *Wilson and *Turner, and in 1836 *Constable wrote that 'He has been deemed the most perfect landscape painter the world ever saw, and he fully merits the distinction.' However, it was also in England that the first serious critical attack was made on Claude, in 1846 by *Ruskin, who considered his work artificial and lacking in invention. By 1900 his reputation had greatly declined, and it did not seriously revive until after the Second World War.

Claude glass. A small tinted mirror, with a slightly convex surface, used for reflecting landscapes in miniature so as to show their broad tonal values, without distracting detail or colour. The device is named after *Claude, who is said to have used one, and was particularly popular in the 18th century, when it was much employed by cultural travellers as well as by artists (the poet Thomas Gray is known to have had one). Its use continued into the 19th century, a notable devotee being *Corot, who regarded tonal unity in painting as supremely important.

Clausen, Sir George (1852–1944). British painter (mainly of landscapes and scenes of rural life), born in London, the son of a decorative painter of Danish descent. His training included a few months at the *Académie Julian, Paris, in 1883 and his work was influenced by French *plein-air painting. He was particularly interested in effects of light, often showing figures set against the sun, but he always retained a sense of solidity of form. With other like-minded painters he was a founder of the *New English Art Club in 1886. From 1904 to 1906 he was professor of painting at the *Royal Academy. His lectures were published as *Six Lectures on Painting* (1904) and *Aims and Ideals in Art* (1906); a collected edition appeared as *Royal Academy Lectures on Painting* in 1913. In them he urged the traditional study of the Old Masters.

Clement VII, Pope. *See* MEDICI.

Clemente, Francesco. *See* NEO-EXPRESSIONISM.

Clerck, Hendrik de (c.1570–1630). Flemish painter. Early in his career he visited Italy (he is documented in Rome in 1587), then settled in Brussels, where he was appointed court painter to the Archduke Ernest in 1594 and later continued in the service of his successor, the Archduke Albert. He is said to have been the pupil of the *Mannerist painter Maerten de *Vos and he carried the Mannerist tradition far into the 17th century. Much of his output consisted of altarpieces and other pictures

for churches in Brussels and its neighbourhood; a characteristic example is the *Holy Kinship* (1590, Mus. Royaux, Brussels), his earliest dated work, with its Italianate figures clad in restless draperies and placed in a coldly classical building. He also painted historical and mythological scenes.

Clodion (real name Claude Michel) (1738–1814). French sculptor (known by the diminutive form of his first name), who created some of the most charming works of his age. The son-in-law of Pajou and the nephew of L.-S. *Adam, he trained with the latter and briefly with *Pigalle. He produced a few large-scale works, but he excelled chiefly in small statuettes and terracotta figures and groups. They are often of light-hearted classical subjects—nymphs and satyrs and so on—and have the wit and verve of the best *Rococo art. After the Revolution he changed his style completely to suit the sterner *Neoclassical taste; his later work included carvings on the Arc de Triomphe du Carrousel (1806–9) in Paris, which was built to commemorate Napoleon's victories.

Cloisonnism (from Fr., *cloison*: 'partition'). Style of painting associated with some of the painters who worked at *Pont-Aven at Brittany in the 1880s and 1890s, characterized by dark outlines enclosing areas of bright, flat colour, in the manner of stained glass or cloisonné enamel. *Anquetin and *Bernard first developed the style, and *Gauguin also worked in it. The term was coined by the critic Édouard Dujardin in 1888.

Cloisters, The. *See* METROPOLITAN MUSEUM OF ART.

Close, Chuck (1940–). American painter. His early work was *Abstract Expressionist, but he soon turned to *Superrealism, becoming well known for huge portrait heads (mainly of friends), seen frontally like gigantic passport photographs—his self-portrait (1968) in the Walker Art Center, Minneapolis, is almost 3 m (10 ft) high. Originally he worked in black and white, but in about 1970 he turned to colour. He works from photographs, dividing them into a grid and then transferring the grid to the canvas. In some of his later work he has deliberately emphasized the grid, creating 'low resolution' images resembling a computer scan or a face seen through frosted glass. In 1988 Close was partly paralysed following an injury to a spinal blood vessel, but he resumed painting with the aid of a brace support on his wrist.

Clouet, Jean (d. 1540/1). French painter of Netherlandish descent. He was celebrated in his lifetime, but no documented works survive. A handful of portraits, however, including *Man Holding Petrarch's Works* (Royal Coll., Windsor), and a number of drawings (mainly in the Musée Condé, Chantilly) are attributed to him on fairly strong circumstantial evidence. The paintings belong to the tradition of Netherlandish *naturalism that dominated French portraiture at this time, but the drawings are more personal and often of very high quality. They have been compared to those of Clouet's contemporary Hans *Holbein the Younger, with which they share a keenness of observation; whereas Holbein's drawings are overwhelmingly linear, however, Clouet's are subtly modelled in light and shade with a delicate system of *hatching that recalls *Leonardo, whose work he could well have known. Jean's son, **François** (c.1510–72), succeeded him as court painter in 1541. His work is somewhat better documented than his father's, but his career is still very obscure (they were known by the same nickname, 'Janet', which has caused much confusion, and one of the finest works attributed to him, the celebrated portrait of Francis I in the Louvre, showing the king in a lavish gold doublet, has also been given to Jean). François, too, was mainly a portraitist, his signed works including *Pierre Quthe* (1562, Louvre, Paris), much more Italianate than any of his father's paintings, and *Lady in her Bath* (c.1570, NG, Washington). This mysterious and captivating work has been traditionally identified as representing Diane de Poitiers, mistress of Henry II, but it is more probably a likeness of Marie Touchet, mistress of Charles IX. A number of drawings, mostly in the Musée Condé, are also attributed to him.

Clovio, Giulio (c.1498–1578). Italian *illuminator and painter, born in Croatia, which at this time was part of Venetian territory. He moved to Italy in 1516 and spent most of his career in Rome, although he also worked in several other cities. Clovio was the outstanding Italian illuminator of the 16th century and enjoyed a very high contemporary reputation—his friend *Vasari described him as a '*Michelangelo of small works'. His illuminations do indeed make frequent use of motifs from the work of Michelangelo and *Raphael, adapting the fashionable *Mannerist style to a miniature scale. From 1540 he worked mainly for Cardinal Alessandro *Farnese, to whom he recommended the young El *Greco. El Greco painted Clovio's portrait (c.1570, Mus. di Capodimonte, Naples), showing him holding the *Farnese Hours* (c.1546, Pierpont Morgan Lib., New York), the manuscript that is generally regarded as his masterpiece. In addition to illuminations, he sometimes painted small independent pictures (*Pietà*, 1551, Uffizi, Florence).

Coade stone. An artificial stone manufactured in London in the late 18th and early 19th centuries, used for figure sculpture, monuments, architectural dressings, and decorative work. Essentially a type of clay, fired in a kiln at high temperature, it was named after Eleanor Coade (1733–1821), who set up in business in Lambeth in 1769. She claimed that it resisted frost and therefore retained sharpness of outline better than natural stone, and time has proved her right. It was mixed into a kind of paste and formed into the required shape with moulds, so popular designs could be more or less mass produced. The business was an immediate success; Robert Adam was one of the notable architects who used the material and several good sculptors, particularly John *Bacon the Elder, worked for the firm. Monuments made of Coade stone exist in many English churches, and some garden sculpture remains. Mrs Coade's successor in the business, her distant relative William Croggon, died bankrupt in 1835 and Coade stone soon vanished from the market.

Cobra. A group of *Expressionist painters formed in Paris in 1948 by a number of Netherlandish and Scandinavian artists. The name derived from the first letters of the capital cities of the three countries of the artists involved—Copenhagen, Brussels, and Amsterdam. The Dutchman Karel *Appel, the Belgian *Corneille, and the Dane Asger *Jorn were the leading figures among the founders. Those who joined later included Pierre *Alechinsky and the Scottish painter William Gear (1915–97). The aim of the Cobra painters was to exploit free expression of the unconscious, unimpeded and undirected by the intellect. In their emphasis on spontaneous gesture, they had affinities with the American *Action Painters, but they differed in their strange and fantastic imagery, related in some cases to Nordic mythology and folklore, in others to various magical or mystical symbols of the unconscious. Their approach was similar to the exponents of *Art Informel, but was more savage and vigorously expressive. The group arranged Cobra exhibitions at Copenhagen (1948), Amsterdam (1949), and Liège (1951), before disbanding in 1951.

Cock, Jan Wellens de (d. c.1526). Netherlandish painter, perhaps to be identified with a 'Jan van Leyden' who became a master in the Antwerp painters' guild in 1503. He is a shadowy figure and the reconstruction of his oeuvre is controversial, but he is noteworthy as one of the earliest followers of *Bosch, his penchant seemingly being small pictures of hermits and saints in weird landscapes. He had two artist sons, **Matthys** (c.1509–c.1548) and **Hieronymus** or **Jerome** (c.1510–70), both of whom worked in Antwerp. Matthys was renowned in his day as a landscapist and is mentioned by *Vasari as well as van *Mander, but little is known for certain of his work. Jerome was an etcher and the leading print publisher of his time in northern Europe; his business was called 'Aux Quatre Vents' (At the Sign of the Four Winds). Pieter *Bruegel was much employed by him in the earlier part of his career, when he excelled at prints in the tradition of Bosch.

Cockerell, Sir Sydney. See FITZWILLIAM MUSEUM.

Codazzi, Viviano. See LAER.

Codde, Pieter (1599–1678). Dutch *genre and portrait painter, active in his native Amsterdam. His genre pictures are mainly scenes of fashionable life (with ladies and cavaliers drinking or making music) or of military life (typically soldiers in guardrooms or plundering). His best works are usually on a small scale, marked by subtle silvery-grey tonalities, but he achieved one memorable feat on a much larger scale. In 1637 he was called upon to finish the group portrait of the Amsterdam civic guards

known as the *Meagre Company* (Rijksmuseum, Amsterdam) that Frans *Hals began in 1633 and refused to finish because he would not come to Amsterdam for sittings, and Codde succeeded so well in capturing Hals's spirit and the touch of his brush that experts still disagree where the work of the one ends and the other begins. Codde also wrote poetry.

Coecke van Aelst, Pieter (1502–50). Netherlandish painter, architect, sculptor, designer of tapestries and stained glass, writer, and publisher. He was probably a pupil of Bernard van *Orley in Brussels, but he was active mainly in Antwerp, where he became a member of the painters' guild in 1527. Sometime before then he had probably been to Rome and in 1533–4 he visited Constantinople. His mission to gain business there for the Brussels tapestry works was unsuccessful, but the drawings he made on his journey were later published by his widow Mayken Verhulst as woodcut illustrations in *Les Mœurs et fachons de faire des Turcz* (The Manners and Customs of the Turks, 1553). He ran a large workshop and was regarded as one of the leading Antwerp painters of his day, but his work is fairly run-of-the-mill and he is generally more important for his publishing activities. Like his paintings, his books are saturated in Italian influence, and the translation that he and his widow issued of the architectural treatise of Sebastiano Serlio (1549–53) played a large part in spreading *Renaissance ideas in the Netherlands (it was from this edition, too, rather than from the Italian original, that the English translation of 1611 was made). Pieter *Bruegel the Elder was his son-in-law, and, according to van *Mander, his pupil, but there is no trace of Coecke's influence in his work.

Coello, Claudio (1642–93). Spanish painter, the last important master of the Madrid School of the 17th century. He was primarily a religious painter, but he also produced portraits. His masterpiece, *Charles II Adoring the Host* (1685–90), a huge canvas in the sacristy of the *Escorial, combines a mystical religious subject with realistic portraiture and is an outstanding example of *Baroque *illusionism, mirroring the architecture of the building in which it hangs. He had other noteworthy successes, particularly in work he carried out for Toledo Cathedral, but he died a disappointed man because he was passed over in favour of the Italian Luca *Giordano for the commission to carry out a huge programme of decoration at the Escorial. Coello had travelled to Italy as a young man and also studied the work of *Titian in the royal collection, and his skill as a colourist and painterly brushwork reflect the influence of the great Venetian masters.

Coldstream, Sir William (1908–87). British painter, mainly of portraits, but also of landscape and still life. He studied at the *Slade School, 1926–9, and worked on documentary films for the GPO, 1934–7. In 1937 he was one of the founders of the *Euston Road School, which helped to establish a tradition of sober figurative painting of which he was one of the main representatives. In 1939 he joined the Royal Artillery and in 1943–5 he was an *Official War Artist, working in the Near East and then Italy. After the war he taught at Camberwell School of Art, 1945–9, then was professor at the Slade School, 1949–75. He exerted an important influence not only through his teaching but also through his appointment as chairman of the National Advisory Council on Art Education in 1959. The Coldstream Report of 1960 helped to change the structure of art school teaching in Britain, introducing the compulsory study of art history for art students and eventually leading to degree status being awarded to recognized art school courses. Coldstream's own work was typically austerely naturalistic: 'I find I lose interest unless I let myself be ruled by what I see.' Kenneth *Clark had been an early supporter, but he came to see Coldstream's attitude to art as one of 'dismal rectitude'.

Cole, Sir Henry. *See* VICTORIA AND ALBERT MUSEUM.

Cole, Thomas (1801–48). The outstanding American landscape painter of the first half of the 19th century, a founder of the *Hudson River School. His family emigrated to America from England in 1818 and he became passionately devoted to the natural scenery of his new country. He studied at the Pennsylvania Academy of the Fine Arts in Philadelphia, 1823–5, then settled in New York, where he was an immediate success, his work being bought by *Dunlap,

*Durand, and *Trumbull. He soon began making sketching trips in the Hudson River Valley, and he settled there, in the village of Catskill, in 1836. In 1829–32 he visited Europe, and it was partly the influence of *Turner and John *Martin that encouraged him to turn from the depiction of natural scenery towards grandiose historical and allegorical themes, notably in two great series of paintings: *The Course of Empire* (1836, New-York Historical Society) and *The Voyage of Life* (1839–40, Munson-Williams-Proctor Inst., Utica). He visited Europe again in 1841–2, and after this he was increasingly attracted to religious subjects.

collage (Fr., *coller*: 'to gum'). A term applied to a type of picture (and also to the technique used in creating such pictures) in which photographs, news cuttings, and other suitable objects are pasted on to a flat surface, often in combination with painted passages. Long popular as a leisure-time occupation for children and amateurs (in scrapbooks for example), it first became an acknowledged artistic technique in the early 20th century, when it took much of its material from the proliferation of mass-produced images in newspapers, advertisements, cheap popular illustrations, etc. The *Cubists were the first to make collage a systematic and important part of their work, and subsequently it has been used in many major art movements, for example *Dada, *Surrealism, and *Pop art. For some artists—notably Kurt *Schwitters—it has been the central concern of their work, and others have created personal versions of it. Examples are Max *Ernst, with his 'collage novels' and *Matisse with his late *gouaches découpées* (paper cut-outs). *See also* MONTAGE and PHOTOMONTAGE.

Collins, William (1788–1847). English painter. He was initially taught by *Morland (of whom his father, a picture dealer, wrote a biography) and specialized in sentimental rustic landscapes and *genre scenes that won him great popularity. As with Morland, his work became very repetitive. He was a lifelong friend of *Wilkie, after whom he named his elder son, the novelist Wilkie Collins, who published a biography of his father in 1848. His second son was **Charles Allston Collins** (1828–73), a friend of *Millais and painter of the well-known *Convent Thoughts* (1851, Ashmolean Mus.,

Oxford, 1851), which *Ruskin rated highly because of its botanical detail, done in a fastidious *Pre-Raphaelite manner. He abandoned painting for writing in the late 1850s and married one of Charles Dickens's daughters in 1860.

Collinson, James (1825–81). English painter. He was one of the original members of the *Pre-Raphaelite Brotherhood (PRB) in 1848, but he left it in 1850 because he felt it was incompatible with his Roman Catholic faith and in 1852 began training to be a Roman Catholic priest. Another change of heart followed, and in 1854 he returned to painting, specializing in pretty and sentimental *genre scenes, the best known of which is *The Empty Purse* of 1857 (versions in Tate, London, and Graves AG, Sheffield). He is probably the least known of the PRB and the most remarkable talent he showed at their meetings was his ability to fall asleep at any time.

Colombe, Michel (c.1430–1514?). French sculptor. He had a great name in his day, but only two works that are certainly by him survive, both from late in his life. They are: the tomb of Francis II of Brittany and Marguerite de Foix (1502–7, Nantes Cathedral), done in collaboration with Jean *Perréal and Girolamo da Fiesole, an Italian sculptor working in France; and a relief of *St George and the Dragon* (1508–9, Louvre, Paris), done for an altarpiece for the chapel of the Château de Gaillon. The altarpiece too was a work of collaboration, for the frame was carved by Jérôme Pacherot, another Italian expatriate. Colombe's fame rests mainly on the *St George*, for it is a captivating work, blending the fantasy of the French *Gothic style with elements of the Italianate *Renaissance taste that was coming into vogue in southern France at this time, yet without copying particular Italian models. His brother **Jean Colombe** (d. c.1495) was a manuscript illuminater; he completed the *Limbourg brothers' *Très Riches Heures*.

Colour Field Painting. A type of abstract painting in which the whole picture consists of large expanses of more or less unmodulated colour, with no strong contrasts of tone or obvious focus of attention. Some Colour Field Paintings use only one colour; others use several that are similar in tone and intensity. This type of painting developed in the USA in the late 1940s and early 1950s, leading pioneers including Barnett *Newman and Mark *Rothko. It is thus an aspect of *Abstract Expressionism and it has also been seen as a type—or precursor—of *Minimal art. From 1952 Helen *Frankenthaler developed Colour Field Painting by soaking or staining diluted paint into unprimed canvas, so that the paint is integral with the surface rather than superimposed on it. The term Colour Stain Painting is applied to works of this type.

Colquhoun, Robert (1914–62). British painter, graphic artist, and designer. In 1933–8 he studied at *Glasgow School of Art, where he became the inseparable companion of his fellow student Robert MacBryde (1913–66). They settled in London in 1941. During the war Colquhoun was an ambulance driver in the Civil Defence Corps by day and painted by night (MacBryde was exempt from military service because of tuberculosis). Within a few years the studio of the Roberts (as they were generally known) at 77 Bedford Gardens, Campden Hill, had become a centre for a group of young artists and writers, among them Keith *Vaughan. Following a successful one-man show in 1943 Colquhoun developed a reputation as one of the outstanding British painters of his generation; his characteristic angular figure compositions owed something to *Cubism, but had an expressive life of their own. After he and MacBryde were evicted from their studio in 1947, however, his fortunes began to decline and he died (of a heart attack) in relative obscurity. Apart from painting, both Colquhoun and MacBryde produced many lithographs and worked together on stage designs.

combine painting. A term coined by Robert *Rauschenberg for a type of work he invented in the early 1950s—a very radical form of *collage—in which a painted surface is 'combined' with various real objects, or sometimes photographic images, attached to it. The most famous example is *Monogram* (1955–9, Moderna Museet, Stockholm), featuring a stuffed goat with a tyre around its middle.

Conca, Sebastiano (1680–1764). Italian painter. He was a pupil of *Solimena in Naples, then in about 1706 moved to Rome, where he became one of the leading decorative painters during the first half of the 18th century, developing an elegant *Rococo style out of the High *Baroque tradition. There are examples of his altarpieces and frescos in several churches in Rome, the *Coronation of St Cecilia* (1721–4) on the ceiling of the nave of S. Cecilia in Trastevere (1725) often being cited as his masterpiece. He also produced pictures of historical and mythological subjects for private collectors. In about 1752 Conca returned to Naples, where he remained active until almost the end of his long life.

Conceptual art. A type of art in which the idea or ideas that a work represents are considered its essential component and the finished 'product', if it exists at all, is regarded primarily as a form of documentation rather than as an artefact. Its origins go back to Marcel *Duchamp, but it was not until the later 1960s that Conceptual art became a recognizable movement and acquired its name. It flourished most vigorously in the early 1970s, becoming an international phenomenon and often overlapping with other art forms and movements that were fashionable at this time, notably *Arte Povera, *Body art, *Land art, and *Performance art. These have all been seen as aspects of the reaction against the *formalism and commercialism of *Minimal art. However, Conceptual art has proved just as susceptible to commercial exploitation as other forms of avant-garde expression, with dealers selling the documentation of Conceptual works to collectors and museums. Such documentation takes varied forms, including photographs, sound and video cassettes, texts, maps, diagrams, and sets of instructions, but some Conceptual works do not have any physicality at all, an example being *Telepathic Piece* (1969) by the American artist Robert Barry (1936–), consisting of a statement that 'during the exhibition I will try to communicate telepathically a work of art, the nature of which is a series of thoughts that are not applicable to language or image'. Although some Conceptual art purports to deal with serious political issues, much of it is concerned with deliberately abstruse analysis of language or with the kind of eccentric private concerns shown by Barry. Exponents and admirers of Conceptual art see such activities as posing questions about

the nature of art and provocatively expanding its boundaries. Robert *Morris, for example, wrote in 1970 that 'The detatchment of art's energy from the craft of tedious object production . . . refocuses art as an energy driving to change perception.' To the uninitiated, however, Conceptual art is as pointless as it is pretentious: in 1972 Keith *Vaughan wrote that 'the term is a contradiction in itself, art being the realization of concepts, not just having them'. The initial wave of enthusiasm for Conceptual art was over by the mid-1970s, but there was a substantial revival of interest in it in the mid-1980s (for example in the work of some of the exponents of *Neo-Geo). The term 'Neo-Conceptual' is sometimes applied to this revival.

Concrete art. Term applied to abstract art that is intended to be totally autonomous, without any figurative meaning or symbolic associations. The name was coined by Theo van *Doesburg, who in Paris in 1930 issued a manifesto called *Art Concret* (it took the form of the first number of a periodical with this title, but no other numbers were issued). Although Concrete art is typically severely geometrical, it is not necessarily so: for example, the sculpture of Max *Bill (an artist particularly associated with Concrete art) often uses graceful spiral or helix shapes.

Condivi, Ascanio (1525–74). Italian painter, sculptor, and writer, a pupil and friend of *Michelangelo. He was an insignificant artist and his only claim to fame is his *Life of Michelangelo*, published in Rome in 1553. Three years earlier the first edition of Giorgio *Vasari's *Lives* had appeared, and Michelangelo seems to have taken exception to some of the statements made there. Condivi's *Life* was meant as a corrective, and he writes not only from intimate personal knowledge, but obviously at times almost at dictation from the master. Johannes *Wilde (*Michelangelo*, 1978) considers that Condivi was a 'simpleton' who could not have composed 'such an eminently readable book' unaided, and thinks that Annibale Caro (1507–66), a humanist man of letters, was probably the ghost writer.

Coninxloo, Gillis van (1544–1606/7). The outstanding member of a large and prolific family of Netherlandish painters, many of whom are not clearly distinguishable personalities. He was born in Antwerp, which he left after it was captured by the Spanish in 1585. Like other Protestant refugees, he fled to Holland, then in 1587 moved to Frankenthal (near Frankfurt) in Germany, where he became the most important figure among a small group of Netherlandish landscape painters, now known as the Frankenthal School. In 1595 he settled permanently in Amsterdam. Coninxloo's early landscapes are panoramic views of vast valleys and great mountain ranges populated by biblical or mythological figures, in the tradition of *Bruegel. In later works, such as the majestic *Forest* (c.1600, KH Mus., Vienna), his field of vision is narrower and he concentrates on the mood evoked by luxuriant nature. Van *Mander described Coninxloo as 'the best landscape painter of his time' and said 'his style is now frequently imitated in Holland'. He was indeed a major figure in the transition from the *Mannerist landscape tradition to the much more realistic idiom characteristic of 17th-century Dutch painters. His younger countrymen Roelandt *Savery and David *Vinckboons, who had come to Holland at about the same time as Coninxloo, were influenced by his late works, and his pupils included Hercules *Segers and Esaias van de *Velde.

Conroy, Stephen. See GLASGOW SCHOOL OF ART.

Constable, John (1776–1837). English painter, ranked with his contemporary *Turner as one of the two greatest figures in the history of British landscape painting. Both of them brought a new freedom and inventiveness to their subject and they had a good deal of mutual respect. However, their temperaments and goals differed greatly and their careers were strongly contrasting. Whereas Turner was precocious and soon achieved critical and financial success, Constable was slow to mature and had difficulty in making a name in England (he was more appreciated in France). He was born at East Bergholt, Suffolk, the son of a prosperous corn merchant, and was trained for a career in the family business. However, his passion for art was so strong that in 1799 his father reluctantly allowed him to become a student at the *Royal Academy Schools in London. He continued studying

there until 1802, and during this time he also had informal tuition from his friend Sir George *Beaumont (whom he first met in 1796). However, he learnt most by copying the work of great landscape masters of the past, so essentially he was self-taught. He continued living in London, but he spent much of his time painting in his home area (now known as 'Constable country') and in 1809 he became engaged to Maria Bicknell, granddaughter of the rector of East Bergholt. Her family disapproved of the match, as Constable's career had made little progress, and he did not marry Maria until 1816, when his father's death made him more financially secure. The marriage was very happy, but Maria died of tuberculosis in 1828, leaving Constable emotionally devastated and with seven young children to care for. In 1824 his most famous work, *The Hay Wain* (1821, NG, London) had won a gold medal at the Paris *Salon, but it was not until 1829, when he was over 50, that he was grudgingly made a full member of the Royal Academy, elected by a majority of only one vote. In 1833, buttressed by this new status, he began lecturing on landscape painting, showing impressive knowledge as well as great love for the subject. Although his skill as a lecturer helped to consolidate his reputation, by the time of his death he still remained only moderately successful. The biography by his friend C. R. *Leslie, published in 1843, helped to establish his posthumous fame.

Constable's early work was strongly influenced by *Gainsborough (likewise a native of Suffolk) and by 17th-century Dutch landscape painting (he revered *Ruisdael in particular). However, he developed a highly personal approach by trying to communicate the feelings he felt in front of nature, conveying a sense—in his own words—of 'light, dews, breezes, bloom'. Just as his contemporary William Wordsworth rejected what he called the 'poetic diction' of his predecessors, so Constable turned away from the pictorial conventions of 18th-century landscape painters, who, he said, were always 'running after pictures and seeking the truth at second hand'. He thought that 'No two days are alike, nor even two hours; neither were there ever two leaves of a tree alike since the creation of the world.' Unlike the much-travelled Turner, he never went abroad, and his finest works are of the places he knew and loved best, particularly Suffolk and Hampstead (at this time a village north of London), where he lived from 1821. To render the changing effects of light and weather he abandoned traditional ideals of smooth finish, using rough, vigorous brushwork to suggest the sparkle of sunlight, the movement of clouds across the sky, or the drama of storms. To many contemporaries his work looked unfinished, but Henry *Fuseli was among those who applauded the freshness of his approach: C. R. Leslie records him as saying, 'I like de landscapes of Constable; he is always picturesque, of a fine colour, and de lights always in de right places; but he makes me call for my greatcoat and umbrella.'

Constable worked extensively in the open air, sketching in oils, but his finished pictures were produced in the studio. For his most ambitious works—'six-footers' as he called them—he followed the unusual technical procedure of making a full-size oil sketch, and recently there has been a tendency to praise these even more highly than the finished works because of their boldness and freedom of brushwork. (The full-size sketch for The Hay Wain is in the V&A, London, which has the finest collection of Constable's work.) In England Constable had no real successor and the many imitators (who included his son **Lionel**, 1825–87) turned rather to the formal compositions than to the more direct sketches. In France, however, he was a major influence on *Romantic painters such as *Delacroix and on the members of the *Barbizon School.

Constructivism. A movement or ideology in abstract art that originated in Russia in about 1914, became dominant there for a few years after the 1917 Revolution, and in the 1920s spread to the West, where it has subsequently been influential on a wide spectrum of artists. Constructivism is typically characterized by the use of industrial materials—such as glass, plastic, and standardized metal parts—arranged in clear formal relationships, but the meaning to be attached to the word varies according to context, and some writers prefer to use the terms 'Soviet Constructivism' (or 'Russian Constructivism') and 'European Constructivism' (or 'International Constructivism') to make a distinction between the original movement and its much more diffuse after-

math. Even in the context of Revolutionary Russia, however, the meaning of the word is far from clear-cut.

The father of Constructivism was Vladimir *Tatlin, who visited Paris in 1914 and on his return to Russia began making abstract Relief Constructions using materials such as sheet metal, wood, and wire. He was influenced by the sculptural experiments of *Picasso, who had used a variety of ingeniously assembled odds and ends, and perhaps also by the *Futurist sculptural manifesto (1913), in which *Boccioni similarly advocated a move away from the traditional techniques of modelling and carving in favour of sculpture that was constructed from various new materials—this was the essential idea behind Constructivism. From his reliefs Tatlin went on to develop small openwork structures (sometimes hanging), and several other artists, including Alexander *Rodchenko, created similar works in the years immediately after the 1917 Revolution. The Revolution created a ferment of enthusiasm in Russia for the building of a better society, with machinery seen as a liberating force, and in this climate Tatlin's idea of investigating and exploiting industrial materials came into its own. Initially Soviet Constructivism was inseparable from politics, and the revolutionary zeal for socially useful art led many Soviet artists to conclude that traditional 'fine art' was dead. In this way, a term that had originated in Tatlin's modest reliefs expanded to embrace the whole of applied art, and 'by 1925 Constructivism had become a blanket term for any angular designs applied to furniture, fabrics, porcelain or theatre sets' (Robert Auty and Dimitry Obolensky, eds., An Introduction to Russian Art and Architecture, 1980).

Many artists who were not prepared to abandon traditional art for industrial design left Russia at this time. Among them were the brothers Naum *Gabo and Antoine *Pevsner, who left in 1922 and 1923 respectively. Although they wanted to reflect modern technology in their work, they rejected the idea that art must serve an obvious social purpose; they thought that 'fine art' could make an important contribution to society by being spiritually uplifting and they conceived a purely abstract type of sculpture that used industrial materials such as plastic and glass. It is from their work that European or International

Constructivism derives and each of them played an important part in spreading their ideals. In England Gabo was co-editor of *Circle* (1937), in which he published his essay 'The Constructive Idea'. The subtitle of *Circle* is *International Survey of Constructive Art*, an indication of the 'international constructive tendency' that was recognized at this time. Among the other contributors to the volume, *Moholy-Nagy was particularly influential in the spread of Constructivism through his teaching at the *Bauhaus and elsewhere. (Meanwhile, Constructivism in the Soviet Union was dead by this time, killed—like all other modern forms of expression—by *Socialist Realism.) Gabo's concept of Constructivism, as expressed in his essay in *Circle*, was vague, being equated with 'creative human genius' in art, science, or any other sphere, and since the Second World War the term has been applied to a very broad range of work. Sometimes it is used as a rough equivalent of 'geometrical abstraction'. In Britain, however, the word is often used to refer specifically to a type of work—reliefs and free-standing constructs in metal or perspex—that became popular with a group of abstract artists in the 1950s and 1960s, including Kenneth and Mary *Martin, and Victor *Pasmore.

consular diptych. See DIPTYCH.

conté crayon. A type of hard crayon, named after Nicolas-Jacques Conté (1755–1805), a French scientist who worked as a portrait painter in his youth and invented the modern graphite *pencil in the early 1790s. Conté crayons are similar to *chalk, but they have a slightly greasy quality that makes them less liable to crumble. Black and warm red are the most common colours. *Seurat made some of his best drawings in black conté crayon.

continuous representation or **continuous narrative.** A pictorial convention whereby two or more consecutive incidents from a narrative are combined in the same image. It is most common in medieval art, but occasionally occurs later. In *Pontormo's *Joseph in Egypt* (c.1518, NG, London), for example, four episodes from Genesis are shown in the same panel and Joseph appears separately in each of them.

contrapposto (It.: 'set against'). Term applied to poses in which one part of a figure twists or turns away from another part. It was originally applied, during the *Renaissance, to a relaxed asymmetrical pose characteristic of much Greek and Roman sculpture in which the body's weight is borne mainly on one leg, so that the hip of that leg rises relative to the other (the *Doryphoros* of *Polyclitus is a classic example). The term is now, however, used in a much broader sense and applied as much to painting as to sculpture. The acknowledged master of contrapposto was *Michelangelo, and his *Mannerist followers (for example *Bronzino) often devised poses of wilful complexity in order to demonstrate their skill in the field.

conversation piece. A portrait showing two or more full-length figures engaged in conversation or other polite social activity, generally in a domestic or landscape setting. Conversation pieces are usually, though not always, fairly small in size. They were especially popular in Britain during the 18th century, when Arthur *Devis, the young *Gainsborough, and *Zoffany were notable practitioners, but the use of the term is not confined to British painting or to this period.

Cook, Beryl (1926–). British *naive painter. She took up painting seriously when she was about 40 and in 1975 had her first exhibition, at the Plymouth Arts Centre. It was a great success and within a few years she was well known through other exhibitions, television appearances, and the publication of the first of several collections of her work in book form (*The Works*, 1978), with the paintings accompanied by her own amusing commentaries. Her chubby, usually jovial characters have also been much used on greetings cards. Cook's subjects are drawn from everyday life and frequently involve the kind of saucy humour associated with seaside holidays (she used to run a boarding house in Plymouth) and tabloid Sunday newspapers (often she incorporates newsprint as a collage element in her work).

Cooper, Douglas (1911–84). British art historian and collector. He lived in France for much of his life and was severely critical of the British for what he regarded as their failure to appreciate or patronize modern art. His main interest was *Cubism, and in

1932 he decided to devote part of his inheritance to forming a collection of its four leading exponents—*Picasso, *Braque, *Gris, and *Léger—in its greatest period, 1907–14. He later added works by other artists, but the Cubists remained the core. In the Second World War he worked in intelligence and helped to identify, protect, and repatriate works of art. Picasso was later a neighbour and visitor in southern France, but their friendship turned to hostility. Cooper, indeed, had a notoriously difficult temperament and enjoyed controversy; in the 1950s he became particularly well known for his attacks on the *Tate Gallery and its director Sir John *Rothenstein. He was a formidable scholar and published substantial books on all four major Cubists.

Cooper, Samuel (1608?–72). English *miniaturist, the nephew and pupil of John *Hoskins. The greatest English miniaturist of the 17th century, Cooper enjoyed a prosperous career and a European reputation (he is said to have travelled on the Continent as a young man). He worked for both sides during the Civil War and Commonwealth, and his sitters included Oliver Cromwell and Charles II. His portraits are almost always of the bust only, but within this limitation his range is remarkable: he presents each sitter (man or woman) with an individuality of characterization that can make the life-size portraits of contemporaries such as *Lely appear doll-like, and his vigorous *Baroque sense of design marks a complete break with the tradition of *Hilliard and Hoskins. His brother **Alexander** (1609–c.1658) was also a miniaturist. He worked mainly on the Continent—in the Netherlands and at the court of Queen Christina in Stockholm.

Coorte, Adriaen (active 1683–1707). Dutch still-life painter, active around Middelburg. Nothing is known of his life, and his work was completely forgotten for more than two centuries after his death. Only a handful of paintings by him survive, but they show him to have been one of the most individual still-life painters of his time. They are the complete opposite of the lavish pieces by such celebrated contemporaries as Jan van *Huysum and Rachel *Ruysch, for they are small in scale and depict a few humble objects, characteristically placed on a bare ledge. The intensity of his scrutiny is such, however, that they take on something of the mystical quality of the still lifes of *Sánchez Cotán or *Zurbarán, and the hovering butterfly that Coorte sometimes incorporates in his work may have allegorical significance. One of his favourite subjects was a bundle of asparagus (examples in the Rijksmuseum, Amsterdam; the Fitzwilliam Mus., Cambridge; and the Ashmolean Mus., Oxford).

Copley, John Singleton (1738–1815). The greatest American painter of the 18th century. He was the stepson of the engraver Peter Pelham (c.1695–1751), from whose large collection of engravings he gained a considerable knowledge of European art, but he was virtually self-taught as a painter. While still in his teens he established his own practice in his native Boston and by his early twenties he was painting portraits that, in their sense of life and character, completely outstripped anything previously produced by Colonial portraitists (*Colonel Epes Sargent*, c.1760, NG, Washington). Though he became extremely successful, Copley was diffident and self-doubtful by nature and came to see himself as a provincial figure, cut off from the great European tradition of painting. For a long while he hesitated to leave the security of Boston (where he earned 'as much as if I were a *Raphael or a *Correggio'), even after his portrait of his half-brother Henry Pelham (*The Boy with a Squirrel*, 1765, MFA, Boston) had been highly praised by both *Reynolds and *West when it was exhibited in London in 1766. He finally left in 1774, when revolutionary activity was beginning to threaten his practice, and settled in London in 1775 after a study trip to Italy.

In England Copley's style changed markedly, as he sacrificed the forthright vigour of his Colonial work for a more fashionable and ornate manner. He continued to paint fine portraits that were more than a match for the work of most of his contemporaries, but it is generally agreed that those he painted in America have greater originality and conviction. In compensation for this decline as a portraitist, he was able to turn his hand to *history painting, in which he had long been eager to make a success but for which the opportunities in America were severely limited. The first major work in this field was *Brook Watson and the Shark*

(1778, NG, Washington; a copy Copley made for himself is in the MFA, Boston, and a smaller variant, 1782, is in the Detroit Inst. of Arts). In this he followed the innovation of his countryman West in using modern dress, and went beyond him in depicting a subject not because it was of historical importance or moral significance, but merely because it was exciting. It was not until a generation later that the French *Romantics took up this revolutionary idea. His other history paintings have more conventional themes, mainly patriotic and military, such as the *Death of Major Peirson* (1783, Tate, London). In such works Copley revealed a magnificent gift for depicting heroic action in multi-figure compositions that none of his British contemporaries could approach, and these paintings won him considerable acclaim. They also brought on him the wrath of the *Royal Academy (of which Copley had become a full member in 1779) when they were shown privately with great success, for this constituted a rival attraction to the Academy's own exhibitions. Copley's success in England, however, was fairly short-lived and his work gradually went out of favour. His final years were marked by a sad decline. *Morse visited him in 1811 and wrote: 'His powers of mind have almost entirely left him; his late paintings are miserable; it is really a lamentable thing that a man should outlive his faculties.' He died leaving debts that had to be paid off by his son and namesake, who was created Baron Lyndhurst and was three times Lord Chancellor.

Coppo di Marcovaldo (documented 1260–76). Italian painter, one of the earliest about whom there is a body of documented knowledge. He served in the army of Florence and evidently settled in Siena after his capture at the Battle of Montaperti (1260). In 1261 he painted the signed and dated *Madonna and Child Enthroned* (called the *Madonna del Bordone*) for S. Maria dei Servi, Siena (still in situ), and between 1265 and 1276 he is documented several times working at Pistoia Cathedral, which has a *Crucifix* that is assumed to be one of two he was commissioned to produce (although the workmanship is thought by some critics to be largely by his son, **Salerno**). On the basis of these two works, other paintings have been attributed to Coppo, notably

a *Madonna and Child Enthroned* in the Cathedral Museum in Orvieto, and a *Crucifix* in the Pinacoteca at San Gimignano. He introduced new solidity and humanity to the *Byzantine tradition, in the way, for example, that he represents the Virgin with her head inclined towards the Child, and with *Guido da Siena he ranks as one of the founders of the Sienese School.

Coques, Gonzales (1618?–84). Flemish *genre and portrait painter, known as the 'little van *Dyck', although his style is much closer to *Terborch. He was born in Antwerp and was mainly active there, but he also travelled to Holland and England. His best works, charming and daintily executed, are small-scale fashionable group portraits such as *A Family Group* (c.1664, NG, London).

Corinth, Lovis (1858–1925). German painter and printmaker. Part of his training was with *Bouguereau in Paris (1884–7), but he was more strongly influenced by the painterly work of French artists such as *Courbet and *Manet, as well as by *Hals, *Rembrandt, and *Rubens. On his return to Germany he lived mainly in Munich before settling in Berlin in 1901. With *Liebermann and *Slevogt (both of whom also lived in Berlin) he was recognized as one of the leading German exponents of *Impressionism and in the first decade of the century he was a great fashionable success. However, in 1911 he was partially paralysed by a stroke and when he began to paint again (with great difficulty) it was in a much looser and more powerful *Expressionist manner, to which he had previously been strongly opposed (he has been described as 'an eleventh-hour convert to modernism'). He was varied and prolific as a painter and printmaker. His paintings included landscapes, portraits, and still lifes, and he had a fondness for voluptuous allegorical and religious subjects (*Temptation of St Anthony*, 1908, Tate, London). His prints were mainly drypoints and in his later years lithographs (which he used for the numerous commissions he had for book illustrations). He also made a few etchings and woodcuts. After the Nazis came to power in 1933 his later works were declared *degenerate. *Kirchner said of Corinth, 'In the beginning, he was only of average stature; at the end he was truly great.'

Cormon, Fernand (pseudonym of Fernand-Anne Piestre) (1845–1924). French painter. He had a successful career both as a painter and a teacher (his pupils included *Matisse, *Toulouse-Lautrec, and van *Gogh), but his reputation has not lasted well. His work included decorations at the Museum of Natural History and the Petit Palais in Paris and some excellent portraits, and he also had a penchant for paintings of prehistoric history (*The Age of Stone*, 1884, Mus. du Prieuré, Saint-Germain-en-Laye).

Corneille (Cornelis van Beverloo) (1922–). Belgian painter, active mainly in Paris. He was a founder member of *Cobra in 1948 and his paintings typically display brilliant colour and vigorous brushwork, with childlike imagery suggesting mythical beings.

Corneille de Lyon (d. 1575). Netherlandish-born painter, active mainly at Lyons in France. He was a native of The Hague (in France he is still often known as 'Corneille de La Haye'), but he had settled in Lyons by 1533 (the first record of him) and in 1540 he became court painter to the Dauphin, later Henry II. Contemporary references to Corneille indicate that he had a considerable reputation as a portrait painter, but only one work survives that is unquestionably from his hand, a portrait of Pierre Aymeric (1534, Louvre, Paris), authenticated by an inscription in the sitter's handwriting on the back of the picture. Many other works in a similar style go under his name. They are mostly small in scale and sharply naturalistic in manner, with the sitter usually set against a plain green or blue background.

Cornelis van Haarlem (Cornelis Cornelisz.) (1562–1638). Dutch painter who ranks with Hendrik *Goltzius and Karel van *Mander as one of the leading representatives of *Mannerism in the Netherlands. He is best known for his large biblical and historical pictures packed with athletic, life-size Italianate nudes in wrenched and sharply foreshortened positions. But he also did a few forceful portraits of individuals and groups that show he was an important forerunner of Frans *Hals. Both facets of his work can best be seen in the Frans Hals Museum in Haarlem, the city where he spent most of his life.

Cornelisz. van Oostsanen, Jacob (also called Jacob van Amsterdam) (*c*.1470–1533).

Netherlandish painter and designer, the best-known member of a family of artists. Born in Oostsanen, he worked mainly in nearby Amsterdam, where he was a successful painter and the leading designer of woodcuts in his period. The woodcuts include a series illustrating Christ's Passion (1512–17) and among the paintings are a *Self-Portrait* (1533, Rijksmuseum, Amsterdam) and an *Adoration of the Shepherds* (1512, Mus. di Capodimonte, Naples), which contains pudgy angels playing toy-like instruments, singing, and decorating an improbable *Renaissance manger with garlands. Although his work is somewhat provincial, he marks the beginning of the great artistic tradition of Amsterdam, and his keenness of observation was to be one of the trademarks of later Dutch art. Jan van *Scorel was possibly his pupil.

Cornelius, Peter (1783–1867). German painter, draughtsman, and teacher. He was born in Düsseldorf, and trained there at the Academy, where his father was a teacher. From the beginning of his career his primary ambition was to produce monumental wall paintings. He moved to Rome in 1811 and the following year became a member of the *Nazarenes. In 1819 he was called to Munich by Crown Prince Ludwig of Bavaria (later Ludwig I), for whom he worked extensively, notably on a series of frescos in the Ludwigskirche (1836–9), including a *Last Judgement* that is larger than *Michelangelo's in the Sistine Chapel. In 1841 he moved to Berlin to work for Frederick William IV of Prussia. His major commission there was for a series of frescos in a mausoleum for the royal family. The project was officially cancelled after the revolution in 1848, but Cornelius continued to work on his drawings for it for the rest of his life. In 1853 to 1861 he lived in Rome again. His style is rather self-conscious in its desire to revive the heroic pictorial language of *Raphael and Michelangelo, and combine it with the didactic philosophy of German *Romanticism, but his work has an impressive epic sweep. Cornelius was director of the academies at Düsseldorf (1821–5) and Munich (from 1825) and he helped to make these institutions the most important centres in Germany for the teaching of *history painting. His work was a major influence in promoting a revival of fresco decoration in Germany and his reputation in the field was such that in 1841 he visited London to give advice on the projected mural decorations for the Houses of Parliament.

Cornell, Joseph (1903–72). American sculptor, one of the pioneers and most celebrated exponents of *assemblage. He had no artistic training, but in about 1931, influenced by *Surrealism, he began making collages, and from these developed the distinctive type of work that he made his own—small wooden boxes, usually glass-fronted, in which he arranged collections of photographs, magazine illustrations, trinkets, and all manner of bric-a-brac. His work is sometimes compared with that of *Schwitters, but whereas Schwitters was fascinated by refuse, Cornell concentrated on fragments of once beautiful and treasured possessions, using the Surrealist technique of irrational juxtaposition to evoke a feeling of nostalgic reverie. From the late 1940s—perhaps influenced by *Mondrian, whom he much admired—his work began to become more abstract. Cornell also painted and from the late 1930s he made several Surrealist films, sometimes using discarded Hollywood movie footage.

Corot, Camille (1796–1875). French painter, mainly of landscapes. His father was a textile merchant and his mother a fashionable dressmaker, and he was expected to follow them into the clothing business. In 1822, however, at the age of 26, he was allowed to give up his commercial career, to which he was ill suited, and devote himself to art, which was his passion; his parents gave him generous financial support, so he was able to follow his own interests without having to worry about earning a living. He studied briefly with Achille-Etna *Michallon (who died soon after their association began) and then with Jean-Victor Bertin (1767–1842). Both his teachers had been pupils of *Valenciennes, and through them Corot inherited the classical tradition of which Valenciennes had been the main upholder in the previous generation. However, he brought a personal poetry to this tradition and an unaffected naturalness reflecting the sketches from nature that formed the basis for his finished pictures; his work has a wonderful feeling of clarity and balance, but he seems

to achieve this instinctively, without any striving for effect. He was based in Paris all his life but travelled a good deal in France and abroad, visiting Switzerland several times and also Italy (1825–8, 1834, and 1843), the Low Countries (1854), and England (1862).

From 1827 Corot exhibited regularly at the *Salon; his reputation grew steadily from the 1830s and by 1850 he was established as a major figure. His initial success was based mainly on a type of picture that was very different from his topographical work—more traditionally Romantic in its evocation of an Arcadian past, and painted in a misty soft-edged style that contrasts sharply with the luminous clarity usually associated with him. Throughout his career Corot also painted figure studies, as well as portraits of friends and relatives, and from the 1850s figure painting (notably of the female nude) assumed greater importance in his output; this aspect of his work has only fairly recently emerged from neglect. His directness of vision and sincerity of feeling were greatly admired by landscape painters of the later 19th century, and he took a lively interest in the work of younger artists: *Daubigny, *Pissarro, and *Sisley were among those who profited from his advice. His popularity with collectors was (and is) such that he is said to be the most forged of all painters (this in addition to an already large output). In his lifetime he was held in great esteem as a man as well as an artist, for he had a noble, generous, almost saintly nature and was completely unspoilt by his success (even the normally caustic *Degas described him as 'an angel who smokes a pipe'); he supported *Millet's widow, for example, and gave a cottage to the poor and almost blind *Daumier.

Correggio (Antonio Allegri) (c. 1490–1534). Italian painter, named after the small town in Emilia where he was born and died. Although he worked mainly in provincial centres, he was one of the most sophisticated artists of his time, blending disparate sources into a potent synthesis, and although his reputation in his lifetime was modest, he had enormous posthumous fame and influence. His early career is poorly documented and his artistic education has to be conjectured on stylistic grounds. He probably received a rudimentary training from his uncle, the painter Lorenzo Allegri (d.1527), but the most obvious source of inspiration for his early development is *Mantegna, and he may well have studied in Mantua (which is fairly near his home town), possibly even with the aged Mantegna himself. His first surviving documented work is the *Virgin of St Francis* (1514–15, Gemäldegalerie, Dresden), commissioned by the church of S. Francesco in Correggio; by the time he painted this he was also influenced by Lorenzo *Costa (in the pearly colouring) and by *Leonardo (in the characteristic pointing finger of St John). Later he absorbed more of Leonardo's introspection and his soft *sfumato, which helped to create his fluid, elegant, and alluring style. Another strong source of influence on Correggio's work comes from Rome; it is now generally assumed that he visited the city early in his career, probably around 1518, although *Vasari implies that he never went there and the impact of *Raphael and *Michelangelo could be accounted for by drawings and prints, which were known all over Italy.

Correggio's most characteristic paintings are altarpieces and small devotional works, often very tender and intimate in feeling. However, he also produced a number of major frescos in Parma, which is about 30 km (20 miles) from his home town. He is first documented there in 1520, but the earliest of his commissions in the city was probably carried out a year or so before this—the fresco decoration of the abbess's room in the convent of S. Paolo. The theme of the paintings is Diana, goddess of chastity and the chase (an unusual subject for a convent, but the abbess was a worldly and intellectual woman); in the vaulted ceiling Correggio uses Mantegna's idea of a leafy trellis framing *putti and symbols of the hunt. This work was followed by two great dome paintings in Parma, in which Correggio developed the *illusionist conception—already used by Mantegna—of depicting a scene as though it were actually taking place in the sky above (*see* SOTTO IN SÙ, DI). The first of the dome paintings, the *Vision of St John the Evangelist on Patmos* (1520–4), is in the church of S. Giovanni Evangelista; the twelve Apostles sit on clouds round the base, while Christ is shown in steep foreshortening ascending to heaven. In the second dome, that of Parma Cathedral, Cor-

reggio painted the *Assumption of the Virgin* (1526–30), using the same principle, but on a larger scale and with still more daring foreshortening. These works reveal Correggio as one of the boldest and most inventive artists of the High *Renaissance. They were too audacious for some contemporaries (a priest at the cathedral described the fresco there as a 'stew of frogs legs'), but they were highly influential on the development of *Baroque dome painting (one of the most important artists in this field, *Lanfranco, was a native of Parma). Other aspects of Correggio's work were even more forward-looking, for his extraordinarily sensuous mythologies, notably the series on the Loves of Jupiter painted for Federigo *Gonzaga in *c*.1530–2 (*Ganymede* and *Jupiter and Io* in the KH Mus., Vienna; *Leda* in the Gemäldegalerie, Berlin; *Danaë* in the Borghese Gal., Rome), foreshadow the paintings of *Rococo artists such as *Boucher. It was at this time that Correggio's renown was at its height; he was ranked almost on the same level as Raphael (*Mengs was named after both of them by his artist father). Subsequently his reputation has declined somewhat, but his place as one of the greatest painters of his age is secure.

Corrente. An anti-Fascist association of young Italian artists formed by Renato *Birolli in Milan in 1938; *Guttuso was among the other founder members. The association had no fixed programme, but it was opposed to the provincialism of the official *Novecento Italiano. The members stood for the defence of 'modern' art at a time when the Nazi campaign against *degenerate art was spreading to Italy. Corrente arranged two exhibitions in Milan in 1939, and it published a fortnightly review of literature, politics, and the arts entitled *Corrente di vita giovanile* (Stream of youthful life), later renamed simply *Corrente*. This ceased publication in 1943 and the activities of the group were dissipated by the Second World War.

Cortese. *See* COURTOIS.

Cortona, Pietro da (Pietro Berrettini) (1596–1669). Italian painter, architect, decorator, and designer, second only to *Bernini as the most versatile genius of the full Roman *Baroque style. He is named after his birthplace, Cortona in Tuscany, where he probably had some training with his father, a stonemason, before settling in Rome in about 1612. His first major works there were frescos in the church of S. Bibiana (1624–6), commissioned by Urban VIII (Maffeo *Barberini), and the patronage of the Barberini family played a major part in his career. For their palace he painted his most famous work, a huge fresco, *Allegory of Divine Providence and Barberini Power*, on the ceiling of the Gran Salone. He began this in 1633, but interrupted the work in 1637 to go to Florence, where he painted two frescos commissioned by the Grand Duke Ferdinand II de' *Medici on the walls of the Sala della Stufa in the *Pitti Palace: the *Golden Age* and the *Silver Age*. After returning to Rome he completed the Barberini ceiling in 1639. One of the key works in the development of Baroque painting, it is a triumph of *illusionism, for the centre of the ceiling appears open to the sky and the figures seen from below (di *sotto in sù) appear to come down into the room as well as soar out of it. It demonstrates Cortona's belief, which came out in a debate with Andrea *Sacchi in the Accademia di S. Luca in about 1636, that a history painting could be compared with an epic and was entitled to use many figures; Sacchi, intent on *classical simplicity and unity, argued for using as few figures as possible. For most of the period from 1640 to 1647 Cortona again worked in Florence, continuing his decorations in the Pitti Palace. He first completed his Four Ages of Man decorations in the Sala della Stufa with the *Bronze Age* and the *Iron Age*, then began a series of allegorical ceiling paintings in five rooms named after the planets (the work was completed by his pupil Ciro Ferri (1634–89)). These paintings are combined with sumptuous *stucco ornamentation, and this form of decoration was widely influential, not only in Italy, but also in France. (Cortona turned down an invitation from Cardinal Mazarin to visit Paris, but his style was taken there by his best pupil, *Romanelli.) From 1647 until his death Cortona again worked in Rome, his major paintings from this period being an extensive series of frescos in S. Maria in Vallicella (the Chiesa Nuova, 1647–65), in which, as in his Pitti decorations, paint and stucco are magnificently combined. Throughout his career he painted easel pictures of religious and mythological subjects, and he also designed cartoons for a number of tapestries on the

history of Constantine (1626–41) for the Palazzo Barberini (now in the Philadelphia Museum of Art), completing a series that had been begun by *Rubens.

Cortona once wrote that architecture was merely a pastime for him, but he ranks among the greatest architects of his period. His masterpiece is the church of SS. Martina e Luca in Rome (1635–50), which was the first Baroque church designed and built as a complete unity. Although his architecture has all the vigour of his painting, there is less correspondence between the two fields than might be imagined. He never decorated any of his own churches, and indeed they were not designed with fresco decoration in mind, making their impact through grandeur of form rather than richness of ornament. His great contemporary reputation sank in the next century with those of many other Baroque artists. In a famous passage in his *Dizionario delle belle arti* (1797), Francesco Milizia wrote: 'Borromini in architecture, Bernini in sculpture, Pietro da Cortona in painting...represent a diseased taste—one that has infected a great number of artists.'

Cosmati work. A type of geometrical decorative inlaywork using coloured marbles and mosaic that flourished mainly in Rome between *c*.1100 and *c*.1300. The term derives from the Cosmatus family, several members of which are documented as creating such work. At one time it was believed they were responsible for all of it, but it has now been established that many other craftsmen were active in this field, some of them belonging to families whose work extended over several generations. Cosmati work was used to adorn church furnishings such as tombs and pulpits and also for architectural enrichment and floors. Several examples are in Westminster Abbey, executed by imported Italian craftsmen.

Cossa, Francesco del (*c*.1435–*c*.1477). Italian painter, active mainly in Ferrara, where with Cosimo *Tura and Ercole de' *Roberti he was the leading artist of the period. His style has many affinities with that of Tura and the same background of development from *Mantegna and *Piero della Francesca, but Cossa's work reveals a more genial and relaxed temperament. This found expression in the delightful frescos of the *Months* in the Palazzo Schifanoia at Ferrara; Cossa, Roberti, and Tura are all thought to have contributed to the scheme, but Cossa seems to have been the principal figure. In the early 1470s he moved to Bologna, where his work included an altarpiece for the Griffoni Chapel in the church of S. Petronio (1473); the central panel is in the National Gallery, London.

Costa, Lorenzo (c.1460–1535). Italian painter. He probably trained in Ferrara and his early work was much influenced by *Tura and Ercole de' *Roberti. In the early 1480s he settled in Bologna, where he entered into partnership with *Francia and worked for the ruling Bentivoglio family. In 1504–5 he painted an *Allegory* for Isabella d'*Este (Louvre, Paris) and in 1507 he succeeded *Mantegna as court painter at Mantua. He was the leading artist there until the arrival of *Giulio Romano in 1524, but little of his large-scale work survives. His mature style is often rather sweetly *Peruginesque, with a delicate feeling for landscape, and has been suggested as one of the sources of *Giorgione's work. There are good examples of Costa's work in the National Gallery, London, including *The Concert*, one of the first examples of a type of picture (a close-up of a group of musicians) that was later to have a considerable vogue.

Cosway, Richard (1742–1821). English painter, mainly of *miniatures. A friend of the Prince of Wales (later Prince Regent), Cosway was by far the most fashionable miniaturist of his day, imparting to sitters an air of great elegance. The larger portraits in oils that he occasionally painted are considered less successful. In 1781 he married Maria Hadfield (1759–1838), who was a miniaturist and etcher.

Cotes, Francis (1726–70). English portrait painter, a pupil of *Knapton. He began as a specialist in *pastel and never altogether gave up the medium, but in the 1760s he turned mainly to oils and became a great fashionable success, the only serious rival to *Gainsborough and *Reynolds. Like them, he was a founder member of the *Royal Academy. His work is charming, vivacious, and totally unintellectual: in the words of Sir Ellis *Waterhouse, 'He went all out for health and youth and fine clothes, a strong likeness and no nonsense.' Cotes died from the effects of a toxic potion

he took to try to cure the gall stones or kidney stones from which he was suffering. His studio in Cavendish Square in London (and something of his position in the market) was later taken over by *Romney.

Cotman, John Sell (1782–1842). English landscape painter (mainly in watercolour) and etcher, born in Norwich. He moved to London in 1798, aged 16, and became a member of Dr *Monro's circle. As far as is known, he had no formal tuition in art, but by 1800 he was already accomplished enough to have six of his watercolours accepted for the annual *Royal Academy exhibition. Between 1800 and 1805 he made several sketching tours to Wales and Yorkshire and these resulted in some of his finest works. They did not bring him much success, however, and in 1806 he returned to his native city, where, together with *Crome, he became the most important representative of the *Norwich School. As well as depicting local scenery, he made several trips to France, which bore fruit in *Architectural Antiquities of Normandy* (1822), one of various books he illustrated with his etchings. In 1834 he moved to London to become professor of drawing at King's College, a position he held until his death. He was delighted to be offered the post, as he often had difficulty in making a living with his work and he was in debt at the time. Throughout his life he was also subject to periods of melancholia and despondency. Cotman's early watercolours, such as the celebrated *Greta Bridge* (c.1805, BM, London; a later version, 1810, is in the Castle Mus., Norwich), include some of the greatest examples of the classic English watercolour technique, showing remarkable boldness and sureness of hand. He used large flat *washes to build up form in clearly defined planes and shapes of almost geometrical simplicity. In his later years, however, his style became much more flamboyant; he sometimes mixed flour or rice paste with his watercolours to produce an *impasto that echoed the effects of oil paint. Throughout his career he also painted in oils, but this side of his work has been overshadowed by his achievements as a watercolourist.

Counihan, Noel. *See* ANGRY PENGUINS.

Courbet, Gustave (1819–77). French painter, one of the most powerful personalities in 19th-century art. He was born at Ornans, at the foot of the Jura Mountains, near the Swiss border, the son of a prosperous farmer. His country upbringing was important to his art, for although he spent most of his career in Paris, he rarely painted urban subjects ('His palette smells of hay', Cézanne said of him). He was a man of independent character and obstinate self-assurance, and claimed to be self-taught. In fact he studied with various minor masters in Ornans, Besançon and Paris, where he moved in 1839, but he learnt more from copying the work of 17th-century *naturalists such as *Caravaggio and *Velázquez in the Louvre. It was largely from them that he derived his very solid and weighty style, with its strong contrasts of light and shade. His earliest pictures (including several narcissistic self-portraits) were in the *Romantic tradition, but with three large canvases exhibited at the *Salon of 1850 he established himself as the leader of the *Realist movement: these are *A Burial at Ornans* (Mus. d'Orsay, Paris), *Peasants at Flagey* (Mus. B.-A., Besançon), and *The Stone Breakers* (formerly in Dresden, but destroyed in the Second World War). The huge burial scene in particular made an enormous impact; it was attacked in some quarters for its alleged crudity and deliberate ugliness, but also hailed for its powerful naturalism (he got the idea for the picture at his grandfather's funeral). Never before had a scene from everyday life been presented in such an epic manner and Courbet was cast in the role of a revolutionary socialist. He gladly accepted this role (although it is unlikely that he painted the picture with political intention) and he became a friend and follower of the anarchist philosopher Pierre-Joseph Proudhon, collaborating on his book *On Art and its Social Significance* (1863). Courbet's boldness and self-confidence are as evident in his technique as in his choice of subjects. He often used a palette knife to apply paint and his work shows an unprecedented relish for the physical substance of his materials.

Courbet's unconventionality and hatred of authority were expressed most forcefully in 1855, when, dissatisfied with the representation allotted to him at the Paris Universal Exhibition, he organized a pavilion for his own work, calling it 'Le Réalisme'. Included in the works he showed here was his most celebrated picture, *The Painter's Studio* (1854–5, Mus. d'Orsay). This huge canvas (6 m (20 ft) wide) was subtitled by Courbet, 'a real allegory [a seeming contradiction in terms] summing up seven years in my artistic life'. He wrote a long (but not very clear) account of it, describing it as 'the moral and physical history of my studio' and saying it showed 'all the people who serve my cause, sustain me in my ideal and support my activity'. In it he presents himself as the artist-hero, and in taking as his subject the activity of creating art he sounded a note that reverberated into the 20th century. Interpretations of the picture have been many and varied, and it has recently been shown that it has covert but carefully thought-out political content, attacking Napoleon III. Subsequently, however, his work became less doctrinaire. His colours were less sombre and he often chose more obviously attractive subjects—landscapes from the Forest of Fontainebleau, the Jura, or the Mediterranean, seascapes, still lifes, or comely and sensual nudes. Following the abdication of Napoleon III in 1870, Courbet was appointed head of the arts commission of the Commune, the short-lived revolutionary government of Paris. When the Commune was suppressed by government troops, he was sentenced to six months' imprisonment for his role in the destruction of the Vendôme Column, a symbol of Bonapartism. He was released in 1872, but the following year he was decreed to be personally responsible for the cost of re-erecting the Column. Unable to pay and fearing arrest, he went into exile in Switzerland. He stayed there for the remaining four years of his life, painting mainly landscapes and portraits.

Courbet's resounding rejection of idealization and his concentration on the tangible reality of things had an enormous influence on 19th-century art: 'Superbly plebeian . . . Courbet acted as the bull that smashed the china shop of polite art, whether academic or preciously avant-gardist, thus enabling a new generation (including the *Impressionists) to concentrate on the problem of expressing visual experience' (Lorenz Eitner, *An Outline of 19th Century European Painting*, 1987). 'Painting', he said, 'is an art of sight and should therefore concern itself with things seen; it should, therefore, abandon both the historical scenes of the *classical school and poetic subjects from *Goethe and Shakespeare favoured by the Romantic school.' When asked to include angels in a painting for a church he replied: 'I have never seen angels. Show me an angel and I will paint one.'

Courtauld, Samuel (1876–1947). British industrialist, collector, and philanthropist. He came from a family of prosperous silk-merchants and was chairman of the textile firm Courtaulds Ltd from 1921 to 1946. He began collecting in 1922, buying mainly *Impressionist and *Post-Impressionist works, and in 1923 he gave the Tate Gallery £50,000 for the purchase of French paintings in his own area of interest (which was poorly represented). This fund was used to buy 23 paintings over the next few years, transforming the Tate's collection (most of the pictures have subsequently been transferred to the National Gallery). His interests also extended to living artists, and in 1925 he joined his friend Maynard Keynes in founding the London Artists' Association to provide financial assistance to young painters and sculptors. In 1931 came his most famous benefaction when he endowed the Courtauld Institute of Art, London, Britain's first specialist centre for the study of the history of art. The Institute opened in 1932 and in the same year Courtauld presented most of his collection to the University of London, together with funds for a building to house them. The co-founders of the Institute were Lord Lee of Fareham (1868–1947), a soldier and politician, who in 1921 had presented his country house—Chequers—to the nation to be the prime minister's country residence, and Sir Robert Witt (1872–1952), a lawyer who formed a library of reproductions of paintings and drawings that is now one of the cornerstones of the Institute's pre-eminence in art-historical studies. Both men left collections to the Courtauld Institute—Lee mainly of paintings, Witt of drawings and watercolours—and there have been several other important bequests, including that of the painter and critic Roger *Fry. The most recent of the major bequests, that of the Anglo-Austrian art historian Count Antoine Seilern (1901–78) in 1978, raised an already outstanding collection to new heights. Seilern's bequest is varied, reflecting his own scholarly interests, but its chief glory is its superlative group of works by *Rubens. The Institute was originally located in Courtauld's former house at 20 Portman Square (a fine 18th-century building by James Wyatt and Robert Adam), while the galleries (opened in 1958) occupied a building about a mile away, next to the *Warburg Institute in Woburn Square. In 1989–90, however, all the Institute's activities and collections were brought together under one roof at Somerset House in the Strand, fulfilling Courtauld's intention that students should work in intimate contact with original works of art.

Courtois, Jacques (1621–76) and **Guillaume** (1628–79). French painters, brothers, active in Italy and often known by the Italian forms of their names, Giacomo and Guglielmo Cortese. They came from Burgundy and both had the nickname 'Il Borgognone' or 'Le Bourguignon'. Jacques was a prolific painter of battle scenes, fairly close in style to those of Salvator *Rosa, but more colourful; his work was influential in popularizing the genre in Italy. Guillaume was a pupil of Pietro da *Cortona and mainly painted altarpieces. He was an outstanding draughtsman and also made a few etchings. Both brothers worked in Rome for much of their careers and they sometimes collaborated.

Cousin, Jean the Elder (c.1490–c.1560). French painter, engraver, and designer, active in his native Sens and from about 1538 in Paris. He had a successful career as a painter and a designer of stained glass and tapestries, but very little surviving work can be securely attributed to him. The only certain documented works are three tapestries from a series on the life of St Mammès, which he contracted to design in 1543 (two are in Langres Cathedral, for which they were woven, the other is in the Louvre, Paris). The painting *Eva Prima Pandora* (Louvre), however, can also be confidently given to him, as the attribution goes back almost to his lifetime, and two windows in Sens Cathedral are also traditionally attributed to him. In 1560 he published a treatise on perspective. A similar pattern emerges with his son **Jean the Younger** (c.1525–c.1595), a painter and engraver. He too worked in Sens and Paris and had a great contemporary reputation, but again little documented work survives. His most important painting is a *Last Judgement* (Louvre); he also produced a book of *emblem drawings entitled *Livre de fortune* (Institut de France, Paris, 1568) and in 1595 published an instructional book on drawing the human figure, *Livre de pourtraicture*, which went through several editions and remained in use until the 19th century. The work of both father and son shows strong Italian influence and is remarkable for its independence from the prevailing style of the School of *Fontainebleau.

Coustou, Guillaume I (1677–1746). The best-known member of a dynasty of French sculptors. He was trained by *Coysevox (his mother's brother), and like him worked a good deal for the court. His vigorous style was formed partly on the example of *Bernini, whose work he saw in Rome, where he worked c.1697–1700. His masterpieces are the celebrated pair of *Horse Tamers* (*The Marly Horses*) (1739–45), made for the royal chateau at Marly, then moved to the Place de la Concorde, Paris, and now in the Louvre. **Nicolas** (1658–1733), Guillaume's brother, was also employed in court circles, and his work can be seen at Versailles and in the Tuileries Gardens in Paris. He was probably the teacher of *Roubiliac. **Guillaume II** (1716–77), the son of Guillaume I, inherited his father's technical skill but little of his originality. Nevertheless, he enjoyed a successful career, his most important work being the monument to Louis de Bourbon (son of Louis XV) and his wife in Sens Cathedral (1766–77). **François** (d. 1690), the father of Guillaume I and Nicolas and the founder of the dynasty, was a minor woodcarver working in Lyons.

Couture, Thomas (1815–79). French historical and portrait painter, a pupil of *Gros and *Delaroche. He is chiefly remembered for his vast 'orgy' picture *The Romans of the Decadence* (Mus. d'Orsay, Paris), which was the sensation of the 1847 *Salon. As with other 'one-hit wonders', his reputation has sunk with that of his big work, which now is often cited as the classic example of the worst type of bombastic academic painting, impeccable in every detail and totally false in overall effect. His more informal works, however, are often much livelier in conception and technique, and as a teacher he encouraged direct study from landscape. *Manet was his best-known pupil, and others included *Fantin-Latour and *Puvis de Chavannes.

Cowie, James (1886–1956). One of the most individual Scottish painters of the 20th century. Whereas the central tradition of modern Scottish painting has been one of rich colouring and lush, free brushwork (see, for example, SCOTTISH COLOURISTS), Cowie worked in a strong, hard, predominantly linear style—highly disciplined rather than intuitive (he made many preparatory drawings and often worked on a picture for several years). He took his subjects from what he saw around him, but he was also inspired by the Old Masters, often using their compositions as a starting point, without actually imitating them. Among his contemporaries he was perhaps closest in spirit to John *Nash, an artist he greatly admired. They shared an ability to infuse the ordinary with a sense of the mysterious. Cowie taught at several art schools in Scotland, his pupils including Robert *Colquhoun, Robert *MacBryde, and Joan *Eardley.

Cox, David (1783–1859). English landscape painter, mainly in watercolour. In his youth he worked as a scene painter in his native Birmingham, then in 1804 moved to London, where he took up watercolour, receiving lessons from John *Varley. He lived in Hereford, 1814–27, and in London, 1827–41, before retiring to Harborne, near Birmingham, from where he made annual sketching tours to the Welsh mountains. In spite of a certain anecdotal homeliness, his style was broad and vigorous, and in 1836 he began to paint on a rough Scottish wrapping paper that was particularly suited to it. A similar paper was made commercially and marketed as 'Cox Paper'. Cox devoted much of his time to teaching and he wrote several instructional books on watercolour; in the last two decades of his life he also worked a good deal in oils. His son, **David Cox the Younger** (1809–85), was also a landscape watercolourist.

Coypel. Dynasty of French painters of which **Noël** (1628–1707) was the head. He worked in an academic style based on the example of *Poussin and *Le Brun, was much employed on the large decorative schemes of Louis XIV, notably at Versailles, and was director of the French Academy in Rome (1672–4) and then of the Académie

Royale in Paris (1695–9). His son **Antoine** (1661–1722) accompanied his father to Rome as a boy (he was a child prodigy) and there is a strong Italian element in his style. This comes out particularly in his most famous work, the ceiling of the chapel at Versailles (1708), which derived from *Gaulli's ceiling in the Gesù in Rome. This and Coypel's decorations at the Palais Royal in Paris (1702–5, destroyed) rank as the two most completely *Baroque schemes found in French art of this period. The Versailles ceiling is more successful than much of Coypel's work, which often combines, in the words of Anthony *Blunt, 'the bombast of the Baroque and the pedantry of the *classical style without the virtues of either'. He became director of the Académie Royale in 1714 and chief painter to the king in 1715. His half-brother **Noël-Nicolas** (1690–1734) painted with much more charm, mainly mythological subjects, but he seems to have had a rather timid personality and did not achieve the worldly success of the other members of the family. Indeed, he was the best painter of the family, but is the least famous. *Chardin was briefly his pupil. Antoine's son **Charles-Antoine** (1694–1752) was a much more forceful character than Noël-Nicolas and had a resoundingly successful career, largely due to his administrative capacity in the various official positions that he held. In 1747 he became director of the Académie Royale and chief painter to the king. He also wrote verse, plays (several of which were performed at court), and art criticism. As a painter he was versatile and prolific, but the weakest member of the family: his *Supper at Emmaus* (1746) in St Merri, Paris, has been described by Sir Michael Levey as 'pathetically inept'.

Coysevox, Antoine (1640–1720). French sculptor, with *Girardon the most successful of Louis XIV's reign. His style was more *Baroque than Girardon's and he overtook his rival in popularity towards the end of the 17th century, as the king's taste turned away from the *classical. By 1679 Coysevox was working at Versailles, where he made numerous statues for the gardens and did much interior decoration, including a large stucco *relief of the *Triumph of Louis XIV* (c.1682) in the Salon de la Guerre. His originality, however, is seen mostly in his portrait busts, which show a naturalism of concep-

tion and an animation of expression that look forward to the *Rococo. This is particularly so with his portraits of friends, but even his formal commissions can be remarkably lively. The Wallace Collection, London, has an outstanding example of both his formal and informal portraits: the bronze *Louis XIV* (c.1686) and the terracotta *Charles Le Brun* (1676).

Cozens, Alexander (1717?–86). English landscape draughtsman. Cozens was one of the first major British artists to work exclusively as a landscapist and he helped to bring intellectual respectability to his speciality by stressing its poetic and imaginative qualities rather than its topographical function. He was born in Russia, the son of a shipbuilder employed by Peter the Great (there is no truth in the legend that Peter was his real father), and although he was educated in England, he later returned to Russia and did not settle in Britain until he was about 30. For much of his career he worked as a fashionable teacher, and he published several treatises. The most famous of these is *A New Method of Assisting the Invention in Drawing Original Compositions of Landscape* (1786), in which he explains his method of 'blot drawing'—using accidental marks on the drawing paper to stimulate the imagination by suggesting landscape forms that could be developed into a finished work (see AUTOMATISM). Cozens mentions that 'something of the same kind had been mentioned by *Leonardo da Vinci, in his Treatise on Painting' and that reading the passage in question 'tended to confirm my own opinion'. He worked almost exclusively in monochrome, and both his 'blot drawings' and his more formal compositions use intense lights and darks with masterly effect to suggest the power and mystery of nature.

His son, **John Robert Cozens** (1752–97), was the outstanding landscape watercolourist of his generation. Much of his work derived from two Continental journeys, in 1776–9 and 1782–3, during which he visited Italy and Switzerland. On the first he was draughtsman to Richard Payne *Knight, and on the second he was part of the entourage of William *Beckford (a former pupil of his father). Throughout his life he was subject to fits of severe depression and in 1794 he became insane, thereafter being cared for by Dr *Monro. His work was more naturalistic than his father's, but nevertheless was more concerned with evocation of mood (typically one of poetic melancholy) than with topographical accuracy. Unlike his father, he does not seem ever to have worked wholly from imagination, but he often transposed landscape features to obtain a more pleasing composition. His work was admired and copied by *Constable (who called him 'the greatest genius that ever touched landscape'), *Girtin, and *Turner.

Cragg, Tony. See NEW BRITISH SCULPTURE.

Cranach, Lucas the Elder (1472–1553). German painter and designer of woodcuts. He takes his name from the small town of Kronach in south Germany, where he was born. Very little is known of his life before he moved to Vienna in 1501/2 and started working for the humanist circles associated with the newly founded university. His stay in Vienna was brief (he left in 1504), but in this period he painted some of his finest and most original works. They include portraits, notably those of Johannes Cuspinian, a lecturer at the university, and his wife Anna (1502–3, Reinhart Coll., Winterthur), and several religious works in which he shows a remarkable feeling for the beauty of landscape characteristic of the *Danube School. The finest example of this manner is perhaps the *Rest on the Flight into Egypt* (Gemäldegalerie, Berlin), which shows the Holy Family resting in the glade of a German pine forest. It was painted in 1504, just before Cranach moved to Wittenberg as court painter to Frederick III (the Wise), Elector of Saxony.

Cranach remained in Wittenberg until 1550, when he followed the Elector John Frederick (the Unfortunate) into exile, to Augsburg, Innsbruck, and finally Weimar. During his time in Wittenberg he became extremely wealthy and one of the city's most respected citizens, serving as burgomaster for several years. His paintings were eagerly sought by collectors, and his busy studio often produced numerous replicas of popular designs, particularly those in which he showed his skill at depicting female beauty—more than ten versions are known of his *Reclining Nymph*. He excelled at such erotic nudes, which are influenced by Italian *Renaissance models but totally different in spirit, and he also had a penchant for pictures of coquettish women wearing large hats, sometimes shown as Judith or the goddesses in the Judgement of Paris. The most innovative works of his Wittenberg period, however, are probably his full-length portraits (*The Duke* and *Duchess of Saxony*, 1514, Gemäldegalerie, Dresden). Wittenberg was at the centre of the Protestant Reformation and Cranach supported the Lutheran cause. He painted several portraits of Luther and also designed the woodcut illustrations for his translation of the New Testament (1522). However, always an astute businessman, he also worked for Catholic patrons. During his later years he was assisted by his son, **Lucas the Younger** (1515–86), who eventually took over the workshop and imitated his father's style so successfully that it is often difficult to distinguish between their hands.

Crane, Walter (1845–1915). British illustrator, designer, painter, writer, and administrator. His career was very varied, but he is best remembered today as an illustrator of children's books, a field in which he was prolific throughout his life. He took this work very seriously, believing that 'We all remember the little cuts that coloured the books of our childhood. The ineffaceable quality of these early pictorial and literary impressions affords the strongest plea for good art in the nursery and the schoolroom.' His work for adults included designing wallpaper, and he was a leading figure in the *Arts and Crafts Movement that tried to rehabilitate good design and craftsmanship. He was greatly interested in art education, serving on various examination boards; in the 1890s he taught in Manchester and Reading, and in 1898–9 he was principal of the *Royal College of Art.

craquelure. A network of small cracks that appears on the surface of a painting when in the course of time the paint or *varnish has become brittle.

Crawford, Thomas (1813/14–57). American sculptor. He moved to Rome in 1835, studied with *Thorvaldsen, and became the most thoroughgoing *Neoclassicist among American sculptors of his generation. Although he settled permanently in Rome (the first American sculptor to do so), he made visits to his native country and attained an extraordinary reputation there, receiving numerous prestigious public commissions. The most notable is the bronze *Armed Liberty* on top of the dome of the Capitol in Washington, which was begun in 1855 and set in place in 1863 after Crawford's early death from cancer.

crayon. *See* CHALK.

crayon manner. An engraving technique, a variant of *etching, used for the reproduction of red or brown chalk drawings. The technique was invented in about 1750 in France, where such drawings were highly popular at the time (*Boucher and *Fragonard were among the artists whose work was reproduced); it was also widely used in England. An offshoot of crayon manner soon developed in the form of pastel manner, in which several plates were inked with different colours to give the appearance of *pastel drawings. The techniques were rendered obsolete by *lithography early in the 19th century.

Credi, Lorenzo di (*c.*1458–1537). Florentine painter. He was a fellow pupil of *Leonardo in *Verrocchio's workshop and he seems to have stayed there until Verrocchio's death in 1488, managing the painting side of his master's varied business. He was a very fine craftsman, but his style lacked individuality. His early work is in an extremely prosaic version of Leonardo's youthful style; later he absorbed some of the ideas of the High *Renaissance. He had several pupils and seems to have had a fairly successful career with his solid, unspectacular skills. It is said that in the 1490s he was influenced by the teachings of Savonarola (*see* BARTOLOMMEO and BOTTICELLI) and destroyed all his pictures with profane subjects.

Creed, Martin. *See* TURNER PRIZE.

Crespi, Daniele (*c.*1597–1630). Milanese painter. Although he died young of the plague, his output was large and his work is considered to be one of the most typical expressions of the zealous spirit of the Counter-Reformation that affected Milan during his time. His acknowledged masterpiece is *St Charles Borromeo at Supper* (*c.*1628, S. Maria della Passione, Milan); in its simple composition and emotional directness it reflects the ideals of painting advocated by the Council of Trent and marks a move from *Mannerism to *Baroque. He was probably a relative of Giovanni Battista *Crespi, whose work influenced him.

Crespi, Giovanni Battista (Il Cerano) (*c.*1575–1632). Italian painter, sculptor, engraver, architect, and writer. His nickname derived from his birthplace, Cerano near Novaro, but he was active mainly in Milan, where he was one of the leading artists of his time. He had settled there by the late 1590s, probably following a period in Rome, and became a protégé of Cardinal Federico Borromeo (cousin of St Charles Borromeo). Borromeo, who was archbishop of Milan and an important art patron, appointed Crespi head of the painting section of the Accademia Ambrosiana, which he founded in 1620, and in 1629 put him in charge of the sculptural decoration of Milan Cathedral. Crespi's paintings, often mystical in feeling, are complex stylistically: there is a strong *Mannerist current in his colouring and in the elegant posturing of his figures, but his work also shows a solidity and a feeling for realistic details that give it a place in the vanguard of the *Baroque.

Crespi, Giuseppe Maria (called 'Lo Spagnuolo') (1665–1747). Bolognese painter. His nickname ('the Spaniard') was given to him in his student days because of his manner of dress. He reacted against the academic tradition in which he was trained (*Cignani was one of his teachers) and is now best known for low-life *genre scenes. They are in the tradition of the everyday-life paintings of the *Carracci, but go far beyond them in their sombre gravity and sense of unvarnished reality (*The Hamlet*, *c.*1705, Pinacoteca Nazionale, Bologna). He also painted many other subjects, and after the death of his wife in 1722 he became very pious and concentrated on religious works. From this time he became reclusive, rarely leaving his house except to go to Mass, but earlier in his career he had travelled a good deal in Italy; he had an international reputation and was particularly influential on Venetian painters, most notably *Piazzetta. Rudolf *Wittkower called him 'the only real genius of the late Bolognese school'.

Crivelli, Carlo (*c.*1430/5–1493/5). Italian painter. He always signed himself as a Venetian, but he is only once recorded in the city (in 1457 when he was fined and sentenced to six months' imprisonment for committing adultery) and he spent most of his career working in the Marches, particularly at Ascoli Piceno; he also lived for some time at Zara in Dalmatia (now Zadar, Croatia), which at this time was part of Venetian territory. Ascoli Piceno was for a time controlled by Naples and in 1490 Crivelli was knighted by Prince Ferdinand of Capua (later Ferdinand II of Naples), an indication of the high contemporary reputation he enjoyed. His paintings are all of religious subjects, done in an elaborate, old-fashioned style that owes much to the wiry Paduan tradition of *Squarcione and *Mantegna and yet is highly distinctive, with a rich vein of fantasy. Their dense ornamentation is often increased by the use of *gesso decoration combined with the paint. The finest collection of his works is in the National Gallery in London and includes the delightful and much-reproduced *Annunciation* (1486). **Vittore Crivelli** (d. 1501/2), Carlo's younger brother, was a faithful but pedestrian follower.

Crome, John (1768–1821). English landscape painter and etcher, with *Cotman the major artist of the *Norwich School. Whereas Cotman was primarily a watercolourist, Crome painted mainly in oils. He was born, worked, and died in Norwich, earning a major part of his living as a drawing master; he made regular trips to London and visited other parts of the country, but his only journey abroad was to Paris in 1814 to see the exhibition of pictures looted by Napoleon. Of humble origin, he was first apprenticed to a coach- and sign-painter and taught himself principally by copying works in the collection of Thomas Harvey, a local collector and amateur painter who befriended him. The Dutch painters *Ruisdael and *Hobbema were particularly influential on him and he also admired *Gainsborough and *Wilson, but his work was based as much on direct observation of nature as on study of the Old Masters. His favourite subjects included heathland, woods, and tranquil stretches of river, and his style was fresh, clear, and unaffected. In addition to his paintings he made 34 etchings, which were posthumously published by his widow and his eldest son **John Bernay Crome** (1794–1842). The elder Crome is sometimes referred to as 'Old Crome' to distinguish

him from his son, who painted in his manner but with less distinction.

Cross, Henri-Edmond. *See* NEO-IMPRESSIONISM.

Crowe, Sir Joseph Archer (1825–96). English journalist, diplomat, and art historian, brother of the painter **Eyre Crowe** (1824–1910). He had a distinguished career as a commercial attaché in Berlin, Paris, and Vienna and was also a war correspondent in the Crimea and elsewhere, but he is best known for his writings on art history done in collaboration with the Italian draughtsman Giovanni Battista Cavalcaselle (1819–97). They met by chance in 1847 and became firm friends when Cavalcaselle was later a political refugee in London; for a time they lived in the same house. Every detail of their books was discussed between them, but Crowe did all the actual writing because Cavalcaselle's English was inadequate; in the words of John *Pope-Hennessy, 'Crowe was the synthesizer and historian, Cavalcaselle was the eye.' Their prodigious output included *The Early Flemish Painters* (1857), *A New History of Painting in Italy* (3 vols., 1864–8), *A History of Painting in North Italy* (2 vols., 1871), *Titian: His Life and Times* (2 vols., 1877) and *Raphael: His Life and Works* (2 vols., 1882). These works, all of which have appeared in subsequent editions, either in English or translation, set new standards of methodical research, bringing to light masses of information, and they are still considered valuable.

Cruikshank, George (1792–1878). English *caricaturist, illustrator, and painter. The son of a caricaturist, **Isaac Cruikshank** (1764–1811), he was highly precocious and was successful whilst still in his teens. By the time *Gillray died in 1815, Cruickshank was already recognized as his successor as the leading political cartoonist of the day (he had completed various works Gillray had been too ill to finish and could imitate his style fluently). The dissolute private life of the Prince Regent was one of his favourite topics, but when his target became king as George IV in 1820, Cruikshank was paid £100 'in consideration of a pledge not to caricature His Majesty in any immoral situation'. From this time he began to turn from political satire to social observation and from prints to book illustrations.

His output in this field was enormous and gained him a European reputation. Among his most famous illustrations are the 24 etchings he made for Dickens's *Oliver Twist* (1837). In 1847 he suddenly took up the cause of temperance, producing moral narratives in series of prints (*The Bottle*, 1847; *The Drunkard's Children*, 1848) and a vast painting *The Worship of Bacchus* (1860–2, Tate, London). His brother, **Robert Cruikshank** (1789–1856), with whom he sometimes collaborated, was a printmaker, illustrator, and painter.

Cubism. A term describing a revolutionary style of painting created jointly by *Braque and *Picasso in the period 1907–14 and subsequently applied to a broad movement, centred in Paris but international in scope, in which their ideas were adopted and adapted by many other artists. These artists were mainly painters, but Cubist ideas and motifs were also used in sculpture, and to a more limited and superficial degree in the applied arts and occasionally in architecture. Cubism was a complex phenomenon, but in essence it involved what Juan *Gris (its leading exponent apart from the two founders) called 'a new way of representing the world'. Abandoning the idea of a single fixed viewpoint that had dominated European painting for centuries, Cubist pictures used a multiplicity of viewpoints, so that many different aspects of an object could be simultaneously depicted in the same picture. Such fragmentation and rearrangement of form meant that a painting could now be regarded less as a kind of window through which an image of the world is seen, and more as a physical object on which a subjective response to the world is created. This new approach proved extraordinarily influential, and John *Golding has described Cubism as 'perhaps the most important and certainly the most complete and radical artistic revolution since the *Renaissance'.

Braque and Picasso met in October 1907. At this time, Braque had recently been overwhelmed by the memorial exhibition of *Cézanne's work at the *Salon d'Automne, and Picasso had spent much of the year working on *Les Demoiselles d'Avignon* (1906–7, MoMA, New York), in which the angular and aggressive forms owed much to the influence of African sculpture. These two sources—Cézanne and *primitive art—were of great importance in the genesis of Cubism. Cézanne's late work, with its subtle overlapping patches of colour, showed how a sense of solidity and pictorial structure could be created without traditional perspective or modelling; and primitive art offered an example of expressively distorted forms and freedom from inhibition. The pictures to which the term 'Cubism' was first applied were a group of landscapes painted by Braque in the summer of 1908, when he was staying at L'Estaque, near Marseilles. They were shown later that year at *Kahnweiler's gallery, and in reviewing this exhibition Louis Vauxcelles (*see* FAUVISM) made reference to Braque's way of reducing 'everything—sites, figures, and houses—to geometric outlines, to cubes'. The following year Vauxcelles used the expression 'bizarreries cubiques' (cubic eccentricities), and by 1911 the term 'Cubism' had entered the English language. The word is undoubtedly apposite for the block-like forms in some of the Braque landscapes that occasioned Vauxcelles's jibes and in a few similar works by Picasso, but it is not really appropriate to their later Cubist pictures, in which the forms tend to be broken into facets rather than fashioned into cubes. However, they soon accepted the term, as did their followers.

Braque and Picasso's mature Cubist work is usually divided into two phases—Analytical Cubism (1909–11) and Synthetic Cubism (1912–14). In the 'Analytical' phase, the relatively solid massing of their earliest Cubist paintings gave way to a process of composition in which the forms of the object depicted are fragmented into a large number of small, intricately hinged planes that fuse with one another and with the surrounding space. This fascination with pictorial structure led to colour being downplayed, and the archetypal Analytical Cubist paintings are virtually monochromatic, painted in muted browns or warm greys. Examples—showing how similar the two artists were in style at this date—are Braque's *The Portuguese* (1911, Kunstmuseum, Basle) and Picasso's *The Accordionist* (1911, Guggenheim Mus., New York). At times they worked in such close harmony—'like mountaineers roped together' in Braque's memorable phrase—that even experts can have difficulty in differentiating their hands. In *The

Portuguese, Braque introduced the use of stencilled lettering, and by the following year he was experimenting with mixing materials such as sand and sawdust with his paint to create interesting textures. He refined this notion again by imitating the effect of wood graining. Later in the same year, 1912, Picasso took this a stage further when he produced his first *collages, and Braque quickly followed with his own type of collage—the *papier collé. These developments—marking a move away from the very cerebral near-abstraction of Analytical Cubism to a more relaxed and decorative art incorporating everyday ephemera—ushered in Synthetic Cubism. This reversed the compositional principle of Analytical Cubism, the image being built up ('synthesized') from pre-existing elements or shapes rather than being created through a process of fragmentation. One consequence of this concern with greater surface richness was that Braque and Picasso reintroduced colour to their paintings. In the Synthetic phase of Cubism, Juan Gris played as important a role as Braque or Picasso, and by this time many other artists had been won over to the movement (including Fernard *Léger, who is often considered the fourth major Cubist). Indeed, Cubism had become the dominant avant-garde idiom in Paris as early as 1911, *Delaunay, *Gleizes, *La Fresnaye, *Metzinger, and *Picabia being among the adherents by this time.

Cubism proved immensely adaptable and was the starting point or an essential component of several other movements, including *Constructivism, *Futurism, *Orphism, *Purism, and *Vorticism, as well as a spur to the imagination of countless individual artists. These included not only painters, but also sculptors, who adapted Cubist ideas in various ways, notably by the opening up of forms so that voids as well as solids form distinct shapes. Picasso himself made Cubist sculpture, and other leading artists who worked in the idiom include *Archipenko (whose international success played a great part in spreading Cubist ideas), *Duchamp-Villon, *Laurens, *Lipchitz, and *Zadkine. Another noted Cubist sculptor was the Czech Otto *Gutfreund, who was part of a remarkable flowering of Cubist art and design in Prague in the years immediately before the First World War. This was the only place where there was a

significant adaptation of Cubism to architecture: several Czech architects broke up the façades of their buildings with abstract, prismatic forms in a way that clearly recalls the fragmentation of Analytical Cubism. In the applied arts, Cubism was one of the sources of *Art Deco, and more generally it has had a huge and varied impact on modern pictorial culture, becoming part of the common currency of ideas: 'Cubist painting gave to artists complete freedom to deal with reality in art in any way they chose. Cubist collage gave them in addition the equally radical freedom to *make* art out of anything they chose. These developments have been enormously fruitful—they have been and they continue to be the basis of much of the best of modern art' (Simon Wilson, *What is Cubism?*, 1983).

Cullen, Maurice (1866–1934) Canadian painter, whose work was influential in introducing *Impressionism to his country. From 1889 to 1895 he lived in Paris and elsewhere in France, with trips to Venice and North Africa; he made two shorter trips to Europe before settling for good in Canada in 1902. His subjects included city scenes (*Old Houses, Montreal*, c.1900, Montreal MFA) and landscapes on the St Lawrence River, in the Laurentian hills, at St John's in Newfoundland (his birthplace), and in the Rocky Mountains. After about 1920 he lived in virtual retirement in a cabin he built at Lac Tremblant in the Laurentians. His friend J. W. *Morrice said of his work: 'he gets at the guts of things.'

Cumberland Market Group. A small group of painters formed in London in 1914, with Robert *Bevan, Harold *Gilman, and Charles *Ginner as the core members; all three had belonged to the recently defunct *Camden Town Group and were at this time members also of its successor, the *London Group. The Cumberland Market Group was named after 49 Cumberland Market in Camden, the address of Bevan's studio, where the members used to meet. They held only one exhibition, at the Goupil Gallery in April 1915, by which time John *Nash had joined the group. It never officially disbanded but lapsed in about 1918.

Currie, Ken. *See* GLASGOW SCHOOL.

Currier and Ives prints. Popular *lithographs published in New York by Nathaniel

Currier (1813–88) and James M. Ives (1824–95). Currier began issuing prints in 1834 and the name 'Currier & Ives' was first used in 1857, when Ives (the firm's bookkeeper) became a partner. They advertised their lithographs as 'Coloured Engravings for the People', and they represented almost every aspect of contemporary America, including sporting, sentimental, patriotic, and political subjects, together with portraits, landscapes, disasters, scenes of city life, railroads, Mississippi steamboats, and so forth. A number of artists, most of whom specialized in particular subjects, were retained by the firm to draw the lithographs in black and white; afterwards the prints were coloured by hand on a production-line system (one assistant to each colour) and sold cheaply to the public by agents, printsellers, and pedlars. The business was carried on until 1907 by the sons of the founders.

Curry, John Steuart (1897–1946). American painter. He was born on a farm in Kansas, and never forgot his Midwestern roots. From 1919 to 1926 he worked as an illustrator for pulp magazines, then spent a year in Europe, before settling in New York, where he was encouraged and supported by Gertrude Vanderbilt *Whitney. He believed that art should grow out of everyday life and be motivated by affection, and his subjects were taken from the Midwest he loved. Two of his most famous works are *Baptism in Kansas* (1928, Whitney Mus., New York) and *Hogs Killing a Rattlesnake* (1930, Art Inst. of Chicago); they show his anecdotal, rather melodramatic style (he often depicted the violence of nature)—sometimes weak in draughtsmanship, but always vigorous and sincere. In the 1930s Curry was recognized—along with *Benton and Grant *Wood—as one of the leading exponents of *Regionalism, and he was given commissions for several large murals; the best known—generally regarded as his masterpieces, even though the scheme was never completed—are in the state capitol in Topeka, Kansas (1938–40); the subjects include the activities of John Brown, the famous campaigner against slavery.

Cuyp. The name of a family of Dutch painters of Dordrecht, of which three members gained distinction. **Jacob Gerritsz. Cuyp** (1594–1652) was the son of a glass painter and according to *Houbraken was a pupil of Abraham *Bloemaert in Utrecht. His output was varied, but he is now best known as a portraitist—his portraits of children are particularly fine. **Benjamin Gerritsz. Cuyp** (1612–52) was the half-brother of Jacob. He is known mainly for paintings of biblical and *genre scenes that use melodramatic light and shade in the manner of the young *Rembrandt. **Aelbert Cuyp** (1620–91) is the most famous member of the family and now one of the most celebrated of all landscape painters, although he also painted many other subjects. He was the son and probably the pupil of Jacob Gerritsz. Cuyp. His early works also show the influence of Jan van *Goyen. Aelbert was born and died in Dordrecht, but he seems to have travelled along his country's great rivers to the eastern part of the Netherlands, and he also painted views of Westphalia. A prodigious number of pictures are ascribed to him, but his oeuvre poses many problems. He often signed his paintings but rarely dated them, and a satisfactory chronology has never been established. Although he had little influence outside Dordrecht, Cuyp had several imitators there, and some of the paintings formerly attributed to him are now given to Abraham Calraet (1642–1722), who signed himself 'AC' (the same initials as Cuyp). In 1658 Cuyp married a rich widow, and in the 1660s he seems to have virtually abandoned painting. He was almost forgotten for two generations after his death, then was rediscovered in the late 18th century, when he started to become particularly popular with British collectors. He is still much better represented in British collections, public and private, than in Dutch museums (there are eleven pictures by him in the National Gallery, London, for example). His finest works—typically river scenes and landscapes with placid, dignified-looking cows—show great serenity and masterly handling of glowing light (usually Cuyp favoured the effects of the early morning or evening sun). He approaches *Claude more closely in spirit than any of his countrymen who travelled to Italy.

D

Dada. A movement in European art (with manifestations also in New York), c.1915–c.1922, characterized by a spirit of anarchic revolt against traditional values. It arose from a mood of disillusionment engendered by the First World War, to which some artists reacted with irony, cynicism, and nihilism. Originally Dada appeared in two neutral countries (Switzerland and the USA), but near the end of the war it spread to Germany and subsequently to a few other countries. The unprecedented carnage of the war led the Dadaists to question the values of the society that had created it and to find them morally bankrupt. Their response was to go to extremes of buffoonery and provocative behaviour to shock people out of corruption and complacency. One of their prime targets was the institutionalized art world, with its bourgeois ideas of taste and concern with market values. The Dadaists deliberately flouted accepted standards of beauty and they exaggerated the role of chance in artistic creation. Group activity was regarded as more important than individual works, and traditional media such as painting and sculpture were largely abandoned in favour of techniques and devices such as *collage, *photomontage, and *ready-mades, in which there was no concern for fine materials or craftsmanship; in literature the nonsense poem was a characteristic form of expression. Although the Dadaists scorned the art of the past, their methods and manifestos—particularly the techniques of outrage and provocation—owed much to *Futurism; however, Dada's nihilism was very different from Futurism's militant optimism.

European Dada was founded in Zurich in 1915 by a group of artists and writers including Jean *Arp, the German painter, sculptor, and film-maker Hans Richter (1888–1976), and the Romanian poet Tristan Tzara (1896–1963). According to the most frequently cited of several accounts of how the name (French for 'hobby horse') originated, it was chosen by inserting a penknife at random in the pages of a dictionary, thus symbolizing the anti-rational stance of the movement. By the end of the war the movement was spreading to Germany, and there were significant Dada activities in three German cities: Berlin, Cologne, and Hanover. In Berlin the movement had a strong political dimension, expressed particularly through the brilliant photomontages of Raoul Hausmann (1886–1971) and John *Heartfeld and through the biting social satire of Otto *Dix and George *Grosz; eventually it gave way to *Neue Sachlichkeit. In Cologne a brief Dada movement (1919–20) was centred on two figures: Arp, who moved there from Zurich when the war ended; and Max *Ernst, who made witty and provocative use of collage and organized one of Dada's most notorious exhibitions, at which axes were provided for visitors to smash the works on show. In Hanover Kurt *Schwitters was the only important Dada exponent but one of the most dedicated of all.

Dada in New York arose independently of the European movement and virtually simultaneously. It was mainly confined to the activities of Marcel *Duchamp, *Man Ray, and Francis *Picabia; their work tends to be more whimsical and less violent than that of their counterparts in Europe, although they still liked to shock. Duchamp was the most influential of all exponents of Dada and Picabia was the most vigorous in promoting its ideas, forming a link between the European and American movements. He founded his Dada periodical *391* in Barcelona and he introduced the movement to Paris in 1919. In Paris the movement was mainly literary in its emphasis, and its tendency towards the fanciful and the absurd formed the basis for *Surrealism, which was officially launched there in 1924 but began to emerge a few years earlier.

Although it was fairly short-lived and confined to a few main centres, Dada was highly influential in its questioning and debunking of traditional concepts and methods, setting the agenda for much subsequent artistic experiment. Its techniques involving accident and chance were of great importance to the Surrealists and were also later exploited by the *Abstract Expressionists. *Conceptual art, too, has its roots in Dada. The spirit of the Dadaists, in fact, has never completely disappeared, and its tradition has been sustained in, for example, *Junk sculpture and *Pop art, which in the USA was sometimes known as *Neo-Dada.

Dadd, Richard (1817–86). English painter who murdered his father in 1843 and spent the rest of his life in Bedlam and Broadmoor asylums. Before his mental breakdown he was considered one of the most promising artists of his generation (his friend *Frith called him 'a man of genius that would assuredly have placed him high in the first rank of painters') and after his incarceration he was encouraged to continue painting. Although most of his work before the murder had been fairly conventional, he had begun to paint fairy and fantasy subjects and in the asylums he developed these along highly imaginative lines: *The Fairy Feller's Master-Stroke* (1855–64, Tate, London) is probably the best known. Dadd was virtually forgotten for many years, but since the 1970s his work has become well known.

Daddi, Bernardo (d. 1348?). Florentine painter, the outstanding painter in Florence in the period after the death of *Giotto (who was possibly his teacher). Daddi ran a busy workshop specializing in small devotional panels and portable altarpieces—types that he helped to popularize. His signed and dated works include a *polyptych of the *Crucifixion with Eight Saints* (1348, Courtauld Gal., London), and the works attributed to him include frescos of the Martyrdoms of Sts Lawrence and Stephen in S. Croce. His style—a sweetened version of Giotto's, combining firm draughtsmanship with lightness and grace—was influential into the second half of the century.

Daguerre, Louis (1787–1851). French artist and inventor. He invented the *diorama (1822) and the daguerreotype, the first practicable photographic process (made public in 1839).

Dahl, Johan Christian (1788–1857). Norwegian landscape painter, active mainly in Dresden, where he became a professor at the Academy in 1824. In spite of his long residency in Germany, he took his subjects mainly from his native country and began its tradition of landscape painting—he is often called the discoverer of the Norwegian landscape. He was a friend of *Friedrich and he shared with him a feeling for *Romantic grandeur in nature, although Dahl's work does not have the mystical element found in Friedrich. Dahl often returned to Norway, and his strong patriotic feelings were expressed not only in his paintings, but also in helping to found (1837) the National Gallery in Christiania (now Oslo), to which he presented his own impressive art collection.

Dahl, Michael (1659?–1743). Swedish portrait painter, active mainly in England. He settled permanently in London in 1689 (following an earlier stay in 1682–5) and became *Kneller's principal rival. His work is less dashing and fluent than Kneller's, but at his best he surpasses him in sincerity and humanity. There are several paintings by him or from his busy studio in the National Portrait Gallery in London.

Dalí, Salvador (1904–89). Spanish painter, sculptor, graphic artist, designer, filmmaker, and writer. After working in a variety of styles, influenced by *Cubism, *Futurism, and *Metaphysical Painting, he had turned to *Surrealism by 1929. In that year he had a sell-out exhibition in Paris; André *Breton wrote the catalogue preface, and this marked Dalí's official membership of the movement. His talent for self-publicity rapidly made him its most famous representative—its symbol in the mind of the general public. Throughout his life he cultivated eccentricity and exhibitionism, claiming that this was the source of his creative energy (one of his most outrageous stunts was delivering a lecture at the London International Surrealist Exhibition in 1936 dressed in a diving suit; he almost suffocated). He adopted the Surrealist idea of *automatism but transformed it into a more positive method that he named 'critical paranoia'. This involved elaborating on the images of his dreams and fantasies and substituting them for—or merging them with—the world of natural appearances. It resulted particularly in the ambiguous double images that play such a large part in his work, in which a form can be read, for example, as part of a landscape or part of a human body.

During the heyday of Surrealism in the 1930s Dalí produced several of the established 'icons' of the movement, using a meticulous academic technique that was contradicted by the unreal 'dream' space he depicted and by the strangely hallucinatory character of his imagery. He described his pictures as 'hand-painted dream photographs' and had certain favourite and recurring images, such as the human figure with half-open drawers protruding from it, burning giraffes, and watches bent and flowing as if made of melting wax (*The Persistence of Memory*, 1931, MoMA, New York). Dalí himself said that the melting watches—one of the most parodied images in 20th-century art—were inspired by eating a ripe Camembert cheese, but some commentators have sought deeper meanings, seeing them, for example, as expressing a fear of impotence. In the late 1930s Dalí made several visits to Italy and adopted a more traditional style; this together with his political views (he was a supporter of General Franco) led Breton to expel him from the Surrealist ranks. He moved to the USA in 1940 and remained there until 1948. During this time he devoted himself largely to self-publicity and making money (Breton coined the anagram 'Avida Dollars' for his name). From 1948 he lived mainly at Port Lligat in Spain, but he also spent much time in Paris and New York. Among his late paintings the best known are probably those on religious themes (*Crucifixion of St John of the Cross*, 1951, St Mungo Mus., Glasgow), although sexual subjects and pictures centring on his wife Gala were also continuing preoccupations. In old age he became one of the world's most famous recluses, generating rumours and occasional scandals to the end.

Apart from painting, Dalí's output included sculpture, book illustration, jewellery design, and work for the theatre. In collaboration with the director Luis Buñuel he also made the first Surrealist films—*Un chien andalou* (1929) and *L'Âge d'or* (1930)—and he contributed a dream sequence to Alfred Hitchcock's *Spellbound* (1945). He also wrote a novel, *Hidden Faces* (1944), and several volumes of flamboyant autobiography. Although he is undoubtedly one of the most famous artists of the 20th century, his status is controversial: many critics consider that he did little if anything of consequence after his classic Surrealist works of the 1930s. There is a museum devoted to Dalí's work in Figueras, his home town

in Spain, and another in St Petersburg, Florida.

Dalmau, Luis (active 1428–61). Spanish painter, first recorded in 1428 in Valencia, where he worked for Alfonso V of Aragon. In 1431 Alfonso sent him to Bruges to study tapestry weaving. After his return to Spain he settled in Barcelona, and his most important work, the *Virgin of the Councillors* (1445, Barcelona Mus.), was painted for the town hall there. Dalmau's visit to Flanders is the first recorded contact of a Spanish painter with the Netherlandish School, and this painting is very strongly influenced by Jan van *Eyck.

Dalou, Jules (1838–1902). French sculptor. Among the French sculptors of his generation Dalou ranks second only to *Rodin. His work was more conventional than Rodin's, sometimes using the heroic language and allegorical devices of *Baroque tradition, but it has a naturalistic warmth that is far removed from the chilliness of much statuary of the time. He had left-wing political views and after supporting the Commune (the short-lived revolutionary government of Paris in 1871) he spent the period 1871–9 in exile in London. On his return to Paris he began work on his best-known achievement, a huge bronze group of the *Triumph of the Republic*, eventually unveiled in 1899 (Place de la Nation, Paris). An even more ambitious work, a vast *Monument to Labour*, was left uncompleted at his death, but clay models for many of the figures are preserved in the Petit Palais, Paris. Dalou's other public statuary included the memorial to *Delacroix in the Luxembourg Gardens, Paris (1890), and he also produced smaller works, including portrait busts.

Dalziel Brothers. Firm of English *wood engravers founded in London in 1839 by **George Dalziel** (1815–1902) and **Edward Dalziel** (1817–1905). Two other brothers, **John** (1822–69) and **Thomas** (1823–1906), worked for the firm, which was the most prolific source of book illustrations in Victorian England, producing more than 50,000 images. *Leighton, *Millais, and *Tenniel were among the artists whose work they engraved. George and Edward collaborated on the book *The Brothers Dalziel: A Record of Fifty Years' Work . . . 1840–1890* (1901).

Danby, Francis (1793–1861). Irish-born painter, active in England. He worked mainly in Bristol and London, but between 1830 and 1838, owing to financial and marital problems, he lived in Paris and Switzerland. His early work was naturalistic, but in the 1820s he turned to melodramatic apocalyptic paintings, such as *The Delivery of Israel out of Egypt* (1825, Harris Mus. and AG, Preston), which were a direct challenge to John *Martin. It is for these that he is chiefly remembered, but his best works are now usually considered to be the romantic landscapes of his later years, with their mood of melancholy and solemn serenity (*Temple of Flora*, 1840, Tate, London). In 1847 he retired to Exmouth, embittered by his failure to achieve financial success or academic honours.

Dance, Nathaniel (1735–1811). English painter, primarily of portraits. He studied under *Hayman and spent the years 1754–65 in Rome, where he was much influenced by the sophisticated portrait style of Pompeo *Batoni. In 1768 he became a foundation member of the *Royal Academy, but on inheriting a fortune in 1776 he retired from professional practice. He became an MP in 1790 and in 1800 he was created a baronet and assumed the surname Dance-Holland. One of his best-known portraits is *Captain Cook* (1766, Nat. Maritime Mus., London). He was the son and brother of architects, both called **George Dance**.

Daniele da Volterra (Daniele Ricciarelli) (*c*.1509–66). Italian *Mannerist painter and sculptor, born in Volterra and perhaps trained in Siena under *Sodoma. In about 1536 he moved to Rome, where he became a friend of *Michelangelo and one of his most gifted and individual followers. Michelangelo helped to gain him commissions and (as with *Sebastiano del Piombo) supplied him with drawings to work from, but Daniele's finest picture owes little to the direct influence of the master. This is his fresco of the *Deposition* (*c*.1545) in the Cappella Orsini in S. Trinità dei Monti, a powerful and moving work, based compositionally on *Rosso Fiorentino's famous painting of the same subject in Volterra, but with an eloquent richness of its own. It was one of the most admired works of its generation in Rome and continued to be influential into the next century: *Domenichino (Hatton

Gal., Newcastle upon Tyne) was among the artists who copied it, and *Rubens was clearly inspired by it in his painting of the subject in Antwerp Cathedral. Daniele was present at Michelangelo's deathbed and his most famous work of sculpture is a bronze bust of him based on the death mask (casts are in the Casa Buonarroti, Florence; the Louvre, Paris; and elsewhere). Ironically, in view of his devotion to the master, Daniele is perhaps best remembered for painting draperies (1564–5) over the nude figures in Michelangelo's *Last Judgement*, a concession to Counter-Reformation prudery that earned him the nickname 'Il Braghettone' (the breeches-maker).

Danti, Vincenzo (1530–76). Italian sculptor, architect, and writer, born in Perugia and active mainly in Florence. His work reveals his admiration for *Michelangelo, whose funeral ceremonies in 1564 he helped to plan. Danti's style, however, is more elegant and much less powerful than the master's. His best-known works are (in Florence) the bronze group of the *Execution of the Baptist* over the south door of the Baptistery (finished 1571), and (in Perugia) the bronze figure of Pope Julius III outside the Cathedral (1555). In 1573 he was appointed Perugia's city architect and he helped found the city's Accademia del Disegno. He was the author of a treatise on proportion (1567), dedicated to the Duke Cosimo I de' *Medici, and he also wrote poetry.

Danube School. Term applied to a number of German and Austrian artists working in the early 16th century who were among the pioneers in depicting landscape (particularly the forests and hills of the Danube Valley) for its own sake (in drawings and prints as well as paintings). *Altdorfer, *Cranach the Elder (in his earlier work), and *Huber are the most important artists covered by the term. They worked independently of one another, so 'Danube School' (Ger. *Donauschule*) is a term of convenience rather than an indication of any group affiliation.

Daret, Jacques (*c*.1405–*c*.1468). Netherlandish painter. He was born in Tournai, where from 1428 to 1432 he was apprenticed along with Rogelet de la Pasture (assumed to be identical with Rogier van der *Weyden) to Robert Campin; the similarity of Daret's style to that of the *Master of Flémalle is one of the main reasons for thinking that Campin and this master are one and the same. Four panels survive from Daret's chief work, an altarpiece for the Abbey of St Vaast in Arras (1432–5), and one of these—the *Nativity* (Thyssen Mus., Madrid)—is obviously based on the Master of Flémalle's painting of the subject in Dijon (Mus. B.-A.). Two of the other three panels from the St Vaast Altarpiece are in Berlin (Gemäldegalerie), and the fourth is in Paris (Petit Palais). Daret's other work included tapestry *cartoons and manuscript *illuminations.

Darwin, Sir Robert ('Robin'). *See* ROYAL COLLEGE OF ART.

Daubigny, Charles-François (1817–78). French landscape painter, one of the earliest exponents of *plein-air painting in France. He came from a family of artists and was taught initially by his father **Edmé-François** (1789–1843), likewise a landscape painter; he also learnt a good deal by copying 17th-century Dutch pictures in the Louvre. Although he is considered a member of the *Barbizon School, he never actually lived in the locality, and his favourite subjects were river—rather than forest —scenes (he often painted from a specially fitted boat). His work, which is notable for the sensitivity with which he depicted the effects of light on trees and water, was an important influence on early *Impressionism. He was influential not only stylistically but also through the support and encouragement he gave to younger painters: as a member of the *Salon jury in 1868, he helped to get the work of several of the Impressionists shown, and it was he who introduced *Monet and *Pissarro to the dealer *Durand-Ruel, when all four of them had taken refuge in England during the Franco-Prussian War of 1870–1.

Daumier, Honoré (1808–79). French *caricaturist, painter, and sculptor. During his lifetime he was known chiefly as a political and social satirist, but since his death he has been increasingly recognized as a painter. In 1830, after learning the still fairly new process of *lithography, he began to contribute political cartoons to the newly launched anti-monarchist weekly *La Caricature*. He was an ardent Republican and in 1832 was

sentenced to six months' imprisonment for his attacks on King Louis Philippe, whom he represented as 'Gargantua swallowing bags of gold extorted from the people'. In 1835 the government prohibited political caricature and Daumier turned to social satire, mainly in *Le Charivari*, but at the time of the 1848 revolution, in which Louis Philippe was deposed, he returned to political subjects. He is said to have produced more than 4,000 lithographs, wishing each time that the one he had just made could be his last. His paintings were probably done for the most part fairly late in his career. He had examples accepted four times by the *Salon, but otherwise he never exhibited them and they remained practically unknown up to the time of an exhibition held at *Durand-Ruel's gallery in 1878, the year before his death. Most of them depict contemporary life and manners with satirical overtones, but he also did a number on literary and mythological themes (*Don Quixote and Sancho Panza*, c.1865, Courtauld Gal., London). His technique was remarkably broad and free. As a sculptor he specialized in caricature heads and figures, and these too are in a very spontaneous style. In particular he created the memorable figure of 'Ratapoil' ('skinned rat'), who embodied the sinister agents of the government of Louis Philippe. (A similar political type in his graphic art was 'Robert Macaire', who personified the unscrupulous profiteer and swindler.) As a caricaturist Daumier stands head and shoulders above all others of the 19th century. The essence of his satire lay in his power to interpret mental states in terms of physical absurdity, but in his directness of vision and lack of sentimentality he has affinities with the *Realism of *Courbet. Although he never made a commercial success of his art, he was appreciated by the discriminating, his friends and admirers including *Baudelaire, *Degas, *Delacroix, and *Forain. In his final years he was almost blind and was saved from destitution by *Corot.

Davey, Grenville. *See* NEW BRITISH SCULPTURE.

David, Gerard (d. 1523). Netherlandish painter. He was born at Oudewater, near Gouda, but he spent almost all his career in Bruges; he had settled there by 1484, when he became a member of the painters' guild, and after the death of *Memlinc in 1494 he became the city's leading painter. At this time the economic importance of Bruges was declining, but it still maintained its prestige as a centre of art and David played an important role in the flourishing export trade in paintings that it developed in the first quarter of the 16th century. Late in his career he probably also ran a workshop in Antwerp (he is thought to be the 'Meester Gheraert van Brugghe' who became a master in the painters' guild there in 1515). His work—extremely accomplished, but conservative and usually rather bland—was very popular and his stately compositions were copied again and again. Among his followers were *Benson and *Ysenbrandt, who carried on his tradition until the middle of the 16th century. Almost all his work was on traditional religious themes, but for Bruges town hall he painted a pair of pictures on an obscure secular legend, *The Judgement of Cambyses* (1498, Groeningemuseum, Bruges), a gory subject (concerning the trial and execution of an unjust judge) to which his reflective style was not ideally suited. They were no doubt intended to rival the judgement paintings by Rogier van der *Weyden and Dirk *Bouts for the town halls of Brussels and Louvain.

David, Jacques-Louis (1748–1825). French *history painter and portraitist. He was the greatest of *Neoclassical painters and one of the most influential European artists of his time. On the advice of the aged *Boucher, a distant relative, he was apprenticed to *Vien in 1766 and in the same year he became a student at the Académie Royale. In 1774 he won the *Prix de Rome at the fifth attempt, and the following year he went to Italy with Vien, who had been appointed director of the French Academy in Rome. David remained in Italy until 1780 and during this period he purged his work of *Rococo mannerisms and developed a heroic style heavily influenced by his study of *antique sculpture and his admiration for *Poussin and *Raphael. After his return to Paris he quickly rose to be the leading painter of the day. His success depended not only on the grandeur and dignity of his work, but also on its moral seriousness, which was in keeping with the spirit of the time. The Rococo style was associated with the frivolity of court life, and as the royal family and the aristocracy became increasingly unpopular, David's sternly Neoclassical paintings could be seen as expressions of the desire for social as well as aesthetic change. The work that more than any other established his pre-eminence was the *Oath of the Horatii* (1785, Louvre, Paris), which shows three ancient Roman brothers dedicating their lives to the state as they prepare to face three enemy champions in mortal combat. It has been described as 'an image of extraordinary lucidity and visual punch ... a clarion call to civic virtue and patriotism' (Hugh Honour, *Neo-Classicism*, 1968), and its ideas of austerity, stoical self-sacrifice, and devotion to duty were repeated in two other celebrated masterpieces, the *Death of Socrates* (1787, Met. Mus., New York) and the *Lictors Bringing Brutus the Bodies of his Sons* (1789, Louvre). These three pictures were acclaimed by critics and public alike and they mark the summit of Neoclassical painting.

After the Revolution in 1789, with which he was entirely in sympathy, David became actively involved in politics (he served on various committees and voted for the execution of Louis XVI) and he used his art directly as propaganda. He made designs for Revolutionary festivals, and his paintings of the time included three pictures of 'martyrs of the Revolution', in which he moved portraiture into the domain of universal tragedy. They were: the *Death of Lepelletier* (1793, destroyed, but known from an engraving), the *Death of Marat* (1793, Mus. Royaux, Brussels), and the *Death of Bara* (1794, Mus. Calvet, Avignon; unfinished). After the fall of his friend Robespierre (1794), however, David was imprisoned for having supported him, narrowly escaping the guillotine; he was released after pleas from his wife, who had previously divorced him because of his Revolutionary sympathies (she was a royalist). They were remarried in 1796, and David's *Intervention of the Sabine Women* (1794–9, Louvre), begun while he was in prison, is said to have been painted to honour her, its theme being one of love prevailing over conflict. It was also interpreted at the time, however, as a plea for reconciliation in the civil strife that France suffered after the Revolution and it was the work that re-established David's fortunes. By the time it was finished, Napoleon had restored order to France. David transferred his allegiance to him ('Bonaparte is my hero', he said after first meeting him in 1798) and became one of the leading artists in depicting his life and legend. Napoleon, in turn, showered David with honours and after he was crowned emperor in 1804 gave him the title of first painter (although he eventually came to prefer the work of *Gros, David's former pupil).

David's commissions from Napoleon included various portraits and a projected series of four huge pictures of events from his life, of which only two were produced: the *Coronation of Napoleon* (1805–7, Louvre) and the *Presentation of the Eagle Standards* (1808–10, Versailles). These two pictures show a change in technique and feeling from his earlier work, severe compositions and cold colours giving way to a new feeling for pageantry and an almost *Romantic warmth and ardour (he hated the Romantic movement, but he influenced it greatly). After the final defeat of Napoleon in 1815, David (who had signed a declaration of loyalty to the emperor) left France and settled in Brussels in 1816. He was now approaching 70 and the paintings from his final decade in exile have generally been regarded as an undistinguished coda to his life, his work weakening as the possibility of exerting a moral and social influence receded. However, the sensuous qualities of his late mythological paintings are now winning appreciation, and he continued to be an outstanding portraitist, although he never surpassed such earlier achievements as the great *Napoleon Crossing the Alps* (1800, KH Mus., Vienna, one of four versions) or the coolly erotic *Madame Récamier* (1800, Louvre). David was the most important teacher of his day and he was loyally supported by his many former pupils (notably Gros, who took over the master's studio in Paris and tried to bring about his return to France, even though David was content in Brussels). His other pupils included *Gérard, *Girodet, and *Ingres, and he also had prominent followers among artists who did not actually study with him, notably *Guérin. These artists, sometimes referred to as the 'School of David', formed the most prestigious group of painters in Europe in the early 19th century; David was perhaps the last great painter to create such a following.

David, Pierre-Jean (1788–1856). French sculptor, known after his birthplace as

David d'Angers. He won the *Prix de Rome in 1811 and from then until 1815 lived in Italy, where he met and admired *Ingres and was also influenced by *Canova and *Thorvaldsen. However, *Neoclassical influence was tempered by a strong inclination towards naturalism, and his contemporaries considered him a *Romantic. His most prestigious commission was the high-relief pedimental sculpture of the Pantheon in Paris, which shows an allegorical figure of France distributing wreaths to great Frenchmen (1830–7), but his best works are to be found among his busts and medallions of famous men. He left a large collection of them to the Musée des Beaux-Arts in his native city.

Davie, Alan (1920–). British painter, graphic artist, poet, musician, silversmith, and jeweller. After service in the army and a short period as a professional jazz musician (he plays several instruments), he travelled in Europe, 1948–9. This gave him the chance to see works by Jackson *Pollock and other American painters in Peggy *Guggenheim's gallery in Venice, and he was one of the first British artists to be affected by *Abstract Expressionism. Other influences on his eclectic but extremely personal style are African sculpture and Zen Buddhism. His work is full of images suggestive of magic or mythology (some based on ancient forms, some of his own invention) and he uses these as themes around which—like a jazz musician—he spontaneously develops variations in exuberant colour and brushwork. From the 1960s he developed an international reputation.

Davies, Arthur Bowen (1862–1928). American painter, printmaker, and tapestry designer. During his lifetime he had a high reputation as an artist, but he is now remembered mainly for his role in promoting avant-garde art (even though his own work was fairly conservative). He was a member of The *Eight and president of the Association of American Painters and Sculptors that was created to organize the *Armory Show; his enthusiasm for the project was largely responsible for the scope of the show and the force of its impact. His own work was varied and embraced remarkably diverse influences (he was a man of wide culture and unlike the other members of The Eight he did not specialize in modern urban scenes). In his early career he showed an enthusiasm for the *Pre-Raphaelites, *Whistler, and *Puvis de Chavannes, and specialized in idyllic landscapes inhabited by dreamlike, visionary figures of nude women or mythical animals (*Unicorns*, 1906, Met. Mus., New York). After the Armory Show his work displayed superficial *Cubist influence, but in the 1920s he returned to a more traditional style.

Davis, Stuart (1894–1964). American painter. He grew up in an artistic environment, for his father was art director of the *Philadelphia Press*, a newspaper that had employed *Glackens, *Luks, *Shinn, and *Sloan—the four artists who were to form the nucleus of The *Eight—and his mother, Helen Stuart Foulke, was a sculptor. In 1910–13 he studied with Robert *Henri in New York, and in 1913 he was one of the youngest exhibitors in the *Armory Show, which made an overwhelming impact on him. After this he began experimenting with a variety of modern idioms and in the 1920s he achieved a sophisticated grasp of *Cubism, but it was only after spending a year in Paris in 1928–9 that he forged a distinctive style. Using motifs from the characteristic environment of American life, he rearranged them into flat poster-like patterns with precise outlines and sharply contrasting colours (*House and Street*, 1931, Whitney Mus., New York). In this way he became the only major artist to treat the subject matter of the *American Scene painters—extraordinarily popular at the time—in avant-garde terms: he was both distinctly American and distinctively modern—a rare combination that won him wide admiration. Later his work became more purely abstract, although he often introduced lettering or suggestions of advertisements etc. into his bold patterns (*Owh! in San Pao*, 1951, Whitney Mus.). The zest and dynamism of such works reflect his interest in jazz.

Davis is generally regarded as the most important American painter to come to maturity between the two world wars and the outstanding American artist to work in a Cubist idiom. He made witty and original use of it and created a distinctive American style, for however abstract his work became he always claimed that every image he used had its source in observed reality: 'I paint what I see in America, in other words I paint the American Scene.' He was an articulate defender of modern art, a major influence on many younger artists, including his friends *Gorky and *de Kooning, and a precursor of *Pop art, forming an important link between the pioneering avant-garde artists of the Armory Show generation and the triumphant New York art scene of the post-war years.

Deacon, Richard. *See* NEW BRITISH SCULPTURE.

Dean, Graham. *See* SUPERREALISM.

De Andrea, John (1941–). American *Superrealist sculptor. As with Duane *Hanson, his figures are made of fibreglass and are realistic to the last detail, but De Andrea specializes in nude figures and his models are usually young and attractive, if rather vapid (*Model in Repose*, 1981, Scottish NG of Modern Art, Edinburgh).

decorative arts. Term generally used more or less synonymously with *applied art but which can also embrace objects made purely for decoration, without any practical purpose.

Degas, Edgar (1834–1917). French painter, draughtsman, printmaker, and sculptor. He was the son of a wealthy art-loving banker and was initially trained for the law. In 1854, however, he began studying with Louis Lamothe (1822–69), a pupil of *Ingres, who handed on the master's tradition of draughtsmanship. Degas also attended the École des *Beaux-Arts, but the most important part of his artistic education was gained through assiduous study of the Old Masters, both in the Louvre and in Italy, where he lived 1856–9 (he had Italian relatives and made several subsequent visits to the country). Most of his early works were portraits or history paintings on classical themes (*Young Spartans Exercising*, c.1860, NG, London), but in 1862 he met *Manet (while copying a *Velázquez in the Louvre) and this helped to bring about a decisive change of direction in his art. Manet introduced him to the circle of the young *Impressionists and during the next few years he abandoned historical pictures and turned to contemporary subjects; they included scenes of the ballet and theatre, café interiors, laundresses at work, and women bathing—no other painter of his time portrayed such a rich variety of themes from contemporary urban society. Degas participated in seven out of the eight Impressionist exhibitions and he figures prominently in all accounts of the movement. However, he was Impressionist only in certain restricted aspects of his work and like Manet (who also came from an upper middle-class background) he stood somewhat aloof from the rest of the group. He had little interest in landscape and therefore did not share the Impressionist concern for rendering the effects of changing light and atmosphere (his favourite outdoor subject was horse racing, but he painted the pictures in the studio and usually left the setting generalized). As with the other Impressionists, he depicted the world around him in a fresh and informal way, and liked to give the suggestion of spontaneous and unplanned scenes, often using unfamiliar viewpoints or figures cut off as if in a snapshot (he was very interested in photography). However, the appearance of spontaneity was an appearance only; in reality his pictures were carefully composed. 'Even when working from nature, one has to compose', he said, and 'No art was ever less spontaneous than mine.'

Up to 1874, because of his prosperous background, Degas never had any need to sell his work, but in that year his father died leaving unexpected debts, which Degas largely paid off himself, selling his house and his picture collection to do so (going far beyond what was legally required of him). Unlike the other Impressionists, however, he never had any difficulty marketing his work (his formidable skill as a draughtsman made him more immediately acceptable to most buyers) and by 1880 he had overcome his financial crisis and was a well-established and prosperous figure in the art world. After the final Impressionist exhibition in 1886 he stopped showing his work in public, selling it selectively through a number of dealers. By this time he had turned 50 and was having serious trouble with his eyesight. Because of this he turned increasingly from oils to pastel, in which he was physically closer to the surface on which he was working; the figures in his later pictures are often shown in intimate close-up, as if he is peering at them from a

very near viewpoint. His failing eyesight and his use of pastel led to a broadening and blurring of form and the use of richer colour, with the somewhat ironic result that in the 1890s—by which time the Impressionist group had broken up—his work came closer in style to mainstream Impressionism than it had ever been before. He experimented boldly with pastels, as he did with other techniques; he sometimes mixed different kinds of paints in the same picture, for example, and he sometimes steamed his pastels, so he could manipulate the colours more fluidly. Degas also made prints in various techniques, and from the late 1860s he produced wax sculptures; as his sight failed, this tactile medium became of more importance to him. Most of his sculptures were small, private works, but a few were more ambitious, including the only one he exhibited in his lifetime, the famous *Little Fourteen-Year-Old Dancer*, dressed in a real tutu, which was shown at the fifth Impressionist exhibition in 1881 (like his other sculptures, it was cast in bronze after his death; one cast is in Tate Modern, London).

After the turn of the century Degas could produce little work and in his final years he was virtually blind. Contrary to what is sometimes said, he was not a misanthrope (he had numerous friends and was good with children, and it was only in old age, when his eyesight made life difficult for him, that he became reclusive and cantankerous). However, he was a formidable personality, feared for his biting wit, and his complete devotion to his art made him seem cold and aloof to many people (as far as is known he never had any kind of romantic or sexual involvement). Among his fellow artists, though, his genius compelled universal respect (*Renoir ranked him above *Rodin as a sculptor, and in 1883 Camille *Pissarro described him as 'certainly the greatest artist of our epoch'). By the time of his death he was almost a national monument and his reputation as one of the giants of 19th-century art has endured undimmed.

degenerate art. A term coined in Germany in the 1930s to discredit all contemporary art that did not correspond to the ideology of the Nazi party. Such art, which included most avant-garde work, was systematically defamed and suppressed in Germany throughout the period when the Nazis ruled the country, 1933–45. Adolf Hitler and Alfred Rosenberg (the chief theoretical spokesman of Nazism) linked art with political doctrines and racial theories, attacking modern art as 'political and cultural anarchy'. Nazi-approved art was thoroughly traditional in concept and technique, and it favoured themes (often militaristic) that glorified Hitler and his ideals of Aryan supremacy. Hitler made his first speech against 'degenerate art' (Ger., *entartete Kunst*) at Nuremberg in 1934, and a series of exhibitions designed to ridicule modern art culminated in an infamous show (also called 'Entartete Kunst') that opened in Munich in 1937 and then went on tour round Germany. The works on display were confiscated from German museums and were mocked by being shown alongside pictures done by inmates of lunatic asylums. The artists represented were mainly German (by birth or residence), but a few foreigners were included. Among the total of over a hundred were many distinguished figures and several of the giants of 20th-century art: *Beckmann, *Ernst, *Grosz, *Kirchner, *Klee, *Kokoschka, *Marc, *Mondrian, *Picasso (the inclusion of Marc caused some embarrassment, for he had been killed in action fighting for Germany—as a volunteer—in the First World War). As a propaganda exercise the exhibition was a huge success, more than two million people visiting it in Munich alone. Living German artists whose work was declared degenerate were forbidden to exhibit or even to work, and people who sympathized with modern art were deprived of their posts in museums and teaching posts. Some of the confiscated works were sold at auction, Nazi officials helped themselves to others, and the 'unsaleable stock' is said to have been burnt in Berlin.

Deineka, Alexander. *See* SOCIALIST REALISM.

de Kooning, Willem (1904–97). Dutch-born painter (and latterly sculptor) who became an American citizen in 1961, one of the major figures of *Abstract Expressionism. He went to America as a stowaway in 1926 and the following year settled in New York. His early work was conservative, but in 1929 he met Arshile *Gorky, who became one of his closest friends and intro-

duced him to avant-garde circles. During the 1930s and 1940s he experimented vigorously and by the time of his first one-man show in 1948 (at the Egan Gallery, New York) he was painting in an extremely energetic abstract style (often in black and white) close to that of Jackson *Pollock. The exhibition established his reputation (although prosperity was still some years away) and after it he was generally regarded as sharing with Pollock the unofficial leadership of the Abstract Expressionist group. Unlike Pollock, de Kooning usually retained some suggestion of figuration in his work, and in 1953 he caused a sensation when his *Women* series (*Women nos I–VI*) was exhibited at his third one-man show, at the Sidney *Janis gallery. *Woman I* (1950–2, MoMA, New York), with its grotesque leer and frenzied brushwork, shocked the public and dismayed those critics who believed in a rigorously abstract art. One of these was Clement *Greenberg, but New York's other most influential critic of avant-garde art—Harold *Rosenberg—supported de Kooning. *Woman I* became one of the most reproduced paintings in the USA and de Kooning was enormously influential on young painters at this time. By the end of the 1950s, however, he was beginning to be regarded as an elder statesman whose best days as a creative force were past. From the 1960s he had honours heaped on him. His paintings continued to mix abstract and semi-figurative work and in 1969 he began making sculpture—figures modelled in clay and later cast in bronze. He continued working well into his eighties, until he was incapacitated by Alzheimer's disease.

His wife, **Elaine de Kooning** (1919–89), was also a painter, notably of *Expressionist portraits, and a writer on art. The couple married in 1943, separated amicably in 1957, and reunited in 1975. A collection of her writings, *The Spirit of Abstract Expressionism*, was published in 1994.

Delacroix, Eugène (1798–1863). French painter, draughtsman, and lithographer. He was one of the towering figures of the *Romantic movement and one of the last major artists to devote a large part of his career to mural painting in the heroic tradition. Lorenz Eitner (*An Outline of 19th Century European Painting*, 1987) describes him as 'the last great European painter to use the repertory of humanistic art with conviction and originality. In his hands, antique myth and medieval history, Golgotha and the Barricade, Faust and Hamlet, Scott and Byron, tiger and Odalisque yielded images of equal power.' He was the son of a diplomat, Charles Delacroix, who at the time of his son's birth was ambassador in The Hague, but it has been suggested that his natural father was the great statesman Talleyrand, a friend of the family. His mother, Victoire Oeben, was the daughter of Jean-François Oeben, one of the most distinguished furniture makers of his day. Delacroix had a good education and grew up with a love of literature and music as well as art. In 1815 he began studying with Pierre-Narcisse *Guérin, who had earlier taught *Géricault (whose work greatly influenced Delacroix), and the following year he enrolled at the École des *Beaux-Arts. His real artistic education, however, was gained by copying Old Masters in the *Louvre, where he delighted particularly in *Rubens and the 16th-century Venetian painters. Throughout his life he remained a keen and perceptive student of his predecessors, and Rubens—with his richness of imagination, warmth of colour, and enormous energy—was a constant source of inspiration. In 1822 his career was brilliantly launched when his first submission to the *Salon, the *Barque of Dante* (Louvre, Paris), a melodramatic scene from Dante's *Inferno*, was the talking point of the exhibition and was bought by the state. Two years later he had another success at the Salon with the *Massacre at Chios* (Louvre), inspired by a Turkish atrocity in the recent Greek War of Independence. It aroused much hostile criticism (*Gros, who had admired the *Barque of Dante*, called it 'the massacre of painting'), but it was awarded a gold medal and once again was bought by the state (with Talleyrand perhaps pulling strings in the background).

The success of the *Massacre at Chios* funded a trip to England in May–August 1825 (Delacroix had earlier met *Bonington and admired *Constable's *Hay Wain*, which had been exhibited to great acclaim in the 1824 Salon). After this visit, English literature became an important source of inspiration in his work for several years: his next major Salon success, for example, the violent and erotic *Death of Sardanapalus* (1827, Louvre), was based on a play by Byron. He was also influenced by contemporary English painting; his portrait of his friend Louis-Auguste Schwiter (1826–30, NG, London) is almost like an act of homage to *Lawrence, of whom he had a high opinion personally as well as professionally. Another major source of imagery in Delacroix's work came from North Africa. In 1832 he visited Spain, Morocco, and Algeria in the entourage of the Comte de Mornay (who headed a diplomatic mission to the Sultan of Morocco), and acquired a rich fund of exotic visual imagery that he exploited for the rest of his life, lion hunting becoming one of his favourite themes (*Lion Hunt*, 1861, Art Inst. of Chicago). In spite of his love of such quintessentially Romantic subjects and his open enmity with *Ingres, who was upheld as the great champion of the classical tradition, Delacroix always regarded himself as part of this tradition, and for his large works he followed the time-honoured course of making numerous preparatory drawings. Although his work often gives the feeling of great spontaneity, he thought deeply about all aspects of his art and craft.

In 1833 Delacroix received a commission to decorate the Salon du Roi in the Palais Bourbon (now the Assemblée Nationale), Paris, and from this point much of his career was devoted to large-scale wall and ceiling painting. He finished the work in the Salon du Roi in 1837 and followed this with decorations in the library of the same building (1838–47). His other major decorative schemes (all in Paris) include those in the Library of the Luxembourg Palace (1841–6), the Galerie d'Apollon in the Louvre (1850), and the Chapelle des Anges of the church of St Sulpice (1853–61), with its celebrated scenes of *Jacob and the Angel* and *Heliodorus Expelled from the Temple*. All these works are in oils (he only once experimented with fresco). In addition to these huge public undertakings, Delacroix continued to produce a wide range of smaller paintings, and he also made lithographs, the best known of which are his illustrations to Goethe's *Faust* (1828) and Shakespeare's *Hamlet* (1843). He was awarded many honours for his work, and his charm, intelligence, and dashing looks meant that he was in demand by fashionable society. However, he was fairly solitary by nature (he never married) and had only a few close friends, including another archetypal Romantic genius, Chopin, of whom he painted a portrait (1838, Louvre) and whom he described as 'the truest artist I have ever met' (he had a piano installed in his studio so the great man could play there). Although he carefully trained the assistants he used on his decorative commissions, he otherwise had few pupils, and none of them attained any independent distinction. Nevertheless, he had enormous influence on a wide range of artists, particularly through his vibrant and uninhibited use of colour. He was 'the supreme colourist of the first half of the nineteenth century' (Lee Johnson, *Delacroix*, 1963), and the artists who were most clearly influenced by this aspect of his work include *Monet, *Renoir, and *Seurat. Among those who copied his work and valued its liberating effect on the imagination were *Cézanne, *Degas, van *Gogh, and *Redon, and among the professed admirers depicted in *Fantin-Latour's *Homage to Delacroix* (1864, Mus. d'Orsay, Paris) are *Baudelaire, *Manet, and *Whistler.

Delacroix's output was enormous. After his death his executors found more than 9,000 separate works in his studio, including several hundred paintings and more than 6,000 drawings. He drew every day, like a musician practising scales, and he prided himself on the speed at which he worked, declaring 'If you are not skilful enough to sketch a man falling out of a window during the time it takes him to get from the fifth storey to the ground, then you will never be able to produce monumental work.' Delacroix also left behind a substantial literary legacy, for few other great painters have written so copiously or so interestingly about art. He was a voluminous letter writer and kept a journal from 1822 to 1824 and again from 1847 until his death—a wonderfully rich source of information and opinion on his life and times. His studio in Paris is now a museum devoted to his life and work, but the Louvre has the finest collection of his paintings.

Delaroche, Paul (1797–1856). French painter, one of the leading pupils of *Gros. He achieved European fame with his melodramatic, Hollywoodesque history scenes, engravings of which hung in thousands of homes. Often he chose subjects from English history, as with three of his most famous works, *Cromwell Gazing at the Body of Charles I* (1831, Mus. B.-A., Nîmes), *The Princes in the Tower* (1831, Louvre, Paris; reduced replica in Wallace Coll., London), and the *Execution of Lady Jane Grey* (1833, NG, London). They are *Romantic in flavour, but academically impeccable in their draughtsmanship and detailing. After a period when such pictures were totally out of favour, his work is once again being treated seriously. Delaroche also painted religious works and portraits, and he was a highly respected teacher, his pupils including *Couture, *Gérôme, and *Millet. In 1835 he married the daughter of Horace *Vernet; her early death in 1845 cast a pall over his final years.

Delaunay, Robert (1885–1941). French painter. Initially he painted in an *Impressionist style, but in 1906 he began the experiments with the abstract qualities of colour that were to provide the central theme of his career. His starting point was *Neo-Impressionism, but instead of using *Seurat's pointillist technique he investigated the interaction of large areas of contrasting colours. He was particularly interested in the interconnections between colour and movement. By 1910 he was making an individual contribution to *Cubism, combining its fragmented forms with vibrant colours (rather than the muted browns and greys typical of *Braque and *Picasso at this time) and depicting the dynamism of city life rather than the standard Cubist repertoire of still life and so on. In particular he did a memorable series of paintings of the Eiffel Tower, in which the huge monument seems to be unleashing powerful bursts of energy (*Eiffel Tower*, 1910, Guggenheim Mus., New York). By 1912 he was painting completely abstract pictures (the first French artist to do so). *Apollinaire gave the name *Orphism to Delaunay's work of this period because of its analogies with the abstract art of music. In 1913 he had a one-man show at the *Sturm Gallery in Berlin, and his work was a major influence on German *Expressionists such as *Klee, *Macke, and *Marc; it also powerfully affected the *Futurists in Italy and the American *Synchromists. Delaunay was notoriously competitive and fully aware of the importance of his work; at about this time he drew up a list of all the artists, no matter how minor, he thought he had influenced. However, the period when he was a key figure in modern art was fairly brief; he lived in Spain and Portugal during the First World War and after his return to Paris in 1920 his work lost its inspirational quality and became rather repetitive. His home became a meeting place for *Dada artists, but Delaunay's own paintings continued to be related to colour theories. His last major works were two large murals (destroyed) for pavilions in the Paris World Fair of 1937.

Delaunay-Terk, Sonia (1885–1979). Russian painter and textile designer, active in Paris, the wife of Robert *Delaunay. She settled in Paris in 1905, married Delaunay in 1910 (after a short-lived marriage of convenience to Wilhelm *Uhde) and became associated with him in the development of *Orphism. During the 1920s she worked mainly as a designer of hand-printed fabrics and tapestries; she made a strong impact on the world of international fashion, designing creations for such famous women as Nancy Cunard and Gloria Swanson. The Depression affected her business, however, and in the 1930s she returned primarily to painting and became a member of the *Abstraction-Création association. After the death of her husband in 1941 she continued to work as a painter and designer.

Delvaux, Paul (1897–1994). Belgian painter. After working in *Neo-Impressionist and *Expressionist manners, he discovered *Surrealism in 1934 and became an instant convert, destroying much of his earlier work. He was never formally a member of the movement, and was not in sympathy with its political aims, but he became one of the foremost upholders of its tradition. Most of his paintings show nude or semi-nude women in incongruous settings. The women are always of the same type—beautiful, statuesque, unattainable dream figures, lost in thought or reverie or even in a state of suspended animation. These dream beauties are often placed in elaborate architectural settings, reflecting both de *Chirico's strange perspectives and Delvaux's interest in the buildings of ancient Rome (he visited Italy in 1938 and 1939). Sometimes he included skeletons in his pictures (influenced by *Ensor) and trains were another recurrent motif. A large retrospective of Delvaux's work was held at the Palais des Beaux-Arts, Brussels, in 1944, and this marked the beginning of his international reputation.

De Maria, Walter (1935–). American sculptor and experimental artist. He was one of the earliest exponents of *Minimal art, producing examples of the type c.1960, before the term was current, and he was also a pioneer of *Land art. Some of his work can also be regarded as *Conceptual art, as for example *Mile Long Drawing* of 1968, two parallel chalk lines 12 ft (3.5 m) apart in the Mojave Desert.

De Morgan, Evelyn (1855–1919). British painter, born Evelyn Pickering; in 1887 she married **William De Morgan** (1839–1917), famous as a designer of pottery, tiles, and ceramics, but also a painter himself (late in life he also became a successful novelist). She specialized in literary subjects, done in a style owing much to the *Pre-Raphaelites and to such *Renaissance artists as *Botticelli (she and her husband spent each winter in Italy for the sake of his health). At the end of her career she painted several allegories relating to the First World War, exhibiting them to raise money for the Red Cross.

Demuth, Charles (1883–1935). American painter and illustrator, a pioneer of modern art in his country. He visited Europe in 1904, 1907–8, and 1912–14, staying mainly in Paris, and during the last of these visits he became seriously interested in avant-garde art, particularly *Cubism. From about 1916 its influence is evident in his paintings of architectural subjects, with which he became one of the leading exponents of *Precisionism. His most personal paintings are what he called 'poster portraits' (pictures composed of words and objects associated with the person 'represented'). The most famous example is *I Saw the Figure Five in Gold* (1928, Met. Mus., New York), a tribute to the poet William Carlos Williams and named after one of his poems. Demuth was lame from childhood and in the last decade of his life was debilitated by diabetes. Often he worked on a small scale in watercolour, rather than in more physically demanding media. The fastidious taste and concentrated energy of his work are suggested by his comment: 'John *Marin [another great American watercolourist] and I drew our inspiration from the same source, French modernism. He brought his up in buckets and spilt much along the way.

I dipped mine out with a teaspoon, but I never spilled a drop.'

Denis, Maurice (1870–1943). French painter, designer, lithographer, illustrator, and writer on art theory. Early in his career he was a *Symbolist and a member of the *Nabis. He was the chief theorist of the group and one of his articles, 'Definition of Neo-Traditionalism' (1890), contains a pronouncement that has become famous as an anticipation of the underlying principle of much modern—especially abstract—art: 'Remember that a picture—before being a war horse or a nude woman or an anecdote —is essentially a flat surface covered with colours assembled in a certain order.' Denis's early work, strongly influenced by *Gauguin, did indeed place great emphasis on flat patterning, but he did not intend to encourage non-representational art, for he was also very much concerned with subject matter; he was a devout Catholic and wanted to bring about a revival of religious painting. He carried out numerous church commissions, typically in a style that was tender and mild, with pale colours and relaxed lines, and he also did a good deal of secular decorative work. His most famous single picture is probably *Homage to Cézanne* (1900, Mus. d'Orsay, Paris) showing Denis himself and a number of *Cézanne's other admirers, including *Bonnard, *Redon, *Sérusier, and *Vuillard, gathered round a still life by the master. His best paintings were done early in his career; after about 1900 they became more classical in style (influenced by visits to Italy) and increasingly bland.

Derain, André (1880–1954). French painter, printmaker, theatrical designer, and sculptor. In the first two decades of the 20th century he was near the centre of avant-garde developments in Paris: he was one of the creators of *Fauvism, an early adherent of *Cubism, and one of the first to 'discover' *primitive art. However, in the 1920s he moved away from his pre-war experimentation to a much more conservative style reflecting his admiration for the Old Masters. The works he painted in this manner (including landscapes, portraits, still lifes, and nudes) made him wealthy and famous (he exhibited widely abroad), but they dismayed many supporters of avant-garde art. He polarized opinion so

much that in January 1931 the periodical *Les Chroniques du jour* published a feature entitled 'André Derain: Pour ou Contre'. Among those quoted in this was Jacques-Émile *Blanche, who—even though he was a fairly conservative painter himself—wrote: 'Youth has departed: what remains is a highly cerebral and rather mechanical art.' The differences of opinion he had provoked in his life continued after Derain's death. Many critics think that his work after the First World War was essentially a long anticlimax, but some admirers have thought extraordinarily highly of him, notably *Giacometti, who wrote in 1957: 'Derain excites me more, has given me more and taught me more than any painter since *Cézanne; to me he is the most audacious of them all.' Two years later the American critic John Canaday (1907–85) summed up the situation in his book *Mainstreams of Modern Art*: 'His detractors think of him as a parasite on both the past and the present, but...some critics award Derain unique status as the only twentieth-century painter to achieve an individual compound of the great tradition of French culture as a whole with the spirit of his own time...This opinion is particularly held in France—where, of course, it is most legitimate.'

desco da parto (It. 'tray of childbirth'). A type of circular or twelve-sided painted wooden tray used in medieval and *Renaissance Italy to present small gifts, sweetmeats, and wine to a mother after childbirth. *Deschi da parto* were often decorated on both sides, typically with an appropriate narrative or symbolic scene on one side and a coat of arms or family device on the other. Many of them were produced in workshops specializing in *cassoni, although they were occasionally commissioned from distinguished artists. One of the best surviving examples of a *desco da parto* is that marking the birth of Lorenzo de' *Medici in 1449 (Met. Mus., New York); it shows the *Triumph of Fame* and was painted by *Masaccio's brother Lo Scheggia.

Desiderio da Settignano (c.1430–64). Florentine sculptor. He came from Settignano, near Florence, a village renowned for its stonecutters. Like most of his contemporaries he formed his style on *Donatello's work of the 1430s. He learnt from him the practice of carving in very low *relief, and the lively, thick-set figures of children on the master's *Singing Gallery* for Florence Cathedral (1433–9) provided models for Desiderio's various reliefs of the *Madonna and Child*. Desiderio's artistic personality, however, was more delicate than Donatello's, and for refinement of handling he is unsurpassed by any Italian sculptor of his period, as is seen particularly in his portrait busts of women, good examples of which are in Florence (Bargello) and Washington (NG). He died young and his only important public work was the tomb of the Florentine humanist and statesman Gregorio Marsuppini (d.1453) in S. Croce. This is architecturally dependent on the tomb of Leonardo Bruni by Bernardino *Rossellino (possibly Desiderio's teacher), executed for the same church about ten years earlier, but is sculpturally richer and more animated.

Despiau, Charles (1874–1946). French sculptor and illustrator. He was one of *Rodin's assistants from 1907 to 1914, after which he turned from his master's intense, vigorous style to a more static, generalized manner in the vein associated with *Maillol. His best-known works are his portrait busts, with their intimate delineation of character (*Head of Madame Derain*, 1922, Philips Coll., Washington). He also made several monuments. In the 1920s and 1930s his reputation stood very high in France, but at the end of his life he was ostracized because of his friendship with the Nazi sculptor Arno Breker (1900–91); they had known each other since before the war and in 1942 Despiau attended an exhibition of the German's work in occupied Paris.

Desportes, Alexandre-François (1661–1743). French painter, mainly of animal and still-life subjects. In his early career he worked much as a portraitist, notably in 1695–6 at the court of Jan Sobieski (John III) in Poland, but on his return to France he took up subjects related to the hunt, especially pictures of dogs with dead game. He became a leading specialist in his field, rivalled only by *Oudry, and his patrons included Louis XIV, Louis XV, and a host of aristocrats (he was also appreciated in England, which he visited in 1712). Although he continued the lavish Flemish tradition exemplified by *Snyders, Desportes was among the first artists of the 18th century to make landscape studies from nature for

his backgrounds—a practice for which he was considered eccentric. His work is well represented in the Louvre (which has his handsome *Self-Portrait as a Huntsman*, 1699) and in the Wallace Collection, London.

Detroy. *See* TROY.

Deutsch, Niklaus Manuel (*c*.1484–1530). Swiss painter, draughtsman, designer, writer, and politician, active mainly in his native Berne. Deutsch was one of the outstanding Swiss artists of his period, but much of his energy was expended in other activities. He fought as a mercenary in Italy in 1516 and 1522 and he took an active part in the political and religious affairs of Berne, serving on the town council for many years; he was a passionate supporter of the Reformation, writing satirical poems against the pope, whom he equated with Antichrist. His paintings are related to *Baldung and *Grünewald in their love of the grotesque (*Temptation of St Anthony*, 1520, Kunstmuseum, Berne). Deutsch also made designs for woodcuts, stained glass, metalwork, and sculpture.

Deverell, Walter Howell (1827–54). British painter, closely associated with the *Pre-Raphaelites (he was proposed for membership of the Brotherhood, to replace *Collinson, but was never actually elected). In 1849 he 'discovered' Elizabeth Siddal, the archetypal Pre-Raphaelite model and *Rossetti's future wife. Deverell was noted for his good looks and charm and Elizabeth was probably in love with him. He died aged 26 from Bright's disease, leaving only a small number of paintings.

Devis, Arthur (1712–87). English painter, active mainly in London but also in his native Preston, the best-known member of a family of artists. He was one of the first specialists in the small *conversation piece and also painted single portraits of similar scale. His sitters are often somewhat artificially posed, with less animation than in *Zoffany's conversation pieces of the next generation. Devis was a minor artist in his day and virtually forgotten until the 1930s, but since then his work has attained considerable popularity because of the doll-like charm of his figures and the delicate detail of his settings. It has also become of interest to social historians, as most of his clients were from the newly prosperous middle class—merchants and country squires. There are good examples of his work in the Harris Art Gallery, Preston. His half-brother **Anthony Devis** (1729–1816) was a landscape painter, and two of Arthur's sons were also artists: **Arthur William Devis** (1763–1822) and **Thomas Anthony Devis** (1757–1810). Arthur William spent the years 1785–95 in India, where he painted portraits and a series of pictures representing the arts, manufactures, and agriculture of Bengal (two examples are in the Ashmolean Museum, Oxford), which were engraved. He lived in London from 1795, working mainly as a portraitist, but also painting the *Death of Nelson* (c.1806, Nat. Maritime Mus., London). Thomas Anthony painted undistinguished portraits and *fancy pictures. Little of his work survives.

De Wint, Peter (1784–1849). English landscape painter of Dutch extraction. From 1802 to 1806 he was apprenticed to the engraver, miniaturist, and painter John Raphael Smith (1752–1812), and he later studied at the *Royal Academy, had advice from John *Varley, and frequented the house of Dr *Monro. Although he painted in oils a good deal, he achieved little success in this field and is best known as one of the finest watercolourists of his generation. His only journey abroad was a short visit to Normandy in 1828, and almost all his work is devoted to the English countryside. He is particularly associated with views of the area around Lincoln (where his wife's parents lived), in which he often uses broad *washes of colour somewhat in the manner of *Cotman. De Wint loved painting—he said 'Mine is a beautiful profession'—and was popular as a teacher.

Diaghilev, Sergei (1872–1929). Russian impresario, famous above all as the founder of the Ballets Russes, through which he exerted great influence on the visual arts as well as on dancing and music. From 1890 to 1896 he studied law in St Petersburg, where he became part of a circle of musicians, painters, and writers including Léon *Bakst and Alexander *Benois. In 1899 he founded the magazine *World of Art*, with the object of interchanging artistic ideas with Western Europe. When it ceased publication in 1904 he concentrated for a while on organizing exhibitions, including one of Russian painting at the 1905 *Salon d'Au-

tomne in Paris—the most comprehensive to have been seen in the West up to that time. In 1907 he organized a series of concerts of Russian music in Paris, and in 1909 he brought a ballet company for the first time (this is usually described as the Ballets Russes, but the name was first used in 1911). The company was a sensational success, as much for the exotic designs of Bakst as for the music and choreography (the dancers included Nijinsky and Pavlova). For the next two decades, until his death in 1929, Diaghilev toured Europe and America with his ballet (he never returned to Russia after the 1917 Revolution and Paris was the main centre of his operations). He was often on the verge of bankruptcy, but he had a remarkable flair for spotting young talent and for integrating various interests and people, enabling him to bring together as his collaborators some of the foremost artistic personalities of his time; the painters who designed sets and costumes for him included *Braque, de *Chirico, *Derain, *Matisse, and *Picasso. He preferred using painters rather than artists who had trained as stage designers, as he thought specialists were likely to be too tied to old ideas.

Diaz de la Peña, Narcisse (1807–76). French painter, born in Bordeaux of Spanish parents who had settled there as political refugees. He began his career (c.1823) as a colourist in a porcelain factory and took up painting in the late 1820s, first exhibiting at the *Salon in 1831. His early paintings included *scènes galantes*, imaginative oriental subjects, and still lifes, usually small in size and rich in colour and texture, but after meeting Théodore *Rousseau in 1836 he became a member of the *Barbizon School of landscape painters. Stylistically, however, he stood somewhat apart from his Barbizon colleagues: his liking for melodramatic lighting contrasts with the sense of quiet communion with nature that was typical of the group and his restless brushwork remained highly distinctive. Indeed, he never lost the Romantic leanings of his youth, and carried on painting mythological scenes (typically featuring nymphs) throughout his career. He achieved success earlier than most of his friends and was generous in helping younger painters by purchasing their work. Several of the *Impressionists were influenced by him, notably *Renoir, who said that meeting Diaz led him to lighten his palette.

Dickinson, Edwin (1891–1978). American painter and draughtsman. He often treated enigmatic or disquieting subject matter and he has been described as 'perhaps the first American artist about whom some knowledge of dream theory is essential for decoding his works' (Matthew Baigell, *A Concise History of American Painting and Sculpture*, 1984). His personal symbolism is seen at its most disturbing and provocative in his self-portraits, in which he sometimes depicted himself as dead. He is best known, however, for large compositions such as *The Fossil Hunters* (1926–8, Whitney Mus., New York). Dickinson often worked on his big pictures for a number of years and said that they were never 'really finished'. He has been called a *Surrealist and also seen as a sophisticated culmination of the 19th-century *Romantic tradition.

Dickinson, Preston (1891–1930). American painter. He spent five years in Europe, 1910–15, and in Paris he was influenced particularly by the structural features of *Cézanne's work and the high-keyed colour of the *Fauves. In the 1920s, however, his work became less experimental as he became associated with the *Precisionists. Like others of the group, he favoured subjects (notably machinery) that were adapted to representation in terms of semi-geometrical abstract design (*Industry*, c.1924, Whitney Mus., New York).

Diderot, Denis (1713–84). French philosopher and writer, perhaps best known as the chief editor of the *Encyclopédie* (1751–72), a work of fundamental importance in shaping the rationalist and humanitarian ideals of the Age of Enlightenment. He was a highly versatile author, his vast output including novels, plays, scientific writings, and criticism. His views on art appear in various places, notably in articles in the *Encyclopédie* and in his reviews of the *Salons from 1759 to 1781, which appeared in the journal *Correspondence littéraire*. They are written in a lively conversational style and formed the model for the criticism of *Baudelaire. His aesthetic views, which are sometimes inconsistent, reflect both his common-sense approach and the 18th-century taste for sentiment. He was enthusiastic about *Greuze because of what seemed his moral seriousness, but he berated *Boucher, whom he regarded as frivolous. Some of his best writing is on *Chardin, whose close scrutiny of the real world set him apart from the prevailing *Rococo artificiality.

Diller, Burgoyne (1906–65). American painter and sculptor. His early work was influenced by *Impressionism and *Cubism, but by the mid-1930s he had become probably the earliest American exponent of *Mondrian's type of geometrical abstraction. He remained committed to this style for the rest of his career, in his sculpture (which is restricted to rectangular elements and primary colours) as well as his painting. He was a member of *American Abstract Artists and from 1935 to 1940 supervisor of the Mural Division of the *Federal Art Project.

diluent. A liquid used to dilute a paint and give it the fluidity the artist desires, for example *turpentine in *oil painting, and water in *watercolour. *See also* VEHICLE.

Dine, Jim (1935–). American painter, printmaker, experimental artist, and poet. In 1959 he was one of the pioneers of *happenings and in the early 1960s he became one of the most prominent figures in American *Pop art (he also made an impact in England, where he lived 1967–71). His Pop canvases were vigorously handled in a manner recalling *Abstract Expressionism, but he often attached real objects to them—generally everyday items such as clothes and household appliances (including a kitchen sink). Characteristically the objects were Dine's personal possessions and his work often has a strong autobiographical flavour. In addition to such *assemblages, he also made free-standing works and *environments, but since the mid-1970s he has concentrated more on traditional two-dimensional work, especially drawings (he has written and illustrated several books of poetry) and prints.

diorama. A form of public entertainment, popular in the 19th century, featuring a large, partially translucent scenic painting, which by means of varied illumination simulated such effects as sunrise, changing weather, etc. By extension the term was also applied to the building in which the display was housed. The diorama was invented by *Daguerre, who gave his first demonstration in Paris in 1822, and the following year he opened one in London; the audience sat in darkness and the spectacle was an ancestor of the cinema. Other cities also had dioramas, but none has survived (although the building that housed the London example still exists, much altered internally). Today the term is more usually applied to various kinds of model, particularly a type of museum display: it consists of a miniature scene, viewed through a window or screen, in which the foreground details, modelled in the round, join imperceptibly with the more distant parts, which are painted in perspective on a vertical panel.

dipper. A small metal container that clips on to the edge of the oil painter's *palette and holds *medium or *diluent. They are often made in pairs—a 'double dipper'. The American term is 'palette cup'.

diptych. A picture or other work of art consisting of two equal-sized parts facing one another like the pages of a book. Diptychs are usually fairly small in size and often the two parts are hinged together so the work could be folded when not in use and easily transported. The type seems to have originated in ivory carvings in the late Roman empire. Initially they were used for writing tablets, the outer surfaces being carved, with wax on the hollowed inner surfaces. They were sometimes used to commemorate family events such as weddings, but they were mainly used to mark the appointment of a new consul; it became the custom for the office holder to distribute such panels as gifts to friends, relatives, and persons of rank. The earliest 'consular diptych' to survive is of 428, and the practice ceased in 541. Because they can be precisely dated by the name of the official they bear, they are important tools in scholarship of the period. Many were later reused for Christian purposes, and in the Middle Ages the diptych became a popular format for portable altarpieces; the Wilton Diptych (see INTERNATIONAL GOTHIC) is the most celebrated example. See also POLYPTYCH and TRIPTYCH.

direct carving. The practice of producing carved sculpture (particularly stone sculpture) by cutting directly into the material, as opposed to having it reproduced from a plaster model using mechanical aids and assistants. Although this might seem a purely technical matter, in the early 20th century it became associated with aesthetic and ethical issues, particularly in Britain and in France. During the 19th century it was customary for sculpture to be exhibited in plaster; it was much more expensive and time-consuming to produce bronze casts or marble carvings, so these were usually made only when firmly commissioned, typically with the aid of a *pointing machine. A successful sculptor could become the administrator of a large studio producing numerous, almost identical versions of popular works (*Rodin employed many assistants, including artists of the calibre of *Bourdelle, *Despiau, and *Pompon, and he rarely touched hammer and chisel himself, only occasionally adding final touches to his works in marble). This kind of procedure was attacked by John *Ruskin, who in 1872 denounced the 'modern system of modelling the work in clay, getting it into form by machinery, and by the hands of subordinates'. Ruskin argued that the sculptor of such works thinks in clay and not in marble, that 'neither he nor the public recognize the touch of the chisel as expressive of personal feeling and that nothing is looked for except mechanical polish'. However, it was not until the early years of the 20th century that his ideas on direct carving were put into practice by sculptors in Britain. Among the most important pioneers were Jacob *Epstein, Eric *Gill, and Henri *Gaudier-Brzeska, who collectively illustrate some of the range of issues involved. For Epstein, the activity of carving was linked to his interest in sculpture from outside the Graeco-Roman tradition, such as that of Assyria and Africa, and it reflected his contact in Paris with *Brancusi and *Modigliani, who had similar interests. For Gill, a return to carving was a return to a medieval practice, through which he hoped to overcome the iniquitous effect of industrialism in dividing the work of the thinker and the maker. For Gaudier-Brzeska, carving was equated with a struggle that was both manual and creative, an aspect of a 'virile' art that contrasted with the 'feminine' modelling that had dominated the previous generation of *New Sculptors.

After the First World War a number of British sculptors, including Barbara

*Hepworth and Henry *Moore, practised direct carving as a dogma (*see* TRUTH TO MATERIAL), while others, such as Frank *Dobson and Leon *Underwood, worked as both carvers and modellers. In France, direct carving moved from being chiefly an avant-garde concern before 1914 to wider acceptance in the 1920s, and at the same time it was taken up in other countries; Fritz *Wotruba was an influential exponent in Austria, for example, as was William *Zorach in the USA. After the Second World War the carving versus modelling debate was rendered largely obsolete by the prevalence of newer techniques, although for many older sculptors the sense of personal engagement with the material through carving still remained of central importance.

Discobolus. See MYRON.

distemper. Type of paint in which the pigment is mixed with water and glue or *size. Its principal use is in stage scenery, as it is cheap but impermanent. Whitewash is a form of distemper.

divisionism. A method of painting in which colour effects are obtained by applying small areas or dots of pure, unmixed colours on the canvas in such a way that to a spectator standing at an appropriate distance they appear to react together, producing greater luminosity and brilliance than would have resulted if the same colours had been physically mixed together. The method was employed empirically by the *Impressionists, but it was not developed systematically and scientifically until *Seurat and the *Neo-Impressionists. Seurat (in common with other contemporaries) spoke of an 'optical mixture', but (contrary to what is usually stated) the dots do not really fuse in the viewer's eye to make different colours, for they remain visible as dots. Rather, they seem to vibrate, creating something of the shimmering effect experienced in strong sunlight. The effect is noted in Ogden Rood's *Modern Chromatics* (1879), a treatise on colour theory well known to Seurat. Camille *Pissarro, who was closely associated with Seurat at this time, said that the optimum viewing distance for a picture painted by the divisionist method was three times the diagonal measurement. The terms divisionism and *pointillism are not always clearly differentiated, but whereas divisionism refers mainly to the underlying theory, pointillism describes the actual painting technique associated with Seurat and his followers. 'Divisionism' (usually with a capital D) was also the name of an Italian movement, a version of *Neo-Impressionism, that flourished in the last decade of the 19th century and the first decade of the 20th century. It was one of the sources of *Futurism.

Dix, Otto (1891–1969). German painter and printmaker. In the 1920s he was, with George *Grosz, the outstanding artist of the *Neue Sachlichkeit movement, his work conveying his disillusionment and disgust at the horrors of war and the depravities of a decadent society with complete psychological truth and devastating emotional effect. *The Match Seller* (1920, Staatsgalerie, Stuttgart), for example, is a pitiless depiction of indifference to suffering, showing passers-by ignoring a blind and limbless ex-soldier begging in the street, and Dix's fifty etchings entitled *The War* (1924) have been described by George Heard Hamilton (*Painting and Sculpture in Europe: 1880–1940*, 1967) as 'perhaps the most powerful as well as the most unpleasant anti-war statements in modern art'. Another favourite theme was prostitution and he was a brilliantly incisive portraitist (*Sylvia von Harden*, 1926, Pompidou Centre, Paris). In 1927 he was appointed a teacher at the Dresden Academy, but his anti-military stance angered the Nazi regime and in 1933 he was dismissed from his academic posts and his work was declared *degenerate. From 1936 he lived quietly in the country near Lake Constance and painted traditional landscapes, yet he still aroused suspicion; in 1939 he was arrested on a charge of complicity in a plot on Hitler's life, but was soon released. He was conscripted into the *Volkssturm* (Home Guard) in 1945 and was a prisoner in France 1945–6; he then returned to Lake Constance. His post-war work—which was much more loosely handled and often inspired by religious mysticism—did not compare in originality or strength with his great achievements of the 1920s, but he remained a highly respected figure, receiving major awards from both East and West Germany.

Dobell, Sir William (1899–1970). Australian painter. In 1929 he won a travelling scholarship that enabled him to study at the *Slade School (he also had some private tuition from *Orpen) and he did not return to Australia until 1938. By this time his style had changed from the carefully studied, solidly constructed naturalism of his early works to a much looser and more *Expressionist manner, sometimes with a satirical air. The rich colours and textures were influenced by art he saw on his travels in Europe, particularly the paintings of *Soutine. He immediately acquired a circle of admiring patrons in Sydney, and in 1944 he became a household name in Australia when he was involved in a cause célèbre for modernism. In January of that year he was awarded the 1943 Archibald Prize for portraiture, given annually by the Art Gallery of New South Wales, Sydney. His winning picture was *Portrait of an Artist* (damaged beyond repair by fire), representing his fellow painter Joshua Smith (1905–95). Two of the unsuccessful competitors contested the award in the Supreme Court of New South Wales, on the grounds that the winning work was not a portrait but a caricature—a 'pictorial defamation of character'. Their suit was dismissed and the case was regarded as a significant victory for the cause of modern art in Australia. Some critics think that this marks the peak of Dobell's career and that much of his later work shows a decline in confidence. However, he continued to be much in demand as a portraitist and also painted landscapes, some of them inspired by visits to the highlands of New Guinea in 1949 and 1950.

Dobson, Frank (1886–1963). British sculptor. His early work consisted mainly of paintings, the few surviving examples showing how impressed he was by the *Post-Impressionist exhibitions organized by Roger *Fry. After the First World War (when he was on active service with the Artists' Rifles), he turned increasingly to sculpture, and during the 1920s and 1930s he gained an outstanding reputation: in 1925 Fry described his work as 'true sculpture and pure sculpture...almost the first time that such a thing has been even attempted in England'. The monumental dignity of his work was in the tradition of *Maillol, and like him Dobson found the female nude the most satisfactory subject for three-dimensional composition, as in *Cornucopia* (1925–7, Univ. of Hull), des-

cribed by Clive *Bell as 'the finest piece of sculpture by an Englishman since—I don't know when'. His work was more stylized than Maillol's, however, and his sophisticated simplifications of form made him one of the pioneers of modern sculpture in Britain. Dobson was also outstanding as a portrait sculptor, his best-known work in this field being the head of Sir Osbert Sitwell in polished brass (1923, Tate, London). He worked in various other materials, including bronze, terracotta, and stone; his craftsmanship in all these materials was superb and he played an important role as a liberal-minded and kind-hearted teacher at the *Royal College of Art, where he was professor of sculpture from 1946 to 1953. With the rise of a younger generation led by Henry *Moore, however, Dobson's prestige as an artist waned; his work was regarded as dated, and the memorial exhibition organized by the *Arts Council in 1966 was poorly received. Since then his reputation has greatly revived and he has again been recognized as one of the outstanding figures in 20th-century British sculpture.

Dobson, William (1611–46). English portrait painter. He was described by John Aubrey in his *Brief Lives* (c.1690) as 'the most excellent painter that England hath yet bred' and he is indeed regarded as the most accomplished native-born painter (other than miniaturists) before *Hogarth. About 60 paintings by him are known, all the securely dated examples being from the years 1642–6, when he was painter to Charles I's wartime court at Oxford. The city surrendered to the Parliamentarians in 1646 and Dobson moved to London. Said to have been 'somewhat loose and irregular in his way of living', he was thrown into prison for debt, and his early death followed shortly after his release. His style is superficially similar to van *Dyck's, but his colouring is richer and his paint texture rougher, very much in the Venetian tradition. He also had an uncompromisingly direct way of presenting character that is considered quintessentially English, as in his most celebrated work, *Endymion Porter* (c.1643, Tate, London). Various paintings by Dobson other than portraits are mentioned by early writers, but only two survive: the *Executioner with the Baptist's Head* (Walker AG,

Liverpool); and an allegory, the *Civil Wars of France* (Rousham House, Oxfordshire).

Documenta. A large international exhibition of contemporary art held at Kassel, Germany, every four or five years since 1955. The first such exhibition was of great cultural and political significance, as it marked Germany's reacceptance of avant-garde art, which had been banned by the Nazis as *degenerate.

Doesburg, Theo van (1883–1931). Dutch painter, designer, architect, and writer on art. His early work was influenced variously by *Impressionism, *Fauvism, and *Expressionism, but in 1915 he met *Mondrian and rapidly underwent a transition to complete abstraction. In 1917 he was one of the founders of De *Stijl and he devoted the rest of his life to propagating the association's ideas and the austerely geometrical style it stood for, seeing himself as a crusader fighting to cleanse the world of cultural impurities. He spent much of the 1920s travelling to promote his beliefs, particularly in Germany, and from 1922 to 1924 he taught intermittently at the *Bauhaus. By the mid-1920s he had abandoned the rigid horizontal–vertical axes insisted upon by Mondrian and introduced diagonals into his paintings in a series of works entitled *Counter-Compositions*; he called this new departure *Elementarism. In 1929 he moved to Paris and designed a house and studio for himself in the suburb of Meudon in a stark and stripped style (1929–31); he thought that an artist's studio should resemble a medical laboratory. In 1930 he published a manifesto of *Concrete art and in 1931, shortly before his death from a heart attack, a meeting of artists in his new studio led to the formation of the *Abstraction-Création association.

Dolci, Carlo (1616–86). Florentine painter, active in his native city for virtually his whole career. He was intensely devout and most of his paintings are of religious subjects, done in a cloyingly sweet and meticulously smooth style. They were enormously popular in his lifetime (many of his favourite compositions exist in multiple versions), but have appealed less to modern taste. His portraits, on the other hand, are now much admired for their sober objectivity. Dolci's work was highly prized by contemporary British visitors to Florence, and one of these, the physician Sir John Finch, made an impressive collection of it. Dolci painted a portrait of Finch and one of his friend Sir Thomas Baines (*c*.1665–70), both in the Fitzwilliam Museum, Cambridge.

Domenichino (Domenico Zampieri) (1581–1641). Bolognese painter and draughtsman. He was a favourite pupil of Annibale *Carracci and one of the most important upholders of the tradition of Bolognese *classicism. After studying with *Calvaert and Ludovico Carracci he moved to Rome in 1602 and joined the group of artists working under Annibale on the decoration of the gallery in the Palazzo *Farnese. His only undisputed work there is the *Maiden with the Unicorn*, a charming, gentle fresco over the entrance of the gallery. For most of the second and third decades of the century he was Rome's leading painter; during this time he painted numerous altarpieces and had a succession of major decorative commissions, among them scenes from the life of St Cecilia in S. Luigi dei Francesi (1613–14). The dignified frieze-like composition of the figures reflects his study of *Raphael's tapestries, and in turn influenced *Poussin. The frescos in the pendentives and apse of S. Andrea della Valle (1624–8), his chief work of the 1620s, show a move away from this strict classicism towards an ampler *Baroque style; but compared with his rival *Lanfranco (who at this time was overtaking him in popularity) Domenichino never abandoned the principles of clear, firm drawing for the sake of more painterly effects. In 1631 he moved to Naples, and in his ceiling frescos of the S. Gennaro chapel in the cathedral he made even greater concessions to Baroque taste. Some Neapolitan artists were jealous of his success and were hostile towards him, leading him to flee the city in 1634 (he had an anxious and timid personality). He returned the following year, but he died (it was rumoured by poisoning) before completing his work in the cathedral.

Although he was renowned mainly for his fresco decorations and altarpieces, Domenichino was also important in other fields, particularly as an exponent of *ideal landscape, in which he formed the link between Annibale Carracci and *Claude (four of his landscapes are in the Louvre). He was one of the finest draughtsmen of his generation (the Royal Library at Windsor Castle has a superb collection of his drawings) and also an excellent portraitist (*Pope Gregory XV and Cardinal Ludovico Ludovisi*, c.1621–3, Mus. B.-A., Béziers,). In the 18th century his reputation was enormous—his *Last Communion of St Jerome* (1614, Pinacoteca, Vatican) was generally regarded as one of the greatest pictures ever painted—but he fell from grace in the 19th century under the scathing attacks of *Ruskin, along with the other Bolognese painters. In the later 20th century his reputation greatly revived.

Domenico Veneziano (d. 1461). Italian painter, an important but enigmatic figure, whose life is poorly documented. His name indicates that he came from Venice, but he is first documented in Perugia, in 1438, and was active mainly in Florence, where he died. *Vasari credits him with introducing *oil painting into Tuscany. Although this is incorrect, it seems to be true that he was responsible for bringing a new interest in colour and texture to a tradition in which draughtsmanship normally ruled supreme. His only documented fresco cycle, on scenes from the life of the Virgin (1439–45) in S. Egidio, Florence, on which *Piero della Francesca was one of his assistants, is destroyed (except for a few fragments), and only two signed works survive. These are a *Virgin and Child Enthroned*, the largest of three much-damaged and repainted fragments from a frescoed street tabernacle (c.1440, NG, London), and the celebrated St Lucy Altarpiece of c.1445, painted for the church of S. Lucia de' Magnoli, Florence (the central panel is in the Uffizi, Florence, and the *predella panels are dispersed in Cambridge (Fitzwilliam Mus.), Washington (NG), and Berlin (Gemäldegalerie)). This is one of the great masterpieces of 15th-century Italian painting; its pearly beauty of colouring, mastery of light, and airy lucidity of spatial construction are reflected in the work of Domenico's assistant Piero, and also, for example, in that of *Baldovinetti. *See also* ANDREA DEL CASTAGNO.

Donatello (Donato di Niccolo) (c.1386–1466). Florentine sculptor. He was the greatest European sculptor of the 15th century and one of a remarkable group of artists—including his friends *Alberti, *Brunelleschi, and *Masaccio—who created the *Renaissance style in Florence. His long career was hugely productive, and he was unrivalled in the variety of his output, his emotional range and depth, his formal inventiveness, and his versatility in the handling of materials, which included bronze, stone, wood, terracotta, and stucco. He worked in Padua, Pisa, Rome, and Siena as well as Florence (he also turned down invitations to work in Mantua, Modena, and Naples), and he had an enormous impact on his contemporaries and artists of the following generation—painters as well as sculptors—through his wide repertoire of pose and expression, his use of *antique motifs, and his sophisticated handling of perspective in his *reliefs; indeed he was unquestionably the most influential Italian artist of his time in any medium. In spite of his fame and success, and the high opinion in which he was held by his eminent patrons, he is said to have lived simply, utterly devoted to his work and preferring criticism to praise, as it inspired him to greater heights.

At the outset of his career Donatello worked as an assistant to *Ghiberti (1404–7), but he developed a style that departed radically from his master's *Gothic elegance. He was unconcerned with the surface polish or linear grace so typical of Ghiberti, and excelled rather in emotional force. His individuality was first revealed in a series of powerfully realistic but deeply spiritual figures (mainly in marble) that he made for the external decoration of Florence Cathedral, the adjacent campanile, and the church of Orsanmichele. The series began with the imperious *St John the Evangelist* (1408–15) for the cathedral (now Cathedral Mus.), included the celebrated *St George* (c.1415–17) for Orsanmichele (now in the Bargello, Florence), and culminated in the uncompromisingly unidealized *Habakkuk* (completed 1436), usually known by its nickname of *Zuccone* ('bald-pate'), for the campanile (now Cathedral Mus.). *Vasari conveys the brilliance of Donatello's characterization in his description of the *St George*: 'The head exhibits the beauty of youth, its spirit and valour in arms, a proud and terrifying lifelikeness, and a marvellous sense of movement within the stone.' With this acute psychological insight went a technique of daring originality that shows how concerned Donatello was with the optical effects in his works. He carefully took into consideration the position from which they would be viewed, adjusting the proportions of a figure when it would be seen from below, for example, and carving with almost brutal power and boldness when it was positioned to be seen at a distance. On the other hand, his relief of *St George and the Dragon* (1417, Bargello), done for the base of his *St George* statue, is executed with great delicacy in the technique Donatello invented called *rilievo schiacciato* (relief so low it is like 'drawing in stone'); originally situated on the north side of Orsanmichele, the relief was seen in a soft, diffused light, so the subtlety of the carving could be appreciated.

In 1430–3 Donatello worked in Rome, and the impact of the antique art he saw there can be seen most clearly in his famous *Cantoria* (singing gallery) for Florence Cathedral (now Cathedral Mus., 1433–9), which makes a lavish show of freely interpreted classical motifs. His bronze statue of David (Bargello), which is credited with being the first free-standing nude statue since antiquity, is also sometimes seen as a response to Donatello's visit to Rome and assigned to the 1430s, but some scholars date it much later. The subject as well as the date is controversial, for it has been proposed that it represents 'Mercury with the Head of Argus' rather than David. From 1443 to 1453 Donatello was based in Padua, where he carried out three major commissions. Two of them were for the church of S. Antonio (the Santo) and they are still there: a life-size bronze *Crucifix* (1443–9), originally made for the rood screen but now placed above the high altar, and the high altar itself (begun 1446), an imposing architectural structure featuring seven free-standing bronze statues, four large reliefs of the *Miracles of St Anthony*, and various other elements (the altar has been remodelled several times and no longer looks as Donatello intended). His third great work in Padua is the famous monument to the condottiere Erasmo da Narni, known as Gattamelata, in the Piazza del Santo (1447–53), which begins the modern tradition of the equestrian statue (*see MARCUS AURELIUS*). It has been imitated many times but never surpassed in grandeur and dignity.

From 1454 until his death Donatello was based mainly in Florence, although he also worked in Siena on an abortive project for a set of bronze doors for the cathedral. In his final years his style became even more emotionally intense. The most important works of this period include the bronze *Judith and Holofernes* (Palazzo Vecchio, Florence), which is an allegory of humility triumphing over pride, and a series of bronze reliefs (mainly of scenes from Christ's Passion) for a pair of pulpits in S. Lorenzo. The harrowing and emaciated *Mary Magdalene* in painted wood (Cathedral Mus.) has also traditionally been considered one of his late works, but there is evidence to suggest it belongs to an earlier period. Although the S. Lorenzo reliefs were unfinished at Donatello's death and were completed by his pupil *Bertoldo di Giovanni, they are essentially the master's work and show how freely he exploited the expressive possibilities of distortion, creating what has been called 'the first style of old age in the history of art'.

In addition to his major independent works, Donatello produced three important tombs in partnership with *Michelozzo di Bartolommeo, and he also made numerous smaller works. They include bronze *plaquettes, reliefs of the *Virgin and Child* in marble and stucco, which became prototypes for the following generation of sculptors, and a portrait bust in painted terracotta (*Niccolò da Uzzano*, Bargello), which is thought to date from the 1430s and is probably the earliest portrait bust of the Renaissance, preceding the first dated example (by *Mino da Fiesole, 1453) by several years.

Dongen, Kees van (1877–1968). Dutch-born painter and printmaker who settled in Paris in 1897 and took French nationality in 1929. His early work was *Impressionist, but he became a member of the *Fauves in 1906 and in 1908 exhibited with the German *Expressionist group Die *Brücke. He had a reputation as a ladies' man, and his work (mainly nudes and female portraits) was often erotic in spirit; in 1913 one of his pictures was removed from the *Salon d'Automne by the police on the grounds of alleged indecency. After the First World War he became internationally famous for his paintings of fashionable life, particularly portraits of insolently glamorous women in which he created a type that has been described as 'half drawing-room prostitute, half sidewalk princess'. He kept the brilliant colouring and bold handling of his Fauve days, but his great facility led to repetition and banality and it is generally agreed that his best work was done before 1920. From 1959 he lived in Monaco.

Donkey's Tail. Title of an exhibition organized in Moscow in 1912 by *Goncharova and *Larionov after they had dissociated themselves from the *Knave of Diamonds group in 1911. They accused that group of being too much under foreign influence, and advocated a nationalist Russian art. At this time Larionov and Goncharova were painting in a 'Neo-primitivist' manner based partly on icon painting and peasant art. The title of the exhibition referred to an incident in 1910 when three pictures painted with a brush tied to a donkey's tail were shown at the jury-free *Salon des Indépendants in Paris (a stunt devised by a journalist to poke fun at modern art; the pictures were hung as works of the fictitious 'Boronali', an anagram of *aliboron*, 'jackass'). At the Moscow exhibition there was an outcry because some of the paintings on view had religious subjects and it was thought to be irreverent to show religious works under such a title (the police ordered several to be removed). Goncharova and Larionov followed it up with the *Target Exhibition in 1913.

Donner, Georg Raphael (1693–1741). The outstanding Austrian *Baroque sculptor, active mainly in Salzburg, Bratislava, and Vienna. His acknowledged masterpieces are the figures from the fountain in the Mehlmarkt, Vienna (1737–9, Österreichisches Barockmuseum, Vienna), and the group of *St Martin and the Beggar* (c.1735, Bratislava Cathedral), in which the saint is dressed in hussar's uniform rather than the traditional armour. These works are in lead, which Donner preferred to the Austrian speciality of wood; his smooth surfaces have led some critics to see his work as presaging *Neoclassicism, although his elongated figures seem to place him closer to Italian *Mannerism. His brother **Matthäus** (1704–56) was also a sculptor.

donor. A term applied to a person who commissions and pays for a work of religious art and has his or her portrait incorporated in it as an act of devotion. By having themselves included in the picture, donors sought to associate themselves in a special way with the sacred figures portrayed there, either in thanks for favours received or in the hope of future protection and salvation. A famous example is *Giotto's portrayal of Enrico Scrovegni in the Arena Chapel, Padua (c.1305); Scrovegni, who had the chapel built and decorated in expiation of his father's sins, is shown kneeling in front of the Virgin Mary and presenting her with a model of the building. In Netherlandish art of the 15th century, a favourite format for donor paintings, popularized by Rogier van der *Weyden, was to show the Virgin and Child on one wing of a *diptych and a portrait of the donor in prayer facing them on the other. None of Rogier's diptychs of this type survives intact, the two panels in all cases having been separated, with one sometimes lost, but a well-known intact example by *Memlinc is the Nieuwenhove Diptych (1487, Memlingmuseum, Bruges).

Doré, Gustave (1832–83). French illustrator, painter, and sculptor. He was the most celebrated book illustrator of the mid-19th century and was so prolific that at one time he employed more than forty wood engravers. His best-known works are lavishly illustrated editions of literary classics, including Dante's *Inferno* (1861), *Don Quixote* (1862), and the Bible (1866)—works that helped to give European currency to the illustrated book of large format. Characteristically his style was rich and exuberant, with a strong vein of grotesque fantasy, but he worked in a more sombre and realistic manner in his illustrations for *London: A Pilgrimage* (1872). In these images he presented the grim life of the poor in a way that was admired by van *Gogh among others. Doré had an amazing appetite for work, and in addition to his huge output of illustrations he produced numerous paintings, including some very large religious compositions that became a popular attraction at the Doré Gallery in New Bond Street, London, open from 1868 to 1892 (examples are in the Petit Palais, Paris). In the 1870s he also took up sculpture, his best-known work in this medium being the monument to the dramatist and novelist Alexandre Dumas in the Place Malesherbes in Paris, erected in 1883.

Doryphorus. See POLYCLITUS.

Dossi, Dosso (Giovanni di Luteri) (*c*.1490?–1541/2). The outstanding painter of the Ferrarese School in the 16th century. His early life and training are obscure, but *Vasari's assertion that he was born around 1474 is now thought unlikely. He is first recorded in 1512 in Mantua (the name 'Dosso' probably comes from a place near Mantua—he is not called 'Dosso Dossi' until the 18th century). By 1514 he was in Ferrara, where he spent most of the rest of his career, collaborating with the poet Ariosto in devising entertainments, triumphs, tapestries, etc. for the *Este court. Dosso painted various kinds of pictures—mythological and religious works, portraits, and decorative frescos—and he is perhaps most important for the part played in his work by landscape, in which he continued the romantic pastoral vein of *Giorgione and *Titian (he is documented in Venice in 1516 and 1518 and may well have made an earlier visit or visits). Dosso's work, however, has a personal quality of fantasy and an opulent sense of colour and texture that give it an individual stamp (*Melissa*, *c*.1523, Borghese Gal., Rome). His brother **Battista Dossi** (*c*.1497–1548) often collaborated with him (even though Vasari said they disliked each other); there is insufficient evidence to know whether Battista made an individual contribution.

dotted manner. *See* MANIÈRE CRIBLÉE.

Dou, Gerrit (1613–75). Dutch painter. He was born and active in Leiden, where he became the first pupil of the young *Rembrandt in 1628. His early work was closely based on his master's, but after Rembrandt moved to Amsterdam in 1631/2, Dou developed a style of his own characterized by minute detail and a surface of almost enamelled smoothness (he had initially trained in his father's profession of glass engraving and this background must have helped instil a love of glossy surfaces). He was astonishingly fastidious about his tools and working conditions, with a particular horror of dust, and sometimes painted with the aid of a magnifying glass. In about 1640 he was visited by *Sandrart, who 'praised the great care that he had lavished on painting a broomstick hardly larger than a fingernail', only for Dou to reply that 'he would need three more days to finish it'. He painted various subjects, but is best known for domestic interiors. They usually contain only one or two figures framed by a window or by the drapery of a curtain, and surrounded by books, musical instruments, or household paraphernalia. He was renowned for his skill with night scenes. With Jan *Steen, Dou was among the founders of the Guild of St Luke at Leiden in 1648. Unlike Steen he was prosperous and respected throughout his life; indeed he had an international reputation and turned down an invitation from Charles II to visit England. His pictures continued to fetch big prices (consistently higher than those paid for Rembrandt's work) until the advent of *Impressionism influenced taste against the neatness and precision of his style. Dou had a workshop with many pupils who perpetuated his style (notably *Schalken), and Leiden continued the *fijnschilder* (fine painter) tradition into the 19th century.

Doughty, Thomas (1793–1856). American painter, one of the first American artists to specialize exclusively in landscapes. Doughty was born in Philadelphia and mainly lived there, but also in Boston and New York, where he died. He was essentially self-taught as a painter. In 1837 and again in 1845 he travelled to Europe, visiting England on both occasions. As one of the first to recognize the American landscape as a viable subject for painting, he is regarded as a forerunner of the *Hudson River School. His best-known painting is probably *In Nature's Wonderland* (1835, Detroit Inst. of Arts). Doughty was also one of the first American exponents of lithography.

Dove, Arthur (1880–1946). American painter, a pioneer of abstract art. For most of his career he earned his living as a commercial illustrator and he was often in great financial difficulty (even though he was supported by *Stieglitz and Duncan *Phillips). He visited Europe in 1907–9, coming into contact with *Fauvism and other avant-garde movements, and in 1910 he painted the first abstract pictures in American art (*Abstraction No 1*–*Abstraction No 6*, priv. coll.), which are somewhat similar to *Kandinsky's work of the same time. He never exhibited these in his lifetime, but he displayed similar work at his first one-man exhibition at Stieglitz's 291 Galley in 1912. Typically his abstractions are based on organic forms, suggesting the rhythms of nature with their pulsating shapes (*Sand Barge*,

1930, Phillips Coll., Washington). During the 1940s he experimented with a more geometric type of abstraction (*That Red One*, 1944, William H. Lane Foundation, Leominster, Mass.). In his later years he took a leading part in the campaign to win artists royalty rights for the reproduction of their work.

Downman, John (*c*.1750–1824). English portrait painter. His best work is on a small scale and he often worked in a distinctive technique using pencil or charcoal lightly tinted with watercolour (four examples of the type are in the Wallace Collection, London). He lived mainly in London, but he travelled widely about the country, often staying in great houses whilst he painted a series of portraits of members of the family.

drapery painter. A specialist in the painting of costume and other accessories employed by a portraitist with a large practice. Such specialist assistants or subcontractors seem to have emerged in the late 17th century, perhaps in the Netherlands, and almost all the leading British portraitists of the early and mid-18th century employed one or more (the main exceptions were *Hogarth and *Gainsborough, who were too individual to subscribe to the idea). The doyen of the draperyman's profession at this time was the Flemish-born Joseph van Aken (*c*.1699–1749), who settled in England in about 1720 and worked for *Highmore, *Hudson, *Knapton, *Ramsay, and others, including provincial painters (they sent their unfinished pictures to his London studio or sometimes painted the head on a separate piece of canvas that could be pasted onto the costumed figure). Van Aken had a repertoire of poses and costumes that his clients evidently used as a kind of pattern book: the same features sometimes occur virtually identically in the work of different painters, leading *Vertue to comment that van Aken 'puts them so much on a level that it is difficult to know one hand from another'. By the end of the century such production line methods were falling out of favour and the separate profession of drapery painter was dying out.

Dreier, Katherine S. (1877–1952). American painter, patron, and collector, a wealthy heiress remembered mainly for her missionary zeal in promoting modern art in the USA. She became an ardent supporter of avant-garde art as a result of the *Armory Show, where she met Marcel *Duchamp, and in 1920 together with him and *Man Ray she founded the *Société Anonyme. 'A domineering woman of tireless energy and Wagnerian proportions, she was the antithesis of Duchamp in every possible way, and they got along famously' (Calvin Tomkins, *The World of Marcel Duchamp*, 1966). In addition to organizing exhibitions (the main business of the Société Anonyme), she did a good deal of lecturing, and she also promoted avant-garde music and dance. Her best-known painting is her portrait of Duchamp (1918, MoMA, New York). Soon after she painted this, her work became abstract, influenced by *Kandinsky.

Drost, Willem (1633–59). Dutch painter, one of the most gifted of *Rembrandt's pupils, but also one of the most enigmatic. Several paintings now given to him were formerly attributed to his master. Among his undisputed works the masterpiece is the sensuous *Bathsheba* (1654, Louvre, Paris), painted in the same year as Rembrandt's famous depiction of the subject (likewise in the Louvre) and evidently inspired by it.

Drouais, François-Hubert (1727–75). French portrait painter. He trained under *Boucher (among others) and became a rival to *Nattier as a fashionable portraitist. His portraits have a gracious and artificial charm and at their best bear comparison with those of Boucher. He was particularly successful with children, but his best-known painting is probably the very grand portrait of Mme de Pompadour in the National Gallery, London (1763–4), completed after the sitter's death. His father and his son were painters. **Hubert Drouais** (1699–1767) had a successful career as a *miniaturist and *pastel portraitist. **Germain Drouais** (1763–88) was J.-L. *David's favourite pupil and won the *Prix de Rome in 1784; David regarded him as his greatest potential rival ('He alone could trouble my sleep'), but he died of smallpox aged 24.

Drummond, Malcolm. *See* CAMDEN TOWN GROUP.

Drury, Alfred. *See* NEW SCULPTURE.

drying oils. Fatty oils of vegetable origin that harden into a solid transparent substance on exposure to air and are much used as *vehicles in paints. Those that have been in commonest use since the Middle Ages are *linseed, *walnut, and *poppy oil. Almond and olive oil are not suitable as they do not harden. Sunflower oil has been used in Russia but has never become popular.

drypoint. A printmaking method in which the design is scratched directly into a copper plate with a sharp tool that is held like a pen. It is a more spontaneous technique than *line engraving, but not so fluent as *etching. A distinctive feature of drypoint is provided by the *burr—the tiny upturned edge of the furrow made by the cutting tool. This produces a soft, rich quality in the print, but because it soon wears down only a limited number of good impressions can be taken. Drypoint, which seems to have originated in the last quarter of the 15th century, has frequently been used in combination with other processes; *Rembrandt, for example, often touched up his etchings in drypoint. He also made a few prints purely in drypoint, notably one of his most celebrated works, *The Three Crosses*, and he sometimes used special papers to bring out the softness of the burr.

Drysdale, Sir Russell (1912–81). Australian painter. He was born in England of a family that had long associations with Australia and he spent several years of his childhood there. The family settled in Melbourne in 1923 and in the late 1930s Drysdale gave up farming to study art. After moving to Sydney in 1940, he devoted himself full-time to painting and his work became well known throughout Australia during the 1940s. It revived the tradition of hardship, tragedy, and melancholy associated with the Australian bush that had been obscured by the much more optimistic interpretation developed during the 1890s by the city-based painters of the *Heidelberg School. However, in place of the basically *Impressionist style of the Heidelberg painters, Drysdale blended *Expressionist and *Surrealist features founded on his knowledge of contemporary European painting. In 1949 Kenneth *Clark, on a visit to Sydney, encouraged Drysdale to exhibit in London and in 1950 he had a one-man show at the Leicester Galleries; this marked the beginning of a new interest in Australian art in

Britain and in Europe—a trend that peaked in the early 1960s. *Dobell and *Nolan were two other artists whose work became well known in the northern hemisphere in this period and together with Drysdale they represented Australia at the 1954 Venice *Biennale. Of these three, Drysdale remained closest to the Australian soil. In the 1950s he travelled widely in the vast tract of Northern Australia, which he described as 'magnificent in dimension, old as time, curious, strange, and compelling'. As well as the landscape, he painted the life of the Aborigines. During the early 1960s he experienced periods of depression accentuated by the death of his son and his wife. He was knighted in 1969.

Dubois, Ambroise. *See* FONTAINEBLEAU, SCHOOL OF.

Dubreuil, Toussaint. *See* FONTAINEBLEAU, SCHOOL OF.

Du Broeucq, Jacques. *See* GIAMBOLOGNA.

Dubuffet, Jean (1901–85). French painter, sculptor, lithographer, and writer. He studied painting as a young man but was engaged mainly in the wine trade until 1942, when he took up art seriously again, his first exhibition coming in 1945. He preferred untrained spontaneity to professional skill and was fascinated by graffiti and by what he called *Art Brut ('raw art'), the products of psychotics or wholly untrained persons. His own work is aggressively reminiscent of such 'popular' art, often featuring subjects drawn from the street life of Paris (*Man with a Hod*, 1956, Tate, London). Frequently he incorporated materials such as sand and plaster into his paintings, and he also produced sculptures made from junk materials. His work initially provoked outrage, but then found acceptance and in some quarters reverence, and it has proved highly influential, foreshadowing many of the trends of the 1960s and beyond. He is one of the key figures in the tendency in contemporary art to depreciate traditional materials, methods, and, standards, and, as he himself said in 1957, to 'bring all disparaged values into the limelight'.

Duccio di Buoninsegna (d.1318/19). The most famous painter of the Sienese School. Little is known of his life: he is first recorded in 1278, records of several commissions survive, and he is known to have been fined on several occasions for various minor offences (one perhaps involving sorcery), but only one fully documented work by him survives. This is the famous *Maestà* commissioned by Siena Cathedral and completed in 1311 (it is usually said to have been begun in 1308, but *Pope-Hennessy has argued that a document of that year is an interim contract, not the initial contract, and that the elaborate double-sided altarpiece must have taken more than three years to paint). Today most of the altarpiece is in the cathedral museum in Siena, but several of the *predella panels are scattered outside Italy—in London (NG), Washington (NG), and elsewhere. It has been described by John White (*Art and Architecture in Italy: 1250–1400*, 1966) as 'probably the most important panel ever painted in Italy. It is certainly among the most beautiful. Compressed within the compass of an altarpiece is the equivalent of an entire programme for the fresco painting of a church.' The whole of the front of the main panel is occupied by a scene of the Virgin and Child in majesty surrounded by angels and saints, and corresponding to this on the back are 26 scenes from Christ's Passion. Originally there were subsidiary scenes from Christ's life above and below the main panel. Although Duccio drew much on *Byzantine tradition, he introduced a new warmth of human feeling that gives him a role in Sienese painting comparable to that of *Giotto in Florentine painting. He recreates the biblical stories with great vividness, and as no one else before him he succeeds in making the setting of a scene—a room or a hillside—a dramatic constituent of the action, so that figures and surroundings are intimately bound together. The other main work attributed to Duccio is the large *Rucellai Madonna* (Uffizi, Florence), which is probably the picture documented as having been painted by him for S. Maria Novella, Florence, in 1285. Several other smaller panels can be attributed to him or his workshop with a fair degree of confidence, but there is no evidence that he ever worked in fresco. His exquisite colouring and supple draughtsmanship set enduring standards in Siena (Simone *Martini was his greatest disciple) and his influence reached as far as France, notably in the work of *Pucelle. It is possible that he visited France:

a 'Duche de Siene' is documented in Paris in 1296 and 1297.

Duchamp, Marcel (1887–1968). French-born artist and art theorist who became an American citizen in 1955, the brother of Raymond *Duchamp-Villon and Jacques *Villon. His output was small (most of his key works are in the Philadelphia Museum of Art) and for long periods he was more or less inactive, but he is regarded as one of the most potent figures in modern art because of the originality and fertility of his ideas. His early works, influenced by *Post-Impressionism and *Fauvism, were unexceptional, but he sprang to notoriety with *Nude Descending a Staircase, No. 2* (Philadelphia), which was the most discussed work at the *Armory Show in 1913. It depicts a stylized, semi-abstract figure walking down a spiral staircase, movement being suggested by the use of overlapping images, in the manner of rapid-fire multiple-exposure photography. The attention the picture received was mainly negative, but the publicity made Duchamp suddenly much better known in the USA than he had ever been in France. This first conspicuous achievement as a painter was also Duchamp's last, for from this point he virtually abandoned conventional media. From 1915 to 1923 he lived mainly in New York, where with *Man Ray and Francis *Picabia he formed the nucleus of the city's *Dada movement. His main contribution to this was the *ready-made, the best-known of which was *Fountain* (1917), consisting of a urinal bowl signed 'R. Mutt', which was rejected by the *Society of Independent Artists. Another of his celebrated provocative gestures was adding a moustache and beard and an obscene inscription to a reproduction of the *Mona Lisa* (1919). During his years in New York Duchamp was engaged intermittently on his most complex and ambitious work—an enigmatic construction on glass entitled *The Bride Stripped Bare by Her Bachelors, Even*, often known for short as 'The Large Glass' (Philadelphia; replica by Richard *Hamilton, 1965–6, in Tate Modern, London). He abandoned it as 'definitively unfinished' in 1923, but it was damaged whilst being transported in 1926 and ten years later he made repairs, incorporating cracks in the shattered glass as part of the image and declaring it completed 'by chance'. Scholars have produced voluminous interpretations of this work, but to many people it is an incomprehensible joke.

In 1923 Duchamp returned to Paris and lived there until 1942 (although he made several visits to New York), devoting much of his time in this period to his passion for chess. He was one of the best players in France and his obsessive devotion to the game ruined his first—rather frivolous—marriage in 1927, of which Man Ray wrote: 'Duchamp spent the one week they lived together studying chess problems, and his bride, in desperate retaliation, got up one night when he was asleep and glued the chess pieces to the board. They were divorced three months later.' (With his aristocratic looks and enormous charm, Duchamp was highly attractive to women, and a friend wrote that he 'could have had his choice of heiresses'; in 1954 he made a happy second marriage to Alexina Sattler, who had previously been the wife of the art dealer Pierre Matisse, son of Henri *Matisse.) In 1942 Duchamp settled permanently in New York, although he regularly visited France. By this time he seemed to have long abandoned art, but he had in fact continued to experiment quietly, for example with rotating coloured discs that anticipate *Kinetic art. He also did a good deal to promote avant-garde art, particularly *Surrealism, in France and the USA, notably through the activities of the *Société Anonyme, but in the exciting post-war New York art world he was for many years a marginal figure. From the late 1950s, however, avant-garde artists began to rediscover his work and ideas and in his final years he was revered as a kind of patron saint of modern art. Near the end of his life he revealed that he had been working in secret for twenty years (1946–66) on a large mixed-media construction called *Étant donnés: 1° La Chûte d'eau, 2° Le Gaz d'éclairage* (Given: 1. The Waterfall, 2. The Illuminating Gas). It features a naturalistic painted sculpture of a nude reclining woman holding a gas lamp, with behind her a simulated landscape, including a trickle of water representing a waterfall; this elaborate tableau is viewed through peepholes in a heavy wooden door. He presented it to the Philadelphia Museum of Art, where it joined the majority of his other works.

Duchamp's iconoclasm and experimental attitude have been enormously influential, most obviously on *Conceptual art, but also for example on *Minimal art and on *Pop art, in which the ready-made has played such a big part. His wit and irony have been sadly lacking in most of his followers, however, and it could be argued that his influence has been disastrous, encouraging people of no discernible talent to believe that anything they do, say, or think is worthy of attention as art.

Duchamp-Villon, Raymond (1876–1918). French sculptor, the brother of Marcel *Duchamp and of Jacques *Villon (he adopted the name Duchamp-Villon in about 1900). After illness forced him to abandon his medical studies at the University of Paris in 1898, he took up sculpture, at which he was self-taught. For the next dozen years or so he experimented with various styles until in about 1910 he became involved with *Cubism. Several other Cubists used to meet in the studios of Duchamp-Villon and Villon and from these meetings the *Section d'Or group emerged. In 1914 Duchamp-Villon enlisted in the army as an auxiliary doctor; he contracted typhoid fever in 1916 and spent his last two years as an invalid before he died in a military hospital. His death cut short a career of great promise, for his major work, *The Horse* (1914), has been described by George Heard Hamilton (*Painting and Sculpture in Europe: 1880–1940*, 1967) as 'the most powerful piece of sculpture produced by any strictly Cubist artist' (there are casts in Tate Modern, London; MoMA, New York; and elsewhere). This 'abstract diagram of the muscular tensions developed by a leaping horse' (Hamilton) has been compared with the work of the *Futurists, particularly that of *Boccioni, who met Duchamp-Villon in 1913. In the success with which it suggests taut energy it certainly achieves at least one of the things the Futurists were aiming at in their attempts to represent 'the dynamics of movement'.

Dufy, Raoul (1877–1953). French painter, graphic artist, and designer. His early work was *Impressionist in style, but he became a convert to *Fauvism in 1905 after seeing *Matisse's *Luxe, calme et volupté* ('this miracle of creative imagination in colour and line') at the *Salon des Indépendants. He exhibited with the Fauves in 1906 and

1907, but in 1908 he worked with *Braque at L'Estaque and abandoned Fauvism for a more sober style influenced by *Cézanne. However, he soon returned to a lighter style and in the next few years developed the highly distinctive personal manner for which he has become famous. It is characterized, in both oils and watercolours, by rapid calligraphic drawing on backgrounds of bright, thinly washed colour and was well suited to the scenes of luxury and pleasure Dufy favoured. He had achieved considerable success by the mid-1920s and the accessibility and joie de vivre of his work helped to popularize modern art. In 1910 Dufy made friends with the fashion designer Paul Poiret, and he did design work for him and for Bianchini-Férier, a silk manufacturer of Lyons. His other work included stage designs, numerous book illustrations, and several murals, the largest of which was The Spirit of Electricity, commissioned for the Pavilion of Light at the 1937 Paris World Fair and now in the Musée d'Art Moderne de la Ville de Paris. In 1952 he was awarded the main painting prize at the Venice *Biennale. His popularity has continued undiminished since his death, not least in Japan, where he is a favourite with collectors.

dugento (It.: '13th century'). See QUATTRO-CENTO.

Dughet, Gaspard (Gaspard Poussin) (1615–75). Franco-Italian landscape painter, draughtsman, and etcher, born in Rome, the son of a French cook and his Italian wife. He never left Italy, spending almost all his life in or near Rome, but he is traditionally considered a member of the French School. In 1630 his sister married Nicolas *Poussin, with whom he studied c.1631–5 and whose surname he adopted. A few paintings have been disputed between the two artists, but usually Dughet's work is fairly distinct in spirit from that of his illustrious brother-in-law. He combined something of Poussin's solidity with the romanticism of *Claude, but he preferred a more rugged type of scenery, and he was particularly fond of the countryside near Tivoli (where he often stayed), with its cliffs, cascades, and dense vegetation (View of Tivoli, c.1645–50, Hatton Gal., Newcastle upon Tyne). Very few of his paintings can be securely dated—the main exceptions are his frescos (c.1647–51) on the history of the

Carmelite Order in S. Martino ai Monti, Rome (these too are landscapes)—and it has proved difficult to establish a chronology for him. However, in spite of the lack of detailed knowledge of his work, it is clear that he enjoyed a successful career and in the 18th century his reputation stood very high, particularly in England. His pictures were avidly sought by English collectors and he influenced painters such as Richard *Wilson and the supporters of the *Picturesque.

Dujardin, Karel (1626–78). Dutch painter and etcher of landscapes, cattle, *genre scenes, portraits, and religious subjects, active mainly in his native Amsterdam. He is best known for his small paintings of humble bucolic scenes set in an Italianate or a Dutch landscape and diffused with a clear, warm light. These works reveal the impact of Nicolaes *Berchem (who was probably his teacher) and his admiration for Paulus *Potter and Adriaen van de *Velde. He was also an excellent portraitist and his large religious pictures show that he was familiar with the pictorial ideas of Italian *Baroque art. It is generally assumed, on such stylistic evidence, that he visited Italy in the 1640s, but there is no documentary proof. He did, however, spend his last four years in Italy, dying in Venice. Like so many of the 17th-century Dutch artists who made the journey to Italy, Dujardin was a Catholic.

Dulac, Edmund (1882–1953). French-born illustrator, designer, painter, and sculptor who settled in England in 1905 and became a British citizen in 1912. Dulac is best known as a book illustrator, particularly of fairy-tale and legendary subjects, in which his sense of fantasy and gifts as a colourist were put to brilliant effect (he was much influenced by Middle and Far Eastern art). He was also a portrait painter, a caricaturist, a sculptor, and a highly versatile designer; his output included much work for the stage, and one of his last commissions was a stamp commemorating the coronation of Queen Elizabeth II in 1953. See also RACKHAM.

Dumonstier. Family of French artists, active in various fields but mainly as portrait painters. About a dozen members of the family are recorded and several of them held court appointments. The earliest of any significance was **Geoffroy** (c.1510–60), and the best-known member of the dynasty was **Daniel** (1574–1645), who continued the tradition of the *Clouets into the middle of the 17th century.

Dunlap, William (1766–1839). American painter, writer, and theatrical manager. He trained as a painter, studying with *West in London 1784–7, but he became fascinated by the theatre during this time, and it was his main profession for the next twenty years. In 1798–1805 and again in 1806–11 he managed the Park Theatre, New York, the interruption being caused by his bankruptcy (he was considered too good-natured to be a successful businessman). He wrote, adapted, or translated (from French and German) about 50 plays and has been described as 'the father of American drama'. In 1817 he returned to painting, hoping (in vain) to make a better living at that profession, and in 1825 he was one of the founders of the *National Academy of Design. His paintings, which included portraits and large religious scenes, are now virtually forgotten, and his most enduring works are two books he produced near the end of his life: *History of the American Theatre* (1832) and *History of the Rise and Progress of the Arts of Design in the United States* (1834). The latter is the most valuable sourcebook on the subject, rich in information and anecdote, and has earned him the nickname 'the American *Vasari'.

Dunoyer de Segonzac, André (1884–1974). French painter, printmaker, and designer. Early in his career he went through a period of *Cubist influence, but after the First World War he became recognized as one of the leading upholders of the naturalistic tradition in a period dominated by anti-naturalistic tendencies. His oil paintings (mainly landscapes, still lifes, and figure compositions) are often sombre in tone and usually executed in thick paint, emphasizing the weight and earthiness of the forms. His watercolours and etchings, however, are more elegant and spontaneous, with a wider range of subject matter, including dancers and boxers. He also did designs for the theatre and ballet. His reputation was at its height in the 1930s: he won first prize at the Carnegie International in Pittsburgh in 1933 and the main painting prize at the Venice *Biennale in 1934.

Dupont, Gainsborough (1754–97). English painter and engraver, the nephew and only assistant of Thomas *Gainsborough. He made copies and *mezzotints of his uncle's pictures, completed others left unfinished at his death, and painted some original works in his manner. The best-known are probably his portraits of actors, examples of which are in the Garrick Club, London, but his landscapes are sometimes regarded as his best works.

Dupré, Jules. *See* BARBIZON SCHOOL.

Duque Cornejo, Pedro. *See* ROLDÁN.

Duquesnoy, François (1597–1643). Flemish sculptor, active mainly in Rome. He settled there in 1618 and with *Algardi became the outstanding sculptor in the city apart from the great *Bernini. In 1627–8 he worked for Bernini on the decoration of the *baldacchino in St Peter's, but his style—like Algardi's—was much more restrained and less *Baroque than the master's. He was indeed a leading figure in circles devoted to classical art (initially he earned his living partly by restoring *antique sculpture and he shared a house for a time with his friend *Poussin). Duquesnoy produced only two major public works—the marble statues of St Susanna (S. Maria di Loreto, 1629–33) and St Andrew (St Peter's, 1629–40)—but his fame was spread by numerous smaller works: reliefs and statuettes of mythological and religious subjects in bronze, ivory, terracotta, and wax. He was particularly renowned for his handling of *putti, and it is curious that someone who so unaffectedly depicted the beauty and charm of children was depressive and perhaps mentally unstable; his biographer *Passeri wrote that he was 'so hesitant and careful in every particular that he wore out his life in irresolution', and the diarist John Evelyn, visiting Rome in 1644, said that he 'died mad' because his *St Andrew* 'was placed in a bad light' (he had died the previous year on his way to Paris to work for Louis XIII). Duquesnoy's father and brother were sculptors: **Jerome I** (c.1570–1641/2) and **Jerome II** (1602–54). His father is remembered mainly for the famous *Manneken-pis* fountain (1619) behind the town hall in Brussels, showing a boy urinating. His brother worked with François in Rome and took a somewhat diluted Baroque style back to

Brussels with him. The tomb of Bishop Anton Trest in Ghent Cathedral (1651–4) is considered his finest work. He moved to Ghent to complete this, but soon after his arrival he was accused of committing sodomy in the cathedral with his pupils and was executed.

Durand, Asher B. (1796–1886). American painter and engraver. His early work was mainly as an engraver and he established his reputation with his print after John *Trumbull's *Signing of the Declaration of Independence* and with portraits of eminent contemporaries. In the 1830s he turned increasingly to painting. At first he worked mainly as a portraitist, but then devoted himself to landscape, becoming a leading figure of the *Hudson River School. Thomas *Cole was a major source of inspiration, and Durand's most famous painting, *Kindred Spirits* (1849, New York Public Lib.), was painted as a memorial to him; it shows Cole (who had died the previous year) and the poet William Cullen Bryant admiring spectacular scenery in the Catskill Mountains, New York State.

Durand-Ruel, Paul (1831–1922). The best-known member of a family of French picture dealers, renowned as the first dealer to give consistent support to the *Impressionists. He took over the family firm in 1865 and established himself as the main dealer of the *Barbizon School painters. It was one of these—*Daubigny—who introduced him to *Monet and *Pissarro when all four had taken refuge in England from the Franco-Prussian War of 1870–1. Durand-Ruel's championship of the Impressionists often brought him near to bankruptcy, but in 1886 he achieved a breakthrough with an exhibition of their work in New York, the success of which encouraged him to open a branch of his firm there. This played a major role in building up some of the great American collections of Impressionists. After Durand-Ruel's death, Monet wrote to the dealer's son: 'I shall never forget all that my friends and I owe to your father, in a very special way.'

Dürer, Albrecht (1471–1528). German printmaker, painter, draughtsman, and writer, the greatest figure of *Renaissance art in northern Europe. He was born in Nuremberg, the son of a goldsmith, Albrecht Dürer the Elder, who trained him in his profession. Both his grandfathers had also been goldsmiths, but from an early age Dürer had intellectual ambitions that reached far beyond the confines of the medieval craftsman's workshop. His godfather was Anton Koberger, Nuremberg's leading publisher, whose books were sent all over Europe, and his best friend from childhood was Willibald Pirckheimer, who became a poet and scholar and had the best private library in Germany. In 1486, aged 15, Dürer left his father's workshop to study with Michael *Wolgemut, the leading local painter. By this time he had already shown remarkable talent as a draughtsman, as is seen in his exquisite silverpoint self-portrait dated 1484 (Albertina, Vienna). (This is the earliest of several memorable self-portraits by Dürer; he was the first artist to produce a series of them at various stages of his life rather than one or two isolated examples, and they show his high conception of the artist's profession as well as his pride in his appearance—typically he presents himself in thought, or as a beautifully dressed and immaculately groomed gentleman, or even as a Christlike figure, rather than as a humble craftsman.) Wolgemut was a prolific book illustrator as well as a painter and Dürer must have learned the technique of *woodcut from him. After completing his apprenticeship he spent the years 1490–4 travelling and gaining experience of the world. In 1492 he visited Colmar, hoping to meet Martin *Schongauer, the most illustrious German painter and engraver of the day. He arrived too late, as Schongauer had recently died, but the master's brothers furnished Dürer with introductions that gained him work as a book illustrator in Basle (a major publishing centre), where he remained for over a year in 1492–3. After visiting Strasbourg, he returned to Nuremberg in 1494 and in the same year made an arranged marriage to the daughter of a local coppersmith. The union was childless and evidently unhappy (his wife had none of his intellectual interests), but it lasted until Dürer's death. A few months after the wedding he left his bride behind to make a study visit to north Italy, mainly Venice.

After his return to Nuremberg in spring 1495, Dürer quickly established himself as the city's leading artist. Although he was also active as a painter, his reputation was made mainly as a printmaker, his first great success being a series of fifteen woodcuts of the *Apocalypse* (1498). Most of his woodcuts were on traditional religious subjects, but they were much more ambitious than the work of his predecessors—large in size, elaborate in technique, vivid in imagery, and rich in human feeling, marking the highest development of the technique before it was virtually superseded by copper engraving. These early works tend to have crowded compositions and emphatic emotions, but Dürer became much more classical and restrained, as he learned to reconcile his native love of precise detail with Italian ideals of grandeur and harmony. In 1505–7 he made a second visit to Italy, again staying mainly in Venice. This time he was something of a celebrity, not the promising youngster of his first trip, and he painted a major altarpiece for the German church of S. Bartolommeo, Venice (*Feast of the Rose Garlands*, 1506, NG, Prague). In richness of colour it was intended to compete with Venetian artists on their own ground or, in Dürer's words, 'to silence those who said that I was good as an engraver but did not know how to handle the colours in painting'. Some of the local artists were evidently jealous of Dürer (he even said that he feared being poisoned by them), but he was warmly treated by Giovanni *Bellini, for whom he had great admiration.

Back in Nuremberg Dürer consolidated his position as Germany's leading artist and by 1509 he was prosperous enough to buy a large house (now a museum dedicated to him). Apart from prints, his work included altarpieces such as the *Adoration of the Trinity* (1511, KH Mus., Vienna). In 1512 the emperor Maximilian I (*see* HABSBURG) visited Nuremberg and he subsequently gave Dürer several commissions (he often failed to pay for these, but in 1515 he directed the civic authorities to give the artist a substantial annual allowance). Dürer's largest project for Maximilian was the design (finished 1515) of an enormous woodcut triumphal arch, laden with history and allegory, glorifying the emperor and his family. At the same time Dürer found creative outlets entirely of his own choosing, notably in three celebrated prints that are sometimes known as the 'Master Engrav-

ings': *The Knight, Death, and the Devil* (1513), showing a Christian soldier passing resolutely through the perils of life; *St Jerome in his Study* (1514); and *Melencolia I* (1514), a brooding, enigmatic allegory. In these prints he attained a mastery of *line engraving that has never been surpassed, achieving a richness of shading and texture that rivalled the effects of painting. He also produced much more modest works for his own satisfaction. Like his contemporary *Leonardo da Vinci, with whom he is often compared, he found visual stimulation all around him and he made many wonderful drawings and watercolours of subjects that few other artists of the time would have noticed (*A Hare*, 1502, Albertina, Vienna).

In 1519 the emperor Maximilian died, and in 1520–1 Dürer journeyed north to meet his successor Charles V, to whom he successfully appealed for a renewal of his annual allowance. He attended Charles's coronation in Aachen and visited various places in the Netherlands, where he was fêted as the acknowledged leader of his profession. The day-to-day diary that he kept on this tour, together with his drawings showing the people and places he saw, is the first record of its kind in the history of art. A good deal of other personal writing by Dürer survives, including letters and a family chronicle that he composed in 1524. These sources reveal much about his personality and beliefs, including his religious views and fears. He thought deeply about religion and became a convert to Lutherism in about 1520, but he was moderate in his opinions, wanting toleration rather than theological conflict. After his return to Nuremberg in 1521 he dedicated much of his time to writing, producing three learned treatises—on measurement (published 1525), fortifications (1527), and proportion in the human body (published soon after his death in 1528). However, he continued his activities as a printmaker and painter, and his final works include two panels of the 'Four Apostles' (1526, Alte Pin., Munich) that are often considered his masterpieces in painting. In these he summed up his life's work: the study of the ideal human figure—here depicted in forms of heroic dignity—and the expression of a deeply felt religious message.

At his death Dürer was acknowledged as the leading artist of his time outside Italy and as the greatest of all printmakers. He was the first artist of the very highest rank to devote the major part of his career to prints, and their portability gave them international currency—*Vasari wrote that they 'astonished the world'. Even in Dürer's lifetime his prints were extensively imitated and forged and they were reprinted and copied for generations afterwards, often as illustrations in prayerbooks and devotional works. A new phase of posthumous fame came in the *Romantic period, when Dürer was acclaimed as a German national hero—the statue of him unveiled in Nuremberg in 1840 was the first such public monument ever erected to an artist. His enormous reputation has endured, and in Germany the 400th anniversary of his death (in 1928) and the 500th anniversary of his birth (in 1971) were celebrated as 'Albrecht Dürer Years'.

Duveen, Joseph (Baron Duveen of Millbank) (1869–1939). English art dealer, patron, and philanthropist. In 1886 he entered the firm of his father, Sir **Joseph Duveen** (1843–1908), and with his enormous energy, larger-than-life personality, and great gift for salesmanship expanded it into the biggest firm of art dealers in the world, operating on an unprecedented scale. He employed Bernard *Berenson to give his seal of authenticity to the *Renaissance paintings he sold and he was the main agent in forming the collections of such fabulously wealthy Americans as *Frick, *Kress, and Andrew *Mellon. Duveen's benefactions to the arts were also on a princely scale. In addition to giving many pictures to national collections, he paid for extensions or new galleries at the *National Gallery, the *National Portrait Gallery, the *Tate Gallery, and the *British Museum (to house the *Elgin Marbles). He also bore the cost of decorations at the *Wallace Collection and of Rex *Whistler's murals at the Tate Gallery and endowed a professorship in the history of art at London University.

Duvet, Jean (c.1485–1561/70). French engraver and goldsmith, sometimes called the Master of the Unicorn from his series of engravings (probably from the 1540s) on the medieval theme of the hunting of the unicorn. Little is known of his life; he lived mainly in Langres and Dijon, but the *Renaissance influence in his early work strongly suggests that he spent some time in Italy. His most famous work, a set of 24 engravings of the *Apocalypse*, published at Lyons in 1561, is, however, completely different in style. The engravings borrow many features from *Dürer's famous woodcuts of the *Apocalypse* (1498), but they are a world apart in spirit, for Duvet treats the subject with a visionary intensity and expressive freedom that anticipate William *Blake (who may well have known Duvet's prints). His work reflects the disturbed religious conditions that prevailed in Langres and is in complete contrast to the mannered elegance of the School of *Fontainebleau, then the dominant force in French art.

Duyster, Willem (1599–1635). Dutch painter of *genre scenes and portraits, active mainly in his native Amsterdam. Most of his paintings depict soldiers, sometimes fighting or looting, but more usually drinking, gaming, or wooing. His delicate skill at painting textiles, his ability to characterize individuals, and his power to express subtle psychological relationships between them, suggest that if he had not been carried off by the plague in his mid-thirties he might well have rivalled *Terborch. There are two examples of his fairly rare work in the National Gallery, London.

Dyce, William (1806–64). Scottish painter, designer, and administrator, active mainly in London. In the 1820s he twice visited Italy, where he was influenced by *Renaissance painting and by the *Nazarenes, with whom he became friendly. Dyce was highly cultured and widely talented (he was an accomplished musician and wrote learned essays on antiquities and a prize-winning paper on electromagnetism), but for some time he was successful mainly as a rather conventional portraitist in Edinburgh. In 1837 he moved to London to work for the newly founded School of Design (which developed into the *Royal College of Art) and he made a tour of state art schools in France and Germany to study their methods. His report on his findings led to his appointment as superintendent (director) of the School in 1840. He resigned in 1843, but he remained a central figure in the art world—indeed 'there was no major [artistic] undertaking in mid nineteenth-century Britain in which he did not play either an executive or advisory role' (David and Francina Irwin,

Scottish Painters at Home and Abroad, 1975). In particular he was a key figure in the revival of fresco painting, which was stimulated mainly by the mural decoration (begun 1843) of the new Houses of Parliament. Dyce's own work there has deteriorated badly, but his *Neptune Resigning to Britannia the Empire of the Sea* (1847, Osborne House, Isle of Wight) is one of the best preserved of all Victorian frescos. This was one of several royal commissions for Dyce, who was a favourite of Prince Albert. In addition to murals, he produced a varied range of easel paintings, from high-minded religious scenes (he was a devout Christian) to the delightfully sentimental *Titian's First Essay in Colour* (1856-7, Aberdeen AG); his *Pegwell Bay, Kent* (1859-60, Tate, London) is considered one of the most remarkable of all Victorian landscapes. Dyce's strong colours, firm outlines, naturalistic detail, and thoughtful sincerity of approach formed a bridge between the Nazarenes and the *Pre-Raphaelites, and *Ruskin said that it was Dyce who gave him his 'real introduction' to the Pre-Raphaelites when, at the 1849 *Royal Academy exhibition, he 'dragged me literally up to the *Millais picture of the Carpenter's Shop, which I had passed disdainfully, and forced me to look for its merits'.

Dyck, Sir Anthony van (1599–1641). Apart from *Rubens, the outstanding Flemish painter of the 17th century, renowned chiefly as one of the greatest of all portraitists. Van Dyck was born in Antwerp, where in 1609 he was apprenticed to Hendrick van *Balen. He was exceptionally precocious and on his earliest dated painting (*Portrait of a Man aged 70*, 1613, Mus. Royaux, Brussels) he has proudly inscribed his own age (14) as well as that of the sitter. From about 1617 to 1620 he was Rubens's chief assistant, but in this period he also painted works of his own and established an independent reputation: in 1620 the Earl of *Arundel's secretary wrote from Antwerp to tell his employer that 'Van Dyck is still with Signor Rubens, and his works are hardly less esteemed than those of his master.' Van Dyck's early work was based very firmly on that of Rubens (there is no trace of influence from van Balen); experts still sometimes have difficulty in differentiating their hands, although van Dyck's style was typically less energetic and more nervously sensitive than that of his supremely robust mentor, reflecting differences in character and constitution (van Dyck was highly strung in temperament and comparatively slight in physique). In addition to learning so much from Rubens's paintings, van Dyck also consciously imitated his aristocratic demeanour and way of life: *Bellori wrote that 'His manners were those of a lord rather than an ordinary man, for he had been accustomed to consort with noblemen in Rubens's studio.' However, he did not have Rubens's prodigious intellectual powers or force of personality and although he was intelligent and charming, he sometimes struck people as haughty (he was certainly vain about his good looks, as his numerous self-portraits testify).

In 1620-1 van Dyck visited London, where he spent a few months in the service of James I, then in 1621 moved to Italy, where he stayed until 1627. At the beginning of this period he was primarily a painter of figure compositions (and he always nursed unfulfilled ambitions to produce grand decorative schemes in the manner of Rubens), but in Italy he turned increasingly to portraiture, a field in which *Titian was his chief inspiration. He travelled a good deal, but worked mainly in Genoa, where he painted a series of grand portraits of the nobility in which he established a distinctive aristocratic type, with slender figure and proud bearing. A superb example is the full-length *Marchesa Elena Grimaldi* (1623, NG, Washington), of which Sir David Piper wrote (*Van Dyck*, 1968): 'this is how one imagines any feminine aristocrat worthy of her rank must feel herself essentially to be, yet did not know it till van Dyck showed her—aloof and formally regal, but endowed with an elegance and grace that are infinitely seductive.'

After leaving Italy, van Dyck worked mainly in Antwerp for the next few years, 1628-32. During this period he painted some of his finest religious works, including a series of major altarpieces for local churches, beginning in 1628 with the *Martyrdom of St Augustine* (church of St Augustine, Antwerp, on loan to the city's Koninklijk Mus.). He was a devout Catholic and his religious pictures are often highly emotional in tone. In 1632 he moved to London to become court painter to Charles I, who knighted him in that year. Van Dyck was based in England for the rest of his life (he married one of the queen's ladies-in-waiting in 1640), but he never really settled there and was always on the lookout for opportunities elsewhere: between 1634 and 1641 he made three visits to the Continent (he was away for about two years in all), and during the second trip he went to Paris in the hope of winning the commission to decorate the Grande Galerie of the Louvre (which went instead to *Poussin). Nevertheless, in spite of his frustrations in England (which included dilatory payments from the king), it is probably for his portraits of Charles, his family, and his courtiers that van Dyck is best remembered; he depicted his royal and aristocratic sitters in images of such beguiling beauty and glamour that it is hard to envisage the era other than through his eyes, and these pictures have had a profound and lasting influence on British art. *Gainsborough, in particular, revered van Dyck, but he was an inspiration to many others until the early 20th century, when society portraiture ceased to be a major form of artistic expression.

The contemporary poet Edmund Waller described van Dyck's studio as a 'shop of beauty', and he is often characterized as a shameless flatterer of his sitters—when Charles I's niece Sophia of Bavaria first met Queen Henrietta Maria in 1641 she wrote: 'Van Dyck's handsome portraits had given me so fine an idea of the beauty of all English ladies that I was surprised to find that the Queen, who looked so fine in painting, was a small woman raised up on her chair, with long skinny arms and teeth like defence works projecting from her mouth.' However, not all his sitters felt that their looks had been enhanced: when the Countess of Sussex saw the portrait van Dyck painted of her in 1639–40 (now lost) she

felt 'quite out of love with myself. The face is so big and fat that it pleases me not at all. It looks like one of the winds puffing—but truly I think tis like the original.'

In addition to his painted portraits, van Dyck planned a series of etchings of famous contemporaries, to be known as the *Iconography*. He etched a few plates himself and had others made from his drawings by various printmakers. The project was unfinished at his death, but 100 etchings were issued as a set in 1645. After he moved to England, he had little time or opportunity to produce paintings other than portraits, but for his own pleasure he made some remarkably fresh and informal drawings and watercolours of the English countryside. This aspect of his work—looking forward to the great English watercolour tradition—is all the more surprising considering that any landscape elements in his oil paintings are usually treated in summary or conventional fashion.

Dying Gaul. Marble statue in the Capitoline Museum, Rome, showing a fallen warrior straining to support himself on one arm as blood gushes from a wound in his side. The statue is first recorded in 1623, in the collection of Cardinal Ludovico Ludovisi in Rome, and thereafter it quickly became one of the most celebrated of *antique works. It is a Roman copy of a Greek work in the *Pergamene style of the late 3rd century BC. Sometimes it is called the 'Dying Gladiator', but this is a misnomer, as the hairstyle and accessories are scrupulously Gallic. It was among the works looted from Italy by Napoleon and was in Paris from 1798 to 1815. Unlike many once-famous antique statues, the *Dying Gaul* is still a highly regarded work, admired particularly for its sense of pathos.

E

Eakins, Thomas (1844–1916). American painter, primarily of portraits, active for most of his life in his native city of Philadelphia; he is regarded by most critics as the outstanding American painter of the 19th century and by many as the greatest his country has yet produced. After studying at the Pennsylvania Academy of the Fine Arts, he moved to Paris and continued his training under *Gérôme, 1866–9. However, he learnt more from a six-month visit to Spain, where he particularly admired the precise and uncompromising sense for actuality he found in *Velázquez and *Ribera. In 1870 he returned to Philadelphia and in 1876 he began teaching there at the Pennsylvania Academy. He was attacked for his radical ideas, particularly his insistence on working from nude models, and in 1886 he was forced to resign after allowing a mixed class to draw from a completely nude male model. Eakins's quest for realism led him to study anatomy and make full use of *Muybridge's photographic researches, but the scientific bent in his work is of less importance than his honesty and depth of characterization. His portraits are often compared with Rembrandt's because of their dramatic play of sombre lighting and sense of inner truth. The most famous of his paintings is *The Gross Clinic* (1875, Thomas Jefferson Univ., Philadelphia), which aroused controversy because of its unsparing depiction of surgery, an experience that was repeated with *The Agnew Clinic* (1889, Univ. of Pennsylvania, Philadelphia). Because of financial support from his father, Eakins could continue on his chosen course despite public abuse, but much of his later career was spent working in bitter isolation. It was only near the end of his life that he achieved recognition as a great master, and in the first two decades of the 20th century his desire to 'peer deeper into the heart of American life' was reflected in the work of the *Ashcan School and other realist painters; Robert *Henri was one of his greatest admirers. In addition to portraits, Eakins painted genre scenes of Philadelphia life (boating and bathing were favourite themes), and he also took photographs and made a few sculptures. His wife, **Susan Hannah Macdowell Eakins** (1851–1938), whom he married in 1884, was likewise a painter and photographer, as well as an accomplished pianist.

Eardley, Joan (1921–63). British painter, born in Sussex but considered Scottish (her mother was Scottish and she lived in Scotland from 1940). One of her teachers was James *Cowie; he perhaps helped to shape her preference for subjects drawn from everyday experience, but her approach was more earthy and sensuous than his. She divided her time between Glasgow (where she painted *kitchen sink subjects) and the fishing village of Catterline, about 30 km (20 miles) south of Aberdeen on the north-east coast. Her favourite subjects in her later years were the village and the sea, especially in stormy weather (she is said to have set off from her Glasgow home as soon as she heard reports of gales). The freely painted, often bleak and desolate works that resulted are among the most powerful and individual landscapes in 20th-century British art. After her early death from breast cancer her ashes were scattered on the beach at Catterline. Her work is well represented in the Scottish National Gallery of Modern Art, Edinburgh.

Earl, Ralph (1751–1801). American painter, active in Connecticut, Massachusetts, New York, and Vermont, and also in England (1778–85), when his loyalty to the British put his life in danger in his homeland. He painted landscapes and battle scenes of the Revolution, but was primarily a portraitist. Although his style became softer and more sophisticated after studying with *West in London, his work generally has a sincerity and freshness of vision that makes him one of the finest American artists of the 18th century. His presentation of character is extremely forthright and his portraits convey the immense pride his New England sitters took in their possessions. Earl's personal life was a disaster. He was imprisoned for debt and died an alcoholic after deserting both of his wives in turn. Other members of his family were artists, notably his brother **James** (1761–96) and his son **Ralph E. W. Earl** (c.1785–1838), who is remembered mainly for his portraits of President Andrew Jackson, whose niece he had married.

Early Christian art. Term generally applied to Christian art from the 3rd century AD until about 750, particularly in Italy and the western Mediterranean. The art of the Eastern empire during this time is termed *Byzantine art, but there is no hard-and-fast demarcation between the two traditions.

Earthwork. *See* LAND ART.

easel. Stand on which a painting is supported while the artist works on it. The oldest representation of an easel is on an Egyptian relief of the Old Kingdom (c.2700–c.2150 BC). *Renaissance illustrations of the artist at work show all kinds of contrivances, the commonest being the three-legged easel of a type still used today, with pegs to support the picture. Lightweight folding easels were not made until the 18th and 19th centuries, when painters took to working out of doors. The studio easel, a 19th-century invention, is a heavy piece of furniture that runs on castors or wheels, and served to impress the clients of portrait painters. Oil painters need an easel that will support the canvas almost vertically or tip it slightly forward to prevent reflection from the wet paint, whereas the watercolourist must be able to lay his paper nearly flat so that the wet paint will not run down. The term 'easel painting' is applied to any picture small enough to have been painted on a standard easel.

Eastlake, Sir Charles Lock (1793–1865). English painter, art historian, and administrator. He studied under *Haydon and achieved early fame with his *Napoleon on Board the Bellerophon* (1815, Nat. Maritime Mus., London), made from sketches when he witnessed Napoleon on board ship (in Eastlake's native Plymouth) en route to exile in St Helena. Using the proceeds from the sale of this work he lived in Rome 1816–30, and there painted picturesque scenes of the Roman Campagna, often peopled by banditti, that became very popular in England. After his return there, however, he turned increasingly to administration and

achieved a remarkable record as a public servant. Most notably he was president of the Royal Academy from 1850 and director of the National Gallery (the first holder of this post) from 1855 until his death. His informed purchases of early Italian paintings for the National Gallery were largely responsible for its outstanding representation in this area. Among his writings are *Materials for a History of Oil Painting* (1847), a pioneering work, and a translation of *Goethe's *Theory of Colours* (1840). His wife, **Elizabeth**, née Rigby (1809–93), was in her own right a figure in the literary-artistic world of the day. She wrote several books on art and also translated Gustav *Waagen's *Treasures of Art in Great Britain* (1854). Eastlake's nephew, **Charles Locke Eastlake** (1836–1906), was keeper of the National Gallery, 1878–98, and published several works on art and decoration, the best known of which was *Hints on Household Taste* (1868), in which he advocated quality of materials and workmanship. It was highly influential in England and even more so in America, although so-called 'Eastlake furniture' often has little to do with his ideas.

Eckersberg, Christoffer Wilhelm (1783–1853). Danish painter. He was one of the leading figures in his country's art in the first half of the 19th century, and is sometimes called 'the father of Danish painting' because of the influence he exerted on his contemporaries. After training in Copenhagen and under J.-L. *David in Paris (1811–13), he continued his studies in Rome (1813–16), where he executed a masterly portrait of his friend *Thorvaldsen (1815, Academy, Copenhagen). In 1816 he returned to Copenhagen and in 1818 he was appointed a professor at the Academy, where he revolutionized teaching by introducing painting from nature into the curriculum. His pupils included J. C. *Dahl and Christen *Købke. In addition to portraits, which were his financial mainstay, Eckersberg painted landscapes, marine subjects, scenes from Danish history, and occasional religious works. His style combines *Neoclassical clarity of form with freshness of observation.

eclectic, eclecticism. Terms in criticism for a person or style that conflates features borrowed from various sources. Such a style often arises from the notion that the excellences of great masters can be selected and combined in one work of art. After *Vasari praised *Raphael for his skill in selecting the best from the art of his predecessors, it became common to use the same formula about other artists. Thus it was said that *Tintoretto had tried to combine the drawing of *Michelangelo with the colour of *Titian. In the 18th century, 'eclectics' became a label for the *Carracci and their Bolognese followers, and gradually the term came to be used mainly pejoratively, implying lack of originality. Such usage has been abandoned in serious criticism, and it is clear that the Carracci never adopted eclecticism as a fundamental principle. As Denis *Mahon has said, 'Annibale Carracci, the greatest member of the family and one of the founders of 17th-century painting, was ...contemptuous of art theory, and (far from being a dispenser of learned recipes and synthetic systems) was in practice one of the most insatiable experimentalists known to the history of art.'

École de Paris (School of Paris). A term that was originally applied to a number of artists of non-French origin, predominantly of Jewish background, who in the years immediately after the First World War lived in Paris and painted in figurative styles that might loosely be called poetic *Expressionism, forming the most distinctive strand in French painting between *Cubism and *Surrealism. *Chagall (Russian), *Foujita (Japanese), *Modigliani (Italian), *Pascin (Bulgarian), and *Soutine (Lithuanian) are among the most famous artists embraced by the term. However, particularly outside France, the meaning of the term was soon broadened to include all foreign artists who had settled in Paris since the beginning of the century (van *Dongen, *Gris, *Picasso, for example), and then it expanded still further to cover virtually all progressive art in the 20th century that had its focus in Paris. In this broadest sense, the term reflects the intense concentration of artistic activity, supported by critics, dealers, and connoisseurs, that made Paris the world centre of advanced art during the first 40 years of the 20th century. After the Second World War, however, New York replaced Paris as the world capital of avant-garde art.

écorché (Fr.: 'flayed'). A representation of a figure with the skin removed, displaying the muscles. Drawings, prints, and statues of such figures, both human and animal (horses were particularly popular), were much used in art teaching from the 16th century. *Stubbs's écorché figures of animals are well known and *Houdon made a celebrated human écorché statue (1767, Schlossmuseum, Gotha).

Eddy, Don. *See* SUPERREALISM.

Edelfelt, Albert (1854–1905). Finnish painter, who with *Gallen-Kallela ranks as his country's leading artist in the 19th century. He trained in Antwerp and then in Paris, where under the influence of his friend *Bastien-Lepage he took up *plein-air naturalism. His paintings gave a fresh interpretation of Finnish country life and he sometimes set biblical scenes in the Finnish landscape (*Christ and Mary Magdalene*, 1890, Atheneum, Helsinki). Much of his later work was on themes from Finnish history, a type of patriotic work that reflected opposition to Russia's growing oppression of his country. Edelfelt was also an outstanding book illustrator and portraitist.

Edelinck, Gerard (1640–1707). Flemish-born engraver who settled in Paris in 1666 and became a French citizen in 1675. He was the son-in-law of *Nanteuil and like him was celebrated as a portrait engraver. His prints after the Old Masters are also highly distinguished, notably that of *Rubens's copy of *Leonardo's *Battle of Anghiari*.

Eeckhout, Gerbrandt van den (1621–74). Dutch painter, born and active in Amsterdam. He was a pupil of *Rembrandt and, according to *Houbraken, his 'great friend'. His religious paintings were deeply influenced by Rembrandt: *St Peter Healing the Cripple* (1667, M. H. de Young Memorial Mus., San Francisco), for example, shows how well he understood the broad touch and warm colours of the master's mature works. Eeckhout's *genre scenes, on the other hand, are close to *Terborch in style (*The Music Lesson*, 1655, Statens Mus., Copenhagen). His other works included portraits and a few landscapes. He also made etchings and was a prolific draughtsman.

Egg, Augustus (1816–63). English painter. He painted historical, anecdotal, and literary themes (he was a friend of Dickens and a talented actor), and under the influence of the *Pre-Raphaelites he also turned to overtly moralizing subjects. His most famous work in this vein is the series of three pictures *Past and Present* (1858, Tate, London), which melodramatically illustrates the dire consequences of adultery.

Eidophusikon. (Gk.: 'image of nature'). An entertainment invented by P. J. de *Loutherbourg in which spectacular scenic effects were created on a small-scale stage set. Loutherbourg first exhibited the Eidophusikon in London in 1781 with immediate popular success (more than 100 paying spectators could be seated in the room in which it was displayed). The stage area in which the spectacle was performed was roughly 2 m (7 ft) wide, 1 m (3 ft) high, and 3 m (10 ft) deep, and the effects were produced by means of lights, gauzes, coloured glass, and smoke; musical accompaniment was provided by a harpsichord. Among the scenes presented were views of London and other cities, a storm at sea (ships, figures, and the like were moved by a system of rods and pulleys), and 'Satan arraying his Troops on the Banks of the Fiery Lake, with the Raising of the Palace of Pandemonium; from Milton'. *Gainsborough and *Reynolds were among the artists who were impressed by the Eidophusikon. Loutherbourg ran it for several seasons, then sold it to an assistant, who took it on a provincial tour.

Eight, The. A group of American painters who exhibited together in 1908, united by opposition to the conservative *National Academy of Design and a determination to bring painting into direct touch with modern life. The eight members were: Arthur B. *Davies, Maurice *Prendergast, Ernest *Lawson, Robert *Henri, George *Luks, William J. *Glackens, John *Sloan, and Everett *Shinn. They banded together when the National Academy of Design rejected work by Glackens, Luks, and Sloan for its 1907 exhibition. Henri, who was the dominant personality of the group and a member of the Academy's jury, withdrew his own work in protest, and Davies was then asked to organize an independent exhibition at the Macbeth Gallery, New York. This took place in February 1908; it was the only exhibition in which The Eight showed together as a group, but it was subsequently circulated to nine other venues over a

period of a year and gained a good deal of publicity for their work and ideals. The members of the group were not unified stylistically, but their predominant theme was contemporary urban life (several of them were part of the broader trend known as the *Ashcan School). Their exhibition is regarded as an important landmark in American art, helping to lead the way to the *Armory Show of 1913.

The Eight was also the name of a group of progressive Czech artists formed in Prague in 1907, and of a group of Hungarian painters, inspired by *Post-Impressionism, founded in Budapest in 1909.

Elementarism. A modified form of *Neo-Plasticism propounded by van *Doesburg in the mid-1920s. While continuing *Mondrian's restriction to the right angle, Elementarism abandoned his insistence on the use of strict horizontals and verticals. By introducing inclined lines and forms, van Doesburg sought to achieve a quality of dynamic tension. Mondrian was so offended by this 'heresy' that he left De *Stijl.

Elgin Marbles. A collection of Greek sculpture and architectural fragments from the Acropolis in Athens acquired by the British diplomat Thomas Bruce, 7th Earl of Elgin (1766–1841), in 1801–3, when he was ambassador to the Sultan of Turkey, who at this time ruled Greece. The collection consists mainly of sculptures from the Parthenon (most of what little has survived), but includes other pieces, notably a *caryatid from the Erechtheum. They were shipped to Britain over a period of several years and part of the collection was first exhibited to selected visitors (including some of the most distinguished artists of the day) in 1807. Before this, original Greek sculpture of the *Classical age had been virtually unknown in Britain (people had been familiar only with Roman and late *Hellenistic copies) and they made an enormous impact. *Flaxman was bowled over, declaring that compared with the figure of Theseus (now usually identified as Dionysus or Herakles) from the Parthenon the *Apollo Belvedere* was 'a dancing master', and *Haydon wrote, 'I consider it truly the greatest blessing that ever happened to this country their being brought here.' When he was asked to restore them, *Canova said that 'it would be a sacrilege in him or any man to presume to touch them with a chisel'. Many other artists expressed similar opinions, but a dissenting voice came from Richard Payne *Knight, who said, 'You have lost your labour, my Lord Elgin. Your marbles are overrated: they are not Greek: they are Roman of the time of Hadrian.' The enormous expense involved in buying and transporting the marbles left Elgin in debt and in 1811 he offered to sell them to the nation for what amounted to the price they had cost him. Eventually, after the deliberations of a special committee of the House of Commons, they were bought for the British Museum in 1816 for £35,000—about half the sum Elgin had spent. The committee rightly dismissed Payne Knight's objections and the sculptures have come to be universally recognized as one of the summits of ancient art. However, they have continued to be the subject of controversy on another count—that of the morality or legality of their removal when Greece was under the dominion of a foreign power. Byron wrote of them as 'poor plunder from a bleeding land' (*Childe Harold's Pilgrimage*, canto ii, 1812), and a campaign to have them restored to Greece is active today. *See also* PHIDIAS.

Elsheimer, Adam (1578–1610). German painter, etcher, and draughtsman, active mainly in Italy. Although he died young and his output was small, he played a key role in the development of 17th-century landscape painting. He was born in Frankfurt, where he absorbed the *Coninxloo tradition, and moved to Italy in 1598. In Venice he worked with his countryman *Rottenhammer, then in 1600 settled in Rome. There his early *Mannerist style gave way to a more direct manner in which he showed great sensitivity to effects of light; his nocturnal scenes are particularly original, bringing out the best in his lyrical temperament, and he is credited with being the first artist to represent the constellations of the night sky accurately (*Flight into Egypt*, 1609, Alte Pin., Munich). In a few of his pictures, figures are the dominant element, but generally they are fused into a harmonious unity with their landscape settings. His paintings are invariably on a small scale and on copper (the only exception is a self-portrait in the Uffizi, Florence, of doubtful attribution); they are exquisitely executed but have a grandeur out of all proportion to their size. Elsheimer's work was highly regarded by discerning contemporaries, but his life was unhappy and he died in poverty (he was evidently imprisoned for debt); *Sandrart says he suffered from melancholia and was often unable to work. His posthumous fame spread quickly, partly through engravings of his pictures made by the Dutch artist Hendrik Goudt (1573–1648), who seems to have been his patron as well as his pupil (Elsheimer himself made a number of etchings). *Rubens was a friend of Elsheimer and after his death lamented his 'sin of sloth, by which he has deprived the world of the most beautiful things'; he also wrote, 'I have never seen his equal in the realm of small figures, of landscapes, and of so many other subjects'. Both Rubens (Staatliche Kunstsammlungen, Kassel) and *Rembrandt (NG, Dublin) made paintings of the Flight into Egypt inspired by Elsheimer's masterpiece, and his influence is apparent in the work of many other 17th-century artists.

emblem. A visual image carrying a symbolic meaning and often accompanied by texts to explain this meaning. In its most typical form the emblem consisted of a picture, a motto, and an explanatory verse called an epigram. For example, one of the most famous emblems depicted a dolphin and an anchor with the motto 'Festina Lente' ('Make haste slowly'), to symbolize the idea that maturity is achieved by a combination of the speed and energy of the dolphin and the steadiness and gravity of the anchor. The aim of the emblem therefore was to give symbolic expression to a moral adage. Printed collections of emblems ('emblem books') enjoyed a great vogue in the 16th and 17th centuries and were often used as sources of pictorial imagery. In particular, *Iconologia* (1593; 1st illustrated edn., 1603) by the Italian writer Cesare Ripa (c.1555–1622) became the standard handbook on *iconography for artists.

Emin, Tracey. *See* YOUNG BRITISH ARTISTS.

emulsion. A liquid in which water is combined with an oily or resinous substance in such a way that they will not separate out. Oil proverbially will not mix with water, but if an emulsifying agent—such as albumen—

is added, it will surround the drops of oil and prevent them from coming together. The *medium of *tempera painting is always an emulsion. The natural emulsions used most commonly in painting are egg yolk and *casein. Both have the advantage that once they have set they are not soluble in water.

enamel. A smooth, glossy material made by fusing glass to a prepared surface, usually of metal, by means of intense heat. The term is also applied to any object made of, or decorated with, this material. The study of enamelling belongs mainly to the history of jewellery and the decorative arts, but in the Middle Ages enamel was sometimes used for major works, for example *Nicolas of Verdun's Klosterneuburg Altar. Today the word 'enamel' is loosely used of any glossy protective covering such as durable paint or varnish applied to the surface of objects made from metal, wood, etc.

encarnado (Spanish: 'flesh-coloured'). Term applied in Spanish art to the painting of the flesh parts of wooden sculptures in more or less naturalistic colours. The term *estofado* (literally 'quilted') is applied to the painting of draperies. In the 16th century the paint of both flesh and draperies was given a glossy finish, but in the 17th century a matt finish was adopted for greater realism. Such work was sometimes done by distinguished painters as well as by specialist craftsmen—*encarnadores* and *estofadores*. For example, *Pacheco often painted figures by *Montañés. *See also* POLYCHROME.

encaustic Technique of painting using *pigments mixed with hot wax. Its name derives from a Greek word meaning 'burnt in' and it was one of the principal painting techniques of the ancient world. *Pliny describes two methods that were already 'ancient' in his day (one of them on ivory), and a third newer method that had been devised since it became the practice to paint ships, and he records that it stood up to sun, salt, and winds. Encaustic painting was the commonest technique in the early centuries of the Christian era but fell into disuse in the 8th or 9th century. Since then various attempts have been made to revive it (e.g. by Julius *Schnorr von Carolsfeld, who painted several scenes in encaustic in the Residenz at Munich in the 1830s). Jasper *Johns has used encaustic in his *Flag*

and *Target* paintings, but the technique finds few exponents today, probably because it is too troublesome.

Engelbrechtsz., Cornelis (c.1460–1527). Netherlandish painter, active in Leiden, where he was the leading artist of his day. Although his style shows the influence of the Italianate tendencies prevalent at Antwerp, Engelbrechtsz.'s work has a deeper intensity of feeling that is *Gothic rather than *Mannerist in spirit. Contorted linear rhythms and resonant colouring characterize his highly personal art, which is closer to the *Master of the Virgo inter Virgines than to any Antwerp artist. The altarpieces of the *Crucifixion* and the *Lamentation* in the Lakenhal Museum, Leiden, are typical of his work. *Lucas van Leyden was his greatest pupil and tends to overshadow his achievements. The other pupils in his large studio included his three sons, **Pieter, Cornelis,** and **Lucas,** as well as Lucas van Leyden's brother, Aertgen.

English, Michael. *See* SUPERREALISM.

engraving. Term applied in its broadest sense to the various processes of cutting a design into a plate or block of metal or wood, and to the prints taken from these plates or blocks (*see* PRINT for a classification of these processes). In everyday usage, the term more usually applies to one of the processes, known more technically as *line engraving.

Ensor, James (1860–1949). Belgian painter and etcher (his father was English and he had British nationality until 1929). One of the most original artists of his time, Ensor had links with *Symbolism, was a major influence on *Expressionism, and was claimed by the *Surrealists as a forerunner, but his work defies classification within any school or group. He was born in Ostend, where his parents kept a souvenir shop, and apart from a period studying at the Academy in Brussels, 1877–80, and a few brief trips abroad, he rarely left his home town. His early works were mainly bourgeois interiors painted in a thick and vigorous technique. When several were rejected by the Salon in Brussels in 1883, Ensor joined the progressive group Les *Vingt. From about this time his subject matter changed and he began to introduce the fantastic and macabre elements that are chiefly associated with his name. He made much use of carnival masks, grotesque figures, and skeletons, his bizarre and monstrous imaginings recalling the work of his Netherlandish forebears *Bosch and *Bruegel. The interest in masks probably originated in his parents' shop, but he was also one of the first European artists who appreciated African art, in which they play such a great part. Through his 'suffering, scandalized, insolent, cruel, and malicious masks', as he called them, he portrayed life as a kind of hideous carnival. Often his work had a didactic or satirical flavour involving social and religious criticism; his most famous painting, the huge *Entry of Christ into Brussels* (1888, Getty Mus., Los Angeles), shows how he imagined Christ might be greeted on a new Palm Sunday. It provoked such an outburst of criticism among his associates in Les Vingt (who refused it for exhibition) that he was almost expelled from the group. From this time he became something of a recluse and his work became even more misanthropic. Nevertheless, from about the turn of the century his reputation grew rapidly, and in 1903 he was made a Knight of the Order of Leopold. The culmination of his career came in 1929, when the inaugural exhibition of the Palais des Beaux-Arts in Brussels was devoted to his work (the *Entry of Christ into Brussels* was shown in public for the first time) and he was created a baron by King Albert. His work changed little after about 1900, however, and he was content to repeat his favourite themes. From 1904 he also gave up printmaking (he was one of the greatest etchers of his time and also made some lithographs). There is a museum of his work in Ostend.

entartete Kunst. *See* DEGENERATE ART.

Environment (or Environmental) art.
An art form in which the artist creates a three-dimensional space in which the spectator can be completely enclosed and involved in a multiplicity of sensory stimulations—visual, auditory, kinetic, tactile, and sometimes olfactory. This type of art was prefigured in the Merzbau of Kurt *Schwitters and in the elaborate decor of some of the *Surrealist exhibitions of the 1930s, as well as in certain types of entertainments at funfairs, but as a movement it originated in the late 1950s and flourished chiefly in the 1960s, when it was closely connected with *happenings. The leading figures who have worked in Environment art include *Kaprow, *Kienholz, and *Oldenburg, and one of the most celebrated works in the genre was created by Niki de *Saint Phalle. The term has been loosely used, and confusingly it has sometimes been applied to *Land art or its analogues —that is, to a category of art that consists in manipulating the natural environment, rather than to an art that *creates* an environment to enfold and absorb the spectator.

Epstein, Sir Jacob (1880–1959). American-born sculptor (and occasional painter and illustrator) who settled in England in 1905 and became a British citizen in 1911. Before then, in 1902–5, he had studied in Paris and visits to the Louvre aroused an interest in ancient and *primitive sculpture that lasted all his life and powerfully affected his work. His first important commission was executed in 1907–8: eighteen over-life-size figures for the façade of the British Medical Association's headquarters in the Strand. The nude figures aroused a furore of abuse on the grounds of alleged obscenity and were mutilated in 1937 when the building was bought by the government of Southern Rhodesia. Such verbal attacks and acts of vandalism were to become a feature of Epstein's career. The next scandal came with his tomb of Oscar Wilde (1912, Père Lachaise Cemetery, Paris), a magnificently bold and original piece featuring a hovering angel inspired by Assyrian sculpture, which was banned as indecent until a bronze plaque had been fixed over the angel's sexual organs. (It was removed in a night raid by a band of artists and poets.) While he was in Paris in connection with the tomb Epstein met *Picasso, *Modigliani, and *Brancusi and was influenced by their formal simplifications. Back in England he became involved with Wyndham *Lewis and the *Vorticists (although he was never a formal member of the movement), and at this time he created his most radical work—*The Rock Drill* (1913–15, Tate, London, and other casts), a robot-like figure that was originally shown mounted on an enormous drill; he said it symbolized 'the terrible Frankenstein's monster we have made ourselves into'. Epstein's later work was generally much less audacious than this, but his public sculptures were still attacked with monotonous regularity, their expressive use of distortion being offensive to conservative critics even when they were immune to charges of indecency. In the face of such controversy Epstein concentrated increasingly on bronze portrait busts, which found a more appreciative audience than his monumental works. Many notable men and women sat for him and he portrayed them with psychological intensity and great mastery of expressive surfaces, carrying on the tradition of *Rodin. It was only after the Second World War that his work began to achieve public acceptance, and in the 1950s he belatedly received a stream of honours (including a knighthood in 1954) and of major commissions, including the enormous bronze group of *St Michael and the Devil* (1958) at Coventry Cathedral.

Erbslöh, Adolf. *See* NEUE KÜNSTLER-VEREINIGUNG.

Ernst, Max (1891–1976). German-born painter, printmaker, collagist, and sculptor who became an American citizen in 1948 and a French citizen in 1958, one of the major figures of *Dada and even more so of *Surrealism. He studied philosophy and psychology at Bonn University, but he became fascinated by the art of psychotics (he visited the insane as part of his studies) and neglected academic work for painting. After serving in the First World War he became with *Arp (his lifelong friend) the leader of the Dada movement in Cologne. In 1920 he organized one of Dada's most famous exhibitions in the conservatory of a restaurant there: visitors entered through the lavatories, and axes were provided so they could smash the exhibits if they felt so inclined. In 1922 Ernst settled in Paris, where he joined the Surrealist movement on its formation in 1924. Even before then, however, he had painted works that are regarded as Surrealist masterpieces, such as *Celebes* (1921, Tate, London), in which an elephant is transposed into a strange mechanistic monster. The irrational and whimsical imagery seen here, in part inspired by childhood memories, occurs also in his highly original collages. In them he rearranged parts of banal engravings from sources such as trade catalogues and technical journals to create strange and startling scenes, showing, for example, a child with a severed head in her lap where a doll might be expected. He also arranged series of such

illustrations with accompanying captions to form 'collage novels'; the best-known and most ambitious is *Une semaine de bonté* (A Week of Kindness), published in Paris in 1934. Another imaginative technique of which he was a leading exponent was *frottage, which he invented in 1925. In 1930 he appeared in the Surrealist film *L'Âge d'or*, created by Luis Buñuel and Salvador *Dalí, and in 1935 he made his first sculpture (he worked seriously but intermittently in this field, characteristically creating totemic-like figures in bronze).

In 1938 Ernst broke with the Surrealist movement, but this did not affect his work stylistically. He was interned for a short while after the German invasion of France and in 1941 moved to New York, remaining in America until 1953 (apart from a visit to France in 1949). While in the USA he collaborated with *Breton and *Duchamp in the Surrealist periodical *VVV*. He settled permanently in France in 1953 and in his late years acquired many honours, including the main painting prize at the Venice *Biennale in 1954. His painting of this time became more lyrical and abstract. Ernst was married four times. His third (very brief) marriage was to Peggy *Guggenheim; his fourth wife (married 1946) was Dorothea Tanning (1910–), one of the outstanding American Surrealist painters. In the late 1930s he lived in Paris with the British-born (later Mexican) Surrealist painter and writer Leonora Carrington (1917–). His son **Jimmy Ernst** (1920–84) was also a painter.

Erté (Romain de Tirtoff) (1892–1990). Russian-born French designer, painter, and sculptor. He was born in St Petersburg into an aristocratic family and in 1912 moved to Paris, where he studied at the *Académie Julian (his adopted name derives from the French pronunciation of his initials, 'r' and 't'). Erté was best known for his fashion illustrations (particularly for the American magazine *Harper's Bazaar*) and for his costume and set designs for theatre, cabaret, opera, ballet, and cinema (he designed costumes for Mata Hari among other celebrities). However, he also painted, and in the 1960s he produced lithographs and made sculpture from sheet metal.

Escher, M. C. (Maurits Cornelis) (1898–1972). Dutch printmaker, working principally in the techniques of woodcut and lithography. His early prints were mainly landscapes and townscapes in a bold but fairly naturalistic style; however, from the mid-1930s he turned increasingly to what he described as 'inner visions'. Many of these were expressed as sophisticated designs in which repeated figures of stylized animals, birds, or fish are arranged in dense, interlocking patterns. From about 1940 the bizarre element in his work became more overtly *Surrealist, particularly in the kind of print for which he is now most famous—views of strange imaginary buildings in which he made brilliant play with optical illusion to represent, for example, staircases that seem to go both up and down in the same direction (*Ascending and Descending*, 1960). Such prints have been of considerable interest to mathematicians as well as to psychologists involved with visual perception. From the 1960s Escher's work has also found a large popular audience, especially among young people, some of whom felt that his images complemented the 'mind-expanding' experiences gained through hallucinogenic drugs.

Escorial. A small village about 50 km (30 miles) north-west of Madrid that gives its name to the monastery-palace built there by Philip II (*see* HABSBURG), one of the great monuments of Spanish architecture and one of the great treasure houses of Spanish art. Philip built the Escorial to honour the wishes of his father, the emperor Charles V (d. 1558), who in his will had specified the creation of a religious foundation in which he was to be buried alongside his wife, Isabella of Portugal (d. 1539). In addition to this function as a royal mausoleum (almost every Spanish monarch from Charles V onwards has been buried there), the Escorial was built as a palace, a monastery, and a seminary, all centred on an imposing domed church. The huge complex was begun in 1563, with Juan Bautista de Toledo as architect; he died in 1567 and was succeeded by Juan de Herrera, under whom it was officially completed in 1584 (although construction went on for some time after this). Externally the Escorial is built of grey granite and is overpoweringly austere, with forms of almost geometric clarity and virtually no ornament. Internally, however, it contains an extraordinary wealth of decoration (including vast areas of wall and ceiling frescos), which engaged

teams of artists long after Philip's death. The plan is a large rectangle, roughly 160 × 200 m (525 × 650 ft) and the layout has been compared to a gridiron; this is the attribute of St Lawrence (a 3rd-century martyr said to be of Spanish origin), to whom the monastery was dedicated in acknowledgement of Philip II's victory over the French at St Quentin on Lawrence's feast day in 1557. Many of the works of art in the Escorial feature the saint, including *Titian's great altarpiece of the *Martyrdom of St Lawrence*, commissioned by Philip in 1564. Philip failed to persuade Titian (his favourite painter) to come to Spain, but he imported many other Italian artists to work at the Escorial, including the painters Luca *Cambiaso, Pellegrino *Tibaldi, and Federico *Zuccaro, and the sculptor Pompeo *Leoni. Such artists formed the main channel through which the *Mannerist style entered Spain. Among the Spanish artists employed by Philip on the decoration of the Escorial were *Navarrete and *Sánchez Coello. El *Greco too painted a major altarpiece for him, the *Martyrdom of St Maurice and the Theban Legion* (1580–2), but Philip disliked it and had it replaced (although it remains in the Escorial). Artists of later generations who made important contributions to the decoration of the building include Claudio *Coello and Luca *Giordano, both of whom worked there in the late 17th century. In the 18th century Charles III used the Escorial as a hunting seat and furnished the hitherto unoccupied state rooms of the palace; many of the tapestries with which the walls were hung were designed by *Goya. Other outstanding works of art in the Escorial include a marble *Crucifix* carved by Benvenuto *Cellini and paintings by *Dürer, *Bosch (a favourite artist of Philip II), *Ribera, and *Velázquez.

Este. Italian family, rulers of Ferrara, Modena, and Reggio from the late 13th century until 1598, when Ferrara was annexed by the papacy, and thereafter of Modena and Reggio until 1796, when the family was deposed by the invading French. Various members were notable patrons of arts and letters. **Leonello** (1407–50; reigned from 1441) made Ferrara into an important cultural centre. He was the friend of *Alberti, and a patron of Jacopo *Bellini, *Piero della Francesca, and *Pisanello; Rogier van der *Weyden painted his illegitimate son **Francesco** (Met. Mus., New York), who spent most of his life in the Netherlands. Leonello's brother **Borso** (1413–71; reigned from 1450) commissioned the outstanding work of 15th-century Ferrarese painting—the series of frescos in the Hall of the Months in the Palazzo Schifanoia, attributed mainly to Francesco del *Cossa. **Isabella** (1474–1539), daughter of **Ercole I** (1431–1505), the half-brother of Leonello and Borso, was the greatest of the Este patrons and one of the most brilliant women of her time. She secured paintings from *Mantegna, *Perugino, *Costa, and later *Correggio to decorate her famous Studiolo in Mantua (she was married to Francesco *Gonzaga) and is said to have implored art dealers not to show her their wares so she would not spend herself even further into debt. A portrait drawing of her by *Leonardo is in the Louvre, Paris. Her brother **Alfonso I** (1476–1534; reigned from 1505) commissioned mythological paintings by Giovanni Bellini and *Titian for his Studiolo. Dosso and Battista *Dossi, *Garofalo, and *Scarsellino were among the other painters employed by the Estes during the 16th century. In the next century they continued their activities in Modena. **Francesco I** (1610–58; reigned from 1629) commissioned portraits of himself from *Bernini and *Velázquez. Both portraits are now in the Galleria Estense in Modena, which houses many other works from the Este collections. However, in 1744 **Francesco III** sold 100 of his most splendid pictures to Augustus III of Poland (as elector of Saxony he had his court in Dresden and these paintings are now among the treasures of the Gemäldegalerie there).

Estes, Richard. *See* SUPERREALISM.

estofado. *See* ENCARNADO.

etching. Term applied to a method of engraving in which the design is bitten into the plate with acid, and also to the print so produced. The design is drawn on a metal (usually copper) plate that has been coated with a waxy, acid-resistant substance. Where the waxy coating is scratched through with the etching needle, the bare metal is exposed, and when the plate is placed in a bath of acid the acid bites only the lines so exposed. The depth to which the lines are bitten (and hence the darkness with which they will print) depends on how long the plate is immersed in the acid, and it is possible to achieve subtle variations of tone by 'stopping out' part of the design (covering it with a protective varnish) while other parts are bitten more deeply. It is a much more spontaneous technique than *line engraving, as it is possible to draw on the waxy ground with virtually the same fluency as with pen or pencil. Etching is thought to have originated in the use of acid to decorate armour. Prints were first made using the technique in the early 16th century, and it reached exalted heights in the 17th century in the hands of *Rembrandt, the greatest of all etchers. By the early 19th century etching was used mainly for commercial illustration, but from the 1860s to the First World War there was a great renewal of interest in it as a medium for original expression, especially in Britain. *Whistler and *Sickert were leading lights of this movement, which is called the Etching Revival. Etching is still a popular technique, *Hockney being a leading contemporary exponent.

Etty, William (1787–1849). English painter, one of the few British artists to specialize almost exclusively in the nude. He was born and died in York, but was active mainly in London, where he trained at the *Royal Academy Schools and then (1807–8) with *Lawrence, who had a great influence on him; this was later modified by the impact of Venetian art, which he admired on a lengthy tour of France and Italy in 1822–4. Etty's paintings are often of mythological or historical subjects, sometimes on an ambitious scale, but he also made life studies in the RA Schools throughout his career, and these are now probably his most admired works. He was often attacked for the alleged indecency of his work, *The Times* considering it 'entirely too luscious for the public eye'. However, by the time of his death he was wealthy and respected. He summed up his attitude to his favourite subject thus: 'Finding God's most glorious work to be Woman, that all human beauty had been concentrated in her, I dedicated myself to painting—not the Draper's or Milliner's work—but God's most glorious work, more finely than ever had been done.' His draughtsmanship is often criticized, but it is generally agreed that he attained a glowing voluptuousness in the painting of flesh that few British artists have approached. The best collection of Etty's work is in York Art Gallery.

Euston Road School. A group of British painters centred round the 'School of Drawing and Painting' that opened in a studio at 12 Fitzroy Street, London, in 1937, and soon transferred to nearby 316 Euston Road. Its founding teachers were William *Coldstream, Victor *Pasmore, and Claude *Rogers; Graham *Bell and Lawrence *Gowing were also leading members of the circle. These artists advocated a move away from modernist styles to a more straightforward naturalism; by encouraging sound skills in representational painting, they hoped to end the isolation of artist from public that avant-garde movements had created. The outbreak of the Second World War in 1939 caused the School to close, but although it was so short-lived, it was influential; the term 'Euston Road' was used for a decade or so afterwards as a generic description for painting done in a style similar to that practised by the founders. Coldstream, through his position as professor at the *Slade School, was the chief upholder of the tradition.

Everdingen, Allart van (1621–75). Dutch landscape and marine painter. He was born in Alkmaar and is said to have been a pupil of *Savery in Utrecht and *Molyn in Haarlem. In 1644–5 he visited Scandinavia, where he developed a taste for subjects inspired by the scenery there—above all mountain torrents—and helped to popularize such themes in the Netherlands. *Ruisdael, in his pictures of majestic waterfalls, was one of the artists influenced by him. Allart was also a fine etcher and a prolific draughtsman. His elder brother **Caesar** (1617–78), who painted portraits and historical pictures, was attracted by the south not the north. Although he never went to Italy, he captured the spirit of Italian art better than many of his countrymen who crossed the Alps: witness his beautiful *Four Muses with Pegasus* (c.1650), part of the decoration of the royal villa—the Huis ten Bosch—at The Hague.

Evergood, Philip (1901–73). American painter. He was educated in England, at Eton and Cambridge (his mother came from a cultured British family), and much of his early life was spent travelling and studying in Europe. His early works were mainly of biblical and imaginative subjects, but after settling in New York in 1931 he became a leading figure among the *Social Realists who used their art as an instrument of protest and propaganda during the Depression years. He was active in several organizations concerned with the civil rights of artists, and under the banner of the *Federal Art Project he produced militant paintings of social criticism, his best-known work in this genre being *American Tragedy* (1937, Whitney Mus., New York), which commemorates a police attack on striking steelworkers in Chicago. Even his allegorical religious painting *The New Lazarus* (1954, Whitney Mus.) has sociological overtones, with its figures of starving children. His style varied, but his inclination for the bizarre and grotesque sometimes brings his work close to *Surrealism, as is seen in what is perhaps his most famous painting, *Lily and the Sparrows* (1939, Whitney Mus.).

Evesham, Epiphanius (1570?–c.1634?). English sculptor. He was the first distinctive personality in English sculpture since the Reformation, but details of his career are scanty. From 1601 to c.1614 he was working as a sculptor and painter in Paris, but though he had a studio of some size and several works in both arts are recorded, none has survived. After his return to England he made a number of tombs that stand out for their humanity, freshness of invention, and refinement of handling at a period when most English tomb sculpture was mass-produced. His signed tomb of Lord Teynham (c.1622, Lynsted, Kent), for example, has, in addition to the recumbent effigy, an imposing kneeling figure of the widow and a series of touching *reliefs of mourning children. *Vertue called him 'that most exquisite artist'.

Eworth (or **Ewouts**), **Hans** (c.1520?–1573?). Netherlandish painter, active mainly in England, where he settled in the 1540s. About 30 of his paintings survive, almost all portraits (there are also a few allegories), dating from 1549 to 1570. He is known also to have painted for pageants and masques. Although his work is uneven, he was the outstanding figure in the history of English painting in the mid-16th century. He painted Queen Mary and Queen Elizabeth I, but his masterpiece is perhaps the striking allegorical portrait of Sir John Luttrell (1550, Courtauld Gal., London).

Execias. The most famous of Greek *black-figure vase painters, active in the second half of the 6th century BC. Among the best-known works with his signature are an amphora (wine jar) showing Achilles and Ajax gaming (versions BM, London, and Vatican Mus.) and a splendid cup showing Dionysus in his boat (Antikensammlungen, Munich). Many of the works signed by Execias contain battle scenes, but he was able to impart an air of dignity and grandeur even to the most ordinary activities, and his greatest gift was perhaps for conveying pathos and psychological insight.

Expressionism. A term used in the history and criticism of the arts to denote the use of distortion and exaggeration for emotional effect. The term is employed in several different ways and can be applied to various art forms. In the pictorial arts, it can be used in its broadest sense to describe art of any time or place that raises subjective feeling above objective observation, reflecting the state of mind of the artist rather than images that conform to what we see in the external world. The paintings of *Grünewald and El *Greco, who conveyed intense religious emotion through distorted, unnaturalistic forms, are outstanding examples of expressionism in this sense (when used in this way the word is usually spelled with a small 'e'). In a narrower sense, the word Expressionism is applied to a broad trend in modern European art in which strong, non-naturalistic colours and distorted or abbreviated forms were used to project inner feelings. This trend traces its origin to van *Gogh, who used colour and line emotionally 'to express...man's terrible passions', and among the other great artists who exemplify it are *Ensor and *Munch. Expressionism in this sense represented a rebellion against the naturalism of 19th-century art, and its insistence on the supreme importance of the artist's personal feelings was one of the foundations of aesthetic attitudes in the 20th century. More specifically, the term Expressionism is applied to one aspect of the trend just described—a movement that was the dominant force in German art

from about 1905 to about 1930. (In the German-speaking countries Expressionism also had a powerful effect on other arts in this period, notably drama, poetry, and the cinema, which often show a common concern with the eruption of irrational forces from beneath the surface of the modern world. Some music, too, is described as Expressionist because of its emotional turbulence and lack of conventional logic, and there are also a few remarkable Expressionist buildings, although the most startling architectural designs remained on paper.) The *Brücke and *Blaue Reiter groups represent the high point of German Expressionism in painting, and led, in the case of *Kandinsky, for example, to abstraction. Expressionism was suppressed by the Nazis when they came to power in 1933, along with all other art they considered *degenerate, but it revived after the Second World War, and Germany has been one of the main homes of its descendant *Neo-Expressionism. In its broadest sense, the influence of Expressionism can be seen in the work of artists of many different persuasions—*Chagall and *Soutine for example—and in movements such as *Abstract Expressionism.

Exter, Alexandra (1882–1949). Russian painter and designer. In 1908 she visited Paris for the first time and from then until the outbreak of the First World War she made regular visits there, forming a link between the Western avant-garde and that in Russia (she knew *Apollinaire, *Braque, and *Picasso, among other luminaries). Her early paintings were influenced by various modernist styles, including *Cubism and *Futurism, and by 1917 she had arrived at complete abstraction, using interpenetrating, semi-geometrical slabs of colour in a manner that is something like a cross between *Delaunay's *Orphism and *Malevich's *Suprematism. From 1917 to 1921 she taught at her own studios first in Odessa (1917–18) and then in Kiev (1918–21). Her pupils, who included Pavel *Tchelitchew, helped her to create huge abstract designs for agit-steamers (propaganda boats) and agit-trains, which the new Soviet government used to celebrate the Russian Revolution and spread knowledge of it. Her most impressive and original work, however, was as a stage designer, particularly for Alexander Tairov's Kamerny (Chamber) Theatre in Moscow between 1916 and 1921. In powerful *Constructivist sets she explored the architectural potential of the stage, avoiding both traditional decorative illusionism and flat stylization. In 1924 she settled in Paris, and she lived in France for the rest of her life. In her later career she was mainly active as a theatre, ballet, and fashion designer. A good collection of her drawings for stage designs is in the Victoria and Albert Museum, London.

ex-voto (Lat.: 'from a vow'). A painting or other work of art made as an offering to God or a saint in gratitude for a personal favour or blessing or in the hope of receiving some miraculous benefit. There is a famous example by Philippe de *Champaigne.

Eyck, Jan van (d. 1441). The most celebrated painter of the Early Netherlandish School. Within a few years of his death he had a reputation on both sides of the Alps as a painter of great stature and importance, and although he is no longer credited with being the 'inventor' of *oil painting, as was long maintained, his fame has continued undimmed to the present day. Nothing is known for certain of his early life and he is first recorded in 1422, working in The Hague at the court of John of Bavaria, Count of Holland. In 1425 John died and later in the same year Jan entered the service of Philip the Good, Duke of Burgundy, in Bruges, moving soon afterwards to Lille. Jan remained in Philip's employment for the rest of his life, serving him as *varlet de chambre* (equerry) as well as painter. Philip evidently held him in personal affection as well as high professional regard, and on several occasions he sent him on diplomatic missions, most notably to Portugal in 1428–9 as part of an embassy that arranged a marriage between Philip and a Portuguese princess. After his return from Portugal, Jan seems to have settled permanently in Bruges, where he bought a house in 1432. It is only from this point that his career as an artist comes into focus, for all his dated paintings belong to the period 1432–9 and there are many difficulties concerning the few works that have sometimes been attributed to his earlier years. The central problem of his career—and one of the most discussed in the history of art—concerns the work that has always been the basis of

his resounding fame, the great altarpiece of the *Adoration of the Lamb* (completed 1432), in Ghent Cathedral. An inscription on the frame states that it was begun by 'the painter Hubert van Eyck, than whom none was greater', and completed by 'Jan, second in art'. Jan's brother **Hubert** (d. 1426?) is such an obscure figure that some scholars have questioned the authenticity of the inscription and doubted Hubert's existence. There is certainly no obvious division between the work of two hands in the altarpiece, but the prevailing opinion now is that the inscription is essentially genuine, although debate continues as to how far work had progressed at Hubert's death. Thus, Jan's contribution to the central masterpiece of Early Netherlandish painting is uncertain. *Dürer called the Ghent Altarpiece 'a stupendous painting' and the comment is appropriate both to the majesty and *iconographical richness of the huge *polyptych, and also to its breathtaking technical mastery. It consists of twelve panels, eight of which are painted on both sides (they are hinged so they can fold over the central section), making twenty images in all. These images are overwhelming in their beauty and brilliance of colour and remarkably wide-ranging in the things they represent: vivid portraits of the *donors, realistic full-length nudes (of Adam and Eve), landscapes, townscapes, interior views, sumptuous costumes and manifold still-life details. Collectively the altarpiece is almost like a manifesto of everything that oil painting could achieve in naturalistic effects.

Apart from the Ghent Altarpiece, about two dozen other paintings are reasonably attributed to Jan. They are all either religious works or portraits, although he is known to have painted pictures of other subjects (including a nude woman at her bath), which are now lost. Outstanding among the surviving works are the famous double portrait *Giovanni Arnolfini and his Wife* (1434, NG, London) and two paintings of the Virgin and Child with donors—the *Madonna with Chancellor Rolin* (c.1435, Louvre, Paris) and the *Madonna with Canon van der Paele* (1436, Groeningemuseum, Bruges). The Louvre painting, with large figures in the foreground set against a distant panoramic landscape, shows Jan's all-embracing vision of the natural world and his mastery of light and space, as well as detail and texture—in Erwin *Panofsky's words, 'his eye operates as a microscope and as a telescope at the same time'. The 'Man in a Red Turban' (1433, NG, London) is generally considered to be a self-portrait. All Jan's single portraits are fairly similar in format, showing the sitter bust-length in three-quarter view against a plain background. They are more objective than those of his great contemporary Rogier van der *Weyden, with the features subjected to relentlessly close scrutiny, but they nevertheless convey a sense of inner life.

Jan stands with the *Master of Flémalle as the founder of the Early Netherlandish School and his technique became the accepted model for his successors. His closest follower and chief successor in Bruges was Petrus *Christus, but his influence was wide (it is seen, for example, in the work of Luis *Dalmau in Spain) and profound. In the Netherlands itself, however, the more emotional style of Rogier van der Weyden came to have even greater influence, and the very perfection of Jan's work must have made him the most daunting of models.

Fabritius, Carel (1622–54). Dutch painter. He was *Rembrandt's most gifted pupil and a painter of outstanding originality and distinction, but he died tragically young when the Delft gunpowder magazine exploded, devastating the town, and only a tiny body of his work survives (much may have perished in the disaster). In his youth he worked as a carpenter and it was once thought that he derived his name from this profession (Lat., *faber*: 'craftsman'), but it is now known that his father, an amateur painter, had used it. He was probably in Rembrandt's studio in the early 1640s and he settled in Delft in about 1650. Although only about a dozen paintings by him are known, they show great variety. His earliest works (*Raising of Lazarus*, c.1645, Nat. Mus., Warsaw) are strongly influenced by Rembrandt, but he broke free from his master and developed a personal style marked by an exquisite feeling for cool colour harmonies and (even though he often worked on a small scale) unerring handling of a loaded brush (*The Goldfinch*, 1654, Mauritshuis, The Hague). These qualities, together with an interest in perspective, occur in the work of *Vermeer, the greatest of Delft painters, and Fabritius certainly influenced him, although it is not likely (as is sometimes maintained) that he was his master, this distinction perhaps belonging to *Bramer. Carel's brother **Barent** (1624–73) was also a painter, but of much lesser quality. He also may have studied with Rembrandt; his output consisted mainly of portraits and religious works.

Faithorne, William (c.1616–91). English engraver. He fought as a Royalist in the Civil War and later spent some time in exile in France, where he worked with *Nanteuil. In about 1650 he returned to London and he became the most distinguished of English 17th-century engravers, especially of portrait heads. He engraved the work of painters (van *Dyck, William *Dobson, *Lely) and also made engravings of his own drawings from the life, many published as frontispieces to books. He

also drew sensitive portrait heads as independent works (*John Aubrey*, 1666, Ashmolean Mus., Oxford). In 1662 he published a translation of *Bosse's *Traité des manières de graver* as *The Art of Graving and Etching*—the first manual on the subject in English. His son **William** (1656–1710) was also an engraver.

Falcone, Aniello (1607–56). Neapolitan painter, one of the leading artists in Naples in the generation before the plague of 1656 (in which he died). He painted numerous religious subjects, including frescos for Neapolitan churches, but he is now remembered mainly as the first specialist in battle pieces, a genre that won him an international reputation and in which he inspired his pupil Salvator *Rosa. His pictures generally show war as a confused struggle between anonymous soldiers, creating a type that the art historian Fritz Saxl (1890–1948) described as 'the battle scene without a hero'. Falcone was also an outstanding draughtsman.

Falconet, Étienne-Maurice (1716–91). French sculptor and writer on art, a pupil of J. B. *Lemoyne. Falconet was perhaps the most quintessentially *Rococo of all French sculptors, his forte being gently erotic figures such as the celebrated marble *Bather* (1757, Louvre, Paris). Like many other of his works, this was reproduced in porcelain by the Sèvres factory, of which he was director from 1757 to 1766, a position that he gained through the influence of his patron Mme de Pompadour. Falconet had other sides to his talent, however, and his masterpiece—the equestrian statue of Peter the Great in St Petersburg—is in a completely different vein. He moved to Russia in 1766, recommended to Catherine II by *Diderot, and stayed for twelve years; the statue was unveiled in 1782, four years after his return to France. The huge horse is represented with its forelegs raised and unsupported—a daring technical feat—and the heroic vigour of the statue gives it a place among the greatest examples of the type. Falconet suffered a stroke in 1783 and thereafter produced no more sculpture, devoting himself to the revision of his writings, a six-volume edition of which had appeared in 1781. His best-known literary work is 'Réflexions sur la sculpture' (1760), originally written for Diderot's *Encyclopédie*. In this, Falconet was one of the first to argue that the modern artists were superior to those of the ancient world (he was a man of humble origins and fierce independence of thought, and it is significant that unlike most of his distinguished contemporaries he never saw the need to visit Italy).

fancy picture. A term applied in the 18th century to certain types of sentimental *genre pictures. The term is difficult to define with precision, but it refers to pictures that have a rather charmingly contrived air, showing figures—particularly children—playing out various roles. *Gainsborough's fancy pictures usually have contemporary pastoral settings, depicting idealized peasants who behave rather more as if they are in the studio than the countryside, whereas *Reynolds favoured classical or allegorical themes, with titles such as *Hope Nursing Love* and *Venus Chiding Cupid*. He often used beggar children from the streets as models for these pictures, fitting in the work in gaps between portrait sessions. His pupil *Northcote wrote that Reynolds used to 'fill his painting room' with such children and 'When any of the great people came, Sir Joshua used to flounce them into another room until he wanted them again.'

Fantastic Realism (Phantastischer Realism). A style of painting that developed in Vienna in the late 1940s. Its exponents, of whom the best known is Ernst Fuchs (1930–), were mainly pupils of Albert Paris Gütersloh (1887–1973), who was a renowned teacher at the Vienna Academy. They shared an interest in the art of the past, notably that of Pieter *Bruegel (supremely well represented in the Kunsthistorisches Museum in Vienna), and their paintings were often literary and anecdotal in character, depicting a fairy-tale world of fantasy and imagination with minute detail.

Fantin-Latour, Henri (1836–1904). French painter and lithographer. He is best known for his luxurious flower pieces, but he produced many other kinds of work, including several group portraits that are important historical documents and show his friendship with leading avant-garde artists and writers. *Homage to Delacroix* (1864, Mus. d'Orsay, Paris) shows Fantin-Latour himself, with *Baudelaire, *Manet, *Whistler, and others grouped round a portrait of *Delacroix; and *A Studio at Batignolles* (sometimes called *Homage to Manet*) (1870, Mus. d'Orsay) shows *Monet, *Renoir, and others in Manet's studio. In spite of his associations with such progressive artists, Fantin-Latour was essentially a traditionalist, and his portraits particularly are in a precise, detailed style. Much of his later career was devoted to *lithography; he greatly admired Richard Wagner and did imaginative lithographs illustrating his music and that of other composers. His wife **Victoria Fantin-Latour** (née Dubourg (1840–1926)) was also a painter, mainly of flower pieces.

Farington, Joseph (1747–1821). English landscape painter and topographical draughtsman, best known today for his copious diary (1793–1821), which contains valuable information about the London art world of the time. Most of the original manuscript is in the Royal Library at Windsor Castle. The full text appeared in sixteen volumes in 1978–84; previous editions had been heavily abridged.

Farnese. Italian family of humanists and patrons of the arts who rose to importance with the election of Cardinal **Alessandro Farnese** (1468–1549) as Pope Paul III in 1534. He was the most important patron of *Michelangelo's later years, commissioning from him the *Last Judgement* in the Sistine Chapel and the *Conversion of St Paul* and the *Crucifixion of St Peter* in his private chapel in the Vatican (the Cappella Paolina), and also appointing him architect to St Peter's. Michelangelo also had a hand in the design of the Palazzo Farnese, the finest palace built in Rome in the 16th century. Pope Paul's grandson (or 'nephew' as he was known), another **Alessandro** (1520–89), was made a cardinal in 1534 and held many lucrative church appointments. Much of his enormous wealth was spent on artistic projects, and he ranks among the greatest patrons of the 16th century. He built up the largest collection of antiquities in Rome (now mainly in the Archaeological Museum in Naples; *see FARNESE BULL; FARNESE HERCULES*), was instrumental in bringing *Titian to Rome (1545–6), encouraged *Vasari to write his *Lives*, engaged Giacomo da Vignola to complete the Palazzo Farnese at Caprarola, and commissioned some of the most important *Mannerist frescos. He gave special support to the Jesuits and built for them the church of Il Gesù, Rome (designed by Vignola, begun 1568), one of the most influential buildings in the history of architecture. Alessandro's great-nephew, Cardinal **Odoardo** (1573–1626), great-great-grandson of Paul III, commissioned Annibale *Carracci to decorate the gallery in the family palace in Rome. The family collections eventually passed to **Elizabeth Farnese** (1692–1766), who married Philip V of Spain in 1715, and then to her son Charles, who was king of Naples from 1734 to 1759 (as Charles VII) and king of Spain from 1759 until his death in 1788 (as Charles III). It was in this way that the Farnese collections moved to Naples, where they remain—in the Archaeological Museum and the Museo di Capodimonte.

Farnese Bull. Ancient marble sculpture group (probably a Roman copy of a Greek original of *c*.150 BC), once part of the *Farnese collection and now in the Archaeological Museum in Naples. The subject, taken from Greek legend, shows the punishment of Dirce, who for her cruelty to Antiope was tied to the horns of a bull by Antiope's sons (Dirce's stepsons) and trampled to death. The figures are life-size, and the group, which was found in the Baths of Caracalla in Rome in 1545, is one of the most spectacular examples of the technical virtuosity and dramatic movement typical of *Hellenistic art; Federico *Zuccaro described it as a 'marvellous mountain of marble'.

Farnese Hercules. Gigantic marble statue of Hercules leaning sideways on his club and resting after his labours, once part of the *Farnese collection and now in the Archaeological Museum in Naples. It is signed by an Athenian sculptor named Glycon and is a copy of a lost original of the 4th century BC, probably by *Lysippus. The figure was discovered in the Baths of Caracalla in Rome in about 1546 and became highly influential and much copied. Its powerful musculature and realistic surface treatment were particularly admired by *Baroque artists.

Fattori, Giovanni. *See* MACCHIAIOLI.

Fautrier, Jean (1898–1964). French painter, sculptor, and printmaker. He is best known for the paintings in his *Hostages* series, inspired by his horror at the brutality and suffering of the Second World War. These strange paintings feature layer upon layer of heavy paint creating a central image that is abstract but suggests a decaying human head. The pale powdery colours evoke death, but the delicacy of the handling gives them a mysterious ambivalence. They were first exhibited at the Galerie René Drouin in Paris in 1945 and were much acclaimed. They have been seen as forerunners of *Art Informel, and with the post-war vogue for this kind of expressive abstraction Fautrier gained a reputation as one of the leading painters of the *École de Paris. In 1960 he won the Grand Prix at the Venice *Biennale. Fautrier's other works included sculpture and prints (notably lithographs illustrating Dante's *Inferno*, 1928), and he developed a novel type of work called 'multiple originals', printing a basic drawing on anything up to 300 canvases and then completing each work by hand. He first exhibited such works in 1950.

Fauvism. Movement in painting based on the use of intensely vivid, non-naturalistic colours; centred on a group of French artists who worked together from about 1905 to 1907, it was the first of the major avant-garde movements in European art in the period of unprecedented experimentation between the turn of the century and the First World War. The Fauves first exhibited together at the *Salon d'Automne of 1905 and their name was given to them by the critic Louis Vauxcelles (1870–1943), who pointed to a Renaissance-like sculpture in the middle of the same gallery and exclaimed: 'Donatello au milieu des fauves!' (Donatello among the wild beasts). *Matisse was the leading figure of the group and the others included *Derain, *Marquet, *Rouault, *Vlaminck, and the Dutch-born van *Dongen. Later they were joined by *Dufy (1906) and *Braque (1907). These artists were influenced in varying degrees by *Cézanne, van *Gogh, *Gauguin, and the *Neo-Impressionists. Their most characteristic subject was landscape and the outstanding feature of their work was extreme intensity of colour, often used arbitrarily for emotional and decorative effect. By 1907 the members of the group were drifting apart. For most of them Fauvism was a temporary phase through which they passed in the development of widely different styles, and their work never again displayed such similarity. Although short-lived, however, Fauvism was highly influential, for example on German *Expressionism and the *Scottish Colourists.

Federal Art Project. A project run by the US Government from 1935 to 1943 with the dual purpose of helping artists through the Depression years and of deploying the artistic potential of the country in the decoration of public buildings and places. There were also a Federal Writers' Project, a Federal Theater Project, and a Federal Music Project, and collectively they are known as the Federal Arts Projects. They were part of the Works Progress Administration (later called Work Projects Administration, both abbreviated to WPA), a work programme for the unemployed carried out as an aspect of President F. D. Roosevelt's New Deal. At its peak the Federal Art Project employed more than 5,000 people, not only decorating public buildings but also producing prints, posters, various works of craft, and setting up community art centres and galleries in areas where art was virtually unknown. The scheme also involved an *Index of American Design*, a gigantic documentation of the decorative arts in America. Virtually all the major American artists of the period were involved in the Federal Art Project, either as teachers or practitioners. It generated a huge amount of work, but most of it was unremarkable in quality.

Feininger, Lyonel (1871–1956). American painter who spent most of his career in Europe. He was born in New York into a German-American musical family. In 1887 he moved to Germany with the intention of studying music, but he turned instead to art. He had drawings published in Berlin's humorous weeklies and by the turn of the century he was Germany's leading political cartoonist. In 1906–8 he lived in Paris and under the influence of Robert *Delaunay turned seriously to painting. By 1912 he had evolved a personal style (influenced by *Cubism but highly distinctive) in which natural forms were treated in terms of a rhythmic pattern of prismatically coloured

interpenetrating planes bounded by straight lines—a manner that he applied particularly to architectural and marine subjects. His work impressed the members of the *Blaue Reiter, who invited Feininger to exhibit with them in 1913. Although he was an alien, he remained in Germany throughout the First World War and afterwards taught at the *Bauhaus from its foundation in 1919 (one of his woodcuts appeared on the cover of its manifesto) until its closure by the Nazis in 1933; he was the only person to be on the staff from start to finish, although he did little teaching in its later years. In 1935 he visited the USA and in 1937 (the year in which the Nazis declared his work *degenerate) he returned there permanently. He settled in New York and adopted the architecture of Manhattan as one of his favourite subjects, working with vigour into his eighties. His son Andreas Feininger (1906–99) was a distinguished photographer and writer on photography.

Feke, Robert (active 1741–51). American Colonial portrait painter. Little is known of his life until 1741, when he executed a large portrait group in Boston, *Isaac Royall and his Family* (Harvard Univ.). Later he worked in Philadelphia, and he is last recorded in 1751. There are about a dozen signed portraits from his hand and about 50 more are reasonably attributed to him. His works are somewhat lacking in characterization, but their strength and clarity of design and delicacy of touch give them a high place among Colonial portraits.

Félibien, André (1619–95). French administrator and writer on art. He is remembered chiefly for his *Entretiens sur les vies et sur les ouvrages des plus excellens peintres anciens et modernes*, first published in 1666–88, often reprinted, and translated into several languages. This massive compilation is a history of European art from antiquity to his own days. It contains the fullest contemporary biography of *Poussin (who became a friend of Félibien when he was secretary to the French ambassador in Rome, 1647–9).

Felixmüller, Conrad. *See* NEUE SACHLICHKEIT.

feminist art. A term applied to art that deals with issues specifically relating to women's identity and experience. As a movement it originated in the late 1960s, in parallel with the militant Women's Liberation Movement. It is not associated with any particular style or medium, but rather is concerned with a range of endeavour aimed at giving women a just place in the world and specifically in the art world, which feminist artists regard as heavily biased in favour of men. Much of this endeavour has been collective—for example in the organization of exhibitions (devoted to reviving the reputations of women artists of the past as well as promoting the work of women artists of the present), in the setting up of courses dealing with women's art, and in the publishing of periodicals, several of which have appeared since the early 1970s. Some feminist art has been fairly traditional in presentation—for example the paintings of Sylvia Sleigh (1916–) (see ALLOWAY), in which long-standing stereotypes of the nude are reversed by presenting males as a subject for female erotic delectation. However, much feminist art uses more avant-garde types of expression; indeed, as many feminist artists feel that traditional forms are tainted by patriarchy, they tend to be interested in newer forms, such as *Performance art and *Video art. The imagery of feminist art often focuses on sexuality, both in celebrating female eroticism and in attacking male sexual violence, and another common theme is matriarchy. Some feminist art, however, is more concerned with technique than imagery. Indeed, an important aspect of the movement has been the desire to revive interest in art forms such as quiltmaking that employ skills traditionally regarded as female and which have generally been given a low status compared with the *fine arts. This return to craft skills is emphasized in what is probably the most famous 'icon' of feminist art, *The Dinner Party* (1974–9, Through the Flower Corporation) by the American Judy Chicago (1939–); more than a hundred women (and also some men) worked on the elaborate china-painting and needlework it involved. It takes the form of an open triangular banquet table, with 39 place settings, each representing a significant woman in Western civilization. *The Dinner Party* has been seen by large audiences at several venues in the USA and elsewhere (its first showing was at the San Francisco Museum of Modern Art in 1979, when it attracted 100,000 visitors in three months).

Fénéon, Félix. *See* NEO-IMPRESSIONISM.

Fergusson, J.D. (John Duncan) (1874–1961). Scottish painter (mainly of landscapes and figure subjects) and occasional sculptor, the best known of the *Scottish Colourists. From about 1895 he made regular visits to Paris and he lived there 1907–14. His early work was *Whistlerian and he then came under the influence of Manet, but by 1907 he had adopted the bold palette of *Fauvism and became the most uncompromising adherent to the style among British artists (*Blue Beads*, 1910, Tate, London). In 1914 the war brought him back to Britain; he lived in London, 1914–29; in Paris, 1929–40; and finally in Glasgow, 1940–61. Soon after his arrival in Glasgow he founded the New Art Club to provide better exhibiting facilities for the city's progressive artists, and out of it grew the New Scottish Group (1942), of which Fergusson was first president. At this time he was also editor of the periodical *Scottish Art and Letters*, and he wrote a book entitled *Modern Scottish Painting* (1943).

Fernández, Alejo (c.1475–1545). Spanish painter, probably of German extraction, as he is referred to as 'Maestro Alexos—pintor Aléman'. He married the daughter of a painter called Pedro Fernández at Cordova and took her name, but he worked mainly in Seville, where he was the leading painter of the first third of the 16th century. His work, which is well represented in Seville Cathedral, was essentially Flemish *Mannerist in style, but it has a personal lyrical quality. One of his finest paintings is the *Virgin of the Navigators* (c.1530–40, Alcázar, Seville), a rare example of a picture reflecting the Spanish conquest of the Americas.

Fernández (or **Hernández**), **Gregorio** (c.1576–1636). Spanish sculptor, active for all his known career in Valladolid, where he is first recorded in 1605. He was one of the great masters of the *polychrome wooden statue, continuing the expressive tradition of *Juan de Juni but in a more realistic manner (he abandoned the earlier practice of lavish use of gold in favour of naturalistic colouring). Among the numerous altarpieces from his workshop are those of S. Miguel, Valladolid (1606), and Plasencia Cathedral (1624–34). He is well represented in Valladolid Museum.

Ferrari, Gaudenzio (c.1470/80–1546). Italian painter and sculptor, active over a wide area of Lombardy and his native Piedmont. His early paintings were strongly influenced by *Leonardo and his Milanese followers, and throughout his life he remained *eclectic, absorbing into his highly charged, emotional style elements from *Pordenone and *Lotto and also, for example, from the engravings of *Dürer. He was prolific and an artist of considerable power and individuality, but his work has remained comparatively little known because much of it is in fairly remote locations. His most remarkable works are the *Stations of the Cross* (c.1520–6) in a series of chapels at the Sanctuary of Sacro Monte, Varallo; here he combined highly realistic life-size sculptures in painted terracotta with a frescoed background.

Ferri, Cirro. *See* CORTONA.

fête champêtre (Fr.: 'outdoor feast'). Type of painting in which figures are shown in an idealized outdoor setting, usually eating, dancing, flirting, or listening to music, and typically evoking a mood of reverie. Since the Gardens of Love represented in medieval manuscripts, the theme has had great popularity in European art, undergoing several transformations. It was particularly favoured in 16th-century Venetian painting and the *Concert Champêtre* in the Louvre (traditionally by *Giorgione, but now usually given to *Titian) is the most celebrated of all examples of the type. The term **fête galante** (courtship party) was invented by the Académie Royale in Paris in 1717 to describe *Watteau's variants on the theme, in which figures in ball dress or masquerade costume disport themselves amorously in a parkland setting.

Feti (or **Fetti**), **Domenico** (c.1589–1623). Italian painter. He was born in Rome, where he studied under *Cigoli, was court painter to Vincenzo *Gonzaga in Mantua from 1613 to 1622, and then moved to Venice. His most characteristic works are of religious themes turned into *genre scenes of contemporary life. Though small in scale, they are broadly painted, with characteristic 'windswept' brushstrokes. Their great popularity is shown by the fact that they often exist in numerous very similar versions. Feti, who was also an excellent

portraitist, was one of a group of non-Venetian artists (including the German *Liss and the Genoan *Strozzi) who revivified painting in the city when there was a scarcity of native talent. Consequently, he is often classed as a member of the Venetian School, even though he spent only a few months there (from September 1622 until his death in April 1623).

Feuchtmayer, Joseph Anton (1696–1770). German *Rococo sculptor and *stuccoist, the most famous member of a family of artists from Wessobrunn in Bavaria. He and his workshop produced a large amount of decorative work for buildings in the Lake Constance area (mainly churches, although he also had secular commissions). The greatest ensemble of his work is in the pilgrimage church of Neu-Birnau (1746–53); it includes his most famous single figure, the *Honey-Licking Putto*.

Feuerbach, Anselm (1829–80). German painter. He studied in Düsseldorf, Antwerp, and Paris (with *Couture), then lived in Italy from 1855 to 1873. His father was a professor of classical archaeology (he had written a book on the *Apollo Belvedere*) and Feuerbach grew up in an atmosphere saturated with the high-minded ideals of humanistic philosophy. He wished to become the founder of a new school that was to combine noble, didactic, and idealistic subjects with a style derived from the *Grand Manner of 16th-century Venetian painting. His subjects are usually taken from Greek antiquity (*Plato's Symposium*, 1869, Kunsthalle, Karlsruhe). Feuerbach's fervent desire to preach a philosophy through pictorial means was usually a source of weakness rather than strength, and his best works are now generally considered to be his portraits of his model and mistress Nanna Risi, which have a statuesque beauty lacking in his more elaborate paintings; she also posed for subject pictures such as *Iphigenia* (1862, Hessisches Landesmus., Darmstadt). Feuerbach moved to Vienna in 1873 to become professor of history painting at the Academy, but he returned to Italy in 1876 following criticism of his work. Throughout his life he complained that he was being misunderstood and not receiving the recognition due to a very great artist. It is this element of self-pity that makes his book *Ein Vermächtnis* (A Testament) one of the most pathetic and repellent autobiographies ever written. It was posthumously published in 1882.

Fielding, Copley (Anthony Vandyke Copley Fielding) (1787–1855). English watercolour painter, the best-known member of a family of artists. He was a pupil of *Varley, whose sister-in-law he married in 1813. Early in his career he specialized in scenes of Wales and the Lake District, but from 1817 he spent much of his time on the south coast because of his wife's health, and turned increasingly to seascapes. He was enormously prolific and much of his later work is repetitive.

Field Painting. A type of painting developed in the USA from about 1950 in which the picture is no longer regarded as a structure of interrelated elements but as a single indivisible expanse. Field Painting has affinities with *Systemic art and with the *all-over style associated with Jackson *Pollock. The term *Colour Field Painting has been used when emphasis is placed on brilliance and saturation of colour. Rather than being a specific style, it may be regarded as an aspect of a very general tendency during the 1950s and 1960s to eschew traditional composition in favour of a single 'total' theme.

figurative art. Art in which recognizable figures or objects are portrayed. The term 'representational art' is used synonymously; the opposite is non-figurative or *abstract art.

Filarete (Antonio Averlino) (c.1400–c.1470). Florentine sculptor, architect, and writer on art. His nickname, which he adopted late in life, is derived from the Greek for 'lover of virtue'. He probably trained with *Ghiberti and his most important work in sculpture—the bronze doors for St Peter's in Rome (c.1433–45)—are heavily indebted to Ghiberti's doors for the Baptistery in Florence, although much less accomplished (*Vasari called them 'deplorable'); they are one of the few parts of Old St Peter's to survive in the present building. In 1448 Filarete fled Rome under suspicion of stealing holy relics. After stays in Florence and Venice, in 1451 he settled in Milan. There he was employed mainly as an architect, his principal work being the Ospedale Maggiore (begun 1457, completed in the 18th century), which helped to introduce the *Renaissance style

to Lombardy and created new standards of comfort and sanitation in hospital design. His novel ideas came out also in his *Treatise on Architecture*, written in 1461–4 but not published until 1896. It includes a vision of an ideal city, Sforzinda (named after his patron, Francesco *Sforza), which is the first symmetrical town-planning scheme of modern times. Among his ingenious proposals for his ideal city was a Tower of Virtue and Vice, a ten-storey structure accommodating a brothel on the ground floor and an astronomical observatory at the top. Vasari described the treatise as 'perhaps the most stupid book ever written'.

Filla, Emil (1882–1953). Czech painter, sculptor, graphic artist, and writer on art. Between 1907 and 1914 he spent much of his time in France, Germany, and Italy, and during this period he turned from his early *Expressionist manner to *Cubism, becoming the pioneer and one of the most distinguished exponents of the style in Czechoslovakia in both painting and sculpture. He spent the First World War in the Netherlands and returned to Prague in 1920. His most characteristic paintings of this time were still lifes, but in the late 1930s he turned to themes of violence, presaging the horrors of the Second World War (during which he was imprisoned in the concentration camp at Buchenwald). His post-war work was more naturalistic in style and included some large landscapes. He wrote numerous articles on art and several books.

fine arts. Term that came into use in the 18th century to describe the 'higher' non-utilitarian arts, as opposed to *applied or *decorative arts. Usually it is taken to cover painting, sculpture, and architecture (even though architecture is obviously a 'useful' art), but it is often extended to cover poetry and music too. *See also* LIBERAL ARTS.

Finiguerra, Maso (1426–64). Florentine goldsmith, engraver, designer, and the most famous craftsman of the day in *niello (a type of decorative metal inlay). *Vasari asserts that Finiguerra was the inventor of copper engraving and although this claim has been discredited, the technique did develop in Italy as an extension of niello work. He is said to have often worked from designs by Antonio *Pollaiuolo.

Fitzwilliam Museum. The museum and art gallery of the University of Cambridge. It was founded in 1816 and is one of the oldest public museums in Great Britain. Like the *Ashmolean Museum in Oxford, it has been built up almost entirely from private benefactions. The founder, the 7th Viscount Fitzwilliam (1745–1816), who had studied at Cambridge, bequeathed to the university a typical gentleman's collection of the 18th century, which included Italian High *Renaissance paintings and the best collection of *Rembrandt etchings then in England. He also left £100,000 for a building, which was begun in 1837 by George Basevi and continued by C. R. Cockerell after Basevi's death in 1845. It opened to the public in 1848, but the grand entrance hall (by E. M. Barry), with its magnificent staircase, was not finished until 1875. Subsequently there have been several extensions to the building. Among the bequests to the museum the most noteworthy after the founder's was that of Charles Brinsley Marlay (1831–1912), which enriched all departments. Among several distinguished directors the most famous was M. R. James (1862–1936), eminent medievalist and celebrated writer of ghost stories, who was in charge from 1893 to 1908. However, the most important administrator in the museum's history was his successor, Sir Sydney Cockerell (1867–1962), who was director from 1908 to 1937. According to the *Dictionary of National Biography*, he 'transformed a dreary and ill-hung provincial gallery into one which set a new standard of excellence which was to influence museums all over the world. This he achieved by the skilful and uncrowded display of pictures against suitable backgrounds, and by the introduction of fine pieces of furniture, Persian rugs, and flowers provided and arranged by lady admirers, fired by his enthusiasm.' In Cockerell's own words, 'I found it a pig stye, I turned it into a palace', and the Fitzwilliam has maintained the reputation he gave it as a pleasurable place to visit. Its collections are now extremely wide-ranging; the areas of greatest richness include Italian painting and Greek coins.

fixative. An adhesive liquid applied to drawings in *chalk, *charcoal, or *pastel (usually by means of spraying) to prevent the *pigments from rubbing off, by binding them together and securing them to the *ground. It is most needed for pastels, but it tends to reduce their brilliance.

Flack, Audrey. *See* SUPERREALISM.

Flandrin, Hippolyte (1809–64). French painter. He was one of the favourite pupils of *Ingres and won the *Prix de Rome in 1832. In Italy he was influenced by the monumental decorative tradition and after his return to Paris in 1838 he became the leading muralist of his day, painting vast compositions in such churches as St Vincent-de-Paul (1849–53) and St Germain-des-Prés (1856–61) in Paris. He was a zealous but rather frigid upholder of Ingres's theories. Flandrin was an excellent portraitist and also painted historical and mythological works. He came from a family of artists. His brothers **Auguste** (1804–43) and **Paul** (1811–1902) were likewise pupils of Ingres, and concentrated mainly on portraiture and landscape respectively; his son **Paul-Hippolyte** (1856–1921) painted religious, historical, and *genre scenes.

Flavin, Dan. *See* LIGHT ART.

Flaxman, John (1755–1826). English sculptor, draughtsman, and designer, an outstanding figure of the *Neoclassical movement. He was the son of a moulder of plaster figures, and after studying at the *Royal Academy Schools (where he met his life-long friend William *Blake) he worked for the potter Josiah Wedgwood from 1775 to 1787. The designs he produced for Wedgwood not only strengthened his interest in *antique art but also developed the innate sensitivity to line that was his greatest gift. In the same period he gradually built up a practice as a sculptor. From 1787 to 1794 Flaxman lived in Rome. While there he drew illustrations, much influenced by Greek vase painting, to the *Iliad* and the *Odyssey*, engraved and published in Rome in 1793, followed by illustrations to Aeschylus (1795) and Dante (1802). These engravings, which are of exceptional purity of outline, were republished in several editions, and won him international fame. His later illustrations to Hesiod (1817) were engraved by Blake. He returned to England in 1794 with a well-established reputation and immediately became a busy sculptor. His monument to the poet William Collins (1795, Chichester Cathedral) and the more important one to Lord Mansfield (1795–1801, Westminster Abbey) were commissioned while he was in Rome. His extensive practice as a maker of monuments included large groups with free-standing figures (*Lord Nelson*, 1809, St Paul's Cathedral), but his most characteristic work appears in simpler and smaller monuments, sometimes cut in low *relief. In these his great gift for linear design was given full play. Flaxman was appointed the first professor of sculpture at the Royal Academy in 1810 and his reputation among Neoclassical sculptors was exceeded only by those of *Canova and possibly *Thorvaldsen. He was one of the first English artists to be famous outside his own country, although his reputation and influence were based principally on engravings after his drawings rather than his sculpture. University College London has a large collection of Flaxman's drawings and models, and examples of his monuments can be seen in churches throughout England.

Flinck, Govert (1615–60). Dutch painter, active mainly in Amsterdam. He studied with *Rembrandt from about 1633 to 1636, and his early work, including portraits, religious subjects, and landscapes, was overwhelmingly influenced by his master (several of his paintings have indeed at some time been assigned to Rembrandt). From the mid-1640s, however, Flinck adopted the elegant style of van der *Helst, with which he had great success. In 1659 he was awarded the most prestigious commission given to any Dutch painter of his time: he was asked to paint twelve pictures for van *Campen's new town hall in Amsterdam, eight of which (each about 5 m (16 ft) high) were to represent the story of the Revolt of the Batavians. However, Flinck died suddenly three months after signing the contract and the commission was divided among Rembrandt, *Lievens, and *Jordaens.

Flint, Sir William Russell (1880–1969). British painter and graphic artist. He was trained as a lithographer and was a prolific book illustrator, but is now best remembered for his watercolours (particularly his mildly erotic nudes), painted in a distinctive and rather flashy style.

Floris (or **Floris de Vriendt**). Netherlandish family of artists active in Antwerp. The most important members were the brothers **Cornelis** (*c.*1514–75) and **Frans** (*c.*1519–70). Both of them spent some time in Rome and returned to Antwerp with a desire to emulate the Italian *Renaissance manner. Cornelis was an architect and sculptor and also published engravings of Italianate motifs, which were used by many northern artists. He is famous principally as the architect of Antwerp Town Hall (1561–5), the finest and most influential building of the 16th century in Flanders. Frans was a painter and studied with Lambert *Lombard before going to Italy, where he was overwhelmed by *Michelangelo's *Last Judgement* (he was in Rome at about the time it was unveiled in 1541). The impression it made on him is reflected in his most characteristic works—large religious and mythological pictures crowded with athletic *Mannerist nudes (*Fall of the Rebel Angels*, 1554, Koninklijk Mus., Antwerp). In his portraits, however, he combined powerful brushwork with forthright characterization in a way that anticipates *Hals (*Old Lady*, 1558, Mus. B.-A., Caen). According to van *Mander, every Flemish youth with artistic leanings studied with him, but in spite of his success he died in debt because of his extravagant lifestyle.

Flötner, Peter (*c.*1490–1546). German sculptor, medallist, designer, and printmaker, active mainly in Nuremberg. He visited Italy early in his career and he was one of the first German sculptors to be strongly influenced by *Renaissance ideas. His best-known work is the Apollo Fountain (1532, Stadtmuseum Fembohaus, Nuremberg), which is classical in inspiration but with a flowing elegance that is Flötner's own.

Fluxus. A loosely organized international group of avant-garde artists set up in Germany in 1962 and flourishing until the early 1970s. There was no common stylistic identity among the members, but they revived the spirit of *Dada and were opposed to artistic tradition and everything that savoured of professionalism in the arts. Their activities were mainly concerned with *happenings (usually called *Aktions* in Germany), street art, and so on. Fluxus festivals were held in various European cities (including Amsterdam, Copenhagen, Düsseldorf, London, and Paris), and also in New York, which became the centre of the movement's activities. The most famous artist involved with Fluxus was Joseph *Beuys; among the others were the Japanese-born American Yoko Ono (1933–), and the German Wolf Vostell (1932–98). The group's chief co-ordinator and editor of its many publications was the Lithuanian-born American George Maciunas (1931–78), who coined its name (Lat., *fluxus*: 'flowing)', suggesting a state of continuous change.

Focillon, Henri (1881–1943). French art historian. He was a celebrated teacher and held various university appointments, notably at the Sorbonne in Paris, where in 1924 he succeeded Émile *Mâle as professor of medieval archaeology. He also taught in the USA. Focillon's work ranged from studies of medieval sculpture to 20th-century painting; he also wrote much on prints (his father was an engraver), notably a book on *Piranesi (1918). His best-known work is *Art d'Occident* (The Art of the West, 1938), a study of *Romanesque and *Gothic art in which he placed great emphasis on the technical aspects of artistic creation, stressing how the artist responds to his raw materials, their potentialities, and limitations. This outlook also finds expression in Focillon's *Vie des formes* (1934), translated as *The Life of Forms in Art* (1942).

Fontainebleau, School of (École de Fontainebleau). Term applied to artists working in a style associated with the French court at Fontainebleau in the 16th century. The palace at Fontainebleau (about 65 km (40 miles) south-east of Paris) was the most brilliant expression of the ambition of Francis I (reigned 1515–47) to glorify the French crown by emulating the lavish patronage of the great humanist princes of Italy. As France lacked an indigenous tradition of mural painting adequate to his grandiose conceptions, he brought in Italian masters to lead the work. The two most important Italians to work at Fontainebleau were *Rosso Fiorentino, who moved to France in 1531, and *Primaticcio, who followed in 1532. The Italian masters succeeded in adapting their own styles to the courtly ideals of the French taste and were assisted by French and Flemish artists. From the combination was born a distinctive *Mannerist style—elegant, sophisticated, and often voluptuous, expressed most characteristically in mural painting combined

with stucco ornament. Much of the stuccowork was in high *relief, but Rosso also developed a distinctive motif known as strapwork, in which the stucco is formed into shapes resembling leather or parchment that has been rolled and cut into decorative patterns; this became a particularly popular form of ornament in England and the Low Countries (Fontainebleau motifs were widely spread through engravings). Primaticcio's distinctive figure style—characterized by long limbs, small heads, and sharp, elegant profiles—became virtually canonical in French art until the end of the 16th century. Other Italian artists who worked at Fontainebleau included Niccolò dell'*Abate and *Cellini, but much of the work associated with the school is by unknown hands, although often of high quality, such as the celebrated painting *Diana the Huntress* (c.1550, Louvre, Paris). The mythological subject matter, elongated elegance, idyllic landscape setting, and air of sophisticated artificiality in this work are wholly typical of the School, the influence of which left few French artists of the time untouched. After the hiatus caused by the Wars of Religion (1562–98) the decorative painting of royal palaces was revived under the patronage of Henry IV (reigned 1589–1610). The name **Second School of Fontainebleau** is usually given to the artists who carried out this work for Henry IV, notably Ambroise Dubois (1542/3–1614), Toussaint Dubreuil (1561–1602), and Martin Fréminet (1567–1619). Their work was accomplished, but without the inventive brilliance of the best work of the First School.

Fontana, Lucio (1899–1968). Italian painter, sculptor, and ceramicist. He worked mainly in Milan, where in 1930 he had his first one-man show at the Galleria del Milione; this was the first exhibition in which abstract sculpture was seen in Italy and Fontana became a leading figure in promoting abstract art in his country. In 1935 he moved to Paris, where he became a member of the *Abstraction-Création association, then in 1940 moved to Argentina (his mother was Argentinian), where in 1946 he issued his *White Manifesto*. This introduced a new concept of art called *Spatialism (Spazialismo), which aimed for co-operation with scientists in synthesizing new ideas and materials. In 1947 he returned to Milan, and in the same year officially launched the Spatialist movement and issued the *Technical Manifesto of Spatialism* (four more Spatialist manifestos followed, the last in 1952). His most characteristic works, which he began producing in 1958, are paintings in which completely plain surfaces are penetrated by gashes in the canvas, but he also made *environments (for example using neon lights in blackened rooms) and carried out various decorative projects.

Fontana, Prospero (*c*.1512–97). Italian painter. He worked in various Italian cities, notably Florence, Genoa, and Rome, assisting *Vasari and other artists on decorative projects, and was also employed at *Fontainebleau (*c*.1560) under *Primaticcio. Most of his career, however, was spent in his native Bologna, where he was the leading painter during the 1570s. He was a favourite artist of Gabriele Paleotti, Bishop of Bologna, one of the churchmen who, in line with the ideals of the Counter-Reformation, called for greater clarity in painting as an aid to devotion, but Fontana's work—elegant but rather spineless—is generally seen as exemplifying everything that the *Carracci opposed in their move towards naturalism. Most of Fontana's work is still in and around Bologna. His daughter and pupil **Lavinia Fontana** (1552–1614) was much esteemed in her day as a portraitist.

Foppa, Vincenzo (1427/30–1515/16). Italian painter, the leading figure in Lombard painting until the arrival of *Leonardo da Vinci in Milan in 1481/2. He was born near Brescia and worked a good deal in the city, but his main places of activity at the height of his career were Pavia and Milan. According to *Vasari he trained in Padua, and his robust style owed much to *Mantegna, not least in his interest in perspective. His major works include frescos in S. Eustorgio, Milan, and S. Maria del Carmine, Brescia.

Forain, Jean-Louis (1852–1931). French painter, lithographer, and caricaturist. In the first half of his career he worked mainly on satirical illustrations for various Paris journals, combining something of the realistic outlook of *Manet and the mordant satire of *Daumier. However he exhibited at four of the *Impressionist exhibitions

between 1879 and 1886, and after the turn of the century he concentrated more on painting. His most distinctive work included some court scenes, two examples of which are in Tate Modern, London: *The Court of Justice* (*c*.1902) and *Counsel and Accused* (1908). Forain was much influenced by his friend *Degas, who said 'he paints with his hand in my pocket'.

Forbes, Stanhope. *See* NEWLYN SCHOOL.

Ford, Edward Onslow. *See* NEW SCULPTURE.

formalism. A term used in the discussion of the arts to describe an approach (on behalf of creator or critic) in which the formal qualities of a work—such as line, shape, and colour—are regarded as self-sufficient for its appreciation, and all other considerations—such as representational, ethical, or social aspects—are treated as secondary or redundant. The idea that formal qualities can have meaning or resonance independently of representative function was essential to the development of *abstract art, and several notable writers on art in the 20th century were basically formalist in outlook, including Clive *Bell, Roger *Fry, and Clement *Greenberg. Many other writers have been strongly opposed to their ideas, believing that form and 'content' are to a large extent interdependent. Formalism has been particularly opposed in Communist countries, especially Stalinist Russia, where art was supposed to serve a moral purpose in the education and inspiration of the masses, and anything that suggested cultural elitism was condemned. The Soviet authorities regarded formalism as a sign of Western decadence—so much so that the word was used virtually as an all-purpose term of abuse for Western art or its influence.

Forum Exhibition (in full, Forum Exhibition of Modern American Painters). An exhibition arranged in New York in 1916 by the critic Willard Huntington Wright with the support of the magazine *Forum*, to which he was a regular contributor. The purpose of the exhibition was to pinpoint the best of American modernist painting in order to convince the public that it could stand up to the European avant-garde, which had made a great impact at the *Armory Show three years earlier. Both

Robert *Henri and Alfred *Stieglitz were on the selection committee. The exhibition consisted of about 200 pictures by seventeen artists, including *Benton (ironically, later a vociferous enemy of modern art), *Dove, *Macdonald-Wright (Wright's brother), *Marin, *Sheeler, and *Zorach. Anticipating that some of the work on show might be too advanced for public taste, Wright wrote in the catalogue: 'Not one man represented in this exhibition is either a charlatan or a maniac', and he vigorously defended abstraction.

Foster, Myles Birket (1825–99). English painter and illustrator. He was trained as a wood engraver and early in his career designed many book illustrations. After c.1858, however, he devoted himself primarily to watercolour painting of rustic subjects in a sweetly sentimental style that has made him a favourite artist for manufacturers of greetings cards.

Foujita, Tsuguharu (or **Léonard**) (1886–1968). Japanese-French painter and graphic artist. He moved to Paris in 1913 and spent most of the rest of his life in the city, with the exception of a long interlude, 1933–50, when he returned to Japan. In the 1920s he developed a distinctive style of delicately mannered *Expressionism, combining Western and Japanese traits, and he became recognized as a leading figure of the group of emigrés who made up the *École de Paris—the only Japanese artist of his time to earn a considerable reputation in Europe. Characteristic works in his prolific output include landscapes, portraits, nudes, pictures of cats (once very popular in reproduction), and compositions in which still life and figures are combined. In 1959 he converted to Roman Catholicism and adopted the first name Léonard in recognition of his admiration for Leonardo da Vinci. From this time he began painting religious subjects, and in his later career he tended to lapse into sentimentality.

Fouquet (or **Foucquet**), **Jean** (c.1420–c.1481). The outstanding French painter of the 15th century, active mainly in his native Tours. Between 1446 and 1448 he was in Rome, where he painted a portrait, now lost, of Pope Eugenius IV. Much has been made of this Italian journey, the influence of which can be seen in the perspective effects and classical architecture of his sub-

sequent paintings, but in certain respects—notably his close, unidealized scrutiny of the human face—his work remained deeply rooted in northern tradition and did not succumb to Italian influence. On his return from Italy, Fouquet worked much for the French court. His first patron was Étienne Chevalier, the royal secretary and lord treasurer, for whom he produced a *Book of Hours (1450–60), now dismembered but mainly in the Musée Condé at Chantilly, and who appears in the Melun Diptych (c.1452), now divided between Antwerp (Koninklijk Mus.) and Berlin (Gemäldegalerie). The figure of the Virgin in the panel in Antwerp is rumoured to be a portrait of Agnès Sorel, Charles VII's mistress, whom Chevalier had also loved. It was not until 1475 that Fouquet became royal painter (to Louis XI), but in the previous year he was asked to prepare designs for the king's tomb, and he must have been the leading court artist for many years. In both his *miniatures and his work on a larger scale in panel paintings, Fouquet's art has the same clarity and dignity, his figures being modelled in broad planes defined by lines of magnificent purity. His sculptural sense of form went with a cool and detached temperament, and in his finest works the combination creates a deeply impressive gravity.

Fragonard, Jean-Honoré (1732–1806). French painter whose scenes of frivolity and gallantry are among the most complete embodiments of the *Rococo spirit; he has been described as the 'fragrant essence' of the 18th century. After a brief period studying with *Chardin, to whom he was temperamentally unsuited, Fragonard became *Boucher's most brilliant pupil and in 1752 won the *Prix de Rome, even though he was not officially qualified to enter the competition as he was not a student at the Académie Royale (Boucher said 'It does not matter; you are *my* pupil'). From 1756 to 1761 he lived in Rome, where he eschewed the work of the approved masters of the High *Renaissance and instead found inspiration in a freer and more colourful tradition, represented above all by *Tiepolo. His best friend in Rome was Hubert *Robert, with whom he spent several weeks at the Villa d'Este, Tivoli, in the summer of 1760; he made some beautiful drawings of the villa's gardens, memories of which occur in paintings throughout his career (he saw the villa again on a second visit to Italy in 1773–4). In 1765 Fragonard became a member of the Académie with *Coroesus Sacrificing Himself to Save Callirhoe* (Louvre, Paris), a mythological scene in the *Grand Manner. Although the picture won lavish praise, he soon abandoned this idiom for the erotic canvases by which he is chiefly known. His delicate colouring, witty characterization, and spontaneous brushwork ensured that even his most intimate or voyeuristic subjects are never vulgar, and his finest works have an irresistible verve and joyfulness (*The Swing*, 1767, Wallace Coll., London). After his marriage in 1769 he also painted children and pictures of domestic life, and his large output included various other subjects, including landscapes, portraits, and occasional religious scenes. He stopped exhibiting at the *Salon in 1767 and almost all his work was done for private patrons. Among them was Mme du Barry, Louis XV's most beautiful mistress, for whom he painted the works that are often regarded as his masterpieces—the four canvases entitled *The Progress of Love* (*c*.1770–3, Frick Coll., New York; he later added other pictures to the series). Mme du Barry, however, returned the pictures and had them replaced with works by *Vien—an early indication that taste in court circles was beginning to turn against Fragonard's light-hearted style. He adapted to some extent to the new *Neoclassical vogue, notably by using more polished brushwork, but after the French Revolution his scenes of frivolous aristocratic pleasure were completely outmoded and he seems to have abandoned painting in about 1792. Jacques-Louis *David, who as a young unknown had been helped by Fragonard, returned the kindness by finding him an administrative job at the *Louvre, which had opened as a national museum in 1793. Fragonard worked there until 1800, then lived the rest of his life in obscurity.

There were several other painters in Fragonard's family, including his sister-in-law Marguerite Gérard (1761–1837), who was regarded as one of the finest women artists in France (her work consisted mainly of portraits and genre scenes), and his son, **Alexandre-Évariste Fragonard** (1780–1850), who specialized in historical subjects. Berthe *Morisot was Fragonard's great-granddaughter.

Frampton, Sir George (1860–1928). British sculptor. Early in his career he was one of the leading avant-garde British sculptors of his day, experimenting with unusual materials and *polychrome and working in a style imbued with elements of *Art Nouveau and *Symbolism (*Mysteriarch*, 1892, Walker AG, Liverpool). Later his work became more traditional and he had a successful career with accomplished but uninspired monuments, the best known of which are *Peter Pan*, erected in Kensington Gardens in 1911, and the Edith Cavell memorial (1920) in St Martin's Place, London. His son **Meredith** (1894–1984) was a painter, primarily of portraits. He gave up painting in 1945 because his sight was failing and was almost entirely forgotten until an exhibition of his work was held at the Tate Gallery in 1982, revealing him as an artist of great distinction. His work is beautifully finished, with a sense of hypnotic clarity (the images seem almost palpable yet at the same time strangely remote), and he excelled in conveying the intellectual qualities of his sitters. He was a slow worker and his output was small.

Francavilla, Pietro. *See* GIAMBOLOGNA.

Francesco di Giorgio (1439–1501). Sienese painter, sculptor, architect, military engineer, and writer, a pupil of the equally versatile *Vecchietta. He painted mainly during the early part of his career and few pictures certainly by him survive; the most important are a signed *Nativity* (*c*.1475) and a documented *Coronation of the Virgin* (1472–4), both in the Pinacoteca in Siena. As a sculptor, his major works are two bronze angels (1489–97) on the high altar of Siena Cathedral. Francesco was widely travelled, and the latter part of his career was spent mainly as an architect and military engineer (he was an expert in fortifications and is said to have exploded the first mine). As a technological innovator he was second only to his friend *Leonardo, whom he certainly influenced. Among his patrons was Federico da *Montefeltro, and Francesco may have had a hand in the designing of his celebrated palace in Urbino. His also designed churches, notably S. Maria del Calcinaio, near Cortona, begun 1484. Francesco wrote a treatise on architecture in the last years of his life; it was not published until 1841.

Francia, Francesco (Francesco Raibolini) (*c.*1450–1517). The outstanding Bolognese painter of his period. He originally trained as a goldsmith and had several other skills, being recorded as a sculptor, miniaturist, and engraver of *nielli. However, from about 1485 he worked mainly as a painter, principally of altarpieces for churches in Bologna and neighbouring towns and of small devotional works; he was also an accomplished portraitist. His softly rounded style was strongly influenced by *Perugino. According to *Vasari, Francia died of 'grief' after seeing *Raphael's *St Cecilia* (*c.*1515, Pinacoteca Nazionale, Bologna), which made his own paintings look hopelessly old-fashioned. There are several examples of his work in the National Gallery, London.

Franciabigio (Francisco di Cristofano) (1484–1525). Florentine painter, a minor master of the High *Renaissance style. He was a pupil of Mariotto *Albertinelli and later shared a workshop with *Andrea del Sarto, who was the dominant influence on his style. His best works are generally considered to be his portraits, particularly those of young men (*A Knight of Rhodes*, *c.*1514, NG, London).

Francis, Sam (1923–94). American painter, one of the leading second-generation *Abstract Expressionists. While serving in the US Army Air Corps he injured his spine in a plane crash and he took up painting in 1944 when he was recovering in hospital. In 1950 he settled in Paris, where he studied under *Léger and was friendly with *Riopelle and other *Art Informel painters; his style was influenced by these artists as well as by Americans such as Jackson *Pollock. He visited Japan several times, and the thin texture of his paint, his drip and splash technique, and his asymmetrical balance of colour against powerful voids (he often left areas of canvas blank) have led critics to speak of influences from Japanese traditions of contemplative art. In 1961 Francis returned to his native California, settling first at Santa Barbara and then in Santa Monica. From the mid-1960s the feeling of oriental simplicity in his painting increased, bringing his work into closer affinity with *Minimal art. Francis carried out several mural commissions, but he often worked on a small scale in watercolour. He also made lithographs (from 1960) and sculpture (from 1965).

Francken. Family of Flemish painters active in the 16th and 17th centuries, mainly in Antwerp. The individual contributions of the many artists in the family are often difficult to distinguish, but the two most important members were **Frans I** (1542–1616) and particularly his son **Frans II** (1581–1642). The father mainly painted religious and historical compositions. His early works were often large in scale; the late ones were small, usually done on copper, and crowded with exotic figures and accessories. Frans II frequently adopted his father's subjects and style, but his range was wider. He painted landscapes and *genre scenes as well as historical pictures, and was also one of the first artists to use the interior of a picture gallery as a subject, giving faithful miniature reproductions of the works in the collection. His paintings were even smaller and more crowded than his father's; they were also more colourful. Frans II was frequently employed by his fellow artists in Antwerp to paint the figures in their landscapes and interiors.

Frankenthaler, Helen (1928–). American painter, an important figure in the transition from *Abstract Expressionism to *Colour Field Painting. In her early work she was influenced by Jackson *Pollock and she developed his drip technique by pouring and running very thin paint—like washes of watercolour—onto canvases laid on the floor. She first used this method in *Mountains and Sea* (1952, artist's collection, on loan to NG, Washington), which is regarded as one of the seminal works of post-war American painting. It particularly impressed Morris *Louis and Kenneth *Noland when they saw it in her studio in 1953. In 1962 Frankenthaler switched from oil to acrylic paint, which allowed her to achieve more richly saturated colour. Her limpid veils of colour float on the surface of the canvas, but they often evoke suggestions of landscape. Since 1960 Frankenthaler has also made aquatints, lithographs, and woodcuts; in 1964 she began to work in ceramics; and in 1972 she made her first sculpture. From 1958 to 1971 she was married to Robert *Motherwell.

Frankenthal School. *See* CONINXLOO.

Fréminet, Martin. *See* FONTAINEBLEAU, SCHOOL OF.

French, Daniel Chester (1850–1931). American sculptor. He made his name with the famous bronze statue of the *Minute Man* (1875), in Concord, Massachusetts, a monument to commemorate the rising of the citizens of the town during the early years of the Revolution (the figure was ready to fight for his country in a minute). After this success, French went on to become the most illustrious sculptor of public monuments of his day, his best-known work being the huge seated marble figure of Abraham Lincoln (dedicated in 1922) on the Lincoln Memorial in Washington.

fresco (It., *fresco*: 'fresh'). A method of wall painting in which powdered *pigments mixed in water are applied to wet plaster freshly laid on the wall. The paint fuses with the plaster, making the picture an integral part of the wall. This technique is also called *buon fresco* or *fresco buono* (true fresco) to distinguish it from painting on dry plaster, which is called by analogy *fresco secco* or simply *secco. Buon fresco* is exceptionally permanent in dry climates, but if damp penetrates the wall, the plaster is liable to crumble and the paint with it. Consequently the art has been practised chiefly in dry countries, particularly in Italy (though less often in watery Venice), and seldom in northern Europe. The technique is of great antiquity, going back to Greek times, and it is also found outside Europe, for example in China and India. *Giotto stands at the head of the glorious Italian tradition of fresco painting, and from his time many of the leading Italian masters produced their most famous works in the medium. It became less common in the 18th century and Giambattista *Tiepolo was the last in the line of great Italian painters who used it. It was revived in the 19th century, notably by German painters such as the *Nazarenes and *Cornelius, but some notable decorators, such as *Delacroix and *Puvis de Chavannes, preferred to use the method of *marouflage. In the 20th century the most famous exponents of fresco were the Mexican muralists *Orozco, *Rivera, and *Siqueiros.

Freud, Lucian (1922–). German-born British painter. He was born in Berlin, a grandson of Sigmund Freud, came to England with his parents in 1931, and acquired British nationality in 1939. His earliest love was drawing, and he began to work full time as an artist after being invalided out of the Merchant Navy in 1942. In 1951 his *Interior at Paddington* (Walker AG, Liverpool) won a prize at the Festival of Britain, and since then he has built up a formidable reputation as one of the most powerful contemporary figurative painters. Portraits and nudes are his specialities, often observed in arresting close-up. He prefers to paint people he knows well: 'If you don't know them, it can only be like a travel book.' His early work was meticulously detailed, so he has sometimes been described as a *Realist (or rather absurdly as a *Superrealist), but the subjectivity and intensity of his work has always set him apart from the sober tradition characteristic of most British figurative art since the Second World War. In his later work (from the late 1950s) his handling became much broader. He is also an outstanding etcher. In 1993 Peter *Blake wrote that since the death of Francis *Bacon the previous year, Freud was 'certainly the best living British painter'.

Freundlich, Otto (1878–1943). German painter, sculptor, and designer (of mosaics, tapestries, and stained glass), active mainly in France. From 1909 to 1914 he spent much of his time in Paris, where he was a member of *Picasso's circle and flirted briefly with *Cubism. In 1918 he was a member of the *Novembergruppe in Berlin and soon afterwards he began producing purely abstract paintings, composing with interlocking swathes of colour. From 1924 to 1939 he lived in Paris, where he was a member of *Cercle et Carré and *Abstraction-Création. In his own country his work was condemned as *degenerate (his sculpture *The New Man* was reproduced on the cover of the catalogue of the infamous 'Degenerate Art' exhibition held in Munich in 1937 and was later destroyed by the Nazis). He did not take up large-scale sculpture until 1928, but his few surviving works in this field are generally considered his finest achievements, notable for their feeling of sombre mystery. After being arrested in the Pyrenees, he died at Maidanek concentration camp in Poland.

Frick, Henry Clay (1849–1919). American industrialist, art collector, and philanthropist. He made an enormous fortune in coke and steel operations and devoted much of his wealth to his passion for art and to philanthropy (he endowed several hospitals for example). Although he sometimes took expert advice (notably from Roger *Fry), Frick essentially relied on his own taste and eye for quality. In addition to paintings, his purchases included drawings, prints, enamels, bronzes, and porcelain. On his death he left his New York mansion and a large fund to form the Frick Collection, which was opened to the public in 1935. It is generally regarded as one of the finest small museums in the world, with a choice collection of works from the Middle Ages to the late 19th century. *Rembrandt's *Polish Rider* and Giovanni *Bellini's *St Francis* are among the celebrated masterpieces in the collection. Frick's will stipulated that further acquisitions could be made and a few pictures have subsequently been added to the collection, maintaining the superb standards he set. Attached to the Frick Collection is the Frick Art Reference Library, which has major collections of books and photographs. It was founded in 1920 by Frick's daughter, **Helen Clay Frick**. In 1970 she established the Frick Art Museum in Pittsburgh, the city where her father had made his fortune.

Friedlaender, Walter (1873–1966). German-American art historian. He had a distinguished academic career in Germany and, as professor at the university of Freibourg, numbered Erwin *Panofsky among his pupils. In 1933 he was dismissed by the Nazis and emigrated to the USA, where he became professor at New York University and exercised a great influence on American art historians. His major publications include *Caravaggio Studies* (1955), *David to Delacroix* (1952), *Mannerism and Anti-Mannerism in Italian Painting* (1957), and monographs on *Poussin in German (1914) and English (1966).

Friedländer, Max J. (1867–1958). German art historian. The successor to Wilhelm von *Bode as director of the Gemäldegalerie in Berlin, he enriched the collection particularly in his own field of Early Netherlandish painting. In 1934 he retired to Holland. His magnum opus is *Die altniederländische Malerei* (14 vols., 1924–37). In a prefatory note to the English edition (*Early Netherlandish Painting*, 16 vols., 1967–76) Erwin *Panofsky described it as 'one of the few uncontested masterpieces produced by our discipline'.

Friedländer covered the same ground in a much briefer format in *Die frühen niederländischen Maler von Van Eyck bis Bruegel* (1916), translated as *From Van Eyck to Bruegel* (1956).

Friedrich, Caspar David (1774–1840). The greatest German *Romantic painter and one of the most original geniuses in the history of landscape painting. He was born at Greifswald, near the Baltic coast, and after studying at the Copenhagen Academy under *Juel and *Abildgaard from 1794 to 1798, he settled permanently in Dresden. There he led a quiet life, interrupted only by occasional excursions to the mountains or to the Baltic coast, single-mindedly pursuing his personal insight into the spiritual significance of landscape. He was intensely introspective and often melancholic (although his marriage at the age of 44 brought him much happiness), and he relied on deep contemplation to summon up mentally the images he was to put on canvas. 'Close your bodily eye, so that you may see your picture first with your spiritual eye,' he wrote, 'then bring to the light of day that which you have seen in the darkness so that it may react on others from the outside inwards.' Friedrich began with topographical drawings in pencil and *sepia wash and did not take up oil painting until 1807. One of his first works in the new medium, *The Cross in the Mountains* (1808, Staatliche Kunstsammlungen, Dresden), caused great controversy because it was painted as an altarpiece, and to use a landscape in this unprecedented way was considered sacrilege by some critics. His choice of subjects often broke new ground and he discovered aspects of nature so far unseen: an infinite stretch of sea or mountains, snow-covered or fog-bound plains in the strange light of sunrise, dusk, or moonlight. Even when he does not use any overt religious symbolism, his landscapes convey a sense of haunting spirituality. Friedrich had a severe stroke in 1835 and returned to his small sepias. Although he enjoyed considerable success and renown earlier in his career, by the time of his death he was virtually forgotten and his immediate influence was confined to members of his circle in Dresden, notably G. F. *Kersting, who sometimes painted the figures in Friedrich's work. It was only at the end of the 19th century, with the rise of *Symbolism, that his greatness began to be recognized. Most of his work is still in Germany; *Winter Landscape* (c.1811), acquired by the National Gallery, London, in 1988, is the first Friedrich oil to enter a British public collection.

Frink, Dame Elisabeth (1930–93). British sculptor and graphic artist. Some of her early work—influenced by *Giacometti—was angular and menacing. During the 1960s her figures—typically horses and riders or male nudes—became smoother, but she retained a feeling of the bizarre in the polished goggles that feature particularly in her over-life-size heads. She worked mainly in bronze and had numerous public commissions, for example *Horse and Rider* (1975) in Piccadilly, London, made for Trafalgar House Investments Ltd. Later in her career she also did numerous portrait busts of distinguished sitters. In addition to sculpture she made prints and drawings.

Frith, William Powell (1819–1909). English painter. He began his career with literary subjects (from Shakespeare, Scott, and other authors), but in the 1850s he turned to contemporary scenes, with which he had great commercial success. His crowded, anecdote-packed pictures of Victorian life, among them *Derby Day* (1858, Tate, London) and *The Railway Station* (1862, Royal Holloway and Bedford New College, Egham), are among the most familiar images of their age. Frith's *My Autobiography and Reminiscences* (1887) and *Further Reminiscences* (1888) give lively accounts of the art world of his time.

Froment, Nicolas (d. 1483/4). French painter. He probably came from northern France, but he worked in Avignon. Two documented works by him survive, both *triptychs: The Raising of Lazarus* (1461, Uffizi, Florence) and *The Burning Bush* (1476, Aix-en-Provence Cathedral). They show that with *Quarton he introduced Netherlandish naturalism to French art. His figures have strong if sometimes clumsy expressions and gestures, while his draperies have a characteristic angularity reminiscent of some of the works of the Spanish and German followers of Rogier van der *Weyden.

Fromentin, Eugène (1820–76). French painter and writer. As a painter he was a specialist in Oriental scenes (he visited North Africa in 1846, 1847–8, and 1852–3); his pictures in this vein were much admired

in his own day but are now virtually forgotten. His reputation instead rests on his book *Les Maîtres d'autrefois* (The Masters of Past Time, 1876), a study of Dutch and Flemish painting, particularly of the 17th century. He also wrote a lyrical novel, *Dominique* (1862).

Fronte Nuovo delle Arti (New Art Front). An association of Italian artists founded in 1946 with the aim of combating the pessimism of the post-war world and revitalizing Italian art, which had not been a leading force in Europe since the heyday of *Futurism. *Birolli and *Guttuso were the best-known figures in the group, which embraced artists of very different styles and ideologies. The split between abstractionists and realists led to the dissolution of the association in 1948.

Frost, Sir Terry (1915–2003). British painter, one of the leading *St Ives painters. He started painting in 1943 when he was a prisoner of war, encouraged by his fellow prisoner Adrian *Heath, then studied at St Ives and under *Coldstream and *Pasmore at the Camberwell School of Art, 1947–50. He began painting in the sober, naturalistic tradition of the *Euston Road School, but he soon turned to abstraction. His work remained based on observations of nature, however, often the harbour at St Ives (where he lived for much of the 1950s and 1960s). Characteristically he used patterns of interlinked shapes—strongly outlined but avoiding geometrical regularity. He taught at various art schools, notably at Reading University, 1965–81. His son **Anthony Frost** (1951–) is also an abstract painter of the St Ives School.

frottage (French: 'rubbing'). A technique of creating an image by placing a piece of paper over some rough surface such as grained wood or sacking and rubbing the paper with a crayon or pencil until it acquires an impression of the surface quality of the substance beneath. The resulting image is usually taken as a stimulus to the imagination, forming the point of departure for a picture expressing unconscious imagery. The technique was invented in 1925 by Max *Ernst; many other *Surrealists adopted it.

Fry, Roger (1866–1934). English critic, painter, and designer. He took a first-class degree in natural sciences at Cambridge in 1888, but was already more interested in art, and in the 1890s he built up a reputation as a writer and lecturer (and a much more modest one as a painter). His success as a public speaker depended partly on his mellifluous voice; George Bernard Shaw said it was one of only two he knew that were worth listening to for its own sake—the other was that of the actor Sir Johnston Forbes-Robertson. Fry was curator of paintings at the *Metropolitan Museum of Art, New York, 1906–10, but in the year he took up this appointment he 'discovered' *Cézanne and turned his attention away from the Italian Old Masters, with whom he had established his scholarly reputation, to become his period's most eloquent champion of modern French painting. After returning to London in 1910 he organized two exhibitions of *Post-Impressionist painting at the Grafton Galleries (1910 and 1912) that are regarded as milestones in the history of British taste. They attracted an enormous amount of publicity, most of it unfavourable, and many people thought that Fry was a charlatan or possibly even insane. Certain young artists were immensely impressed by the exhibitions, however, and Fry became an influential figure among them. They included Vanessa *Bell and Duncan *Grant, both of whom worked for the *Omega Workshops, which Fry founded in 1913. For the rest of his life he kept up a steady output of writing and lecturing (at the time of his death he was Slade professor at Cambridge University). His books include monographs on *Bellini (1899), Cézanne (1927), and *Matisse (1930), an edition of *Reynolds's *Discourses* (1905), and several collections of lectures and essays. In spite of the initial opposition to his ideas, he probably did more than anyone else to awaken public interest and understanding of modern art in England. Kenneth *Clark called him 'incomparably the greatest influence on taste since *Ruskin' and said: 'In so far as taste can be changed by one man, it was changed by Roger Fry.' As a painter Fry was experimental (his work includes a few abstracts), but his best pictures are fairly straightforward naturalistic portraits; his sitters included several of his *Bloomsbury Group friends.

Fuchs, Ernst. *See* FANTASTIC REALISM.

Fuller, Isaac (c.1606–72). English decorative and portrait painter. He is said to have studied in France with *Perrier, then worked in Oxford and London. Fuller painted altarpieces for Oxford colleges (his *Resurrection* in All Souls was described by the diarist John Evelyn in 1644 as 'too full of nakeds for a chapel') and did decorative painting for taverns in London, including mythological scenes for the Mitre Tavern, Fenchurch Street, but these works have disappeared. His largest surviving works are five canvases, each about 3 m (10 ft) wide, showing Charles II's escape after the Battle of Worcester in 1651 (NPG, London). Otherwise, Fuller is remembered for his highly idiosyncratic portraits. He was a notorious drunkard and his self-portraits (NPG, and Bodleian Lib., Oxford) are painted with a bravura worthy of a larger-than-life character.

Funk art. Term applied to a type of art that originated in California (specifically the San Francisco area) around 1960 in which tatty or sick subjects—often pornographic or scatological—are treated in a deliberately distasteful way (the word 'funky' has various meanings, including 'smelly'; when applied to music it can mean 'earthy' or 'authentic'). Such art has been seen as a subversive reaction against the seriousness of *Abstract Expressionism and the New York art scene in general. Although the first funk works were paintings, its most characteristic products are three-dimensional, either sculpture or *assemblages. Edward *Kienholz is the best-known practitioner of the genre.

Fuseli, Henry (Johann Heinrich Füssli) (1741–1825). Swiss-born painter, draughtsman, and writer on art, active mainly in England, where he was one of the outstanding figures of the *Romantic movement. He was the son of a portrait painter, **Johann Caspar Füssli** (1706–82), but he originally trained as a Zwinglian minister; he took holy orders in 1761, but soon abandoned the priesthood. In 1764 he moved to London at the suggestion of the British ambassador in Berlin, who had been impressed by his drawings. *Reynolds encouraged him to take up painting, and he spent the years 1770–8 in Italy, engrossed in the study of *Michelangelo, whose elevated style he sought to emulate for the rest of his life. After his return to England in 1779 he exhibited highly imaginative works such as *The Nightmare* (1781, Detroit Inst. of Arts), the picture that secured his reputation when it was shown at the Royal Academy in 1782 (there is another version in the Goethe-museum, Frankfurt). An unforgettable image of a woman in the throes of a violently erotic dream, this painting shows how far ahead of his time Fuseli was in exploring the murky areas of the psyche where sex and fear meet. His fascination with the horrifying and fantastic also comes out in many of his literary subjects, which formed a major part of his output; he painted several works for *Boydell's Shakespeare Gallery, and in 1799 he followed this example by opening a Milton Gallery in Pall Mall with an exhibition of 47 of his own paintings. From 1799 to 1805 Fuseli was professor of painting at the *Royal Academy and he was re-elected to the post in 1810. He was a popular teacher and a much-respected figure (he was buried in St Paul's Cathedral next to Reynolds), but his work was generally neglected for about a century after his death until the *Expressionists and *Surrealists saw in him a kindred spirit. His work can be clumsy and overblown, but at its best it has something of the imaginative intensity of his friend William *Blake, who described Fuseli as 'The only man that e'er I knew | who did not make me almost spew.' Fuseli's extensive writings on art include *Lectures on Painting* (1801) and a translation of *Winckelmann's *Reflections on the Painting and Sculpture of the Greeks* (1765).

Futurism (Futurismo). Italian avant-garde art movement, launched in 1909, that exalted the dynamism of the modern world; it was literary in origin, but most of its major exponents were painters, and it also embraced sculpture, architecture, music, the cinema, and photography. The First World War brought the movement to an end as a vital force, but it lingered in Italy until the 1930s, and it had a strong influence in other countries. The founder and chief theorist of Futurism was the Italian writer Filippo Tommaso Marinetti (1876–1944), and the main painters involved were *Balla, *Boccioni, *Carrà, *Russolo, and *Severini. The aim

of the movement, which was outlined in various manifestos, was to break with the past and its academic culture and to celebrate modern technology, dynamism, and power. In trying to work out a visual idiom to express such concerns, the Futurist painters at first were strongly influenced by *Divisionism, in which forms are broken down into small patches of colour—suitable for suggesting sparkling effects of light or the blurring caused by high-speed movement. From 1911, however, some of them—influenced by *Cubism—began using fragmented forms and multiple viewpoints, often accentuating the sense of movement by vigorous diagonals. The subjects of the Futurist painters were typically drawn from urban life, and they were often political in intent, but at times their work came close to abstraction. Marinetti had a prodigious talent for publicity (backed by substantial inherited wealth) and Futurism was promoted not only through exhibitions but also by lectures, press conferences, and various attention-seeking stunts, some of which foreshadowed *Performance art. In keeping with this talent for self-promotion, the Futurists had widespread influence in the period immediately before and during the First World War. Stylistically, the influence is clear in *Vorticism in England and *Rayonism in Russia, for example, and in the work of Marcel *Duchamp in France and Joseph *Stella in the USA, whilst the use of provocative manifestos and other shock tactics was most eagerly adopted by the *Dadaists.

Fyt, Jan (1611–61). Flemish painter and etcher, primarily of still life and hunting pieces. He was born and mainly active in Antwerp, where he was a pupil of *Snyders, but he also visited Paris, Italy, and possibly the Netherlands. He had a successful and prolific career and often collaborated with other artists. His most characteristic paintings are in the Snyders tradition, depicting trophies of the hunt, dead stags, hares, and birds, all treated with a vigorous feeling for texture. The rare flower paintings by Fyt are exceptionally fine and perhaps more attuned to modern taste.

G

Gabo, Naum (Naum Neemia Pevsner) (1890–1977). Russian-born sculptor who became an American citizen in 1952, the most influential exponent of *Constructivism. He was the younger brother of Antoine *Pevsner, and adopted another family name, Gabo, in 1915 to avoid confusion between the two. After studying medicine, natural sciences, and engineering in Munich, he was introduced to avant-garde art when he visited his brother in Paris in 1913–14, and in 1915 he began to make geometrical constructions in Oslo, where they had taken refuge during the First World War. In 1917 the brothers returned to Russia and in 1920 they published their *Realistic Manifesto*, which set forth the basic principles of Constructivism. They advocated a pure abstract sculpture, but official policy in the new Soviet Russia increasingly insisted on art being channelled into industrial design and other socially useful work (as exemplified by *Tatlin). Gabo therefore left Russia in 1922 and spent the next ten years in Berlin, where he knew many of the leading artists of the day, particularly those connected with the *Bauhaus. In 1932 he moved to Paris, where he was a prominent member of the *Abstraction-Création group, and in 1935 he settled in England, living first in London (where in 1937 he was co-editor of the Constructivist review *Circle*) and then from 1939 in Cornwall (see ST IVES SCHOOL). In 1946 Gabo moved to the USA, settling at Middlebury, Connecticut, in 1953. In the last three decades of his life he received many prestigious awards and carried out numerous public commissions in Europe and America. He often worked on themes over a long period: his *Torsion Fountain* outside St Thomas's Hospital in London, for example, was erected in 1975, but is a development from models he was making in the 1920s. (Small models are a feature of his work; there are numerous examples in Tate Modern, which has an outstanding collection of Gabo material.)

Gabo never trained as an artist, but came to art by way of his studies of engineering and physical science, and was one of the first artists to embody in his work modern concepts of the nature of space. He was one of the earliest to experiment with *Kinetic sculpture and to make extensive use of semi-transparent materials for a type of abstract sculpture that incorporates space as a positive element rather than displacing or enclosing it. He was throughout his life an advocate of the Constructivist idea not merely as an artistic movement but as the ideology of a way of life.

Gaddi, Taddeo (d. 1366). Florentine painter, the son of a painter and mosaicist **Gaddo Gaddi** (d. *c*.1330). According to Cennino *Cennini, Taddeo was *Giotto's godson and worked with him for 24 years. He was one of the leading Florentine artists of his day and in 1347 he headed a list of the best living painters made for the purpose of choosing a master to paint an altarpiece for S. Giovanni Fuorcivitas, Pistoia. His best-known works were painted for S. Croce, Florence, notably the frescos devoted to the life of the Virgin in the Baroncelli Chapel (*c*.1330), and the panels illustrating the life of Christ (*c*.1335), originally meant for the doors of a sacristy cupboard and now scattered among museums in Florence (Accademia), Munich (Alte Pin.), and Berlin (Gemäldegalerie). Many other panels are attributed to him and he must have had a flourishing workshop. Although transmitting the tradition of Giotto, his style is less heroic and more anecdotal. Gaddi's son **Agnolo** (d. 1396) continued the Giotto tradition but modified it still further in the direction of decorative elegance. He is particularly notable for his cool, pale colours, which influenced the refined late *Gothic art of artists of the next generation such as *Lorenzo Monaco. Agnolo's works include frescos on the story of the Cross in the chancel of S. Croce (*c*.1390) and on the story of the Virgin and her girdle in the Chapel of the Holy Girdle in Prato Cathedral (1392–5). Many panel paintings also are attributed to him.

Gainsborough, Thomas (1727–88). English painter of portraits, landscapes, and *fancy pictures, one of the most individual geniuses in British art. He was born at Sudbury, Suffolk, the son of a cloth merchant, and showed artistic talent from an early age; around 1740 (aged about 13) he moved to London, where he studied with *Gravelot and perhaps also with *Hayman. In 1748 he returned to Sudbury, and in 1752 he set up as a portrait painter in Ipswich, the largest town in the county. His work at this time consisted mainly of heads and half-lengths, but he also produced some small portrait groups in landscape settings, including the celebrated *Mr and Mrs Andrews* (c.1749, NG, London), remarkable for its 'dewy freshness' (Ellis *Waterhouse). In addition he painted pure landscapes (*Cornard Wood*, 1748, NG, London). His patrons in Ipswich were mainly the merchants of the town and local squires, but in 1759 he moved to Bath, where he worked for much more fashionable clients, many of them wealthy visitors to the spa town. From now on all his portraits were life-size and many of them were full-lengths, in which he cultivated a free and elegant manner (*Mary, Countess Howe*, c.1764, Kenwood House, London). In 1768 he was elected a foundation member of the *Royal Academy, and in 1774 he settled permanently in London. Here he further developed the personal style he had evolved at Bath, working with light and rapid brushstrokes and delicate and evanescent colours. He became a favourite painter of the royal family, even though his rival *Reynolds was appointed principal painter to the king. Gainsborough sometimes said that while portraiture was his profession, landscape painting was his pleasure, and he continued to paint landscapes long after he had left a country neighbourhood. He also produced many landscape drawings, some in pencil, some in charcoal and chalk (he liked to experiment technically and sometimes used mixed media, for example combining chalk with oils). In his later years he extended his range to include fancy pictures of pastoral subjects (*Peasant Girl Gathering Sticks*, 1782, Manchester AG). He is only once known to have left England, making a brief visit to the Netherlands in 1783.

Gainsborough's style had diverse sources. His early works show the influence of French engraving and of Dutch landscape painting; at Bath his change of portrait style owed much to a close study of van *Dyck, whose work he saw in nearby country houses (his admiration is most clear in *The Blue Boy*, c.1770, Huntington Art Coll., San Marino); and in his later landscapes he was sometimes influenced by *Rubens (*The Watering Place*, c.1777, NG, London). But he was an independent and highly original artist, able to assimilate to his own ends what he learnt from others, and he always relied mainly on his own resources. With the exception of his nephew Gainsborough *Dupont, he had no assistants and unlike most of his contemporaries he never employed a *drapery painter. He was in many ways the antithesis of Reynolds. Whereas Reynolds was sober-minded and the complete professional, Gainsborough (even though his output was prodigious) was much more easy-going and often overdue with his commissions, writing that 'painting and punctuality mix like oil and vinegar'. Although he was an entertaining letter-writer, Gainsborough, unlike Reynolds, had no interest in literary or historical themes, his great passion outside painting being music (his friend William Jackson the composer wrote that he 'avoided the company of literary men, who were his aversion...he detested reading'). Gainsborough and Reynolds had great mutual respect, however; Gainsborough asked for Reynolds to visit him on his deathbed, and Reynolds paid posthumous tribute to his rival in his Fourteenth *Discourse*. Recognizing the fluid brilliance of his brushwork, Reynolds praised 'his manner of forming all the parts of a picture together', and wrote of 'all those odd scratches and marks' that 'by a kind of magic, at a certain distance...seem to drop into their proper places'. Examples of Gainsborough's work are in many collections in Britain and the USA, including the museum devoted to him in Sudbury, located in the attractive house in which he was born.

Gallego, Fernando (documented 1468–1507). Spanish painter. He worked mainly in Salamanca, where *Palomino says he was born, and was the major Castilian painter of his period. Gallego's sober, impassive style has affinities with that of Dirk *Bouts, and it has been suggested that he visited the Netherlands early in his career. His works include a *triptych of *The Virgin, St Andrew and St Christopher* (c.1470) in the new cathedral of

Salamanca (one of his few signed paintings), an altarpiece of *San Idelfonso* (*c*.1475–80) in the cathedral of Zamora, and ceiling frescos on astrological subjects (*c*.1480, much repainted) in the Old Library in the University of Salamanca. Gallego had considerable influence in Castile. One of his followers, **Francisco Gallego**, was presumably a relative.

Gallen-Kallela, Akseli (1865–1931). Finnish painter, graphic artist, designer, and architect. A major figure in the *Art Nouveau and *Symbolist movements, Gallen-Kallela travelled widely and was well known outside Finland, particularly in Germany (he had a joint exhibition with *Munch in Berlin in 1895 and exhibited with Die *Brücke in Dresden in 1910). He was deeply patriotic (he volunteered to fight in the War of Independence against Russia in 1918, even though he was in his fifties) and he was inspired mainly by the landscape and folklore of his country, above all by the Finnish national epic *Kalevala* ('Land of Heroes'). His early work was in the 19th-century naturalistic tradition, but in the 1890s he developed a flatter, more stylized manner, well suited to the depiction of heroic myth, with bold simplifications of form, strong outlines, and vivid—sometimes rather garish—colours. Apart from easel paintings, Gallen-Kallela did a number of murals for public buildings (including the Finnish National Museum, Helsinki, 1928). His work also included book illustrations (notably for an edition of *Kalevala*, 1922) and designs for stained glass, fabrics, and jewellery. He is regarded not only as his country's greatest painter, but also as the chief figure in the creation of a distinctive Finnish art, and he was given a funeral befitting a national hero. His former home (which he designed himself) at Tarvaspää near Helsinki is now a museum dedicated to him.

Gambart, Ernest (1814–1902). Belgian-born picture dealer and print publisher who settled in London in 1840 and became a dominant figure in these fields. In the three decades between his arrival in England and his retirement to the Continent in 1871, 'Gambart, more than any other individual, transformed the London art world. He founded a system for the promotion and sale of pictures on an international scale; contributed increasingly to the status of the artist in society; and brought the London, if not the European, art trade from infancy to maturity … [He] became a print publisher of international repute, who exploited the possibilities of the print so as to raise it to the level of pure popular art' (Jeremy Maas, *Gambart: Prince of the Victorian Art World*, 1975).

Gardner, Isabella Stewart (1840–1924). American socialite and art collector. She married into a prominent Boston family and spent most of her life in that city, where she patronized numerous artistic causes (including the Boston Symphony Orchestra) and dazzled and occasionally mildly scandalized polite society (for example by attending boxing matches). Her interest in art was guided by Bernard *Berenson, one of her protégés, who helped her to assemble a superb collection of Italian Renaissance paintings, including *Titian's *Rape of Europa*, which has often been claimed as the greatest painting in America. Other highlights of her collection include some outstanding 17th-century Dutch paintings and her full-length portrait (1888) by *Sargent (to whom she had been introduced in London by Henry James). The portrait shows off her celebrated figure (she wears her pearls round her waist rather than her neck) and was considered rather shocking —in the spirit of Sargent's earlier *Madame X* (some contemporaries assumed that he and Mrs Gardner were lovers, but this seems unlikely). Her husband, the financier Jack Gardner, died in 1898, and the following year she began building Fenway Court in Boston as both a home and a museum. The building, which was formally opened in 1903, is modelled on a Venetian Renaissance palace and incorporates various architectural fragments that she bought on her numerous trips to Europe. She supervised the construction with immense care, acting virtually as site foreman. In her will she left the Isabella Stewart Gardner Museum to Boston as a public institution, with the proviso that the collection should be maintained exactly as she had arranged it. The British art historian Sir Philip Hendy, who published a catalogue of the Gardner Museum in 1931, described it as 'probably the finest collection of its compact size in the world'. In addition to paintings, sculpture, drawings, and prints, it contains objects of many other types, including furniture, textiles, ceramics, glassware, manuscripts, and books.

Garofalo (Benvenuto Tisi) (1481?–1559). Italian painter, active mainly in Ferrara. His nickname is said to come from his liking for including a gillyflower (It., *garofano*) in a corner of his paintings. According to *Vasari he twice visited Rome, and his work—derivative but beautifully crafted—was heavily influenced by *Raphael. He was the first to paint in such a manner in Ferrara and was influential in spreading the High *Renaissance style. His output was large and varied (frescos, altarpieces, small devotional works, also a few mythologies); there are many examples in Ferrarese churches and, for example, in the National Gallery, London. In about 1550 he went blind.

Gaudí, Antoni. See ART NOUVEAU.

Gaudier-Brzeska, Henri (Henri Gaudier) (1891–1915). French sculptor and draughtsman, active in England for most of his short career and usually considered part of the history of British rather than French art. In 1910 he took up sculpture in Paris without formal training, and in the same year he met Sophie Brzeska, a Polish woman twenty years his senior, with whom he lived from that time, both of them adopting the hyphenated name. In 1911 they moved to London, which Gaudier had visited briefly in 1906 and 1908, and lived for a while in extreme poverty. He became a friend of Wyndham *Lewis and other leading literary and artistic figures, and his work was shown in avant-garde exhibitions, such as the *Vorticist exhibition of 1915. In 1914 he enlisted in the French army and was killed in action the following year, aged 23. Gaudier developed with astonishing rapidity from a modelling style based on *Rodin towards a highly personal manner of carving in which shapes are radically simplified in a manner recalling *Brancusi (*Red Stone Dancer*, c.1913, Tate, London). In England, only *Epstein was producing sculpture as stylistically advanced as Gaudier-Brzeska at this time. In his lifetime his work was appreciated by only a small circle, but since his death he has become widely recognized as one of the outstanding sculptors of his generation and has acquired something of a legendary status as an unfulfilled genius. In addition

to his sculptures he left behind some splendid animal drawings.

Gauguin, Paul (1848–1903). French *Post-Impressionist painter, printmaker, sculptor, and ceramicist, born in Paris, the son of a journalist from Orléans and a Peruvian Creole mother. He spent his childhood in Lima, joined the merchant marine in 1865, and from 1872 worked successfully as a stockbroker. In the early 1870s he became a keen amateur painter and in 1874 he saw the first *Impressionist exhibition. At about the same time he met *Pissarro, who encouraged him, and began to make a collection of Impressionist pictures. He had a landscape accepted by the *Salon in 1876 and his work was shown in the fifth to eighth (and last) Impressionist exhibitions (1880–6). In 1883 he gave up his employment to become a full-time artist, but had little success and sold his collection to support himself and his family. After the last Impressionist exhibition he moved to Brittany, abandoning his family, and until 1890 he spent much of his time at *Pont-Aven, where he became the pivot of a group of artists who were attracted by his powerful personality and stimulating ideas about art. The most important work he produced there was *The Vision after the Sermon*, also known as *Jacob Wrestling with the Angel* (1888, NG, Edinburgh), in which he broke away completely from the Impressionist style, using areas of pure, flat colour for expressive and symbolic purposes. In 1887–8 he visited Panama and Martinique, and in 1888 he spent a short time at Arles with van *Gogh, a visit that ended in a disastrous quarrel as van Gogh suffered one of his first attacks of madness.

Gauguin had had a taste for colourful, exotic places since his childhood in Peru and in 1891 he left France for Tahiti. In the account he wrote of his life there, *Noa Noa* (1st pub. 1897), he said: 'I have escaped everything that is artificial and conventional. Here I enter into Truth, become one with nature. After the disease of civilization, life in this new world is a return to health.' His theory and practice of art reflected these attitudes. He was one of the first to find visual inspiration in the arts of ancient or primitive peoples (*see* PRIMITIVISM), and he reacted vigorously against the naturalism of the Impressionists and the scientific preoccupations of the *Neo-Impressionists. As well as using colour unnaturalistically for its decorative or emotional effect, he employed emphatic outlines forming rhythmic patterns suggestive of stained glass or Japanese colour prints (*see* UKIYO-E). Gauguin also produced woodcuts in which the black and white areas formed almost abstract patterns and the tool marks were incorporated as parts of the design. Along with those of Edvard *Munch, these prints played an important part in stimulating the major revival of the art of woodcut in the 20th century. Gauguin's other work included woodcarving and pottery. In Tahiti he endeavoured to 'go native' and despite the constant pressure of poverty he painted his finest pictures there. His colours became more resonant, his drawing more grandly simplified, and his expression of the mysteries of life more profound. In 1893 poverty and ill health forced him to return to France, but he had a financial windfall when an uncle died and he was back in Tahiti in 1895. At the end of 1897 he painted his largest and most famous picture, the allegory of life *Where Do We Come From? Who Are We? Where Are We Going?* (MFA, Boston), before attempting suicide (although he had deserted his family he had been devastated that year by the news of the death of his favourite daughter). In September 1901 he settled at Dominica in the Marquesas Islands, where he died two years later. Until his death he worked continuously in the face of poverty, illness (he had syphilis), and lack of recognition. During his time in the South Seas he was often unable to obtain proper materials and was forced to spread his colours thinly on coarse sacking, but from these limitations he forged a style of rough vigour wholly appropriate to the boldness of his vision.

Gauguin was by no means forgotten in France during his years in the South Seas, but at the time of his death few would have agreed with his self-assessment: 'I am a great artist and I know it. It is because I am that I have endured such suffering.' His reputation was firmly established, however, when 227 of his works were shown at the *Salon d'Automne in Paris in 1906, and his influence has been enormous. The *Nabis were formed under his inspiration, he was a leading figure of the *Symbolist movement and one of the sources for *Fauvism. Later, he was one of the major influences on the general non-naturalistic trend of 20th-century

art. Because of the romantic appeal of his life and personality, particularly his willingness to sacrifice everything for his art, Gauguin (like his friend van Gogh) has also been an inspiration for popular and fictional biography, including the novel *The Moon and Sixpence* (1919) by Somerset Maugham, and the opera (1957) of the same title by John L. Gardner.

Gaulli, Giovanni Battista (Il Baciccio) (1639–1709). Italian painter; the name 'Baciccio', by which he is often known, is a dialect contraction of his forenames. He was born in Genoa and active mainly in Rome, where he settled in 1657 and became a friend and protégé of *Bernini (his portrait of Bernini (*c*.1675, NG, Edinburgh) became a kind of official likeness of the Grand Old Man, serving as the basis for the frontispiece engraving of *Baldinucci's biography of 1682). Gaulli achieved success as a painter of altarpieces and portraits (he painted each of the seven popes from Alexander VII to Clement XI as well as many cardinals), but he is remembered mainly for his decorative work and above all for his *Adoration of the Name of Jesus* (1674–9) on the ceiling of the nave of the Gesù. This is one of the supreme masterpieces of *illusionistic decoration, ranking alongside *Pozzo's slightly later ceiling in S. Ignazio, and it appears in countless books as an archetypal example of Counter-Reformation art. The *stucco figures that are so brilliantly combined with the painted decoration (from the ground it is not always possible to tell which is which) are the work of Bernini's pupil Antonio Raggi (1624–86).

Gear, William. *See* COBRA.

Geertgen tot Sint Jans (*c*.1460–*c*.1490). Netherlandish painter, active in Haarlem, where he was the outstanding artist of his day. Almost nothing is known of his career, but van *Mander says that he was a pupil of *Ouwater and that he died when he was about 28. His name means 'Little Gerard of the Brethren of St John', after the Order in Haarlem of which he was a lay brother. For the monastery church of the Brethren he painted his only documented work, a *triptych of the *Crucifixion*, of which two large panels (originally two sides of a wing) survive (KH Mus., Vienna): the *Lamentation of Christ* and the *Burning of the Bones of St John* *the Baptist*. Certain features of these paintings—particularly the slender, doll-like figures with smooth, rather egg-like heads—are highly distinctive, and a small oeuvre of about fifteen paintings has been attributed to Geertgen on stylistic grounds. Unlike the Vienna panels, most of the other pictures given to him are fairly small. They include such remarkably beautiful works as the *Nativity* (NG, London), a radiant nocturnal scene, and *St John the Baptist in the Wilderness* (Gemäldegalerie, Berlin), which shows an exquisite feeling for nature. The vein of tender melancholy that pervades Geertgen's work, the beguilingly innocent charm of his figures, and his sensitivity to light are perhaps the salient qualities that make him one of the most irresistibly attractive artists of the Early Netherlandish School.

Gelder, Aert de (1645–1727). Dutch painter, active mainly in his native Dordrecht. After studying there with *Hoogstraten, he became one of *Rembrandt's last pupils in Amsterdam. He was not only one of the most talented of Rembrandt's pupils, but also one of his most devoted followers, for he was the only Dutch artist to continue working in his style into the 18th century, remaining completely resistant to new trends. His religious paintings, in particular, with their imaginative boldness and preference for oriental types, are very much in the master's spirit, although de Gelder often used colours—such as lilac and lemon yellow—that were untypical of Rembrandt, and his palette was in general lighter. One of his best-known works, *Jacob's Dream* (Dulwich Picture Gal., London), was long attributed to Rembrandt.

Generalić, Ivan (1914–92). Yugoslav (Croatian) *naive painter, the best-known member of the school of peasant painters associated with his native village of Hlebine. Unlike most naive painters, Generalić had a wide repertory. Most of his pictures depict scenes from village life—weddings, funerals, farm work, fairs, and so on—but he also painted landscapes, portraits, still lifes, and imaginative subjects. Some of his pictures are idyllic in mood, but in others there is an element of grotesque fantasy or of *Surrealist strangeness. Usually he painted on glass and his pictures often have a kind of inner glow. After the Second World War he became internationally recognized as one of the finest of all naive artists, his work featuring in numerous group and solo exhibitions and winning him various awards. In spite of his success, he continued to live the life of a peasant and to paint only in his spare time.

genre. Term in art history and criticism for paintings or other works depicting scenes from daily life. It may be applied to appropriate art of any place or period, but most commonly suggests the type of domestic subject matter favoured by Dutch 17th-century artists. In a broader sense, the term is used to mean a particular branch or category of art; landscape and portraiture, for example, are genres of painting, and the essay and the short story are genres of literature.

Gentile da Fabriano (d. 1427). Italian painter, named after his birthplace, Fabriano in the Marches. His birthdate has been traditionally estimated as *c*.1370, but expert opinion now inclines to put it about fifteen years later. Gentile carried out important commissions in several major Italian art centres and was recognized as one of the foremost artists of his day, but most of the work on which his great contemporary reputation was based has been destroyed. It included frescos in the Doges' Palace in Venice (1408) and for St John Lateran in Rome (1427). In between he worked in Florence, Siena, and Orvieto. His major surviving work is the celebrated altarpiece of the *Adoration of the Magi* (1423, Uffizi, Florence), painted for the church of S. Trinità in Florence, which places him alongside *Ghiberti as one of the greatest exponents of the *International Gothic style in Italy. It is remarkable not only for its exquisite decorative beauty but also for the naturalistic treatment of light in the *predella, where there is a night scene with three different light sources. Gentile had widespread influence (much more so initially than his great contemporary *Masaccio), notably on Jacopo *Bellini, who probably worked with him in Florence, *Pisanello, who completed work in Rome he left unfinished at his death, and Fra *Angelico, who was his greatest heir.

Gentileschi, Orazio (1563–1639). Italian painter. He was born in Pisa, but in about

1576 he settled in Rome. After working in a *Mannerist style he became one of the closest and most gifted of *Caravaggio's followers. He was one of the few *Caravaggisti who were friends of the master, and in 1603 he and Caravaggio and two other artists were sued for libel by Giovanni *Baglione. Gentileschi's work does not have the power and uncompromising naturalism of Caravaggio, tending rather towards the lyrical and refined. His graceful figures are stately and clearly disposed, with sharp-edged drapery—qualities recalling his Tuscan heritage. In 1621 he moved to Genoa, where he stayed until 1623; while there he painted an *Annunciation* (Gal. Sabauda, Turin) that is often considered his masterpiece. After working for Marie de *Médicis in Paris, he settled in England in 1626 and became court painter to Charles I. He was held in great esteem in England and remained until his death. His travels were a factor in spreading the Caravaggesque manner, but by the end of his career he had long abandoned heavy *chiaroscuro in favour of light colours. His major works in England were a series of ceiling paintings (1635–8) commissioned by Charles I for the Queen's House at Greenwich, now in Marlborough House, London. His daughter **Artemisia Gentileschi** (1593–1652/3) was one of the greatest of Caravaggesque painters and a formidable personality. She showed remarkable talent whilst still in her teens, built up a European reputation, and lived a life of independence rare for a woman of the time. Up to about 1630 she worked mainly in her native Rome, apart from the years 1612–20, when she lived in Florence (in 1616, aged only 23, she became the first ever female member of the city's Accademia del Disegno). In about 1630 she settled in Naples, but in 1638–41 she visited England, presumably initially to see her ailing father. Although she had doubtless been trained by Orazio, her powerful and dramatic style was very different to his. It is seen at its most characteristic in paintings of *Judith and Holofernes*, a subject she made her own (one of the finest examples is in the Uffizi, Florence). Her predilection for the bloodthirsty theme has been related to events in her own life. At the age of 17 she was allegedly raped by Agostino *Tassi and was tortured during his ensuing trial; thus the fierce intensity with which she depicted a woman decapitating a man has been seen as pictorial 'revenge' for her sufferings.

Gérard, François (1770–1837). French painter, born in Rome, where his father worked for the French ambassador to the Vatican (his mother was Italian). His family returned to Paris in 1782 and in 1786 Gérard began studying with J.-L. *David, becoming one of his favourite pupils. In the *Salon of 1796 he won acclaim with his portrait *Jean-Baptiste Isabey and his Daughter* (Louvre, Paris) and by the turn of the century he was established as France's leading society portraitist. He also produced historical and mythological pictures, notably *Psyche Receiving Cupid's First Kiss* (1798, Louvre). He successfully negotiated the various political changes of the day and received numerous honours, culminating in 1819 when he was made a baron. His style derived from David but was much less taut and heroic, tending at times towards a mannered gracefulness.

Gérard, Marguerite. *See* FRAGONARD.

Gerhaert, Nicolaus (d. 1473?). Sculptor, perhaps of Netherlandish origin, active in Germany and Austria, an artist of great power and originality. He is first recorded in 1462 in Trier and is known to have worked also in Strasbourg and Vienna; several signed or documented works survive, in sandstone and marble (woodcarvings have also been attributed to him), but the details of his life are mostly obscure. His work is extraordinarily vivid and unconventional, capturing an intense feeling of inner life, as in the celebrated sandstone *Bust of a Man* (Mus. de l'Œuvre Notre-Dame, Strasbourg), which is usually considered to be a self-portrait. The voluminous style of his draperies and his boldness of approach suggest that he was trained in a Burgundian workshop where Claus *Sluter's style was still predominant, although he is sometimes called Nicolaus 'of Leyden', implying that he came from Leiden in the northern Netherlands. His work had considerable influence in central Europe.

Géricault, Théodore (1791–1824). French painter and lithographer, one of the prime movers and most original figures of *Romanticism. He studied in Paris with Carle *Vernet and Pierre *Guérin, but was influenced more by making copies of the Old Masters in the *Louvre, developing in particular a passion for *Rubens. In 1816–17 he visited Italy and there became an enthusiastic admirer of *Michelangelo and the *Baroque. After his return to Paris he began work on the picture for which he is most famous, the *Raft of the Medusa* (Louvre, Paris), which caused a sensation at the 1819 *Salon; although it was awarded a medal, it created a furore both on account of its realistic treatment of a horrific event and because of its political implications (it depicts the ordeal of the survivors of the shipwreck of the *Medusa* in 1816, a disaster ascribed by some to government incompetence). The huge picture, which was remarkably original in treating a contemporary event with epic grandeur, also attracted great attention in England, where Géricault spent the years 1820–2 (more than 50,000 visitors paid to see it when it was exhibited in London). During his stay in England he painted jockeys and horse races (*Derby at Epsom*, 1821, Louvre) and was one of the first to bring English painting to the attention of French artists (he was particularly enthusiastic about *Bonington and *Constable). Géricault was a passionate horseman and his death at the age of 32 was hastened by a riding accident. In his temperament and lifestyle as well as his work he ranks as an archetypal Romantic artist. His tempestuous career lasted little more than a decade and in that time he displayed a meteoric and many-sided genius (his teacher Guérin said that he had 'the stuff of several painters' in him). His love of stirring action, his sense of swirling movement, his energetic handling of paint, and his taste for the macabre were all to become features of Romanticism. He was, at the same time, forward-looking in his realism: he made studies from corpses and severed limbs for the *Raft of the Medusa* and painted an extraordinary series of portraits of mental patients in the clinic of his friend Dr Georget, one of the pioneers of humane treatment for the insane (*A Kleptomaniac*, c.1822–3, Mus. B.-A., Ghent). His work had enormous influence, most notably on *Delacroix.

Gérôme, Jean-Léon (1824–1904). French painter and (in his later career) sculptor. He was a pupil of Paul *Delaroche and inherited his highly finished academic style, with which he had a career of great public success. Lorenz Eitner writes that 'In the variety and sensationalism of his subjects ...

Gérôme ... surpassed all his rivals at the *Salon—murder in the Roman Senate and carnage in the gladiatorial arena; luscious nudity at the slave auction or the harem bath; Bonaparte contemplating the Sphinx, and Molière breakfasting with Louis XIV—all served equally well for his carefully plotted picture-plays, graced with sex, spiced with gore, and polished into waxwork lifelikeness by a technique that his admirers took for realism' (*An Outline of 19th Century European Painting*, 1987). Gérôme had considerable influence as an upholder of academic tradition and enemy of progressive trends in art; he opposed, for example, the acceptance by the state of the *Caillebotte bequest of *Impressionist pictures.

Gerstl, Richard (1883–1908). Austrian painter. His early painting was in the style of the Vienna *Sezession, but by 1905 he had developed a highly personal type of *Expressionism. His finest works are portraits, including two groups of the family of the composer Arnold Schoenberg (Österreichische Gal., Vienna), notable for their psychological intensity. He was a tormented character, and after running off with Schoenberg's wife he committed suicide. His work, which anticipates that of such painterly Expressionists as *Kokoschka, remained little known until the 1930s, when he was hailed as an 'Austrian van *Gogh'.

Gertler, Mark (1891–1939). British painter. He was born in the East End of London to poor Polish-Jewish immigrant parents and he spoke only Yiddish up to the age of 8. In 1908–12 he studied at the *Slade School, where he won several prizes. After the First World War he spent a good deal of time in the south of France for the sake of his delicate health (he had tuberculosis). Gertler was influenced by *Post-Impressionism, but his style was highly individual, with strong elements of eastern European folk art. His favourite subjects included female portraits, still lifes, and nudes, such as the earthy and voluptuous *Queen of Sheba* (1922, Tate, London), painted in his characteristic feverishly hot colours. His best-known work is perhaps *Merry-Go-Round* (1916, Tate, London), a powerful image—probably a satire on militarism—in which figures spin on fairground horses in a mad, futile whirl. Gertler had many admirers, including distinguished figures in the literary world; D. H. Lawrence made him the model for the sculptor Loerke in *Women in Love* (1920). The word 'genius' was frequently applied to him, and he was seen by many as the acceptable face of modernism. However, he began to lose popularity in the early 1930s, when he adopted a more avant-garde style characterized by a flatter sense of space and a greater emphasis on surface pattern. He had always been subject to fits of depression, and after the failure of an exhibition at the Lefevre Gallery, London, in 1939, he committed suicide.

gesso. Brilliant white preparation of powdered chalk mixed with glue, used during the Middle Ages and the *Renaissance as a *ground to prepare a panel or canvas for painting or gilding. The gesso was applied in several layers, with the proportion of chalk to glue progressively increasing. When applied to frames and furniture it could be painted and gilded in the same way, and was often modelled (*gesso rilievo*). In the 20th century the term 'gesso' came to be used loosely for any white substance that can be mixed with water to make a ground; in reference to sculpture it often means *plaster of Paris.

gestural painting. A term describing the application of paint with expansive gestures so that the sweep of the artist's arm is deliberately emphasized. It carries an implication that the artist's actions express his or her emotions and personality, just as in other walks of life gestures express a person's feelings. The term has been applied particularly to *Abstract Expressionism and is sometimes used more or less as a synonym for *Action Painting. However, it can also apply to figurative painting, notably *Neo-Expressionism.

Getty, J. Paul (1892–1976). American oil magnate and art collector. Reputedly the richest man in the world, he amassed a large collection of works of art, his main areas of interest being, as he wrote in his book *The Joys of Collecting* (1966), 'Greek and Roman marbles and bronzes; Renaissance paintings; sixteenth-century Persian carpets; Savonnerie carpets and eighteenth-century French furniture and tapestries'. The J. Paul Getty Museum was opened in 1954 in a wing of his home in Malibu, Los Angeles, and in 1974 a new museum, housed in a re-creation of a Roman villa, was opened

nearby. One of the archetypes of the eccentric, parsimonious millionaire, Getty lived in England from the 1950s and never saw his creation. On his death it became the most richly endowed museum in the world, and its spectacular purchases (*see* LYSIPPUS), aroused fears that it would monopolize the world market for masterpieces. In 1997 a second Getty Museum opened at Brentwood, Los Angeles; this now houses all the collections other than antiquities, which remain at Malibu. The new museum is part of the enormous Getty Center, which houses various facilities for art research and education. **Sir Paul Getty** (1932–2003), one of Getty's five sons by his five wives, spent much of his life in England and was a princely benefactor to British art institutions: most notably he gave £50,000,000 to the National Gallery, London, in 1985. He adopted British nationality in 1998.

Ghe, Nikolai. *See* WANDERERS.

Gheeraerts, Marcus the Younger (1562–1636). Flemish-born portrait painter, active in England. He settled there in 1568 with his father **Marcus the Elder** (*c*.1530–*c*.1590), an engraver and painter who had fled from Bruges because of religious persecution. Marcus the Younger was probably the leading society portraitist in London at the peak of his career (his popularity declined after about 1615). About 30 paintings can be confidently assigned to him on the basis of signatures or inscriptions, the best-known among them being the splendid full-length portrait of Elizabeth I known as the 'Ditchley' portrait (*c*.1592, NPG, London), in which the queen is shown standing on a map of England. Many other portraits have been attributed to him, but it is not easy to disentangle his work from that of some of his contemporaries.

Gheyn, Jacob de II (1565–1629). Dutch draughtsman, engraver, and painter. He was born in Antwerp and was probably a pupil of his father **Jacob de Gheyn I** (1537/8–81?), a glass painter and engraver. From *c*.1585 to 1590 he studied with Hendrick *Goltzius in Haarlem. He worked in various other Dutch towns, notably for the court at The Hague, where he designed the grotto (the earliest in the Netherlands) and other ornamentation of Buitenhof, the garden of Prince Maurice. His drawings and engravings are of greater importance than his paintings, for in their liveliness and informality they are outstanding documents of the period of transition from *Mannerism to *naturalism in Dutch art. His son **Jacob de Gheyn III** (c.1596–1641) was also an engraver, specializing in mythological subjects.

Ghezzi, Pier Leone. See CARICATURE.

Ghiberti, Lorenzo (1378?–1455). Florentine sculptor, goldsmith, and designer, one of the most important artists of his period. He came to prominence in 1401 when he competed successfully (defeating *Brunelleschi, Jacopo della *Quercia, and four other artists) for a commission, offered by the merchant guild, to make a pair of gilded bronze doors for the Baptistery of Florence. His competition *relief of the *Sacrifice of Isaac* is in the Bargello, Florence. Work on the doors lasted until 1424 and in 1425 he was asked to make a second pair for the same building, which occupied him until 1452. Both sets of doors are divided into panels showing biblical scenes or figures in high reliefs. The two commissions had immense prestige, and Ghiberti's workshop became a kind of academy for a whole generation of artists, attracting some of the best talent of the day: *Donatello, *Masolino, and *Uccello were among those who had at least part of their training there. Although the two sets of doors dominated his career, Ghiberti was involved in numerous other projects; indeed, he boasted that 'Few works of importance were made in our city that were not designed or devised by my hand.' He served on the committee in charge of the architectural works of Florence Cathedral, designed stained-glass windows, goldsmiths' work, and reliquaries (none of his work in precious metals survives), and made three over-life-size bronze statues for the church of Orsanmichele: *St John the Baptist* (1413–17), *St Matthew* (1419–22), and *St Stephen* (c.1425–9). The *St John* was the first bronze statue of such size to be produced since antiquity. In addition to his own works, Ghiberti said he gave help to 'many painters, sculptors, and stonecarvers', for whom he made 'models in wax and clay'.

Ghiberti was also a writer, leaving a lengthy incomplete manuscript entitled *Commentaries*. It contains a survey of ancient art based on *Pliny and observations on the science of optics, as well as valuable records of Italian painters and sculptors of the 14th century, and also Ghiberti's autobiography, the first by an artist that has survived. The same interest in the new humanist ideals that is reflected in Ghiberti's writings also prompted him to collect *classical sculptures. However, in spite of the prominent place that he occupies in the classical revival, his style was deeply rooted in the tradition of *Gothic craftsmanship. His first pair of Baptistery doors was modelled on the pattern of Andrea *Pisano's earlier doors for the same building, and its 28 panels (20 showing episodes from the life of Christ and 8 depicting saints) have much of the spirit of *International Gothic about them, with their emphasis on graceful lines, lyrical sentiment, and close attention to landscape detail. These traits survive in Ghiberti's second pair of doors, but they are here subordinated to the new principles of the *Renaissance. The doors are divided into ten large panels in which episodes from the Old Testament are represented on carefully constructed *perspective stages. As the reliefs were designed by 1437, they must rank among the most 'advanced' works of Florentine art of their time, particularly in the mastery of composition within a spatial framework. The fame of these doors has always stood high. *Michelangelo's dictum, recorded by *Vasari, that they were worthy to form the Gates of Paradise secured their prestige even in times less sympathetic to *quattrocento art.

Ghirlandaio, Domenico (c.1449–94). Florentine painter. According to *Vasari he trained with *Baldovinetti and it has been suggested that he also spent some time in *Verrocchio's workshop. His style was solid, prosaic, and rather old-fashioned (especially when compared with that of his great contemporary *Botticelli), but he was an excellent craftsman and good businessman and had one of the most prosperous workshops in Florence. In this he was assisted by his younger brother **Davide** (1452–1525); another brother, **Benedetto** (c.1458–97), seems to have spent much of his career in France. Domenico's largest undertaking was the fresco cycle in the choir of S. Maria Novella, Florence, illustrating scenes from the lives of the Virgin and St John the Baptist (1485–90). This was commissioned by Giovanni Tornabuoni, a partner in the

*Medici bank, and Ghirlandaio depicts the sacred story as if it had taken place in the home of a wealthy Florentine burgher. It is this talent for portraying the life and manners of his time (he often included portraits in his religious works) that has made Ghirlandaio popular with many visitors to Florence. But he also had considerable skill in the management of complex compositions and a certain grandeur of conception that sometimes hints at the High *Renaissance. Ghirlandaio worked on frescos in Pisa, San Gimignano, and Rome (in the Sistine Chapel) as well as in Florence, and his studio produced numerous altarpieces. He also painted portraits, the finest of which is *Old Man and a Boy* (c.1485, Louvre, Paris); this depicts the man's diseased features with ruthless realism, but has a remarkable air of tenderness. Ghirlandaio's son **Ridolfo** (1483–1561) was a friend of *Raphael and a portrait painter of some distinction. He probably had his initial training from his father, but Domenico's most famous pupil was *Michelangelo.

Giacometti, Alberto (1901–66). Swiss sculptor and painter, active mainly in Paris. He was the son of **Giovanni Giacometti** (1868–1933), a painter influenced by *Impressionism and *Post-Impressionism. After short periods at the École des Arts et Métiers, Geneva, and in Italy, he moved to Paris, where he worked under *Bourdelle from 1922 to 1925. He abandoned naturalistic sculpture in 1925, however, and went through a period of restless experimentation. From 1930 to 1935 he participated in the *Surrealist movement, developing a highly individual attenuated manner exemplified in the cage-like construction of *The Palace at 4 a.m.* (1933, MoMA, New York). In 1935, however, he abandoned Surrealism and began to work again from the model. From 1941 to 1944 he lived in Geneva to escape the German occupation of France, but he then returned permanently to Paris, and in 1947 he began evolving the style for which he became famous, characterized by human figures of extremely elongated proportions and emaciated, nervous character (*Man Pointing*, 1947, Tate, London). These fragile, isolated figures often have a suggestion of existentialist tragedy, and Giacometti was indeed a friend of the existentialist philosopher Jean-Paul Sartre,

who wrote on his work, notably the introduction to the catalogue of his exhibition at the Pierre Matisse Gallery, New York, in 1948. It was this exhibition that established Giacometti's post-war reputation, and his work soon had widespread influence, which can be seen, for example, in some of the entries for the 'Unknown Political Prisoner' competition of 1953 (*see* BUTLER, REG). He impressed many people not only through the quality of his work, but also by his force of personality, integrity, and devotion to his work. Simone de Beauvoir, Sartre's companion, wrote: 'Success, fame, money—Giacometti was indifferent to them all.' He is generally considered one of the outstandingly original sculptors of the 20th century, and from the late 1950s his reputation as a painter began to increase. Most of his paintings and drawings are portraits of his family and friends; his brother **Diego** (1902–85), who was a skilled technician and a lifelong assistant, was a favourite model and the subject of dozens of sculptures, paintings, and drawings (in his own right he is notable as the designer of furniture and light fittings for the Musée Picasso in Paris, 1984–5). Their cousin **Augusto Giacometti** (1877–1947) was a painter, one of the first to produce pure abstracts.

Giambologna (Giovanni Bologna, originally Jean Boulogne) (1529–1608). Flemish-born Italian sculptor. He was the greatest sculptor of the age of *Mannerism and for about two centuries after his death his reputation was almost equal to that of *Michelangelo. Virtually all his career was spent in Florence, but he was admired throughout Europe and patrons and collectors of his work included several popes, the Holy Roman emperors Maximilian II and Rudolf II (*see* HABSBURG), and kings of France (Henry IV) and Spain (Philip III). Giambologna was born in Douai (now in France) and trained under Jacques Du Broeucq (c.1505–84). In 1550 he went to Italy to further his studies and spent two years in Rome, where he met the elderly Michelangelo. He intended returning to Flanders, but on the way he visited Florence and settled there for life. The work that made his name, however, was for Bologna—the Fountain of Neptune (1563–6), with its impressive nude figure of Neptune, which he had designed for a similar fountain in Florence (*Ammanati defeated him in the competition). Even before working on the fountain in Bologna, however, Giambologna had begun in Florence the first of a series of celebrated marble groups demonstrating his formidable mastery of complex twisting poses: *Samson Slaying a Philistine* (c.1561–2, V&A, London); *Florence Triumphant over Pisa* (completed 1575, Bargello, Florence); *The Rape of a Sabine* (1581–2, Loggia dei Lanzi, Florence); *Hercules and the Centaur* (1594–1600, Loggia dei Lanzi). These were made for members of the *Medici family, his greatest patrons (he was court sculptor to three successive Medici Grand Dukes of Tuscany: Cosimo I, Francesco I, and Ferdinando I). His monument to Cosimo I (1587–95) was the first equestrian statue made in Florence and an immensely influential design, becoming the pattern for similar statues all over Europe, including two from his own workshop: that to Henry IV in Paris (destroyed), which was completed after Giambologna's death by his colleague Pietro Francavilla (1548–1615); and that to Philip III in Madrid, which was installed after the master's death by his most important pupil, Pietro *Tacca.

It was for the Medici also that Giambologna made his largest work—the colossal (about 10 m (33 ft) high) figure of the mountain god Appennino (1577–81) in the gardens of the family's villa at Pratolino. Constructed of brick and stone, the god crouches above a pool and seems to have emerged from the earth. Giambologna, however, was as happy working on a small scale as in a monumental vein. His bronze statuettes were enormously popular (they continued to be reproduced almost continuously until the 20th century) and being portable helped to give his style European currency. The most famous of them is *Mercury* (originally made c.1565), of which several versions and many copies exist. It is such a potent image of speed and grace that it has been adapted in several ways in the modern world, for example as the symbol of Interflora. Many of Giambologna's preliminary models also survive (uniquely for an Italian sculptor of his period), giving insight into his creative processes. The best collection is in the Victoria and Albert Museum.

Gibbings, Robert (1889–1958). British wood engraver, book designer, and travel writer. He founded the Society of Wood Engravers in 1919, and from 1924 to 1933 he ran the Golden Cockerel Press, one of the most distinguished private presses of the day, illustrating many of its books himself and also employing engravers such as Eric *Gill and Eric *Ravilious. He went through a nudist phase at about this time and sometimes typeset in the nude. Gibbings's books typically combine topographical impressions, personal anecdote, and observations of nature, illustrated with his own engravings; they include two on the River Thames—*Sweet Thames Run Softly* (1940) and *Till I End My Song* (1957).

Gibbons, Grinling (1648–1721). Anglo-Dutch woodcarver and sculptor, born in Rotterdam, the son of English parents who had business interests there (his father was a draper). He settled in England c.1667 and was 'discovered' by John Evelyn (*Diary*, 18 Jan. 1671). Evelyn introduced him to King Charles II and to Sir Christopher Wren, who employed him on decorations at Hampton Court and St Paul's Cathedral. In 1693 he was appointed royal master carver. Gibbons was unsurpassed in his day for naturalistic decorative carving of fruits, flowers, and shells, strung together in garlands and festoons, with small animals, cherubs' heads, etc. Because of his fame an enormous amount of work has been attributed to him, but he lived in a great age of English craftsmanship and much of the carving that is connected with his name was done by artists influenced by his style. Apart from his work for Wren, his documented commissions include outstanding ensembles at Burghley House, Lincolnshire, and Petworth House, Sussex. His virtuosity in wood was not equalled in marble or bronze, and George *Vertue said of him: 'He was a most excellent carver in wood, he was neither well skill'd or practized in Marble or Brass for which works he employd the best artists he coud procure.' In about 1684 he took as partner Artus III *Quellin, who is thought to have been mainly responsible for some of the figure sculpture for which Gibbons was officially credited.

Gibson, Charles Dana (1867–1944). American illustrator and painter. He studied at the *Art Students League of New York, 1884–5, and in the 1890s became a great success with pen-and-ink drawings contributed to such magazines as *Collier's Weekly*, *Harpers*, and *Life*. He specialized in scenes of fashionable social life and achieved immortality with his creation of the 'Gibson Girl', a type (modelled on his wife) representing an ideal of American womanhood—feminine and gracefully attired, but a lover of sports and the outdoor life. His work was immensely popular until about 1914, influencing fashions in women's clothes and hairstyles, and he earned a fortune. He also tried to gain recognition as a portrait painter, but he was much less successful in this field.

Gibson, John (1790–1866). British *Neoclassical sculptor. His early years were spent as a monumental mason in Liverpool, where he became a protégé of the banker and connoisseur William Roscoe. In 1817 he moved to London, where he met *Flaxman, on whose encouragement he went to Rome that year with an introduction to *Canova, whose pupil he became. Later he was also taught by *Thorvaldsen. He spent nearly all the rest of his life in Rome apart from occasional visits to England, the longest being from 1844 to 1847. Gibson won recognition internationally as one of the outstanding Neoclassical sculptors, and in his enthusiasm for Greek art he experimented with the ancient practice of colouring statues (*see* POLYCHROMY), arousing much controversy. His best-known work of this type is the *Tinted Venus* (1851–6, Walker AG, Liverpool). He left most of the fortune he made from his work to the *Royal Academy.

Gilbert, Sir Alfred (1854–1934). British sculptor and metalworker. He studied at the *Royal Academy Schools and the École des *Beaux-Arts, Paris (1875–8), after which he spent six years in Rome. He returned to England in 1884 and worked on several major projects, the best known of which is his Shaftesbury Memorial Fountain in Piccadilly Circus (1887–93). The celebrated figure of Eros that surmounts the fountain is cast in aluminium, one of the earliest examples of the use of this metal in sculpture. Its light weight allowed Gilbert to achieve a much more delicately poised pose than if he had been restricted to the traditional medium of bronze. Although Gilbert was hardworking, respected, and sought-after, he was unworldly and a hopeless businessman; his refusal to delegate work or compromise

his standards meant that he took on more work than he could handle and he sometimes lost money on commissions. In 1901 he became bankrupt, and in 1909 he moved into self-imposed exile in Bruges, where he did little work. In 1926, however, he returned to London, and in 1926–8 he completed his masterpiece, the tomb of the Duke of Clarence in St George's Chapel, Windsor Castle, which he had begun in 1892. The sinuous and labyrinthine detailing, crafted with consummate skill, reveals Gilbert as one of the major practitioners of *Art Nouveau, although he was disparaging about the style. Characteristically the tomb is in a variety of materials: marble, bronze, aluminium, brass, and ivory. His final major work was the bronze memorial to Queen Alexandra at Marlborough Gate, London (1926–32); on its completion he was knighted. His reputation sank after his death because he was so clearly outside the mainstream of 20th-century art (stylistically the Alexandra memorial looks more like a work of the 1890s than the 1930s), but he is now regarded as the greatest British sculptor of his generation. *See also* NEW SCULPTURE.

Gilbert & George (Gilbert Proesch, 1943– , and George Passmore, 1942–). British artists (Gilbert is Italian-born) who met whilst studying at St Martin's School of Art in London in 1967 and since 1968 have lived and worked together as self-styled 'living sculptures': 'Being living sculptures is our life blood, our destiny, our romance, our disaster, our light and life.' They initially attracted attention as *Performance artists, their most famous work in this vein being *Underneath the Arches* (1969), in which—dressed in their characteristic neat suits and with their hands and faces painted gold—they mimed mechanically to the 1930s music-hall song of the title. Although they gave up such 'living sculpture performances' in 1977, they still see themselves as living sculptures, considering their whole lifestyle a work of art. Since the early 1970s their work has consisted mainly of photo-pieces—large and garish arrangements of photographs, usually in black and white and fiery red, and often violent or homoerotic in content, with scatological titles. The images are often drawn from the street life of the East End of London in which they live. Gilbert & George have become the most famous British avant-garde artists of their generation. Their work has been shown worldwide and has attracted an enormous amount of commentary. In 1986 they won the *Turner Prize. Critical opinion on them is sharply divided, however: to some they are geniuses, to others tedious poseurs.

Gill, Eric (1882–1940). British sculptor, engraver, typographer, and writer. He began to earn his living as a letter cutter in 1903 and carved his first figure piece in 1910. In 1913 he became a convert to Roman Catholicism and was commissioned to make fourteen relief carvings of the *Stations of the Cross* for Westminster Cathedral (1914–18). These and the *Prospero and Ariel* group on Broadcasting House, London (1929–31), are his best-known sculptures. Gill was one of the chief protagonists in the movement for the revival of *direct carving, and his work usually has an impressive simplicity of conception; he wrote that his 'inability to draw naturalistically was, instead of a drawback, no less than my salvation. It compelled me ...to concentrate upon something other than the superficial delights of fleshly appearance ... to consider the significance of things.' In life, as in his work and writing, he was an advocate of a romanticized medievalism, and he tried to revive a religious attitude towards art and craftsmanship. His unconventionality was well known in his own time (he disliked trousers, for example, preferring to wear smocks), but the most bizarre and unpleasant aspects of his life were not revealed until the publication of Fiona MacCarthy's biography in 1989: he had incestuous relationships with two of his sisters and two of his daughters and sexual congress with a dog. Apart from religion, sex is the main subject of his work. Gill was an important figure in book design and typography as well as sculpture. He illustrated many books, and his 'Perpetua' and 'Gill Sans-Serif' typefaces are among the classics of 20th-century typography. His books include *Christianity and Art* (1927), *Art* (1934), and *Autobiography* (1940).

Gillot, Claude (1673–1722). French painter, draughtsman, and etcher. Few of his paintings survive, but his interest in scenes from the popular theatre (*Quarrel of the Cabmen*, Louvre, Paris) was inherited by his pupil *Watteau. His work survives

mainly in the form of drawings and etchings, and he excelled at designs in the elegant *Rococo manner of *Audran.

Gillray, James (1756–1815). English *caricaturist. He was one of the greatest of all caricaturists and probably the first significant artist to devote himself almost exclusively to this field. Initially he trained as a commercial engraver and although he later studied at the *Royal Academy Schools, he seems to have been largely self-taught as an artist. By the mid-1780s his vividness and fecundity of imagination had gained him recognition as the leading caricaturist in Britain and he made a small fortune for the printseller Hannah Humphrey, above whose London shop he lived and for whom he worked almost exclusively from about 1790 (they were rumoured to be lovers). His most characteristic works are his political cartoons, in which he satirized George III and other members of the royal family. Another frequent target was Napoleon, whom he depicted as a belligerent midget. Gillray drank heavily and from about 1810 had fits of madness; he died insane. *See also* CRUIKSHANK.

Gilman, Harold (1876–1919). British painter of interiors, portraits, and landscapes. In 1907 he met *Sickert and became one of the leading figures in his circle; he was a founder member of the *Camden Town Group in 1911 and of the *London Group (of which he was first president) in 1913. His early work was rather sombre, but under the influence of Sickert he adopted a higher colour register and a technique of using a mosaic of opaque touches. From Sickert also he derived his taste for working-class subjects. After Roger *Fry's first *Post-Impressionist exhibition (1910) and a visit to Paris (1911) he used very thick paint and bright (sometimes garish) colour. He was one of the most gifted English painters of his generation and one of the most distinctive in his reaction to Post-Impressionism, but his career was cut short by the influenza epidemic of 1919.

Gilpin, Sawrey (1733–1807). English animal painter. He began his career as an apprentice to Samuel *Scott, the marine painter, but turned to the painting of horses, making a name with 'portraits' of celebrated racers. In occasional large canvases he contrived his own blend of horse and history painting (*The Election of Darius*, *c*.1772, York AG). His son, **William Sawrey Gilpin** (1762–1843), began his career as a watercolourist but turned to landscape gardening, a field in which he had great success, in spite of his lack of professional training. The Revd **William Gilpin** (1724–1804), brother of Sawrey, was a writer, draughtsman, and printmaker, one of the most important advocates of the *Picturesque.

Ginner, Charles (1878–1952). British painter. He grew up in France (his father, a doctor, practised there) and settled in London in 1910. He was already a friend of *Gilman and *Gore and through them he was drawn into *Sickert's circle, becoming a founder member of the *Camden Town Group in 1911 and the *London Group in 1913. His Continental background made him a respected figure among his associates, who were united by an admiration for French painting. Ginner was primarily a townscape and landscape painter and he is known above all for his views of London (often drab areas, although he also depicted the hustle and bustle of places such as Leicester Square and Victoria Station). He painted with thick, regular brushstrokes and firm outlines, creating a heavily textured surface and a feeling of great solidity. Once he had established his distinctive style (by about 1911) it changed little and he became one of the main upholders of the Camden Town tradition after the First World War (ironically, unlike other members of the group, he never actually lived in Camden Town). He worked for the Canadian War Records Commission in the First World War and was an *Official War Artist in the Second.

Giordano, Luca (1634–1705). Neapolitan painter, the most important Italian decorative artist of the second half of the 17th century. He was nicknamed '*Luca Fa Presto*' (Luke work quickly) because of his prodigious speed of execution and huge output. His early works were in the *tenebrist manner of *Ribera (perhaps his teacher), but his style became much more colourful under the influence of such great decorative painters as *Veronese, whose works he saw on his extensive travels. Indeed, he absorbed a host of influences and was said to be able to imitate other artists' styles with ease. His work was varied also in subject matter, although he was primarily a religious and mythological painter. In addition to the frescos for which he is principally famed, he produced a large number of easel paintings and was a prolific draughtsman. He worked mainly in Naples, but also extensively in Florence and Venice, and he was widely influential in Italy. In 1692 he was called to Spain by Charles II (*see* HABSBURG) and stayed there for ten years, painting in Madrid, Toledo, and the *Escorial. His last works, after his return to Naples, included the decoration of the dome of the Treasury Chapel of the Certosa di S. Martino (1704). He died a very wealthy man and one of the most famous artists in Europe. In his personal self-confidence and courtliness, and in the open, airy compositions and light luminous colours of his work, Giordano presages such great 18th-century painters as *Tiepolo.

Giorgione (Giorgio da Castelfranco) (*c*.1477–1510). Venetian painter. Almost nothing is known of his life and only a handful of paintings can be confidently attributed to him, but he holds a momentous place in the history of art. He had achieved legendary status soon after his early death (evidently from plague) and through succeeding centuries he has continued to excite the imagination in a way that few other painters can match. The extraordinary discrepancy between his enormous fame and the tiny size of his oeuvre is explained by the fact that he initiated a new conception of painting. He was one of the earliest artists to specialize in *cabinet pictures for private collectors rather than works for public or ecclesiastical patrons, and he was the first painter who subordinated subject matter to the evocation of mood—it is clear that his contemporaries sometimes did not know what was represented in his pictures. *Vasari, who says that Giorgione earned his nickname—meaning 'Big George'—'because of his physical appearance and his moral and intellectual stature', ranked him alongside *Leonardo as one of the founders of 'modern' painting.

Giorgione was born in Castelfranco, about 40 km (25 miles) north-west of Venice, and according to Vasari he trained with Giovanni *Bellini (although it has also been suggested that *Carpaccio may have been his teacher). He had two important public commissions in Venice: in 1507–8 he painted a canvas (now lost without trace) for the audience chamber of the Doges' Palace; and in 1508 (together with *Titian) he painted frescos on the exterior of the Fondaco dei Tedeschi (the German warehouse), now known only through engravings and ruinous fragments. Apart from this, the only certain contemporary documentation on any of his surviving paintings is an inscription on the back of a female portrait known as *Laura* (KH Mus., Vienna), which says it was painted by 'Master Zorzi da Castelfranco' in 1506; it also records that Giorgione was a colleague of Vincenzo *Catena, a partnership about which nothing else is known. (An inscription on *Portrait of a Man* in the San Diego Museum of Art is more doubtful.) The main document for reconstructing Giorgione's oeuvre is a series of notes by the Venetian collector and connoisseur Marcantonio Michiel (c.1484–1552), written intermittently between 1521 and 1543. Michiel, who is a scrupulous and reliable source, mentions a number of paintings by Giorgione, four or five of which can be plausibly identified with extant works: *The Tempest* (Accademia, Venice), *The Three Philosophers* (KH Mus.), *Sleeping Venus* (Gemäldegalerie, Dresden), *Boy with an Arrow* (a copy?, KH Mus.), and (an oblique and less explicit reference than the others) *Christ Carrying the Cross* (S. Rocco, Venice). Michiel says that *The Three Philosophers* was finished by *Sebastiano del Piombo and that the *Sleeping Venus* (the work that founded the tradition of the reclining female nude) was finished by Titian. The problem of attribution was, then, complicated from the start by the fact that some of Giorgione's paintings were completed after his death by other hands, and confusion soon arose: in the first edition of his *Lives* (1550) Vasari attributed the S. Rocco painting to Giorgione, but in the second edition (1568) he gave it in one place to Giorgione and in another to Titian, even though 'many people believed it was by Giorgione'. Distinguishing between the work of Giorgione and the young Titian continues to be one of the knottiest problems in connoisseurship, the celebrated *Concert Champêtre* in the Louvre being the picture most hotly disputed between them.

Among the other paintings given to Giorgione are the *Castelfranco Madonna*, in the cathedral of his home town (first mentioned by *Ridolfi in 1648 and accepted by almost all critics), and several male portraits, including a self-portrait in the Herzog-Anton-Ulrich Museum in Brunswick (perhaps a copy). Giorgione is said to have been handsome and amorous, and he initiated a type of dreamily romantic portrait that became immensely popular in Venice. The powerful influence that his work exerted in the generation after his death (even the venerable Bellini succumbed to it) is one of the main factors in making the construction of a catalogue of his work so difficult, for there are scores of paintings of the period, particularly pastoral landscapes, that can be described as Giorgionesque, and many are of high quality. The problems of *iconography that Giorgione's paintings present are sometimes every bit as difficult as those of attribution. The most famous instance is *The Tempest*, one of his most enigmatic and poetic creations. Michiel saw it in 1530 and described it as a 'little landscape with the tempest with the gipsy and soldier', so he evidently did not know what subject, if any, was represented. X-rays have shown that Giorgione radically altered the figures in a way that suggests he was here indulging his imagination rather than illustrating a particular theme, although many ingenious attempts have been made to unravel a subject. This creation of the 'landscape of mood', in which he used colour and atmosphere with great subtlety, was his most momentous contribution to the history of art—an innovation of great originality and influence. Apart from the artists already mentioned, *Palma Vecchio and Dosso *Dossi were among the contemporaries who fell under Giorgione's spell, and among later artists *Watteau was his most sensitive heir.

Giottesques. A term applied to the 14th-century followers of *Giotto. The best-known artists embraced by the term are the Florentines Bernardo *Daddi, Taddeo *Gaddi, *Maso di Banco, and to a lesser extent the *Master of St Cecilia. Giotto's most loyal follower was Maso, who concentrated on the essential and maintained the master's high seriousness.

Giottino. *See* MASO DI BANCO.

Giotto di Bondone (*c*.1270–1337). Florentine painter and architect. Giotto is
regarded as the founder of the central tradition of Western painting because his work
broke away decisively from the stylizations
of *Byzantine art, introducing new ideals of
naturalism and creating a convincing sense
of pictorial space. His momentous achievement was recognized by his contemporaries
(Dante praised him in a famous passage of
The Divine Comedy, saying he had surpassed
his master *Cimabue), and to succeeding
generations it was clear that a new artistic
era began with him: in about 1400 Cennino
*Cennini wrote that 'Giotto translated the
art of painting from Greek into Latin and
made it modern.' He was the first artist
since antiquity to achieve widespread
fame, the demand for his services coming
from all over Italy: early sources suggest
that he worked in Assisi, Bologna, Ferrara,
Lucca, Milan, Naples, Padua, Ravenna,
Rimini, Rome, Urbino, and Verona, as well
as Florence, and according to *Vasari he also
visited Avignon in France, where he is said
to have carried out commissions for Pope
Clement V (reigned 1305–14). However,
these early references tend to be frustrat-
ingly vague, many of the works they refer
to are unidentifiable or have been destroyed, and no surviving painting can be
given to Giotto on the basis of unimpeachable contemporary documentation. His
work, indeed, poses some formidable problems of attribution, but it is universally
agreed that the fresco cycle in the Arena
Chapel at Padua is by him (he is credited
with it in two separate literary references
dating from *c*.1313), and it forms the
starting point for any consideration of his
work. The Arena Chapel (so-called because
it occupies the site of a Roman arena) was
built by Enrico Scrovegni (*see* DONOR), one of
Padua's leading citizens, in expiation for the
sins of his father, a notorious usurer mentioned by Dante. It was begun in 1303 and
Giotto's frescos are usually dated *c*.1303–6.
They run right round the interior of the
chapel, which is virtually devoid of architectural ornament and clearly was conceived
with painted decoration in mind (Giotto
himself may well have been involved in
the design of the building); the west wall is
covered with a *Last Judgement*, there is an
Annunciation over the chancel arch, and the
main wall areas have three tiers of paintings
representing scenes from the life of the
Virgin and her parents, St Anne and St
Joachim, and events from the ministry and
Passion of Christ. Below these scenes are
figures personifying Virtues and Vices,
painted to simulate stone *reliefs—the first
*grisailles. The figures in the main narrative
scenes are about half life-size, but from reproductions it is easy to imagine they
are much bigger, because Giotto's conception is so grand and powerful. His figures
have a completely new sense of three-
dimensionality and physical presence, and
in portraying the sacred events he creates a
feeling of moral weight rather than divine
splendour. He seems to base the scenes on
personal experience, and no artist has surpassed his ability to go straight to the heart of
a story and express its essence with gestures
and expressions of unerring conviction.

The other major fresco cycle associated
with Giotto's name is that on the life of St
Francis in the Upper Church of S. Francesco
at Assisi. This was first specifically given to
him by Vasari and the attribution was not
doubted until the 19th century; subsequently the question of its authorship has
become one of the most controversial issues
in the history of art. The St Francis frescos are
clearly the work of an artist of great stature
(their intimate and humane portrayals have
done much to determine posterity's mental
image of the saint), but they are more anecdotal and less powerful than the Arena
Chapel frescos—stylistic differences that to
many critics seem so pronounced that they
cannot accept a common authorship. Other
authorities, however, argue that the differences can be explained by Giotto maturing
as his career progressed (the Assisi frescos
are probably earlier than the Arena Chapel
frescos, but their dating too is contentious).
Attempts to attribute other frescos at Assisi
to Giotto have met with similar controversy
(*see also* MASTER OF THE LEGEND OF ST FRANCIS
and MASTER OF ST CECILIA). There is a fair
measure of agreement, however, about the
frescos associated with Giotto in S. Croce in
Florence. He probably painted in four
chapels there, and work survives in the
Bardi and Peruzzi chapels, generally dated
to the 1320s. The frescos are in very uneven
condition (they were whitewashed in
the 18th century), but some of those in the
Bardi Chapel on the life of St Francis remain
deeply impressive. Among Giotto's other

major works was an external mosaic for Old St Peter's, Rome, showing Christ walking on the waters and popularly known as the *Navicella* ('little boat'—a reference to the vessel carrying the Apostles, which symbolizes the Church, in which the faithful find refuge). The mosaic was saved when Old St Peter's was demolished and part of it is displayed in the portico of the present church, but it has been so heavily restored that it can no longer be regarded as Giotto's work. It is not known when he visited Rome, but during his stay he would have seen the work of Pietro *Cavallini, which was as important an influence on him as that of Cimabue, who is traditionally (and highly plausibly) said to have been his teacher. The best documented period of Giotto's career is the time (1328–33) he spent at the court of Robert of Anjou, King of Naples. He had an honoured place in the royal household, but only small fragments survive of the paintings he carried out for Robert (Vasari says they included 'portraits of many famous men', including a self-portrait—among his rare secular works). In 1334, following his return from Naples, he was appointed city architect in Florence and in this role began the celebrated campanile (bell tower) of the cathedral (the design was altered after his death, but his essential concept was followed and the building is sometimes called 'Giotto's Tower').

The panel paintings associated with Giotto are not as controversial as the frescos, but they nevertheless present numerous problems. Several panels bear his signature, but it is generally agreed that the signature is a trademark showing that the works came from his shop rather than an indication of his personal workmanship. Similarly, the Stefaneschi Altarpiece (Vatican Mus.) is connected with Giotto in a credible early source, but it is now regarded as having only tenuous links with him. On the other hand, the *Ognissanti Madonna* (c.1305–10, Uffizi, Florence) is neither signed nor firmly documented (it is first recorded in 1418), but it is a work of such grandeur and humanity that Giotto's authorship has never been seriously questioned. Among the other panels attributed to him, the finest is the *Crucifix* in S. Maria Novella, Florence. In the generation after his death Giotto had an overwhelming influence on Florentine painting; this declined with the growth of *International Gothic, but his work was later an inspiration to *Ma-

saccio, and even to *Michelangelo. These two giants were his true spiritual heirs.

Giovanni di Paolo (active 1417; d. 1482). One of the most attractive and idiosyncratic painters of the Sienese School, sometimes called Giovanni dal Poggio, from the district of the city where he lived. Little is known of his life, but there is a considerable number of surviving works by him—all small-format religious panels (the earliest known dates from 1426). He may have been taught by *Taddeo di Bartolo and was influenced notably by *Gentile da Fabriano and *Sassetta, but his style is highly personal and engaging, with rather whimsical figures inhabiting strange landscapes. After centuries of neglect his reputation was revived by *Berenson, who called him 'the El *Greco of the *quattrocento'.

Girardon, François (1628–1715). French sculptor. He ranked with *Coysevox as the outstanding sculptor of Louis XIV's reign, but his style was more restrained and *classical, embodying the ideas of the Academy. Much of his work was done for Versailles, where he collaborated with *Le Brun; it includes a marble group of *Apollo Tended by the Nymphs* (1666–75) that is regarded as one of the most purely classical works of French 17th-century sculpture. (The group was originally in a grotto room, but is now in the palace gardens.) His other work includes the marble monument to Cardinal Richelieu (1675–94) in the church of the Sorbonne, Paris. He also made a bronze equestrian statue of Louis XIV (1683–92) for the Place Vendôme in Paris, but this was destroyed during the French Revolution. Girardon died on the same day as Louis XIV.

Girodet, Anne-Louis (1767–1824). French painter and illustrator, usually known as Girodet-Trioson, a name he took in honour of a surgeon, Dr Trioson, who adopted him after he was orphaned at an early age and who was probably his natural father. He studied with J.-L. *David, won the *Prix de Rome in 1789, and spent the years 1790–5 in Italy. In style and technique he followed David, but in his choice of themes and his emotional treatment of them he was *Romantic in spirit. He was particularly interested in unusual colour effects and melodramatic lighting, as in the *Sleep of Endymion* (1791) and the *Entombment of Atala*

(1808), both in the Louvre. Girodet often favoured literary themes, but he also won renown for his paintings glorifying Napoleon (*Revolt of Cairo*, 1810, Versailles Mus.) and he was a fine portraitist. One of his best-known portraits, *Mademoiselle Lange as Danaë* (1799, Minneapolis Inst. of Arts), caused a scandal because of its scurrilous sexual allusions (the woman portrayed was a well-known actress with whom Girodet had quarrelled). His book illustrations included work for editions of Racine and Virgil. In 1815 he inherited a fortune when Dr Trioson died and thereafter devoted himself mainly to writing unreadably boring poems and treatises on aesthetics.

Girtin, Thomas (1775–1802). English painter and printmaker, one of the supreme masters of the watercolour landscape. His earlier works were tinted drawings in the 18th-century topographical tradition, but by the end of his short life he had developed a technique that revolutionized watercolour painting. He used strong colour in broad *washes, influenced to some extent by J. R. *Cozens, but going beyond him in the boldness of his compositions, the grandeur with which he created effects of space, and the power with which he suggested mood. His work stands at the beginning of the classic English tradition of watercolour painting, freed from its dependence on line drawing, and *Turner acknowledged his friend's greatness with the words 'If Tom Girtin had lived, I should have starved.' Girtin made tours in various parts of Britain, and spent six months in Paris in 1801–2, making a series of etchings of the city that were posthumously published in 1803. In 1802 he exhibited an enormous panorama of London, painted in oils, the *Eidometropolis*; this is no longer extant, but sketches for it survive. He died of tuberculosis.

gisant. French term used from the 15th century onwards for a recumbent effigy on a funerary monument. In *Renaissance monuments *gisants* often formed part of a lower register, where the deceased person was represented as a corpse (sometimes in decomposition), while on the upper part he or she was shown *orant* (praying), as if alive.

Gislebertus (active first half of 12th century). French *Romanesque sculptor. He was one of the great geniuses of medieval art, but his name has survived only because he carved his signature—'*Gislebertus hoc fecit*' (Gilbert made this)—beneath the feet of the central figure of Christ in the tympanum of the west doorway of Autun Cathedral in Burgundy. The unusually prominent position of his signature suggests that his greatness was appreciated in his own time. The tympanum represents the Last Judgement; it is a huge work (over 6 m (20 ft) wide at the base) and a masterpiece of expressionistic carving, conveying with visionary intensity both the horror of the damned and the bliss of the elect. Most of the rest of the sculptural decoration of the cathedral can be confidently attributed to Gislebertus. It includes the carving of 60 or so capitals and a large-scale reclining nude figure of Eve that is without parallel in medieval art (this piece, a fragment of the north doorway, is now in the Musée Rolin, Autun). These carvings display Gislebertus' great fecundity of imagination and range of feeling. It has been surmised that he was trained in the workshop responsible for the decoration of the abbey of Cluny, the most influential of all Romanesque monasteries, and that he worked at the cathedral at Vézelay before going to Autun (all three places are in Burgundy). He was already a mature artist when he started at Autun, where he worked *c*.1125–35, and his style changed little while he was there. His influence was felt in the sculpture of various Burgundian churches, and many of his ideas had a long-term effect on the development of French *Gothic sculpture.

Giulio Romano (1499?–1546). Italian painter, architect, and designer, born in Rome (he was the only major *Renaissance artist who was a native of the city) and active mainly in Mantua. In his youth he was *Raphael's chief pupil and assistant (although exactly what part he played in his workshop is uncertain) and later one of the outstanding figures of *Mannerist art and architecture. It is not known when Giulio began working for Raphael, but it was probably in about 1515, when he was still very young; after the master's death in 1520 he became his main artistic executor, completing a number of his unfinished works, including the decorations of the Villa Madama. His independent works of this time include the *Holy Family* (*c*.1522) in S. Maria dell'Anima, Rome, and the design of some pornographic prints that caused such a scandal that their engraver Marcantonio *Raimondi was imprisoned (their notoriety was sustained by the sonnets that the poet Pietro Aretino wrote inspired by them soon after their publication). Giulio had moved to Mantua in 1524 and escaped Raimondi's fate. He remained there for the rest of his life and dominated the artistic affairs of the *Gonzaga court. The great monument to his genius is the Palazzo del Tè, begun in 1526 for Federico Gonzaga. This was one of the first Mannerist buildings, deliberately flouting the canons of classical architecture as exemplified by *Bramante in order to shock or surprise the spectator. The same tendency is continued in Giulio's fresco decoration in the palace, especially in the Sala dei Giganti, where the whole room is painted from floor to ceiling to give an overall illusionistic effect, and the spectator feels overwhelmed by the rocks and thunderbolts hurled down on the rebellious Titans who attempted to storm Olympus. Giulio painted several other frescos in the Palazzo del Tè and in the Sala di Troia of the Ducal Palace at Mantua that testify to his classical learning and exuberant invention. His muscular style owed much to *Michelangelo as well as to Raphael, but was less daunting than that of either and proved widely influential. Indeed, he became one of the most famous painters of his day and has the distinction of being the only modern artist mentioned by Shakespeare; he called him 'that rare Italian master Julio Romano', but mistakenly imagined him a sculptor (*The Winter's Tale*, v. ii).

Giusti, Giovanni (1485–1549). Italian-born sculptor who settled at Tours in France in about 1504, changing his name to Jean Juste. He was a leading figure in the introduction of the *Renaissance style to France. His masterpiece is the tomb of Louis XII and Anne of Brittany (abbey of Saint-Denis, near Paris, 1517–31). He was probably assisted in the work by his brother **Antonio** (1479–1519), who settled with him in France. It features seated figures of the twelve Apostles in purely Italian style, allegorical figures of the Virtues, and *reliefs depicting the king's Italian victories.

Giustiniani. Prominent Italian family, branches of which were established in many parts of Italy, especially Genoa and Venice, where they played important roles in politics, literature, and religion. For the arts the most interesting member of the family was the enormously wealthy Marchese **Vincenzo** (1564–1637). He owned the finest collection of *antique sculpture in Rome—published in the *Galleria Giustiniana* (1631), the first ever illustrated catalogue of an art collection—and was an enthusiastic and discriminating patron of painters, especially *Caravaggio (he owned no fewer than fifteen pictures by him) and his northern followers.

Glackens, William James (1870–1938). American painter and draughtsman. His early career was spent mainly as a newspaper illustrator in his native Philadelphia, but he was encouraged to take up painting by Robert *Henri, whom he met in 1891. In 1896 he settled in New York and in 1908 he was one of the group of painters who exhibited together as The *Eight. He is considered one of the central figures of the *Ashcan School, but he was less concerned with *Social Realism than with representing the life of the people as a colourful spectacle, and he was heavily influenced by the *Impressionists. By the time of the *Armory Show (1913), which he helped to organize, Glackens was painting in a style reminiscent of the early *Renoir. From 1912 he was employed as art consultant by Dr Albert C. *Barnes and toured Europe buying paintings that formed the nucleus of the celebrated Barnes Foundation at Merion, Pennsylvania. In 1917 he was elected first president of the *Society of Independent Artists.

glair. A term for white of egg when used as the *medium in *illuminating manuscripts, in *tempera painting, and in gilding with gold dust. It is also used as an adhesive substance to fix gold leaf.

Glasgow School. A term that has been applied to several groups of artists whose activities have centred on Glasgow. The first and largest of these groups was a loose association of artists active from about 1880 to the turn of the century; there was no formal membership or programme, but the artists involved (who preferred to be known as the Glasgow Boys) were linked by a desire to move away from the conservative and parochial values they thought were represented by the Royal Scottish Academy in Edinburgh. Sir James Guthrie (1859–1930) and Sir John *Lavery were probably the best-known members of the group. Several of them had worked in France and were proponents of open-air painting. The heyday of the group was over by 1900 and it did not survive the First World War, but it rejuvenated Scottish art, breaking ground where the *Scottish Colourists were soon to follow. A slightly later group, active from about 1890 to 1910, created a distinctive version of *Art Nouveau. Its most important member was the architect and designer Charles Rennie Mackintosh (1868–1928). More recently, the term 'Glasgow School' (or facetiously 'Glasgow pups') has been applied to a group of figurative painters working in the city from the 1980s. They include Ken Currie (1960–), Peter Howson (1958–), and Adrian Wiszniewski (1958–), all of whom were students at *Glasgow School of Art at much the same time.

Glasgow School of Art. Art school founded in 1840 as the School of Design in Ingram Street, Glasgow. In 1869 it moved to its present site in Sauchiehall Street, and in 1896 the architect Charles Rennie Mackintosh (see GLASGOW SCHOOL) won a competition to design a new building. This was erected in 1897–9, with a library block and other extensions added in 1907–9. Together they form one of the most original and dramatic works of architecture of the period anywhere in Europe. At this time the School was enjoying its golden age, under the directorship (1885–1918) of the painter Francis ('Fra') Newbery (1855–1946), who had admirable skill as an administrator and a flair for recognizing and encouraging talent. He had good connections abroad and helped the School to win an international reputation. It continues to enjoy high status and produced a particularly outstanding crop of graduates in the 1980s, including the painters Steven Campbell (1953–), Stephen Conroy (1964–), and Alison Watt (1965–). Their work marks a return to an interest in figurative art after the 'anything goes' 1970s.

glass prints (or *clichés-verres*). Prints made by exposing sensitized photographic paper to the sun beneath a glass plate on which the design has been drawn. Such prints resemble *etchings. The medium was popular in France from about 1850 to 1870, when it was used by several distinguished artists, above all *Corot, and it has occasionally been used subsequently.

glaze. A transparent or semi-transparent layer of paint applied over another layer so as to modify its colour; the light passing through is reflected back by the under surface and altered by the glaze. The effect produced by glazing differs from any obtainable by directly mixing colours together, for the technique imparts a special depth and luminosity. From the 15th to the 19th century most oil paintings were built up as an elaborate structure of superimposed layers, glazes, and *scumbles over an underpainting, but since *alla prima painting became the norm such a highly deliberate, craftsmanly approach has fallen into disfavour.

Gleizes, Albert (1881–1953). French painter, printmaker, and writer. His early work was *Impressionist in style, but in 1909 he took up *Cubism. In 1912 he was among the founders of the *Section d'Or group and in 1912 he wrote with *Metzinger the book *Du Cubisme* (an English translation, *Cubism*, appeared in 1913). This was the first book on the movement and it remains Gleizes's main claim to fame. Much of his later career was devoted to trying to achieve a synthesis of medieval and modern art, expressing Christian ideas through pseudo-Cubist forms. In this he is generally reckoned to have been conspicuously unsuccessful and his modest reputation as a painter rests on his pre-war work. He expounded his views in several books and pamphlets.

Gleyre, Charles (1806–74). Swiss painter, active mainly in Paris, where he enjoyed a successful career, particularly with anecdotal scenes, sometimes in an *antique setting, and portraits. He was a renowned teacher and when *Delaroche closed down his teaching studio in 1843, the majority of his students transferred to Gleyre. He taught *Whistler and several of the *Impressionists—*Bazille, *Monet, *Renoir, and *Sisley—and although his own paintings were conventional, he encouraged open-air painting (see PLEIN AIR). Renoir, however, said that his main strength as a teacher was that he left his pupils 'pretty much to their own devices'. Gleyre closed his studio in 1864 because of an eye ailment.

Gobelins. French tapestry manufactory, named after a family of dyers and cloth-makers who set up business on the outskirts of Paris in the 15th century. Their premises became a tapestry factory in the early 17th century, and in 1662 it was taken over by Louis XIV, who appointed *Le Brun its director. For Louis it made not only tapestries but also every kind of product (except carpets, which were woven at the Savonnerie factory) required for the furnishing of the royal palaces—its official title was 'Manufacture royale des meubles de la Couronne'. The celebrated tapestry designed by Le Brun of *Louis XIV Visiting the Gobelins* (c.1667, Gobelins Mus., Paris) gives a good idea of the range of its activities. In 1694 the factory was closed because of the king's financial difficulties, and although it reopened in 1699, thereafter it made only tapestries. For much of the 18th century it retained its position as the foremost tapestry manufactory in Europe. *Oudry and *Boucher successively held the post of director (1733–70). The Gobelins continues in production today and also houses a tapestry museum.

Godefroid de Clair (Godefroid de Huy). *Mosan goldsmith and enamellist, active in the mid-12th century. He may have trained in the workshop of *Rainer of Huy. Early sources praise his great skill and suggest he was a prolific artist, but his career is obscure and most of the numerous attributions to him of reliquaries and *enamels are highly speculative. Peter Lasko (*Ars Sacra: 800–1200*, 1972) considers that 'On the whole, the introduction of the personality of Godefroid has hindered rather than helped our understanding of the development of the Mosan style.'

Godward, J. W. *See* ALMA-TADEMA.

Goes, Hugo van der (d. 1482). Netherlandish painter, one of the greatest and most individual of his period. Nothing is known of his life before 1467, when he became a master in the painters' guild at Ghent. He had numerous commissions from the town of Ghent for work of a temporary nature such as processional banners, and in 1475 he became dean of the painters'

guild. At about the same time he entered a monastery near Brussels as a lay brother, but he continued to paint and also to travel. In 1481 he suffered a mental breakdown (he had a tendency to acute depression) and although he recovered, died the following year. An account survives of his illness written by Gaspar Ofhuys, a monk at the monastery; Ofhuys was evidently jealous of Hugo and his description has been called by Erwin *Panofsky 'a masterpiece of clinical accuracy and sanctimonious malice'. No paintings by Hugo are signed and the only work attributed to him on solid early evidence is his masterpiece, a large *triptych of the Nativity (c.1475–8, Uffizi, Florence). This was commissioned by Tommaso Portinari, the representative of the *Medici bank in Bruges, for the church of the Hospital of S. Maria Nuova in Florence, and its masterful handling of the oil technique made a powerful impact on Italian painters. There is a great variety of surface ornament and detail, but this is combined with lucid organization of the figure groups and a convincing sense of spatial depth. As remarkable as Hugo's skill in reconciling grandeur of conception with keen observation is his psychological penetration in the depiction of individual figures, notably the awestruck shepherds. Other works have been convincingly attributed to Hugo on the basis of similarity of style with the Portinari Altarpiece. They include two large panels painted c.1478 for the church of Holy Trinity in Edinburgh: the *Holy Trinity Adored by Sir Edward Bonkil* (the provost of the church) and the *Royal Family of Scotland* (Royal Coll., on loan to NG of Scotland). His last work is perhaps the *Death of the Virgin* (Groeningemuseum, Bruges), a painting of remarkable tension and poignancy that seems a fitting swansong for such a tormented personality.

Goethe, Johann Wolfgang von (1749–1832). German writer, scientist, patron, and amateur artist, one of the giants of European culture. He was born in Frankfurt and spent most of his life in Weimar. Throughout his career he devoted much time to the study of painting and was a prolific draughtsman. Although his own talent as an artist was modest, his writings were influential on the visual arts, particularly in the growth of *Romanticism. Initially he stressed the role of passion in art, but after visiting Italy in 1786–8 he gained a greater appreciation of the *classicism of the *Renaissance. His writings on art included a book on theory of colour (*Zur Farbenlehre*, 1810; translated into English by *Eastlake in 1840), in which he purported to refute the *Optics* of Newton, and a translation into German of *Cellini's *Autobiography* (1798). Many other pieces were published in two journals Goethe founded as mouthpieces for his views: *Die Propyläen* (1798–1800) and *Über Kunst und Altertum* (On Art and Antiquity, 1816–32). He was a friend and patron of numerous artists, including *Friedrich and *Tischbein, and his imaginative works were an inspiration to many others: *Delacroix, for example, produced a set of lithographs (1828) illustrating his *Faust*.

Gogh, Vincent van (1853–90). Dutch painter and draughtsman, active for much of his brief career in France, with *Cézanne and *Gauguin the greatest of *Post-Impressionist artists. His uncle was a partner in the international firm of picture dealers Goupil and Co. and in 1869 van Gogh went to work in the branch at The Hague. In 1873 he was sent to the London branch and fell unsuccessfully in love with the daughter of his landlady. This was the first of several disastrous attempts to find happiness with a woman, and his unrequited passion affected him so badly that he was dismissed from his job. He returned to England in 1876 as an unpaid assistant at a school, and his experience of urban squalor awakened a religious zeal and a longing to serve his fellow men. His father was a Protestant pastor, and van Gogh began to train for the ministry, but he abandoned his studies in 1878 and went to work as a lay preacher among the impoverished miners of the grim Borinage district in Belgium. In his zeal he gave away his own worldly goods to the poor and was dismissed for his literal interpretation of Christ's teaching. He remained in the Borinage, suffering acute poverty and a spiritual crisis, until 1880, when he found that art was his vocation and the means by which he could bring consolation to humanity. From this time he worked at his new 'mission' with single-minded intensity, and although he often suffered from extreme poverty and undernourishment, his output

in the ten remaining years of his life was prodigious: about a thousand paintings and a similar number of drawings. The spontaneous, irrational side of his character has often been stressed, but he was a cultivated and well-read man, who in spite of his speed of work thought deeply about his paintings and planned them carefully.

From 1881 to 1885 van Gogh lived in the Netherlands, sometimes with his parents, sometimes in lodgings, supported by his devoted brother **Theo** (1857–91), a picture dealer in Paris who regularly sent him money from his own small salary as well as art materials and prints. Their correspondence is an extraordinarily rich source of information on van Gogh's life and art. Initially he confined himself to drawings, often using charcoal or boldly handled black chalk, but he took up oils in 1882. In keeping with his humanitarian outlook he painted peasants and workers, the most famous picture from this period being *The Potato Eaters* (1885, Van Gogh Mus., Amsterdam). Of this he wrote to Theo: 'I have tried to emphasize that those people, eating their potatoes in the lamp-light have dug the earth with those very hands they put in the dish, and so it speaks of manual labour, and how they have honestly earned their food.' In 1885 van Gogh moved to Antwerp on the advice of Anton *Mauve (a cousin by marriage), and studied for some months at the Academy there. Academic instruction had little to offer such an individualist, however, and in February 1886 he moved to Paris, where he met *Degas, Gauguin, *Pissarro, *Seurat, and *Toulouse-Lautrec. At this time his painting underwent a violent metamorphosis under the combined influence of *Impressionism and Japanese woodcuts (*see* UKIYO-E), losing its moralistic flavour. Van Gogh became obsessed by the symbolic and expressive values of colours and began to use them for this purpose rather than, as did the Impressionists, for the reproduction of visual appearances, atmosphere, and light. 'Instead of trying to reproduce exactly what I have before my eyes,' he wrote, 'I use colour more arbitrarily so as to express myself more forcibly.' Of his *Night Café* (1888, Yale Univ. AG), he said: 'I have tried to express with red and green the terrible passions of human nature.' For a time he was influenced by Seurat's delicate *pointillist manner, but he abandoned this for broad, vigorous, and swirling brush-strokes.

In February 1888 van Gogh settled at Arles in the south of France, where he painted more than 200 canvases in fifteen months. During this time he lived in poverty and suffered recurrent nervous crises with hallucinations and depression. He became enthusiastic for the idea of founding an artists' co-operative at Arles and in October he was joined by Gauguin. However, as a result of a quarrel between them van Gogh suffered a crisis in which he cut off part of his left ear (24 December 1888), an event commemorated in his *Self-Portrait with Bandaged Ear* (1889, Courtauld Gal., London); epilepsy and schizophrenia are among the causes that have been suggested to account for his mental disturbances. In May 1889 he went at his own request into an asylum at St Rémy, near Arles, but during the year he spent there he continued a fervent output of tumultuous pictures such as *Starry Night* (1889, MoMA, New York). He produced 150 paintings (as well as drawings) in the course of this year. In 1889 Theo married and in May 1890 van Gogh moved to Auvers-sur-Oise, to the north of Paris, to be near him, lodging with the patron and connoisseur Dr Paul Gachet. There followed another tremendous burst of activity and during the last 70 days of his life he painted 70 canvases. But his spiritual anguish and depression became more acute and on 29 July 1890 he died from the results of a self-inflicted bullet wound; Theo died six months later and was buried alongside him in Auvers. Van Gogh sold almost nothing during his lifetime and was little known to the art world at the time of his death, but his fame grew rapidly thereafter. His influence on *Expressionism, *Fauvism, and early abstraction was enormous, and it can be seen in many other aspects of 20th-century art. His passionate life and unswerving devotion to his ideals have made him one of the great cultural heroes of modern times, providing the most auspicious material for the 20th-century vogue in romanticized psychological biography, notably Irving Stone's novel *Lust for Life* (1934) and the Hollywood film of the same name (1956).

golden section. A proportion in which a straight line or rectangle is divided into two unequal parts in such a way that the ratio of the smaller to the greater part is the same as that of the greater to the whole. Like the mathematical value pi, it cannot be expressed as a finite number, but an approximation is 8 : 13 or 0.618 : 1. The proportion has been known since antiquity and has been said to possess inherent aesthetic value because of an alleged correspondence with the laws of nature or the universe. It was much studied during the *Renaissance, and Luca Pacioli, the most famous mathematician of his day and a friend of *Leonardo and of *Piero della Francesca, wrote a book on it called *Divina proportione* (1509). In accordance with the tendencies of the time, Pacioli's book, illustrated with drawings by Leonardo, credits this 'divine proportion' with various mystical properties and exceptional beauties both in science and in art.

Golding, John (1929–). British painter and art historian. He is probably best known as an eminent scholar of 20th-century art, particularly for his standard book *Cubism: A History and an Analysis, 1907–1914* (1959; rev. edns. 1968 and 1988), but he has also made a reputation as an abstract painter. He taught history of art at the *Courtauld Institute 1962–81 and in 1976–7 he was *Slade professor at Cambridge University. He began painting seriously in the late 1950s (his first one-man exhibition was in 1962) and gradually devoted more of his time to it. In 1971 he started to teach at the *Royal College of Art and in 1981–6 (having given up his post at the Courtauld Institute) was senior tutor there. His abstracts are typically large in format, with broad expanses of glowing colour; he sees them as 'basically reflective or contemplative'.

Goldsworthy, Andy (1956–). British sculptor and *Land artist. He works mainly with found natural materials such as leaves, pebbles, twigs, and even snow and ice, typically using no tools other than objects that come easily to hand. Many of his sculptures are inherently short-lived and are recorded by him in colour photographs, which have been acquired by many public collections. He says that 'each work grows, stays, decays—integral parts of a cycle which the photograph shows at its height, marking the moment when it is most alive. There is an intensity about a work at its peak which I hope is expressed in the image. Process and decay are implicit.' In addition to his transient sculptures, Goldsworthy has produced more permanent pieces, including two large earthworks in County Durham, and he has published several books documenting his output. He was born in Cheshire, grew up in Yorkshire, and has spent much of his life in Scotland, but he works internationally, his projects taking him to Japan and the Canadian Arctic for example.

Goldwater, Robert. *See* BOURGEOIS.

Goltzius, Hendrick (1558–1617). Dutch printmaker, draughtsman, and painter of German descent, one of the most influential figures of his time in northern European art. He was the best-known line engraver of his day (he also made a few etchings) and the leader of a group of *Mannerist artists who worked in Haarlem, where he founded some kind of 'academy' (perhaps a life class) with *Cornelis van Haarlem and Karel van *Mander. In 1590–1 he visited Rome and after this his style became more *classical. Goltzius's right hand was crippled, but in spite of this handicap he was renowned for his technical virtuosity and for his skill in imitating the work of other great engravers such as *Dürer and *Lucas van Leyden. In his early career much of his work was reproductive, but he also produced many original compositions, including a splendid series on *Roman Heroes* (1586). His portrait drawings were also outstanding, and the landscape drawings he made after 1600 mark him as a forerunner of the great 17th-century landscape artists. His paintings are generally less interesting than his drawings and much less advanced stylistically.

Gombrich, Sir Ernst (1909–2001). Austrian-born British art historian. He settled in England in 1936 and began a long association with the *Warburg Institute in the University of London, where he was director and professor of the history of the classical tradition from 1959 to 1976. He was also *Slade professor at both Oxford and Cambridge. His scholarly work, which shows a remarkable ability to combine great breadth of learning with lucidity and wit, was devoted largely to the theory of art, the psychology of pictorial representation, and Renaissance symbolism, and won him a position of the highest esteem in his profession. His writings bore witness to his interest in scientific method and helped to promote interchange between art history and other disciplines. Gombrich's best-known book, however, is a popular work, *The Story of Art*, which was first published in 1950 and has ever since held its place as the most congenial introduction to the history of art. It reached its sixteenth English edition in 1995 and has been translated into twenty languages. Among his other books the best known is probably *Art and Illusion* (1960 and subsequent editions). This highly influential work deals with conventions of representation and examines how styles change and develop, challenging many orthodox views and received opinions about visual perception. In *Thinkers of the Twentieth Century* (ed. Elizabeth Devine *et al.*, 1983) J. M. Massing wrote: 'For his scholarly method, his theoretical approach and his defence of cultural values, Gombrich will be remembered as one of the leading art historians of this century. Through his study of the psychology of perception, he is also one of the very few to have widened our understanding of the visible world.'

Gonçalves, Nuno (active 1450–71). Portuguese painter, first recorded in 1450, when he was appointed court painter by Alfonso V. No works certainly by his hand survive, but there is strong circumstantial evidence that he was responsible for the *St Vincent* *polyptych (*c.*1460–70, Mus. Nacional de Arte Antiga, Lisbon), the outstanding Portuguese painting of the 15th century. The style is rather dry, but powerfully realistic, and the polyptych contains a superb gallery of highly individualized portraits of members of the court, including a presumed self-portrait. There are affinities with contemporary Burgundian and Flemish art, especially the work of *Bouts.

Goncharova, Natalia (1881–1962). Russian-French painter, designer, printmaker, and illustrator, born into a distinguished family (she was related to the poet Pushkin). In Moscow in 1900 she met her fellow student Mikhail *Larionov, who became her lifelong companion. In the years leading up to the First World War they were among the most prominent figures in Russian avant-garde art, taking part in and often helping to organize a series of major exhibitions in Moscow. Her early paintings were *Impressionist, but from

1906 she began to develop a *primitivist style combining her interest in peasant art and icon painting with influences from modern French art, particularly *Fauvism and *Cubism, to which was later added *Futurism. By the time of the *Target Exhibition of 1913 she was painting in a near-abstract *Rayonist style (*Cats*, 1913, Guggenheim Mus., New York). In 1915 she left Russia with Larionov and after settling in Paris in 1919 she devoted herself mainly to designing settings and costumes for the theatre, particularly *Diaghilev's Ballets Russes. Goncharova and Larionov became French citizens in 1938 and were married in 1955. By this time they had been virtually forgotten, but there was a great revival of interest in them in the early 1960s.

Goncourt, Edmond de (1822–96) and **Jules de** (1830–70). French writers, brothers, who worked in close collaboration. They wrote on various artistic topics, their most important work of criticism being a book made up of a collection of articles, *L'Art du dix-huitième siècle* (1875), which helped to revive the reputation of 18th-century French artists such as *Watteau. The brothers inherited a substantial fortune when their aristocrat mother died in 1848, and their lives were divided between writing and self-indulgence; the *Journal* that they began in 1851, and which Edmond continued after Jules died until his own death, provides a richly detailed record of Paris in the second half of the 19th century. Edmond's books on Utamaro (1891) and Hokusai (1896) helped to popularize Japanese art (*see* UKIYO-E). The brothers also wrote novels and painted. The Académie Goncourt, founded under Edmond's will, is a body of ten men or women of letters that awards an annual prize (the Prix Goncourt) for imaginative prose.

Gonzaga. Italian family, rulers of Mantua from 1328 to 1707, who at several different periods attracted to their court some of the greatest Italian and other European artists. Under **Ludovico** (1412–78; reigned from 1444) *Mantegna was appointed court painter and *Alberti began the church of S. Andrea. The presence of Isabella d'*Este, who married **Francesco II** in 1490, helped to make Mantua one of the greatest centres of art collecting and patronage. Under **Federico II** (1500–40; reigned from 1519)

*Giulio Romano built and decorated the Gonzaga pleasure house, the Palazzo del Tè, and turned Mantua into one of the main centres of *Mannerist art. **Vincenzo I** (1562–1612; reigned from 1587) was one of the greatest collectors of his day and *Rubens's chief patron during his years in Italy. **Ferdinando** (1587–26; reigned from 1612) employed van *Dyck, Domenico *Feti, Francesco *Albani, and other artists. Most of the family collections were sold by **Vincenzo II** in 1627, principally to Charles I of England, and important Gonzaga patronage came to an end after Mantua was sacked by Austrian troops in 1630.

González, Julio (1876–1942). Spanish sculptor, draughtsman, metalworker, and painter, the leading pioneer in the use of iron as a sculptural medium. He learnt to work metals under his father, a goldsmith and sculptor, but his early career was spent mainly as a painter. In about 1900 he moved to Paris and formed a lifelong friendship with *Picasso, whom he had earlier met in his native Barcelona. He initially supported himself mainly by making metalwork and jewellery, and it was not until the late 1920s, when he was already 50, that he devoted himself wholeheartedly to sculpture and turned to welded metal as a material. His best-known work, *Montserrat* (1937, Stedelijk Mus., Amsterdam), is a fairly naturalistic piece, showing a woman with a child in her arms, and commemorates the suffering of the people of Spain in the civil war (Montserrat is Spain's holy mountain). More usually, however, his sculptures are semi-abstract, as in his series of *Cactus People*, formidable pieces with some of Picasso's savage humour. González's work had great influence, notably on Picasso, to whom he taught the techniques of iron sculpture, and on a generation of British and American artists exemplified by Reg *Butler and David *Smith. His brother **Joan González** (1868–1908) was a draughtsman and painter.

Gordon, Douglas. *See* TURNER PRIZE.

Gore, Spencer (1878–1914). British painter of landscapes, music-hall scenes, interiors, and occasional still lifes. He was the son of Spencer Walter Gore, who won the first Wimbledon tennis championship in 1877, and nephew of Charles Gore, bishop of

Oxford. In 1896–9 he studied at the *Slade School, where he was a particular friend of Harold *Gilman. In 1904 he visited *Sickert in Dieppe; this marked the beginning of his close acquaintance with recent French painting (he returned to France in 1905 and 1906), and his enthusiasm helped to decide Sickert to return to Britain in 1905. For the rest of his short career Gore was part of Sickert's circle, becoming a founder member successively of the *Allied Artists' Association in 1908, the *Camden Town Group (of which he was first president) in 1911, and the *London Group in 1913. His early work was *Impressionist in style, but he was strongly influenced by Roger *Fry's *Post-Impressionist exhibitions (Gore's own work was included in the second in 1912) and his later pictures show vivid use of flat, bright colour and boldly simplified forms. He died of pneumonia aged 35 and was much lamented by his many friends in the art world. Sickert said Gore was 'probably the man I love and admire most of any I have known', and his obituary in the *Morning Post* remarked that 'his personal character was so exceptional as to give him a unique influence in the artistic affairs of London in the last dozen years'. His son **Frederick Gore** (1913–) is also a painter.

Gorky, Arshile (Vosdanig Manoog Adoian) (1904–48). American painter, born in Turkish Armenia, who formed a link between European *Surrealism and American *Abstract Expressionism. He emigrated to the USA in 1920 and adopted the pseudonym Arshile Gorky, the first part of the name being derived from the Greek hero Achilles, the second part (Russ. 'the bitter one') from the Russian writer Maxim Gorky, to whom the painter sometimes claimed he was related (evidently not realizing that the writer's name, too, was a pseudonym). In 1925 he settled in New York, where he first studied and then taught at the Grand Central School of Art. Gorky took a romantic view of his vocation and is said to have hired a Hungarian violinist to play during his classes to encourage his students to put emotion into their work. His early paintings were strongly influenced by *Cézanne (whom he considered 'the greatest artist that has lived') and he also fell under the spell of *Picasso, as can be seen both in the haunting *The Artist and his Mother* (c.1926–9,

Whitney Mus., New York) and in his experimentation with *Cubism at this period. Much of his work of the 1930s represents an attempt to synthesize the flatness of Cubist structure (in which he was influenced also by Stuart *Davis) with the improvisatory fluidity and energy of *Surrealist *automatism. In the early 1940s he came into contact with the European Surrealists who had emigrated to New York to escape the Second World War and under their influence (particularly that of *Matta and *Miró) he created the distinctive style of his last phase, featuring delicately drawn shapes, suggestive of living organisms, floating in brilliant colour. However, just as Gorky began to emerge as a powerful original voice in American art, he suffered a tragic series of misfortunes. In 1946 a fire in his Connecticut studio destroyed a large proportion of his recent work, and in the same year he was operated on for cancer. In 1948 he broke his neck in an automobile accident, and when his wife left him soon afterwards he hanged himself. Gorky has been called both the last of the great Surrealists and the first of the Abstract Expressionists, and his work in the 1940s was a potent factor underlying the emergence of a specifically American school of abstract art. He was particularly influential on his friend *de Kooning.

Gormley, Antony (1950–). British sculptor. His work has been mainly concerned with the human figure and is often based on moulds from his own body. He won the *Turner Prize in 1994 and achieved much wider fame in 1998 when his enormous *Angel of the North* was erected near Gateshead, overlooking the A1 trunk road, and thereafter quickly became one of Britain's most instantly recognizable sights. Made of steel, it stands 20 m (66 ft) high and has a wingspan of 54 m (177 ft). It was commissioned by Gateshead Metropolitan Borough Council in 1994, and its creation and erection was a complex industrial undertaking.

Gossaert, Jan (also called Mabuse) (c.1478–1532). Netherlandish painter, probably from Maubeuge (now in France), from which his name 'Mabuse' derives. In 1503 he became a master in the Antwerp painters' guild, and a few years afterwards he entered the service of Philip of Burgundy (illegitimate son of Duke Philip the Good and later bishop of Utrecht). In 1508–9 he was part of Philip's retinue when he visited Rome as ambassador to the Vatican. After his return to the Netherlands, Gossaert seems to have settled in Zeeland, although it is not known in which town he made his home. His work before his Italian journey is in the tradition of Hugo van der *Goes and Gerard *David, whose influence can still be seen in the *Adoration of the Magi* (NG, London), probably painted soon after his return. His later work, however, was transformed by the experience of Italy, although the motifs he learned there were never thoroughly digested and coexisted with Flemish forms and details. *Vasari acclaimed him for being the first 'to bring the true method of representing nude figures and mythologies from Italy to the Netherlands', but in, for example, *Neptune and Amphitrite* (1516, Gemäldegalerie, Berlin), the life-size muscle-bound figures are in fact closer to *Dürer than to any Italian contemporary, and the curious classical temple in which they stand has bizarrely hybrid architectural elements. Gossaert was highly thought of by his contemporaries. His commissions took him to various towns in the Netherlands, his patrons included Margaret of Austria (*see* HABSBURG) and Christian II of Denmark, and his work was widely influential. However, to modern eyes there seems justice in Dürer's assessment of him as better in execution than in invention ('nit so gut im Haupstreichen als im Gemäl'). Jan van *Scorel was Gossaert's pupil for a short time.

Gotch, Thomas Cooper. *See* NEWLYN SCHOOL.

Gothic. Style of architecture and art that succeeded *Romanesque and prevailed in Europe (particularly northern Europe) from the mid-12th century to the 16th century. Like many other stylistic labels, the word was originally a term of abuse; it was coined by Italian artists of the *Renaissance to denote the type of medieval architecture they condemned as barbaric (implying, quite wrongly, that this architecture was created by the Gothic tribes who had destroyed the classical art of the Roman empire). The Gothic style is still characterized chiefly in terms of architecture—in particular by the use of pointed arches, flying buttresses, and elaborate tracery. By

extension, however, the term 'Gothic' is applied to the ornament, sculpture, and painting of the period in which Gothic architecture was built; it has less precise meaning in these contexts, although a swaying elegance is often considered typical of Gothic figures, which are generally much more naturalistic and less remote than those of the Romanesque period.

Gottlieb, Adolph (1903–74). American painter, one of the leading *Abstract Expressionists. His early work was *Expressionist and in 1935 he was one of the founding members of the Expressionist group The *Ten. In 1936 he worked for the *Federal Art Project. Some of his landscapes of the late 1930s were influenced by *Surrealism, and from the early 1940s this tendency was enhanced by contact with expatriate European Surrealists and by an interest in Freudian psychology. His personal style began to emerge in 1941 and from then until the end of his life he worked on three main series: *Pictographs* (1941–51), *Imaginary Landscapes* (1951–7, and again in the mid-1960s), and *Bursts* (1957–74). The *Pictographs* use a loose grid- or compartment-like arrangement with schematic shapes or symbols suggesting some mythic face; the *Imaginary Landscapes* feature a zone of astral shapes against a foreground of heavy *gestural strokes; and the *Bursts*, becoming still freer, suggest solar orbs and astral bodies hovering above violently coloured terrestrial explosions. Gottlieb also designed stained glass and other works for churches and synagogues, suggesting a religious mood without any specific representation.

gouache. Opaque *watercolour, sometimes also known as *body colour. It differs from transparent watercolour in that the *pigments are bound with glue and the lighter tones are obtained by the admixture of white pigment. Its degree of opacity varies with the amount of white that is added, but in general it is sufficient to prevent the reflection of the *ground through the paint and it therefore lacks the luminosity of transparent watercolour painting. It is, however, easier to use, and trials and errors can be painted over. The colours sold as poster paints by commercial colourmen are usually a form of gouache.

Goudt, Hendrik. *See* ELSHEIMER.

Goujon, Jean (c.1510–68?). French sculptor. He ranks second only to Germain *Pilon as the greatest French sculptor of the 16th century and he created a distinctive *Mannerist style as sophisticated as the finest works of painting and decoration of the contemporary School of *Fontainebleau. Nothing is known of his early life and he is first recorded in 1540 as the carver of the impressive columns supporting the organ loft in the church of St Maclou at Rouen. The pure *classicism of these columns has caused some critics to assume that he had earlier visited Italy. He had moved to Paris by 1544, when he was working on the screen of St Germain-l'Auxerrois, in collaboration with the architect Pierre Lescot. Low-*relief panels (now in the Louvre) from this screen show that Goujon had evolved a style of extreme grace and delicacy, owing something to the influence of Benvenuto *Cellini. The style is seen at its most mature in his decorations (now in the Louvre) for the Fontaine des Innocents, Paris (1547–9). The six relief panels of nymphs from this fountain, with their exquisitely carved rippling draperies, are generally considered his masterpieces. Goujon's most extensive undertaking was on the sculptural decoration of the *Louvre; he worked there from 1549 to 1562 in collaboration with Lescot, mainly on decorative panels forming part of the architectural scheme. Unfortunately all Goujon's work there has been heavily restored, including the famous *caryatids (1550–1) in the Salle des Caryatides. Using caryatids on a monumental scale was a novelty, perhaps inspired by his reading of Vitruvius (he made illustrations for the first French translation of his treatise in 1547). There is no indication of any work executed after 1562 and it is possible that Goujon left France because of religious persecution and died in Bologna (there is some doubt concerning the documentation).

Gower, George (d. 1596). English portrait painter. He was appointed serjeant-painter to Queen Elizabeth in 1581 and seems to have been the leading English portraitist of his day. His Sir Thomas Kytson and Lady Kytson (1573, Tate, London) show his clear and individual, if unsubtle, style. Gower was a gentleman by birth and his Self-Portrait (1579, priv. coll.) shows his coat of arms outweighed in a balance by a pair of dividers, a symbol of the painter's craft.

Gowing, Sir Lawrence (1918–91). British painter and writer on art. He had a distinguished academic career, during which he was deputy director of the Tate Gallery (1965–7) and a professor at several universities (notably at the *Slade School, 1975–85), and he wrote books and catalogues, valued for their critical insights, on numerous artists, among them *Cézanne, *Matisse, and *Vermeer. As a painter he began as a pupil of *Coldstream working in the *Euston Road tradition, and much of his subsequent work was in this sombre vein. His work also included abstracts, however, and in 1976 he began producing large pictures in which he traced the outline of his own naked body stretched on the canvas, the paint being applied by an assistant.

Goya, Francisco de (1746–1828). Spanish painter, printmaker, and draughtsman. He was the most powerful and original European artist of his time, but his genius was slow in maturing and he was well into his thirties before he began producing work that set him apart from his contemporaries. Born at Fuendetodos in Aragon, the son of a gilder, he trained initially with a local painter in Saragossa, then in 1763 moved to Madrid, where he continued his studies under Francisco *Bayeu (he twice failed in attempts to enrol at the Academy of San Fernando). After a visit to Italy (c.1768–71), he worked in Saragossa, then after marrying Bayeu's sister in 1773 he settled in Madrid in 1774. Bayeu secured him employment making designs for the royal tapestry factory, and this took up most of his working time from 1775 to 1780 (he continued the work more sporadically until 1792). Goya made 63 tapestry designs in all (most of them are in the Prado, Madrid). Although they are usually referred to as *'cartoons', they are in fact finished oil paintings, many of them of impressive size (the largest are more than 6 m (20 ft) wide). The subjects range from idyllic scenes to realistic incidents of everyday life; they are conceived in a lively and romantic spirit and executed with *Rococo decorative charm, but they are sometimes spiced with a sardonic humour that looks forward to Goya's later work.

During the 1780s Goya progressed steadily in his career, becoming a sought-after portraitist, achieving success as a religious painter, and winning a series of official distinctions. He was elected to the Academy of San Fernando in 1780 and became deputy director of painting in 1785; in 1786 he was appointed one of the painters to the king and in 1789 he was promoted to the more prestigious post of painter to the royal household (he marked his elevation by adding the aristocratic 'de' to his name). A more important turning point in his career than any of these appointments, however, was the mysterious, traumatic, and near-fatal illness he experienced in the winter of 1792-3 (syphilis and lead poisoning from paint are among the causes that have been suggested). The illness paralysed him and partially blinded him for a while and left him stone deaf for the rest of his life. Whilst convalescing in 1793 he painted a series of small pictures as a kind of therapy, 'to occupy my imagination, vexed by consideration of my sufferings, and ... to make observations that normally are given no place in commissioned works, where caprice and invention cannot be developed'. This marks the beginning of his preoccupation with the morbid, bizarre, and menacing that was to be such a feature of his mature work. It was given vivid expression in the first of his great series of prints, *Los Caprichos* (Caprices), issued in 1799. The set consists of 80 plates dealing with the ills and disorders of society.

In 1795 Goya succeeded Bayeu as director of painting at the Academy of San Fernando and in 1799 he was appointed principal painter to the royal household, producing his most famous portrait group, the *Family of Charles IV* (Prado), in the following year. The weaknesses of the royal family are revealed with unsparing realism, though evidently without deliberate satirical intent. Goya's early portraits had followed the manner of *Mengs, but stimulated by the study of *Velázquez's paintings in the royal collection he developed a much more natural, lively, and personal style, showing increasing mastery of pose and expression, heightened by dramatic contrasts of light and shade. From about the same date as the royal group portrait are the celebrated pair of paintings the *Clothed Maja* and *Naked Maja* (Prado), whose erotic nature led Goya to be summoned before the Inquisition. Popular legend has it that they represent the Duchess of Alba, the beautiful widow whose

relationship with Goya caused scandal in Madrid.

During the French occupation of Spain (1808-13) Goya retained his appointment of royal painter under Joseph Bonaparte (installed as king by his brother Napoleon), but his activity as a painter of court and society decreased, and—like many others—he may have been torn between welcoming the regime (which potentially brought freedom from royal tyranny) and feeling patriotic abhorrence against foreign military rule. He never openly expressed his political opinions and to a certain extent he was prepared to bend with the prevailing wind for the sake of his career (during the occupation he painted the Duke of Wellington, Napoleon's eventual conqueror, as well as supporters of the French). After the restoration of Ferdinand VII in 1814 Goya was exonerated from the charge of having 'accepted employment from the usurper' by claiming he had not worn the medal awarded him by the French, and he painted for the king two powerful and harrowing pictures of Spain's 'glorious insurrection', the bloody uprising of the citizens of Madrid against the occupying forces—*The Second of May, 1808* and *The Third of May, 1808* (both 1814, Prado). Even more savage are the 65 etchings *Los desastres de la guerra* (The Disasters of War, 1810-14), which depict atrocities committed by both French and Spanish.

Goya virtually retired from public life after 1815, subsequently working for himself and friends. He kept the title of court painter but was superseded in royal favour by Vicente *López y Portaña. Towards the end of 1819 he fell seriously ill for the second time (a remarkable self-portrait in the Minneapolis Institute of Arts shows him with the doctor who nursed him). Earlier that year he had bought a country house in the outskirts of Madrid, the Quinta del Sordo (House of the Deaf Man); and it was here, after his recovery, that he executed fourteen large murals (now in the Prado) known as the *Black Paintings* (1820-3) on account of their nightmarish subjects as well as their dark tonality. Painted almost entirely in blacks, greys, and browns, they feature religious and mythological scenes as well as ones entirely from Goya's imagination; they are executed with an almost ferocious intensity and freedom of handling and have been seen as reflections on death. By the time he completed these extraordinary works, many Spanish liberals were leaving the country because of the oppressive regime of Ferdinand VII, and in 1824 Goya obtained permission to visit France, ostensibly for reasons of health, and settled at Bordeaux. He made two brief visits to Spain, on the first of which (1826) he officially resigned as court painter and was granted a pension. In these last years he took up the new medium of *lithography (in four bullfighting scenes known collectively as the *Bulls of Bordeaux*, 1824–5), while his final paintings illustrate his progress towards a style anticipating *Impressionism in its freedom and lightness of touch.

Goya's output was enormous: there are about 700 surviving paintings by him, some 300 prints, and nearly 1,000 drawings. He was exceptionally versatile and his work expresses a very wide range of emotion. His technical freedom and originality likewise are remarkable—he sometimes manipulated paint with knives or fingers (and with more unconventional tools, including sponges and a wooden spoon, if Théophile Gautier's account in *Voyage en Espagne*, 1845, is to be believed), and in his prints he often used more than one technique on the same plate, especially combining *etching with *aquatint. In his own day he was chiefly celebrated for his portraits (which account for more than half of his painted output), but his enormous reputation now rests equally on work that was virtually unknown to his contemporaries: the *Disasters of War* etchings were not published until 1863 and the *Black Paintings* were not publicly exhibited until the 1870s.

Goyen, Jan van (1596–1656). Dutch painter, one of the foremost pioneers of realistic landscape painting in the Netherlands. His earliest works are heavily indebted to his master Esaias van de *Velde, but he then created a distinctive type of monochrome landscape in browns and greys with touches of vivid blue or red to catch the eye. He was one of the first painters to capture the quality of the light and air in a scene and to suggest the movement of clouds. Most of his paintings seem to be based on drawings made as he travelled about the countryside, and he evidently used the same drawings again and again because the same themes and motifs recur repeatedly in his works: gnarled oaks, wide plains, usually seen from

a height, low horizons, and clouded skies are typical of his repertoire. His finest work has a sense of poetic calm as well as great freshness and luminosity of atmosphere. Van Goyen worked in his native Leiden, Haarlem, and The Hague, where he died. He was hugely prolific and had many pupils and imitators. With Salomon van *Ruysdael, whose paintings are often virtually indistinguishable from his, he was the outstanding master of the 'tonal' phase of Dutch landscape painting, when the depiction of atmosphere was the artist's prime concern.

Gozzoli, Benozzo (Benozzo di Lese) (c.1421–97). Florentine painter. He probably trained under Fra *Angelico and he later worked as his assistant in Rome (1447) and Orvieto (1448). His reputation rests on only one work—but one of the most enchanting in all Italian *Renaissance art: the decoration of the chapel of the Palazzo *Medici in Florence with frescos of the *Journey of the Magi* (1459–61). This is the most glittering fresco cycle of the century, recalling, and perhaps consciously rivalling, *Gentile da Fabriano's *Adoration of the Magi* of 1423. Its secular outlook is far removed in spirit from the work of his master Fra Angelico. The rest of Benozzo's career was busy but fairly unremarkable. His biggest undertaking was a fresco cycle of Old Testament scenes in the Campo Santo in Pisa; he began work on it in 1467 and spent most of the rest of his life in Pisa. The frescos were badly damaged by bombing in the Second World War. Benozzo also painted altarpieces, one of which (*Madonna and Child with Saints*, 1461–2) is in the National Gallery, London.

Graf, Urs (c.1485–1529/30). Swiss draughtsman, printmaker, designer, goldsmith, and painter, active mainly in Basle. He is best known for his drawings, which survive in considerable number, often signed and dated. They are done in a bold and energetic style, with virtuoso curling strokes of the pen; favourite subjects are soldiers (Graf himself spent some time as a mercenary in Italy), peasants, and flamboyantly dressed ladies of easy virtue. Graf also designed stained glass, made woodcuts, and executed the earliest extant dated etching, *Girl Washing her Feet* (1513).

Graffiti art. A style of painting based on the type of spray-can vandalism familiar in cities all over the world and specifically in the New York subway system; the term can apply to any work in this vein, but refers particularly to a vogue in New York in the 1980s (several commercial galleries specialized in it at this time and a Museum of American Graffiti opened there in 1989). The best-known figures of Graffiti art were Jean-Michel Basquiat (1960–88) and Keith Haring (1958–90), both of whom enjoyed huge reputations (and prices) during their brief careers, which were ended for Basquiat by a drugs overdose and for Haring by AIDS. Basquiat was a genuine street artist who 'crossed over' into the gallery world; Haring had an art school training but adopted a primitivistic style based on graffiti. Robert *Hughes satirized them as 'Keith Boring and Jean-Michel Basketcase'.

Graham, Maria. *See* CALLCOTT.

Grand Manner. Term applied to the lofty and rhetorical manner of *history painting that in academic theory was considered appropriate to the most serious and elevated subjects. The classic exposition of its doctrines is found in *Reynolds's Third and Fourth *Discourses* (1770 and 1771), where he asserts that 'the *gusto grande* of the Italians, the *beau idéal* of the French, and the *great style, genius*, and *taste* among the English, are but different appellations of the same thing'. Cecil Gould (*An Introduction to Italian Renaissance Painting*, 1957) rightly points out that 'the Grand Manner is an attitude rather than a style' and goes on to give a lucid exposition of some of its characteristics. 'The general aim is to transcend Nature ... The Subject itself must be on an elevated and elevating plane ... Similarly, the individual figures in such a scene must be shown purged of the grosser elements of ordinary existence ... Landscape backgrounds or ornamental detail must be reduced to a minimum and individual peculiarities of human physiognomy absolutely eliminated. Draperies should be simple, but ample and noble, and fashionable contemporary costume absolutely shunned. Alternatively, the figures should be nude.' The idea of the Grand Manner took shape in 17th-century Italy, notably in the writings of *Bellori. His friend *Poussin and the great Bolognese painters of the 17th century were regarded as outstanding exponents of the

Grand Manner, but the greatest of all was held to be *Raphael.

Grand Tour. An extensive Continental journey, chiefly through France, the Netherlands, and above all Italy, sometimes in the company of a tutor, to complete the education of an aristocrat or gentleman. The origins of the Grand Tour go back to the 16th century, but its heyday was the 18th century, when it was an almost obligatory part of the tutelage of the sons (or at least eldest sons) of noble families in Britain (similar tours were also undertaken by young men from other countries, but they are associated above all with British travellers). The traveller was usually aged between 17 and 22 and the tour typically lasted a year or longer. Such tours laid the basis for many art collections among the landed gentry, helping to spread the fashion for *Neoclassicism and an enthusiasm for Italian painting. Among the native artists who catered for this demand were *Batoni, *Canaletto, *Panini, and *Piranesi, and British artists (such as Gavin *Hamilton, William *Kent, and Joseph *Nollekens) were sometimes able to support themselves while in Italy by working for the dealers and restorers who supplied the tourist clientele, particularly in Rome. There was also a flourishing market in guidebooks (*see* RICHARDSON). Between 1792 and 1815 the French Revolutionary and Napoleonic Wars virtually ended foreign travel, and although the Grand Tour resumed after this, its golden age was over. By the middle of the 19th century, railways were beginning to open up Europe to middle-class travellers and the Grand Tour was defunct.

Granet, François-Marius (1775–1849). French painter and museum official. Granet was a pupil of J.-L. *David and subsequently spent the years 1802–19 in Rome (he returned to Italy several times thereafter). He made a speciality of sombre tonal effects and changing light in dimly lit interiors, his pictures recalling 17th-century Dutch interiors rather than expressing the *Neoclassical tradition in which he was trained. His *Choir of the Capuchin Church in Rome* (Met. Mus,. New York) was exhibited at the 1819 *Salon with such success that he made more than a dozen replicas of it. Granet also painted Italian landscapes, constructed with firm, cubic volumes, in which some critics have seen a foreshadowing of *Cézanne. In 1826 he became a curator at the *Louvre and in 1833 he was appointed curator of the newly established museum at Versailles. During the Revolution of 1848 he retired to his native Aix-en-Provence, where he founded the museum that bears his name. It contains a celebrated portrait of him by *Ingres.

Grant, Duncan (1885–1978). British painter and designer. Through the writer Lytton Strachey (his cousin) he became a member of the *Bloomsbury Group, and he was also familiar with avant-garde circles in Paris (he met *Matisse in 1909 and *Picasso soon afterwards). Up to about 1910 his work—which included landscapes, portraits, and still lifes—was fairly sober in form and restrained in colour, but he then underwent a rapid development to become one of the most advanced of British artists in his response to modern French painting (he was included in Roger *Fry's second *Post-Impressionist exhibition in 1912). From about 1913 he was also influenced by African sculpture, and he was one of the first British artists to produce completely abstract pictures. However, this extreme avant-garde phase was fairly-short-lived and he soon reverted to a figurative style. In 1913 he began working for the *Omega Workshops, and having discovered a taste and talent for interior decoration, he sought similar commissions when the Workshops closed in 1919. In this field he worked much in collaboration with Vanessa *Bell, with whom he lived from 1916. He was at the height of his popularity and esteem in the 1920s and 1930s, but after the Second World War his work went out of fashion. However, he lived long enough to see a great revival of interest in the Bloomsbury Group, which brought a renewed appreciation of his own work. Apart from paintings, his work included designs for textiles, pottery, stage scenery, and costumes.

Grant, Sir Francis (1803–78). Scottish painter, one of the most fashionable portrait painters of his day. His best works are generally considered to be his smaller sporting *conversation pieces. In 1866 he succeeded *Eastlake as president of the *Royal Academy.

graphic art. Term current with several meanings in the literature of the visual arts. In the context of the *fine arts, it usually refers to those arts that rely essentially on line or tone rather than colour—i.e. drawing and the various forms of engraving. Some writers, however, exclude drawing from this definition, so that the term 'graphic art' is used to cover the various processes by which prints are created. In another sense, the term—sometimes shortened to 'graphics'—is used to cover the entire field of commercial printing, including text as well as illustrations.

Grasser, Erasmus (c.1450–1518). German sculptor, active mainly in Munich. He worked in an animated and expressive late *Gothic style and was the leading sculptor of his day in south Bavaria, with a flourishing workshop and numerous pupils. His best-known works are ten (originally sixteen) limewood figures of morris dancers for the ballroom of the old town hall in Munich (1480, Stadtmuseum, Munich). Grasser was also an architect and hydraulic engineer.

Gravelot (pseudonym of Hubert-François Bourguignon) (1699–1773). French draughtsman, engraver, and painter, active for several years (1732–45) in London, where he became the leading book illustrator of the day. He worked on more than 50 English books, including John Gay's *Fables* (1738) and Samuel Richardson's *Pamela* (1742), one of the first novels to be illustrated. On *Pamela* he worked in collaboration with his friend *Hayman. His other friends included *Hogarth and he taught at the *St Martin's Lane Academy, where *Gainsborough was among his pupils. Although not an artist of outstanding talent, he played an important role in introducing the French *Rococo style to England.

Greaves, Derrick. *See* KITCHEN SINK SCHOOL.

Greaves, Walter. *See* WHISTLER, J. M.

Greco, El (c.1541–1614). Cretan-born painter, sculptor, and architect who settled in Spain and is regarded as the first great genius of the Spanish School. His real name was Domenikos Theotocopoulos and it was thus that he signed his paintings throughout his life, always in Greek characters, and sometimes followed by *Kres* (Cretan). To avoid the tongue-twisting name, he was known in Spain as Domenico

Griego or simply El Griego (the Greek). Evidently it was not until after his lifetime that the curious form 'El Greco' was adopted (curious because 'El' is Spanish and 'Greco' is Italian). Little is known of his early years, and only a few works survive by him in the *Byzantine tradition of *icon painting, notably the signed *Dormition of the Virgin* discovered in 1983 (church of the Dormition, Syros). In 1567 or 1568 he moved to Venice (Crete was then a Venetian possession), and late in 1570 he is described as 'recently arrived' in Rome. The *miniaturist Giulio *Clovio, who became a friend of El Greco there, referred to him as a 'disciple' of *Titian, but of all Venetian painters *Tintoretto influenced him most, with his sense of movement and dramatic lighting (El Greco's turbulent skies are often particularly reminiscent of Tintoretto).

It is generally presumed that El Greco remained in Rome until 1576 (when he is first recorded in Spain), but there is little documentation on his time in the city, and it has been suggested that he returned to Venice for a while. Clovio was an influential friend, and through him El Greco gained accommodation in the Palazzo *Farnese; however, he received no public commissions in Italy and worked on a fairly small scale. Among his surviving pictures of the period are two paintings of the *Purification of the Temple* (Minneapolis Inst. of Arts, and NG, Washington), a favourite theme with him, and a portrait of Clovio (Mus. di Capodimonte, Naples). Accomplished though they are, they give little hint of the explosion of genius that occurred after he settled in Spain. He is documented in Madrid in 1576, and by the following year he was in Toledo, where he lived for the rest of his life. His decision to move there was presumably influenced by the young Spanish priest Luis de Castilla, part of his circle in Rome, whose father was dean of Toledo Cathedral and a man of considerable influence. El Greco quickly gained major commissions in his new home, beginning with the high altarpiece of the church of S. Domingo el Antiguo (1577). The central part of the altarpiece, a 4 m (13 ft) high canvas of the *Assumption of the Virgin* (Art Inst. of Chicago), was easily his biggest work to date, but he carried off the dynamic composition triumphantly. A succession of great altarpieces followed throughout his career, the

two most famous being *El Espolio* (Christ Stripped of His Garments) (1577–9, Toledo Cathedral) and the *Burial of Count Orgaz* (1586–8, S. Tomé, Toledo). These two mighty works convey the awesomeness of great spiritual events with a sense of mystic rapture, and in his late work El Greco went even further in freeing his figures from earthbound restrictions; the *Adoration of the Shepherds* (1612–14, Prado, Madrid), painted for his own tomb, is a prime example. His style has something in common with Italian *Mannerism in its use of elongated figures and non-rational space, but his flame-like forms, electric colours, and ecstatic emotion are intensely personal. Toledo at this time was the spiritual capital of Spain, with more than a hundred religious establishments, so El Greco had little need to look beyond it for commissions; he attempted to win royal favour but failed, as Philip II (*see* HABSBURG) rejected an altarpiece he painted for the *Escorial.

Although he was primarily a religious painter, El Greco excelled also as a portraitist. His sitters were mainly ecclesiastics (*Felix Paravicino*, 1609, MFA, Boston) or gentlemen, although one of his most beautiful works is a portrait of a lady (*c*.1577–80, Pollok House, Glasgow), traditionally identified as a likeness of Jeronima de las Cuevas, his common-law wife. He also painted two views of Toledo (Met. Mus., New York, and Mus. del Greco, Toledo), both late works, and a mythological painting, *Laocoön* (*c*.1610, NG, Washington), that is unique in his oeuvre. The unusual choice of subject is perhaps explained by the local tradition that Toledo had been founded by descendants of the Trojans. El Greco also designed complete altar compositions, working as architect and sculptor as well as painter, for instance at the Hospital de la Caridad, Illescas (1603). *Pacheco, who visited El Greco in 1611, refers to him as a writer on painting, sculpture, and architecture, and an inventory of his books drawn up after his death indicates he had wide intellectual interests. He had a strong sense of professional pride and expected to be well rewarded for his work; on several occasions he engaged in legal disputes over payments, and the failure of one such lawsuit seems to have caused him financial difficulties near the end of his life. His workshop produced a great many replicas of his paintings, but his work was so personal that his influence was slight, his only followers of note being his son **Jorge Manuel Theotocopoulos** (c.1578–1631) and Luis *Tristán. At the time of his death he was famous and respected, but his reputation soon declined and in 1724 *Palomino described his work as 'contemptible and ridiculous, as much for his disjointed drawing as for the unpleasant colour'. By the time the *Prado opened in 1819 he was so little regarded that it did not display a single example of his work. Interest in his art revived at the end of the 19th century and his great popular fame has come in the wake of modern art, particularly *Expressionism, of which he has been seen as a forerunner. The strangeness of his art has inspired various theories, for example that he was mad or suffered from astigmatism, but his rapturous paintings make complete sense as an expression of the religious fervour of his adopted country.

Greek Revival and **Greek Taste.** See NEO-CLASSICISM.

Green, Anthony (1939–). British painter. He specializes in scenes from his own middle-class domestic life portrayed with loving attention to detail and an engaging sense of whimsy. Often he uses oddly *shaped canvases that accentuate his strange perspective effects, and his subjects are frequently erotic as well as humorous. His work, which is often on a large scale, is instantly recognizable and is generally highly popular with the public at the *Royal Academy summer exhibition, for he vividly communicates the loving feeling he puts into his paintings.

Green, William. See ACTION PAINTING.

Greenaway, Kate (1846–1901). English painter, illustrator, and writer, famous for her illustrations in children's books. Her delicate skill and fragile sentimentality, often imitated but never matched, won her many distinguished admirers, including *Ruskin, and (perhaps for her feeling for flat pattern) *Gauguin. She often illustrated her own texts, issuing for example a series of *Kate Greenaway's Almanacks*, and her work became so popular that the quaint clothes that are such a feature of her illustrations influenced children's costume.

Greenberg, Clement (1909–94). American art critic. With Harold *Rosenberg he was his country's most influential writer on contemporary art in the post-war years when American painting and sculpture first achieved a dominant position in world art. His approach to criticism is sometimes described as *formalist, and the artists to whose works he gave the most powerful advocacy were chiefly uncompromising abstractionists—most famously Jackson *Pollock and David *Smith, and later the *Post-Painterly Abstractionists (Greenberg coined this term) and the British sculptor Anthony *Caro. In painting he laid particular stress on the flatness of the picture surface and the rejection of any kind of illusionistic modelling, and he opposed the mere 'novelty' art of painters such as *Rauschenberg. Although he regarded aesthetic judgements as autonomous, he also believed that history possessed order and purpose (the result of early contacts with Marxism) and this allowed him to endow his 'disinterested aesthetic' verdicts on art with a claim for historical certainty. His influence was at its height in the 1950s and 1960s, but thereafter it waned in the face of such developments as *Conceptual art and *New Figuration. His best-known book is probably *Art and Culture* (1961), an anthology of his writings; his other books include monographs on *Miró (1948), *Matisse (1953), and *Hofmann (1961).

Greene, Balcomb. See AMERICAN ABSTRACT ARTISTS.

Greenough, Horatio (1805–52). American *Neoclassical sculptor who spent the greater part of his working life in Italy (1825–6, 1828–51). He is sometimes described as the first professional American sculptor and his major work, the colossal marble figure of George Washington (1833–41), was the first important state commission given to an American sculptor. It was originally placed in the rotunda of the Capitol in Washington, but is now in the National Museum of American History. The seated figure is based on *Phidias' celebrated statue of Zeus at Olympia, but the head follows *Houdon's portrait of Washington—an uneasy mixture of idealism and naturalism. Greenough's work is in general rather uninspiring, and the essays he wrote on art in the final decade of his life are considered more interesting; his views on architecture have been claimed as precursors of modern functionalism. His brother, **Richard Saltonstall Greenough** (1819–1904), was also a sculptor, best known for his statue of Benjamin Franklin (1855) outside Boston City Hall.

Greuze, Jean-Baptiste (1725–1805). French painter. He had a great success at the 1755 *Salon with a group of paintings including *Father Reading the Bible to his Children* (Louvre, Paris) and he went on to win enormous popularity with similar sentimental and melodramatic genre scenes. His work was praised by *Diderot as 'morality in paint' and as representing the highest ideal of painting in his day. He also wished to succeed as a history painter, but when he presented his *Septimius Severus Reproaching Caracalla* (1769, Louvre) to the Académie Royale as his reception piece he was accepted only as a genre painter, causing him acute embarrassment. Much of his later work consisted of titillating pictures of young girls, which contain thinly veiled sexual allusions under their surface appearance of mawkish innocence: *The Broken Pitcher* (Louvre), for example, alludes to loss of virginity. With the swing of taste towards *Neoclassicism his work went out of fashion and after the Revolution in 1789 he sank into obscurity. At the very end of his career he received a commission to paint a portrait of Napoleon (1804–5, Versailles), but he died in poverty. His huge output is particularly well represented in the Louvre, the Wallace Collection in London, the Musée Fabre in Montpellier, and in the museum dedicated to him in Tournus, his native town.

Grien, Hans Baldung. *See* BALDUNG.

Grimaldi, Giovanni Francesco (1606–80). Italian landscape painter, born in Bologna and sometimes called Il Bolognese. He developed an attractive landscape style in the manner of the mature Annibale *Carracci, and his work, which was popular with collectors and much engraved, helped to spread the tradition of *ideal landscape in Europe. Grimaldi worked mainly in Rome, painting frescos as well as easel paintings, notably at the Villa Doria Pamphili, where he was also employed as an architect. In 1649–51 he worked in Paris.

Grimmer. Two Netherlandish painters, **Jacob** (*c*.1526–90) and his son **Abel**

(*c*.1570–*c*.1619), whose styles are so similar that it is often difficult to distinguish between their works. They worked in Antwerp, mainly painting landscape and *genre subjects in an attractive style, full of lively anecdote, that places them among the best followers of *Breugel. Jacob's work was praised by van *Mander and others.

Grimshaw, Atkinson (1836–93). English painter. He specialized in a distinctive type of nocturnal townscape, usually featuring gaslights and wet streets, and *Whistler said of him, 'I considered myself the inventor of Nocturnes until I saw Grimmy's moonlit pictures.' Grimshaw's paintings, however, unlike Whistler's, are sharp in focus and rather acidic in colouring, although often remarkably atmospheric. They were very popular (in spite of the fact that he rarely exhibited at the *Royal Academy) and he was much imitated, not least by two of his sons, **Arthur** (1864–1913) and **Louis** (1870–1944?). Their father worked in his native Leeds and in other northern towns, as well as in London.

Gris, Juan (1887–1927). Spanish painter, sculptor, illustrator, and designer, active mainly in Paris, where he settled in 1906. In his early years there he earned his living mainly with humorous drawings for various periodicals and he did not begin painting in earnest until 1910. By this time he was strongly influenced by his fellow Spaniard *Picasso and his serious painting was almost entirely in the *Cubist manner. He made such rapid strides that by 1912 he was becoming recognized as the leading Cubist painter apart from the founders of the movement, Picasso and *Braque. His work stood out at the *Section d'Or exhibition in that year, attracting the attention of collectors and dealers (Gertrude *Stein was among those who bought his paintings and *Kahnweiler gave him a contract). In 1913–14 he developed a personal version of Synthetic Cubism, in which *papier collé played an important part. He said that he conceived of his paintings as 'flat, coloured architecture' and his methods of visual analysis were more systematic than those of Picasso and Braque. His subjects were almost all taken from his immediate surroundings (mainly still lifes, with occasional landscapes and portraits), but he began with the image he had in mind rather than with an object in the external world: 'I try to make concrete that which is abstract... *Cézanne turns a bottle into a cylinder, but I make a bottle—a particular bottle—out of a cylinder.' In 1919 Gris had his first major one-man exhibition (at the Galerie de l'Effort Moderne in Paris), but in the following year he suffered a serious attack of pleurisy and from then on his health was poor; for this reason he spent much of his time in the south of France. In this last period of his life his style became more painterly (*Violin and Fruit Dish*, 1924, Tate, London). Apart from paintings, his work included polychrome sculpture, book illustrations, and set and costume designs for *Diaghilev. He wrote a few essays on his aesthetic ideas and a collection of his letters, edited and translated by Douglas *Cooper, was published in 1956.

grisaille. A painting done entirely in shades of grey or another neutral greyish colour. The idea was evidently first used in stained glass. The earliest known examples in painting are among *Giotto's frescos in the Arena Chapel, Padua (*c*.1305), where they imitate the appearance of stone sculpture. Grisaille was sometimes also used for underpainting or for oil sketches (notably in the work of *Rubens). *See also* CAMAIEU.

Gromaire, Marcel. *See* LURÇAT.

Gropius, Walter (1883–1969). German-born architect, designer, and teacher who became an American citizen in 1944. In 1919 he founded the *Bauhaus, of which he was principal until 1928, when he resumed his architectural practice in Berlin. In 1934, after the Nazis had come to power, he left Germany for England, where he practised in partnership with the British architect Maxwell Fry. In 1937 he settled in the USA, where he taught at Harvard until 1951. He remained active until the end of his life and had an exceptional list of notable buildings to his credit. Although Gropius's practical work was in the field of architecture, his influence upon modernist trends in all the visual arts has probably not been exceeded by that of any other man. Nowhere else have so many major artists of outstanding originality been brought into collaboration as those whom Gropius gathered at the Bauhaus.

Gros, Antoine-Jean (1771–1835). French painter. He trained with his parents, both of whom were *miniaturists, and then with J.-L. *David. Although he revered David and became one of his favourite pupils, Gros had a passionate nature and he was drawn more to the colour and vibrancy of *Rubens and the great Venetian painters than to the *Neoclassical severity of his master. From 1793 to 1800 he worked in Italy, where he met Napoleon and was commissioned to paint portraits documenting his campaigns. After his return to Paris he continued this vein in huge paintings such as the *Battle of Eylau* (1808, Louvre, Paris) that are among the most stirring images of the Napoleonic era. Compared with the contemporary war scenes of *Goya, they are glamorous lies, but they are painted with such skill and panache that they cannot but be admired on their own terms. When David went into exile in 1816 after the fall of Napoleon, he entrusted his studio to Gros, who subsequently tried to work in a more consciously Neoclassical style. He never again approached the quality of his Napoleonic pictures, however (although he continued to paint excellent portraits), and haunted by a sense of failure, unhappily married, and in poor health, he drowned himself in the Seine. In spite of the sad end to his career, Gros is regarded as the most gifted of David's immediate followers and an important figure in the development of *Romanticism; the colour and drama of his work influenced *Géricault, *Delacroix, and his pupil *Bonington amongst others.

Grosvenor Gallery, London. A commercial gallery founded in 1877 by the wealthy dilettante painter Sir Coutts Lindsay (1824–1913) and Charles E. Hallé, son of the famous musician Sir Charles Hallé. *Whistler showed eight paintings at the opening exhibition, and *Ruskin's notorious outburst against one of them led to the libel trial that caused the painter's financial ruin. The other artists who showed at the gallery included such distinguished academics as *Leighton and *Poynter, but it became particularly associated with the Aesthetic Movement (*see* AESTHETICISM) and was memorably satirized in Gilbert and Sullivan's *Patience* (1881): 'A greenery-yallery, Grosvenor Gallery, Foot-in-the-grave young man' (an allusion to the deathly pallor possessed by many of the figures in works by painters such as *Burne-Jones). In

1888 the Grosvenor Gallery was taken over by the New Gallery; by this time it 'had become little more than an overflow from the *Royal Academy' (Dennis Farr, *English Art 1870–1940*, 1978).

Grosz, George (1893–1959). German-born painter and draughtsman who became an American citizen in 1938. He began as a *caricaturist and through his drawings he expressed his disgust at the depravity of the Prussian military caste. During the First World War he twice served in the German army and each time was discharged as being unfit for service. In 1917, with *Heartfield, he Anglicized his name (adding an 'e' to 'Georg') as a protest against the hatred being whipped up against the enemy. The most famous of the satirical anti-war illustrations he made at this time is the drawing *Fit for Active Service* (1918, MoMA, New York), in which a fat, complacent doctor pronounces a skeleton fit for duty. From 1917 to 1920 Grosz was a prominent figure in the *Dada movement in Berlin, and in the 1920s, with *Dix, he became the leading exponent of the *Neue Sachlichkeit. In 1917 he published the first of several collections of drawings, through which he established an international reputation. The most famous are *The Face of the Ruling Class* (1921) and *Ecce Homo* (1927). In these and in his paintings he ruthlessly denounced a decaying society in which gluttony and depravity are placed beside poverty and disease; prostitutes and profiteers were frequently among his cast of characters. Grosz often used watercolour, and in spite of the nastiness of the subject matter and the bluntness of his satire, his works in this medium are remarkable for the sheer beauty and delicacy of their technique. His more conventional works of this time include a number of incisive portraits. He was prosecuted several times for obscenity and blasphemy, and in 1933, despairing at the political situation in Germany, he moved to America to take up the offer of a teaching post at the *Art Students League of New York. In America he largely abandoned his satirical manner for more romantic landscapes and still lifes, with from time to time apocalyptic visions of a nightmare future. Although he won several honours in his later years, he regarded himself as a failure because he was unable to win recog-

nition as a serious painter rather than a brilliant satirist, and he painted several self-portraits showing how isolated and depressed he was in his adopted country (*The Wanderer*, 1943, Memorial AG, Univ. of Rochester, New York). His autobiography, *A Little Yes and a Big No*, was published in New York in 1946. He returned to Berlin in 1959, saying, 'my American dream turned out to be a soap bubble', and died there shortly after his arrival, following a fall down a flight of stairs.

grotesque. A term originally used in the visual arts to describe a type of fanciful wall decoration (painted, carved, or moulded in *stucco) characterized by the use of interlinked floral motifs, animal and human figures, masks, etc., often arranged in an vertical, column-like format. Such decoration was inspired by the ornament found in the excavated rooms (popularly called *grotte*: 'grottoes') of certain ancient Roman buildings, notably the Golden House of Nero in Rome, which began to be uncovered at the end of the 15th century. During the 16th century this kind of decoration spread from Italy to most of the countries of Europe. In France the word *grotesque* was applied as an adjective to literature and even to people fairly early in the 17th century, and later in the same century this meaning spread to England, and the word began to assume its current sense in everyday parlance, suggesting the ridiculous, absurd, monstrous, or abnormal.

ground. The surface or *support on which a painting or drawing is executed, typically paper for watercolours, for example, and canvas for oils; or, more specifically, a preparatory coating applied to such a surface before the picture is begun. The purpose of the ground in the second, more technical, sense is to isolate the paint from the support so as to prevent chemical interaction, to render the support less absorbent, to provide a satisfactory surface for painting or drawing on, and to heighten the brilliance of the colours. *Gesso is the ground that occurs most often in the literature of art history. In *etching the ground is the acid-resisting mixture which is spread over the plate before work is begun.

Groupe de Recherche d'Art Visuel (GRAV). A group of *Kinetic artists formed in Paris in 1960. The members, who included Julio *Le Parc and *Vasarely's son Yvaral, adopted a scientific approach and investigated the use of modern industrial materials for artistic purposes. As well as creating individual works, they often worked together on anonymous collective projects, and it was one of their aims to produce art that called for involvement from the spectator. The group had its base at the Galerie Denise René, but on various occasions it attempted to bring art into the life of the streets. It disbanded in 1968.

Group of Seven. Group of 20th-century Canadian painters, based in Toronto, who found their main inspiration in the landscape of northern Ontario and created the first major national movement in Canadian art. The group was officially established in 1920, when it held its first exhibition in the Art Gallery of Toronto, the seven painters involved being Franklin Carmichael (1890–1945), Lawren *Harris, A. Y. *Jackson, Frank Johnston (1888–1949), Arthur Lismer (1885–1969), J. E. H. MacDonald (1873–1932), and Frederick Varley (1881–1969). Some members of the group had, however, been working together since 1913, and Tom *Thomson, who was one of the early leaders, had died in 1917. Other artists joined after the 1920 exhibition. The members made group sketching expeditions and worked in an *Expressionist style characterized by brilliant colour and bold brushwork. After initial critical abuse, they won public favour and Emily *Carr was inspired by their example. The group's last exhibition was held in 1931 and two years later it disbanded and was superseded by the *Canadian Group of Painters; thereafter the members worked more as individuals and developed separately.

Gruber, Francis (1912–48). French painter. His early work was often of visionary subjects, but from about 1933 he began to paint mainly from the model in the studio; he also did still lifes, views through windows, and from 1937 landscapes painted out of doors. Gruber's mature style was grave and melancholy, featuring long, drooping figures, and he is regarded as the founder of the 'Misérabiliste' strain in French painting, later particularly associated with *Buffet. A typical work is *Job* (1944, Tate, London), painted for the 1944

*Salon d'Automne, which was known as the Salon of the Liberation because it was held soon after Paris was freed from the German occupation; the picture symbolizes oppressed peoples who like Job in the Bible had endured a great deal of suffering. In spite of the tuberculosis that caused his early death, Gruber worked with great energy and had a substantial output.

Grünewald, Mathis (c.1475/80–1528). German painter, the greatest of *Dürer's contemporaries. His real name was Mathis Gothardt or Neithardt, but this was not discovered until the 1930s. The origin of the nickname Grünewald ('greenwood') is unknown, but it was evidently not used before the 17th century, notably by *Sandrart, who published the first biography of the artist in his *Teutsche Akademie* (1675). This haziness about his identity reflects the isolation and individuality of his work and the obscurity into which he fell after his death; he had no known pupils and (unlike most of his German contemporaries) he did not make woodcuts or engravings, which would have spread his name. He was successful for most of his career, working as court painter to two successive archbishops of Mainz, but his reputation did not long survive, and in 1597, when the emperor Rudolf II (*see* HABSBURG) tried to buy his masterpiece, the Isenheim Altarpiece, the name of the painter had already been forgotten. The surviving documentation on him is meagre and sometimes confusing, for it appears that some references that have previously been assumed to allude to him are in fact concerned with other artists called 'Master Mathis' (the name was fairly common at the time). He spent much of his career in Aschaffenburg, a town near Frankfurt, and it is there that he is first firmly documented in 1504/5. By 1510 he was working for the archbishop of Mainz, Uriel von Gemmingen, whose official residence was in Aschaffenburg. Von Gemmingen died in 1514 and Grünewald was also employed by his successor Albrecht von Brandenburg (who was also archbishop of Magdeburg). In addition to being a painter, he is known to have worked as a hydraulic engineer and supervisor of architectural works. The little that is recorded of his personal life comes from Sandrart, who says he was melancholy and withdrawn and made an unhappy marriage

late in life. There is no documentary con-
firmation of his marriage, but he is known
to have had an adopted son called Andreas
Neithardt, whose surname the painter
sometimes used for himself in documents
relating to the boy, thus creating one of the
sources of confusion about the painter's
identity.

Grünewald's work forms a complete contrast to that of Dürer. Whereas Dürer—an
intellectual imbued with *Renaissance
ideas—had limitless curiosity about the
visual world, Grünewald concentrated exclusively on religious themes, and in particular the Crucifixion, a subject he was to
make his own. His most famous treatment
of it is the central panel of his masterpiece,
the altarpiece for the hospital church of the
Anthonite abbey at Isenheim in Alsace,
completed in about 1515 and now in the
Musée d'Unterlinden, Colmar. The hospital
at Isenheim cared particularly for plague
victims, and the concentration on Christ's
appalling physical agonies, his body grue-
somely mangled and torn, must have bol-
stered the faith of the sick by reminding
them that he too had suffered horribly
before triumphing over death. In the *Resurrection*, Christ displays his nail and lance
wounds, but the lacerations that cover his
body in the *Crucifixion* have disappeared,
affirming that the patients at the hospital
could be cleansed of their diseases and sins.
The altarpiece is marked by extreme emotional intensity, brought about by expressive distortion and by colouring of an
extraordinary incandescent beauty. Grünewald was familiar with Renaissance ideas of
*perspective, but spiritually he belongs to
the late medieval world. His other work includes *Crucifixions* in Basle (Öffentliche
Kunstsammlung), Karlsruhe (Staatliche
Kunsthalle), and Washington (NG), and several drawings survive.

The end of Grünewald's career was
marked by a decline in his fortunes. He
had Protestant sympathies, and following
the Peasants' War, in which Archbishop Albrecht's palace was besieged, he left his service and moved to Frankfurt. There he made
a meagre living at a variety of jobs, including selling artists' colours and a curative
balm, the latter presumably something he
had learnt about at Isenheim. In 1527 he
became convinced his life was in danger
and fled to Halle, where he died of plague

the following year. His effects included
'much Lutheran trash'. Although his influence can be seen in the paintings of contemporaries such as *Baldung and *Ratgeb, it
was not until the advent of *Expressionism
in the early 20th century that his work
started to arouse widespread interest and
he began his rise to his present pinnacle of
esteem as one of the most awe-inspiring
artists of his, or any other, time.

Guardi, Francesco (1712–93). Venetian
painter, the best-known member of a family
of artists. He is now famous for his views of
Venice, indeed next to *Canaletto he is the
most celebrated view-painter (*see* VEDUTA) of
the 18th century, but he produced work on
a great variety of subjects and seems to have
concentrated on views only after the death
of his brother **Gianantonio** (1699–1760).
Until then Francesco's personality was
largely submerged in the family studio, of
which Gianantonio was head and which
handled commissions of every kind. Francesco's career was unsuccessful in worldly
terms; he was still working for other artists
when he was over 40, he never attracted the
attention of foreign visitors in the way Canaletto did, and he died in poverty. Recognition of his genius came in the wake
of *Impressionism, when his vibrant and
rapidly painted views were seen as having
qualities of spontaneity, bravura, and atmosphere lacking in Canaletto's sharply defined and deliberate works. Francesco was
enormously prolific and his work is in many
public collections in Italy, Britain, and elsewhere. Few works from the Guardi studio
are signed, dated, or reliably documented,
and there has been a good deal of scholarly
controversy about certain works. The major
problem concerns the authorship of paintings representing the Story of Tobit that
decorate the organ loft of S. Raffaele in
Venice. Critical opinion is divided as to
whether these brilliant works, painted
with brushwork of breathtaking freedom,
are by Francesco or Gianantonio (there is
dispute also over the dating), but if they
are indeed by the latter, he too must rank
as a major figure. Giambattista *Tiepolo
was married to the sister of the Guardi
brothers, and it was possibly through his
influence that Gianantonio became a founder member of the Venetian Academy in
1756. Francesco was not elected until 1784,

during the presidency of his nephew Gian-domenico Tiepolo. After Francesco's death, the studio was inherited by his son **Giacomo Guardi** (1764–1835), who produced a large number of Venetian views, mainly drawings.

Guercino (Giovanni Francesco Barbieri) (1591–1666). One of the outstanding Italian painters and draughtsmen of the 17th century; his nickname Guercino ('Squinter') was given to him because of an eye defect that is said to have been caused by a childhood accident. He was born at Cento near Bologna and seems to have been mainly self-taught. His early work drew on a variety of north Italian sources, notably Ludovico *Carracci and Venetian painting, to create a highly individual style characterized by dramatic and capricious lighting, strong colour, and broad, vigorous brushwork. In 1621 one of his patrons, Cardinal Alessandro Ludovisi, became Pope Gregory XV and summoned him to Rome. Among other commissions there he painted the celebrated ceiling fresco of *Aurora* (1621) in the Casino of the Villa Ludovisi for Gregory's nephew, Cardinal Ludovico Ludovisi. This exuberant work, with its illusionistic architectural framework designed by Agostino *Tassi, is much more *Baroque in style than Guido *Reni's treatment of the subject of a decade earlier. On the death of the pope in 1623 Guercino returned to Cento, but his short stay in Rome introduced a more classical feeling to his work. This trend became more pronounced after he moved to Bologna in 1642 to take over the mantle of Reni, who died in that year. For the next quarter of a century, until his own death, he was Bologna's leading painter, and his late works can be remarkably similar to Reni's—calm and light in colouring, with little of the lively movement of his early style (*St Luke Displaying a Painting of the Virgin*, 1652, Nelson–Atkins Mus., Kansas City, Missouri). Guercino was one of the most brilliant draughtsmen of his age. In addition to preparatory studies for his paintings, he made many informal drawings for his own pleasure (including landscapes, genre scenes, and caricatures) and these—usually executed in pen and brown ink—often show remarkable freedom and vitality. The finest collection of his drawings is in the Royal Library at Windsor Castle.

Guérin, Pierre-Narcisse (1774–1833). French painter. He was one of the most successful French artists of his time, but his reputation did not long survive his death. In 1797 he won the *Prix de Rome, and his later distinctions included becoming director of the French Academy in Rome in 1822 and being created a baron in 1829. His style was derived mainly from J.-L. *David (who said, 'I think he has been eavesdropping at the door of my studio'), but his scenes from classical history and mythology are less severe and more stagy. Next to David he was the most sought-after teacher of his period, his many pupils including *Géricault and *Delacroix, and he was an important figure in the transition from *Neoclassicism to *Romanticism. As a teacher he laid particular emphasis on the painted sketch and was instrumental in establishing a sketch competition as a preliminary to the Prix de Rome.

Guggenheim, Solomon R. (1861–1949). American industrialist, collector, and philanthropist, a member of a famous family of financiers whose fortunes were based on the mining and smelting of metals. Like other members of his family, he devoted much of his vast wealth to philanthropy and in 1937 he founded the Solomon R. Guggenheim Foundation 'for the promotion and encouragement of art and education in art'. In 1943 he commissioned Frank Lloyd Wright to design a museum in New York City to house his collection, and the Solomon R. Guggenheim Museum was opened in 1959, a decade after the founder's death. It is renowned not only for the outstanding collection of late 19th-century and 20th-century art it contains, but also for the radical nature of the architecture, which marks a complete departure from traditional museum design; the exhibition space is a continuous spiral ramp, six 'storeys' high, encircling an open central space. It is architecturally exhilarating, but its suitability for displaying paintings and sculptures has been much questioned. Guggenheim's niece, **Peggy Guggenheim** (1898–1979), was a noted patron, collector, and dealer, who played an important role in promoting avant-garde art, in particular by helping to introduce *Surrealism to the USA and by furthering the career of many leading *Abstract Expressionists. She spent much of her life in Europe, but during its brief existence (1942–7) her Art of This Century gallery in New York was the main showcase for Abstract Expressionism in its formative period. Notorious for her loose living, she had affairs with several artists and in 1941 married and divorced Max *Ernst. Her own superb collection is open to the public in Venice under the administration of the Solomon R. Guggenheim Foundation. In 1997 a new Guggenheim Museum opened in Bilbao, Spain. Designed by the American architect Frank Gehry, it is one of the most spectacular buildings of the age—huge, eccentrically shaped, and clad largely in titanium. It is intended particularly for the display of works that are too large to be shown in the Guggenheim Museum in New York.

Guglielmo della Porta (d. 1577). Italian sculptor. He is first documented in Genoa, in 1534, but he spent most of his career in Rome. *Vasari says he moved there in 1537, but he is not documented in the city until 1546. The following year he succeeded *Sebastiano del Piombo as keeper of the papal seals. Guglielmo had a prolific and varied career, his work including several papal busts and a number of tombs in Roman churches, the most important being that of Paul III in St Peter's (1549–75). He also produced numerous small devotional and pagan statuettes and worked as a restorer and copier of *antique works. The major influence on his style was *Michelangelo and he had a penchant for reclining figures in the manner of the master's *Day* and *Night*, *Dawn* and *Evening* in the Medici Chapel, Florence.

Guido da Siena. Sienese painter active during the 13th century. Nothing is known of his life, and his only certain work is a *Madonna and Child* in the Palazzo Pubblico, Siena. The picture bears an inscription with the date 1221, but this has been the subject of much controversy, as stylistically the painting seems to belong about half a century later. It has been suggested that the inscription may have some commemorative purpose, the significance of which is now lost, rather than being a record of the date of execution. Although the painting is majestic in effect and follows *Byzantine conventions of *iconography, the figures to some extent relax the stiff linear patterns that had been conventional in central Italian painting up to that time. On the basis of this picture a number of other panels, most of which are in the Siena Pinacoteca, have been assigned to Guido or his school. Despite his great obscurity, he is regarded as sharing with *Coppo di Marcovaldo the honour of founding the Sienese School.

Guillaumin, Armand (1841–1927). French landscape painter, one of the minor figures of the *Impressionist group. Lack of success made him take a post with the department of bridges and causeways until he won a prize in a lottery in 1891 and was able to devote all his time to painting. Often his paintings are of industrial subjects, but he also painted seascapes. His style was bold and often brilliantly coloured. He was the last survivor of those who participated in the first Impressionist exhibition in 1874, dying the year after *Monet.

gum. A sticky liquid exuded by certain trees and shrubs, various types of which have been used in making paints from ancient times. The most commonly used is gum arabic, obtained from a species of acacia, which is the normal binding agent for watercolours.

Gunn, Sir James (1893–1964). British portrait painter. Gunn enjoyed a successful career with portraits of eminent soldiers, academics, judges, and so on, painted in a solid, forthright style. He was a more interesting painter in less traditional work, notably his portrait of the blind composer Delius (City AG, Bradford), which was the public's choice as 'picture of the year' at the *Royal Academy in 1933. Also well known is Gunn's *Conversation Piece at the Royal Lodge, Windsor, 1950* (NPG, London), showing George VI, Queen Elizabeth (the Queen Mother), and Princesses Elizabeth (later Elizabeth II) and Margaret.

Günther, Ignaz (1725–75). German sculptor. After a varied training culminating in several months at the Vienna Academy, he settled in Munich in 1754. He was one of the great woodcarvers of his age (occasionally he worked in other materials), combining an elegant *Rococo style with a highly emotional religious feeling. In 1759–62 he produced his chief work, the almost entire furnishing of the church at Rott-am-Inn.

Guston, Philip (1913–80). American painter. After travelling in Mexico in 1934, studying the work of *Orozco and *Rivera in particular, he settled in New York and from 1934 to 1941 worked as a muralist on the *Federal Art Project. In 1941 he moved to Iowa City to teach at the State University there, and from 1945 to 1947 he was artist-in-residence at Washington University, St Louis. After leaving New York he switched from mural to easel painting, and during the 1940s his work changed in another fundamental way, moving from social and political subjects to abstraction; by 1950 (when, after travels in Europe, he settled in New York again) he had eliminated all figurative elements from his work. His most characteristic paintings feature luminous patches of overlapping colours delicately brushed in the central area of a canvas of light background (*Dial*, 1956, Whitney Mus., New York). This manner of his has been described as 'Abstract Impressionism' and he was associated with the more lyrical wing of *Abstract Expressionism—he was the only member of the group who had already had a successful career as a figurative painter. During the 1960s shades of grey encroached on the earlier brilliant colours and vague naturalistic associations crept in, until in the 1970s he returned to figurative painting in a satirical, garishly coloured, cartoon-like style that has been seen as the source of *New Image Painting. His works in this manner included scenes of fantastic social comment, involving, for example, the Ku Klux Klan.

Gütersloh, Albert Paris. *See* FANTASTIC REALISM.

Gutfreund, Otto (1889–1927). Czech sculptor. After training in Prague, he spent several months in Paris, 1909–10. He studied under *Bourdelle but he was inspired more by paintings he saw by *Braque and *Picasso and he became one of the first artists to try to apply the principles of *Cubism to sculpture. On his return to Prague in 1911 he joined the Group of Plastic Artists (see ČAPEK), whose members attempted to fuse Cubism with *Expressionism. An example of his work from this time is *Cubist Bust* (1912–13, Tate, London). After the First World War he developed a more naturalistic style based on folk art. He committed suicide by drowning.

Guthrie, Sir James. *See* GLASGOW SCHOOL.

Guttuso, Renato (1912–87). Italian painter. He was a forceful personality and Italy's leading 20th-century exponent of *Social Realism; he never subordinated artistic quality to political propaganda, but his art was often the direct expression of his hatred of injustice and of the abuse of power. In 1931 he abandoned legal studies for painting, in which he was mainly self-taught. He settled in Rome in 1937 and in the following year became a founder member of the anti-Fascist association *Corrente. Fascism was not his only target, however, for he also pilloried the Mafia and in 1943 published a series of drawings protesting against the massacres that took place under the German occupation of Italy. After the war (in which he worked with the Resistance) he became a member of the *Fronte Nuovo delle Arti in 1946. His post-war works were often inspired by the struggles of the Sicilian peasantry, and his other subjects included the 1968 student riots in Paris, a city he often visited. Many of his paintings were large, with allegorical overtones, typically painted in a vigorous *Expressionist style.

Guys, Constantin (1802–92). French illustrator. In the earlier part of his career he travelled widely and adventurously, fighting in the Greek War of Independence in the 1820s, for example, and in 1855 he covered the Crimean War as a correspondent for the *Illustrated London News*. After he settled in Paris in the late 1850s, however, he became famous for his vigorous drawings of fashionable life, which were published in various journals. He seems to have been self-taught as an artist. In 1863 *Baudelaire immortalized him as 'The Painter of Modern Life' in his celebrated essay of that name. Many of the leading avant-garde painters of the day admired his work, including *Degas and *Manet, and because of his realistic approach to contemporary subjects and his liveliness of touch he has been seen as a precursor of *Impressionism. In spite of his renown, he had difficulty earning a living with his work and died in poverty at the age of 89.

H

Habsburg (or **Hapsburg**). One of the major ruling dynasties of European history, the members of which have included several important art patrons and collectors. The family can be traced back to the 10th century and it established a hereditary monarchy in Austria in the 13th century. From 1452 it held the title of Holy Roman Emperor almost continuously until the empire was dissolved by Napoleon in 1806. The family's territories reached their greatest extent in the early 16th century under Charles V, who—as a result of diplomacy, marriage, and conquest—ruled one of the largest empires ever created: in addition to its heartland in central Europe, it included Spain, the Kingdom of Naples and other parts of Italy, and most of the Netherlands, as well as vast colonial possessions in the Americas. When Charles abdicated in 1556 the empire was divided between his son Philip, who inherited Spain, the New World colonies, the Italian possessions, and the Netherlands, and his brother Ferdinand, who inherited the rest (the 'Austrian' territories), as well as the title of emperor. The Habsburgs ruled in Spain until 1700 and in Austria until 1918, when the upheavals of the First World War brought the dynasty to an end.

Maximilian I (1459–1519), who became emperor in 1493 and reigned until his death, was one of the most cultured rulers of his time (he was himself an accomplished writer) and the first of the great Habsburg patrons. He is sometimes known as the 'Last Knight', because in certain respects he represents a final flowering of the ways of the medieval world (he was, for example, his period's leading patron of armourers, and the graceful style of German armour characteristic of the time is known as Maximilian after him). In other ways, however, he was forward-looking, notably in his appreciation of the power of the printing press and the propaganda value of art. The most remarkable example of his use of visual propaganda was a huge woodcut triumphal arch, made up of more than a hundred blocks, celebrating his family's achievements; 700 copies were produced for distribution throughout

the empire. *Dürer, the designer-in-chief, finished his work in 1515, but the cutting of the blocks took two more years, and the printing was not finished until 1518. Among the other artists who worked for Maximilian were Hans *Burgkmair the Elder and Bernhard *Strigel. They often had to wait a long time for payment, for Maximilian was constantly in financial trouble. His tomb (or more strictly monument, as he is buried elsewhere) in the Hofkirche, Innsbruck, was begun in 1508 as a vast dynastic memorial, but the design was much truncated by the time it was completed more than half a century later. Various artists worked on it, including Peter *Vischer the Elder.

Maximilian was succeeded by his grandson **Charles** (1500–58), who ruled the empire as Charles V, 1519–56, and was also king of Spain as Charles I, 1516–56; he relinquished both titles two years before his death and retired to a life of religious devotion. By this time his unwieldy empire was becoming ungovernable, in the face of numerous problems, not least the spread of Protestantism. Charles had wide-ranging interests, and he collected maps, globes, and scientific instruments, as well as pictures, tapestries, books, arms and armour, coins, jewellery, and even featherwork from the Americas. His favourite painter was *Titian, who twice visited the imperial court at Augsburg, and the other artists he patronized included the sculptor Leone *Leoni and the architect Pedro *Machuca.

Charles's aunt, **Margaret of Austria** (1480–1530), and his sister, **Mary of Hungary** (1505–58), were successively regent of the Netherlands (1507–30 and 1530–56 respectively). Both of them were art lovers and each of them owned Jan van *Eyck's '*Arnolfini Marriage*' (1434, NG, London) for a time; Mary also owned another celebrated masterpiece of Early Netherlandish painting —Rogier van der *Weyden's *Descent from the Cross* (c.1440, Prado, Madrid). Bernard van *Orley served as court painter to both of them. Charles's nephew, **Maximilian II** (1527–76), who became emperor in 1564, was a devotee of the arts and learning and one of the main patrons of Giuseppe *Arcimboldo.

Arcimboldo also worked for Maximilian's son, **Rudolf II** (1552–1612), who became emperor in 1576 and was the most remarkable of all Habsburg patrons and collectors; he was indeed one of the most impassioned art lovers in history. Politically his career was a disaster: he was subject to fits of morbid depression and spent long periods in semiseclusion, making him incapable of governing effectively (in 1611 he was forced to abdicate as king of Bohemia in favour of his brother Mathias). However, his fervour for art and science turned his capital Prague into one of the leading cultural centres of Europe. His patronage attracted a roster of distinguished artists, scientists, and scholars to the city (including the astronomers Tycho Brahe and Johann Kepler) and his collection of pictures was one of the greatest ever assembled. The artists who worked for him in Prague included Hans von *Aachen, Roelandt *Savery, Bartholomeus *Spranger, and Adriaen de *Vries. He also commissioned work from some of the leading Italian masters of the day, including *Barocci, *Tintoretto, and *Veronese. Among earlier artists he particularly loved the work of *Bruegel and Dürer. In addition to paintings and sculptures, he collected applied art and curiosities of all kinds.

Rudolf's collections were dispersed after his death, but several of the paintings he owned are in the *Kunsthistorisches Museum, Vienna, which is the greatest monument to the artistic interests of the Habsburgs. The real father of its picture collection was Archduke **Leopold William** (1614–62). He was governor of the Spanish Netherlands from 1646 to 1656 and during this period at the hub of the international art market he bought pictures on a grand scale, taking advantage of the political upheavals of the time (including the dispersal of the collection of Charles I of England after his execution in 1649). His court painter, David *Teniers the Younger, produced several pictures showing his remarkable collection. It was particularly rich in Italian (especially Venetian) pictures of the 16th century and in Flemish pictures of the 15th to the 17th century.

Among the later Habsburg patrons were **Maria Theresa** (1717–80; Holy Roman Empress 1740–65), who bought numerous pictures, particularly by *Rubens, and patronized *Bellotto, and her son **Joseph II** (1741–90; reigned from 1765), who opened the imperial collections to the public in 1781. Joseph was succeeded by his brother **Leopold II** (1747–92). He reigned for only two years before his death, but earlier, as Grand Duke Pietro Leopoldo, he had played an important role in the artistic life of Florence (see UFFIZI).

The Habsburg monarchs of Spain included two patrons and collectors who rank among the greatest in history, **Philip II** (1527–98; reigned from 1556) and his grandson **Philip IV** (1605–65; reigned from 1621). Philip II, the son of Charles V, lived an austere life in many ways—he was intensely religious and obsessively devoted to bureaucratic paperwork—but he also had a genuine passion for art. The greatest artistic memorial of his reign is the *Escorial, the huge monastery-palace near Madrid, begun in 1563. Philip imported many Italian artists to work on its decoration, and he also collected pictures on a scale that had not previously been seen in Spain. By the end of his life he owned about 1,500 and they were the basis of the Spanish royal collection that now forms the heart of the *Prado. His favourite living artist was Titian and he was the most important patron of his later career. Among earlier painters, he particularly admired *Bosch. In addition to paintings he also collected books and manuscripts, as well as sculpture, tapestries, arms and armour, antiquities, and other objects. At the beginning of his reign, Spain was at the height of its power and wealth, but he suffered various setbacks in his later years, including the defeat of the Spanish Armada in 1588, and by the end of his life the country was in decline.

Under Philip IV this political decline accelerated, but his reign witnessed a glorious flowering of Spanish art. His favourite artist was *Velázquez, who produced numerous portraits of him and his family, and he employed many other eminent artists of this golden age, particularly on the decoration of royal buildings. In addition to the Escorial, these included the Buen Retiro palace, built in Madrid in the 1630s, and the Torre de la Parada, a hunting lodge near Madrid that Philip enlarged in 1635–7. Rubens and his collaborators produced more than a hundred paintings for the Torre de la Parada, and so much art was required to furnish the Buen Retiro that large numbers of pictures were commissioned from the Netherlands and Italy (*Claude was among the artists involved) as well as from Spanish painters, including *Mayno (who had taught Philip drawing when he was a child), *Pereda, and *Zurbarán. Philip also bought pictures by earlier artists, including works by some of the greatest Renaissance masters, notably *Raphael and Titian.

Philip was succeeded by his sickly son **Charles II** (1661–1700; reigned from 1665), whose mental and physical infirmities reflected generations of Habsburg inbreeding. He inherited some of the family love of art, and his court painters included *Carreño de Miranda, *Coello, and *Palomino. In 1692 he brought Luca *Giordano to Spain to work at the Escorial. By the time Charles died childless in 1700, Spain's power had declined so much that Louis XIV of France was able to install his grandson (Charles's great-nephew) as Philip V, bringing the Spanish Habsburg line to an end and provoking the War of the Spanish Succession.

Hackaert, Jan (1628–c.1685). Dutch landscape painter, active mainly in his native Amsterdam. Most of his work consists of Italianate landscapes and woodland scenes. He travelled in Switzerland in the 1650s, but there is no documentary evidence that he visited Italy; however, he captured the golden Italian sunlight so successfully that his *Lake of Zurich* (c.1673, Rijksmuseum, Amsterdam) was long thought to be a view of Lake Trasimene in Umbria. The figures in his paintings are often the work of other artists, notably *Berchem and Adriaen van de *Velde.

Hackert, Jakob Philipp (1737–1807). German landscape painter, active in Italy from 1768. In 1786 he became court painter to Ferdinand IV of Naples. He was a sensitive upholder of the *ideal landscape tradition of *Claude, which he seasoned with touches of *Romanticism. Much of his large output was devoted to views of famous sites, which were eagerly sought by foreign visitors to Italy. *Goethe met Hackert in 1787 and edited his memoirs (published 1811). His work is exceptionally well represented at Attingham Park in Shropshire. He came from a family of artists and often collaborated with his brother **Johann Gottlieb Hackert** (1744–73).

Hadfield, Maria. *See* COSWAY.

Haecht, Willem van. *See* VERHAECHT.

Hague School. Informal group of Dutch artists who worked mainly in The Hague between about 1860 and 1900. The group is particularly associated with landscapes and beach scenes, but the members also painted street scenes, views of everyday life, and church interiors. In some ways this was a *Romantic revival of the 17th-century tradition, and this romantically nostalgic strain—particularly in pictures made during the first years the group worked together—is one of the things that distinguishes them from their French counterparts, the painters of the *Barbizon School and the *Impressionists. They shared with the great Dutch landscapists of the 17th century a special sensitivity in recording light and atmospheric effects. Leading members of the Hague School included *Bosboom, *Israëls, the *Maris brothers, *Mauve, *Mesdag, and *Weissenbruch. The group was the leading force in Dutch painting in the late 19th century and van *Gogh was strongly influenced by Mauve and Israëls.

Hals, Frans (1582/3–1666). Dutch painter. He was born in Antwerp, the son of Flemish parents who moved to Holland after the city was captured by the Spaniards in 1585. His parents had settled in Haarlem by 1591 and he spent the rest of his long life there. He was twice married, had at least ten children, and was constantly in financial trouble. *Houbraken says he was 'filled to the gills every evening', but there is no real foundation for the popular image of him as a drunken wife-beater. His second wife, however, was more than once in trouble for brawling. During his last years he was destitute and the municipal authorities of Haarlem awarded him a small annual stipend four years before his death.

Hals was the first great artist of the 17th-century Dutch School and is regarded as one of the most brilliant of all portraitists. Almost all his works are portraits and even those that are not (some *genre scenes, and an occasional religious picture) are portrait-like in character. He is said to have been taught in Haarlem by Karel van *Mander, but there is no discernible influence from him in Hals's early works, which are not numerous or well documented. The earliest dated picture associated with him is *Jacobus Zaffius* (1611, Hals Mus., Haarlem; perhaps a copy), and on stylistic evidence a few other paintings can be dated around the same time. Nothing he did before 1616 anticipated the way he shattered well-established traditions that year with his life-size group portrait of the *Banquet of the Officers of the St George Militia Company* (Hals Mus.). There is no real precedent in either his own work or that of his predecessors for the vigorous composition and characterization of this picture, which has become a symbol of the strength and healthy optimism of the men who established the new Dutch Republic. It demonstrates to the full his remarkable ability—his greatest gift as a portraitist—to capture a sense of fleeting movement and expression and thereby convey a compelling feeling of life.

From 1616 onwards there are numerous dated or documented works by Hals and his artistic development is clear. He was at the height of his popularity in the 1620s and 1630s. During these decades he made five large group portraits of civic guards; one (finished by Pieter *Codde) is in the Rijksmuseum and the others are in the museum named after Hals in Haarlem, the only place where one can get a comprehensive view of his range and power. In the 1630s his compositions became simpler and monochromatic effects took the place of the bright colours of the earlier paintings (*Lucas de Clercq* and *Feyntje van Steenkiste*, 1635, Rijksmuseum, Amsterdam). The group portrait of the *Regents of the St Elizabeth Hospital* (1641, Hals Mus.) sets the key for the sober restraint of the late period, when his pictures became darker and his brushstrokes more economical. His career culminated in his group portraits of the *Regents* and the *Regentesses of the Old Men's Alms House* (*c.*1664, Hals Mus.), which rank among the most moving portraits ever painted. By this time Hals was using in his commissioned portraits the bold brushwork and the *alla prima* technique that early in his career he reserved for genre pictures. No drawings by him are known and he presumably worked straight on to the canvas.

Hals had two painter brothers and five painter sons, but the only artist of substance among them was his brother **Dirk** (1591–

1656), who painted charming small interior scenes. Apart from his sons, Hals taught numerous pupils, including (with varying degrees of certainty) Judith *Leyster, Jan Miense *Molenaer, Adriaen van *Ostade, Adriaen *Brouwer, and Philips *Wouwerman. His reputation did not long outlive him, however, and it was only in the second half of the 19th century that there was a renewed appreciation of his genius. The spontaneity of his work appealed to the generation of the *Impressionists, and from about 1870 to about 1920 he was one of the most popular of the Old Masters, becoming a model for society portraitists. Lord Hertford's purchase of his most famous work, *The Laughing Cavalier* (1624, Wallace Coll., London), in 1865 for the then enormous sum of 51,000 francs (more than six times the auction estimate) was a milestone in the revival of his fortunes, and the buoyant confidence of his paintings later made him a particular favourite with the new generation of fabulously rich American collectors—self-made men—who were beginning to dominate the picture market. This explains why so many works by him are in American collections.

Hamilton, Gavin (1723–98). Scottish painter, archaeologist, and picture-dealer. From 1748 he lived mainly in Rome, where he was a leading member of the *Neoclassical circle of *Mengs and *Winckelmann. As an artist he concentrated on *history paintings, and he is one of the few British artists (with *Barry and the Anglo-Americans *Copley and *West) to make a significant contribution in this field. He was particularly drawn to Homeric subjects, in his treatment of which he was influenced by *Poussin as well as by the *antique (*Achilles Lamenting the Death of Patroclus*, 1763, NG, Edinburgh). His pictures in this vein were never very numerous and today are generally regarded as ponderous, but they became well known through engravings, and greatly influenced the development of the Neoclassical style amongst both his contemporaries and the younger generation, including J.-L. *David. His occasional portraits generally appeal more to modern taste (*The 8th Duke of Hamilton with Dr John Moore and Ensign John Moore*, 1775–7, NPG, Edinburgh). Hamilton met and encouraged virtually all the British artists who visited Rome in the second half of the 18th century, but he remained better known on the Continent than in Britain, where his name was more familiar for his lucrative activities in selling Old Masters and classical antiquities. From about 1769 he directed archaeological excavations himself, notably at Hadrian's Villa at Tivoli. Gavin Hamilton is not to be confused with **Gawen Hamilton** (c.1697–1737), a minor portrait painter remembered for his *Conversation of Virtuosi at the Kings Armes* (1735, NPG, London), which shows himself and several other artists of the day.

Hamilton, Richard (1922–). British painter, printmaker, teacher, exhibition organizer, and writer, one of the leading pioneers of *Pop art. As a young man he worked in advertising and commercial art and he is best known for his montages featuring scenes from the fields of advertisement and contemporary life, notably *Just what is it that makes today's homes so different, so appealing?* (1956, Kunsthalle, Tübingen). This photomontage is sometimes considered to be the first Pop art work. Hamilton has had a distinguished career as a teacher, notably at King's College, Newcastle upon Tyne (which later became Newcastle University), 1953–66, and has organized several exhibitions, including 'The Almost Complete Works of Marcel *Duchamp' at the Tate Gallery, London, in 1966. An anthology of his writings, *Collected Works*, appeared in 1982. *See also* INDEPENDENT GROUP.

Hammershøi, Vilhelm (1864–1916). Danish painter, active mainly in his native Copenhagen. He painted portraits, architectural subjects (including two murals for Copenhagen Town Hall), and landscapes, but is best known for his quiet interior scenes. They are painted in muted colours, and have a certain affinity with *Vermeer, often featuring a single standing or seated figure. Most of Hammershøi's paintings are in Denmark, but two of his interiors are in Tate Modern, London.

Hanson, Duane (1925–96). American sculptor. Hanson was probably the best-known exponent of *Superrealism in sculpture, producing minutely detailed fibreglass resin figures dressed in real clothes and accompanied by real props. He commented pungently on the depressing or tasteless aspects of everyday American life, his subjects including down-and-outs, exhausted shoppers, or, in one of his most famous works, a pair of fat, ageing, and garishly dressed sightseers (*Tourists*, 1970, Scottish NG of Modern Art, Edinburgh).

happening. A form of entertainment, often carefully planned but usually including some degree of spontaneity, in which an artist performs or directs an event combining elements of theatre and the visual arts. The term was coined in 1959 by Allan *Kaprow, to whom the concept of the happening was bound up with his rejection of traditional principles of craftsmanship and permanence in the arts. Happenings had close affinities with *Performance art (the two terms have sometimes been used more or less synonymously) and they were not restricted like environments to the confines of a gallery or some other specific site. The composer and artist John Cage (1912–92), one of Kaprow's teachers, organized a performance at *Black Mountain College in 1952 that has sometimes been described as the first happening. Kaprow's own first happening was *Intermission Piece*, staged at the Reuben Gallery, New York, in 1959; in October of the same year he performed *18 Happenings in 6 Parts* at the same venue, and this was the first event to be actually titled a happening. Apart from Cage and Kaprow, the artists chiefly responsible for the development of the form in the USA include Jim *Dine, Roy *Lichtenstein, Claes *Oldenburg, and Robert *Rauschenberg. Outside America, the happening was widely exploited during the 1960s and 1970s—in Japan, for example, and in Europe. The term has often been used to cover staged demonstrations for political or social propaganda, as for example in the work of the *Fluxus group (whose happenings in Germany were usually called *Aktions*).

Hard-Edge Painting. A type of abstract painting in which forms, although not necessarily geometrical, have sharp contours and are executed in flat colours. It was one of the types of painting that developed as a reaction against the spontaneity and painterly handling of *Abstract Expressionism (*see* POST-PAINTERLY ABSTRACTION). Major exponents have included Ellsworth *Kelly and Kenneth *Noland. The term was coined by the American critic Jules Langsner in 1958.

Haring, Keith. *See* GRAFFITI ART.

Harnett, William Michael (1848–92). American still-life painter. He was born in Ireland and brought to America as a child, living first in Philadelphia and then from 1869 in New York (with the exception of a stay in Europe, 1880–6). He specialized in elaborate *trompe-l'œil compositions, often involving firearms or musical instruments (*After the Hunt*, 1885, California Palace of the Legion of Honor, San Francisco). Although his works were long popular with the public, they were generally dismissed by critics as mere sleight of hand until about 1940, when they began to win favour for their strength of composition.

Harpignies, Henri (1819–1916). French landscape painter (and occasional print-maker). He did not take up painting ser-iously until 1846, but he was then very prolific and won considerable success and fame. He is sometimes classed with the *Barbizon School, but his work shows more specifically the influence of *Corot.

Harris, Lawren Stewart (1885–1970). Canadian painter, active mainly in Toronto and (from 1940) in Vancouver. From 1904 to 1908 he studied in Berlin, where his work was influenced by *Expressionism. Early in his career his favourite subjects were city-scapes and views of houses, but in about 1911 he also took up landscape and from 1920 (when he was one of the founder members of the *Group of Seven) this became his main interest. Harris was a fol-lower of Theosophy and he used spectacular scenery as a way of expressing spiritual values. To this end he sought out the most overpowering landscapes he could find—in the Rockies and even the Arctic. The tran-scendental quality in his work was main-tained when he turned to abstraction in the 1930s. In the later part of his career he became a patriarchal figure in Canadian painting.

Hartley, Marsden (1877–1943). American painter, whose work represents a diverse yet also highly personal response to Euro-pean modernism. In 1909 he was given a one-man exhibition by *Stieglitz, and in 1912 help from Stieglitz and Arthur B. *Davies enabled him to travel to Europe— the beginning of the almost compulsive travels that lasted throughout his life (he was a lonely, reclusive, rather haunted char-acter who never achieved much worldly success). Apart from a visit to New York in 1913, he lived in Europe until 1916. During these years he created a distinctive semi-abstract manner seen most famously in *Painting No. 5* (1914–15, Whitney Mus., New York); this work represents a remarkably personal synthesis of modernist trends, being more closely structured and objective than German *Expressionism and more freely patterned and highly coloured than French *Cubism. In 1916 Hartley returned to America, and in 1918 said that he had grown weary of 'emotional excitement in art'. He turned to landscape as his principal subject, working in a more representational but still highly formalized style. In 1921 he returned to Europe, stayed there for a decade, then continued his wandering life in the early 1930s, visiting Mexico in 1932, for example, when he painted a series of pictures of the volcano Popacatepetl. In 1934 he settled in his native Maine. The work of his final years (usually rugged mountain and coastal scenes) was character-ized by blunt, block-like forms, showing a powerful feeling for the beauty and grand-eur of nature.

Hartung, Hans (1904–89). German-born abstract painter and printmaker who settled in Paris in 1935 and became a French citizen in 1946. During the Second World War he fought in the French Foreign Legion; he was badly wounded in 1944 and had a leg amputated without anaesthetic. Hartung was an individualist who pursued his own path, unconcerned with fashion and sus-tained by what he called 'stubborn staying power'. He had begun painting abstracts in 1922, when he was only 17, and he de-veloped a sensuous, freely improvised style that anticipated post-war developments. It was only after the war that he made a repu-tation and was hailed as one of the pioneers of *Art Informel. His fame was at its peak around 1960, in which year he was joint winner of the main painting prize at the Venice *Biennale. In some of his paintings the vibrant thick black lines and blotches have a kinship with the work of Franz *Kline, but Kline is more brusquely ener-getic and less subtle.

Hassam, Childe (1859–1935). American painter and printmaker. He was one of his country's earliest and most accomplished exponents of *Impressionism, which he discovered on his second visit to Europe in 1886–9. On his return to America he settled in New York, and the life of the city became one of his main sources of subject matter; scenes of rainy streets were something of a speciality. Another favourite theme was a woman in an interior. His early paintings are fresh and clear but sometimes rather slick and saccharine. After the turn of the century, his style tended towards greater simplification and flatness in composition and his colour became lusher—somewhat in the manner of *Bonnard. Hassam was immensely prolific in oils, watercolour, pastel, and a variety of drawing media; in his fifties he also took up printmaking seriously, producing a large number of etchings and lithographs (notably harbour scenes in a style reminiscent of *Whistler). He received many honours and died a wealthy man, although by this time he was seen in artistic circles as a very conservative figure. *See also* TEN, THE.

hatching. The use of closely spaced parallel lines to suggest shading. The technique is found mainly in drawing and engraving, but is also used, for example, in *tempera painting. When intersecting sets of lines are used, the term cross-hatching is applicable.

Hausmann, Raoul. *See* DADA and PHOTO-MONTAGE.

Haworth, Jann. *See* BLAKE, SIR PETER.

Haydon, Benjamin Robert (1786–1846). English painter and writer, a mediocre artist but a fascinating personality. Inspired by *Reynolds's *Discourses*, he aimed to bring a new seriousness to British art by producing historical and religious work in the *Grand Manner and through them to educate and improve public taste. His life, which was punctuated by bankruptcy, imprisonment, and disputes with patrons, was a story of bombastic frustration and stubborn opposition to the establishment (particularly the *Royal Academy), as he fought continuously for personal recognition and argued for the social purpose of art. However, his talents fell far short of his lofty ambitions, his multi-figure compositions degenerating into turgid melodrama. His great monument, rather, is the massive collection of

autobiographical writings he left behind him (various editions have been published), which gives fascinating insights into the contemporary artistic scene and paints a vividly detailed picture of his disturbed mind and tragicomical life. He was closely linked with the *Romantic movement in literature, particularly with William Wordsworth, who wrote a sonnet to him, and with John Keats, painting portraits of both of them (NPG, London), and but for his lack of talent he would exemplify all the traits traditionally ascribed to the Romantic concept of genius. In true Romantic fashion his death came by suicide.

Hayez, Francesco (1791–1882). Italian painter, active mainly in Milan. Hayez was the most important figure in the transition from *Neoclassicism to *Romanticism in Italian painting, but his Romantic leanings come out mainly in subject matter rather than in technique, the clear outlines he favoured revealing his training in Rome in the circle of *Canova and *Ingres. He painted religious, historical, and mythological works in a vein owing something to *Delacroix and *Delaroche, and portraits that are sometimes thought worthy of comparison with those of Ingres. Many of the most eminent Italians of the day sat for him. For many years he taught at the Brera in Milan (he became director in 1860) and he exercised great influence on his pupils. The Brera has an outstanding collection of his work.

Hayman, Francis (*c.*1708–76). English painter and book illustrator. He was the most versatile British painter of his period, his work including subjects from literature and the theatre (notably Shakespeare), scenes of rural folklore, and portraits (his *conversation pieces anticipated those of *Gainsborough, who early in his career probably worked with him). Hayman also had the reputation of being 'unquestionably the best historical painter in the kingdom before the arrival of *Cipriani' (Edward Edwards, *Anecdotes of Painters...*,1808), but little of his work in this vein survives. In addition he was a prolific designer of book illustrations, sometimes collaborating with *Gravelot. His biggest undertaking (*c.*1741) was the painting of about 50 large pictures to decorate the supper boxes and pavilions at Vauxhall Gardens, the fashionable

London pleasure resort. Few of these survive intact (two are in the Victoria and Albert Museum, London), but several are known through drawings and engravings; the subjects included children's games, popular festivities, and scenes from plays. Amiable and popular with his fellow artists, Hayman was president of the *Society of Artists, 1766–8, and became a foundation member of the *Royal Academy in 1768; he was appointed librarian in 1771. His best work has a certain *Rococo charm, but there is some justification in Horace *Walpole's comment that his paintings are 'easily distinguishable by the large noses and shambling legs of his figures'.

Hayter, Sir George (1792–1871). English historical and portrait painter. The son of a *miniaturist, **Charles Hayter** (1761–1835), he studied at the *Royal Academy Schools and in Rome. In 1837 he was appointed portrait and history painter to Queen Victoria, and on the death of *Wilkie in 1841 he was made 'principal painter in ordinary to the queen'. He is known chiefly for his royal portraits and his huge groups (*House of Commons, 1833*, 1833–43, NPG, London), unexciting in their handling, but composed with dexterity and accomplished grandiloquence. In spite of his royal favour he was never a member of the Royal Academy, seemingly because, after an unfortunate early marriage, he lived with a woman who was not his wife.

Hayter, S. W. (Stanley William) (1901–88). British printmaker and painter, a descendant of Sir George *Hayter. He spent most of his life in Paris, where in 1927 he founded an experimental workshop for the graphic arts—Atelier 17—that played a central role in the 20th-century revival of the print as an independent art form. (The name was adopted in 1933 when Hayter moved his establishment from its original home to 17 rue Campagne-Première.) In 1940–50 he lived in New York, taking Atelier 17 with him. Hayter was a chemist by training and had an unrivalled knowledge of the technicalities of printmaking, on which he wrote two major books, *New Ways of Gravure* (1949) and *About Prints* (1962). Although his historical importance has long been acknowledged (probably no modern British artist has been so influential internationally), it is only recently that his own work has won

him belated recognition as one of the outstanding graphic artists of his time. His prints are varied in technique and style, but most characteristically are influenced by the abstract vein of *Surrealism and are notable for their experiments with texture and colour.

Hazlitt, William (1778–1830). English critic. He is known mainly for his literary criticism, but he also wrote much on the fine arts and he ranks as the most important British writer on the subject between *Reynolds and *Ruskin. Early in his career he worked briefly as a portraitist (*Charles Lamb*, 1804, NPG, London), but he lived mainly by journalism, writing for numerous newspapers and journals. He was a *Romantic in outlook, placing more importance on the role of genius in artistic creation than on rules or theories. Thus he admired Reynolds's paintings, but attacked his ideas. A notable feature of Hazlitt's writing is that (unlike most previous art criticism) it was written for the general reader rather than for the connoisseur or practising artist.

Heartfield, John (Helmut Herzfelde) (1891–1968). German designer, painter, and journalist, a leading light of *Dada in Berlin, best known as one of the pioneers and perhaps the greatest of all exponents of *photomontage. With *Grosz he Anglicized his name during the First World War as a protest against German nationalistic fervour and his finest works are brilliantly satirical attacks—often in the form of book covers and posters—against militarism and Nazism. Harassed by the Nazis he left Germany in 1938 and moved to London, where his work included designs for Penguin Books. He returned to Germany in 1950 and died in Berlin, his native city.

Heath, Adrian (1920–92). British abstract painter. In 1949 and 1951 he visited St Ives, where he met Ben *Nicholson, and he formed a link between the *St Ives School and London-based *Constructivists such as Victor *Pasmore and Kenneth and Mary *Martin, with whom he was also associated. During the early 1950s he was an important figure in promoting abstract art—by organizing collective exhibitions at his London studio (at 22 Fitzroy Street) in 1951, 1952, and 1953, and by writing a short popular book on the subject, *Abstract Painting: Its*

Origin and Meaning (1953), which begins with the sentence: 'There seems to be little understanding of the values of abstract painting and consequently no general appreciation of its qualities.' Heath's paintings of this time featured large, block-like slabs of colour, heavily brushed. He also made a few constructions. Later his paintings became freer and more dynamic.

Heckel, Erich (1883–1970). German painter and graphic artist, one of the founders of Die *Brücke. His work was somewhat more lyrical than that of the other members of the group and he showed a special concern for depicting sickness and inner anguish. His landscapes, too, sometimes have a decorative quality foreign to most German *Expressionism. During the First World War, when he worked as a medical orderly in Flanders, his work became more melancholic and tragic. After the war, however, his painting lost much of its intensity, with pastel tones replacing the bold, sometimes harsh colours he had earlier used. In 1937 his work was declared *degenerate by the Nazis and in 1944 his Berlin studio was destroyed in an air raid. Heckel then moved to Hemmenhofen on Lake Constance. From 1949 until his retirement in 1955 he taught at the Karlsruhe Academy. Apart from *Kirchner, Heckel was the most prolific printmaker among the Brücke artists, producing more than 400 woodcuts, about 400 lithographs, and nearly 200 etchings, mainly in the period 1903–23.

Heda, Willem Claesz. (*c*.1594–1680/2). Dutch still-life painter, active in his native Haarlem. He and Pieter *Claesz. are the most important representatives of *ontbijt* (breakfast piece) painting in the Netherlands. His overall grey-green or brownish tonalities are very similar to those of Claesz., but Heda's work was usually more highly finished and his taste was more aristocratic. He showed a preference for ham, mincemeat pie, and oysters, and after 1629 never included a herring in his pictures. His son **Gerrit** (d. before 1702) was his pupil and a close imitator of his style.

Heem, Jan Davidsz. de (1606–83/4). One of the greatest Dutch still-life painters. He was born in Utrecht and active mainly in Antwerp, where he settled in about 1635. His early pictures are in the style of Balthasar van der *Ast and he also studied the restrained and simple works of the Haarlem still-life artists *Claesz. and *Heda. In Antwerp, however, he turned to a different idiom, producing splendid flower pieces and large compositions of exquisitely laid tables in the opulent spirit of Flemish *Baroque art. His work formed a link between the Dutch and Flemish still-life traditions and he is claimed by both schools. He came from a large family of painters and his many followers in Flanders and Holland included his sons **Cornelis de Heem** (1631–95) and **Jan Jansz. de Heem** (1650–after 1695).

Heemskerck, Maerten van (1498–1574). Netherlandish painter and draughtsman, born at Heemskerck and active mainly in nearby Haarlem, where he was the leading artist of the day. The most important part of his training was with Jan van *Scorel in Utrecht, *c*.1527–9. Although Heemskerck was only three years younger than Scorel and was a mature man when he entered his studio (he had already studied with two other teachers), the experience left a distinctive mark on him. In some pictures, particularly portraits, experts still have difficulty differentiating their hands. As a rule, however, Heemskerck's paintings are more crowded and nervous than Scorel's balanced and harmonious compositions. Equally significant for Heemskerck's development was a visit to Italy (1532–6), where he was overwhelmed by *Michelangelo and deeply impressed by the remains of ancient buildings and sculpture, of which he made sensitive drawings (some of them in a sketchbook that is now in the Kupferstich-kabinett, Berlin); he later included a view of the Colosseum in the background of his arresting *Self-Portrait* (1553, Fitzwilliam Mus., Cambridge). After his return to the Netherlands, the impact of Michelangelo (and of the *Laocoön) is clearly seen in such forceful, emotive works as the *Crucifixion* (1540, Linköping Cathedral). Later his style became more restrained, but sometimes no less eloquent, as in the *Lamentation* (1566, Prinsenhof Mus., Delft), a work of great pathos. In addition to his paintings, Heemskerck made designs for hundreds of prints, and through these he played a major role in disseminating *Mannerism in northern Europe.

Heidelberg School. Group of Australian painters who worked together at Heidelberg, Victoria (at the time a village, now a suburb of Melbourne), from 1886 to about 1900. Tom *Roberts (the dominant figure) and Arthur *Streeton were among the members. The work of the group, based on the *Impressionist ideal of painting in the open air, featured local subject matter and was associated with the emergence of a distinctive Australian literature. By 1900 the group had broken up, many of the leading members having gone to Europe, but its vision of Australian life and landscape came to dominate the country's painting in the early 20th century and inspired many other artists in later decades.

Heizer, Michael. *See* LAND ART.

Held, Al (1928–). American painter. His early work was in the prevailing *Abstract Expressionist idiom, being particularly influenced by Jackson *Pollock. From about 1960, however, he began to develop a more individual style characterized by clean-edged, bold, brightly coloured geometrical forms. It had affinities with *Hard-Edge Painting, but Held's work was distinguished by his use of very heavily textured paint. He often worked on a huge scale, giving his paintings an extremely forceful physical impact. In 1967 he began making black-and-white paintings, using white linear structures on a black ground or black lines on a white ground to create overlapping and interlocking box-like forms that demonstrate his interest in Renaissance perspective. In the 1980s he reintroduced colour with a vengeance, as in his 17 m (55 ft) long mural *Mantegna's Edge* (1983, Southland Center, Dallas), a work of tremendous high-keyed vigour.

Hellenistic. A term applied to Greek culture in the late 4th to late 1st century BC, conventionally from 323 BC, when Alexander the Great died, to 27 BC, when Augustus became the first Roman emperor. During this period Greece itself had lost its political importance as Rome rose to power, but Greek culture was adopted by diverse peoples in the Mediterranean world and beyond. Hellenistic art is more varied in inspiration than that of the *Classical age which preceded it, and the sculpture of the period is often remarkable for its technical bravura and overt display of emotion, as in the celebrated *Laocoön*, the most famous of Hellenistic works of art. After original

Greek works of the Classical period became widely known in the course of the 19th century much Hellenistic art was generally dismissed as decadent, but it is now recognized as a rich field of study.

Helst, Bartholomeus van der (*c*.1613–70). Dutch portrait painter, born in Haarlem and active in Amsterdam. In the 1640s he took over from *Rembrandt as the most popular portraitist in the city, his detailed, tasteful, and slightly flattering likenesses appealing more to the fashionable burghers than the master's work, which was becoming more individual and introspective. Van der Helst was highly influential during his lifetime. For example, Rembrandt's talented pupils *Bol and *Flinck abandoned the style of their master in order to follow his more popular manner. His reputation endured into the next century and as late as 1781 *Reynolds wrote that his *Banquet of the Amsterdam Civic Guard in Celebration of the Peace of Münster* (1648, Rijksmuseum, Amsterdam) 'is, perhaps, the first picture of portraits in the world', adding that it as far exceeded his expectations as Rembrandt's *Night Watch* fell below them.

Hemessen, Jan Sanders van (active 1519–56). Netherlandish painter, born in Hemessen and active mainly in nearby Antwerp, where he was the outstanding artist between the death of *Massys in 1530 and the emergence of *Bruegel in the 1550s. After visiting Italy early in his career, he was established in Antwerp by 1524. Like his contemporary *Marinus van Reymerswaele he specialized in scenes exposing human vanities and follies, such as greed and loose living (*The Prodigal Son*, 1536, Mus. Royaux, Brussels). The figures in these compositions are muscular and strongly three-dimensional, placed close to the *picture plane. Although the subjects are often religious, the pictures typically have a strong feeling of everyday life and they helped to found the Flemish tradition of *genre painting. Hemessen also painted portraits, as did his daughter and pupil **Catharina van Hemessen** (1528–after 1587).

Henri, Robert (1865–1929). American painter, teacher, and writer, a major figure in combating conservative attitudes in American art in the early 20th century. From 1886 to 1888 he trained at the Pennsylvania Academy of the Fine Arts,

Philadelphia, under Thomas Anshutz (1851–1912), who passed on the tradition of Thomas *Eakins, an artist Henri came to admire deeply. In 1888–91 he lived in Paris, studying mainly at the *Académie Julian. After returning to Philadelphia he became the leader of a circle of young arists— *Glackens, *Luks, *Shinn, *Sloan—that later became the nucleus of The *Eight and the *Ashcan School. In 1895–7 and 1898–1900 he again lived in Paris, then in 1900 settled in New York. There he became an outstanding teacher, first at the New York School of Art, 1902–9, then at his own school, 1909–12, at the Modern School of the Ferrer Center (a radical educational establishment), 1911–18, and finally at the *Art Students League, 1915–28. The essence of his teaching was that art should grow from life, not from theories. He said that he wanted his own paintings to be 'as clear and as simple and sincere as is humanly possible', and he was a powerful force in turning young American painters away from academism to look at the rich subject matter provided by modern urban life; indeed he was 'regarded by many of his contemporaries as the most influential single force affecting the development of American art in the generation preceding the *Armory Show of 1913' (William Innes Homer, *Robert Henri and his Circle*, 1969). Henri was open-minded about the new developments seen at the Armory Show but he was not interested in experiment for experiment's sake and his own painting was little affected by it. His early work had been *Impressionist, but in the 1890s he adopted a darker palette, with rapid slashing brushwork geared to creating a sense of vitality and immediacy. From 1909 his work became more colourful again. Apart from scenes of urban life, he painted many portraits, and also landscapes and seascapes (which have been rather neglected). He made frequent visits to Europe and found inspiration there for figure studies of picturesque characters—Irish peasants, gypsies, and so on. His paintings are dashing but rather superficial and they are generally regarded as much less important than his teaching and crusading. Henri wrote numerous articles on art and in 1923 published *The Art Spirit*, a collection of his letters, lectures, and aphorisms, in which art is seen as an expression of love for life.

Hepworth, Dame Barbara (1903–75). British sculptor, one of the most important figures in the development of abstract art in Britain. She trained at Leeds School of Art, where she became a friend of Henry *Moore, and at the *Royal College of Art. Her early sculptures were quasi-naturalistic and had much in common with Moore's work (*Doves*, 1927, Manchester AG), but she already showed a tendency to submerge detail in simple forms, and by the early 1930s her work had become entirely abstract. She worked both in wood and stone, and she described an important aspect of her early career as being 'the excitement of discovering the nature of carving'. In this preference for *direct carving she was again united with Moore, but whereas his abstractions always remained based on natural forms, Hepworth's were often entirely unrepresentational in origin. Yet she consistently professed a *Romantic attitude of emotional affinity with nature, speaking of carving both as a 'biological necessity' and as an 'extension of the telluric forces which mould the landscape'.

From 1925 to 1931 Hepworth was married to the sculptor John Skeaping (1901–80). In 1931 she met Ben *Nicholson, who became her second husband in 1938, and through him she became aware of contemporary European developments. They joined *Abstraction-Création in 1933, and *Unit One in the same year. During the 1930s Hepworth, Nicholson, and Moore worked in close harmony and became recognized as the nucleus of the abstract movement in England. In 1939 Hepworth moved to St Ives in Cornwall with Nicholson and lived there for the rest of her life (see ST IVES SCHOOL). During the late 1930s and 1940s she began to concentrate on the counterplay between mass and space in sculpture. In 1931 in *Pierced Form* (destroyed during the Second World War) she first introduced into England the use of the 'hole', and she now developed this with great subtlety, making play with the relationship between the outside and inside of a figure, the two surfaces sometimes being linked with threaded string, as in *Pelagos* (1956, Tate, London). *Pelagos* also shows her sensitive use of painted surface to contrast with the natural grain of the wood. In all her work she displayed a deep understanding of the quality of her materials and superb standards of craftsmanship. By the 1950s she was one of the most internationally famous of sculptors and she received many honours and prestigious public commissions, among them the memorial to Dag Hammarskjöld—*Single Form*—at the United Nations in New York (1963). She now worked more in bronze, especially for large pieces, but she always retained a special feeling for direct carving. Hepworth died tragically in a fire at her studio in St Ives, which is now a museum dedicated to her work. Her obituary in the *Guardian* described her as 'probably the most significant woman artist in the history of art to this day'.

Herkomer, Sir Hubert von (1849–1914). German-born painter, printmaker, designer, teacher, and writer who settled in England in 1857 with his father (a woodcarver) and became a British citizen. He established his reputation with *The Last Muster—Sunday at the Royal Hospital, Chelsea* (1875, Lady Lever AG, Port Sunlight), a work appealing to the public taste for patriotic sentiment, and then became a successful and prolific portrait painter. His best-known works today, however, are his scenes of social concern, which were then still something of a novelty in English art (*On Strike*, 1891, RA, London). Herkomer was a versatile artist and a man of many parts. He composed operas, which were performed at his private theatre at Bushey, Hertfordshire, and as well as performing in them and designing the sets, he experimented with new forms of stage lighting; he also designed sets for the cinema. From 1883 to 1904 he ran his own art school at Bushey (William *Nicholson was one of his pupils) and he lectured widely. His books include the autobiographical *My School and My Gospel* (1908).

Hermitage, St Petersburg. Russia's pre-eminent collection of art and antiquities, one of the world's greatest museums. It takes its name from a pleasure pavilion (now known as the Little Hermitage) created for Catherine the Great in the late 1760s as an extension to the recently built Winter Palace, providing a place to entertain friends and display some of her art treasures ('hermitage' meaning 'place of retreat'). In 1787 she completed another similar extension (now known as the Old Hermitage). Catherine was one of the most

voracious collectors of all time and at her death in 1796 the imperial collections contained about 4,000 pictures, as well as many other treasures. In 1837 the Winter Palace was ravaged by fire, but the Little and Old Hermitages were saved. The palace was extensively reconstructed in sumptuous style and Nicholas I added a custom-built museum, designed by the German architect Leo von Klenze. This building, known as the New Hermitage, was opened to the public in 1852. After the 1917 Revolution the imperial collections were nationalized and the whole vast palace complex was gradually turned into a museum, known as the State Hermitage. Its representation of Western painting is rich in virtually every period and school, but perhaps most notably in 17th-century Dutch and Flemish painting and in French painting of the late 19th and early 20th centuries (almost all the great figures of *Impressionism and *Post-Impressionism are well represented). Many of the French paintings come from the collections of two Moscow businessmen who were among the outstanding collectors and patrons of their time: Ivan Morozov (1871–1921) and Sergei Shchukin (1851–1936). They commissioned new works as well as buying through dealers. *Matisse was a particular favourite of both men, and Shchukin's interest also extended to *Cubism. After the Revolution their collections were nationalized and later distributed between the Hermitage and the Pushkin Museum in Moscow. Although primarily famous for its paintings, the Hermitage includes much else, notably extensive collections of Central Asian and Oriental art.

Heron, Patrick (1920–99). British painter, writer, and designer. His early paintings were influenced by *Braque and *Matisse, but in 1956 he turned to abstraction; in the same year he settled in Cornwall, becoming a member of the *St Ives School. His abstracts were varied, including stripe paintings—vertical and horizontal—as well as looser formats with soft-edged shapes, but all his work is notable for its vibrancy of colour. He wrote several books, including *The Changing Forms of Art* (1955), *The Shape of Colour* (1973), and studies of *Vlaminck (1947), *Hitchens (1955), and Braque (1958).

Herrera, Francisco the Elder (c.1590–1654). Spanish painter and engraver, a representative of the transition from *Mannerism to *Baroque. He spent most of his career in his native Seville and with his older contemporary *Roelas, under whose influence he developed, he helped to prepare the way for the naturalistic style characteristic of the following generation of painters in the city. *St Basil Dictating his Rule* (*c.*1639, Louvre, Paris), which is generally considered his masterpiece, shows his work at its most bold and vigorous. In about 1650 Herrera moved to Madrid, where he died. According to *Palomino, Herrera was a 'harsh and ill-tempered man' whose pupils never stayed with him very long. *Velázquez is said to have been one of these short-lived pupils, as was his son, **Francisco Herrera the Younger** (1627–85), a painter and architect. After fleeing from home, he evidently spent several years in Italy, although there is no documentary evidence for his visit. He worked for several years in Seville but mainly in Madrid, where he was appointed a royal painter to Charles II (*see* HABSBURG) in 1672 and royal architect in 1677. His greatest achievement was the design (subsequently modified) of the church of El Pilar at Saragossa, begun in 1681. His work as a painter, airy and colourful, owed much to the example of Murillo.

Herring, John Frederick, Sen. (1795–1865). British painter, the best-known member of a family of sporting and animal artists. He had great success as a painter of racehorses, regularly doing portraits of the winners of the Derby and St Leger, and his work enjoyed wide popularity in engravings. His three painter sons included **John Frederick, Jun.** (d. 1907), and he also had a painter brother, **Benjamin Herring, Sen.** (1806–30). It is often not easy to distinguish between the work of the various members of the family.

Heyden, Jan van der (1637–1712). Dutch painter, draughtsman, printmaker, and inventor, active in Amsterdam. He painted some landscapes and still lifes, but is renowned mainly as one of the greatest of all townscape painters. His views of Amsterdam and other towns are done with loving attention to detail, with precise rendering of foliage, bricks, and architectural detail. However, this treatment never appears dull or dry, for the detail is underpinned by dignified composition and his handling of

colour and light is highly attractive. In spite of the seemingly objective nature of his work, van der Heyden often took liberties with topographical accuracy and he also painted *capriccios. Painting was only a part of his activity, for he was also involved in civic administration in Amsterdam. In 1669 it became the first European city to enjoy street lighting when it adopted the oil lamps he proposed. The fire hose is also said to have been his invention and features in his *Brandspuiten-boek* ('Fire Engine Book', 1690), which is illustrated with plates from his own drawings, some of which he etched and engraved himself. His varied activities made him a wealthy man.

Heysen, Sir Hans (1877–1968). German-born Australian landscape painter in oils and watercolour. His family emigrated to Australia when he was 6 and he worked mainly in or near Adelaide. Robert *Hughes (*The Art of Australia*, 1970) writes: 'Heysen's large body of work was immensely popular; it has most of the textbook virtues and, for many years, no Australian business firm was considered quite solid unless it had a Heysen in its boardroom ... The only deficiency of his art is that it has no imagination ... He was, in fact, the Alfred *Munnings of the gum-tree.' His work is represented in all Australian state galleries and many provincial galleries.

Hicks, Edward (1780–1849). The best-known American *naive painter of the 19th century, active in Bucks County, Pennsylvania. He was a coach- and sign-painter early in life, but for many years he devoted himself to preaching—the pleasure he derived from painting conflicted with his austere Quaker outlook and caused him much conscience-searching. Some of his pictures are farm scenes or landscapes, but he is best known for his many versions (he reputedly made more than 100) of *The Peaceable Kingdom*. Exemplifying the pacifism of the Quaker society in which he lived, they depict with a vivid and charming literalness the prophecy in Isaiah 11 that all men and beasts will live in peace.

Highmore, Joseph (1692–1780). English painter (mainly of portraits) and writer. He studied at *Kneller's Academy and had a considerable practice as a portraitist by the 1720s. His early work is in the manner of

*Richardson, but from the 1730s his portraits became more elegant as he responded to the *Rococo influences that began to pervade English painting at this time. Some of his more informal works, however, have a directness and freshness that recall *Hogarth (*Mr Oldham and Friends*, c.1750, Tate, London). Highmore was a friend of the novelist Samuel Richardson and in 1743–4 painted a series of twelve illustrations to *Pamela* (Tate; Fitzwilliam Mus., Cambridge; NG of Victoria, Melbourne) which link him with *Hayman and Hogarth as one of the initiators of a British school of narrative painting. He also painted several portraits of Richardson (two are in the NPG, London). In 1762 he gave up painting and retired to Canterbury to devote himself to writing, including a good deal on artistic topics.

Hildebrand, Adolf von (1847–1921). German sculptor and writer on art. He spent much of his career in Italy and is regarded as one of the main upholders in his period of the classical tradition in sculpture. His most characteristic works were nude figures—timeless and rather austere, in the high-minded tradition of Greek art—although he also made several large monuments, including a statue of the composer Johannes Brahms in Meiningen (1898). He is now, however, better known for his treatise *Das Problem der Form in der bildenden Kunst* (1893) than for his highly accomplished but rather bland sculpture. The book went through many editions (an English translation, *The Problem of Form in Painting and Sculpture*, was published in 1907) and it was influential in promoting a move against surface naturalism in sculpture.

Hilliard, Nicholas (c.1547–1619). The most celebrated of English *miniaturists. He was the son of an Exeter goldsmith and himself trained in this craft, completing a seven-year apprenticeship in London in 1569. It is not known how he learnt miniature painting, but by 1572 he was working for Elizabeth I (his first surviving portrait of her, dating from that year, is in the NPG, London). Later he also worked for James I, but after the turn of the century his position as the leading miniaturist in the country was challenged by his former pupil Isaac *Oliver; these two were head and shoulders above their contemporaries. In his treatise *The Arte of *Limning* (written in about 1600

but not published until 1912) Hilliard declared himself as a follower of *Holbein's manner of limning. In particular he avoided the use of shadow for modelling and in his treatise he records that this was in agreement with Queen Elizabeth's taste—'for the lyne without shadows showeth all to good jugment, but the shadowe without lyne showeth nothing'. But whereas for Holbein a miniature was always a painting reduced to a small scale, Hilliard developed in the miniature an intimacy and subtlety peculiar to the art. He combined his unerring use of line with a jeweller's exquisiteness in detail, an engraver's elegance in calligraphy, and a unique realization of the individuality of each sitter. His miniatures are often freighted with enigmatic inscription and allegory (e.g. a hand reaching from a cloud), but this usually heightens the vividness with which the sitter's face is impressed. Apart from the Queen herself, many other great Elizabethans sat for him, including Sir Francis Drake, Sir Walter Raleigh, and Sir Philip Sidney. The best collection of his miniatures is in the Victoria and Albert Museum, including the celebrated *Young Man Leaning on a Tree among Roses* (c.1587). Hilliard is known also to have worked on a large scale and among the paintings attributed to him are portraits of Elizabeth I in the National Portrait Gallery, London, and the Walker Art Gallery, Liverpool. In spite of his success, he had considerable financial problems and in 1617 was briefly imprisoned for debt. His son **Laurence** (c.1582–1647/8) was also a miniaturist.

Hilton, Roger (1911–75). British painter of German extraction (Aby *Warburg was his father's cousin). He trained at the *Slade School, and in the 1930s also studied in Paris under *Bissière. In 1950 he began painting abstracts; initially he was influenced by developments in Paris (to which he regularly returned), but on a visit to the Netherlands in 1953 he was inspired more by *Mondrian. From 1955 he reintroduced a sense of a shallow pictorial space, and from 1956, when he began making visits to St Ives (see ST IVES SCHOOL), there are suggestions of beaches, boats, rocks, and water in his work. In 1961 he returned to overt figuration with a series of exuberant, jokey female nudes. These dismayed some of his admirers, who regarded him as a standard-bearer for abstraction, but they are now among his most popular works (*Oi yoi yoi*, 1963, Tate, London). For the last few years of his life he was bedridden with a muscular disease, but his ill health was belied in the series of colourful, good-humoured gouaches he did in this period.

Hirshfield, Morris. *See* JANIS.

Hirst, Damien (1965–). British sculptor, painter, and designer, whose flair for self-publicity has helped him become the most famous and controversial British artist of his generation. Whilst still a student at Goldsmiths College, London, he made a name for himself by organizing a exhibition of student work ('Freeze', 1988). From his youth he had a fascination with death, and his most famous work is *The Physical Impossibility of Death in the Mind of Someone Living* (1991, priv. coll.), consisting of a dead tiger-shark balanced and weighted so that it floats in preserving fluid in a large tank made of glass and steel. In 1995 he was awarded the *Turner Prize. The work he showed at the exhibition of shortlisted candidates' work at the Tate Gallery was *Mother and Child Divided*, consisting of four tanks containing the severed halves of a cow and calf. According to the accompanying catalogue, 'Hirst strips the closest of bonds between living creatures to its starkest reality', but many people hated the work, and a letter to *The Times* suggested that the Tate authorities must be suffering from mad cow disease. *See also* YOUNG BRITISH ARTISTS.

history painting. A term applied to pictures showing figures involved in momentous or morally edifying scenes, treated in a suitably grand and noble way. The term derives from the Latin *historia* ('story' or 'narrative') and is applied not only to pictures representing actual historical events but also to appropriate subjects from legend and literature. Thus scenes from the Bible, Greek mythology, Dante, or Shakespeare would usually come under the heading 'history painting', whereas scenes drawn from a domestic novel might be considered as *genre pictures, even if set in a period before the painter's own. In conventional academic theory, history painting was considered the highest branch of art, to which the *Grand Manner was appropriate. Its status derived not only from its elevating aims, but also from the fact that it was considered the most difficult branch of painting to master, involving the skilful arrangement of numerous figures with convincing gestures and expressions. The American painters *West and *Copley were pioneers in painting history pictures in modern dress.

Hitchens, Ivon (1893–1979). British painter, mainly of landscapes. He created a highly distinctive style, on the borderline between abstraction and figuration, in which broad, fluid areas of vibrant colour, typically on a canvas of wide format, evoke but do not represent the forms of the English countryside that were his main inspiration. From 1940, after his London studio was destroyed by bombing, he lived in Sussex. By this time his characteristic manner was fully developed and subsequently his work altered little, apart from the fact that his palette changed from naturalistic browns and greens to much more vivid colours such as bright yellows and purples. Contrary to what often happens when an artist remains constant in one style over a period of decades, Hitchens's work did not become stereotyped or banal. In addition to landscapes he painted flowers and figures, and he did several large murals, for example at the University of Sussex (1963).

Hoare, William (*c*.1707–92). English portrait painter. He spent the formative years of his career in Italy (1728–37), but his style is a continuation of *Richardson's. By 1738 he had settled in Bath, and until the arrival of *Gainsborough in 1759 he was the leading portrait painter there. Sir Ellis *Waterhouse has described his style as 'serious, but a little blank'. He worked much in *pastel, and in this was followed by his daughter **Mary** (*c*.1753–1820), also a portraitist.

Hobbema, Meindert (1638–1709). Dutch landscape painter. He worked in his native Amsterdam, where he was the friend and only documented pupil of Jacob van *Ruisdael. Some of his pictures are very like Ruisdael's, but he was brighter in temperament and narrower in range, painting favourite subjects—particularly watermills and trees around a pool—over and over again. In 1668 he began working for Amsterdam customs and excise, supervising the weighing and measuring of imported wine, and thereafter seems to have painted only in his spare time. However, his most famous work, *The Avenue at Middelharnis* (NG, London), dates from 1689; it is considered the swansong of the great age of Dutch landscape. Hobbema has long been a popular artist in England (his influence is clear in *Gainsborough's early landscapes) and he is outstandingly well represented in English collections.

Höch, Hannah. *See* PHOTOMONTAGE.

Hockney, David (1937–). British painter, draughtsman, printmaker, photographer, designer, and writer, active mainly in the USA. After a brilliant prize-winning career as a student at the *Royal College of Art, Hockney had achieved considerable success by the time he was in his mid-twenties, and he has since consolidated his position as by far the best-known and most critically acclaimed British artist of his generation. His phenomenal success has been based not only on the flair and versatility of his work, but also on his colourful personality, which has made him a recognizable figure even to people not particularly interested in art. In 1961 he emerged as one of the leaders of British *Pop art at the *Young Contemporaries exhibition. Hockney himself disliked the label 'Pop', but his work of this time makes many references to popular culture (notably in the use of graffiti-like lettering) and is often jokey in mood. His first retrospective exhibition came as early as 1970, at the Whitechapel Art Gallery, London (it subsequently toured to Hanover, Rotterdam, and Belgrade). By this time he was painting in a weightier, more traditionally representational manner, in which he did a series of large double-portraits of friends, including the well-known *Mr and Mrs Clark and Percy* (1970–1, Tate, London). These portraits are notable for their airy feeling of space and light and the subtle flattening and simplification of forms, as well as for the sense of stylish living they capture. Hockney often paints the people and places he knows best (his art is frequently autobiographical) and has memorably celebrated his romance with Los Angeles (he first visited the city in 1963 and settled there in 1976), particularly in his many paintings featuring swimming pools (*A Bigger Splash*, 1967, Tate, London). In these works he skilfully exploited the qual-

ities of the new *acrylic paint. Hockney has also been outstanding as a graphic artist; his work in this field includes etched illustrations to Cavafy's *Poems* (1967) and *Six Fairy Tales of the Brothers Grimm* (1969), as well as many individual prints, often on homoerotic themes. In the 1970s he also came to the fore as a stage designer, notably with his set and costume designs for Stravinsky's *The Rake's Progress* and Mozart's *The Magic Flute*, produced at Glyndebourne in 1975 and 1978 respectively. The broader style demanded by stage design has been reflected in his subsequent easel paintings. In the 1980s he experimented a good deal with photography, producing, for example, photographic collages and—since 1986—prints created on a photocopier. Hockney is a perceptive commentator on art and has published several books on his own life and work, as well as *Secret Knowledge: Rediscovering the Lost Techniques of the Old Masters* (2001), in which he argues that the use of optical aids such as the *camera lucida and *camera obscura has been much more common in European art than previously thought.

Hodges, William (1744–97). English painter, mainly of landscapes. He was the pupil and assistant of Richard *Wilson, 1758–65, and became a skilful imitator of his style. His work took on a more personal character when he travelled as draughtsman with Captain James Cook on his second voyage to the South Pacific in 1772–5, and his finest paintings are those based on drawings he made of such exotic places as Tahiti and Easter Island (examples are in the National Maritime Museum, London). In 1779–84 he worked in India (where he earned a good deal of money) and in 1790 he visited the Continent, going as far as Russia. He did pictures for *Boydell's Shakespeare Gallery and also some allegorical subjects, but in 1795 he abandoned painting and opened a bank in Dartmouth. It failed shortly before he died.

Hodgkin, Sir Howard (1932–). British painter and printmaker, regarded as one of the outstanding colourists in contemporary art. His paintings, which are usually fairly small, sometimes look completely abstract, but in fact he bases his work on specific events, usually an encounter between people. He has travelled widely, making several visits to India, and his preference for flat colours and decorative borders reflects his admiration for Indian miniatures. A well-known figure in the art world, he has been a Trustee of the Tate Gallery and the National Gallery, and in 1985 he was awarded the *Turner Prize.

Hodgkins, Frances (1869–1947). New Zealand painter, active mainly in England, where she settled in 1913 after some time alternating between the two hemispheres. She was the daughter of **William Matthew Hodgkins** (1833–98), a barrister and amateur painter who had emigrated from England in 1859 and took a lead in the artistic life of Dunedin. Her father taught her watercolour painting, but she did not begin to paint in oils until 1915. Until that time her work had been conventional, but she gradually developed a more individual style, echoing *Matisse and *Dufy (she spent a good deal of time in France), in its use of vibrant colour. She mainly painted landscapes and still lifes. Her later paintings approach abstraction in a manner akin to *Hitchens's work.

Hodler, Ferdinand (1853–1918). Swiss painter, born in Berne and active mainly in Geneva. He ranks alongside *Böcklin as the outstanding Swiss artist of his time, but his early work was rather unimaginatively naturalistic, his landscapes amounting to ambitious colour postcards for tourists. However, in 1890, with his brooding *Night* (Kunstmuseum, Berne), Hodler began a sudden change of style. This picture, depicting a black-shrouded, phantom-like presence amid a number of semi-naked sleeping figures, set the pattern for his most characteristic works—allegories featuring stately groups of flat, stylized figures composed into a rhythmic and repetitive pattern of lines, forms, and colours. Often the same basic figure is repeated throughout the picture with only slight variations. Hodler called his method 'Parallelism'; he used the same principles in scenes from Swiss history and landscapes. By the turn of the century he had become immensely popular throughout the German-speaking world. In the last decade of his life he returned more to landscape painting. As well as being a major figure of *Symbolism and *Art Nouveau, Hodler has been seen as one of the harbingers of *Expressionism.

Hofmann, Hans (1880–1966). German-born painter and teacher who became an American citizen in 1941. From 1904 to 1914 he lived in Paris, where he knew many of the leading figures of *Fauvism, *Cubism, and *Orphism. In 1915 he founded his own art school in Munich and taught there successfully until 1932, when he emigrated to the USA (following visits in 1930 and 1931, during which he taught at the University of California, Berkeley). He founded the Hans Hofmann School of Fine Arts in New York in 1934 (followed the next year by a summer school at Provincetown, Massachusetts) and became a teacher of great influence on the minority group of American artists who practised abstract painting during the 1930s. Hofmann continued teaching until 1958, when he closed his schools so that he could concentrate on his own painting. This was to counter opinions that he was merely an academic figure and a symbol of the avant-garde rather than a significant creative artist himself. In the course of his career he experimented with many styles, and was a pioneer of the technique of dribbling and pouring paint that was later particularly associated with Jackson *Pollock. His later works, in contrast, feature rectangular blocks of fairly solid colour against a more broken background. As a painter and teacher he was an important influence on the development of *Abstract Expressionism. The essence of his approach was that the picture surface had an intense life of its own.

Hogarth, William (1697–1764). English painter and engraver. He trained as an engraver of silver plate and by 1720 had set up his own business in London, doing various kinds of commercial work. In his spare time he studied painting, first at the *St Martin's Lane Academy and later under Sir James *Thornhill, whose daughter he married in 1729. By the early 1730s he had achieved some success as a painter of *conversation pieces and at about the same time he invented the idea of using a sequence of anecdotal pictures 'similar to representations on the stage' to point a moral and satirize social abuses. *A Harlot's Progress* (6 scenes, c.1731; destroyed by fire) was followed by *A Rake's Progress* (8 scenes, c.1735, Soane Mus., London) and *Marriage à la Mode* (6 scenes, c.1743, NG, London), each of them unfolding a cautionary tale of vanity, corruption, and betrayal leading to decline and death. Hogarth produced all three series with a view to engraving them, and the prints had a wide sale and were popular with all classes. They were indeed so successful that unauthorized copies were marketed and Hogarth's campaigning against the profiteers led to the Copyright Act of 1735. He wrote of his 'modern moral subjects' that 'I have endeavoured to treat my subjects as a dramatic writer: my picture is my stage, and men and women my players.' However, he was much more than a preacher in paint. His satire was directed at pedantry and affectation as well as at immorality, and he saw himself to some extent as a defender of native common sense against a fashion for French and Italian mannerisms. In spite of his xenophobia, he made some attempts to show he could paint in the Italian *Grand Manner (*Sigismunda*, 1759, Tate, London). These, however, are generally considered his weakest works, and apart from his morality subjects he excelled mainly in portraiture. *Captain Coram* (1740, Coram Foundation, London), which he regarded as his highest achievement in this field, shows that he could paint a portrait in the *Baroque manner with complete confidence and without artificiality. However, wealthy clients generally preferred bland flattery to Hogarth's robust directness, so he was not financially successful as a portraitist. In 1735 he established an academy in St Martin's Lane (a successor to the one at which he had studied), and this became an important forerunner of the *Royal Academy. In 1753 he published *The Analysis of Beauty*, a treatise on aesthetic theory written with the conviction that the views of a practising artist should carry greater weight than the theories of the connoisseur or dilettante. It reveals him as an original if somewhat muddled thinker.

Hogarth was far and away the most important British artist of his generation. He was equally outstanding as a painter and engraver and by the force of his pugnacious personality as well as by the quality and originality of his work he freed British art from its domination by foreign artists. Because so much of his work has a 'literary' element, his qualities as a painter have often been overlooked, but his more informal pictures in particular show that his

brushwork could live up to his inventive genius. The vigour and spontaneity of *The Shrimp Girl* (c.1740, NG, London), for example, have made it deservedly one of the most popular British paintings of the 18th century.

Holanda (or **Hollanda**), **Francisco de** (1517–84). Portuguese draughtsman, *miniaturist, painter, architect, and writer on art, the son of a Netherlandish miniaturist, **Antonio de Holanda** (d. 1557), who spent part of his career in Lisbon. In 1538–40 Francisco visited Italy, where he produced a volume of drawings (now in the Escorial, near Madrid) documenting various sights he saw there, including fortifications and antiquities. Although he became court painter in Lisbon, his influence in propagating the Italianate style in Portugal was exercised mainly through his writings. In 1548 he completed a manuscript entitled *Da pintura antigua* (Of Ancient Painting); this was the first treatise on painting written in the Iberian peninsula, but it was not published until 1890–6. It contains four dialogues (Eng. trans., 1928) in which Holanda purportedly discusses theories of art with *Michelangelo, the miniaturist Giulio *Clovio, and others. As an appendage Holanda completed in 1549 ten dialogues entitled *Do tirar polo natural* (On Drawing from Nature).

Holbein, Hans (c.1497–1543). German painter and designer, chiefly celebrated as one of the greatest of all portraitists. He trained in his native Augsburg with his father, **Hans Holbein the Elder** (c.1465–1524), one of the leading artists of the day there; his brother, **Ambrosius** (c.1494–c.1519), was also a painter. By 1515 the brothers had moved to Basle. There Hans quickly found employment as a designer for printers, and in 1516 he painted portraits of Jacob Meyer, mayor of the city, and his wife (Öffentliche Kunstsammlung, Basle). From 1517 to 1519 he worked in Lucerne, assisting his father on the decoration of a house for the city's chief magistrate (only a fragment of the work survives, in the Lucerne museum). It is possible that during this time Holbein crossed the Alps to Lombardy, for on his return to Basle, where he was to remain until 1526, his work had more dignity and authority and his modelling had become softer. The harrowing *Christ in the Tomb* (1521 or 1522,

Öffentliche Kunstsammlung, Basle), for example, has a power of expression combined with a mastery of *chiaroscuro that almost rivals *Leonardo.

Holbein was now the leading artist in Basle, producing a highly varied output, including portraits, altarpieces, murals, and designs for stained glass. He also continued to work for printers, producing between about 1523 and 1526 his best-known work in this field, the series *Dance of Death*. This was not published until 1538 but then enjoyed enormous popularity, running into many editions. His most notable portraits in these years are three of Erasmus, all dating from *c*.1523 (Louvre, Paris; Earl of Radnor Coll., Longford Castle, Wiltshire; and Öffentliche Kunstsammlung, Basle). In them, perhaps by the sitter's wish, he used the formula of the scholar in his study, first devised by Quentin *Massys, also for a portrait of Erasmus. A visit to France in 1524 gave Holbein further knowledge of *Renaissance painting, especially through the works of *Raphael in the royal collection, and the effect may be seen in the *Meyer Madonna* (1526, Schlossmuseum, Darmstadt). Mother and Child alike have an ideal beauty that is quite un-German, though the *donor portraits have a splendid naturalism.

The disturbances of the Reformation meant a decline of patronage in Basle, and in 1526, armed with an introduction from Erasmus to Sir Thomas More, Holbein sought work in England. His great group portrait of the More family (lost, but later copies in NPG, London, and Nostell Priory, Yorkshire) is a landmark in European art, for no previous artist had produced a group portrait of full-length figures in their own home. A number of single portraits of eminent sitters also date from this visit and Holbein seems to have prospered financially. However, in 1528 he returned to Basle, probably because there was a risk of losing his citizen's rights if he was absent too long. He bought a house in the city soon after his return and again was in demand for a variety of work. His biggest commission in Basle was the decoration of the council chamber of the town hall with murals (of which only fragments remain) on the theme of Justice; they were begun in 1521 and completed after his return from England. While he had been away the religious strife in Basle had intensified, and in 1532

he returned to England, leaving behind his wife and two children. He saw them only once more, on a brief visit to Basle in 1538, and was based in London for the rest of his life.

England too had changed since his first visit. More had resigned as lord chancellor and gone into retirement and members of his circle who had patronized Holbein were similarly out of favour. He found new patrons among the prosperous German merchant community in London, and in about 1533 he painted a portrait of Thomas Cromwell (Frick Coll., New York), soon to be Henry VIII's secretary. Cromwell may have obtained for Holbein the commission for his celebrated double portrait *The Ambassadors* (1533, NG, London), and almost certainly helped him to gain royal patronage. By 1536 he was working for the king, and in the next year he produced the work that his contemporaries regarded as the masterpiece of his English years, the wall painting in Whitehall Palace of Henry VIII with his father and mother and his third wife, Jane Seymour. Though the picture perished in a fire in 1698, part of the *cartoon survives (NPG, London) and the massively assertive full-length figure of the king is well known through copies. Visitors to Whitehall Palace are said to have been 'abashed' and 'annihilated' by this overpowering image of royal authority. The only portrait of the king indisputably from Holbein's hand is a bust-length picture in the Museo Thyssen-Bornemisza, Madrid, a type of which numerous replicas exist. The king also twice sent Holbein abroad to produce portraits of prospective brides—*Christina, Duchess of Milan* (1538, NG, London) and *Anne of Cleves* (1539, Louvre). Numerous other members of the court are portrayed in paintings and in drawings, a superb collection of which is in the Royal Library at Windsor Castle. Holbein also made many designs for the royal household, ranging from substantial architectural elements to buttons, but there are no surviving objects based on his drawings. At about the time he entered royal service he also took up *miniature painting, to which his exquisitely detailed craftsmanship was eminently suited. Holbein's portraits were much copied, but none of his followers in England approached the penetration of his characterization or the virtuosity of his technique. Only in miniature painting did he have a worthy successor in *Hilliard.

Hollar, Wenceslaus (or **Wenzel**) (1607–77). Bohemian etcher and watercolourist. He was born in Prague and had part of his training in the workshop of *Merian in Frankfurt. In 1636, while working in Cologne, he met the Earl of *Arundel; he accompanied Arundel on a diplomatic mission through central Europe and returned with him to England. Hollar remained in England for most of the rest of his life (he lived in Antwerp 1644–52 and went on an expedition to Tangier 1668–9); during the Civil War he fought on the Royalist side. He was one of the outstanding draughtsmen and etchers of the 17th century and his views of London form an invaluable record of its appearance before the Great Fire of 1666. His prolific output also included many other subjects.

Homer, Winslow (1836–1910). American landscape, marine, and *genre painter. Next to *Eakins and the expatriate *Whistler, he is probably regarded as the greatest American painter of his period. He came to painting from illustration (chiefly for *Harper's Weekly*) and *Prisoners from the Front* (1866, Met. Mus., New York), one of his first major oils, has a quality of vivid, unromanticized reportage: 'When I have selected the thing carefully, I paint it exactly as it appears.' In 1867 he visited Paris; he was impressed by *Manet's work, but he explored the rendering of light and colour in a different way from the *Impressionists—instead of blurring forms, he sought luminosity within a firm construction of clear outline and broad planes of light and dark (*Long Branch, New Jersey*, 1869, MFA, Boston). The sea was Homer's favourite subject, and after living at Cullercoats on the rugged coast of north-east England in 1881–2, he settled at Prout's Neck on the Maine coast, where he lived in isolation. His pictures of the Maine coast, showing the power and solitude of the sea and the contest of man with the forces of nature, are his best-known works. He was an artist of considerable originality and power who created an imaginative vision of nature that has come to be seen as a reflection of the American pioneering spirit. He used watercolour with the force and authority of oil (*Inside the Bar, Tynemouth*, 1883, Met. Mus.).

Hondecoeter, Melchior d' (1636–95). Dutch painter, the best-known member of a family of artists. He was the Netherlands' most renowned painter of birds, winning an international reputation with his vigorous and brightly coloured canvases. They show both domestic and exotic birds, often in vigorous movement and sometimes pointing a moral. Hondecoeter also painted still lifes. He was a prolific artist and is represented in many museums. His father, **Gysbert** (1604–53), was also a bird painter, and his grandfather, **Gillis** (d. 1638), was a landscapist. Melchior trained with his father and with his uncle, Jan Baptist *Weenix; he worked in Utrecht, The Hague, and Amsterdam.

Hone, Nathaniel (1718–84). Irish *miniaturist and portrait painter, who settled permanently in London after studying in Italy, 1750–2, and became a foundation member of the *Royal Academy in 1768. He is now remembered mainly for one painting, *The Conjurer* (1775, NG, Dublin), in which he satirized *Reynolds's practice of borrowing poses from the Old Masters. The picture was accepted at the RA, but was withdrawn after Angelica *Kauffmann (whose name had been linked romantically with Reynolds's) objected that a nude figure in the background was meant to represent her. (Hone painted out the nude figures, but they can be seen in his sketch for the picture (Tate, London).) In protest at the removal of his painting Hone exhibited it in a one-man show in St Martin's Lane, the first of its kind recorded in Britain. Hone's sons, **Horace** (*c*.1755–1825) and **Camillus** (1759–1836), were also painters, as was a brother, **Samuel** (1726–?). Camillus was the subject of some of his father's best portraits.

Evie Hone (1894–1955), a descendant of Nathaniel, was one of the outstanding stained-glass designers of the 20th century. Her masterpiece is the huge east window of Eton College Chapel, commissioned in 1949 to replace glass destroyed by bombing in the Second World War and completed in 1952.

Honthorst, Gerrit van (1592–1656). Dutch painter of biblical, mythological, and *genre scenes, and of portraits. He was a pupil of *Bloemaert in his native Utrecht, but his style was formed by a long stay in Italy, where he probably spent most of the second decade of the century. On his return to Utrecht in 1620 he became, along with *Baburen and *Terbrugghen, one of the leading followers of *Caravaggio in the Netherlands. The candlelight effects he favoured in his early pictures (*Christ before the High Priest*, c.1617, NG, London) earned him the nickname 'Gherardo delle Notti' (Gerard of the Night Scenes). In the late 1620s, however, he abandoned his Caravaggesque style for a lighter manner in which he achieved international success (rare for a Dutch artist) as a court portraitist. His distinguished patrons included Christian IV of Denmark and Charles I of England; he spent most of 1628 in England, where he painted several portraits, including one of Charles (NPG, London). From 1637 to 1652 he was court painter in The Hague.

Hooch, Pieter de (1629–84). Dutch *genre painter. He was born in Rotterdam, is said to have studied in Haarlem (as a pupil of *Berchem), and spent the last two decades of his life in Amsterdam, but he is particularly associated with Delft. His period of residence there was fairly brief (c.1655–c.1661), but during this time he painted the pictures on which his reputation rests—a small number of tranquil masterpieces that perfectly evoke the well-being of his peaceful and prosperous country. Typical subjects include a sunny yard (*Courtyard of a House in Delft*, 1658, NG, London) or light streaming into the interior of a corner of a burgher's house (*The Pantry*, c.1658, Rijksmuseum, Amsterdam). There is a kinship of spirit with his great Delft contemporary *Vermeer, and de Hooch sometimes approaches him in delicate observation of light and lucidity of composition, although not in beauty of brushwork. After de Hooch moved to Amsterdam in the early 1660s, however, the quality of his paintings was less remarkable than their quantity. Instead of the simple brick and plaster settings of his earlier groups he chose sumptuous marble interiors, and towards the end these backgrounds acquired something of the harsh quality of a stage backdrop. He died in a madhouse.

Hoogstraten, Samuel van (1627–78). Dutch painter, printmaker, and writer on art. He painted *genre scenes in the style of de *Hooch and *Metsu, and portraits, but he is best known as a specialist in *perspective effects, notably in his *peep-show boxes, which show a painted toy world viewed through a small opening. Only in his early works can it be detected that he was a pupil of *Rembrandt. Hoogstraten visited London, Rome, and Vienna, worked in Amsterdam and The Hague as well as his native Dordrecht, and was a man of many parts. He was an etcher, poet, director of the mint at Dordrecht, and art theorist. His *Inleyding tot de hooge schoole der schilderkonst* (Introduction to the Art of Painting, 1678) contains one of the rare contemporary appraisals of Rembrandt's work.

Hope, Thomas (1769–1831). British collector, patron, and writer. He was born in Amsterdam to a wealthy banking family, and travelled extensively before and after settling in England in 1795. In 1801 he was described as being reputedly 'the richest, but undoubtedly far from the most agreeable man in Europe', and he used his great wealth to spend lavishly on art for his London mansion in Duchess Street (to which the public could buy admission tickets) and his country seat at Deepdene, Surrey. He was a devotee of *Neoclassicism, and the artists he patronized included *Canova, *Flaxman, and *Thorvaldsen. Hope also had notable collections of paintings and antique statuary. He trained craftsmen to make furniture from his own Greek and Egyptian designs, and his publications included *Household Furniture and Interior Decoration* (1807).

Hopper, Edward (1882–1967). American painter and etcher. He spent almost all his career in New York, but he travelled extensively in the USA, making long journeys by car. His main training was at the New York School of Art, where Robert *Henri was one of his teachers. Between 1906 and 1910 he made three trips to Europe (mainly Paris), but these had little influence on his style. In 1913 he exhibited (and sold) a picture at the *Armory Show, but from then until 1923 he earned his living entirely by commercial illustration. After turning to painting fulltime in 1924, however, he enjoyed a fairly rapid rise to recognition as the outstanding exponent of *American Scene Painting (he was given a retrospective exhibition by the *Museum of Modern Art in 1933 and this set the seal on his reputation). Hopper's distinctive style was formed by the mid-1920s and thereafter changed little. The central theme of his work is the loneliness of city life, generally expressed through one or two figures in a spare setting—his best-known work, *Nighthawks* (1942, Art Inst. of Chicago), has an unusually large 'cast' with four. Typical settings are motel rooms, filling stations, cafeterias, and almost deserted offices at night. He was the first artist to seize on this specifically American visual world and make it definitively his own. However, although his work is rooted in a particular period and place, it also has a peculiarly timeless feel and deals in unchanging realities about the human condition. He never makes feelings explicit or tries to tell a story; rather he suggests weariness, frustration, and troubled isolation with a poignancy that rises above the specific. Hopper himself enjoyed solitude (although he was happily married to another ex-student of Henri) and he disliked talking about his work. When he did, he discussed it mainly in terms of technical problems; one of his best-known pronouncements is that he wanted only to 'paint sunlight on the side of a house'. Of *Nighthawks* he said: 'I didn't see it as particularly lonely...Unconsciously, probably, I was painting the loneliness of a big city.' Deliberately so or not, in his still, reserved, and blandly handled paintings he exerts a powerful psychological impact that makes him one of the great painters of modern life. Hopper worked in watercolour as well as oil and also made etchings, beginning in 1915—in fact his individual vision emerged in this medium before it did in painting. His best-known print is *Evening Wind* (1921), establishing a theme that would later often recur in his paintings—the female nude in a city interior. He virtually abandoned printmaking in 1923, but in spite of his short career in the medium he has been described as 'undoubtedly the greatest American etcher of this century' (Frances Carey and Antony Griffiths, *American Prints 1879–1979*, 1980).

Hoppner, John (1758–1810). British portrait painter. He trained as a chorister in the Chapel Royal, St James's Palace, and later received an allowance from George III to study at the Royal Academy Schools. The royal favour he was shown led to rumours that he was the king's illegitimate son. In 1789 he was appointed portrait painter to the Prince of Wales (later George IV) and after the death of *Reynolds, he and *Lawrence were the leading portraitists in the country. Hoppner rarely achieved striking individuality (his portraits often recall Reynolds and *Romney and later Lawrence and *Raeburn), but his best work, particularly when depicting women and children, has great charm.

Hoskins, John (*c.*1595–1665). The leading English portrait *miniaturist between *c.*1620 and *c.*1640 (from the death of *Hilliard to the emergence of Samuel *Cooper, Hoskins's nephew and pupil). His early work is a development of Hilliard's style. He later became a specialist in miniature versions of van *Dyck's large-scale portraits, but his work often has a charm and originality of its own. His son, **John Hoskins the Younger** (*c.*1620–after 1692), was also a miniaturist.

Houbraken, Arnold (1660–1719). Dutch painter and writer on art. His paintings are now forgotten, but he is important for his large biographical work *De groote schouburgh der Nederlantsche konstschilders en schilderessen* (The Great Theatre of Netherlandish Men and Women Painters, 3 vols., 1718–21). This was intended as a sequel to van *Mander's *Schilder-boeck* of 1604 and is the most important sourcebook on 17th-century Dutch art. Arnold's son **Jacobus** (1698–1780) was a leading portrait engraver. His work includes engraved plates after his father's designs for the *Groote schouburgh*.

Houdon, Jean-Antoine (1741–1828). French sculptor. A pupil of Michel-Ange *Slodtz, Jean-Baptiste *Lemoyne, and Jean-Baptiste *Pigalle, he won the *Prix de Rome in 1761. During his stay in Rome, 1764–8, he produced two works that made his reputation: a male *écorché figure (1767, Schloss-museum, Gotha), casts of which were widely used in art academies, and *St Bruno* (1767, S. Maria degli Angeli), executed in a direct and unpretentious classical style. After returning to Paris in 1768, he was successful in the popular mythological idiom, becoming a member of the Academy in 1777 with his *Morpheus* (Louvre, Paris). His greatest strength, however, was with portraits, in which he showed a brilliant gift for catching lively gesture and expression. By the mid-1780s he was acknowledged as the leading portrait sculptor of Europe and in 1785 he visited America in connection with his statue of George Washington (marble original, 1788, in Virginia State Capitol, Richmond; bronze copy outside the NG, London). His other well-known works include several portraits of Voltaire (e.g. in the Comédie-Française, Paris, and V&A, London). During the French Revolution he narrowly escaped imprisonment and although he found favour again under Napoleon (a terracotta bust of him, 1806, is in the Musée des Beaux-Arts, Dijon), he produced little of importance after the turn of the century. He last exhibited in 1814 and in his final years his mind was impaired following a stroke.

Howson, Peter. *See* GLASGOW SCHOOL and OFFICIAL WAR ART.

Huber, Wolfgang (or **Wolf**) (*c*.1490–1553). Austrian painter, printmaker, and architect, active mainly in Passau in Germany, where he was court painter and architect to the prince-bishop. He was first and foremost a poetic interpreter of landscape and is usually counted among the masters of the *Danube School. His landscape drawings are particularly delicate and his religious paintings and portraits sometimes have landscape backgrounds.

Hudson, Thomas (1701–79). English portrait painter, a pupil of Jonathan *Richardson the Elder, whose daughter he married. From the mid-1740s to the mid-1750s he was the leading fashionable portraitist in London, rivalled only by *Ramsay. His studio produced a great deal of work, with much help from specialist assistants (*see* DRAPERY PAINTER), and he has been described by Sir Ellis *Waterhouse as 'the last of the conscienceless artists, of whom *Lely was the first in England, who turned out portraits to standard patterns and executed comparatively little of the work themselves'. Hudson went into semi-retirement in the late 1750s, when his former pupil *Reynolds was rapidly rising in success. His other pupils included John Hamilton *Mortimer and Joseph *Wright.

Hudson River School. Term applied retrospectively to a number of American landscape painters, active *c*.1825–*c*.1875, who were inspired by pride in the beauty of their homeland. The early leaders and the three most important figures in the group were Thomas *Cole, Thomas *Doughty, and Asher B. *Durand, who painted the Hudson River Valley, the Catskill Mountains, and other remote and untouched areas of natural beauty. These three artists and many of those who followed had studied in Europe and part of their inspiration came from painters of the grandiose and spectacular such as *Turner and John *Martin. The patriotic spirit of the painters of the Hudson River School won them great popularity in the middle years of the century. Painters of a similar outlook who found their inspiration in the Far West are known collectively as the *Rocky Mountain School.

Huet, Christophe (1700–59). French *Rococo painter, engraver, and designer, best known for paintings and engravings involving animals, dressed up and acting like humans (*see* SINGERIE). Several other members of his family were artists, notably his nephew **Jean-Baptiste Huet** (1745–1811), a painter and engraver, mainly of animal subjects.

Hughes, Arthur (1832–1915). English painter and illustrator. In the 1850s he was one of the most distinguished of the *Pre-Raphaelite sympathizers, remarkable for his lyrical delicacy of colour and drawing. Two paintings are particularly well known: *April Love* (1856, Tate, London), which *Ruskin called 'exquisite in every way', and *The Long Engagement* (1859, City AG, Birmingham). After about 1870, however, his work declined in quality, although he did some good book illustrations. He was shy and withdrawn and in later life he lived in suburban obscurity.

Hughes, Robert (1938–). Australian art critic. In 1964 he moved to Europe (first to Italy, then England) and in 1970 settled in New York as art critic of *Time* magazine. His books include *The Art of Australia* (1966; rev. 1970), *Heaven and Hell in Western Art* (1969), and *Nothing If Not Critical: Selected Essays on Art and Artists* (1990). He has also made films for television, notably two much-praised series: *The Shock of the New* (1980) and *American Visions* (1996), both with accompanying books. He writes mainly on 20th-century art and has a richly deserved reputation as a witty and penetrating observer of the contemporary art scene.

Huguet, Jaime (active 1448, d. 1492). Spanish painter, the most prominent figure in the Catalan School during the second part of the 15th century. For most of his career he worked in Barcelona, where he had settled by 1448. He continued the Catalan tradition of Bernardo *Martorell, but was highly individual in his characterization. His studio produced many sumptuous composite altarpieces of the type that became typical in Spanish art and his work exercised a wide influence on the painting of Catalonia and Aragon.

Hume, Gary. *See* YOUNG BRITISH ARTISTS.

Humphry, Ozias (1742–1810). English portrait painter. He worked for a time as a *miniaturist in Bath, but settled in London in 1764 on the encouragement of *Reynolds. In 1772 a riding accident that affected his eyes made him abandon miniatures and after a visit to Italy in 1773–7 (he made the outward journey with *Romney), he practised in oils. From 1785 to 1788 he was in India, where he resumed miniature painting, but again he found the work too great a strain for his eyes. He then took up pastel and in this medium was highly successful (being given the title of 'Portrait Painter in Crayons to His Majesty' in 1792) until he went blind in 1797.

Hundertwasser, Fritz (Friedrich Stowasser) (1928–2000). Austrian painter and graphic artist. He took the name Hundertwasser in 1949, translating the syllable *-sto* (which means 'hundred' in Czech) into the German *hundert*. From about 1969 he signed his work 'Friedensreich Hundertwasser', symbolizing by the word 'Friedensreich' (Kingdom of Peace) his boast that by his painting he would introduce the observer into a new life of peace and happiness. He often added 'Regenstag' (Rainy Day) to the name—making it in full 'Friedensreich Hundertwasser Regenstag'—on the ground that he felt happy on rainy days because colours then began to sparkle and glow. This exaggerated concern with the name is a symptom of the braggadocio, conceit, and talent for self-advertisement that are apparent in his work as well as his life. Standing outside most contemporary artistic movements, though borrowing from many, he worked mainly on a small scale, often in watercolour. His work has sometimes been compared with that of *Klee and *Klimt, but although it is in the same tradition of figurative fantasy it lacks their elegance and wit. In his concern with the dehumanizing aspects of 20th-century society, he was an outspoken critic of modern architecture and his work included the design of an idiosyncratic, multicoloured, fairy-tale-like housing unit in Vienna (completed 1986).

Hunt, William Holman (1827–1910). English painter, co-founder of the *Pre-Raphaelite Brotherhood in 1848. He was the only member of the Brotherhood who throughout his entire career remained faithful to Pre-Raphaelite aims, which he summarized as finding serious and genuine ideas to express, direct study from nature in disregard of all arbitrary rules, and envisaging events as they must have happened rather than in accordance with artistic conventions. Hunt's work was remarkable for its minute precision, its accumulation of incident, and its didactic emphasis on moral or social symbolism, and he made three visits to the Middle East so he could paint biblical scenes with accurate local detail. One of the most famous paintings that resulted from his fanatical devotion to authenticity is *The Scapegoat* (1854–5, Lady Lever AG, Port Sunlight), showing the outcast animal on the shore of the Dead Sea. His colour tends to be painfully harsh and his sentiment mawkish, but he created some of the most enduring images of the Victorian age, among them *The Hireling Shepherd* (1851, Manchester AG), *The Awakening Conscience* (1853, Tate, London), and *The Light of the World* (1851–3, Keble College, Oxford; a smaller version, 1853–7, is in Manchester AG, and a larger replica, 1900–4, is in St Paul's Cathedral, London). Like the other Pre-Raphaelites, Hunt suffered critical attacks early in his career, but the moral earnestness of his work later made it immensely popular with the Victorian public and he earned a fortune from the sale of engravings of his paintings. In old age he became a patriarchal figure in the art world and he was awarded the Order of Merit in 1905. In the same year he published his autobiographical *Pre-Raphaelitism and the Pre-Raphaelite Brotherhood*, which is a basic sourcebook on the subject, though somewhat biased.

Hunter, Leslie. *See* SCOTTISH COLOURISTS.

Huntington, Henry E. (1850–1927). American businessman, collector, and philanthropist. He made an enormous fortune, mainly in the railway industry, but by about 1910 he had retired from most of his business interests to devote himself to collecting art and books. In the remaining years of his life he built up a huge library of early books that ranks in importance with those of the great national collections. With art he was more selective, concentrating on British paintings of the late 18th and early 19th centuries. In 1919 he signed a deed creating what is now the Huntington Library, Art Collections and Botanical Gardens at his home at San Marino, California, his aim being 'to promote and advance learning, the arts and sciences, and to promote the public welfare by founding, endowing and having maintained a library, art gallery, museum and park'. The chief glory of the art collection is the array of full-length British portraits in the main gallery—probably the finest group of such works to be seen anywhere in the world, including *Gainsborough's *Blue Boy* (c.1770) and Reynolds's *Mrs Siddons as the Tragic Muse* (1784). Since Huntington's death the collection has expanded and now also has a good representation of American and French paintings. Huntington's cousin (later also his stepson), **Archer M. Huntington** (1870–1955), a poet, Spanish scholar, and philanthropist, founded the Hispanic Society of America, New York, in 1908 and commissioned *Sorolla y Bastida to paint mural panels for the interior. Archer's wife, **Anna Hyatt Huntington** (1876–1973), was a sculptor of animal subjects in a traditional style. Her work includes an equestrian statue of El Cid outside the Hispanic Society of America (another cast is in Seville). She continued working almost up to her death at the age of 97.

Huysum, Jan van (1682–1749). Dutch painter, born and active in Amsterdam, with Rachel *Ruysch the most distinguished flower painter of his day. He had a European reputation and was much imitated, his light colours and intricate, flamboyant compositions becoming characteristic of 18th-century Dutch flower painting. Occasionally he painted subjects other than flowers—mainly landscapes, although there is also a self-portrait in the Ashmolean Museum, Oxford. He was a pupil of his father, **Justus van Huysum the Elder** (1659–1716), and he had three painter brothers: **Justus the Younger** (c.1684–1707), **Michiel** (d. 1759), and **Jacob** (c.1687–1740). Father and sons were all flower painters, apart from Justus the Younger, who specialized in battle scenes.

Hyperrealism. *See* SUPERREALISM.

Hyppolite, Hector. *See* NAIVE ART.

Ibbetson, Julius Caesar (1759–1817). English painter. His unusual Christian names were given to him because of his Caesarean birth. He specialized in fairly small landscapes with figures and animals, and his style has been characterized by Sir Ellis *Waterhouse as 'more natural than de *Loutherbourg's, and more civilized than *Morland's'; Benjamin *West called him 'the *Berchem of England'. Ibbetson worked mainly in his native Yorkshire, but also at times in London, Scotland, and the Lake District, and in 1787–8 he was draughtsman on a British mission to China, during which he visited Java. He worked in watercolour as well as oil and also made etchings. In 1803 he published a manual on painting. Like his friend Morland, Ibbetson is said to have been given to dissipation, but his work did not obviously suffer because of this in the way that Morland's did.

ICA. *See* INSTITUTE OF CONTEMPORARY ARTS.

icon. (From Gk., *eikōn*: 'likeness'). An image of a saint or other holy personage, particularly when the image is regarded by the devotee as sacred in itself and capable of facilitating contact between him or her and the personage portrayed. The term has been applied particularly to sacred images of the *Byzantine Church and the Orthodox Churches of Russia and Greece.

iconography. The aspect of art history dealing with the identification, description, classification, and interpretation of the subject matter of the figurative arts. In his book *Studies in Iconology* (1939) Erwin *Panofsky proposed that the term 'iconology' should be used to distinguish a broader approach towards subject matter in which the scholar attempts to understand the total meaning of the work of art in its historical context. However, in practice an exact distinction between the two terms is rarely made, and 'iconography' is the much more commonly used of the two. The term 'iconography' can also be applied to collections (or the classification) of portraits. Van *Dyck, for example, made a series of etchings of famous contemporaries entitled *Iconography*.

iconostasis. In *Byzantine and Russian churches, an *icon-covered screen separating the sanctuary from the main body of the building.

ideal. A conception of something that is perfect, referring in the visual arts to works that attempt to reproduce the best of nature, but also to improve on it, eliminating the inevitable flaws of particular examples. The notion derives ultimately from Plato, according to whom all perceptible objects are imperfect copies approximating to unchanging and imperceptible Ideas or Forms. This idea reappeared with the revival of Platonism in the Italian *Renaissance, and throughout much of subsequent European art the model of ideal beauty was supplied by classical statuary (*see* ANTIQUE). Its most influential formation was in a lecture by *Bellori delivered before the Accademia di S. Luca (*see* ACADEMY) in Rome in 1664, and published as a preface to his *Lives* in 1672. To Bellori, the contemporary artist who best exemplified the doctrine was *Poussin, whose example greatly influenced the French Académie Royale in the 17th century. The doctrine provided the philosophical justification for the *Grand Manner, and was the basis of criticism of anti-idealistic artists such as *Caravaggio and *Rembrandt, who were thought to have broken the 'rules' of good art. Although the doctrine has been responsible for much arid art, it has also been an inspiration to such great artists as *Raphael, who said, 'To paint a beautiful woman I must see several, and I have also recourse to a certain ideal in my mind', and Guido *Reni, who said 'The beautiful and pure *idea* must be in the mind, and then it is no matter what the model is.'

ideal landscape. A type of landscape painting, invented by Annibale *Carracci in the first decade of the 17th century, in which natural elements are composed into a grand and highly formalized arrangement suitable as a setting for small figures from serious religious or mythological subjects. It was an extraordinarily influential invention, developed most memorably by *Claude and *Poussin.

illuminated manuscripts. Books written by hand, decorated with pictures and ornaments of different kinds. The word 'illuminated' comes from a usage of the Latin word *illuminare* in connection with oratory or prose style, where it means 'to adorn'. The decorations are of three main types: (a) *miniatures* or small pictures incorporated into the text or occupying the whole page or part of the border; (b) *initial letters* either containing scenes (historiated initials) or with elaborate decoration; (c) *borders*, which may consist of miniatures but more often are composed of decorative motifs. They may enclose the whole of the text space or occupy only a small part of the margin of the page. Manuscripts are for the most part written on *parchment or vellum. From the 14th century paper was used for less sumptuous copies. Although a number of books have miniatures and ornaments executed in outline drawing only, the majority are fully coloured. After the introduction of printing in the mid-15th century the illuminated book became outmoded, although fine examples were produced well into the 16th century. During the 15th and 16th centuries illuminations were often added to printed books.

illusionism. Term applied in its broadest sense to the basic principle of *naturalistic art whereby verisimilitude in representation causes the spectator in various degrees to seem actually to be seeing the object represented, or the space in which it is represented, even though with part of his mind he knows that he is looking at a pictorial representation. In a somewhat narrower sense 'illusionism' refers to the use of pictorial techniques such as *perspective and foreshortening to deceive the eye (if not the mind) into taking that which is painted for that which is real, or in architecture and stage scenery to make the constructed forms seem visually more extensive than they are. Two specific forms of illusionism in painting are *quadratura, in which painted architecture appears to extend the real space of a room, and *trompe-l'œil, in which the spectator is genuinely, if mo-

mentarily, tricked into thinking that a painted object is a real one.

impasto. Thickly applied opaque paint (usually oil paint) showing the marks of the brush or other instrument of application.

Imperial War Museum. *See* OFFICIAL WAR ART.

Impressionism. A movement in painting that originated in France in the 1860s and had an enormous impact on Western art over the following half-century. The Impressionists were not a formal group with clearly defined principles and aims; rather they were a loose association of artists linked by some community of outlook who banded together for the purpose of exhibiting. The central figures were (in alphabetical order) *Cézanne, *Degas, *Manet, *Monet, Camille *Pissarro, *Renoir, and *Sisley. Monet, Renoir, and Sisley met as students, and the others came into contact with them through the artistic café society of Paris. There were friendly ties of varied degrees of intimacy linking each of them to most of the others, but Degas and even more Manet were set somewhat apart because they came from a higher stratum of society than the others, and the artists' commitment to Impressionism varied considerably (Manet was much respected as a senior figure, but he never exhibited with the group). They were united, however, in rebelling against academic conventions to try to depict their surroundings with spontaneity and freshness, capturing an 'impression' of what the eye sees at a particular moment, rather than a detailed record of appearances. Their archetypal subject was landscape (and painting out of doors, directly from nature, was one of the key characteristics of the movement), but they treated many other subjects, notably ones involving everyday city life. Degas, for example, made subjects such as horse races, dancers, and laundresses his own, and Renoir is famous for his pictures of pretty women and children.

The Impressionists' desire to look at the world with a new freshness and immediacy was encouraged by photography and by scientific research into colour and light. In trying to capture the effects of light on varied surfaces, particularly in open-air settings, they transformed painting, using bright colours and sketchy brushwork that seemed bewildering or shocking to traditionalists. The name 'Impressionism', in fact, was coined derisively, when it was applied to a picture by Monet, *Impression: Sunrise* (1872, Mus. Marmottan, Paris), which was shown at the first Impressionist exhibition, held in Paris in 1874. There were seven more Impressionist exhibitions (1876, 1877, 1879, 1880, 1881, 1882, and 1886), and after the final one the group broke up, only Monet continuing to pursue Impressionist ideals rigorously. Although the Impressionists at first had a generally hostile reception and several of them endured great financial hardship early in their careers, they began to achieve substantial success in the 1880s (helped by the dedicated promotion of *Durand-Ruel) and during the 1890s their influence was widely felt. Few artists outside France adopted Impressionism wholesale, but many lightened their palettes and loosened their brushwork as they synthesized its ideas with their local traditions. Indeed its impact was so enormous that much of the history of late 19th-century and early 20th-century painting is the story of developments from it or reactions against it. The *Neo-Impressionists, for example, tried to give the optical principles of Impressionism a scientific basis, and the *Post-Impressionists began a long series of movements that attempted to free colour and line from purely representational functions. Similarly, the *Symbolists wanted to restore the emotional values they thought the Impressionists had sacrificed by concentrating so strongly on the fleeting and the casual.

imprimatura. A thin layer of transparent colour applied to a white *ground to reduce its absorbency and tone down its brightness.

Independent Group. A small and informal discussion group that met intermittently between 1952 and 1955 at the *Institute of Contemporary Arts, London. Its members included Lawrence *Alloway, Richard *Hamilton, and Eduardo *Paolozzi. The issues they discussed included advertising and mass culture, and the first phase of British *Pop art grew out of the group.

Indiana, Robert (1928–). American painter, sculptor, and graphic artist. His ori-

ginal name was Robert Clark, but he adopted the name of his native state as his own. He is regarded as one of the leading American *Pop artists, and although he has done some figurative paintings he is best known for pictures involving geometric shapes emblazoned with lettering and signs. His vivid colours often create effects of visual ambiguity reminiscent of those of *Op art.

Informalism. *See* ART INFORMEL.

Ingres,   Jean-Auguste-Dominique (1780–1867). French painter, born at Montauban, the son of a minor painter and sculptor, **Jean-Marie-Joseph   Ingres** (1755–1814). After early training in the Toulouse Academy he moved to Paris in 1797 to study in Jacques-Louis *David's studio. He won the *Prix de Rome in 1801, but because of the unsettled political situation in France his departure for Italy was postponed until 1806. In the interval he produced his first portraits. These fall into two categories: portraits of himself and his friends, often *Romantic in spirit (*Self-Portrait*, 1804, Mus. Condé, Chantilly), and portraits of well-to-do clients characterized by purity of line and enamel-like colouring (*Mlle Rivière*, 1805, Louvre, Paris). Their expressive contours have a sensuous beauty of their own beyond their function to contain and delineate form, and this was characteristic of Ingres's painting throughout his life.

During his first years in Rome Ingres continued to execute portraits and began to paint bathers, a theme that was to become one of his favourites (*Valpinçon Bather*, 1808, Louvre). When his four-year scholarship ended, he decided to stay in Rome, where he earned his living mainly with pencil portraits of members of the French colony. However, he also received more substantial commissions, including two decorative paintings for Napoleon's palace in Rome (*Triumph of Romulus over Acron*, 1812, École des Beaux-Arts, Paris; and *Ossian's Dream*, 1813, Mus. Ingres, Montauban). In 1820 he moved from Rome to Florence, where he remained for four years, working mainly on his *Raphaelesque *Vow of Louis XIII*, commissioned for the cathedral of Montauban. Ingres's work had often been severely criticized in Paris because of its 'Gothic' distortions, and when he accompanied this painting to the *Salon of 1824 he was surprised to find it acclaimed and himself set up as the leader of the academic opposition to the Romanticism exemplified by Delacroix (whose *Massacre at Chios* was shown at the same Salon). Ingres stayed in Paris for the next ten years and received the official success and honours he had always craved. During this period he devoted much of his time to executing two large works: the *Apotheosis of Homer*, for a ceiling in the *Louvre (installed 1827), and the *Martyrdom of St Symphorian* (shown at the 1834 Salon) for the cathedral of Autun. After the latter painting was badly received, however, he accepted the directorship of the French Academy in Rome, a post he held from 1835 to 1840. He was a model administrator and teacher, greatly improving the academy's facilities, but he produced few major works in this period. In 1841 he returned to France, once again acclaimed as the champion of traditional values. He was heartbroken when his wife died in 1849, but he made a happy second marriage in 1852, and he continued working with great energy into his eighties. In this final period he produced some of his best portraits (*Madame Moitessier*, 1856, NG, London), and one of his acknowledged masterpieces dates from the last years of his life, the extraordinarily sensuous *Turkish Bath* (1863, Louvre). At his death he left a huge bequest of his work (several paintings and more than 4,000 drawings) to his home town of Montauban and they are now in the museum bearing his name there.

Ingres is a puzzling artist and his career is full of contradictions. By the end of his life he was perceived as the great upholder of the French classical tradition, yet he had spent much of his early career obstinately persisting with work that was unappreciated in Paris. In his way of life he was bourgeois, but as *Baudelaire remarked, his finest works 'are the product of a deeply sensuous nature'. The central contradiction of his career is that although he was held up as the guardian of classical rules and precepts, it is his personal obsessions and mannerisms that make him such a great artist. His technique as a painter was academically unimpeachable—he said paint should be as smooth 'as the skin of an onion'—but he was often attacked for the expressive distortions of his draughtsmanship; critics said,

for example, that the abnormally long back of *La Grande Odalisque* (1814, Louvre) had three extra vertebrae. Unfortunately his influence was mainly seen in those shortcomings and weaknesses that have come to be regarded as the hallmark of inferior academic work; he had scores of admiring pupils, but *Chassériau was the only one to attain distinction. In terms of calligraphic draughtsmanship, his true successors were *Degas and *Picasso.

ink. Coloured fluid used for writing, drawing, or printing. Inks usually have staining power without body, but printers' inks—pigments mixed with oil and varnish—are opaque. The use of inks goes back in China and Egypt to at least 2500 BC. The earliest known type was produced from lampblack (a pigment made from soot) ground into a solution of glue or gums. These materials could be moulded into dry sticks or blocks, which were then mixed with water for use. Ink brought from China or Japan in such dry form came to be known in the West as 'Chinese ink' or 'Indian ink'. The names are also given to a similar preparation used today. Other materials that have been used to make ink include plant dyes, soot (*see* BISTRE) and fluids from marine creatures (*see* SEPIA). Most modern inks use soluble synthetic dyes as the colouring agent.

Innes, J. D. (James Dickson) (1887–1914). British painter, mainly of landscapes (particularly mountain scenes) but also occasionally of figure subjects. He often painted with his friend Augustus *John, particularly in their native Wales in 1911 and 1912. His early work was in an *Impressionist manner influenced by *Steer, but he developed a more expressive *Post-Impressionist style combining hot colour and decorative pattern. He usually painted on a fairly small scale, often on wooden panels; he also worked a good deal in watercolour.

Inness, George (1825–94). American landscape painter. He was largely self-taught, learning a good deal during several lengthy visits to Europe (the *Barbizon School in particular had a powerful impact on him). His early work was influenced by the detailed handling and *Romantic approach of the *Hudson River School, but his style became much freer and more atmospheric, and he turned away from grandiose scenes to intimate subjects lacking in conventional picturesque appeal. He was a deeply spiritual man and some of his later work has a mystical, *Symbolist flavour. At the beginning of his career he worked in New York, but in 1859 he moved to the village of Medfield, near Boston, where he found the isolation more conducive to his work; later he settled in New Jersey. Inness is considered by many to be the greatest American landscape painter of the 19th century. His son, **George Inness, Jr.** (1854–1926), was also a painter and published an account of his father's career (1917).

Inshaw, David. *See* BLAKE, SIR PETER.

installation. A term that can be applied very generally to the disposition of objects in an exhibition (the hanging of paintings, the arrangement of sculptures, and so on), but which also has the more specific meaning of a one-off work (often a large-scale *assemblage) conceived for and usually more or less filling a specific interior (generally that of a gallery). This type of work has various precedents, including the room-filling *Merz* constructions of Kurt *Schwitters, but it was not until the 1970s that the term came into common use and not until the 1980s that certain artists started to specialize in this kind of work, creating a genre of 'Installation art'. In the 1970s installations were often impermanent and could be seen as part of the movement against the collectable art 'object' that was so fashionable at the time. However, many installations are now intended for permanent display, and even some of the most unlikely works have proved collectable. The best-known example is *20:50* (1987) by the British sculptor Richard Wilson (1953–), which consists of a room filled with used sump oil; this was created for the Matt's Gallery, London, but it was subsequently resited at the Royal Scottish Academy, Edinburgh, and it is now in the Saatchi Collection, London.

Institute of Contemporary Arts (ICA), London. Cultural centre founded by Roland *Penrose and Herbert *Read in 1947 to encourage new developments in the arts and cater for some of the functions fulfilled by the *Museum of Modern Art in New York—organizing exhibitions, lectures, films, and so on. Its original home was in Dover Street,

but it moved to Nash House, the Mall, in 1968. Many leading artists have been members of the ICA and it has played an important role in certain developments; for example, in the 1950s it was the cradle of British *Pop art (*see* INDEPENDENT GROUP).

intaglio. Carving or engraving on a small scale, as for example on a gemstone or seal, in which the design is hollowed into the surface—the opposite of *cameo, in which the design projects above the surface. In the graphic arts, 'intaglio printing' refers to any process of printmaking in which the parts of the plate or block that will take the ink are recessed into it rather than raised above it ('relief printing'). *Etching is thus a form of intaglio printing (*see* PRINT).

intarsia. Method of creating a picture or design on a wooden surface (typically wall panelling or a piece of furniture) by attaching small pieces of variously coloured woods to it. Intarsia was popular in *Renaissance Italy; the most famous examples of the technique decorate the studiolo of Federico da *Montefeltro in the Ducal Palace, Urbino.

International Gothic. Style in painting, sculpture, and the decorative arts that spread widely over western Europe between *c.*1375 and *c.*1425. The style was characterized by aristocratic elegance and delicate naturalistic detail and was formed by a blending of elements from Italy and northern Europe, a situation encouraged by the cultural rivalry of major courts and the growing frequency with which leading artists travelled between them. Lombardy, Franco-Flemish Burgundy, and Bohemia were among the most important centres of the style, major exponents of which included *Gentile da Fabriano, *Pisanello, and the *Limbourg brothers. Elements of the style are present in the work of many of the leading artists of the early *Renaissance, such as Fra *Angelico, *Ghiberti, and *Uccello. In the context of English art, the finest work in the style is the celebrated Wilton Diptych (NG, London), which testifies to how genuinely international the International Gothic style was, for although it is a painting of extraordinary beauty and must be from the hand of an artist of the highest rank, authorities disagree as to his likely nationality (English, French, Italian, and Bohemian have been proposed). It shows

Richard II being presented to the Virgin and Child by John the Baptist, Edward the Confessor, and Edmund the Martyr (his patron saints), but its purpose and significance are uncertain. It probably dates from late in Richard's reign (heraldic evidence suggests it cannot be earlier than *c.*1395), and was presumably commissioned by him.

Intimisme. A type of painting featuring intimate domestic scenes, more or less *Impressionist in technique, particularly associated with *Bonnard and *Vuillard, who practised it from the 1890s (this is when the term was first used). Whereas the Impressionists usually aimed at accurately reflecting the colours of the natural world, the Intimistes often exaggerated and distorted colour to express mood, conveying the warmth and comfort of an untroubled domestic life.

intonaco. In *fresco painting, the final layer of plaster on the wall; the paint is applied to it while the plaster is still wet.

Isenbrandt Adriaen. *See* YSENBRANDT.

Israëls, Jozef (1824–1911). Dutch painter. He studied in Amsterdam and Paris and began his career as a portrait and historical painter, but in the 1850s he turned to the kind of work for which he is principally known—scenes of fishermen and peasants and the milieu in which they lived. In 1870 he moved from Amsterdam to The Hague and thereafter became one of the leading members of the *Hague School. He has been called 'the Dutch *Millet' and he won great popularity because of his piously sentimental approach; indeed, in his time he was the most famous living Dutch artist, with an international reputation. His son, **Isaac** (1865–1934), also worked mainly in The Hague, but in a style almost completely independent of his father's. His pictures of the social life of his time are influenced by *Breitner and characterized by the vivid colours and vigorous brushwork of the *Impressionists.

Itinerants. *See* WANDERERS.

Itten, Johannes (1888–1967). Swiss painter, designer, writer on art, teacher, and administrator. In 1916 he opened his own school of art in Vienna, then from 1919 to 1923 he taught at the *Bauhaus, where he was in charge of the 'preliminary course', obligatory for all students. In 1923 he left the Bauhaus and opened another school of his own in Berlin, then from 1932 to 1938 he taught at the Krefeld School of Textile Design. In 1938 he settled in Zurich, where he held four posts concurrently—as director of the School of Arts and Crafts, the Museum of Arts and Crafts, the Rietberg Museum, and the School of Textile Design. He held the first three posts until 1953 and retired from the fourth in 1961. Itten wrote several books on art theory and his work as a painter consisted mainly of geometrical abstractions exemplifying his researches into colour. However, he is best remembered as a teacher, especially for his preliminary course at the Bauhaus, which had a great influence on instruction in other art schools. He emphasized the importance of knowledge of materials, but also encouraged his pupils to develop their imaginations through, for example, automatic writing (*see* AUTOMATISM). His mystical ideas were opposed to the technological outlook of *Gropius (their quarrels caused Itten's departure from the Bauhaus) and he had a reputation as a crank (he followed an obscure faith called Mazdaznan, shaved his head, and wore a long robe), but he influenced many of his students. Frank Whitford (*Bauhaus*, 1984) describes him as 'a perplexing mixture of saint and charlatan'.

Ivanov, Alexander (1806–58). Russian painter. He was born in St Petersburg and studied there at the Academy under his father, the painter **Andrei Ivanov** (1772–1848). Most of his career was spent in Rome, where he settled in 1831. Initially he was preoccupied with subjects from the classical world, but partly under the influence of the *Nazarenes (he was a friend of *Overbeck) he turned to religious painting, and his fame is inseparable from his main work, which occupied him for twenty years, *Christ's First Appearance to the People* (1837–57, Tretyakov Gal., Moscow). This enormous painting achieved European celebrity long before its completion, but it had a disappointing reception when it was finally exhibited in St Petersburg in 1858, its *Raphaelesque composition being at odds with the naturalistic setting and details, the result of hundreds of preparatory studies. Ivanov accompanied the painting to St Petersburg and died there of cholera a few months afterwards. He had no immediate followers, but the moral sincerity of his work was influential on many Russian painters, notably *Kramskoi and *Repin; when Repin first saw *Christ's First Appearance to the People* in 1867 he pronounced it 'the greatest work in the whole world, by a genius, born in Russia'.

ivory. A hard, smooth, creamy white substance obtained from the tusks or teeth of certain animals, widely used as a carving material from prehistoric times onwards. Elephant tusks have been the commonest source of ivory, but mammoth tusks (from deposits in Siberia), hippopotamus teeth, and walrus tusks have been much used; carvings made from narwhal and rhinoceros horn, stag-horn, and even bone, have also been embraced by the term. True ivory is an excellent material for high-quality, small-scale sculpture, for it can be easily worked with saws, chisels, drills, and rasps, and it can take a fine polish and detailed surface treatment. Unless separate pieces are joined together, the size and shape of a carving are limited by the dimensions of the tusk, the curvature of which has sometimes been exploited to give a graceful swing to the figure, notably in *Gothic statuettes of the Virgin. Though ivory was often painted in the Middle Ages, its natural lustre, translucence, and satin smoothness have always been appreciated. In the ancient world it was classed with gold and precious stones as a luxury material, and the Greeks used it for colossal *chryselephantine (gold and ivory) cult statues. After the 14th century ivory-carving declined steadily in Europe, but the art revived in the 17th century.

Jack of Diamonds. *See* KNAVE OF DIA-MONDS.

Jackson, A. Y. (Alexander Young) (1882–1974). Canadian landscape painter, active mainly in Toronto, where he settled in 1913 after extensive travels in Europe. He was one of the leading artists in the *Group of Seven and in the later years of his long career became a venerated senior figure in Canadian painting. Jackson visited virtually every region of Canada, including the Arctic, and responded particularly to the hilly region of rural Quebec along the St Lawrence River. From 1921 he visited the area almost every spring, and the canvases he prepared from sketches made there are generally regarded as his finest works. Their easy, rolling rhythms and rich colouring influenced many other Canadian landscape painters.

James, M. R. *See* FITZWILLIAM MUSEUM.

Jamesone, George (1589/90–1644). Scottish portrait painter, active in Aberdeen and Edinburgh. His name has been indiscriminately attached to a great number of Scottish portraits of the period, as he is virtually the only 17th-century Scottish painter about whom anything is known. A now discounted tradition has it that he trained with *Rubens and he has been flatteringly called 'the Scottish van *Dyck', but his style was closer to Cornelius *Johnson's. It is difficult to assess, however, as many of the works that are certainly by him are in a bad state of preservation. John Michael *Wright was his pupil.

Janis, Sidney (1896–1989). American art dealer and writer on art. Between the departure of Peggy *Guggenheim from the USA in 1947 and the rise of Leo *Castelli in the 1960s he was the most important figure in promoting the work of avant-garde American artists, particularly the *Abstract Expressionists. He was also interested in *naive art and in 1939 'discovered' one of the outstanding American naive painters, Morris Hirshfield (1872–1946). Janis wrote *They Taught Themselves: American Primitive Painters of the 20th Century* (1942), *Abstract and Surrealist Art in America* (1944), and (with his wife Harriet) *Picasso: The Recent Years, 1939–1946* (1946).

Janssen, Abraham (*c*.1575–1632). Flemish figure and portrait painter, active mainly in Antwerp. In 1598 and 1601 he is documented in Rome and by 1602 he was back in Antwerp. A second visit to Italy has been postulated, for although in 1601 he was painting in a *Mannerist style (*Diana and Callisto*, MFA, Budapest), by 1610 (*Scaldis and Antwerpia*, Koninklijk Mus., Antwerp) his work had become much more solid, sober, and classical, suggesting close knowledge of *Caravaggio in particular. For the next decade Janssen was one of the most powerful and individual painters in Flanders, but during the 1620s his work became less remarkable as he fell under the all-pervasive influence of *Rubens. His pupils included Gerard *Seghers and Theodoor *Rombouts.

Jawlensky, Alexei von (1864–1941). Russian *Expressionist painter, active mainly in Germany. Originally he was an army officer, but in 1906 he resigned his commission and moved to Munich to devote himself completely to art. Munich was to be his home until the outbreak of the First World War, but he travelled a good deal in this period, notably making several visits to France (he was the first of his Munich associates to have direct contact with advanced French art). In 1905 he met *Matisse in Paris and was influenced by the strong colours and bold outlines of the *Fauves. He combined them with influences from the Russian traditions of icon painting and peasant art to form a highly personal style that expressed his passionate temperament and mystical conception of art. A mood of melancholy introspection—far removed from the ebullience of Fauvism—is characteristic of much of his work and it has been said that he 'saw Matisse through Russian eyes'. In 1909 he was one of the founders of the *Neue Künstlervereinigung, and apart from *Kandinsky he was the outstanding artist of the group. His most characteristic works of this period are a series of powerful portrait heads, begun in 1910 (*Alexander Sacharoff*, 1913, Städtisches Mus., Wiesbaden). On the outbreak of war in 1914 Jawlensky took refuge in Switzerland, where he remained until 1921. His work there included a series of 'variations' on the view from a window—small, semi-abstract landscapes with a meditative, religious aura. Like Kandinsky and others, Jawlensky believed in a correspondence between colours and musical sounds and he named these pictures *Songs without Words*. In 1918 he began a series of nearly abstract heads, in which he reduced the features to a few curves and lines. Unlike Kandinsky, however, he always based his forms on nature. From 1921 he lived in Wiesbaden, and in 1924 he joined with Kandinsky, *Klee, and *Feininger to form the *Blaue Vier. From 1929 he suffered from arthritis and by 1938 this had forced him to abandon painting completely.

Jervas, Charles (*c*.1675–1739). Irish painter, active mainly in London. His surname was pronounced, and often spelled, Jarvis. After studying with *Kneller he spent ten years in Italy, mainly Rome, before settling in London in 1709. Jervas had a great reputation and succeeded Kneller as principal painter to George II in 1723, but his fame depended on his friendship with various literary figures, who trumpeted his praises, rather than on the quality of his work, which does not rise above the level of that of any other of Kneller's pupils or followers. He has perhaps more claim to literary distinction, for he made a well-regarded translation of Cervantes's *Don Quixote*, posthumously published in 1742. His conceit was enormous: once, having copied a painting by *Titian, he looked from one to the other and said complacently 'Poor Little Tit! How he would stare!'

Jeune Peinture Belge. An avant-garde artists' association founded in Brussels in 1945 with the aim of holding exhibitions of contemporary Belgian art throughout Europe. The members of the group (who included *Alechinsky and *Bury) were strongly individualistic and had no common programme, but they were basically abstract in their outlook and were influenced particularly by the expressive abstraction of the post-war *École de Paris. The group dissolved in 1948.

John, Augustus (1878–1961). British painter and draughtsman. He studied at the *Slade School, 1894–8. In his early days there 'he appeared a neat, timid, unremarkable personality' (*DNB*), but after injuring his head diving into the sea while on holiday in Pembrokeshire in 1897 he became a dramatically changed figure, described by Wyndham *Lewis as 'a great man of action into whose hands the fairies had placed a paintbrush instead of a sword'. He grew a beard and became the very image of the unpredictable bohemian artist. His work, too, changed dramatically: previously it had been described by *Tonks as 'methodical', but it became vigorous and spontaneous, especially in his brilliant drawings—his draughtsmanship was already legendary by the time he left the Slade. In the first quarter of the 20th century John was identified with all that was most independent and rebellious in British art and he became one of the most talked-about figures of the day. In 1911–14 he led a nomadic life, sometimes living in a caravan and camping with gypsies. As well as romanticized pictures of gypsy life he painted deliciously colourful small-scale landscapes, sometimes working alongside his friend J. D. *Innes. During the same period he also painted ambitious figure compositions, with stylized forms that bring him close to French *Symbolist painters (*The Way Down to the Sea*, 1909–11, Lamont AG, Exeter, New Hampshire). In the First World War he was an *Official War Artist. It is as a portraitist, however, that John is best remembered. He was taken up by society and painted a host of aristocratic beauties as well as many of the leading literary figures of the day. Increasingly, however, the painterly brilliance of his early work degenerated into flashiness and bombast, and the second half of his long career added little to his achievement, although he remained a colourful, newsworthy figure until the end of his life. He was one of the few British artists who have become familiar to the general public, and his image changed from that of rebel to Grand Old Man (he was awarded the Order of Merit in 1942). He wrote two volumes of autobiography, *Chiaroscuro*, 1952, and *Finishing Touches*, posthumously published in 1964. A new edition entitled *The Autobiography of Augustus John* appeared in 1975.

John, Gwen (1876–1939). British painter. She was the sister of Augustus *John, but his complete opposite artistically, as she was in personality, living a reclusive life and favouring introspective subjects. After studying at the *Slade School, 1895–8, she took lessons in Paris from *Whistler, and adopted from him the delicate greyish tonality that characterizes much of her work. In 1899 she returned to London, but in 1904 she settled permanently in France, living first in Paris (earning her living modelling for other artists—including *Rodin, who became her lover), then from 1911 in Meudon, on the outskirts of the city. In 1913 she became a Catholic, and she said 'My religion and my art, these are my life.' Most of her paintings depict single figures (typically girls or nuns) in interiors, painted with great sensitivity and an unobtrusive originality (*Self-Portrait*, c.1900, NPG, London). She had only one exhibition devoted to her work during her lifetime (at the New Chenil Galleries, London, in 1936) and at the time of her death was little known. However, her brother's prophecy that one day she would be considered a better artist than him has been fulfilled, for as his star has fallen hers has risen, and since the 1960s she has been the subject of numerous books and exhibitions.

Johns, Jasper (1930–). American painter, sculptor, and printmaker. His career has been closely associated with that of his friend Robert *Rauschenberg, and they are considered the leading figures in the move away from *Abstract Expressionism to the types of *Pop art and *Minimal art that succeeded it. In the early 1950s he worked as a commercial artist in New York, doing display work for shop windows. He began to emerge on the art scene in 1955 and had his first one-man show at Leo *Castelli's gallery in New York in 1958. This was an enormous success, and since then he has become one of the most famous (and wealthy) living artists. Much of his work has been done in the form of series of paintings presenting commonplace two-dimensional objects—for example *Flags*, *Targets*, and *Numbers*—and his sculptures have most characteristically been of equally banal subjects such as beer cans or brushes in a coffee tin. Such works—at one and the same time laboriously realistic and patently artificial—are seen by his admirers as brilliant explorations of the relationship between art and reality; to others, they are as uninteresting as the objects depicted.

Johnson, Cornelius (Cornelis Jonson van Ceulen) (1593–1661). Anglo-Dutch portrait painter. He was born in London of Flemish parents and perhaps trained in Holland. By about 1618 he was in practice in London and he worked there until 1643, when he left England because of the Civil War and settled in Holland. There are several hundred portraits by him, mainly of people from the upper (but not the highest) levels of society. He was a conservative artist but a sensitive one, with a delicate feeling for colour and characterization.

Johnston, Frank. *See* GROUP OF SEVEN.

Jones, Allen (1937–). British painter, printmaker, sculptor, and designer, one of the most committed exponents of *Pop art. Although he has worked primarily as a painter, printmaker, and designer, he is best known to the public for a distinctive type of sculpture in which figures of women—more or less life-size, dressed in fetishistic clothing, and with what Jones calls 'high definition female parts'—double as pieces of furniture; for example, a woman on all fours supporting a sheet of glass on her back becomes a coffee table, and a standing figure with outstretched hands becomes a hatstand. He began making such sculptures in the late 1960s and continues to do so, although in a manner that he calls 'less aggressive' and 'easier to take' (they have come in for a good deal of criticism for alleged demeaning of women as sex objects; an article in the feminist journal *Spare Rib* in 1973 suggested that they expressed a castration complex). His work as a designer has included sets and costumes for the erotic review *Oh! Calcutta!* (1969).

Jones, David (1895–1974). British painter, draughtsman, printmaker, and writer. A convert to Roman Catholicism in 1921, he met Eric *Gill in 1922 and under his influence achieved a sense of purpose (his studies at the Camberwell School of Art, 1909–15, had left him, as he said, 'completely muddle-headed as to the function of art in general'). Gill not only introduced him to wood engraving, but also guided him in rejecting the current concern with formal properties in favour of an art that aspired to reveal universal and symbolic truths behind the appearance of things. He worked mainly in pencil and watercolour, his subjects including landscape, portraits, still life, animals, and imaginative themes; Arthurian legend was one of his main inspirations. As a writer he is best known for In Parenthesis (1937), a long work of mixed poetry and prose on the subject of the First World War (in which he had fought). T. S. Eliot declared this to be a work of genius and it was awarded the Hawthornden Prize. After the Second World War Jones retired to Harrow and devoted himself mainly to calligraphic inscriptions in the Welsh language (he was of Welsh extraction).

Jones, Inigo (1573–1652). English architect, stage designer, draughtsman, and painter. Jones was one of the greatest of English architects and certainly the most influential, introducing a pure classical style based on the work of the Italian architect Andrea Palladio to a country where *Renaissance influence had previously been fairly superficial. It was not until he was in his forties, however, that he showed his genius as an architect, and the first known mention of him as an artist is as a 'picture maker' in 1603. No paintings certainly by him are known, but his drawings survive in large numbers (the finest collection is at Chatsworth). They are mainly costume and scenery designs for the court masques, on which he worked from 1605 to 1640, and in which he introduced movable scenery and the proscenium arch into England. His lively and fluent style as a draughtsman reflects two lengthy visits to Italy (c.1600 and 1613–14), the second of them accompanying the great collector the Earl of *Arundel. He advised Arundel on the purchase of Italian antiques while developing his own knowledge of Italian and *antique architecture, and his knowledge as well as his skills gave him immense prestige in England at the courts of James I and Charles I. His principal collaborator in the masques was the formidable Ben Jonson, with whom he had a running feud about the rival claims of words and spectacle. Few of Jones's buildings survive in anything like their original state. The two most important are in London: the Queen's House at Greenwich (1616–35), for which Orazio *Gentileschi

provided decorations, and the Banqueting House in Whitehall (1619–22), with its painted ceiling by *Rubens.

Jones, Thomas (1742–1803). Welsh landscape painter, a pupil of Richard *Wilson. He painted some ambitious *classical landscapes in Wilson's manner, but he is now best known for his remarkably fresh and unaffected oil sketches done in and around Naples and Rome during a period in Italy, 1776–83 (good examples are in the National Museum and Gallery, Cardiff). They are among the earliest British examples of this kind of open-air sketch and have a directness that looks forward to *Corot.

Jongkind, Johan Barthold (1819–91). Dutch landscape painter and etcher, active mainly in France, where he was a precursor of *Impressionism. Although he was better appreciated during his lifetime than van *Gogh, in some ways his career is similar to that of his more famous countryman. Both artists made a greater impression abroad than in their own country; both failed to adjust to the society of their time; both endured much poverty and were troubled by serious psychological problems; and sensational aspects of their lives—in Jongkind's case it was alcoholism—have interfered with a balanced appraisal of their achievement. Jongkind studied in The Hague under *Schelfhout. From 1846 he spent much of his time in France and from 1860 he made his home there permanently. He worked and exhibited with members of the *Barbizon School, and during the 1860s he played an important part in the development of Impressionism; his friend *Monet acknowledged him, together with *Boudin, as the most significant formative influence on his work. Jongkind's output was varied, but he is perhaps best known for his atmospheric coastal and river scenes.

Joos van Cleve (c.1490–1540/1). Netherlandish painter, born presumably at Cleves in the lower Rhine region and active mainly in Antwerp, where he became a member of the painters' guild in 1511. He seems to have become one of the city's leading painters, but his eclectic style and the lack of documented works mean that his career is ill-defined. There is a flavour of *Leonardo in some of his paintings, and he may have visited Italy. Almost certainly he worked in

France in the early 1530s, and he possibly visited England at about the same time, as a portrait of Henry VIII (*c*.1536) in the Royal Collection is attributed to him. According to van *Mander he collaborated with Joachim *Patinir: a *Rest on the Flight into Egypt* (Mus. Royaux, Brussels) is possibly a joint work. The large output from his studio consisted mainly of religious works, particularly pictures of the Virgin and Child and the Holy Family. Joos's son, **Cornelis van Cleve** (1520–67), was also a painter. He was known as 'Sotte Cleve' (Mad Cleve) after becoming insane in 1556—a result of failing to win the patronage of Philip II of Spain (*see* HABSBURG).

Joos van Wassenhove (active *c*.1460–80). Netherlandish painter, part of whose career was spent in Italy, where he was known as Giusto da Guanto (Justus of Ghent). He became a member of the Antwerp painters' guild in 1460, but by 1464 he had moved to Ghent, where he was a friend of Hugo van der *Goes. At some time after 1469 he moved to Rome, and by 1473 he had settled in Urbino, where he worked for Duke Federico da *Montefeltro. Joos's only documented work is the *Communion of the Apostles* (also known as the *Institution of the Eucharist*, 1473–4), which is still at Urbino, in the Galleria Nazionale. Like Hugo's Portinari Altarpiece, it was an important work in spreading knowledge of the Netherlandish oil technique in Italy. Of the other works attributed to Joos, the most important are a series of 28 *Famous Men* (Gal. Naz., Urbino, and Louvre, Paris), commissioned for the Ducal Palace. Their authorship is controversial, and they may have been a work of collaboration between Joos and the Spanish painter Pedro *Berruguete.

Jordaens, Jacob (1593–1678). Flemish painter, the pupil and son-in-law of Adam van *Noort. Early in his career he often assisted *Rubens, but he had a flourishing studio of his own by the 1620s, and after Rubens's death in 1640 he was the leading figure painter in Flanders. His style was heavily indebted to Rubens, but was much more earthbound, using thick *impasto, strong contrasts of light and shade, and colouring that is often rather lurid. His physical types, too, are coarser than Rubens's and his name is particularly associated with large canvases of hearty rollicking peasants. Two of his favourite subjects, which he depicted several times, are 'The Satyr and the Peasant', based on one of Aesop's fables, and 'The King Drinks', which depicts a boisterous group enjoying an abundant Twelfth Night feast. Jordaens's prolific output, however, included many other subjects, including religious works and portraits, and he also etched and made designs for tapestries. He rarely left his native Antwerp, but he received commissions from several courts in northern Europe, the most important being *The Triumph of Frederick Hendrik* (1651–2), an enormous composition painted for the Huis ten Bosch, the royal villa near The Hague. In about 1655 Jordaens became a convert to Protestantism; he continued to paint pictures for Catholic churches, but the work of the last two decades of his life is more subdued.

Jorn, Asger (Asger Oluf Jørgensen) (1914–73). Danish painter, sculptor, printmaker, ceramicist, designer, collector, and writer, active in Paris for much of his career. He was one of the founders of the *Cobra group in 1948, and his most characteristic works are highly coloured abstracts executed with violently expressive brushwork.

Joseph II, Emperor. *See* HABSBURG.

Jouvenet, Jean (1644–1717). French painter, the outstanding member of a family of artists from Rouen. He moved to Paris in 1661 and became one of *Le Brun's assistants. His early works, including decorations for the Salon de Mars at Versailles (1671–4), were usually imitative of his master's style, although he was also influenced by Eustache *Le Sueur (*St Bruno in Prayer*, Nationalmuseum, Stockholm). He worked on numerous major decorative schemes throughout his career, but he is now best remembered as the leading French religious painter of his generation, creating many altarpieces (some of huge size) for churches in Paris and elsewhere. His later work was marked both by *Baroque emotionalism and by a realistic treatment of details foreign to the principles encouraged by the Académie Royale. It is recorded, for example, that before painting his *Miraculous Draught of Fishes* (*c*.1706, Louvre, Paris) he studied fishing scenes on the spot at Dieppe. Throughout his career he also painted portraits. In 1713 his right hand was paralysed, but he learnt to paint with his left.

Juan de Flandes (d. *c*.1519). Netherlandish painter active in Spain, where he is first documented in 1496. He was one of a number of north European artists employed by Queen Isabella of Castile. A portable altarpiece he painted for her in a delicate miniaturistic style was once much renowned, but it is now dismembered and the surviving 27 panels (out of the original 47) are widely scattered (one is in the NG, London). After Isabella's death in 1504 he worked for churches in Salamanca and Palencia.

Juan de Juanes. *See* MAÇIP.

Juan de Juni (*c*.1507–77). French sculptor, active in Spain from *c*.1533. He worked in León and Salamanca before settling in Valladolid in 1540. A prolific sculptor of religious subjects, he excelled in the dramatic expression of emotion, and is generally ranked next to Alonso *Berruguete as the outstanding Spanish sculptor of his period. Berruguete himself called him 'the best foreign carver in Castile'. Juni's most famous works are probably the two groups of the *Entombment* in Valladolid Museum (1545) and Segovia Cathedral (1571).

Judd, Donald (1928–94). American sculptor, designer, and writer on art, one of the leading exponents of *Minimal art. From 1959 to 1965 he earned his living as an art critic, working mainly for *Arts Magazine*. He began his career as a practising artist as a painter, but in the early 1960s he took up sculpture with heavily textured monochrome reliefs. In 1963 he began making the type of work for which he is best known—arrangements of identical rectangular box-like shapes cantilevered ladder-like from a wall. Initially he worked mainly in wood, but after a successful exhibition at the Green Gallery, New York, in 1963–4 he began having them industrially manufactured in various metals (or sometimes coloured perspex). In 1970 he began making works for the specific space in which they were to be exhibited, and in 1972 he began producing outdoor works. In spite of great financial success, Judd (who was notoriously touchy) disliked the New York 'art crowd' and in 1973 moved to Marfa, Texas, where he converted the buildings of an old army base into studios and installation spaces. In the 1980s he began designing furniture in a similar style to his sculptures. His *Complete Writings* have been published in two volumes (1976 and 1987).

Juel, Jens (1745–1802). Danish painter. He had a distinguished career both in Denmark and in his travels throughout Europe—he studied in Hamburg and between 1772 and 1779 he worked successively in Dresden, Rome, Paris, and Geneva. After settling in Copenhagen he became court painter (1780) and a professor at the Academy (1784), although he had little interest in teaching. Juel painted landscapes, *genre scenes, and still lifes (particularly flowers), but he is most renowned for his sensitive portraits.

Jugendstil. *See* ART NOUVEAU.

Julian, Rodolphe. *See* ACADÉMIE.

Julius II, Pope. *See* ROVERE.

Junk art. Art constructed from the waste products of urban life. In so far as Junk art represented a revolt against traditional materials and a desire to show that works of art can be constructed from the humblest and most worthless things, it may be plausibly traced back to *Cubist collages, *Duchamp's *ready-mades, and the work of Kurt *Schwitters. However, it is not until the 1950s that it is possible to speak of a Junk movement, particularly with the work of Robert *Rauschenberg, who used rags and tatters of cloth, torn reproductions, and other waste materials in his *combine paintings. Lawrence *Alloway, in 1961, was the first to apply the name 'Junk art' to such works, and the term was then extended to sculpture made from scrap metal, broken machine parts, used timber, and so on. Californian *Funk art sometimes made use of similar materials. The Junk art of the USA had analogies in the work of *Tàpies and others in Spain, *Burri and *Arte Povera in Italy, and similar movements in most European countries and in Japan, where debris from the Second World War was sometimes converted to artistic use.

Juste, Jean. *See* GIUSTI.

Justus of Ghent. *See* JOOS VAN WASSENHOVE.

K

Kahlo, Frida (1907–54). Mexican painter. In 1925, at a time when she was preparing to enter medical school, she suffered appalling injuries in a traffic accident, leaving her a permanent semi-invalid, often in severe pain. During her convalescence she began painting portraits of herself and others. She remained her own favourite model and her art was usually directly autobiographical. In 1928 she married Mexico's most famous artist, Diego *Rivera, who was twice her age and twice her size. Their relationship was often strained, but it lasted to her death, through various separations, divorce and remarriage (1939–40), and infidelities on both sides (one of her lovers was Leon Trotsky, who was assassinated in 1940 while living in Mexico City). Kahlo was mainly self-taught as a painter. She was influenced by Rivera, but more by Mexican folk art, and her work has a colourful, almost *naive vigour, tinged with *Surrealist fantasy. Her paintings of her own physical and psychic pain are narcissistic and nightmarish, but also—like her personality—fiery and flamboyant. They were widely shown in Mexico and she had successful exhibitions in Paris and New York in 1938 and 1939 respectively, but during her lifetime she was overshadowed by her husband. Since her death, however, her fame has grown and she has become something of a feminist heroine, admired for her refusal to let great physical suffering crush her spirit or interfere with her art and her left-wing political activities. Her house in the suburb of Coyoacán, Mexico City, was opened as a museum dedicated to her in 1958.

Kahnweiler, Daniel-Henri (1884–1979). German-born art dealer, publisher, and writer, who became a French citizen in 1937. In 1907 he opened a gallery in Paris. His first purchases were of *Fauvist works, but he is best known as the friend and promoter of the *Cubists. In 1912 *Braque and *Picasso signed contracts giving Kahnweiler exclusive rights to buy their entire outputs. He was also a friend and supporter of Juan *Gris, of whom he wrote a standard biography (1947). As a publisher he brought out numerous books illustrated by his artist friends.

Kalf, Willem (1619–93). Dutch painter, one of the most celebrated of all still-life painters. He was born in Rotterdam and from about 1640 to 1646 worked in Paris. On his return to the Netherlands he lived in Hoorn and then in 1653 settled in Amsterdam. His early works were modest kitchen and courtyard scenes, but he soon became the outstanding exponent of a type of still life in which fruit and precious objects—porcelain, oriental rugs, Venetian glass—are arranged in grand *Baroque displays. He was an art dealer as well as a painter, so he may have used objects he had in stock as models. His pictures have often been compared with those of *Vermeer because of his masterly handling of texture and his ability to manipulate warm and cool colours (he frequently contrasts the reddish browns in a carpet with the yellow of a peeled lemon and the blue and white of porcelain).

Kandinsky, Wassily (1866–1944). Russian-born painter, printmaker, designer, teacher, and art theorist, who became a German citizen in 1927 and a French citizen in 1939, one of the most important figures in the development of *abstract art. He abandoned a promising university career teaching law, partly under the impact of an exhibition in Moscow of French *Impressionists, at which one of *Monet's *Haystack* pictures made a powerful impression on him, and in 1896 he moved to Munich to study painting. Munich was to be the centre of his activities until 1914, but he travelled widely in this period and spent a year in Paris, 1906–7. His pictures at the turn of the century combined features of *Art Nouveau with reminiscences of Russian folk art, to which he added a *Fauve-like intensity of colour. In 1909 (the year in which he was one of the founders of the *Neue Künstlervereinigung) he began a series of *Improvisations*, in 1910 of *Compositions*, and in 1911 of *Impressions*; in these he eliminated all representational content to arrive—in about

1910—at pure abstraction. The choice of names, deriving from musical terminology, was significant, for like the *Symbolists he was interested in analogies between colours and sounds (a great lover of music, he played the cello and piano and was a friend of Arnold Schoenberg, whose revolutionary atonality he equated with his own experiments). Kandinsky himself described how he came to recognize that colour and line in themselves could be sufficient vehicles for the expression of emotions: he returned to his studio one evening and failed to recognize one of his own paintings that was lying on its side, seeing in it a picture 'of extraordinary beauty glowing with an inner radiance ... Now I knew for certain that the subject matter was detrimental for my paintings'. He discussed the issue of abstraction in his book *Über das Geistige in der Kunst* (Concerning the Spiritual in Art), which was published late in 1911 (it bears the date 1912) and is the best known of his writings. His views about the nature of art were influenced by mysticism and Theosophy; he did not completely repudiate representation, but he held that the 'pure' artist seeks to express only 'inner and essential' feelings and ignores the superficial and fortuitous.

In 1911 Kandinsky was one of the founders of the *Blaue Reiter, and the brief lifetime of this group (broken up by the First World War) marked a period of intense achievement and growing fame for him. A major work from this period is *Composition VI* (1913, Hermitage, St Petersburg), a huge, gloriously coloured apocalyptic vision. On the outbreak of the war in 1914 Kandinsky returned to Russia, where he was highly active as a teacher and administrator in various cultural organizations instituted by the new Soviet regime. However, he was out of sympathy with the growing tide of ideas that subordinated fine art to industrial design in the service of the proletariat (even though he made designs for cups and saucers himself), and in 1922 he accepted an offer to take up a teaching post at the *Bauhaus, where he remained until it was closed by the Nazis in 1933. His painting of this period became more geometrical, but in addition to circles and triangles he used arrow-like forms and wavy lines in a manner that ran counter to the typical Bauhaus concern with geometrical purity (*Swinging*, 1925, Tate, London). In 1926, to mark his sixtieth birth-

day, an exhibition of his work toured Germany, and by this time he was an internationally renowned figure (his reputation was spread in the USA by the *Blaue Vier). He left Germany for France in 1933 and settled at Neuilly-sur-Seine, a suburb of Paris. The paintings of his last period represent something of a synthesis between the organic style of his Munich period and the more geometrical manner of his Bauhaus period, but there was also a new element of fantasy in the use of amoeba-like forms that show the influence of *Surrealism (*Sky Blue*, 1940, Pompidou Centre, Paris). Examples of his paintings are in many of the world's leading collections, with particularly rich representations in, for example, the Lenbachhaus, Munich (*see* LENBACH); the Guggenheim Museum, New York; and the Pompidou Centre, Paris (many presented by his widow).

Kane, John (1860–1934). American *naive painter, born in Scotland. He emigrated to the USA in 1879 and moved around a good deal working at various labouring jobs. However, he considered Pittsburgh his home. In 1891 he lost a leg when he was struck by a train, but he became so agile with his artificial limb that few realized he was disabled. He took to drink after his son died soon after birth in 1904 and his wife consequently left him, taking their two daughters with her. Kane then led a wandering life, scraping a living by housepainting and carpentry. His first oil paintings were done *c*.1910; he produced portraits—an intense *Self-Portrait* (1929, MoMA, New York) is his best-known work—landscapes, interiors, and cityscapes of industrial Pittsburgh, combining meticulous observation with naive stylization and imaginative reconstruction. In 1927 he achieved sudden fame, at the age of 67, when one of his paintings was accepted for the Carnegie International Exhibition in Pittsburgh. Kane was the first American naive painter to achieve such recognition; some people thought his picture was a hoax, but in the remaining seven years of his life he achieved considerable acclaim and became something of a celebrity (in consequence of which he was reunited with his wife). His autobiography *Sky Hooks* (named after the supports of a housepainter's scaffold) was posthumously published in 1938.

Kanoldt, Alexander. *See* NEUE KÜNSTLER-VEREINIGUNG.

Kapoor, Anish (1954–). British abstract sculptor, born in India, the son of a Hindu father and Jewish-Iraqi mother. He settled in London in 1973. Although his sculpture is not obviously indebted to his Asian background, he feels an affinity with the spirituality of Indian art: 'I don't want to make sculpture about form . . . I wish to make sculpture about belief, or about passion, about experience that is outside of material concern.' His early work was predominantly in fairly lightweight materials, including wood and mixed media, and was often brightly coloured, but in the late 1980s he changed direction. Having acquired a large ground-floor studio where he could handle heavy materials, he turned to working in stone. Typically his sculptures from this time have consisted of large, rough-hewn blocks; he has also made smooth, organic pieces in cast metal. Kapoor was Britain's representative at the Venice *Biennale in 1990 and in 1991 he was awarded the *Turner Prize.

Kaprow, Allan (1927–). American artist and art theorist, best known as the main creator of *happenings. His studies included a period with the musician John Cage (*see* BLACK MOUNTAIN COLLEGE), from whom he took over the idea of chance and indeterminacy in aesthetic organization. In the mid-1950s he gave up painting for *assemblages and then *environments, and in 1958 he published an article in *Art News* in which he argued for the abandonment of craftsmanship and permanence in the fine arts and advocated the incorporation of perishable materials. His first happenings took place at the Reuben Gallery, New York, in 1959. Kaprow has been an evangelic promoter of his ideas through his teaching at various universities and his voluminous output of writings, as well as through his own performances.

Karlowska, Stanislava de. *See* BEVAN.

Kauffer, E. McKnight (1890–1954). American-born painter and designer, active mainly in England, where he settled in 1914. He was a member of Wyndham *Lewis's Group X and of the *Cumberland Market Group, but he abandoned painting in 1921 and is best known for his brilliant

and witty poster designs, notably for the London Transport Board and the Great Western Railway. In 1940 he returned to the USA and settled in New York. His work in America included posters (for government agencies during the Second World War and afterwards for American Airlines) and also book jackets and illustrations.

Kauffmann, Angelica (1741–1807). Swiss painter, active mainly in Italy and England. From an early age she travelled with her father, the painter **Joseph Johann Kauffmann** (1707–82), in Switzerland and Italy, and she formed her style in Rome. In 1766 she moved to London, where her work and her person were vastly admired. A foundation member of the *Royal Academy in 1768, she was a close friend of the president, Sir Joshua *Reynolds, their relationship giving rise to gossip and to a satirical picture by Nathaniel *Hone. (*Canova, *Goethe, and *Winckelmann were among the other distinguished men who were charmed by her.) Kauffmann began in England as a fashionable portraitist, but then devoted herself more to historical scenes and also did decorative work for Robert Adam and other architects. Although her work owes much to the *Neoclassical tradition, it has a prettiness that can be described as *Rococo. At its best it has great charm, but it can be rather insipid, and she was much more successful with ladylike decorative vignettes than with scenes from Homer or Shakespeare. In 1767 she married an unscrupulous adventurer from whom she was quickly estranged. Following his death in 1780 she married the decorative painter Antonio Zucchi (1726–95) and settled with him in Italy, where she continued her successful career, mainly in Rome.

Kelly, Ellsworth (1923–). American painter, sculptor, and printmaker. In the mid-1950s he became recognized as one of the leading exponents of the *Hard-Edge style that was one of the reactions against *Abstract Expressionism. His paintings are characteristically very clear and simple in conception, sometimes consisting of a number of individual panels placed together, identical in size but each painted a different uniform colour (he started using this formula in 1952). He was also one of the first artists to develop the idea of the *shaped canvas. Kelly has also worked in various printmaking techniques and in sculpture (using painted cut-out metal forms—often industrially manufactured—related to those in his paintings).

Kelly, Sir Gerald (1879–1972). British painter. One of the leading society portraitists of his day, he had many distinguished friends, among them Somerset Maugham, whose portrait by Graham *Sutherland he wittily attacked. From 1949 to 1954 he was president of the *Royal Academy; in this position he devoted much of his time to organizing loan exhibitions, and became well known for his appearances in related television programmes. His popularity helped to revitalize the Academy's image after the damage done by his predecessor, the arch-conservative *Munnings. Apart from portraits, Kelly painted landscapes and also pictures of Asian dancing girls (he had spent some time in Burma) that were once very popular in reproduction.

Kelmscott Press. A private printing press founded in 1890 by William *Morris at Hammersmith and named after the village near Oxford where he had lived since 1871. Between 1891 and 1898, two years after Morris's death, the press issued more than fifty titles, including editions of several of Morris's own works. Deeply influenced by his study of early printing, Morris himself designed most of the type, borders, ornaments, and title-pages. The press's greatest book, and by common consent one of the world's masterpieces of book production, is the 1896 edition of Geoffrey Chaucer's works, with illustrations by *Burne-Jones. Although short-lived, the Kelmscott Press had enormous influence on the private presses that followed in its wake.

Kempeneer, Pieter de (c.1503–c.1580). Netherlandish painter and tapestry designer, active for much of his career in Spain, where he was known as Pedro de Campaña. He is documented in Seville from 1537 to 1561 and in the later part of this period he was the leading painter in the city (several examples of his work are in the cathedral). Before arriving in Spain he is said to have spent several years in Italy. This has been doubted, as the fairly superficial Italian influence in his *Mannerist style could have been gained from prints. By 1563

he was back in Brussels, his native city, designing tapestry cartoons. He is also said to have worked as an architect and sculptor.

Kemp-Welch, Lucy. *See* OFFICIAL WAR ART.

Kennington, Eric (1888–1960). British painter, sculptor, and draughtsman. He was an *Official War Artist in the First and Second World Wars and is best known for his paintings and drawings of the daily life of ordinary soldiers and airmen. Between the wars he worked mainly as a portraitist but also did book illustrations, including those for T. E. Lawrence's *Seven Pillars of Wisdom* (1926). His sculptures include the Monument to the 24th Division in Battersea Park, London (1926) (the writer Robert Graves was the model for one of the three soldiers); figures (in carved brick) for the Shakespeare Memorial Theatre in Stratford-upon-Avon (1930); and the recumbent effigy of T. E. Lawrence on his tomb in St Martin's church, Wareham, Dorset (1940).

Kent, William (1685–1748). English architect, designer, landscape gardener, and painter, the most versatile British artist of his time. He began his career as a painter and spent a decade (1709–19) in Italy, mainly Rome, where in 1717 he painted a ceiling in the church of S. Giuliano dei Fiamminghi (offering to work without payment for the chance to establish his reputation). As a guide and art dealer for Englishmen on the *Grand Tour he met the architect and patron Lord Burlington, with whom he returned to London in 1719. From then until Kent's death in 1748 the two were inseparable partners. Initially Kent was employed mainly as a decorative painter (notably at Burlington House and Kensington Palace, both in London), but his talent in this field was described by Horace *Walpole as 'below mediocrity' and he turned increasingly to architecture and design. His biggest architectural commission was Holkham Hall, Norfolk, begun in 1734 for the 1st Earl of Leicester, whom he had initially met in Rome. Externally it is in a severe Palladian style, but the opulent interior has been described by Nikolaus *Pevsner as 'more consistently palatial than that of almost any other house in England'. Kent was the first British artist to envision an interior and its furnishings as a unified scheme and he designed some impressively grand furniture, including the magnificent state bed (1732) at Houghton Hall, Norfolk. His other work as a designer was highly varied; it included book illustrations, sculpture (notably the Shakespeare monument (1740) in Westminster Abbey, carved by Peter *Scheemakers), and a state barge for Frederick Lewis, Prince of Wales (1731–2, Nat. Maritime Mus., London). In his later years he worked mainly as a garden designer, in which field he was a key figure in the development of the informal style later particularly associated with Capability Brown. Although he was a painter of little talent, Kent has the distinction of painting the earliest medieval history subjects in British art—a series of three pictures for Queen Caroline depicting scenes from the life of Henry V (c.1730, Royal Coll.). There is no attempt to recreate the scenes accurately, and in fact there is some doubt whether one of the pictures is intended to represent the Battle of Agincourt (1415) or the Battle of Crécy (1346).

Kersting, Georg Friedrich (1785–1847). German painter. After studying at the Copenhagen Academy 1805–8, he settled in Dresden, where he specialized in small portraits set in delicately rendered interiors. They include three similar pictures showing his friend *Friedrich in his studio (1811, Kunsthalle, Hamburg; 1812, Staatliche Museen, Berlin; 1819, Kunsthalle, Mannheim).

Kessel, Jan van (1626–79). Flemish still-life and flower painter active in Antwerp, where he became a member of the painters' guild in 1645. He continued the traditions of his grandfather, Jan 'Velvet' *Brueghel, and was also influenced by Daniel *Seghers. Van Kessel painted garlands and bouquets of flowers, but is best known for small, jewel-like pictures, often on copper, of insects or shells against a light background, depicted with vivid colour and great exactitude of detail. Good examples of his large output are in Oxford (Ashmolean Mus.), Cambridge (Fitzwilliam Mus.), and Madrid (Prado).

Ketel, Cornelis (1548–1616). Dutch portrait and history painter. He worked mainly in his native Gouda and in Amsterdam, where he died, but also in France and in England (1573–81). Van *Mander, who was well informed about him, mentions that he painted a portrait of Queen Elizabeth I for the Earl of Hertford in 1578, and this has been identified with a picture in the Siena Pinacoteca. Ketel's finest works are his group portraits (examples in the Rijksmuseum, Amsterdam), which prefigure those of Frans *Hals.

Kettle, Tilly (1735–86). English portrait painter. After working in the Midlands and London, he became one of the first British painters to risk a long visit to India, where he spent the years 1769–76 and made a fortune painting nabobs and princes. He died at Aleppo on his way out a second time, having found it much harder to achieve success in England. Kettle's style was derivative from those of *Reynolds, *Cotes, and *Romney.

Key, Willem (c.1515–68). Netherlandish painter, mainly of portraits. He was probably a pupil of Lambert *Lombard c.1540 in Liège. In 1542 he became a master in the painters' guild in Antwerp, where he spent the rest of his working life. **Adriaen Thomasz. Key** (c.1544–after 1589), was probably his pupil and perhaps a distant relative (although not his nephew, as previously believed). He became a master in the Antwerp guild in 1568. Both artists were highly regarded in their day and did assured and solid portraits of famous people. Their religious works are less well known, and many of Willem's are known to have perished at the hands of iconoclasts.

Keyser, Hendrick de (1565–1621). The outstanding Dutch sculptor and one of the leading Dutch architects of his period. Most of his career was spent in Amsterdam, where he was appointed municipal sculptor and architect in 1594. His most important buildings are the Zuiderkerk (South church, 1606–14), Holland's first large Protestant church, and the Westerkerk (West church, 1620–38), which broke with the *Mannerist tradition, looking forward to the *classicism of Jacob van *Campen. The splendid towers of these two churches are still among Amsterdam's chief landmarks. As a sculptor, de Keyser excelled particularly as a portraitist in a soberly realistic style (*Unknown Man*, 1608, Rijksmuseum, Amsterdam), but his best-known work is the tomb of William the Silent (1614–21) in the Niewe Kerk at Delft. **Thomas de Keyser** (c.1597–1667), Hendrick's son and pupil, was Amsterdam's municipal architect from 1662 until his death (he added the cupola to van Campen's town hall), but he is better known as a portrait painter. He was, indeed, Amsterdam's leading portraitist before being overtaken in popularity by *Rembrandt in the 1630s. His life-size portraits look stiff compared with Rembrandt's and he is more attractive and original on a small scale. *Constantin Huygens and His Clerk* (1627, NG, London) is an excellent example of his small portraits of full-length figures in an interior, forerunners of the *conversation piece. His small equestrian portraits were also a new type (*Pieter Schout*, 1660, Rijksmuseum). Two other sons of Hendrick, **Pieter** (1595–1676) and **Willem** (1603–after 1678), were sculptors. Willem worked for some years in England, probably with Nicholas *Stone, Hendrick's son-in-law and former pupil.

Kiefer, Anselm (1945–). German painter. Early in his career he was a *Conceptual artist, but he turned to painting and has become one of the leading exponents of *Neo-Expressionism, with an international reputation. He produces large, heavily worked canvases, often with objects or vegetable matter (such as plants or straw) attached to them (he has also mixed blood with his paint). Sometimes the surface is further 'distressed' by such means as scorching it with a blowtorch. Many of his pictures refer to German history or Nordic mythology and show an attempt to come to terms with his country's Nazi past. Another subject that has interested him is the Chinese Communist leader Mao Zedong (*Let a Thousand Flowers Bloom*, 2000, Tate, London).

Kienholz, Edward (1927–94). American sculptor specializing in life-size tableaux. Typically he created situations of a bizarre and gruesome character in which death and decay are common themes (his work is sometimes categorized as *Funk art). A much reproduced example is *The State Hospital* (1964–6, Moderna Museet, Stockholm), showing a mentally ill patient strapped to his bed with his own self-image (in a thought bubble) strapped to the bed above. Both figures are modelled with revolting realism but have glass bowls for heads. H. H. Arnason (*A History of Modern Art*, 1969) describes the work as 'one of the most horrifying concepts created by any modern artist'.

Kinetic art. (from Gk., *kinesis*: movement). Term applied to art that moves or appears to move. In its broadest sense the term can encompass a great deal of phenomena, including cinematic motion pictures, *happenings, and the animated clockwork figures found on clock towers in many cities of Europe. More usually, however, it is applied to sculptures such as *Calder's mobiles that are moved either by air currents or by some artificial means—usually electronic or magnetic. In addition to works employing actual movement, there is another type of Kinetic art that produces an illusion of movement when the spectator moves relative to it (and *Op art paintings are sometimes included within the field of Kinetic art because they appear to flicker). The idea of moving sculpture had been proposed by the *Futurists as early as 1909, and the term 'kinetic' was first used in connection with the visual arts by *Gabo and Antoine *Pevsner in their *Realistic Manifesto* in 1920. Gabo produced an electrically driven oscillating wire construction in this year, and at the same time Marcel *Duchamp was experimenting with *Rotative Plaques* that incorporated movement. Various other works over the next three decades are explorations in the same vein, such as *Moholy-Nagy's *Light-Space-Modulator* (1922–30, Busch-Reisinger Mus., Harvard Univ.), one of a series of constructions he made using reflecting metals, transparent plastics, and sometimes mechanical devices to produce real movement. However, for many years Calder was the only leading figure who was associated specifically with moving sculpture (and many people regarded him as eccentric), and it was not until the 1950s that the phrase 'Kinetic art' became a recognized part of critical vocabulary; the exhibition 'Le Mouvement' at the Denise René Gallery, Paris, in 1955 was a key event in establishing it as a distinct genre. The artists represented in the exhibition included *Agam, *Bury, Calder, Duchamp, *Tinguely, and *Vasarely.

King, Sir Phillip (1934–). British sculptor. He is probably the most renowned of the generation of avant-garde British sculptors (mainly, like himself, pupils of *Caro) who came to prominence at the *New Generation exhibition in 1965. His work at this time was characteristically in smooth, man-made materials such as plastic or fibre-glass, often brightly coloured, with the cone shape being a favourite motif (*And the Birds Began to Sing*, 1964, Tate, London). At the end of the decade he began using more rugged materials, including steel and wood. With Bridget *Riley he represented Britain at the Venice *Biennale of 1968 and his work has been included in many other international exhibitions. He has taught at various art schools in Britain and elsewhere and from 1980 to 1990 he was professor of sculpture at the *Royal College of Art. He was president of the *Royal Academy, 1999–2004.

Kip, Johannes (1653–1722). Dutch topographical engraver who settled in England in about 1690. He is best known for his engravings of country houses in the sumptuous *Britannia Illustrata* (1708 and subsequent volumes). They are of modest artistic merit but have great historical interest.

Kiprensky, Orest (1782–1836). Russian painter, active for much of his career in Italy. He was the leading Russian portraitist of the *Romantic era; in his work he combined the then fashionable attitude of 'Byronic' melancholy with an elegance that earned him the nickname 'the Russian van *Dyck'.

Kirchner, Ernst Ludwig (1880–1938). German *Expressionist painter, printmaker, and sculptor, the dominant figure in the *Brücke group. Like the other members of the group, he was influenced by *Post-Impressionism, particularly *Gauguin and van *Gogh, by *Fauvism, and by *Munch. He also claimed that he was the first of the group to appreciate Polynesian and other *primitive art (which he saw in the Zwinger Museum in Dresden), but this had little obvious effect on his work. His paintings consisted mainly of figure compositions, including portraits and nudes (he often spent the summer months in seclusion in the country or on the coast, where he could draw and paint nude models in natural movement). There is often an explicit erotic quality in his work and sometimes a feeling of malevolence. His forms are typically harsh and jagged, and his colours dissonant. From 1910 he began to spend much of his time in Berlin and he settled there in 1911. During the next few years his work developed more independ-

ently of the other members of Die Brücke, and his criticisms of his associates were an important factor in the the break-up of the group in 1913. His most celebrated paintings of this period are a series of street scenes of Berlin that are regarded as marking one of the high points of Expressionism. In a style that had become more spiky and aggressive he depicted the pace, the glare, and the tension of big city life (*Street, Berlin*, 1913, MoMA, New York). Kirchner was drafted into the German army in 1915, but he was soon discharged after a mental and physical collapse. In 1916 he was hit by a car in Berlin and during his long period of recuperation he settled in Frauenkirch, near Davos, in Switzerland, which became his home for the rest of his life. By 1921 he had recovered from heavy dependence on drugs, but he never fully regained mental equilibrium. When he started painting again he concentrated on mountain landscapes and peasant scenes, his work gaining in serenity what it lost in vigour. From the late 1920s his style began to move towards abstraction, as he painted less directly from nature. Many exhibitions of his work were held in the 1930s, in Germany and elsewhere, but in the middle of the decade he was overcome again by mental anxiety and physical deterioration. The inclusion of his work in the Nazi exhibition of *degenerate art in 1937 caused him acute distress and the following year he shot himself. Throughout his career, printmaking (in woodcut, etching, and lithography) was as important to him as painting and he ranks as one of the 20th century's greatest masters in this field. He also made wooden sculpture, rough-hewn and harshly coloured.

Kitaj, Ron B. (1932–). American painter, printmaker, and draughtsman, active mainly in England, where he has been one of the most prominent figures of the *Pop art movement. Before studying at the *Royal College of Art in 1959–61 Kitaj had travelled widely (he was a merchant seaman, then served in the US army) and his wide cultural horizons gave him an influential position among his contemporaries (he studied with *Hockney and Allen *Jones), particularly in upholding his preference for figuration in opposition to the prevailing abstraction. After a visit to Paris in 1975 he was inspired by *Degas to take up pastel, which he has used for much of his subsequent work. Late 19th-century French art has been a major source of inspiration, as has a preoccupation with his Jewish identity, and he has said: 'I took it into my cosmopolitan head that I should attempt to do *Cézanne and Degas and Kafka over again, after Auschwitz.' Unlike the majority of Pop artists, Kitaj has had relatively little interest in the culture of the mass media and has evolved a multi-evocative pictorial language, deriving from a wide range of visual and literary sources—indeed he has declared that he is not a Pop artist. Typically his work uses broad areas of flat colour within a strong linear framework, creating an effect somewhat akin to comic strips.

kit-cat. A canvas measuring 36×28 in. (91×71 cm). The name derives from *Kneller's portraits of the Kit-Cat Club (c.1702–21, NPG, London), all but one of which (there are 42) are of this size. Members of the club, which was founded in the late 17th century and included many of the leading Whigs of the day, met originally at a tavern near Temple Bar in London kept by Christopher ('Kit') Cat (or Kat), who served mutton pies known as 'Kit-cats'. The kit-cat size canvas is particularly suited to life-size portraits showing the sitter's head and shoulders and one or both hands, and Kneller's portraits did much to popularize the format.

Kitchen Sink School. A group of British *Social Realist painters active in the 1950s who specialized in drab working-class subjects, notably interior scenes and still lifes of domestic clutter and debris; the term was coined by the critic David Sylvester (1924–2001) in an article in the December 1954 issue of the journal *Encounter*. The main artists covered by the term were John *Bratby, Derrick Greaves (1927–), Edward Middleditch (1923–87), and Jack Smith (1928–), who were supported by the Beaux Arts Gallery in London (they became known as the Beaux Arts Quartet) and by the left-wing critic John Berger (1926–); in 1956 they exhibited together at the Venice *Biennale. By their choice of dour and sordid themes and their harsh aggressive style they expressed the same kind of dissatisfaction with the social and moral values of postwar British society as the 'Angry Young

Men' in literature (writers such as John Osborne, whose *Look Back in Anger* was first produced in 1956, were sometimes referred to as 'kitchen sink dramatists'). The mood did not last and from the late 1950s the painters of the Kitchen Sink School developed in different ways, Bratby, for example, emphasizing his *Expressionist handling and Smith eventually turning to abstraction. Berger denounced his former protégés.

Kitson, Linda. *See* OFFICIAL WAR ART.

Klee, Paul (1879–1940). German-Swiss painter, printmaker, teacher, and writer on art, one of the most individual and best-loved figures in 20th-century art. From 1898 to 1901 he studied in Munich, principally at the Academy under Franz von *Stuck. After travelling in Italy, 1901–2, he lived in Berne for the next four years, then in 1906 moved to Munich after marrying the German pianist Lily Stumpf (both Klee's parents were musicians and he was himself a violinist of professional standard). In 1911 he became friendly with *Jawlensky, *Kandinsky (whom he had first met as a student ten years earlier), *Macke, and *Marc, and in the following year he took part in the second *Blaue Reiter exhibition. Also in 1912 he visited Paris for the second time (he had earlier been there with Louis *Moilliet in 1905); he met *Delaunay on this occasion and saw *Cubist pictures. At this point he was principally an etcher, his most notable prints including a series of eleven *Inventions* (1903–5)—bizarre and satirical works with freakishly distorted figures. However, in 1914 he visited Tunisia with Macke and Moilliet and was dramatically awakened to the beauty of colour. Two weeks after arriving he wrote: 'Colour possesses me. I no longer need to pursue it: it possesses me forever, I know. Colour and I are one—I am a painter.' During the war he served in the Germany army, engaged for part of the time on painting aeroplane wings. After the war he returned to Munich, and a large exhibition of his work there in 1919 secured his reputation and led *Gropius to invite him to teach at the *Bauhaus; he took up the appointment in 1921 and remained with the school for the next ten years, proving an inspired, undogmatic teacher who was enormously popular with his students. However, he found the internal disputes at the school increasingly tiresome and in 1931 he moved to the Düsseldorf Academy. He was dismissed from this post by the Nazis in 1933 and left Germany for Berne; four years later works by him were included in the notorious exhibition of *degenerate art.

Although Klee was not politically inclined, his mood during his last years was one of profound disappointment. In 1935 he suffered the first symptoms of the illness that killed him—a rare debilitating skin disease called scleroderma—and although he remained highly productive to the end, his earlier playfulness gave way to a preoccupation with malign and malevolent forces. His exquisitely sensitive line grew deliberately rough and crude and his sense of humour became macabre; his imagery was haunted by premonitions of death, as in *Death and Fire* (1940, Paul Klee Foundation, Kunstmuseum, Berne), one of his starkest and most powerful works. It depicts a ghastly, ashen face, the features of which are made up of letters forming the word *Tod* (Ger.: 'death'). Klee was one of the most inventive and prolific of modern masters, his complete output being estimated at some 9,000 works. He usually worked on a small scale; initially he painted only in watercolour, but he took up oils in 1919 and sometimes used both media in one painting. It is impossible to categorize his work stylistically, for he moved freely between figuration and abstraction, absorbing countless influences and transforming them through his unrivalled imaginative gifts as he explored human fantasies and fears. In spite of this variety, his work—in whatever style or medium—is almost instantly recognizable as his, revealing a joyous spirit that is hard to parallel in 20th-century art. Various collections of his writings (including his notebooks and diaries) have been published. The best-known individual work is *Pädagogisches Skizzenbuch*, published in 1925 and translated into English as *Pedagogical Sketchbook* (1953).

Klein, Yves (1928–62). French painter and experimental artist, one of the most influential figures in European avant-garde art in the post-war period. Both his parents were painters, but he had no formal artistic training, and for much of his short life he earned his living as a judo instructor (in 1952–3 he lived in Japan, where he obtained

the high rank of black belt, fourth dan). In the mid-1950s he began exhibiting 'monochromes', pictures in which a canvas was uniformly painted a single colour, usually a distinctive blue that he called 'International Klein Blue'. He used this also for other works including sculptured figures, and reliefs of sponges on canvas. In a lecture given at the Sorbonne in 1959, Klein explained his theory of monochrome painting as an attempt to depersonalize colour by ridding it of subjective emotion and thus giving it a metaphysical quality. Klein also made pictures by a variety of unorthodox methods, including the action of rain on prepared paper (these he called *Cosmogonies*), the use of a flame-thrower (*Peintures de feu*), or imprints of the human body (*Anthropométries*). In 1958 he created a sensation (and almost a riot) at the Galerie Iris Clert in Paris by an 'exhibition of emptiness'—an empty gallery painted white. It was called *Le Vide* (The Void). In 1960 he gave his first public exhibition of the *Anthropométries*: naked women smeared with blue pigment dragged each other over canvas laid on the floor to the accompaniment of his *Symphonie monotone*—a single note sustained for ten minutes and alternating with ten minutes' silence. Critical reception was very mixed. He became a celebrity in Europe, but an exhibition at the Leo *Castelli gallery in New York in 1961 was a dismal failure. Klein died young of a heart attack, but he produced a large amount of work and had wide influence, particularly on the development of *Minimal art. A great showman, he exemplifies the tendency in 20th-century art for the personality of the artist to assume greater importance than the things he makes—a tendency continued most notably by Joseph *Beuys.

Klimt, Gustav (1862–1918). Austrian painter, draughtsman, and designer, one of the leading figures in one of the most exciting epochs of Vienna's cultural history. Early in his career he was highly successful as a painter of lavish decorative schemes in the grandiose tradition of *Makart, whose staircase decoration in the Kunsthistorisches Museum in Vienna he completed after Makart's death in 1884. In spite of his official academic successes, Klimt was drawn to avant-garde art, and his work was influenced by *Impressionism, *Symbolism, and *Art Nouveau. Discontent with the conservative attitudes of the Viennese Artists' Association led him and a group of friends to resign in 1897 and set up their own organization, the *Sezession, of which he was elected president. In a short time Klimt thus went from being a pillar of the establishment to a hero of the avant-garde, and this new role was confirmed when his enormous allegorical mural paintings for Vienna University were denounced as nonsensical and pornographic. (Klimt was given the commission in 1894 and abandoned it in 1905; the paintings—entitled *Jurisprudence, Medicine,* and *Philosophy*—were destroyed by fire in 1945.) Although official commissions dried up after this, he continued to be much in demand with private patrons, as a portraitist as well as a painter of mythological and allegorical themes. He was highly responsive to female beauty (he was a great womanizer) and in both his portraits and his subject pictures he stresses the allure and mystery of womanhood. Notable examples are the magnificent full-length portrait of his sister-in-law and close friend Emilie Flöge (1902, Historisches Mus. der Stadt, Vienna) and *Judith I* (1901, Österreichische Galerie, Vienna), one of the archetypal images of the femme fatale. Characteristically, the figures in Klimt's paintings are treated more or less naturalistically but embellished—in the background or their clothing—with richly decorative patterns recalling butterfly or peacock wings, creating a highly distinctive style of extraordinarily lush sensuality. The erotic aspect of his work is even more pronounced in his drawings, most of which were done as independent works rather than as preparatory studies for paintings; typically they show naked or semi-naked women in a state of sexual arousal. In addition to paintings and drawings, he did a good deal of design work for the *Wiener Werkstätte. Most of this was fairly modest, but the great exception was the major commission of his later years—the mosaics (executed 1909–11) for the dining room of the Palais Stoclet in Brussels, a luxury home built at huge expense for the young Belgian industrialist Adolphe Stoclet, who had just inherited the family fortune. Klimt had a great reputation in his day and was influential on some of his Viennese contemporaries, notably *Kokoschka

and *Schiele, but his work was too personal to find much of a following.

Kline, Franz (1910–62). American painter, generally considered one of the most individual of the *Abstract Expressionists. He began as a representational painter, notably of urban landscapes, but turned to abstraction at the end of the 1940s. This change of direction reflected the influence of *de Kooning and was also stimulated by his seeing some of his own drawings enlarged by a projector, an experience that made him realize their potential as abstract compositions. Once he had embarked on this new path he very quickly developed a highly individual style, converting the brushstrokes of these drawings into large-scale abstract paintings, using bold black patterns on a white ground reminiscent of oriental calligraphy, but with a distinctive rough vigour (he used commercial paints and house-painter's brushes, sometimes up to 8 in. (20 cm.) wide). Towards the end of his life he sometimes incorporated vivid colours but for the most part remained loyal to his characteristic black-and-white style. He died of heart disease.

Klinger, Max (1857–1920). German painter, sculptor, and printmaker. He studied in Karlsruhe and Berlin, then after brief periods in Brussels, Berlin, and Munich, he spent the years 1883–6 in Paris, 1886–8 in Berlin, and 1888–93 in Rome. After his return to Germany in 1893 he settled in his native Leipzig, where his home became one of the centres of the city's cultural life. His work reveals a powerful imagination and an often morbid interest in themes of love and death. As a painter he is best known for his enormous *Judgement of Paris* (1885–7, KH Mus., Vienna), in which the frame is part of the decorative scheme. As a sculptor he experimented with *polychromy in the manner of Greek *chryselephantine statues; the culmination was his statue of Beethoven (1899–1902, Mus. der Bildenden Künste, Leipzig) in white and coloured marbles, bronze, alabaster, and ivory. It is as a printmaker, however, that Klinger is now best known and most clearly showed his originality, especially in *Adventures of a Glove* (3 series, begun 1881), a grotesque exploration of fetishism that antedated the publication of Freud's theories. These etchings concern a hapless young man and his involvement with an elusive lost glove that has clearly sexual connotations. Together with other works of Klinger, they have been claimed as forerunners of *Surrealism, and his influence can be seen in the work of de *Chirico (one of his greatest admirers), *Dalí, and *Ernst, amongst others.

Knapton, George (1698–1778). English portrait painter, a pupil of *Richardson. He was in Italy 1725–32 and in 1736 he became a foundation member of and official painter to the Society of Dilettanti, a social club for gentlemen who had visited that country. His 23 portraits of his fellow members (1741–9, several still in the possession of the Society) are considered his finest works. Most of them show the members in fancy dress. These portraits are in oil, but otherwise Knapton worked mainly in pastel. He had a great reputation as a connoisseur and from 1765 until his death he was Keeper of the King's Pictures. By the time of this appointment he seems to have given up painting. *Cotes was his most important pupil.

Knave of Diamonds or **Jack of Diamonds.** An artists' association, formed in Moscow in 1910, that was for a time the most important of the avant-garde groups in Russia. There are various explanations of how the name came about, one being that it refers to the diamond markings on the uniforms of civil prisoners; the artists involved thus wanted to indicate that they were revolutionaries. In 1911 *Goncharova and *Larionov broke away from the group, accusing it of being too dominated by the 'cheap orientalism of the Paris School' and the 'Munich decadence', and founded their own association, the *Donkey's Tail, to promote an art based on native inspiration. The Knave of Diamonds held regular exhibitions up to 1917, then broke up.

Kneller, Sir Godfrey (originally Gottfried Kniller) (1646–1723). German-born painter who settled in England and became the leading portraitist there in the late 17th and early 18th centuries. He studied in Amsterdam under *Bol, a pupil of *Rembrandt, and later in Italy, before moving to England, probably in the mid-1670s. The opportune death of serious rivals (notably *Lely in 1680) and his own arrogant self-assurance enabled him to establish himself as the dominant

court and society painter by the beginning of the reign of James II (1685). On the accession of William III and Mary II in 1688 he was appointed their principal painter jointly with John *Riley (becoming sole bearer of the title when Riley died in 1691), in 1692 he was knighted, and in 1715 he was created a baronet by George I, an unprecedented honour for a painter. Kneller's output was vast and he made extensive use of assistants. Sitters were required to pose only for a drawing of the face and efficient formulas were worked out for the accessories. He is said sometimes to have accommodated as many as fourteen sitters in a day, but the idea of his running a kind of picture factory has been exaggerated. The average portrait turned out from his studio was slick and mechanical (and the heavy wigs then fashionable make for great monotony in male portraits), but Kneller was capable of work of much higher quality when he had a sitter to whom he especially responded; outstanding examples are *The Chinese Convert* (1687, Kensington Palace, London) and *Matthew Prior* (1700, Trinity College, Cambridge). Many other examples of his work, including the portraits of the *Kit-Cat Club, are in the National Portrait Gallery, London. His style was less elegant and more forthright than Lely's, but the influence of his mass-produced work was stultifying. He was the last foreign-born artist to dominate English painting, but it needed a *Hogarth and a *Reynolds to break through the conventions he had popularized.

Knight, Dame Laura (née Johnson, 1877–1970). British painter. In the first half of the century she was one of the most highly regarded of British artists and in 1936 she became the first woman to be elected a *Royal Academician since the original women members Angelica *Kauffmann and Mary *Moser. At the height of her considerable fame (she was regarded as a 'character'—the nearest equivalent to a female Augustus *John) she won great popularity for her colourful scenes of circus life and the ballet, but these now often seem rather corny. On the other hand, her early *Newlyn School landscapes, which at their best have a sparkling sense of joie de vivre, have recently come back into favour. Some of the work she did as an *Official War Artist during the Second World War is also now highly regarded. In 1946 she went to Nuremberg to make a pictorial record of the War Criminals' Trial; she made scores of sketches and produced a large painting (Imperial War Mus., London). Her husband **Harold Knight** (1874–1961) was also a painter, mainly of portraits.

Knight, Richard Payne (1751–1824). English collector, connoisseur, and writer. His collections were highly varied, but particularly outstanding were his drawings and antique coins and bronzes, which he bequeathed to the *British Museum. He was a leading advocate of the *Picturesque, and his country house, Downton Castle, Herefordshire (1774–8), which he helped to design himself, was novel in being in a pseudo-medieval 'castellated' style and deliberately irregular in plan and outline. His writings include *An Account of the Remains of the Worship of Priapus* (1786), which some contemporaries attacked as obscene, and *An Analytical Inquiry into the Principles of Taste* (1805). *See also* ELGIN MARBLES.

Knüpfer, Nicolaus. *See* STEEN.

Købke, Christen (1810–48). Danish painter, a pupil of *Eckersberg. Although he visited Italy in 1838–40, this had little influence on his work, which was rooted in his native land. He concentrated on everyday scenes in and around Copenhagen and on portraits of family and friends, displaying great sensitivity in his treatment of colour and light and a warm intimacy of characterization. Købke was little appreciated in his lifetime, but he began to win recognition at the end of the 19th century and is now considered the outstanding Danish painter of his period.

Koch, Joseph Anton (1768–1839). Austrian painter, active mainly in Rome, where he settled in 1795. He was influenced by *Carstens and worked with the *Nazarenes on the decorations of the Casino Massimo (1825–9) in Rome, choosing Dante's *Inferno* for his subject, but he is now best known for his landscapes. They were directly descended from the heroic and *ideal landscape of *Poussin, but have a distinctive *Romantic flavour, particularly in his paintings of mountains.

Koekkoek, Barend Cornelis (1803–62). The best-known member of a family of Dutch painters. He spent much of his career in Germany, where he found inspiration for his *Romantic views of forests and mountains; they are painted in a precise and detailed style, often with rosy light effects recalling the work of Jan *Both. His work was highly popular in his lifetime, leading to many imitations and forgeries. Other members of his large and prolific family specialized mainly in seascapes.

Kokoschka, Oskar (1886–1980). Austrian *Expressionist painter, printmaker, and writer (he became a Czech citizen in 1937 and a British citizen in 1947 but reverted to Austrian nationality in 1975). His formative years where spent in Vienna, where in 1909 he began to make an impact with his 'psychological portraits', in which the soul of the sitter was thought to be laid bare. A good example is his portrait of the architect Adolf Loos (1909, Staatliche Museen, Berlin), showing the sensitive, quivering line through which Kokoschka captured what he called the 'closed personalities, so full of tension' of his sitters. Later his brushwork became much broader and more broken, with high-keyed flickering colours. In 1915 he was badly wounded whilst serving in the Austrian army, and in 1917—still recuperating—he settled in Dresden, where he taught at the Academy from 1919 to 1924. After this he embarked on a period of wide travel that lasted for seven years, and during this time he turned more from portraits to landscapes, including a distinctive type of townscape seen from a high viewpoint (*Jerusalem*, 1929–30, Detroit Inst. of Arts). In 1931 he returned to Vienna, but he was outspokenly opposed to the Nazis (who later declared his work *degenerate) and he moved to Prague in 1934 and then to London in 1938. By this time he had an international reputation, but his work was as yet little known in England and he was poor throughout the war years. After the war his fortunes soon improved and he came to be generally regarded as one of the giants of modern art. From 1953 he lived mainly at Villeneuve in Switzerland, and from 1953 to 1963 he ran a summer school at Salzburg. In his later years he continued to paint landscapes and portraits, but his most important works of this time are allegorical and mythological pictures, including the *Prometheus* ceiling (1950) for the house of Count Seilern (*see* COUR-TAULD) at Princes Gate in London, and the *Thermopylae* triptych (1954) for Hamburg University. Kokoschka remained steadfastly unaffected by modern movements throughout his long life, pursuing his highly personal version of pre-1914 Expressionism. Unlike many other Expressionists, however, he was essentially optimistic in outlook. His writings include an autobiography (1971), and several plays, notably *Mörder Hoffnung der Frauen* (Murderer Hope of Women), an early example of Expressionist theatre that caused outrage when it was first performed in 1908 because of its violence.

Kollwitz, Käthe (née Schmidt, 1867–1945). German graphic artist and sculptor. She came from a family of strong moral and social convictions, and after marrying a doctor of similar outlook, Karl Kollwitz, in 1891, she moved to one of the poorer quarters of Berlin, where she gained first-hand knowledge of the wretched conditions in which the urban poor lived. The two series of etchings that established her reputation were inspired by a spirit of protest against working conditions of the day, although their subjects are set in the past—*Weavers' Revolt* (1893–7) and *Peasants' War* (1902–8). After about 1910 lithography replaced etching as her preferred medium (she also made woodcuts), and after the First World War she turned from illustrating particular subjects to depicting abstract concepts and great timeless themes such as the Mother and Child. Her work is uncompromisingly serious and often deeply pessimistic in spirit, and many of her later drawings and prints are pacifist in intention (her son was killed in the First World War and her grandson in the Second World War). Appropriately, her best-known sculpture is a war memorial—that at Dixmuiden, Flanders, completed in 1932. In line with her left-wing views Kollwitz visited the Soviet Union in 1927, but she subsequently became disillusioned with Soviet Communism. In 1919 she had been made the first ever woman member of the Berlin Academy, but when Hitler came to power in 1933 she was forced to resign. She suffered harassment, but she was never declared a *degenerate artist (in fact the Nazis sometimes used her images—without her name or authorization—in their propaganda), and she continued to produce outstanding work. Her masterpiece is arguably the series of eight lithographs on the subject of Death (1934–5), memorably showing the powerful breadth of her style, in which all accidentals and inessentials are eliminated. In its poignant concern for suffering humanity, her work represents one of the high points of German *Expressionism and of 20th-century graphic art. 'I should like', she wrote in 1922, 'to exert influences in these times when human beings are so perplexed and in need of help.'

Koninck (or **de Koninck**), **Philips** (1619–88). Dutch painter, the best-known member of a family of artists. He studied with his brother **Jacob** (*c.*1615–after 1690) in Rotterdam, and *Houbraken says he was also a pupil of *Rembrandt in Amsterdam, where he settled in 1641. Although he painted various subjects (the poet Vondel praised his portraits and history pictures) his fame now rests on his landscapes. He specialized in extensive views—powerful and majestic works that rival the similar scenes of *Ruisdael; the National Gallery in London has four outstanding examples. Like many Dutch painters he had a second occupation; he ran a prosperous shipping firm and evidently painted little in the last decade of his life. His wealth enabled him to collect drawings. He was a prolific draughtsman himself and his sketchy penmanship can be deceptively close to Rembrandt's. **Salomon Koninck** (1609–56), a relative (perhaps a cousin) of Philips and Jacob, was also a painter and likewise active in Amsterdam. He was a follower of Rembrandt, imitating him in pictures of hermits, old men, and philosophers in their studies, as well as in religious scenes, and exaggerating the master's early predilection for rich exotic costumes, emphatic gestures, and dramatic contrasts of light and shadow. His work is fairly rare; there are examples in the Rijksmuseum, Amsterdam, and the Mauritshuis, The Hague.

Koons, Jeff. *See* NEO-GEO.

kore (pl. **korai**; Gk.: 'maiden'). Term applied to the draped standing female statues characteristic of the *Archaic period. *See also* KOUROS.

Kossoff, Leon (1926–). British painter, born of Russian-Jewish immigrant parents in the East End of London, an area that has provided the chief subject-matter of his paintings. His training included evening classes under David *Bomberg, 1950–2, and his work has close affinities with that of another Bomberg student, Frank *Auerbach—in choice of subject, emotional treatment of it, and use of extremely heavy *impasto. Kossoff generally retains a firmer sense of structure than Auerbach, however, often using thick black outlines, and unlike him does not approach abstraction. His reputation was slow to grow, but there was a major retrospective exhibition of his work at the Tate Gallery, London, in 1996. *See also* SCHOOL OF LONDON.

Kosuth, Joseph (1945–). American experimental artist, a well-known exponent of *Conceptual art. He has been much concerned with linguistic analysis of concepts of art, his best-known work being *One and Three Chairs* (1965, MoMA, New York), which presents an actual chair alongside a full-scale photograph of a chair and an enlarged photograph of a dictionary definition of a chair. 'Actual works of art', he said, 'are little more than historical curiosities.'

kouros (pl. **kouroi**; Gk.: 'young man'). Term applied to the nude standing male statues typical of the *Archaic period. *See also* KORE.

Kraft, Adam (d.1509). German sculptor, active in Nuremberg, where he is first recorded in 1490. He was a virtuoso stone-carver and his most celebrated work, the tabernacle in St Lawrence, Nuremberg (1493–6), is a gigantic stone imitation (*c*.18 m (60 ft) high) of a subtle piece of goldsmith's work. The richly decorated structure houses a multitude of human figures, animals, amphibia, etc. One of the supporting figures at the base is said to be a self-portrait of Kraft.

Kramskoi, Ivan (1837–87). Russian painter. In 1863 he led a revolt of fourteen students at the St Petersburg Academy; they left together in protest because they thought its approach was out of touch with modern life, and in 1870 they formed the nucleus of the *Wanderers, of which Kramskoi was a leading light. A sensitive and highly principled man, he believed that 'only a sense of social purpose can give an artist strength and multiply his powers

...only confidence that the artist's work is needed and appreciated by society can help those exotic plants called pictures to ripen'. He was one of the outstanding Russian portraitists of his time and also painted deeply serious religious works. The most famous is *Christ in the Wilderness* (1872, Tretyakov Gal., Moscow), of which Tolstoy said, 'This is the best Christ I know.' His style was clear and sharply focused, perhaps reflecting the fact that he had been a photographic retoucher in his youth. Kramskoi was a hero and intellectual father to a generation of Russian painters, including *Repin, who called him a 'mighty man'.

Krasner, Lee. *See* POLLOCK.

Kress, Samuel H. (1863–1955). American businessman, art collector, and philanthropist. He became immensely wealthy from his chain of stores and in 1929 he established the Samuel H. Kress Foundation 'to promote the moral, physical and mental welfare of the human race'. His philanthropic work included contributions to medical research and restoring historic buildings in Europe after the Second World War, but he is best known for donations of works of art to American museums. Above all, his donation of 375 paintings and eighteen sculptures to the newly formed National Gallery of Art in Washington in 1939 (together with subsequent gifts) formed one of the cornerstones of the collection. Kress was a friend of Bernard *Berenson and his main field of interest was Italian *Renaissance painting.

Krieghoff, Cornelius (1815–72). Dutch-born Canadian painter. He studied in Düsseldorf, went to New York *c*.1835, and from 1840 spent most of his career in Canada (mainly in Montreal and Quebec), although he also had periods in Europe and the USA (he died in Chicago). His pictures of the Indians, French-Canadian life, and the landscape, done in a colourful, detailed, and often anecdotal style, proved highly popular, and he has been much imitated and forged.

Krohg, Christian (1852–1925). Norwegian painter, active mainly in Christiania (now Oslo), although he had a lengthy stay in Paris from 1902 to 1909. He took his subjects mainly from ordinary life—often from its sombre or unsavoury aspects. In particular, he is well known for his paintings of prostitutes, and he wrote a controversial novel on the same subject (*Albertine*, 1886). His work was often attacked by conservative critics, but his vigorous and forthright tackling of modern issues made him a hero to many Norwegian artists of a younger generation, most notably *Munch. His son **Per Krohg** (1889–1965) was also a painter. In his early work he specialized in scenes of city life, using bright *Fauvist colours (he studied under *Matisse in Paris) and exaggerated gestures that sometimes border on caricature (*Kiki of Montparnasse*, 1928, NG, Oslo). From about 1930, however, his style became more naturalistic and he worked mainly as a muralist, decorating many public buildings, particularly in Oslo. Father and son both held the post of director of the Academy of Fine Arts in Oslo, Christian from 1909 until his death, Per from 1955 to 1958.

Krøyer, P. S. (Peder Severin) (1851–1909). The most famous Danish painter of his period. After studying at the Copenhagen Academy he travelled extensively in Europe 1875–81. During this period he spent two years in Paris, 1877–9, and he was influenced by French *plein-air painting, showing a particular interest in capturing complex effects of light—the fusion of daylight and lamplight, for example. From 1882 he spent much of his time at the village of Skagen on the Jutland coast, where he was a prominent figure in a colony of artists; his work is well represented in the museum there. The pictures he painted at Skagen include poetic views of figures on the beach in the blue light of summer evenings. He was also a successful portraitist. From 1900 his career was marred by mental illness.

Kubin, Alfred (1877–1959). Austrian draughtsman, illustrator, painter, and writer. From 1906 he lived mainly at Zwicklédt in Upper Austria, although he travelled a good deal. He was a friend of *Kandinsky and showed his work in the second *Blaue Reiter exhibition in 1912, but his preoccupations were very different to those usually associated with the group. His work shows a taste for the morbid and fantastic, which he combined with pessimistic social satire and allegory. Often he depicted weird creatures in the kind of murky nightmare world associated with Odilon *Redon, whom he met in

1905. Kubin's imagery reflects his disturbed and traumatic life (he had an unhappy childhood, attempted suicide on his mother's grave in 1896, and in 1903 underwent a mental breakdown after the death of his fiancée). He was obsessed with the theme of death (he is said to have liked to watch corpses being recovered from the river) and with the idea of female sexuality as a symbol of death. In 1909 he wrote a fantastical novel *Die andere Seite* (The Other Side) and he illustrated many books, often ones whose subject matter matched his own macabre interests, such as the stories of Edgar Allan Poe. From the 1920s his reputation was widespread and he was influential on the *Surrealists. His spidery style changed little throughout his career.

Kunsthistorisches Museum, Vienna. Museum of painting, sculpture, and decorative arts (the name means 'Art History Museum') based on the accumulation of treasures by members of the imperial *Habsburg dynasty from the 16th century onwards. The imperial collections were first opened to the public in 1781 in the Belvedere Palace, which became informally known as the Belvedere Gallery. The present museum, a huge structure in neo-Renaissance style, was built in 1872–82. It is one of a series of very grand buildings arranged around the Ringstrasse, the great circular boulevard created on the line of the city's ancient ramparts, which were demolished in 1858–64. The architects of the museum were Gottfried Semper and Karl von Hasenauer, and the extremely lavish decoration includes murals by *Makart on the main staircase. The collection of Old Master paintings in the Kunsthistorisches Museum is one of the most celebrated in the world, particularly rich in works by the great 16th-century Venetians (*Giorgione, *Titian, *Tintoretto, *Veronese), and by *Bruegel, *Dürer, van *Dyck, *Rubens, and *Velázquez. There are also major holdings in other areas, including antiquities, sculpture, and coins.

Kunstkammer. German term (literally 'art chamber') used to describe a type of collection of pictures and curios popular with princely collectors in the 16th and 17th centuries. The pieces in such collections (which were by no means confined to Germany) might include anything from a watch to a fossil. In 16th- and 17th-century inventories the term *Kunstkammerstück* means an object of art, a jewel, or a devotional article of particularly notable character or quality ordered specially for display in the *Kunstkammer*.

Kupka, František (Frank, François) (1871–1957). Czech painter and graphic artist, active mainly in France, a pioneer of *abstract art. He studied in Prague and Vienna, and settled in Paris in 1895 or 1896, working first mainly as a satirical draughtsman and book illustrator; his paintings of the time were influenced by *Symbolism and then *Fauvism. From an early age he had been interested in the supernatural (later in Theosophy), and from this grew a concern with the spiritual symbolism of colour. It became his ambition to create paintings whose colours and rhythms would produce effects similar to those of music, and in his letters he sometimes signed himself 'colour symphonist'. From 1909 (inspired by high-speed photography) he experimented—in a manner similar to that of the *Futurists—with ways of showing motion, and by 1912 this had led him to complete abstraction in *Amorpha: Fugue in Two Colours* (NG, Prague). This created something of a sensation when exhibited at the *Salon d'Automne in 1912. As with *Delaunay and the *Orphists, to whom his work is closely related, Kupka excelled at this stage in his career in the creation of lyrical colour effects. At the outbreak of the First World War he volunteered for military service; he fought on the Somme and he also did a good deal of propaganda work such as designing posters. After the war the Prague Academy appointed him a professor in Paris with the brief of introducing Czech students there to French culture. In 1931 he was one of the founder members of the *Abstraction-Création group. His later work was in a more geometrical abstract style. Although Kupka gradually established a considerable reputation, his pioneering role in abstraction was not generally realized until after his death.

L

Lachaise, Gaston (1882–1935). French-born sculptor who emigrated to the USA in 1906 and became an American citizen in 1916, one of the pioneers of modern sculpture in his adopted country. He settled first in Boston, then in 1912 moved to New York, where he became assistant to Paul *Manship. Lachaise was a consummate craftsman in stone, metal, and wood (his father was a cabinetmaker), but his most characteristic works are in bronze. He did a number of portrait busts remarkable for their psychological insight and he earned a good deal of his living from decorative animal sculptures, but he is best known for his female nudes—monumental and anatomically simplified figures, with voluptuous forms and a sense of fluid rhythmical movement (*Standing Woman*, 1912–27, Whitney Mus., New York). Their smooth modelling links them with the work of *Nadelman, who was also at this time helping to lead American sculpture away from the 19th-century academic tradition, but Lachaise's figures are more powerful than those of Nadelman and have an overt sexuality that has caused them to be compared with the nudes of *Renoir. The inspiration for the figures—Lachaise's embodiment of female beauty—was Isabel Dutaud Nagle, a married American woman with whom he fell in love when he was about 20; she was the reason for his move to America and he was eventually able to marry her in 1917.

Laer, Pieter van (1599–*c*.1642). Dutch painter, active for much of his career (*c*.1625–38) in Rome. There he was nicknamed 'Il Bamboccio' (which may be translated as 'Little clumsy one'), as he was crippled or deformed in some way. His self-portrait in the Pallavicini Gallery in Rome suggests that he bore his handicap with good humour, and he was one of the leaders of the *Schildersbent, a fraternal organization set up by the Netherlandish artists in Rome to protect their interests. Van Laer was the first artist to specialize in scenes of street life in Rome. His work proved popular with collectors and he inspired numerous

followers who were known as the 'Bamboccianti'. They were mainly other Northerners working in Rome, such as the Flemings Jan Miel (1599–1663) and Michiel *Sweerts, but also included Italians such as Michelangelo *Cerquozzi and Viviano Codazzi (1611–72). Their pictures are called *bambocciate* (the singular is *bambocciata*—Italian for 'childishness') or in French *bambochades*; an English equivalent—bambocciade—exists, but it is rarely used. In about 1638 van Laer returned to his native Haarlem. He is said to have set off for Rome again in 1642, and to have disappeared soon afterwards.

La Fosse, Charles de (1636–1716). French painter, one of the pre-eminent decorative artists of Louis XIV's reign. He was a pupil of *Le Brun and his assistant at Versailles, but his style was more strongly affected by his stay in Italy (1658–63), where he absorbed the *Baroque manner of Pietro da *Cortona and was influenced by the colour and warmth of such north Italian artists as *Correggio and *Veronese. In the 1680s he turned more to *Rubens as a source of inspiration. From 1689 to 1692 La Fosse worked in London for the 1st Duke of Montagu on the decoration of Montagu House (formerly on the site of the British Museum), then returned to Paris to decorate the church of the Invalides. Originally he was commissioned to paint the entire building, but eventually he did only the dome and pendentives (1702–4), in a style that heralds something of the lightness and elegance of the ensuing *Rococo. La Fosse's work was much more free and colourful than that of most of his contemporaries, and Anthony *Blunt described him as 'almost the only 17th-century French artist whom *Watteau may have studied with profit'.

La Fresnaye, Roger de (1885–1925). French painter. In 1912–14 he was a member of the *Section d'Or group, and his work shows an individual response to *Cubism; his paintings were more naturalistic than those of *Braque and *Picasso, but he adopted something of their method of analysing forms into planes. The effect in

La Fresnaye's work, however, is more decorative than structural, and his prismatic colours reflect the influence of *Delaunay, as in his most famous and personal work, *The Conquest of the Air* (1913, MoMA, New York), in which he portrays himself and his brother in an exhilaratingly airy setting with a balloon ascending in the background. La Fresnaye's health was ruined during his service in the army during the First World War and he never again had the energy for sustained work. In his later paintings he abandoned Cubist spatial analysis for a more linear style.

Laguerre, Louis (1663–1721). French decorative painter, active for almost all his career in England. After working for a short time under Charles *Le Brun in Paris he moved to England in 1683/4, initially collaborating with *Verrio but soon branching out on his own, working mainly in country houses, notably Burghley House, Chatsworth, and Blenheim Palace. He was a better painter than Verrio (although still unexceptional judged by European standards) and was also a more attractive personality, but he never achieved the extravagant worldly success of the Italian. From about 1710 *Thornhill began to succeed him in popularity. Late in his career Laguerre turned increasingly to portraits and history paintings.

La Hyre, Laurent de (1606–56). French painter, active in his native Paris. He painted religious and mythological scenes, portraits, and landscapes and also made engravings. His earlier work owed much to *Primaticcio and the *Fontainebleau schools, but from about 1638 his style became more classical, under the influence of Nicolas *Poussin and then of Philippe de *Champaigne. *The Birth of Bacchus* (1638, Hermitage, St Petersburg) is a good example of his work—obviously indebted to Poussin, but showing a certain individuality in the soft and romantic treatment of the landscape.

Lairesse, Gérard de (1640–1711). Dutch painter, etcher, and writer on art. Born in Liège, he settled in Amsterdam in about 1665 and became the leading decorative painter in Holland in the second half of the 17th century, working in an academic *classical style that inspired his overenthusiastic contemporaries to call him 'the Dutch

*Raphael' and 'the Dutch *Poussin'. In about 1690, however, he suddenly went blind and thereafter devoted himself to art theory. His lectures were collected in two books—*Grondlegginge der teekenkonst* (Principles of Drawing, 1701) and *Het groot schilderboek* (The Great Book of Painters, 1707)—which went through many editions and translations during the 18th century. Lairesse's writings reveal the same academic approach as his paintings and he somewhat naively confessed that he had a special preference for *Rembrandt until he learned 'the infallible rules of art'. Rembrandt had painted a portrait of the young Lairesse in 1665 (Met. Mus., New York), sympathetically showing his disease-ravaged face (he was disfigured by congenital syphilis, which probably caused his blindness).

Lam, Wifredo (1902–82). Cuban painter. His father was Chinese and his mother of mixed African, Indian, and European origin, and Lam's career was appropriately cosmopolitan. After studying in Havana, he settled in Madrid in 1924, then in 1938 moved to Paris, where he became a friend of *Picasso. He also met André *Breton (whose book *Fata Morgana* he illustrated in 1940) and in 1939 joined the *Surrealists. In 1941 Lam sailed from Marseilles for Martinique on the same ship as *Masson, Breton, and many other intellectuals who were fleeing the Germans. After his return to Cuba in 1942 he came increasingly under the spell of African and Oceanic sculpture, and following visits to Haiti in 1945 and 1946 he also began incorporating images of Voodoo gods and rites in his work. In 1952 he returned to Paris and from the 1960s also spent much of his time at Albisola Mare, near Genoa. In the 1970s he began making bronze sculpture. Lam's work successfully reconciles the artistic vigour of Latin America with the European avant-garde and with the powerful mystique of African and Oceanic tradition, fusing human, animal, and vegetable elements in menacing semi-abstract images. He won numerous prestigious prizes and his work is included in many leading collections.

Lamb, Henry (1883–1960). British painter, mainly of portraits. Under parental pressure he studied medicine, but abandoned it in 1904 to become an artist. (On the outbreak of the First World War, however, Lamb returned to his medical studies, qualifying at Guy's Hospital, London, in 1916 and then serving as a medical officer in France, Macedonia, and Palestine; he was gassed and won the Military Cross. He also worked as an *Official War Artist, as he did again in the Second World War.) Lamb was associated with the *Bloomsbury Group and is best known for his sensitive portraits of fellow members, painted in the restrained *Post-Impressionist style that characterized his work throughout his career. Above all he is remembered for his portrait of Lytton Strachey (1914, Tate, London), in which he 'has relished emphasizing Strachey's gaunt, ungainly figure, and the air of resigned intellectual superiority with which he surveys the world from that incredible slab-like head' (*DNB*); Sir John *Rothenstein described it as 'one of the best portraits painted in England in this century'. Apart from portraits, Lamb also painted landscapes and (especially in later life when his health was failing) still lifes.

Lambert, George (1700–65). The leading English landscape painter of his day. He began his career working in the style of John *Wootton and also learned something of the principles of *ideal landscape composition from studying the work of Gaspard *Dughet. As well as painting handsome works essentially in Dughet's manner, Lambert also did more realistic topographical views. Sir Ellis *Waterhouse has written of him: 'Lambert was the first native painter to apply the rules of art to the English rural scene, and, in this sense, *Wilson followed him.' The figures in Lambert's paintings were done by other artists—sometimes, according to plausible tradition, by *Hogarth. He also collaborated with Samuel *Scott (who painted the shipping) in views of the East India Company's settlements (1732, India Office Library, London).

Lamothe, Louis. *See* DEGAS.

Lancret, Nicolas (1690–1743). French painter. He studied under Claude *Gillot, who slightly earlier had taught *Watteau, and he became a great admirer of Watteau's work, imitating the style and themes he had made popular. In 1719 he was received into the Académie Royale in Paris as a painter of *fêtes galantes—a category that had been created especially for Watteau only two years earlier. Although his work is prosaic compared with Watteau's, it has great charm and he had a successful career.

Land art (or **Earth art** or **Earthworks**). Terms applied to a type of art that uses as its raw materials earth, rocks, soil, and so on. The terms are not usually clearly differentiated, although 'Earthworks' generally refers to very large constructions. Land art emerged as a movement in the late 1960s and has links with several other movements that flourished at that time: *Minimal art in that the shapes created are often extremely simple; *Arte Povera in the use of 'worthless' materials; *happenings and *Performance art because the work created was often impermanent; and *Conceptual art because the more ambitious earthwork schemes frequently exist only as projects. There are affinities also with the passion at this time for the study of prehistoric mounds and ley lines—part of the hippie back-to-nature ethos that expressed a disenchantment with the sophisticated technology of urban culture. The desire to get away from the traditional elitist and money-orientated gallery world was also very much typical of the time, although large earthworks have in fact necessitated very hefty expenditure, and far from being populist and accessible, such works are usually in remote areas; some are intelligible only from the air and therefore can rarely be appreciated other than by people rich enough to own or hire aeroplanes. Moreover, in spite of the desire to sidestep the gallery system, dealers have proved capable of exploiting this kind of art, just like any other, and some land artists at least have made handsome livings from it.

The artist associated more than any other with large-scale earthworks in situ was Robert *Smithson, whose *Spiral Jetty* (1970) in the Great Salt Lake, Utah, is easily the most reproduced work of this kind. The most ambitious of all such enterprises is probably the Roden Crater Project by James Turrell (1941–), involving the reshaping of an extinct volcano in Arizona (begun in the mid-1970s). Most of the other leading exponents are—like Smithson and Turrell—Americans. They include Alice Aycock (1946–), whose work has included underground mazes, and Michael Heizer (1944–), whose best-known work is *Double Negative* (1969–70) in the Nevada desert—

two massive cuts 30 ft (9 m) wide and 50 ft (15 m) deep in an area where he said he found 'that kind of unraped, peaceful religious space artists have always tried to put in their work'. Some critics, however, consider that earthworks can themselves constitute a type of rape or violation.

*Christo is sometimes grouped with land artists, although his work really defies classification. The leading British exponents are Andy *Goldsworthy and Richard *Long.

Landseer, Sir Edwin (1802/3–73). English painter, sculptor, and engraver, mainly of animal subjects. He was the son of an engraver and writer, **John Landseer** (1769–1852), and was an infant prodigy. His career was a story of remarkable social as well as professional success; he was the favourite painter of Queen Victoria (who considered him 'very good looking although rather short') and his friends included Dickens and Thackeray. The qualities in his work that delighted the Victorian public, however, have subsequently caused his reputation to plummet, for although he had great skill in depicting animal anatomy, he tended to humanize his subjects to tell a sentimental story or point a moral. His most familiar works in this vein include *The Old Shepherd's Chief Mourner* (1837, V&A, London), *Dignity and Impudence* (1839, Tate, London), and *The Monarch of the Glen* (1850, Guinness plc, Edinburgh). Other paintings by Landseer have been attacked for their cruelty (he made many visits to the Scottish Highlands and frequently painted scenes of deer-hunting). Apart from animal subjects, he also painted portraits and historical scenes. Although he had no previous experience as a sculptor, in 1858 he was commissioned to make four huge bronze lions for the base of Nelson's Column in Trafalgar Square, London; they were cast by *Marochetti and unveiled in 1867. By this time Landseer's health had broken down (it was for this reason that he declined the presidency of the *Royal Academy in 1865), and in his last years he suffered from bouts of madness, aggravated by alcohol. His brother **Thomas** (1798–1880) was an engraver, whose prints played a great part in popularizing Edwin's work. Another brother, **Charles** (1800–79), bequeathed £10,000 to the Royal Academy to found Landseer scholarships.

Lane, Sir Hugh (1875–1915). Irish dealer, patron, collector, and administrator. He made his fortune as a picture dealer in London and had no particular interest in Ireland until about 1900, when through the influence of Sarah *Purser and the playwright Lady Gregory (his aunt) he became caught up in the rising tide of nationalism in the arts. He commissioned John Butler *Yeats to paint a series of eminent contemporary Irishmen (it was completed by *Orpen, a distant cousin and close friend of Lane's) and he helped to found Dublin's Municipal Gallery of Modern Art, opened in temporary premises in 1906. In addition to giving and lending numerous works to the gallery, he offered to bequeath his finest late 19th- and early 20th-century French paintings to Dublin, on condition that a suitable gallery were built to house them. This caused arguments with Dublin's city authorities, however, and he moved the pictures to the National Gallery in London. Lane was killed when the *Lusitania* (on which he was returning from business in the USA) was torpedoed by a German submarine. A codicil to his will expressed his intention of returning the French pictures to Dublin, but it was unwitnessed, creating a long-term legal dispute about their ownership. In 1959 an agreement was eventually reached whereby the paintings were divided into groups to be shown alternately in Dublin and London. This agreement has subsequently been somewhat modified. The Municipal Gallery of Modern Art was given a permanent home in Dublin in 1933, and in 1979 it was renamed the Hugh Lane Municipal Gallery of Modern Art.

Lanfranco, Giovanni (1582–1647). Italian painter, who with *Guercino and Pietro da *Cortona ranks as one of the founders of the High *Baroque style of painting. He was born in Parma, where he trained under Agostino *Carracci before going to Rome in 1602 to assist Annibale Carracci in the Palazzo Farnese. After Annibale's death in 1609, he returned for a while to Emilia, but by about 1612 was back in Rome, where he gradually superseded his arch-rival *Domenichino as the leading fresco decorator in the city. Their work can be compared in the church of S. Andrea della Valle: Domenichino painted the apse and the pendentives of the dome, but Lanfranco was awarded the commission for the *Assumption of the Virgin* (1625–7) in the dome itself. This fresco is one of the key works of Baroque art and it ended the dominance of Bolognese classicism in Rome. The heroic figure style derives from the Carracci, but the *illusionistic foreshortening is based on *Correggio's dome paintings in Lanfranco's native Parma, here carried to new extremes. *Bellori compared the way in which Lanfranco handles the multitude of figures to the harmonious blending of voices in a choir, and the dynamic design became a pattern for illusionistic decorators throughout Europe. Between 1634 and 1646 Lanfranco was based in Naples, where he produced numerous frescos in the cathedral and other major churches. His work was an inspiration to such Neapolitan masters as Mattia *Preti, Luca *Giordano, and *Solimena. He returned to Rome in 1646, the year before his death; his final (unfinished) work, a fresco of *S. Carlo Borromeo in Glory* in the apse of S. Carlo ai Catinari, exemplifies the airy luminosity of his late style. Lanfranco is much less renowned as an easel painter, but he created some outstanding works in this field also. Particularly remarkable are his *Ecstasy of the Blessed Margaret of Cortona* (1622, Pitti, Florence), which possibly influenced *Bernini's *St Teresa*, and *St Mary Magdalen Transported to Heaven* (c.1605, Mus. di Capodimonte, Naples), a bizarre and highly original work in which the rapturous saint is carried by angels above a poetically evoked view of the Roman Campagna.

Lanyon, Peter. *See* ST IVES SCHOOL.

Lanzi, Luigi (1732–1810). Italian art historian, archaeologist, and philologian. He was appointed curator of the antiquarian collections of the *Uffizi, Florence, in 1775, and he ranks second only to *Winckelmann as a pioneer in the systematic study of ancient art. However, he is best known for his history of Italian painting from the 13th century until his own time, *Storia pittorica della Italia . . .* (1792; 2nd edn., 1795–6; 3rd edn. 1809). Lanzi classified his material by regional schools and based his work on a thorough knowledge of previous writings on the subject and of the paintings themselves (he visited churches and collections throughout central and northern Italy in the course of his work). His methodical arrangement and his synthesis of solid research with sensitive

analysis of style make his work a landmark in art-historical writing, and Rudolf *Wittkower has described it as 'still unequalled for knowledge of the material and breadth of approach'. There have been numerous editions since Lanzi's death, including an English translation in 1828. His other writings included a scholarly but controversial work on the Etruscan language (1789) and a book on ancient vases (1806) in which he correctly perceived that vases traditionally called Etruscan were in fact Greek in origin.

Laocoön. An antique marble group (Vatican Mus.) representing the Trojan priest Laocoön and his two sons being crushed to death by serpents as a penalty for warning the Trojans against the wooden horse of the Greeks, an incident related by Virgil in the *Aeneid* 2, 199–231. It is usually dated to the 2nd or 1st century BC or the 1st century AD, although whether it is an original *Hellenistic piece or a Roman copy has long been a matter of dispute. *Pliny states that in his time it stood in the palace of the emperor Titus in Rome, records that it was made by the sculptors Hagesander, Polydorus, and Athenodorus of Rhodes, and describes it as 'a work to be preferred to all that the arts of painting and sculpture have produced'. This praise echoed long after the sculpture had disappeared, and its dramatic rediscovery in a vineyard in Rome in 1506 made an overwhelming impression, notably on *Michelangelo, who went to see it immediately. Its liberating influence for the expression of the emotions continued to be important for *Baroque sculpture, and until the 19th century it was ranked (with the *Apollo Belvedere and the *Belvedere Torso) as one of the greatest works of antiquity. (As early as about 1530 *Titian satirized the adulation it received in a woodcut showing the figures changed to monkeys.) It was given a new aesthetic significance by *Winckelmann, who saw it as a supreme symbol of the moral dignity of the tragic hero and the most complete exemplification of the 'noble simplicity and quiet majesty' that he regarded as the essence of Greek idealistic art and the key to true beauty. In 1766 G. E. *Lessing chose *Laokoon* as the title of the book in which he attacked Winckelmann's ideas. The sculpture was one of the prizes taken from Italy by Napoleon and was in Paris 1798–1815. Although no longer considered one of the world's greatest master-pieces, the *Laocoön* has slipped in esteem much less than some once-revered antique statues; it continues to be a work with a powerful hold over the imagination and still finds a place in almost all general histories of art. It has been restored several times since its discovery, and a complete renovation was made in the 1950s, when Laocoön's original right arm was returned to the figure and replaced in its correct position behind his head.

Study of the *Laocoön* was revolutionized in 1957 by one of the most spectacular archaeological discoveries of the 20th century, when several groups of marble figures representing events in Homer's *Odyssey* were found at Sperlonga near Naples; the names Hagesander, Polydoros, and Athenodoros are inscribed on one of the groups (now in the museum at Sperlonga), which are close in style to the *Laocoön*. The cave in which these sculptures were found was evidently used as a banqueting hall by the emperor Tiberius (reigned AD 14–37), and there is other evidence linking them with the 1st century AD, so this date is now finding favour among classical archaeologists for the *Laocoön* also.

Largillière (or **Largillierre**), **Nicolas de** (1656–1746). French painter, mainly of portraits. He spent his youth in Antwerp and from 1675 to 1679 he worked in England, assisting *Lely and *Verrio. After settling in Paris in 1679 he soon established his position as a leading portraitist, rivalled only by *Rigaud, his almost exact contemporary. The two men were friends and seldom in direct competition, for Largillière specialized in portraits of the rich middle classes and Rigaud painted the aristocracy. Largillière's successful career continued into old age: he was director of the Académie Royale (*see* ACADEMY) in his eighties (1734–5 and 1738–42). His output of portraits was prodigious (contemporary sources indicate he painted about 1,500), and he also did religious works (once highly regarded), still lifes, and landscapes. At his best, his paintings are vigorous, forthright, and colourful; at his worst, they are pompous and vacuous.

Larionov, Mikhail (1881–1964). Russian painter and designer, one of the leading figures in the development of modernism in Russia in the period before the First World War. His early work was influenced by *Impressionism, but from 1908, together with Natalia *Goncharova (his lifelong companion and collaborator), he developed a style known as Neo-Primitivism, in which he blended *Fauvist colour with elements drawn from Russian folk art. Together they were involved in a series of avant-garde groups and exhibitions, notably the *Knave of Diamonds group, founded in 1910, the *Donkey's Tail exhibition in 1912, and the *Target Exhibition in 1913, at which Larionov launched *Rayonism, a near abstract movement that was a counterpart to Italian *Futurism. In May 1914 Larionov and Goncharova accompanied *Diaghilev's Ballets Russes to Paris. They returned to Russia in July on the outbreak of the First World War, and Larionov served in the army and was wounded. After being invalided out, he and Goncharova left Russia permanently in 1915, moving first to Switzerland and then settling in Paris in 1919 (they became French citizens in 1938). In Paris he practically abandoned easel painting and concentrated on theatrical designing for the Ballets Russes. After Diaghilev's death in 1929 Larionov took up painting again, but he gradually sank into obscurity and his final years were marred by illness and poverty. His reputation was revived shortly before his death with retrospective exhibitions (jointly with Goncharova) in London (Arts Council, 1961) and Paris (Mus. d'Art Moderne de la Ville de Paris, 1963).

Larkin, William (d. 1619). English portrait painter. He emerged from total obscurity in 1952 with the publication of his only securely attributed works—a pair of small oval portraits at Charlecote Park, Warwickshire. Subsequently, on circumstantial evidence, several other portraits have been attributed to him; they are in a very different vein to the Charlecote pictures—full-lengths featuring elaborate Turkey carpets, dazzling metallic curtains, and poses of a starched magnificence, notably a breathtaking group at Ranger's House, London. If they are indeed all by Larkin he was the genius of Jacobean painting; Ellis *Waterhouse considered the Ranger's House portraits to be the work of 'at least three different hands' (one of them perhaps Isaac *Oliver's), but technical examination in the 1980s indicated they are all from the same studio.

Laroon, Marcellus (1679–1772). English painter, the son of a Franco-Dutch painter of the same name (d. 1701/2) who moved to England as a young man and was one of *Kneller's assistants. The younger Laroon was a colourful character who in his long and strenuous life was a musician, singer, soldier, and man of pleasure; he drew and painted 'for diversitions', to use the words of *Vertue, and did not concentrate on art until he retired from the army in 1732. He painted portraits, *conversation pieces, and *genre scenes, usually fanciful in character. His nearly monochromatic, feathery style added a touch of French daintiness to the stolid English manner and he anticipated *Gainsborough by his lightness of touch. After a long period of neglect, he was rediscovered in the 20th century.

Larsson, Carl (1853–1919). Swedish painter, illustrator, printmaker, and writer. His work included numerous portraits and book illustrations, as well as several large-scale murals (the best known are those on Sweden's artistic history in the Nationalmuseum, Stockholm, 1896), but he is now remembered mainly for the house he created in the village of Sundborn in Dalarna (Dalecarlia) and for his watercolours of the idyllic life he enjoyed there with his wife **Karin** (1853–1928), a textile designer. The house—called Lilla Hyttnäs—was opened as a museum in 1942. To Swedes it epitomizes a healthy, happy society, and it has exercised a lasting influence on Scandinavian interior design.

Lassaw, Ibram. See ABSTRACT EXPRESSIONISM.

Lastman, Pieter (c.1583–1633). Dutch painter, highly esteemed in his day but now remembered mainly as the most significant of *Rembrandt's teachers. Most of his career was spent in his native Amsterdam, but in about 1603–7 he was in Italy, where *Caravaggio and *Elsheimer made a strong impact on his style. He specialized in small-scale religious, historical, and mythological scenes and often chose unusual subjects that showed off his learning (*The Roman Women and Children Beseeching Coriolanus not to Attack Rome*, 1625, Trinity College, Dublin). The glossy colours, the animated gestures and facial expressions, and the dramatic lighting of Rembrandt's early works all owe much to Lastman, and his *Balaam and the Ass* (1626, Mus. Cognacq-Jay, Paris), for example, is clearly based on a prototype by his master (1622, priv. coll.). Lastman also taught Rembrandt's friend Jan *Lievens.

László, Philip de (1869–1937). Hungarian-born portrait painter (and occasional sculptor) who settled in London in 1907 and became a British citizen in 1914 (although he was interned during the First World War). He trained in Budapest, Munich, and Paris (at the *Académie Julian) and already had an international reputation as a society portraitist when he moved to England. There his career continued in its successful course, his sitters including Edward VII and numerous members of the aristocracy (examples are in the NPG, London). According to the *Dictionary of National Biography*, he had 'a pleasing, courteous, and exuberant manner, and was very popular in society'. He was a fast and fluent worker and his style was elegant but superficial.

La Thangue, H. H. (Herbert Henry) (1859–1929). British painter. He had his main training at the *Royal Academy in London and the École des *Beaux-Arts in Paris. In 1887 he described the Academy as 'the diseased root from which other evils grow', and he was one of the leading figures in founding the *New English Art Club in opposition to it and in introducing the ideals of French *plein-air painting to Britain. He lived in the countryside (first in Norfolk, then in Sussex), and *Clausen wrote of him: 'Sunlight was the thing that attracted him: this and some simple motive of rural occupation, enhanced by a picturesque surround.' From about 1898 he turned to peasant scenes set in Provence or Italy, places where he often stayed. As the countryside changed, his work became increasingly nostalgic, as he hankered after what *Munnings called a 'quiet old world village where he could live and find real country models'.

La Tour, Georges de (1593–1652). French painter, active at Lunéville in the Duchy of Lorraine. He had a successful career (his paintings were owned by Louis XIII, Cardinal Richelieu, and the Duke of Lorraine), but his name sank into oblivion after his death and it was not until the 20th century that he was rediscovered and hailed as the most inspired of *Caravaggesque painters.

Little is recorded of his life (although he is known to have been arrogant and unpopular with his neighbours) and it is a matter of dispute whether he gained his knowledge of Caravaggio's style via painters of the Utrecht School such as *Honthorst or by travelling to Italy. Like Honthorst he is particularly associated with nocturnal scenes and with the use of a candle as the light source in a painting. La Tour's handling of light is more subtle and sensitive, however, and he is grander in conception and more sombre in mood. In his mature work he smoothed the forms of his figures until they approached geometric simplicity and achieved a feeling of monumental stillness that is considered to represent the spirit of 17th-century French *classicism no less than the paintings of Philippe de *Champaigne and *Poussin in their different fields. Only three of La Tour's paintings are dated—the *Payment of Taxes* (1634?, Picture Gal., Lviv, Ukraine); *Penitent St Peter* (1645, Cleveland Mus. of Art); the *Denial of St Peter* (1650, Mus. B.-A., Nantes)—and there is much scholarly debate about his chronology. The works associated with the beginning of his career are daylit scenes of such subjects as peasants and card-sharpers; they are very different in spirit from the calm and majestic religious images of his maturity and have become controversial as regards attribution as well as dating. It has been argued (and hotly disputed) that the *Fortune Teller* (Met. Mus., New York) is a modern fake, and although the status of most of the other early works as authentic (and high-quality) 17th-century French paintings is not denied, their attribution to La Tour (which rests almost entirely on stylistic evidence) has been questioned. Another problem in La Tour studies is that many of his undeniably authentic compositions exist in more than one version, and the studio replicas (as they appear to be) are sometimes of extremely high quality: the versions of *St Sebastian Tended by St Irene* in the Louvre, Paris, and the Gemäldegalerie, Berlin, for example, are each extraordinarily beautiful. La Tour's son **Étienne** (1621–92) worked in his father's studio and may have been responsible for some of the replicas. No independent works certainly by him are known, but the *Education of the Virgin* (Frick Coll., New York), signed 'de la Tour', has been attributed to him.

La Tour, Maurice-Quentin de (1704–88). With *Perronneau the most celebrated and the most successful French *pastel portraitist of the 18th century. His portraits are remarkable for their beauty of colour, their mastery of texture, and above all their brilliant handling of expression, which gives them a feeling of great vivacity. La Tour himself said, 'I penetrate into the depths of my subjects without their knowing it, and capture them whole.' He portrayed many of the most famous men and women of his day and in 1750 he became portraitist to Louis XV. He made a fortune from his work and late in life he used much of it for philanthropic purposes, in both Paris and his native St-Quentin. The museum there has a good collection of his work.

Laurana, Francesco (*c.*1430–1502?). Italian sculptor, born near Zara in Dalmatia, at that time subject to Venice. He is first recorded in 1453 in Naples, where he was one of several sculptors who worked on the decorations to the triumphal arch of Alfonso I that forms the entrance to Castelnuovo. By 1461 he was working in Provence and thenceforward he divided his time between France and Italy, mainly the south of Italy, including Sicily, although he is thought to have visited Urbino, and was possibly related to Luciano Laurana, the chief architect of the celebrated Ducal Palace there. In France his most important work was the chapel of St Lazare (1475–81) in the Old Cathedral at Marseilles, described by Anthony *Blunt as 'probably the earliest purely Italian work on French soil'. He is best known, however, for his female portrait busts of royal and aristocratic sitters. In these remarkably sensitive works the forms of the face are subtly generalized in a search for basic geometric shapes, and their simple naturalism was sometimes enhanced by heightening the marble with colour, as in the bust of Isabella of Aragon (*c.*1470) in the Kunsthistorisches Museum, Vienna.

Laurens, Henri (1885–1954). French sculptor, printmaker, designer, and illustrator, born in Paris, where he trained as an ornamental stonemason. His early work shows the influence of *Rodin, but in 1911 he became a friend of *Braque (he later met *Gris, *Léger, and *Picasso) and he was one of the first artists to adapt the *Cubist style to sculpture. He made collages, reliefs, and constructions of wood and metal, mainly still lifes using the familiar Cubist repertory of bottles, glasses, and fruit. Much of his work was coloured, but he retained a genuine sculptor's feeling for mass, and his distrust of intellectual speculation preserved his independence from Cubist theorizing. In the mid-1920s he moved away from his geometrical style to one that featured curved lines and voluptuous forms, notably in female nudes. Many of his fellow artists regarded him as one of the greatest sculptors of his time, but financial success and official recognition were slow in coming. When he failed to win the first prize for sculpture at the 1948 Venice *Biennale, *Matisse was so disgusted that he offered to share his own painting prize with him. In 1953, however, Laurens won the Grand Prix at the São Paulo Bienale. Apart from sculpture, his work included stage design for *Diaghilev and numerous book illustrations.

Lavery, Sir John (1856–1941). British painter, mainly of portraits. He was born in Belfast and studied in Glasgow, in London, and then in the early 1880s in Paris (at the *Académie Julian and elsewhere). Between 1885 and 1896 he lived mainly in Glasgow (see GLASGOW SCHOOL), then settled in London, although he travelled a good deal and often wintered in Morocco, where he bought a house in about 1903. Lavery had an immensely successful career as a fashionable portraitist (particularly of women), painting in a dashing and fluid, if rather facile, style. He also painted interiors, landscapes, and outdoor scenes such as tennis and bathing parties, and he was an *Official War Artist, 1917–18. His reputation did not long survive his death, but there has recently been a revival of interest in his work.

Lawrence, Sir Thomas (1769–1830). The outstanding English portrait painter of his generation. Lawrence was a child prodigy and was almost entirely self-taught. He was also handsome and charming, and after a resounding early triumph with his portrait of Queen Charlotte (1789–90, NG, London) he never looked back in terms of professional and social success. On the death of *Reynolds in 1792 he succeeded him as official painter to George III, and in 1794, aged 25, he became the youngest person to be elected a Royal Academician (although Mary *Moser was a founder member when even younger). On the death of *Hoppner in 1810 he was recognized as the leading portrait painter of the time, and also to some extent as head of the profession of painting in Britain. The high point of his career came in 1818, when he was sent to Europe as the envoy of the Prince Regent (later George IV) to paint the heads of state and military leaders who were involved with the allied victory over Napoleon. As a preliminary gesture he was knighted, and on his return in 1820 he succeeded *West as president of the *Royal Academy. The portraits painted on this tour are now in the Waterloo Chamber, Windsor Castle. Lawrence was devoted to the memory and example of Reynolds and in some respects he was the last of the great portrait painters in the 18th-century tradition. In others he was a *Romantic, responding to the glamour of the historic years through which he lived. His fluid and lush brushwork won the admiration of French painters when his work was exhibited at the Paris *Salon of 1824 and after *Delacroix visited London in the following year he paid Lawrence the compliment of painting a portrait in his style (Louis-Auguste Schwiter, 1826–30, NG, London). Lawrence's reputation declined after his death, however, and has never revived to its former heights. He was constantly in debt in spite of his success and took on too many commissions, so his work is uneven and sometimes careless (and like Reynolds he was a failure as a history painter), but at his best he has a feeling for paint that few British artists can rival. Lawrence was a man of great taste and made a superb collection of Old Master drawings, particularly rich in works by *Michelangelo and *Raphael (these are now among the greatest treasures of the Ashmolean Museum in Oxford). He played a part in founding the *National Gallery and in securing the *Elgin Marbles for the nation, and was noted for the unselfish help he gave to young artists.

Lawson, Ernest (1873–1939). American painter, the least distinguished and most orthodox member of The *Eight. Unlike the other members of the group he was primarily a landscapist (although he did also paint urban scenes), and his work was essentially *Impressionist in style.

lay figure. A doll-like model of the human figure, jointed so that it can be given all kinds of poses. It may be anything from a few inches in height to life-size. Articulated dolls and marionettes were known in antiquity, but the first description of an artist's lay figure is given by *Filarete in his *Treatise on Architecture* (1461–4). Although *Vasari mentions a life-size wooden model made by Fra *Bartolommeo, early lay figures were mostly small and were called manikins. Some 18th-century portrait painters used life-size figures, completely jointed and covered with fabric. They could arrange the costumes on it and work on that part of the picture in the absence of the sitter.

Lear, Edward (1812–88). English artist, author, and traveller. Although he is now remembered principally for his nonsense poems and as the popularizer of the limerick, he earned his living mainly through drawing and painting. He began his career as a draughtsman for the Zoological Society, but when the exacting work began to affect his eyesight he turned to topographical painting in the 1830s, initially in watercolour and later in oils. His style is very clear and brightly lit. He travelled widely and published several illustrated accounts of his journeys. In 1871 he settled in San Remo, Italy.

Le Brun, Charles (1619–90). French painter, designer, and art theorist, the dominant artist of Louis XIV's reign. He trained under *Vouet and quickly made a name for himself, winning a commission from Cardinal Richelieu when he was barely out of his teens; the only surviving picture from this commission (for the Palais Cardinal in Paris) is *Hercules and the Horses of Diomedes* (c.1640, Castle Mus., Nottingham). In 1642 Le Brun went to Rome in company with *Poussin, who was returning from his visit to Paris, and remained there until 1646. After his return to Paris he was soon busy with varied commissions and during the 1650s he established himself as the leading decorative painter in France. In 1662 he was raised to the nobility and named first painter to the king, and in 1663 he was made director of the *Gobelins factory and of the Académie Royale. For the next two decades, until the death of his patron Jean-Baptiste Colbert (Louis XIV's chief minister) in 1683, Le Brun was virtually the dictator of the visual arts in France. He not only supervised all the great royal commissions, but also turned the Académie into a channel for imposing a codified system of artistic orthodoxy (*see* ACADEMY). His lectures, formulated on the *classicism of Poussin, came to be accepted as providing the official standards of artistic correctness and gave authority to the view that every aspect of artistic creation can be reduced to teachable rule and precept. In 1698 his small illustrated treatise *Méthode pour apprendre à dessiner les passions . . .* was posthumously published; in this, again following theories of Poussin, he purported to codify the visual expression of the emotions in painting. The treatise went through numerous editions in French and other languages and remained a standard textbook for art students until well into the 19th century. Despite the classicism of his theories, Le Brun's own talents lay rather in the direction of flamboyant and grandiose decorative effects. Among the most outstanding of his works for the king were the Galerie d'Apollon at the *Louvre (1663), and the famous Galerie des Glaces (Hall of Mirrors) (1679–84) and the Escalier des Ambassadeurs (Great Staircase) (1671–8, destroyed in 1752) at Versailles. Because his artistic domination became so closely identified with the political despotism of Louis XIV, Le Brun's posthumous reputation suffered, but it rose again in the second half of the 20th century, a major exhibition of his work at Versailles in 1963 being a landmark in demonstrating the range and quality of his work. In addition to his achievements as a decorative painter, he was a fine portraitist and an extremely prolific draughtsman.

Leck, Bart van der (1876–1958). Dutch painter and designer. After working for eight years in stained-glass studios, he studied painting in Amsterdam, 1900–4. His early work was influenced by *Art Nouveau and *Impressionism, but from about 1910 he developed a more personal style characterized by simplified and stylized forms: his work remained representational, but he eliminated perspective and reduced his figures (which included labourers, soldiers, and women going to market) to sharply delineated geometrical forms in primary colours. In 1916 he met *Mondrian and in 1917 was one of the founders of De *Stijl. At this time his work was purely abstract, featuring geometrically disposed bars and rectangles in a style close to those of Mondrian and van *Doesburg. However, he found the dogmatism of the movement uncongenial and left it in 1918, reverting to geometrically simplified figural subjects. In the 1920s he became interested in textile design and during the 1930s and 1940s he extended his interests to ceramics and interior decoration, experimenting with the effects of colour on the sense of space. His work can best be seen at the Rijksmuseum Kröller-Müller, Otterlo.

Le Clerc, Jean. See SARACENI.

Le Corbusier (Charles-Édouard Jeanneret) (1887–1965). Swiss-born architect, painter, designer, and writer who became a French citizen in 1930. Although chiefly celebrated as one of the greatest and most influential architects of the 20th century, Le Corbusier also has a niche in the history of modern painting as one of the founders of *Purism. Up to 1929 he painted only still life, but from that time he occasionally introduced the human figure into his compositions. He adopted the pseudonym Le Corbusier in 1920, but continued to sign his paintings 'Jeanneret'. The pseudonym derives from the name of one of his grandparents and is also a pun on his facial resemblance to a raven (Fr., *corbeau*). Apart from paintings and architecture, his enormous output included drawings, book illustration, lithographs, tapestry designs, furniture, and numerous books, pamphlets, and articles.

Leduc, Ozias (1864–1955). Canadian painter, active mainly in his native St Hilaire, Quebec. His career was devoted principally to church decoration, but he also painted portraits, genre scenes, and still life—mostly for his own pleasure or for friends. In 1897 he visited Paris, and his later work was affected by *Symbolist ideas. He lived modestly and unambitiously away from the main centres of art, but he was an inspiration to many of those who knew him, notably Paul-Émile *Borduas.

Lee, Arthur Hamilton (Viscount Lee of Fareham). See COURTAULD.

Leech, John (1817–64). English *caricaturist and illustrator, one of the leading artists of *Punch* from its foundation in 1841 until his death. He made over 3,000 pictures for

Punch alone (including political cartoons and scenes of everyday life) and he was also particularly associated with the sporting novels of R. S. Surtees. The other books he illustrated included R. H. Barham's *The Ingoldsby Legends* (1840) and Charles Dickens's *Christmas Books* (1843). Dickens said of his pictures that they were 'always the drawings of a gentleman'; and he more than any other set the gentlemanly tone for *Punch*.

Le Fauconnier, Henri (1881–1946). French painter, mainly of figure subjects, including nudes and allegories. From about 1910 he was influenced by *Cubism, but in about 1914 he moved to a more *Expressionist style, although he still retained structural features derived from Cubism. He spent the First World War in the Netherlands, where he laid the basis of a European reputation and exercised considerable influence on the development of northern Expressionism (his work is better represented in Dutch collections than it is in French). After his return to Paris in 1920 he gradually abandoned his Expressionist manner for a more restrained and austere style. He is not now generally highly regarded as a painter, but he played an important role in spreading the mannerisms of Cubism.

Léger, Fernand (1881–1955). French painter and designer. After passing through various early influences he turned to *Cubism in 1909. Although he is regarded as one of the major figures of the movement, he always stood somewhat apart from its central course; he disjointed forms but did not fragment them in the manner of *Braque and *Picasso, preferring bold tubular shapes (he was for a time known as a 'tubist'). During the First World War he served as a sapper in the front line, then as a stretcher-bearer, and his experiences were 'a complete revelation to me as a man and a painter'. They enlarged his outlook by bringing him into contact with people from different social classes and walks of life and also by underlining his feeling for the beauty of machinery. Henceforward he made it his ambition to create an art that would be accessible to all ranks of modern society. After being gassed, he spent more than a year in hospital and was discharged in 1917. During the next few years, his work showed a fascination with machine-like forms, and even his human figures were depicted as almost robot-like beings (*The City*, 1919, Philadelphia Mus. of Art). In 1920 he met *Le Corbusier and *Ozenfant, who shared his interest in a machine aesthetic, and in the mid-1920s his work became flatter and more stylized, in line with their *Purist style. He used bold, poster-like contrasts of form and colour, with strong black outlines and extensive areas of flat, uniform colour. In the interwar years he expanded his range beyond easel painting with murals (sometimes completely abstract) and designs for the theatre and cinema. He was also busy as a teacher and travelled extensively, making three visits to the USA in the 1930s. The contacts that he made during these visits stood him in good stead when he lived in America during the Second World War.

His work of the war years included pictures of acrobats, cyclists, and musicians, and after his return to France in 1945 he concentrated on the human figure rather than the machine. He joined the French Communist Party soon after his return and favoured proletarian subjects. Some of his pictures in this vein were very big, especially *The Great Parade* (1954, Guggenheim Mus., New York), and in his later career he also worked a good deal on large decorative commissions, notably stained-glass windows and tapestries for the church at Audincourt (1951) and a glass mosaic for the University of Caracas (1954). Many honours came to him late in life, including the Grand Prix at the 1955 São Paulo *Bienal. Shortly before his death he bought a large house at Biot, a village between Cannes and Nice, and his widow built a museum of his work here, opened in 1960. In the catalogue of the exhibition 'Léger and Purist Paris' (Tate Gallery, London, 1970), John *Golding wrote of Léger: 'No other major twentieth-century artist was to react to, and to reflect, such a wide range of artistic currents and movements. Fauvism, Cubism, *Futurism, Purism, *Neo-Plasticism, *Surrealism, *Neoclassicism, *Social Realism, his art experienced them all. And yet he was to remain supremely independent as an artistic personality.' However, despite Léger's centrality in modern art, Edward Lucie-Smith thinks that he 'still ranks as an underappreciated artist, one who is on the whole more respected than loved. His work has a

deliberate harshness which repels many spectators' (*Lives of the Great Twentieth Century Artists*, 1986). Certainly he never achieved the popularity with ordinary working-class people that he aimed for.

Legros, Alphonse (1837–1911). French-born painter and printmaker who settled in England in 1863 (encouraged by *Whistler) and became a British citizen in 1881, although he never acquired fluency in English. His chief importance was as an influential teacher (particularly of etching) at the *Slade School, where he was professor 1876–92 in succession to *Poynter. He encouraged a respect for the tradition of the Old Masters.

Lehmbruck, Wilhelm (1881–1919). German sculptor. His early work was in a fairly conservative academic manner, but when he was living in Paris from 1910 to 1914 he developed a much more personal style, influenced by the formal simplifications of *Archipenko, *Brancusi, and *Modigliani, although still essentially in the tradition of *Rodin and *Maillol. It is exemplified in the extremely attenuated forms, angular pose, and melancholic expression of his *Kneeling Woman* (1911, MoMA, New York). On the outbreak of the First World War he returned to Germany and worked in a hospital, the suffering he witnessed being reflected in the poignancy of his last works. The war brought him to a state of acute depression and he committed suicide in 1919. Lehmbruck often worked in marble, but he was by temperament a modeller rather than a carver, working in clay over a spindly armature, and several of his works were cast in artificial stone to preserve the texture of the clay. With *Barlach he ranks as the outstanding German *Expressionist sculptor. Lehmbruck also made etchings and lithographs, painted, and wrote poetry. There is a museum dedicated to him in his native Duisburg.

Leibl, Wilhelm (1844–1900). German painter, one of the leading exponents of *Realism in his country. He studied at the Academy in Munich and in 1869 he met *Courbet, who was visiting the city for an international exhibition. Later that year he moved to Paris to work with Courbet, but the outbreak of the Franco-Prussian War in 1870 forced him to return to Germany.

However, he continued to exhibit his work in Paris and during his lifetime he had a higher reputation in France than in his own country. Disgusted with the intrigues of the Munich art world, from 1873 Leibl withdrew to the Bavarian countryside, where he found his favourite models in simple country folk, as in his best-known work *Three Women in Church* (1878–82, Kunsthalle, Hamburg). This is in the hard, objective manner of his so-called *'Holbein period'; later his technique became more fluid. Leibl also painted a number of portraits. His work is well represented in the Wallraf-Richartz-Museum in Cologne, his birthplace.

Leighton, Frederic (Baron Leighton of Stretton) (1830–96). English painter and sculptor, one of the dominant figures of late Victorian art. He travelled widely in Europe as a boy and his artistic education was gained successively in Frankfurt, Rome, and Paris. It was not until 1859 that he settled in England, but he had earlier made his name with *Cimabue's Celebrated Madonna is Carried in Procession through the Streets of Florence*, which he painted in Rome; it was exhibited at the 1855 *Royal Academy exhibition and bought by Queen Victoria (it is now on loan from the Royal Collection to the National Gallery, London). In spite of this success, Leighton was for several years regarded as an alien presence in the British art world, but from the mid-1860s he enjoyed a degree of worldly success that was matched perhaps only by *Millais, his almost exact contemporary: he became president of the Royal Academy in 1878, was made a baronet in 1886, and a few days before he died was raised to the peerage, the first English artist to be so honoured. Intelligent, cultured, and of distinguished appearance (although rather austere), he was one of the chief adornments of London society. His varied output included portraits and book illustrations, but he is best known for his paintings of classical Greek subjects, the finest of which are distinguished by magnificently opulent colouring as well as splendid draughtsmanship (*Garden of the Hesperides*, 1892, Lady Lever AG, Port Sunlight). As a sculptor he is best known for the bronze *Athlete Struggling with a Python* (1874–7), which can be seen in Leighton House (on loan from Tate Britain), the sumptuously decorated house and studio he built in Holland Park Road, Kensington, now a Leighton museum.

Lely, Sir Peter (1618–80). Painter of Dutch origin who spent almost all his career in England and was naturalized in 1662. His family name was originally van der Faes, and the name Lely is said to have come from a lily carved on the house in The Hague where his father was born. Lely was born at Soest in Westphalia (where his father, a captain of infantry, was stationed) and trained in Haarlem. He moved to England in the early 1640s (early biographers say 1641 or 1643), and although he first painted figure compositions in landscapes (*Sleeping Nymphs*, c.1650, Dulwich Picture Gal.), he soon turned to the more profitable field of portraiture. Fortune shone on him, for within a few years of his arrival the best portraitists in England disappeared from the scene: van *Dyck and William *Dobson died in 1641 and 1646 respectively, and Cornelius *Johnson returned to Holland in 1643. In 1654 he was described as 'the best artist in England'. Lely portrayed Charles I and his children, Oliver Cromwell and his son Richard, and other leading figures of the Interregnum, but he is associated chiefly with the Restoration court of Charles II. He was made principal painter to the king in 1661 and was able to enjoy a lavish lifestyle, described in the *Diary* of Samuel Pepys, who called him 'a mighty proud man, and full of state'. With the aid of a team of assistants he maintained an enormous output, and his fleshy, sleepy beauties clad in exquisite silks and his bewigged courtiers have created the popular image of Restoration England. Van Dyck was the strongest influence on his style, but Lely was more earthy and less refined. Much of his work is repetitive (it is sometimes hard to tell sitters apart), but he was a fluent and lively colourist and had a gift for impressive composition. He completely dominated English painting in his time, and his tradition of society portraiture, developed by *Kneller, *Jervas, and *Richardson, endured well into the 18th century until it was challenged by *Hogarth. He was a notable connoisseur and amassed one of the finest collections of Old Master drawings ever assembled; it was sold after his death.

Lemoyne. Family of French sculptors. **Jean-Louis Lemoyne** (1665–1755) was a pupil of *Coysevox and is remembered mainly for portrait busts in his master's manner. His brother **Jean-Baptiste the Elder** (1679–1731) was a figure and portrait sculptor of no great distinction. Jean-Louis's son, **Jean-Baptiste the Younger** (1704–78), was the outstanding member of the family and worked a good deal for Louis XV. He did much large-scale work at Versailles and elsewhere, but is renowned particularly for the vivacity of his portraits. Among his pupils were *Falconet, *Houdon, and *Pigalle.

Lemoyne (or **Lemoine**), **François** (1688–1737). French painter. He was one of the leading decorative artists of the day, continuing the grand tradition of *Le Brun but adapting it to the lighter taste of the court of Louis XV, to whom he became official painter in 1736. Much of his work can be seen at Versailles, notably in the Salon d'Hercule. He was a man of wide pictorial culture, learning from *Rubens in his use of colour and from 17th-century Bolognese painters in his clarity and grace of drawing. The easy fluency of his style belies his disturbed personality: he committed suicide a few hours after completing *Time Revealing Truth* (1737, Wallace Coll., London). *Boucher was his most important pupil.

Lempicka, Tamara de (née Tamara Gorska) (1898?–1980). Painter of Polish-Russian birth active mainly in Paris and the USA. According to her own account she was born in Warsaw in 1898, but there is evidence to indicate that the place of her birth (and upbringing) was Moscow and that she deducted a few years from her age. In 1916 she married Tadeusz Lempicki, a Russian lawyer and socialite, and in 1918 they fled the Russian Revolution to Paris, where she studied with Maurice *Denis and André *Lhote. She quickly established a reputation as a painter of portraits, mainly of people in the smart social circles in which she moved—writers, entertainers, the dispossessed nobility of eastern Europe. Her style owes something to the 'tubism' of *Léger, but is very distinctive in its hard, streamlined elegance and sense of chic decadence—better than anyone else she represents the *Art Deco style in painting. Apart from portraits, her main subjects were hefty erotic nudes and still lifes of calla lilies. She received considerable critical acclaim and also became a social celebrity, famed for her aloof Garboesque beauty, her parties, and her love affairs (with women as well as men). In 1939 she moved to the USA with her second husband Baron Raoul Huffner, repeating her artistic and social success in Hollywood and New York. By the 1950s, however, her work was going out of fashion. She tried painting pictures in a different, much looser style, but these were coolly received. Interest in her earlier work began to revive in the 1970s and by the 1990s she had again become something of a stylish icon, with her paintings fetching huge prices in the saleroom and featuring in television advertisements as symbols of the high life.

Le Nain, Antoine (d. 1648), **Louis** (d. 1648), and **Mathieu** (c.1607–77). French painters, brothers, who were born at Laon but had all moved to Paris by 1630. The traditional birthdates for Antoine and Louis are 1588 and 1593 respectively, but it is now thought likely that they were born around 1600, so that all three brothers were of much the same age. Mathieu was made painter to the city of Paris in 1633, and all three were foundation members of the Académie Royale (see ACADEMY) in 1648. Apart from this, little is known of their careers and the attribution of works to one or other of them is fraught with difficulty and controversy, for such paintings as are signed bear only their surname, and, of those that are dated none is later than 1648, when all were still alive. The finest and most original works associated with the brothers—powerful and dignified *genre scenes of peasants—are conventionally given to Louis; Antoine has been credited with a group of richly coloured family scenes, mainly on copper; and in a third group, traditionally attributed to Mathieu, are paintings of a more *eclectic style, chiefly portraits and group portraits in a manner suggesting influence from Holland. All these pictures are fairly small, but there are also some slightly larger paintings, mainly of religious subjects, associated with the brothers. Examples of all these types are in the Louvre, Paris. Early accounts of the brothers, as well as technical examination of the pictures, indicate that they sometimes collaborated, making the issue of assigning works to individual hands even more difficult. In 1978–9 a major exhibition in Paris brought together most of the pictures associated with the brothers, but it raised as many problems as it solved. It also, however, confirmed the stature of 'Louis', whose sympathetic and unaffected peasant scenes are the main reason why the Le Nains have attracted so much attention.

Lenbach, Franz von (1836–1904). German painter, active mainly in Munich but also in Italy, Vienna, and elsewhere. He painted various subjects, but is remembered chiefly as the most successful German portraitist of his day. His rich Venetian technique combined with his solid, respectful characterization appealed greatly to the prosperous ruling classes of Germany. He painted about a hundred portraits of Bismarck, whom he first met in 1878 and with whom he had a reserved friendship. Lenbach was a dominant figure in Munich's artistic life in the late 19th century; his splendid house there, which he designed himself, is now a museum.

Leo X, Pope. *See* MEDICI.

Leochares. Greek (probably Athenian) sculptor active in the mid-4th century BC. He is recorded in several ancient sources but is an elusive figure. In about 350 BC he is thought to have worked with *Scopas and two other sculptors on the friezes of the celebrated Mausoleum of Halicarnassus, but it is not possible confidently to assign any of the surviving portions (BM, London) to him. He is also said to have worked for Philip of Macedon and his son Alexander the Great. On rather tenuous evidence, the original of the *Apollo Belvedere* is sometimes attributed to Leochares, and a seated marble figure of the goddess Demeter (the *Demeter of Cnidus*, BM) has been proposed as a work from his own hand. It is considered one of the finest Greek sculptures to survive from the 4th century.

Leonard, Michael. *See* SUPERREALISM.

Leonardo da Vinci (1452–1519). Florentine artist, scientist, and thinker, the most versatile genius of the Italian *Renaissance. He was born in or near the small town of Vinci, a day's journey from Florence, the illegitimate son of a notary and a peasant girl. In 1472 he was enrolled as a painter in the fraternity of St Luke in Florence, after serving an apprenticeship with *Verrocchio. *Vasari attributed to Leonardo one of the angels in Verrocchio's *Baptism of Christ* (*c.*1470, Uffizi, Florence), and the head of the angel on the left of the picture does indeed far surpass its companion in spirituality and beauty of technique, giving the first demonstration of the combined languor and intensity that is so characteristic of Leonardo's work. Verrocchio is said to have been so impressed that he gave up painting to concentrate on sculpture, and it is possible that he was content to entrust the painting side of his business to Leonardo, who was still living in his master's house in 1476. Leonardo remained in Florence until about 1482, when he settled in Milan. Several pictures are reasonably attributed to the period before this move, among them an exquisite *Annunciation* (*c.*1473, Uffizi), usually regarded as his earliest surviving independent painting, and a portrait of Ginevra de' Benci (NG, Washington), probably painted *c.*1476 for the Venetian ambassador Bernardo Bembo. The most important work of the period is an altarpiece of the *Adoration of the Magi* (Uffizi), commissioned in 1481 by the monks of S. Donato a Scopeto near Florence and left unfinished when Leonardo moved to Milan. This painting and the numerous preparatory drawings for it show the astonishing fecundity of his mind. The range of gesture and expression was unprecedented, and such features as the contrasting figures of wise old sage and beautiful youth who stand at either side of the painting, and the rearing horses in the background, became permanent obsessions in his work.

Leonardo lived in Milan until 1499 (when the city was captured by French invaders), working mainly at the court of Duke Ludovico *Sforza (Il Moro). He is said to have been initially recommended as a musician (he was a virtuoso performer on the *lira da braccio*, an instrument somewhat like a large viola), and in a letter to the duke listing his accomplishments he gives some idea of his versatility, writing of himself first and foremost as a designer of instruments of war and adding his attainments as an artist almost as an afterthought. This many-sidedness comes out in his notebooks, which are filled with technological schemes and investigations of all kinds into the natural world;

Kenneth *Clark called him 'the most relentlessly curious man in history'. The price he paid for his versatility was a tendency to leave tasks uncompleted, as his restless mind wandered to some new venture; as Vasari wrote, he 'could have profited more if he had not been so changeable and unstable, for he was able to study many things, but as soon as he had started, he abandoned them'. Although he surpassed all of his contemporaries in the sheer beauty of his technique as a painter, this 'mechanical' aspect of his work was much less appealing to him than solving problems of composition and characterization in his drawings, of which there is a wonderful collection at Windsor Castle (he was the greatest and most prolific draughtsman of his time, using chalk, ink, and metalpoint with equal skill). His dilatoriness dismayed his patrons and he left a high proportion of his pictures unfinished. This stress on the intellectual aspects of painting was one of the most momentous features of Leonardo's career, for he was largely responsible for establishing the idea of the artist as a creative thinker, not simply a skilled craftsman (*see* LIBERAL ARTS).

Leonardo's two main artistic undertakings in Milan were a project for a huge equestrian statue (about three times life-size) to Ludovico Sforza's father, which got as far as a full-size model of the horse but is now known only in preliminary drawings, and the wall painting of the *Last Supper* (*c*.1495–7), in the refectory of the monastery of S. Maria delle Grazie. The *fresco method of mural painting was not flexible or subtle enough for the slow-working Leonardo, so he adopted an experimental technique that quickly caused the picture to deteriorate disastrously. In spite of its sad condition, it has for five centuries been perhaps the most revered painting in the world. There have been many attempts to restore it, the most recent (which has proved highly controversial) being unveiled in 1999. Leonardo's other works in Milan included portraits, notably the superb picture of Duke Ludovico's mistress Cecilia Gallerani known as the *Lady with an Ermine* (*c*.1490, Czartoryski Gal., Cracow) and an altarpiece of the *Virgin of the Rocks*, which exists in two problematically related versions, the earlier (Louvre, Paris) probably painted *c*.1483–5, the later (NG, London) probably in the 1490s, although it

was evidently not finished until 1508. There may have been some studio assistance in the London version, but the finest passages, notably the heads of the Virgin and the angel, with their exquisitely curled hair and heavy-lidded eyes, can be by no one but Leonardo himself. The larger, bolder forms of the London picture show Leonardo's move towards the more monumental style of the High Renaissance, of which he was the main creator; incidental detail is reduced to create a greater unity of form and atmosphere.

Between 1499, when he abandoned Milan, and 1516/17, when he left Italy for France, Leonardo moved about a good deal. In 1500 he visited Venice, in 1502–3 he worked as a military engineer for Cesare Borgia, in 1508–13 he was based again in Milan, and in 1513 he moved to Rome, but the artistic activity of his later years was chiefly centred in Florence in the years 1500–8. From this time dates his portrait of *Mona Lisa* (begun *c*.1503, Louvre), in which he showed a subtlety and naturalness of pose and expression that make most earlier portraits look rigid, and the wall painting of the *Battle of Anghiari* (1503–6), in the Palazzo Vecchio, Florence, where he worked in rivalry with *Michelangelo. The battle piece was abandoned unfinished and the remains were painted over by Vasari in 1557, but something of its appearance is known from copies; fittingly, the most famous is a drawing by *Rubens (Louvre) (a copy of a copy), for Leonardo's painting anticipated the dynamism of the *Baroque and influenced battle painters up to the 19th century. During this intermittent period in Florence Leonardo also worked out variations on a theme that fascinated him and presented a great challenge to his skill in composing closely knit groups of figures— the Virgin and Child with St Anne. In addition to various sketches, there survive a painting of the subject in the Louvre and the incomparably beautiful *cartoon (which includes also the infant John the Baptist) in the National Gallery, London; the exact dates of these two famous works are controversial. During his subsequent period based in Milan (1508–13) Leonardo's main artistic project was for another equestrian statue, ironically to Gian Giacomo Trivulzio, the Italian general who had led the French army that drove Ludovico Sforza

Leoni, Leone

338

from the city. This got no further than drawings, and Leonardo received no important
commissions after moving to Rome, where
Pope Leo X (Giovanni de' *Medici) was wary
of him because of his reputation for failing
to complete work. In 1516 or 1517 he
accepted an invitation from Francis I to
move to France, and he died at Cloux, near
Amboise, in 1519. The last paintings from
his hand are probably two pictures of St
John the Baptist (one later converted into a
Bacchus), both in the Louvre (c.1510–15).
They show the enigmatic smile, the dense
shadow, the pointing finger, and the thick
curling hair that rapidly became clichés in
the work of his followers.

Leonardo's work marked the greatest advance in naturalism in painting since *Masaccio, and he had enormous influence (as is
indicated by the large number of contemporary copies and adaptations of his pictures). His heroic figures and beautifully
balanced compositions (particularly his use
of pyramidal grouping) were the basis of the
High Renaissance style, influencing particularly his two greatest contemporaries, Michelangelo and *Raphael, and his subtle
modelling through light and shade (see SFU-
MATO) showed the potentialities of the *oil
medium, which he was one of the first Italians to exploit. *Correggio and *Giorgione
were among those most deeply influenced
by this aspect of his work, and they also
responded to his sense of fantasy and mystery. Leonardo's writings on painting were
influential too; they were first published
from his scattered notes as the *Treatise on
Painting* (in Italian and French) in 1651, but
they were well known before then. In sculpture and architecture no work that is indisputably by him survives, but his expertise
and ideas were important in both fields. He
is one of the very few artists whose reputation has from his own time onward always
remained at the highest level, even though
his output of completed works was small—a
reflection of his remarkable personal mag-
netism, his extraordinary force of intellect,
and his virtually single-handed creation of
the idea of the artist as genius.

Leoni, Leone (c.1509–90). Italian *Mannerist sculptor who worked in many parts of
Italy and in the service of the emperor
Charles V (see HABSBURG) in Germany and
the Netherlands. He was trained in gold-
smithery, but none of his works in that

medium survives. From 1538 to 1540 he
worked as a coin engraver in the papal
mint, but he was then condemned to the
galleys for attacking and maiming the
papal jeweller. He was released in 1541
and for most of the rest of his life was master
of the imperial mint in Milan. In 1549 and
1556 he visited the imperial court in Brussels and in 1551 the imperial court in Augsburg. He also worked for Charles's son,
Philip II of Spain; his own son, **Pompeo
Leoni** (c.1533–1608), settled in Spain in
1556 and gave the finishing touches to
works his father sent there. The most important commission was a group of fifteen
bronze statues (installed 1591) for the high
altar of the *Escorial, to which Pompeo later
added several others. Pompeo also executed
several tombs in Spain on his own account,
and was, like his father, a goldsmith and
medallist. Again like his father, he had a
dangerous brush with authority, being
briefly imprisoned by the Inquisition for
unorthodox views.

Leopold II, Emperor. See HABSBURG.

Leopold William, Archduke. See HABS-
BURG.

Le Parc, Julio (1928–). Argentinian
painter, sculptor, and experimental artist,
regarded as one of the leading exponents of
*Kinetic art. In 1958 he settled in Paris and
in 1959 became a founder member of the
*Groupe de Recherche d'Art Visuel. Le Parc
professes to adopt a rational and objective
attitude to his work, repudiating the ideas
of artistic creativity or symbolic meaning
and working according to scientific principles. He often uses the idea of spectator
participation, but tries to eliminate subjective response on the part of the spectator,
looking for an objective and predictable perceptual response to a planned stimulus.
Much of his work consists of devices for
disorienting the spectator (distorting glasses and so on), but he has also made some
outstanding *mobiles, using perspex or metallic elements to scatter or reflect the light.

Lépicié, Nicolas-Bernard (1735–84).
French painter. His output included portraits and historical subjects, but he is best
known for his domestic *genre scenes,
which have something of the tranquil
beauty of *Chardin and something of the
sentimentality of *Greuze (*The Reading*

Lesson, *c.*1774, Wallace Coll., London). His father **François-Bernard** (1698–1755) was an engraver and writer on art. In 1737 he was appointed secretary and official historian of the Académie Royale and he played an important role in its administration.

Leslie, C. R. (Charles Robert) (1794–1859). British painter and writer on art of American parentage. In his day he was well known for his paintings of literary themes, but he is now remembered mainly as a writer, above all for his *Memoirs of the Life of John Constable* (1843), which is regarded as one of the classics of artistic biography (Constable was a close friend).

Lessing, Gotthold Ephraim (1729–81). German writer. He was a man of formidable intellect and great versatility who played a leading role in the development of German theatre, but he is known mainly for his treatise on aesthetics, *Laokoon* (1766). This takes as its starting point a passage in *Winckelmann's writings in which he discussed the celebrated antique statue *Laocoön*. Winckelmann contrasted what he considered the stoical beauty of Laocoön in the sculpture with the loud cries that Virgil causes him to utter in the *Aeneid*, interpreting the alleged difference (to most people he appears to be howling with pain in the sculpture too) as a superior serenity in Greek art. Lessing dissented, and argued that each art achieves its effects by the means appropriate to its medium and that the artist must exploit the potentialities of his medium to the full, whilst respecting its limitations. The impact of Lessing's book stemmed from its emphasis on the aesthetic functions of art in contrast with the traditional view of art as the handmaid of religion and philosophy, with a duty primarily to instruct. *See also* THEOPHILUS.

Lessing, Karl Friedrich (1808–80). German painter, the great-nephew of Gotthold Ephraim *Lessing. In 1826 he settled in Düsseldorf and he became one of the leading figures in the tradition of history painting associated with the city. He combined earnestly melodramatic poses with studiously correct historical detail, so that many of his pictures look like scenes from plays or pageants. His best-known works have subjects taken from the Hussite Rebellion of the 15th century (*Hussite Sermon*, 1836, Kunstmuseum, Düsseldorf) and were

identified with the spirit of rebellion against the political and religious repression of the day. Lessing also painted landscapes. In 1858 he became director of the gallery at Karlsruhe, and settled there permanently.

Lessore, Thérèse. *See* SICKERT.

Le Sueur, Eustache (1616–55). French painter, active throughout his career in his native Paris. He was a pupil of *Vouet, whose influence is strong on his early works (*Presentation of the Virgin*, *c.*1640, Hermitage, St Petersburg). In the 1640s he was profoundly affected by the paintings of *Poussin (who visited Paris 1640–2) and his work became more *classical. He lacked Poussin's heroic grandeur, but he added a tenderness of his own to the master's manner, as in his most important works, a series of paintings (begun 1645) illustrating the life of St Bruno, done for the Charterhouse of Paris and now in the Louvre. In the last years of his life his chief model became *Raphael, particularly through engravings of his tapestry designs. Le Sueur was a founder member of the French Académie Royale (*see* ACADEMY) in 1648. In his own day he was almost as well thought of as Poussin, and in the 18th century he was known as 'the French Raphael', but his reputation declined in the 19th century and he now has the status of an attractive minor master.

Le Sueur, Hubert (*c.*1580–after 1658). French sculptor, active for much of his career in England, where he is first recorded in 1626. He worked a good deal for Charles I, and his most famous work is the equestrian statue of the king (1633) at Charing Cross in London. This shows the skill as a bronze caster for which he was renowned, but also his smooth, lifeless surfaces, which give his works, in the words of Margaret Whinney (*Sculpture in Britain 1530–1830*, 1964), 'a curious, inflated appearance, as if they were not modelled, but blown up from within'. He was remarkably conceited, on occasions signing himself '*Praxiteles Le Sueur', but Charles recognized him as a second-rate artist and sometimes reduced the prices he asked for his work. By 1643 Le Sueur was back in Paris. His main influence in England was in popularizing the portrait bust.

Leutze, Emanuel Gottlieb (1816–68). German-born painter who lived in America from 1825 to 1841 and again from 1859 until his death and is usually considered a member of the American School. He is remembered mainly for his *Washington Crossing the Delaware* (1851, Met. Mus., New York), painted in Düsseldorf, where he spent most of his career, and for another work that similarly appeals more for its patriotic sentiments than for its aesthetic merits—his large mural *Westward the Course of Empire Takes its Way* (1861-2) in the Capitol at Washington. His portraits and rare landscapes are more distinguished, but remain little known.

Levitan, Isaak. *See* WANDERERS.

Lewis, John Frederick (1804-76). English painter, mainly in watercolour, son of the engraver and landscape painter **Frederick Christian Lewis** (1779-1856). He travelled extensively and spent the years 1841-51 in Cairo. His colourful and highly detailed scenes of life in the harem and bazaar were a huge success in London, and after his return there in 1851 he concentrated on them exclusively, playing a major part in creating the vogue for 'Oriental' subjects. Several other members of the family were painters, including his brother, **Frederick Christian Lewis, Jun.** (1813-75). He worked in India for many years and is sometimes known as 'Indian Lewis' to distinguish him from his brother.

Lewis, Wyndham (1882-1957). British painter, novelist, and critic, born of a British mother and a wealthy American father on his yacht off Nova Scotia. He came to England as a child, studied at the *Slade School, 1898-1901, then lived on the Continent for seven years, mostly in Paris. In 1909 he returned to England and in the years leading up to the First World War emerged as one of the chief figures in British avant-garde art. From 1911 he developed an angular, machine-like, semi-abstract style that had affinities with both *Cubism and *Futurism. He worked for a short time with Roger *Fry at the *Omega Workshops, but after quarrelling with him in 1914 he formed the Rebel Art Centre, from which grew *Vorticism, a movement of which he was the chief figure and whose journal *Blast* he edited. He served with the Royal Artillery, 1915-17, and as an *Official War Artist, 1917-18, carrying his Vorticist style

into works such as *A Battery Shelled* (1918, Imperial War Mus., London). In 1919 he founded Group X as an attempt to revive Vorticism, but this failed, and from the late 1920s he devoted himself mainly to writing, in which he often made savage attacks on his contemporaries (particularly the *Bloomsbury Group). His association with the British Fascist Party and his praise of Hitler alienated him from the literary world. The best-known paintings of his later years are his incisive portraits, more naturalistic than his earlier works but still with a bold, hard simplification of form; the rejection of that of T. S. Eliot (Durban AG) caused Augustus *John to resign in disgust from the *Royal Academy in 1938.

Lewis was the most original and idiosyncratic of the major British artists working in the first decades of the 20th century, and he was among the first artists in Europe to produce completely abstract paintings and drawings. He built his personal style on features taken from Cubism and Futurism but did not accept either. He accused Cubism of failure to 'synthesize the quality of LIFE with the significance or spiritual weight that is the mark of all the greatest art' and of being mere visual acrobatics. The Futurists, he wrote, had the vivacity that the Cubists lacked, but they themselves lacked the grandness and the 'great plastic qualities' that Cubism achieved. His own work, he declared, was 'electric with a mastered and vivid vitality'. He wrote several books, including novels, notably *Tarr* (1918), and collections of essays and criticism. *Blasting and Bombardiering* (1937), *Wyndham Lewis the Artist* (1939), and *Rude Assignment* (1950) are autobiographical.

LeWitt, Sol (1928-). American sculptor, graphic artist, writer, and *Conceptual artist. His career did not take off until the early 1960s, when he turned to sculpture and became one of the leading exponents of *Minimal art. His 'structures', as he prefers to call them, characteristically involve permutations of simple basic elements, sometimes arranged in box- or table-like constructions. He is also an exponent of Conceptual art; in 1968, for example, he fabricated a metal cube and buried it in the ground at Visser House at Bergeyk in the Netherlands, documenting photographically the object's disappearance (this has also been considered an example of *Land art). LeWitt has also written numerous articles on Conceptual art. His other work includes prints in various techniques.

Leyster, Judith (1609–60). Dutch painter of *genre scenes, portraits, and still lifes. She was probably a pupil of Frans *Hals in Haarlem, where she was born and spent her early career. After her marriage to Jan Miense *Molenaer in 1636 she moved to Amsterdam, where she shared a studio with her husband, using the same models and props. Leyster was one of Hals's best followers and her work has sometimes passed as his, an example being the *Lute Player* in the Rijksmuseum, Amsterdam. Her monogram includes a star, a play on 'Ley/ster' (lodestar).

Lhote, André (1885–1962). French painter, sculptor, teacher, and writer on art. He worked initially as a commercial woodcarver and was largely self-taught as a painter. His early work was *Fauvist in spirit, but from 1911 he adopted *Cubist mannerisms in his varied range of subjects, including landscapes, still lifes, interiors, mythological scenes, and portraits. Lhote, however, was more important as a teacher and critic than as a practising artist. In 1922 he opened his own school in Paris, the Académie Montparnasse, and through this had an extensive influence on younger artists, French and foreign; he founded a South American branch on a visit to Rio de Janeiro in 1952. His writings included treatises on landscape painting (1939) and figure painting (1950).

liberal arts. In the context of *Renaissance art, a term applied to pursuits that were considered primarily as exercises of the mind rather than of practical skill and craftsmanship. The concept of a distinction between 'liberal' (worthy of a free man: Lat., *homo liber*) and 'vulgar' arts goes back to classical antiquity, and survived in one form or another up to the Renaissance, forming the basis of secular learning in the Middle Ages. In the early Renaissance the lowly position accorded to the visual arts was increasingly contested, providing a theoretical basis for the social struggle that took place to raise them from the status of manual skill to the dignity of a liberal exercise of the spirit. The most formidable champion of the visual arts was *Leonardo,

who more than anyone else was responsible for creating the idea of the painter as a creative thinker. By about 1500 painting and sculpture were generally accepted as liberal arts by Italian humanists (significantly so in Baldassare Castiglione's influential *Book of the Courtier* of 1528, which was translated into English in 1561). However, as Anthony *Blunt points out (*Artistic Theory in Italy 1450–1600*), 'As soon as the visual arts became generally accepted as liberal, the protagonists began to quarrel among themselves about which of them was the noblest and most liberal.' The acceptance came later in other parts of Europe than in Italy.

Libre Esthétique, La. *See* VINGT.

Lichtenstein, Roy (1923–97). American painter, sculptor, and printmaker. In the late 1950s his style was *Abstract Expressionist, but in the early 1960s he changed to *Pop art and his first one-man exhibition in this style, at the Leo *Castelli gallery, New York, in 1962, was a sensational success. In common with other Pop artists, Lichtenstein adopted the images of commercial art, but he did so in a highly distinctive manner. He took his inspiration from comic strips but blew up the images to a large scale, reproducing the primary colours and dots of the cheap printing processes (*Whaam!*, 1963, Tate, London). The initial stimulus is said to have come from one of his young children, who pointed to a comic book and challenged, 'I bet you can't paint as good as that.' Despite their use of such kitsch material, his paintings show an impressive feeling for composition and colour and Lichtenstein enjoyed continued critical success as well as popular appeal. In the mid-1960s he began producing Pop versions of paintings by modern masters such as *Cézanne and *Mondrian, and also started making screenprints. In the 1970s he expanded his range to include sculpture, mostly in polished brass and imitating the *Art Deco forms of the 1930s. His later work included several large commissions for public places.

Liebermann, Max (1847–1935). German painter (of portraits, figure subjects, and landscapes), etcher, and lithographer, active mainly in his native Berlin. From 1873 to 1878 he lived mainly in Paris, and together with *Corinth and *Slevogt he came to be considered one of the leading German representatives of *Impressionism. In 1899 he became first president of the Berlin *Sezession, but he did not keep abreast of developments and a decade later he was regarded as a pillar of the traditionalism against which the German *Expressionists were in revolt. He was one of the dominant figures in the German art world and in the later part of his career he accumulated many honours. When the Nazis came to power, however, he was required—as a Jew—to resign as president of the Prussian Academy and from his other prestigious positions. His widow committed suicide in 1943 rather than suffer at the hands of the Gestapo.

Lievens, Jan (1607–74). Dutch painter and printmaker. He was extremely precocious, and after training in Amsterdam with *Lastman he is said to have begun practising independently in his native Leiden when he was barely into his teens. From c.1625 to 1631/2 he worked in close collaboration and friendly rivalry with *Rembrandt. They shared the same models (and probably a studio) and contemporaries sometimes had difficulty distinguishing between their hands (a few works are still disputed between them). The diplomat and connoisseur Constantijn Huygens visited them in 1629 and thought they showed equal promise of greatness. He wrote that Rembrandt surpassed Lievens in vivacity of expression, but that Lievens was superior in 'a certain grandeur of invention and boldness of subjects and forms'. That this was not excessive praise is borne out by Lievens's marvellously melodramatic *Raising of Lazarus* (1631, Brighton Mus. and AG), in which the only parts of Lazarus shown are his arms emerging from the tomb. After the paths of the two young artists separated in 1631/2, however, Lievens did not sustain his early brilliance, although in his later years he was more successful than Rembrandt in worldly terms. In 1632–5 he visited England, then from 1635 to 1644 he lived in Antwerp, where he adopted a more elegant and facile style, influenced by van *Dyck, that brought him a good deal of work as a fashionable portraitist. In 1644 he returned to the Netherlands and was based in Amsterdam for the rest of his life, although he made visits to other Dutch cities and to Germany. It is not known whether he had any contact with his old friend Rembrandt when both were living in Amsterdam. In addition to his work as a painter, Lievens was a talented etcher and also made some woodcuts.

Light art. A general term for works that use artificial light (usually electric) as an artistic medium of its own or as an important constituent of a piece. The idea can be traced back to the 18th century, when the French scientist Louis-Bertrand Castel became interested in the relationship between sound and colour (both of which, he argued, were products of vibration) and constructed various 'ocular harpsichords', some of which incorporated coloured glass. However, his theories do not seem to have been followed up until the 20th century. Various artists in the first half of the century experimented with artificial light, for example *Moholy-Nagy, but it was not until the 1960s that it is possible to think of Light art constituting a movement. During this decade there were several large exhibitions devoted to Light art in Europe and the USA, and it often overlapped with other genres, particularly *Kinetic art, but also for example *Minimal art, notably in the work of the American sculptor Dan Flavin (1933–96), who typically used arrangements of fluorescent tubes. In the 1960s, also, lasers and holography (which was made possible by lasers) became available to the artist. Lasers have been used most characteristically to create spectacular nocturnal displays. Many artists, including Salvador *Dalí, have experimented with holograms, and they have been sold by leading dealers such as Leo *Castelli, but in the art world holography is generally regarded as a curiosity rather than a serious means of expression. The term *Luminism is sometimes used as an alternative to 'Light art'. However, this usage is potentially confusing, as the word already has other meanings in art-historical writing.

Lightfoot, Maxwell Gordon. *See* CAMDEN TOWN GROUP.

Limbourg, de. Netherlandish manuscript *illuminators, the brothers **Herman**, **Jean** (Jannequin), and **Pol** (Paul), all three of whom died in 1416, presumably victims of the plague or other epidemic. Pol was probably the head of the workshop, but it is not possible to distinguish his hand from those of his brothers. The Limbourgs came from Nijmegen and were nephews of Jean *Malouel. In 1402 Jean and Pol were working for Philip the Bold, Duke of Burgundy, and after Philip's death in 1404 all three Limbourgs worked for his brother Jean, Duc de Berry, remaining in his service until their deaths and holding privileged positions at his court, which moved with him around France from one magnificent residence to the next. He was one of the most extravagant patrons and collectors in the history of art, and the Limbourgs illuminated two manuscripts for his celebrated library: the *Belles Heures* (c.1408, Met. Mus., New York) and the *Très Riches Heures* (Mus. Condé, Chantilly), which was begun c.1413 and left unfinished at their deaths (it was completed by the French illuminator Jean *Colombe about seventy years later). The *Très Riches Heures* (see BOOK OF HOURS) is by common consent one of the supreme masterpieces of manuscript illumination and the archetype of the *International Gothic style. Its most original and beautiful feature is the series of twelve full-page illustrations of the months (the first time a calendar was so lavishly treated), full of exquisite ornamentation and beautifully observed naturalistic detail. The *miniatures are remarkable, too, for their mastery in rendering space, strongly suggesting that one or more of the brothers had visited Italy, and they occupy an important place in the development of the northern traditions of landscape and *genre painting.

limner. A word for a painter that has been used in various ways in different contexts. In the Middle Ages it was applied to manuscript *illuminators, and from the 16th century it was used of painters of *miniature portraits (Nicholas *Hilliard's treatise is called *The Arte of Limning*). In terms of American art, it denotes the anonymous and often itinerant painters, particularly portraitists, of the 17th and 18th centuries. Limners in this last sense are sometimes given invented names in the same manner in which the term 'Master of' is used in European painting—the Schuyler Limner, named after one of the families he portrayed, is an example.

Lindner, Richard (1901–78). German-born painter who became an American citizen in 1948. He fled from the Nazi regime in 1933 and settled in Paris, then moved to the USA in 1941. At first he worked as a magazine and book illustrator (in Germany he had been art director of a publishing firm), and he did not begin to paint seriously until the early 1950s. His most characteristic works take their imagery from New York life, often with overtly erotic symbolism, and are painted with harsh colours and hard outlines. The effects he created owed something to *Expressionist exaggeration, *Surrealist fantasy, and *Cubist manipulations of form, but his style is vivid and distinctive and anticipates aspects of *Pop art.

Lindsay. Family of Australian artists. The members included five of the children of Dr R. C. Lindsay of Creswick, Victoria: **Percy Lindsay** (1870–1952), painter and graphic artist; **Sir Lionel Lindsay** (1874–1961), art critic, watercolour painter, and graphic artist in pen, etching, and woodcut, who helped to create an interest in the collection of original prints in Australia; **Norman Lindsay** (1879–1969), painter, graphic artist, critic, and novelist; **Ruby Lindsay** (1887–1919), graphic artist; and **Sir Daryl Lindsay** (1889–1976), painter and director of the National Gallery of Victoria from 1942 to 1956. Norman's son **Raymond** (1904–60) and Daryl's wife **Joan** (1896–1984) were also painters. For over half a century this family, through one or other of its members, played a leading role in Australian art. The most interesting character among them was Norman Lindsay, who according to Robert *Hughes (*The Art of Australia*, 1970) 'has some claim to be the most forceful personality the arts in Australia have ever seen'. He believed that the main impulse of art and life was sex, and his work was often denounced as pornographic. However, when he saw some of Lindsay's works at an exhibition of Australian art in London in 1923, Sir William *Orpen commented that they were 'certainly vulgar, but not in the least indecent. They are extremely badly drawn, and show no sense of design and a total lack of imagination.' Norman's son **Jack Lindsay** (1900–90) was a writer who settled in England in 1926. His books include several biographies of major artists.

Lindsay, Sir Coutts. See GROSVENOR GALLERY.

line engraving. Term applied to a method of making prints (and the print so made) in which the design is cut directly into the surface of a metal (usually copper) plate. In normal parlance the word *'engraving' usually refers to line engraving, but it is also used as a generic term, covering a variety of printmaking processes (see PRINT). The line engraver cuts the design into a smooth metal plate with a tool called a *burin. Characteristically, line engravings have a quality of metallic hardness and austere precision, compared with the easy, spontaneous drawing of the *etcher or *lithographer. The essential nature of the medium is linear, though shading and tone may be suggested by parallel strokes, cross-*hatching, or textures compounded of various dots and flicks. Line engraving seems to have originated towards the middle of the 15th century in the workshops of goldsmiths, arising independently in Italy (*see* NIELLO) and Germany, though perhaps slightly earlier in the latter country. Martin *Schongauer, who died in 1491, was the first major artist to work mainly as an engraver, and the medium had its finest flowering in the early 16th century in the work of Albrecht *Dürer and *Lucas van Leyden. Active at the same time was Marcantonio *Raimondi, who was the great pioneer in the use of engraving as a means of reproducing the works of other artists. This soon became the primary function of line engraving, and it was the principal method of reproductive printing until the 19th century, when it was challenged by *wood engraving in the popular market and then superseded by photomechanical processes. In the 20th century, however, line engraving was revived as a means of original expression, the most important impetus coming from S. W. *Hayter.

Linnell, John (1792–1882). English painter. He made his reputation and his fortune as a fashionable portraitist, but was devoted to landscape painting. His wealth enabled him to patronize William *Blake, and some of his early landscapes have something of the visionary quality of the master and of Samuel *Palmer, who married Linnell's daughter in 1837. In the 1840s Linnell gave up portraiture and after settling at Redhill in 1851 most of his prolific output was devoted to idyllic scenes in Surrey, done in a lush and more conventional pastoral idiom

than his early work. Such works were highly popular and he became immensely wealthy. In spite of his success he was denied membership of the *Royal Academy, this being a reflection of his unpopularity with his fellow artists (his admiration for Blake was the saving grace in an otherwise unsavoury character).

linocut. A term applied to the technique of making a print from a thick piece of linoleum and to the print so made. Linoleum was invented in the 1860s, but it was not used for printing (in the manufacture of wallpaper) until the 1890s. The technique is essentially a development of the *woodcut, the earliest of printmaking methods, but linocuts are much simpler to make because the material is soft and grainless and therefore easier to cut, using knives and gouges. For this reason linocutting is particularly associated with the art education of children, but it has also been used by numerous eminent artists from the beginning of the 20th century. Erich *Heckel, who was making linocuts by 1903, was probably the first major figure to take up the technique, and later practitioners included *Matisse and *Picasso. Because the surface can be cut rapidly and spontaneously, linocut is particularly appropriate for big prints boldly conceived, and it is also well suited to colour prints, since a number of large blocks may be used without undue expense (Picasso, however, used a method of printing in several colours successively from one block).

linseed oil. Oil from the seeds of flax, the commonest *medium in *oil painting. Many modern painters have used raw linseed oil diluted with *turpentine as a medium, but the Old Masters generally preferred polymerized oil, known as 'stand oil', which was prepared by heating linseed oil or drying it in the sun. Linseed oil tends to turn yellow with age, but has less tendency to crack than either *walnut or *poppy oil.

Liotard, Jean-Étienne (1702–89). Swiss painter (mainly in pastels) and printmaker. He travelled widely in Europe and also spent four years in Constantinople (1738–42), after which he adopted Turkish dress and beard; his eccentric appearance, which was a useful form of self-publicity, is familiar from his numerous self-portraits (after his marriage he reluctantly shaved off the beard to please his wife). His delicate and polished style brought him fashionable success as a portraitist in Paris, the Netherlands, and England, which he visited in 1754–5. The best collection of his work is in the Musée d'Art et d'Histoire in Geneva, his native city.

Lipchitz, Jacques (1891–1973). Lithuanian-born sculptor who became a French citizen in 1925 and an American citizen in 1958. After studying engineering in Lithuania he moved to Paris in 1909; by about 1912 he was part of a circle of avant-garde artists including *Matisse, *Modigliani, and *Picasso, and from 1914 he became one of the first sculptors to apply the principles of *Cubism in three dimensions (*Man with Guitar*, 1916, MoMA, New York). During the 1920s his style changed, as he became preoccupied with open forms and the interpenetration of solids and voids, and from about 1930 he began to use allegorical subject matter drawn from the Bible or classical mythology. In 1941 he moved to the USA, where he returned to greater solidity of form, but with a desire for greater spirituality. At times the tortured, bloated forms of his late work look rather like inflated shrubbery, as in *Prometheus Strangling the Vulture* (1944–53, Walker Art Center, Minneapolis). His later work included several large public commissions, for example *Peace on Earth* (1967–9, Los Angeles Music Centre). This, like most of his work, is in bronze, but he also made stonecarvings.

Lippi, Filippino (c.1457–1504). Florentine painter, the son and pupil of Filippo *Lippi, who died when the boy was about 12. Filippino ('little Filippo') later studied with *Botticelli and learned much from his expressive use of line, but Filippino's style, although sensitive and poetic, is more robust than his master's. His first major commission (c.1485) was the completion of *Masaccio's fresco cycle in the Brancacci Chapel of S. Maria del Carmine, a task he carried out with such skill and tact that it is sometimes difficult to tell where his work begins and that of more than half a century earlier ends. Among his other frescos, the most important are cycles on the life of St Thomas Aquinas (1488–93) in the Caraffa Chapel, S. Maria sopra Minerva, Rome, and on the lives of St Philip and St John (c.1495–

1502) in the Strozzi Chapel, S. Maria Novella, Florence. In these he created picturesque, and even bizarre effects that reveal him as one of the most inventive of late *quattrocento painters. Filippino also painted many altarpieces, the most famous of which is the *Vision of St Bernard* (c.1485, Badia, Florence), an exquisitely tender work, full of beautiful detail. Although he is now somewhat overshadowed by Botticelli, Filippino enjoyed a great reputation in his lifetime, being described by Lorenzo de' *Medici as 'superior to *Apelles'.

Lippi, Fra Filippo (c.1406–69). Florentine painter. He was brought up as an unwanted child in the Carmelite friary of S. Maria del Carmine, where he took his vows in 1421. Unlike the Dominican Fra *Angelico, however, Lippi was a reluctant friar and had a scandalous love affair with a nun, Lucrezia Buti, who bore his son Filippino *Lippi and a daughter Alessandra. The couple were released from their vows and allowed to marry, but Lippi still signed himself 'Frater Philippus'. His biography (romantically embroidered to include capture by Moorish pirates) is one of the most colourful in *Vasari's *Lives* and has given rise to the picture of a worldly *Renaissance artist, rebelling against the discipline of the Church—an image reflected in Robert Browning's poem about Lippi ('Fra Lippo Lippi' in *Men and Women*, 1855). He must certainly have had a more eventful life than most, but there is little documentary evidence of his character and personality. Vasari writes that Lippi was inspired to become a painter by watching *Masaccio at work in the Carmine church, and his early work, notably the *Tarquinia Madonna* (1437, Gal. Naz., Rome) is certainly overwhelmingly influenced by him. From about 1440, however, his style changed direction, becoming more linear and preoccupied with decorative motifs— thin, fluttering draperies, brocades, etc. Lippi is associated particularly with paintings of the Virgin and Child, which are sometimes in the form of *tondi, a format he was among the first to use—a beautiful example (c.1453), showing the wistful delicacy and exquisite pale lighting that characterizes his best work, is in the Pitti, Florence. Another formal innovation with which Lippi is closely associated is the *sacra conversazione*—his Barbadori Altarpiece (begun

1437, Louvre, Paris) is sometimes claimed as the earliest example of the type. As a fresco painter Lippi's finest achievement is his cycle on the lives of St Stephen and St John the Baptist (1452–66) in Prato Cathedral. Lippi was highly regarded in his day (he was patronized by the *Medici, who came to his aid when he was imprisoned and tortured for alleged fraud) and his influence is seen in the work of numerous artists, most notably *Botticelli, who was probably his pupil. Four centuries later he was one of the major sources for the second wave of *Pre-Raphaelitism.

Lipton, Seymour. *See* ABSTRACT EXPRESSIONISM.

Lismer, Arthur. *See* GROUP OF SEVEN.

Liss (or **Lys**), **Johann** (c.1597–1631). German painter, active mainly in Italy. Apart from *Elsheimer, he was the most brilliant German painter of the 17th century. He trained in the Netherlands (probably in Amsterdam, possibly with *Goltzius) and visited Paris before moving to Italy c.1620. Venice seems to have been the main centre of his activity, but he also worked in Rome, and *Caravaggesque influence is clearly seen in such vivid and strongly lit works as *Judith and Holofernes* (c.1622, NG, London). His work enjoyed considerable popularity in Venice (where there was a dearth of talented native painters at this time) and his *Vision of St Jerome* in the church of S. Nicolo da Tolentino (c.1628) was much copied. It shows the remarkably free brushwork and brilliant use of high-keyed colour that were the salient features of his style and which were influential on Venetian painting when its glory revived in the 18th century. It was formerly assumed that Liss perished in the Venetian plague of 1629–30, but it is now known that he died in Verona in 1631.

Lissitzky, El (Eliezer Markowich) (1890–1941). Russian painter, designer, graphic artist, and architect. He studied engineering in Darmstadt and architecture in Moscow. In 1919 he became professor of architecture and graphic art at the art school in Vitebsk run by *Chagall. One of his other colleagues there was *Malevich, whose advocacy of the use of pure geometric form greatly influenced Lissitzky, notably in his series of abstract paintings to which he gave the collective name 'Proun' and which he referred to as 'the interchange station between painting and architecture'. They do indeed look like plans for three-dimensional constructions, and at the same time Lissitzky made ambitious architectonic designs that were never realized. In 1921 he was sent to Berlin to arrange and design a major exhibition of abstract art at the Van Diemen Gallery—the show that first comprehensively presented the modern movement in Russia to the West (it was later shown also in Amsterdam). While in Berlin he made contact with van *Doesburg and members of De *Stijl and with *Moholy-Nagy, who spread Lissitzky's ideas through his teaching at the *Bauhaus. In 1923 he went with *Gabo to a Bauhaus exhibition at Weimar and there met *Gropius. From 1923 to 1925 he lived in Switzerland, and (after a short visit to Russia) from 1925 to 1928 in Hanover. He returned to Russia in 1928 and settled in Moscow. By this time he had abandoned painting and devoted himself mainly to typography and industrial design. His work included several propaganda and trade exhibitions, notably the Soviet Pavilion of the 1939 World's Fair in New York, and his dynamic techniques of *photomontage, printing, and lighting had wide influence. For a considerable time Lissitzky was the best known of the Russian abstract artists in the West. In his mature work he achieved a fusion between the *Suprematism of Malevich (often using his diagonal axis), the *Constructivism of *Tatlin and *Rodchenko, and features of the *Neo-Plasticism of *Mondrian.

lithography. A method of printing from a design drawn directly onto a slab of stone or other suitable material. The most recent of the major graphic techniques, it was invented in 1798 by Aloys *Senefelder. The process is based on the antipathy of grease and water, the design being drawn with a greasy crayon. After this has been chemically fixed, the stone is wetted and then rolled with oily ink, which adheres only to the greasy drawing, the rest of the surface, being damp, repelling the ink. Prints can then be taken in a press. Only certain types of stone are suitable for use in lithography, and zinc (from about 1830) and aluminium (from about 1890) have been employed as substitutes. The results they produce are usually identical. Colour lithography, using a different stone for each ink, was introduced in the 1830s. Many distinguished artists of the 19th and 20th centuries have worked in the lithographic technique (beginning with *Goya in his old age), attracted by the freedom it allows (the artist need do nothing more than draw on the stone—the printer can handle all the technicalities), and *Daumier was the first great figure to execute the major part of his life's work in lithography. *Toulouse-Lautrec was another outstanding master of the process; he invented a novel method of creating a speckled effect by spattering ink on the stone with a toothbrush.

Llanos, Fernando. *See* YAÑEZ.

Lochner, Stefan (d. 1451?). German painter. The works associated with him have long been regarded as the finest paintings produced in Cologne in the mid-15th century, but there has recently been some doubt about the artist's identity. A painter called Stefan Lochner is first documented in Cologne in 1442 and evidently died there in 1451, but there are no signed or documented works by him. In 1520 *Dürer visited the city and saw 'with wonder and astonishment' an unspecified altarpiece by 'Master Stefan'. The altarpiece that Dürer saw is usually identified as a large triptych of the *Adoration of the Magi*, painted for Cologne's town hall but now in the city's cathedral, and the 'Master Stefan' has been assumed to be Lochner. However, certain works attributed to the same hand as the altarpiece are now thought to date from after 1451, Lochner's date of death. In spite of the difficulties, Lochner's name is still usually retained for convenience. The work associated with him is characterized by exquisite colouring and delicate sentiment.

Loggan, David (1634–92). British engraver and draughtsman. He was born in Poland, of Anglo-Scottish descent, and moved to London in the late 1650s. He is best known for his topographical books on the universities, *Oxonia Illustrata* (1675) and *Cantabrigia Illustrata* (1690), but he also made sensitive portrait drawings.

Lohse, Richard (1902–88). Swiss painter and printmaker. In his early works he experimented with various subjects and styles, but in the 1940s he became one of the leading representatives of *Concrete

art. His paintings are mathematically based, often featuring chequerboard or grid-like patterns, but they are not cold or analytical in effect; indeed his work is particularly noted for its beauty and refinement of colour, and has a certain resemblance to *Op art of the kind associated with Bridget *Riley. From about 1950 he gained an international reputation.

Lomazzo, Giovanni Paolo (1538–1600). Milanese painter and writer. At the age of 33 he went blind and thereafter devoted himself to writing, publishing two treatises on art: *Trattato dell'arte de la pittura, scoltura, et architettura* (1584) and *Idea del tempio della pittura* (1590). The *Trattato* was the largest and most comprehensive treatise on art published in the 16th century and has been described as 'the Bible of *Mannerism'. It is divided into seven books, whose themes are Proportion, Motion, Colour, Light, *Perspective, Practice, and History, the last containing a guide to Christian and classical *iconography. Throughout the book runs the assumption that the arts can be taught by detailed precepts. It was widely influential and an English translation by the Oxford physician Richard Haydocke was published in 1598, entitled *A Tracte Containing the Artes of Curious Paintinge, Carvinge & Buildinge*. The translation adds details of English artists such as *Hilliard not mentioned in Lomazzo's original. Lomazzo's second treatise is a shorter and more abstract work; he also wrote poetry and treatises on other subjects. An example of his rare surviving paintings is a self-portrait (1568) in the Brera, Milan.

Lombard, Lambert (1505/6–66). Netherlandish painter, draughtsman, engraver, architect, and antiquarian, active mainly in his native Liège. He trained in Antwerp and was influenced by *Gossaert and Jan van *Scorel. A man of scholarly inclinations, Lombard visited Rome in 1537–8 and made drawings of the *antique, some of which were engraved in the workshop of Jerome *Cock. He corresponded with *Vasari, providing him with information about Netherlandish artists, and Vasari said of him: 'Of all the Flemish artists I have named none is superior to Lambert Lombard of Liège, a man well versed in letters, a painter of judgement, a learned architect and—by no means his least title to merit—the master of

Frans *Floris, and Willem *Key.' This opinion was confirmed by van *Mander, who wrote in 1604: 'One can confidently rank him among the best Netherlandish painters, past and present.' Few paintings survive to bear witness to his high contemporary reputation, but his work is known from drawings (almost 500 by him are preserved), copies, and engravings. A formidable *Portrait of the Artist* in the Musée de l'Art Wallon, Liège (another version is in the Staatliche Kunstsammlungen, Kassel) is among the best paintings given to him, but some critics think it is by his pupil Frans Floris. The portraits associated with Lombard—lively and strongly characterized—generally appeal more to modern taste than his somewhat academic religious paintings.

Lombardo. Family of Italian artists, the leading Venetian sculptors of their period: **Pietro** (*c*.1435–1515) and his sons **Tullio** (*c*.1455–1532) and **Antonio** (*c*.1458–1516). Pietro, who came from Lombardy, settled in Venice in about 1467. He was an architect as well as a sculptor, and his church of S. Maria dei Miracoli (1481–9) is one of the gems of Venetian *Renaissance architecture; his sons assisted him on its sculptural decoration. Of his numerous tombs in Venetian churches, the best known is that of Doge Pietro Mocenigo (*c*.1476–81, SS. Giovanni e Paolo). His style is distinguished by polished mastery of marble cutting and an interest in the *antique, features that recur in the work of Tullio. Tullio's most imposing work is the Vendramin monument (*c*.1488–94) in SS. Giovanni e Paolo; the figure of Adam from this—a sensuously beautiful free-standing nude—is in the Metropolitan Museum, New York. Antonio has less substance as an independent artist. His work included a series of mythological reliefs in marble for Alfonso d'*Este (mainly in the Hermitage, St Petersburg).

London, School of. *See* SCHOOL OF LONDON.

London Group. An exhibiting society of British artists formed in 1913 by an amalgamation of the *Camden Town Group with several smaller groups and various individuals. The first president was Harold *Gilman. Initially it was dominated by *Futurists and those who would soon be called *Vorticists, among them *Bomberg, *Epstein (who suggested the name), *Nevinson, and *Wadsworth. It soon became less aggressively avant-garde, although it still represented advanced taste. Several artists associated with the *Bloomsbury Group joined in the early years, including Roger *Fry (1918), who wrote that the London Group had 'done for *Post-Impressionism in England what the *New English Art Club did in a previous generation for *Impressionism'. By the Second World War the group had lost its place as a significant force in British art, but it still exists.

Long, Edwin. *See* ALMA-TADEMA.

Long, Richard (1945–). British avant-garde artist whose work brings together sculpture, *Conceptual art, and *Land art. Since 1967 his artistic activity has been based on long solitary walks that he makes through landscapes, initially in Britain, and from 1969 also abroad, often in remote or inhospitable terrain. Sometimes he collects objects such as stones and twigs on these walks and brings them into a gallery, where he arranges them into designs, usually circles or other fairly simple geometrical shapes (*Circle of Sticks*, 1973; *Slate Circle*, 1979; both Tate, London). He also creates such works in their original settings, and documents his walks with photographs, texts, and maps. Long has an international reputation (as early as 1976 he represented Britain at the Venice *Biennale) and has attracted a great deal of commentary, much of it laudatory, although the critic Peter Fuller described his work as 'the barren arrangement of gathered stones'. In 1989 Long won the *Turner Prize.

Longhi, Pietro (1701–85). Venetian painter. Although he carried out some fresco commissions he is known principally as a painter of small *genre scenes of contemporary patrician and low life. These charming and often gently satirical scenes were very popular, although surprisingly he does not seem to have been patronized by English visitors to Venice. A prolific artist, Longhi occasionally painted more than one version of his own compositions, and these again were often duplicated by pupils and followers. His son **Alessandro Longhi** (1733–1813) was a successful portraitist. He was the official portrait painter to the Venetian Academy, so that he was in a good position for compiling his book *Compendio delle vite de' pittori veneziani istorici* (1762), a collection of biographies of Venetian artists; each subject is illustrated by a portrait that Longhi etched himself.

Longhi, Roberto (1890–1970). Italian art historian. Longhi was a scholar of great industry, and published much new material, particularly in the area with which he is most associated—*Caravaggio and Caravaggism (he catalogued the great exhibition of the work of Caravaggio and the *Caravaggisti held in Milan in 1951, which is regarded as a landmark in this field). He was involved with various periodicals, and in 1950 founded a new journal, *Paragone*, in Florence, where he was a professor at the university. His villa in Florence is now an art-historical foundation, housing his picture collection and his library of books.

Loo, Carle van (Carle Vanloo) (1705–65). French painter of Flemish descent, the most illustrious member of a family of artists. He won the *Prix de Rome in 1724 (he was in Italy 1727–34) and enjoyed a career of unbroken success, ending his life as first painter to the king (1762) and director of the Académie Royale (1763). Industrious and versatile, he was primarily a history painter but also produced works in several other genres, including portraits, landscapes, and hunting scenes. His eclectic style was fluent but rather bland. Some of his contemporaries considered him the greatest painter in Europe, but after his death his work soon went out of favour, seeming flimsy and superficial to *Neoclassical taste, and his reputation did not seriously revive until the later 20th century.

Lopes, Gregório (*c*.1490–*c*.1550). Portuguese painter, court painter to Manuel I and John III. Among Portuguese painters of his period he was the most directly inspired by *Renaissance influence. Most of his surviving works (mainly altarpieces) are in the Museu Nacional de Arte Antiga, Lisbon.

López y Portaña, Vicente (1772–1850). Spanish painter. He painted many different subjects but was primarily a portraitist, continuing the tradition of *Mengs into the 19th century; his sitters included many of the leading Spanish personalities of his period. In 1814 he was appointed principal

court painter to Ferdinand VII (jointly with the elderly *Goya), in 1817 director of the Academy of San Fernando, and in 1823 curator of the *Prado.

Lorenzetti, Pietro (active 1320–45) and **Ambrogio** (active 1319–48). Sienese painters, brothers. They were among the outstanding Italian artists of their time, but their lives are poorly documented—it is possible that both died in the Black Death of 1348. Pietro is usually said to have been the elder brother, but the evidence is not conclusive. His first dated work is of 1320—a *polyptych of the *Virgin and Child with Saints* in the Pieve di S. Maria at Arezzo; Ambrogio's earliest reliably attributed work is of a year earlier—a *Virgin and Child* for a church at Vico l'Abate (Museo Diocesano, Florence). Apart from collaborating in a cycle on the life of Mary, which they painted in fresco on the façade of Siena's public hospital in 1335 (now lost), the brothers worked independently. They shared a certain affinity of style, however, the weightiness of their figures showing the influence of *Giotto and clearly setting them apart from the elegance of their greatest Sienese contemporary, Simone *Martini. Ambrogio was the more innovative of the brothers, and his greatest work, the fresco series *Good and Bad Government* in the Palazzo Pubblico in Siena (1338–9), is one of the most remarkable achievements in 14th-century Italian art. In it he broke new ground in the naturalistic painting of landscape and townscape, and the talkative crowds of figures show he was an acute observer of his fellow men. Ambrogio's other dated work includes altarpieces of the *Presentation in the Temple* (1337–42, Uffizi, Florence) and the *Annunciation* (1344, Pinacoteca, Siena). Pietro's work is noted for its emotional expressiveness, his fresco of the *Descent from the Cross* in the Lower Church of S. Francesco at Assisi having remarkable pathos and dramatic power. The extent and the date of Pietro's contribution at Assisi are matters of controversy, but his other work includes dated altarpieces of the *Virgin and Child Enthroned* (1340, Uffizi) and the *Birth of the Virgin* (1342, Cathedral Mus., Siena).

Lorenzo Monaco (*c*.1370–*c*.1425). Italian painter. He evidently came from Siena, but all his known professional activity was in

Florence. In 1391 he took his vows as a monk of the Camaldolese monastery of S. Maria degli Angeli. He rose to the rank of deacon, but in 1402 he was enrolled in the painters' guild under his lay name, Piero di Giovanni (Lorenzo Monaco means 'Laurence the Monk'), and was living outside the monastery. The monastery was renowned for its manuscript *illuminations and several *miniatures in books in the Laurentian Library in Florence have been attributed to him, but he was primarily a painter of altarpieces, good examples of which are in the National Gallery in London and the Uffizi in Florence. His only known works in fresco are the scenes of the life of the Virgin in the Bartolini chapel of S. Trinità, Florence. His style is distinguished by luminous beauty of colouring and a graceful, rhythmic flow of line. He stands in complete contrast to his great contemporary *Masaccio and represents the highest achievement of the last flowering of *Gothic art in Florence.

lost wax. See CIRE PERDUE.

Lotto, Lorenzo (c.1480–1556/7). Venetian painter. According to his own testimony he was born in Venice, and *Vasari suggests that he was trained there, but he worked in many other places, had an idiosyncratic style, and stands somewhat apart from the central Venetian tradition. He is first recorded in 1503 in Treviso, where he was based until 1506. He then had a period in central Italy, during which he worked for Julius II (Giuliano della *Rovere) in the Vatican (nothing survives by him there). From 1513 to 1525 he worked mainly in Bergamo, then returned to Venice. He remained there until 1532, then was peripatetic for the rest of his career, working mainly in various towns in the Marches. In 1554, when he was partially blind, he became a lay brother at the monastery at Loreto, where he died. (These movements are unusually well documented because his account book for the period 1538–54 survives, together with numerous letters from the earlier part of his career.) Lotto's rootless existence reflects his anxious, difficult temperament, and his work is extremely uneven. It draws on a wide variety of sources, from northern Europe as well as Italy, but at the same time shows acute freshness of observation. He is now perhaps best known for his portraits, in which he often conveys a mood of psychological unrest (*Young Man in his Study*, c.1527, Academy, Vienna), but he worked mainly as a religious painter. An outstanding example of how original and poetic his altarpieces could be is the *Annunciation* (c.1527, Pinacoteca Civica, Recanati), a bizarre and captivating work full of brilliant colours and lighting effects, odd expressions and poses, and unusual and beautifully painted details, including a startled cat.

Louis, Morris (Morris Louis Bernstein) (1912–62). American painter, a major pioneer of the movement from *Abstract Expressionism to Colour Stain Painting (see COLOUR FIELD PAINTING). Almost all his career was spent first in Baltimore and then from 1947 in nearby Washington. He isolated himself from the New York art world, concentrating on his own experiments and supporting himself by teaching. However, it was a visit to New York in 1953 with Kenneth *Noland that led to the breakthrough in his art. He and Noland went to Helen *Frankenthaler's studio, where they were immensely impressed by her painting *Mountains and Sea*, and Louis immediately began experimenting with her technique of applying liquid paint to unprimed canvas, allowing it to flow over and soak into the canvas so that it acted as a stain and not as an overlaid surface. He was secretive about his technical methods and it is uncertain how he achieved his control over the flow of colour, but towards the end of his life he suffered from severe back problems caused by his constant bending and stooping over the canvas. Whatever his methods, the effect was to create suave and radiant flushes of colour, with no sense of brush gesture or hint of figuration. His method was exacting, allowing no possibility for alteration or modification. For this reason, perhaps, he destroyed much of his work of this period.

Louis painted various series of pictures in his new technique, the first of which was *Veils* (1954; he did another series in 1957–60). The other major series were *Florals* (1959–60), *Unfurleds* (1960–1), and *Stripes* (1961–2). The *Veils* consist of subtly billowing and overlapping shapes filling almost the entire canvas, but his development after that was towards rivulets of colour arranged in rainbow-like bands, often on a predominantly bare canvas. It was not until 1959 that his career began to take off and he had little time to enjoy his success before dying of lung cancer. However, his reputation now stands very high and he has had enormous influence on the development of Colour Stain Painting. In the introduction to the catalogue of the 1974 Arts Council exhibition of his work, John Elderfield wrote: 'Morris Louis is one of the very few artists whose work has really changed the course of painting ... With Louis, fully autonomous abstract painting came into its own for really the first time, and did so in paintings of a quality that matches the level of their innovation.'

Loutherbourg, Philippe Jacques de (1740–1812). French painter, stage designer, and illustrator, active mainly in England. He was born in Strasbourg, the son of an engraver and miniaturist. In 1755 he moved to Paris, where he trained under Carle van *Loo and Giovanni Battista Casanova (1728–95) (brother of the famous amorist), a painter of battle, hunting, and equestrian scenes. During the 1760s he enjoyed considerable success at the *Salon, mainly with landscapes. In 1771 he settled in London, armed with an introduction to the actor-manager David Garrick, for whom he became a highly inventive designer of spectacular stage sets at Drury Lane Theatre. After Garrick's retirement in 1776, Loutherbourg continued under his successor Richard Brinsley Sheridan, but in 1781 he left Drury Lane and launched his own theatrical entertainment, the *Eidophusikon. This was a popular success, and in the 1780s Loutherbourg also made an impact as a landscape painter at the *Royal Academy exhibitions (he became an RA in 1781). He travelled widely in England and Wales, and although his landscapes can be rather stagy, they are also lively, and their feeling for *Picturesque and *Sublime qualities provided an influential alternative to the dominance of the Italianate tradition. In 1786 he became involved with the occultist Count Cagliostro and in 1788–9 he abandoned painting for faith-healing; however, he was forced to give up the practice because of public opposition and thereafter he returned successfully to art. In his later work he turned more to history painting, including battle scenes and biblical sub-

jects. He made numerous book illustrations and also published two collections of engravings of his work: *The Picturesque Scenery of Great Britain* (1801) and *The Romantic and Picturesque Scenery of England and Wales* (1805).

Louvre, Paris. The national museum and art gallery of France. The first building on the site, begun *c*.1190 by Philip II as a fortress and arsenal, held the royal treasures of jewels, armour, illuminated manuscripts, etc. It was enlarged and beautified by Charles V (reigned 1364–80), and his successor Charles VI used it as a residence for visiting royalty. Francis I began to demolish it in the 1520s and in 1546 he commissioned the architect Pierre Lescot to build a new palace of four wings around a square court, roughly of the same size as the old castle and on the same site. Only the west and half of the south wings were completed by Lescot, but his work forms the heart of the present vast structure, and his elegant and sophisticated classical style set the tone for all the future additions to the Louvre, which were made by virtually every French monarch up to Napoleon III in the mid-19th century (although for much of the early 18th century it was neglected, after Louis XIV had moved the court to Versailles). In 1699 one of the infrequent exhibitions of the Académie Royale (*see* ACADEMY) was held in the Louvre, and from 1737 the palace's Salon Carré became the venue for more regular exhibitions—hence the term *Salon. In 1784 Louis XVI began converting the Grande Galerie into a museum to display the royal collection (Hubert *Robert was in charge), and as a result of the democratic fervour of the Revolution the Louvre was opened as the first national public gallery in 1793 (though as a public museum it was preceded by others, including the *Ashmolean Museum in Oxford and the *Vatican Museums). It was originally called the Muséum Central des Arts, but in 1803 Napoleon renamed it the Musée Napoléon and exhibited there the works of art he had looted from conquered territories. Most were returned after his fall from power. In 1851 his nephew Napoleon III opened new rooms, housing *Rubens's Marie de *Médicis cycle (transferred from the Luxembourg Palace) and other works. Subsequently there have been various other additions, including a spectacular glass pyramid (1985–9) in the main courtyard serving as a new entrance to the museum; it was designed by the American architect I. M. Pei. In addition to one of the world's greatest collections of paintings, the Louvre houses many other treasures, including large holdings of Greek and Roman antiquities. Among the famous ancient statues are the *Borghese Warrior*, the *Venus de Milo*, and the *Victory of Samothrace*. To relieve congestion after the Second World War a special museum for Impressionist art was formed at the Jeu de Paume in the gardens of the Tuileries. The paintings from the Jeu de Paume, together with certain other works from the Louvre, have now been moved to the *Musée d'Orsay.

Lowry, L. S. (Laurence Stephen) (1887–1976). British painter. He lived all his life in or near Manchester (mainly in Salford) and worked as a rent collector and clerk for a property company until he retired in 1952. His painting was done mainly at night after his day's work, but he was not a *naive painter, having studied intermittently at art schools from 1905 to 1925. The most important of his teachers—at Manchester School of Art—was Adolphe Valette (1876–1942), a French painter who settled in Manchester in 1905 and whose work includes some memorably atmospheric views of the city. Lowry, too, concentrated on urban subjects, but his style was very different to Valette's and much more in the tradition of certain painters of the *Camden Town Group. His most characteristic pictures feature firmly drawn backgrounds of industrial buildings, often bathed in a white haze, against which groups or crowds of figures, painted in his distinctive stick-like manner, move about their affairs. Many of them record his immediate surroundings, but others are semi-imaginary views. There is sometimes an element of humour, but the prevailing feeling is generally what Sir John *Rothenstein calls 'a kind of gloomy lyricism' (Lowry was a solitary character and said, 'Had I not been lonely I should not have seen what I did'). His first one-man exhibition, at the Reid and Lefevre Gallery, London, in 1939, established his name outside his home area for the first time, and his reputation steadily increased thereafter, although he continued to lead a spartan life. In 1976, a few months after his death, a comprehensive retrospective exhibition of his work at the Royal Academy brought considerable divergence of opinion among critics. Some thought of him as a great artist with an important original vision. Others represented him as a very minor talent, although interesting as a social commentator. The best collection of his work is in the Lowry, a large arts centre that opened in Salford in 2000.

Lucas, Sarah. *See* YOUNG BRITISH ARTISTS.

Lucas van Leyden (1494?–1533). Netherlandish engraver and painter, born and mainly active in Leiden. He was the pupil of his father, from whose hand no works are known, and of Cornelis *Engelbrechtsz., but both these were painters whereas Lucas himself was principally an engraver. How he learnt engraving is unknown, but he was highly skilled in that art at a very early age; the earliest dated print by him (*Mohammed and the Murdered Monk*, 1508) was made when he was perhaps only 14, yet it reveals no trace of immaturity in inspiration or technique. In 1514 he became a member of the Leiden painters' guild. He seems to have travelled a certain amount, and on a visit to Antwerp in 1521 he met *Dürer, who drew his portrait (Mus. B.-A., Lille). An unbroken series of dated engravings makes it possible to follow his career as a printmaker and to date many of his paintings, but no clear pattern of stylistic development emerges. Dürer was the single greatest influence on him, but Lucas was less intellectual in his approach, tending to concentrate on the anecdotal features of the subject and to take delight in *caricatures and *genre motifs. Van *Mander characterizes him as a pleasure-loving dilettante, who sometimes worked in bed, but he left a large œuvre, in spite of his fairly early death, and must have been a prodigious worker. Lucas had a great reputation in his day (*Vasari even rated him above Dürer in certain respects) and he is universally regarded as one of the greatest figures in the history of *graphic art (he made etchings and woodcuts as well as engravings and was a superb draughtsman). His status as a painter is less elevated, but he was undoubtedly one of the outstanding Netherlandish painters of his period. He was a pioneer of the Netherlandish genre tradition, as witness his *Chess Players* (c.1508, Gemäldegalerie, Berlin)—which actually represents a variant game called 'courier'—and his *Card Players* (c.1517, Wilton House, Wiltshire), while his celebrated *Last Judgement* *triptych (1526–7, Lakenhal Mus., Leiden) shows the heights to which he could rise as a religious painter. It eloquently displays his vivid imaginative powers, his superb skill as a colourist, and his deft and fluid brushwork. Lucas left no pupils or direct followers, but his work was a stimulus to an even greater Leiden-born artist, *Rembrandt.

Luchism. *See* RAYONISM.

Luini, Bernardino (c.1480–1532). Milanese painter, one of the most prominent of *Leonardo's followers in Lombardy. Little is known of his life, but his prolific output indicates that he must have enjoyed a successful career (he was unusual among Leonardo's followers in that he painted numerous frescos as well as easel pictures). His work is well represented in the Brera in Milan and many of his frescos and altarpieces are in Lombard churches. He also painted mythological subjects (*Cephalus and Procris*, c.1522, NG, Washington). Luini sentimentalized Leonardo's style, and this helped to win him great popularity with the Victorians. His best work is of high quality, but he ran a busy workshop and some of his followers and copyists vulgarized his style into almost a parody of Leonardo, with sickly smirks and exaggerated *chiaroscuro.

Luks, George (1867–1933). American painter and graphic artist. In 1894, after a decade's travel in Europe, he became an illustrator on the *Philadelphia Press* and made friends with other newspaper artists—*Glackens, *Shinn, and *Sloan— who introduced him to Robert *Henri. In 1896 Luks moved to New York, where he turned more to painting and became a member of The *Eight and the *Ashcan School. A flamboyant character who identified himself with the poorer classes and made a pose of bohemianism, he was much given to tall tales and sometimes posed as 'Lusty Luks', an ex-boxer. His work was uneven and unpredictable. It had vigour and spontaneity but often lapsed into superficial vitality. One of his best-known works is *The Wrestlers* (1905, MFA, Boston), which shows his preference for earthy themes and admiration for the bra-

vura painterly technique of artists such as *Manet. Luks taught for several years at the *Art Students League and also ran his own school.

Luminism. Term coined by John Baur, director of the Whitney Museum in New York, to describe an aspect of mid-19th-century American landscape painting in which the study of light was paramount. He defined Luminism as 'a polished and meticulous realism in which there is no sign of brushwork and no trace of impressionism, the atmospheric effects being achieved by infinitely careful gradations of tone, by the most exact study of the relative clarity of near and far objects, and by a precise rendering of the variations in texture and color produced by direct or reflected rays' ('American Luminism', *Perspectives USA*, Autumn 1954). At their most characteristic, Luminist paintings are concerned chiefly with the depiction of water and sky. Leading Luminists included *Bingham and *Durand, and aspects of the trend can be seen in the work of the *Hudson River School. By about 1880 Luminism was becoming outmoded by French influences.

In the field of 20th-century art the term 'luminism' has also been used in completely different senses: as a name for *Neo-Impressionism in Belgium and as a term applied to works of art incorporating electric light (*see* LIGHT ART).

Lurçat, Jean (1892–1966). French painter and designer. For a time he was influenced by *Cubism, but more important and lasting influences on his painting came from his extensive travels during the 1920s in the Mediterranean countries, North Africa, and the Middle East. His pictures were dominated by impressions of desert landscapes, reminiscences of Spanish and Greek architecture, and a love of fantasy that led him to join the *Surrealist movement for a short period in the 1930s. Lurçat is chiefly remembered, however, for his work in the revival of the art of tapestry. His designs combined exalted themes from human history with fantastic representations of the vegetable and insect worlds, and he succeeded in reconciling the stylizations of medieval tapestry with modern modes of abstraction. In 1939 he was appointed designer to the tapestry factory at Aubusson and together with Marcel Gromaire (1892–1971) he brought about a renaissance in its work. He made more than a thousand designs, the most famous probably being the huge *Apocalypse* for the church of Notre-Dame-de-Toute-Grâce at Assy (1948). From 1930 onwards he also produced coloured lithographs, stage designs, and book illustrations, and in the 1960s he renewed his painting activities. Lurçat also wrote poetry and books on tapestry.

lyrical abstraction. A rather vague term, used differently by different writers, applied to a type of expressive but non-violent abstract painting flourishing particularly in the 1950s and 1960s; the term was evidently coined by the French painter Georges *Mathieu, who spoke of 'abstraction lyrique' in 1947. European critics often use it more or less as a synonym for *Art Informel or *Tachisme; Americans sometimes see it as an emasculated version of *Abstract Expressionism. To some writers it implies particularly a lush and sumptuous use of colour.

Lysippus. Greek sculptor from Sicyon, near Corinth, active in the middle and later 4th century BC. He was one of the most famous of Greek sculptors, with a long and prolific career (he worked from perhaps as early as *c.*360 BC to as late as *c.*305 BC and *Pliny said he made 1,500 works—all in bronze). Nothing is known to survive from his own hand, but some idea of his style can be gained from Roman copies of his work, the best and most reliable being the *Apoxyomenos* (a young athlete scraping himself with a strigil) in the Vatican Museums. The figure is tall and slender, bearing out the tradition current in antiquity that Lysippus introduced a new scheme of proportions for the human body to supersede that of *Polyclitus, and the pose—with one arm outstretched—is novel. Lysippus was famous also for his portraits of Alexander the Great, who is said to have let no other sculptor portray him; several copies survive, including examples in the British Museum, London, and the Louvre, Paris. Among his other works was a colossal statue of Hercules at Sicyon, which was probably the original of the celebrated *Farnese Hercules* in the Archaeological Museum in Naples. It shows the realism that was said to be another hallmark of his work. Of the works associated with him on stylistic grounds, the best-known is a bronze statue of a victorious athlete found in the Adriatic Sea in 1964; this was bought by the *Getty Museum, Los Angeles, in 1977 for $3,900,000, then the highest price ever paid for a piece of sculpture, and it is now sometimes known as 'the Getty Victor'. Even from the second-hand evidence that survives, it is clear that Lysippus was an outstandingly original sculptor whose stylistic innovations, like those of his great contemporary *Praxiteles, became common currency in the Greek world: J. J. Pollitt (*Art in the Hellenistic Age*, 1986) describes him as 'probably the single most creative and influential artist of the entire *Hellenistic period'.

Mabuse. *See* GOSSAERT.

MacBryde, Robert. *See* COLQUHOUN.

Macchiaioli. Group of Italian painters, active mainly in Florence *c*.1855–65, who were in revolt against academic conventions and emphasized painterly freshness through the use of spots or patches (*macchie*) of colour. The name Macchiaioli (spot-makers) was applied facetiously to them in 1862 and the painters themselves adopted it. They were influenced by the *Barbizon School, but they painted *genre scenes, historical subjects, and portraits as well as landscapes. Leading members included, Giovanni Fattori (1825–1908) and Telemaco Signorini (1835–1901). *Boldini and de *Nittis sympathized with their ideas. The Macchiaioli met with little critical or financial success, but they are now considered the most important phenomenon in 19th-century Italian painting. Sometimes they are even claimed as proto-*Impressionists, but the differences between the two groups are as striking as the similarities; there is often a strong literary element in the work of the Macchiaioli, for example, and however bright their lighting effects, they never lost a sense of solidity of form.

MacColl, D. S. (Dugald Sutherland) (1859–1948). British painter, critic, lecturer, and administrator. From 1890 to 1895 he was art critic of the *Spectator* and from 1896 to 1906 of the *Saturday Review* (and again from 1921 until 1930, when he moved to the newly founded *Week-End Review*). In these positions he helped to influence public taste in favour of *Impressionism, and his book *Nineteenth Century Art* (1902) contains one of the earliest balanced assessments of the movement. He did not care for the *Post-Impressionists, however, and thought that *Cézanne must have suffered from an eye defect. MacColl was keeper of the *Tate Gallery, 1906–11, and of the *Wallace Collection, 1911–24, one of the founders of the *National Art Collections Fund in 1903, and a vigorous controversialist; in the *Dictionary of National Biography* he is described as

'highly versatile, volcanically energetic, utterly honest and self-confident'. As a painter he concentrated on landscape watercolours, although he also did portraits in oils, including one of Augustus *John (1907, Manchester AG). His books include *Confessions of a Keeper* (1931) and *Philip Wilson *Steer* (1945).

McCubbin, Frederick (1855–1917). Australian painter, born in Melbourne, where he spent most of his life. In the 1890s he was a member of the *Heidelberg School, and he is best known for the scenes of pioneer life he painted at this time (*Bush Burial*, 1890, Geelong AG). After a visit to Europe late in life in 1906, his work was more directly influenced by *Impressionism. From 1886 until his death he taught drawing at the Melbourne National Gallery School. His son **Louis** (1890–1952) was also a painter. His major work is a huge mural of battle scenes for the Australian National War Museum in Canberra (1920–9). From 1936 to 1950 he was director of the National Gallery of South Australia.

MacDonald, J. E. H. *See* GROUP OF SEVEN.

Macdonald, Jock (1897–1960). Canadian painter, born in Scotland. He emigrated to Canada in 1926 to teach at the new Vancouver School of Decorative and Applied Arts. His early work was in the *Group of Seven tradition, but in 1934 he painted his first abstract work, *Formative Colour Activity* (NG, Ottawa). In the late 1930s he became a friend of Emily *Carr, and in 1940 of Lawren *Harris, who encouraged him in his abstract experiments. These included *automatic paintings in a *Surrealist vein. During the last five years of his life Macdonald's output was prodigious, as he threw himself into experimenting with various techniques and media. He taught at several art colleges in the course of his career and played a leading role in advancing the cause of modern art in Canada.

Macdonald-Wright, Stanton (1890–1973). American painter, designer, and experimental artist, remembered chiefly as a pioneer of abstract art. In 1907 he moved to Paris, where he met Morgan *Russell in 1911; together they evolved *Synchromism—a style of painting based on the abstract use of colour. They first exhibited works in this style in 1913 and claimed that they, rather than *Delaunay and *Kupka (whose work of the time was very similar), were the originators of a new type of abstract art. In 1914–16 Macdonald-Wright lived in London, then returned to the USA. In 1919 he moved to California, where he abandoned Synchromism and became involved with experiments with colour film and various other projects. He was deeply interested in Oriental art and from 1958 he spent part of every year in a Zen monastery in Japan. His brother, Willard Huntington Wright (1888–1939), began his career as an art and literary critic (see FORUM EXHIBITION), but turned to crime fiction in the 1920s; under the pen name S. S. Van Dine, he made a fortune as the author of a series of books featuring the supersleuth Philo Vance, whose scholarship and urbanity were modelled on his own.

McEvoy, Ambrose (1878–1927). English painter. He began as a painter of restful interiors, but from about 1915 he gained great success as a portraitist. His most characteristic pictures are of beautiful society women, often painted in watercolour in a rapid, sketchy style. They can be merely flashy or cloyingly sweet (during the First World War one critic joked that at a time of sugar shortage McEvoy was 'a positive asset to the nation'), but the finest have something of the romantic air of refinement of *Gainsborough, an artist he greatly admired. His wife **Mary McEvoy** (1870–1941), whom he married in 1902, was a painter of interiors with figures, flowers, and portraits.

Mach, David. See NEW BRITISH SCULPTURE.

Machuca, Pedro (d. 1550). Spanish architect and painter, active mainly in Granada. He worked in Italy in his early career (which is ill documented) and was one of the first Spanish artists to break entirely with medieval tradition and become steeped in *Renaissance ideas. His earliest dated work, the *Virgin with the Souls of Purgatory* (1517, Prado, Madrid), was painted in Italy and is thoroughly *Raphaelesque in style. Ma-

chuca was back in Spain by 1520; he continued painting, but after Charles V (see HABSBURG) appointed him architect of his new palace in Granada (begun 1527), he devoted himself mainly to this great building. It is strongly Italianate in style; indeed the majestic circular courtyard expresses the ideals of the High Renaissance more completely than any surviving building of the same date in Italy.

Maçip (or **Masip**), **Vicente** (c.1475–1550). Spanish painter, one of a dynasty of artists working in Valencia. Little is known of his life, but his major work, the main altarpiece of Segorbe Cathedral (1528–30), shows him to have been a leading representative of the Italianate style. During his later years he collaborated with the outstanding member of the family, his son and follower **Juan** (known as Juan de Juanes, c.1510–79). Juan's work combines figures in the Italian *Mannerist style with a polished Netherlandish technique. He was the leading painter of his time in Valencia and had many followers.

Maciunas, George. See FLUXUS.

Macke, August (1887–1914). German *Expressionist painter. His training included a period studying with *Corinth in Berlin. Between 1907 and 1912 he visited Paris several times and he came closer in spirit to French art than any other German painter of his time, evolving a personal synthesis of *Impressionism, *Fauvism, and *Orphism (he met Robert *Delaunay in 1912). His subjects were generally light-hearted, without any of the angst associated with other Expressionists, and although his colour was bright it was never strident; often he showed people enjoying themselves. In 1909–10 he met *Kandinsky and Franz *Marc in Munich and in 1911 he joined them in forming the *Blaue Reiter, but apart from a few experiments his work moved less towards abstraction than that of other members of the group. Early in 1914 he made a trip with Paul *Klee and Louis *Moilliet to Tunisia, and the watercolours he did there are considered his finest achievements. He was killed in action in the First World War.

Mackennal, Sir Bertram. See NEW SCULPTURE.

Mackintosh, Charles Rennie. See GLASGOW SCHOOL.

Maclise, Daniel (1806–70). Irish painter and *caricaturist, active in London from 1827. An outstanding draughtsman, Maclise became the leading British history painter of his period, his most prestigious commissions being two enormous murals in the House of Lords: the *Meeting of Wellington and Blücher at Waterloo* (completed 1861) and the *Death of Nelson at Trafalgar* (completed 1865). They were done in the *water-glass technique and are poorly preserved (a sketch for the *Nelson* in the Walker Art Gallery in Liverpool gives an idea of the original colouring), but they are powerful works—fully coherent in spite of the huge numbers of figures involved—and they remain the most stirring examples of his heroic powers of design. Maclise was handsome, charming, and popular with fellow artists, and *Frith wrote that he was spoken of in academic circles as 'out and away the greatest artist that ever lived'. Grandiose history painting was only one side to his talent, however, for he also excelled as a caricaturist, and is particularly noted for a series of character portraits of literary men and women. There are several examples of his conventional portraits in the National Portrait Gallery, London, including a well-known one of his close friend Charles Dickens (1839).

McQueen, Steve. *See* TURNER PRIZE.

McTaggart, William (1835–1910). The leading Scottish landscape painter of his period. He has been called 'the Scottish *Impressionist', but although he was much concerned with light and atmosphere, the sense of the drama of nature in his work brings him closer in spirit to *Constable. His brushwork was free and fervent and he often depicted rough seas and scudding clouds. He was an influential figure, his followers including his grandson, **Sir William MacTaggart** (1903–81).

Maddox, Conroy. *See* SURREALISM.

Maderno, Stefano (c.1576–1636). Italian sculptor. He was one of the leading sculptors in Rome during the papacy of Paul V (1605–21) before *Bernini came into the ascendancy, working on statues and *reliefs in numerous churches, notably the chapel that the pope had built (the Cappella Paolina, begun 1605) in S. Maria Maggiore. One of his sculptures has attained lasting fame; the recumbent figure of St Cecilia (1600) in

S. Cecilia in Trastevere, a lyrical and poignant work that is said to show the body of the Early Christian martyr in the exact position in which it was discovered in the church in 1599.

Maes, Nicolaes (1634–93). Dutch painter. He was born in Dordrecht and in about 1648 became a pupil of *Rembrandt in Amsterdam, staying there until 1653, when he returned to his native town. In his early years he concentrated on *genre pictures, rather sentimental in approach, but distinguished by deep glowing colours he had learnt from his master. Old women sleeping, praying, or reading the Bible were favourite subjects. In the later 1650s, however, Maes began to turn more to portraiture, and from about 1660 he worked exclusively in this field. His style changed too, becoming closer to van *Dyck than to Rembrandt. He abandoned the reddish tone of his earlier manner for a wider, lighter, and cooler range (greys and blacks in the shadows instead of brownish tones). In 1673 he moved permanently to Amsterdam and had great success with this kind of picture. Maes was a fairly prolific painter and is well represented in, for example, the National Gallery, London, and the museum at Dordrecht.

Maestà (It.: 'Majesty'). Term used to describe a representation of the Virgin and Child in which the Virgin is enthroned as Queen of Heaven, often surrounded by a court of saints and angels. The most famous example is by *Duccio.

Mafai, Mario. *See* SCIPIONE.

Maffei, Francesco (c.1605–60). Italian painter, born in Vicenza and active for much of his career in Venice. He had a refreshingly individualistic style, carrying on the great painterly tradition of *Tintoretto and *Bassano, reinforced by the example of *Liss, *Feti, and *Strozzi, to which he added his own note of mysterious and sometimes bizarre fantasy. He painted religious and mythological scenes and also allegorical portraits of local officials.

Magic(al) Realism. Term coined by the German critic Franz Roh in 1925 to describe the aspect of *Neue Sachlichkeit characterized by sharp-focus detail. In the book in which he originated the term—*Nach-Expressionismus, Magischer Realismus, Probleme* *der neuesten Europäischen Malerie* (Leipzig, 1925)—Roh also included a rather mixed bag of non-German painters as 'Magic Realists', among them *Miró and *Picasso. Subsequently critics have used the term to cover various types of painting in which objects are depicted with photographic naturalism but which, because of paradoxical elements or strange juxtapositions, convey a feeling of unreality, infusing the ordinary with a sense of mystery. The paintings of *Magritte are a prime example. In the English-speaking world the term gained currency with an exhibition entitled 'American Realists and Magic Realists' at the Museum of Modern Art, New York, in 1943. The director of the museum, Alfred H. *Barr, Jr., wrote that the term was 'sometimes applied to the work of painters who by means of an exact realistic technique try to make plausible and convincing their improbable, dreamlike or fantastic visions'.

Magnasco, Alessandro (1667–1749). Italian painter, known as Lissandrino (little Alessandro) on account of his small stature. He was born and died in Genoa, but spent most of his working life in Milan. At the beginning of his career he was a portraitist, but virtually nothing is known of this aspect of his career. Later he turned to the type of work for which he is now known—highly individual melodramatic scenes set in storm-tossed landscapes, ruins, convents, and gloomy monasteries, peopled with small, elongated figures of monks, nuns, gypsies, mercenaries, witches, beggars, and inquisitors. His brushwork is nervous and flickering and his lighting effects macabre. He was prolific and his work is rarely dated or datable. Marco *Ricci and Francesco *Guardi were among the artists influenced by him.

Magritte, René (1898–1967). Belgian painter, one of the leading exponents of *Surrealism. Apart from three years living in a suburb of Paris (1927–30), his entire career was spent in Brussels, where he lived a life of bourgeois regularity (the bowler-hatted figure who so often features in his work is to some extent a self-portrait). After initially working in a *Cubist-Futurist style, he turned to Surrealism in 1925 under the influence of de *Chirico and by the following year had already emerged as a highly individual artist with *The Menaced Assassin* (MoMA, New York), a picture that

displays the startling and disturbing juxtapositions of the ordinary, the strange, and the erotic that were to characterize his work for the rest of his life. Apart from a period in the 1940s when he experimented first with pseudo-*Impressionist brushwork and then with a *Fauve technique, he worked in a precise, scrupulously banal manner (a reminder of the early days when he made his living designing wallpaper and drawing fashion advertisements) and he always remained true to Surrealism. He had a repertory of obsessive images that appeared again and again in ordinary but incongruous surroundings. Enormous rocks that float in the air and fishes with human legs are typical leitmotivs. He repeatedly exploited ambiguities concerning real objects and images of them (many of his works feature paintings within paintings), inside and out-of-doors, day and night. In a number of paintings, for example, he depicted a night scene, or a city street lit only by artificial light, below a clear sunlit sky. He also made Surrealist analogues of a number of famous paintings—for example *David's *Madame Récamier* and *Manet's *The Balcony*, in which he replaced the figures with coffins. Late in life he also made wax sculptures based on such paintings, and some of them were cast in bronze after his death (*Madame Récamier*, Pompidou Centre, Paris). He also made prints and a few short comic films, using his friends as actors. His work was included in many Surrealist exhibitions, but it was not until he was in his fifties that he began to achieve international success and honours. By the time of his death his work had had a powerful influence on *Pop art, and it has subsequently been widely imitated in advertising. In the fertility of his imagery, the unforced spontaneity of his effects, and not least his rare gift of humour, he was one of the very few natural and inspired Surrealist painters. J. T. Soby (*René Magritte*, 1965) summed this up felicitously when he wrote: 'In viewing Magritte's paintings ... everything seems proper. And then abruptly the rape of commonsense occurs, usually in broad daylight.'

mahlstick. *See* MAULSTICK.

Mahon, Sir Denis (1910–). British art historian and collector. A private scholar with private means, he has devoted himself single-mindedly to the study of 17th-century Italian (particularly Bolognese) painting, and has not only built up a choice collection in this field, but also played a greater part than anyone else in the re-habilitation of such once-scorned artists as the *Carracci, *Guercino, and *Reni. He is also a leading *Poussin scholar. His publications include *Studies in Seicento Art and Theory* (1947), a brilliant pioneering work, and catalogues of Carracci drawings (1956) and Guercino paintings (1968) and drawings (1969) for major exhibitions of their work in Bologna.

Maiano, Benedetto da (*c*.1442–97). One of the leading Florentine sculptors of his generation, a member of a family of artists from Maiano, near Florence, a village renowned for its quarries. He often worked with his brothers **Giuliano** (*c*.1432–90), who was primarily an architect, and **Giovanni I** (*c*.1439–78), and he also sometimes collaborated with the painter Domenico *Ghirlandaio, whose essentially conservative outlook and high standards of craftsmanship were similar to his own. Nothing is documented of Benedetto's training. He is first recorded as a woodcarver, in 1467, and he continued working in wood throughout his career, but his most important works are in marble and he perhaps learnt his skills with this material from Antonio *Rossellino. His masterpiece is the pulpit in S. Croce, Florence (*c*.1475–80), which features five relief panels on the life of St Francis (terracotta models for three of the panels are in the V&A, London). The pulpit was commissioned by the Florentine merchant Pietro Mellini, of whom Benedetto carved a portrait bust (1474, Bargello, Florence). He also produced a bust of the banker Filippo Strozzi (1475, Louvre, Paris); the terracotta model for this is in the Skulpturengalerie, Berlin, and this is the only instance of a 15th-century portrait bust in which both model and finished marble survive. Benedetto's son, **Giovanni II** (*c*.1487–*c*.1542), was also a sculptor. From about 1520 to about 1536 he worked in England (possibly recruited by *Torrigiano) and he helped to introduce *Renaissance influence to the country. His most important documented works in this respect are eight terracotta roundels of Roman emperors (1521) made for Cardinal Wolsey for the external decor-ation of his palace at Hampton Court (still in situ). The superb wooden screen (*c*.1533–6) at King's College Chapel, Cambridge, has been attributed to him.

Maillol, Aristide (1861–1944). French sculptor, painter, illustrator, and tapestry designer. His early career was spent mainly as a tapestry designer, but he also painted, exhibiting with the *Nabis. Although he first made sculpture in 1895, it was only in 1900 that he decided to devote himself to it after serious eyestrain made him give up tapestry. In 1902 he had his first one-man exhibition, which drew praise from *Rodin; in 1905 came his first conspicuous public success at the *Salon d'Automne; and after about 1910 he was internationally famous and received a constant flow of commissions. With only a few exceptions, he restricted himself to the female nude, expressing his whole philosophy of form through this medium. Commissioned in 1905 to make a monument to the 19th-century revolutionary Louis-Auguste Blanqui, and asked by the committee what form he proposed to give it, he replied: 'Eh! une femme nue.' More than any other artist before him he brought to conscious realization the concept of sculpture in the round as an independent art form stripped of literary associations and architectural context, and in this sense he forms a transition between Rodin and the following generation of modernist sculptors. However, he rejected Rodin's emotionalism and animated surfaces; instead, Maillol's weighty figures, often shown in repose, are solemn and broadly modelled, with simple poses and gestures. His work consciously continued the classical tradition of Greek and Roman sculpture (Maillol visited Greece in 1908), but at the same time has a quality of healthy sensuousness (his peasant wife sometimes modelled for him). Maillol took up painting again in 1939 when he returned to his birthplace, Banyuls, but apart from his sculpture the most important works of his maturity are his book illustrations. His finest achievements in this field are the woodcut illustrations (which he cut himself) for an edition of Virgil's *Eclogues* (begun 1912 but not published until 1926), which show superb economy of line. A museum dedicated to Maillol opened in Paris in 1995 and his work can also be seen in many important collections of modern art.

Makart, Hans (1840–84). Austrian painter. He studied under *Piloty in Munich and from 1869 worked in Vienna, where he was enormously successful and became a leading society figure. His pictures, often vast in size, were characteristically of mythological, historical, and allegorical subjects, treated in the manner of grand opera or Hollywood epics in an exuberant, somewhat *Rubensian style. They were produced in a huge studio that was one of the sights of Vienna (Makart liked to paint in front of visitors). His decorative commissions included murals in the *Kunsthistorisches Museum. Makart's work had great influence in Austria and Germany, notably on the early work of *Klimt, but his reputation soon declined after his death.

Malatesta, Sigismondo (1417–68). Italian nobleman, ruler of Rimini from 1432 until his death. A brilliant and totally unscrupulous condottiere, he is the archetype of the megalomaniac, paganizing tyrant once thought to be characteristic of the Italian *Renaissance. His contemporaries accused him of incest, murder, and rape, amongst other crimes, and he was publicly consigned to hell while still alive—the only man ever to suffer this fate—by Pope Pius II. However, he was also a noted patron of art and scholarship. In particular, his name is indissolubly linked to one of the most remarkable artistic projects of the 15th century—the conversion (begun 1447) of the church of S. Francesco in Rimini into a memorial to himself and his mistress (later wife) Isotta degli Atti. *Alberti was responsible for the exterior cladding of the building in a noble classical style and *Agostino di Duccio and *Piero della Francesca were among the artists who worked on the decoration of the interior. The scheme was never completed, but under Sigismondo's direct inspiration it became the most self-conscious return to the *antique yet seen, and even in its unfinished state it is one of the gems of Renaissance art. Much of the sculpted ornament makes allusion to classical literature and philosophy, prompting Pius II's remark that the church was 'so full of pagan images that it seems like a temple for the worshippers of demons and not for Christians'. However, it was not until the 18th century that the building was dubbed the Tempio Malatestiano—the name by which it is still known.

Mâle, Émile (1862–1954). French art historian. A pioneer in the study of French medieval art, he became professor of the history of art at the Sorbonne in 1912. The best known of his books is probably *L'Art religieux du XIIIe siècle en France* (1902), translated as *The Gothic Image* (1913). His work is distinguished not only by great learning but also by literary merit, his style being praised by Marcel Proust amongst others.

Malevich, Kasimir (1878–1935). Russian painter, designer, and writer, with *Mondrian the most important pioneer of geometric *abstract art. He began working in an unexceptional *Post-Impressionist manner, but by 1912 he was painting peasant subjects in a massive 'tubular' style similar to that of *Léger as well as pictures combining the fragmentation of form of *Cubism with the multiplication of the image of *Futurism (*The Knife Grinder*, 1912, Yale Univ. AG). Malevich, however, was dissatisfied with representational art or—as he put it—fired with the desire 'to free art from the burden of the object'. He was a devout Christian, with mystical leanings, and he thought that by abandoning the need to depict the external world he could break through to a deeper level of meaning and 'swim in the white free abyss' (he often used the analogy of flight and space when discussing his paintings). His first abstract work was a backdrop for the Futurist opera *Victory over the Sun*, produced in the Luna Park Theatre, St Petersburg, in December 1913; his original drawing (now in the Theatrical Mus., St Petersburg) shows a rectangle divided almost diagonally into a black upper segment and a white lower one. He claimed that he made a picture 'consisting of nothing more than a black square on a white field' as early as 1913, but Suprematist paintings were first made public in Moscow in 1915 (there is often difficulty in dating his work and also in knowing which way up his paintings should be hung, photographs of early exhibitions sometimes providing conflicting evidence). For a time Malevich moved away from absolute austerity, tilting rectangles from the vertical, adding more colours, and introducing a suggestion of the third dimension and even a degree of painterly handling, but around 1918 he returned to his purest ideals with a series of *White on White* paintings. After this he seems to have realized he could go no further along this road and virtually gave up abstract painting, turning more to teaching, writing, and making three-dimensional models that were important in the growth of *Constructivism. In 1919, at the invitation of *Chagall, he started teaching at the art school at Vitebsk, where he exerted a profound influence on *Lissitzky, and in 1922 he moved to Petrograd (Leningrad), where he lived for the rest of his life. He went to Warsaw and Berlin in 1927, accompanying an exhibition of his works, and visited the *Bauhaus. In the late 1920s he returned to figurative painting, but he was out of favour with a political system that now demanded *Socialist Realism from its artists and he ran into trouble with the authorities. However, he remained a revered figure among artists. Malevich wrote various theoretical tracts and several collections of his writings have been published. His influence on abstract art—in the West as well as Russia—was enormous.

Malouel, Jean (d. 1415). Netherlandish painter, the uncle of the *Limbourg brothers. From 1397 he was court painter to Philip the Bold, Duke of Burgundy, and his successor John the Fearless. No documented works by him survive, but he has been proposed as the author of several paintings, including a *tondo of the Trinity in the Louvre, Paris. It has all the refinement of French court art combined with a strength of modelling and a realistic naturalism derived from Flanders. See also BELLECHOSE.

Malton, Thomas. See TURNER.

Malvasia, Count Carlo (1616–93). Italian writer and antiquarian. His major work, Felsina pittrice: vite dei pittori bolognesi (1678), is the most important source for knowledge of the great period of the Bolognese School that began with the *Carracci (Felsina was the Etruscan name for Bologna). It contains a particularly revealing biography of his friend *Reni. Malvasia also wrote a guide to the paintings of Bologna (1686), one of the first books of its kind.

Mamontov, Savva. See ABRAMTSEVO.

Mancini, Antonio. See BOLDINI.

Mander, Karel van (1548–1606). Netherlandish painter and writer on art, active mainly in Haarlem. He is sometimes known as the 'Dutch *Vasari', for his fame rests primarily on his work as a biographer of artists, published in Het schilder-boeck (The Book of Painters) in 1604. The most important part of the book is made up of about 175 biographies of Netherlandish and German artists from the van *Eycks to van Mander's own younger contemporaries. This is the first systematic account of the lives of northern European artists, and our only source of information about some of them. The book also contains the lives of Italian artists from *Cimabue up to his own time. Most of this material is a condensed translation into Dutch of Vasari, but it also has valuable information collected by van Mander himself when he was in Italy in 1573-7 or from friends and correspondents; he was sufficiently up to date to mention *Caravaggio, 'who is doing extraordinary things in Rome'. Another part of the book is a long poem that gives practical advice to artists and sums up much of the theory and practice of 16th-century Netherlandish art. About 30 of van Mander's own pictures survive; they are mainly of religious and allegorical subjects, characterized by elongated *Mannerist forms. With *Cornelis van Haarlem and Hendrick *Goltzius, he is said to have founded an academy in Haarlem. Frans *Hals was probably his pupil.

Manessier, Alfred (1911–93). French painter, lithographer, and designer of tapestries and stained glass, a pupil of *Bissière. During the 1930s his work was influenced by *Cubism and *Surrealism, but after staying at a Trappist monastery in 1943 he became deeply committed to religion and turned to expressing spiritual meaning through abstract art. Characteristically his paintings feature rich colours within a loose linear grid, creating an effect reminiscent of stained glass (a medium in which he did some of his best work). After the Second World War Manessier came to be regarded as one of the leading exponents of expressive abstraction in the *École de Paris and won numerous awards, notably the main painting prize at the 1962 Venice *Biennale.

Manet, Édouard (1832–83). French painter and printmaker. He was the son of a senior civil servant in the Ministry of Justice and inherited considerable wealth when his father (who disapproved of his choice of career) died in 1862. His upper middle-class background was important, for although he was seen as an artistic rebel, he always sought traditional honours and success and he cut an impeccable figure as a man about town. He trained under *Couture, 1850–6, but his own style was based mainly on a study of the Old Masters at the *Louvre, and particularly Spanish painters such as *Velázquez (his greatest artistic hero) and *Ribera. During the 1850s he visited museums in the Netherlands, Germany, Austria, and Italy and it is one of the ironies of Manet's career that a painter with such reverence for the art of the past should be so much attacked for his modernity. His first taste of official disfavour came when his first submission to the *Salon—*The Absinthe Drinker* (1859, Ny Carlsberg Glyptotek, Copenhagen)—was rejected. He had two paintings accepted in 1861, but then in 1863 his *Déjeuner sur l'herbe* (Mus. d'Orsay, Paris) caused a scandal. It was turned down by the Salon and was shown instead at the *Salon des Refusés, set up specially for such rejected paintings. Its hostile reception was based on moral as well as aesthetic grounds, for nudity was considered acceptable only if it was sufficiently remote in time or place and this showed a naked woman having a picnic with two contemporary, clothed men. Manet caused even greater outrage two years later when his *Olympia* (1863, Mus. d'Orsay) was exhibited at the Salon. The reclining nude figure was based on *Titian's *Venus of Urbino* (which Manet had copied in Florence ten years earlier), but her blatant sexuality was thought an affront to accepted standards of decorum, and one critic wrote: 'Art sunk so low does not even deserve reproach.' Manet was denounced also for his bold technique, in which he eliminated the fine tonal gradations of academic practice and created vivid contrasts of light and shade: 'The shadows are indicated by more or less large smears of blacking', wrote another critic; 'The least beautiful woman has bones, muscles, skin, and some sort of colour. Here there is nothing…but the desire to attract attention.' From this time, Manet reluctantly found himself acquiring a reputation as a leader of the avant-garde. He was a respected and admired member of the group of young *Impressionists who met at the Café Guerbois and elsewhere. But despite their admiration for him, Manet stood somewhat aloof from the group (although he enjoyed going to the races with *Degas, who was also from the upper middle class) and did not participate in the Impressionist exhibitions. He did, however, adopt the Impressionist technique of painting out of doors (encouraged by Berthe *Morisot, who became his sister-in-law in 1874), and his work became freer and lighter in the 1870s under their influence. In the late 1870s Manet became ill with a disease diagnosed as locomotor ataxia (associated with the late stages of syphilis), which caused him bouts of great pain and extreme tiredness. Increasingly he preferred to work in pastels, which were less physically demanding than oils, but his last great painting, *A Bar at the Folies-Bergère* (1882, Courtauld Gal., London), is unsurpassed in 19th-century art for sheer beauty of technique. He died in appalling pain a week after having a gangrenous leg amputated. The official honours he had craved—in the form of a second-class medal at the Salon and membership of the Legion of Honour—came too late (1881) to be enjoyed.

Manet was a complex and many-sided artist. He painted a great variety of subjects (he was also a skilled etcher and lithographer) and rarely repeated himself. His approach was completely undogmatic and he was reluctant to theorize; his friend Émile Zola wrote of him, 'In beginning a picture, he could never say how it would come out.' His work often has a feeling of complete freshness and spontaneity, yet he would often repaint and rework pictures or even cut them into fragments. His greatest strength was with modern-life subjects (he sketched constantly in the boulevards and cafés of Paris), but although he is accused by some critics of having no imagination, of being able to paint something only if he had it in front of him, his pictures are far from being straight transcriptions of nature. They are, indeed, sometimes enigmatic and elusive, as with *A Bar at the Folies-Bergère*, and seem to be more concerned with the act of painting than with the ostensible subject. It is partly in this freedom from the traditional literary, anecdotal, or moralistic associations of painting that he is seen as one of the founders of 'modern' art, and it is significant that the official title of the first *Post-Impressionist Exhibition, organized by Roger *Fry in 1910, was 'Manet and the Post-Impressionists'.

Manfredi, Bartolommeo (1582–1622). Italian painter, born near Mantua and active mainly in Rome, where he was one of the most important of *Caravaggio's followers. He painted various subjects but is best known for low-life scenes of taverns, card-playing, soldiers in guardrooms, etc., and it was he rather than Caravaggio himself who was mainly responsible for popularizing this kind of work, particularly with painters from France and the Netherlands who visited Italy. In spite of his contemporary reputation, no works survive that are signed or documented as his, and several of the 40 or so paintings now given to him were formerly attributed to Caravaggio.

manière criblée (Fr.: 'sieved manner') (or **dotted manner**). A technique used in some *metal cuts, in which dots were stamped with a punch over selected parts of the plate to create a textured effect in those areas, the dots showing as white against the inked background. The technique was uncommon after the end of the 15th century, but there was something of a revival in the late 18th century.

Mannerism. Term used in the study of the visual arts (and by transference in the study of literature and music) with a confusing variety of critical and historical meanings. Even more than with most stylistic labels, there is little agreement amongst scholars as to its delimitations, and John Shearman begins his book on the subject (*Mannerism*, 1967) with the frank admission: 'This book will have at least one feature in common with all those already published on Mannerism; it will appear to describe something quite different from what all the rest describe.' The word derives from the Italian *maniera* ('style' or 'stylishness'), and it was popularized mainly by the writings of *Vasari, who used it as a term of praise, signifying qualities of grace, poise, facility, and sophistication—characteristics that are indeed apparent in much of the art that he admired from his own time. From the 17th century, however, most critics thought that Italian art of Vasari's period marked a decline from the peaks of grandeur and harmony reached during the High *Renaissance by *Leonardo, *Michelangelo, and

*Raphael, and the term 'Mannerism' came to suggest an art characterized by artificiality, superficiality, and exaggeration, feebly plagiarizing and distorting the work of the masters. From being a stylistic label the term expanded its meaning to become a period label, so that 'Mannerism' came to designate the era in Italian art between the High Renaissance and the *Baroque—that is, from about 1520 to about 1600. The term is still applied mainly to Italian art and architecture, but it is also used of art in other countries.

It was not until the 20th century—and particularly the period between the two world wars—that a more sympathetic attitude towards Mannerist art emerged, and the word began to be used neutrally, without the implication of decadence that it had long carried. At this time, after the revolutionary achievements of early 20th-century art, Mannerist art was looked at with new eyes, and the work of artists who had long been ignored or disparaged began to seem exciting and original to modern taste. The qualities associated with Mannerist art include tension, emotionalism, elongation of the human figure, strained poses, unusual or bizarre effects of scale, lighting, or perspective, and vivid—sometimes harsh or lurid—colours. Often the subject is approached in an unconventional way, with the artist drawing attention to his learning or virtuosity. In the hands of the greatest Mannerist artists (for example *Pontormo or *Parmigianino) such preoccupations led to works that are not only highly sophisticated, but also powerful, disturbing, and moving. The work of less accomplished Mannerists (for example Vasari as a painter) often degenerated, however, into insipid or frenzied gesturing and grimacing.

With Mannerism no longer receiving blanket condemnation, more subtle issues occupied the minds of historians, for example to what extent the term could be applied to art outside Italy (e.g. El *Greco in Spain, the School of *Fontainebleau in France, and *Hilliard in England) or to architecture (where what might be taken in one context as playful or capricious disregard for the rules of classical architecture might in another be regarded as provincial clumsiness). While some critics wish to expand the use of the term, others wish to contract it, and still others seek to distinguish what they regard as the central elements of the style within the general period label by using the term *'maniera'*. The following sentence from S. J. Freedberg's *Painting in Italy: 1500-1600* (1971) in the Pelican History of Art series shows how potentially bewildering the terminology can be: 'The first generation of Mannerism, its inventors, thus could achieve *maniera*, but this requires to be distinguished not only chronologically but in degree and in some respects of kind from the "high Maniera" or Maniera proper.' Thus while the term 'Mannerism' can generally be taken to imply an elegant, refined, artificial, self-conscious, and courtly style, the shade of meaning to be attached to it varies very much according to the context and the outlook of the writer using it.

Man Ray (1890–1976). American painter, photographer, draughtsman, sculptor, and film-maker. He was born Emmanuel Radinsky, but he was known only as Man Ray from about the age of 15 because other youngsters jeered at his foreign-sounding name. After seeing the *Armory Show in 1913 he began painting in a *Cubist style. In 1915 he began a lifelong friendship with Marcel *Duchamp, collaborating with him and *Picabia in founding the New York *Dada movement. He also collaborated with Duchamp and Katherine *Dreier in forming the *Société Anonyme in 1920. In 1921 he settled in Paris, where he continued his Dada activities and then became a member of the *Surrealist movement. For several years he earned his living mainly as a fashion and portrait photographer, but he painted regularly again from the mid-1930s. In 1940 he went back to America to escape the Nazi occupation of Paris and settled in Hollywood, then in 1951 returned permanently to Paris. From the 1940s photography took a secondary place in his activities, but it is as a photographer that his reputation is now most secure. In the 1920s and 1930s he was one of the most imaginative artists in this field, particularly for his exploitation of the 'Rayograph' (also known as photogram), a photograph produced without a camera by placing objects directly on sensitized paper and exposing them to light, and for his development of the technique of 'solarization' (the complete or partial reversal of the tones of a photographic image). In addition to his celebrity as a photographer, he

gained an international reputation as one of the most prominent figures of Dada and Surrealism. Several of his 'objects' have become icons of the movements, notably *Gift* (1921), consisting of a flat iron with a row of nails sticking out of its smooth face (the original is no longer extant; a reconstruction is in the Museum of Modern Art, New York).

Manship, Paul (1885–1966). American sculptor, active mainly in New York. He worked in an elegant, streamlined style, his beautifully crafted figures characterized by clarity of outline and suave generalized forms, and he achieved great success as a sculptor of public monuments. One of his best-known works is the gilded bronze *Prometheus* (1933) in Rockefeller Center Plaza, New York. Manship was also an excellent portraitist. Because of the stylization of his work, derived partly from his interest in archaic sculpture, he had for a time a reputation as a pioneer of modern sculpture in America, but his modernism was fairly superficial and by about 1940 he was being labelled an academic artist.

Manson, J. B. *See* CAMDEN TOWN GROUP.

Mantegna, Andrea (*c.*1431–1506). Italian painter and printmaker. He was the pupil and adopted son of *Squarcione in Padua, growing up in a humanist atmosphere that was to colour his whole approach to art. Squarcione exploited his pupils for his own ends and in 1448, when he was only about 17, Mantegna gave an early indication of his formidable strength of character by taking him to court and forcing him to recognize his independence. He was remarkably precocious, and the distinctive style he created at the beginning of his career changed little over the next half-century. It was a style characterized by sharp clarity of drawing, colouring, and lighting, a passion for archaeology that fed on the abundance of classical remains in northern Italy, and a mastery of perspective and foreshortening unequalled in the 15th century. These qualities were evident in his first major commission (1448), the decoration of the Ovetari Chapel of the Eremitani Church in Padua with frescos on the lives of St Christopher and St James (almost completely destroyed by bombing in the Second World War), and they can also be seen in the celebrated *Agony* *in the Garden* (*c.*1460–5, NG, London). For all his learning, however, Mantegna was never dry. His work, indeed, often shows wit and fancifulness, and he was a delightful painter of animals—witness the rabbits in the *Agony in the Garden*.

In 1460 Mantegna moved to Mantua as court painter to Ludovico *Gonzaga, and apart from a visit to Rome in 1488–90 he remained there for the rest of his life. He was held in the highest esteem by Ludovico, by his son and successor Federico, and by Isabella d'*Este, who married Federico's successor, Francesco. At this time Mantua was becoming one of the leading centres of humanist culture in Europe, and Mantegna glorified the Gonzaga family and court in his most famous work—the fresco decoration (1465–74) of the Camera degli Sposi (Bridal Chamber) in the Ducal Palace. Group portraits of the Gonzaga family, arranged in various courtly scenes, line the walls and above them are bust medallions of the Caesars, indicating that the reigning house was worthy to continue the traditions of the Roman empire. The most remarkable feature of the room, however, is the *illusionistic painting of the architecture (particularly of the ceiling), which appears to extend the real space of the room. This was the first time since antiquity that such a scheme had been carried out and Mantegna's work became the foundation for much subsequent decorative painting (*see* QUADRATURA). Mantegna's other great undertaking for the Gonzaga was a series of nine paintings of the *Triumphs of Caesar* (*c.*1480–1500, Royal Coll., Hampton Court, London); it is often said that they were done for Francesco, but in fact it is not known which member of the family commissioned them. These large and fragile canvases have suffered dreadfully at the hands of 'restorers' in former centuries, but they were successfully cleaned in the 1960s and 1970s, and although they are battered and faded they still give a superb picture of Mantegna's magnificent powers of invention and design and rank alongside *Raphael's tapestry *cartoons as one of the greatest ensembles of *Renaissance art outside Italy.

Besides such large commissions, Mantegna painted many smaller works, including altarpieces, devotional pictures, portraits, and allegories. He also produced engravings of outstanding quality (they are the finest of their time in Italy) and was one of the first artists to use such prints to disseminate his compositions (initially he probably cut the plates himself but later relied on specialist assistants). In addition he designed his own house in Mantua, and it is generally thought that he modelled the bronze bust of himself in his memorial chapel in the church of S. Andrea (a cast of the bust is in the National Gallery, London). By the time of his death he was a widely venerated figure and his reputation has remained high. His influence was profound, not only on Italian artists such as his brother-in-law Giovanni *Bellini, but also, for example, on *Dürer, one of the many northern artists who found his version of the *antique particularly easy to assimilate.

Manzoni, Piero (1933–63). Italian experimental artist. Until 1956 he painted in a traditional style (mainly landscapes), but he then turned to avant-garde work. In 1957 he began to produce *Achromes*, textured white paintings influenced by *Burri and *Klein (whom he met in 1957), and from 1959 he devised a series of provocative works and gestures that included signing people's bodies and designating them works of art, a block on which is inscribed upside down 'The base of the world' (1961, Herning Park, Denmark), and cans of his own excrement. He is regarded as one of the forerunners of *Arte Povera and *Conceptual art. His early death was caused by cirrhosis.

Manzù, Giacomo (1908–91). Italian sculptor. From the age of 11, he worked successively for a woodcarver, a gilder, and a stucco-worker, but he was virtually self-taught as an artist. His early work was influenced by Egyptian and Etruscan art, but he then turned to a more *Impressionistic style owing much to the example of *Rodin and Medardo *Rosso. In the 1940s he simplified his style, so that although the surface of his work is often animated, the feeling it produces is one of classic calm. His sculpture included nudes, portraits, and scenes from everyday life, but he was best known for religious subjects. In 1938 he produced his first figure of a cardinal, a type of work that became particularly associated with him. These figures have been variously interpreted as expressions of an anticlerical attitude or as glorifications of ecclesiastical dignity, but Manzù himself always said that he regarded them as still lifes with no deeper significance than a plate of apples, representing 'not the majesty of the church but the majesty of form'. His most famous work is the set of bronze doors he made for St Peter's in Rome after winning an international competition in 1950 (they were not completed until 1964). In 1958 he also completed a set of doors for Salzburg Cathedral and in 1968 one for the church of St Lawrence in Rotterdam. These works have been much praised and show the possibility of producing sculpture that fits within a traditional religious context and yet is in a modern and personal idiom. Manzù also worked as an etcher, lithographer, and painter.

maquette. A small preliminary model, typically in clay or wax, for a work of sculpture. The word implies something in the nature of a rough sketch, not so fully worked out as a *bozzetto*.

Maratta (or **Maratti**), **Carlo** (1625–1713). Italian painter, the leading painter in Rome in the latter part of the 17th century. A pupil of Andrea *Sacchi, he continued the tradition of the classical *Grand Manner, based on *Raphael, and he gained an international reputation particularly for his paintings of the Madonna and Child, which are reworkings of types established during the High *Renaissance. However, the rhetorical splendour of his work is thoroughly in the *Baroque idiom, and the numerous altarpieces he painted for Roman churches (many still in situ) give wholehearted expression to the dogmas of the Counter-Reformation. Maratta was also an accomplished fresco painter and the finest portraitist of the day in Rome. He had a large studio and his posthumous reputation suffered when the inferior works of his many pupils and imitators were confused with his own paintings.

marble. A word sometimes loosely applied to any stone that will take a good polish so that it is suitable for decorative work; more strictly, it refers to limestones whose structure has been recrystallized by heat or pressure, rendering the stone particularly hard and dense. Marbles are widely distributed and occur in a great variety of colours and patterns, but certain types have been par-

ticularly prized by sculptors. In the ancient world the most famous of Greek marbles was the close-grained, golden-toned Pentelic, which was quarried at Mount Pentelicon in Attica. The *Elgin Marbles are carved in Pentelic. Also widely used were the somewhat coarser-grained translucent white marbles from the Aegean islands of Paros and Naxos. Parian marble was used for the celebrated Mausoleum at Halicarnassus. The pure white Carrara marble, quarried at Massa, Carrara, and Pietra Santa in Tuscany from the 3rd century BC, is the most famous of all sculptors' stones. It was used for the *Apollo Belvedere*, and was much favoured in the *Renaissance, particularly by *Michelangelo, who often visited the quarries to select material for his work. *Neoclassical sculptors also favoured Carrara marble because of its ability to take a sleek surface, but it can look rather 'dead' compared with some of the finest Greek marbles.

Marc, Franz (1880–1916). German painter, active mainly in his native Munich. His early work was in an academic style, but visits to Paris in 1903 and 1907 introduced him to *Impressionism and *Post-Impressionism. He was particularly impressed by the work of van *Gogh, under whose influence his style moved towards *Expressionism. In 1910 he met August *Macke, who became his closest friend, and also *Kandinsky; with them he was a leading member of the *Blaue Reiter group, founded in 1911. Marc was of a deeply religious disposition (in 1906 he visited Mount Athos in Greece with its famous monasteries) and was troubled by a profound spiritual malaise; through painting he sought to uncover mystical inner forces that animate nature. His ideas were expressed most intensely in paintings of animals, for he believed that they were both more beautiful and more spiritual than man. Using non-naturalistic symbolic colour and simplified, rhythmic shapes, he tried to paint animals not as we see them, but as they feel their own existence (*Blue Horses*, 1911, Minneapolis Inst. of Arts). In 1912 Marc saw an exhibition of *Futurist paintings in Berlin and also met *Delaunay in Paris. These events helped to move his work towards abstraction, as in *Animal Destinies* (1913, Kunstmuseum, Basle), which uses panic-stricken animals to symbolize a world on the edge of destruction; on the back of the picture he wrote: 'Und alles Sein ist flammend Leid' (And all being is flaming suffering). By 1914, his paintings had become still more abstract, losing almost entirely any representational content, as in *Fighting Forms* (1914, Neue Pin., Munich), an image of convulsive fury in which there are the merest suggestions of beak- and claw-like forms. These last paintings are considered among the culminating works of German Expressionism. Marc was killed in action in the First World War.

Marcus Aurelius. Over-life-size bronze statue (Capitoline Mus., Rome) of the emperor Marcus Aurelius on horseback, probably made during his reign (AD 161–80). It is the only bronze equestrian statue to survive from antiquity (although another one, the *Regisole*, survived in Pavia until 1797) and one of the few famous *antique statues that always remained unburied and visible after the fall of the Roman empire. During the Middle Ages it was commonly thought to represent Constantine, the first Christian emperor, and this perhaps saved it from destruction. The history of the statue can be traced back to about the 10th century, although early references to it are vague. For centuries it stood outside the Lateran Palace in Rome, but in 1538 Pope Paul III (Alessandro *Farnese) had it transferred to the Capitoline Hill, where *Michelangelo made it the focal point of the piazza he created there; he also designed a new base for the statue. It remained in the open air until 1981, when—because it was being damaged by atmospheric pollution—it was transferred to the Capitoline Museum. A full-size copy was erected in the piazza in 1997, as part of the celebrations to mark the 2,750th anniversary of the traditional date of the foundation of Rome. The original statue was too fragile for a cast to be taken from it, so the copy was made with the aid of moulds created from computerized photographs. From the 15th century the *Marcus Aurelius* was one of the most copied and reproduced of ancient works—in statuettes, engravings, and other forms. It influenced the two greatest equestrian monuments of the *Renaissance—*Donatello's *Gattamelata* and *Verrocchio's *Colleoni*—and many others subsequently. Such influence has usually been generalized rather than precise, but it is fairly specific in Sir Richard

*Westmacott's two equestrian statues of George III (1818–22, Monument Place, Liverpool, and 1824–30, Windsor Great Park, Berkshire).

Marées, Hans von (1837–87). German painter, active mainly in Italy (he lived there 1864–9 and settled permanently in 1873). Like his friends *Böcklin, *Feuerbach, and *Hildebrand, he was one of the Germanic artists working in Italy who turned to the tradition of *ideal art at a time when naturalism was becoming dominant in their own countries. He devoted himself mainly to the theme of the human figure in a landscape setting (*Three Youths under Orange Trees*, 1875–80, Neue Pin., Munich). In 1873 he carried out a major commission to paint a series of large frescos in the Zoological Institute in Naples, but he lacked self-confidence, and died disappointed and practically unknown. It was only at the beginning of the 20th century that the statuesque dignity of his work became appreciated and was hailed as a symbol of a new spirit of modernity in German art.

Margaret of Austria. *See* HABSBURG.

Margarito (or **Margaritone**) **of Arezzo** (active *c*.1262). Italian painter from Arezzo. He is one of the very few 13th-century Italian painters and the only early Aretine by whom we have signed works (examples are in the NG, London, and the NG, Washington). His paintings are clumsy, but they have something of the vividness and lucid brevity of a comic strip. *Vasari, who also came from Arezzo, included a biography of Margarito in his *Lives* (saying he was an architect as well as a painter), and this is virtually the only source of knowledge on him, although a document of 1262 probably refers to him.

Maria Theresa, Empress. *See* HABSBURG.

Marin, John (1870–1953). American painter and printmaker. From 1905 to 1910 he lived in Europe, mainly Paris, where he was influenced by *Whistler's watercolours and etchings, but he first came into contact with avant-garde movements after his return to America, when he became a member of *Stieglitz's circle. The *Armory Show also made a great impact on him. Responding especially to German *Expressionism and the late work of *Cézanne, he developed a distinctive semi-abstract style that he used most characteristically in powerful watercolours of city life and the Maine coast (where he often painted in the summer). His oil paintings (which became more important in his work from the 1930s) are often similar in effect to watercolours, leaving parts of the canvas bare. Marin also made etchings, especially early in his career. From the 1920s he enjoyed a high reputation. He was an individualist, belonging to no movement, and one of the finest watercolourists of the 20th century.

Marinetti, Filippo Tommaso. *See* FUTURISM.

Marini, Marino (1901–80). One of the outstanding Italian sculptors of the 20th century, also a painter, lithographer, and etcher. His travels (particularly his visits to Paris) brought him into contact with many distinguished modern artists (*Braque, *Giacometti, *Gonzales, *Maillol, *Picasso —to name but a few), but he did not ally himself with any avant-garde movements, remaining essentially isolated in his artistic aims. Although he experimented with various materials, he worked mainly in bronze and concentrated on a few favourite themes, most notably the 'Horse and Rider', a subject in which he seemed to express an obscure but poignant tragic symbolism (*Horseman*, 1947, Tate, London). His other subjects include female nudes and he also made numerous portrait busts, remarkable for their psychological penetration and sensuous exploitation of the surface qualities of the material. Often he *polychromed his bronzes, sometimes working with corrosive dyes. In 1952 he won the main sculpture prize at the Venice *Biennale, setting the seal on his international reputation. There are Marini museums in Florence, Milan, and Pistoia and his work is represented in many major collections of modern art.

Marinus van Reymerswaele (*c*.1490–1567?). Netherlandish painter, presumably from Roymerswaele (once in Zeeland but now under the sea). He specialized in two types of picture, both with more or less life-size half-length figures: representations of St Jerome in his study (influenced by *Dürer) and *genre scenes of bankers, usurers, misers, and tax-collectors. The genre scenes show the sin of avarice and the vanity of earthly possessions; according to a Flemish proverb a banker, a usurer, a tax-collector, and a miller were the four evangelists of the devil. These paintings must have been very popular, for they exist in numerous versions and copies, but it is not known what kind of clientele bought pictures of such unpleasant characters, grotesquely presented in a manner deriving (via *Massys) from *Leonardo's *'caricatures'. A 'Marinus . . . of Romerswael' is mentioned in Middelburg in 1567, when he was condemned to walk in a penitential procession for taking part in the looting of a church, but he may not be identical with the painter, who is described as deceased in another document of that year.

Maris. Family of three brothers who played a leading part in Dutch painting during the second half of the 19th century. **Jacob** (Jacobus Hendricus) (1837–99) was one of the leaders of the *Hague School, specializing in views of the Dutch countryside and scenes in Dutch towns. **Matthias** (Matthijs, Thijs) (1839–1917) began in similar fashion, but came to specialize in figure compositions of visionary subjects. In 1869 he moved to Paris and then in 1877 to London, where he lived for the rest of his life and was influenced by the *Pre-Raphaelites in his choice of poetic subjects, although not in style. **Willem** (1844–1910) was a pupil of his two brothers and was influenced by *Mauve. His subjects are almost entirely confined to meadows and cattle. In his later years he became a leader of Dutch *Impressionism, urging his pupils— among them *Breitner—to paint in the open air and to use vivid colours.

Marlow, William (1740–1813). English landscape and marine painter, a pupil of Samuel *Scott and possibly also of Richard *Wilson. His early landscapes were topographical views, including pictures of country houses, but after a visit to the Continent (1765–6) he painted largely from his memories of France and Italy. In the 1780s he went into semi-retirement, devoting himself to making scientific instruments. *See also* CAPRICCIO.

Marmion, Simon (d. 1489). Franco-Flemish manuscript *illuminator and painter. In 1449–54 he lived in Amiens, where he may have been born, and he joined the Tournai painters' guild in 1468, but most of his working life was spent in Valenciennes, where he is first documented in 1458. He had a great reputation in his day, but no works certainly from his hand survive. The main paintings attributed to him are two wings of an altarpiece (1455–9) from the abbey of St Bertin, St Omer (Gemäldegalerie, Berlin; fragments from the altarpiece are in the NG, London). Several manuscripts also are attributed to him. His style was very tender, with delicate, almost pastel colouring, and does not belong to the mainstream of either French or Netherlandish art.

Marochetti, Carlo (1805–67). Italian sculptor. He had an internationally successful career, being made a baron in his native country, awarded the Legion of Honour in France, and patronized by Queen Victoria and Prince Albert in England, where he settled in 1848. His dramatic style, exemplified in his equestrian statue of Richard the Lionheart (1851–60) outside the Houses of Parliament, was, however, considered rather flashy by some English critics. *See also* LANDSEER.

marouflage. Term for gluing a *canvas on to a wall, whether before painting it or afterwards. In French *maroufle* means a sticky mixture of the remains of paint left in the artist's pots, and *maroufler* may describe almost any operation that might be carried out with this glue, for example lining one canvas with another to strengthen it.

Marquet, Albert (1875–1947). French painter and draughtsman. He was one of the *Fauves, and for a time his boldness of colour almost matched that of *Matisse (his lifelong friend). However, he soon abandoned Fauvism and turned to a comparatively naturalistic style. He painted some fine portraits and did a number of powerful female nudes (1910–14), but he was primarily a landscapist. His favourite—eventually almost exclusive—themes were ports and the bridges and quays of Paris, subjects he depicted with unaffected simplicity and great sensitivity to tone. Marquet was an outstanding draughtsman and from 1925 worked mainly in watercolour. He travelled widely and built up an international reputation, but he lived very quietly (he was timid in personality) and refused all honours.

Marsh, Reginald (1898–1954). American painter. Until 1930 he worked mainly as a newspaper illustrator, but he took up painting seriously after a study trip to Paris in 1925–6, and in the 1930s he became well known for his paintings depicting shabby and tawdry aspects of life in New York. His favourite subjects included Coney Island, the amusement arcades of Times Square, and the cheap and grubby streetlife of the Bowery district (*Tattoo and Haircut*, 1932, Art Inst. of Chicago). Although he was capable of bitter satire against the complacency of the wealthy, his work generally shows a love of depicting teeming life through ugly but colourful subjects rather than a desire for social protest. His aim was to represent contemporary subjects in the manner of the Old Masters and he worked mainly in *tempera, also experimenting with other venerable techniques. He came from a wealthy family and to some extent his work expressed a rejection of the affluent and genteel circumstances in which he grew up.

Marshall, Benjamin (1768–1835). English sporting painter, one of the best followers of *Stubbs. He was briefly a pupil of the portrait painter L. F. *Abbot, but from *c.*1792 he turned to animal painting. In 1812 he settled at Newmarket, famous for its racecourse, but he returned to London in 1825. There are examples of his work in Tate Britain.

Martin, John (1789–1854). English *Romantic painter and *mezzotint engraver, celebrated for his melodramatic scenes of cataclysmic events crowded with tiny figures placed in vast architectural or landscape settings. He caught the public imagination with spectacular paintings such as *Joshua Commanding the Sun to Stand Still* (1816, United Grand Lodge of Great Britain, London), the work that made his reputation, and in 1821 *Lawrence referred to him as 'the most popular painter of the day'. His work was indeed truly popular, for he made his living mainly through the sale of prints of his pictures rather than the paintings themselves. He became famous in France as well as Britain, he was knighted by Leopold I of Belgium (1833), and his influence was felt by American artists such as *Cole. However, while he pleased a large public and was regarded by some admirers as one of the greatest geniuses who ever lived, Martin was reviled by *Ruskin and other critics, who considered his work vulgar sensationalism. Few artists, indeed, have been subject to such extremes of critical fortune, and he later sank so much in esteem that very large and once famous paintings by him were sold in the 1930s for as little as £2. By the 1970s his reputation had greatly revived. Martin made mezzotints not only as a means of reproducing his paintings but also as original compositions. Particularly noteworthy are his illustrations to the Bible and John Milton's *Paradise Lost*, which show that although he had great weaknesses as an artist, especially in his drawing of the human figure, he also had a vividness and grandiloquence of imagination not unworthy of such elevated subjects. He is sometimes called 'Mad Martin', but the sobriquet is undeserved and applies more to his brother Jonathan, who was insane and set fire to York Minster. John Martin was eminently sane and in the 1830s almost bankrupted himself with extremely ambitious but entirely practical plans for improving the water supply and sewage system of London. His schemes did not come to fruition, but they reveal a heroic desire to put the architectural visions of his paintings into a concrete form. His work is best represented in Tate Britain, London, and in the Laing Art Gallery in Newcastle upon Tyne, near his native Haydon Bridge.

Martin, Kenneth (1905–84). British painter and sculptor. In 1930 he married Mary Balmford (a fellow student at the *Royal College of Art), whose artistic development as **Mary Martin** (1907–69) had very close affinities with his own. In the 1930s he painted in a naturalistic style, but during the 1940s his work became less representational until in 1948–9 he produced his first abstract pictures. His wife soon followed suit and in the early 1950s they began making abstract constructions. With Victor *Pasmore and others they became recognized as leaders of the *Constructivist movement that burgeoned in England in the 1950s. Kenneth Martin's contribution came not only through his work, but also by writing and organizing exhibitions. Mary Martin had numerous major commissions, among them a screen for Musgrave Park Hospital, Belfast (1957).

Martin, Sir Leslie. *See* CIRCLE.

Martini, Simone (*c.*1285–1344). Next to *Duccio, the most distinguished painter of the Sienese School. Nothing certain is known of him before 1315. *Vasari says that he was a pupil of *Giotto, but the prevailing opinion is that he probably trained in Duccio's circle; certainly he learnt much from the decorative use of outline, colour, and patterning characteristic of Duccio's work. The main features of his style are present in his earliest surviving work, the large fresco of the *Maestà* (1315; reworked 1321) in the Palazzo Pubblico in Siena: the sumptuous materials and the aloofness of the Madonna derive from the *Byzantine style of the older generation; the decorative line, gesture, and expression are informed by the gracious *Gothic fashion that was now current in Siena; and the use of foreshortening to create depth shows the awakening desire for more lifelike effects. Two years later he painted an altarpiece (1317, Mus. di Capodimonte, Naples) for Robert of Anjou (king of Naples, 1309–43) showing his elder brother St Louis of Toulouse, newly canonized, resigning his crown to him. The *predella scenes contain the boldest compositions in perspective that had been produced up to that date. Perhaps at about the same time (although the evidence for the dating is inconclusive) he carried out the fresco decoration of the chapel of S. Martino in the lower church of S. Francesco, Assisi.

The next major work associated with Simone is a fresco, bearing the date 1328, on the wall opposite his *Maestà* in the Palazzo Pubblico in Siena, commemorating the condottiere Guidoriccio da Fogliano, who in that year had won a great victory for the Sienese and liberated the town of Montemassi, depicted in the background. This highly original work, which shows the general riding in stately but solitary triumph, is generally regarded as one of the first equestrian portraits since antiquity; however, it has recently been the subject of great controversy, some scholars considering that it is not by Simone and appreciably later than assumed (this opinion is based on technical evidence allegedly showing that part of the fresco lies on top of another fresco known to date from 1363). The work that is generally regarded as the epitome of Simone's style is the *Annunciation* (1333, Uffizi, Florence), although this is jointly signed with his brother-in-law Lippo *Memmi. It is a ravishing blend of fragile grace and sweet sentiment and for sheer beauty of craftsmanship is unsurpassed in its age. Simone's work is more fully Gothic in spirit than that of any other major Italian painter; it is not surprising that he was appreciated in France, and from about 1335 until his death he worked at the papal court in *Avignon. During this period he painted the unusual subject *Christ Reproved by his Parents* (1342, Walker AG, Liverpool) and the frontispiece to a Virgil manuscript belonging to the poet Petrarch (Ambrosiana Lib., Milan). He also did a portrait of Petrarch's beloved Laura; it is lost, but mentioned in one of the poet's sonnets. Simone's style and compositions were taken over by *illuminators from France and Flanders and generations of Italian panel and fresco painters copied him too. He was one of the main sources of the *International Gothic style.

Martorell, Bernardo (d. 1452). Spanish painter and *illuminator. He worked in Barcelona (where he is first documented in 1427) and was the outstanding painter in Catalonia in the second quarter of the 15th century, the successor to *Borrassá, who perhaps taught him. Only one surviving work is securely documented—the altarpiece of *St Peter of Púbol* (1437–42, Gerona Mus.)—but on stylistic grounds a group of paintings formerly given to 'the Master of St George' has been attributed to him. The group includes (and formerly took its identity from) an altarpiece of *St George*; the central panel is in the Art Institute of Chicago and the four wings are in the Louvre, Paris. Martorell's work, influenced by Franco-Flemish painting and illumination, was essentially *International Gothic in style, but reveals a distinctive personality, particularly in its vigorous sense of drama and delicate handling of light. Among painters of the next generation, *Huguet was most obviously indebted to him.

Mary of Hungary. *See* HABSBURG.

Marzal de Sax, Andrés (active 1393–1410). Painter of German origin (Sax indicating Saxony) who worked in Valencia, Spain. Only one fragment survives of his documented works—the *Incredulity of St Thomas* in Valencia Cathedral, part of an altarpiece he completed for the cathedral in 1400. Among the works given to him on stylistic

grounds the most important is the huge and sumptuous *St George* altarpiece (V&A, London), featuring the varied tortures of the saint in grisly detail. The somewhat rough vigour of Marzal de Sax's style had considerable influence in Valencia; he is last mentioned in 1410, impoverished and ill, receiving free lodging from the city in recognition of the quality of his work and his generosity in training local painters.

Masaccio (Tommaso di Ser Giovanni di Mone Cassai) (1401–28/9). Florentine painter. Although he died aged only 26 or 27, he brought about a revolution in painting and he ranks alongside his friends *Alberti, *Brunelleschi, and *Donatello as one of the founding fathers of the *Renaissance. His affectionate nickname, which may be translated as 'Hulking Tom' or 'Sloppy Tom', was given to him, so *Vasari says, because he was so completely absorbed in art that 'he refused to give any time to worldly matters, even to the way he dressed'. He became a member of the painters' guild in Florence in 1422, but nothing is known of his training, the tradition that he was taught by *Masolino, later his collaborator, now being discounted. The earliest work attributed to him is the S. Giovenale *Triptych (1422, S. Pietro, Cascia di Reggello), which is somewhat uncouth but reveals a totally individual spirit in its rejection of all *Gothic elegance and concentration on the weight and bulk of the figures. Instead of learning from contemporary painters, Masaccio looked back to *Giotto for inspiration, recapturing the gravity of feeling and grandeur of form that characterized his work. But whereas Giotto set his figures in space intuitively, Masaccio grappled with and solved the problem of creating a completely coherent and consistent sense of three dimensions on a two-dimensional surface, his work thus becoming part of 'the bed-rock of European art' (in Kenneth *Clark's phrase). His enormous achievement was based on his mastery of the new science of *perspective and his use of a single consistent light source to define the structure of the body and its draperies. Among contemporary artists he was closest in spirit to Donatello. Both artists were less concerned with surface appearances and isolated detail than with the underlying construction of objects and both excelled at the depiction of emotion with great force and directness.

Masaccio has left three great works to posterity in which he enunciated his new principles: a *polyptych (1426) for the Carmelite church in Pisa (the central panel is in the National Gallery in London, and the other ten surviving panels—probably representing about half the original total—are in the Gemäldegalerie, Berlin; the Getty Museum, Los Angeles; the Museo di Capodimonte, Naples; and the Museo Nazionale, Pisa); a fresco cycle, done in collaboration with Masolino, on the life of St Peter (with additional scenes of the *Temptation of Adam and Eve* and the *Expulsion from Paradise*) in the Brancacci Chapel of S. Maria del Carmine, Florence (c.1425–8); and a fresco of the *Trinity* in S. Maria Novella, Florence (c.1428). Masaccio moved to Rome in 1428, leaving the frescos in the Brancacci Chapel unfinished, and died so suddenly that Vasari said 'there were some who even suspected he had been poisoned'. Vasari adds that 'during his lifetime he had made only a modest name for himself', and certainly many of his Florentine contemporaries and successors were unmoved by his innovations. He was a great inspiration to the progressive masters of the next generation, however (Fra *Angelico, Filippo *Lippi, *Piero della Francesca), and Vasari records a whole roster of major artists, including *Leonardo, *Michelangelo, and *Raphael, who studied his work with profit.

Masaccio's younger brother, **Giovanni di Ser Giovanni** (1406–86), was also a painter, known by the nickname Lo Scheggia ('The Splinter'); this presumably indicates he was slight in stature or marks his connections with woodworking (his grandfather made wooden boxes and much of his own work consisted of decorating objects such as *cassoni and *deschi da parto).

Masereel, Frans (1889–1972). Belgian graphic artist and painter, active mainly in France. He was a prolific illustrator of books and periodicals. Much of his work was motivated by social concern, one of his chief themes being the suffering caused by war. He often used the formula of *Romans in Beelden* (novels in pictures), which are series of woodcuts telling a story without a text.

Maso di Banco (active second quarter of the 14th century). Florentine painter. Almost nothing is known of his career (*Vasari does not mention him by name and attributes some of his work to an obscure—possibly fictitious—artist called Giottino: 'little Giotto'). However, Maso is now regarded as the greatest of *Giotto's followers on the strength of *Ghiberti's testimony that he was the painter of the frescos illustrating the legend of St Sylvester in the Bardi Chapel of S. Croce, Florence. The stately figures here are sometimes even more massive than Giotto's and the lucid and beautifully coloured compositions are of almost geometric clarity (although it has been argued that some of the effect of monumental simplicity may be due to restoration). On stylistic grounds other works have been attributed to Maso, including panels in Budapest (MFA), Chantilly (Mus. Condé), and New York (Brooklyn Mus. and Met. Mus.).

Masolino da Panicale (Tommaso di Cristofano) (c.1383?–c.1440?). Italian painter, an enigmatic and intriguing figure. He presumably came from Panicale in Umbria, and he worked in various places in Italy (and also in Hungary), but he is regarded as a member of the Florentine School. According to *Vasari he trained as a sculptor and goldsmith under *Ghiberti, but his early life is obscure. For a short period his career was closely linked to that of *Masaccio, but the exact nature of their association remains ill-defined (the nickname Masolino, meaning 'Little Tom', almost suggests that he and Masaccio—'Big' or 'Hulking Tom'—were thought of as a kind of double act). The tradition that he was Masaccio's master is now dismissed, for he became a member of the painters' guild in Florence only in 1423 (a year after Masaccio) and although he was evidently almost two decades older, it was he who was influenced by Masaccio rather than the other way round. On stylistic grounds they are thought to have collaborated on the *Madonna and Child with St Anne* (c.1425, Uffizi, Florence), and Vasari records that they worked together on the decoration of the Brancacci Chapel of S. Maria del Carmine in Florence (c.1425–8). Masolino's style was softer and more graceful than Masaccio's and there is a fair measure of agreement about the division of hands in the chapel. The contrast in style is seen most clearly in the frescos of the *Temptation* *of Adam and Eve* and the *Expulsion from Paradise*: Masolino's nude figures in the *Temptation* have an almost doll-like daintiness, whereas Masaccio's in the *Expulsion* are massively powerful and convey a feeling of tragic intensity. After Masaccio's early death in 1428 Masolino's style became more decorative. At his best he was a painter of great distinction, his masterpiece perhaps being the fresco of the *Baptism of Christ* (*c*.1435) in the Baptistery at Castiglione d'Olona, near Como, a graceful and lyrical work that is a world away from Masaccio's sombre *Baptism of the Neophytes* in the Brancacci Chapel.

Masson, André (1896–1987). French painter, printmaker, sculptor, stage designer, and writer, one of the major figures of *Surrealism. During the First World War he was seriously wounded and deeply scarred emotionally. His pessimism was accompanied by a profound and troubled curiosity about the nature and destiny of man and an obscure belief in the mysterious unity of the universe; he devoted the whole of his artistic activity to penetrating and expressing this belief. In the early 1920s he was influenced by *Cubism, but in 1924 he joined the Surrealist movement and remained a member until 1929, when he left in protest against *Breton's authoritarian leadership. His work belonged to the spontaneous, expressive, semi-abstract variety of Surrealism, and included experiments with automatic drawings (*see* AUTOMATISM), chance effects, and unusual materials (he sometimes incorporated sand in his paintings). Themes of metamorphosis, violence, psychic pain, and eroticism dominated his work. In 1934–6 he lived in Spain until the Civil War drove him back to France and in 1941–5 he took refuge from the Second World War in the USA. There his work formed a link between Surrealism and *Abstract Expressionism. In 1945 he returned to France and two years later settled at Aix-en-Provence, where he concentrated on landscape painting, achieving something of the spiritual rapport with nature seen in some Chinese paintings.

Massys (or **Matsys** or **Metsys**), **Quentin** (*c*.1466–1530). Netherlandish painter, born in Louvain and active in Antwerp, where he was the leading painter of his day. He became a master in the painters' guild

there in 1491, but his early career is obscure and his training is a matter of conjecture (van *Mander says he was self-taught, and according to another early account he originally followed his father's trade as a blacksmith but took up art to woo his sweetheart away from a painter she admired). His first dated works are the altarpieces of *St Anne* (1507–9, Mus. Royaux, Brussels) and the *Lamentation* (1508–11, Koninklijk Mus., Antwerp). Massys continued the tradition of the great masters of 15th-century Netherlandish art, but he was also clearly aware of Italian art (particularly the work of *Leonardo) and may well have crossed the Alps at some point in his career. In his exquisite *Madonna and Child with Angels* (*c*.1505, Courtauld Gal., London), for example, the *iconographic type of the standing Virgin goes back to Jan van *Eyck, but the *putti holding a garland reveal *Renaissance influence. The landscape backgrounds of some of his religious works were evidently done by his friend Joachim *Patinir. Massys also painted portraits and *genre scenes. The satirical quality in his pictures of bankers, tax-collectors, and avaricious merchants has been linked with the writings of the great humanist Erasmus. Certainly the two met, for Massys painted a pair of portraits of Erasmus (Royal Coll.) and his friend Petrus Aegidius (Earl of Radnor Coll., Longford Castle, Wiltshire) as a gift for Sir Thomas More in 1517. They instituted a new type—the scholar in his study—that influenced *Holbein among others. Massys had two painter sons, **Jan** and **Cornelis**.

Master E. S. (sometimes called the Master of 1466 from the date on one of his engravings). German engraver working in the mid-15th century, named after the monogram on several of his surviving prints. He was the most prolific and influential of the early German engravers, working on profane and fantastic subjects as well as religious images and producing more than 300 known prints (about a third of them survive in unique copies). Earlier engravers had been content with pure outline, but E. S. managed to create rich tonal effects by the ingenious use of *hatching and crosshatching.

Master Francke. German painter, active in Hamburg in the early 15th century. His major surviving work is an altarpiece (now fragmentary) for the guild of merchants trading with England (1424, Kunsthalle, Hamburg), showing scenes from Christ's Passion and incidents from the life of St Thomas à Becket. Francke was a leading exponent of *International Gothic in northern Germany and he had wide influence there and along the shores of the Baltic.

Master of . . . Term used in art history to label the author of anonymous works or groups of works for convenience in discussing them. This use of invented names is more common in the study of painting and printmaking than of sculpture, and historians of architecture hardly ever resort to it. It began in Germany in the early 19th century with the description of Early Netherlandish painting. Initially the choice of names was often more lyrical than descriptive, as with the 'Master of the Pearl of Brabant', named after a small gem-like altarpiece (Alte Pin., Munich), now usually attributed to Dieric *Bouts. Nowadays invented names tend to be more prosaic and more directly appropriate. Often the anonymous master is named after a particular picture and/or the collection to which it belongs, e.g. 'Master of the Louvre Annunciation'. Alternatively, the name can refer to some aspect of the artist's style, as in the 'Master of the Anaemic Figures' (a 15th-century Spanish painter), who shows that the designation 'master' is used neutrally and is not a term of approbation. The practice of creating artistic personalities in this way has been overdone, but is often useful.

Master of Alkmaar (active early 16th century). Netherlandish painter named after the altarpiece of the *Seven Works of Mercy* painted for the church of St Lawrence in Alkmaar in 1504 and now in the Rijksmuseum, Amsterdam. The painter has been plausibly identified with Cornelis Buys, who was the brother of Jacob *Cornelisz. van Oostsanen. The figure style is reminiscent of *Geertgen tot Sint Jans and the altarpiece is important as an early instance of the characteristically Dutch delight in the representation of everyday life.

Master of Flémalle. Netherlandish painter named after three paintings in the Städelsches Kunstinstitut in Frankfurt that in the 19th century were wrongly said to have come from an 'abbey of Flémalle,

near Liège' (no such abbey ever existed). Scholarly opinion now generally identifies him with Robert Campin (c.1375–1444), who settled in Tournai in about 1405 and became the city's leading painter. None of Campin's documented pictures survive, and the identification of him with the Master of Flémalle depends on the similarity between the paintings given to the Master and those of Jacques *Daret and Rogier van der *Weyden, for Daret was Campin's pupil and Rogier almost certainly was. The once popular hypothesis that the Master of Flémalle's paintings are early works by Rogier now has few adherents. While there may still be doubt about the Master of Flémalle's identity, there is no argument about his achievement, for he made a radical break with the elegant *International Gothic style and ranks with Jan van *Eyck as one of the founders of the Early Netherlandish School of painting. None of the paintings given to him are dated—with the exception of the wings of the Werl altarpiece of 1438 in the Prado, a doubtful attribution—but it seems likely that his earliest works antedate any surviving picture by van Eyck. The earliest of all is generally thought to be the *Entombment* (Courtauld Gal., London) of about 1420. This still has the decorative gold background of medieval tradition, but the influence of Claus *Sluter is clear in the sculptural solidity and dramatic force of the figures. The most famous work associated with the Master of Flémalle is the Mérode Altarpiece (Met. Mus., New York), and he is indeed sometimes referred to as the Master of Mérode. However, the attribution of this painting has also been questioned. Among the other works associated with him are the *Marriage of the Virgin* (Prado, Madrid), the *Nativity* (Mus. B.-A., Dijon), and the *Virgin and Child before a Firescreen* (NG, London), which shows the homely detail and down-to-earth naturalism characteristic of the artist (the firescreen behind the Virgin's head doubles as a halo). The National Gallery also has three portraits attributed to the Master of Flémalle. In spite of the many problems associated with him, he ranks as a very powerful and important artistic personality.

Master of Mary of Burgundy. Netherlandish manuscript illuminator, active in the last quarter of the 15th century. He is named after a *Book of Hours painted for Mary of Burgundy, who married the emperor Maximilian I (*see* HABSBURG) in 1477 and died in 1482 (Österreichische National-bibliothek, Vienna). This is among the finest illuminated books of the period, with many charming everyday-life and still-life details, and other high-quality works in a similar style have been attributed to him, including a Book of Hours in the Bodleian Library, Oxford. It has been suggested that he is to be identified with Sanders *Bening.

Master of Moulins (active *c*.1480–*c*.1500). French or Netherlandish painter, named after a *triptych of the *Madonna and Child with Saints and Donors* (*c*.1498) in Moulins Cathedral. The style of this work is highly distinctive, and has enabled a considerable oeuvre to be built up around it. The Master of Moulins's sculptural precision of form (recalling *Fouquet), the poise of his figures, his brilliant palette, the harmony of his compositions, and his taste for splendid and meticulous details make him one of the outstanding painters of his period in northern Europe. Various suggestions have been made for identifying him with named artists; these include Jean *Perréal, who had the biggest contemporary reputation of any French artist of this period, but the most plausible candidate is now thought to be Jean Hey, a Netherlandish painter who is known to have worked in France around 1500.

Master of St Cecilia (active *c*.1300). Italian painter named after the St Cecilia Altarpiece (Uffizi, Florence), which came from the church of S. Cecilia, Florence, destroyed by fire in 1304. Presumably he was a Florentine, but nothing is known about him. Other works have been attributed to him because of their resemblance to the Uffizi picture, the most important being the first scene and the three concluding scenes of the great fresco cycle of the life of St Francis in the Upper Church of S. Francesco at Assisi (*see* MASTER OF THE LEGEND OF ST FRANCIS). The painter of these scenes resembles *Giotto in lucidity of presentation and the solid drawing of his figures, but he is more genial in feeling. His figures are more vivacious, his colour warmer and sweeter. Some critics have attempted to identify him with the famous but elusive *Buffalmacco.

Master of St George. *See* MARTORELL.

Master of St Giles (active *c*.1480–*c*.1500). French or Netherlandish painter named after two panels representing scenes from the life of St Giles (NG, London). Other paintings in the same style have been grouped round them. Their attention to detail and their meticulous finish have prompted the view that the artist was trained in the Netherlands, but the inclusion of views of Paris in some of his works indicates that he worked there, whatever his origin. His work is of high quality and he must have been one of the best painters of the day in northern France.

Master of Segovia. *See* BENSON.

Master of the Brunswick Monogram (active *c*.1520–40). Netherlandish painter, named after a picture in the Herzog-Anton-Ulrich Museum in Brunswick of the *Parable of the Great Supper* (Luke 14). There is no agreement as to how the interlinked letters of the monogram should be read. A dozen or so small pictures have been attributed to the same hand; about half depict religious subjects in the open air, and most of the others are brothel scenes. The quality of the pictures is uniformly high. The artist's observation of nature, his fine drawing, and ability to integrate figures into a landscape make him an important forerunner of Pieter *Bruegel. Suggestions have been made for identifying him with various named painters, including Jan Sanders van *Hemessen.

Master of the Housebook (late 15th century). German (or according to some authorities Netherlandish) printmaker and draughtsman, so called from a number of drawings contained in a kind of commonplace book in Castle Wolfegg in Germany. He has also been called the Master of the Amsterdam Cabinet, since the largest collection of his prints (all drypoints) is in the Print Room of the Rijksmuseum. They often represent very worldly subjects and are done in a lively sketchy manner. *Dürer must have known them, as their influence can be traced in several of his early drawings. A few paintings have also been attributed to this master. Various suggestions have been made for identifying him with named artists, but none has met with general acceptance.

Master of the Legend of St Francis. A name for the main painter of the famous cycle of frescos on the nave walls of the Upper Church of S. Francesco in Assisi, depicting the life of St Francis and probably dating from about 1300, although some critics put them as late as the 1330s. This cycle was praised by *Vasari as one of the principal works of *Giotto and figures as such in much art-historical literature, but many scholars now challenge the attribution, feeling that Giotto's undoubted works in the Arena Chapel at Padua differ so thoroughly from those of Assisi in both sentiment and formal organization that it is hard to imagine that he should have painted both. There are 28 scenes in the cycle; the first one and the last three differ in style from the rest and have been attributed to the *Master of St Cecilia.

Master of the Life of the Virgin or **Master of the Life of Mary** (active *c*.1460–90). German painter, named after a series of eight panels illustrating the life of the Virgin, of which the *Presentation in the Temple* is in the National Gallery, London, and the remainder in the Alte Pinakothek, Munich. He was one of the outstanding Cologne painters of his time, and his affinities with Dirk *Bouts and Rogier van der *Weyden suggest that he trained in the Netherlands. None of the pictures attributed to him is dated, but a *Crucifixion* in the hospital church at Cues on the Moselle, generally accepted as his work, is probably from about 1465.

Master of the Playing Cards (active mid-15th century). German engraver, named after a set of playing cards depicting human figures, animals, flowers, etc., now mainly divided between the Kupferstichkabinett in Dresden and the Bibliothèque Nationale in Paris. They have been dated as early as the 1430s and he was one of the first distinct artistic personalities in the history of engraving. More than a hundred prints have been attributed to him, his style being characterized by closely observed naturalistic detail and the use of short, densely packed parallel strokes to create shading.

Master of Třeboň or **of Wittingau.** Bohemian painter, active in the late 14th century, named after his main work, three panels (*c*.1380–90) from an altarpiece originally in the monastery at Třeboň (Wittingau in German) in the Czech Republic and now in the National Gallery, Prague. He was the outstanding Bohemian painter of his time and because of his combination of elegant forms and naturalistic details he is sometimes claimed as a pioneer of the *International Gothic style.

Master of the Virgo inter Virgines (active *c*.1480–1500). Netherlandish painter, named after a picture representing the Virgin Mary with the virgin saints Barbara, Catherine, Cecilia, and Ursula (Rijksmuseum, Amsterdam). He is thought to have worked in Delft, for his style is reflected in the woodcut illustrations (which he presumably designed) to several books published there between 1482 and 1498. About twenty paintings have been attributed to him, revealing a very distinctive and distinguished artist, who obtained his highly emotional effects through intense colours, desolate landscapes, and gaunt figures. His work is sometimes awkward but always sincere and involving. Two of his finest paintings are the *Crucifixion* (Bowes Mus., Barnard Castle) and the *Entombment* (Walker AG, Liverpool).

Master of Vyšší Brod (or of **Hohenfurth**). Bohemian painter, so called after his main work, a large altarpiece with scenes from the life of Christ (*c*.1350, NG, Prague) painted for the monastery of Vyšší Brod (Hohenfurth in German) in the Czech Republic. The anonymous master combined knowledge of Italian painting with Bohemian traditions to create the courtly style characteristic of Prague in the third quarter of the 15th century.

masterpiece. A term now loosely applied to the finest work by a particular artist or to any work of art of acknowledged greatness or of pre-eminence in some particular field or respect. Originally it meant the piece of work by which a craftsman, having finished his training, gained the rank of 'master' in his guild.

Master Theodoric (active mid-14th century). Bohemian painter. He is first certainly documented in 1359, when he is described as court painter to the emperor Charles IV in Prague. However, he may well be identical with a Theodoric who in 1348 became first head of the newly founded painters' guild in Prague. In 1367 he was rewarded for his only documented work—the extraordinarily rich decoration of the Chapel of the Holy Cross in Karlstein Castle near Prague. The decoration features more than a hundred panels of saints, prophets, and angels, most of them still in situ, together with frescos and coloured stone inlays. His figures are rather heavy in form but softly modelled, and he is regarded as one of the originators of the 'Soft Style' that was characteristic of much central European painting in the late 14th and early 15th centuries.

Mateo de Compostela (active late 12th century). Spanish *Romanesque architect and possibly sculptor. An inscription dated 1188 on the Portico de la Gloria at the cathedral of Santiago de Compostela names Mateo as the director of works. It has usually been assumed that he was the sculptor as well as the architect of the portico (which features the greatest ensemble of Spanish sculpture of this period), but this is by no means certain.

Mathieu, Georges (1921–). French painter. In the 1950s he gained an international reputation as one of the leading exponents of expressive abstraction. This was partly because of a flair for publicity that has led to him being described as 'the Salvador *Dalí of *Art Informel'. He works rapidly, often on a large scale, with sweeping, impulsive gestures, sometimes squeezing paint straight from the tube on to the canvas. He regards himself as a traditional history painter working with abstract means, and he has painted dressed in armour in front of an audience.

Matisse, Henri (1869–1954). French painter, sculptor, draughtsman, printmaker, and designer, one of the most illustrious artists of the 20th century. From the 1920s he enjoyed an international reputation alongside *Picasso as the foremost painter of his time. Unlike Picasso, he was a late starter in art, and he was not quite so prolific or versatile, but for sensitivity of line and beauty of colouring he stands unrivalled among his contemporaries. He began studying art in 1891 after abandoning a legal career. His early pictures—mainly still lifes and landscapes—were sober in

colour, but in the summer of 1896, painting in Brittany, he began to adopt the lighter palette of the *Impressionists. In 1899 he started to experiment with the *Neo-Impressionist technique, which he still used five years later in one of his first major works—the celebrated *Luxe, calme et volupté* (1904–5, Mus. d'Orsay, Paris), exhibited at the *Salon des Indépendants in 1905 and bought by *Signac. During this period he had been painting with *Marquet, and had met *Derain and through him *Vlaminck; in 1905, together with these and other friends from student days, he took part in the exhibition at the *Salon d'Automne that launched *Fauvism. In the same year (Matisse's annus mirabilis) he acquired his first important patrons—the expatriate Americans Gertrude, Leo, and Michael *Stein—and they were soon followed by others. Previously he had struggled to earn a living, but he was now free from financial worries and could afford to travel (before the First World War he visited Germany, where his work was becoming influential among the *Expressionists, Morocco, Russia, and Spain). His growing reputation also attracted many pupils to the art school he ran in Paris from 1907 to 1911.

Matisse had met Picasso as early as 1906, and during the second decade of the century he was influenced by *Cubism (or rather responded to its challenge) and painted some of his most austere and formal pictures (*Bathers by a River*, 1916–17, Art Inst. of Chicago). In the 1920s, however, he returned to the luminous serenity that characterized his work for the rest of his long career. From 1916 he spent most of his winters on the Riviera, mainly at Nice and also at Vence. The luxuriously sensual works he painted there—odalisques, still lifes of tropical fruits and flowers, and glowing interiors—are irradiated with the strong sun and rich colours of the south. During the 1930s he travelled widely again, but in 1940 he settled permanently in the south of France to escape the German occupation of Paris. Following two major operations for duodenal cancer in 1941, he was confined to bed or a wheelchair, but he worked until the end of his life and one of his greatest and most original works was created in 1949–51, when he was in his eighties. This is the Chapel of the Rosary at Vence, a gift of thanksgiving for a woman who had nursed him after his operations, then become a nun at this Dominican convent. Matisse designed every detail, including the priests' vestments. The stained-glass windows show his familiar love of colour, but the walls feature murals of pure white ceramic tiles decorated with black line drawings of inspired simplicity. Matisse was not a believer, but he created here one of the most moving religious buildings of the 20th century and expressed what he called 'the nearly religious feeling I have for life'.

In his bedridden final years Matisse also embarked on another kind of highly original work, using brightly coloured cut-out paper shapes (*gouaches découpées*) arranged into purely abstract patterns (*L'Escargot*, 1953, Tate, London). 'The paper cut-out', he said, 'allows me to draw in the colour. It is a simplification for me. Instead of drawing the outline and putting the colour inside it—the one modifying the other—I draw straight into the colour.' The colours he used in his cut-outs were often so strong that his doctor advised him to wear dark glasses. They must rank among the most joyous works ever created by an artist in old age. Unlike many of his great contemporaries, Matisse did not attempt to express in his work the troubled times through which he lived. 'What I dream of', he wrote, 'is an art of balance, of purity and serenity devoid of troubling or disturbing subject matter ... like a comforting influence, a mental balm—something like a good armchair in which one rests from physical fatigue.'

Matisse made sculptures at intervals throughout his career, the best known probably being the four bronzes called *The Back I–IV* (1909–*c*.1929, casts in Tate, London, and elsewhere), in which he progressively removed all detail, paring the figure down to massively simple forms. He also designed sets and costumes for *Diaghilev and was a brilliant book illustrator. His work is represented in most important collections of modern art, the finest holdings being at the *Barnes Foundation in Merion, Pennsylvania; the Hermitage, St Petersburg; and the Pushkin Museum, Moscow. There are also Matisse museums in Le Cateau (his birthplace) and Nice.

His son **Pierre Matisse** (1900–89), an art dealer, settled in the USA in 1925 and became an American citizen in 1942. His gallery in New York (opened 1932) dealt particularly in the work of leading *Surrealists, but he also represented artists as varied as *Balthus, *Chagall, and *Giacometti.

Matta (Roberto Matta Echaurren) (1911–2002). Chilean painter and sculptor active mainly in Paris, but also in Italy and the USA. He trained as an architect but turned to painting in 1937 and in the same year joined the *Surrealist movement. In 1939 he fled from Europe to New York, where with other émigrés including *Breton, *Ernst, *Masson, and *Tanguy he formed a strong and influential Surrealist presence. He played a particularly significant role in encouraging *Gorky, *Pollock, and others to experiment with *automatic techniques. From about 1944 he began to create his most characteristic works—large canvases bordering on abstraction that evoke fantastic subjective landscapes and take as their theme the precariousness of human existence in a world dominated by machines and hidden forces. In 1948 he broke with the Surrealists and returned to Europe, but his work continued in a similar vein. He lived in Rome in the early 1950s, then mainly in Paris, although he travelled widely. In 1957 he began making sculpture.

Matteo di Giovanni (active 1452–d. 1495). Italian painter. He was a native of Borgo San Sepolcro, *Piero della Francesca's home town, and he painted the wings and *predella (Pinacoteca, Sansepolcro) of the altarpiece of which Piero's *Baptism of Christ* (NG, London) was the centre panel. However, he spent most of his career in Siena, where he seems to have been one of the most popular and prolific painters of the second half of the 15th century. His style was elegant, linear, and decorative.

Maulbertsch (or **Maulpertsch**), **Franz Anton** (1724–96). The outstanding Austrian decorative painter of the 18th century. He was based in Vienna for most of his career, but he was active (and extremely productive) over a wide area of central Europe; most of his works (altarpieces as well as frescos) are still in the churches and secular buildings in Austria, the Czech Republic, Hungary, and Slovakia for which they were painted. Maulbertsch's vivacious, colourful, and emotional style was almost completely resistant to *Neoclassical influences, representing the last glorious flowering of the *Baroque and *Rococo tradition. His painterly dash is even more apparent in his oil sketches, which are well represented in the Barockmuseum, Vienna, and he was also an outstanding etcher.

maulstick (**mahlstick** or **rest-stick**). A wooden rod about 1 m (3 ft) long with a padded knob at one end, used by painters to support and steady the brush hand, particularly when working on detailed passages. Maulsticks are first recorded in the 16th century, and from the 17th century they often appear in artists' self-portraits.

Mauritshuis. The royal picture gallery in The Hague, opened to the public in 1820. The building, designed by Jacob van *Campen in 1633 as a palace for Count Johan Maurits of Nassau-Siegen (Maurice of Nassau), is one of the masterpieces of Dutch architecture. It houses one of the world's choicest collections of 17th-century Dutch painting (with pictures also from the 15th, 16th, and 18th centuries), including such celebrated works as *Rembrandt's *Anatomy Lesson of Dr Tulp* and *Vermeer's *View of Delft*.

Mauve, Anton (1838–88). Dutch painter, one of the leading artists of the *Hague School. He concentrated on small pictures of unpretentious subjects—dunes, meadows, and beaches—painted in light, silvery tones. His sincere and modest spirit made a deep impression on van *Gogh, who was a cousin of Mauve's wife and spent some time working with him in 1881–2. Mauve was a prolific and popular artist and is represented in many museums in the Netherlands and elsewhere.

Maximilian I, Emperor. *See* HABSBURG.

Maximilian II, Emperor. *See* HABSBURG.

Mayno (or **Maino**), **Juan Bautista** (1578–1641). Spanish painter. According to *Palomino he was a pupil of El *Greco in Toledo, but there is no suggestion of this in Mayno's clear and firm style, which was formed in Italy (his stay is not precisely documented, but he seems to have spent most of the first decade of the 17th century there). Paintings such as the *Adoration of the Shepherds* (1611, Prado, Madrid) show echoes of *Caravaggio (no other Spanish artist was so directly influenced by him) and of Guido *Reni, who is said to have been a friend of Mayno. In 1613 he took holy orders and subsequently did little painting, but after moving from Toledo to Madrid in about 1620 he was drawing master to the future Philip IV (*see* HABSBURG). The most important painting of his later career is the *Recovery of Bahía* (1634–5, Prado), part of a series of battle pictures for the Buen Retiro Palace that also included the *Surrender of Breda* by his friend *Velázquez.

Mazo, Juan Bautista Martínez del (c.1612/15–67). Spanish painter. He was a pupil of *Velázquez, married his daughter in 1633, and succeeded him as court painter in 1661. His life is fairly well documented, but his work is not. Among his very few signed paintings is a portrait of Queen Mariana (1666, NG, London), and many of the works attributed to him were formerly given to Velázquez, whose mature style he imitated with great assurance. In addition to portraits he painted some excellent landscapes.

Mazzoni, Sebastiano (c.1611–78). Italian painter, poet, and architect, born in Florence and active mainly in Venice, where he settled in 1646/8. He was one of the most individualistic of Italian *Baroque painters, often choosing unusual subjects and expressing a vivid sense of movement with his brilliantly free brushwork. His work looks forward to 18th-century Venetian painting and he may have been Sebastiano *Ricci's first teacher.

Meckenem, Israhel van the Younger (c.1440/50–1503). German engraver, the son of an engraver of the same name, active c.1450–65. He is thought to have trained with his father and probably with *Master E. S., whose work he copied. His oeuvre is bigger than that of any other 15th-century engraver; about 600 plates are attributed to him, and in some instances over a hundred prints have been preserved from each plate. Like many early engravers, he also worked as a goldsmith. Although he was a minor figure as a creative artist (much of his work consisted of copies), he is important in showing the growing popularity of engraving. He was the first artist to engrave his own features (in a double portrait together with his wife, c.1490) and looks a very shrewd individual.

Medici. Italian family of bankers and merchants that ruled Florence and later Tuscany for most of the period from 1434 to 1737 and was famous for its patronage of learning and the arts throughout the *Renaissance. Unlike most of the great Italian ruling dynasties, the Medici were not primarily military men, gaining their power through wealth and political astuteness rather than force. Their influence extended beyond the city and the region, for the family produced three popes and two queens of France.

The Medici name appears in Florentine records as early as the 12th century, but the real founder of the family fortune was **Giovanni di Bicci de' Medici** (1360–1429), who became one of the leading bankers in Italy and in 1421 was appointed gonfalonier (head of Florence's governing council). He also began the family tradition of art patronage, notably by commissioning *Brunelleschi to build the Old Sacristy of the church of S. Lorenzo in 1419. His son **Cosimo** (1389–1464) was effectively ruler of Florence from 1434, although in theory he was an ordinary citizen of the republic. His major artistic undertaking was the building of the family palace (now known as the Palazzo Medici-Riccardi), designed by *Michelozzo and begun in 1445. The other artists he employed included *Donatello and *Uccello, and he was an important collector of manuscripts, founding what is now the Laurentian Library in Florence. His son **Piero** (1416–69), known as Piero the Gouty, is best remembered in artistic terms for commissioning Benozzo *Gozzoli's celebrated frescos in the family palace. Piero's son and successor, **Lorenzo the Magnificent** (1449–92), was the most famous member of the family. A poet and scholar, he had a great interest in the classical world and made a fine collection of antiquities, including sculpture, gems, and cameos. He also patronized some of the best contemporary artists, including the young *Michelangelo, who was treated almost like an adopted son (he lived in the Medici Palace for a time and had access to Lorenzo's sculpture garden, which served as a kind of informal art *academy). Lorenzo's most important architectural commission was the Villa Medici at Poggio a Caiano, near Florence, designed by Giuliano da Sangallo and built in the 1480s. For another villa,

near Volterra, he commissioned paintings from *Botticelli and other artists. This building has been destroyed, but Botticelli produced other work for the Medici: his *Primavera* and *Birth of Venus* were certainly owned by the family and were perhaps painted for Lorenzo's second cousin, **Lorenzo di Pierfrancesco** (1463–1503). Lorenzo the Magnificent was succeeded by his son **Piero** (1471–1503), who was exiled from Florence in 1494 after being forced to make humiliating concessions to Charles VIII of France, who had invaded Italy. The Medici were absent from Florence until 1512, when Piero's brother **Giuliano** (1479–1516) returned and assumed power. From 1527 to 1530 the family was again expelled, then **Alessandro** (1511–37), an illegitimate descendant of Lorenzo the Magnificent, regained control and assumed the title of duke of Florence. A despotic ruler, he was assassinated in 1537 and succeeded by a distant cousin **Cosimo** (1519–74), who restored stability to the city. In 1557 Cosimo gained control of Siena and most of its dependent territories, giving him dominion over much of the region, and in 1569 Pope Pius V awarded him the hereditary title of Grand Duke of Tuscany. Unlike some other Medici rulers, Cosimo was not a connoisseur, but he appreciated the propaganda value of art and he spent lavishly on glorifying himself and his family and on embellishing Florence. *Bronzino was his favourite artist, and the others he employed included *Ammanati, *Cellini, *Giambologna, *Pontormo, and *Vasari, who designed the *Uffizi, originally used as offices but soon adapted to include gallery space for the family art collections. Its great collection of artist's self-portraits was founded by Cardinal **Leopoldo de' Medici** (1617–75), who in this way made perhaps the most distinctive contribution to the arts of any of the later members of the family. Cosimo's descendants ruled until 1737, when the last Medici Grand Duke, **Gian Gastone**, died without a male heir and was succeeded by a distant relative, Francis Stephen, Duke of Lorraine. At this point Gian Gastone's sister, **Anna Maria Luisa** (1667–1743), presented the family collections to the city of Florence.

The three Medici popes were Leo X (reigned 1513–21), Clement VII (1523–34), and Leo XI (reigned very briefly in 1605); the first two were notable art patrons. Leo X (born **Giovanni de' Medici** in 1475) was the second son of Lorenzo the Magnificent. As pope he continued his predecessor Julius II's projects in the rebuilding of St Peter's and the decoration of the Vatican Stanze (*see* RAPHAEL). His extravagant spending (on war and personal pleasures as well as art) left the papal treasury in heavy debt. Clement VII (born **Giulio de' Medici** in 1478) was a nephew of Lorenzo the Magnificent. The artists he patronized included Cellini, Michelangelo, and *Sebastiano del Piombo. The two Medici queens of France were **Catherine de' Medici** (1519–89), known in France as Catherine de Médicis, and **Maria de' Medici** (1573–1642), known in France as Marie de Médicis. Catherine was the wife of Henry II and after his death in 1559 she was regent or adviser to three of their sons who became king in turn: Francis II, Charles IX, and Henry III. The artists she patronized included Niccolò dell'*Abate, Germain *Pilon, and Francesco *Primaticcio. Maria was the second wife of Henry IV and after his death in 1610 she became regent for their son Louis XIII. *Rubens painted a great cycle of paintings glorifying her life (1622–5, Louvre, Paris). The image it presents of her is far from the truth, for she was politically inept and ended her life in exile.

Medici Venus. Marble statue of naked Venus (Uffizi, Florence), first recorded for certain in 1638 in the Villa Medici in Rome. It is signed 'Cleomenes son of Apollodorus', but in the 18th century its fame as a model of female beauty was so great that the signature's authenticity was doubted and the statue was attributed to such illustrious names as *Phidias and *Praxiteles (to whose *Aphrodite of Cnidus* it bears some resemblance in pose). Several other statues of similar type exist, but in spite of the *Medici Venus*'s quite severe restorations, it far outdid its rivals in fame, and it was one of the greatest prizes that Napoleon brought to France when Italy was under his dominion (it was in Paris 1803–15). As late as 1840 it was described by *Ruskin as 'one of the purest and most elevated incarnations of woman conceivable', but its reputation has since crumbled, Martin Robertson (*A History of Greek Art*, 1975) describing it as being 'among the most charmless remnants of antiquity'. It is now considered to be a copy of *c*.100 BC deriving from an original of the time of Praxiteles.

medium. Term used to refer to the material or form of expression used by an artist; thus painting, sculpture, and drawing are three different media, and bronze, marble, and wood are three of the media of sculpture. In a more restricted sense, the term refers to the substance with which *pigment is mixed to make paint; for example, gum arabic in *watercolour, egg yolk in *tempera, *linseed oil (most usually) in *oil painting. *See also* VEHICLE.

Meegeren, Han van. *See* BREDIUS.

megilp. A painting *medium consisting of mastic varnish mixed with *linseed oil. It makes paint glossy and easy to manipulate, for which reason it was popular in the 18th and 19th centuries; however, it is a dangerous aid, in time rendering the paint yellow and brittle.

Meissonier, Ernest (1815–91). French painter, illustrator, and sculptor. He was immensely successful with his small-format, nigglingly detailed historical paintings and historical *genre pieces (particularly scenes in *Three Musketeers* vein or from the Napoleonic campaigns) and from the 1840s he received the highest official honours, including the Grand Cross of the Legion of Honour in 1889—he was the first painter to win this award. Astonishingly conceited as well as mean-spirited, he cultivated a huge white beard and liked to be photographed or painted in attitudes of fiercely profound thought, as in his self-portrait of 1889 in the Musée d'Orsay, Paris. He did his best work when he was at his least pretentious. His landscapes are attractive descriptive exercises and his *Rue de la Mortellerie* (1848, Mus. d'Orsay), which shows a corpse-strewn Paris street during the revolutionary events of 1848, has genuine pathos and impressed *Delacroix. There are large collections of Meissonier's work in the Musée d'Orsay and in the Wallace Collection, London.

Meit, Conrad (*c*.1475–1550/1). German sculptor, born at Worms. From about 1506 to 1510 he worked in Wittenberg at the court of Frederick the Wise, elector of Saxony, collaborating with *Cranach. Soon afterwards he moved to the Netherlands, where he was court sculptor to the *Habsburg rulers for most of his career. His work included a number of large monuments, but his most characteristic sculptures are small figures and portraits, most notably sensuous free-standing nudes such as the well-known alabaster *Judith with the Head of Holofernes* (*c*.1510–15, Bayerisches Nationalmuseum, Munich). In these he created a distinctive type of German *Renaissance sculpture, combining Italian idealism with northern particularity of detail.

Meléndez, Luis (1716–80). Spanish painter, active in Madrid. He painted various subjects, but from the 1760s he specialized in still life and is regarded as the finest Spanish painter in this field in the 18th century (he is sometimes called 'the Spanish *Chardin'). However, he spent much of his life in poverty. His work is rare outside Spain, but there are examples of his still lifes in London (NG) and York (City AG), and there is a striking self-portrait of 1746 in the Louvre, Paris. Several other members of his family were painters, including two sisters.

Mellan, Claude (1598–1688). French engraver. One of the most renowned engravers of his period, he was best known for his portraits, but he also made prints after *Poussin and *Vouet, for example. He was a technical virtuoso and instead of using cross-*hatching he obtained his effects of light and shade by varying the thickness of his lines. The most famous example of his prowess is his *Sudarium of St Veronica* (1642), a portrait of Christ made up of a single continuous spiral line that goes round from the centre to the edge like the groove on a gramophone record. Mellan also painted, but few of his pictures survive.

Mellon, Andrew W. (1855–1937). American businessman, public official, art collector, and philanthropist. A banker and steel, coke, and oil magnate, he became secretary to the US treasury (1921–32), ambassador to England (1932–3), and one of the richest men in the world. In 1937, shortly before his death, he donated his collection (particularly rich in Dutch and English painting) to the nation, together with funds to build a gallery to house them, thus creating the National Gallery of Art in Washington (opened 1941). His son, **Paul**

Mellon (1907–99), was also one of the greatest collectors of his generation, his main field of interest being British art. In 1966 he founded the Yale Center for British Art at New Haven. Opened in 1977, the Center is not only a major gallery, but also a research institution, with important collections of books and photographs. Its sister institution, the Paul Mellon Centre for Studies in British Art, was established in London in 1970. It is an educational charity whose purpose is to advance the study of British art, mainly by sponsorship of publications and support of research.

Melozzo da Forlì (1438–94). Italian painter from Forlì in the Romagna, active mainly in Loreto, Rome, and Urbino. He was an attractive and idiosyncratic painter who achieved a high reputation in his time, but little of his work survives intact and he has been a neglected figure until fairly recently. His style was indebted to *Piero della Francesca and he was renowned for his skill in *perspective and *illusionism; he was, indeed, credited with being the inventor of the extreme form of foreshortening known as *di *sotto in sù*, of which *Mantegna was another great exponent. Melozzo's skill in this field is seen in his fresco of the *Ascension* (1478–80) for the dome of SS. Apostoli in Rome, fragments of which are in the Quirinal Palace and the Vatican.

Memlinc (or **Memling**), **Hans** (*c*.1430/40–94). Netherlandish painter, active in Bruges from 1465. He was born in Seligenstadt, near Frankfurt, but nothing of his German heritage survives in his paintings, which show close connections with Rogier van der *Weyden, by whom—according to plausible tradition—he was taught. His softened and sweetened version of Rogier's style (there is some influence also from *Bouts) made him the most popular Netherlandish painter of his day. Whereas Rogier excelled in the depiction of intense emotion, Memlinc's impeccably crafted paintings are quiet, restrained, pious, and beautifully balanced. Tax records indicate that he was one of Bruges's wealthiest citizens and his large output shows he must have had a busy workshop. His style changed very little and it is difficult to place undated paintings in a chronological scheme. He painted numerous portraits and showed rather more originality in this field than in religious painting. Among his patrons were Italians then living in Bruges (*Tommaso Portinari* and his wife *Maria Portinari*, c.1468, Met. Mus., New York), and his portraits seem to have influenced artists such as Giovanni *Bellini in northern Italy. Gerard *David was among the local artists who continued his tradition. Memlinc's work is in many major collections, but it can be best seen in the museum devoted to him in Bruges.

Memmi, Lippo (active 1317–47). Sienese painter, Simone *Martini's brother-in-law and most able follower. They jointly signed the celebrated *Annunciation* (1333, Uffizi, Florence) and their respective shares in it are uncertain. Several other works are signed by Memmi, including *Madonnas* in the Gemäldegalerie, Berlin, and S. Maria dei Servi, Siena, showing his refined draughtsmanship, delicate palette, and extremely sensitive modelling. He was not an innovator, but an indication of the high quality of his work is that several paintings are disputed between him and Simone.

Meneses Osorio, Francisco. *See* MURILLO.

Mengs, Anton Raphael (1728–79). German painter, the son of a court painter in Dresden, **Ismael Mengs** (1688–1764). His father brought him up with harsh severity to be a great painter, on the models particularly of *Correggio and *Raphael (from whom he gained his Christian names). In 1740 he was taken to Rome and there established a reputation as a youthful prodigy. He returned to Germany in 1744 and in the next few years achieved success as a portraitist in Dresden. In 1748–9 he made another visit to Rome, during which he married an Italian girl, and in 1752 he settled in the city, becoming a close friend of *Winckelmann, who provided much of the theoretical inspiration for his work. It was for Winckelmann's patron, Cardinal Alessandro *Albani, that Mengs painted his most famous work, the ceiling fresco *Parnassus* (1761) in the Villa Albani (now the Villa Torlonia), Rome. The fresco now seems flimsy and simpering, but it was the basis of Mengs's enormous contemporary reputation (he was widely regarded not only as a leader of the *Neoclassical movement, but also as the greatest living painter).

It breaks completely with *Baroque *illusionism, treating the scene exactly as if it were to be seen at normal eye level, and is full of allusions to the *antique and the High *Renaissance. In 1761–9 and 1774–7 he worked as court painter in Spain, carrying out a large amount of decoration in the Royal Palace, Madrid. His frescos there are dull and sterile, but it is a sign of the move in taste towards Neoclassicism that certain of his works were preferred to those of his rival Giambattista *Tiepolo, now regarded as an incomparably greater artist. Mengs was influential through his writings on art (which appeared in or soon after his lifetime in English, French, German, Italian, and Spanish) as well as his paintings. Today his portraits are considered more successful than his history paintings, and he was *Batoni's main rival as the leading portraitist in Rome.

Menpes, Mortimer. *See* WHISTLER, J.M.

Menzel, Adolph (1815–1905). German painter and printmaker, active mainly in Berlin, where in 1832 he took over his dead father's lithographic business. He was extremely industrious and achieved fame with 400 illustrations (wood engravings from his lively drawings) for Franz Kugler's *History of Frederick the Great* (1840–2). In painting he worked on similar themes and with comparable success, creating the popular image of the founder of the Prussian state. From the 1860s he turned to subjects from modern life and was one of the first German painters to depict the picturesque qualities of industry (*The Steel Mill*, 1872–5, Alte NG, Berlin). Today, however, Menzel is most highly regarded not for the works that brought him contemporary acclaim, but for a series of informal landscapes and interiors dating from the 1840s that remained virtually unknown in his lifetime. They are remarkably free and fresh in technique, unorthodox in composition, and both bold and refined in their treatment of light, presaging the developments of *Impressionism (*The Artist's Sister with a Candle*, 1847, Neue Pin., Munich). His attitude towards these paintings was strange; he kept them hidden and referred to Impressionism as 'the art of laziness', and when he visited Paris in 1855, 1867, and 1868 the artist he most admired was the tiresomely meticulous *Meissonier.

Merian, Matthäus (1593–1650). German printmaker and publisher, active mainly in Frankfurt, where he ran an enormously prolific business. It published thousands of prints, many of them views of European towns for various topographical books. Much of this output came from the hands of assistants, among them Wenceslaus *Hollar. Merian's daughter **Maria Sibylla Merian** (1647–1717) trained as a flower painter. From 1685 she lived mainly in Amsterdam and in 1699–1701 she visited Surinam in South America, returning with numerous drawings and specimens of insects, including butterflies. In 1705 she published a book on these, illustrated with hand-coloured engravings that are remarkable for their scientific accuracy as well as their delicate beauty. Her brother, **Matthäus Merian the Younger** (1621–87), ran the family business in Frankfurt after his father's death.

Merz. *See* SCHWITTERS.

Mesdag, Hendrik Willem (1831–1915). Dutch painter and collector. He abandoned the family profession of banking in 1866 and became one of the leading artists of the *Hague School, particularly noted for his beach and sea scenes. His best-known work is the vast panorama (1881) of the fishing village of Scheveningen—about 120 m (400 ft) in circumference—housed in a specially designed building in The Hague. The Mesdag Museum, in the same city, contains his excellent collection of paintings, rich in works by members of the *Barbizon and Hague Schools, which he presented to the nation in 1903.

Mesens, E. L. T. (1903–71). Belgian musician, poet, collagist, exhibition organizer, and dealer. His interest in the visual arts developed under the influence of *Duchamp and *Picabia, whom he met in Paris in 1921, and he was influenced towards *Surrealism by the paintings of de *Chirico. He became a friend and champion of *Magritte and a highly active figure in the Surrealist movement, although more as an organizer than an artist. In 1938 he settled in London and became director of the London Gallery in Cork Street, the headquarters of Surrealism in England, organizing exhibitions of the work of many European artists there (including *Ernst, *Schwitters, and *Tan-

guy); he also edited the gallery's publication, the *London Bulletin*, an important documentary source for the period (it ran for twenty issues, 1938–40). He returned to Belgium in the 1950s. In his own work as an artist, Mesens was best known for his collages, which he created from an assortment of materials—tickets, ribbons, pieces of paper and print, etc. He made extensive use of printed words to create disconcerting or amusing ambiguities and suggested meanings, some of which might almost be regarded as anticipations of *Conceptual art.

Meštrović, Ivan (1883–1962). Yugoslavian (Croatian)-born sculptor who became an American citizen in 1954. He studied at the Academy in Vienna, 1900–4, and in 1908–9 lived in Paris, where he met *Rodin. After returning to Yugoslavia he worked in a style that was basically classical but furbished with a superficial air of modernity. He spent the First World War in Rome, Geneva, Paris, and London, and in 1919 returned to Yugoslavia, where he received many public commissions, including an enormous mausoleum outside Belgrade in commemoration of the Unknown Soldier (1934), one of the many works in which he expressed his ardent patriotism. From 1943 to 1946 he lived in Switzerland, then settled in the USA, where he was professor of sculpture at Syracuse University, New York, 1947–55, and at the University of South Bend, Indiana, from 1955 until his death. His work in the USA included a number of monuments. The great reputation he enjoyed in his lifetime has declined since his death, the rhetoric of his large-scale works now seeming rather ponderous; his smaller, more lyrical pieces have dated less. There are Meštrović museums in Split (his former house, which he designed himself) and Zagreb.

metal cut. A print made from a metal plate in which the parts of the design that take the ink are raised in *relief (as in a *woodcut) rather than incised into the plate as in a *line engraving. Prints done in the *manière criblée* are examples of the type and William *Blake used a personal version of the technique in his illuminated books.

metalpoint. Method of drawing using a small metal-tipped rod on paper or other material that has been coated with a special *ground. This coating is slightly granular, causing a trace of the metal to rub off on it. The metal may be copper, gold, lead, or (most commonly) silver, which gives an attractive fine grey line that oxidizes to a light brown. Often the ground is tinted with pigment, increasing the opportunity for delicate colouristic effects. The strength of tone can hardly be varied at all, so the technique depends on the quality of the drawn line and is best suited to work on a small scale. It demands great certainty of purpose and hand, for the line cannot be removed except by disturbing the ground. Silverpoint first appeared in medieval Italy and was particularly popular in the 15th century; *Dürer and *Leonardo were perhaps the greatest exponents of the medium. It went out of fashion in the 17th century, probably because the graphite *pencil was coming in, but was revived in the 18th century by *miniature painters, especially in France.

Metaphysical Painting. A style of painting invented by de *Chirico in about 1913 and practised by him, *Carrà (from 1917), *Morandi (from 1918), and a few other Italian artists until about 1920. The term (*Pittura Metafisica*) was coined by de Chirico and Carrà in 1917, when both were patients at a military hospital in Ferrara. The meaning attached to the word 'metaphysical', which occurs in the titles of several pictures by de Chirico particularly, was never precisely formulated, but the style is characterized by images conveying a sense of mystery and hallucination. This was achieved partly by unreal perspectives and lighting, partly by the adoption of a strange iconography involving, for example, the use of tailor's dummies and statues in place of human figures, and partly by an incongruous juxtaposition of realistically depicted objects in a manner later taken over by some of the *Surrealists. However, the dreamlike quality conveyed by Metaphysical Painters differed from that of the Surrealists because of their concern with pictorial structure; their works often have an architectural sense of repose deriving from Italian *Renaissance art.

Metropolitan Museum of Art, New York. The largest and most comprehensive collection of art in the USA and one of the greatest in the world. It was founded in 1870 by a group of art collectors, civic leaders, and philanthropists, and after two temporary locations for the museum, it opened at its present site in Central Park in 1880. The building was designed by Calvert Vaux (one of the designers of Central Park) in Gothic style, and the grandiose classical façade overlooking Fifth Avenue was added in the early 20th century. There have been numerous other extensions over the years, and the original building now forms only a small part of the vast structure. The museum is owned by the city, but is supported mainly by private endowment, and the history of its foundation and growth illustrates the rapid rise of New York at the end of the 19th century as the financial and cultural capital of North America, and the growing economic supremacy of America over Europe. In the first half-century or so of its existence, at a time when the major public collections in Europe were engaged in consolidation, relying largely on their purchase grants and other state aid, the Metropolitan Museum was being built up out of the private fortunes of great businessmen, who collected for prestige rather than out of connoisseurship, but collected only first-class works of art. It has also benefited from a number of endowed purchase grants, many of them unconditional, and its collections are now rich in virtually every field of the *fine and *applied arts from all parts of the world. Notable scholars who have been employed at the museum include Roger *Fry, John *Pope-Hennessy, and Wilhelm *Valentiner. Much of the collection of medieval art is housed in a separate building called the Cloisters in Fort Tryon Park, overlooking the Hudson River. Opened in 1938, the Cloisters is a medieval-style structure, largely made up of parts of *Romanesque and *Gothic buildings transported from Europe. Many of the works it houses were collected by the American sculptor George Grey Barnard (1863–1938), who lived in France for much of his career.

Metsu, Gabriel (1629–67). Dutch painter, active in his native Leiden, then in Amsterdam, where he had settled by 1657. *Houbraken says he was a pupil of *Dou, but Metsu's early works are very different from his—typically historical and mythological scenes, broadly rather than minutely painted. Metsu also painted portraits and still lifes, but his most characteristic works are *genre scenes, some of which rank among the finest of their period. He concentrated on scenes of genteel middle-class life, fairly close to de *Hooch and *Terborch in style, but with a personal stamp. One of his best-known pictures, *The Sick Child* (c.1660–5, Rijksmuseum, Amsterdam), is often compared with *Vermeer's work because of its strength of design. His masterpiece, however, is perhaps *Woman Reading a Letter* (c.1660–5, NG, Dublin), in which the secondary figure of a maid examines a picture on the wall—a telling indication of the wide social appeal of art in 17th-century Holland. Metsu's paintings are rarely dated, so his development and relationships with other artists are difficult to trace.

Metzger, Gustav. *See* AUTO-DESTRUCTIVE ART.

Metzinger, Jean (1883–1956). French painter and writer on art. After passing through *Neo-Impressionist and *Fauvist phases he became one of the earliest devotees of *Cubism and a central figure of the *Section d'Or group. However, he is remembered less for his paintings than as the co-author with *Gleizes of *Du Cubisme* (1912), the first book to be published on the movement.

Meulen, Adam Frans van der (1632–90). Flemish painter and tapestry designer, active mainly in France. He moved to Paris in 1664, became an assistant to *Le Brun, and was made one of Louis XIV's court painters, specializing in military scenes. He accompanied the king on his campaigns, and his paintings and designs for *Gobelins tapestries are accurate historical documents of the battles they represent. His work of this type is well represented at Versailles. He also made much less grandiose pictures of such subjects as hunting parties and landscapes.

Meunier, Constantin (1831–1905). Belgian sculptor and painter, well known for his sincere but rather heavy-handed glorification of the nobility of labour in his treatment of such subjects as miners, factory workers, and stevedores. In the early 20th century he had considerable influence on younger sculptors interested in *Social Realist subjects. There is a museum of his work in Brussels and his most ambitious work,

the *Monument of Labour* (erected after his death), is in the Place de Trooz there.

Meyer, Hannes. *See* BAUHAUS.

mezzotint (It., *mezzotinto*: 'half-tint'). A printmaking method that produces subtly graduated tones rather than lines; the term also applies to a print made by this method. A metal (usually copper) plate is laboriously roughened with a serrated steel tool called a rocker, creating a texture somewhat like that of fine sandpaper over the whole surface. If inked and printed from in this condition, the plate would produce solid black. The design is formed by scraping away the textured *burr to varying degrees. When the plate has been inked and then wiped, the ink is retained where the plate is rough and will print an intense black, but where it has been smoothed, less ink is held and a lighter tone results (for the highlights the burr is completely removed and the metal polished smooth). Mezzotint was invented in the Netherlands in the early 1640s by Ludwig von *Siegen and soon spread to England, where it became an extremely popular method for reproducing paintings, especially portraits. Its heyday was the 18th century, but memorable use was made of it in the following century by John *Martin, one of the few eminent artists to make original creative use of the medium rather than reproducing someone else's designs. Like *drypoint, mezzotint yields only a small number of good impressions before the burr wears down. The technique virtually died out in the later 19th century with the development of photographic methods of reproduction, but it is still used by some printmakers who value its rich tonal qualities.

Michallon, Achille-Etna (1796–1822). French landscape painter, the first artist to win the *Prix de Rome in the historical landscape category that was established in 1817. He was a pupil of J.-L. *David and *Valenciennes and in his turn taught *Corot, who was influenced by his severe compositions and cool colour harmonies. His early death was caused by pneumonia.

Michel, Georges (1763–1843). French landscape painter. He achieved little recognition in his lifetime, but he is now regarded as an important forerunner of the *Barbizon School. His paintings were influenced by

17th-century Dutch artists (he worked as a copyist and restorer of their work), but they have a modest directness reflecting the many studies he made in the open air (*see* PLEIN AIR). He lived in Paris all his life and most of his work depicts scenes within a few miles of the city.

Michelangelo (Michelangelo Buonarroti) (1475–1564). Florentine sculptor, painter, architect, draughtsman, and poet, one of the giants of the *Renaissance and, in his later years, one of the forces that shaped *Mannerism. Michelangelo's career lasted more than 70 years and for most of that time he was the dominant figure in Italian art. His contemporaries regarded him with awe, and the word *terribilità*, which may be translated as 'frightening power', was often applied to his work. He was the subject of two detailed biographies in his lifetime, both of them by people who knew him well (*Vasari and *Condivi), and because of these and other sources (including his own letters, about 500 of which survive), more is known about him—his personal qualities as well as the details of his career—than about any previous artist. He was utterly devoted to art and religion, living frugally in spite of his fame. However, although he was scornful of the conventional trappings of success, he was sure of his own worth and was concerned about his place in society. He tended to be suspicious and withdrawn, and had a sharp temper and a sarcastic tongue, but he was affectionate and generous to his family and friends. His father, a member of the gentry, claimed noble lineage and throughout his life Michelangelo was touchy on the subject; pride of birth had much to do with the family opposition to his choice of an artistic career as well as with Michelangelo's own insistence on the status of painting and sculpture among the *liberal arts. In 1488 he was apprenticed to the painter Domenico *Ghirlandaio, but the following year he transferred to a kind of informal *academy sponsored by Lorenzo de' *Medici and overseen by the sculptor *Bertoldo di Giovanni. Michelangelo later claimed to be largely self-taught and this is probably true as far as marble carving is concerned (Bertoldo was a specialist in bronze), but Ghirlandaio was an excellent craftsman and in his workshop Michelangelo probably at least laid the foundations of his technical skill in fresco painting. Stylistically, however, he learned much more from the austere grandeur of *Giotto and *Masaccio (his earliest surviving drawings, done *c.*1490, include copies of figures from their frescos).

After the death of Lorenzo de' Medici in 1492 the political situation in Florence became unstable, and in October 1494 Michelangelo left for Bologna, where he carved three small figures for the shrine of St Dominic (*see* NICCOLÒ DELL'ARCA). He returned briefly to Florence in 1495 but in June 1496 moved to Rome, where he remained for the next five years and where he carved the two statues that established his fame when he was still in his early twenties—*Bacchus* (*c.*1496–7, Bargello, Florence) and the *Pietà* (1498–9, St Peter's, Rome). The latter is the masterpiece of his early years—a tragically expressive and yet beautiful and harmonious solution to the problem of representing a full-grown man lying dead in the lap of a woman. There are no marks of suffering—as were common in northern representations of the period—and the carving has a flawless beauty and polish demonstrating his absolute technical mastery. For unclear reasons, Michelangelo returned to Florence in 1501, leaving unfinished an altarpiece of the *Entombment* commissioned by the church of S. Agostino, Rome (NG, London), one of only two or three surviving panel paintings by him. He remained in Florence until the spring of 1505, the major completed work of the period being the marble *David* (1501–4, Accademia, Florence), which has become a symbol of Florence and Florentine art (it was originally intended for the cathedral but was instead set up outside the Palazzo Vecchio, the seat of government, David being regarded as a virtuous fighter for freedom, as the citizens of the Florentine republic liked to see themselves). Soon after the *David* was completed, Michelangelo received another great commission from the Florentine government—a huge mural of the *Battle of Cascina* for the new Council Chamber in the Palazzo Vecchio; here he worked in rivalry with *Leonardo, who was engaged on the *Battle of Anghiari* for the same room. Neither painting came to fruition, but Michelangelo completed the full-size *cartoon or part of it, and during its brief life this was highly influential (Vasari says that it was 'torn apart and divided into many pieces' because it was 'placed too freely in the hands of artists'). It is now known through a copy of the central section, as well as from some magnificent preliminary drawings (for example in the British Museum, London).

Michelangelo left the battlepiece unfinished when Pope Julius II (Giuliano della *Rovere) summoned him to Rome in 1505 to make his tomb. However, the following year Julius began the rebuilding of St Peter's, which deflected his attention from the tomb, and at his death in 1513 little had been accomplished on it. Afterwards the project dragged on for decades, causing Michelangelo to lament, 'I have wasted all my youth chained to this tomb.' It was originally conceived on the most grandiose scale, but was whittled down in successive contracts with Julius's heirs, and of the monument finally erected in S. Pietro in Vincoli, Rome, in 1545 only three figures, including the celebrated *Moses* (c.1515), are from Michelangelo's own hand. (Two figures of *Slaves*, c.1513, carved by Michelangelo for the tomb are now in the Louvre, Paris.) The other great work commissioned from Michelangelo by Julius—the frescoing of the ceiling of the Sistine Chapel (1508–12)—was equally daunting, but was brought to sublime fruition. Michelangelo, who always regarded himself as a sculptor first and foremost, was reluctant to undertake the work, but he made of it his most heroic achievement, not only for its quality as a work of art, but also in terms of the endurance and stamina he showed in completing so quickly and virtually unaided such a huge and physically uncomfortable task. There is still much debate about the exact interpretation of the scores of figures that adorn the ceiling, but the main images represent scenes from Genesis, from the Creation to the Drunkenness of Noah, forming the background to the frescos on the life of Moses and of Christ on the walls below by a number of 15th-century artists (*see* PERU-GINO). Prophets and Sibyls who foretold Christ's birth are at the sides of the ceiling, and at each corner of the central scenes are figures of beautiful nude youths (usually called the *Ignudi*). Their exact significance is uncertain, but as Kenneth *Clark wrote, 'Their physical beauty is an image of divine perfection; their alert and vigorous movements an expression of divine energy.'

From the moment of its completion the ceiling has always been regarded as one of the supreme masterpieces of pictorial art (the cleaning in the 1980s revealed anew the beauty of the colouring), and Michelangelo, at the age of 37, was recognized as the greatest artist of his day, a position he retained unchallenged until his death half a century later.

In 1516 Michelangelo was commissioned by Julius II's successor, Leo X (Giovanni de' Medici), to design a façade for the Medici parish church in Florence, S. Lorenzo, which had been left unfinished by *Brunelleschi. The project came to nothing and wasted a good deal of Michelangelo's time, but it led to two other works for S. Lorenzo—the Medici Chapel, or New Sacristy, planned as a counterpart to Brunelleschi's Old Sacristy, and the Biblioteca Laurenziana, which houses the Medici collection of books and manuscripts. Neither project was completed in accordance with Michelangelo's plans, but they nevertheless rank among his finest creations. He began work on the Medici Chapel in 1519, broke off when the Medici were expelled from Florence in 1527, restarted in 1530, and left the work incomplete in 1534 when he settled permanently in Rome. The powerful architectural forms of the building are conceived as the setting for the wall tombs of Giuliano and Lorenzo de' Medici, who are characterized in their marble figures as representatives of the Active and Contemplative Life; below them are allegorical reclining figures symbolizing Day and Night (for *Vita activa*) and Dawn and Evening (for *Vita contemplativa*). Anthony *Blunt has written of the Medici Chapel sculptures: 'there is still that superhuman quality visible in the Sistine frescoes . . . but in addition there is a feeling of brooding, of sombre disquiet, which becomes from this time a hall-mark of Michelangelo's work. They are no longer only symbols of eternal beauty; they also reflect the tragedy of human destiny.'

In the 30 years that remained to him in Rome, Michelangelo worked mainly for the papacy. He was at once commissioned to paint the *Last Judgement* in the Sistine Chapel and began the actual painting in 1536. It was unveiled on 31 October 1541, 29 years to the day after the unveiling of the Sistine Ceiling but a whole world away from it in feeling and meaning, with its massive and menacing figures and mood of wrathful desolation. In the interval the world of Michelangelo's youth had collapsed in the horror of the Sack of Rome (1527), and its confident humanism had been found insufficient in the face of the rise of Protestantism and the new, militant spirit of the Counter-Reformation. For Paul III (Alessandro *Farnese), who commissioned the *Last Judgement*, Michelangelo also executed his final works in painting, the *Conversion of St Paul* and the *Crucifixion of St Peter* (1542–50), frescos in the Cappella Paolina (Paul's private chapel) in the Vatican. The figures here are even more blunt, heavy, and unconcerned with physical allure, totally repudiating his own early ideals. Something of the same deep and troubled spirituality is seen in Michelangelo's late drawings of the Crucifixion and in two sculptures known as Pietàs (although they might more accurately be described as representing the Deposition). One (now in Florence Cathedral) was intended for his own tomb and contains a self-portrait as Nicodemus; it was begun *c.*1546 and mutilated and abandoned by Michelangelo in 1555. The other (Castello Sforza, Milan) was his last work, left unfinished at his death.

For the last twenty years of his life, however, Michelangelo devoted most of his attentions to architecture, and in this field his stature is just as great as in sculpture and painting (no other artist has approached this domination in the three major visual arts). His most important commission—indeed the most important in Christendom—was the completion of St Peter's, which had been begun under Julius II in 1506. When Michelangelo became architect in 1546, the building had advanced little since *Bramante's death in 1514. As with the Sistine Ceiling, he was initially unwilling to undertake the task, but he then proceeded with formidable energy and by the time of his death, work had advanced so far that the drum of the dome was nearly complete. Michelangelo also designed the dome itself, but as executed after his death it is probably a good deal steeper in outline than he intended. The addition of a long nave in the early 17th century altered Michelangelo's plan for a centralized church, but nevertheless the exterior of the building owes more to him than to any other architect and forms a fitting conclusion to his titanic

career. In architecture, Michelangelo's decorative vocabulary soon attained widespread currency, but it was only in the 17th century that his massive and dynamic style was fully appreciated and emulated; it is fitting that *Bernini, the great sculptor-architect of the age, should complete St Peter's with his glorious piazza. In painting and sculpture, Michelangelo's means of expression was limited almost entirely to the heroic male figure, usually nude, but in this domain he reigned supreme as no artist has done before or since, and for centuries afterwards it was virtually impossible for any artist to work in the field without referring, consciously or unconsciously, to his example.

Michelozzo di Bartolommeo (sometimes incorrectly called Michelozzo Michelozzi) (1396–1472). Florentine architect and sculptor. As a sculptor he worked for *Ghiberti (on both his sets of doors for the Florentine Baptistery) and in partnership with *Donatello (1425–*c.*1433). With Donatello he produced three major tombs—those of the anti-pope John XXIII (1424–8, Baptistery, Florence), Cardinal Rinaldo Brancacci (1426–8, S. Angelo a Nilo, Naples), and Bartolommeo Aragazzi (1427–38, Montepulciano Cathedral, but now disassembled; two angels are in the V&A, London). His style was vigorous and forthright. In his later career Michelozzo worked mainly as an architect, and he ranks as one of the leading figures of the generation after *Brunelleschi, whom he succeeded as *capomaestro* at Florence Cathedral (1446). His most famous building is the Palazzo Medici-Riccardi in Florence (begun 1445), often described as the first *Renaissance palace. Michelozzo was influential in spreading the Renaissance style; he worked in Milan, Yugoslavia, and the island of Chios.

Michiel, Marcantonio. *See* GIORGIONE.

Middleditch, Edward. *See* KITCHEN SINK SCHOOL.

Miel, Jan. *See* LAER.

Miereveld (or **Miereveldt**), **Michiel van** (1567–1641). Dutch portrait painter, active mainly in his native Delft and in The Hague. He was court painter to the House of Orange, highly successful, and very prolific: *Sandrart reports that Mierevelt himself estimated that he made about 10,000 portraits. Even though this figure must be a considerable exaggeration, his portraits certainly tend to be dull and formulaic; however, they are meticulously crafted and of great value as historical records.

Mieris, Frans van (1635–81). Dutch painter, the most distinguished member of a family of artists active in Leiden. He was one of the best pupils of Gerrit *Dou and followed his master in choice of subjects (mainly domestic *genre scenes) and in his highly polished technique. The tradition was continued by his sons **Jan** (1660–90) and **Willem** (1662–1747) and by Willem's son **Frans II** (1689–1763).

Mies van der Rohe, Ludwig. *See* BAUHAUS.

Mignard, Pierre (1612–95). French painter, one of the most successful of *Vouet's pupils. His career culminated in 1690, when, on the death of *Le Brun, he became director of the Académie Royale and first painter to the king. He was one of the principal supporters of de *Piles and the 'Rubénistes' in their battle against the *classicism of the 'Poussinistes' (*see* POUSSIN). His own historical and religious paintings, however, did not exemplify his theories, being more in the classical tradition of *Domenichino and Poussin (he spent much of his career in Italy, 1635–57). His best works are his portraits; he painted many of the members of Louis XIV's court, sometimes fitting out his sitters with allegorical trappings. Pierre's brother, **Nicolas** (1606–68), also trained with Vouet and had a successful career painting portraits and religious subjects.

Millais, Sir John Everett (1829–96). English painter and book illustrator. A child prodigy who was hard-working as well as naturally gifted, he became the youngest ever student at the *Royal Academy Schools when he was 11, and although he suffered some temporary setbacks in his twenties, his career was essentially one of the great Victorian success stories. In 1848, with *Rossetti and Holman *Hunt, he founded the *Pre-Raphaelite Brotherhood and had his share of the abuse heaped against the members until *Ruskin stepped in as their champion. (In 1855 Millais married Effie Gray, formerly Ruskin's wife, after this

first marriage had been annulled.) In the 1850s his style changed, as he moved away from the brilliantly coloured, minutely detailed Pre-Raphaelite manner to a broader and more fluent way of painting—with a family to support he said he could not afford to spend a whole day working on an area 'no larger than a five shilling piece'. His subjects changed also, from highly serious, morally uplifting themes to scenes that met the public demand for sentiment and a good story. Many of them featured children, whom he painted with great affection, often modelling them on his own family; *The Boyhood of Raleigh* (1870, Tate, London), for example, shows his two eldest sons. He became enormously popular, not only with subject pictures such as this (colour reproductions of his best-loved works sold in hundreds of thousands), but also as a portraitist and book illustrator; his drawings for the novels of Anthony Trollope were such a success that Trollope said they influenced the way he developed the characters in sequels. Millais lived in some splendour on his huge income and was loaded with honours; most notably, in 1885 he was created a baronet (a rare distinction for a painter) and in the year of his death he was elected president of the Royal Academy. To some contemporaries it seemed that he wasted his talents pandering to public taste, and many 20th-century critics presented him as a young genius who sacrificed his artistic conscience for money. Millais, an easy-going and much-liked man, certainly enjoyed his success, but he was far from being a cynic. He was always proud of his skills (near the end of his career he wrote, 'I may honestly say that I have never consciously placed an idle touch upon canvas'), and few of his contemporaries could match his late works for sheer beauty of handling (*Bubbles*, 1886, A. & F. Pears Ltd.).

millboard. *See* CARDBOARD.

Miller, Lee. *See* MAN RAY and PENROSE.

Milles, Carl (1875–1955). Sweden's greatest sculptor. From 1897 to 1904 he lived in Paris, where he worked for a time as assistant to *Rodin, then moved to Munich (1904–6), where he was influenced by *Hildebrand. In the following two years he lived in Rome, Stockholm, and Austria, then settled at Lidingö, near Stockholm, in

1908. His travels had given him a wide knowledge of ancient, medieval, and Renaissance art, as well as of recent developments, and he forged from these varied influences an eclectic but vigorous style. He is best known for his numerous large-scale fountains, distinguished by rhythmic vitality and inventive figure types (he liked to fuse classical and Nordic types such as tritons and goblins), and sometimes by a grotesque humour. From 1931 to 1945 he was professor of sculpture at the Cranbrook Academy at Bloomfield Hills, Michigan; his work in the USA includes fountains in Chicago, Kansas City, New York, and St Louis. He became an American citizen in 1945 but returned to Sweden in 1951 and died at Lidingö, where his home is now an open-air museum of his work, known as Millesgården.

Millet, Francisque (Jean-François) (1642–79). French landscape painter of Flemish birth. He worked mainly in Paris, but he is said to have visited England and Holland. No signed or documented paintings are known, but several are authenticated by early engravings. His work was influenced by *Poussin and *Dughet, sometimes enlivened by romantic touches in the manner of Salvator *Rosa, as in *Mountain Landscape with Lightning* (NG, London), one of the most original works of an artist usually content to be an able follower. His son **Jean** (*c*.1666–1723) was a landscape painter, and he too had a painter son, **Joseph** (*c*.1688–1777).

Millet, Jean-François (1814–75). French painter, draughtsman, and printmaker, born into a prosperous and cultured farming family at Gruchy, near Cherbourg, in Normandy. After studying with local painters, he moved to Paris in 1837 and for two years continued his training under *Delaroche at the École des *Beaux-Arts. His early work consisted of portraits and then small mythological and pastoral scenes, but with *The Winnower* (NG, London), exhibited at the *Salon in 1848, he turned to the pictures of rustic life from which his name is now inseparable. *The Winnower* perfectly caught the spirit of the time, for earlier in the year in which it was shown, King Louis Philippe had been deposed, helping to create a taste for pictures of ordinary people such as this (it was indeed bought by a minister in the new republican government).

Critics of the time tended to interpret Millet's work in terms of their own social views, so whereas republicans thought he was showing the dignity of working people in a progressive spirit, conservatives regarded his paintings as coarse and subversive, the peasantry being to them a potential source of civil unrest. Millet himself, however, saw his work in aesthetic and personal rather than political terms, and the feeling of sad solemnity that so often characterizes it is an expression of his own melancholic temperament. In 1854 he commented: 'I must confess, at the risk of being taken for a socialist, that it is the treatment of the human condition which touches me most in art . . . I never see the joyous side; I do not know where to find it, for I have never seen it. The happiest thing I know is the calm and the silence one so deliciously experiences in the forest or in the fields.' This 'calm and silence' he expressed through figures of great strength and dignity, reflecting his admiration for Old Masters such as *Poussin.

In 1849 Millet settled at *Barbizon, where he remained for the rest of his life apart from the period of the Franco-Prussian War (1870–1), when he took refuge in Cherbourg. Late in his career he turned increasingly to pure landscape, influenced by Théodore *Rousseau, one of his closest friends. Rousseau sometimes helped Millet financially, for he spent much of his career in poverty, but in the 1860s—his work now being much less controversial—he began to prosper and to build an international reputation (he became especially popular with American collectors). By the time of his death he was a celebrated figure, and he had considerable influence on late 19th-century art. *Seurat, for example, greatly admired the grand simplicity of his draughtsmanship, and van *Gogh copied reproductions of his work when he was teaching himself to draw. As well as achieving great respect among fellow artists, Millet also pleased a large popular audience, above all with *The Angelus* (1859, Mus. d'Orsay, Paris), which became perhaps the most widely reproduced painting of the 19th century. This had a harmful effect on his subsequent critical fortunes, for largely on the strength of it he was pigeon-holed for much of the 20th century as a purveyor of pious sentimentality (it shows a farmer and his wife pausing in their work to pray as a church bell tolls the evening Angelus). A major exhibition of his work in Paris and London in 1975–6 was a landmark in his critical rehabilitation.

Mills, Clark (1810–83). American sculptor, a jack-of-all-trades, who was self-taught as an artist. In 1848 he won a competition for the monument to President Andrew Jackson in Lafayette Square, Washington, and worked for five years on this, the first equestrian statue in the USA. He built his own foundry to cast the statue, which daringly has the rearing horse supported only by its hind legs, and eventually succeeded at the seventh attempt. The ecstatic response when the statue was unveiled in 1853 brought him great financial rewards and the commission for an equestrian statue to George Washington in Washington Circle (1860). He spent his final years under a cloud, however, suspected of dishonesty in handling the metal assigned to him.

miniature. A term applied to two different kinds of pictures: first, representational images (as distinct from decorative motifs) in *illuminated manuscripts; and secondly, very small independent paintings, particularly portraits that can be held in the hand or worn as a piece of jewellery. The word derives from the Latin *minium*, the red lead used to emphasize initial letters in manuscripts, decorated by the *miniator*. However, on account of a mistaken etymology, the word has become connected with 'minute' (small). What we today call a 'miniature' was called *historia* in the Middle Ages and the portraits painted by *Hilliard and others were named 'limnings' or 'pictures in little' by the Elizabethans. They were painted on vellum (*see* PARCHMENT), or occasionally on ivory or card, and in the 17th and 18th centuries there was a vogue for miniatures done in an *enamelling technique. The portrait miniature developed from a fusion of the traditions of medieval illumination and the *Renaissance medal and flourished from the early 16th century to the mid-19th century, when photography virtually killed it as a serious art form.

Minimal art. A type of abstract art, particularly sculpture, characterized by extreme simplicity of form and a deliberate lack of expressive content; it emerged as a trend in the 1950s and flourished particularly in the 1960s and 1970s. The roots of Minimal art can be traced to the geometrical abstractions of *Malevich and the *readymades of *Duchamp in the second decade of the 20th century, but as a movement it developed mainly in the USA and its impersonality is seen as a reaction against the emotiveness of *Abstract Expressionism. According to *The Tate Gallery: An Illustrated Companion* (1979), 'The theory of minimalism is that without the diverting presence of "composition", and by the use of plain, often industrial, materials arranged in geometrical or highly simplified configurations we may experience all the more strongly the pure qualities of colour, form, space and materials.' Minimal art has close links with *Conceptual art (Minimalist sculpture often has a strong element of theoretical demonstration about it, with the artist leaving the fabrication of his designs to industrial specialists), and sometimes there are affinities with other contemporaneous movements, such as *Land art. There is even a kinship with *Pop art in a shared preference for slick, impersonal surfaces (some Minimal artists, however, have used 'natural' materials such as logs rather than machine-finished products). The leading Minimalist sculptors include Carl *Andre, Don *Judd, and Tony *Smith. Minimalist painters (for whom the immediate precedents were *Albers and *Reinhardt) include Frank *Stella (in his early work) and *Hard-Edge abstractionists such as Ellsworth *Kelly and Kenneth *Noland.

Minne, Georg. *See* SYMBOLISM.

Mino da Fiesole (*c.*1429–84). Florentine sculptor. According to *Vasari he was a pupil of *Desiderio de Settignano, but this seems unlikely, as Desiderio was about the same age—possibly even a year or so younger. Mino is remembered mainly for his portrait busts. Whereas Desiderio's are all of women, Mino's are almost all of men; the earliest—that of Piero de *Medici (1453, Bargello, Florence) is the first dated portrait bust of the *Renaissance (although an undated example by *Donatello probably precedes it). Mino also worked as a tomb sculptor, but much of his work in this field has been altered or destroyed or is of uncertain attribution because he collaborated with other sculptors. The one that most clearly shows his own workmanship is that of Count Hugo of Tuscany (completed 1481, Badia, Florence), which Vasari describes as 'the most beautiful work that he ever produced'. Mino had three documented stays in Rome (1454, 1463, and 1474–80) and also worked briefly in Naples (1455). His reputation was at its height in the 19th century, when his delicate carving of marble was much admired.

Minton, John (1917–57). British painter, illustrator, and designer. In 1938–9 he spent a year in Paris, where he shared a studio with Michael *Ayrton. Among the artists whose work he saw in Paris, he was particularly influenced by the brooding sadness of *Berman and *Tchelitchew. From 1943 to 1946 he had a studio in London at 77 Bedford Gardens (the house in which *Colquhoun and MacBryde lived) and from 1946 to 1952 he lived with Keith *Vaughan. Minton was a leading exponent of *Neo-Romanticism and an influential figure as a teacher at Camberwell School of Art (1943–7), the Central School of Arts and Crafts (1947–8), and the *Royal College of Art (1948–56). He was extremely energetic, travelling widely and producing a large body of work as a painter (of portraits, landscapes, and figure compositions), book illustrator, and designer. After about 1950, however, his work went increasingly out of fashion. He made an effort to keep up with the times with subjects such as the *Death of James Dean* (1957, Tate, London), but stylistically he changed little. He committed suicide with an overdose of drugs.

Mir Iskusstva. *See* WORLD OF ART.

Miró, Joan (1893–1983). Spanish painter, sculptor, printmaker, and designer. He first visited Paris in 1919 and from then until 1936 (when the Spanish Civil War began) his regular pattern was to spend the winter in Paris and the summer at his family's farm near Barcelona. His early work shows the influence of various modern movements—*Fauvism, *Cubism (he was a friend of Pablo *Picasso), and *Dadaism—but he is particularly associated with the *Surrealists, whose first manifesto he signed in 1924. Throughout his life, whether his work was purely abstract or whether it retained figurative suggestions, Miró remained true to the basic Surrealist principle of releasing the creative forces of the unconscious mind

from the control of logic and reason. However, even though André *Breton wrote that he was 'probably the most Surrealistic of us all', Miró was never a formal member of the movement and always stood somewhat apart because of the variety, geniality, and lack of attitudinizing in his work, which shows none of the superficial devices beloved of other Surrealists. One of the works in which he first displayed an unmistakable personal vision is *Harlequin's Carnival* (1924–5, Albright-Knox AG, Buffalo), featuring a bizarre assembly of insect-like creatures dancing and making music—a scene inspired by 'my hallucinations brought on by hunger'. Much of his work has the delightful quality of playfulness seen in this picture, but he was inspired to much more sombre and even savage imagery by the Spanish Civil War, during which he designed propaganda posters for the Republicans fighting against Franco.

Miró settled in Paris in 1936 because of the Civil War, but in 1940 he returned to Spain to escape the German occupation of France and thereafter lived mainly on the island of Majorca. It was from about this time that he began to achieve international recognition. For the rest of his long life he worked with great energy in a wide variety of fields. In 1944 he began making ceramics and slightly later he took up sculpture, initially small terracottas but eventually large-scale pieces for casting in bronze. He visited the USA for the first time in 1947 and did a large mural for the Terrace Hilton Hotel in Cincinnati. This fulfilled his desire to communicate with a large public, and several of the major works of his later year were in a similar vein, notably a mural for Harvard University in 1950 (now replaced by a ceramic copy; the original is in MoMA, New York) and two vast ceramic wall decorations, *Wall of the Sun* and *Wall of the Moon* (installed 1958), for the Unesco Building in Paris. Another aspect of his desire to make his art widely accessible is his productivity as a printmaker (etchings and lithographs). He continued to explore new techniques into his old age, taking up stained-glass design when he was in his eighties. In spite of the worldwide fame he acquired, he was a modest, retiring character, utterly devoted to his work, and in one of his rare public statements he criticized Picasso for what seemed to him like a mania for publicity.

The Foundation Joan Miró was opened in 1975 on the heights of Montjuic overlooking Barcelona. It is designed both as a memorial museum housing a collection of Miró's works and as a centre of artistic activity.

misericord. In Christian church architecture, a bracket or ledge projecting from the underside of a hinged tip-up seat in the choir, against which an elderly or infirm clergyman could lean and rest during long services whilst still appearing to stand. The term, which derives from the Latin *misericordia* ('compassion'), is first recorded in Germany in the 11th century, but the earliest surviving examples date from the early 13th century. Misericords are often richly carved, and England has a particularly impressive tradition in them. The subject matter of the carving is predominantly secular and frequently humorous, illustrating fables and proverbs for example, but there is often a moral attached. Misericords were at their peak of development in the 14th and 15th centuries in England, but they continued to be produced into the 17th century.

mobile. Term coined by Marcel *Duchamp in 1932 to describe the motor- or hand-powered *Kinetic sculptures of Alexander *Calder and soon extended to those he produced where the movement is caused by air currents. Typically they consisted of flat metal parts suspended on wires. Many other sculptors (notably Lynn *Chadwick) have experimented with the genre, and mobiles have also been adopted as articles of interior decoration and (on a miniature scale) as playthings for babies.

modello. A preparatory drawing or painting for a larger work, particularly one made to be shown to a patron. Since the object was to impress the patron and give him a clear idea of the picture that the artist had in mind, a *modello* was more elaborate and fully worked out than a sketch or *bozzetto*. *Rubens's work is particularly rich in *modelli*.

Modersohn-Becker, Paula (1876–1907). German painter, born Paula Becker. In 1898 she joined the artists' colony at *Worpswede and in 1901 she married **Otto Modersohn** (1865–1943), another member of the group. Her early work—mainly landscapes and scenes of peasant life—was in the lyrical, rather sentimental manner associated with Worpswede at this time, but she developed a massively powerful style through which she expressed a highly personal vision of the world. Her artistic evolution was influenced by four visits she made to Paris between 1900 and her early death in 1907. The work of *Gauguin and van *Gogh in particular helped her to find the 'great simplicity of form' for which she had been searching, and in her mature work she concentrated on single figures, including self-portraits and portraits of peasants. In her self-portraits she typically shows herself with wide, staring eyes and often in the nude. Although she had a weak physical constitution, she worked with great discipline and perseverance, and in a career that lasted only a decade she produced a substantial output of paintings and drawings as well as a few etchings. She died of a heart attack three weeks after giving birth to her first child. She was little known at the time of her death (she had sold only a handful of pictures), but is now regarded as one of the outstanding German artists of her time. Her symbolic use of colour and pattern, her subjective outlook (she wrote that 'the principal thing is my personal feeling'), and the almost primitive force of some of her work give her a place among the most important precursors of *Expressionism.

Modigliani, Amedeo (1884–1920). Italian painter, sculptor, and draughtsman, active mainly in Paris. Although virtually his whole career was spent in France, he laid the foundations of his style in Italy with his study of the masters of the *Renaissance. In particular he is often seen as a spiritual heir of *Botticelli because of the linear grace of his work, and his reclining nudes continue a tradition begun by *Giorgione and *Titian. He moved to Paris in 1906; apart from visits to his family in Italy and a year spent at Nice and Cagnes, 1918–19, this was his home for the rest of his life, and he became a familiar figure in the café and night life of Montmartre. Initially he was strongly influenced by *Cézanne, from whom he learnt much about simple dignity of composition and subtle handling of colour harmonies. However, in 1909 he met *Brancusi and under his influence devoted himself mainly to stonecarving until 1914, when the war made it impossible for him to get materials. He then returned to painting and his finest pictures were produced in the last five years of his short life. Both as a sculptor and as a painter his range was limited. Almost all his two dozen or so surviving sculptures are heads and the great majority of his paintings are portraits or female nudes. Common to virtually all his work are extremely elongated, simplified forms and a superb sense of rhythmic vitality, but there is a great difference in mood between, for example, his sculptures (*Head*, *c*.1911–12, Tate, London), which have the primitive power of the African masks that inspired them, and his gloriously sensual nudes (*Reclining Nude*, *c*.1919, MoMA, New York), which were censured for their open eroticism (the only one-man exhibition he held in his lifetime, at the Galerie Berthe Weill, Paris, in 1917, was closed by the police because of the 'filth' on display). Modigliani's early death from tuberculosis was hastened by his notoriously dissolute lifestyle, and his mistress Jeanne Hébuterne, pregnant with their second child, committed suicide the day after he died. At this time he was beginning to make a name among enthusiasts of modern art but was virtually unknown to the world at large; his posthumous fame was established by an exhibition at the Galerie Bernheim-Jeune, Paris, in 1922 and a colourful biography by the poet and critic André Salmon (1881–1969) published in 1926—*Modigliani, sa vie et son œuvre*. His reputation as one of the outstandingly original artists of his time is now secure, but his fame rests even more on his reputation as the 'bohemian par excellence: in the popular imagination he is the archetypal romantic genius, starving in a garret, the victim of drugs and alcohol, an inveterate womanizer, but painting and carving obsessively.

Moholy-Nagy, László (1895–1946). Hungarian-born painter, sculptor, experimental artist, and writer who became an American citizen in 1944. After qualifying in law at Budapest University and serving in the First World War, he moved to Vienna in 1919 and then in 1921 to Berlin, where he painted abstract pictures influenced by *Lissitzky (himself newly arrived from Russia). He also experimented with *collage and *photomontage and in 1922 had his first one-man exhibition, at the *Sturm Gallery.

From 1923 to 1928 he taught at the *Bauhaus, taking over from *Itten the running of the preliminary course. The difference in approach between these two highly distinctive characters is summed up by Frank Whitford (*Bauhaus*, 1984): 'Even Moholy's appearance proclaimed his artistic sympathies. Itten had worn something like a monk's habit and had kept his head immaculately shaved with the intention of creating an aura of spirituality and communion with the transcendental. Moholy sported the kind of overall worn by workers in modern industry. His nickel-rimmed spectacles contributed further to an image of sobriety and calculation belonging to a man mistrustful of the emotions, more at home among machines than human beings.' Although he was regarded as a brilliant teacher, his assertiveness and his rejection of a spiritual dimension in art made him unpopular with some of his colleagues. He resigned when Hannes Meyer replaced Gropius as director in 1928, then worked for some years in Berlin, chiefly on stage design and experimental film. In 1934 he left Germany because of the Nazis, moving to Amsterdam and then in 1935 to London, where he worked on designs for the science fiction film *Things to Come* (1936), produced by his fellow Hungarian Alexander Korda, and contributed to the *Constructivist review *Circle* (1937). In 1937 he emigrated to Chicago, where he became director of the short-lived New Bauhaus (1937–8), then founded his own School of Design (1939; it changed its name to the Institute of Design in 1944), directing it until his death. He was one of the most influential teachers of the 20th century and one of the most inventive and versatile of Constructivist artists, pioneering especially in his use of light, movement (*see* KINETIC ART), photography, film, and plastic materials. His views, emphasizing the Constructivist doctrine that so-called *fine art must be integrated with the total environment, were most fully expressed in his posthumously published book *Vision in Motion* (1947).

Moilliet, Louis (1880–1962). Swiss painter and designer of stained glass. In 1911 he introduced *Klee (a friend since schooldays) to the *Blaue Reiter circle, and in 1914 he visited Tunisia with Klee and *Macke. After the First World War he travelled extensively, especially in the Mediterranean. As a painter he worked mainly in watercolour in a style influenced by *Orphism. The same feeling for colour comes out in the stained glass windows he designed for Swiss churches, notably the Lucaskirche at Lucerne (1934–6) and the Zwinglikirche at Winterthur (1943–4).

Mola, Pier Francesco (1612–66). Italian *Baroque painter. Although he spent most of his life in Rome, his style, characterized by warm colouring and soft modelling, was formed mainly on the example of *Guercino and Venetian art (his early career is not well documented, but he probably spent much of the period 1633–47 in north Italy). He painted frescos in Roman churches and palaces, and his best-known painting is the striking *Barbary Pirate* (1650, Louvre, Paris), but his most characteristic works are fairly small canvases with religious or mythological figures set in landscapes (two examples are in the National Gallery, London). They are somewhat reminiscent of Francesco *Albani, but much freer, and closer in spirit to Salvator *Rosa; with the latter, Mola was one of the chief representatives of a distinctively romantic strain in Roman painting in the mid-17th century.

Molenaer, Jan Miense (*c*.1610–68). Dutch painter, active in his native Haarlem and in Amsterdam, where he moved in 1636 after marrying Judith *Leyster; both belonged in their youth to the circle of Frans *Hals. He and his wife probably collaborated and sometimes it is difficult to differentiate their work. Molenaer, however, was more prolific and more versatile. His *genre scenes range from pictures of the indecorous activities of peasants to exquisitely finished interiors showing well-to-do families. He also painted portraits and religious scenes. His early works (which are considered his best) have a grey-blond tonality and touches of bright colour; his later ones are darker, in the manner of *Brouwer or *Ostade. He had two painter brothers, **Bartholomaeus** (d. 1650) and **Claes** (d. 1676), both active in Haarlem.

Molyn, Pieter de (1595–1661). Dutch landscape painter, active mainly in Haarlem. With Jan van *Goyen, and Salomon van *Ruysdael, also active in Haarlem, he ranks as one of the pioneers of naturalistic landscape painting in Holland. It is not known if these three painters worked together, if they arrived at similar solutions independently, or if one of them began experiments with monochromatic pictures of dunes and cottages and the others followed his lead. However, Molyn's *Sand Dune* (1626, Herzog-Anton-Ulrich Mus., Brunswick) is earlier than any comparable dated picture by van Goyen or Ruysdael. Molyn's later career was less distinguished, and he seems then to have worked more as a draughtsman than a painter. He also produced a few etchings.

Momper, Joos (or **Jodocus**) **II de** (1564–1635). Flemish landscape painter, the outstanding member of a family of artists. He worked in his native Antwerp, where he became a master in the painters' guild in 1581, but mountains are so much a prevailing theme in his work that it seems likely he crossed the Alps to Italy at some time in his career (frescos in the church of S. Vitale in Rome have recently been attributed to him). His chief inspiration was *Bruegel and his work stands halfway between the constructed landscapes of the 16th century and the naturalistic landscapes of the 17th century. Judging by the great number of extant pictures in his manner, his work must have enjoyed great popularity. They vary greatly in quality, but the best works that are indisputably from his own hand, for example the majestic *Winter Landscape with the Flight into Egypt* (Ashmolean Mus., Oxford), show that he was one of the greatest landscape painters of his period and worthy to be mentioned in the same breath as Bruegel. His style seems to have changed little and his work is difficult to date. Figures in his paintings are often the work of other artists, notably Jan 'Velvet' *Brueghel.

Mondrian, Piet (1872–1944). Dutch painter, one of the most important figures in the development of *abstract art. His early paintings were naturalistic and direct, often delicate in colour, but between 1907 and 1910 his work took on a *Symbolist character, partly under the influence of *Toorop and perhaps partly owing to his conversion to Theosophy. Between 1912 and the outbreak of the First World War in 1914 he divided his time between Paris and the Netherlands, and in this period he was strongly influenced by *Cubism, painting a series of pictures on the theme of a tree in which the image became progressively more fragmented and abstract (*Flowering Apple Tree*, 1912, Gemeente Mus., The Hague). By 1914 he had virtually eliminated curved lines from his work, using a structure that was predominantly horizontal and vertical, with the merest suggestion of natural forms underlying the patterning. In 1915 he met Theo van *Doesburg, and two years later he joined him in founding the association De *Stijl; it promoted a new kind of rigorously geometrical abstract painting of which Mondrian became the main exponent. In this style, which he named *Neo-Plasticism, he limited himself to straight lines and basic colours to create an art of great clarity and discipline that he thought reflected the laws of the universe, revealing immutable realities behind the ever-changing appearances of the world. Typically he used a bold grid of black lines (all completely straight and either strictly horizontal or strictly vertical) to form an asymmetrical network of rectangles of various sizes that were painted with a narrow range of colours (the three primaries—blue, red, and yellow—plus black, white, and initially grey, although this was later dropped).

From 1919 to 1938 Mondrian lived in Paris, where in 1931 he joined the *Abstraction-Création group. For many years he had struggled to earn a living, but in the 1920s he gradually became known to an international circle of admirers, including the American Katherine *Dreier (from 1926). In 1938 he left Paris because of the threat of war, and for the next two years he lived in London, near Naum *Gabo and Ben *Nicholson. After the house next door to his studio was hit by a bomb, he moved to New York in 1940 and spent his remaining years there, adapting well to his new home even though he was now almost 70. In America he developed a more colourful style, with syncopated rhythms that reflect his interest in jazz and dancing (*Broadway Boogie-Woogie*, 1942–3, MoMA); he was noted for his immaculate tidiness and rather fussy lifestyle, but he had a passion for social dancing and took lessons in fashionable steps. His enormous influence was not limited to artists whose style and aesthetic outlook were similar to his own. He also had a powerful impact on much industrial, dec-

orative, and advertisement art from the 1930s onwards; indeed Ian Dunlop writes that 'it is no exaggeration to say that his effect on the look and style of contemporary life has been greater than that of any modern artist, even of such supreme masters as *Matisse and *Picasso' (*Piet Mondrian*, 1967). This influence was spread by his writings (including numerous articles in the periodical *De Stijl*) as well as his paintings.

Monet, Claude (1840–1926). French *Impressionist painter. He is regarded as the archetypal Impressionist in that his devotion to the ideals of the movement was unwavering throughout his long career, and it is fitting that one of his pictures—*Impression: Sunrise* (1872, Mus. Marmottan, Paris)—gave the group its name. His youth was spent in Le Havre, where he first excelled as a *caricaturist but was then converted to landscape painting by his early mentor *Boudin, from whom he derived his enthusiasm for painting out of doors. In 1859 he studied in Paris at the *Académie Suisse and formed a friendship with *Pissarro. After two years' military service in Algiers, he returned to Le Havre and met *Jongkind, to whom he said he owed 'the definitive education of my eye'. Then, in 1862, he entered the studio of *Gleyre in Paris and there met *Renoir, *Sisley, and *Bazille, with whom he was to form the nucleus of the Impressionist group. Monet's devotion to painting out of doors is illustrated by the famous story concerning one of his most ambitious early works, *Women in the Garden* (1866–7, Mus. d'Orsay, Paris). The picture is about 2.5 m (8 ft) high and to enable him to paint all of it outside he had a trench dug in the garden so the canvas could be raised or lowered by pulleys to the height he required. *Courbet visited him when he was working on it and said Monet would not paint even the leaves in the background unless the lighting conditions were exactly right. However, although he always liked to maintain this image as an outdoor painter, he later came to rely more and more on studio work.

During the Franco-Prussian War (1870–1) Monet took refuge in England with Pissarro: he painted the Thames and London parks, and met the dealer *Durand-Ruel, who was to become one of the great champions of the

Impressionists. From 1871 to 1876 he lived at Argenteuil, a village on the Seine near Paris, and here were painted some of the most joyous and famous works of the Impressionist movement, not only by Monet, but by his visitors *Manet, Renoir, and Sisley. In 1878 he moved to Vétheuil and in 1883 he settled at Giverny, also on the Seine, but about 65 km (40 miles) from Paris. Early in his career he had experienced extreme poverty, but in the 1880s he began to prosper. By 1890 he was successful enough to buy the house at Giverny he had previously rented and in 1892 he married his mistress, with whom he had begun an affair in 1876, three years before the death of his first wife. From 1890 he concentrated on series of pictures in which he painted the same subject at different times of the day in different lights—*Haystacks* or *Grainstacks* (1890–1) and *Rouen Cathedral* (1891–5) are the best known. He continued to travel widely, visiting London and Venice several times (and in 1895 Norway, where he painted with his beard 'covered in icicles'), but increasingly his attention was focused on the celebrated water garden he created at Giverny, which served as the theme for the series of paintings of waterlilies (*Nymphéas*) that began in 1899 and grew to dominate his work completely (in 1914, by now wealthy and famous, he had a special studio built in the grounds of his house so he could work on the huge canvases). From 1908 he was troubled by failing eyesight (he had a cataract operation in 1923), but he painted until the end, completing a great decorative scheme of waterlily paintings that he donated to the nation in 1926, the year of his death. They were installed in the Orangerie, Paris, in 1927. In these late works his style had become so loose and free that the forms almost disappear in a blur of vibrant brushstrokes. It has even been suggested that they anticipate *Abstract Expressionism, but the subject matter always remained important to Monet.

monotype. A method of making an image (on the borderline between painting and printmaking) in which a design is painted (usually in oil colours) on a flat sheet of metal or glass and is then transferred directly to a sheet of paper; the term is also applied to the print so made. With glass plates, pressure has to be applied to the back of the paper by hand; in other cases monotypes may be printed in a press. Strictly speaking, only one print may be taken by this process (hence the term 'monotype'); in practice the colour on the slab may be reinforced after printing and another one or two impressions taken, although they will differ considerably from the first. Various modifications of the principle are known. G. B. *Castiglione is generally credited with the invention of the monotype in the 1640s. William *Blake and Edgar *Degas are among the artists who have made memorable use of the technique.

Monro, Dr Thomas (1759–1833). English collector, patron, and amateur painter, a physician by profession. He played an important role in encouraging some of the outstanding watercolour painters of his period, his protégés including *Cotman, *De Wint, *Girtin, *Turner, and many others. They used his houses in London and Bushey, Hertfordshire, as places to meet and work, and were given the run of his superb collection. Late in life Turner recalled how he and Girtin had often made 'drawings for good Dr Monro at half a crown apiece and a supper'.

montage (Fr.: 'mounting'). A pictorial technique in which a number of cut-out illustrations, or fragments of them, are arranged together and mounted on a suitable background; the term also refers to the picture so created. Ready-made images alone are used and they are generally chosen for their subject and message; in both these respects montage can be distinguished from *collage, in which materials of varied kinds can be used, often primarily with an interest in their decorative qualities. Montage is now associated particularly with advertising, but it has also been used by artists. *Photomontage is montage using photographic images only. In cinematic usage, the term 'montage' refers to the assembling of separate pieces of film into a sequence or superimposed image.

Montagna, Bartolomeo (*c*.1450–1523). Italian painter. He probably trained in Venice, but he worked mainly in Vicenza, where he was the leading painter of his day, producing many altarpieces for local churches. His style has been well characterized by S. J. Freedberg (*Painting in Italy: 1500–1600*, 1971) as 'gloomily impressive'.

Montañés, Juan Martínez (1568–1649). The greatest Spanish sculptor of the 17th century, known as 'el dios de la madera' (the god of wood) on account of his mastery as a carver. He was active mainly in Seville, his most famous work being the *Christ of Clemency* (1603–6) in the cathedral there, which shows the new naturalism he brought to the *polychromed wooden statue (*Pacheco often painted his figures). In this he occupied a role comparable to Gregorio *Fernández in Valladolid, but Montañés was more aristocratic in style, tempering *Baroque emotionalism with a classical *sense of dignity. In 1635–6 he was in Madrid to undertake his only recorded secular work, a portrait head (now lost) of Philip IV (*see* HABSBURG) to serve as model for the equestrian statue of the king executed by Pietro *Tacca in Florence, and it was on this occasion that *Velázquez painted his well-known portrait of Montañés (Prado, Madrid). His work influenced painters such as *Zurbarán as well as sculptors such as *Cano (whom he probably taught), and his style was spread by his flourishing workshop.

Montefeltro. Italian noble family that ruled Urbino from 1234 with short intervals until 1508, when the line became extinct. For most of this period Urbino was of only local importance, but under **Federico da Montefeltro** (1422–82; ruled from 1444) the city had a brief golden age as one of the most important centres of *Renaissance culture. Federico fulfilled the ideal of the Renaissance prince, for he was a brave soldier and a humane ruler as well as an enlightened patron of literature and the arts. His library was the finest in Italy and his palace is one of the most beautiful buildings of the Renaissance. For us he chiefly survives—broken nose, warts, and all—in the famous portrait (Uffizi, Florence) by *Piero della Francesca, who was one of the leading lights of his court. Federico's ideals lived on in his son **Guidobaldo** (1472–1508), whose court is commemorated in Castiglione's famous book *The Courtier* (1528). Guidobaldo was deposed by Cesare Borgia in 1502, but recovered Urbino the following year. When he died childless in 1508, the dukedom

passed to his nephew Francesco Maria I della *Rovere.

Monticelli, Adolphe (1824–86). French painter, active in his native Marseilles and in Paris. He was a pupil of Paul *Delaroche, but he learned more from his studies of Old Masters in the Louvre; he was also influenced by his friends *Delacroix and *Diaz de la Peña. His subjects included landscapes, portraits, still lifes, fêtes galantes in the spirit of *Watteau, and scenes from the circus, painted in brilliant colours and thick impasto that influenced van *Gogh. He enjoyed great success in Paris in the 1860s, but after the outbreak of the Franco-Prussian War in 1870 he returned to Marseilles and led a retiring life. His work is represented in many French museums, and he has been much forged.

Moore, Albert (1841–93). English painter, son of a portrait painter, **William Moore** (1790–1851). His early works were in a *Pre-Raphaelite vein, but in the mid-1860s, under the influence particularly of the *Elgin Marbles, he turned to classical subjects. He specialized in elaborately, and sometimes diaphanously, draped female figures, singly or in groups—'subjectless' pictures akin to those of his friend *Whistler. The two men met in 1865 and influenced each other. Like Whistler, Moore was a colourist of great sensitivity, although his colours tend to be much higher keyed, and he ranks with him as one of the leading figures of *Aestheticism. Four of Moore's brothers were artists, most notably **Henry** (1831–95), a successful marine painter.

Moore, George. *See* ACADEMY.

Moore, Henry (1898–1986). British sculptor, draughtsman, and printmaker. He is regarded as one of the greatest sculptors of the 20th century and from the late 1940s until his death he was unchallenged as the most celebrated British artist of his time. He was born in Yorkshire, the son of a miner, and after service in the British army in the First World War, he trained at Leeds School of Art and from there obtained a scholarship to the *Royal College of Art in 1921. After completing his training in 1924, he taught there until 1931. From 1932 to 1939 he was the first head of sculpture in a new department at Chelsea School of Art. During the 1930s he lived in Hampstead in the same area as Ben *Nicholson, Barbara *Hepworth, the critic Herbert *Read, and other leading figures of the avant-garde. In 1940, after the bombing of his studio, he moved to Much Hadham in Hertfordshire, where he lived for the rest of his life. Most of Moore's early work was carved, rejecting the academic tradition of modelling in favour of the doctrine of *truth to material, according to which the nature of the stone or wood—its shape, texture, and so on—was part of the conception of the work. He also rejected the *classical and *Renaissance notion of beauty and put in its place an ideal of vital force and formal vigour that he found exemplified in much ancient sculpture (Mexican, Sumerian, etc.), which he studied in the British Museum, and also in the frescos of *Giotto and *Masaccio, which he saw in Italy in 1925 in the course of a travelling scholarship. During the 1930s his work was more directly influenced by European avant-garde art, particularly the *Surrealism of *Arp. Although he produced some purely abstract pieces, his work was almost always based on forms in the natural world —often the human figure, but also, for example, bones, pebbles, and shells. The reclining female figure and the mother and child were among his perennial themes.

By the late 1930s Moore was well known in informed circles as the leading avant-garde sculptor in England (Kenneth *Clark and Jacob *Epstein were among his early supporters), and his wider fame was established by the poignant drawings he did as an *Official War Artist (1940–2) of people sheltering from air raids in underground stations. Subsequently his reputation grew rapidly (particularly after he won the International Sculpture Prize at the 1948 Venice *Biennale), and from the 1950s he carried out many public commissions in Britain and elsewhere. During this time there were major changes in his way of working. Bronze took over from stone as his preferred medium and he often worked on a very large scale. There was a tendency also for his works to be composed of several elements grouped together rather than made up of a single object. Some critics discerned a falling away of his powers in his later work, marked in particular by a tendency towards inflated rhetoric, but for others he remained a commanding figure to the end. A man of great integrity and un-

affected charm, Moore was held in almost universally high esteem. He held broad socialist principles, was pleased to find that his work could be appreciated by a wide audience and not just an elite, and gave his time generously to serve on public bodies. The tributes paid after his death made it clear that he was widely regarded not only as one of the greatest artists of the century, but also as one of the greatest Englishmen in any field. He was a lucid and perceptive commentator on his own and other people's sculpture, and his writings have been collected as *Henry Moore on Sculpture* (1966). His huge output is represented in collections of modern art throughout the world; among the cities with particularly fine holdings are Leeds (City Art Gallery), London (Tate), Toronto (Art Gallery of Ontario), and Washington (Hirshhorn Museum and Sculpture Garden).

Moorman, Charlotte. *See* VIDEO ART.

Mor, Anthonis (c.1517/20–1576/7). Netherlandish portrait painter, a pupil of Jan van *Scorel in his native Utrecht. He was the most successful court portraitist of his day, leading an international career that took him to England, Germany, Italy, Portugal, and Spain. In England he painted a portrait of Mary Tudor (1554, Prado, Madrid, and other versions), for which he is said to have been knighted—he is sometimes known as Sir Anthony More (it is thus that he appears in the *Dictionary of National Biography*) and the Spanish version of his name, Antonio Moro, is also commonly used. His work shows little variation throughout his career; sitters are shown life-size or a little larger, half-, three-quarter-, or full-length, turned slightly to the side, with an air of unruffled dignity. His composition is simple and strong and his grasp of character firm but undemonstrative. He owed much to *Titian, but his surfaces are more detailed and polished in the northern manner. Mor had great influence on the development of royal and aristocratic portraiture, particularly in Spain, where his ceremonious but austere style ideally suited the rigorous etiquette of the court. *Sánchez Coello was his pupil. From 1567 he worked mainly in Antwerp, where he died.

Morales, Luis de (d. c.1586). Spanish painter. He worked for most of his life in

Badajoz, a town on the Portuguese border, and his style—formed away from the influence of the court or great religious and artistic centres such as Seville—is highly distinctive. His pictures are usually fairly small and he concentrated on devotional images such as the *Mater Dolorosa* or *Ecce Homo*, painted with intense spirituality. The piety of his work has earned him the nickname 'El Divino'. His style owes something to Netherlandish art, but his misty modelling seems to derive more from *Leonardo da Vinci.

Morandi, Giorgio (1890–1964). Italian painter and etcher. He was born in Bologna and lived there all his life. Apart from brief associations with *Futurism and *Metaphysical Painting, he stood aloof from modern aesthetic experiments. Early in his career (and again in the 1940s) he painted landscapes, but he came to specialize almost exclusively in still life, eschewing literary and symbolic content, and using subtle combinations of colour within a narrow range of tones. His style has something in common with *Purism, but is more subtle and intimate; the greatest influence on his work was *Cézanne, whom he revered. After the Second World War Morandi gained an international reputation, and his work won great respect among younger Italian artists for its poetic quality and devotion to purely aesthetic values.

Moreau, Gustave (1826–98). French painter, one of the leading *Symbolist artists. He was a close friend of Théodore *Chassériau and was influenced by his exotic *Romanticism, but Moreau went far beyond him in his feeling for the bizarre and developed a style that is highly distinctive in subject and technique. Typically his pictures are mystically intense images treated with an extraordinary sensuousness, his paint encrusted and jewel-like. Often the subjects are religious or mythological (Orpheus was a favourite theme), but sometimes they more vaguely evoke long-dead civilizations. Although he had some success at the *Salon, Moreau was highly sensitive to criticism and for long periods did not exhibit his work. He had no need to sell his paintings, as he had private means, and much of his life was spent in seclusion. Nevertheless, his paintings became well known, partly because they appealed

strongly to some of the leading writers of the day; most notably, there is a lengthy description of his work in J. K. Huysman's novel *A rebours* (1884), one of the key texts of the Symbolist movement. In 1892, Moreau became a professor at the École des *Beaux-Arts and proved an inspired teacher, bringing out his pupils' individual talents rather than trying to impose his own ideas on them. His pupils included *Marquet and *Matisse, but his favourite was *Rouault, who became the first curator of the Moreau Museum in Paris (the artist's house), which Moreau left to the nation on his death. The bulk of his work is preserved there. Much of it consists of small pictures and watercolours, as he executed comparatively few major oils.

Moreelse, Paulus (1571–1638). Dutch painter and architect, active in his native Utrecht, where he was the first dean of the painters' guild, founded in 1611. He painted various types of picture, including portraits (similar to those of his teacher *Miereveld, but less severe) and religious works. More interesting than these are his Arcadian scenes with shepherds and shepherdesses; he was one of the first Dutch artists to paint such pictures. As an architect he designed the Catherine Gate (destroyed) and possibly the façade of the Meat Market in Utrecht. He served on the town council and was involved in founding Utrecht's university in 1636.

Morelli, Giovanni (1816–91). Italian critic. He trained as a physician and spent most of his career as a politician, but from 1873 he began to write articles on Italian art. These were written in German (he was educated in Switzerland and Germany), and at first he published them as supposed translations from the Russian of Ivan Lermolieff (an anagram of his surname with a Russian termination). They appeared in English in various books, beginning with *Italian Masters in German Galleries* (1883). Morelli concentrated mainly on the problems of attribution and claimed to have reduced the matter to scientific principles. He maintained that an artist's method of dealing with subordinate details, such as fingernails or ears (here his anatomical training was useful), is tantamount to a signature and that by systematic study of such details attribution can be put beyond doubt. This method, still sometimes referred to as 'Morellian criticism', was influential on connoisseurs such as *Berenson, but it has proved much less productive of scientific certainty than Morelli hoped; it is now felt that we recognize the work of individual artists more by general effect than by details, and that the details rather than the general effect are what an imitator will be able to reproduce most convincingly. Morelli himself made some brilliant attributions, but also some noteworthy blunders. A devoted patriot, he declined the directorship of the *Uffizi because he did not want to be distracted from his political duties, and he helped to secure legislation restricting the export of works from Italy. His own collection of pictures was left to the Pinacoteca of his adopted city of Bergamo.

Moretto da Brescia (Alessandro Bonvicino) (*c.*1498–1554). Italian painter, active mainly in his native Brescia and the neighbourhood. *Ridolfi says he was a pupil of *Titian, and certainly his influence is apparent in Moretto's work. He was the leading Brescian painter of his day, mainly producing altarpieces and other religious works, the best of which display an impressive gravity and a poetic feeling for nature (*St Giustina with a Donor*, *c.*1530, KH Mus., Vienna). However, his portraits, although much less numerous, are considered to be generally of higher quality and of greater importance historically. It seems likely that he introduced the independent full-length portrait to Italy, for although *Vasari credits Titian with this distinction, Moretto's *Portrait of a Gentleman* of 1526 in the National Gallery, London, antedates any known example by Titian by several years. The National Gallery has an outstanding collection of works by Moretto, including two other portraits, which show the thoughtful qualities he passed on to his pupil *Moroni.

Morgan, J. Pierpont (1837–1913). American financier, industrialist, and art collector. The son of a financier and head of one of the most powerful banking houses in the world, Morgan used his personal fortune to spend lavishly on works of art. His main collecting interests were manuscripts and rare books and after his death his son, also **J. Pierpont Morgan** (1867–1943), endowed the Pierpont Morgan Library in New York as a research institute and

museum in memory of his father. It has superb collections of *illuminated manuscripts and Old Master drawings and also contains stained glass, sculpture, and metalwork. The Metropolitan Museum in New York also received an important bequest from the elder Morgan, who was chairman of its governing board for many years.

Morisot, Berthe (1841–95). French *Impressionist painter. *Fragonard was her great-grandfather and she was brought up in a highly cultured atmosphere. She was a pupil of *Corot, but the chief formative influence on her work was *Manet, whom she met in 1868, and whose brother she married in 1874. In her turn she is said to have persuaded Manet to experiment with the Impressionist 'rainbow' palette and with *plein-air painting. After Manet's death in 1883 she came under the influence of *Renoir. Her pictures were regularly accepted for the *Salon, but she was a strong opponent of conventional academic teaching and a champion of Impressionist ideals; she participated in all the Impressionist exhibitions except the fourth (1879), when she was prevented from taking part by ill health. She specialized in gentle domestic scenes, painted in a delicate, feathery technique, and was also an excellent marine painter. Her watercolours are as accomplished as her oils, and in addition she produced pastels, drypoints, and lithographs. She was renowned for her beauty and charm and often posed for Manet.

Morland, George (1763?–1804). English painter, mainly of scenes from rural life, the son and pupil of **Henry Morland** (1716?–97), a painter of portraits and *fancy pictures who was also a dealer, forger, and restorer. George was precocious and a fluent worker and produced a huge amount of work, in spite of leading a dissolute life and often being drunk, in hiding from his creditors, or in prison. His name is particularly associated with small scenes of middle- and lower-class rural life, usually drawn more from the tavern and the stable than the cottage. The quality of his work is uneven, but at his best he showed a spirited technique and a sure sense of tone. His paintings became extremely popular and he was much imitated and forged; numerous prints were made after his work, some of them by his brother-in-law William

*Ward. With *Wheatley and *Ibbetson he established the village scene in the English painter's repertory.

Morley, Malcolm (1931–). British painter, active mainly in the USA. In the 1960s he turned from abstract to figurative work and became one of the pioneers of *Superrealism. From about 1970, however, his paintings became increasingly loose in handling, often depicting animals in lush landscapes. In 1984 he was the first winner of the *Turner Prize, awarded for 'the greatest contribution to art in Britain in the previous twelve months', a decision that occasioned much controversy as Morley had been living in New York since 1958.

Moroni, Giovanni Battista (c.1520/4–1578). Italian painter. He trained under *Moretto in Brescia and worked mainly in his home town of Albino and in nearby Bergamo. His style was based closely on that of his master, but whereas his religious paintings are unexceptional, his portraits are worthy successors to Moretto's. They are remarkable for their psychological penetration, dignified air, and exquisite silvery tonality. The National Gallery, London, has the best collection of his work, including the celebrated portrait known as '*The Tailor*' (c.1570).

Morozov, Ivan. See HERMITAGE.

Morrice, James Wilson (1865–1924). Canadian landscape and figure painter, active mainly in Paris, where he settled in 1890. He was friendly with many leading artists, notably *Whistler, who was an influence on his early work; later his style became mildly *Fauvist. He was widely travelled and made several return visits to Canada, playing an important role in introducing modern trends to his country.

Morris, Robert (1931–). American artist and writer. He is regarded as one of the most prominent exponents and theorists of *Minimal art, and has also worked in other fields, including *Conceptual art, *Land art, and *Performance art. His most characteristic sculptures consist of large-scale, hard-edged geometric forms, but he has also made 'anti-form' pieces in soft, hanging materials.

Morris, William (1834–96). English designer, craftsman, writer, painter, and social reformer. As a student at Oxford University he formed a lifelong friendship with *Burne-Jones and began to write poetry and to study medieval architecture. In 1856 he was apprenticed to the architect G. E. Street, but soon left to paint under *Rossetti's guidance—his only completed oil painting, *Queen Guenevere* (1858, Tate, London), is strongly *Pre-Raphaelite. In 1859, Morris married Jane Burden, who appears in numerous paintings by Rossetti as an archetypal femme fatale; Morris's architect friend Philip Webb built the famous Red House, Bexleyheath, for the couple. With Webb, Rossetti, Burne-Jones, Ford Madox *Brown, P. P. Marshall (a surveyor), and Charles Faulkner (an accountant), Morris founded the manufacturing and decorating firm of Morris, Marshall, Faulkner & Co. in 1861 (reorganized in 1875 as Morris & Co). After a shaky start, the firm prospered, producing furniture, tapestry, stained glass, furnishing fabrics, carpets, and much more. Morris's wallpaper designs are particularly well known (they are still produced commercially today) and Burne-Jones did some superb work for the firm, particularly in stained glass and tapestry design. Morris repudiated the concept of *fine art and his company was based on the ideal of a medieval guild, in which the craftsman both designed and executed the work. As a socialist he wished to produce art for the masses, but there was an inherent flaw in his ambition, for only the rich could afford his expensive hand-made products. His ideal of universal craftsmanship and his glorification of manual skill thus proved unrealistic in failing to come to terms with modern machine production. However, his work bore lasting fruit, in England (see ARTS AND CRAFTS MOVEMENT) and abroad, in the emphasis it laid on the social importance of good design and fine workmanship in every walk of life. He also played an important part in the development of the private printing press, through the founding of the *Kelmscott Press. Morris's homes at Walthamstow in London and Kelmscott Manor in Oxfordshire contain good examples of work designed by him and his associates.

Morse, Samuel F. B. (1791–1872), American painter and inventor. He had ambitions as a history painter and studied with *West during a period in London, 1811–15, but for financial reasons he had to work mainly as a portraitist. After his return to the USA he lived in Boston and then in New York, where he was a founder member of the *National Academy of Design and its first president from 1826 to 1845. Disenchanted by his failure to achieve major commissions as a history painter, however, he turned to invention, and in the 1830s conceived the idea of the telegraph and developed the Morse Code, which eventually made him a fortune. His first telegraph line was established between Washington and Baltimore in 1844, by which time he had abandoned painting as a profession.

Mortimer, John Hamilton (1740–79). English painter. He studied under *Hudson and became a lifelong friend of his fellow pupil Joseph *Wright. Like Wright, he painted portraits as well as subject pieces of a pioneering *Romantic nature. His *conversation pieces bear comparison with those of *Zoffany, but he found his true bent in the 1770s with pictures representing the exploits of soldiers and banditti in the 'savage' style of Salvator *Rosa (*Bandit Taking Up his Post*, *c.*1775, Detroit Inst. of Arts). Many of his paintings have disappeared and are now known only through engravings. Mortimer led an eccentric and disorderly life, but he became more settled after marrying in 1775 and his early death cut short the career of one of the most individual British painters of his generation.

mosaic. The art of making patterns and pictures by arranging small (usually multi-coloured) pieces of glass, marble, and other suitable materials and fixing them into a bed of cement or plaster. It was first developed extensively by the Romans in pavements. But it is also well suited to the adornment of walls and vaults, and great use was made of wall mosaic by the Christian churches of Italy and the *Byzantine empire throughout the Middle Ages. As an exterior decoration it has sometimes appeared on the façades of medieval churches and in modern architecture (*see* o'GORMAN). More rarely it has been made into portable pictures, or inlaid in furniture and small objects, as in the Aztec art of Mexico.

Mosan School. Tradition of manuscript illumination, metalwork, and enamelwork flourishing from the late 11th to the early 13th century in the valley of the Meuse (or Maas). The river rises in France and empties into the Rhine estuary in the Netherlands, but in the context of medieval art the term Mosan refers to the stretch of river and its tributaries in present-day Belgium, particularly the area around Liège and the Benedictine monastery of Stavelot. The most important artists of the school are *Godefroid de Clair, *Nicolas of Verdun, and *Rainer of Huy. The Mosan style is part of *Romanesque art, but is distinctive because of its more naturalistic, if idealized, attitude towards the human figure. In Rainer of Huy's font at Liège, for example, the figures are three-dimensional and well proportioned and their draperies are notably *antique-like. Mosan art is also noteworthy for its sheer sumptuousness, and Mosan metalworkers in particular were famed throughout Europe; Abbot *Suger employed a number at Saint-Denis.

Moser, Lukas (active 1432). German painter, known only from one work, the *Magdalen* altarpiece in the church at Tiefenbronn (signed and dated 1432—not 1431, as had previously been read). The altarpiece is remarkably advanced stylistically, showing a detailed naturalism in the treatment of figures and landscape and an interest in light that have much in common with the paintings of *Witz, who worked in nearby Switzerland. Also remarkable is an enigmatic inscription on the frame (perhaps no more than the lament of an underpaid artist): 'schri kunst schri und klag dich ser din begert iecz niemen mer' ('Cry out, art, cry out and wail! No one wants you now').

Moser, Mary (1744–1819). English flower painter, the daughter of **George Moser** (1706–83), a Swiss goldsmith, enameller, and medallist who settled in London in about 1726. Like her father, she was a foundation member of the *Royal Academy in 1768 (Angelica *Kauffmann was the only other woman so honoured). Only 24 at the time, she was the youngest ever RA, and in 1805 she was proposed as a candidate for the presidency. Her flower pieces in the Dutch manner were highly popular.

Moses, Grandma (née Anna Mary Robertson) (1860–1961). The most famous of American *naive painters. She took up painting in her seventies (initially copying postcards and *Currier and Ives prints) after arthritis made her unable to continue with embroidery, with which she had regularly won prizes at country fairs. Her first exhibition was held in a drugstore at Hoosick Falls, NY, in 1938. She was then 'discovered' by a collector, Louis J. Caldor, and had a one-woman show in New York in 1940 at the age of 80. Thereafter she rapidly became famous and something of a national institution, her work being widely reproduced, notably on Christmas cards. In 1949 she was received at the White House by President Harry Truman and in 1960 Governor Nelson Rockefeller proclaimed her 100th birthday, 7 September, 'Grandma Moses Day' in New York State. She produced more than a thousand pictures (working on a sort of production-line system, three or four at a time, painting first the skies and last the figures), her favourite subjects being scenes of what she called the 'old-timey' farm life she had known in her younger days. Examples are in many American collections, notably the Bennington Museum, Vermont.

Mostaert, Jan (c.1475–1555/6). Netherlandish painter. He worked mainly in Haarlem and the influence of *Geertgen tot Sint Jans can clearly be seen in his rather stiff and gangling figures. Most of his paintings are religious works or portraits (for a period of unknown duration, probably c.1516–26, he worked as court portraitist to Margaret of Austria, Regent of the Netherlands; see HABSBURG). However, his most remarkable painting is 'West Indies Landscape' (c.1545, Frans Hals Mus., Haarlem), which is now thought to represent New Mexico. He presumably based it on written accounts.

Motherwell, Robert (1915–91). American painter, collagist, writer, editor, and teacher, one of the pioneers and principal exponents of *Abstract Expressionism. He took up painting seriously in 1941 after studying philosophy at Stanford and Harvard universities and the erudite approach of his writings played a large part in setting the serious intellectual tone of the Abstract Expressionist movement. Motherwell was unusual among Abstract Expressionists in that his painting was essentially abstract from the beginning of his career. However, his work was deeply influenced by *Surrealism (particularly in the use of *automatism)

and there is often a suggestion of figuration in the large amorphous shapes of his paintings. Moreover, the intellectual sensibilities he brought to his work are reflected in the inspiration from literature, history, or his personal life. For example, he painted a series of works (more than a hundred pictures) entitled *Elegy to the Spanish Republic*. By the late 1960s his style had moved towards *Colour Field Painting. He was an extremely prolific artist and also displayed great energy as a writer, teacher, and lecturer. From 1958 to 1971 he was married to Helen *Frankenthaler.

Mucha, Alphonse (1860–1939). Czech painter and designer, active for much of his career in Paris. He settled there in 1888, and it was his centre of activity until about 1905, when he began to spend an increasing amount of time in his homeland. His output was highly varied, but he is best known for his luxuriously flowing poster designs, which rank among the most distinctive products of the *Art Nouveau style. They often feature beautiful women, but have nothing of the morbid sexuality typical of the period. Some of the best known were made in the 1890s for the celebrated actress Sarah Bernhardt. Mucha also designed sets, costumes, and jewellery for her. He was successful in the USA as well as Europe, making four journeys there between 1903 and 1922; a Chicago industrialist and Slavophile, Charles Richard Crane, sponsored a series of twenty huge paintings entitled *Slav Epic* (1909–28, Moravsky Krumlov Castle). Although he is so strongly associated with Paris, Mucha was an ardent patriot, and after Czechoslovakia became independent in 1918 he did a good deal of work for the new nation (giving his services free), including designing its first banknotes and stamps. After his death his work was long out of fashion, but interest in him has revived so strongly that in the popular imagination he is now one of the symbols of the turn-of-the-century era.

Müller, Otto. See BRÜCKE.

Mulready, William (1786–1863). Irish-born painter, active in England, the pupil and brother-in-law of John *Varley. After undistinguished beginnings with historical *genre and landscape he turned with great success to scenes of contemporary life in the vein made popular by *Wilkie. *The Fight Interrupted* (1816, V&A, London), which shows a vicar intervening between two boys who have come to blows, made his reputation and set the course for his career. At first his meticulous brushwork showed the influence of 17th-century Dutch painting, but in the 1820s he began to develop a more distinctive technique, using light colours over a white ground. This, together with his clear draughtsmanship and the poetic quality of some of his later paintings (*The Sonnet*, 1839, V&A), has led him to be seen as a precursor of the *Pre-Raphaelites, although they themselves regarded his work as trivial. Mulready made numerous book illustrations and also designed the first penny postage envelope (issued 1840).

multiples. A term designating works of art other than prints or cast sculpture that are designed to be produced in a large—potentially limitless—number of copies. Whereas prints and casts of sculptures are copies of an original work hand-made by the artist, multiples are different, for the artist often produces only a blueprint or set of specifications for an industrial process of manufacture in materials such as plastic. Multiples were first made in the 1960s, *Le Parc and *Oldenburg being early exponents. In theory, they represented a democratization of art, but in practice they are too expensive for a mass market and have been sold through galleries rather than high street shops. By about 1980 the idea seemed to be dying out, but there was a revival of interest in the 1990s.

Multscher, Hans (d. *c.*1467). German sculptor, active in Ulm, where he is first documented in 1427. The solid *naturalism of his style, reminiscent of *Sluter, suggests that he trained in the Netherlands or northern France. He ran a large workshop, which was influential in spreading this manner in southern Germany. Paintings were often integral to his altarpieces, but it is a matter for debate whether he practised painting himself. Among his most important works was the high altar (1456–8) for the church at Sterzing in the Tyrol (now in Italy and known as Vipiteno), parts of which are in the Multscher museum there.

Munch, Edvard (1863–1944). Norwegian painter and printmaker, his country's greatest artist. He began painting in a conventional naturalistic manner, but by 1884 he was part of the world of bohemian artists in Christiania (now Oslo) who had advanced ideas on ethics and sexual morality, Christian *Krohg being his early mentor. In 1885 he made the first of several visits to Paris, where he was influenced by the *Impressionists and *Symbolists and, above all, by *Gauguin's use of simplified forms and non-naturalistic colours. Soon after his return he painted the first work in which he showed a distinctly personal vision, *The Sick Child* (1885–6, NG, Oslo). Munch had endured a traumatic childhood (his mother and eldest sister died of consumption when he was young, and as a result his grief-stricken father became almost dementedly pious): 'Illness, madness, and death were the black angels that kept watch over my cradle', he wrote, and in his paintings he gave expression to the neuroses that haunted him. Certain themes—jealousy, sickness, the awakening of sexual desire—occur again and again, and he painted extreme psychological states with an unprecedented conviction and an intensity that sometimes bordered on the frenzied.

In 1892 Munch was invited to exhibit at the Verein Berliner Künstler (Association of Berlin Artists) and his work caused such an uproar in the press that the exhibition was closed. The scandal made him famous overnight in Germany, so he decided to base himself there and from 1892 to 1908 he lived mainly in Berlin (although he moved around restlessly, staying in boarding houses, and made frequent visits to Norway as well as journeys to France and Italy). During this period—the heart of his creative life—he devoted much of his time to an ambitious open-ended series of pictures that he called the 'Frieze of Life'—'a poem of life, love and death'. The most famous of the paintings from the series, *The Scream* (1893, NG, Oslo), and several others were translated by Munch into etching, lithography, or woodcut. He was one of the greatest of all printmakers, and his woodcuts, together with those of Gauguin, played a major part in the 20th-century revival of the technique; they are often in colour and exploit the grain of the wood to create a sense of rough, intense vigour. In 1908 Munch suffered what he called 'a complete mental collapse', the legacy of heavy drinking, overwork, and a wretched love affair, and after recuperating he made his home permanently in Norway, where he was by now an honoured figure. He realized that his mental instability was part of his genius ('I would not cast off my illness, for there is much in my art that I owe to it'), but he made a conscious decision to devote himself to recovery and abandoned his familiar imagery. The anguished intensity of his art disappeared and his work became much more extroverted. He announced this change of direction in a series of murals decorating the Assembly Hall of Oslo University (1910–16); they are concerned with what Munch called 'great eternal forces' (*History* and *The Sun* are two of the titles) and they are strong and fresh in colour and optimistic in spirit. In 1916 he bought a large house called Ekely, at Skøyen on the outskirts of Oslo, and he spent most of the rest of his life there, leading an increasingly isolated existence, although he continued to travel a good deal. His subjects in his later years, during which he kept up a prodigious output, included landscapes, portraits (he made much of his living through commissions), and workmen, often seen trudging through snow. However, he sometimes returned to the themes that haunted his youth, and occasionally he rekindled the passion and profundity of his early years, as in the last of his numerous self-portraits, *Between the Clock and the Bed* (1940–2, Munch Mus., Oslo), in which he shows himself old and frail, hovering on the edge of eternity. At his death he left a huge body of his work to the City of Oslo to found the Munch Museum (opened in 1963 to mark the centenary of his birth).

Munch ranks as one of the most powerful and influential of modern artists. His impact was particularly strong in Scandinavia and Germany, where he and van *Gogh are regarded as the two main sources of *Expressionist art. The intensity with which he communicated mental anguish opened up new paths for art. 'Just as *Leonardo da Vinci studied human anatomy and dissected corpses', he said, 'so I try to dissect souls.'

Munkácsy, Mihály (1844–1900). Hungarian painter. After training in Budapest, Munich, and Düsseldorf, he lived mainly in Paris. He had a resounding early success when he won a gold medal at the 1870 *Salon with the *Last Day of a Condemned Man* (NG, Budapest) and won an international reputation with *Milton and his Daughters* (1877–8, New York Public Lib.). These theatrical costume pieces were enormously popular with rich collectors and Munkácsy became one of the wealthiest artists of his day. His best works are now, however, considered to be his landscapes, in which although he did not paint out of doors, he continued the tradition of the *Barbizon School. He despised the *Impressionists, but his work is often very free in handling. Munkácsy is generally regarded as Hungary's greatest painter; appropriately the best collection of his work is in the National Gallery in Budapest.

Munnings, Sir Alfred (1878–1959). English painter, a specialist in scenes involving horses. He was at the height of his popularity in the interwar years, when he cut a figure in fashionable society and was often invited to the grandest country houses to paint the owners with their horses (he was also besieged with commissions when he visited the USA in 1924). From 1944 to 1949 he was president of the *Royal Academy and he became notorious for a splenetic speech attacking modern art that he delivered at the RA annual dinner in 1949. It was broadcast live on radio and was a national talking point the next day. His successor as PRA, Sir Gerald *Kelly, did much to restore the damage done to the Academy's prestige. Munnings was an artist of considerable natural ability, but he became rather slick and repetitive and his continued popularity is more with lovers of horses and the countryside than with lovers of painting. His work can best be seen at Castle House, Dedham, Essex, his home from 1919, which his widow converted into a Munnings Museum.

Münter, Gabriele. *See* NEUE KÜNSTLERVEREINIGUNG.

Murillo, Bartolomé Esteban (1617/18–82). Spanish painter, active for almost all his life in his native Seville. His early career is not well documented, but he started working in a naturalistic *tenebrist style, showing the influence of *Zurbarán. After making his reputation with a series of eleven paintings on the lives of Franciscan saints for the Franciscan monastery in Seville (1645–6, the pictures are now dispersed in Spain and elsewhere), he displaced Zurbarán as the city's leading painter and was unrivalled in this position for the rest of his life. His pre-eminence was acknowledged in 1660 when an academy of painting was founded in Seville (the first in Spain) and Murillo, together with Francisco *Herrera the Younger, was appointed joint president. Most of his paintings are of religious subjects, appealing strongly to popular piety and illustrating the doctrines of the Counter-Reformation Church, above all the Immaculate Conception, which was his favourite theme. His mature style was very different to that seen in his early works; it is characterized by idealized figures, soft, melting forms, delicate colouring, and sweetness of expression and mood. The term *estilo vaporoso* ('vaporous style') is often used of it. Murillo also painted *genre scenes of beggar children that have a similar sentimental appeal, but his fairly rare portraits are strikingly different in feeling—much more sombre and intellectual (an outstanding self-portrait, *c*.1670, is in the NG, London). He died from the effects of injuries he sustained when he fell from scaffolding whilst painting a huge altarpiece of the *Mystic Marriage of St Catherine* for the Capuchin church in Cadiz; the picture, completed by his pupil Francisco Meneses Osorio (*c*.1640–1721), is now in the city's Museo de Bellas Artes. Murillo had many assistants and followers, and his style continued to influence Sevillian painting into the 19th century. His fame in the 18th century and early 19th century was enormous. With *Ribera he was the only Spanish painter whose work was widely known outside Spain and he was ranked by many critics amongst the greatest artists of all time. Later his reputation plummeted, and he was dismissed as facile and sugary, but now that his own work is being distinguished from that of his numerous imitators his star is rising again.

Musée du Luxembourg, Paris. *See* POMPI-DOU CENTRE.

Musée National d'Art Moderne, Paris. *See* POMPIDOU CENTRE.

Musée d'Orsay, Paris. The French national museum of *fine and *applied arts from 1848 to 1914, opened in 1986. It is housed in a large building that was originally a railway station, the Gare d'Orsay (1897–1900). The main train service to it closed in 1939 and the building was subsequently put to various uses (for example as a theatre) before it was decided to transform it into a museum. Structural work began in 1979, and in 1980 the Italian architect Gae Aulenti began the conversion of the interior; her design has proved controversial, as some critics feel that it clashes with and obscures the handsome original fabric of the building and provides an unsympathetic setting for many of the works on show. The collections cover the era between the territories of the *Louvre and the *Pompidou Centre. Not surprisingly, the museum is particularly strong in French art, and at its heart is the superb collection of *Impressionist and *Post-Impressionist paintings formerly housed in the Jeu de Paume. The Musée d'Orsay also houses pictures transferred from the Louvre and decorative art from other state collections.

Museum of Modern Art, New York. The world's pre-eminent collection of art from the late 19th century to the present day, privately founded in 1929 by a group of collectors. It operated first in rented premises, holding loan shows, but the nucleus of a permanent collection was established with the bequest of Lillie P. Bliss (one of the founders), who died in 1931. The present building, in 53rd Street, was opened in 1939 and it has subsequently expanded greatly in size in various stages (in 1966 it took over the adjacent premises when the *Whitney Museum moved from them to its new home). Apart from its unrivalled holdings of painting, sculpture, and the graphic arts, the museum has collections of photographs, films, and architectural documentation, and a large library. Through its permanent collections, exhibitions, and many other activities it exercises a strong influence both on taste and on artistic production. The many publications it has produced include some of the standard texts on modern art, several of them written by Alfred H. *Barr, Jr., the first director of the museum.

Muybridge, Eadweard (1830–1904). British-born photographer and pioneer of motion photography who emigrated to the USA in about 1852. He became director of photographic surveys to the US Government, and while surveying the Pacific coast in 1872, he was asked by the railroad magnate Leland Stanford, then Governor of California, to photograph a horse in motion, evidently to settle a bet as to whether a horse ever had all four legs off the ground simultaneously. Muybridge experimented with a battery of cameras with high-speed shutters operated by the horse itself passing across trip threads (he worked at Stanford's stud farm, and at his expense), and succeeded in proving that all four legs of a horse are indeed at times in the air simultaneously. He published his photographs in *The Horse in Motion* (1878), and then went on to study the movement of other animals, including humans, publishing his results in volumes such as *Animal Locomotion* (1887). In 1880 he invented the zoopraxiscope to project the pictures and recreate the movements he had photographed, and this he showed to scientific bodies all over Europe and America. This predecessor of the modern cinema caused a sensation. Muybridge's photographs were much used as a source by artists, among them *Eakins and the *Futurists.

Myron. Greek sculptor active in Athens in the mid-5th century BC. He was one of the leading Greek sculptors of the period and is celebrated for his bronze *Discobolus* (Discus Thrower), which survives in Roman marble copies; the best of them is in the Terme Museum in Rome. As an example of compositional equilibrium it achieved a fame comparable to the *Doryphorus* of *Polyclitus. Copies also exist of Myron's group of *Athena and Marsyas*, but no visual record survives of the work for which he was most renowned in his own time—the bronze *Cow* in the market place at Athens, which was said to

display remarkable naturalism. *See also* SEVERE STYLE.

Myslbek, Josef Václav (1848–1922). The leading Czech sculptor of the late 19th and early 20th centuries. He created numerous statues of national heroes in Prague, most notably the famous St Wenceslas Monument in Wenceslas Square, which was conceived in 1887 but not completed until 1923, the year after Myslbek's death. His work is in the *Renaissance tradition but has a suitably Romantic Slavonic ardour; *Rodin admired his richly worked bronze surfaces.

Mytens, Daniel (*c.*1590–1647). Anglo-Dutch portrait painter. He was born in Delft and trained in The Hague (probably under *Miereveld), but almost all of his known career was spent in England, where he is first recorded in 1618 working for the Earl of *Arundel. By 1620 he was employed by James I and in 1625 he was appointed 'one of our picture drawers' by Charles I. Mytens introduced a new elegance and grandeur into English portraiture, especially in his full-lengths, and he was the dominant painter at court until the arrival of van *Dyck in 1632. Van Dyck completely outclassed him, however, and he returned to The Hague in about 1634. Few paintings are known from his final years, but he continued to work as Arundel's agent. His finest picture is acknowledged to be *The First Duke of Hamilton* (1629, NPG, Edinburgh), described by Sir Ellis *Waterhouse as 'the great masterpiece of pre-Vandyckian portraiture in England'. Mytens belonged to a dynasty of painters active into the 18th century. Among the other members was his great-nephew, **Daniel Mytens the Younger** (1644–88), also a portraitist.

Nabis. A group of painters, mainly French, active in Paris in the 1890s; their outlook was essentially *Symbolist and they were particularly influenced by *Gauguin's expressive use of colour and rhythmic pattern. The name Nabis (Hebrew: 'prophets') was coined in reference to the missionary zeal with which they promoted Gauguin's teachings. *Sérusier, who met Gauguin at Pont-Aven in 1888, was the driving force behind the group and with *Denis was its main theorist. Other members included *Bonnard, *Maillol (before he turned to sculpture), Ranson (*see* ACADÉMIE), *Vallotton, *Vuillard, and Vuillard's brother-in-law, Ker-Xavier Roussel (1867–1944). They were active in design (of posters, stained glass, and theatrical decor) and book illustration as well as painting. Group exhibitions were held between 1892 and 1899, after which the members gradually drifted apart. Several of them, however, continued Nabis ideas into the 20th century, notably Denis and Sérusier, whose work remained esoteric in spirit and bound up with their religious beliefs.

Nadelman, Elie (1882–1946). Polish-born sculptor who became an American citizen in 1927. After brief studies in his native Warsaw and in Munich, he settled in Paris in 1903 or 1904 and lived there until 1914. With the outbreak of the First World War, Nadelman moved to London and then New York. He had a successful one-man show at *Stieglitz's gallery in 1915 and was befriended by Paul *Manship and Gertrude Vanderbilt *Whitney among others. His patrons included Helena Rubinstein (he had known her in Paris), who commissioned him to make sleek marble heads for her beauty salons. He married a wealthy widow in 1919 and his work has a witty sophistication appropriate to the high society world he moved in, as with the delightful bowler-hatted bronze *Man in the Open Air* (1915, MoMA, New York). With his humour went a bold simplification and distortion of forms that places him alongside *Lachaise as one of the pioneers of modern sculpture in America. The Depression had a disastrous effect on his market and his career virtually ended when much of his work was accidentally destroyed in 1935.

naive art. Term applied to painting (and to a much lesser degree sculpture) produced in more or less sophisticated societies but lacking conventional expertise in representational skills. Colours are characteristically bright and non-naturalistic, perspective non-scientific, and the vision childlike or literal-minded. The term *'primitive' is sometimes used more or less synonymously with naive, but this can be confusing, as 'primitive' is also applied loosely to paintings of the pre-Renaissance era as well as to art of 'uncivilized' societies. Other terms that are sometimes used in a similar way are 'folk', 'popular', or 'Sunday painters', but these too have their pitfalls, not least 'Sunday painter', for many amateurs do not paint in a naive style, and naive artists (at least the successful ones) often paint as a full-time job. Sophisticated artists may also deliberately effect a naive style, but this 'false naivety' (*faux naïf*) is no more to be confused with the spontaneous quality of the true naive than the deliberately childlike work of say *Klee or *Picasso is to be confused with genuine children's drawing. Naive art has a quality of its own that is easy to recognize but hard to define. Scottie *Wilson summed it up when he said 'It's a feeling you cannot explain. You're born with it and it just comes out.'

Naive art, as the term is now generally understood, developed in the 19th century (before then, pictures that have a naive quality might more reasonably be classified as folk art or simply as amateurish works) and the first notable exponent was perhaps the American Edward *Hicks. It was not until the early years of the 20th century, however, that there has been a vogue for naive art. Henri *Rousseau was the first naive painter to win serious critical recognition and he remains the only one who is regarded as a great master, but many others have won an honourable place in modern art. The critic Wilhelm *Uhde was chiefly responsible for putting naive painters on the map in the years after the First World War. At first their freshness and directness of vision appealed mainly to fellow artists, but a number of major group exhibitions in the 1920s and 1930s helped to develop public taste for them, notably 'Masters of Popular Painting: Modern Primitives of Europe and America' at the Museum of Modern Art, New York, in 1938. Most of the early naive painters to make reputations were French (mainly because Uhde was active in discovering and promoting them in France); they included *Bauchant, *Bombois, *Séraphine, and *Vivin. In Britain the best-known figures include Beryl *Cook and Alfred *Wallis (two painters who show the huge difference of approach and style that can exist between artists given the same label). L. S. *Lowry is also often claimed as a naive painter, but some critics regard him as outside this classification because of his many years of study at art school. In the USA the leading figures include John *Kane and Grandma *Moses. The richest crop of naive painters, however, has been in Croatia, with Ivan *Generalić outstanding. Haiti is also particularly noteworthy in that naive painting has been the country's central tradition in modern art; the leading figures include Hector Hyppolite (1894–1948) and Wilson Bigaud (1931–).

Nanni di Banco (d. 1421). Florentine sculptor, one of the major figures of the transition from *Gothic to *Renaissance. Much of his work was designed for one or other of two architectural settings in Florence, the cathedral and the church of Orsanmichele, which together formed the chief source of demand for sculpture in the city during the first quarter of the 15th century, and he often worked alongside *Donatello. His work has a Gothic elegance, but also shows the influence of the *antique; his masterpiece, the group of the *Quattro Santi Coronati* (Four Crowned Saints) at Orsanmichele, for example, features grave and dignified figures modelled on Roman senator statues. Because this and other major works are of controversial dating, however, it is uncertain whether he was in advance of Donatello in his use of *classical exemplars.

Nanteuil, Robert (*c*.1623–78). French engraver, draughtsman, and pastellist, almost exclusively of portraits. He is considered the greatest European portrait engraver of the 17th century, and in France stands as the counterpart of Philippe de *Champaigne among painters. He often engraved the work of Champaigne and other painters, but also made original compositions, in which he showed both great technical mastery and penetrating characterization. Louis XIV appointed him royal draughtsman in 1658 and he made many pastel portraits as well as engravings of the king and royal family. His other sitters included some of the leading Frenchmen of his time.

Nash, Paul (1889–1946). English painter, book illustrator, writer, photographer, and designer. Nash was one of the most individual British artists of his period, taking a distinguished place in the English tradition of deep attachment to the countryside whilst at the same time responding imaginatively to European modernism. He saw himself as a successor of William *Blake and *Turner. After training at the *Slade School he served in the First World War, was wounded, and worked as an *Official War Artist, creating memorable images of the devastation the war wrought on the countryside. In the 1920s and particularly in the 1930s he was influenced by *Surrealism (above all by de *Chirico, an exhibition of whose work he saw in London in 1928) and often concentrated on mysterious aspects of the landscape (*Monster Field*, 1939, Durban AG). For much of this time he lived in rural areas (Kent, Sussex, Dorset), basing his work on scenes he knew well but imaginatively transforming them. In 1933 he was the prime mover in the formation of *Unit One, and he helped to organize and exhibited in the International Surrealist Exhibition in London in 1936. In the Second World War he was again an Official War Artist. He was already very sick with the asthmatic condition that killed him, but he produced one of the best-known works to be inspired by the conflict, *Totes Meer (Dead Sea)* (1940–1, Tate, London), which portrays shot-down aircraft with their wings looking like undulating waves. Nash was regarded as one of the finest book illustrators of his time; he also designed scenery, fabrics, and posters, and was a photographer and writer, his books including a guide to Dorset (1936). His brother **John** (1893–1977) was also a painter and illustrator, excelling in meticulous flower drawings for botanical publications. Like Paul he was an Official War Artist in both world wars.

Nasmyth, Alexander (1758–1840). Scottish painter. He worked mainly in his native Edinburgh, but he was a pupil and assistant of *Ramsay in London 1774–8, and in 1782–4 he visited Italy. There he became interested in landscape painting, which eventually took over from portraiture as his main concern. In his landscapes he blended *classical elements stemming from *Claude with naturalistic observation and became the founder of the Scottish landscape tradition, influencing many younger painters. He was a man of wide culture, interested in science as well as art, and he worked as a stage designer and architectural consultant. One of his friends was the poet Robert Burns, whose portrait he painted against a romantic landscape background (1787, NPG, Edinburgh). Nasmyth had several artist sons and daughters, of whom the most important was his eldest child, **Patrick** (1787–1831). He worked mainly in London and achieved great popularity with his large output of landscapes in the manner of the 17th-century Dutch masters, earning the nickname 'the English *Hobbema'.

National Academy of Design, New York. A professional association of artists founded in New York in 1825 in opposition to the conservative American Academy of the Fine Arts (which ran from 1802 to 1841; *see* TRUMBULL). The National Academy was originally called the Society for the Improvement of Drawing; it adopted its present name in 1828. For most of the 19th century it was the leading art institution in America, its annual exhibitions helping to make New York the country's major art centre. *Morse was first president, and most ambitious artists of the time sought membership. However, its views became unprogressive, prompting certain artists to break away (notably to found The *Eight in 1908). Today it exists mainly as a historical institution.

National Art Collections Fund. The UK's largest art charity, founded in 1903 to assist public collections to acquire works of art they would not otherwise be able to afford. The founders, who included Roger

*Fry and D. S. *MacColl, shared a concern about the amount of art leaving the country, and the Fund's first conspicuous achievement came in 1906 when, by means of a public appeal, it bought *Velázquez's *Rokeby Venus*, which was in danger of being sold abroad, and presented it to the *National Gallery, London. Many similar successes have followed, most memorably that with *Leonardo da Vinci's *cartoon of the *Virgin and Child with St Anne and St John the Baptist*: in 1962 financial problems forced the *Royal Academy to sell the cartoon, its greatest treasure, and the Fund's campaign to secure it for the National Gallery caught the public imagination to such an extent that an estimated 300,000 people made contributions to the purchase price. Most of the Fund's work deals with more modest art, however, and by the time of its centenary in 2003 it had helped more than 600 museums, galleries, and historic houses throughout the UK to make more than 400,000 acquisitions, ranging from prehistoric artefacts to contemporary experimental pieces. More broadly, the Fund aims to increase public enjoyment and understanding of art and has, for example, played a leading role in the campaign to abolish admission charges to national museums, which achieved its aim in 2001. The Fund is supported mainly by members' subscriptions.

National Gallery, London. The British national collection of European paintings from *c*.1300 to *c*.1900 (it also includes a few earlier pictures and has recently started to acquire works from the early 20th century). It was founded in 1824 when the government purchased 38 paintings from the collection of John Julius Angerstein, a Russian-born merchant who had died the previous year. Initially they were displayed in his former house at 100 Pall Mall, but further acquisitions (including the bequest of Sir George *Beaumont) soon necessitated larger premises, and the present building in Trafalgar Square, designed by William Wilkins, was opened in 1838. In its early days the gallery was run in rather haphazard fashion, but Charles *Eastlake, director 1855–65, brought professionalism, flair, and drive to its administration (other notable directors have included Edward *Poynter and Kenneth *Clark). The gallery shared the premises with the *Royal Academy until 1869, by which time it had grown into one of the great collections of the world. Since then there have been various enlargements of the building and in 1991 a major extension was opened—the Sainsbury Wing, the gift of Sir John, Simon, and Timothy Sainsbury. This wing now houses the gallery's early paintings, up to about 1510. The collection as a whole now has about 2,200 pictures. This is a fairly small number compared with some of the great Continental galleries based on former royal collections, but the National Gallery's paintings surpass those of any other gallery in giving a balanced view of the mainstream of European painting from *Giotto to *Cézanne. Best represented of all are the early Italian and Dutch Schools. The representation of the British School is selective because of the existence of *Tate Britain as a separate national gallery of British art. Other well-known national galleries, with their dates of foundation, are: the National Gallery of Scotland in Edinburgh (1859); the National Gallery of Victoria in Melbourne (1859); the National Gallery of Ireland in Dublin (1864); the National Gallery of Canada in Ottawa (1880); the National Gallery of Art in Washington (1937; *see* MELLON); and the Australian National Gallery in Canberra (1976).

National Portrait Gallery, London. The national collection of portraits of eminent British men and women. It was founded in 1856 at the urging of the historian and politician Philip Henry Stanhope, 5th Earl Stanhope, who was the first chairman of the trustees. The collection was originally housed at 29 Great George Street, Westminster, and the present premises, adjoining the National Gallery, were opened in 1896. The criterion for inclusion in the gallery is the celebrity of the sitter rather than the quality of the portrait, so the pictures in the collection vary enormously in artistic merit, from an acknowledged masterpiece such as *Holbein's cartoon of Henry VIII to the amateurish representation of the three Brontë sisters by their brother Branwell. Nevertheless, because portraiture has played such a great part in the history of British art, many illustrious artists are well represented. Recently the NPG has begun to commission portraits of living sitters, and since 1980 it has organized a series of annual portrait awards for artists under 40

years old. From the 1970s it has collaborated with several historic houses outside London, in which works from the gallery are displayed in appropriate period settings: the main ones are Montacute House in Somerset, Beningbrough Hall in Yorkshire, and Bodelwyddan Castle in Wales. The Scottish National Portrait Gallery was established in Edinburgh in 1882, and the National Portrait Gallery in Washington in 1962.

Nattier, Jean-Marc (1685–1766). French portrait painter. His father, **Marc** (*c.*1642–1705), was a painter and his mother, **Marie** (née Courtois) (*c.*1655–1703), was a *miniaturist. He was one of the most successful artists at the court of Louis XV, excelling in the vogue for painting women in mythological or allegorical fancy dress—or undress—transforming his sitters into goddesses (*Mlle de Lambesc as Minerva*, 1732, Louvre, Paris). The pastel-like delicacy of his handling led to the accusation that he 'painted with make-up'. His portraits are little concerned with individual characterization, but they show fluency, vivacity, and a relaxed charm. Towards the end of his career taste began to turn against him and some of his later work shows signs of fatigue. His brother **Jean-Baptiste** (1678–1726) was also a painter; he committed suicide after being expelled by the Académie Royale.

naturalism. Term denoting an approach to art in which the artist endeavours to represent objects as they are empirically observed, rather than in a stylized or conceptual manner. *Bellori (1672) was the first to apply the term to a particular type of painting in discussing the followers of *Caravaggio, with reference to their doctrine of copying nature faithfully whether it seems to us ugly or beautiful. Naturalism, however, is not incompatible with the *idealization of nature, for Greek sculpture may be naturalistic in its command of anatomy but idealistic in that it sets up a standard of physical beauty remote from the everyday world. Nor need the term imply minute attention to detail, although this is often part of a naturalistic approach. The shade of meaning to be attached to the word can thus vary greatly according to context; when used in its broadest sense it may suggest little more than that a work is representational rather than *abstract. The terms 'naturalistic' and 'realistic' are often used more or less synonymously, but *Realism with a capital R has a specific meaning in the history of art and should not be used loosely.

Navarrete, Juan Fernández de (c.1538–79). Spanish painter from Navarre, called 'El Mudo' (the mute) because he was deaf and dumb. He spent several years in Italy (where according to *Palomino he was a pupil of *Titian) and returned to Spain in about 1565. In 1568 he was appointed a court painter to Philip II (see HABSBURG) and he spent most of the rest of his life painting altarpieces for the *Escorial. His work was important in spreading Italian influence in Spain.

Nazarenes. A group of young, idealistic German painters of the early 19th century who believed that art should serve a religious or moral purpose and desired to return to the spirit of the Middle Ages. The nucleus of the group was established in 1809 when six students at the Vienna Academy formed an association called the Brotherhood of St Luke (Lukasbrüder), named after the patron saint of painting. The name Nazarenes (first used c.1817) was given to them facetiously because of their devout way of life and adoption of flowing biblical hairstyles. They wished to revive the working environment as well as the spiritual sincerity of the Middle Ages, and lived and worked together in a quasi-monastic fashion. In 1810 *Overbeck, *Pforr, and two other members moved to Rome, where they occupied the disused monastery of S. Isidoro. Here they were joined by Peter *Cornelius and others. One of their aims was the revival of monumental *fresco painting and they obtained two important commissions that made their work internationally known (Casa Bartholdy, 1816–17, the paintings are now in the Alte Nationalgalerie, Berlin; and Casino Massimo, 1817–29, in situ). Stylistically they were much indebted to *Perugino and their work is clear and prettily coloured, but often insipid. In general, modern taste has been more sympathetic towards the Nazarenes' simple and sensitive landscape and portrait drawings than to their ambitious and didactic figure paintings. They broke up as a formal group in the 1820s, but their ideas continued to be influential and the name was applied to younger

followers until about 1850. In 1819 Cornelius had moved to Munich, where he attracted a large number of pupils and assistants who in turn carried his style to other German centres. The studio of Overbeck (the only Nazarene to remain permanently in Rome) was a meeting place for artists from many countries (the Russian *Ivanov was his friend, for example); *Ingres admired him and Ford Madox *Brown visited him. William *Dyce introduced some of the Nazarene ideals into English art and there is a kinship of spirit with the *Pre-Raphaelites.

NEAC. See NEW ENGLISH ART CLUB.

Neeffs (or **Neefs**), **Pieter the Elder** (c.1578–1656/61). Flemish painter, active in Antwerp. Most of his pictures are interiors of *Gothic churches, some of them night scenes illuminated by artificial light. They are generally small, painted on copper, and executed in a precise, neat way—similar in style to those of the *Steenwycks, but more mechanical. His son **Pieter Neeffs the Younger** (1620–after 1675) painted the same subjects, and it is very difficult to distinguish between their hands. Another son, **Lodewijk** (1617–49?), was also a painter, but little is known of his work.

Neer, Aert (or **Aernout**) **van der** (1604?–77). Dutch landscape painter, active in his native Amsterdam. He had two specialities: moonlit scenes, of which he is the acknowledged master among Dutch painters; and winter landscapes with skaters, as an exponent of which he is in the first rank. In both types he displayed his mastery of light effects and subtle modulations of colour. He was a prolific painter and his work was much copied and imitated, but he had difficulty earning a living as an artist. In 1658 he opened a wine shop in Amsterdam, but this venture was a failure and in 1662 he became bankrupt. Two of his sons were artists. **Eglon** (c.1634–1703) is best known for *genre pieces done in the style of *Terborch and *Metsu. He was conspicuously more successful than his father and from 1690 worked as court painter in Düsseldorf. The few works that can be attributed to **Jan** (c.1638–65) show that he was an imitator of his father.

Neoclassicism. The dominant movement in European art and architecture in the late

18th and early 19th centuries, characterized by a desire to recreate the spirit and forms of the art of ancient Greece and Rome. A new and more scientific interest in *classical antiquity, greatly stimulated by the discoveries at Pompeii (where excavations began in 1748) and Herculaneum, was one of the features of the movement, and it is also seen as a reaction against the light-hearted and frivolous *Rococo style. The order, clarity, and reason of Greek and Roman art appealed greatly in the Age of Englightenment, and the Neoclassical style could have moral as well as aesthetic implications, particularly in France, where it is associated with the Revolution and a desire to restore ancient Roman values into civil life. It is, indeed, in the paintings of J.-L. *David, with their antique grandeur and simplicity of form, and their heroic severity of tone, that Neoclassicism finds its purest expression, but the style was born and had its focal point in Rome. *Mengs and *Winckelmann were in the vanguard of the movement there, and other leading figures from all over Europe—*Canova, *Flaxman, Gavin *Hamilton, *Thorvaldsen—spent the main or important parts of their careers in the city. Many American artists worked there too—notably the sculptor Horatio *Greenough, who was a pupil of Thorvaldsen—and took the Neoclassical style back to their country. Because Neoclassicism placed respect for approved models above personal expression it was a style that particularly lent itself to this kind of international currency. The 18th century saw a great growth in the publication of lavishly illustrated volumes on classical art, architecture, and antiquities, and this helped to spread the ideals of the movement. There was, however, considerable stylistic variation within Neoclassicism; Angelica *Kauffmann, for example, painted in a delicate and pretty manner that is far removed from David's severity. Moreover, there is no firm dividing line between Neoclassicism and *Romanticism, even though in some ways they appear to be at opposite spiritual poles. In the revival of interest in antique art, archaeological zeal could easily give way to a nostalgic yearning for a lost Golden Age, and the term 'Romantic Classicism' is sometimes used to characterize an aspect of Neoclassicism in which an interest in antiquity is tinged with Romantic feeling. In fact the antipathy between Classics and Romantics (exemplified by *Ingres and *Delacroix, for example) was unknown before the 19th century, and it was only in the mid-19th century, at a time when the antique revival style was out of fashion, that the word 'Neoclassicism' was coined—originally a pejorative term with suggestions of lifelessness and impersonality. These negative connotations have clung tenaciously to the term, and the ardent aspirations of the founders of Neoclassicism have been obscured by the fact that the more decorative aspects of the movement—Wedgwood pottery, for example—have become more closely associated with the word in the public consciousness than have the great masterpieces of David and Canova.

Neoclassicism is related to but can be distinguished from Greek Taste, which was a fairly superficial fashion for Greek-inspired decoration, and from the Greek Revival, which in architecture was a movement expressing a new interest in the simplicity and gravity of ancient Greek buildings. It began seriously in the 1790s and culminated in the 1820s and 1830s. Greek architecture became widely known in the West only around 1750-60 and in the early days of Neoclassicism it was regarded as primitive and few architects cared to imitate it.

In the context of modern art, the term Neoclassicism has been applied to a revival of the spirit of classicism among avant-garde artists in the second and third decades of the 20th century, marking a return to restraint after a period of unprecedented experimentation. Other terms for this phenomenon include 'the New Classicism', 'the classical revival', 'the return to order', and 'the call to order' (this last being the title of a book by Jean Cocteau, published in 1926— *Le Rappel à l'ordre*).

Neo-Dada. A term that has been applied to various styles, trends, or works that are perceived as reviving the methods or spirit of *Dada. It has been used as a synonym for *Pop art, for example, and has been applied to the work of Jasper *Johns.

Neo-Expressionism. Movement in painting (and to a lesser extent sculpture) emerging in the late 1970s, characterized by intense subjectivity of feeling and aggressively raw handling of materials. Neo-Expressionist paintings are typically large and rapidly executed, sometimes with materials such as straw or broken crockery embedded in their surfaces. They are usually figurative, often with violent or doom-laden subjects, but the image is sometimes almost lost in the welter of surface activity. To some extent Neo-Expressionism marked a return to more traditional forms after the 'anything goes' experimentation of the 1970s. Perhaps partly for this reason it was welcomed by art dealers and collectors, but critical reaction to the movement has been very mixed. Several exponents, above all Julian *Schnabel, have become rich and famous, but to many critics their work seems deliberately bad, ignoring all conventional ideas of skill; indeed the term 'Bad Painting' (from the title of an exhibition at the New Museum, New York, in 1978) has been applied to certain works in the vein (Punk Art and Stupid Painting are alternative terms). Distinguishing between good 'Bad Painting' (i.e. that which deliberately cultivates crudeness for its emotional value) and bad 'Bad Painting' (something that is just a mess) is an unenviable critical task. Neo-Expressionism has flourished mainly in Germany (where its exponents are sometimes called Neue Wilden—'New Wild Ones'), Italy, and the USA. Leading exponents include: in Germany, Georg *Baselitz and Anselm *Kiefer; in Italy, Sandro Chia (1946–) and Francesco Clemente (1952–); in the USA, David Salle (1952–) and Julian Schnabel. *See also* NEW IMAGE PAINTING.

Neo-Geo. Term (short for Neo-Geometric Conceptualism) applied to the work of a group of American artists active in New York in the mid-1980s who employed a variety of styles and media but were linked by the fact that their paintings, sculpture, or other products were predominantly cool and impersonal, in reaction to the emotionalism of *Neo-Expressionism. Jeff Koons (1955–), who exhibited consumer products such as vacuum cleaners in a reworking of *Dada *ready-mades, is the best-known figure of the group. Many critics have seen their work as cynical and empty ('dead on arrival' is one memorable description), but Neo-Geo has been a hit with certain collectors, most notably Charles *Saatchi, who has bought it in bulk.

Neo-Impressionism. A movement in French painting—both a development from *Impressionism and a reaction against it—in which the Impressionist approach to depicting light and colour was made more rational and scientific. Georges *Seurat was the founder of the movement and far and away its outstanding artist. His friend Paul *Signac was its main theoretician, and Camille *Pissarro was briefly a leading adherent. All three showed Neo-Impressionist pictures at the final Impressionist exhibition in 1886 (the term Neo-Impressionism was coined by the critic Félix Fénéon (1861–1944) in a review of this exhibition). The theoretical basis of Neo-Impressionism was *divisionism, with its associated technique of *pointillism—the use of dots of pure colour applied in such a way that when seen from an appropriate distance they achieve a maximum of luminosity. In each painting the dots were of a uniform size, chosen to harmonize with the scale of the work. In Seurat's paintings, this approach combined solidity and clarity of form with a vibrating intensity of light; in the hands of lesser artists, it often produced works that look rigid and contrived. As an organized movement Neo-Impressionism was short-lived, but it had a significant influence on several major artists of the late 19th and early 20th centuries, notably *Gauguin, van *Gogh, and *Matisse, who worked with Signac and another Neo-Impressionist, Henri-Edmond Cross (1856–1910), at St Tropez in 1906.

Neo-Plasticism. Term coined by Piet *Mondrian for his style of austerely geometrical abstract painting and more broadly for the philosophical ideas about art that his work embodied. He claimed that art should be 'denaturalized', by which he meant that it must be purely abstract, with no representational relation to the natural world. To this end he limited the elements of pictorial design to the straight line and the rectangle (the right angles in a strictly horizontal–vertical relation to the frame) and to the primary colours—blue, red, and yellow—together with black, white, and grey. In this way he thought that one might escape the particular and achieve expression of an ideal of universal harmony. Mondrian took the term *nieuwe beelding* (which might be translated as 'new image creation') from the writings of Dr Matthieu Schoenmaekers, a Dutch author of popular books on philosophy and religion, whom he admired for a time but later considered to be a charlatan. The Dutch term was rendered in French by Mondrian himself as *néo-plasticisme*, and this in turn was translated into English as Neo-Plasticism.

Neo-Romanticism. A movement in British painting and other arts *c.*1935–55, in which a number of loosely affiliated artists looked back to certain aspects of 19th-century *Romanticism, particularly the 'visionary' landscape tradition of William *Blake and Samuel *Palmer, and reinterpreted them in a more modern idiom. The term was coined by the critic Raymond Mortimer in 1942. Painters and graphic artists representative of the movement include John *Minton, John *Piper, and Graham *Sutherland, who all worked in a landscape tradition that was regarded as distinctly national, and projected a Romantic image of the countryside at a time when it was under threat from Nazi Germany. Other artists whose work has been dubbed Neo-Romantic include the poet Dylan Thomas, the film director Michael Powell, and photographers such as Bill Brandt and Edwin Smith. The term Neo-Romanticism has also been applied to certain painters working in France in the 1930s, notably *Berman and *Tchelitchew, who typically painted dreamlike imaginary landscapes with rather mournful figures. Their work influenced the British Neo-Romantics. In the 1980s 'Neo-Romanticism' was one of the many terms used as a synonym for *Neo-Expressionism, but it did not catch on in this sense.

Neroccio dei Landi (1447–1500). Sienese painter and sculptor. He was probably a pupil of *Vecchietta and worked in partnership with *Francesco di Giorgio in the early 1470s. Most of his paintings are representations of the Virgin and Child with Saints, but one of his finest works is a *Portrait of a Lady* (*c.*1490, NG, Washington). He continued the elegant and refined Sienese tradition that stretched back to *Duccio and his work is particularly noted for its delicate colouring. His work as a sculptor included commissions for Siena Cathedral.

Netscher, Caspar (1635/9?–84). Dutch painter. *Houbraken makes inconsistent statements about his birthplace, mentioning both Heidelberg and Prague, and there

is similar doubt about his birthdate. Most of his career was spent in The Hague, where he settled in 1661/2, but he trained in Deventer with *Terborch. From his master he took his predilection for depicting costly materials—particularly white satin. He painted *genre scenes and some religious and mythological subjects, but from about 1670 he devoted himself almost exclusively to portraits, often for court circles in The Hague. His reputation was such that Charles II invited him to England (*Vertue says that he came, de *Piles and Houbraken that he declined). His work, elegant, Frenchified, small in scale, and exquisitely finished, influenced Dutch portraiture into the 18th century, his followers including his sons **Constantijn** (1688–1723) and **Theodoor** (1661–1732).

Neue Künstlervereinigung München (NKV) ('New Artists' Association of Munich'). An association of artists founded in Munich in 1909 to provide a more liberal alternative to existing exhibiting venues, particularly the *Sezession. *Kandinsky was elected president; Alexander Kanoldt (1881–1939) was secretary and Adolf Erbslöh (1881–1947) was chairman of the exhibition committee. Other members included *Jawlensky, *Kubin, Kandinsky's lover Gabriele Münter (1877–1962), and Jawlensky's lover Marianne von Werefkin (1870–1938). They were strongly influenced by *Fauvism and the three exhibitions that they held (1909, 1910, and 1911) were far too advanced for the critics and public and were met with torrents of abuse. The second exhibition was European in character, including works by the Russians David and Vladimir *Burliuk; by *Le Fauconnier, *Picasso, and *Rouault; and by members of the Fauves (*Braque, *Derain, van *Dongen, *Vlaminck), some of whom had already moved on to *Cubism. Franz *Marc came to the NKV's defence after this exhibition and it was in this way that he met Kandinsky. When Erbslöh rejected an abstract painting submitted by Kandinsky for the third exhibition, Kandinsky resigned and with Marc founded the *Blaue Reiter. They moved so quickly that the Blaue Reiter's first exhibition opened on the same day as the NKV's last and stole its thunder.

Neue Sachlichkeit (New Objectivity). Movement in German painting in the

1920s and early 1930s reflecting the resignation and cynicism of the post-war period. The name was coined in 1923 by Gustav Hartlaub, director of the Kunsthalle, Mannheim, and used as the title of an exhibition he staged there in 1925, featuring 'artists who have retained or regained their fidelity to positive tangible reality'. The movement was not characterized by a unified style or by any kind of group affiliation, but its major trend involved the use of meticulous detail and violent satire to portray the face of evil. This marked a continuation of the interest in social criticism that had characterized much of *Expressionism, but Neue Sachlichkeit rejected the abstract tendencies of the *Blaue Reiter, in which Expressionism had reached its high point just before the First World War. *Dix and *Grosz were the greatest figures of the movement, which was dissipated in the 1930s with the rise of the Nazis. Other artists associated with Neue Sachlichkeit include Conrad Felixmüller (1897–1977), Christian Schad (1894–1982), and Rudolf Schlichter (1890–1955).

Nevelson, Louise (1899–1988). Russianborn American sculptor, painter, and printmaker. Her family emigrated to the USA in 1905 and she settled in New York in 1920. Her serious study of art began at the *Art Students League in 1929–30 and she then studied under Hans *Hofmann in Munich. In 1932–3 she worked with Ben *Shahn as assistant to Diego *Rivera on his frescos in New York. She started to make sculpture in 1932 and in 1944 began experimenting with abstract wooden assemblages. It was towards the end of the 1950s that she began the 'sculptured walls' for which she became internationally famous. These are wall-like *reliefs made up of many boxes and compartments into which abstract shapes are assembled together with commonplace objects such as chair legs, bits of balustrades, and other 'found objects' (*An American Tribute to the British People*, 1960–4, Tate, London). These constructions, painted a uniform black, or later in her career white or gold, won her a reputation as a leader in both *assemblage and *environment sculpture. They have great formal elegance, but also a strange ritualistic power. In the late 1960s she started working in a greater variety of materials and also began to receive

commissions for large open-air and environmental sculptures, which she executed in aluminium or steel.

Nevinson, C. R. W. (Christopher Richard Wynne) (1889–1946). British painter and printmaker. As a student at the *Académie Julian, Paris, in 1912–13 Nevinson met several of the *Futurists and he became the outstanding British exponent of their style. His work included landscapes, urban scenes, figure compositions, and flowers, but he found his ideal subjects during the First World War. He served in France with the Red Cross and the Royal Army Medical Corps, 1914–16, before being invalided out, and his harsh, steely images of life and death in the trenches received great acclaim when he held a one-man exhibition at the Leicester Galleries, London, in 1916. Stylistically they drew on certain *Cubist as well as Futurist ideas, but they are closer to the work of the *Vorticists (with whom he had exhibited in 1915). In 1917 Nevinson returned to France as an *Official War Artist, and he was the first to make drawings from the air. Some of his work was considered too unpleasant for public viewing and was censored, but a second one-man exhibition at the Leicester Galleries in 1918 was another triumph. At the end of the war Nevinson renounced Futurism and his later, more conventional paintings are generally regarded as an anticlimax; an example is *Twentieth Century* (1932–5, Laing AG, Newcastle upon Tyne), an ambitious but rather turgid attempt to portray a world on the brink of catastrophe.

Newbery, Francis ('Fra'). *See* GLASGOW SCHOOL OF ART.

New British Sculpture. A term sometimes applied to the work of a loosely connected group of British sculptors who emerged in a series of exhibitions at the beginning of the 1980s, notably 'Objects and Sculpture' shown at the *Institute of Contemporary Arts and the Arnolfini Gallery, Bristol, in 1981. There is no single common factor linking these sculptors, but predominantly their work is abstract (although sometimes with human associations), using industrial or junk material, and most of them are represented by the same dealer—the Lisson Gallery, London. Among the leading figures are: Tony Cragg

(1949–), Grenville Davey (1961–), Richard Deacon (1949–), Anish *Kapoor (each of these four has won the *Turner Prize), David Mach (1956–), Julian Opie (1958–), Richard Wentworth (1947–), Alison Wilding (1948–), and Bill Woodrow (1948–). Most of these are well represented in the *Saatchi Collection.

New Contemporaries. *See* YOUNG CONTEMPORARIES.

New English Art Club (NEAC). Artists' society founded in London in 1886 in reaction against the conservative and complacent attitudes of the *Royal Academy. The founders—largely artists who had worked in France and had been influenced by *plein-air painting—included *Clausen, *Sargent, *Steer, *La Thangue and *Tuke. There were about 50 members when the inaugural exhibition was held in April 1886 at the Marlborough Gallery. In 1889 the NEAC came under the control of a minority group led by,*Sickert, who had joined in 1888; he and his associates were influenced by *Impressionism, and in 1889 they held an independent exhibition under the name 'The London Impressionists'. Sickert resigned in 1897 (he returned in 1906) and from then up to about the First World War the NEAC was effectively controlled by Frederick Brown (*see* SLADE), Henry *Tonks, and Steer. In this period it contained most of the best painters in England. From about 1908, however, it began to lose initiative to progressive groups such as the *Allied Artists' Association and the *Camden Town Group. After the war the NEAC occupied a position midway between the Academy and the avant-garde groups. With the gradual liberalization of the Academy exhibitions its importance diminished, but it still exists.

New Figuration. A very broad term for a general revival of figurative painting in the 1960s following a period when abstraction (particularly *Abstract Expressionism) had been the dominant mode of avant-garde art in Europe and the USA. The term is said to have been first used by the French critic Michel Ragon, who in 1961 called the trend 'Nouvelle Figuration'.

New Generation. The title of four exhibitions, sponsored by the Peter Stuyvesant [tobacco company] Foundation, held at the Whitechapel Art Gallery, London, in 1964,

1965, 1966, and 1968, with the aim of introducing young British painters and sculptors to the public. *Op and *Pop art were well represented, but the series is best remembered for the 1965 exhibition, which featured a group of sculptors who were seen as creating a new school of British abstract sculpture, largely under the influence of Anthony *Caro (most of them had been his pupils at St Martin's School of Art). Subsequently their work has been referred to as 'New Generation Sculpture'. The leading figures were Phillip *King, Tim Scott (1937–), and William *Tucker. William *Turnbull is generally grouped with them, even though he did not train at St Martin's or show at the New Generation exhibition. Their work had in common a liking for simple shapes and strong colours—sometimes close to *Minimal art, sometimes with a Pop flavour.

New Image Painting. A vague term applied since the late 1970s to the work of certain painters who employ a strident figurative style, often with cartoon-like imagery and abrasive handling owing something to *Neo-Expressionism. The term was given currency by an exhibition entitled 'New Image Painting' at the Whitney Museum, New York, in 1978. The accompanying catalogue unhelpfully informs us that the New Image painters 'felt free to manipulate the image on canvas so that it can be experienced as a physical object, an abstract configuration, a psychological associative, a receptacle for applied paint, an analytically systemized exercise, an ambiguous quasi-narrative, a specifically nonspecific experience, a vehicle for formalist explorations or combinations of any'. Philip *Guston, who in the 1970s abandoned *Abstract Expressionism for a comic-strip style of figuration, is regarded as the progenitor of New Image Painting. Other American artists who have been labelled New Image Painters include Jennifer Bartlett (1941–), Jonathan Borofsky (1942–), and Susan Rothenberg (1945–). In Britain the term 'New Image' has been applied particularly to painters of the 1980s *Glasgow School.

Newlyn School. A name applied to the painters who worked in the Cornish fishing village of Newlyn from the 1880s, particularly those directly linked with Stanhope Forbes (1857–1947), who was the founder and leader of the school. One of the attractions of Newlyn was the mild climate, which made it particularly suitable for outdoor work, and Forbes and his associates were among the pioneers of *plein-air painting in Britain. Apart from Forbes and his wife Elizabeth Armstrong (1859–1912), the artists most closely associated with Newlyn in its heyday include: Frank Bramley (1857–1915); Thomas Cooper Gotch (1854–1931), better known for his later work, particularly his allegorical pictures of children; and Henry Scott *Tuke. Many of the Newlyn artists were members of the *New English Art Club, but they also showed their work at the *Royal Academy. The golden period of Newlyn was over by the turn of the century; thereafter it was vulgarized by an influx of inferior talent, and *St Ives came to have a greater attraction for 20th-century artists. However, distinguished painters continued to be associated with Newlyn: Harold and Laura *Knight lived there, 1907–18, for example, and Dod Procter (1892–1972) and her husband Ernest Procter (1886–1935) studied with Forbes and settled in the village after their marriage in 1912.

Newman, Barnett (1905–70). American painter, one of the leading figures of *Abstract Expressionism and one of the initiators of *Colour Field Painting. During the 1930s he had a hard time financially: the Depression almost ruined his father's clothing business, and unlike most American painters of the time Newman did not work for the *Federal Art Project, being unwilling to accept State handouts. Part of his living came from teaching art in high schools. He destroyed most of his early work and stopped painting in the early 1940s, but he began again in 1944, and in the second half of the 1940s evolved a distinctive style of mystical abstraction—he considered 'the sublime' to be his ultimate subject matter. The work with which he announced this style was *Onement I* (1948, MoMA, New York), a monochromatic canvas of dark red with a single stripe of lighter red running down the middle. Such stripes (or 'zips' as Newman preferred to call them) became a characteristic feature of his work. By the time he painted *Onement I* Newman already had a reputation as a controversialist and a spokesman for avant-garde

art (in catalogue essays and in articles in journals). In 1949 he painted his first wall-size pictures (he was one of the pioneers of the very large format) and in 1950 he had his first one-man exhibition, at the Betty *Parsons gallery. This was coolly received by critics and fellow artists, and by the mid-1950s his very spare style had separated him from the predominantly *gestural idiom of his colleagues. For a time he became a somewhat marginalized figure and he stopped painting in 1956. He had a heart attack in 1957, but in the following year a resurgence began with a series of paintings in black and white, and in the last decade of his life his reputation and his output soared. From 1965 he made steel sculptures (vertical strips recalling his paintings) and in his late years he also experimented with *shaped canvases, painting several triangular pictures.

New Realism. A vague term, of dubious value, that has been used in at least three distinct senses in connection with art of the 1960s and later. First, it has been used in a way similar to the term *New Figuration to describe a revival of figurative art after a dominant period of abstraction; whereas 'New Figuration' has been used very broadly, however, 'New Realism' has often been applied more specifically to works that are objective in spirit, particularly *Superrealist pictures or those of Philip *Pearlstein. In a second sense, 'New Realism' has been used as a straight translation of the French term 'Nouveau Réalisme' and applied to works incorporating three-dimensional objects, usually mass-produced consumer goods, in *assemblages or attached to the surface of a painting. Thirdly —and perplexingly—it has been used as a synonym for *Pop art.

New Sculpture, the. A trend in British sculpture between about 1880 and 1910 characterized chiefly by an emphasis on naturalistic surface detail and a taste for the spiritual or *Symbolist in subject matter, in reaction against the blandness of much Victorian sculpture. The name was coined by the critic Edmund Gosse in a series of four articles, 'The New Sculpture, 1879–1894', published in the *Art Journal* in 1894. Leading representatives of the trend include Gilbert Bayes (1872–1953), Alfred Drury (1856–1944), Edward Onslow Ford

(1852–1901), Sir George *Frampton, Sir Alfred *Gilbert, the Australian-born Sir Bertram Mackennal (1863–1931), Sir William Reynolds-Stephens (1862–1943), Sir Hamo *Thornycroft, Albert Toft (1862–1949), and Derwent Wood (1871–1926). Their archetypal product was the 'ideal' free-standing figure, often with imagery drawn from mythology or poetry. Most typically these ideal figures were in bronze, but polychromy—using such materials as ivory and coloured stones—was also a feature of the New Sculpture. Although the New Sculpture did not survive the First World War as a major force, some of the practitioners went on working in the idiom long after this.

New York Realists. Informal name given during the early years of the 20th century to Robert *Henri and his disciples, whose work included scenes of unidealized contemporary urban life.

New York School. Name applied to the innovatory painters, particularly the *Abstract Expressionists, who worked in New York during the 1940s and 1950s and whose critical and financial success helped the city to replace Paris as the world's leading centre of avant-garde art.

Niccolò dell'Arca (d.1494). Italian sculptor. He was probably of south Italian origin, but his known career was spent in Bologna, where he is first documented in 1462. His name comes from his work on the Arca di S. Domenico (Shrine of St Dominic) in S. Domenico Maggiore, Bologna, for which he carved a marble canopy and small free-standing figures (1469 onwards). The work was unfinished at his death and *Michelangelo carved three missing figures. Niccolò's greatest work is a highly emotional group of the *Lamentation over the Body of Christ* in S. Maria della Vita, Bologna, executed in terracotta and originally painted. It is of uncertain date. According to tradition the figure of Nicodemus is a self-portrait.

Nicholson, Ben (1894–1982). British painter and maker of *reliefs, one of his country's most distinguished pioneers of abstract art. From his father, Sir William *Nicholson, he inherited a feeling for simple and fastidious still lifes, which with landscapes made up the bulk of his early work. They show him responding to the innovations of *Cubism, using the standard

Cubist repertoire of objects such as jugs and glasses and arranging them as flat shapes on the picture plane. Nicholson was also influenced by the *naive painter Alfred *Wallis, whose work he discovered in 1928 and whose roughly textured surfaces he emulated. From the early 1930s he turned to abstraction, partly because of the influence of Barbara *Hepworth (they shared a studio from 1932 and married in 1938) and partly because of the impact of several visits he made to Paris at this time. He joined the *Abstraction-Création association in 1933 and became friendly with several leading avant-garde artists, *Mondrian's work in particular coming as a revelation to him. In 1933 he made his first abstract relief and in 1934 his first strictly geometrical 'white relief' in painted wood, using only straight lines and circles. Such works were the most uncompromising examples of abstract art made by a British artist up to that date (*White Relief*, 1935, Tate, London). He also did paintings in a similar intellectual vein but with a poetic refinement of colour that offsets their severity of composition (*Painting*, 1937, Tate). By this time Nicholson was recognized as being at the forefront of the modern movement in England. He was a member of *Unit One (1933), and one of the editors of *Circle* (1937). In 1939 he and Hepworth moved to Cornwall, where they became the nucleus of the *St Ives School. They divorced in 1951 and in 1958 Nicholson settled in Switzerland with his third wife, the Swiss photographer Felicitas Vogler. After the Second World War he won an international reputation, accompanied by many awards. He returned to England in 1971. His late work moved freely between abstraction and figuration and included large, free-standing reliefs, notably one in marble in the garden of Sutton Place, Surrey (1982). Nicholson's first wife, **Winifred Nicholson** (1893–1981), was a painter of distinction. She is best known for her flower paintings, but she also did other subjects and abstracts, all her work showing her joy in colour and light.

Nicholson, Sir William (1872–1949). British painter and graphic artist. He is perhaps best remembered for his brilliant early work as a poster designer, done in collaboration with his brother-in-law James *Pryde under the name 'J. & W. *Beggarstaff'. As a painter he was successful mainly as a portraitist, but he is now particularly admired for his still lifes, typically small, unpretentious, and sensitively handled.

Nicolas of Verdun (active late 12th century–early 13th century). *Mosan goldsmith, enameller, and metalworker. He is considered the greatest goldsmith and enameller of his day and a major figure in the transition from *Romanesque to Gothic. Two signed works by him survive: an *enamelled pulpit frontal made for the abbey church at Klosterneuburg, near Vienna (completed in 1181, damaged in 1320, and then remodelled into its present *triptychaltar form); and the Shrine of St Mary for Tournai Cathedral (1205). Among the works attributed to him the most important is the Shrine of the Three Kings, made for Cologne Cathedral in about 1190, which is the largest and most sumptuous reliquary of the period. All three works still belong to the churches for which they were commissioned. The Klosterneuburg Altar is his masterpiece, featuring 45 enamel plaques in an elaborate *typological programme, events from the New Testament being paralleled by ones in the Old Testament. His figure style is expressive and dynamic, with individualized faces and richly articulated drapery suggesting influence from the *antique.

niello. A black substance (typically sulphur, silver, lead, and copper) used as a decorative inlay on metal surfaces; the term can also be used to refer to the process of making such an inlay, and to a surface or object so decorated. Niello prints are impressions taken from such surfaces and are invariably Italian work of the second half of the 15th century. They were probably initially taken as proofs by niellists who wanted to see their work clearly. But it appears that these craftsmen then took to engraving plates with the express purpose of taking impressions from them, and many early examples of Italian *line engraving show the influence of the niello craft. Maso *Finiguerra, whom *Vasari credits with the invention of line engraving, was both niellist and line engraver.

Nittis, Giuseppe de (1846–84). Italian painter, mainly of landscapes and scenes of city life. Early in his career he was associated

with the *Macchiaioli. He settled in Paris in 1868, became a friend of *Degas and *Manet, and took part in the first *Impressionist exhibition in 1874 (because de Nittis had already enjoyed some success at the *Salon, Degas thought that the presence of his work among the Impressionists would mean that critics 'won't be able to say that ours is an exhibition of rejected artists'). The best collection of his work is in the Pinacoteca Communale at Barletta, his native town.

NKV. *See* NEUE KÜNSTLERVEREINIGUNG.

Nolan, Sir Sidney (1917–92). The most internationally famous of Australian painters. He turned from odd jobs to art after attending night classes in his native Melbourne, and became a full-time painter when he was 21. His early work was abstract, but while serving in the Australian army (1941–5) he painted a series of landscapes of the Wimmera District of Victoria that gave the first unmistakable signs of the originality of his vision, capturing the heat and emptiness of the bush. In 1946 he began a series of paintings on the notorious bushranger Ned Kelly, who had become a legendary figure in Australian folk history, and it was with these works that he made his name. He returned to the Kelly theme throughout his career and he also drew on other events from Australian history. In such works Nolan created a distinctive idiom to express this novel Australian subject matter and memorably portrayed the hard, dry beauty of the desert landscape. Technically, his work is remarkable for the lush fluidity of his brushwork and sometimes he painted on glass or other smooth materials. Nolan first visited Europe in 1950 and from 1955 he lived mainly in England. He also worked in Paris and the USA and travelled extremely widely (the Australian airline Qantas commissioned him to fly around the world gathering material for a series of paintings to decorate their offices). Apart from Australian themes, he was inspired by journeys to Antarctica and New Guinea, for example, as well as by literary subjects such as the legend of Leda and the Swan.

Noland, Kenneth (1924–). American abstract painter and sculptor. In 1949 he settled in Washington, where he became a close friend of Morris *Louis. On a visit to

New York in 1953 they were greatly impressed by Helen *Frankenthaler's *Mountains and Sea* and they began experimenting with the kind of pouring and staining techniques she pioneered. They became the leading figures of a group of *Colour Field Painters known as the Washington Color Painters, but from the late 1950s Noland tended to use more precisely articulated geometrical forms, and in the 1960s he became one of the chief exponents of *Hard-Edge Painting. Initially he used concentric circles on a square canvas. This was followed by a chevron motif, sometimes on a diamond or lozenge-shaped canvas, and this again was gradually lengthened into horizontal stripes running across a canvas of a very long rectangular format. In 1966 he began to make sculpture, influenced by his friend Anthony *Caro.

Nolde, Emil (1867–1956). German painter and printmaker, one of the most powerful representatives of *Expressionism. Born of a peasant family, he was originally trained as a woodcarver and came late to artistic maturity. His studies took him from his native north Germany to Munich and Paris, and from 1906 to 1907 he was a member of the *Brücke in Dresden, but he was essentially an isolated figure, standing apart from his great German contemporaries. He moved around a good deal in Germany and was well travelled elsewhere (in 1913–14 he visited Russia, the Far East, and the South Sea islands as part of an ethnographic expedition), but at times he lived almost like a hermit. His travel broadened his knowledge of the kind of *primitive art that was then beginning to excite avant-garde artists, but Nolde had already established the essential features of his style before his contact with such art, and when the term 'primitive' is applied to his work it refers to its brutal force, not to any exotic trappings. He was a deeply religious man and is now famous for his paintings of Old and New Testament subjects, in which he expresses intense emotion through violent colour, radically simplified drawing, and grotesque distortion. The majority of his pictures, however, were landscapes, and he was also one of the outstanding 20th-century exponents of flower painting, working with gloriously vivid colour, often in watercolour. He was also a prolific etcher and lithographer. Although

he was a member of the Nazi Party, he was declared a *degenerate artist by the Nazis and in 1941 forbidden to paint. He did, however, execute small watercolours in secret (these are called the 'unpainted pictures') and from these made larger oils after the war. From 1926 he lived at Seebüll, where there is now a Nolde Foundation that has an outstanding collection of his work.

Nollekens, Joseph (1737–1823). English sculptor, the son of a Flemish painter of the same name (1702–48) who settled in London in 1733. The younger Nollekens was a pupil of *Scheemakers. From 1762 to 1770 he worked in Rome, making a handsome living by copying, restoring, faking, and dealing in *antique sculpture. He also made a few portrait busts including that of Laurence Sterne (1766, NPG, London), a splendid character study in the antique manner, and on his return to England it was chiefly as a portraitist that he built up his great reputation and fortune (he left £200,000 at his death). His finest portraits are vivacious and brilliantly characterized, but there are many inferior studio copies of his more popular works. He also made statues in a slightly erotic antique manner, and produced numerous funerary monuments. Nollekens and his wife were well-known figures in London's artistic circles and were notorious skinflints. The life by his pupil and disappointed executor J. T. Smith (1766–1833), *Nollekens and his Times* (1828), gives a remarkable picture of their meanness and has been described by Rupert Gunnis (*Dictionary of British Sculptors 1660–1851*, 1953) as probably 'the most candid, pitiless and uncomplimentary biography in the English language'.

Non-Objective art. General term for abstract art that is intended to be completely non-representational, rather than derived (however remotely or obliquely) from appearances in the world around us; most commonly it is applied to severely geometrical works. The term was coined by *Rodchenko, who used it in the title of some of his paintings (*Non-Objective Painting: Black on Black*, 1918, MoMA, New York), and it is also particularly associated with *Malevich.

Noort, Adam van (1562–1641). Flemish history and portrait painter, remembered chiefly as one of the teachers of *Rubens.

Too little is known of the style of either man at the time to estimate what influence he may have had. Another famous pupil was *Jordaens, who became van Noort's son-in-law in 1616.

Northcote, James (1746–1831). English painter and writer. He was born in Plymouth and was largely self-taught until he moved to London in 1771 and became the pupil and assistant of *Reynolds, a fellow Devonian. From 1777 to 1780 he was in Italy, where he gained ambitions to be a history painter; however, his exercises in this field, notably for *Boydell's Shakespeare Gallery, are ponderous and awkward. As a portraitist he was an uninspired follower of Reynolds, and it is as a writer that he has the main claim to distinction; he was something of a character and a lively commentator on the artistic scene. *Memoirs of Sir Joshua Reynolds* (1813; supplement 1815) is his major publication.

Norwich School. A group of English landscape painters associated with the Norwich Society of Artists, which was founded in 1803. It held annual exhibitions in 1805–25 and again in 1828–33 after it had been reformed as the Norfolk and Suffolk Institution for the Promotion of the Fine Arts—the first instance of a provincial institution holding regular exhibitions. John *Crome was a founder member and became president in 1808; when he died in 1821, *Cotman took over the role. The Norwich artists, who included amateurs as well as professionals, consisted almost entirely of landscape painters in oil and watercolour; they concentrated on local scenery and often sketched out of doors, but they also found inspiration in 17th-century Dutch painting.

Nost (originally **van Ost**), **John** (d. 1711/13). Flemish-born sculptor who settled in England in about 1678. By 1686 he was foreman to Artus III *Quellin, whose widow he later married. He is chiefly notable as a maker of lead garden statues, some based on Italian or *antique models but others of his own creation. Examples remain at Melbourne Hall, Derbyshire, Hampton Court, and other places. His tombs are less interesting. His son—not, as long thought, his nephew—of the same name (d. 1780) settled in Dublin in about 1750 and became the leading sculptor of the day there.

Notke, Bernt (d. *c*.1509). German sculptor, the leading woodcarver in the Baltic area during his period. He worked mainly in Lübeck, where he is first recorded (as a painter) in 1467, but his masterpiece was executed in Sweden, where he was summoned *c*.1483 to make a monument commemorating a victory by the regent, Sten Sture, over the Danes. The victory was attributed to the assistance of St George, and Notke's stirring group of *St George and the Dragon* (completed 1489) in the Storkyrka (Stockholm's main church) is one of the greatest of all votive images. Its spiky forms represent the most expressionistic strain in late *Gothic art and the vividly naturalistic details include the use of real elk antlers for the dragon's horns.

novecento (It.: '20th century'). *See* QUATTROCENTO.

Novecento Italiano (Italian 20th Century). Association of Italian artists, founded in 1922; it aimed to reject European avant-garde movements and revive a naturalistic type of art based on classical Italian tradition. The Novecento had no clear artistic programme (although it wished to revive large-scale figurative compositions) and numbered within its ranks artists of very different styles and temperaments, among them *Carrà and *Marini. Increasingly it came to be associated with Fascist propaganda and during the 1930s it was the main bastion of reactionary attitudes. It disbanded in 1943.

November Group. An association of Finnish *Expressionist artists founded in Helsinki in November 1917. This was only a month after the declaration of independence from Russia and the members of the November Group were sometimes aggressively nationalistic in outlook, creating a distinctively Finnish form of Expressionism. Tyko *Sallinen was the leading figure of the group.

Novembergruppe. A group of radical left-wing German artists formed in Berlin in December 1918; it was named after the revolution that had broken out in Germany the previous month, at the end of the First World War, and the professed aim of the Novembergruppe was to bring about national renewal by means of a closer relation between progressive artists and the public. Max *Pechstein was among the prime

movers. In 1919 the founders of the association created the Arbeitsrat für Kunst
(Workers' Council for Art) in an attempt to
bring about a dialogue between art and the
masses, but this collapsed in 1921 and interest and support came mainly from the
middle classes. Artistically the group
covered a wide spectrum of ideas and styles.
Through its numerous exhibitions it did a
good deal to foster an artistic revival, and
many of its aims were more fully realized at
the *Bauhaus. The group disbanded in 1929.

objet trouvé (Fr.: 'found object'). An object found by an artist and displayed with no, or minimal, alteration as (or as an element in) a work of art. It may be a natural object, such as a pebble, a shell, or a curiously contorted branch, or a man-made object such as a piece of pottery or old piece of ironwork or machinery. The essence of the matter is that the finder-artist recognizes such a chance find as an 'aesthetic object' and displays it for appreciation by others as he would a work of art. The practice began with the *Dadaists (especially Marcel *Duchamp) and was particularly cultivated by the *Surrealists. Subsequently, found material has been much used in *assemblage. *See also* READY-MADE.

Ochtervelt, Jacob (1634–82). Dutch *genre painter. He was born and mainly active in Rotterdam, but he is said to have been a pupil of *Berchem in Haarlem, and from 1674 he lived in Amsterdam. Apart from a few portraits and some early hunting-party and 'merry-company' scenes, his paintings are almost all elegant upper-class interiors, in which he showed off a skill in painting silks and satins to rival that of *Terborch. His figures are extremely refined, but there is often a sexual element in his paintings—a couple eating oysters (believed to be an aphrodisiac) was a favourite subject.

O'Conor, Roderic (1860–1940). Irish painter and etcher, active for most of his life in France (mainly Paris), where he settled in 1883 after studying in London and Antwerp. He was strongly influenced by *Gauguin and van *Gogh, and by the early 1890s was painting in a full-blooded *Post-Impressionist style marked by bold colour—often used non-naturalistically—and thick brushwork. He lived a fairly reclusive life (although he was friendly with many British visitors to France, including Clive *Bell and Roger *Fry) and he was virtually unknown in the British and Irish art worlds. It was only after his death that he was recognized as the outstanding pioneer of Post-Impressionism among English-speaking artists. He did, however, notably influence Matthew *Smith, whom he met in 1919. O'Conor was mainly a landscapist, but he also painted still lifes, portraits, interiors, and figure subjects.

Official War Art. Art sponsored by the British Government during the First and Second World Wars to make a visual record of all aspects of the war effort for information and propaganda purposes. In the First World War the work was directed by the Ministry of Information, which was advised by a committee drawn from distinguished figures in the art world and public life, among them Campbell Dodgson, keeper of prints and drawings at the British Museum, and Eric MacLagan, later director of the Victoria and Albert Museum. In 1916 the Ministry launched the Official War Artists scheme, under which artists were recruited, with appropriate military ranks, to serve as chroniclers (the Germans already had a similar scheme in operation). The first artist to be commissioned was Honorary 2nd Lieutenant Muirhead *Bone, who left for France on 16 August 1916 and toured the front in a chauffeur-driven car. Many others soon followed, among them some of the most illustrious British artists of the time. They included men who had already been serving in the armed forces, such as Paul *Nash, C. R. W. *Nevinson, and Stanley *Spencer, and others who were too old for active duty. The works produced varied enormously in style and quality (the committee was admirably broad in its choice of artists) and included imaginative evocations of the war as well as sober factual records. There were many portraits of participants, but two of the most notable portraitists who worked as Official War Artists—*Orpen and *Sargent—showed a different and unexpected side to their talents, powerfully depicting the horrors they saw.

In the autumn of 1939, soon after the outbreak of the Second World War, the Ministry of Information appointed Kenneth *Clark chairman of a small group that became known as the War Artists' Advisory Committee (Muirhead Bone was one of the members). It met weekly at the National Gallery, of which Clark was director, and its functions were principally 'to draw up a list of artists qualified to record the War at home and abroad ... [and] ... to advise on the selection of artists from this list for war purposes and on the arrangement for their employment'. Clark regarded his work on the committee as 'my only worthwhile activity' during the war: 'We employed every artist whom we thought had any merit, not because we supposed that we would get records of the war more truthful or striking than those supplied by photography, but because it seemed a good way of preventing artists being killed' (*Ravilious was one of the rare fatalities). Several painters who had been Official War Artists in the First World War were employed in the same capacity in the Second, among them Nash and Spencer, but the Committee mainly employed men of a younger generation. The terms in which they were employed varied: some were given salaried posts for a specific period, while others were given one-off commissions. The Committee also encouraged artists, whether serving or civilian, to submit pictures for consideration. Generally the commissions in the Second World War were on a smaller scale than those in the First, with many works being executed in watercolour (Spencer's huge canvases of shipbuilding on the Clyde are a conspicuous exception). Henry *Moore's drawings of Londoners sheltering from air raids in Underground stations are perhaps the best known of all the works produced under the auspices of Clark's Committee.

In both wars women were employed as Official War Artists on the home front, notably the animal painter Lucy Kemp-Welch (1869–1958) in the First and Laura *Knight in the Second. A huge number of works was produced. The largest collection (about 10,000 items) is in the Imperial War Museum, London, which was opened in 1920 and moved to its present home (the former Royal Bethlehem Hospital) in 1936. The Tate has another major collection, and many provincial museums have good examples.

Since the Second World War the tradition of Official War Art has been maintained on a lesser scale by the Artistic Records Committee of the Imperial War Museum. Linda Kitson (1945–) went on its behalf to the Falkland Islands during the war there against Argentina in 1982, for example, and Peter Howson (1958–) went to Bosnia in 1993. His exhibition 'War in Bosnia' at the Imperial War Museum the following year attracted considerable attention because of its unsparing depiction of atrocities: 'Now that I've actually seen dead bodies, and guts and brains, and starving children, it has made the work authentic.'

offset. A reproduction, also called a counterproof, made from a drawing by dampening it and/or a sheet of paper and pressing them together by machine or hand. The image is therefore reversed left to right and is also fainter than the original. Offsets were often made for working purposes by designers of ornament who needed to have a copy of a design in reverse, or to complete one half of a symmetrical design, and they have also been used to create forgeries.

Ofili, Chris. *See* TURNER PRIZE and YOUNG BRITISH ARTISTS.

O'Gorman, Juan (1905–82). Mexican architect and painter. Early in his career he designed a series of houses in Mexico City (notably those for himself and for Diego *Rivera) that were among the first in the Americas to show the functionalist ideas of *Le Corbusier. In the 1930s, however, he abandoned architecture for painting. His work was strongly nationalistic and his anti-fascist, anti-church frescos at Mexico City airport (1937–8) were destroyed in 1939 during a political swing to the right. In the 1950s he returned to architecture, now advocating a more 'organic' approach inspired in part by Frank Lloyd Wright. His most celebrated work in this vein is the Library of the National University in Mexico City (1951–3), in which a modern structural design is completely covered externally in mosaics of his own design that symbolically represent the history of Mexican culture. In 1953–6 O'Gorman built a second home for himself outside Mexico City. This too was lavishly decorated in mosaics externally and internally and it was designed to harmonize with the lava formation of the landscape. He committed suicide.

oil paint. Paint in which *drying oils are used as the medium; *linseed oil is the best known, but others that have been used in painting include *poppy oil and *walnut oil. It was long believed that oil painting was invented by Jan van *Eyck in the early 15th century, but it is now known that its origins are older and obscurer (the treatise of *Theophilus, written probably in the 12th century, describes 'grinding colours with oil'). There is no doubt, however, that van Eyck revolutionized the technique and brought it to a sudden peak of perfection. He showed the medium's flexibility, its rich and dense colour, its wide range from light to dark, and its ability to achieve both minute detail and subtle blending of tones. Other painters soon took up his innovations—first in northern Europe, then in Italy—and from the 16th century oil colour has been the dominant medium in Europe for serious painting (other than for murals, in which *fresco continued to be the norm). Its success has been largely on account of its versatility and ability to show an artist's personal 'handwriting', for it can attain any variety of surface from porcelain smoothness to violent *impasto. Its versatility was increased still further in the 19th century with the invention of the collapsible metal tube (devised in 1841), which made it convenient to work out of doors. In the 20th century, however, *acrylic became a serious rival to oil paint.

O'Keeffe, Georgia (1887–1986). American painter. One of the pioneers of modernism in America, she was a member of the circle of *Stieglitz, whom she met in 1916 and married in 1924. She is best known for her near-abstract paintings based on enlargements of flower and plant forms, works of great elegance and rhythmic vitality, whose sensuous forms are often sexually suggestive (*Black Iris*, 1926, Met. Mus., New York). In the 1920s she also painted townscapes of New York in a manner close to that of the *Precisionists and landscapes done in broad, simple forms. From the 1930s she spent each winter in New Mexico and she settled there after Stieglitz's death in 1946, the desert landscape appearing frequently in her paintings (bleached animal bones were a favourite subject). She began to travel widely in the 1950s and many of her later paintings were inspired by views of the earth, sky, and clouds seen from an aeroplane. She became partially blind in 1971 and did little work thereafter. A museum dedicated to her opened in Santa Fe in 1997.

Oldenburg, Claes (1929–). Swedish-born sculptor and graphic artist who became an American citizen in 1953. He was educated at Yale University and studied at the Art Institute of Chicago (earning his living with part-time jobs as a reporter and illustrator), then in 1956 settled in New York. There he came into contact with a group of young artists, including *Dine, *Kaprow, and *Segal, who were in revolt against *Abstract Expressionism and from c.1958 he became interested in arranging *happenings, *environments, 'situations', etc. His inspiration was drawn largely from New York's street life—shop windows, graffiti, advertisements, and so on—and in 1961 he opened 'The Store', at which he sold painted plaster replicas of foods and other domestic objects. This led to the work with which his name is most closely associated—giant-size sculptures of foodstuffs and 'soft sculptures' of normally hard objects (*Dual Hamburger*, 1962, MoMA, New York). With these he was hailed as one of the leaders of American *Pop art. Oldenburg is also well known for his projects for colossal monuments—for example, *Lipsticks in Piccadilly Circus, London* (1966, Tate, London), consisting of a magazine cutting of an array of lipsticks pasted on to a picture postcard. The first of these projects to be realized was a giant lipstick erected at Yale University in 1969. Since 1976 he has concentrated almost exclusively on such large-scale projects, in collaboration with his second wife, the Dutch writer Coosje van Bruggen.

oleograph. A coloured lithograph impressed with a canvas grain and varnished to make it look like an oil painting. Oleographs were popular—but often considered rather vulgar—in the second half of the 19th century.

Olitski, Jules (1922–). Russian-born American painter and sculptor, one of the leading figures of *Post-Painterly Abstraction, specifically of *Colour Field Painting. His early paintings were influenced by *Fauvism and they were followed by heavily textured abstracts, but in 1960 the direction of his work changed radically when he began experimenting with stain techniques in the manner of *Frankenthaler and *Louis. In 1964 he began using a spray gun and in the second half of the 1960s he developed the type of painting for which he is best known—vast canvases covered with luscious mists of atmospheric colour; he said that ideally he would like 'nothing but some colours sprayed into the air and staying there'. Sometimes there are some heavier touches at the edges of the canvas in a sort of ironic reference to *Abstract Expressionism, and in the 1970s Olitski returned to a more textural handling of paint, often reducing his colour to delicate modulations of greys and brown. He took up sculpture seriously in 1968 and has worked mainly with painted metal.

Oliver, Isaac (c.1565–1617). English *miniaturist of French origin, the son of a refugee Huguenot goldsmith who settled in England in about 1568. Although he was naturalized in 1606, he always considered himself French and his command of written English was shaky. He trained under *Hilliard (whose main rival he later became) and by 1590 was established in his own practice. Hilliard continued to receive royal favour under James I, but Oliver was made *limner to the Queen, Anne of Denmark, in 1604, and he was also patronized by Henry, Prince of Wales, and his circle. His style was more naturalistic than Hilliard's, using light and shade to obtain modelling and generally dispensing with the emblematic trappings so beloved of the Elizabethan age. In 1596 he is documented in Venice, and unlike Hilliard he produced copies of Renaissance pictures in miniature. Contemporary sources indicate that he probably also painted life-size portraits, and he has been proposed as the author of some of the pictures more usually attributed to William *Larkin. His son, **Peter Oliver** (1594?–1647), was also a miniaturist; he began as a portraitist but from the 1620s specialized in miniature copies after the Old Masters.

Omega Workshops. Decorative arts company founded by Roger *Fry in London in 1913 with the twin aims of improving the standard of design in Britain and providing work for the young avant-garde artists in his circle. (Omega is the last letter of the Greek alphabet and it has been suggested that Fry chose the name to indicate its products were 'the last word' in design, but in fact he seems to have picked it because it was anonymous but easy to remember and in addition to being a word was a sign that could be used as a trademark.) Fry disliked the smooth finish of machine products, and Omega works characteristically have the irregularities of hand craftsmanship, although the furniture it sold was originally bought ready-made and then painted on the premises, and its linens were expertly printed in France. Its other products included ceramics and carpets. The favourite Omega motifs included flowers, nudes, and abstract patterns, and colour was often very bright; *Cubism and *Fauvism were strong influences. Apart from Fry himself, the designers most closely associated with Omega were Vanessa *Bell and Duncan *Grant, and several other distinguished artists worked for the enterprise, including Paul *Nash and William *Roberts. However, all the work was sold anonymously. Artists were paid a regular wage, the financing coming from Fry himself and from subscribers, including George Bernard Shaw. The Workshops made a promising start, but the First World War had a disastrous effect on sales (Fry in any case had little business aptitude) and in June 1919 Omega's remaining stock was sold off; the company was officially liquidated in 1920. The best idea of Omega furnishings in a contemporary setting can be gained at Charleston, the country home of Bell and Grant at Firle in Sussex. There are also good examples in London at the Courtauld Gallery and the Victoria and Albert Museum.

Ono, Yoko. See FLUXUS.

Oostsanen. See CORNELISZ. VAN OOSTSANEN.

Op art (abbreviation of Optical art on the analogy of Pop art). A type of abstract art that exploits certain optical phenomena to cause a work to seem to vibrate, pulsate, or flicker. It flourished mainly in the 1960s; the term was first used in print in the American magazine *Time* in October 1964 and had become a household phrase by the following year, partly through the attention given to the exhibition 'The Responsive Eye' held at the Museum of Modern Art, New York, in 1965. This was the first international exhibition with a predominance of Op paintings. The development of Op art as a recognizable movement had begun a few years earlier than this, in about 1960, the works and theories of Josef *Albers being among the main sources. The devices employed by Op artists (after-images, effects of dazzle and vibration, and so on) are often elaborations on the well-known visual illusions to be found in standard textbooks of perceptual psychology, and maximum precision is sought in the control of surfaces and edges in order to evoke an exactly prescribed retinal response. Many Op paintings employ repeated small-scale patterns arranged so as to suggest underlying secondary shapes or warping or swelling surfaces. This kind of work can retain much of its effect in reproduction, but Op art also embraces constructions that depend for their effects on light and/or movement, so Op and *Kinetic art sometimes overlap. The two most famous exponents of Op art are Bridget *Riley and Victor *Vasarely. Their work illustrates the considerable impact that Op made on fashion and design in the 1960s—its instant popular success (accompanied by a fairly cool critical reception) is hard to parallel in modern art. Op art became something of a craze in women's fashion and in 1965 Riley unsuccessfully tried to sue an American clothing company that used one of her paintings as a fabric design. One of Vasarely's designs was used on the plastic carrier bags of France's chain of COOP stores. Among other exponents of Op art the best known is probably the American Richard Anuszkiewicz (1930–), a former pupil of Albers; his work is typically concerned with radiating expanses of lines and colours.

Opie, John (1761–1807). English painter. He was something of a child prodigy and was discovered by the political satirist John Wolcot (better known by his pen name Peter Pindar), who in 1781 successfully launched him in London as an untaught genius ('The Cornish Wonder'). At this time Opie was painting strongly modelled portraits and rustic *fancy pictures with rich *Rembrandtesque lighting. He soon lost the rugged freshness of his early work and his later paintings were undistinguished and repetitive. His career continued to flourish, however, and he became professor of painting at the *Royal Academy in 1805, his lectures being posthumously published

in 1809 (prefaced with a memoir by his wife, the novelist and poet Amelia Opie). Apart from portraits and *genre scenes, he also painted history pictures, notably for *Boydell's Shakespeare Gallery.

Opie, Julian. See NEW BRITISH SCULPTURE.

Oppenheim, Meret (1913–85). German-Swiss painter, sculptor, and maker of objects, born in Berlin. In 1932 she moved to Paris, where she was introduced to the *Surrealist group by *Giacometti and became for a while the model and disciple of *Man Ray. He described her as 'one of the most uninhibited women I have ever known' and she became celebrated among the Surrealists as the 'fairy woman' whom all men desire. She had a long career, but she is remembered mainly for one early work: *Object* (1936, MoMA, New York), a fur-lined tea cup and saucer. This became famous as a symbol of artistic anarchy after being shown at major Surrealist exhibitions in London and New York in 1936.

***orant.** See GISANT.

Orcagna, Andrea (Andrea di Cione) (d. c.1368). The leading Florentine artist of the third quarter of the 14th century, a painter, sculptor, architect, and administrator. His nickname 'Orcagna' was evidently local slang for 'Arcangelo' ('Archangel'). In 1343/4 he was admitted to the painters' guild in Florence and in 1352 to that of the masons. His only certain work as a painter is the altarpiece of *The Redeemer with the Madonna and Saints* (1354–7) in the Strozzi Chapel of S. Maria Novella. This is the most powerful Florentine painting of its period, and in spite of the massiveness of the figures it represents a reversion from *Giotto's naturalism to the hieratic ideals of *Byzantine art. Colours are resplendent, with lavish use of gold, and the figures are remote and immobile. Among paintings attributed to Orcagna, the most important is a fragmentary fresco trilogy of the *Triumph of Death, Last Judgement*, and *Hell* in S. Croce. As a sculptor and architect he is known through one work, the tabernacle in Orsanmichele (finished 1359), a highly elaborate ornamental structure housing a painting of the *Virgin Enthroned* by Bernardo *Daddi. Orcagna was *capomaestro* of Orvieto Cathedral from 1358 to 1362, supervising the mosaic decoration of the façade. He was also an adviser on the construction of Florence Cathedral. During 1368 he fell mortally ill while painting the *St Matthew* altarpiece (Uffizi, Florence) and this work was finished by his brother **Jacopo di Cione** (d. 1398/1400), who worked in his style and continued it to the end of the century. Another brother, **Nardo di Cione** (d. 1365/6), was also a painter. *Ghiberti attributes to him the series of frescos of the *Last Judgement, Hell*, and *Paradise* in the same chapel in S. Maria Novella that houses Andrea's great altarpiece. A fourth brother, **Matteo di Cione** (d. *c*.1390), was a sculptor, but almost nothing is known of his work.

Orchardson, Sir William Quiller (1832–1910). Scottish painter of *genre subjects and portraits, active in London from 1862. He made his name with historical costume pieces, but later did his most memorable work in modern-day scenes of upper-class married life. In these he used large empty spaces to create feelings of psychological tension or despair. The best-known are *The First Cloud* (1887, Tate, London) and a pair representing *A Marriage of Convenience* (1883, Glasgow AG, and 1886, Aberdeen AG).

Ordóñez, Bartolomé (d. 1520). Spanish sculptor, active mainly in Barcelona. On stylistic grounds, he is presumed to have trained in Florence, perhaps with Andrea *Sansovino, and he was certainly in Italy in 1517–18 and 1520. His main work there is the marble altarpiece of the Caracciolo Chapel in the church of S. Giovanni a Carbonara, Naples, where he perhaps worked in collaboration with Diego de *Siloe (there is evidence that the altarpiece was made *c*.1515, but some authorities connect it with Ordóñez's visit to Italy in 1517–18). By 1519 he was working on the decoration of the choir stalls in Barcelona Cathedral, and in the same year he began work on two tombs—that of Philip I and Joanna of Castile (Chapel Royal, Granada) and that of Cardinal Francisco Jiménez de Cisneros (S. Ildefonso, Alcalá de Henares). He died at Carrara (*see* MARBLE) in Italy before these were finished, but his will indicates that he had completed major parts, including the effigies of Philip and Joanna. Although he died young (he was perhaps born *c*.1485), his elegant and imaginative work played an important role in introducing the High *Renaissance style to Spain.

Orley, Bernard (or **Barend**) **van** (*c*.1490–1542). Netherlandish painter of religious subjects and portraits and designer of tapestries and stained glass. He was the leading artist of his day in Brussels, becoming court painter to Margaret of Austria (*see* HABSBURG), regent of the Netherlands, in 1518 and to her successor Mary of Hungary in 1532. His work is full of Italianate motifs, often rather ill-digested. There is no evidence that he visited Italy, and his knowledge presumably came from engravings and from *Raphael's tapestry *cartoons, which were in Brussels *c*.1516–19; he has (very flatteringly) been called 'the Raphael of the Netherlands'. His best-known work is the turbulent *Job* altarpiece (1521, Mus. Royaux, Brussels, 1521). As a portraitist his style was quieter and more thoughtful (*Georg Zelle*, 1519, Mus. Royaux, Brussels). None of van Orley's paintings bears a date later than 1530; after that time he was chiefly occupied with designing tapestries and stained-glass windows.

Orozco, José Clemente (1883–1949). Mexican painter, with his contemporaries *Rivera and *Siqueiros one of the trio of politically and socially committed muralists who were the dominant force in modern Mexican art. Following the first outburst of revolutionary activity in Mexico in 1910 (which was to last on and off until 1920), Orozco took up work as a political cartoonist. In 1912 he began a series of watercolours called 'House of Tears' dealing with prostitutes (a favourite symbol of human degradation for Orozco). The angry reaction of critics and moralists to these works was one of his reasons for leaving for the USA, where he spent three unhappy and unproductive years, 1917–20. His career as a muralist began after he returned to Mexico in 1920. The country was now relatively stable under the government of Alvaro Obregón, who encouraged nationalistic subjects as a way of creating a positive identity for the country after years of turmoil. Orozco's first frescos were in the Escuela Nacional Preparatoria (National Training School), 1923–4. They were controversial because of their caricatural style, and all except *Maternity* and *The Rich Banquet while the Workers Quarrel* were subsequently destroyed or altered. In 1927 to 1934 (broken by a brief trip to Europe in 1932) he again worked in the USA. This time he was much more successful, carrying out a number of important mural commissions, most notably a cycle for Dartmouth College, New Hampshire: *The Coming* and *The Return of Quetzalcoatl* (1932–4). This huge scheme showed his outlook crystallizing into a contrast between a pagan paradise and a capitalist hell. Unlike Rivera and Siqueiros, Orozco did not align himself with a political movement, but his work had an intense humanitarian mission. He returned to Mexico in 1934 with a big reputation after his success in the USA, and he spent most of the rest of his life engaged on mural projects in Mexico City and Guadalajara, the country's second city. In his last years his work became ever more violent in expression, moved by a passionate concern for the suffering and miseries of mankind. His studio in Guadalajara is now a museum dedicated to him.

Orpen, Sir William (1878–1931). British painter, chiefly famous as one of the leading fashionable portraitists of his day. Orpen was a child prodigy and had a brilliant student career at the *Slade School. He worked mainly in London but he kept up links with his native Ireland, teaching part-time at the Metropolitan School in Dublin, 1902–14. His style had much in common with that of his friend Augustus *John, being vigorous and painterly but sometimes rather flashy. He was at his best when he was away from his standard boardroom and drawing-room fare, and his numerous self-portraits are often particularly engaging, as he pokes fun at himself in character roles. Up to the First World War he had a steady rise in worldly success and after the war he earned an average of about £35,000 a year, rising to over £50,000 a year in 1929—a colossal sum then. In 1920 a story appeared in London newspapers that he had refused an offer of £1,000,000 to work for a dealer in the USA, and he was one of the few British artists of his time capable of attracting public attention in such a way. Apart from portraits, Orpen also painted genre subjects, landscapes, interiors, nudes, and allegories, and he did memorable work as an *Official War Artist in France (he also attended the 1919 Peace Conference in Paris and painted a large group portrait showing the *Signing of the Peace in the Hall of Mirrors, Versailles, 28 June, 1919* (Imperial War Mus., London)).

His reputation faded badly after his death but revived greatly in the 1970s.

Orphism (or **Orphic Cubism**). Terms coined by *Apollinaire to describe a type of painting—a development from *Cubism—practised by Robert *Delaunay and some of his associates between 1911 and the outbreak of the First World War in 1914. The reference to Orpheus, the singer and poet of Greek mythology, reflected the desire of the artists involved to bring a new element of lyricism and colour into the austere intellectual Cubism of *Picasso, *Braque, and *Gris. Apart from Delaunay, the artists whom Apollinaire mentioned as practitioners of Orphism were Marcel *Duchamp, Fernand *Léger, and Francis *Picabia (all members of the *Section d'Or), but František *Kupka, another member of their circle, was in fact closer in style to Delaunay than these three. By 1912 both Delaunay and Kupka were painting completely non-representational pictures characterized by intensely vibrant fragmented colours. Despite its short life, Orphism was highly influential, notably on several major German painters, particularly *Klee (who visited Delaunay in 1912), *Macke, and *Marc. It was also closely related to *Synchromism.

Orsi, Lelio (*c*.1511–87). Italian *Mannerist painter, active mainly in his birthplace Novellara, near Parma, and in nearby Reggio Emilia. His large-scale work in fresco has almost all perished and he is now known mainly by *cabinet pictures of religious subjects (*The Walk to Emmaus*, *c*.1570, NG, London). He was influenced by various sources (*Correggio, *Giulio Romano, *Michelangelo, *Parmigianino, and perhaps also German woodcuts), but his style has a leaning towards the bizarre, with dramatic stage-lighting effects, that gives it a distinctly personal touch. Orsi was an outstanding draughtsman and also worked as an architect.

Os, van. Dutch family of painters active during the late 18th and 19th centuries, mainly in The Hague. **Jan** (1744–1808) was the founder. He and his daughter **Maria Margaretha** (1780–1862) and his son **Georgius** (1782–1861) specialized in painting flowers and fruits in the lavish detailed manner of Jan van *Huysum. Another of Jan's sons, **Pieter Gerardus**

(1776–1839), specialized in landscapes with cattle. His son and pupil, **Pieter Frederik** (1802–92), taught *Mauve.

Osona, Rodrigo de (d. 1518). Spanish painter. He was one of the leading painters of his day in Valencia, introducing both Netherlandish and Italian *Renaissance influence to the area. His most important work is a *Crucifixion* (1476) in the church of S. Nicolás, Valencia. On the basis of an altarpiece of the *Adoration of the Magi* (V&A, London) signed 'the son of Master Rodrigo', several works have been attributed to **Rodrigo de Osona the Younger** (d. *c*.1514). He continued his father's style in a weaker, more Italianate manner.

Ostade, Adriaen van (1610–85). Dutch painter, draughtsman, and etcher, active in his native Haarlem. Although he turned his hand to many subjects, he was principally a *genre painter. According to *Houbraken, he and Adriaen *Brouwer (whose work is similar) were fellow pupils of Frans *Hals. Ostade's early pictures depict lively scenes of peasants carousing or brawling in crowded taverns or hovels. In his later works (after *c*.1650) his peasants learn better manners and the rooms they live in are tidier. These later pictures are lighter in key and more colourful; thus they follow the general trend of Dutch painting around this time. Ostade was successful, prolific, and much imitated. He is said to have taught Jan *Steen and his other pupils included his brother **Isaak van Ostade** (1621–49), who likewise worked in Haarlem. As well as painting genre scenes in the manner of Adriaen, Isaak was an outstanding exponent of the winter landscape, and his early death cut short a career of great promise. Good examples of the work of both brothers are in the National Gallery, London.

ottocento (It.: '19th century'). *See* QUATTROCENTO.

Ottonian art. Term applied to art of the Holy Roman empire in the 10th century and most of the 11th century. The period is named after Otto the Great, who was crowned king of the Germans in 936 and was Holy Roman emperor from 963 until his death in 973. He re-established a strong royal authority after the fall of the Carolingian empire. The Ottonian period saw the revival of large-scale bronze casting (*see* BERNWARD OF HILDESHEIM) and of life-size sculpture (in the celebrated Gero Crucifix of *c*.970 in Cologne Cathedral), but the most typical sculptural products of the time were in ivory and metalwork, notably for book covers and altar reliefs. Though wall paintings still survive, the character of Ottonian art is better seen in a rich store of *illuminated manuscripts. In spite of differences in local schools, all Ottonian illumination has certain things in common, notably the pre-eminence given to the human figure, which is often imbued with strong expression and marked by exaggerated gestures. Ottonian art was one of the sources out of which *Romanesque grew.

Oudry, Jean-Baptiste (1686–1755). French painter, tapestry designer, and illustrator. He was a pupil of *Largillière and painted some portraits, but he is renowned chiefly as one of the outstanding animal painters of the 18th century. With *Desportes he was his period's foremost exponent of hunting scenes and still lifes with dead game. Some of his best work was done as a tapestry designer, and he was head of the Beauvais and *Gobelins factories from 1734 and 1748 respectively. He also did book illustrations, notably for an edition of La Fontaine's *Fables* (1755–9). His son **Jacques-Charles** (1722/3–78), a flower and animal painter, sometimes collaborated with him.

Ouwater, Albert van (active mid-15th century). Netherlandish painter. There is no known contemporary information on him (an alleged documentary reference to him in 1467 is now thought to be a misreading), and knowledge of his life depends on the account in van *Mander's *Schilder-boeck* (1604). According to this, Ouwater was the founder of the Haarlem School and the teacher of *Geertgen tot Sint Jans. Van Mander also praised Ouwater's skill as a landscapist, so it is ironic that the only painting that can be identified as his from the descriptions of his work in the *Schilder-boeck* is an interior scene—the *Raising of Lazarus* (*c*.1440–50, Gemäldegalerie, Berlin). The thoughtful, unemotional style of this picture has some affinities with the work of Dirk *Bouts, who was probably a native of Haarlem.

Ovenden, Annie and **Graham.** *See* BLAKE, SIR PETER.

Ovens, Juriaen. *See* CAMPEN.

Overbeck, Friedrich (1789–1869). German painter, the leading member of the *Nazarenes. He moved to Rome in 1810 and was based there for the rest of his life, although he made several visits to Germany. In 1813 he was converted to Roman Catholicism and apart from a few portraits (there is a self-portrait in the Uffizi, Florence) his work was almost exclusively on religious themes. He painted in a consciously archaic style—clear and sincere but rather pallid—based on the work of *Perugino and the young *Raphael. His best-known painting is perhaps the *Rose Miracle of St Francis* (1829, Porziuncola Chapel, S. Maria degli Angeli, Assisi). The high-minded and didactic tone of his work won it a more sympathetic acceptance (particularly in England) than its artistic quality alone merited. William *Dyce and Ford Madox *Brown were among his supporters and there were affinities between his aspirations and those of the *Pre-Raphaelite Brotherhood.

Ozenfant, Amédée (1886–1966). French painter, writer, and teacher. In 1918 he met *Le Corbusier, with whom he founded *Purism, but he is more important as a writer and teacher than as a painter. He lived in London, 1935–9, then in New York, 1939–55, founding art schools in both cities. After returning to France he settled in Cannes, where he directed a studio for foreign art students. His most important book is *Art* (1927), translated as *Foundations of Modern Art* (1931; enlarged edn., 1952). This is a study of the interrelationship of all forms of human creativity, including science and religion, and is one of the most widely read books by any modern artist.

P

Pacheco, Francisco (1564–1644). Spanish painter and writer, active in Seville. He was a man of great culture, a poet and scholar as well as a painter, and his house was the focus of Seville's artistic life. As a painter he was undistinguished, working in a stiff academic style (though his portraits are fresher than his religious works). He was an outstanding teacher, however, for (in spite of his own limitations) he was sympathetic to the more naturalistic style that was then developing. Moreover, he was generous enough in spirit to acknowledge openly that his greatest pupil, *Velázquez (who became his son-in-law in 1618), was a much better painter than himself: 'I consider it no disgrace for the pupil to surpass the master.' Alonso *Cano was his other outstanding pupil, and Pacheco often collaborated with the great sculptor *Montañés, painting his wooden figures. In 1649 his book *Arte de la pintura* (Art of Painting) was posthumously published; part theoretical, part biographical, this is a major source of information for the period (it includes accounts of his meeting with El *Greco in Toledo in 1611 and of Velázquez's early career). Pacheco was an official overseer of religious images for the Inquisition and the highly detailed *iconographical prescriptions in his book were often strictly adhered to by contemporary artists.

Pacher, Michael (d. 1498). Austrian painter and sculptor, active mainly at Bruneck in the Tyrol, where he is first documented in 1467 (although there are records of lost works dating back to 1462). He worked mainly for local churches, carrying out the carving as well as the painting of his altarpieces, and much of his work is still in situ. His most celebrated work is the St Wolfgang altarpiece (1471–81) in the church of St Wolfgang on the Abersee, a huge *polyptych with some astonishingly intricate woodcarving and painted wings. Although Pacher's sculpture is thoroughly late *Gothic in spirit, his painting is strongly influenced by Italian art. He is particularly close to *Mantegna, especially in

the way dramatic effects are obtained by using a low viewpoint and setting the figures close to the picture plane. There is no documentary evidence that Pacher visited Italy, but because of its proximity to the Tyrol it seems likely that he did. His work had wide influence and before *Dürer he was the most important interpreter of *Renaissance ideas for painting in the German-speaking world. His son **Hans Pacher** was a painter, and Michael sometimes collaborated with a **Friedrich Pacher**, who was perhaps also a relative (although the surname is not uncommon).

Paik, Nam June. See VIDEO ART.

pala. An Italian term for an altarpiece consisting of a single large painting, as distinct from a *polyptych with many panels.

Palacios, Francisco de. See PEREDA.

Palamedesz., Anthonie (1601–73). Dutch portrait and *genre painter, active mainly in his native Delft. He was a pupil of *Miereveld and Dirk *Hals and his paintings resemble those of his masters—his portraits rather wooden, his 'merry company' groups of soldiers, cavaliers, and their ladies livelier and pleasantly coloured. His younger brother **Palamedes I Palamedesz.** (1607–38) and his son **Palamedes II Palamedesz.** (1633–1705) were both painters.

palette. A flat board, usually rectangular, ovoid, or kidney-shaped, on which artists arrange their paints ready for use; early examples sometimes had a handle, rather like a table-tennis bat, but a thumb-hole is now standard. Palettes first appeared *c.*1400; before then individual containers (sometimes shells) were used for mixing colours. For oil painting, mahogany is traditionally considered the best material for palettes, although other close-grained hardwoods have been used. Materials such as porcelain or ivory have been used by watercolour or *miniature painters and also sometimes by oil painters—*Millais, for example, used a porcelain palette early in his career, when he painted with fastidious detail and wished to avoid muddying his colours. For many artists, choice of their pigments and the order in which they are set out on the palette is a very important and personal matter and much advice was published on how to 'set' a palette in handbooks of the 18th and 19th centuries. By extension, the term 'palette' thus refers to the range of colours characteristic of an artist: *Caravaggio has a dark or restricted palette, *Monet a bright or rich palette.

palette knife. A thin, flexible, dull-edged blade, set in a handle, used for mixing paint, scraping it off the *palette or canvas, and also as a painting instrument (although more delicate tools—'painting knives', shaped like miniature trowels—are often preferred for this purpose). Palette knives became popular in the 18th century, ordinary knives being used for the purpose before this. Today the blades are invariably made of steel, but other materials, including ivory, have been used in the past. *Courbet is sometimes credited with inventing the specialized painting knife, but *Constable had earlier used a similar implement.

Palma Giovane (Giacomo or Jacopo Palma) (*c.*1548–1628). Venetian painter, great-nephew of *Palma Vecchio. He is said to have been a pupil of *Titian, but this tradition has been doubted (it is probably based on the fact that he completed the *Pietà* that Titian left unfinished at his death). In the late 1560s and early 1570s he worked in central Italy, mainly Rome, but thereafter he spent the rest of his life in Venice, and after the death of *Tintoretto in 1594 he was the leading painter in the city. His style was influenced by several of his great Venetian predecessors—*Veronese as well as Titian and Tintoretto—and by central Italian *Mannerism. He was extremely prolific, fulfilling many commissions from abroad as well as for Venetian churches, and his later work is often mechanical. As well as religious pictures, he painted historical and mythological works, and he also made etchings.

Palma Vecchio (Giacomo or Jacopo Palma) (*c.*1480–1528). Italian painter, born near Bergamo, but active for all his known career in Venice, where he is first documented in 1510. His original surname was Negreti, but he was using the name Palma by 1513. He is called Palma Vecchio (Old Palma) to distinguish him from *Palma Giovane (Young Palma), his great-nephew. Nothing is known of his training, and there is indeed very little secure knowledge about his life and works, none of his pictures being dated or reliably signed and very few of them being certainly identifiable from early sources. His style is distinctive, however, and in practice the definition of his oeuvre is much less problematic than with many of his contemporaries. He painted a few altarpieces for Venetian churches, but most of his work was done for private clients, his speciality being half-length portrayals of beautiful and voluptuous blonde-haired women, sometimes in religious or mythological guise. In opulence of colour and beauty of handling they show the influence of the early work of *Titian, and the finest, such as the celebrated *La Bella* (Thyssen Mus., Madrid), are worthy of his name. Palma also painted some *Giorgionesque reclining nudes and some male portraits. His work was influential on painters of the next generation in Venice, notably *Bonifazio Veronese.

Palmer, Erastus Dow (1817–1904). American sculptor. Self-taught, he rarely left Albany in his native New York State, and he was the most successful American sculptor of his period to work in the USA rather than in Europe. He began with *cameo portraits and had a flourishing business with portrait busts and bas-*reliefs on religious subjects, but his most celebrated work, now as in his own day, is the *White Captive* (1858, Met. Mus., New York). Inspired by *Powers's *Greek Slave*, it shows a naked young girl who has been captured by Red Indians and is sustained by her Christianity—this accompanying storyline undoubtedly contributed to its popularity. The statue is fresher in observation than Powers's *Greek Slave*, for although the marble surfaces are impeccably smooth, the chubby proportions of the figure are unidealized and the strikingly characterized head is a portrait of Palmer's daughter. From the 1860s he worked increasingly in bronze.

Palmer, Samuel (1805–81). English landscape painter and etcher. He was precocious, exhibiting landscape drawings at the *Royal Academy when he was only 14. In 1822 he met John *Linnell, who introduced him to William *Blake in 1824. Palmer had had visionary experiences from childhood and the effect of Blake upon him was to intensify an inherent mystical bent. In 1826 he moved to Shoreham, near Sevenoaks, Kent, where he was the central figure of the group of artists known as the *Ancients and produced what are now his most famous works—landscapes charged with a sense of pantheistic fecundity and other-worldly beauty. In about 1832 what he called his 'primitive and infantine feeling' for landscape began to fade, and after returning to London in 1835, marrying Linnell's daughter in 1837, and spending a two-year honeymoon in Italy, the break with his visionary manner was complete. His later paintings were in a much more conventional topographical or pastoral mode, highly-wrought and often sentimental in feeling. In his etchings, however, something of his early genius remained; at his death he was working on an edition of Virgil's *Eclogues*, translated and illustrated by himself. His early work was virtually forgotten until the 1920s, but it subsequently influenced modern romantic landscape artists such as Paul *Nash and Graham *Sutherland (*see* NEO-ROMANTICISM).

Palomino, Antonio (1655–1726). Spanish painter and writer on art, active mainly in Madrid, where in 1688 Charles II (*see* HABSBURG) appointed him one of his court painters. He was famous in his day for frescos in churches in Madrid and elsewhere, but he is now best known for his book *El museo pictórico y escala óptica* ('The Pictorial Museum and Optical Scale', vol. 1, 1715; vols. 2 and 3, 1724). The first two volumes are devoted respectively to the theory and the practice of art, and the third volume is a collection of biographies, the most important source for the history of Spanish art from the 16th to the early 18th century. It earned Palomino the nickname 'the Spanish *Vasari'.

panel. Term in painting for a *support of wood, metal, or other rigid material, as distinct from *canvas. Until the introduction of canvas in the 15th century, nearly all movable paintings in Europe were executed on wood, and even up to the beginning of the 17th century it is probable that as much painting was done on the one support as on the other. Painters who worked on a small scale often used copper panels (*Elsheimer is a leading example), and in the colonial art of South America copper and tin and even lead and zinc were used. On a larger scale, slate has occasionally been used as a support, for example by *Rubens for his altarpiece for S. Maria in Vallicella (the Chiesa Nuova) in Rome; the picture he originally painted, on canvas (*Virgin and Child Adored by St Gregory and Other Saints*, 1607, Mus. B.-A., Grenoble), was said to reflect the light unpleasantly and slate was used for the replacement to produce a more matt finish (1608, in situ). The choice of wood for panels depended mainly on local availability. In Italy, poplar was most commonly used, and oak was preferred in northern Europe. Many other types were used, however; analysis of the contents of art galleries has yielded a long list, including beech, cedar, chestnut, fir, larch, linden, mahogany, olive, and walnut. Today cedar, teak, and dark walnut are favourites, and modern painters have also used plywood, fibreboard, and other synthetic materials as supports (*see also* ACADEMY BOARD).

Panini (or **Pannini**), **Giovanni Paolo** (or **Gianpaolo**) (1691–1765). Italian painter. He was born in Piacenza, where he trained as a *quadraturista* and stage designer. In 1711 he settled in Rome, where he became the pre-eminent painter of real and imaginary views of the city. He was the first painter to make a special feature of ruins—an aspect of his work that links him with Hubert *Robert and *Piranesi—and he also did paintings of public festivities and events of historical importance. Panini taught perspective at the French Academy in Rome and his influence was strong with French as well as Italian artists. He was a prolific painter and many galleries have examples of his work.

Panofsky, Erwin (1892–1968). German-American art historian, a professor at Hamburg University 1926–33, until dismissed by the Nazis. In 1934 he settled in the USA, where he had been a visiting professor at New York since 1931, and was then visiting professor at Princeton University, 1934–5, and from 1935 professor at the Institute for Advanced Study, Princeton. Kenneth *Clark described him as 'unquestionably the greatest art historian of his time', and he is renowned particularly for his immensely learned contributions to the study of *iconography. His books include *Studies in Iconology* (1939), *Albrecht Dürer* (1943), *Early Netherlandish Painting* (1953), and *Tomb Sculpture* (1964). Panofsky enjoyed teaching and was influential through his work in the classroom and lecture hall as well as through his writings. Many scholars have tried to emulate his way of analysing works of art as part of a broad philosophical, intellectual, and cultural pattern, but few have rivalled his learning or finesse, and some of his followers have been accused of 'over-interpreting' pictures in their desire to uncover 'hidden symbolism'.

panorama. 'A picture of a landscape or other scene, either arranged on the inside of a cylindrical surface round the spectator as a centre (a *cyclorama*), or unrolled or unfolded and made to pass before him, so as to show the various parts in succession' (*OED*). In 1787 a patent for such a 360-degree painting was granted to Robert Barker (1739–1806), an Irish-born painter working in Edinburgh, and the type soon became a popular form of entertainment: 'Panorama painting seems all the rage', *Constable wrote in 1803. Panoramas were indeed a kind of forerunner of the popular cinema and tended to be remarkable for sheer spectacle rather than artistic merit. Distinguished artists were sometimes associated with them, however, notably *Girtin, who made a panorama of London, now lost, and *Mesdag, whose panorama of Scheveningen can still be seen in The Hague. In more general parlance, the term 'panorama' is used of any wide, uninterrupted view over a scene, particularly a landscape.

pantograph. An instrument, known since the 17th century, for copying a drawing or design, either same size or on a larger or smaller scale. By a simple system of levers, the outline of the original work traced with a point attached to one arm can be repeated on to another surface by a drawing instrument that is attached to another arm.

Paolozzi, Sir Eduardo (1924–). British sculptor and printmaker of Italian parentage. He had his first one-man exhibition as a sculptor in 1947 and in the same year he began making *collages using cuttings from American magazines, etc. (*I was a Rich Man's Plaything*, 1947, Tate, London). Pao-

lozzi regarded these collages as 'ready-made metaphors' representing the popular dreams of the masses, and they have been seen as forerunners of *Pop art (he eventually amassed a large collection of pulp literature, art, and artefacts, which he presented to the University of St Andrews). From the 1950s he has worked primarily as an abstract sculptor, often on a large scale. His work of the 1950s was characteristically heavy and bulky, often incorporating industrial components, showing his interest in technology as well as in popular culture. In the 1960s his work became more colourful, including large totem-like figures made up from casts of pieces of machinery and often brightly painted. In the 1970s he made solemn machine-like forms and also box-like low *reliefs, both small and large, in wood or bronze, sometimes made to hang on the wall, compartmented and filled with small carved items. His more recent work has included several large public commissions, for example mosaic decorations for Tottenham Court Road underground station in London (installed 1983–5). Paolozzi has taught at various art schools and universities in Britain, Europe, and the USA. He was knighted in 1989 and has been awarded many other honours. *See also* INDEPENDENT GROUP.

paper. A material made from the pulp of wood or other fibrous substances, manufactured in thin sheets as a surface for writing, drawing, or printing. Paper was invented in China about 2,000 years ago and was first made in Europe in the 11th century, in Spain. Other European countries followed, and by the end of the 14th century France, southern Germany, Italy, and Switzerland had well-developed paper industries. The first record of a papermill in England dates from 1494. The growing availability of paper (in place of the much more expensive *parchment) was a great stimulus to the development of drawing during the *Renaissance. Until 1800 European paper was made entirely of rags pulped in water, and drawing paper of the best quality is still made by hand in the traditional way. Writing papers, less expensive drawing papers, and some book papers are machine-made of a mixture of cotton, hemp, esparto, and wood, with a good deal of china clay added to make them smooth and opaque, *size to make them non-absorbent, and starch to make them stiff. Cheaper papers are machine-made wholly of wood. Oriental papers made of bamboo, rice straw, and mulberry bark are imported for artists' use.

papier collé (Fr.: 'pasted paper'). A type of *collage in which pieces of decorative or printed paper are incorporated into a picture or—when stuck on a ground such as canvas—themselves constitute the picture. The technique was invented by *Braque in September 1912 in his *Fruit-Dish and Glass* (priv. coll.) and was almost immediately adopted by *Picasso. *Gris too made extensive use of papier collé, and *Matisse's use of cut-out paper shapes in his late work is a development of the technique.

papyrus. A writing material made from the stem of the marsh plant of the same name, growing in antiquity principally in Egypt and now in the Sudan. Its use in Egypt goes back to at least the third millennium BC and it was the standard writing material in ancient Greece and throughout the Roman empire. From the 4th century AD it was increasingly replaced by *parchment.

parchment. Writing material made from the skins of sheep or calf, less frequently pig, goat, and other animals; it has also been used for painting, and occasionally for printing and bookbinding. *Pliny says that it was invented in the 2nd century BC in Pergamum; hence the name 'parchment' (from Lat., *pergamena*: 'of Pergamum'). Skin had been used as a writing material before this, but the refined methods of cleaning and stretching involved in making parchment enabled both sides of a leaf to be used, leading eventually to the supplanting of the manuscript roll by the bound book. Vellum is a fine kind of parchment made from the delicate skins of young (sometimes stillborn) animals. *Paper began to replace parchment from about the 14th century in Europe, but parchment is still used for certain kinds of documents, and the name is often applied to high-quality writing paper.

Pareja, Juan de. *See* VELÁZQUEZ.

Paris, Matthew (d. 1259). English chronicler and manuscript illuminator. He became a monk at the monastery of St Albans in 1217 and was appointed monastery chronicler in 1236. In 1248 he was sent to Norway to reform the monastery of St Benet-Holme, but this is his only recorded visit abroad (the surname Paris is found elsewhere in England in the 13th century and does not necessarily imply that he had any French associations). Matthew carried on the abbey's *Chronica Majora* from 1235 until his death (it is now divided between Corpus Christi College, Cambridge, and the BL, London) and also wrote a summary of the chief events between 1200 and 1250 that is known as the *Historia Minor* or *Historia Anglorum* (BL). His historical manuscripts are almost unique in being illustrated with numerous marginal scenes and symbols from his own hand. He also composed several Lives of the Saints (the *Life of St Alban*, Trinity College, Dublin, is autograph) in which the illustrations occupy the upper half of the page and are of equal importance with the text. The frontispiece to his *Historia Anglorum* is his only signed work—a self-portrait showing him on his knees dedicating the manuscript to the Virgin. It is a tinted outline drawing, and because of his fame there has been a mistaken tendency to assign all mid 13th-century English work of this character to St Albans in general and, if at all plausible, to his hand.

Paris, School of. *See* ÉCOLE DE PARIS.

Parler, Peter (*c*.1330–99). German architect and sculptor, the most famous member of a dynasty of masons active in the 14th century and early 15th century. In the 1350s he settled in Prague, where he was architect to the cathedral (much of the present structure was designed by him). He also built the celebrated Charles Bridge over the River Vltava. As a sculptor he is best known for a series of portrait busts in the triforium of the cathedral, including a self-portrait and one of the emperor Charles IV.

Parmigianino (Girolamo Francesco Maria Mazzola) (1503–40). Italian *Mannerist painter, draughtsman, and printmaker, born in Parma, from which he takes his nickname. He was precociously gifted, and as early as 1522–3 he painted highly accomplished frescos in two chapels in S. Giovanni Evangelista, Parma; they show his admiration for *Correggio, who was working in the same church at this time. The originality and sophistication he displayed from the beginning, particularly his love of unusual spatial effects, is most memorably seen in his celebrated *Self-Portrait in a Convex Mirror* (1524, KH Mus., Vienna), in which *Vasari said he looks 'so beautiful that he seemed an angel rather than a man'. In 1524 Parmigianino moved to Rome, possibly via Florence, and his work became both grander and more graceful under the influence of *Raphael and *Michelangelo. The *Vision of St Jerome* (1526–7, NG, London) is his most important work of this time, showing the disturbing emotional intensity he created with his elongated forms, disjointed sense of space, chill lighting, and lascivious atmosphere. Parmigianino left Rome after it was sacked by German troops in 1527 and moved to Bologna. In 1530 he returned to Parma and contracted to paint frescos in S. Maria della Steccata. He failed to complete the work, however, and in 1539 was imprisoned for breach of contract. Vasari says he neglected the work because he was infatuated with alchemy—'he allowed his beard to grow long and disordered ... he neglected himself and grew melancholy and eccentric'. His later paintings show no falling off in his powers, however, and his work reaches its apotheosis in his celebrated *Madonna of the Long Neck* (c.1535, Uffizi, Florence). The forms of the figures are extraordinarily elongated and tapering and the painting has a refinement and grace that place it among the archetypal works of Mannerism. Parmigianino's range extended beyond religious works. He painted a highly erotic *Cupid Carving his Bow* (1535, KH Mus., Vienna), and was one of the subtlest portraitists of his age (two superb examples are in the Mus. di Capodimonte, Naples). The landscape backgrounds to his religious works have a mysterious and visionary quality that influenced Niccolò dell'*Abate and through him French art (*see* FONTAINEBLEAU, SCHOOL OF). Parmigianino, whose draughtsmanship was exquisite, also made designs for engravings and *chiaroscuro woodcuts and seems to have been the first Italian artist to produce original etchings from his own designs.

Parrhasius. Greek painter from Ephesus, active in the later 5th century BC. He is said to have been particularly skilful in the use of contour and in depicting character through facial expression, and his mastery of illusionism is recorded in one of *Pliny's most famous anecdotes. It concerns a contest Parrhasius had with *Zeuxis, who painted some grapes so naturalistically that birds came to peck at them. Victory seeming to be his, he called on Parrhasius to draw back the curtain concealing his picture, but this turned out to be a painted curtain. Zeuxis conceded the contest: he had deceived the birds, but Parrhasius had deceived him.

Parrish, Maxfield (1870–1966). American painter and illustrator. He studied at the Pennsylvania Academy of the Fine Arts with the author-illustrator Howard Pyle (1853–1911), celebrated for his children's books. In 1895 Parrish designed a cover for *Harper's Weekly* and thereafter rapidly made a name for himself with illustrations, posters, and advertisements. His greatest fame and popularity came with colour prints designed for the mass market. Sentimental scenes such as the *Garden of Allah* (copyrighted 1919) and *Dawn* (1920) sold by the million. They are in a lush and romantic style, set in an escapist world combining elements of the *Arabian Nights*, Hollywood, and classical antiquity, with languorous maidens and idyllic landscape backgrounds. His draughtsmanship and detailing are immaculate and his colouring distinctively high-keyed and luminous. Many of his advertisements were in a similar vein. In the 1930s his style went out of fashion and he retired to paint landscapes, working up to his death at the age of 95. Shortly before this there was a revival of interest in his work, which had long been dismissed as kitsch; in 1964, for example, the Metropolitan Museum, New York, bought his painting *Errant Pan* (c.1915).

Parsons, Betty (1900–82). American art dealer, collector, painter, and sculptor. After Peggy *Guggenheim closed her New York gallery in 1947, Parsons became for a few years the leading dealer of the *Abstract Expressionists, until several of the major figures left her for Sidney *Janis in the early 1950s. She continued to support avant-garde art, and by the time her New York gallery closed in 1977 she had represented many of the most famous names in American art over the previous three decades, especially *Colour Field and *Minimal painters. Her own work as an artist was predominantly abstract.

Pascin, Jules (Julius Pincas) (1885–1930). Bulgarian-born painter and draughtsman. He led a wandering life, and although he acquired American citizenship when he moved to New York during the First World War, he is chiefly associated with Paris, where he belonged to the circle of émigré artists who gravitated around *Chagall, *Modigliani, and *Soutine. His work includes portraits of his friends, café scenes, and flower pieces, as well as a few large paintings with biblical themes, but the bulk of his output consists of erotically charged studies of nude (or very flimsily dressed) teenage girls. They have been compared to the work of *Degas and *Toulouse-Lautrec, but Pascin's paintings are less penetrating and more obviously posed. He can be rather repetitive, but his best art has great delicacy of colour and handling and a poignant sense of lost innocence. Pascin's art brought him financial success, but he led a dissolute life and was emotionally unstable; on the day on which a major exhibition of his art was due to open at the Galerie Georges Petit in Paris he committed suicide in his studio (slashing his wrists and then hanging himself).

Pasmore, Victor (1908–98). British painter and maker of constructions who is unusual in having achieved eminence as both a figurative and an abstract artist. After early experiments with abstraction he reverted to naturalistic painting, and in 1937 he combined with William *Coldstream and Claude *Rogers in forming the *Euston Road School. Characteristic of his work at this time and in the early 1940s are some splendid female nudes and lyrically sensitive Thames-side landscapes that have been likened to those of *Whistler (*Chiswick Reach*, 1943, NG, Ottawa). In the late 1940s he underwent a dramatic conversion to pure abstract art, and by the early 1950s he had developed a personal style of geometrical abstraction. As well as paintings he made abstract *reliefs, partly under the influence of Ben *Nicholson. His earlier reliefs had a hand-made quality but later, through the introduction of transparent perspex, he gave them the impersonal precision and finish of machine products. Through work in this vein he came to be regarded as one of the leaders of *Constructivism in Britain. Later paintings are less austere and more organic. Pasmore was an influential teacher, notably at King's College, Newcastle upon Tyne (now Newcastle University), where he was head of the painting department, 1954–61. The 'basic design' course he taught there (based on *Bauhaus ideas) spread to many British art schools. He was also much concerned with bringing abstract art to the general public. In 1955, for example, he was appointed consulting director of architectural design for Peterlee New Town, County Durham, and designed an urban centre in the form of a Pavilion that integrated architectural design with abstract relief painting. In his later career Pasmore was also a prolific printmaker. He won many honours and Kenneth *Clark described him as 'one of the two or three most talented English painters of this century'.

Passarotti, Bartolommeo (1529–92). Italian painter. After spending much of his early career in Rome (*c.*1551–*c.*1565) he settled in his native Bologna, where he had a large studio that became the focal point of the city's artistic life. The religious paintings that were the basis of his success are fairly conventional, and he is now remembered mainly for his pioneering *genre scenes of butchers' shops (one of the few surviving examples is in the Galleria Nazionale, Rome). They reflect the influence of northern painters such as *Aertsen and in their lively observation marked a break with the prevailing *Mannerism. Annibale *Carracci (whose brother Agostino studied with Passarotti) was influenced by these genre scenes in his early career, although Annibale's approach was more serious. In addition to his religious and genre works, Passarotti painted fine portraits throughout his career. His son **Tiburzio** (d. *c.*1612) imitated his style, and he in turn had two artist sons, **Gaspare** and **Archangelo**.

Passeri, Giovanni Battista (*c.*1610–79). Italian painter and writer on art. He is of no significance as a painter, but he is important for his collection of biographies of contemporary artists, *Vite de' pittori, scultori ed architetti che anno lavorato in Roma morti dal 1641 fino al 1673*, not published until 1772. His accounts are detailed and on the whole accurate, forming one of the most important sources for the study of Roman *Baroque art.

pastel. A drawing or painting material consisting of a stick of colour made from powdered *pigments mixed with just enough *resin or *gum to bind them. Pastel is applied directly to paper, with no diluent, and a significant difference between this and other methods of painting is that the colour as applied represents the final result —no allowance has to be made for changes during drying. Pastel has the disadvantage, however, of being very fragile and easily dislodged from the paper. This can be counteracted by using a *fixative, but fixing is apt to reduce the brilliance of the colour. As they are so delicate, pastels are usually used on a small scale, and they have been especially popular for portraits. They were first used in the late 15th century and their heyday was the 18th century. The medium had a second great flowering in the late 19th century, when several of the *Impressionists, most notably *Degas, took it up. *See also* CHALK.

pastel manner. *See* CRAYON MANNER.

Pasternak, Leonid (1862–1945). Russian painter and draughtsman. He was a friend of many literary, musical, and political personalities, notably Leo Tolstoy, whose works he illustrated (*War and Peace*; *Resurrection*), and whom he portrayed on many occasions. In 1921 he left the Soviet Union and settled in Berlin, where he worked mainly as a portraitist (his sitters included Max *Liebermann and Albert Einstein). He left Germany because of the rise of Nazism and settled in England in 1938, spending his last years in Oxford. The celebrated writer Boris Pasternak was his son.

pastiche (or **pasticcio**). A work of art that imitates the style of another work, artist, or period; more specifically, in the visual arts, a picture or other work that (often with fraudulent intent) imitates the style of a particular artist by borrowing and rearranging motifs from his authentic works.

Patch, Thomas (1725–82). English painter and engraver who lived in Italy from 1747. In Rome he first made a reputation as a view painter, especially among English tourists, but after settling in Florence in 1755 he was best known for good-humoured *caricature *conversation pieces and it is for these that he is chiefly remembered today. Patch knew *Reynolds, who included a portrait of him in his own caricature of *Raphael's *School of*

Athens (1751, NG, Dublin), and it is uncertain who influenced whom in the genre.

Patel, Pierre (*c*.1605–76). French landscape painter, active in Paris. He was a pupil of *Vouet but worked in the manner of *Claude, with whose paintings his own have sometimes been confused (although Patel's style is harder). Much of his work was done in the form of panels set into the decoration of rooms; two examples (*c*.1647) from the Cabinet de l'Amour of the Hôtel Lambert, Paris, are in the Louvre. His son, **Pierre-Antoine** (1648–1707), painted in the same vein as his father. Both men often featured classical ruins in their paintings, looking forward to the *Picturesque.

Patenier. *See* PATINIR.

Pater, Jean-Baptiste (1695–1736). French painter, the only pupil of *Watteau (a fellow native of Valenciennes), with whom he had a somewhat touchy relationship. An unlikely legend has it that Watteau dismissed him from his studio (*c*.1713) because he thought he was a threat to his own pre-eminence; whatever the reason for their differences, they were reconciled soon before Watteau's death. Like Watteau's other chief imitator, *Lancret, Pater repeated the master's type of fêtes galantes (*see* FÊTE CHAMPÊTRE) in a fairly stereotyped fashion. He showed more originality in scenes of military life and groups of bathers (in which he gave freer rein to the suggestiveness often seen in his fêtes galantes). Examples of all types of his work are in the Wallace Collection, London.

Pater, Walter (1839–94). English critic and essayist. A bachelor don at Brasenose College, Oxford, he lived uneventfully with his two spinster sisters and was the unlikely standard-bearer for *Aestheticism, which set a supreme value upon the enjoyment of beauty. His best-known book is *Studies in the History of the Renaissance* (1873), which includes essays on *Winckelmann, the then neglected *Botticelli, and *Leonardo, with his celebrated evocation of the *Mona Lisa*: 'She is older than the rocks among which she sits.' This volume (which concludes 'To burn always with this hard gemlike flame, to maintain this ecstasy, is success in life'), though attacked by some as unscholarly and morbid, had a profound influence on the undergraduates of the day and was acclaimed by Oscar Wilde as 'the holy writ of beauty'.

patina. Incrustation, usually green, on the surface of a metal (typically bronze) object, caused by corrosion. Such discoloration occurs naturally with age through exposure to the atmosphere and can be accelerated or modified when an object is buried in the sea or soil, where various substances present will cause chemical reactions. Patination can produce an attractive mellowing effect, and since the *Renaissance bronze statues have often been artificially patinated, usually by treatment with acid. By extension, the term 'patina' can be applied to any form of surface discoloration or mellowing, for example dirty varnish on a painting.

Patinir, Herri. *See* BLES.

Patinir (or **Patenier,** or **Patinier**), **Joachim** (d. 1524). Netherlandish painter, a pioneer of landscape as an independent genre. Although landscape never constitutes the entire subject of his pictures, it dwarfs the figures in his religious and mythological scenes and he has been described as the first landscape specialist in European art. Nothing is known of his early life, but in 1515 he became a member of the painters' guild in Antwerp. When *Dürer visited the city in 1521 he became friendly with Patinir and described him as a 'good landscape painter' (perhaps the first occurrence of this term). There are only a very few signed paintings, but many others have been attributed to him or his busy workshop. Patinir also painted landscape backgrounds for other artists, including his friend Quentin *Massys (who after Patinir's death became guardian of his children); the most securely authenticated instance of such collaboration is the *Temptation of St Anthony* (Prado, Madrid), which in a 1574 inventory of the *Escorial is described as having 'the figures by Master Quentin and the landscape by Master Joachim'. Patinir's work combines naturalistic observation of detail with a wonderful sense of fantasy, forming a link between *Bosch and *Bruegel.

Paton, Sir Joseph Noel (1821–1901). Scottish painter. A friend of *Millais (a fellow student at the *Royal Academy), he had a kinship with the *Pre-Raphaelites

early in his career. He painted mythological and historical scenes and later gained great success with his rather portentous and sentimental religious pictures, which went on tour and were much reproduced. His brother, **Waller Hugh Paton** (1828–95), was also a painter, mainly of landscapes in watercolour.

Paul III, Pope. *See* FARNESE.

Paul V, Pope. *See* BORGHESE.

Pausanias (2nd century AD). Greek traveller and geographer, the author of a *Description of Greece* in ten books that is the single most important literary source for the history of Greek art (painting and sculpture as well as architecture). It is a guidebook written for tourists—simple, unpretentious, detailed, and in the main reliable, as is frequently attested by the remains of the monuments he describes. Occasionally he has lapses: he saw several statues said to be the work of the legendary Daedalus and accepted that he really existed. Sir James Frazer, who produced one of the several English translations of the work (6 vols., 1898), said of Pausanias: 'without him the ruins of Greece would for the most part be a labyrinth without a clue, a riddle without an answer.'

Peake, Mervyn (1911–68). British writer and illustrator, born in China, the son of medical missionaries. He is now best known as a novelist, but he studied at the *Royal Academy Schools and spent much of his career teaching drawing in London art schools. His reputation rests mainly on his trilogy of novels *Titus Groan* (1946), *Gormenghast* (1950), and *Titus Alone* (1959), a work of grotesque Gothic fantasy to which his vividly imaginative drawing style was well matched (originally, however, the books were published without his accompanying illustrations). Peake illustrated numerous other books, including Stevenson's *Treasure Island* (1949) and several by himself (among them an instructional manual, *The Craft of the Lead Pencil*, 1946). In 1946 he was commissioned by the Ministry of Information to make drawings of people liberated from Belsen concentration camp—an experience that left him emotionally scarred. In the last decade of his life he was gradually incapacitated by Parkinson's disease. Peake is described in the *Dictionary of National*

Biography as 'Tall, thin, dark, and haggard ... gentle, gracious, unworldly, and unpractical'.

Peale, Charles Willson (1741–1827). American painter, inventor, naturalist, and patriot, the founder and most distinguished member of a family of artists. Peale was a highly versatile craftsman, and early in his career he worked as a saddler, watchmaker, silversmith, and upholsterer, as well as a sign painter. He received advice and encouragement from *Copley and spent two years in London (1767–9), where he studied under *West. In 1776 he settled in Philadelphia, where he became the most fashionable portraitist in the Colonies, Copley having left for England in 1774. He fought as a colonel of the militia in the War of Independence and became a Democratic member of the Pennsylvania Assembly. In 1782 he built an exhibition gallery next to his studio, the first art gallery in the United States, and there displayed his own portraits of leading personalities of the Revolutionary War (he painted George Washington several times). This expanded into a natural history museum, which attained a vast size and included as its star exhibit the first mastodon skeleton to be exhumed in America. Two of his most famous paintings celebrate his scientific interests—*The Exhumation of the Mastodon* (1806) in the Peale Museum, Baltimore, and *The Artist in his Museum* (1822) in the Pennsylvania Academy of the Fine Arts, an institution he helped to found in 1805. His inventions included new types of spectacles and false teeth. As a painter, Peale generally worked in a solid, dignified style, but his most celebrated work is a witty piece of *trompe-l'œil. This is *The Staircase Group* (1795, Philadelphia Mus. of Art), a life-size portrait of two of his sons mounting a staircase, with a real step at the bottom and a real door jamb as a frame; George Washington is said to have been deceived into doffing his hat to the boys' images. Peale married three times and had seventeen children, of whom several became artists. They included **Raphaelle** (1774–1825), one of America's most distinguished still-life painters, **Rembrandt** (1778–1860), a gifted though uneven portraitist, and **Titian Ramsay II** (1799–1885), who continued his father's tradition as an artist-naturalist. Apart from his portraits, Rembrandt won fame with *The Court of Death* (1821, Detroit

Inst. of Arts), a huge, melodramatic allegory that toured the country with success for over half a century. Charles Willson's brother **James** (1749–1831) was also a painter and his son and four daughters carried on the family tradition. The Peales were largely responsible for establishing Philadelphia as one of the country's leading cultural centres.

Pearlstein, Philip (1924–). American painter, a leading proponent of the return to naturalism and interest in the human figure that was one aspect of the move away from the dominance of *Abstract Expressionism. His early works (mainly landscapes) were painted with vigorous *gestural handling, but in the 1960s he developed a cooler, more even type of brushwork. He specializes in starkly unidealized portrayals of the nude figure (singly or in pairs), usually set in domestic surroundings. Because of the clarity of his compositions and the relentlessness of his scrutiny, he is sometimes described as a *Superrealist, but his work has an individuality that puts him outside this classification. He uses harsh lighting, oblique angles, and cropping of the image (heads are often excluded and the body is seen in voyeuristic close-up) in a way that suggests candid photography, but his pictures do not try to counterfeit the effect of photographs; the handling of paint is smooth—but vigorous rather than finicky.

Pechstein, Max (1881–1955). German *Expressionist painter and printmaker. He studied in Dresden and in 1906 became a member of Die *Brücke. In 1908 he settled in Berlin; his energy and charm quickly made him a leading figure in the city's artistic life and in 1910 he was elected president of the Neue *Sezession. In 1913–14, showing an interest in the exotic shared with other Expressionists, Pechstein visited the Palau Islands in the Pacific and he painted bright and lively anecdotal pictures depicting the paradisal life of the island fishermen in a near-*Fauvist manner. His other subjects included nudes, landscapes, portraits, and opulent flower pieces. He was the most French in spirit of the German Expressionists (he was particularly influenced by *Matisse) and probably because his work was decorative rather than emotionally intense, he was the first member of

Die Brücke to achieve success and general recognition; the 1920s marked the height of the fashion for his work. Since then his reputation has faded whilst those of his former colleagues have grown. In 1918 he was one of the founders of the *Novembergruppe and he taught in the Berlin Academy from 1923, being dismissed in 1933 by the Nazis and reinstated in 1945. His later work became repetitive and the high quality of his work during his Brücke period is sometimes forgotten.

peep-show box. An enclosed cabinet with scenes painted on the interior surfaces in such a way that when viewed through a small opening or eyepiece they give a strong illusion of three-dimensional reality. *Alberti may have been the inventor of the peep-show box, for some such device is ascribed to him in a contemporary, anonymous biography, but they had their greatest popularity in 17th-century Holland. Six examples survive from this time, three of them by Samuel van *Hoogstraten (the best, *c.*1655–60, is in the NG, London).

Peeters, Bonaventura the Elder (1614–52). Flemish marine painter. He was virtually the only noteworthy practitioner in the genre in his country, seascapes being much more a Dutch than a Flemish speciality. He is best known for his depictions of storms and shipwrecks, but he also produced various other types of marine pictures, including imaginary Mediterranean port scenes. Several other members of the family were artists, including his sister **Catharina** (1615–76), a seascape and still-life painter, but **Clara Peeters** (1594?–1657?), an outstanding (albeit obscure) Antwerp still-life painter, was no relation.

peintre-graveur. A French term for an artist who makes original prints from his own designs, as opposed to reproductive prints of another artist's work.

Pelham, Peter. *See* COPLEY.

Pellegrini, Giovanni Antonio (1675–1741). Venetian painter, the brother-in-law of Rosalba *Carriera. Pellegrini played a major part in the spread of the Venetian style of large-scale decorative painting in northern Europe, working in Austria, England, France, Germany, and the Netherlands. He was in England from 1708 to 1713 (and briefly in 1719). He and Marco *Ricci were the first Venetian artists to work there; they arrived together, accompanying Charles Montagu (later the 1st Duke of Manchester), the British ambassador to Venice. Pellegrini's work in England included murals at Montagu's country seat, Kimbolton Castle, Cambridgeshire, and the dome paintings (destroyed by fire in 1940) at Castle Howard, Yorkshire. His airy, *illusionistic compositions, with their bright flickering colour and purely decorative intention, set a new standard of *Rococo elegance for English decoration, but he was an extremely prolific painter and by European standards most of his work is routine. *Thornhill defeated him in competition for the commission to decorate the dome of St Paul's Cathedral, London.

pen. Writing and drawing instrument used with ink or a similar coloured fluid. From Early Christian times until the 19th century the standard form of pen in Europe was the quill, made from bird feathers, and most of the pen drawings of the Old Masters were done with such instruments. Goose, swan, and turkey quills have commonly been used for writing and crow quills provide a very fine point for drawing. The reed pen, made from stems of bamboo-like grasses, was already in use in classical antiquity and is probably older than the quill. The point is much coarser, producing a bold, angular line, sometimes slightly blurred at the edges. For drawing it has been used much less than the quill, though *Rembrandt, for example, was a master of the broad energetic technique appropriate to it. The metal pen dates back at least to Roman times, but steel nibs of the modern type were not made until late in the 18th century and began to replace the quill only after machine methods of producing them were developed in the 1820s. No other drawing tool can produce such a variety of texture as the pen or reveal so intimately the personal 'handwriting' of an artist. It is the ideal medium for rapidly noting down the first idea and has been used in this way by draughtsmen as different as *Pisanello, *Michelangelo, *Dürer, and Rembrandt. However, it has also been used with great effect in a careful, calligraphic manner, as in *Botticelli's illustrations to Dante's *Divine Comedy.*

pencil. Writing or drawing instrument consisting of a slender rod of graphite or similar substance encased in a cylinder of wood (or less usually metal or plastic). Although the material is graphite (a form of carbon), the term 'lead' pencil came into use because it superseded the lead point (*see* METAL POINT). The first known reference to a wooden pencil dates from the 1560s, but instruments of predetermined hardness or softness were not produced until 1790, when Nicolas-Jacques *Conté undertook to solve the problem of making pencils when France was cut off from the English supply of graphite (the mines in Borrowdale, Cumbria, which had opened in 1664, being the main source). He found that the graphite could be eked out with clay and fired in a kiln, and that more clay meant a harder pencil. Conté obtained a patent for his process in 1795. It was only then that the pencil became the universal drawing instrument that it is today. *Ingres, who often used pencil with great delicacy in his portrait drawings, was one of the first to show its potential. Although the *Oxford English Dictionary* records the usage of the phrase 'a pencil of black lead' as early as 1612, until the end of the 18th century the word 'pencil' more commonly meant a brush (particularly a small brush). 'Pencilling' could mean 'colouring' or 'brushwork' as well as 'drawing'.

Pencz, Georg (Jörg Bencz) (*c.*1500–50). German painter and engraver of religious and mythological subjects and portraits. He is first documented in 1523 in Nuremberg, where he is presumed to have studied with *Dürer, who strongly influenced him. In 1525 he was expelled from Nuremberg with the *Beham brothers, two other 'godless artists', for their radical Protestant views, but the sentence was soon revoked and he returned to the city. On stylistic evidence he is thought to have visited Italy in the late 1520s and again *c.*1540. The sharp outlines and glossy textures of his portraits show, in particular, a kinship with *Bronzino (*Man Holding a Mirror*, 1544, Hessisches Landesmuseum, Darmstadt). In 1550 he was appointed painter to Duke Albrecht of Prussia, but he died on the way to take up the post.

Penni, Giovanni Francesco (*c.*1496–*c.*1536?). Italian painter. He was born in Florence and died in Naples, but worked mainly in Rome, where he and *Giulio Romano were *Raphael's main assistants (he was nicknamed Il Fattore, which might be translated as 'right-hand man'). Various parts of works by the master have been attributed to him (*Vasari says he was employed on the tapestry *cartoons for the Sistine Chapel), but he is a shadowy figure. After Raphael's death he collaborated with Giulio. A rare signed work by Penni is the *Portrait of a Young Man* (NG, Dublin).

Penny, Edward. See WEST.

Penrose, Sir Roland (1900–84). British writer, exhibition organizer, and artist. As an artist he holds a distinguished place among British *Surrealists (he produced collages and 'objects' as well as paintings), but he is remembered mainly for the missionary zeal with which he promoted Surrealism and contemporary art in general in England. He was one of the organizers of the 1936 International Surrealist Exhibition in London, and he was closely involved with many leading artists, including *Ernst, *Miró, and above all *Picasso, who became a lifelong friend. During the Second World War he was a camouflage instructor. In 1947 he was co-founder (with Herbert *Read) and first chairman of the *Institute of Contemporary Arts. His books include *Picasso: His Life and Work* (1958; 3rd edn. 1981), regarded as a standard work on the artist. Penrose's second wife, whom he married in 1947, was the American photographer Lee Miller (1907–77), who had formerly been a pupil and favourite model of *Man Ray.

pentimento. (It.: 'repentance'). Term describing a part of a picture that has been overpainted by the artist but which has become visible again (often as a ghostly outline) because the upper layer of pigment has become semi-transparent with age. The presence of pentimenti is often used as an argument in matters of attribution, as it is felt that such evidence of an artist's second thoughts is much more likely to occur in an original painting than in a copy.

Peploe, S. J. See SCOTTISH COLOURISTS.

Pereda, Antonio de (1611–78). Spanish painter, active mainly in Madrid. He began as a history painter—his *Relief of Genoa* (1634–5, Prado, Madrid) was painted for Philip IV's (*see* HABSBURG) Buen Retiro Palace in Madrid as part of the same series as

*Velázquez's *Surrender of Breda*—but he is now best known for his still lifes. The most famous painting associated with him is *The Knight's Dream* (also called *The Dream of Life* or *Life is a Dream*, *c.*1650, Academy, Madrid), a splendidly sensuous composition, full of brilliantly painted still-life details, in which worldly pleasures and treasures are seen to be as insubstantial as a dream. It was a key work in the development of the moralizing still life in Spain, influencing *Valdés Leal in particular. However, the attribution to Pereda has recently been questioned, and Francisco de Palacios (1622/5–52) has been suggested as the author.

Peredvizhniki. *See* WANDERERS.

Performance art. An art form combining elements of theatre, music, and the visual arts. It is related to the *happening (the two terms are sometimes used synonymously), but Performance art is usually more carefully programmed and generally does not involve audience participation. The tradition of Performance art can be traced back to the *Futurists, *Dadaists, and *Surrealists, who often staged humorous or provocative events to promote their work or ideas, then through such activities as Georges *Mathieu painting in front of an audience in the 1950s and Yves *Klein directing nude models smeared with paint in the early 1960s. However, it was only in the later 1960s and particularly in the 1970s that Performance art became recognized as a category of art in itself. 'At that time', RoseLee Goldberg writes, 'Conceptual art was in its heyday and performance was often a demonstration, or an execution, of [its] ideas . . . Art spaces devoted to performance sprang up in the major international art centres, museums sponsored festivals, art colleges introduced performance courses, and specialist magazines appeared' (*Performance Art: From Futurism to the Present*, 1988). The form and tone of Performances have varied enormously. Some practitioners have cultivated sadomasochism and scatology (the abuse of the performer's body is something that often occurs also in *Body art, with which Performance art sometimes overlaps). In Britain, however, the field has more often been characterized by whimsicality (in the 1970s there was a fad for Performance groups with quaint names and for wacky newsworthy stunts).

Performance art has also been used as an adjunct to rock music (the American Laurie Anderson (1947–) is the most noted exponent) and as a vehicle for political dissent, as well as for the exploration of private fantasies. Among the artists particularly associated with Performance art are Joseph *Beuys and *Gilbert and George.

Pergamene School. A trend in *Hellenistic sculpture, associated with the city of Pergamum in Asia Minor, whose great period coincided with the Attalid dynasty (241–133 BC). Works of the Pergamene School are characterized by an exaggeration of the general tendency of Hellenistic sculpture towards emotional display and virtuoso naturalistic detail. They include a series of *Dying Gauls (the most famous is in the Capitoline Museum, Rome) that have been identified as copies of statues dedicated by Attalus I to celebrate a victory over the Gauls, and the Great Altar of Zeus (*c.*180–150 BC, Pergamum Museum, Berlin), which features relief carvings of the fight between gods and giants depicted with an extraordinary sense of movement and dramatic tension. It is perhaps the 'Satan's seat' of Revelation 2: 13. Other Hellenistic works from places other than Pergamum (above all the celebrated *Laocoön) are clearly similar in their restless energy, and some scholars deny that there is adequate reason for recognizing a separate Pergamene School. However, T. B. L. Webster in his *Hellenistic Poetry and Art* (1964) maintains that although the artists employed by the Attalid kings came from various places, they 'achieved a unity of style which justifies the name Pergamene'.

Perino del Vaga (Piero Buonaccorsi) (*c.*1501–47). Florentine painter. He took his name (del Vaga) from a minor painter with whom he worked after studying with Ridolfo *Ghirlandaio. In about 1517 he moved to Rome, where he became one of *Raphael's assistants working on the Vatican Loggie. After the Sack of Rome in 1527 he moved to Genoa, where he was based until the late 1530s and where his *Mannerist style had great influence. His major work there was a series of mythological frescos in the Palazzo Doria. During this period he also worked in Pisa. By 1538 he was back in Rome, where he became the principal decorative artist employed by Pope Paul III

(Alessandro *Farnese), his work for him including frescos on the history of Alexander the Great (1545–7) in the Sala Paolina of the Castel S. Angelo. Perino's style derives from Raphael and *Giulio Romano, but is ornamental rather than monumental. He was one of the leading decorative artists of his generation, and his work has been aptly described by S. J. Freedberg (*Painting in Italy: 1500–1600*, 1971) as 'intelligent but facile'. He also did a number of devotional pictures in a Raphaelesque vein, notably the unfinished *Holy Family* (Courtauld Gal., London).

Permeke, Constant (1886–1952). Belgian painter and sculptor, one of the leading exponents of *Expressionism in Belgium in the period between the two world wars. In 1914 he was badly wounded serving in the Belgian army and was evacuated to England. He returned to Belgium in 1919 and lived in Antwerp and Ostend before building his own house and studio at Jabbeke, near Bruges, now a Permeke museum (he called his home De Vier Windstreken: 'The Four Corners of the Earth'). His subjects were taken mainly from the life of the coastal towns of Belgium and he is best known for his strong and solemn portrayals of sailors and fishermen with their women (*The Fiancés*, 1923, Mus. Royaux, Brussels). From 1935 he also made sculpture.

Permoser, Balthasar (1651–1732). German sculptor. He worked in Italy 1675–89 and his lively *Baroque style was much influenced by *Bernini. In 1689 he became court sculptor in Dresden and spent most of the rest of his life there. His most important work was the sculptural decoration of the Zwinger—Augustus the Strong's pleasure palace in Dresden, designed by the architect M. D. Pöppelmann (begun 1711, badly damaged in the Second World War). Permoser carved in wood and ivory as well as stone and also made ingenious use of coloured marble (*Damned Soul*, c.1715, Mus. der Bildenden Künste, Leipzig). *Roubiliac is said to have studied with him.

Perov, Vasily. *See* WANDERERS.

Perréal, Jean (also called **Jean de Paris**) (c.1450/60–1530). French painter, architect, sculptor, and designer. He was the most renowned French artist of his time, painter to three successive kings (Charles VIII, Louis XII, and Francis I), but few works survive

that can be confidently associated with him. They are mainly manuscript illuminations, but a portrait of Louis XII (c.1514) in the Royal Collection is attributed to him by some authorities (others consider it a copy). These works show Perréal as a master of scrupulous *naturalism, and it has been suggested that he is to be identified with the *Master of Moulins. Perréal travelled to Italy several times and on one of these journeys he met *Leonardo, who mentions him in his notebooks.

Perrier, François (c.1590?–1649). French history painter and engraver. He had two stays in Rome (c.1625–8 and 1635–45) and his style was formed on the example of *Lanfranco (in whose studio he worked during his first visit), Pietro da *Cortona, and the *Carracci. His decorative work helped to introduce the grand *Baroque style to France, but almost all of it has been destroyed or altered. However, his influence can be seen in the work of Charles *Le Brun, who was briefly his pupil.

Perronneau, Jean-Baptiste (1715?–83). French painter and engraver. He worked principally as a portraitist and mainly in *pastel. In this medium he was overshadowed in his lifetime by Maurice-Quentin de *La Tour, whose style was more vivacious; however, posterity has judged the more sober but more penetrating Perronneau to be at least his equal. From about 1755 he led a wandering life, visiting England, the Netherlands several times (he died in Amsterdam), Italy, Poland, and Russia. He was a prolific artist and is represented in many galleries in France and elsewhere.

perspective. Method of giving a sense of depth on a flat or shallow surface, utilizing such optical phenomena as the apparent convergence of parallel lines and diminution in size of objects as they recede from the spectator. Perspective is by no means common to the art of all epochs and all peoples. For example, the pictorial art of the ancient Egyptians, although a richly developed tradition, did not take account of the optical effects of recession. Systematic, mathematically founded perspective, based initially on a fixed central viewpoint, was developed in Italy in the early 15th century, when it was invented by *Brunelleschi, described by *Alberti in his treatise *De pictura*, and put into majestic practice by *Masaccio. Various names are given to this type of perspective—geometric, linear, mathematical, optical, *Renaissance or scientific perspective—which remained one of the foundations of European painting until the late 19th century. In pre-Renaissance Europe and in the East, more intuitive systems of representing spatial recession were used. In medieval paintings, for example, lines that would in strict perspective converge are often shown diverging (this 'inverted perspective' can look much more convincing in practice than it sounds in theory); and in Chinese art 'parallel perspective' was a common convention in the depiction of buildings. See also AERIAL PERSPECTIVE.

Perugino, Pietro (Pietro Vannucci) (c.1450–1523). Italian painter, active mainly in Perugia, from which his nickname derives. His early career is obscure, but he seems to have formed his style chiefly in Florence, where *Vasari says he studied with *Verrocchio—this would have been at about the same time that *Leonardo da Vinci was training with him (he is also said to have been a pupil of *Piero della Francesca; this could have preceded his training in Florence). In 1472 he was enrolled as a painter in the fraternity of St Luke in Florence (the same year as Leonardo) and in 1475 he was back in Perugia. By 1481 he was sufficiently well known to be commissioned to paint frescos on the walls of the newly built Sistine Chapel, Rome, for Pope Sixtus IV (Francesco della *Rovere), along with *Botticelli, Domenico *Ghirlandaio, and Cosimo *Rosselli (*Signorelli later completed the work). Vasari says that Botticelli was head of the team, but some modern scholars think that Perugino was more likely to have been leader, partly because of the prominence of his contributions. His main work there is *Christ Delivering the Keys to St Peter*; he also did the frescoed altarpiece, but this was destroyed to make way for *Michelangelo's *Last Judgement*. His reputation firmly established, he had commissions from various places in central Italy, and in the 1490s he maintained a workshop in Florence as well as in Perugia. In 1500 he was described as the best painter in Italy (by Agostino *Chigi), and he was indeed at his peak at about this time. He was a fine portraitist as well as a fresco painter, but today

he is best known for his altarpieces, which are usually gentle, pious, and rather sentimental in manner. His style does not seem to have been a reflection of his personality, for Vasari says he 'was not a religious man' and that he 'would have gone to any lengths for money'. In about 1505 he left the competitive atmosphere of Florence, where his work now seemed old-fashioned, and settled permanently in Perugia, although he returned to Rome in about 1508 to paint a ceiling for Pope Julius II (Giuliano della Rovere) in the Stanza dell'Incendio in the Vatican. His later work is often routine and repetitive, but at his best, as in the Vatican fresco, he has the authority of a great master. The harmony and spatial clarity of his compositions and his idealized physical types strongly influenced the young *Raphael, who worked with him early in his career, so Perugino can be seen as one of the harbingers of the High *Renaissance. A second wave of his influence came in the 19th century, when he was glorified by the *Pre-Raphaelites.

Peruzzi, Baldassare (1481–1536). Sienese architect, painter, and stage designer, active mainly in Rome, where he settled in 1503. He worked under *Bramante on St Peter's, and eventually became architect to the building after *Raphael's death in 1520. Amongst High *Renaissance architects he ranks almost alongside these two great contemporaries, but his style was very different—sophisticated and delicate rather than monumental and grave. In spite of his genius he had little material success, according to *Vasari because of his 'retiring nature'. His greatest work—indeed the greatest secular building of the High Renaissance—is the Villa Farnesina (begun c.1506) in Rome, built for the banker Agostino *Chigi. The Farnesina contains decorations by Raphael, *Sebastiano del Piombo, and *Sodoma, as well as Peruzzi's own masterpiece in painting—the Sala delle Prospettive (c.1517), a brilliant piece of feigned architectural painting that confirms early accounts of his skill in perspective and stage design.

Peters, Matthew William (1741/2–1814). English painter of portraits, *genre and historical scenes, and *fancy pictures. He studied with *Hudson in the late 1750s and between c.1762 and 1784 he made several visits to Italy and Paris. Foreign influence is clearly seen in the richness of his technique (admirers called him 'the English *Titian') and in the pin-up type of picture of pretty women—distinctly reminiscent of *Greuze—with which he caused mild scandal and attained great popularity in engravings. He was ordained a priest in 1782 and retired from professional practice in 1788, but he continued to paint for his own pleasure. His later works include some mawkish religious paintings and some dull pictures for *Boydell's Shakespeare Gallery.

Peterzano, Simone. *See* CARAVAGGIO.

Peto, John Frederick (1854–1907). American still-life painter. With his friend *Harnett he is now considered the outstanding American still-life painter of his period, but he was little known during his lifetime and after his death was completely forgotten until rediscovered in the 1940s by the critic Alfred Frankenstein. His style was strongly influenced by Harnett (whose signature has sometimes been fraudulently added to paintings by Peto), but his work was softer and more anecdotal, often depicting discarded objects. Peto worked in his native Philadelphia, then from 1889 in seclusion at Island Heights, New Jersey.

Pevsner, Antoine (1886–1962). Russian-born sculptor and painter who became a French citizen in 1930. He was the elder brother of Naum *Gabo and like him one of the pioneers and chief exponents of *Constructivism. Between 1911 and 1914 he made lengthy visits to Paris, where *Archipenko and *Modigliani were among his friends. After two years in Norway with Gabo he returned to Russia in 1917. In 1920 he was co-signatory of Gabo's *Realistic Manifesto*, which set forth the ideals of Constructivism, and in 1922 he helped to organize a major exhibition of Soviet art in Berlin. He left Russia in 1923 because the authorities were turning against the 'pure' art in which he was interested in favour of utilitarian work, and later that year he settled permanently in Paris. Up to this time he had been a painter, but he now turned to sculpture, at first working mainly in plastic, then in welded metal. Initially his sculptures retained vestiges of representation, as in his witty *Portrait of Marcel Duchamp* (1926, Yale Univ. AG), but by 1927 he had arrived at pure abstraction. His later work was char-acterized by bold spiralling forms (*Dynamic Projection in the 30th Degree*, 1950–1, Baltimore Mus. of Art). Pevsner was a founder member of *Abstraction-Création and was influential in transmitting Constructivist ideas to other artists in the group. By the end of his career he was a much-honoured figure.

Pevsner, Sir Nikolaus (1902–83). German-born British art historian. He worked at the Gemäldegalerie in Dresden and taught at Göttingen University (1929–33) before moving to England because of the rise of Nazism. As well as teaching at Birkbeck College in the University of London, he was *Slade professor at both Cambridge (1949–55) and Oxford (1968–9). He is best known for his writings on architecture, above all for the celebrated series of county-by-county guides *The Buildings of England* (46 vols., 1951–74), which he conceived, edited, and largely wrote himself. Companion series on the buildings of Ireland (from 1979), Scotland (1978), and Wales (1979) are in course of publication. The four series are now known collectively as the Pevsner Architectural Guides. Pevsner's many other books included important studies on painting, sculpture, and design as well as architecture. They include *Academies of Art, Past and Present* (1940), *An Outline of European Architecture* (1942 and numerous other editions), and *The Englishness of English Art* (1956). He also conceived and edited the Pelican History of Art (which began publication in 1953), the largest, most comprehensive, and most scholarly history of art ever published in English, many of the individual volumes of which have become classics. Anthony *Blunt, Sir Ellis *Waterhouse, and Rudolf *Wittkower are among the scholars who have written volumes in the series.

Pforr, Franz (1788–1812). German painter. He was one of the founders of the *Nazarenes and moved to Rome with other members of the group in 1810. Two years later he died of tuberculosis. His work evokes a fairy-tale type of medievalism, with bright colours and picturesque details. It is best represented in the Städelsches Kunstinstitut of his native Frankfurt.

Phalanx. An association of artists organized in Munich in 1901 in opposition to the conservative views of the Academy and the *Sezession. *Kandinsky was one of the founders of the association and its leading figure, becoming president in 1902. For the first group exhibition in August 1901 he designed a magnificent poster in *Art Nouveau style showing Greek warriors advancing across a battlefield in phalanx formation. The militaristic name of the association was chosen to suggest its aggressive, progressive spirit. Eleven more exhibitions followed before Kandinsky dissolved Phalanx in 1904 because of lack of public support. The exhibitions featured not only work by members, but also by 'guest' artists, notably French *Post-Impressionists and *Neo-Impressionists at the tenth exhibition in 1904. This was the most important of the exhibitions, confirming Kandinsky's internationalism and having a marked effect on several young artists, notably *Kirchner. In 1902–3 Phalanx ran an art school; one of the first students was Gabriele Münter, who became Kandinsky's mistress.

Phidias (d. *c*.430 BC). Greek sculptor, active mainly in Athens, the most famous artist of the ancient world. No work survives that is certainly from his own hand, but through copies, descriptions, and above all the surviving sculpture of the Parthenon at Athens, which Phidias supervised, a fair idea can be gained of his style. In antiquity he was most celebrated for two enormous *chryselephantine cult statues—of Athena, inside the Parthenon, and of Zeus in the temple dedicated to the god at Olympia. The statue of Zeus, a seated figure about 12 m (40 ft) high and one of the Seven Wonders of the World, is known through reproductions on Roman coins. The statue of Athena (dedicated 438 BC), a standing figure about 9 m (30 ft) high, is known through several (much smaller) copies. Phidias also made two bronze statues of Athena for the Acropolis in Athens: the huge *Athena Promachos* (champion), in which the goddess was shown holding a spear; and the *Lemnian Athena* (so called because it was dedicated by Athenian colonists going to Lemnos between 451 and 448 BC). The *Athena Promachos* is represented on coins and the *Lemnian Athena* can be partially reconstructed from what are thought to be two fragmentary copies: a remarkably sensitive head in Bologna (Mus. Civico Archeologico) and a substantially complete figure in Dresden (Albertinum). Other copies have been cred-

ibly associated with works of Phidias mentioned in ancient sources, and recently the two bronze statues of warriors found in the sea near Riace in 1972 ('The Riace Bronzes') have been linked with his name because of their superlative quality; they are now in the archaeological museum at Reggio di Calabria. The greatest testimony to his genius, however, is the sculpture of the Parthenon (447–432 BC), the most ambitious sculptural undertaking of the age, consisting originally of a low-*relief frieze about 160 m (525 ft) long, 92 metopes (decorative panels) in high relief, and groups of free-standing figures on both pediments. Much of the sculpture still survives, mainly in the British Museum, London (*see* ELGIN MARBLES). The quality is variable, as a team of sculptors was involved, and Phidias could not have carved more than a tiny fraction of the work himself, but the finest parts exemplify the harmony and serene majesty that earned the raptures of ancient commentators and stand as the greatest surviving examples of the *Classical period in Greek art.

In spite of his fame and the prominent works on which he was employed, there is much that is enigmatic about Phidias' career, not least about the end of his life. When the great statesman Pericles, his friend and patron, fell out of favour, Phidias was accused of misappropriating gold supplied to him for the statue of Athena. Then, according to Plutarch, having cleared himself of this charge, he was thrown into prison for impiety on the ground that he had introduced portraits of Pericles and himself on the shield of the goddess (a copy of the shield—the 'Strangford Shield'—is in the British Museum). Plutarch says that Phidias died in prison, but according to another ancient source he escaped and went to Olympia to work on his statue of Zeus, the date of which is uncertain. In 1954–8 Phidias' workshop at Olympia was excavated. Moulds, scraps of ivory, and other fragments were discovered, and—remarkably—a cup bearing the inscription 'I belong to Phidias'—the great man's tea-mug, as it were. This poignant relic is in the Olympia Museum.

Philip II, King of Spain. *See* HABSBURG.

Philip IV, King of Spain. *See* HABSBURG.

Phillip, John (1817–67). Scottish painter, active mainly in London. He began as a specialist in paintings of Scottish life and character in the manner of *Wilkie, but following visits to Spain in 1851, 1856, and 1860 he became celebrated for picturesque Spanish *genre scenes and was known as 'Spanish' Phillip or 'Phillip of Spain'. His style was fluent and colourful, often with a picture postcard flavour. He also painted portraits.

Phillips, Duncan (1886–1966). American collector and writer on art. His family had made a fortune in steel and glass and he devoted much of his substantial inheritance to collecting. Mainly he bought the work of late 19th- and 20th-century artists, and when he opened his Washington home to the public (three afternoons a week) in 1921 it represented the first permanent museum of modern art in the USA. It proved so popular that Phillips made the house over completely as a gallery and moved to another home. The Phillips Collection retains its intimate, domestic air, and is widely regarded as one of the world's finest small museums. Its star exhibit is *Renoir's celebrated *Luncheon of the Boating Party* (1880–1). As a writer on art Phillips is best known for his book *The Leadership of Giorgione* (1937). He also edited a short-lived periodical, *Art and Understanding* (1929).

Phillips, Peter (1939–). British painter. He studied at the *Royal College of Art, 1959–62, and with his fellow students Derek *Boshier, David *Hockney, Allen *Jones, and R. B. *Kitaj he emerged as one of the leading exponents of British *Pop art at the *Young Contemporaries exhibition in 1961. Typically his imagery is drawn from modern American culture—juke boxes, pinball machines, automobiles, film star pin-ups, and so on—painted in the tight, glossy manner of commercial art. However, the images are usually set into bold heraldic frameworks or fragmented into sections and reorganized, so that illusionism and abstraction are combined.

Photographic Realism. *See* SUPERREALISM.

photomontage. Term applied to a technique of making a pictorial composition from parts of different photographs and to the composition so made. The technique has antecedents in the 19th century, particularly in the work of O. G. Rejlander

(1813–75), a Swedish photographer and painter active in England. He tried to expand the expressive range of photography by experimenting with double exposures and printing from several negatives onto a single sheet, as in his elaborate allegory *The Two Ways of Life* (1857), printed from 30 negatives onto two sheets joined together. However, as the term is now understood, photomontage involves cutting out, arranging, and pasting down pre-existing photographic images rather than the manipulation of negatives taken for a particular purpose. Photomontage in this sense was largely the creation of the *Dadaists (specifically the Berlin Dadaists), who used the technique for political propaganda, social criticism, and generally to assist the shock tactics in which they indulged. Raoul Hausmann (1886–1971) claimed to have invented photomontage in 1918; this is a dubious claim, but certainly he ranks with *Heartfield and Hannah Höch (1889–1978) as one of the main pioneers and most brilliant exponents of the technique. Photomontage has also been memorably used by, for example, Max *Ernst and other *Surrealists and by *Pop artists such as Richard *Hamilton, but it is now mainly associated with advertising.

Piazzetta, Giovanni Battista (1683–1754). Venetian painter and draughtsman. After preliminary training in Venice he spent about two years in Bologna, where he was strongly influenced by G. M. *Crespi. By 1705 he had returned to Venice and spent the rest of his life there. He was one of the most individual Venetian painters of his period, his sombre and dramatic style looking back to work done a century earlier by *Feti, *Liss, and *Strozzi. Unlike several of his leading contemporaries, he preferred to paint in oils rather than fresco; he was a notoriously slow worker, but his pictures seem fresh and spontaneous rather than laboured. He had a large family and although he was not without wealthy patrons (*Algarotti among them) he relied much on drawings and book illustrations to earn money. As a painter he did religious and historical works and portraits, as well as some hauntingly enigmatic *genre scenes that reflect his admiration for Crespi. In 1750 Piazzetta became the first director of the Venice Academy of Fine Arts, but in his last years he was eclipsed by the new generation. The young *Tiepolo was greatly influenced by him, but later the influence was reversed, as Piazzetta's style became softer and lighter—more *Rococo—in feeling.

Picabia, Francis (1879–1953). French painter, designer, writer, and editor. His talent as an artist was modest, but his restless and energetic personality gave him a significant role successively in the *Cubist, *Dadaist, and *Surrealist movements, and through his publications he helped to disseminate avant-garde ideas. A private income enabled him to carry on his activities without having to worry about earning a living, as well as to indulge his love of fast cars, fast women, and wild living in general. Early in his career he was a successful painter of *Impressionist landscapes. In 1908–9 he experimented with *Neo-Impressionism, and then with *Fauvism and Cubism. In 1911 he met Marcel *Duchamp, who was to be the most important influence on his career, and with him became an exponent of *Orphism. He painted his first purely abstract works in 1912. In 1913 he visited New York as spokesman for the Cubist pictures in the *Armory Show, and he returned to the USA in 1915–16, when he, Duchamp, and *Man Ray were involved in the first stirrings of Dada. After moving to Barcelona (where he lived 1916–17), he launched a magazine entitled *391* (1917–24). In 1917 he spent six months in New York, then lived in Zurich (1918–19) before returning to Paris, where he helped to launch the Dada movement. However, in 1921 he denounced Dada for being no longer 'new', and became involved with André *Breton and the nascent Surrealist movement. In 1924 he attacked this, too, but some of his later works are in a Surrealist idiom. From 1925 to 1945 he lived mainly on the Côte d'Azur, experimenting with various styles. In 1945 he settled permanently in Paris and in his final years returned to abstract painting. Apart from his contributions to avant-garde magazines, Picabia published various pamphlets and wrote poetry. He also conceived the fantasy ballet *Relâche* (1924), with music by Erik Satie, together with the film *Entr'acte* (directed by René Clair), which was used to fill the intermission between the ballet's two acts. Among Picabia's paintings, the most highly

regarded today are those in his 'machinist' style, in which mechanistic and *biomorphic forms are combined in dynamic compositions. The most famous is *I See Again in Memory My Dear Udnie* (1914, MoMA, New York).

Picasso, Pablo (1881–1973). Spanish painter, sculptor, printmaker, draughtsman, ceramicist, and designer, active mainly in France, the most famous, versatile, prolific, and influential artist of the 20th century. Although it is conventional to divide his work into certain phases, all such divisions are to some extent arbitrary, as his energy and imagination were such that he often worked simultaneously on a wealth of themes and in a variety of styles. He said: 'The several manners I have used in my art must not be considered as an evolution, or as steps toward an unknown ideal of painting. When I have found something to express, I have done it without thinking of the past or future. I do not believe I have used radically different elements in the different manners I have used in painting. If the subjects I have wanted to express have suggested different ways of expression, I haven't hesitated to adopt them.'

Picasso was the son of a painter and drawing master and was absorbed in art from childhood (his first word is said to have been 'piz', baby talk for lapiz, 'pencil'). In 1900 he made his first visit to Paris and by this time had already absorbed a wide range of influences. Between 1900 and 1904 he alternated between Paris and Barcelona, and these years coincide with his Blue Period, when he took his subjects from social outcasts and the poor, and the predominant mood of his paintings was one of slightly sentimentalized melancholy expressed through cold and ethereal blue tones (*La Vie*, 1903, Cleveland Mus. of Art). He also made a number of powerful etchings in a similar vein (*The Frugal Repast*, 1904). In 1904 he settled in Paris and quickly became part of a circle of avant-garde artists and writers. A brief phase in 1904–5 is known as his Rose Period. The predominant blue tones of his earlier work gave way to pinks and greys and the mood became less austere. His favourite subjects were acrobats and dancers, particularly the figure of the harlequin. In 1906 he met *Matisse, but although he seems to have admired the work being done by the *Fauves, he did not share their interest in the decorative and expressive use of colour (indeed his work often shows little concern with colour, and it is significant that—unlike most painters —he liked to work at night by artificial light). The period around 1906–7 is sometimes called Picasso's Negro Period, because of the impact that African sculpture made on his work, but *Cézanne was an equally powerful influence at this time, when he was engrossed in the analysis of form. His explorations climaxed in Les Demoiselles d'Avignon (1906–7, MoMA, New York), which in its distortions of form and disregard of any conventional idea of beauty was as violent a revolt against tradition as the paintings of the Fauves in the realm of colour. At the time, the picture was incomprehensible even to other avant-garde artists, including Matisse and *Derain, and it was not publicly exhibited until 1916 or reproduced until 1925. It is now seen not only as a pivotal work in Picasso's personal development but also as the most important single landmark in the development of 20th-century painting. It was the herald of *Cubism, which he developed in close association with *Braque and then *Gris from 1907 up to the First World War.

During the war Picasso continued working in Paris, but in 1917 he went to Rome with his friend Jean Cocteau to design costumes and scenery for the ballet Parade, which was being produced by *Diaghilev. Picasso fell in love with one of the dancers, Olga Koklova, and married her in 1918; they moved into a grand apartment in a fashionable part of Paris, as the bohemian days of his youth were left behind. The visit to Italy was an important factor in introducing the strain of monumental classicism that was one of the features of his work in the early 1920s (Mother and Child, 1921, Art Inst. of Chicago), but at this time he was also involved with *Surrealism—indeed André *Breton hailed him as one of the initiators of the movement. However his predominant interest in the analysis and synthesis of form was at bottom opposed to the irrational elements of Surrealism, its exaltation of chance, or its fascination with material drawn from dreams or the unconscious. Following his serene classical paintings, Picasso entered on a period when his work was characterized by violent emotions

and expressionist distortion, the elements of the human face often being rearranged to convey intensity of feeling. This phase began with The Three Dancers (1925, Tate, London), a savage parody of classical ballet, painted at a time when his marriage was becoming a source of increasing unhappiness and frustration (he could not obtain a divorce, so he remained officially married to Olga until her death in 1955; he remarried in 1961). The period culminated in his most famous work, Guernica (1937, Centro Cultural Reina Sofía, Madrid), produced for the Spanish Pavilion at the Paris Exposition Universelle of 1937 to express horror and revulsion at the destruction by bombing of the Basque capital Guernica during the civil war (1936–9). It was followed by a number of other paintings attacking the cruelty and destructiveness of war, including The Charnel House (1945, MoMA, New York): 'Painting is not done to decorate apartments', he said; 'it is an instrument of war against brutality and darkness.' Picasso remained in Paris during the German occupation, but from 1946 he lived mainly in the south of France, where he added pottery to his many other activities. His later output as a painter does not compare in momentousness with his pre-war work (indeed some critics think there was a sad decline in his powers), but it remained prodigious in terms of sheer quantity. It included a number of variations on paintings by other artists, including 44 on Las Meninas of *Velázquez (the theme of the artist and his almost magical powers is one that exercised him greatly throughout his long career). In his old age he was haunted by the idea of death, and images of physical decay and the contrast between youth and age occur frequently in his work, as if he hoped to ward off his own end through the potency of his art. Some of his late paintings are aggressively sexual in subject and almost frenzied in brushwork (Reclining Nude with Necklace, 1968, Tate); they have been seen as sources for *Neo-Expressionism.

Picasso's status as a painter has perhaps overshadowed his work as a sculptor, but in this field too (although his interest was sporadic) he ranks as one of the outstanding figures in 20th-century art. He was one of the first artists to make sculpture that was assembled from varied materials rather than modelled or carved (in this way he helped to inspire *Constructivism), and he made brilliantly witty use of found objects (*see* OBJET TROUVÉ). The most celebrated example is *Head of a Bull, Metamorphosis* (1943, Mus. Picasso, Paris), made of the saddle and handlebars of a bicycle. Alan Bowness has written (*Modern Sculpture*, 1965), 'Picasso's sculpture sparkles with bright ideas—enough to have kept many a lesser man occupied for the whole of a working lifetime... it is not inconceivable that the time will come when his activities as a sculptor in the second part of his life are regarded as of more consequence than his later paintings.' As a graphic artist (draughtsman, etcher, lithographer, linocutter), too, Picasso ranks with the greatest of the century, showing a remarkable power to concentrate the impress of his genius in even the smallest and slightest of his works. His emotional range is as wide as his varied technical mastery; by turns tragic and playful, his work is suffused with a passionate love of life, and no artist has more devastatingly exposed the cruelty and folly of his fellow men or more rapturously celebrated the physical pleasures of love. There are several museums devoted to him in France and Spain, the largest being in Barcelona and Paris, and other examples of his huge output (which has been estimated at 20,000 works) are in collections throughout the world. Just as this extraordinary oeuvre has been more discussed than the work of any other modern artist, so Picasso's personal life has inspired a flood of writing, particularly regarding his relationships with women. He once characterized them as either 'goddesses or doormats' and he has been criticized for allegedly demeaning them in his work (especially his later erotic paintings) as well as mistreating them in person.

picture plane. In the imaginary space of a picture, the plane corresponding to the physical surface of the work. *Perspective appears to recede from the picture plane, and objects painted in *trompe l'œil may appear to project from it.

Picturesque. Term covering a set of aesthetic ideas about landscape, both real and painted, that flourished in Britain in the late 18th and early 19th centuries. Devotees of the Picturesque found pleasure in roughness and irregularity, and they tried to es-

tablish it as a critical category between the 'Beautiful' and the '*Sublime'. Picturesque scenes were thus neither serene (like the Beautiful) nor awe-inspiring (like the Sublime), but full of variety, curious details, and interesting textures—medieval ruins were quintessentially Picturesque. Natural scenery tended to be judged in terms of how closely it approximated to the paintings of favoured artists such as Gaspard *Dughet, and in 1801 the *Supplement* to Samuel Johnson's *Dictionary* by George Mason defined Picturesque as: 'what pleases the eye; remarkable for singularity; striking the imagination with the force of painting; to be expressed in painting; affording a good subject for a landscape; proper to take a landscape from'. The Picturesque Tour in search of suitable subjects was a feature of English landscape painting of the period, exemplified, for example, in the work of *Girtin and (early in his career) of *Turner, and the Picturesque generated a large literary output; much of it was pedantic and obsessive and it became a popular subject for satire.

Pierce (or **Pearce**), **Edward** (*c*.1635–95). English sculptor and mason, son of a painter (d. 1658) of the same name, some of whose decorative work survives at Wilton House, Wiltshire. Little is known of his early career, but from 1671 he was much employed by Christopher Wren on the rebuilding of the City of London churches, both as a mason and as a stonecarver. He was a woodcarver too, and his work in this field is of such quality that it has sometimes been credited to Grinling *Gibbons. There are also a few portrait busts by Pierce, the most notable being the life-size marble of Wren (*c*.1673, Ashmolean Mus., Oxford), brilliantly characterized and more convincingly *Baroque than anything else of the date in English art. It is generally considered the best piece of English sculpture of the 17th century, but it has been suggested that the workmanship does not live up to the boldness of the conception and that Pierce is here perhaps copying a lost bust by *Coysevox. Pierce also worked as an architect, the Bishop's Palace, Lichfield (1686–7), being his chief documented building. There are several drawings by him in the British Museum, London.

Piero della Francesca (*c*.1415–92). Italian painter, virtually forgotten for centuries after his death, but now regarded as one of the supreme artists of the *Renaissance. He was born and died in Borgo San Sepolcro (now Sansepolcro) in Umbria and spent much of his life there. Evidently he had great affection for his home town, for he took an active part in its civic affairs (he twice served as a town councillor) and the surrounding countryside often features in the backgrounds of his paintings. At various times he also worked in Arezzo, Ferrara, Florence, Rimini, Rome, and Urbino, but his career is scantily documented and it is not possible to follow his movements in detail. (Arezzo and Urbino are close to Sansepolcro and Piero probably spent a good deal of time in both places, but he is only once actually documented in either, in Urbino in 1469.) He is first heard of in 1431, when he received payment for painting some candle poles used in processions, and between 1432 and 1438 is several times recorded working with an obscure local painter, Antonio d'Anghiari, who was perhaps his teacher. In 1439 he is documented outside Sansepolcro for the first time, assisting *Domenico Veneziano on frescos (now lost) in S. Egidio, Florence. This is the only time he is recorded in Florence, but he must have been well acquainted with the city, for his paintings show that he had carefully studied the work of his great Florentine predecessors and contemporaries. He is perhaps closest in spirit to *Masaccio, with whom he shared a sense of massive dignity and deep spiritual authority, but he had more interest in colour than Masaccio, and in this respect is closer to Fra *Angelico and *Masolino, as well as Domenico Veneziano. His fascination with perspective was something he shared with *Uccello. Piero refined and unified the discoveries these artists had made in the previous twenty years and created a style in which monumental, meditative grandeur and almost mathematical lucidity are combined with limpid beauty of colour and light.

Piero's first surviving documented work is the *polyptych of the *Madonna della Misericordia* (Pinacoteca, Sansepolcro), commissioned in 1445 but not completed until about 1460. Such a lengthy period of gestation was typical of Piero, who was a habitually slow worker. This meant that the traditional method of *fresco painting, demanding swiftness and sureness of hand,

was not ideally suited to him, and he experimented with ways of modifying the technique. He sometimes applied wet cloths to the plaster at night so that—contrary to normal fresco practice—he could work for more than one day on the same section, and he also tried using some kind of oil medium. His major work in fresco is the great series, on the Legend of the True Cross in the choir of S. Francesco at Arezzo (c.1450–c.1465). The subject was a medieval legend of great complexity, but Piero made from its fanciful details some of the most solemn and serene images in Western art—even the two battle scenes have a feeling of grim deliberation rather than violent movement. These frescos were painted for a wealthy local family and several of Piero's other paintings were done for religious institutions in his home town. However, he also worked for illustrious patrons further afield. They included Leonello d'*Este in Ferrara, Sigismondo *Malatesta in Rimini, and Pope Pius II in Rome. Nothing survives of his work in Ferrara or Rome, but his fresco of *Sigismondo Malatesta Venerating St Sigismund* (1451, Tempio Malatestiano, Rimini) provides one of the rare firm dates in his career. The most important of his patrons was Federico da *Montefeltro and Piero probably spent much of his later career working at his court in Urbino. There he painted the portraits of Federico and his wife (c.1465–75, Uffizi, Florence) and the celebrated *Flagellation* (still at Urbino, in the Ducal Palace). The *Flagellation* (c.1450–60) is his most enigmatic work, and it has called forth varied interpretations: *Gombrich suggested that the subject is rather 'The Repentance of Judas' and *Pope-Hennessy that it is 'The Dream of St Jerome'.

Piero is last mentioned as a painter in 1478 (in connection with a lost work) and his two final works are probably the *Madonna and Child with Federico da Montefeltro* (c.1475, Brera, Milan) and the unfinished *Nativity* (NG, London). Thereafter he seems to have devoted himself to mathematics and perspective (three treatises by him survive on these subjects). *Vasari said Piero was blind when he died, and failing eyesight may have been his reason for giving up painting, but in a legal document of 1487 he writes in his own clear hand that he is 'sound in mind, in intellect and in body'. His paintings had considerable influence, notably on *Signorelli (in the weighty solemnity of his figures) and *Perugino (in the spatial clarity of his compositions). Both are said to have been Piero's pupils. However, after his death, Piero was remembered mainly as a mathematician rather than as a painter, and even Vasari, who as a native of Arezzo must have known the frescos in S. Francesco well, is lukewarm in his enthusiasm for his work. Most of his major paintings were in locations that were off the beaten track and they were more or less neglected for centuries (although for an instance of his work influencing a 17th-century painter see TOURNIER). The process of rediscovery did not seriously begin until the later 19th century and it was not until the 20th century that he was widely acclaimed.

Piero di Cosimo (1461?–1521?). Florentine painter, a pupil of Cosimo *Rosselli, whose Christian name he adopted as a patronym. There are no signed, documented, or dated works by him, and reconstruction of his oeuvre depends on the account given in *Vasari's *Lives*. It is one of Vasari's most entertaining biographies, for he portrays Piero as a highly eccentric character who lived on hard-boiled eggs, 'which he cooked while he was boiling his glue, to save the firing'. The paintings for which he is best known are appropriately idiosyncratic—fanciful mythological inventions, inhabited by fauns, centaurs, and primitive men. There is sometimes a spirit of low comedy about these delightful works, but in the so-called *Death of Procris* (NG, London) he created a poignant scene of the utmost pathos and tenderness. He was a wonderful painter of animals and the dog in this picture, depicted with a mournful dignity, is one of his most memorable creations. Piero also painted portraits, the finest of which is that of Simonetta Vespucci (Musée Condé, Chantilly), in which she is depicted as Cleopatra with the asp around her neck. His religious works are somewhat more conventional, although still distinctive, and Frederick Hartt (*A History of Italian Renaissance Art*, 1970) has written that 'His whimsical Madonnas, Holy Families, and Adorations provide a welcome relief from the wholesale imitation of *Raphael in early Cinquecento Florence.' One of his outstanding religious works is the *Immaculate Conception* (Uffizi, Florence), which seems to have

been the compositional model for the *Madonna of the Harpies* by his pupil *Andrea del Sarto.

Pietà (It.: 'pity'). Term applied to a painting or sculpture showing the Virgin Mary supporting the body of the dead Christ on her lap. Other figures, such as St John the Evangelist or Mary Magdalene, may also be included. The theme originated in Germany in the 13th century and was more popular in northern Europe than in Italy. However, the most celebrated of all Pietàs is that by *Michelangelo in St Peter's, Rome, and one of the most sublime is by *Titian (Accademia, Venice), said to have been painted for his own tomb. The subject is not always clearly distinguished from the scene known as the Lamentation. However, whereas the Lamentation represents a specific moment from Christ's Passion, between the Descent from the Cross and the Entombment, the Pietà is a timeless devotional image.

Pigalle, Jean-Baptiste (1714–85). French sculptor. He studied under J.-B. *Lemoyne and then in Rome (1736–40). In his early career he endured poverty and sickness (his studies in Rome were made at his own expense and he walked there from Paris), but after he was received into the Académie Royale in 1744 with his rapturously acclaimed *Mercury* (Louvre, Paris; terracotta model in the Met. Mus., New York), he rapidly went on to become one of the leading French sculptors of his period (in terms of worldly success he probably outdid all his contemporaries). He was a superb craftsman and highly versatile and inventive, equally adept at small *genre pieces and the most grandiloquent tomb sculpture. As a portraitist he was noted for his warmth and vivacity. His most famous works are the startling nude figure of Voltaire (1770–6, Louvre) and the spectacular and majestic tomb of Maurice of Saxony (designed 1753) in St Thomas, Strasbourg.

pigment. Any substance used as a colouring agent, particularly the finely ground particles that when held in suspension in a *medium constitute a paint. Most pigments are now manufactured synthetically, but in the past they have been made from a great variety of mineral, plant, and animal sources: the brown colour *sepia, for example, comes from the inky secretions of the cuttlefish, and ultramarine blue was originally made from the semi-precious stone lapis lazuli. The history of pigments is a highly specialized field with little practical importance today for artists who use commercial paints, but it is often vitally important to the expert in relation to authentication and attribution.

Piles, Roger de (1635–1709). French writer on art, amateur painter, and diplomat. De Piles was employed by Louis XIV on various confidential missions (he was imprisoned as a spy in Holland, 1692–7) and his travels enabled him to study the arts at first hand in various European countries. His best-known book is *Cours de peinture par principes avec une balance des peintres* (1708), which has become notorious for the section (the 'balance des peintres') in which he awarded marks to great artists of the past for their skill at composition, drawing, colour, and expression, then added up the scores to form a sort of league table of genius (his criticism, however, is usually much less crude than this). *Raphael and *Rubens come out with the joint highest marks in his scheme, and his admiration for the latter was shown in the famous controversy of the 'Rubénistes' against the 'Poussinistes' (*see* POUSSIN) that split the Académie Royale (*see* ACADEMY) in the second half of the 17th century. De Piles took the side of the Rubénistes, who believed that colour is of prime importance in painting, in opposition to those who upheld the academic emphasis on drawing. He also recognized the value of genius, imagination, and 'enthusiasm', as opposed to skills that can be learnt.

Pillement, Jean-Baptiste (1728–1808). French painter and designer. As a painter he is best known for his charming landscapes, which are strongly indebted to *Boucher but more atmospheric. His importance, however, lies more in the engravings made after his drawings, which were popular throughout Europe and of influence in spreading the *Rococo style, particularly the taste for *chinoiserie. Pillement himself was well travelled, visiting Austria, England, Poland, Portugal, and Spain.

Pilon, Germain (*c.*1525–90). The most powerful and original French sculptor of the 16th century. He was born in Paris, the son of a sculptor, **André Pilon**, and spent most of his career there. His first known work is the group of *Three Graces* on the monument for the heart of Henry II (1561–2, Louvre, Paris), which shows that his early manner was based on the elegant decorative style of the School of *Fontainebleau, in particular *Primaticcio's *stuccowork. Although his work never lost its tendency towards graceful *Mannerist elongation, it developed in the direction of greater naturalism and emotional intensity. These qualities are seen most memorably in his marble *gisants* on the tomb of Henry II and Catherine de' *Medici at Saint-Denis Abbey (1563–70), poignant works in which the semi-nude figures are shown relaxed in death. The kneeling effigies of Henry and Catherine on the upper tier of the tomb are of bronze and Pilon excelled in this medium as well as marble, both as a portrait sculptor (*Charles IX*, *c.*1574, Wallace Coll., London) and a medallist—he was appointed controller general of the Paris mint in 1572. Pilon's early work was influential on his successors, but the deeply felt emotion of his later style proved too personal to inspire imitation. Several examples of his sublime late work are in the Louvre, notably the tomb of Valentine Balbiani (*c.*1580).

Piloty, Karl von (1826–86). German painter, active in his native Munich, where in 1856 he became a professor at the Academy and in 1874 its director. He was highly successful with large, opulent history paintings in which the settings, furnishings, and costumes were reconstructed with great accuracy. They gave the public the same kind of feast for the eye as Hollywood epics and now have a distinctly hollow ring. His pupils included *Makart.

Pintoricchio (or **Pinturicchio**) (Bernardino di Betto) (*c.*1454–1513). Italian painter. He was born in Perugia and in 1481–2 he assisted the city's leading painter, *Perugino, with his frescos in the Sistine Chapel, Rome. His style was strongly influenced by Perugino, especially in his sweet, elegant figure types, but Pintoricchio lacked Perugino's lucidity of design and was more interested in decorative effects. His chief works are frescos in the Borgia rooms in the Vatican (1492–5) and the colourful *Scenes from the Life of Aeneas Sylvius Piccolomini* (i.e. Pope Pius II) in the Piccolomini Library of Siena Cathedral (1503). In these he showed the brilliant colours, ornamental detail, and fanciful charm that make him at his best, in the words of Frederick Hartt (*A History of Italian Renaissance Art*, 1970), 'one of the most endearing masters of the *Quattrocento . . . a kind of Perugian Benozzo *Gozzoli'. Pintoricchio was a prolific painter of panels as well as frescos—there are several examples of his work in the National Gallery, London.

Piper, John (1903–92). English painter, printmaker, draughtsman, designer, and writer. He reluctantly became an articled clerk in his father's legal firm, but took up the study of art after his father's death in 1926, first at the Richmond School of Art and then at the *Royal College of Art. From 1928 to 1933 he wrote as an art critic for the *Listener* and the *Nation* and was among the first to recognize such contemporaries as William *Coldstream, Ivon *Hitchens, Victor *Pasmore, and Ceri *Richards. By the mid-1930s he was one of the leading British abstract artists, but by the end of the decade he had become disillusioned with non-representational art and reverted to naturalism. He concentrated on landscape and architectural views in an emotionally charged style that continued the English *Romantic tradition (*see* NEO-ROMANTICISM). Some of his finest works were done as an *Official War Artist when he made pictures of bomb-damaged buildings. A similar stormy atmosphere pervades his famous views of country houses of the same period. Piper's work diversified in the 1950s and he became recognized as one of the most versatile British artists of his generation. He did much work as a designer of stage decor and of stained glass (notably at Coventry Cathedral) and was a prolific printmaker. In addition he made book illustrations and designed pottery and textiles. As a writer he is probably best known for his book *British Romantic Artists* (1942). He also compiled architectural guidebooks to several English counties, usually in collaboration with the poet John Betjeman.

Piranesi, Giovanni Battista (1720–78). Italian etcher, designer, archaeologist, and architect, born near Venice but active for almost all his career in Rome, where he settled in 1740. In Venice he had studied perspective and stage design and in Rome he achieved great popularity with his spectacular etchings of the ancient and modern city—the *Vedute*—published from 1745 onwards. He often altered the scale of buildings to make them look even grander than they are in actuality (Horace *Walpole said he 'conceived visions of Rome beyond what it boasted even in the meridian of its splendour') and his work played a major role in shaping the popular mental image of the city. Even more dramatic and original are his images of *Carceri d'invenzione*, fantastic imaginary prisons, begun *c.*1745 and reworked in 1761. These striking and obsessive works were later claimed by the *Surrealists as an anticipation of their ideas and their influence can be seen in 20th-century horror movies. Only one building was erected to Piranesi's designs (S. Maria del Priorato, Rome, 1764–6), but he was important as an architectural polemicist, most notably in his *Della magnificenza ed architettura de' Romani* (1761), in which he championed the superiority of Roman architecture over Greek. He influenced not only architects, but also stage designers and painters of *capricci such as his friend Hubert *Robert, and he had a powerful impact on the literary imagination. William *Beckford, for example, said that in writing his Gothic novel *Vathek* (1786) 'I drew chasms, and subterranean hollows, the domain of fear and torture, with chains, racks, wheels and dreadful engines in the style of Piranesi.' His etchings continued to be published for many years after his death and his work was continued by his son **Francesco** (1758–1810).

Pisanello (Antonio Pisano) (*c.*1394–1455?). Italian painter, draughtsman, and medallist. He presumably came from Pisa (hence his nickname—'the little Pisan'), but he spent his early years in Verona, a city with which he kept up his association for most of his life. His successful career also took him to Rome, Naples, and several courts of northern Italy, particularly those of the *Este (Ferrara) and *Gonzaga (Mantua). With *Gentile da Fabriano, Pisanello is regarded as the foremost exponent of the *International Gothic style in Italian painting, but most of his major works have perished, including frescos in the Doges' Palace, Venice (in which he collaborated with Gentile), and in St John Lateran, Rome (in which he completed work left unfinished by Gentile at his death). His surviving documented frescos are the *Annunciation* (*c*.1426, S. Fermo, Verona) and *St George and the Princess of Trebizond* (*c*.1433–8, S. Anastasia, Verona), and attributed to him are some fragments of murals showing scenes of war and chivalry in the Ducal Palace in Mantua, uncovered in 1968 and one of the most spectacular art discoveries of recent years. A handful of panel paintings is also given to him, including two in the National Gallery, London. On the other hand, a good many of his drawings survive, those of animals being particularly memorable. They show his keen eye for detail and his ability to convey an animal's personality. Pisanello was also the inventor of the portrait medal and arguably the greatest of all exponents of this art form, his work having an extraordinary dignity and strength considering the small size of the objects. His first medal commemorated a visit to Italy by the Byzantine emperor John VIII in 1438, and he subsequently made about twenty others, mainly for the ruling families of the courts at which he worked.

Pisano, Andrea (*c*.1290–1348/9?). Italian sculptor and architect, not related to Nicola and Giovanni *Pisano. He probably came from Pontedera, near Pisa (he is sometimes called Andrea da Pontedera), but he is first documented in Florence in 1330, when he began work on a pair of bronze doors for the Baptistery. The doors, finished in 1336, are the first of the three great sets for the Baptistery (the other two are by *Ghiberti), and represent twenty scenes from the life of St John the Baptist and eight Virtues—melodious in line and with a jeweller's refinement of handling. By 1340 Andrea was architect to Florence Cathedral (succeeding *Giotto) and the only other works certainly by him or from his workshop are *reliefs and statues for the cathedral's campanile. In their clear-cut designs the reliefs show the influence of Giotto's painting. In 1347 Andrea was appointed master of works at Orvieto Cathedral, where he was succeeded by his son **Nino** (d. 1368) in 1349. Nino is known from documents to have been active as a goldsmith and architect, but all his surviving works are sculptures in marble. He was much less distinguished as an artist than his father, but noteworthy in being one of the first sculptors to specialize in free-standing life-size statues.

Pisano, Nicola (d. 1278/84) and **Giovanni** (d. 1314/19). Italian sculptors and architects, father and son. They were the greatest sculptors of their period and stand at the head of the tradition of Italian sculpture in the same way that *Giotto stands at the head of the tradition of Italian painting. They often worked together, but their styles are distinctive. Nicola came from Apulia, where the emperor Frederick II (d. 1250) had encouraged a *classical revival, and his first known work, the pulpit in the Baptistery at Pisa (dated 1260 Pisan style, i.e. 1259) shows his brilliant adaptation of *antique forms to a new context. He transformed a Dionysus into Simeon at the Presentation of Christ, a nude Hercules into a personification of Christian Fortitude, and a Phaedra into the Virgin Mary. Instead of following the *Romanesque convention of separating episodes into compartments arranged in bands, he combined them into the formal unity of single pictures on each side of the pulpit with great power and dramatic effect. Several of the figures were directly inspired by ancient sarcophagi that Nicola saw in the Campo Santo in Pisa, but they are much more than simple borrowings, for he made them the vehicle for expressing richly varied human feeling. Nicola followed the Pisa pulpit with a similar but more complex work for Siena Cathedral (1265–8). The carving is deeper, the contrasts between light and shadow sharpened, the *reliefs more densely packed and full of movement. By then Nicola had a large workshop, his assistants including his son Giovanni and *Arnolfo di Cambio. His last great project was the large fountain in the public square of Perugia, which he and Giovanni finished in 1278. The dozens of reliefs are a typical medieval mixture—biblical scenes, heraldic beasts, personifications of seasons and places, and local dignitaries—but the vigour and spontaneity of the carving express a new freedom and naturalness.

By 1284 Nicola was dead. Between the Perugia fountain and this date, Giovanni, alone or in collaboration with his father, had carved the sculpture for the outside of the Pisa Baptistery (now in the Museo Nazionale). Here for the first time in Tuscany a scheme of monumental statuary was incorporated into an architectural setting. Giovanni developed this much further in Siena, where from 1284 onwards he designed the façade of the cathedral and carried out much of the sculptural decoration (some of the figures have been transferred to the cathedral museum and a magnificent fragment is in the Victoria and Albert Museum). It is the most richly decorated of all the great Italian *Gothic cathedral façades, and the statuary has tremendous energy and inner life. Giovanni's last two great works were pulpits for S. Andrea, Pistoia (1300–1), and Pisa Cathedral (1302–10). They are based on those of his father, but more elegant in style (showing French Gothic influence) and also more emotionally charged. The Pisa pulpit was damaged in a fire in 1599, then dismantled and reassembled, some parts being dispersed; several museums, including the Metropolitan Museum, New York, have fragments that are said to come from it. Giovanni also made a number of free-standing statues, the best known of which is the *Madonna and Child* on the altar of the Arena Chapel in Padua (c.1305). Its grandeur and humanity suggests a close kinship with Giotto, amid whose celebrated frescos it stands.

Pissarro, Camille (1830–1903). French painter, printmaker, and draughtsman, born on St Thomas in the West Indies, where his parents (a French Jewish father and a Creole mother) ran a prosperous general store. He was educated at boarding school in Paris, but he then returned to the Caribbean and did not settle in France until 1855. Before this he had been mainly self-taught, but he now studied at the École des *Beaux-Arts and the *Académie Suisse, as well as copying in the Louvre. In 1859 he met *Monet, and with him became a central figure of *Impressionism. Pissarro in fact was the only artist who participated in all eight Impressionist exhibitions and he was a much-respected father figure to his colleagues (he was about a decade older than most of the other members of the group). His talents as a teacher made him influential even among artists of greater stature than himself—*Cézanne and *Gauguin, for example, spoke glowingly of him. During the Franco-Prussian War of 1870–1, when his home at Louveciennes was overrun by the German invaders and many of his paintings were destroyed, he joined Monet in England. In 1872 he settled at Pontoise,

where he introduced Cézanne to painting out of doors. From 1884 he lived at Eragny in Normandy, although he travelled a good deal. In 1885 he met *Seurat and for several years afterwards he experimented with *Neo-Impressionism; in about 1890, however, he reverted to his Impressionist style, though with freer brushwork than in his early work. By this time, following early hardships, he was beginning to prosper, and by the end of his career his work was selling well in Germany and the USA as well as France. From about 1895 deterioration of his eyesight caused him to give up painting out of doors and many of his late works are urban scenes painted from windows (usually of hotels) in Paris and elsewhere. Although he is best known for his landscapes and city views, he painted various other subjects, including portraits, still lifes, and *genre scenes. In addition to a large output of paintings and drawings, he was the most prolific printmaker among the Impressionists, working in a variety of techniques and sometimes mixing them. The best representation of his paintings is in the Musée d'Orsay, Paris. There is another good collection of his work (including numerous drawings) in the Ashmolean Museum, Oxford.

Pissarro had five painter sons, of whom the most important was the eldest, **Lucien** (1863–1944). He took part in the final Impressionist exhibition (1886) and with Seurat in the second *Salon des Indépendants, adopting the *pointillist technique for a time. In 1890 he settled in England, and he became a British citizen in 1916. From 1905 he was part of *Sickert's circle and he was a member of the *Camden Town Group and afterwards of the *London Group. He was a distinguished book illustrator and from 1894 to 1914 ran the Eragny Press, one of the best of the private presses that flourished at this period. A modest and unassuming character, he has been overshadowed by his more famous father, but he was an important figure in helping to introduce Impressionism and Neo-Impressionism to England. His daughter, **Orovida Pissarro** (1893–1968), often known simply as 'Orovida', was a painter and etcher, mainly of animal subjects.

Pitti Palace, Florence. Art gallery, originally built as a palace for Luca Pitti, a wealthy rival of the *Medici. Construction work began in about 1457, so the traditional attribution of its design to *Brunelleschi (who died in 1446) is unlikely; it has also been attributed to *Alberti. The Pitti family had taken up residence by 1469, but their fortunes later declined and the building remained unfinished. In 1550 it was bought by Eleonora of Toledo, the wife of Cosimo de' Medici (later the first Grand Duke of Tuscany). It now became the main Medici residence and from 1560 it was enlarged by *Ammanati. At about the same time the land around the building was developed into the Boboli Gardens. Most of the present vast structure dates from the 16th and 17th centuries, although additions continued to be made into the 19th century. The interior includes opulent decoration by Pietro da *Cortona. After the Medici dynasty came to an end in the 18th century, the family collections became state property and the Pitti was opened as a public gallery in 1833. Among its treasures are about 500 paintings from the Medici collections, mainly from the 16th and 17th centuries; in quality they rival the masterpieces in its sister institution, the *Uffizi. The Pitti also contains a good representation of Italian pictures of the 18th, 19th, and 20th centuries, and collections of costume and of precious objects such as jewels, cameos, and ivories.

Pittoni, Giambattista (1687–1767). Venetian painter of religious, historical, and mythological pictures. He had a highly successful career and ranks as one of the best contemporaries of *Tiepolo, whom he succeeded as president of the Venetian Academy in 1758. As far as is known, Pittoni never left Italy, but he nevertheless received important foreign commissions from the Swedish, Austrian, and German courts. He also painted altarpieces for churches in numerous Italian towns and he had a reputation for being diligent and dependable. His early work was much indebted to *Piazzetta and Sebastiano *Ricci, but his style later became lighter and more colourful under the influence of Tiepolo.

Place, Francis (1647–1728). English gentleman draughtsman and printmaker, active mainly in York. In 1665 he met *Hollar in London (where he had initially intended to study law) and this seems to have been the decisive factor in his taking up art seriously. His early topographical and architectural drawings are near to Hollar's in style, but his later drawings rely on a fuller use of *wash, anticipating the technique that became characteristic of 18th-century watercolour painting. Place also made portraits and was a pioneer of the *mezzotint technique. His work is best represented in York Art Gallery.

Plamondon, Antoine (1804–95). Canadian painter of portraits, religious subjects, and figure compositions, active mainly in Quebec. He was the first Canadian to study in France after Quebec was ceded to Britain in 1763, training in Paris, 1826–30. His portraits, which are his best work, are painted in an austerely classical style. He also executed numerous church commissions in Quebec.

plaquette. A type of small decorative *relief in metal (usually bronze or lead, sometimes silver) made in multiple copies. Plaquettes originated in Italy in the 1440s, flourished there for about a century, and were popular in France, Germany, and the Netherlands into the 17th century. They were almost always cast by the *cire-perdue process and new editions could be made from the wax image of an existing plaquette; if this wax were altered a new 'state' would result. A very few were struck like coins. After casting, the best plaquettes were usually chiselled and chased, and finished with a *patina or gilding. They were used to decorate such objects as sword-hilts, inkwells, or caskets; small ones served as buttons. Because they were easily transportable they helped to disseminate the taste of the *Renaissance—like the engravings of which they are the three-dimensional counterpart. *Flötner's plaquettes, for example, helped to make his designs common property among German artists. *Donatello is the greatest name connected with the art (there are several plaquettes by or attributed to him), but most examples are of unknown authorship.

plaster of Paris. A fine white or pinkish powder, made from gypsum (see ALABASTER), that when mixed with water forms a quick-setting paste that dries to form a uniform, solid, and inert mass. It is used in sculpture for making moulds and casts.

Plastov, Arkady. See SOCIALIST REALISM.

plein air (Fr.: 'open air'). Term used to characterize paintings (usually landscapes) done outdoors rather than in the studio, or more generally to describe pictures that give a strong feeling of the open air. Although there are earlier instances, painting outdoors did not become common until the 19th century, when the development of portable equipment made it much easier in practical terms. It became a central feature of *Impressionism and is especially associated with *Monet.

Pleydenwurff, Hans (d. 1472). German painter and designer of stained glass, the leading painter of his day in Nuremberg, where he was active from about 1450. His work shows a move away from the *International Gothic style to a more naturalistic idiom influenced by Netherlandish painting. A large *Crucifixion* (*c.*1470, Alte Pin., Munich) is characteristic of his refined style. Michael *Wolgemut married his widow and took over his workshop. Pleydenwurff's son **Wilhelm** (d. 1494) was a painter and designer of woodcuts, also active in Nuremberg.

Pliny the Elder (Gaius Plinius Secundus) (AD 23/24–79). Roman writer. As a sideline to his career in public office, Pliny produced (among many other things) the *Historia Naturalis* (Natural History), a massive compilation in 37 books intended to embrace not only the whole of the natural sciences but also their application to the arts and crafts of civilized life. His only extant work, it has been condemned as uncritical, unreliable, and superficial, but it contains a great deal that is interesting and entertaining. Much of its information would have been completely lost but for Pliny's labours, and the material on painting and sculpture is especially interesting because earlier treatises on classical art have perished. It is typical of Pliny's thirst for knowledge that he perished through asphyxiation when making observations of the eruption of Vesuvius that destroyed Pompeii and Herculaneum.

pochade. See BONINGTON.

Poelenburgh, Cornelis van (1594/5–1667). Dutch painter, mainly of landscapes. He studied in his native Utrecht with *Bloemaert and from about 1617 to 1626 was in Rome, becoming one of the leading members of the first generation of Dutch painters of Italianate landscapes. His paintings are typically small scale (he often worked on copper) with biblical or mythological figures set in Arcadian landscapes, sometimes scattered with antique remains. They are strongly influenced by *Elsheimer, but cooler in colour than the German artist's work and without his sense of mystery. After returning to Utrecht Poelenburgh enjoyed a career of great success. He was *Rubens's guide when he visited the city in 1627, was popular in aristocratic and even royal circles (he visited England in 1637 at the invitation of Charles I), and was imitated until the early 18th century. There are examples of his work (and of the work of imitators) in the Fitzwilliam Museum, Cambridge, including his portrait of Jan *Both, in whose landscapes he sometimes painted the figures (an example of their collaboration is in the NG, London).

pointillism. Technique of using regular small touches of pure colour in such a way that when a picture is viewed from a suitable distance they seem to react together optically, creating more vibrant colour effects than if the same colours were physically mixed together. The term ('peinture au point') was coined in 1886 by the French critic Félix Fénéon in reference to *Seurat's *La Grande Jatte*, but Seurat, and also *Signac, preferred the broader term *divisionism. *See also* NEO-IMPRESSIONISM.

pointing. A method of creating an exact copy of a statue or of enlarging a model into a full-size sculpture by taking a series of measured points on the original and transferring them by means of mechanical aids to the copy or enlargement. The ancient Greeks devised elementary methods of pointing using callipers, and some kind of mechanical device was in use by the 1st century BC, when the copying of Greek statues for Roman patrons had become an industry. Various techniques of transfer, using for example a frame and plumb line, have been used since the *Renaissance, but it was not until the late 18th and early 19th century that sophisticated pointing machines became established in the sculptor's workshop (*see* BACON, JOHN). Such devices typically consisted of an upright stand carrying movable arms, each arm having attached to it an adjustable measuring rod that showed the depth to which each point must be drilled. Sometimes hundreds and even thousands of points would be taken. In the late 19th and early 20th centuries most stone sculpture was produced by this mechanical method, but thereafter sculptors increasingly rejected it in favour of *direct carving.

Poliakoff, Serge (1906–69). Russian-born painter, printmaker, and designer who settled in Paris in 1923 and became a French citizen in 1962. For many years he earned his living as a guitarist, but he began to study painting in 1930, attending various art schools, including the *Slade School during a two-year stay in London, 1935–7. His early work was figurative, but after his return to Paris in 1937 he met *Kandinsky and Robert and Sonia *Delaunay, and under their influence he turned to abstraction. During the 1950s he gained recognition as one of the leading abstract painters in the *École de Paris; his pictures characteristically feature bold irregular slabs of mat, roughly textured colour (*Abstract Composition*, 1954, Tate, London). He adopted an almost religious attitude towards painting, saying: 'You've got to have the feeling of God in the picture if you want to get the big music in.'

Polidoro da Caravaggio (Polidoro Caldara) (*c*.1499–1543?). Italian painter, named after his birthplace, Caravaggio in Lombardy. At an early age he moved to Rome, where he assisted *Raphael in the decoration of the Vatican Loggie and then achieved great success painting palace façades with monochrome scenes imitating *classical sculpture. They have almost all perished (only the heavily restored decoration of the Palazzo Ricci remains in situ), but they became well known through engravings and drawings and were much imitated. Polidoro's other claim to fame is his decoration of the chapel of Fra Marino Fetti in S. Silvestro al Quirinale (*c*.1525) with two murals of scenes from the life of St Mary Magdalene and St Catherine of Siena; here he gave an entirely new prominence to the landscape, which dominates the figures. In this he was influenced by ancient Roman painting and foreshadowed the classical landscapes of *Claude and *Poussin. Polidoro fled Rome after the sack of the city in 1527, moving to Naples and then Messina; *Vasari says that he was

murdered there by an assistant for the sake of his money.

Pollaiuolo, Antonio (*c*.1432–98) and **Piero** (*c*.1441–*c*.1496). Florentine artists, brothers, who jointly ran a flourishing workshop, first in their native city and then from about 1484 in Rome. Both of them are recorded as being painters and sculptors and there are considerable problems in attempting to disentangle their individual contributions to their output. However, Antonio was evidently the dominant figure and primarily a goldsmith and worker in bronze, whilst Piero was mainly a painter. Several documented paintings by Piero are known, all of fairly mediocre quality, but none by Antonio, and as certain pictures from the studio of the two brothers are so much better than Piero's independent works, it is generally assumed that Antonio had a major involvement in them. The most important of these pictures is the *Martyrdom of St Sebastian* in the National Gallery, London, probably painted in 1475. The figures of the archers in the foreground reveal a mastery of anatomy paralleled in certain bronzes generally accepted as Antonio's (e.g. the *Hercules and Antaeus*, *c*.1475–80, in the Bargello, Florence), in his only surviving engraving (*Battle of the Nude Men*, *c*.1460), and in his numerous pen drawings, in which his typically wiry figures are seen in vigorous and expressive movement. His main contribution to Florentine painting lay in his searching analysis of the human figure in movement or under conditions of strain, but he is also important for his pioneering interest in landscape, seen in the National Gallery *St Sebastian* and other works. He is said to have anticipated *Leonardo in dissecting corpses in order to study the anatomy of the body. Antonio's two principal public works were the bronze tombs of Pope Sixtus IV (Francesco della *Rovere) (signed and dated 1493) and Pope Innocent VIII (*c*.1492–8), both in St Peter's, Rome. The latter contains the first sepulchral effigy that simulated the living man.

Pollock, Jackson (1912–56). American painter, the commanding figure of the *Abstract Expressionist movement. In 1929–31 he studied at the *Art Students League of New York under Thomas Hart *Benton and was influenced not only by Benton's restlessly energetic style, but also by his image as a virile, hard-drinking macho-man (Pollock began treatment for alcoholism in 1937 and in 1939 he started therapy with Jungian psychoanalysts, using his drawings in sessions with them). During the 1930s he painted in Benton's *Regionalist vein, and he was influenced also by the work of the Mexican muralists (he attended an experimental workshop run by *Siqueiros in New York in 1936) and by certain aspects of *Surrealism, particularly the use of mythical or totemic figures as archetypes of the unconscious. From 1935 to 1942 he worked for the *Federal Art Project, and in 1943 he was given a contract by Peggy *Guggenheim; his first one-man show was held at her Art of This Century gallery in that year. A characteristic work of this time is The She-Wolf (1943, MoMA, New York), a semi-abstract picture with vehemently handled paint and ominous imagery recalling the monstrous creatures of *Picasso's Guernica period. By the mid-1940s Pollock's work had become completely abstract, and the 'drip and splash' type of *Action Painting for which he is best known emerged in 1947. Instead of using the traditional easel, he laid his canvas on the floor and poured and dripped his paint from a can (using commercial enamels and metallic paint because their texture was better suited to the technique); instead of using brushes, he manipulated the paint with 'sticks, trowels or knives' (to use his own words), sometimes obtaining textured effects by the admixture of 'sand, broken glass or other foreign matter'. As he worked, Pollock moved around (and sometimes through) his paintings, creating a novel *all-over style that avoided any points of emphasis and abandoned traditional ideas of composition; the design of the painting had no relation to the size or shape of the canvas—indeed in the finished work the canvas was sometimes docked or trimmed to suit the image. The drip paintings were first publicly shown at Betty *Parsons's New York gallery in 1948. Initially they shocked most observers, but some people were stunned by their energy and passion, which opened up new paths for painting: Willem *de Kooning commented, 'Jackson's broken the ice.'

Pollock's drip period lasted only from 1947 to 1952 (afterwards he went back to quasi-figurative work), but it is on the paintings of these five years that his enormous reputation rests. Among the most celebrated are Autumn Rhythm (1950, Met. Mus., New York) and Lavender Mist (1950, NG, Washington), which Robert *Hughes describes as 'his most ravishingly atmospheric painting'. Pollock's novel methods gave rise to a good deal of mockery (he was nicknamed 'Jack the Dripper'), but he was supported by advanced critics, particularly Clement *Greenberg and Harold *Rosenberg, and as early as 1949 the French painter Georges *Mathieu said that he considered him the 'greatest living American painter'. By 1960 he was generally recognized as the most important figure in the most important movement in the history of American painting, but a movement from which artists were already in reaction. His unhappy personal life and his premature death in a car crash contributed to his status as one of the legends of modern art; he was the first American painter to become a 'star'.

In 1945 Pollock married Lee Krasner (1908–84), who was an Abstract Expressionist painter of some distinction, although it was only after her husband's death that she received serious critical recognition. She was also an important source of encouragement and support to Pollock, whose attitude to his work fluctuated from supreme confidence to dismal uncertainty.

polychrome. Term meaning 'many coloured', applied in art-historical writing particularly to sculpture painted in this fashion. Until the *Renaissance the practice was extremely common, whether the colours were conventionalized, as in much ancient art, or more or less naturalistic, as became more common during the Middle Ages, but because of fading of the pigments the colouring is rarely obvious today. Spain later had a rich tradition of polychrome sculpture (see ENCARNADO).

Polyclitus (active c.450–c.420 BC). One of the most celebrated of Greek sculptors. He was probably a native of Argos, although *Pliny says he came from Sicyon. No original works by him survive, but several are known through Roman copies. He is now most famous for his Doryphorus (Spear Carrier), the best copy of which is in the Archaeological Museum in Naples. In this figure he is said to have embodied the system of mathematical proportions on which he wrote a book, and the statue—long regarded as a standard for ideal male beauty—is sometimes referred to as 'The Canon'. Copies also exist of a *Diadumenus* (a youth wreathing a band round his head) by Polyclitus and of an Amazon with which, according to Pliny, he defeated *Phidias in a competition. In antiquity his greatest work was held to be the colossal *chryselephantine statue of Hera in her temple—the Heraeum—near Argos. It is now known only through descriptions and representations on coins, but ancient writers compared it favourably with Phidias' statue of Zeus at Olympia. Strabo said the Zeus was more magnificent but the Hera more beautiful in workmanship.

polyptych. A picture or other work of art made up of four or more linked parts (usually wooden panels). It was a popular form for altarpieces from the 14th century to the early 16th century. Italian polyptychs of this time typically include a *predella beneath the main panel or tier, the whole enclosed in an elaborate frame. In northern Europe, polyptychs often had panels hinged together and painted on both sides, so that they could be folded to create different pictorial compositions (sometimes ones that were appropriate for particular liturgical seasons or events). Jan van *Eyck's Ghent Altarpiece and *Grünewald's Isenheim Altarpiece are among the famous examples of this type. *See also* DIPTYCH and TRIPTYCH.

Pomarancio, Il. *See* RONCALLI.

Pompidou Centre (in full, Centre National d'Art et de Culture Georges-Pompidou). Cultural centre in Paris named after Georges Pompidou (1911–74), the president of France from 1967 to 1974. In 1969 he expressed a 'passionate wish' for 'a place where the plastic arts, music, cinema, literature, audio-visual research, etc. would find a common ground'. The site chosen for the Centre was the Plateau Beaubourg (hence its colloquial name 'Beaubourg Centre'), a once thriving area near the centre of Paris that had become derelict between the world wars. An international competition for the building produced almost 700 submissions, including bizarre ideas such as a giant egg and an enormous hand extended towards the sky, each finger being intended to house a separate department. The winning design was submitted by the Italian-British team of Renzo Piano and Richard Rogers (later Lord Rogers). Their huge building was constructed in 1971–7 and soon became one of the most famous sights of the city. A leading example of 'high-tech' architecture, it has been described as looking like a 'crazy oil refinery' and has attracted extremes of praise and censure. The large plaza in front of the building is conceived as part of the Centre and is the main forum for the city's street performers. Also outside the building is the ebullient Beaubourg Fountain (1980) by Jean *Tinguely and Niki de *Saint Phalle. The Centre is divided into various departments, including a library, an industrial design centre, and an institute for the development and promotion of avant-garde music. The largest of the departments and the main reason for the Centre's popularity is the national collection of modern art—the Musée National d'Art Moderne—which was formerly housed in the Palais de Tokyo. It was opened there in 1947, but its origins are much older, for it is the heir to the Musée du Luxembourg, opened in 1818 as a showcase for the work of living artists. Its collection of modern art is exceeded in scope and quality probably only by that of the *Museum of Modern Art in New York.

pompier, l'art. A term applied pejoratively to French academic art (more particularly pretentious *history painting) of the late 19th century. It is said to derive from the habit of posing nude models wearing firemen's helmets to substitute for ancient military headgear (Fr., *pompier* 'fireman').

Pompon, François (1855–1933). French sculptor. Much of his career was spent working as an assistant to other sculptors (including *Rodin) and recognition came to him late in life after his *Polar Bear* (Pompidou Centre, Paris) was a great success at the 1922 *Salon d'Automne. The work became enormously popular, reproduced in a variety of forms, and Pompon was hailed as the greatest animal sculptor since *Barye.

Pont-Aven, School of. Term applied to a group of painters associated with *Gauguin during his periods of work at the town of Pont-Aven in Brittany (1886, 1888–9, 1894), and inspired by his anti-naturalistic style. Émile *Bernard was among them, and he and Gauguin together developed *Synthetism.

Pontormo (Jacopo Carucci) (1494–1556). Italian painter, born in the Tuscan village of Pontormo, near Empoli, and active in and around Florence. According to *Vasari, he studied successively with *Leonardo da Vinci, *Albertinelli, *Piero di Cosimo, and *Andrea del Sarto, whose workshop he is said to have entered in 1512. Andrea was certainly a major influence on his early work. Pontormo was precocious (he was praised by *Michelangelo whilst still a youth) and by the time he painted his *Joseph in Egypt* (NG, London) in about 1518 he had already created a distinctive style—full of restless movement and disconcertingly irrational effects of scale and space—that put him in the vanguard of *Mannerism. The emotional tension evident in this work reaches its peak in Pontormo's masterpiece, the altarpiece of the *Entombment* (*c.*1526–8) in the Capponi Chapel of S. Felicità, Florence. Painted in extraordinarily vivid colours and featuring deeply poignant figures who seem lost in a trance of grief, this is one of the high points of Mannerism. Pontormo was primarily a religious painter, but he was also an outstanding portraitist (he was a major influence on his pupil and adopted son *Bronzino) and in 1520–1 for the *Medici villa at Poggio a Caiano he painted a memorable mythological work (*Vertumnus and Pomona* according to Vasari, but the identification is disputed) in which an apparently idyllic scene reveals a strong undercurrent of neurosis. In Pontormo's later work his style was enriched by the study of Michelangelo and *Dürer's prints, but this stage of his career is known mainly through his superb drawings (best represented in the Uffizi), as the great fresco scheme in S. Lorenzo, Florence, that occupied him from 1546 until his death, was destroyed in the 18th century. Pontormo's diary for part of 1554–6 survives, giving a day-to-day account of his progress. It tells us much of his neurotic character—melancholy and introspective, dismayed by the slightest illness.

Pop art. A movement based on the imagery of consumerism and popular culture, flourishing from the late 1950s to the early 1970s, chiefly in the USA and Britain. The term was coined *c.*1955 by Lawrence *Allo-

way. Comic books, advertisements, packaging, and images from television and the cinema were all part of the iconography of the movement. In the USA Pop art was initially regarded as a reaction from *Abstract Expressionism because its exponents brought back figural imagery and made use of *Hard-Edge techniques. It was seen as a descendant of *Dada (in fact Pop art is sometimes called *Neo-Dada) because it debunked the seriousness of the art world and embraced the use or reproduction of commonplace subjects (comic strips, soup tins, highway signs) in a manner that had affinities with *Duchamp's *ready-mades. The most immediate inspiration, however, was the work of Jasper *Johns and Robert *Rauschenberg, both of whom began to make an impact on the New York art scene in the mid-1950s. They opened a wide new range of subject matter with Johns's paintings of flags, targets, and numbers and his sculptures of objects such as beer cans and Rauschenberg's *collages and *combine paintings featuring Coca-Cola bottles, stuffed birds, and photographs from magazines and newspapers. While often using similar subject matter, Pop artists generally favoured commercial techniques in preference to the painterly manner of Johns and Rauschenberg. Examples are Andy *Warhol's screenprints of soup tins and so on, Roy *Lichtenstein's paintings in the manner of comic strips, and Mel *Ramos's brash pin-ups. Claes *Oldenberg, whose subjects include ice-cream cones and hamburgers, has been the major Pop art sculptor. John Wilmerding (*American Art,* 1976) writes that Pop art 'cannot be separated from the culmination of affluence and prosperity during the post-World-War-II era. America had become a ravenously consuming society, packaging art as well as other products, indulging in commercial manipulation, and celebrating exhibitionism, self-promotion, and instant success ... Pop's mass-media orientation may further be related to the acceleration of uniformity in most aspects of national life, whether restaurants or regional dialects. Shared by all Americans were the principal preoccupations of Pop art—sex, the automobile, and food.'

In Britain, too, Pop art revelled in a new glossy prosperity following years of post-war austerity. British Pop was nurtured by the *Independent Group and the work that is often cited as the first fully-fledged Pop art image was produced under its auspices—Richard *Hamilton's collage *Just what is it that makes today's homes so different, so appealing?* (1956, Kunsthalle, Tübingen). However, British Pop art first made a major impact at the *Young Contemporaries exhibition in 1961 (at about the same time that American Pop art became a force). The artists in this exhibition included Derek *Boshier, David *Hockney, Allen *Jones, R. B. *Kitaj, and Peter *Phillips, who had all been students at the *Royal College of Art. In the same year the BBC screened Ken Russell's *Monitor* film 'Pop goes the easel', in which Peter *Blake was one of the featured artists. Although there are exceptions (notably the erotic sculptures of Allen Jones), British Pop art was generally less brash than American, expressing a more romantic view of the subject matter in a way that can now strike a note of nostalgia. Much of the imagery, however, came directly from the American world of pin-ups and pinball machines. Richard Hamilton defined Pop art as 'popular, transient, expendable, low-cost, mass-produced, young, witty, sexy, gimmicky, glamorous, and Big Business', and it was certainly a success on a material level, getting through to the public in a way that few modern movements do and attracting big-money collectors. However, it was scorned by many critics. Harold *Rosenberg, for example, described Pop as being 'Like a joke without humour, told over and over again until it begins to sound like a threat ... Advertising art which advertises itself as art that hates advertising.'

Pope-Hennessy, Sir John (1913–94). British art historian. He was director of the *Victoria and Albert Museum, 1967–73; director of the *British Museum, 1974–6; and from 1977 to 1987 consultative chairman, department of European paintings, *Metropolitan Museum, New York, and professor of fine arts at New York University. His many publications made him perhaps the doyen in the field of Italian Renaissance art among English writers. They include the magisterial *An Introduction to Italian Sculpture* in three parts (all of which have subsequently appeared in revised editions), *Italian Gothic Sculpture* (1955), *Italian Renaissance Sculpture* (1958), and *Italian High Renaissance and Baroque Sculpture* (1963), an edition of *Cellini's *Autobiography* (1949), and monographs on *Giovanni di Paolo (1937), *Sassetta (1939), *Uccello (1950; rev. 1972), Fra *Angelico (1952; rev. 1974), *Raphael (1970), Luca della *Robbia (1980), and Cellini (1985). His autobiography, *Learning to Look*, was published in 1991.

poppy oil. Oil extracted from poppy seeds, one of the most popular of the *drying oils used as a *medium for *oil painting. It is less viscous than *linseed and *walnut oil and does not easily turn rancid. It is, however, slow drying. This turned out to be an advantage rather than a disadvantage when *alla prima* painting came into vogue about the middle of the 19th century and for a time during the second half of that century poppy oil was much used by commercial colourmen.

Porcellis, Jan (c.1584–1632). Dutch painter, etcher, and draughtsman of marine subjects. Porcellis was Flemish by birth, but he spent most of his career in Holland, working in various towns before settling at Zouterwoude, near Leiden. He was regarded as the greatest marine painter of his day and his work marks the transition from the busy and brightly coloured seascapes of the early 17th century, with their emphasis on the representation of ships, to monochromatic paintings that are essentially studies of sea, sky, and atmospheric effects. His favourite theme was a modest fishing boat making its way through a choppy sea near the shore. *Rembrandt and Jan van de *Cappelle collected his works. His son **Julius** (c.1609–45) was also a marine painter.

Pordenone (Giovanni Antonio de Sacchis) (c.1483?–1539). Italian painter, named after the town of his birth, Pordenone, near Venice, and active in various parts of northern Italy. After working in a provincial style at the very start of his career (his master is unknown and *Vasari says he was self-taught), by the beginning of the second decade of the 16th century he had come close to the contemporary Venetian (specifically *Giorgionesque) manner of painting. In the second half of the decade, however, he was in central Italy, and his style changed under the impact particularly of *Michelangelo, acquiring great weight and solidity. Pordenone was influenced also by the illusionism of *Mantegna and by German prints, and the style he forged from these diverse influences was highly distinctive and original. He always retained something of provincial uncouthness—at times vulgarity—but he was, in Vasari's words, 'very rich in invention...bold and resolute', and he excelled at dramatic spatial effects. These qualities are seen at their most forceful in his fresco of the *Crucifixion* (1520-1) in Cremona Cathedral; the densely packed, bizarrely expressive figures are seen as if on a stage through a painted proscenium arch and they lunge violently out into the spectator's space. From 1527 Pordenone lived mainly in Venice and in the 1530s he was the most serious rival to *Titian. His major works in Venice have been destroyed, however. He died in Ferrara, where he had gone to design tapestries for Ercole II d'*Este.

Portinari, Cândido (1903-62). Brazilian painter of Italian descent. He is best known for his portrayals of Brazilian workers and peasants, but he dissociated himself from the revolutionary fervour of his Mexican contemporaries, and painted in a style that shows affinities with *Picasso's 'classical' works of the 1920s (which he saw during a three-year period he spent in Europe, 1928-31). In the 1940s his work took on greater pathos and he also turned to biblical subjects. He gained an international reputation and his major commissions included murals for the Hispanic section of the Library of Congress in Washington (1942) and for the United Nations Building in New York (two panels representing War and Peace, 1953-5).

Posada, José Guadalupe (1851-1913). Mexican graphic artist. His enormous output was largely devoted to political and social issues, revealing, for example, the dreadful conditions in which the poor lived. From 1890 his studio in Mexico City functioned as an open shop fronting the street, where he turned out sensational broadsheets and cheap cartoons that spread among the illiterate throughout the country. His work had the vigour and spontaneous strength of genuinely popular art, with the inborn Mexican taste for the more gruesome aspects of death—one of his recurring motifs is the *calavera* or animated skeleton. He made a major impression on *Orozco and *Rivera during their student days.

Post, Frans (*c.*1612-80). Dutch landscape painter, active mainly in his native Haarlem. In 1637-44 he was a member of the Dutch West India Company's voyage of colonization to Brazil, where he produced 'the first firmly documented landscapes painted in the New World by a trained European artist' (Seymour Slive, *Dutch Painting 1600-1800*, 1995). He observed the unfamiliar flora and fauna with an appropriate freshness, creating scenes of remarkable vividness and charm, and he continued to paint Brazilian landscapes after his return to the Netherlands (indeed he is not known to have painted any other type of picture). Because of his *'naive' style, he has been called the Henri *Rousseau of the 17th century, and he was virtually forgotten or regarded as a curiosity until the 20th century. Examples of his fairly rare work are in the Louvre, Paris, the National Gallery of Ireland, Dublin, and Ham House, London. His brother **Pieter** (1608-69) was one of the outstanding Dutch architects of the 17th century (the Huis ten Bosch near The Hague is his most famous work) and also occasionally painted.

Post-Impressionism. Term applied to various trends in painting, particularly in France, that developed from *Impressionism or in reaction against it in the period *c.*1880-*c.*1905. Roger *Fry coined the term as the title of an exhibition, 'Manet and the Post-Impressionists', which he organized at the Grafton Galleries, London, in 1910. The exhibition was dominated by the work of *Cézanne, *Gauguin, and van *Gogh, who are considered the central figures of Post-Impressionism. These three artists varied greatly in their response to Impressionism: Cézanne, who wished 'to make of Impressionism something solid and enduring, like the art of the museums', was preoccupied with pictorial structure; Gauguin renounced 'the abominable error of naturalism' to explore the symbolic use of colour and line; and van Gogh's uninhibited emotional intensity was the fountainhead of *Expressionism. Georges *Seurat, a figure of almost equal importance, concentrated on a more scientific analysis of colour (*see* NEO-IMPRESSIONISM). The general drift of Post-Impressionism was to lead away from the naturalism of Impressionism towards the series of avant-garde movements (such as *Fauvism and *Cubism) that revolutionized European art in the decade leading up to the First World War. (Some writers extend the notion of Post-Impressionism to cover these developments, making the term embrace the period c.1880–c.1914, but this makes an already broad concept less rather than more useful.)

Fry organized his first Post-Impressionist exhibition at short notice and in an almost casual atmosphere, but he brought together a highly impressive (if far from balanced) collection of pictures, mainly loaned by leading French dealers. The exhibition created what the Daily Mail called 'an altogether unprecedented artistic sensation' or what *Sickert more succinctly described as a 'rumpus'. The reviews were mainly unpleasant, sometimes viciously so. Some visitors were angry (Duncan *Grant recalled people shaking their umbrellas at the pictures) and others mocked. The prevailing opinion was that the pictures on show were childish, crude, and the product of moral degeneracy or mental derangement. Duncan Grant, however, said that he and Vanessa *Bell were 'wildly enthusiastic' about the exhibition, and it powerfully affected the work of several of the painters in Sickert's circle (see CAMDEN TOWN GROUP), in general encouraging the use of strong, flat colours.

Post-Painterly Abstraction. A term coined by the critic Clement *Greenberg to characterize a broad trend in American painting, beginning in the 1950s, in which abstract painters reacted in various ways against the *gestural 'painterly' qualities of *Abstract Expressionism. Greenberg used the term as the title of an exhibition he organized at the Los Angeles County Museum of Art in 1964. He took the word 'painterly' (Ger., malerisch) from Heinrich *Wölfflin, who had discussed it in his book Principles of Art History. By it he understood 'the blurred, broken, loose definition of colour and contour'; Post-Painterly Abstractionists, in contrast, moved towards 'physical openness of design, or toward linear clarity, or toward both'. The characterization was never a very exact one, but essentially it described a rejection of expressive brushwork in favour of broad areas of unmodulated colour. The term thus embraces more precisely defined types of abstract art including *Colour Field Painting and *Hard-Edge Painting. Leading figures of the trend include Helen *Frankenthaler, Al *Held, Ellsworth *Kelly, Morris *Louis, Kenneth *Noland, Jules *Olitski, and Frank *Stella.

Potter, Paulus (1625–54). Dutch painter and etcher of animals in landscapes, active in Delft, The Hague, and Amsterdam. His best-known work, the life-size Young Bull (1647, Mauritshuis, The Hague), was in the 19th century one of the most famous of all Dutch paintings. Subsequent taste has found its detailed and precise manner rather dry and laboured and preferred his more characteristic works, which are much smaller. His speciality was scenes of cattle and sheep in sunlit meadows.

pouncing. A method of transferring a drawing or design to another surface (typically a *cartoon to a wall for *fresco painting) by making a series of pinpricks along the outlines of the drawing, then dabbing pounce (a fine powder of charcoal or similar substance) through them, thus creating a dotted replica of the outlines on the surface below.

Pourbus. Family of Netherlandish painters, distinguished mainly as portraitists. **Pieter** (c.1523–84) spent most of his life in Bruges, where he became a member of the painters' guild in 1543 and at about the same time married the daughter of Lancelot *Blondeel. He was a civil engineer, surveyor, and cartographer as well as a painter. Van *Mander wrote, 'I have never seen a better equipped studio than his.' As well as portraits he painted religious and allegorical scenes, one of the most splendid of which is the Allegory of True Love (c.1547, Wallace Coll., London). Pieter's son, **Frans the Elder** (1545–81), was active in Antwerp, where he was a pupil and follower of Frans *Floris (he married a daughter of Cornelis Floris). The most famous member of the family is his son **Frans the Younger** (1569–1622), who was one of the principal court portraitists of Europe. After spending a year working for the Archduke Albert and the Infanta Isabella in Brussels, from 1600 to 1609 he was employed in Mantua (at the same time as *Rubens) by Vincenzo I *Gonzaga. In 1609 he was called to Paris by Maria de' *Medici and worked as her court painter until his death. His style—more concerned with the meticulous reproduction of rich costumes and jewellery than with interpretation of character—was typical of international court portraiture of the day.

Poussin, Gaspard. *See* DUGHET.

Poussin, Nicolas (1594–1665). French painter and draughtsman, active mainly in Rome. Although he spent almost all his career in Italy, he is regarded not only as the greatest French painter of the 17th century, but also as the mainspring of the *classical tradition in French painting. He was born in Les Andelys, Normandy, and his interest in art was given direction when Quentin Varin (c.1570–1634), a mediocre late *Mannerist painter, visited the town in 1611–12 to carry out a church commission. Soon afterwards Poussin moved to Paris, where he probably spent most of his time until his departure for Rome in 1623, although these years are poorly documented and he may have travelled around France a good deal. The only surviving works from this period that are certainly by him are a series of mythological drawings (1622–3, Royal Library, Windsor Castle) commissioned by the Italian poet Giovanni Battista Marino, who at this time lived in Paris. Encouraged by Marino, Poussin set out for Rome (he had already made two unsuccessful attempts to get there) and arrived in March 1624. Apart from an interlude in Paris in 1640–2, he lived in Rome for the rest of his life and his art was largely shaped by the cultural traditions of his adopted city.

Poussin initially endured hardship in Rome, but Marino's influence gained him an introduction to Cardinal Francesco *Barberini, for whom he painted the *Death of Germanicus* (1626–8, Minneapolis Inst. of Arts), generally regarded as his first masterpiece. The cardinal's secretary, Cassiano dal Pozzo (1588–1657), became Poussin's most important patron in Rome. He was not particularly wealthy, but he had a huge collection of prints and drawings relating to his passion for antiquity, and Poussin absorbed a great deal from this 'paper museum', as Pozzo called it. In the ancient world he found guiding moral principles as well as stylistic models—*Reynolds described him as having 'a mind thrown back two thousand years and, as it were, naturalized in antiquity'. In such an intellectual climate, his style began to shed an earlier tendency towards Mannerist elongation, becoming more classical, but for a time he was also influenced by the dynamic *Baroque style that was then emerging. This is seen most clearly in the only picture he painted for a public setting in Rome, the altarpiece of the *Martyrdom of St Erasmus*, commissioned by Cardinal Barberini for St Peter's (1628–9, Vatican Mus.). His most personal work of this period is the *Inspiration of the Poet* (c.1628, Louvre, Paris), classical in design but Venetian in its rich colouring.

In about 1629 Poussin became seriously ill (*Passeri says he was stricken by venereal disease) and was nursed back to health by the family of Jacques Dughet, a French cook working in Rome, whose daughter he married in 1630. The illness coincided with a change of direction in his work. He abandoned the competition for public commissions (his altarpiece for St Peter's had been coolly received) and henceforth concentrated on pictures of fairly modest size for private collectors whose interests were similar to his own (several of them were indeed his friends). In the early 1630s he specialized in literary subjects from Ovid and Tasso, treated with a lyrical warmth (*Rinaldo and Armida*, c.1630, Dulwich Picture Gal., London), and he also painted some full-blooded bacchanalian scenes. From the mid-1630s, however, he put more stress on clarity of design, and *Raphael replaced Titian as his chief inspiration among *Renaissance painters. In addition to his pagan subjects, he painted religious themes, and he seems to have been able to reconcile Christian beliefs with certain philosophical ideas of the ancient world, particularly the Stoical ideal that virtuous equanimity sustains a wise person in any misfortune. He lived a quiet, simple life, in spite of his growing success, and although he had been something of a hothead in his youth, he came to believe that 'peace and tranquillity of mind are possessions without equal.'

By the later 1630s Poussin had a high reputation in France as well as Italy, and in 1640 he reluctantly succumbed to official pressure and returned to Paris to work for Louis XIII. He was commissioned to superintend the decoration of the Grande Galerie of the *Louvre (work wholly alien to his temperament), to paint altarpieces, and to design frontispieces for the royal press. His visit was ruined by jealousy and intrigue, and in September 1642 he returned to sculptors. His preference for working in marble made the material popular again after it had long been eclipsed by bronze.

Precisionism. A movement in American painting, originating c.1915 and flourishing in the interwar period, particularly the 1920s, in which urban and especially industrial subjects were depicted with a very smooth and precise technique, creating clear, sharply defined, sometimes quasi-*Cubist forms. The terms 'Cubist-Realists', 'Immaculates', and 'Sterilists' have also been applied to Precisionist painters. They were not a formal group, but they often exhibited together. *Demuth, *O'Keeffe, and *Sheeler were among the leading figures. In Precisionist painting the light is typically brilliantly clear (although George Ault (1891–1948) was best known for his night scenes) and forms are often chosen for their geometric interest. Human presence is excluded and there is no social comment. Rather, the American industrial and technological scene is endowed with an air of epic grandeur. The degree of Cubist influence varied greatly. Some of Sheeler's paintings are in an almost photographically realistic style, whereas other works are semi-abstract. Precisionism was influential in both imagery and technique on American *Magic Realism and *Pop art.

predella. A small painting or series of paintings arranged horizontally beneath the main part of an *altarpiece. Predellas are most commonly found in Italian polyptychs of the 14th and 15th centuries.

Predis (or **Preda**), **Ambrogio de** (c.1455– after 1508). Milanese painter. He was court painter to Ludovico *Sforza and worked mainly as a portraitist, but he is chiefly remembered for his association with *Leonardo da Vinci, for whom he worked as assistant on the *Virgin of the Rocks* (NG, London). The wings of this altarpiece, depicting angels with musical instruments, are of much lower quality than the centre panel and are presumed to be by Ambrogio and/or his elder half-brother **Evangelista de Predis** (d. 1490/1). The National Gallery also has two portraits attributed to Ambrogia (one of them dated 1494), showing a rather wooden imitation of Leonardo's style.

Preece, Patricia. *See* SPENCER.

Prendergast, Maurice (1859–1924). Canadian-born American painter and printmaker. He was a member The *Eight, but stood somewhat apart from the rest of the group. Boston was his home for most of his life and he spent much of his career travelling and painting abroad; it was only in 1914 that he moved to New York, the centre of The Eight's activities. The main thing he had in common with other members was a desire to revive American art from academic stagnation, and his work is remarkable for its brilliant decorative colour. His paintings were often of people enjoying themselves in innocent pleasures (*Central Park in 1903*, 1903, Met. Mus., New York). He was one of the first American artists to be influenced by *Post-Impressionism, notably in the way in which he emphasized flat pattern. In 1913 he showed seven works in the *Armory Show and at this time he stood out as one of the most stylistically advanced American artists. Most of his paintings were in watercolour, but in later years he turned increasingly to oils. He also made about 200 *monotypes (mainly between 1891 and 1902), an unusually large oeuvre for this medium.

Pre-Raphaelite Brotherhood (PRB). The name adopted in 1848 by a group of young English artists who shared a dismay at what they considered the moribund state of British painting and hoped to recapture the sincerity and simplicity of early Italian art (i.e. before the time of *Raphael, whom they saw as the fountainhead of academism). The nucleus of the group was formed by three fellow students at the *Royal Academy—John Everett *Millais, William Holman *Hunt, and Dante Gabriel *Rossetti (to whom, son of an Italian ex-revolutionary, the sealing of the group into a secret Brotherhood was due). The other four original brethren were James *Collinson, the sculptor Thomas *Woolner, and the art critics W. M. Rossetti (1829–1919) and F. G. Stephens (1828–1907). Ford Madox *Brown was closely allied with them, though not at any time a member of the Brotherhood. The movement had a strong literary flavour from the start, and the members published a short-lived journal called *The Germ* (4 issues, 1850). They chose religious or other morally uplifting themes and had a desire for fidelity to nature that they expressed through detailed, rather literal-minded observation of flora, etc., and the use of a clear, bright, sharp-focus technique. The kind of pictures they hated were academic 'machines' and trivial *genre scenes. The initials PRB were first used on Rossetti's picture *The Girlhood of Mary Virgin* (Tate, London), exhibited in 1849, and were adopted by the other members of the Brotherhood. When their meaning became known in 1850 the group was subjected to furious criticism and abuse. Charles Dickens led the attack in his periodical *Household Words*, calling Millais's *Christ in the House of His Parents* (1849–50, Tate) 'mean, odious, revolting and repulsive'. He was outraged by the implied rejection of Raphael (still unquestioningly thought of by many critics as the greatest painter who ever lived), and he regarded the claim to go behind Raphael as an anti-progressive reversion to primitivism and ugliness. The fortunes of the Pre-Raphaelites improved after they were publicly defended by *Ruskin in 1851, and they attracted numerous followers, including *Deverell and *Hughes. By 1853, however, the group had virtually dissolved. Apart from their youthful revolutionary spirit (they were very young in 1848) and their romantic if uninformed medievalism, the prime movers had little in common as artists and they went their separate ways. Of the original members only Hunt remained true to PRB doctrines. Millais adopted a much looser style and went on to become the most popular and successful painter of the day. Curiously, however, it was Rossetti, the least committed to PRB ideals (he never cultivated painstaking detail), who continued the name. Although his later work, made up principally of languorous depictions of femmes fatales, is entirely different from his early Pre-Raphaelite pictures, the name stuck to him and to his followers such as *Burne-Jones and *Morris. Thus in the popular imagination the term 'Pre-Raphaelite' conjures up pictures of medieval romance, and ironically a movement that began as a rebellion against artificiality and sentimentality is now itself identified with a kind of escapism. This second wave of pseudo-medieval Pre-Raphaelitism began in the 1860s and survived into the 20th century, in the work, for example, of Evelyn *De Morgan.

Preti, Mattia (Il Cavaliere Calabrese) (1613–99). Italian *Baroque painter. He came from Taverna in Calabria (hence his nickname) and his prolific career took him to many different parts of Italy (and according to an early biographer to Spain and Flanders). His early work includes groups of musicians and card-players, strongly *Caravaggesque in style, but later he excelled mainly in frescos on religious subjects. In this field his main model was *Lanfranco, whom he succeeded in the decoration of S. Andrea della Valle in Rome (1650–1). After the plague of 1656 carried off virtually a whole generation of artists in Naples, Preti worked with great success there, gaining many important commissions. They included a series of seven frescos commemorating the plague for the city gates; they no longer survive, but two *modelli for them are in the Museo di Capodimonte in Naples and give some idea of how powerful the huge frescos must have been. In 1661 Preti moved to Malta, where he lived for the rest of his life. Several churches on the island, including the cathedral of Valletta, have decorations by him.

Primary Structures. A type of abstract sculpture that became fashionable in the mid-1960s, characterized by a preference for extremely simple geometrical shapes and frequently a use of industrially fabricated elements. The term was popularized by an exhibition entitled 'Primary Structures' at the Jewish Museum, New York, in 1966. Among the artists who worked in this vein were Carl *Andre, Donald *Judd, Sol *LeWitt, Robert *Morris, and Tony *Smith. Primary Structures comes within the scope of *Minimal art and the two terms have sometimes been used synonymously.

Primaticcio, Francesco (1504/5–70). Italian painter, architect, and decorator, mainly active in France. He was born in Bologna and developed his all-round skills as *Giulio Romano's assistant in Mantua. In 1532 he was called to France by Francis I and worked with *Rosso Fiorentino at Fontainebleau. Together they were mainly responsible for establishing the distinctive French type of *Mannerism associated with the School of *Fontainebleau. Their respective shares in the creation of the new manner—particularly the highly influential combination of paintings with *stucco ornament—

are uncertain. Rosso is often accorded primacy, but *Vasari said, 'the first works in stucco that were done in France, and the first labours in fresco of any account, had their origin, it is said, in Primaticcio'. His elongated figure style also had wide influence in France. Primaticcio took over the direction of the work at Fontainbleau on Rosso's death in 1540 and in the 1540s he twice visited Rome to buy antiquities or have casts made for Francis. In his later years he turned more to architecture.

priming. A coating applied to a canvas, panel, or other *support to prepare the surface for painting; more specifically, the final thin layer of this coating. In the broader sense, the term is synonymous with *ground.

primitive. Term used with various meanings in the history and criticism of the arts. In its widest sense it is applied to art of societies outside the great Western, Near Eastern, and Oriental civilizations, even though much of it was produced by highly sophisticated peoples. Pre-Columbian art, North American Indian art, African art south of the Sahara, and Oceanic art are the main areas embraced by the term. By extension it has been applied to other fields of art that appear unsophisticated relative to some particular standard. Thus the term was once widely used of pre-*Renaissance European painting, particularly of the Italian and Netherlandish schools, but this usage (as in the expression 'the Flemish primitives') is now much less common and no longer has derogatory implications. The term 'primitive' is also used more or less as a synonym for *naive.

In the context of modern art the term 'primitivism' refers to the use by Western artists of forms or imagery derived from the art of so-called primitive peoples (in the first sense mentioned above), especially those who had been colonized by Western countries. For centuries such art was valued mainly for its ethnographic interest or (in the case of articles made from precious materials) for its monetary worth. However, in the 1890s *Gauguin had tried to escape 'the disease of civilization' among the natives of Tahiti, and in the next generation many avant-garde artists followed his example in cultivating primitive art as a source of inspiration, finding in it a vitality and sincerity that they thought had been polished out of Western art. Usually they followed Gauguin in spirit rather than body, although *Nolde and *Pechstein, for example, visited Oceania. Many artists collected African works, notably *Picasso, and their influence is clear in his *Les Demoiselles d'Avignon*. Other artists studied primitive art in museums—Henry *Moore, for example, was impressed by the powerful block-like forms of Mayan sculpture he saw in the British Museum.

print. A picture or design made (usually on paper) from an inked impression of an engraved metal plate, wooden block, etc. Prints are made by a great variety of processes, but they fall into three main groups, depending on whether the ink is carried (a) on raised parts of the printing surface (relief methods), (b) in grooves made in the surface (intaglio methods), or (c) on the surface itself (planographic or surface methods). It is fairly common for different processes to be combined in one print, and in *Baxter prints, for example, intaglio and relief methods are used together.

(a) *Relief Methods*. In these, the parts of the wood block or metal plate that are to print black are left in relief and the remainder is cut away. The principal methods are *woodcut, *wood engraving, and *linocut. To these may be added certain techniques such as *metal cut, *manière criblée, and *relief etching, in which metal plates are engraved and printed like woodcuts.

(b) *Intaglio Methods*. In intaglio printing the principle is the reverse of that in the relief methods; the surface of the plate does not print, the ink being held only in the engraved furrows. The main techniques are: *line engraving, in which the design is engraved on the metal plate with a *burin; *drypoint, where the lines are drawn by scratching the plate with a strong steel needle; *etching, *softground etching, and *aquatint, where the designs are bitten into the plate by means of acid. In addition there are the mainly reproductive (and mainly defunct) processes of *mezzotint, *stipple engraving, and *crayon manner. The various intaglio processes have often been used in combination with one another on the same plate. *Rembrandt, for example, frequently combined etching and drypoint.

(c) *Planographic Methods*. In these the design is neither raised in relief or incised.

The main method is *lithography, in which the design is printed from a perfectly flat slab of limestone or a prepared metal plate. The process utilizes the antipathy of grease and water to separate those areas that receive and those areas that reject the printing ink. *Stencilling and *screenprinting are sometimes considered planographic methods, although they really form a separate category because the image is created through a barrier rather than printed from a surface.

The *monotype and the *glass print are traditionally grouped with prints, although the former is really a type of painting and the latter a type of photograph. The term 'print' is also more loosely applied to reproductions of works of art made by photomechanical methods.

Prix de Rome. A scholarship, founded concurrently with the French *Academy in Rome (1666), that enabled prizewinning students at the Académie Royale de Peinture et de Sculpture in Paris to spend a period (usually three to five years) in Rome at the state's expense, engaged in study and creative work. The award soon acquired great prestige and was regarded as a stepping stone to the highest honours. Competition rules were complex and they varied over the years, but as many as six painters and four sculptors might be staying as prizewinners in Rome at any one time (prizes for architects were added in the 18th century and for engravers and musicians in the 19th century). In some years, the Grand Prix was not awarded, as none of the entrants was thought good enough, but lesser prizewinners could still qualify to stay in Rome. The rules were sometimes bent: in 1752 *Fragonard won the Grand Prix even though he was not a student at the Académie. Unsuccessful competitors could try again: J.-L. *David won at the fifth attempt in 1774. After a hiatus during the French Revolution, the Prix de Rome continued under the auspices of the École des *Beaux-Arts, which effectively replaced the Académie, and it maintained its prestige well into the 19th century. However, in the 20th century it came to be regarded as a relic from another age and it was abolished in 1968. Similar scholarships have been awarded by other academies, including the *Royal Academy in London.

Procaccini, Giulio Cesare (1574–1625). Italian painter and sculptor, the most distinguished member of a family of artists. He was born in Bologna and worked mainly in Milan, where the family settled when he was a child, and also in Modena and Genoa. Early in his career he was primarily a sculptor, but after about 1600 he concentrated on painting and became one of the leading painters in Milan. His style was eclectic but often very powerful, combining something of the emotional tension of *Mannerism with the dynamism and sense of physical presence of the *Baroque. His colours tend to be acidic, his handling of light and shade dramatic. Many of his paintings are still in Milan, but two large scenes from Christ's Passion (perhaps part of a series) are in Edinburgh (NG) and Sheffield (Graves AG). His father, **Ercole** (1520–95), and his brothers, **Camillo** (c.1555–1629) and **Carlo Antonio** (1571–1630?), were also painters.

Procter, Dod and **Ernest**. *See* NEWLYN SCHOOL.

Prout, Samuel (1783–1852). English painter, best known for his watercolour views of *Picturesque buildings and streets in Normandy. Many of them appeared as engravings in illustrated books and they helped to build up the British *Romantic image of the Continent. His work was greatly admired by *Ruskin.

provenance. The record of the ownership of a movable work of art. An unbroken provenance accounts for the whereabouts of a work from the time of its creation to the present day, and the nearer a work's pedigree approaches this ideal, the more secure its attribution is likely to be.

Provost, Jan (c.1465–1529). Netherlandish painter, active mainly in Bruges, where he settled in 1494. He was perhaps a pupil of *Marmion, whose widow he married soon after the master's death in 1489. His style was fairly close to Gerard *David, then the leading painter in Bruges, but Provost, although clumsier, was more inventive. *Dürer was his guest when he visited Bruges in 1521.

Prud'hon, Pierre-Paul (1758–1823). French portrait and historical painter. His main training was at the Dijon Academy, from which he won a scholarship to Rome in 1784. He became a friend of *Canova there and formed his style on the example of the *sfumato and sensuous charm of *Leonardo and *Correggio. In 1788 he returned to Paris and after working in obscurity for some time he flourished under Napoleon, becoming a favourite of both his empresses, Josephine and Marie Louise. In addition to painting portraits of the imperial court (*Josephine at Malmaison*, 1805, Louvre, Paris), he designed decorations for important ceremonies, including Napoleon's marriage to Marie Louise in 1810. He remained in official favour after the fall of Napoleon in 1815, but he painted little in his final years. He had a neurotic personality and the shock of the suicide of his mistress—his pupil Constance Mayer—in 1821 hastened his own death. Among the leading French painters of his generation, Prud'hon was the most independent in spirit—the only one who did not fall under the dominant influence of J.-L. *David. He belongs to both the 18th and the 19th centuries. In his elegance, his grace, and his exquisite fancy he recalls the epoch of Louis XVI (David referred to him slightingly as 'the *Boucher of his time'), but his deep personal feeling aligns him with the *Romantics. *Gros said of him: 'He will bestride the two centuries with his seven league boots.' Among his best-known pictures are *Justice and Divine Vengeance Pursuing Crime* (1808, Louvre) and *Venus and Adonis* (1810–12, Wallace Coll., London). Prud'hon was one of the finest draughtsmen of his time (especially in his nude studies), typically working with black and white chalk on blue or grey paper. However, many of his paintings are in poor condition because of his use of *bitumen.

Pryde, James (1866–1941). British painter and designer. In the 1890s he designed posters with his brother-in-law William *Nicholson (as 'J. & W. *Beggarstaff') and these are probably his most famous works. Pryde sometimes supplemented his income at this time by taking small parts on the stage. As a painter he is best known for dramatic and sinister architectural views, with figures dwarfed by their gloomy surroundings. They have something of the spirit of *Piranesi's prison etchings, but they are broadly brushed. Pryde—'tall and handsome', but 'dilatory, extravagant, and unproductive for long periods' (*DNB*)—pro-

duced little after 1925. However, in 1930 he designed the sets for Paul Robeson's memorable *Othello* at the Savoy Theatre, London.

psalter. A manuscript (particularly one for liturgical use) or a printed book containing the text of the Psalms. It was the most popular type of *illuminated book from the 11th to the 14th century. Thereafter the *Book of Hours became the most important channel for illuminations.

Pucelle, Jean (d. 1334). French manuscript *illuminator. Little is known of his career, but his large workshop dominated Parisian painting in the first half of the 14th century. His work commanded high prices and—unusually for the time—his reputation endured after his death. Among the manuscripts attributed to him is the *Book of Hours of Queen Jeanne d'Evreux (1325–8, Met. Mus., New York). Certain features of his work—particularly his mastery of space—indicate that he probably travelled in Italy early in his career, and he was also familiar with Netherlandish developments.

Puget, Pierre (1620–94). The greatest French sculptor of the 17th century. He worked mainly in his native Marseilles and in Toulon, for although he sought success at court, his work was much too impassioned to fit into the scheme of *Le Brun's artistic dictatorship. Moreover, he was arrogant and headstrong in temperament and he fell victim to the intrigues of fellow artists. His *Baroque style was formed in Italy, where he worked from about 1638 to 1643; for part of this time he is said to have been an assistant to Pietro da *Cortona in Florence and Rome, presumably as a stuccoist. Subsequently he made several visits to Genoa, where he established a considerable reputation. His first major work was a pair of *atlas figures for the entrance to Toulon Town Hall (1656) and in these (now in the Musée Naval) he showed the physical vigour and emotional intensity that were the hallmarks of his style. These characteristics occur most memorably in his celebrated *Milo of Crotona* (1671–82, Louvre, Paris), which was one of his few works accepted for the palace at Versailles. Puget spent his final years embittered by his failures. He worked as a painter, architect, and decorator of ships as well as a sculptor, and he was an outstanding draughtsman. His son **François** (1651–1707) was a painter, working mainly in Toulon and Marseilles. He did a few religious works but was mainly a portraitist; his sitters included his father (Louvre).

Purism. A movement in French painting advocating an art of clarity and objectivity in tune with the machine age; its founders and sole exponents were Amédée *Ozenfant and *Le Corbusier, who met in Paris in 1918, and it flourished from then until 1925. Feeling that *Cubism—'the troubled art of a troubled time'—was degenerating into an art of decoration, they regarded their association as 'a campaign for the reconstitution of a healthy art', aiming to 'inoculate artists with the spirit of the age'. They set great store by 'the lessons inherent in the precision of machinery' and held that emotion and expressiveness should be strictly excluded from art, apart from the beauty of functional efficiency—the 'mathematical lyricism' that is the proper response to a well-composed picture. Their characteristic paintings are still lifes—cool, clear, almost diagrammatically flat, and impersonally finished. Despite the anti-emotionalism of this functionalist outlook, Ozenfant and Le Corbusier advocated Purism with missionary fervour and dogmatic certainty—in their book *Après le Cubisme* (1918) and other writings. However, they seemed to realize that it represented something of a dead end pictorially and moved on to much looser styles. The movement's main sequel is to be found in Le Corbusier's architectural work and theories and more generally in the field of design, where there is some kinship with the contemporary ideals of the *Bauhaus.

Purser, Sarah (1848–1943). Irish painter, designer, patron, collector, and administrator. She was a successful society portraitist, who in her own words 'went through the British aristocracy like the measles', but she is more important for her other roles in Irish art. She knew everyone who mattered (from 1911 she held regular social gatherings for Dublin's intelligentsia at her home, Mespil House) and in 1924 she founded the Friends of the National Collections of Ireland. One of its aims was to campaign for the return of Sir Hugh *Lane's pictures from London to Dublin and she helped to secure Charlemont House as the home for what

became the Hugh Lane Municipal Gallery of Modern Art. Perhaps most importantly, she was the founder of the stained-glass workshop An Túr Gloine (The Tower of Glass), which operated in Dublin from 1903 to 1944; the work it produced, which can be seen in so many Irish churches, is her finest memorial. With the exception of Harry *Clarke, most of the leading Irish stained-glass designers of the day worked there at one time or another, among them Evie *Hone.

putto (It.: 'little boy'). Term applied to a representation of a chubby, naked child, sometimes winged, appearing—usually as a subsidiary figure—in a work of art. Putti have been a frequent motif of decorative art since classical antiquity and may have a pagan, human, or divine status. They derived from a type of figure used in ancient art to represent Eros, the Greek god of love, and from the *Renaissance onwards a putto has often been used to represent his Roman counterpart, Cupid. More commonly, however, putti are anonymous figures, pictured attending classical gods, or, for example, the Virgin Mary.

Puvis de Chavannes, Pierre (1824–98). The foremost French mural painter of the second half of the 19th century. He decorated many public buildings in France (for example, the Panthéon, the Sorbonne, and the Hôtel de Ville, all in Paris) and also Boston Public Library (*Abbey and *Sargent did murals here too). His paintings were done on canvas and then affixed to the walls (*see* MAROUFLAGE), but their pale colours imitated the effect of *fresco. He had only modest success early in his career (when a private income enabled him to work for little payment), but he went on to achieve an enormous reputation, and he was respected even by artists of very different aims and outlook from his own. *Gauguin, *Seurat, and *Toulouse-Lautrec were among his professed admirers. His reputation has since declined, his idealized depictions of antiquity or allegorical representations of abstract themes now often seeming rather anaemic. He remains important, however, because of his influence on younger artists. His simplified forms, respect for the flatness of the picture surface, rhythmic line, and use of non-naturalistic colour to evoke the mood of the painting appealed to both the *Post-Impressionists and the *Symbolists. In addition to murals he produced easel paintings and pastels, and he was a prolific draughtsman. According to some accounts he was the father of *Utrillo.

Pyle, Howard. *See* PARRISH.

Pynacker, Adam (*c.*1620–73). Dutch landscape painter, active in Schiedam, near Rotterdam, and possibly in Delft before settling in Amsterdam in about 1661. According to *Houbraken he spent three years in Italy (perhaps *c.*1645–8) and he was one of the outstanding Dutch exponents of Italianate landscapes. His style resembles that of Jan *Both and Jan *Asselyn, but his mature work often has a distinctive and attractive silvery tonality. A splendid example of his

work, showing his ability to compose boldly on a large scale, is *Landscape with Sportsmen and Game* (*c.*1665, Dulwich Picture Gal., London), which features some unnaturally (but attractively) blue leaves, caused by yellow pigment fading in the greens.

Pynas, Jan (*c.*1582–1631) and **Jacob** (*c.*1592–1650?). Dutch painters, brothers. Jan visited Italy *c.*1605–7 (he was there at the same time as *Lastman) and again about ten years later. On stylistic grounds it is likely that Jacob too went there at some time. Both of them produced small-scale history paintings in the manner of *Elsheimer, and both of them usually signed their works 'J. Pynas', causing difficulties in differentiating their hands. *Rembrandt is said to have studied briefly with Jacob.

quadratura. A type of *illusionistic decoration in which architectural elements are painted on walls and/or ceilings in such a way that they appear to be an extension of the real architecture of the room into an imaginary space. It was common in Roman art, was revived by *Mantegna in the 15th century, and reached its peaks of elaboration in *Baroque Italy. The greatest of all exponents of *quadratura* was probably *Pozzo, in whose celebrated ceiling in S. Ignazio, Rome, architecture and figures surge towards the heavens with breathtaking bravura. Especially when applied to ceilings, *quadratura* demands formidable skill with perspective, for the painted architecture can all too easily look as if it is collapsing, and—unlike Pozzo—many artists relied on specialists called *quadraturisti* for this part of their work. Agostino *Tassi, for example, painted the architectural setting for *Guercino's famous *Aurora*, and Giambattista *Tiepolo worked much in collaboration with the brilliant *quadraturista* Gerolamo Mengozzi Colonna (*c*.1688–1766).

quadro riportato (It.: 'carried—or transferred—picture'). Term applied to a ceiling picture that is painted without *illusionistic foreshortening, as if it were to be viewed at normal eye level. *Mengs's *Parnassus* (1761) in the Villa Albani (now Villa Torlonia), Rome, is a famous example—a kind of *Neoclassical manifesto against *Baroque illusionism.

Quarton (or **Charonton**), **Enguerrand** (d. 1466?). French painter, active in Provence. His career is unusually well documented for a provincial artist of his date: he worked in Aix, Arles, and Avignon, and there are various records of him dating from 1444 to 1466, in which year he perhaps died in an outbreak of the plague in Provence. However, there are only two extant works that are certainly by him: the *Virgin of Mercy* (1452) in the Musée Condé at Chantilly, painted in collaboration with an obscure artist called Pierre Villatte, and the *Coronation of the Virgin* (1454) in the Musée Municipal at Villeneuve-lès-Avignon. They are highly impressive works, uniting Flemish and Italian influence whilst having something of the monumental character of the sculpture of Quarton's region. Indeed, they show Quarton to have been a painter of such commanding stature that there is an increasing tendency to attribute to him the celebrated *Avignon Pietà* (*c*.1460, Louvre, Paris), the greatest French painting of the period (*see* AVIGNON, SCHOOL OF). Several *illuminated manuscripts have also been attributed to Quarton.

quattrocento. Term (literally 'four hundred') applied to the 15th century (the 1400s) in Italian art. It can be used as a noun ('painting of the quattrocento') or as an adjective ('quattrocento sculpture'). Terms used in the same way for other centuries are: dugento (or duecento) for the 13th century; trecento for the 14th century; cinquecento for the 16th century; seicento for the 17th century; settecento for the 18th century; ottocento for the 19th century; and novecento for the 20th century.

Quellin (or **Quellinus**), **Artus I** (**Arnoldus**) (1609–68). Flemish sculptor, the most distinguished member of a family of artists. He was born in Antwerp, where he trained with his father, **Erasmus I** (*c*.1584–1640). In 1634 he moved to Rome, where he worked in the studio of François *Duquesnoy. He was back in Antwerp in 1639, and by 1648 he had moved to Amsterdam, where from *c*.1650 to 1664 he directed the sumptuous sculptural decoration of the new town hall (now royal palace). His dignified style was singularly appropriate for van *Campen's great building, and the decoration forms the most impressive sculptural ensemble of the time in northern Europe. Quellin also produced tomb sculpture and portrait busts. His collaborators at Amsterdam town hall included his cousin, **Artus II Quellin** (1625–1700), whose independent work was more *Baroque in style. The commanding figure of *God the Father* (1682) adorning the rood screen in Bruges Cathedral is perhaps his finest work. **Artus III Quellin** (1653–86), usually called Arnold, son of Artus II, settled in England in about 1680. By 1684 he was working with Grinling *Gibbons, and the drop in quality of Gibbons's large-scale figure work (not his forte) after Quellin's death indicates that the latter was probably the dominant personality in producing such fine statues as the bronze *James II* (1686) outside the National Gallery in Trafalgar Square. Quellin's outstanding independent work is the tomb of Thomas Thynne (1682, Westminster Abbey), which features a *relief of Thynne's murder in his coach in Pall Mall. Other members of the Quellin family included Artus I's two brothers, **Erasmus II** (1607–78), a painter who often collaborated with *Rubens, and **Hubert** (1619?–87), an engraver who produced numerous prints after works by his relatives.

Quercia, Jacopo della (*c*.1374–1438). The greatest sculptor of the Sienese School, the son of an undistinguished goldsmith and woodcarver, **Piero di Angelo** (Quercia, from which Jacopo takes his name, is a district of Siena). Like his father, he carved in wood and also worked in bronze, but marble was his preferred material. He was one of the outstanding figures of his generation in Italian sculpture, the only non-Florentine who can be mentioned in the same breath as *Donatello and *Ghiberti, but his career is difficult to follow, as he worked in numerous places and sometimes left one commission unfinished while he took up another elsewhere. Contrary to *Vasari's assertion that he led a 'well-ordered life', he seems to have been inveterately dilatory. He is first firmly documented in 1401, unsuccessfully competing for the commission (won by Ghiberti) for the Baptistery doors in Florence. His first surviving works are generally agreed to be a marble statue of the Virgin and Child, commissioned in 1403 for Ferrara Cathedral (now Cathedral Mus.), and the tomb of Ilaria del Carretto, wife of the ruler of Lucca, Paolo Guinigi (*c*.1406, Lucca Cathedral), which was eulogized by *Ruskin. There are Renaissance *putti and swags round the base of the tomb, but the serene and graceful effigy is in the northern manner and suggests that Jacopo had knowledge of work done in the circle of Claus *Sluter in Burgundy. His major work for his native city was a fountain called the *Fonte Gaia* (commissioned in 1408, executed in 1414–19), which is now—much damaged—in the loggia of the Palazzo Pubblico (a copy stands in the Piazza del Campo, where the original was first located). Its *relief carvings include some beautifully draped female figures and a terribly battered but still awesomely powerful panel of the *Expulsion from Paradise*. Between 1417 and 1430 Jacopo worked on reliefs for the font in the Baptistery at Siena (Donatello and Ghiberti were also involved in this commission), and in 1425 he began his last great work (left unfinished at his death), the sculptural decoration of the main doorway of S. Petronio, Bologna. The principal feature of the doorway is a series of relief panels with subjects taken from Genesis and the Nativity of Christ. The figures—usually only two or three to a relief, in contrast to the crowded panels of Ghiberti—have a directness and strength that won the admiration of *Michelangelo, who visited Bologna in 1494. Several of the motifs are to be found, reinterpreted, on the Sistine Ceiling.

Quinn, Marc. *See* YOUNG BRITISH ARTISTS.

R

Rackham, Arthur (1867–1939). British illustrator, celebrated for his work in children's books. He established his reputation with *Fairy Tales of the Brothers Grimm*, published in 1900, and from then until the First World War he had his golden period, when Edmund *Dulac was his only serious rival in his field. They were very different in style. Dulac was much more painterly, using strong expressive colour, whereas Rackham relied on wiry line and subtle, muted colour. He said he believed in 'the greatest stimulating and educative power of imaginative, fantastic and playful pictures and writings for children in their most impressionable years', and he worked in a striking vein of Nordic fantasy, creating a bizarre world populated by goblins, fairies, and weird creatures (he looked rather like a gnome himself). After the First World War the market for expensive children's books declined, but he continued to prosper from gallery sales of his work.

Raeburn, Sir Henry (1756–1823). The leading Scottish portrait painter of his period, active mainly in his native Edinburgh. On leaving school he was apprenticed to a goldsmith and he appears to have been largely self-taught as a painter. In 1784–6 he visited Italy (going via London, where he is said to have met *Reynolds), but his distinctive style was already formed by this time—one of his finest works, the *Revd Robert Walker Skating* (NG, Edinburgh), is traditionally said to date from 1784. He painted directly on to the canvas without preliminary drawings, and his vigorous, bold handling—sometimes called his 'square touch'—could be extraordinarily effective in conveying the character of rugged Highland chiefs or bluff legal worthies. He also had a penchant for vivid and original lighting effects (*William Glendonwyn*, *c*.1795, Fitzwilliam Mus., Cambridge) and could be remarkably sensitive when painting women (*Isabella McLeod, Mrs James Gregory*, *c*.1798, Fyvie Castle, Aberdeenshire, NT). At times, however, his technical facility degenerated into empty virtuosity. In 1822, on the occasion of George IV's visit to Edinburgh, he was knighted and appointed His Majesty's *Limner for Scotland. Since he had all the sitters he needed in Scotland, there was no need for him to compete with *Lawrence and *Hoppner in London (although he did consider moving there after Hoppner's death in 1810), and in the history of British portraiture he is an isolated and perhaps underrated figure.

Raffaellino del Garbo. *See* ANDREA DEL SARTO.

Raggi, Antonio. *See* GAULLI.

Raimondi, Marcantonio (*c*.1480–1527/ 34). Italian engraver, a pioneer in the use of prints to reproduce the work of other artists. He was born near Bologna, studied there with *Francia, and from about 1506 to 1508 lived in Venice, where he learned much from *Dürer's engravings (Dürer, indeed, brought legal proceedings against him for plagiarism). In about 1510 he settled in Rome, and thereafter worked mainly for *Raphael, his engravings helping to spread the master's style throughout Europe. Apart from his association with Raphael, Raimondi is best known for a series of erotic engravings (after designs by *Giulio Romano) that led to his imprisonment in 1524. He left Rome after the Sack of 1527 and died in obscurity.

Rainer (or **Renier**) **of Huy.** *Mosan metalworker active in the early 12th century. Nothing is known of his life, but in a 14th-century chronicle he is credited with one of the great masterpieces of his period—a bronze font (1107–18) originally made for Notre-Dame des Fonts, Liège, and now in St Bartholomew, Liège. It is a large bowl supported on ten (originally twelve) oxen (a reference to the 'sea of cast metal ... mounted on twelve oxen' made for King Solomon (1 Kings 7: 23–5)) and adorned with scenes appropriate to the sacrament of baptism. The figures are much more naturalistic and classical than in most *Romanesque art. Very little other work can be attributed to Rainer or his workshop, but his masterpiece had great influence on Mosan art. It has recently been suggested, however, that he is more or less a mythical figure and that the font was made in the imperial foundry in Constantinople.

Ramos, Mel (1935–). American painter. Ramos is usually described as a *Pop artist, but his smooth, impersonal handling (in oils and watercolour) brings him also within the orbit of *Superrealism. He specializes in paintings of nude women of the calendar pin-up or 'playmate' type. Sometimes they are posed with oversized products such as pieces of cheese and sometimes they allude to the work of leading painters of the past (more rarely the present). The jokey quality of his work is reflected in his titles: two typical series are 'You Get More Spaghetti with Giacometti' and 'You Get More Salami with Modigliani'.

Ramsay, Allan (1713–84). Scottish painter, active mainly in London, where he was the outstanding portraitist from about 1740 to the rise of *Reynolds in the mid-1750s. He studied in Edinburgh and London, and then from 1736 to 1738 in Italy (including a period with *Solimena in Naples), and when he returned to London he brought a cosmopolitan air to British portraiture. His pictures of women have a decidedly French grace (*The Artist's Wife*, *c*.1755, NG, Edinburgh) and in this field he continued to be a serious rival to Reynolds. He was preferred to Reynolds by the royal family and in 1767 was appointed principal painter to George III. However, after injuring his right arm in an accident in 1773 he gave up painting (although his studio continued to produce replicas of royal portraits) and devoted himself to his other interests. He was the son of the poet Allan Ramsay, and he inherited his father's literary inclinations. Political pamphleteering, classical archaeology (he revisited Rome in 1754–7 and 1775–7), and conversation took up much of his later years. He was a prominent figure in literary circles and Samuel Johnson said of him: 'You will not find a man in whose conversation there is more instruction, more information, and more elegance.'

Ranson, Paul. *See* ACADÉMIE.

Raphael (Raffaello Santi) (1483–1520). Italian painter, draughtsman, architect, and designer, the artist who most completely expresses the ideals of the High *Renaissance. He was born in Urbino, the son of the painter and writer Giovanni *Santi, through whom he must have gained early familiarity with the humanist court of Federico da *Montefeltro. This cultured background stood him in good stead throughout his career, for unlike many artists he was renowned for his social poise. *Vasari says that 'Raphael came to be of great help to his father in the numerous works that Giovanni executed in the state of Urbino', but Santi died in 1494, when Raphael was only 11, and the overwhelming influence on his early work was *Perugino. He took from him not only general qualities such as sweetness of expression and elegance of drawing, but also such characteristic details as daintily crooked little fingers and wispy background trees. According to Vasari, Raphael was Perugino's pupil, but this is perhaps not strictly true. He was highly precocious and working as an independent artist by 1500; his close contact with Perugino seems to have come a little later (*c*.1502–3), when he was probably his colleague rather than assistant. By the time he was 21 he had already outstripped Perugino, as is clearly seen by comparing Raphael's *Marriage of the Virgin* (1504, Brera, Milan) with Perugino's slightly earlier painting of the same subject (Mus. B.-A., Caen). The two compositions are closely similar in many ways, but Raphael far surpasses Perugino in lucidity and grace.

In his early career Raphael had commissions from various places in Umbria. From 1504 to 1508 he spent much of his time in Florence, and these years are usually referred to as his Florentine period, although he never took up permanent residence in the city. The experience of Florence greatly affected his art: he moved away from Perugino's manner and his work became grander and more sophisticated under the inspiration of *Leonardo, *Michelangelo, and also Fra *Bartolommeo (whose 'pleasing manner of colouring' is cited by Vasari as an influence). To this period belong some of Raphael's most celebrated depictions of the Virgin and Child (*Madonna of the Meadow*, 1505, KH Mus., Vienna). In these and his paintings of the Holy Family he showed his developing mastery of composition and expression (from Leonardo he particularly learned how to group figures fluently and compactly). He paints the sacred figures as splendid, healthy human beings, but with a serenity, a sense of some deep inner integrity, that removes any doubt as to the holiness of the subject. This sense of well-being distinguishes the art of Raphael from the more disturbingly intellectual work of Leonardo or the overwhelmingly powerful creations of Michelangelo, and evidently reflects his own balanced nature. Unlike his two great contemporaries, he was not a solitary genius but a sociable and approachable figure, whom Vasari describes as 'so gentle and so charitable that even animals loved him'. He must, however, have had considerable toughness to produce the large amount of work he did in a short lifetime.

In 1508, Raphael moved to Rome, where Pope Julius II (Giuliano della *Rovere) entrusted him with the fresco decoration of the Stanza della Segnatura, one of a suite of rooms he was having remodelled in the Vatican. It is not known how Raphael (still only 25) came to the attention of the pope, but he was perhaps recommended by *Bramante, who was a distant relative. Raphael had never before worked on a project of such size and prestige and he had little experience in fresco, but he fulfilled the commission triumphantly and he spent most of the rest of his career in the service of Julius and his successor Leo X (Giovanni de' *Medici). The Stanza della Segnatura was probably used by Julius as his private library and its decoration is based on a complex theological programme concerning the relationship between classical learning and Christian thought. On one main wall, in the celebrated painting known as The School of Athens, are shown the great thinkers of the ancient world, led by Plato and Aristotle, arranged in a majestic architectural setting, a masterpiece of *perspective drawing. Opposite, in the painting called the Disputà (the Disputation over the Sacrament), the doctors of the church adore the Sacrament, while above them the Trinity is surrounded by the saints and martyrs. After the completion of the Stanza della Segnatura in 1511 or 1512 Raphael was entrusted with decorating three adjacent rooms in the Vatican, but by the time he had completed the first of these—the Stanza d'Eliodoro—in 1514, his services were so much in demand that he had to leave the execution of his work in-

creasingly to assistants (of whom *Giulio Romano was the most distinguished). The *cartoons for tapestries of the Acts of the Apostles for the Sistine Chapel (1515–16, Royal Coll., on loan to V&A, London), for example, rank among his noblest designs, but probably little of the actual brushwork is from his own hand. In the Stanze and the cartoons Raphael showed a prodigious ability to arrange groups of varied figures into grandly harmonious compositions and—like Michelangelo's Sistine Ceiling—these works have had a profound and enduring influence on the whole European tradition of *history painting.

Apart from Julius II and Leo X, Raphael's most important patron in Rome was the enormously wealthy Agostino *Chigi. Raphael's work for him included fresco decoration at his villa (now known as the Villa Farnesina), just outside the city walls of Rome, and the design of his burial chapel in the church of S. Maria del Popolo. Most of the work at the Farnesina was carried out by assistants, but the celebrated Galatea (c.1512) was painted by Raphael himself. For the Chigi Chapel (begun c.1512) he designed the entire scheme, comprising architecture, sculpture, painting, mosaic, stuccowork, and marble inlay. The richness of effect was an important source for similar works in the *Baroque era, and it is fitting that the chapel (left unfinished when Chigi and Raphael died within a week of each other in 1520) was completed by *Bernini. In addition to his great decorative schemes, Raphael painted many portraits and it is in these that the quality of his own workmanship in his later years is best seen. They rival Leonardo in subtlety of characterization and *Titian in richness of colouring, show great inventiveness in creating psychological situations, and provide a remarkable record of the intellectual circles in which he moved (Baldassare Castiglione, c.1515, Louvre, Paris). His portrait of Julius II (1511, NG, London) established a type for papal portraits that endured for about two centuries. Other important works from his Roman period that are largely from his own hand are the Sistine Madonna (c.1512–14, Gemäldegalerie, Dresden), his most famous painting of the Virgin and Child, and the great altarpiece of the Transfiguration (Pinacoteca, Vatican), on which he was working at his death, and which—in its agitated movement and emotion—is regarded as one of the well-springs of the Mannerist style. From about 1512 he began to work as an architect, and after the death of Bramante in 1514 he was placed in charge of the rebuilding of St Peter's. Raphael ranks second only to him among High Renaissance architects, but it is difficult to appreciate his status, as little of his work survives as he designed it. His huge workload increased further in 1517 when Leo X appointed him Rome's superintendent of antiquities, in which capacity he planned a detailed survey of the city's ancient monuments.

Vasari says that Raphael's early death from fever (on his thirty-seventh birthday) 'plunged the entire papal court into grief'. He was rich, famous, and honoured, and his influence was widely spread even during his own lifetime through the engravings of Marcantonio *Raimondi. His posthumous reputation was even greater, for until well into the 19th century he was regarded by almost all critics as the greatest painter who had ever lived—the artist who expressed the basic doctrines of the Christian Church through figures that have a physical beauty worthy of the *antique. He became the ideal of all *academies and *Reynolds said of him: 'It is from his having taken so many models that he became himself a model for all succeeding painters: always imitating and always original.' In the later 19th century and particularly the 20th century there was a reaction against such adulation. The modern world likes its artistic heroes to show human frailties and preferably to be eccentrics or rebels, and Raphael—with his obliging personality, efficient management skills, and career of unbroken success—is completely lacking in this kind of appeal. Nevertheless, although his reputation is slightly less exalted than it once was, he remains one of the brightest beacons of European art.

Ratcliffe, William. *See* CAMDEN TOWN GROUP.

Ratgeb, Jörg (*c*.1480–1526). German painter, active in Swabia. His few surviving paintings show him to have been closer in spirit to *Grünewald than practically any of his contemporaries. The most important is the Herrenberg Altarpiece (1519, Staatsgalerie, Stuttgart), which has some harrowing Passion scenes. Ratgeb himself met a grue-some end—executed at Pforzheim for his part in the Peasants' Revolt.

Rauschenberg, Robert (1925–). American painter, printmaker, designer, and experimental artist. With his friend Jasper *Johns, whom he met in 1954, he is regarded as one of the most influential figures in the move away from the *Abstract Expressionism that had dominated American art in the late 1940s and early 1950s. He studied at various art schools, most notably *Black Mountain College. In the mid-1950s he began to incorporate three-dimensional objects into what he called *'combine paintings'. The best-known example is probably *Monogram* (1955–9, Moderna Museet, Stockholm), which features a stuffed goat with a rubber tyre around its middle, splashed with paint in a manner recalling *Action Painting. Other objects he used included Coca-Cola bottles, fragments of clothing, electric fans, and radios, and because of his preoccupation with such consumer products he has been hailed as one of the pioneers of *Pop art. In 1958 he had a one-man show at Leo *Castelli's gallery and from this time his career began to take off. By the early 1960s he was building up an international reputation, and in 1964 he was awarded the Grand Prize at the Venice *Biennale. This caused great controversy, the Vatican newspaper *L'osservatore romano* describing the award as 'the total and general defeat of culture'. In the 1960s Rauschenberg returned to working on a flat surface and was particularly active in the medium of *screenprinting. He has been interested in combining art with new technological developments and in 1966 he helped to form EAT (Experiments in Art and Technology), an organization to help artists and engineers work together. In 1985 he launched Rauschenberg Overseas Cultural Interchange (ROCI), an exhibition dedicated to world peace that toured the world and included works created specifically for each place visited.

Raverat, Gwen (1885–1957). British printmaker, theatre designer, painter, and writer, born in Cambridge, the daughter of Sir George Darwin, professor of astronomy, and granddaughter of Charles Darwin. She studied at the *Slade School, but was mainly self-taught in wood engraving, which was her primary activity. Her best-known works are her book illustrations, notably of collections of poems by her cousin Frances Cornford. Her style was bold and vigorous and she was uninterested in technical virtuosity. Although she was art critic for *Time and Tide* from 1928 to 1939, she did not consider herself a writer and was surprised at the success of *Period Piece* (1952), an account of her childhood with her own illustrations, which became a bestseller on both sides of the Atlantic.

Ravilious, Eric (1903–42). British watercolour painter, printmaker, and designer. In addition to paintings, his highly varied output included book illustrations and book-jackets, and designs for furniture, glass, textiles, and the Wedgwood pottery factory (notably a mug commemorating Edward VIII's coronation; this was withdrawn following Edward's abdication, but the design was used in revised form for the coronations of George VI and Elizabeth II). He was one of the outstanding wood engravers of his time, his book illustrations in this medium making striking use of bold tonal contrasts and complex patterning. In 1940–2 he was an *Official War Artist, and he produced some memorable watercolours of naval scenes off Norway (*Norway, 1940*, Laing AG, Newcastle upon Tyne). His plane disappeared on a flying patrol near Iceland, in 1942, and he was officially presumed dead the following year.

Ray, Man. *See* MAN RAY.

Rayonism (Russ., 'Luchism'). A type of abstract or semi-abstract painting practised by the Russian artists *Goncharova and *Larionov and a few followers from about 1912 to 1914 and representing their own adaptation of *Futurism. Rayonism was launched at the *Target Exhibition in Moscow in 1913. In the same year Larionov published a manifesto on the subject, stating that 'Rayonism is a synthesis of *Cubism, Futurism and *Orphism', and Rayonist pictures do indeed combine something of the fragmentation or splintering of form of Cubism, the dynamic movement of Futurism, and the colour of Orphism. The style was bound up with a very unclear theory of invisible rays, in some ways analogous to the 'lines of force' that were postulated by the Futurists. In early Rayonist paintings an underlying subject is broken up into bundles of slanting

lines, but in later ones the lines take over the picture completely, so that there is no discernible naturalistic starting point and the work becomes completely abstract. Rayonism was short-lived, as both Goncharova and Larionov virtually abandoned easel painting after they left Russia in 1915 and they had no significant followers.

Read, Sir Herbert (1893–1968). British poet and critic, who throughout the middle third of the 20th century was virtually unchallenged as his country's foremost advocate and interpreter of modern art. After serving with distinction in the army in the First World War he worked at the Treasury, then in the ceramics department of the Victoria and Albert Museum, 1922–31, before becoming professor of fine arts at Edinburgh University, 1931–3. By this time he had published several collections of his verse as well as various art-historical studies (including *English Stained Glass*, 1926, still a standard work), critical works on English literature, and the first of his philosophical works on art, *The Meaning of Art* (1931). In 1933 he returned to London as editor (1933–9) of the *Burlington Magazine*, Britain's foremost scholarly art journal, and his attention turned increasingly to contemporary art: in 1933 he published *Art Now*, the first comprehensive defence in English of modern European art, and in 1934 he edited the modernist manifesto *Unit One*. At this time he lived near Henry *Moore, Barbara *Hepworth, and Ben *Nicholson, and he acted as the public mouthpiece of the group of artists of which they were the centre. He was interested in *Surrealism as well as abstraction and was one of the organizers of the 1936 International Surrealist Exhibition in London. In 1947 he was co-founder (with Roland *Penrose) of the *Institute of Contemporary Arts in London. Among his many books the most influential was probably *Education through Art* (1943), which used the insights of psychoanalysis to promote the idea of teaching art as an aid to the development of the personality. His other books include *A Concise History of Modern Painting* (1959) and *A Concise History of Modern Sculpture* (1964), both of which have been frequently reprinted. By the time he wrote them he was becoming disenchanted with contemporary artistic developments, but he was known as 'The Pope of Modern Art' and was regarded as 'an international authority and indeed something of a sage. It was not a role to which he ever pretended, for he was a man of conspicuous modesty' (*DNB*).

Read, Nicholas. *See* ROUBILIAC.

ready-made. A name given by Marcel *Duchamp to a type of work he invented consisting of a mass-produced article isolated from its functional context and displayed as a work of art. His first ready-made (1913) was a bicycle wheel, which he mounted on a kitchen stool. Strictly speaking, this was a 'ready-made assisted', but other 'pure' ready-mades soon followed, notably *Bottle Rack* (1914), *In Advance of the Broken Arm* (a snow shovel, 1915), and the celebrated *Fountain* (1917), consisting of a urinal which he signed 'R. Mutt' (the name of a firm manufacturing sanitary ware); most of the originals have disappeared, but several replicas exist. The ready-made can be considered a type of *objet trouvé (found object), although Duchamp himself made a clear distinction between them, pointing out that whereas the objet trouvé is discovered and chosen because of its interesting aesthetic qualities, its beauty and uniqueness, the ready-made is one—any one—of a large number of indistinguishable mass-produced objects. Therefore the objet trouvé implies the exercise of taste in its selection, but the ready-made does not. In creating such works he demonstrated his belief in the absurdity of life and aesthetic values. The ready-made was one of *Dada's most enduring legacies to modern art. It was much used in *Pop art, for example, and Robert *Rauschenberg called *Bicycle Wheel* 'one of the most beautiful pieces of sculpture I've ever seen'.

realism. Term used with various meanings in the history and criticism of the arts. In its broadest sense the word is used as vaguely as *naturalism, implying a desire to depict things accurately and objectively. Often, however, the term carries with it the suggestion of the rejection of conventionally beautiful subjects, or of idealization, in favour of a more down-to-earth approach, often with a stress on low life or the activities of the common man. In a more specific sense, the term (usually spelled with a capital R) is applied to a movement in 19th-century (particularly French) art characterized by a rebellion against the traditional historical,

mythological, and religious subjects in favour of unidealized scenes of modern life. The leader of the Realist movement was *Courbet, who said, 'painting is essentially a concrete art and must be applied to real and existing things'. The term *Social Realism has been applied to 19th- and 20th-century works that are realistic in this second sense and make overt social or political comment. It is to be distinguished from *Socialist Realism, the name given to the type of art that was officially promoted in the Soviet Union and some other Communist countries; far from implying a critical approach to social questions, it involved toeing the Party line in an academic style. *Magic Realism and *Superrealism are names given to two 20th-century styles in which extreme realism—in the sense of acute attention to detail—produces a markedly unrealistic overall effect. Since the 1950s the term 'realism' has also been used in a completely different way, describing certain types of art that eschew conventional illusionism. This usage is found mainly in the terms *New Realism and *Nouveau Réalisme, which have been applied to works made of materials or objects that are presented for exactly what they are and are known to be. *See also* VERISM.

Recco, Giuseppe (1634–95). Neapolitan still-life painter, the outstanding member of a family of artists. He is best known for pictures of fish, painted in an impressively grand style, but more austere than those of *Ruoppolo, with whom he ranks as the most distinguished Italian still-life painter of his period.

red-figure vase painting. One of the two major divisions of Greek vase painting, the other being *black-figure. In the red-figure technique, the background was painted black, leaving the figures in the unpainted red colour of the pottery. Details of the figure could thus be added with a brush rather than incised through the black paint, allowing much greater flexibility and subtlety of treatment. Because of this advantage the red-figure technique, which developed in Athens from about 530 BC, gradually superseded the black-figure technique.

Redgrave, Richard (1804–88). English painter, writer, and art administrator. He began as a painter of anecdotal literary subjects, often in 18th-century costume, but in the 1840s he became a pioneer of scenes of contemporary social concern (*The Poor Teacher*, 1845, Shipley AG, Gateshead). 'It is one of my most gratifying feelings', he wrote, 'that many of my best efforts in art have aimed at calling attention to the trials and struggles of the poor and the oppressed.' Much of his later career was taken up with administration—the posts he held included Surveyor of the Queen's Pictures and keeper of pictures at the South Kensington (later Victoria and Albert) Museum—and as a painter he turned mainly to landscapes done in his spare time. His brother, **Samuel Redgrave** (1802–76), was a writer on art, the author of a still-useful *Dictionary of Artists of the English School* (1874). The brothers collaborated on *A Century of Painters of the English School* (1866), a valuable source of information on 18th- and 19th-century British artists, many of whom they knew personally.

Redon, Odilon (1840–1916). French painter, draughtsman, and printmaker, one of the outstanding figures of *Symbolism. He led a retiring life, first in his native Bordeaux, then from 1870 in Paris, and until he was in his fifties he worked almost exclusively in black and white—in charcoal drawings and lithographs. In these he developed a highly distinctive repertoire of weird subjects—strange amoeboid creatures, insects, and plants with human heads and so on, influenced by the writings of Edgar Allen Poe. He remained virtually unknown to the public until the publication of J. K. Huysmans's celebrated novel *A rebours* in 1884; the book's hero, a disenchanted aristocrat who lives in a private world of perverse delights, collects Redon's drawings, and with his mention in this classic expression of decadence, Redon too became a figurehead of the movement. During the 1890s he turned to painting and revealed remarkable powers as a colourist that had previously lain dormant. Much of his early life had been unhappy, but after undergoing a religious crisis in the early 1890s and a serious illness in 1894–5, he was transformed into a much more buoyant and cheerful personality, expressing himself in radiant colours in visionary subjects, flower paintings, and mythological scenes (the Chariot of Apollo was one of his favourite themes). He showed

equal facility in oils and pastel and after 1900 he carried out a number of large decorative schemes. His flower pieces, in particular, were much admired by *Matisse, and the *Surrealists regarded Redon as one of their precursors. By the end of his life he was a distinguished figure, although still a very private person.

Redouté, Pierre-Joseph (1759–1840). French botanical illustrator of Flemish birth, the best-known member of a family of artists. He settled in Paris in 1782 and throughout his career he successfully negotiated France's varied political upheavals, becoming official flower painter in turn to Queen Marie Antoinette, both Napoleon's empresses (Josephine and Marie Louise), and Queen Marie Amélie (wife of King Louis Philippe). His large output included black-and-white illustrations for serious scientific treatises, but he is best known for lavish colour plates in deluxe books, notably *Les Roses* (1817–24). He was highly extravagant and died in debt in spite of his successful career.

Regionalism. A movement in American painting, flourishing chiefly in the 1930s, concerned with the depiction of scenes and types from the American Midwest. The term is often used more or less interchangeably with *American Scene Painting, but Regionalism can be more precisely thought of as the Midwestern branch of this broader category. Like all American Scene Painters, the Regionalists were motivated by a patriotic desire to establish a genuinely American art by using local themes and repudiating avant-garde styles from Europe. Specifically they were moved by a nostalgic desire to glorify, or at least to record, rural and small-town America, and it was on this that their widespread popularity depended. The period when they flourished coincided with the Great Depression, and at this time of profound national doubt, they reasserted America's faith in itself, giving the public pictures with which they could readily identify. Their work was often produced under the auspices of the *Federal Art Project and it was supported by the fanatically patriotic critic Thomas Craven. The three major Regionalists were Thomas Hart *Benton, John Steuart *Curry, and Grant *Wood, who were all Midwesterners but differed greatly in temperament and style. They scarcely knew one another personally, but the idea of a group identity was skilfully promoted by Maynard Walker, a Kansas art dealer. Walker got a Benton self-portrait on to the cover of the Christmas 1934 issue of *Time* magazine and this largely created the image of Regionalism in the public eye; as Benton put it, 'A play was written and a stage erected for us. Grant Wood became the typical Iowa small towner, John Curry the typical Kansas farmer, and I just an Ozark hillbilly. We accepted our roles.' On the fringes of the Regionalist movement were Charles *Burchfield and Ben *Shahn. Burchfield's work has a streak of fantasy absent from that of the others, and Shahn was driven by a spirit of social protest. Specifically local styles did not develop anywhere and Regionalism died out in the 1940s in the more international spirit that prevailed during and after the Second World War.

Rego, Paula (1935–). Portuguese-born British painter of figure, animal, and fantasy subjects. She studied at the *Slade School, where she met her husband, the painter Victor Willing (1928–88). In the 1980s Rego became well known for her enigmatic figurative paintings, which often have a feeling of caricature as well as of fantasy. In 1990 she was appointed the first associate artist of the National Gallery, London. She painted murals in the restaurant of the gallery's new Sainsbury Wing in 1991, and in 1992 she became the first living artist to be given an exhibition in the gallery.

Reinhardt, Ad (1913–67). American painter. From the beginning of his career his painting was abstract, but it changed radically in style over the years. During the 1930s he worked in a crisp, boldly contoured geometrical style that owed something to both *Cubism and to the *Neo-Plasticism of *Mondrian. In the 1940s he passed through a phase of *all-over painting which has been likened to that of Mark *Tobey, and in the late 1940s he was close to certain of the *Abstract Expressionists, particularly *Motherwell, with whom he jointly edited the book *Modern Artists in America* (1950), based on conversations with contemporary artists. During the 1950s he turned to monochromatic paintings. At first they were usually red or blue, but from the late 1950s he devoted himself to all-black paintings with geometrical designs of squares or oblongs

barely perceptibly differentiated in value from the background colour—works that were influential on the development of *Minimal art. His reduction of his work to 'pure aesthetic essences' reflects his belief in the complete separation between art and life—'Art is Art. Everything else is everything else.' Reinhardt's views were extremely uncompromising and he was a noted critic of trends in modern art of which he did not approve, as a polemical writer, as a lecturer, and as a satirical cartoonist.

Rejlander, O.G. *See* PHOTOMONTAGE.

relief (or **relievo**) (from It. *rilevare*: to raise). Term applied to sculpture that projects from a background surface rather than standing freely. Since ancient times such sculpture has been particularly used for architectural decoration, but many sculptors have also made reliefs as independent works. According to the degree of projection, reliefs are usually classified as high (*alto rilievo*), medium (*mezzo rilievo*), or low (*basso rilievo* or bas-relief). The name *rilievo schiacciato* is given to a form of very low relief invented by *Donatello and memorably used also by *Desiderio da Settignano.

relief etching. A method of *etching in which the parts of the design that take the ink are raised above the surface of the plate rather than incised into the plate (as in conventional etching). The design is drawn on the plate in an acid-resisting *varnish. The plate is then immersed in acid, which eats away the unprotected parts so that the design stands out in relief and prints can be taken in the same way as from a *woodcut block. The method dates from the 18th century, but was little used except by William *Blake, who called it 'woodcut on copper'. In the 20th century the process was revived by S. W. *Hayter and Joan *Miró.

Rembrandt (Rembrandt Harmensz. van Rijn) (1606–69). Dutch painter, etcher, and draughtsman, his country's greatest artist. He was born in Leiden, the son of a prosperous miller. After attending a Latin school he registered at the city's university in 1620, but probably never actually studied there. At about this time he was apprenticed to the mediocre local painter Jacob van Swanenburgh (*c.*1571–1638), with whom he is said to have studied for about three years. However, much more important for Rembrandt's development were six months spent in Amsterdam with Pieter *Lastman, c.1624. From Lastman he took not only his predilection for mythological and religious subjects, but also his manner of treating them, with exaggerated gestures and expressions, vivid lighting effects, and a meticulous, glossy finish, as in his earliest dated work—the *Stoning of St Stephen* (1625, Mus. B.-A., Lyons). *Houbraken says that Rembrandt also studied with Jacob *Pynas and Joris van Schooten (1587–1651), but this can have been only briefly, for by 1625 he was working as an independent master in Leiden. There he had a close association with his friend Jan *Lievens, but they parted company when Rembrandt moved to Amsterdam (his home for the rest of his life) in 1631/2. The paintings of his Leiden period are mainly figure subjects, often involving old men depicted as philosophers or biblical characters. He also did portraits of himself and of members of his family, but it is not until 1631 that he painted his earliest known formal commissioned portraits, notably that of Nicolaes Ruts, a prosperous Amsterdam merchant (Frick Coll., New York). Rembrandt no doubt realized that here he had a recipe for success, as this type of work dominated his output in his early years in Amsterdam. It was the busiest period of his life, as he quickly established himself as the leading portraitist in the city. The work that most clearly demonstrated his superiority to rivals such as Thomas de *Keyser is the *Anatomy Lesson of Dr Tulp* (1632, Mauritshuis, The Hague), which brought a wholly new vitality to the group portrait. Rembrandt's great energy in his early years in Amsterdam comes out also in his religious works. The most important commission he received during the 1630s was from the Stadholder (head of state) Prince Frederick Henry of Orange for five pictures depicting scenes of Christ's Passion (Alte Pin., Munich), and the *Baroque tendencies of his work at this time are even more emphatically expressed in his sensational, life-size *Blinding of Samson* (1636, Städelsches Kunstinstitut, Frankfurt). Rembrandt's success in the 1630s was personal as well as professional. In 1634 he married Saskia van Uylenburgh, cousin of a picture-dealer associate, and from the evidence of his wonderfully tender portraits of her it

must have been a blissful union. In 1639 he bought an imposing house (now a Rembrandt museum), and he spent lavishly on works of art and anything else that took his fancy or looked as if it might be useful as a prop—armour, old costumes, etc. His domestic happiness was, however, marred by a succession of infant deaths: of the four children Saskia bore him, only his son Titus (1641–68), who became one of his favourite models, lived longer than two months.

Saskia died in 1642, and in this year Rembrandt finished his most famous picture, *The Night Watch* (Rijksmuseum, Amsterdam), which Jacob Rosenberg, in his standard monograph on the artist, calls 'a thunderbolt of genius'. The erroneous title dates from the late 18th century when the painting was so discoloured with dirty varnish that it looked like a night scene. Its correct title is *The Militia Company of Captain Frans Banning Cocq and Lieutenant Willem van Ruytenburch*, and it is the culminating work of the Dutch tradition of civic guard portraits (a genre particularly associated with Frans *Hals). It is also the most ambitious picture of any kind painted by a Dutch artist up to this date, and Rembrandt showed remarkable originality in making a pictorial drama out of an insignificant event. To do this he subordinated the individual portraits to the demands of the composition, and according to popular legend the sitters who had paid for the picture were appalled at this and demanded that Rembrandt make radical changes, paint a new picture, or refund their money. Rembrandt's refusal is supposed to have been his downfall and to have led him into penniless obscurity. There is, however, no basis in fact for the story, which seems to be a 19th-century invention; indeed all the available evidence suggests that the picture was well received by contemporaries. Samuel van *Hoogstraten, for example, wrote: 'It is so painter-like in thought, so dashing in movement, and so powerful' that the pictures beside which it hung were made to seem 'like playing cards'.

Nevertheless, in the 1640s Rembrandt's worldly success did decline as the direction of his art changed. Formal portraiture took up much less of his time and he concentrated more on religious painting, while his style grew less flamboyant and more introspective. The change has been explained as a response to the death of Saskia (and of his mother in 1640), and religion may well have been a solace to him in this difficult period. At the same time, some of his market in portraiture must have gone to pupils such as *Bol and *Flinck, who imitated his style so well. It seems just as likely, however, that Rembrandt was tired of routine portraiture and wanted to return to his first love—painting subjects from the Bible. In the 1640s he also developed an interest in landscape and it has been suggested that he spent more time in the countryside during this period to escape from the domestic problems he encountered after Saskia's death. A widow called Geertge Dircx was employed as Titus's nurse, and she sued Rembrandt for breach of promise after his affections turned to Hendrickje Stoffels, a servant some twenty years his junior who entered the household in about 1645. After some unpleasant legal action Rembrandt succeeded in having Geertge shut up in a reformatory and the litigation did not end until her death in 1656. Hendrickje remained with Rembrandt for the rest of her life and bore him two children, including a daughter, Cornelia, born in 1654, who was the only one of his children to outlive him. Rembrandt's portrayals of Hendrickje are just as loving as those of Saskia, but he was unable to marry her because of a restrictive clause in Saskia's will.

After he turned his back on fashionable portraiture, Rembrandt's extravagance led him into financial difficulties, which became acute by the early 1650s. In 1656 he was declared insolvent (by convincing the authorities that he had acted honestly and in good faith he avoided the worse fate of bankruptcy, which carried the possibility of imprisonment); his collections were sold and by 1660 he had to leave his house and move to lodgings in a poorer district of the city. Houbraken says that 'in the autumn of his life he kept company mainly with common people and such as practised art', but the romantic image of him as a pauper and a recluse is grossly exaggerated. He continued to be a respected figure who received important commissions (his patrons included the Sicilian nobleman Don Antonio Ruffo), and Hendrickje and Titus established an art firm with Rembrandt technically their employee, a device that protected him from his creditors. Indeed, with some

weight thus lifted from his shoulders, Rembrandt may well have felt renewed energy, and there are more dated paintings from 1661 than from any year since the early 1630s. In 1661–2 he painted two of his greatest works—*The Sampling Officers of the Cloth-Makers' Guild* (sometimes called *The Syndics*, Rijksmuseum) and *The Conspiracy of Claudius Civilis*, painted for Amsterdam Town Hall, but for unknown reasons removed in 1663 and cut down (evidently by Rembrandt himself)—the magnificent fragment is now in the Nationalmuseum, Stockholm. Rembrandt's final years were clouded by the deaths of Hendrickje in 1663 and Titus in 1668, but his art was in no way impaired. On the contrary, his work seemed to grow in human understanding and compassion to the very end, and his last self-portraits, the culmination of an incomparable series that began 40 years earlier, show him facing his hardships with the utmost dignity—someone who has no illusions about life, but equally no bitterness. Two self-portraits date from the last year of his life (NG, London, and Mauritshuis), but the painting that best stands as his spiritual testimony is perhaps *The Return of the Prodigal Son* (*c*.1669, Hermitage, St Petersburg), a work of the utmost tenderness and poignancy, described by Kenneth *Clark as 'a picture which those who have seen the original . . . may be forgiven for claiming as the greatest picture ever painted'. The emotional depth and range of Rembrandt's work was matched by the expressive mastery of his technique. Even as a young man, when surface polish and attention to detail were a necessary part of his skill as a fashionable portraitist, he had experimented boldly in his more private works, sometimes, for example, using the butt end of the brush to scrape through the paint. When he began to paint more to please himself in the 1640s, his handling grew much broader, and Houbraken wrote that 'in the last years of his life, he worked so fast that his pictures, when examined from close by, looked as if they had been daubed with a bricklayer's trowel'.

It is not only the quality of Rembrandt's work that sets him apart from all his Dutch contemporaries, but also its range. Although portraits and religious works bulk largest in his output, he made highly original contributions to other genres, including still life (*The Slaughtered Ox*, 1655, Louvre, Paris), and he painted some pictures, such as *The Polish Rider* (c.1655, Frick Coll., New York), that virtually defy classification. Rembrandt was prodigious, too, as an etcher and draughtsman. He is universally regarded as the greatest of all exponents of etching (and *drypoint), capable of expressing the airy breadth of the Dutch countryside with a few quick strokes, but also prepared to radically rework a complex religious scene such as *The Three Crosses* perhaps a decade after he had begun it in 1653 to create one of the most awesome of all images of Christ's Passion. His drawings were done mainly as independent works rather than as studies for paintings and often with the thick bold strokes of the reed pen, of which he was an unsurpassed master.

Rembrandt was a great teacher; Gerrit *Dou became his first pupil in 1628 and Aert de *Gelder, who was with him in the 1660s, continued his master's style into the 18th century. Between these two, Rembrandt taught such illustrious figures as Carel *Fabritius (his greatest pupil), Philips de *Koninck, and Nicolaes *Maes. He continued to have many admirers after his death, and his work often fetched high prices in the 18th century. He was generally regarded as incomparable in his mastery of light and shade, but most critics considered him a flawed genius, whose failing was his 'vulgarity' and lack of decorum. It was during the age of *Romanticism, when it was felt that artists should give expression to their innermost feelings and flout conventions, that his reputation began to rise towards its present supremely exalted heights. In 1851 *Delacroix suggested that one day Rembrandt would be rated higher than *Raphael—'a piece of blasphemy that will make every good academician's hair stand on end'; his prophecy came true within 50 years.

Remington, Frederic (1861–1909). American painter, sculptor, illustrator, and writer, the most famous portrayer of the 'Wild West'. He was a burly, athletic man and after studying art at Yale University he travelled widely in the West, prospecting and cow-punching as he worked to establish himself with his illustrations. Reproductions in *Harper's Weekly* and other popular journals made him a household name, and

with his success he was able to turn more to painting and sculpture. In 1885 he settled in New York, but he continued to make visits to the West. His love of horses was so great that he had barn doors built in his studio so he could bring them inside. Remington travelled to Europe and North Africa as well as in America, and he wrote as well as working as an artist. He covered the Indian Wars of 1890–1 and the Spanish-American War (in Cuba) of 1898 as a newspaper correspondent and he published eight books, including *The Way of an Indian* (1906). There is a collection of his work at the Remington Art Memorial, Ogdensburg, New York State.

Renaissance. Term meaning 'rebirth' applied to an intellectual and artistic movement that began in Italy in the 14th century, culminated there in the 16th century, and influenced other parts of Europe in a great variety of ways. The notion of a rebirth refers to a revival of the values of the classical world, and the concept was used as early as the 15th century, by Italians who thought they were living at a time when the qualities of ancient art and literature were blossoming anew after centuries of barbarism. In the following century *Vasari gave the idea of such a revival a systematically developed form; he thought that art had declined in the Middle Ages, had been set once again on its true path by *Giotto, and had risen to its greatest heights in the work of his friend and hero *Michelangelo. To modern historians this picture seems much too simplistic, and the Renaissance is seen more as a period of gradual change than as a sudden break with the past. Nevertheless, the intellectuals of the Renaissance were the first people to conceive a period identity for themselves, and this in itself gives the label a certain coherence. Scholars may debate endlessly over the exact interpretation of many aspects of the period, but in the general historical scheme of things, the Renaissance has come to represent the time when 'Medieval' turns into 'Modern' and the religion-dominated world of the Middle Ages gives way to a culture more concerned with the individual.

In the visual arts, the revival of the antique can be seen most clearly in architecture, for classical architecture uses a 'vocabulary' of forms that distinguishes it unambiguously from the Gothic style, and there can be no doubt that *Brunelleschi is entitled to rank as the first Renaissance architect. He was interested in Roman buildings probably more for what he could learn about engineering problems than for stylistic reasons, and he was undogmatic and unarchaeological in his use of antique detail, but he had an instinctual understanding of classical design, and his buildings—based on simple mathematical ratios—have a lucidity and harmony worthy of comparison with the finest ancient models. In sculpture, the beginnings of the Renaissance are sometimes traced as far back as Nicola *Pisano in the late 14th century because he is known to have been directly influenced by Roman sarcophagi. However, it is not until *Donatello, in the early 15th century, that we find a sculptor who had thoroughly assimilated the spirit of ancient sculpture, rather than simply borrowing motifs from it. In painting, it is harder to define the Renaissance in terms of antique influence, as very little ancient painting survived compared with the fairly abundant remains of Roman architecture and sculpture to be found in Italy. From the writings of ancient authors, however, classical painters were known to have excelled in fidelity to nature, so this quality was seen as a keynote of Renaissance painting. Because Giotto made such great advances in naturalism he is sometimes put at the head of the Renaissance tradition in painting, but it is more consistent to give this position to *Masaccio, who brought a new scientific rigour to the problems of representation.

Masaccio, like his friends Brunelleschi and Donatello, was a Florentine, and it is thus reasonable to see Florence as the cradle of the Renaissance, and the period around 1425, when they were producing some of their most innovative works, as a major turning point in European art. Florence continued to be of pre-eminent importance throughout the 15th century, but in the 16th century Rome and Venice were equally significant centres for the arts. The culmination of the Renaissance came in the period from about 1500 to 1520—a time that is now known as the High Renaissance. During this time the three most famous artists of the age—*Leonardo, Michelangelo, and *Raphael—produced works that have for centuries been regarded as touchstones of perfection and the fulfilment of all

the ideals that artists had pursued since Giotto. In architecture, *Bramante represents a similar peak, and his noble and grave designs were regarded in his own time as having recaptured the majesty of Roman buildings.

The ideals and imagery of the Italian Renaissance did not generally begin to spread to the rest of Europe until about 1500. Albrecht *Dürer was the outstanding artist of the 'Northern Renaissance', making it his mission to transplant the new Italian ideas onto German soil. His work was of enormous importance in spreading Italian ideas, and during the 16th century it became a normal part of the career of ambitious young artists from northern Europe to follow in his footsteps across the Alps. By this time, however, Italian art had entered the phase called *Mannerism, and much Italian-inspired art of this period in Germany, France, and the Netherlands can be classified as Mannerist rather than Renaissance. Most northern artists imitated only the superficial characteristics of Italian art, and only a few—such as Jan van *Scorel—absorbed something of the order, poise, and dignity associated with the High Renaissance. Although Italian artists worked in England (notably Pietro *Torrigiano and Giovanni II da *Maiano), Renaissance influence there was fairly limited during the 16th century, being confined mainly to decorative motifs (and many of these were used in debased or misunderstood forms). It was not until the 17th century that there emerged an English artist—Inigo *Jones—who thoroughly understood Renaissance ideals, and by this time Italian art had progressed through Mannerism to the *Baroque.

Reni, Guido (1575–1642). Bolognese painter, draughtsman, and occasional etcher. From about 1584 to 1593 he was a pupil of *Calvaert, then transferred to the academy run by the *Carracci, where he absorbed their tradition of clear, firm draughtsmanship. By 1601 he had moved to Rome and he was based there until 1614, although he made frequent visits to Bologna. He flirted briefly with the *Caravaggesque manner (*Crucifixion of St Peter*, 1603, Pinacoteca, Vatican), but *Raphael and the *antique were the main inspiration for his graceful classical style, as is seen in his most celebrated work, *Aurora* (1614,

Casino dell' Aurora, Palazzo Rospiglioso-Pallavacini, Rome), a captivatingly beautiful ceiling fresco painted for Cardinal Scipione *Borghese. Reni was also a favourite artist of Borghese's uncle, Pope Paul V, but in spite of his success in Rome he settled in Bologna in 1614 and seldom left the city again. After Ludovico Carracci's death in 1619, he was unrivalled as Bologna's most important artist; indeed by this time he was probably the most sought-after painter in Italy. The products of his large studio (mainly religious works) were sent all over Europe and *Rubens was the only contemporary painter who had a more glittering international clientele. Reni cut an impressive, aristocratic figure, always fashionably and expensively dressed and usually attended by servants. He earned a huge amount of money from his work, but he was often in debt because of his addiction to gambling. This was one aspect of his complex and decidedly odd character, which is described in detail by his friend and biographer *Malvasia. Because of this remarkable account, more is known about Reni's inner life than that of any previous artist. In spite of his love of gambling, he was deeply religious and also rather prim, hating to hear anyone swearing or even making double entendres. He was devoted to his mother, but otherwise was fearful and suspicious of women: 'It was generally thought that he was a virgin... When observing the many lovely young girls who served as his models, he was like marble' (it has been suggested that he was a repressed homosexual). He was renowned for his generosity to friends, colleagues, pupils, and good causes (to which he often gave money anonymously), but he was notoriously touchy, falling out with several of his fellow artists, including *Albani, *Domenichino, and two of his teachers—Calvaert and Ludovico Carracci. Other quirks were a fear of witchcraft and a dread of being poisoned.

The great reputation Reni enjoyed in his lifetime was maintained in the 18th and early 19th centuries, many critics ranking him second only to Raphael. He was known as 'the Divine Guido' and was lauded for the celestial grace of his work. However, he fell from favour under the scornful attacks of *Ruskin (who detested the Bolognese painters in general), and was long dismissed as vulgar and sentimental. Until well into the 20th century a just appreciation of his stature was impeded by the failure to distinguish between his own works and those by his countless (often extremely insipid) imitators. The great exhibition devoted to him in Bologna in 1954 was a turning point in his critical fortunes, and his status as one of the greatest Italian painters of the 17th century is now firmly re-established. His late works in particular show a beauty of colouring that sets him apart from any of his contemporaries. In his early career he had typically used strong, rich colours, but he came to favour cooler harmonies, with prominent use of ice blue, apple green, pink, and pearly grey, and in the 1630s his tonality lightened even further, his pictures taking on a soft (sometimes almost ethereal), silvery glow. At the same time his brushwork became looser and the mood of his pictures more languid. These changes, particularly the less detailed handling, may have been partly a consequence of the speed at which he worked to pay off his gambling debts (he was once so desperate for money that he hired himself out by the hour), but the best of his late works have an exquisite delicacy and refinement. The largest and finest collection of his paintings is in the Pinacoteca Nazionale in Bologna.

Renier of Huy. *See* RAINER OF HUY.

Renoir, Pierre-Auguste (1841–1919). French *Impressionist painter, born at Limoges into a poor family. In 1854 he began work as a painter in a porcelain factory in Paris, gaining experience with the light, fresh colours that were to distinguish his Impressionist work and also learning the importance of good craftsmanship. His predilection for light-hearted themes was also influenced by the great *Rococo masters, whose work he studied in the Louvre. In 1862, having saved enough to pay for professional tuition, he became a pupil in *Gleyre's studio; there he formed lasting friendships with *Monet, *Sisley, and *Bazille, and with them created the early nucleus of the Impressionist group. His relationship with Monet was particularly close at this time, and their paintings of the beauty spot called La Grenouillère done in 1869 (an example by Renoir is in the Nationalmuseum, Stockholm) are regarded as the classic early statements of the Impressionist style. Like Monet,

Renoir endured much hardship early in his career, but in the late 1870s he began to achieve success as a portraitist (he was well suited to this work temperamentally, as his shy but friendly personality put sitters at their ease). In 1881 the dealer Paul *Durand-Ruel began buying his work regularly and henceforth he was free of major financial worries. By this time Renoir had 'travelled as far as Impressionism could take me', and a visit to Italy in 1881–2 inspired him to seek a greater sense of solidity in his work. The change in attitude is clearly seen in *The Umbrellas* (NG, London), which was begun before the visit to Italy and finished afterwards; the two little girls on the right are painted with the feathery brushstrokes characteristic of his Impressionist manner, but the figures on the left are done in a crisper and drier style, with duller colouring. In the mid-1880s Renoir experimented for a while with this *manière aigre* (harsh or sour manner) as he called it, but he then developed a softer and more supple kind of handling combined with warmer colour. At the same time he began to turn from contemporary themes to more timeless subjects, particularly nudes, but also pictures of young girls in unspecific settings. As his style became grander and simpler he also took up mythological subjects (*The Judgement of Paris, c.*1913–14, Hiroshima Mus. of Art), and the female type he preferred became more mature and ample. In the 1890s Renoir began to suffer from rheumatism, and from 1903 (by which time he was world-famous) he lived in the warmth of the south of France. The rheumatism eventually crippled him (by 1912 he was confined to a wheelchair), but he continued to paint until the end of his life, and in his last years he also took up sculpture, directing assistants (usually Richard Guino, a pupil of *Maillol) to act as his hands (*Venus Victorious*, 1914, Tate, London). The house at Cagnes-sur-Mer in which he spent his final years is now a museum devoted to him.

Renoir is one of the best-loved artists of the 19th century, for his subjects—pretty children, flowers, beautiful scenes, above all lovely women—have instant appeal, and he communicated the joy he took in them with great directness. 'Why shouldn't art be pretty?', he said; 'There are enough unpleasant things in the world.' He was one of the great worshippers of the female form,

and he said, 'I never think I have finished a nude until I think I could pinch it.' His output was enormous (about 6,000 paintings) and examples are in collections all over the world. One of his sons was the celebrated film director Jean Renoir (1894–1979), who wrote a lively and touching biography published in both French and English (*Renoir, My Father*) in 1962.

Repin, Ilya (1844–1930). The most celebrated Russian painter of his day and a central figure in his country's cultural life. Although *Bryulov and *Ivanov had earlier gained great renown in the West with a classical and a biblical picture respectively, Repin was the first Russian painter to achieve European fame with specifically Russian themes. In addition to portraits of a host of celebrities, he painted colourful scenes of Russian history, pictures of peasant life, and contemporary subjects in which he attacked political abuses and social ills; his friend Tolstoy said that he 'depicts our national way of life much better than any other artist'. His main training was at the St Petersburg Academy, where he won a scholarship that enabled him to travel in Europe, 1873–6. He spent most of this time in Paris and returned there several times, becoming a highly respected figure in France (he was made a member of the Legion of Honour in 1901). Repin had mixed feelings about the *Impressionists, who became a great artistic talking point during his scholarship period in Paris (their first group exhibition was in 1874). He admired their lively use of light and colour but thought their work was lacking in serious moral purpose. The importance he attached to such moral values was clearly evident in his first great success, *Barge Haulers on the Volga* (1870–3, Russian Mus., St Petersburg), which won a medal at an international exhibition in Vienna in 1873. He showed his social conscience in revealing the appalling working conditions of the barge haulers, but the picture also celebrates their dignity and fortitude. In 1878–83 Repin lived in Moscow, then settled in St Petersburg, but he spent a good deal of time travelling in remote areas of Russia to gather material for his paintings. He was at his peak in the 1880s, when he produced most of his finest works, including *The Zaporozhian Cossacks Writing a Mocking Letter to the Turkish Sultan*

(1880–91, Russian Mus.), a characteristically full-blooded evocation of Russian history; *They Did Not Expect Him* (1884, Tretyakov Gal., Moscow), showing the unexpected return of a political exile from Siberia; and *Modest Musorgsky* (1881, Tretyakov Gal.), which is often considered his greatest achievement as a portraitist. Although he sometimes worked painstakingly for years on his big historical paintings, the portrait of Musorgsky was a brilliant impromptu performance, produced in a few hours during a temporary improvement in the health of the dying composer; Musorgsky himself referred to the 'fearsome sweeps' of Repin's brush.

In 1894 Repin began teaching at the St Petersburg Academy and became a revered figure among his pupils. Following the 1905 revolution he resigned his post as he did not want to be associated with a government he considered 'behind the times, stupid and ready for a complete downfall'. He returned in 1906 after pleas from his pupils but resigned for good in 1907. In 1899 he had bought a country estate at Kuokkala, which is near St Petersburg but at this time was part of Finland. After Finland declared independence from Russia in 1917 and closed the border, Repin found himself cut off from his native country and never returned. He remained highly respected there, however, and after Stalin's imposition of *Socialist Realism in the 1930s he was extolled as an 'artist-democrat' and held up as a model for Soviet painters. Kuokkala is now part of Russia and has been renamed Repino in his honour; his home there is now a museum dedicated to him.

repoussoir (from Fr. *repousser*: 'to push back, set off'). A figure or object in the foreground of a picture (and usually at the side) used to 'push back' the principal scene or episode, thereby increasing the sense of depth.

reredos. *See* ALTARPIECE.

resin. A sticky substance, insoluble in water, used in art particularly as a constituent of *varnish. Resins are secreted by many trees and plants; those used by painters in the past are not always easy to identify, but they include both soft resins from living trees (such as mastic, dammar, sandarac, Canada balsam, and *turpentine), and hard

fossil resins (such as copal and amber). Resins can now also be made synthetically.

retable. *See* ALTARPIECE.

Rethel, Alfred (1816–59). German painter and printmaker. His biggest work, a cycle of frescos from the life of Charlemagne (Town Hall, Aachen), was once much admired as a great achievement of heroic *history painting, but today seems hollow and theatrical. The cycle was begun in 1847 but left unfinished because of the madness that ended Rethel's career in 1853. He is now mainly remembered for his series of wood engravings *Another Dance of Death* (1849), much in the spirit of *Holbein's famous depictions of the subject, but satirizing the revolutionary events of 1848, with Death seen as the embodiment of anarchy. In 1851 he returned to the theme of death, but in a personal rather than political vein, with a pair of prints that were once extremely popular—*Death as an Avenger* and *Death as a Friend*.

Rewald, John (1912–94). German-born American art historian, a professor at the University of Chicago 1963–71 and thereafter at the City University, New York. He was the doyen of the field of *Impressionist and *Post-Impressionist scholarship, and is famous for two magisterial works, *The History of Impressionism* (1946; 4th edn. 1973) and *Post-Impressionism: From Van Gogh to Gauguin* (1956; 3rd edn. 1978). These show his total command of the voluminous material and his remarkable powers of organization and exposition in forming it into a highly readable narrative, and are, by common consent, among the greatest works of art history ever written (even though some critics have accused him of being strong on facts but weak on interpretation); *The History of Impressionism* used to enjoy the 'distinction' of being the book most frequently stolen from the *Courtauld Institute library. Rewald's other writings include studies of many leading 19th-century French artists, particularly *Cézanne (he received a gold medal from Cézanne's home town, Aix-en-Provence, in 1984), and two collections of his articles have appeared, *Studies in Impressionism* (1985) and *Studies in Post-Impressionism* (1986).

Reynolds, Sir Joshua (1723–92). English painter and writer on art. Reynolds was the leading portraitist of his day, the first

president of the *Royal Academy, a major
art theorist, and perhaps the most important figure in the history of British painting,
for through his social and intellectual eminence he raised his profession to a new level
of dignity. He was born at Plympton in Devonshire, the son of a scholarly clergyman,
and was brought up in an atmosphere of
learning (he said he owed his 'first fondness'
for art to Jonathan *Richardson the Elder's
Essay on the Theory of Painting, which he read
in his father's library). From 1740 to 1743 he
studied painting in London under *Hudson
(likewise a Devonshire man), then set up
independently as a portraitist a year before
his apprenticeship was due to end (the
parting was amicable—he and Hudson
remained on good terms). In 1750-2 he
spent two and a half years in Italy (mainly
Rome), where he made an intensive study of
the *antique and the great masters of the
16th and 17th centuries (whilst copying
*Raphael in the wintry chill of the Vatican
he caught a cold that left him hard of hear-
ing for the rest of his life). He not only
absorbed the formal language of his models,
but also developed a deliberate cult of learning and classical allusion that coloured his
whole approach to art. In tune with established art theory, he thought that *history
painting was the highest branch of art, but
he believed that portraiture could rise above
its traditional status as mere 'face-painting'
by making reference to the great art of the
past. Thus, in the work that established his
reputation after he settled in London in
1753—*Commodore Keppel* (1753-4, Nat. Maritime Mus., London)—the sitter's heroic attitude is based directly (albeit in reverse) on
that of the *Apollo Belvedere*, then regarded
as the matchless ideal of male beauty.
However, his approach involved far more
than simply borrowing poses from approved models, for he tried to create an
image that was in keeping with the character and status of each particular sitter. In the
Keppel portrait, for example, he not only
alludes to an ancient statue, but also depicts
a contemporary man of action with great
verve.

Reynolds quickly achieved a leading position in his profession. He had 150 sitters a
year by 1758, and by 1764 was earning the
enormous annual sum of £6,000. His success was achieved through hard work and
careful business management as well as

talent: on the day he was knighted (21
April 1769) his visit to St James's Palace
was fitted in between two sittings with
clients. Moreover, although he always
retained traces of his provincial origins
(notably his Devonshire accent), he was
completely at home with his eminent
sitters. His pupil James *Northcote said
that 'His general manner, deportment and
behaviour were amiable and prepossessing;
his disposition was naturally courtly. He . . .
contrived to move in a higher sphere of
society than any other English artist had
done before. Thus he procured for the Professors of the Arts a consequence, dignity
and reception which they never possessed
in this country.' Reynolds's elevation of the
status of the artist depended, then, not only
on the intellectual quality of his work, but
also on his social acceptability, and it is significant that his friends were mainly men of
letters—notably Samuel Johnson and Oliver
Goldsmith—rather than other painters
(James Boswell dedicated his celebrated
Life of Johnson to Reynolds). On the foundation of the Royal Academy in 1768, he was
the obvious choice for president, and he
arranged for Johnson and Goldsmith to be
appointed to the honorary positions of professors of ancient history and literature. Between 1769 and 1790 he delivered a series of
lectures to the Academy's students, and
these fifteen *Discourses* are one of the most
impressive bodies of writing ever made by a
practising artist, forming the classic expression of the academic doctrine of the *Grand
Manner (each *Discourse* was published separately and the first collected edition
appeared in 1797). In 1789 failing eyesight
forced Reynolds to give up painting and by
the time of his death he was almost completely blind. He bore his final illness with
what his friend Edmund Burke called a
'mild and cheerful fortitude' and was buried
in St Paul's Cathedral with ceremonial
never before accorded a British painter: his
ten pallbearers were made up of three
dukes, three earls, two marquesses, a viscount and a baron.

As a portraitist Reynolds is remarkable
above all for his versatility—his inexhaustible range of response to the individuality of
each sitter: man, woman, or child. The celebrated remark of his rival *Gainsborough,
'Damn him! How various he is!', is echoed in
the praise of *Ruskin: 'Considered as a

painter of individuality in the human form and mind, I think him the prince of portrait painters. *Titian paints nobler pictures and van *Dyck had nobler subjects, but neither of them entered so subtly as Sir Joshua did into the minor varieties of human heart and temper.' His huge output necessitated the employment of assistants and *drapery painters, and his experimentation with *bitumen has resulted in some of his pictures being in poor condition, but there is nevertheless much beauty of handling in his work, and his finest pictures rank among the great masterpieces of British portraiture. On the other hand, his history paintings, dating mainly from the end of his career, are generally considered ponderous failures (Hester Thrale—a friend of Dr Johnson—said he had 'a rage for sublimity ill-understood'). Reynolds's work is in numerous public collections, great and small, in Britain and elsewhere, and many of his best pictures are still in the possession of the families for which they were painted. His output was so varied that no single collection can be regarded as fully representative. **Frances Reynolds** (1729–1807), Sir Joshua's sister and for many years his housekeeper, was an amateur painter, but evidently not a very good one, for he said of her copies of his work: 'They make other people laugh and me cry.'

Reynolds-Stephens, Sir William. *See* NEW SCULPTURE.

Riace Bronzes. *See* PHIDIAS.

Ribalta, Francisco (1565–1628). Spanish painter, an important figure in the transition from *Mannerism to a more naturalistic style. He spent most of his early career in Madrid, but by 1599 he had settled in Valencia. Up to about 1620 his work was *eclectic, but he then developed a more personal and powerful style, with dramatic lighting that echoes *Caravaggio (*Christ Embracing St Bernard*, 1625–7, Prado, Madrid). *Zurbarán was among the artists who were influenced by him. His son **Juan** (1596/7–1628) was an able painter in his father's style, but died young.

Ribera, José (or **Jusepe**) **de** (1591–1652). Spanish painter, etcher, and draughtsman, active for all his known career in Italy, where he was called 'Lo Spagnoletto' (the little Spaniard). He is recorded in Parma in

1611 and Rome in 1613, but little is known of his life before he settled in Naples (at the time a Spanish possession) in 1616. Naples was then one of the main centres of the Caravaggesque style, and Ribera is often described as a follower of *Caravaggio. However, although his early work is markedly *tenebrist, it is much more individual than that of most Caravaggesque artists, particularly in his vigorous and scratchy handling of paint, and his later works are far removed from Caravaggio in style—rich in colour and soft in modelling. Similarly, his penchant for the typically Caravaggesque theme of bloody martyrdom has been overplayed, enshrined as it is in Byron's lines: 'Spagnoletto tainted | His brush with all the blood of all the sainted' (*Don Juan*, xiii. 71). He did paint some powerful scenes in this vein, notably the celebrated *Martyrdom of St Philip* (1639, Prado, Madrid; formerly identified as the *Martyrdom of St Bartholomew*), but his treatment is invariably dignified rather than merely gory. Moreover he was capable of great tenderness, as in the *Adoration of the Shepherds* (1650, Louvre, Paris), and his work is remarkable for his feeling for individual humanity. This feature is evident in his secular pictures as well as his religious works, for example in the *Clubfooted Boy* (1642, Louvre). His range of secular subjects was fairly wide, for he was the first Spanish painter to show much interest in mythological themes (*Apollo and Marsyas*, 1637, Mus. Royaux, Brussels) and he also created a novel type of picture showing philosophers as beggars or vagabonds (*Archimedes*, 1630, Prado). He was the leading painter in Naples in his period (Velázquez visited him during his second visit to Italy and probably during his first) and his work was influential in Spain (where much of it was exported) as well as in Italy. *Giordano was perhaps among his pupils. His reputation remained high after his death, and until the Napoleonic Wars he and *Murillo were virtually the only Spanish painters whose work was widely known outside their native country.

Ricci, Sebastiano (1659–1734). Italian decorative painter. He was born at Belluno in the Veneto and is considered a member of the Venetian School, but before he settled permanently in Venice in 1717 he led a peripatetic life, working in numerous Italian cities and also in England, Flanders, France, and Germany. His unsettled existence is a reflection not only of the demand for his talents but also of his penchant for illicit love affairs, which often led to his having to move in haste, and once almost resulted in his execution. In view of this it is not surprising that his work is uneven and sometimes shows signs of carelessness, but he had a gift for vivid, fresh colouring, and his itinerant career was important in spreading knowledge of Italian decorative painting. He was in England in 1711/12–16. Little of the decorative work he did there survives except the *Resurrection* in the apse of the chapel at Chelsea Hospital and some large but damaged canvases on the staircase at Burlington House (now the Royal Academy). He is, however, extremely well represented in the Royal Collection. **Marco Ricci** (1676–1730), Sebastiano's nephew, was also born at Belluno and similarly travelled extensively. He made two visits to England (1708 and 1711/12–16), and during the second worked in partnership with his uncle; the collaboration continued after they returned to Venice. Examples of their joint works are in the Royal Collection. Marco was primarily a landscape painter, working in a freely handled style that owed something to *Magnasco.

Riccio, Il (Andrea Briosco) (1470–1532). Italian sculptor, born at Trento, and active in and around Padua; his nickname means 'curly head'. He was trained as a goldsmith by his father, but he turned to sculpture and studied with Bartolommeo Bellano (c.1440–96/7), who is said to have been one of *Donatello's assistants. Although he worked in terracotta, Riccio was primarily a virtuoso in bronze and his masterpiece is the huge (nearly 4 m (13 ft) high) Easter candlestick (1507–16) in the Santo (S. Antonio) at Padua, which with its relief scenes of classically draped figures, its satyrs, sphinxes, and decorative conceits, is an endlessly inventive work. He is best known, however, for small bronze pieces, including statuettes and items such as inkstands and oil lamps. They are done in an *antique manner and greatly appealed to humanist circles in Padua and Venice (he was on friendly terms with leading scholars). Riccio was much imitated, but works from his own hand are distinguished by a vivacity and delicacy of surface that none of his rivals could match.

Richards, Ceri (1903–71). British painter, printmaker, designer, and maker of reliefs, born at Dunvant, near Swansea, into a Welsh-speaking family. From 1924 he spent most of his life in London, but he remained close to his Welsh roots. His output was many-sided, and Sir John *Rothenstein writes that 'Richards's work is widely admired but there is little consensus of opinion about its essential character.' In 1936 he took part in the International *Surrealist Exhibition in London and he said that Surrealism 'helped me to be aware of the mystery, even the "unreality", of ordinary things'. At this time he was also strongly influenced by *Picasso, notably in a series of semi-abstract relief constructions begun in 1933. After the Second World War his painting drew inspiration from the large exhibition of Picasso and *Matisse at the Victoria and Albert Museum in 1945. His best-known works include the *Cathédrale engloutie* series, based on a Debussy prelude (which Richards used to play on the piano) and '*Do not go gentle into that good night*' (1956, Tate, London), based on a poem by Dylan Thomas (whom he once met). Richards's work also included book illustrations, theatre designs, mural decorations for ships of the Orient line, and designs for stained glass and furnishings for the Blessed Sacrament Chapel in Liverpool Roman Catholic Cathedral (1965).

Richardson, Jonathan the Elder (1665–1745). English portrait painter, writer, and collector. John *Riley's most important pupil, he was one of the leading portraitists in the generation after *Kneller's death. This period, however, has been described by Sir Ellis *Waterhouse as 'the most drab in the history of British painting', and Richardson is now remembered more for his writings than his pictures. His most important book is *An Essay on the Theory of Painting* (1715), which was the first significant work of art theory written in English; it was an immediate success and its claims for the intellectual seriousness of painting inspired the young *Reynolds. *An Account of Some of the Statues, Bas-Reliefs, Drawings, and Pictures in Italy* (1722), which he wrote in collaboration with his son, **Jonathan the Younger** (1694–1771), also a portraitist, was much used as a guidebook by young Englishmen making the *Grand Tour. Richardson the

Elder was an excellent draughtsman (a self-portrait in black and red chalk, *c.*1735, is in the NPG, London) and he made a superb collection of Old Master drawings.

Richier, Germaine (1902–59). French sculptor. She had a traditional training as a carver, working under *Bourdelle from 1925 to 1929, but from about 1940 she began to create a distinctive type of bronze sculpture. Her figures became long and thin, combining human with animal or insect (and sometimes vegetal) forms. The surfaces of these powerful and disquieting works have a tattered and lacerated effect, creating a macabre feeling of decomposition, and she was one of the pioneers of an open form of sculpture in which enclosed space becomes as important as the solid material. Such figures were often extremely difficult to cast and she showed great technical resourcefulness in bringing them to completion. The public sometimes found her work shocking, especially her *Crucified Christ* (1950, church of Notre-Dame-de-Toute-Grâce, Assy), which caused a storm of controversy. Nevertheless, her international prestige grew steadily in the years after the Second World War. Late in her career she also produced engravings and paintings.

Richmond, George (1809–96). The best-known member of a family of English painters. He was a pupil of his father, the *miniaturist **Thomas Richmond, Sen.** (1771–1837), and also studied at the *Royal Academy, where he became a friend of Samuel *Palmer. With Palmer and others he was one of the group of William *Blake's followers known as the *Ancients. However, his imitation of Blake's mannerisms was heavy-handed (*The Eve of Separation*, 1830, Ashmolean Mus., Oxford). From about 1830 he turned from poetic and religious themes to portraiture and became a great fashionable success. He was highly prolific, his account books listing about 2,500 portrait paintings and drawings. His brother, **Thomas Richmond, Jun.** (1802–74), and his son, **Sir William Blake Richmond** (1842–1921), were also painters. Thomas specialized in portraits, but William had a varied output and was also a sculptor and a designer (notably of numerous mosaics in St Paul's Cathedral, London).

Richter, Hans. *See* DADA.

Ricketts, Charles (1866–1931). British painter, designer, sculptor, collector, and writer on art. In 1882, whilst studying wood engraving at Lambeth School of Art, he met fellow student Charles Shannon (1863–1937), a painter and engraver who became his lifelong companion. Kenneth *Clark writes that 'Ricketts did most of the talking. Shannon was quiet and recessive, but his rare interpolations showed good sense and considerable learning. One could see that Ricketts turned to him as to a reasonable wife.' Ricketts initially made his mark in book production, first as an illustrator, then as the driving force behind the Vale Press (1896–1904), one of the finest private presses of the day. After the closure of the Press (following a disastrous fire), Ricketts turned to painting and occasional sculpture, and in 1906 he began to make designs for the theatre. His paintings—typically rather melodramatic, heavy-handed figure subjects—have not worn well, but his colourful stage designs are still much admired. He had a great reputation as a connoisseur and in 1915 turned down the offer of the directorship of the National Gallery. Later he regretted this decision, but he served on various committees and put much energy into trying to combat modernism in art. Most of the highly varied collection he made with Shannon was bequeathed to the Fitzwilliam Museum in Cambridge, although the gem of the collection—*Piero di Cosimo's *Fight between Lapiths and Centaurs*—went to the National Gallery. Ricketts's main books were *The Prado and its Masterpieces* (1903), *Titian* (1910), and *Pages on Art* (1913); *Self-Portrait* (taken from his letters and journals) was posthumously published in 1939.

Ridolfi, Carlo (1594–1658). Italian painter and writer. He is insignificant as an artist, but he is remembered as the biographer of *Tintoretto (1642) and author of *Le miraviglie dell'arte* (The Marvels of Art), published in two volumes in 1648. This is a source of great importance for the history of Venetian art, which was somewhat scantily treated by *Vasari. Ridolfi was also a notable collector of drawings; many of those he owned are now at Christ Church, Oxford.

Riemenschneider, Tilman (*c.*1460–1531). German sculptor, active in Würzburg, where he settled in 1483. With

*Stoss, he was the outstanding German late *Gothic sculptor, and his workshop was large and productive (his activities are exceptionally well documented for the time). He worked a good deal in stone, but he was primarily a woodcarver, and he was evidently the first German sculptor to leave his wooden figures un-*polychromed (although they were not entirely uncoloured, as he used pigmented varnish and picked out details such as eyes and lips in colour). His style was intricate, but also balanced and harmonious, with none of the extreme emotionalism often seen in German art of the period. He held various offices in city government, and in 1525 he was briefly imprisoned and perhaps tortured because he was one of the councilmen who refused to support the use of force against the rebels in the Peasants' War. Much of Riemenschneider's work is still in the churches for which it was created, notably the magnificent Holy Blood altarpiece (1501–5) in the Jakobskirche, Rothenburg ober der Tauber. He is also well represented in the Bayerisches Nationalmuseum, Munich, and the Mainfränkisches Museum, Würzburg. Two of his sons, **Jörg** and **Hans**, were sculptors, and two others, **Bartholomäus** (a pupil of *Dürer) and **Tilman**, were painters.

Rietveld, Gerald. See STIJL.

Rigaud, Hyacinthe (1659–1743). French portrait painter, the friend and rival of *Largillière. He was born in Perpignan and after working in Montpellier he settled in Paris in 1681. His reputation was established in 1688 with a portrait (now lost) of Monsieur, Louis XIV's brother, and he became the outstanding court painter of the latter part of Louis's reign, retaining his popularity after the king's death. He was less interested in showing individual character than in depicting the rank and condition of the sitter by nobility of attitude and expressiveness of gesture. These qualities are seen most memorably in his celebrated state portrait of Louis XIV (1701, Louvre, Paris), one of the classic images of royal majesty. Louis so admired this portrait that although he had intended it as a present for Philip V of Spain, he kept it himself. Rigaud's unofficial portraits, such as *The Artist's Mother* (1695, Louvre), are much more informal and show a debt to *Rembrandt, several of whose works he owned. The output from

Rigaud's studio was vast and examples are in many collections.

Rijksmuseum, Amsterdam. The Dutch national art collection. Its origins go back to a National Art Gallery, opened in 1800 in the Huis ten Bosch, a 17th-century palace on the outskirts of The Hague. At this time Holland was under French rule and the creation of such a museum was typical of the centralizing reforms beloved of Napoleon. In 1808 the gallery was relocated to Amsterdam and renamed the Royal Museum—the 'royal' referring to Louis Bonaparte (Napoleon's brother), who had been created king of Holland in 1806. It was housed in the town hall (renamed by Louis the royal palace). After Louis abdicated in 1810 it was renamed the Great Dutch Museum, and after the French were expelled in 1813 it was renamed the National Museum. In 1815 it was given its present title of State Museum (Rijksmuseum), and in 1817 it opened in a new home, a 17th-century building called the Trippenhuis (Trip House), named after its original owners. The idea of the museum was to assemble Netherlandish paintings of national importance and also to stimulate contemporary art. The Trippenhuis proved too small for the growing collection, but it was not until 1877 that a new purpose-built museum was begun. This building, the present Rijksmuseum, opened in 1885. Designed by P. J. H. Cuypers, the outstanding Dutch architect of the 19th century, it is in an eclectic style mixing Gothic and Renaissance features and is of immense size—at the time it opened it was the largest building in the country. In 1895 it transferred its pictures by living artists to Amsterdam's newly opened Stedelijk Museum (Municipal Museum) and from this point it virtually gave up collecting modern works. The most important official in the history of the museum has been Frederick Schmidt-Degener (1881–1941), who was director from 1922 until his death. He modernized its displays and began the acquisition of foreign works of art. Since the Second World War the Rijksmuseum has also greatly expanded its coverage of sculpture and applied art, but it remains chiefly famous for its collection of 17th-century Dutch paintings—the largest and most comprehensive in the world. Associated with the Rijksmuseum is the Rijksprentenkabinet, which has an outstanding collection of prints and drawings.

Riley, Bridget (1931–). British painter and designer, rivalled only by *Vasarely as the most celebrated exponent of *Op art. Her interest in optical effects came partly through her study of *Seurat's technique of *pointillism, but when she took up Op art in the early 1960s she worked initially in black and white. She turned to colour in 1966. By this time she had attracted international attention (one of her paintings was used for the cover to the catalogue of the exhibition 'The Responsive Eye' at the Museum of Modern Art, New York, in 1965, the exhibition that gave currency to the term 'Op art'), and the seal was set on her reputation when she won the International Painting Prize at the Venice *Biennale in 1968. Her work shows a complete mastery of the effects characteristic of Op art, particularly subtle variations in size, shape, or placement of serialized units in an all-over pattern. It is often on a large scale and she frequently makes use of assistants for the actual execution. Although her paintings often create effects of vibration and dazzle, her decorative scheme for the interior of the Royal Liverpool Hospital (1983) uses soothing bands of blue, yellow, pink, and white and is reported to have caused a drop in vandalism and graffiti. She has also worked in theatre design, making sets for a ballet called *Colour Moves* (first performed at the Edinburgh Festival in 1983). Unusually, the sets preceded the composition of the music and the choreography. Riley has travelled widely (a visit to Egypt in 1981 was particularly influential on her work, as she was inspired by the colours of ancient Egyptian art) and she has studios in London, Cornwall, and Provence.

Riley, John (1646–91). English portrait painter. His early career is obscure, but he emerged as the most distinguished figure in English portraiture in the brief interval between the death of *Lely in 1680 and the dominance of *Kneller. Although he was appointed principal painter to William III and Mary II jointly with Kneller in 1688, his finest works are not court portraits but depictions of sitters from humble callings: the two best known are *The Scullion* (Christ Church, Oxford) and *Bridget Holmes* (1686, Royal Coll.), a full-length portrayal of a

nonagenarian royal housemaid who brandishes her broom at a mischievous pageboy. Riley was generally more successful painting men than women (he was no rival to Lely in depicting fine clothes and soft complexions) and his unassuming sincerity of presentation exemplifies a typically English approach to portraiture that he passed on to his pupil Jonathan *Richardson the Elder.

Rimmer, William (1816–79). English-born American sculptor, painter, teacher, and writer. His family emigrated when he was a small child and eventually settled in Boston, which with New York was his main place of work. Rimmer was an offbeat character and had an eccentric career. He believed he was the rightful heir to the French throne and taught himself medicine, being licensed as a physician in 1855. As an artist too he was self-taught, and although he showed brilliantly precocious talent with his gypsum figure of *Despair* (c.1830, MFA, Boston), he struggled for recognition, and for years earned his living mainly as a sign and scenery painter and as a cobbler. In his later years, however, he became famous as a teacher, notably for his instructional books, *Elements of Design* (1864) and *Art Anatomy* (1877). Rimmer's output as an artist was very small, but he was the most powerful and original American sculptor of his time; his work excels in dramatic force and vividly displays his anatomical mastery (*Falling Gladiator*, 1861; original plaster, Nat. Mus. of American Art, Washington; bronze, MFA, Boston). As a painter, his best-known work is the nightmarish *Flight and Pursuit* (1872, MFA, Boston), which, like his sculptures, shows the freshness and unconventionality of his approach and the richness of his imagination.

Riopelle, Jean-Paul (1923–2002). Canadian painter, sculptor, and printmaker. Riopelle was considered the leading Canadian abstract painter of his generation, although he spent most of his career in Paris. His early works were landscapes, but he turned to abstraction under the influence of *Borduas and became a member of his group Les *Automatistes in 1946 before settling in Paris in 1947. His paintings of the late 1940s were in a lyrical manner, but in the 1950s his work became tauter, denser, and more powerful, the paint often applied with a palette knife, creating a rich mosaic-like effect (*Pavane*, 1954, NG, Ottawa). Later his handling became more calligraphic. Riopelle was a prolific artist and at home in various media. In spite of his long residence in France, he kept up a close association with his native country and from 1970 he spent a good deal of time in his native Montreal.

Ripa, Cesare. *See* EMBLEM.

Rivera, Diego (1886–1957). Mexican painter, the most celebrated figure in the revival of monumental fresco painting that is his country's most distinctive contribution to modern art. He visited Paris in 1909 and after a brief return to Mexico he settled there from 1911 to 1920. During this time he became one of the lions of café society and was friendly with many leading artists. He became familiar with modern movements, but although he made some early experiments with avant-garde idioms, notably *Cubism, his mature art was firmly rooted in Mexican tradition. At about the time of the Russian Revolution he had become interested in politics and in the role art could play in society. In 1920–1 he visited Italy to study Renaissance frescos (already thinking in terms of a monumental public art), then returned to his homeland, eager to be of service to the Mexican Revolution. In 1920 Alvaro Obregón, an art lover as well as a reformist, had been elected president of Mexico, and Rivera, who was an extremely forceful personality, swiftly emerged as the leading artist in the programme of murals he initiated glorifying the history and people of the country in a spirit of revolutionary fervour. Many examples of his work are in public buildings in Mexico City, and they are often on a huge scale, a tribute to his enormous energy. His most ambitious scheme, in the National Palace, covering the history of Mexico, was begun in 1929; it was still unfinished at his death, but it contains some of his most magnificent work. Rivera's murals were frankly didactic, intended to inspire a sense of nationalist and socialist identity in a still largely illiterate population; their glorification of creative labour or their excoriation of capitalism can be crude, but his best work has astonishing vigour. He showed formidable skill in choreographing his incident-

and figure-packed compositions, in combining traditional and modern subject matter, and in blending stylized and realistic images.

In 1927 Rivera visited the Soviet Union and in 1930–4 he worked in the USA, painting several frescos that were influential on the muralists of the *Federal Art Project. His main work in American was a series, *Detroit Industry* (1932–3), in the Detroit Institute of Arts (commissioned by William *Valentiner); another major mural, *Man at the Crossroads* (1933), in the Rockefeller Center, New York, was destroyed before completion because he included a portrait of Lenin. It was replaced by a mural by *Brangwyn. Throughout his career he also painted a wide range of easel pictures, in some of which he experimented with the *encaustic (wax) technique. Rivera was an enormous man, and although he was notoriously ugly he was irresistibly attractive to women. He had numerous love affairs and was married three times, his second wife (and his third, for they divorced and remarried) being the painter Frida *Kahlo. Her parents said 'it was like a marriage between an elephant and a dove.'

Rivers, Larry (1923–2002). American painter, sculptor, printmaker, and designer, a leading figure in the revival of figurative art that was one aspect of the reaction against the dominance of *Abstract Expressionism. He was a professional jazz saxophonist in the early 1940s and began painting in 1945, studying at the Hans *Hofmann School, 1947–8, and then at New York University under *Baziotes in 1948. His work of the early and mid-1950s continued the vigorous painterly handling associated with Abstract Expressionism, but was very different in character. Some of his paintings were fairly straightforwardly naturalistic, but others looked forward to *Pop art in their quotations from well-known advertising or artistic sources, their use of lettering, and their deadpan humour. An example is *Washington Crossing the Delaware* (1953, MoMA, New York), based on the picture by *Leutze. In the late 1950s and 1960s his work came more clearly within the orbit of Pop, sometimes incorporating cut-out cardboard or wooden forms, electric lights, and so on, but his sensuous handling of paint set him apart from other Pop artists.

Rivers also made sculpture, collages, and prints, designed for the stage, acted, and wrote poetry.

Robbia, Luca della (c.1400–82). Florentine sculptor, the most famous member of a family of artists. Nothing is known of his early career, and he was a mature artist by the time of his first documented work—a *Cantoria* (Singing Gallery, 1431–8) for Florence Cathedral, now in the Cathedral Museum. It is a work of considerable originality as well as enormous charm, antedating by a year or two the companion gallery by *Donatello (now also in the Cathedral Museum). Its marble *reliefs of angels and children singing, dancing, and making music reflect *antique prototypes, but are conceived in a more cheerful, less heroic spirit than Donatello's figures. In his own time Luca had the reputation of being one of the leaders of the modern (i.e. *Renaissance) style, comparable to Donatello and *Ghiberti in sculpture and *Masaccio in painting, but he is now remembered mainly for his development of coloured, glazed *terracotta as a sculptural medium—in particular for his highly popular invention of the type of the half-length Madonna and Child in white on a blue ground. The family workshop seems to have kept the technical formula a secret and it became the basis of a flourishing business; among the major works by Luca in the medium are the roundels of Apostles (c.1450) in *Brunelleschi's Pazzi Chapel in S. Croce. Luca's business was carried on by his nephew **Andrea** (1435–1525), and later by Andrea's five sons, of whom **Giovanni** (1469–after 1529) was the most important. The famous roundels of infants on the façade of the Foundling Hospital in Florence (1463–6) were probably made by Andrea. His successors tended to sentimentalize Luca's warm humanity, and in course of time the artists' studio became a potters' workshop-industry.

Robert, Hubert (1733–1808). French landscape painter. From 1754 to 1765 he lived in Italy (mainly Rome), where he became a friend of *Fragonard and made a large number of drawings that were a source for his pictures after his return to Paris. Like Fragonard, he had a lively touch and in their drawings they are sometimes so close in style that it is difficult to distinguish their hands. However, whereas Fragonard was primarily a figure painter, Robert became the chief pioneer and leading exponent of scenes involving ruined buildings (he was nicknamed 'Robert des Ruines'). Some of his paintings are fairly accurate depictions of real architecture, but he also produced various types of imaginary ruinscapes, including pictures in which he showed contemporary buildings as they might look after falling into decay. His work was much in demand—part of the vogue for rather artificial, idealized landscape that was one aspect of *Rococo taste. As well as delicacy and charm, however, his paintings have grandeur and he could work convincingly on a large scale; many of his pictures were intended for a specific decorative context in grandiose interiors. In 1784 Louis XVI appointed him keeper of his pictures and gave him responsibility for creating a museum at the *Louvre. However, he fell foul of intrigue during the Revolution and was imprisoned in 1793–4, narrowly escaping execution (he owed his life to a mistake whereby another person of the same name was guillotined in his stead). After his release he returned to his successful career and is said to have died 'brush in hand'.

Roberti, Ercole de' (c.1450–96). Italian painter, active mainly in Ferrara. He succeeded *Tura as court painter to the *Este in 1486, but little is known of his life. Earlier he appears to have assisted *Cossa for some years, and with Cossa and Tura he ranks as the leading artist of the 15th-century Ferrarese School. His only surviving documented painting is the altarpiece with a *Madonna Enthroned with Saints* (1480) painted for S. Maria in Poroto at Ravenna and now in the Brera, Milan. Other works, however, can be confidently given to him because of his distinctive style. He inherited the tradition of Tura and Cossa, with their precise line and metallic colours against elaborately fanciful ornamentation, but he developed this manner with great originality, modifying it with a subtlety of handling that seems to derive from Giovanni *Bellini. His work is often remarkable for its almost mystical intensity of feeling, as in his *Pietà* in the Walker Art Gallery, Liverpool.

Roberts, David (1796–1864). Scottish painter. He was apprenticed to a house painter, then worked as a scene painter for theatres in Edinburgh and Glasgow. In 1822 he settled in London and worked at the Drury Lane Theatre with his friend Clarkson *Stanfield. From 1833 he travelled widely in Europe and the Mediterranean basin and made a fortune with his topographical views. He worked in oil and watercolour and published lavishly illustrated books, among them the six-volume *Views in the Holy Land, Syria, Idumea, Arabia, Egypt and Nubia* (1842–9). His work can be monotonous when seen en masse, but at his best he combines bold design with precise observation.

Roberts, Tom (1856–1931). British-born Australian painter, active mainly in and around Melbourne. He was the most important figure in introducing *Impressionism to Australia and he is regarded as the father of the country's indigenous tradition of landscape painting. Much of his career was spent in Europe and he first acquired some knowledge of Impressionism in 1883 in Spain, where he met artists who had studied in Paris. After returning to Melbourne in 1885 he was soon the leading figure of the *Heidelberg School, whose work was based on open-air painting. In addition to landscapes (and portraits—with which he earned a major part of his living), Roberts painted scenes of rural genre and history (including outlaw life). He continued to make journeys to Europe, where he exhibited with modest success at the *Royal Academy, the Paris *Salon, and elsewhere. By the time of his death, however, 'he had been overshadowed by the more prolific, and by then shallower, talents of his old friend, Arthur *Streeton' (Robert *Hughes, *The Art of Australia*, 1970).

Roberts, William (1895–1980). British painter, chiefly of figure compositions and portraits. After travelling in France and Italy, he worked briefly for the *Omega Workshops, then in 1914 joined the *Vorticist movement. His style at this time showed his precocious response to French modernism and was close to that of *Bomberg in the way he depicted stiff, stylized figures through geometrically simplified forms. After the First World War (in which he served in the Royal Artillery and as an *Official War Artist) his forms became rounder and fuller in a manner reminiscent of the 'tubism' of *Léger. Often his paintings showed groups of figures in everyday settings, his most famous work being *The*

Vorticists at the Restaurant de la Tour Eiffel: Spring 1915, 1961–2, Tate, London), an imaginative reconstruction of his former colleagues celebrating at a favourite rendezvous to mark the publication of the first issue of *Blast*. In response to the exhibition 'Wyndham *Lewis and the Vorticists' at the Tate Gallery in 1956, Roberts wrote a series of pamphlets (1956–8) disputing Lewis's claim (in the catalogue introduction) that 'Vorticism, in fact, was what I, personally, did, and said, at a certain period.' However, in 1974 Roberts issued another pamphlet in which he strangely contradicted his earlier statements, declaring that the term Vorticism 'should only be used in reference to his [Lewis's] own work; and that the term Cubist should be employed to describe the abstract painting of his contemporaries of the 1914 period'.

rocaille. Term applied from the mid-16th century onwards to fancy rock-work and shell-work for fountains and grottoes, and later to ornament based on such forms. The word *Rococo derives from it and the two terms have sometimes been used synonymously by French art historians.

rocker. *See* MEZZOTINT.

Rockwell, Norman (1894–1978). American illustrator and painter. He studied at various art schools in New York and by the time he was 18 was a full-time professional illustrator. In 1916 he had a cover accepted by the *Saturday Evening Post*, the biggest-selling weekly publication in the USA (its circulation was then about 3,000,000), and hundreds of others followed for this magazine until it ceased publication in 1969. He also worked for many other publications. Rockwell's subjects were drawn from everyday American life and his style was anecdotal, sentimental, and lovingly detailed; he described his imagery as 'this best-possible-world, Santa-down-the-chimney, lovely-kids-adoring-their-kindly-grandpa sort of thing'. Such work brought him immense popularity, making him something of a national institution. For most of his career critics dismissed his work as corny, but he began to receive serious attention as a painter late in his career. In his later years, too, he sometimes turned to more serious subjects, producing, for example, a series on racism for *Look* magazine. From 1953 until his death he lived at Stockbridge, Massachusetts, where there is a museum devoted to him.

Rocky Mountain School. Term applied retrospectively to 19th-century American artists who painted the Rocky Mountains in a reverential spirit similar to that adopted by the *Hudson River School. Alfred *Bierstadt is the best-known artist embraced by the term.

Rococo. Style of art and architecture, characterized by lightness, grace, playfulness, and intimacy, that emerged in France *c.*1700 and spread throughout Europe in the 18th century. The Rococo was both a development from and a reaction against the weightier *Baroque style, and initially it was expressed mainly in interior decoration. It shared with the Baroque a love of complexity of form, but instead of a concern for solidity and mass, there was a delicate play on the surface, with sombre colours and heavy gilding giving way to lighter tones and delicate ornament. The word is said to have been coined in the 1790s by a pupil of J.-L. *David as a combination of *barocco* (Baroque) and *rocaille; like many stylistic labels in the history of art, it was originally a term of abuse, meaning 'tastelessly florid or ornate', but it is now used without any pejorative connotations.

In painting, the first great master of the Rococo style was *Watteau and the painters who most completely represent the lighthearted (often gently erotic) spirit of the mature Rococo style are *Boucher and *Fragonard. *Falconet is perhaps the best representative of the style in French sculpture, but generally the Rococo spirit is seen more clearly in small porcelain figures than in large-scale statues (Falconet himself was director of the famous porcelain factory at Sèvres). In architecture the Rococo style was much more suitable for interiors, with asymmetrical curves and pretty decorative motifs prevailing, than for exteriors, but something of the Rococo spirit—of its refinement and charm—can be seen even in such a regular and relatively unadorned building as Ange-Jacques Gabriel's Petit Trianon (1763–9) at Versailles.

From Paris the Rococo was disseminated by French artists working abroad and by engraved publications of French designs. It spread to Germany, Austria, Russia, Spain, and northern Italy (*Tiepolo, Pietro *Longhi, *Guardi). In England it had somewhat less of a vogue, although a substantial exhibition of English Rococo art was held at the Victoria and Albert Museum in 1984 and there are clear reflections of the style even in the work of so xenophobic an artist as *Hogarth. *Gainsborough's delicacy of characterization and sensitivity of touch (although completely personal) are also thoroughly in the Rococo spirit. In each country the style took on a national character and in addition many local variants may be distinguished. Outside France, it had its finest flowering in Germany and Austria, where it merged with a still vigorous Baroque tradition. In churches such as Vierzehnheiligen (1743–72) by Balthasar Neumann, the Baroque qualities of spatial variety and of architecture, sculpture, and painting working together are taken up in a breathtakingly light and exuberant manner. The Rococo flourished in central Europe until the end of the century (as in the work of *Maulbertsch), but in France and elsewhere the tide of taste had begun to turn from frivolity towards the sternness of *Neoclassicism by the 1760s.

Rodchenko, Alexander (1891–1956). Russian painter, sculptor, industrial designer, and photographer, one of the leading *Constructivists. His output was large and his artistic evolution was rapid, as he moved from *Impressionistic pictures in 1913 to pure abstracts, made with a ruler and compass, in 1916. He was influenced by *Malevich's *Suprematism, his *Black on Black* (1918, MoMA, New York) being a response to Malevich's *White on White* paintings. Rodchenko, however, was without Malevich's mystical leanings, and he coined the term *'Non-objective' to describe his own more scientific outlook. In 1917 he began making three-dimensional constructions under the influence of *Tatlin, and some of these developed into graceful hanging sculptures. Like Tatlin and other Constructivists, however, Rodchenko came to reject pure art as a parasitic activity, and after 1922 he devoted his energies to industrial design, typography, film and stage design, propaganda posters, and photography. It was perhaps in photography that he made his most original and enduring contribution to art. Although his photographs were geared towards reportage and creating a pictorial record of the new Russia, many of them are outstanding for their 'abstract' qualities, partly created by his novel exploitation of unusual angles and viewpoints; his dramatic use of light and shadow influenced, for example, the great Soviet film director Sergei Eisenstein. In the mid-1930s, after Stalin's imposition of *Socialist Realism, Rodchenko returned to easel painting. Initially he produced circus scenes, but in 1943 he began to paint abstract 'drip' pictures that—amazingly—prefigure those of Jackson *Pollock. Rodchenko's wife, Varvara Stepanova (1894–1958), was a painter and designer.

Rodin, Auguste (1840–1917). French sculptor and draughtsman, one of the greatest and most influential European artists of his period. He was the first sculptor since the heyday of *Neoclassicism to occupy a central position in public attention and he opened up new possibilities for his art in a manner comparable to that of his great contemporaries in painting—*Cézanne, *Gauguin, and van *Gogh. His beginnings, however, were not auspicious. He came from a poor background, was rejected three times by the École des *Beaux-Arts, and for many years worked mainly as an ornamental mason. In the winter of 1875-6 he visited Italy, where (as he later wrote to *Bourdelle) '*Michelangelo freed me from academism.' Michelangelo was the inspiration for his first major work, a male nude, *The Age of Bronze*, which was exhibited at the 1877 *Salon. (Like many of Rodin's statues, this exists in several casts; the Rodin Museum in Paris has examples of virtually all his work. There is also a Rodin museum in Philadelphia.) It caused a sensation because the *naturalistic treatment of the naked figure was so different from the idealizing conventions then current—he was even accused of having cast it from a live model. Three years later, in 1880, his reputation now established, Rodin was commissioned by the state to make a bronze door for a proposed Musée des Arts Décoratifs. He never finished the huge work—*The Gates of Hell*—in a definitive way (he worked on it intermittently until 1900 and the museum never came into being in its proposed form), but he poured some of his finest creative energy into it, and many of the nearly 200

figures that are part of it formed the basis of famous independent sculptures, most notably *The Kiss* and *The Thinker*. The several casts of the complete structure that exist were made after Rodin's death. Rodin's overall design is a kind of *Romantic reworking of *Ghiberti's *Gates of Paradise* for the Florence Baptistery, the twisted and anguished figures, irregularly arranged, reminiscent of Michelangelo's *Last Judgement* and Gustav *Doré's illustrations for the *Divine Comedy*. The modelling is often rough and 'unfinished' and anatomical forms are exaggerated or simplified in the cause of intensity of expression.

These traits were taken further in some of Rodin's monuments, beginning with the famous group of *The Burghers of Calais* (1885–95), commissioned by the city of Calais for a site in front of the town hall (there are several other casts, including one in Victoria Tower Gardens, London). In the figures of the six hostages who face the threat of death, Rodin showed a variety of responses—including anguish as well as courage—to an extreme emotional crisis. The civic authorities had wanted something in a more traditional heroic-patriotic vein, and the monument was eventually unveiled only after years of wrangling. Even worse hostility was aroused a few years later by his statue of Balzac. This was commissioned by the Société des Gens de Lettres in 1891, but Rodin's design was so radical—an expression of the elemental power of genius rather than a portrait of an individual—that it was rejected, and the monument was not finally cast and set up until 1939—at the intersection of the boulevards Raspail and Montparnasse in Paris. It ranks as the most original piece of public statuary created in the 19th century, and *Brancusi wrote that it was 'indisputably the starting point of modern sculpture'. Rodin himself described it as 'the sum of my whole life'. In spite of the controversy his work caused, by 1900 Rodin was widely regarded as the greatest living sculptor, and in that year a pavilion was devoted to his work at the Paris World Fair. From this point he created no more major monuments, his sculpture consisting mainly of portrait busts, including many of eminent personalities. In his later years he was also a prolific draughtsman, mainly of the female nude, some of the drawings being highly erotic. (He was famed for his

voracious sexual appetite, but this was ex-
cused as an aspect of his Olympian stature;
his lovers included Gwen *John.) He left his
collection of his own work to the state to
found the Musée Rodin in Paris, opened in
1919. His villa at Meudon (now a suburb of
Paris) is an outstation of the museum. Rodin
is buried in the garden at Meudon, with a
cast of *The Thinker* overlooking his grave.

Although the literary and symbolic significance he attached to his work has been
out of keeping with the conception of 'pure'
sculpture that predominated in the 20th
century, Rodin's influence on the development of modern art has been immense, for
single-handedly he revived sculpture from a
period of relative stagnation when it had
lagged behind the momentous achievements of contemporary painters and made
it once again a vehicle for intense personal
expression. His sense of movement and
energy and his use of the partial figure (particularly the torso) as a legitimate subject
were among his most potent legacies.

Roelas, Juan de (*c.*1560–1625). Spanish
painter. Roelas was a priest and virtually all
his work was done for churches and religious houses in and around Seville, where
he was the leading painter of his period. He
has been called 'the Spanish *Tintoretto'
and 'the Spanish *Veronese', and the painterly richness of his large multi-figure compositions suggests he had studied in Italy.
His work, however, has a religious fervour
that is typically Spanish rather than Italian,
and his blending of mysticism with *naturalism was deeply influential in Seville. Most
of his work remains there; his masterpiece
is perhaps the huge *Martyrdom of St Andrew*
(1609, Mus. B.-A., Seville).

Roerich, Nikolai (1874–1947). Russian
painter, designer, archaeologist, anthropologist, and mystical philosopher. He was
a prolific painter of landscapes and of imaginary historical scenes that evoke a colourful pagan image of Russia's past. They
reveal the same feeling for exotic splendour
and bold, sumptuous colour that he displayed in his set and costume designs for
*Diaghilev's Ballets Russes, notably for Stra-
vinsky's *Rite of Spring* (1913), for which Roerich created the scenario with the composer.
A man of immense energy, Roerich combined his career as an artist with one as an
archaeologist and anthropologist. In 1925–8

he led a 26,000-km (16,000-mile) expedition
in Central Asia, and his investigations still
form 'the bedrock of anthropological studies' in the region (*The Times Atlas of World
Exploration*, 1991). From 1928 until his
death he directed a Himalayan research station in the Kulu Valley in India, and many of
his later paintings feature mountain landscapes. He had a deep interest in esoteric
religions and the mysteries of nature, and
he developed a philosophy in which art
should unite humanity. There are Roerich
museums in Moscow and New York (he
lived in the USA, 1920–3), but the best collection of his work is in the Russian
Museum, St Petersburg.

Roger of Helmarshausen. *See* THEOPHI-
LUS.

Rogers, Claude (1907–79). British painter
of portraits, landscapes, and genre scenes.
With William *Coldstream and Victor *Pasmore he founded the *Euston Road School
in 1937 and he became one of the leading
upholders of its sober figurative tradition,
although in his later work the underlying
abstract quality of the composition became
of more importance. Much of his career was
devoted to teaching, notably at the Slade
School, 1949–63, and Reading University,
where he was professor of fine art, 1963–72.

Rohlfs, Christian (1849–1938). German
painter and printmaker. Until he was over
50 he worked in a fairly traditional *naturalistic manner, but he then discovered the
work of the *Post-Impressionists, in particular van *Gogh, whose brilliant colour and
intense feeling were a revelation to him,
and he became one of the pioneers of *Expressionism in Germany. His favourite
themes were visionary views of old German
towns, colourful landscapes, and flower
pieces. He received considerable acclaim
for work in his new style, but in 1937 he
was declared a *degenerate artist by the
Nazis and forbidden to paint.

Roldán, Pedro (1624–99). Spanish *Baroque sculptor. He trained in Granada but
worked mainly in his native Seville, where
he became the leading sculptor of his
period. His work was often *polychromed
by *Valdés Leal, as for example with his
group of the *Entombment* (1670–2), which
forms the centrepiece of the high altar of
the church of the Hospital de la Caridad,

Seville. Roldán's daughter and pupil, **Luisa** (1650–c.1704), was also a sculptor, principally active in Cadiz and Madrid. She was the only woman to hold the position of royal sculptor, to Charles II (see HABSBURG). Roldán's grandson, Pedro Duque Cornejo (1678–1757), was Seville's foremost sculptor of the early 18th century.

Romanelli, Giovanni Francesco (c.1610–62). Italian painter and tapestry designer. He was Pietro da *Cortona's outstanding pupil, and like his master a protégé of the *Barberini family. Romanelli's graceful style was less energetic than Cortona's (he owed much to his first teacher *Domenichino) and his restrained type of Baroque proved particularly popular and influential in France, where he worked 1646–7 and 1655–7. He introduced to Paris Cortona's characteristic manner of decoration, consisting of paintings combined with richly gilded *stuccowork, and this was one of the sources for the great schemes of *Le Brun at Versailles and elsewhere. Examples of Romanelli's decorative work survive in the Bibliothèque Nationale (painted for Cardinal Mazarin, 1646–7) and (much altered) in the Salle des Saisons of the Louvre (painted for Anne of Austria, mother of Louis XIV, 1655–7).

Romanesque. Style of art and architecture prevailing throughout most of Europe in the 11th and 12th centuries, the first style to achieve such international currency. The dominant art of the Middle Ages was architecture, and 'Romanesque', like *'Gothic', is primarily an architectural term that has been extended to the other arts of the period. As the name suggests, it indicates a derivation from Roman art, and sometimes 'Romanesque' is used to cover all the developments from Roman architecture in the period from the collapse of the Roman empire until the flowering of the Gothic—roughly AD 500–1200. More usually, however, it is applied to a distinctive style that emerged, almost simultaneously, in several countries—France, Germany, Italy, Spain—in the 11th century. It is characterized most obviously by a new massiveness of scale, reflecting the greater political and economic stability that followed a period when Christian civilization seemed in danger of extinction. Romanesque painting and sculpture are generally strongly styl-

ized, with little of the *naturalism and humanistic warmth of *classical or later Gothic art. The forms of nature are freely translated into linear and sculptural designs that at times are majestically calm and severe and at others are agitated by a visionary excitement. Because of its expressionistic distortion, Romanesque art, as with other great non-naturalistic styles of the past, has had to wait for the revolution in sensibility brought about by modern art in order to be widely appreciated.

Romantic Classicism. *See* NEOCLASSICISM and ROMANTICISM.

Romanticism. Movement in the arts flourishing in the late 18th and early 19th centuries. Romanticism is so varied in its manifestations that a single definition is impossible, but its keynote was a belief in the value of individual experience. In this it marked a reaction from the rationalism of the Enlightenment and the orderliness of the *Neoclassical style. The Romantic artist explored the values of intuition and instinct, exchanging the public discourse of Neoclassicism, the forms of which had a common currency, for a more private kind of expression. Romanticism is commonly seen as the antithesis of *classicism, and the two concepts are sometimes used in a very general sense to designate polarities in attitude that may be seen in the art of any age—thus *Raphael might be described as a 'classical' artist, whereas his contemporary *Giorgione is a 'romantic' one. However, the exponents of both Romanticism and classicism share a concern with the *ideal rather than the real, and that there is sometimes no firm dividing line between the two approaches is shown by the use of the term 'Romantic Classicism' to describe certain works that show a Romantic response to antiquity. Both Romanticism and classicism embrace concepts of nobility, grandeur, virtue, and superiority. But where the classical seems a possible ideal that will adapt man to his society and mould that society into an orderly setting for him, the Romantic envisages the unattainable, beyond the limits of society and human adaptability. The classical hero accepts the fate over which he has no control and triumphs nobly in this acquiescence, otherwise he would not be a hero. The Romantic hero pits himself against a hostile environment and at no time comes to terms with it even if he reaches his goal, otherwise he would not be Romantic.

Romanticism represents an attitude of mind rather than a set of particular stylistic traits and involves the expression of an idea that tends to have a verbal rather than a visual origin. It lends itself more easily to expression through music and literature than through the visual arts, as a sense of the infinite and the transcendental, of forces exceeding the boundaries of reason, must necessarily be vague—suggestive rather than concrete, as it must be in painting and even more so in sculpture. Almost by definition, the leading Romantic artists differ widely from one another—William *Blake and *Turner in Britain, *Delacroix and *Géricault in France, *Friedrich and *Runge in Germany. The movement of which they were a part died out in the mid-19th century, but in a broader sense the Romantic spirit has lived on, representing a revolt against conservatism, moderation, and insincerity and an insistence on the primacy of the imagination in artistic expression.

Rombouts, Theodoor (1597–1637). Flemish painter, mainly of religious and *genre scenes. He was a pupil of *Janssen in his native Antwerp, then from about 1616 to about 1625 he was in Italy. There his work became strongly *Caravaggesque and he established himself as one of the leading Flemish exponents of the style. Later, he fell under the all-pervasive influence of *Rubens and his work became much lighter in tonality.

Romney, George (1734–1802). English painter, mainly of portraits. Born in Lancashire, the son of a builder and cabinetmaker, he worked in the north of England until 1762, when he settled in London. There he became the most successful portraitist of the day apart from *Reynolds and *Gainsborough. His posthumous reputation was once almost the equal of theirs, but later faded considerably. Much of his work is now considered facile and repetitive compared with that of his two great contemporaries, and he was probably at his best with portraits of young people, when his delicate colour sense and graceful line were used to good effect. As with many successful portraitists, his heart lay elsewhere

and he had aspirations to be a history painter. In 1773–5 he visited Italy and this made a lasting effect on him, but his plans for grandiose literary and historical works rarely advanced beyond his sepia drawings (a large collection is in the Fitzwilliam Museum, Cambridge), although he painted for *Boydell's Shakespeare Gallery. Introspective and nervous by temperament, Romney was attracted to literary circles and associated little with his fellow artists, never exhibiting at the *Royal Academy. His friends among artists tended to be others of literary inclination, such as *Flaxman. In 1781 Romney met Emma Hart, later Lady Hamilton, Nelson's mistress, and became infatuated with her, painting her many times in various guises. His final years were marred by ill health and depression and in 1799 he retired to Kendal in Cumberland. There he was cared for by his wife, whom he had rarely seen since settling in London. Romney's output was large and his paintings are in many collections in Britain and the USA (in the early 20th century he was a particular favourite of American collectors and his work often fetched huge sums at this time).

Ronald, William (William Ronald Smith) (1926–). Canadian-American painter and radio and television presenter, a leading figure in the development and acceptance of abstract art in Canada. In 1955 he moved from Toronto to New York, where he enjoyed considerable success among the second generation of *Abstract Expressionists. He lived in the USA until 1965, becoming an American citizen in 1963, but he retained a large following in Toronto and exerted a strong influence on painters there. With the decline of Abstract Expressionism his popularity waned, but after his return to Canada he achieved success as a radio and television personality, presenting chat shows and programmes on art and current affairs. He also developed a kind of roadshow performance in which he painted on stage before an audience to the accompaniment of rock music.

Roncalli, Cristoforo (c.1552–1626). Italian painter also called Il Pomarancio (after his birthplace, Pomarance, near Volterra). With *Cesari he was one of the leading fresco decorators of his time in Rome. Although he adapted somewhat to the innovations of the *Carracci, he remained essentially in the *Mannerist tradition and his work is generally undistinguished. His unbiased, commonsense views on art, however, commended him to Vincenzo *Giustiniani, one of the most enlightened patrons of his time; Roncalli became his artistic adviser and made a tour of northern Europe with him in 1606.

Rooker, Michael 'Angelo' (1746?–1801). English painter. He studied engraving with his father **Edward** (1724?–1774), who specialized in architectural subjects, and painting with Paul *Sandby (who evidently dubbed him 'Angelo'). From about 1788 he made regular sketching tours in the southern and midland counties and he was one of the most industrious watercolour topographers of his time. From 1779 to 1800 he was scene painter at the Haymarket Theatre in London.

Rops, Félicien (1833–98). Belgian printmaker (and occasional painter), active mainly in Paris (he settled at Essonnes, very near the city, in 1874). Rops was a friend of *Baudelaire, who helped to launch him in the Paris art world, and in his work he similarly showed a fascination with evil and vice, particularly with the idea of woman as a corrupter of man. He was much admired by *Symbolist writers and a good deal of his output was done as illustrations to esoteric and erotic literature. Some of his work is frankly pornographic or blasphemous (for example, he showed Mary Magdalene masturbating at the foot of the cross), but in spite of his disdain for conventional morals, he became famous and successful. Technically he was one of the most resourceful printmakers of his period, mixing different techniques (such as *aquatint with *mezzotint) and experimenting with various types of acids and varnishes. In 1886 he became a member of the avantgarde Brussels group Les *Vingt and his work was notably influential on *Ensor.

Rosa, Salvator (1615–73). Italian painter and etcher, a fiery and flamboyant character who was a poet and actor as well as an artist. After training in his native Naples, he spent most of his career in Rome, except for the 1640s, when he lived mainly in Florence; his decision to move there was probably connected with the scandal he caused by publicly satirizing the great *Bernini. Rosa was a prolific artist and painted various subjects (including spirited battle pieces in which he surpassed his teacher *Falcone), but he is best known for the creation of a new type of wild and savage landscape. His craggy cliffs, jagged, moss-laden trees, and rough bravura handling create a dank and desolate air that contrasts sharply with the serenity of *Claude or the classical grandeur of *Poussin (a situation summed up in the famous lines from James Thomson's *The Castle of Indolence* (1748): 'Whate'er Lorraine light-touched with softening hue, | Or savage Rosa dashed, or learned Poussin drew'). He is also well known for his macabre subjects (notably witches), but he himself set most store by his large historical and religious compositions, which are now considered his least attractive works. His most ambitious etchings, dating mainly from the 1660s, were done to publicize these paintings. Rosa's colourful personality and unswerving belief in his own genius made him a prototype of the *Romantic artist and his fame was greatest in the 18th and 19th centuries (the story that he was a bandit seems to be a 19th-century invention). He was highly influential on the development of the *Picturesque and the *Sublime, and he had a great vogue in England, where *Mortimer was particularly taken with his pictures of bandits. *Ruskin, however, was largely responsible for the fall of his reputation, condemning his landscapes as artificial.

Rose + Croix, Salon de la. *See* SALON DE LA ROSE + CROIX.

Rosenberg, Harold (1906–78). American writer, one of the most influential critics in the field of contemporary art from the 1950s until his death. Early in his career he wrote poetry and essays on literary and general cultural issues, and his first important work devoted to the visual arts was an article in *Art News* in 1952 in which he coined the term *Action Painting. He was one of the major champions of *Abstract Expressionism, writing monographs on *Gorky (1962), *de Kooning (1974), and *Newman (1978). Unlike his rival Clement *Greenberg, who was concerned only with formal values, Rosenberg had an ethical and political conception of art, believing that the critic should less 'judge it' than 'locate it', subordinating visual analysis to intellectual understanding. He thought that authentic modern art should be perpetually disruptive and he attacked the manipulative fashions created by both the market place and the museum. *Pop art, for example, he treated with disdain.

Roslin, Alexander (1718–93). Swedish portrait painter, active mainly in France. He left his country in 1745, worked at the courts of Bayreuth (1745–7) and Parma (1751–2), and in 1752 settled in Paris. There he rapidly became one of the leading portraitists of the day, esteemed particularly for his skilful rendering of expensive fabrics and delicate complexions ('Satin, skin? Go to Roslin'). In the 1770s he visited Moscow, St Petersburg, Vienna, and Warsaw (as well as Stockholm), but in spite of his international travels his elegant work was entirely French in style. His wife, **Marie-Suzanne Giroust** (1734–72), was a pastellist and miniaturist. One of Roslin's finest works is an enchanting portrait of her entitled *The Lady with a Fan* (1768, Nationalmuseum, Stockholm).

Rosselli, Cosimo (1439–1507). Florentine painter. His successful career (the high point of which was painting frescos in the Sistine Chapel, 1481–2, together with *Botticelli, *Ghirlandaio, and *Perugino) was based on his facility and high standards of craftsmanship rather than on any great distinction or originality as an artist. His pupils included Fra *Bartolommeo and *Piero di Cosimo.

Rossellino, Bernardo (c.1409–64) and **Antonio** (c.1427–79). Florentine sculptors, brothers. The family name was Gambarelli, but Antonio's nickname (Rossellino means 'little redhead') is now applied to both of them. They had three other brothers who also worked as sculptors, and all five of them seem to have worked together under Bernardo's management. He was an architect as well as a sculptor and he combined both arts in his chief work—the tomb of the great humanist Leonardo Bruni, chancellor of the Florentine Republic, in S. Croce, Florence (c.1444–7). It is based on the monument of the antipope John XXIII (Baldassare Cossa) by *Donatello and *Michelozzo in the Baptistery in Florence, and although less powerful is more graceful and harmoni-

ous; the pilasters framing the serene reclining effigy have a dignity and elegance almost worthy of *Brunelleschi. It became the model for the niche tomb for the rest of the century.

Antonio was trained by his brother, and his most ambitious work—the tomb of the Cardinal Prince of Portugal in S. Miniato al Monte, Florence (1461–6)—is based on Bernardo's Bruni tomb. It is more elaborate and concerned with movement than Bernardo's masterpiece, but also a less coherent design, and Antonio was a more distinguished artist when working on a smaller scale. He was a fine portraitist (*Giovanni Chellini*, 1456, V&A, London) and also made charming reliefs and statuettes of the Madonna and Child, in which he continued the tradition of Luca della *Robbia in stressing the naturalness and humanity of the Virgin (perhaps the finest of his reliefs is that in the Metropolitan Museum, New York, known as the *Altman Madonna*).

Rossetti, Dante Gabriel (1828–82). English painter and poet. He came from a remarkable and talented family: his father was an exiled Italian patriot and Dante scholar, his sister the poet Christina Rossetti, and his brother the critic William Michael Rossetti. Growing up in modest circumstances but a strongly literary environment, he at first found it hard to decide whether he should devote himself to poetry or painting. Although painting became his profession (following the advice given to him by the poet and critic Leigh Hunt: 'If you paint as well as you write, you may be a rich man'), he continued to write poetry and make translations from the Italian, and he has a secure place in literary history. In 1848 he founded the *Pre-Raphaelite Brotherhood with *Hunt, *Millais, and others. His *Girlhood of Mary Virgin* (1849, Tate, London), the first picture to be exhibited bearing the Brotherhood's initials, was warmly praised and sold well, but the subsequent abuse that the Pre-Raphaelites received hurt him so much that he rarely again exhibited in public. In the 1850s he virtually gave up oils and concentrated on watercolours of medieval subjects. These found ready buyers (often contacts of *Ruskin, whom he met in 1854), and Rossetti, who was a hard and skilful businessman, proved Leigh Hunt's prediction true—by the 1860s he was earning the very substantial sum of £3,000 a year.

In 1860 Rossetti married the beautiful but sickly Elizabeth Siddal, the archetypal Pre-Raphaelite 'stunner', after a long and sometimes vexed liaison. Her melancholy face haunted his imagination, and he portrayed 'Guggums' (as he called her) again and again—'It is like a monomania with him', wrote Ford Madox *Brown in 1855. Rossetti immortalized her mainly in drawings, for in spite of the hatred for academic discipline that made him so disdainful of the official art world, he was an outstanding draughtsman. Elizabeth died from an overdose of laudanum, possibly deliberate, in 1862, and Rossetti was devastated; as a gesture of his grief he had the only complete manuscript of his poems placed in her coffin, but he was persuaded to have them exhumed in 1869 and they were published the following year. Rossetti also painted the intensely spiritual *Beata Beatrix* (Tate) as a memorial to Elizabeth, expressing his love for her as a parallel to Dante's for Beatrice (the picture is dated 1864, but was worked on over a period of several years). By the time of Elizabeth's death Rossetti had returned to oil painting, and in the last two decades of his life his subject matter was confined almost exclusively to beautiful women, portrayed in a richly sensuous manner and often evoking literary or mythological references. Elizabeth was replaced as his favourite model by William *Morris's wife Janey, who became in Rossetti's pictures one of the archetypal femmes fatales—all cascading curls, pouting lips, and smouldering eyes. Rossetti had met Morris and *Burne-Jones in 1856 and entered into partnership with them in 1861 (in the decorative arts firm later known as Morris & Co.), but both business and personal relationships became strained; Rossetti was in love with Janey and he and Morris parted acrimoniously in 1875. In his later years Rossetti became an eccentric recluse (he had a menagerie of unusual animals, including a wombat, the death of which occasioned a poem); he fought a losing battle against drugs and alcohol and he died paralysed and prematurely aged. He was nevertheless a commanding personality and his work was highly influential: his romantic medievalism inspired the second wave of Pre-Raphaelitism associated with Burne-Jones and other followers, and his femmes fatales appealed to the *Symbolists and had a legion of descendants during the turn-of-the-century taste for 'decadence'.

Rosso, Medardo (1858–1928). Italian sculptor. He was virtually self-taught, for he was dismissed from the Brera Academy in Milan in 1883 after only a few months' training when he appealed for drawing to be taught from the nude model rather than casts of statues. In 1884 he first visited Paris, and he lived there from 1889 to 1897, the period of his most intense creative activity. It is indeed with French rather than Italian art that his work has affinity, for he created a sculptural equivalent of *Impressionism, depicting everyday subjects and capturing a feeling of movement, atmosphere, and transitory effects of light. His favourite medium was wax, which he used with great subtlety to express his view that matter was malleable by atmosphere: 'We are mere consequences of the objects which surround us.' His subjects included portraits and single figures and groups in contemporary settings (*The Bookmaker*, 1894, MoMA, New York; *Conversation in a Garden*, 1893, Gal. Naz. d'Arte Contemporanea, Rome). In his early days in Paris Rosso struggled to earn a living (he made funerary monuments for his basic income), but his career blossomed in the 1890s, partly because of the patronage of Henri Rouart (a wealthy industrialist and friend of *Degas), who helped Rosso find clients as well as purchasing works himself. *Rodin, too, tried to help him, but Rosso was suspicious of him and thought he was trying to steal his ideas (it has been suggested that the 'Impressionistic' handling of Rodin's celebrated Balzac monument is indebted to Rosso). In 1897 Rosso returned to Italy and thereafter made almost no new sculpture, devoting his time instead to organizing exhibitions of his work throughout Europe. Through these his work became extremely well known, and after Rodin's death in 1917, *Apollinaire spoke for many when he described him as 'beyond doubt the greatest living sculptor'. His reputation remains high and he is considered one of the most original artists of his time (not even Rodin challenged so decisively the traditional preoccupations of sculpture). He was particularly influential on the *Futurists, who took over and developed many of his ideas.

Rosso's output was fairly small; replicas of several of his works and a collection of his drawings are in the Museo Medardo Rosso at Barzio in Italy.

Rosso Fiorentino (Giovanni Battista di Jacopo) (1494–1540). Florentine painter and decorative artist; the name by which he is known means 'the red-headed Florentine'. *Vasari says that he 'would not bind himself to any master' (a story that fits in with his individuality of temperament), but in his youth he learned most from *Andrea del Sarto, and together with Andrea's pupil *Pontormo (Rosso's friend and close contemporary) he was one of the leading figures in the early development of *Mannerism. His work was highly sophisticated and varied in mood, ranging from the refined elegance of the *Marriage of the Virgin* (1523, S. Lorenzo, Florence) to the violent energy of *Moses Defending the Daughters of Jethro* (c.1523, Uffizi, Florence) and to the disquieting intensity of the *Deposition* (1521, Pinacoteca Communale, Volterra). In 1523 Rosso left Florence for Rome, where he stayed until the Sack of 1527, and he then worked briefly in several Italian towns until 1530, when he was invited to France by Francis I. With *Primaticcio he was the most important artist to work on the decoration of the royal palace at Fontainebleau and one of the creators of the distinctive style of French Mannerism associated with the School of *Fontainebleau. Rosso's principal work there is the Gallery of Francis I. Many engravings were made from his designs and his influence on French art was great. Vasari, whose biography of Rosso includes an entertaining story about his pet baboon, says that he killed himself in remorse after falsely accusing a friend of stealing money from him; there is no supporting evidence for this story, but nothing to contradict it either.

Roszak, Theodore. *See* ABSTRACT EXPRESSIONISM.

Rothenberg, Susan. *See* NEW IMAGE PAINTING.

Rothenstein, Sir William (1872–1945). British painter, printmaker, draughtsman, writer, and teacher. He studied for a year at the *Slade School (1888–9) under Alphonse *Legros and afterwards at the *Académie Julian in Paris. There he was encouraged by

*Degas and *Pissarro, and he was also friendly with *Whistler. His best works are generally thought to be his early Whistlerian paintings such as *The Doll's House* (1899, Tate, London), which shows Augustus *John and Rothenstein's wife as characters in a tense scene from Ibsen's play *A Doll's House*. From about 1898, however, he specialized in portraits of the celebrated and those who later became celebrated. In his later career he was much more renowned as a teacher than a painter. His outlook was conservative (he regarded pure abstraction as 'a cardinal heresy') and as principal of the *Royal College of Art, 1920–35, he exercised an influence second only to that of *Tonks at the Slade School in earlier decades. His books included three volumes of memoirs (1931–9). His brother **Albert** (1881–1953) was a painter, designer, and prolific book illustrator. In 1914 he changed his surname to Rutherston because of anti-German feeling. William's son, **Sir John Rothenstein** (1901–92), had a distinguished career as an art historian (he was director of the Tate Gallery, 1938–64, and wrote numerous books); another son, **Michael Rothenstein** (1908–93), was a painter, printmaker, and writer on art.

Rothko, Mark (1903–70). Russian-born American painter, one of the outstanding figures of *Abstract Expressionism and one of the creators of *Colour Field Painting. He emigrated to the USA as a child in 1913. After dropping out of Yale University in 1923 he moved to New York and studied at the *Art Students League under Max *Weber, but he regarded himself as essentially self-taught as a painter. In the 1930s and 1940s he went through phases influenced by *Expressionism and *Surrealism, but from about 1947 he began to develop his distinctive mature style. Typically his paintings feature large rectangular expanses of colour arranged parallel to each other, usually in a vertical format. The edges of these shapes are softly uneven, giving them a hazy, pulsating quality, and they seem to gently hover or float over the canvas. The paintings are often very large and the effect they produce is generally one of calmness and contemplation, but in spite of their tranquillity, they cost Rothko enormous emotional effort: 'I'm not an abstract artist…I'm not interested in the relationship of colour or form or anything else.

I'm interested only in expressing basic human emotions—tragedy, ecstasy, doom and so on. And the fact that a lot of people break down and cry when confronted with my pictures shows that I can communicate these basic human emotions... The people who weep before my pictures are having the same religious experience as I had when I painted them.'

Rothko was poor for much of his career (from 1929 to 1959 he earned at least part of his living by teaching art), but his reputation grew in the 1950s and in 1961 he was given a major retrospective exhibition at the Museum of Modern Art, New York, that sealed his success. In spite of his soaring fame (and the money it brought), Rothko was plagued by depression. He had a prickly temperament, drank heavily, took barbiturates to excess, was fearful and suspicious of younger artists, had two unhappy marriages, and felt he was misunderstood (he disliked having his paintings discussed in *formalist terms). His early works had often been bright and vivid in colour, but from the 1950s they became increasingly sombre, typically employing blacks, browns, and maroon. He regarded his fourteen paintings for a non-denominational chapel in Houston, Texas (now known as the Rothko Chapel), 1967–9, as his masterpieces. His last paintings were a series of stark black on grey canvases that evoke his painful state of mind leading up to his suicide (he slashed his veins in his studio).

Rottenhammer, Hans (or **Johann**) (1564–1625). German painter, active for much of his career in Italy. He moved there in about 1589, worked in Rome in the early 1590s, then settled in Venice, where he lived 1596–1606. He specialized in mythological scenes in landscape settings, working on a small scale and often on copper, and his paintings form a link between the styles of Paul *Bril, whom he knew in Rome, and Adam *Elsheimer, who was his assistant in Venice (Rottenhammer's workshop became something of a magnet for German artists visiting the city). After his return to Germany he settled in Augsburg. He became one of the leading artists there, but he died in poverty, mainly because of overindulgence in alcohol.

Rouault, Georges (1871–1958). French painter, draughtsman, printmaker, and designer who created a personal kind of *Expressionism that gives him a highly distinctive place in modern art. From 1885 to 1890 he was apprenticed to a stained-glass maker, his work including the restoration of medieval glass; the vivid colours and strong outlines characteristic of the medium left a strong imprint on his work. In 1892 he became a fellow pupil of *Matisse and *Marquet under Gustave *Moreau at the École des *Beaux-Arts. He was Moreau's favourite pupil and in 1898 became the first curator of the Musée Moreau in Paris. At about the same time he underwent a psychological crisis and although he continued to associate with the group of artists around Matisse who were later known as *Fauves, he did not adopt their brilliant colour or characteristic subjects; instead he painted characters such as clowns, prostitutes, and outcasts in sombre but glowing tones. These subjects expressed his hatred of cruelty, hypocrisy, and vice, showing the ugliness and degradation of humanity with passionate conviction. Initially such work disturbed the public, but Rouault achieved financial security after *Vollard became his agent in 1917 and during the 1930s he gained international popularity. From about 1940 he devoted himself almost exclusively to religious art. In addition to his large output of paintings, drawings, and large (in various techniques, often done as book illustrations), his work also included ceramics and designs for tapestry, for stained glass, and for *Diaghilev's ballet *The Prodigal Son* (1929), for which the music was written by Prokofiev. By the time of his death he was a much-honoured figure and he was given a state funeral.

Roubiliac, Louis-François (1702–62). French-born sculptor, active in England for virtually his entire career. Little is known of his life before he settled in London in the early 1730s, although he is said to have trained under Balthasar *Permoser in Dresden and Nicolas *Coustou in Paris. He made his reputation with a full-length seated marble statue of the composer Handel (1738, V&A, London), remarkable for its lively informality, and quickly became recognized as the most brilliant portrait sculptor of the day. His busts have great vivacity, stressing small forms and rippling movement in a manner very different from the broader treatment of his contemporary Michael *Rysbrack. He was especially successful with portraits of old and ugly men, and in his series of busts at Trinity College, Cambridge, and the celebrated statue of Newton (1754–5) there, he showed an unusual gift for producing lively portraits of men long dead. Roubiliac was also outstanding as a tomb sculptor, several notable examples being in Westminster Abbey, including the wonderfully dramatic tomb of Lady Elizabeth Nightingale (1758–61), who is shown being attacked with a spear by Death (a hideous skeleton emerging from a vault), while her husband vainly tries to keep him at bay (the skeleton was carved by Roubiliac's assistant Nicholas Read (c.1733–87)). The Nightingale monument clearly shows the influence of *Bernini, whose work deeply impressed Roubiliac when he visited Rome in 1752: he said that compared with Bernini's, his own sculptures looked 'meagre and starved, as if made of nothing but tobacco pipes'. Roubiliac is generally regarded as one of the greatest sculptors ever to work in England, certainly the greatest of his period. He had a vivid imagination, he was a superb craftsman, and, as Gerald Randall observes (*Church Furnishing and Decoration in England and Wales*, 1980), 'Unlike even the best of his rivals, Roubiliac seems to have been incapable of indifferent work, and even his most modest commissions are designed and executed with a master's touch.'

Rousseau, Henri (known as Le Douanier Rousseau) (1844–1910). French painter, the most celebrated of *naive artists. His nickname refers to the job he held with the Paris municipal toll-collecting service (1871–93), although he never actually rose to the rank of *Douanier* (customs officer). Before this he had served in the army, and he later claimed to have seen service in Mexico, but this story seems to be a product of his imagination. He began to paint as a hobby, self-taught, when he was about 40, and from 1886 he exhibited regularly at the *Salon des Indépendants. In 1893 he took early retirement so he could devote himself to art. His character was extraordinarily ingenuous and he suffered much ridicule (although he sometimes interpreted sarcastic remarks literally and took them as praise) as well as enduring great poverty. However, his faith in his own

abilities never wavered. He tried to paint in the academic manner of such traditionalist artists as *Bouguereau and *Gérôme, but it was the innocence and charm of his work that won him the admiration of the avant-garde. He was 'discovered' by *Vollard and members of his circle in about 1906–7, and in 1908 *Picasso gave a banquet, half serious half burlesque, in his honour. Rousseau is now best known for his jungle scenes, the first of which was *Tiger in a Tropical Storm (Surprised!)* (1891, NG, London) and the last *The Dream* (1910, MoMA, New York). These two paintings are works of great imaginative power, in which he showed his extraordinary ability to retain the utter freshness of his vision even when working on a large scale and with loving attention to detail. He claimed such scenes were inspired by his experiences in Mexico, but in fact his sources were illustrated books and visits to the zoo and botanical gardens in Paris. His other work ranges from the jaunty humour of *The Football Players* (1908, Philadelphia Mus. of Art) to the mesmeric, eerie beauty of *The Sleeping Gypsy* (1897, MoMA). Rousseau was buried in a pauper's grave, but his greatness began to be widely acknowledged soon after his death.

Rousseau, Théodore (1812–67). French landscape painter, the central figure of the *Barbizon School. He was one of the pioneers of landscape painting in the open air (*see* PLEIN AIR), and because of the non-academic outlook of his work it was for several years consistently rejected by the *Salon, earning him the nickname 'le grand refusé' (the period during which his paintings were turned down, 1836–41, was, however, shorter than is sometimes imagined and he had earlier had several pictures accepted and even won a medal, in 1834). He first made a lengthy stay in the Forest of Fontainebleau in 1834 and he settled in Barbizon in 1848. Acclaim began to come in the 1850s, but he did not achieve financial security until near the end of his life. During the later 19th century his reputation stood very high (he was widely regarded as one of the greatest of all landscape painters), but it has subsequently declined.

Roussel, Ker-Xavier. *See* NABIS.

Rovere. Italian family that included two popes and three dukes of Urbino, all of them art patrons. The family achieved prominence when **Francesco della Rovere** (1414–84) became pope in 1471 as Sixtus IV. He was a scholar and was strict in his personal life, but he was ruthless in pursuing his aims and unscrupulous in advancing his relatives (he made six of his nephews cardinals). As a patron, he played a key role in the transformation of Rome from a medieval to a Renaissance city, laying out new streets and widening old ones, building the Ponte Sisto over the Tiber, and restoring old buildings and founding new ones, notably the churches of S. Maria del Popolo and S. Maria della Pace. His most famous foundation is the chapel named after him in the Vatican, the Sistine Chapel. It was built in 1477–80 and the celebrated fresco decorations by *Botticelli, *Perugino, and other artists were begun in 1481. His huge expenditure, on war as well as art, left the papal treasury depleted.

Sixtus's tomb, by Antonio *Pollaiuolo, was commissioned after his death by his nephew **Giuliano della Rovere** (1453–1513), who in 1503 became pope as Julius II. He was one of the most formidable personalities among all the popes ('hated by many and feared by all') and the greatest patron of his time, employing *Bramante, *Michelangelo, and *Raphael to create some of the central works of European art: the new St Peter's (begun 1506), the ceiling of the Sistine Chapel (1508–12), and the decoration of the Vatican Stanze (begun 1508). Howard Hibbard (*Michelangelo*, 1975) writes that 'If, as many believe, this was the greatest assembly of talent ever to work for one man at the same time, we must hail Julius as the most perspicacious as well as the most fortunate patron the world has ever known.' His political policies were aimed at making the papacy the most important power in Italy and he personally led campaigns that greatly expanded its territories (his choice of papal name reflected his admiration for the military prowess of Julius Caesar). In spite of his costly wars and his huge outlay on rebuilding St Peter's, because of his skilful administration he left the papacy more prosperous than he found it. Julius's interest in art extended to collecting *antique sculpture, and he placed several of his finest pieces (including the *Apollo Belvedere* and the *Laocoön*) in the Belvedere Courtyard of the Vatican, where artists and scholars were allowed to see them; this was the origin of the *Vatican Museums.

Julius's nephew, **Francesco Maria I della Rovere** (1490–1538), became duke of Urbino in 1508, when he succeeded his childless uncle, Guidobaldo da *Montefeltro, who had adopted him as his heir. His favourite painter was *Titian, who painted portraits of him and his wife, Eleonora *Gonzaga (*c.*1536–8, both Uffizi, Florence). Francesco Maria's son, **Guidobaldo della Rovere** (1514–74), was also a great admirer of Titian and owned his celebrated *Venus of Urbino* (1538, Uffizi); the title is misleading, as the picture hung in the Ducal Palace in Pesaro, which was part of Guidobaldo's territories. His son **Francesco Maria II della Rovere** (1549–1631) employed numerous artists and was in particular a major patron of Federico *Barocci.

Rowlandson, Thomas (1756/7–1827). English *caricaturist. Rowlandson ranks with James *Gillray as one of the founders and supreme figures of the English caricature tradition. However, whilst Gillray was a political satirist, Rowlandson excelled in comic subjects and his work is essentially jolly rather than abrasive. He trained at the *Royal Academy, 1772–7, and began his career as a painter, mainly of portraits, but he turned to caricature to supplement his income (he was a notorious gambler), and finding his sideline highly successful he gave his career over to it completely. His talent for exuberant and flowing line had affinities with the French *Rococo style (Rowlandson had a French aunt and visited Paris during his student years), but his rollicking humour and delicate tonal effects were distinctively English; the marvel of his art is that there is no inconsistency between the bawdiness or boisterousness of the subject matter and the beauty of his technique. Usually he made his caricatures in ink tinted with watercolour, and engravings were produced from them by specialist printmakers. He created an instantly recognizable gallery of social types, such as the old maid, the hack writer, and the crabbed antiquarian, and his buxom wenches have their descendants in the fat ladies of today's saucy seaside postcards. From 1797 much of his work was produced for Rudolph Ackermann (1764–1834), a major publisher of prints. He issued several collections of Rowlandson's work in book form, including *The Comforts of Bath* (1798) and three featuring Dr Syntax (1812–22), a grotesque and pedantic old schoolmaster. Rowlandson's output was huge, but it was only towards the end of his career that the quality of his work suffered because of overproduction.

Royal Academy of Arts (RA), London. The national art *academy of England, founded in 1768 with George III as its 'patron, protector and supporter'. Its main —interlinked—aims were to raise the status of British artists, to provide a venue for regular exhibitions (which have indeed been held every year since 1769), and to establish a sound system of training for students. The *Society of Artists was a forerunner in these aims, but it was soon eclipsed by the RA. *Reynolds was the first president and other foundation members included the architect Sir William Chambers (who was treasurer), *Gainsborough, *West, Richard *Wilson, and the sculptor Joseph *Wilton. Engravers were initially admitted only as Associates of the Royal Academy (ARAs), but from 1853 they were eligible for full membership (the category of ARA was abolished in 1992). The RA was initially based in Pall Mall, but in 1771 its art school transferred to Old Somerset House in the Strand, and in 1780 the whole institution was given rooms in the new Somerset House, a huge government office block designed by Chambers. In 1837 the RA moved to Trafalgar Square, where it shared premises with the *National Gallery in a building newly erected for this dual purpose. However, it eventually proved too small to accommodate both institutions, and in 1869 the RA moved to its present home in Burlington House, Piccadilly. Throughout this first century of its existence, it had had no real rival as an art school and in general enjoyed great prestige. However, in the late 19th century it was increasingly seen as a bastion of conservatism; the *Slade School (founded 1871) and the *Royal College of Art (given its present name in 1896) became more important as teaching institutions, and organizations such as the *New English Art Club (1886), and later the *London Group (1913), were preferred as exhibiting venues by progressive artists. Adventurous work was rarely shown at the RA's exhibitions (where trad-

itionalism ruled to such an extent that top hats and tailcoats were required dress on Private View Days until 1940), and in the 1930s there were several notable instances of leading artists (*Sickert, Stanley *Spencer, Augustus *John) resigning their membership because of outmoded views and taste. After the presidency (1944–9) of *Munnings, who was notorious for his opposition to modern art, the RA's policy became more liberal, and the gap between official and progressive art narrowed. As an art school it has also won back much of its former prestige. But something of the reputation for stuffiness continued up to the 1970s, and the RA's aim at its inception to provide exhibitions of the best contemporary work from year to year has been challenged by commercial galleries and by bodies such as the *Arts Council. The annual summer exhibition still remains a popular social event, however, and the RA regularly organizes major loan exhibitions (the first was in 1870).

Royal College of Art (RCA), London. Britain's pre-eminent training school for artists and designers. Since 1967 it has been a postgraduate university institution, but it has had many changes of status, name, and location since it was founded in 1837 at Somerset House as the School of Design (William *Dyce was a key figure in its early days). Originally it taught industrial design, the fine arts being the province of the *Royal Academy. In 1852 it moved to Marlborough House and was renamed the Central School of Practical Art. It became part of the Government Department of Science and Art in 1853 and in 1857, renamed the National Art Training School, it moved to South Kensington with the Museum of Ornamental Art (later the *Victoria and Albert Museum). In 1863 it moved to new buildings in Exhibition Road, and in 1896 it was renamed the Royal College of Art by Queen Victoria and allowed to grant diplomas. Walter *Crane was principal in 1898–9. By the turn of the century the RCA had turned much more to fine art, away from industrial design, and by the 1920s it rivalled the *Slade School as the most important art school in the country; William *Rothenstein was principal at this time and the students included Barbara *Hepworth and Henry *Moore. By the end of the Second World War the RCA had become rather stagnant, but it was given new life by Sir Robert ('Robin') Darwin (1910–74), who was head from 1948 to 1971 (in 1967 his title changed from principal to rector). Darwin introduced new departments, including fashion design and photography, aligned the RCA more closely with industry (he aimed to 'provide courses of a thoroughly practical nature in all primary industrial fields'), and revitalized the teaching staff (he said that when he joined, 'two of the five professors were alleged not to have exchanged a word for fifteen years'). His overall concern was to make the RCA a 'magnet for talent'. It was during Darwin's long period in charge—generally reckoned the RCA's golden age—that it moved to its present home, a new eight-storey building in Kensington Gore (1961). Its absolute peak of esteem perhaps came in the late 1950s and early 1960s with the generation of students who were largely responsible for launching British *Pop art, including David *Hockney and Allen *Jones.

Rubens, Sir Peter Paul (1577–1640). Flemish painter, draughtsman, designer, and diplomat, the greatest and most influential figure in *Baroque art in northern Europe. He was born at Siegen in Westphalia, the son of a scholarly lawyer from Antwerp who moved to Germany to escape religious persecution (he had Protestant sympathies). In 1587, soon after his father's death, he returned to Antwerp with his mother; he had been baptized a Calvinist in Germany, but he became a devout Catholic. From about 1590 he studied successively with three fairly undistinguished masters: Tobias *Verhaecht (a distant relative), Adam van *Noort, and Otto van *Veen. The first two could teach him no more than the local tradition, but van Veen was a man of some culture, who had spent several years in Rome, and he no doubt inspired his pupil with a desire to visit Italy. Rubens became a master in the Antwerp painters' guild in 1598, and after working with van Veen for two more years he set out for Italy in 1600. Very little of his early work survives, and his style was largely formed in Italy, where he was based until 1608. Soon after his arrival he began working for Vincenzo *Gonzaga, Duke of Mantua, visiting most of the principal art centres of Italy to make copies for the ducal collection (he also

went to Spain, 1603–4, when he accompanied gifts from Vincenzo to Philip III). The most significant parts of his stay in Italy were spent in Genoa and above all Rome. In Genoa he painted some stately aristocratic portraits (*Marchesa Brigida Spinola-Doria*, 1606, NG, Washington) that inspired van *Dyck when he worked in the city, and in Rome he absorbed the lessons of the *antique, the great masters of the *Renaissance, and Annibale *Carracci, basing his dignified and powerful style on these sources, but adding a distinctive energy and warmth of his own.

On learning that his mother was seriously ill, Rubens returned to Antwerp in 1608, but she died before he arrived. Italy had become his spiritual home (he usually signed himself 'Pietro Pauolo') and he considered returning for good, but his success in Antwerp was so immediate and great that he remained there, and in spite of his extensive travels later in his career he never saw Italy again. In 1609 he was appointed court painter to the Archduke Albert and his wife the Infanta Isabella, the Spanish governors of the Netherlands (Isabella was the daughter of Philip II of Spain—*see* HABSBURG); he was allowed to remain in Antwerp, even though the court was in Brussels. In the same year he married the 17-year-old Isabella Brant, the daughter of an eminent Antwerp lawyer. The portrait of himself and his wife that he painted to mark the union (Alte Pin., Munich) gives a wonderful picture of Rubens on the threshold of his prodigious career—handsome, vigorous, and dashingly self-confident. In the next few years he established his reputation as the pre-eminent painter in northern Europe, his first two resounding successes being the huge *triptychs of the *Raising of the Cross* and the *Descent from the Cross* (1610–11 and 1611–14, Antwerp Cathedral), which showed his mastery of *history painting in the *Grand Manner and the immense vigour of his style.

The demand for Rubens's work was extraordinary, and he was able to meet it only because he ran an extremely efficient studio. It is not known how many pupils or assistants he had, because as court painter he was exempt from registering them with the guild. The idea of his running a sort of picture factory has been exaggerated, but even a man of his seemingly inexhaustible intellectual and physical stamina (he habitually rose at 4 a.m.) could not carry out all the work involved in his massive output with his own hands. He both collaborated with established artists (Jan 'Velvet' *Brueghel, *Jordaens, Daniel *Seghers, *Snyders, and others) and retouched pictures by pupils, the degree of his intervention being reflected in the price. Generally his assistants (of whom van Dyck was the most illustrious) did much of the work between the initial oil sketch and the master's finishing touches. Modern taste has tended to admire these sketches and his drawings (in which his personal touch is evident in every stroke of brush, chalk, or pen) more than the large-scale works, but Rubens himself would surely have found this attitude hard to comprehend, for the sheer size and grandeur of the finished paintings gives them an extra, symphonic dimension. His capacity for collaboration and delegation was an expression of his warm and well-balanced personality as well as of his management skills; he was generous towards his fellow artists and in spite of his immense worldly success he aroused little professional jealousy.

Rubens not only painted virtually every type of subject then known, but also designed tapestries, book illustrations, and decorations for festivals, as well as giving visual directives for sculptors, metalworkers, and architects. 'My talents are such', he wrote in 1621, 'that I have never lacked courage to undertake any design, however vast in size or diversified in subject.' So huge was his output, indeed, that it is difficult to put a figure on it: the *Corpus Rubenianum*, the first complete catalogue of his work using all the resources of modern scholarship, began publication in 1968 and is still incomplete (34 volumes are scheduled). His biggest commission in Flanders was for the decoration of the Jesuit church in Antwerp (a building he may also have had a hand in designing), but almost all his work there was destroyed by fire in 1718. From outside Flanders, those who sought his services included the royal families of France, England, and Spain. For Marie de *Médicis (mother of Louis XIII of France) he did a series of 25 enormous paintings on her life (1622–5, Louvre, Paris); for Charles I of England he painted a series of canvases representing the reign of his father James I

(completed 1635) for the ceiling of the Banqueting House in London (the only one of his major decorative schemes still in situ); and for Philip IV of Spain he produced more than a hundred mythological and animal pictures (1636–8, mainly executed by collaborators) for a royal hunting lodge, the Torre de la Parada, near Madrid. Some of the paintings were destroyed in 1710 when the building was sacked during the War of the Spanish Succession, but many are now in the Prado, Madrid, and more than fifty of Rubens's oil sketches also survive.

After the death of the Archduke Albert in 1621, Rubens became a trusted adviser to the Infanta Isabella. In that year a twelve-year truce between the Spanish Netherlands (Flanders) and its northern neighbour the Dutch Republic (Holland) came to an end and Rubens was entrusted with diplomatic missions aimed at securing a lasting peace between the countries. In this he was unsuccessful, but he did play an important role in the preliminary stage of ending hostilities between Spain (Flanders' overlord) and England (Holland's ally). He visited Spain in 1628–9 (when he met *Velázquez) and England in 1629–30, and he was knighted by the kings of both countries (Charles I in 1630, Philip IV in 1631) for his part in the peace negotiations. In his diplomatic role his courtly manners and linguistic skills were put to good advantage—apart from Flemish and Italian, he knew French, German, Latin, and Spanish. Rubens found the political work a solace following the death of his beloved wife in 1626, but after he remarried in 1630 he had a desire to 'remain home all my life', and although he stayed reluctantly involved in diplomacy until Isabella's death in 1633, he never went abroad again. His new wife, 16 when he married her, was Hélène Fourment, daughter of a rich silk merchant and the niece of his first wife. The second marriage was as happy as the first, and Rubens's love of his family shines through many of his late paintings (*Hélène Fourment with Two of her Children*, c.1636, Louvre). In 1635 he bought a country house, the Château de Steen, between Brussels and Malines, and in his final years he developed a new passion for painting landscapes—wonderfully ripe works that led *Constable to extol 'the joyous and animated character' he impressed on 'the level, monotonous scenery of Flanders', and to declare that 'In no branch of the art is Rubens greater than in landscape.' Superb examples are in the National Gallery and the Wallace Collection, London.

In his lifetime Rubens was described as 'prince of painters and painter of princes' and at his death he was mourned not just as a supreme artist but also as one of the great men of the age. His influence in 17th-century Flanders was overwhelming, and it was spread elsewhere in Europe by his journeys abroad and by pictures exported from his workshop, and also through the numerous engravings he commissioned of his work. In later centuries, his influence has also been immense, perhaps most noticeably in France, where his greatest admirers included *Watteau, *Delacroix (who called him 'that Homer of painting, that father of warmth and enthusiasm'), and *Renoir. Because of the unrivalled variety of his work, artists as different in temperament as these three could respond to it with equal enthusiasm.

Rublev, Andrei (c.1360–1430). The most famous of Russian *icon painters. The 600th anniversary of his birth was celebrated by Soviet Russia in 1960, but the date is not firmly documented and there is little secure knowledge of his life or works. In 1405 he worked as assistant to *Theophanes in the Cathedral of the Annunciation in the Kremlin at Moscow, but it has not been possible to distinguish his share there or in the Cathedral of the Dormition at Vladimir, where he is also said to have painted murals. The work that stands at the centre of his œuvre is the celebrated icon of the Old Testament Trinity (that is, the three angels who appeared to Abraham) in the Tretyakov Gallery, Moscow (c.1411). In its gentle, lyrical beauty this marks a move away from the hieratic *Byzantine tradition, and other icons in a similar style have been attributed to Rublev.

Rude, François (1784–1855). French *Romantic sculptor. He was a fervent admirer of Napoleon Bonaparte and his emotionally charged work expresses the martial spirit of the Napoleonic era more fully than that of any other sculptor. In 1812 he won the *Prix de Rome, but he was unable to take it up because of the Napoleonic Wars, and after Napoleon's final defeat in 1815 he joined

J.-L. *David in exile in Brussels. On his return to Paris in 1827 he became highly successful with public monuments, most notably his celebrated high *relief on the Arc de Triomphe, *Departure of the Volunteers in 1792*, popularly known as *La Marseillaise* (1833–6). None of Rude's other works matches the fire, dynamism, and heroic bravura of this glorification of the French Revolution, but he created another strikingly original work in his monument *Napoleon Awakening to Immortality* (1845–7) in the Parc Noisot at Fixin, near his native Dijon, which shows the emperor casting off his shroud. In spite of the dramatic movement of his work, it always has a solidity that reveals his classical training and his lifelong admiration for the *antique.

Rudolf II, Emperor. See HABSBURG.

Ruisdael, Jacob van (1628/9?–82). The greatest and most versatile of all Dutch landscape painters. He was born in Haarlem, where he probably received training from his father **Isaac,** who was a painter as well as a frame maker and picture dealer (no works by him are known to survive). His uncle Salomon van *Ruysdael (this distinction in spelling occurs consistently in their own signatures) presumably also played a part in his artistic education. Ruisdael was extremely precocious, however; his earliest known paintings date from 1646 and already reveal a mature and distinctive artistic personality. He was also versatile and prolific (about 700 paintings are reasonably attributed to him, together with 100 or so drawings and a dozen etchings): he painted forests, grain fields, beaches and seascapes, watermills and windmills, winter landscapes and Scandinavian torrents influenced by Allart van *Everdingen (he did not visit Scandinavia himself); he could conjure poetry from a virtually featureless patch of duneland as well as from a magnificent panoramic view. Even more than his range, however, it is the emotional force of his work that distinguishes him from his contemporaries. He moved away decisively from the 'tonal' phase of Dutch landscape represented by his uncle; in place of subtle atmospheric effects he favoured strong forms and dense colours and his brushwork is vigorous and *impasted. His emotional, subjective approach is most memorably expressed in *The Jewish Cemetery* (c.1660, versions in Detroit Inst. of Arts and Gemälde-galerie, Dresden), where tombstones and elegiac ruins, symbols of man's transitory and ephemeral existence, are contrasted with nature's power of renewal.

Early in his career Ruisdael seems to have travelled a fair amount in search of subjects, but he never ventured far from home. His most ambitious journey was probably made in 1650 with his friend Nicolaes *Berchem and took him just over the German border, resulting in several pictures of Bentheim Castle in Westphalia. In the most famous of these views (1653, NG, Dublin), the castle heroically crowns the top of a steep, rugged hill, transformed by Ruisdael's imagination from the mild slope it is in actuality. In about 1656 he moved to Amsterdam, where he lived for the rest of his life (although he was buried in St Bavo's Cathedral in Haarlem). He evidently had a fairly prosperous career, but little is known about his life and it was long thought he had died insane in the workhouse at Haarlem, a fate that is now known to have befallen his cousin and near-namesake Jacob van *Ruysdael. There is still uncertainty, however, concerning the story, reported by *Houbraken and supported by some tantalizing evidence, that Ruisdael practised as a surgeon. It seems unlikely that he could have found the time for this (he is said to have taken a medical degree at Caen in Normandy in 1676, when he was in his late forties), but other prolific Dutch painters, for example *Steen (who ran a tavern), managed to pursue two careers. Ruisdael's only documented pupil was *Hobbema, but his influence was resounding, both on his Dutch contemporaries and on artists in other countries in the following two centuries—*Gainsborough, *Constable, and the *Barbizon School for example. Examples of his work are in many public collections, the finest representation being in the National Gallery, London.

Runciman, Alexander (1736–85) and **John** (1744–68/9). Scottish painters, brothers, who specialized in religious, literary, and historical subjects in a proto-*Romantic manner. John, the more gifted, died young in Italy, where both brothers had gone in 1767 (his death has been variously attributed to consumption, nervous depression, and suicide). His masterpiece, *King Lear in the*

Storm (1767, NG, Edinburgh), has freshness and originality, with nothing of the staginess of most 18th-century Shakespearian pictures. Alexander's major work, the decoration (1772) of Penicuik House near Edinburgh with subjects from Ossian and Scottish history, ranked with *Barry's paintings in the Society of Arts as the most ambitious British decorative scheme of the time, but it was destroyed by fire in 1899. Some of its compositions survive in his drawings and etchings. He also painted landscapes and portraits.

Runge, Philipp Otto (1777–1810). German painter and draughtsman. Although he made a late start to his career and died young (of consumption), he ranks second only to *Friedrich among German *Romantic artists. He studied at the Copenhagen Academy (1799–1801), then moved to Dresden, where he knew Friedrich. In 1803 he moved to Hamburg, where he spent most of the rest of his life. Runge was of a mystical, pantheistic turn of mind and in his work he tried to express notions of the harmony of the universe through symbolism of colour, form, and numbers. To this end he planned a series of four paintings called *The Times of the Day*, designed to be seen in a special building and viewed to the accompaniment of music and poetry. He painted two versions of *Morning* (1808 and 1809, Kunsthalle, Hamburg), but the others did not advance beyond drawings. Runge was also one of the best German portraitists of his period; several examples are in Hamburg. His style was rigid, sharp, and intense, at times almost *naive. In 1810 he published *Farben-Kugel* (Colour Sphere) after doing several years of research on colour, during which he corresponded with *Goethe.

Ruoppolo, Giovanni Battista (1629–93). Neapolitan still-life painter. He specialized in pictures of flowers and food (especially fruit and seafood), depicted in an exuberant and succulent style. With *Recco he was the finest Italian still-life painter of his period. His nephew **Giuseppe Ruoppolo** (d. 1710) painted in his style but was much less accomplished.

Rupert, Prince (1619–82). Bohemian-born soldier and amateur artist. Famous as a dashing cavalry commander for his uncle

Charles I in the English Civil War, he also took a serious interest in science and the arts. He was an amateur etcher and introduced *mezzotint engraving to England, having perhaps learnt the technique from its inventor Ludwig von *Siegen (Rupert was himself long credited as the inventor). He demonstrated the technique to the diarist John Evelyn, who publicized it in his book *Sculptura* (1662).

Ruralists, Brotherhood of. *See* BLAKE, SIR PETER.

Rusconi, Camillo (1658–1728). Italian sculptor. He was the outstanding sculptor in Rome during his period, a figure comparable to his friend *Maratta in painting. The vigour and boldness of his style derive from *Bernini, but Rusconi was more restrained and classical. His most important works are four over-life-size marble statues of Apostles in St John Lateran (1708–18) and the tomb of Pope Gregory XIII (1715–23) in St Peter's.

Rush, William (1756–1833). American sculptor, active in his native Philadelphia. His father was a ship's carpenter and Rush worked mainly in wood, progressing from ships' figureheads to free-standing figures, such as those of Comedy and Tragedy (1808) for the new Chestnut Street Theater, Philadelphia (now the Forrest Home for Aged Actors). His work is vigorous and naturalistic and he marks the transition from the unselfconscious folk carver to the professional artist. He was one of the prime movers in the foundation of the Pennsylvania Academy of the Fine Arts (1805), which has many examples of his work. Thomas *Eakins, another native of Philadelphia, greatly admired Rush's work.

Ruskin, John (1819–1900). English writer, artist, social reformer, and philanthropist. He was the most important English art critic of the 19th century, with a remarkable hold over public opinion, and also a talented and prolific draughtsman and watercolourist, mainly of landscape and architectural subjects. His father was a wealthy wine merchant who liked paintings and encouraged his son (his only child) in his intellectual interests; his mother too was devoted to him, but in a repressive, puritanical way. He was educated at home and travelled a good deal in Britain and on the Continent with his parents, developing an ardent love

of nature (he was deeply interested in botany and geology) as well as a feeling for art. From 1837 to 1842 he studied at Oxford University, where he won the Newdigate prize for poetry in 1839 (the following year his studies were interrupted when he had a breakdown, evidently partly caused by a frustrated passion for the daughter of one of his father's business associates). His father gave him a generous allowance, so after graduating he was able to devote himself to writing and lecturing and also could afford to buy paintings, notably works by *Turner, who was his greatest artistic hero (Ruskin first met him in 1840 and became a friend and eventually executor of his will).

Most of Ruskin's art criticism was written early in his career; after about 1855 he concentrated more on economic and political questions. It is, however, difficult to separate his thought into different strands, as he was so concerned with the relationship between art, morality, and social justice; his lectures as the first *Slade professor of fine art at Oxford (1870–7, 1883–4), for example, were as much about sociology as art. Although he later modified his views, the key ideas in his most influential works of art criticism were sincerity and truth to nature. He thought that good art is essentially moral and that bad art is insincere and immoral. When he defended the *Pre-Raphaelites against vicious attacks in 1851, it was mainly their 'labour and fidelity' he praised, and when he dismissed the 17th-century Bolognese painters such as the *Carracci and *Domenichino as 'art-weeds' it was largely because of what he perceived as their lack of genuine feeling: 'There is no entirely sincere or great art in the 17th century.' In architecture he loved the *Gothic style and believed that the key to the beauty of medieval buildings was the delight that craftsmen took in their creation. These views were particularly influential on William *Morris and the *Arts and Crafts movement. In line with his opinions on the dignity and value of manual labour, he regarded factories as degrading places and he tried to improve the conditions in which the working class lived. Many of his social ideas, such as his advocacy of old age pensions, later became commonly accepted. By the end of his life he had disposed of all his large inheritance in philanthropic work and maintained himself on the proceeds of his writings.

Ruskin's personal life was deeply unhappy. His marriage of six years was annulled in 1854 on the grounds of non-consummation (his ex-wife married *Millais the following year) and in middle and old age he made many young girls the objects of his unhealthy affection. He proposed to one of them, the 18-year-old Rose La Touche, in 1866, but was refused; she died mad in 1875. In 1878 he lost a famous libel case against *Whistler, whom he had accused of 'flinging a pot of paint in the public face', and just before it came to court he showed the first signs of the mental illness that made his final years wretched. After 1889, living in isolation in the Lake District, where he was cared for by his cousin, Joan Severn, Ruskin wrote nothing and rarely spoke. His house, Brantwood, overlooking Lake Coniston, is now a memorial to him.

Ruskin's literary output was enormous; the standard edition of his complete works occupies 39 volumes (1903–12). His most important books dealing specifically with art are: *Modern Painters* (5 vols., 1843–60, epilogue 1888), which began as a defence of Turner and expanded into a general survey of art; *The Seven Lamps of Architecture* (1849); and *The Stones of Venice* (3 vols., 1851–3). He is accorded a distinguished place amongst English prose writers of the 19th century, and his finest flights of rhetoric, such as his descriptions of the *Tintorettos in the Scuola di S. Rocco in Venice, are classics of their kind.

Russell, Morgan (1886–1953). American painter, active mainly in Paris, a pioneer of abstract art. He was born in New York, where he studied sculpture at the *Art Students League and painting under Robert *Henri. In 1908 he settled in Paris, where he briefly attended *Matisse's art school. By 1910 he was devoting himself increasingly to painting, and in 1911 he met Stanton *Macdonald-Wright, with whom he developed theories about the analogies between colours and musical patterns. In 1913 they launched *Synchromism, one of the earliest abstract movements, and Russell's *Synchromy in Orange: To Form* (1913–14, Albright-Knox AG, Buffalo) won him considerable renown in Paris. His later work, in which he reintroduced figurative elements,

was much less memorable. He lived in Paris until 1946, then returned to the USA.

Russolo, Luigi (1885–1947). Italian painter and musician. He signed both the *Futurist painters' manifestos in 1910, but he is remembered mainly as 'the most spectacular innovator among the Futurist musicians' (*New Grove Dictionary of Music and Musicians*, 1980). In 1913 he published a manifesto, of *L'arte dei rumari* (The Art of Noises, expanded in book form in 1916), and later in the same year he demonstrated the first of a series of *intonarumori* ('noise-makers'), which produced a startling range of sounds. In 1913–14, he gave noise concerts in Milan (causing a riot), Genoa, and London. Others followed after the First World War. Several leading composers, notably Ravel and Stravinsky, thought they opened up interesting possibilities, and Russolo has been regarded as a pioneer of today's electronic music. Unfortunately his compositions and machines have been destroyed. As a painter Russolo made rather crude use of the Futurist device of 'lines of force' in his early work; after the war his style became more naturalistic.

Rutter, Frank. *See* ALLIED ARTISTS' ASSOCIATION.

Ruysch, Rachel (1664–1750). Dutch still-life painter, with van *Huysum the most celebrated exponent of flower pieces in her period. The daughter of a botanist and the pupil of Willem van *Aelst, she worked mainly in her native Amsterdam, but also in The Hague (1701–8) and Düsseldorf, where from 1708 to 1716 she was court painter to the Elector Palatine. Her richly devised bouquets are painted in delicate colours with meticulous detail, and are worthy of the finest tradition of Dutch flower painting. She continued to use the dark backgrounds characteristic of van Aelst and the older generation long after van Huysum and other contemporaries had gone over to light backgrounds.

Ruysdael, Salomon van (1600/3?–70). Dutch landscape painter, active in Haarlem, where he became a member of the painters' guild in 1623. His earliest works show the influence of Esaias van de *Velde and in the 1630s he was so close in style to Jan van *Goyen that it is sometimes difficult to differentiate between the work of the two artists. Both of them excelled in atmospheric, virtually monochromatic river scenes and they are the leading masters of this type of picture. In the 1640s his landscapes became somewhat more solid and colourful, perhaps reflecting influence from his nephew, Jacob van *Ruisdael. Late in his career he occasionally painted still lifes. He was prolific and many galleries have examples of his work. His son **Jacob van Ruysdael** (*c*.1630–81) was also a landscape painter. An example of his rare work is *A Waterfall by a Cottage* (NG, London), which shows he worked in a style similar to that of his illustrious cousin and near-namesake, with whom he has sometimes been confused in documentary references.

Ryder, Albert Pinkham (1847–1917). American painter of imaginative subjects. He lived and worked most of his life as a solitary and dreamer in New York, and his methods and approach were largely self-taught. His pictures reflect a rich inner life, with a haunting love of the sea (he was born at the fishing port of New Bedford, Mass.) and a constant search to express the ineffable: 'Have you ever seen an inch worm crawl up a leaf or twig, and then clinging to the very end, revolve in the air, feeling for something to reach something? That's like me. I am trying to find something out there beyond the place on which I have a footing.' This imaginative quality and eloquent expression of the mysteriousness of things is expressed typically through boldly simplified forms and eerie lighting (*The Race Track* or *Death on a Pale Horse*, Cleveland Mus. of Art). In spite of his self-imposed isolation Ryder's works became well known in his lifetime and he has been much imitated and faked. His own paintings have often deteriorated because of unorthodox technical procedures. He was greatly admired by Jackson *Pollock, and the critical and popular favour Ryder enjoyed in the 1950s and 1960s was linked to the success of *Abstract Expressionism.

Rysbrack, Michael (1694–1770). Flemish-born sculptor (a member of an Antwerp

family of artists), who settled in England in about 1720. He soon achieved success and for most of the 1720s and 1730s he was the leading sculptor in the country. His best-known work is perhaps the monument to Sir Isaac Newton (designed by William *Kent) in Westminster Abbey (1731), with its eloquent reclining figure of the great scientist, and his most prestigious commission (won in preference to *Scheemakers) is the monument to William III in Queen Square, Bristol (1733–5), generally regarded as the finest equestrian statue made in England in the 18th century. However, from about 1740 (the year of Scheemakers's acclaimed Shakespeare monument in Westminster Abbey), Rysbrack began to lose ground to Scheemakers and also to *Roubiliac. He was a versatile and prolific artist, hard-working and widely admired. His output included tombs, statues, and portraits (often in the form of busts in the *antique manner, a fashion he introduced to England), and he also made architectural elements such as chimney pieces. His style was vigorous and dignified, less sombre than that of Scheemakers. He did not match the brilliant vivacity that characterizes Roubiliac's work, but he could sometimes rival him in beauty of handling.

Rysselberghe, Théo van (1862–1926). Belgian painter, designer, and sculptor. In 1883 he became a founder member of the avant-garde group Les *Vingt; it encouraged an interest in innovative art largely through contact with France, and Rysselberghe, who met *Seurat in Paris, became the leading Belgian exponent of *Neo-Impressionism. He moved to Paris in 1898 and became friendly with the *Symbolist circle of writers and artists; his painting *A Reading* (1903, Mus. voor Schone Kunsten, Ghent) shows several leading literary figures including André Gide and Maurice Maeterlinck. In 1910 he settled in Provence, where he abandoned Neo-Impressionism for a broader style of painting. His work is well represented in the Rijksmuseum Kröller-Müller at Otterlo.

S

Saatchi, Charles (1943–). Iraqi-born British businessman and art collector. In 1970 he was co-founder with his brother Maurice of Saatchi & Saatchi, which became the world's largest advertising agency. He has devoted much of his enormous wealth to buying contemporary art on a huge scale, and in 1985 the Saatchi Collection opened to the public in a new gallery in St John's Wood, north London. It moved to a more central location, in County Hall, in 2003. His patronage has been welcomed by many, but others have been critical of the way in which his bulk buying has given him such power in the art market. He helped to create the boom in *Neo-Expressionism and *Neo-Geo, for example, and he has been the chief patron of the *Young British Artists.

Sacchi, Andrea (1599?–1661). Italian painter, one of the leading artists of his day in Rome. He was a pupil of Francesco *Albani, but he was inspired chiefly by *Raphael, and with the sculptors *Algardi and *Duquesnoy he became the chief exponent of the style sometimes called 'High *Baroque Classicism'. In defence of the *classical principles of order and moderation, Sacchi engaged in a debate in the Accademia di S. Luca with Pietro da *Cortona on the question of whether history paintings should have few figures (as Sacchi maintained) or many (Cortona). Sacchi's ideas were more immediately influential, but his ponderous ceiling fresco of *Divine Wisdom* (1629–33) in the Palazzo Barberini in Rome is completely outshone by Cortona's exhilarating ceiling of the Gran Salone in the same building. Sacchi, indeed, was at his best on a much smaller scale—in altarpieces such as the grave, introspective *Vision of St Romuald* (1631, Pinacoteca, Vatican), in portraits, and not least in his drawings. His most important pupil was *Maratta. Sacchi also worked as an architect, designing the Chapel of St Catherine of Siena (1637–9) in the Sacristy of S. Maria sopra Minerva, a work of refined classical purity.

sacra conversazione (It.: 'holy conversation'). A representation of the Virgin and Child with Saints in which all the sacred personages are disposed in a single pictorial space rather than in the separate compartments of a *polyptych. Usually the figures are shown silently communing rather than conversing. The type originated in Italy in the first half of the 15th century: Filippo *Lippi's Barbadori Altarpiece (begun 1437, Louvre, Paris) is perhaps the first dated example.

Saenredam, Pieter (1597–1665). Dutch painter of architectural subjects, particularly church interiors, active mainly in Haarlem. He was the son of an engraver and mapmaker, **Jan Saenredam** (*c*.1565–1607), and a friend of the architect Jacob van *Campen, who made a drawing of Saenredam (1628, BM, London), which shows that he was dwarf-like and evidently hunchbacked. Saenredam was the first painter to concentrate on accurate depictions of real buildings rather than the fanciful inventions of the *Mannerist tradition. His pictures were based on painstaking drawings, but they never seem pedantic or niggling and are remarkable for their delicacy of colour and airy grace. The Cathedral of St Bavo (where he is buried) and the Grote Kerk in Haarlem were favourite subjects, but he also travelled to other Dutch towns to make drawings, and Utrecht is represented in several of his paintings. He also made a few views of Rome based on drawings in a sketchbook by Maerten van *Heemskerck (now in the Kupferstichkabinett, Berlin) that he (or someone in his circle) owned. His work had great influence on Dutch painting.

Saftleven, Cornelis (1607–81) and **Herman II** (1609–85). Dutch painters, brothers, the best-known members of a family of artists. Cornelis, who was active mainly in Rotterdam, was highly versatile, his output including landscapes, portraits, religious and mythological subjects, peasant scenes in the tradition of *Brouwer and *Teniers, images of Hell, and allegorical and satirical pictures, sometimes with animals dressed as humans. Herman, who was active mainly in Utrecht, painted religious subjects but is best known for his imaginary river views, done in a distinctive misty blue tonality (*View on the Rhine*, 1656, Dulwich Picture Gal.).

Sage, Kay (1898–1963). American *Surrealist painter, mainly self-taught as an artist. The daughter of wealthy parents, she spent much of her life in Italy (she was married to an Italian prince, 1925–35), and Giorgio de *Chirico was an early influence on her work. In 1937 she moved to Paris, where she met Yves *Tanguy in 1939. He followed her to the USA in 1940 and they married later that year. From the time of her return to America, architectural motifs became prominent in her work—strange steel structures depicted in sharp detail against vistas of unreal space—and her pictures also included draperies from which faces and figures sometimes emerged mistily (*Tomorrow is Never*, 1955, Met. Mus., New York). Sage also made mixed-media constructions and wrote poetry. Tanguy's sudden death in 1955 cast a shadow over her last years and she committed suicide.

Saint-Gaudens, Augustus (1848–1907). The leading American sculptor of his period. Saint-Gaudens was born in Dublin in a French father and an Irish mother who settled in America when he was a baby. He began his career as a *cameo-cutter in New York, then studied for three years in Paris (1867–70) and three in Rome (1870–3), returning to America in 1874. His first important commission was the Admiral Farragut Monument (1878–81) in Madison Square Park, New York, and following its successful reception he quickly achieved a leading reputation among American sculptors and retained this throughout his life. Saint-Gaudens was an energetic artist and he produced a large amount of work in spite of the high standards of craftsmanship he set himself. His preferred material was bronze and he excelled particularly at memorials. Although his style is generally warmly naturalistic, his most celebrated work, the Adams Memorial (1886–91) in Rock Creek Cemetery, Washington, is a powerful allegorical figure. It commemorates the wife of a friend of Saint-Gaudens who had committed suicide, and the mysterious female figure, swathed in magnificent voluminous draperies, has been interpreted as 'Grief', although the sculptor himself saw the elegiac work as embodying 'the Peace of God'. Saint-Gaudens was a highly import-

ant figure in the development of American sculpture: he turned the tide against *Neoclassicism and made Paris, rather than Rome, the artistic mecca of his countrymen.

St Ives School. A loosely structured group of artists, flourishing particularly from the late 1940s to the early 1960s, who concentrated their activities in the Cornish fishing port of St Ives. Like *Newlyn, St Ives had been popular with artists long before this (for example, *Sickert and *Whistler painted there together in the winter of 1883–4), but it did not become of more than local importance in painting and sculpture until Barbara *Hepworth and Ben *Nicholson moved there in 1939, two weeks before the outbreak of the Second World War. They were anxious that their children should be safely outside London, and their friend Adrian *Stokes, who lived at Carbis Bay (virtually a suburb of St Ives), invited the family to stay with him. Hepworth lived in St Ives for the rest of her life (her studio is now a museum of her work) and Nicholson (who had discovered Alfred *Wallis on a day trip to St Ives in 1928) lived there until 1958. They formed the nucleus of a group of avant-garde artists who made the town an internationally recognized centre of abstract art, and it is to these artists that the term 'St Ives School' is usually applied, even though many of them had little in common stylistically, apart from an interest in portraying the local landscape in abstract terms. The one with the greatest international prestige was Naum *Gabo, who lived in St Ives from 1939 to 1946. After the war a number of abstract painters settled in or near the town or made regular visits. The residents included Terry *Frost and Patrick *Heron; the visitors included Roger *Hilton (who eventually settled in St Ives in 1965), Adrian *Heath, and Victor *Pasmore. Peter Lanyon (1918–64) was the only notable abstract artist to be born in St Ives. The heyday of the St Ives School was over by the mid-1960s, but the town continued to be an artistic centre. In 1993 the *Tate Gallery opened a branch museum there, housing changing displays of the work of 20th-century artists associated with the town. The building includes a stained-glass window commissioned from Patrick Heron.

St Martin's Lane Academy. A name of two successive organizations in St Martin's

Lane, London, that were important training grounds for English artists in the half-century before the *Royal Academy was established in 1768. They were founded in 1720 and 1735 respectively and each was a drawing and painting class rather than a professional institution. The first St Martin's Lane Academy grew out of another academy (London's first) established in 1711 in Great Queen Street, of which *Kneller was the head. *Thornhill replaced Kneller in 1716, and in 1720, when Thornhill himself was deposed by the French-born Louis Chéron (1660–1725) and John *Vanderbank, the academy moved to St Martin's Lane. It became defunct after a few years, but *Hogarth reconstituted it in 1735 and it remained active until his death in 1764. He described the room in which it met as 'big enough for a naked figure to be drawn after by thirty or forty people'.

Saint Phalle, Niki de (1930–2002). French sculptor, graphic artist, and film-maker, one of the great entertainers of modern art. In 1952 she started painting without formal artistic training and she first came to public prominence in 1960 with 'rifle-shot' paintings that incorporated containers of paint intended to be burst and spattered when shot with a pistol. After she separated from her husband in 1960 she lived with Jean *Tinguely, with whom she collaborated on numerous projects, notably the enormous sculpture *Hon* (Swedish: 'She') erected at the Moderna Museet, Stockholm, in 1963 (destroyed). It was in the form of a reclining woman (more than 25 m (80 ft) long) whose interior was a giant *'environment' reminiscent of a funfair; visitors entered through the vagina. The attractions inside included a milk bar in the breasts and a cinema showing Greta Garbo movies. Externally the figure was gaudily painted in a manner similar to that of her series of *Nanas*—grotesque fat ladies. Her other works included *happenings and films, and from 1979 she worked on a huge sculpture garden at Garavicchio in Italy. Other projects of her later years included a touching book on AIDS addressed to her son (*AIDS: You Can't Catch it Holding Hands*, 1987) and a giant figure of the Loch Ness monster, made for an exhibition of her work in Glasgow in 1992.

Salle, David. *See* NEO-EXPRESSIONISM.

Sallinen, Tyko (1879–1955). The outstanding Finnish *Expressionist painter. He was the son of a tailor who belonged to a strict fundamentalist religious sect (the Hihhulit), and the unhappy background of his early years later formed the basis for some of his paintings. After spending several years as an itinerant jobbing tailor in Sweden, he studied art in Helsinki and in 1909 and 1914 visited Paris, where he was influenced by avant-garde French painting, particularly *Fauvism. Its influence can be seen in what is probably his most famous picture, *Washerwomen* (1911, Ateneum, Helsinki), a work that caused an outcry because of its bold colours and very rough handling. Sallinen's favourite subjects were scenes of Finnish peasant life such as this and also views of the harsh Karelian landscape. He was the leading figure of the *November Group and became regarded as the nationalist Finnish painter par excellence.

Salmon, André. *See* MODIGLIANI.

Salon. France's official art exhibition, first held in 1667 and originally limited to members of the Académie Royale de Peinture et de Sculpture (*see* ACADEMY). The name derives from the fact that from 1737 the exhibitions were held in the Salon Carré in the *Louvre (various other venues had previously been used). For many years their frequency was irregular (though with stretches when they were held annually or biennially); from the 1830s they were mainly annual. The jury system of selection was introduced in 1748. As these were the only public exhibitions in Paris, conservative academic art gained a stranglehold on publicity; dissatisfaction with this situation led to the *Salon des Refusés in 1863. In 1881 the École des *Beaux-Arts relinquished control of the Salon and a group of artists organized the Société des Artistes Français to take responsibility for the show, with a jury elected from each previous year's exhibitors. It still remained hostile to avant-garde art, and from this time a number of competing exhibitions were established, undermining what prestige the Salon still retained. The *Salon des Indépendants, for example, appeared in 1884, and the *Salon d'Automne in 1903.

Salon d'Automne. Annual exhibition founded in Paris in 1903 as a more progressive alternative to the official *Salon and other current exhibiting venues, including the *Salon des Indépendants; it was held in the autumn (October or November), so as not to clash with these other shows, which took place mainly in spring and summer. The early Salons d'Automne played an important role in establishing the reputations of *Cézanne and *Gauguin. There was a small Gauguin exhibition in 1903 (the inaugural show) and a major retrospective in 1906; Cézanne was strongly represented in 1905 and was given a memorial exhibition in 1907. However, the Salon d'Automne is famous above all for the sensational launch of *Fauvism at the 1905 exhibition.

Salon de la Rose + Croix. Art exhibition held annually in Paris from 1892 to 1897. It was organized by the Rosicrucians, an esoteric brotherhood (allegedly founded in the 15th century by one Christian Rosenkreuz) that in the late 19th century had close connections with the *Symbolist movement. The order's symbol, reflecting the name, was a rose and cross combined. Joséphin Péladan (1859–1918), a man of letters who called himself Sâr (i.e. High Priest) Péladan, founded a lodge of the brotherhood in France and this organized the exhibitions. They became a focal point of Symbolism, and the catalogue to the first exhibition said its objects were 'to destroy *Realism and to bring art closer to Catholic ideas, to mysticism, to legend, myth, allegory, and dreams'.

Salon des Indépendants. Annual exhibition held in Paris by the Société des Artistes Indépendants, an association formed in 1884 by *Seurat and other artists in opposition to the official *Salon. There was no selection committee and anyone could exhibit on payment of a fee. This meant that many interesting avant-garde works were shown, but also that they ran the risk of being swamped by a sea of mediocrity. It became the main showcase for the *Post-Impressionists (Henri *Rousseau was also a regular exhibitor) and was a major art event in Paris up to the First World War. By then, however, it had been challenged by the smaller but more discriminating *Salon d'Automne.

Salon des Refusés. Exhibition held in Paris in 1863 to show work that had been refused by the selection committee of the official *Salon. In that year there were particularly strong protests from artists whose work had been rejected, so the emperor Napoleon III, 'wishing to let the public judge the legitimacy of these complaints', ordered this special exhibition. It drew huge crowds, who came mainly to mock, and *Manet's *Déjeuner sur l'herbe* was subjected to particular ridicule. Other major artists represented included *Cézanne, Camille *Pissarro, and *Whistler. In spite of the unfavourable reaction to the works shown there, the Salon des Refusés was of great significance in undermining the prestige of the official Salon. After this, artists began to organize their own exhibitions (notably the *Impressionists in 1874) and art dealers became of increasing importance. The Salon des Refusés is thus regarded as a turning point in the history of art and 1863 has been described as 'the most convenient date from which to begin any history of modern painting' (Alan Bowness, *Modern European Art*, 1972).

Salviati, Francesco (Francesco de' Rossi) (1510–63). Florentine *Mannerist painter, a pupil of *Andrea del Sarto. In about 1530 he moved to Rome and he adopted the name by which he is now known from his main patron there, Cardinal Giovanni Salviati; he lodged in the cardinal's palace and it was for him that he painted the work that established his reputation—the fresco of the *Visitation* (1538) in S. Giovanni Decollato. In 1539 he moved to Venice, but he had left the city by 1541; the rest of his career was mainly divided between Rome and Florence, but he also worked in France in 1556–7. Salviati was one of the leading fresco decorators of his day, specializing in learned and elaborate multi-figure compositions, typically Mannerist in their artificiality and abstruseness, and similar in style to those of his friend *Vasari. He was an artist of higher calibre than Vasari, but he had a difficult temperament and many of his projects were disrupted when he alienated patrons or fellow artists. His finest works are perhaps the frescos on the story of the Roman general Furius Camillus (1543–5) in the Sala dell' Udienza of the Palazzo Vecchio, Florence, intended as an allegory of the reign of Duke Cosimo I de' *Medici. Salviati's work also included portraits (Flor-

531

entine in their direct characterization but north Italian in their richness of colour), altarpieces, and designs for tapestry. **Giuseppe Salviati** (*c*.1520–*c*.1575) was his pupil. He was born Giuseppe Porta, but borrowed his master's borrowed name. He worked mainly in Venice, painting numerous altarpieces and also decorations for civic buildings.

Samaras, Lucas (1936–). Greek-born sculptor and experimental artist who settled in the USA in 1948 and became an American citizen in 1955. His work has been extremely varied in scale, medium, and approach. In 1959 he took part in Kaprow's first *happening and his own work of this time included figures made from rags dipped in plaster and pastels combining *Surrealist fantasy with *Pop art imagery. During the 1960s he worked a good deal with *assemblages, creating bizarre and sometimes sinister objects studded with nails and pins. He also experimented with light and reflection, notably in his *Mirrored Room* (1966), an *environment with mirrors in which the spectator was reflected endlessly. Perhaps his best-known works are his 'Autopolaroids'—photographs of the most intimate parts of his own body that he began making in 1970 and which brought him considerable notoriety.

Sánchez Coello, Alonso (1531/2?–88). Spanish painter of Portuguese parentage, principally a portraitist. He studied under Anthonis *Mor in Flanders in the early 1550s and from 1559 worked at the court of Philip II of Spain (*see* HABSBURG), becoming a personal favourite of the king, who was godfather to his two daughters. His dignified and sober style was strongly influenced by Mor, but was more sensuous, showing his admiration for *Titian, and he is regarded as the founder of the great tradition of Spanish formal portraiture. He also painted religious works, but these are much less distinguished.

Sánchez Cotán, Juan (1560–1627). Spanish painter. He was a still-life painter in Toledo until 1603, when he retired from secular life to become a lay brother at the Carthusian monastery in Granada. The religious works he painted after this date are unexceptional, but as a still-life painter he ranks with the great names of European art.

Characteristically he depicts a few simple fruits or vegetables, arranged on a ledge or shelf with an almost geometric clarity and standing out against a dark background (*Quince, Cabbage, Melon, Cucumber*, *c*.1600, San Diego Mus. of Art). Each form is scrutinized with such intensity that the pictures take on a mystical quality, conveying a feeling of wonder and humility in front of the humblest items in God's creation. Sánchez Cotán's austere style had considerable influence on Spanish painting, notably on *Zurbarán.

Sandby, Paul (1730/1–1809). English topographical watercolourist and printmaker. Like his brother **Thomas** (1721–98) before him, he trained as a military draughtsman at the Tower of London. Both brothers saw service in Scotland, Thomas during the 1745–6 Jacobite rebellion, and Paul after it, when he worked on a survey of the Highlands as part of the government campaign to subdue the area. In about 1752 Paul returned to London, where he lived for a time with his brother. He also spent time with him at Windsor Great Park, where Thomas had held the position of deputy ranger since 1746 (they produced many views of Windsor and its environs, and the Royal Library at Windsor Castle has an outstanding Sandby collection). Thomas also worked as an architect and landscape gardener, his most important project at Windsor being the creation of Virginia Water, the largest artificial lake in the country (he earned the unfortunate nickname 'Tommy Sandbag' after a dam he constructed burst in a storm in 1768). The brothers have much in common as watercolourists, but Paul was the better artist and also more versatile, his output including lively figure compositions as well as an extensive range of landscape subjects. In his later work he often used *body colour (he also sometimes painted in oils) and he was the first professional artist in England to publish *aquatints (1775). *Gainsborough singled him out as the only contemporary English landscape artist who painted 'real views from nature' instead of artificial *Picturesque compositions and he helped to win prestige for the medium of watercolour. Both brothers were founder members of the *Royal Academy in 1768 and Thomas was its first professor of architecture.

Sandrart, Joachim von (1606–88). German painter and writer on art. He travelled widely and was the most highly regarded German artist of his day, but he is now remembered almost exclusively for his treatise *Teutsche Academie der Edlen Bau-, Bild- und Mahlerey-Künste* (German Academy of the Noble Arts of Architecture, Sculpture and Painting), published in Nuremberg in 1675–9 (a Latin edition followed in 1683). This treatise, organized into three main parts, is a sourcebook of major importance. The first part is an introduction to the arts of architecture, painting, and sculpture put together largely from material taken from earlier sources such as *Vasari and van *Mander. The second part, consisting of biographies of artists, likewise contains much material borrowed from previous writers but also much that is original, in particular about German artists and on contemporary artists whom the author knew personally (including *Claude and *Poussin). The third part contains information about art collections and a study of *iconography; remarkably Sandrart also included in his book a chapter on Far Eastern art. Sandrart was the first director (1662) of the Academy at Nuremberg (the earliest such in Germany).

sanguine. A dark red colour; the word is often particularly applied to *chalk of this colour.

Sansovino, Andrea (*c.*1467/70–1529). Italian sculptor and architect, named after his birthplace at Monte San Savino, near Arezzo. He called himself a Florentine, but although much of his sculpture is in Florence, his fame rests on what he did elsewhere, notably in Rome. His major works there include the companion tombs of Cardinal Ascanio Sforza and Cardinal Girolamo Basso della Rovere (1505–9, S. Maria del Popolo) and the group of the *Virgin and Child with St Anne* (1512, S. Agostino), which display classical dignity and grace combined with human tenderness. Sansovino spent much of the period 1513–27 in Loreto in charge of the sculpture (and for part of the time the architecture also) of the shrine of the Holy House, originally designed by *Bramante. In the 1490s he twice visited Portugal, but no work that is certainly by him survives there. Jacopo *Sansovino was Andrea's main pupil.

Sansovino, Jacopo (Jacopo Tatti) (1486–1570). Florentine sculptor and architect, active mainly in Venice. He trained under Andrea *Sansovino, whose name he adopted as a sign of his admiration. In 1505/6 he followed Andrea to Rome, where he moved in the circle of *Bramante and *Raphael and worked on the restoration of ancient sculpture. From *c.*1510 to 1518 he was again in Florence, where he shared a studio with *Andrea del Sarto, and he then returned to Rome until the Sack of 1527, when he moved to Venice. There he was appointed state architect (1529), formed a close friendship with *Titian, and became a dominant figure in the art establishment. Sansovino played a major role in introducing the High *Renaissance style to Venice in both architecture and sculpture, and his sculptures are often important decorative elements of his buildings. His most celebrated work, one of Venice's most familiar sights, is the glorious Library of San Marco (begun 1537). As a sculptor he is best known for the colossal marble figures of Mars and Neptune (1554–66) in the courtyard of the Doges' Palace, although the carving was done by assistants. Sansovino's sculptural style was firmly rooted in his study of antiquity, but it was in no way academic and possessed great vitality. He studied assiduously from the life as well as from the *antique, and legend has it that the model for his marble *Bacchus* (1511–12, Bargello, Florence) went mad through being made to pose for hours on end with his arm raised and one day was found in this position standing naked on top of a chimney. Sansovino's son **Francesco** (1521–83) was a scholar of diversified interests. His *Venetia città nobilissima* (Venice, Most Noble City), published in 1581, is an important sourcebook—the first attempt to give a systematic account of a city's artistic heritage.

Santi, Giovanni (d. 1494). Italian painter and writer, the father of *Raphael, active mainly in Urbino, where he worked for the court. He was 'a mediocre painter but an intelligent man' (*Vasari) and no doubt gave his illustrious son his introduction to humanist culture. Santi is now remembered less for his paintings than for a long rhymed chronicle about Federico da *Montefeltro, Duke of Urbino, which he wrote in 1484–7 and presented to the young Guidobaldo da

Montefeltro in about 1492. This work is undistinguished as literature, but it contains a good deal of useful information about court life, Federico's military campaigns, and artistic matters. Santi's house in Urbino is now a museum—the Casa di Raffaello. It contains a small fresco of the *Virgin and Child* that some authorities consider to be Santi's portrayal of Raphael and his mother, and others claim as a very early work by Raphael himself.

Saraceni, Carlo (1579–1620). Italian painter. He was born and died in Venice but spent almost all his career in Rome. There he formed his style under the influence of *Caravaggio and *Elsheimer, painting small luminous pictures of figures in landscapes as well as much larger altarpieces, including the replacement for Caravaggio's *Death of the Virgin*, which the church of S. Maria della Scala had rejected in 1606. Caravaggio's picture is now in the Louvre, Paris, and Saraceni's is still in the church. He painted several other smaller variants or versions of it, so the design was evidently popular. His style was sensitive and poetic, showing a delicate feeling for colour and tone. His liking for turbans, tasselled fringes, and stringy drapery folds may have influenced Dutch artists in Rome such as *Lastman and *Pynas, and through them *Rembrandt. He also possibly had some influence in Lorraine, through his pupil, the French Caravaggesque painter Jean Le Clerc (*c.*1587–1633). Le Clerc was also an engraver; his prints include one of his master's *Death of the Virgin* (after a small version on copper, now in the Alte Pinakothek, Munich, rather than the large altarpiece in Rome).

Sargent, John Singer (1856–1925). American painter, chiefly famous as the outstanding society portraitist of his age: *Rodin called him 'the van *Dyck of our times'. He was born in Florence, the son of prosperous and cultured parents who had settled in Europe, and he had an international upbringing and career—indeed, he has been described as 'an American born in Italy, educated in France, who looks like a German, speaks like an Englishman, and paints like a Spaniard' (William Starkweather, 'The Art of John S. Sargent', *Mentor*, Oct. 1924). His 'Spanishness' refers to his deep admiration for *Velázquez, for although he was

encouraged to paint directly by his teacher *Carolus-Duran, with whom he studied in Paris 1874–6, the virtuoso handling of paint that characterized his style derived more particularly from Old Masters such as Velázquez and *Hals (he visited Madrid in 1879 and Haarlem in 1880 to study their work). In 1884 he became famous when his portrait of Madame Virginie Gautreau (Met. Mus., New York) caused a sensation at the Paris *Salon because of what was felt to be its provocatively erotic character. It was exhibited as *Madame X*, but the sitter, a society beauty of strikingly unconventional looks, was unmistakable, and her mother wrote to Sargent imploring him to withdraw the picture, which she said had made her daughter a laughing stock (he refused to do so). The scandal persuaded Sargent to move to London, and he remained based there for the rest of his life; he continued to travel extensively, however, and often visited America. The lavish elegance of his work brought him unrivalled success, and his portraits of the wealthy and privileged convey with brilliant bravura the glamour and opulence of high society life. Even in his lifetime he was deprecated by some critics for superficiality of characterization, but although psychological penetration was certainly not his strength, he was admirably varied in his response to each sitter's individuality.

As with many successful portraitists, Sargent's heart lay elsewhere; indeed he came to hate portraiture, calling it 'a pimp's profession'. In 1907—at the height of his career—he announced that he would paint 'no more mugs', and although he was occasionally persuaded to relent, essentially he kept his word and in the remaining eighteen years of his life he produced only about two dozen commissioned portraits. Despite his sophistication and charm and the entrée to high society that his success gave him, he was a very private person, who never married and led a quiet life. With portraiture behind him, he was free to produce work for his own satisfaction. He loved painting landscape watercolours, showing a technique as dashing in this medium as in his oil paintings, and from the 1890s he devoted much of his energies to ambitious allegorical murals in the Public Library and Museum of Fine Arts in Boston: 'Landscape I like, but, most of all, decoration, where the really aesthetic side of art counts for so much more.' For the Library his subject was the History of Religion (his friend E. A. *Abbey painted a series on the quest for the Holy Grail for the same building at the same period). Sargent began work in 1890 and the paintings (in oil on canvas) were installed in stages between 1895 and 1916. They led to the commission from the Museum, for which he painted subjects from classical mythology between 1916 and 1925, completing the work shortly before his death. (As models for the Danaides he used dancing girls from the chorus line of the Ziegfeld Follies.) His murals are in a high-flown, sometimes rather dreary *Symbolist manner and have evoked mixed reactions. A very different side to his talents is revealed in the enormous *Gassed* (1918–19, Imperial War Mus., London), which he painted as an *Official War Artist. It has remarkable tragic power and is one of the greatest pictures inspired by the First World War. Sargent's reputation plummeted after his death but has soared again since the 1970s.

Sarrazin (or **Sarazin**), **Jacques** (1592–1660). The leading French sculptor of the mid-17th century. He was in Rome from about 1610 to 1628, during which time he formed his style on the example of the *antique and classicizing artists such as *Domenichino and *Duquesnoy. On his return to Paris he established himself as head of his profession, and his workshop became the main training ground for sculptors of the following generation. Much of his best work was done as architectural decoration, the finest example being his *caryatids on the Pavillon de l'Horloge at the *Louvre (1639–42). He also supervised the decoration (1652–60) of the Château de Maisons, the masterpiece of François Mansart, the greatest French architect of the 17th century. Although it does not rank on the same level, Sarrazin's dignified work forms a kind of sculptural parallel to the architecture of Mansart or the paintings of *Poussin.

Sassetta (Stefano di Giovanni) (active 1423; d. 1450). Sienese painter; the name Sassetta was evidently first used in the 18th century and is of unknown origin, but it is now the accepted designation. His work continues Sienese tradition in its beautiful colouring and elegant line, but he was also influenced by the *International Gothic style and by contemporary Florentine developments, combining them into a highly personal manner expressive of his mystical imagination. With *Giovanni di Paolo he ranks as the outstanding Sienese painter of the 15th century. His most important work was the St Francis altarpiece (1437–44) painted for the church of S. Francesco at Borgo San Sepolcro and now dispersed. The central panel, *St Francis in Ecstasy* (Berenson Coll., Florence), has a monumental dignity that must have impressed *Piero della Francesca (a native of San Sepolcro), and some of the other panels (seven are in the National Gallery, London) show him at his most lyrical. Sassetta's reputation did not long survive his death and he was not rediscovered until the early 20th century.

Sassoferrato (Giovanni Battista Salvi) (1609–85). Italian painter, known by the name of his town of birth—Sassoferrato—and active in nearby Urbino and other cities of central Italy, notably Rome (where he is said to have been a pupil of *Domenichino) and Perugia. He did some portraits, but specialized in religious works painted in an extremely sweet, almost *Peruginesque style. They are very clearly drawn and pure in colouring and totally un-*Baroque in feeling—indeed, they have a deliberately archaic quality that brings the paintings of the *Nazarenes to mind. Little is known of his life (in the 18th century it was evidently generally believed he was a contemporary of *Raphael) and few of his pictures are dated or datable; they seem to have been in great demand, however, as his compositions often exist in numerous very similar versions. Most of them were presumably done for private collectors, as few are in churches. Examples of his work are in many galleries (including the National Gallery and Wallace Coll., London), and a fine collection of his drawings (virtually his entire surviving output as a draughtsman) is in the Royal Library at Windsor Castle.

Saura, Antonio (1930–98). Spanish painter, draughtsman, and printmaker, active mainly in Madrid. He was self-taught and began painting during a long illness in 1947. His early work was *Surrealist and while he was living in Paris from 1953 to 1955 he met the founder of the movement, André *Breton. Back in Spain, however, he quickly abandoned Surrealism for a violently expressive semi-abstract style that has been seen as one of the most forceful protests against the Franco regime (his change of direction was partly inspired by the brutal suppression of student demonstrations soon after his return to Madrid). The stormy atmosphere and thickly textured figures in his work create a feeling of tortured humanity (*Great Crucifixion*, 1963, Boymans Mus., Rotterdam).

Savery, Roelandt (1576?–1639). Flemish-born Dutch painter, draughtsman, and etcher of landscapes, animal subjects, and still life, the most distinguished member of a family of artists. He was born in Courtrai, grew up in Amsterdam, and in 1619 settled in Utrecht, but he is best known for his association with Prague, where he worked for the emperor Rudolf II (*see* HABSBURG) from 1603 to 1613. Rudolf's famous menagerie allowed him to study in detail the exotic animals that became the trademark of his work. He painted and drew creatures such as pelicans, ostriches, camels, and the now extinct dodo, and was one of the first artists in the Netherlands to do pictures of animals alone. His favourite subjects, however, were Orpheus and the Garden of Eden, which allowed him to include any number of colourful beasts. Savery's bright and highly finished style is similar to that of Jan 'Velvet' *Brueghel, but is somewhat more archaic. His rare flower paintings are sometimes of outstanding quality, and with *Bosschaert (likewise Flemish-born) he was an influential early exponent of this genre in Holland. *Houbraken says that Savery died insane. His brother **Jacob Savery** (*c*.1565–1603) was a painter, draughtsman, and etcher. He was influenced by Pieter *Bruegel and numerous drawings formerly attributed to Bruegel are now considered to be deliberate forgeries by Jacob; other 'Bruegel' drawings are thought to be by Roelandt.

Saville, Jenny. *See* YOUNG BRITISH ARTISTS.

Savoldo, Giovanni Girolamo (active 1506–48). Italian painter, perhaps born in Brescia, first documented in Parma in 1506, and active mainly in Venice. His output was small, his career was fairly undistinguished, and he was virtually forgotten after his death, but he is now regarded as a highly attractive minor master whose work stands somewhat apart from the main Venetian tradition. His forte was night scenes, in which he gave his lyrical sensibility and liking for unusual light effects full play. One of the best-known examples is *Mary Magdalen Approaching the Sepulchre*, of which several versions exist, one in the National Gallery, London. The writer Pietro Aretino described Savoldo as 'decrepit' in 1548 and he is not heard of thereafter.

Saxl, Fritz. *See* FALCONE.

Scarsellino, Lo (Ippolito Scarsella) (*c*.1551–1620). The leading Ferrarese painter of his period. He produced a good deal of large-scale work, including frescos, but he is now remembered mainly for his small mythological or religious scenes set in landscapes, several of which are in the Borghese Gallery, Rome. Their romantic feeling and spirited technique recall Venetian painting (he is said to have studied with *Veronese) and they were particularly influential on the young *Guercino.

Schad, Christian. *See* NEUE SACHLICHKEIT.

Schadow, Johann Gottfried (1764–1850). German sculptor, draughtsman, printmaker, and writer on art. In 1785–7 he lived in Rome, then settled in his native Berlin. His style was essentially *Neoclassical (he became a friend of *Canova in Rome), but it retained a degree of *Baroque liveliness. He was active mainly as a portraitist and tomb sculptor, but his best-known work is the *quadriga* (four-horse chariot) (completed 1791) surmounting the Brandenburg Gate in Berlin, which was badly damaged in the Second World War and has been replaced by a copy. His finest achievement is perhaps the charming and sensitive group of the *Princesses Luise and Frederika of Prussia* (1795–7, Alte NG, Berlin). From 1815 until his death he was director of the Berlin Academy and his later years were mainly devoted to teaching, administration, and writing on art theory. He had three artist sons: **Felix Schadow** (1819–61), a painter, **Rudolf Schadow** (1786–1822), a sculptor, and, most importantly, **Wilhelm von Schadow** (1788–1862), who was a painter and writer on art. In 1810–19 he lived in Rome, where he became a member of the *Nazarenes. From 1826 to 1859 he was director of the Düsseldorf Academy, which he helped to make into a leading centre of history painting. In 1845 he was ennobled and added the aristocratic 'von' to his name.

Schalken, Godfried (1643–1706). Dutch painter of biblical, allegorical, and anecdotal subjects and of portraits, active mainly in Dordrecht. He was taught there by *Hoogstraten and in Leiden by *Dou, and he was one of Dou's most distinguished successors in the *fijnschilder* (fine painter) tradition. His surfaces are as smooth, glossy, and delicately finished as Dou's, but Schalken differed from his master in his lighting effects (he had a liking for the red glow of candlelight) and in his penchant for scenes involving coquettish women. From 1692 to 1697 Schalken lived in London, where he painted a portrait of William III by candlelight (Rijksmuseum, Amsterdam). As with Dou, Schalken's great reputation lasted throughout the 18th century.

Scheemakers, Peter (1691–1781). Flemish sculptor, active mainly in England, where he settled around 1720. Apart from a visit to Rome (1728–1730) he was based in London until 1771, when he retired to his native Antwerp. In the 1730s he became the main rival to *Rysbrack, whose prices he undercut. Rysbrack defeated him in competition for the equestrian statue of William III in Bristol, but Scheemakers gained a great success in 1740 with his Shakespeare monument (designed by William *Kent) in Westminster Abbey and thereafter received numerous commissions and ran a large studio with many assistants. He was, indeed, perhaps the most prolific of mid-18th-century sculptors, particularly as a maker of monuments, ranging from small tablets to large multi-figure compositions. He also made portrait busts, and these, like his monuments, are often severely classical, reflecting his love of the *antique. Scheemakers' brother **Henry** (d. 1748) and his son **Thomas** (1740–1808) were also sculptors working in England.

Scheffer, Ary (1795–1858). Dutch-born painter and lithographer who spent virtually all his career in Paris and became a French citizen in 1850. His work was immensely popular in his lifetime, but is now generally considered sentimental. Early in his career he favoured literary themes (*Francesca da Rimini*, 1835, Wallace Coll., London,

and other versions), but later he turned to mawkishly treated religious subjects (*St Augustine and St Monica*, 1854, NG, London, and other versions). He also painted many portraits. His work is well represented in the museum at Dordrecht, his native town.

Scheggia, Lo. *See* MASACCIO.

Schelfhout, Andreas (1787–1870). Dutch landscape painter in oils and watercolour, a forerunner of the *Hague School. He is best known for carefully depicted winter scenes reminiscent of those made by 17th-century Dutch artists, but he also painted seascapes and other subjects. His work was influential particularly on *Jongkind, his most famous pupil.

Scheyer, Galka. *See* BLAUE VIER.

Schiavone, Andrea (Andrea Meldolla) (*c.*1510/15–1563). Italian painter and etcher. His nickname 'Schiavone' means 'Slav', reflecting the fact that he came from Zara, Dalmatia (then under Venetian jurisdiction). He worked mainly in Venice, where he was on friendly terms with *Titian (who along with *Parmigianino was one of the main influences on his style). His most characteristic works were fairly small religious or mythological pictures for private patrons, done in a vigorous, painterly style that had considerable influence on the next generation.

Schiele, Egon (1890–1918). Austrian painter and draughtsman. He studied at the Vienna Academy and in 1907 met *Klimt, who encouraged him and was a strong influence on his early *Art Nouveau style. By 1909, however, he had begun to develop his own highly distinctive style, which is characterized by an aggressive linear energy expressing acute nervous intensity. He painted portraits, landscapes, and semi-allegorical works, but he is best known for his drawings of nudes (including self-portraits), which have a disturbing and explicit erotic power —in 1912 he was briefly imprisoned on indecency charges, and several of his drawings were burnt. The figures he portrays are typically lonely or anguished, their bodies emaciated and twisted, expressing an aching intensity of feeling. His work was much exhibited, and he was beginning to receive international acclaim when he died (three days after his wife) in the influenza epidemic of 1918. He has since come to be recognized as one of the greatest masters of *Expressionism and only Klimt and *Kokoschka are better known among modern Austrian artists.

Schildersbent (Dutch: 'Band of Painters'). A fraternal organization founded in about 1620 for social fellowship and mutual assistance by a number of Dutch and Flemish artists living in Rome. Its members called themselves *Bentvueghels* ('birds of a flock') and they had individual *Bentnames*—for example Pieter van *Laer, one of the early leaders, was called Bamboccio. In 1720 Pope Clement XI banned the Schildersbent's drunken initiation rituals, which parodied the ceremony of baptism, and the organization was disbanded.

Schinkel, Karl Friedrich (1781–1841). German architect, painter, and designer, active mainly in Berlin. Schinkel was the greatest German architect of the 19th century, but until 1815, when he gained a senior appointment in the Public Works Department of Prussia, he worked mainly as a painter and stage designer. His paintings are highly *Romantic landscapes, somewhat in the spirit of *Friedrich, although more anecdotal in detail (*Gothic Cathedral by a River*, 1813–14, Alte NG, Berlin). He continued working as a stage designer until the 1830s, and in this field ranks among the greatest artists of his period. His most famous designs were for Mozart's *Magic Flute* (1815, Schinkelmuseum, Berlin), in which he combined the clarity and logic of his architectural style with a feeling of mystery and fantasy.

Schjerfbeck, Helene (1862–1946). Finnish painter. In the 1880s she travelled widely, working mainly in France but also in *St Ives and St Petersburg, making a name with open-air scenes notable for their fresh colouring. From about 1900 her health (always delicate) began to fail badly (although she lived into her eighties) and she adopted a solitary life at Hyvinkaa, almost forgotten, developing a much more simplified style. Her subtle colour harmonies recall those of *Whistler, and after her work was exhibited in 1937 she was recognized as one of the pioneers of modernism in Finland. Her work included landscapes, still lifes, figure compositions, and

portraits, notably a long series of self-portraits that are regarded as being among her finest achievements.

Schlemmer, Oskar (1888–1943). German painter, sculptor, stage designer, and writer on art. From 1920 to 1929 he taught at the *Bauhaus, in the metalwork, sculpture, and stage-design workshops. During this time he did much work for the theatre, notably designs for the *Constructivist *Triadic Ballet*, to music by Paul Hindemith, which was performed at the Bauhaus in 1923. After leaving the Bauhaus he taught in Breslau and Berlin, but in 1933 he was dismissed by the Nazis, who declared his work *degenerate. He lived in Switzerland from 1933 to 1937 and from 1940 spent most of his time in Wuppertal. Schlemmer had a mystical temperament and his ideas on art were complex. He rejected what he considered the soullessness of pure abstraction, but he wished to submit his intuition to rational control. Some of his early work was influenced by *Cubism and he showed a deep concern for pictorial structure. Characteristically his paintings represent rather mechanistic human figures, seen in strictly frontal, rear, or profile attitudes set in a mysterious space (*Group of Fourteen Figures in Imaginary Architecture*, 1930, Wallraf-Richartz-Mus., Cologne). His cool, streamlined forms are seen also in his sculpture.

Schlichter, Rudolf. *See* NEUE SACHLICHKEIT.

Schlüter, Andreas (c.1660–1714). German sculptor and architect, active mainly in Berlin. The greatest *Baroque sculptor in northern Germany and also an outstanding architect, he played a leading role in establishing Berlin as an important art centre, but his career was dogged by ill fortune, and few of his major works survive. The most important is the splendid equestrian monument to Frederick William, the Great Elector (1696–1703, Charlottenburg Castle, Berlin). After a series of structural problems with his buildings (probably mainly caused by marshy ground), Schlüter lost his appointment as royal architect in 1707 and had a nervous breakdown. In 1713 he accepted an invitation from Peter the Great to work in the recently founded St Petersburg, but he died soon after arriving.

Schmidt-Degener, Frederick. *See* RIJKS-MUSEUM.

Schmidt-Rottluff, Karl (né Schmidt) (1884–1976). German *Expressionist painter, printmaker, and sculptor, born at Rottluff near Chemnitz (he added the 'Rottluff' to his name in 1906). In 1905 he was one of the founders of Die *Brücke. He was the most independent member of the group, taking a limited part in its activities, and his style was harsher than that of the other members. It was particularly forceful in his woodcuts, which are amongst the finest representatives of Expressionist graphic art. In 1906 he stayed with *Nolde on the island of Alsten, Norway, and in 1907 he painted with *Heckel at Dangast on the coast north-west of Bremen. Apart from landscapes such as the ones he painted in these places, his work included portraits, figure compositions, and still lifes. In 1911, with the other members of Die Brücke, Schmidt-Rottluff moved to Berlin, where he lived for most of the rest of his life. In the 1910s and 1920s he was influenced by the stylized forms of African sculpture (*Dr Rosa Schapire*, 1919, Tate, London). Later his style became somewhat more naturalistic. His work was declared *degenerate by the Nazis and in 1941 he was forbidden to paint. In 1947 he became a professor at the Berlin Hochschule für Bildende Künste. The Brücke-Museum in Berlin was founded on his initiative in 1967 and he gave 60 of his own works to the collection. There are good collections of his graphic work in the Victoria and Albert Museum, London, and the Leicestershire Museum and Art Gallery, Leicester.

Schnabel, Julian (1951–). American painter (and latterly sculptor and film director). His paintings are characteristically large and in a *Neo-Expressionist vein; often they are on unusual materials such as carpet or velvet, and some of them are encrusted with broken crockery (*Humanity Asleep*, 1982, Tate, London) or incorporate other three-dimensional objects (sometimes the supports themselves are three-dimensional, with central projections like a chimney breast). In the 1980s he enjoyed a meteoric rise as the most touted figure in the international art world, treated more like a pop star than a painter, and many critics feel that the huge prices his works have fetched depend more on media hype

and the investment value of contemporary art than on any intrinsic merit. Robert *Hughes, for example, writes that 'Schnabel's work is to painting what Sylvester Stallone's is to acting—a lurching display of oily pectorals—except that Schnabel makes bigger public claims for himself.' In 1983 he began making sculpture, and in 1996 he made his debut as a movie director with *Basquiat*, about the *Graffiti artist Jean-Michel Basquiat.

Schnorr von Carolsfeld, Julius (1794–1872). German painter and draughtsman, the most distinguished member of a family of artists. After studying at the Vienna Academy, he moved to Rome in 1818 and joined the *Nazarenes, taking part in their fresco decoration of the Casino Massimo. In 1827 he moved to Munich, where he was employed by Ludwig I on vast mural schemes in his palace, the Residenz, illustrating scenes from the legend of the Nibelung and from German history (the work was not completed until 1867). In 1846 Schnorr became a professor at the Academy in Dresden and the following year director of the Gemäldegalerie there. Because of his administrative duties and trouble with his eyesight he did comparatively little creative work in his later years. His last major project, on which he worked for many years and which brought him international recognition, was a series of illustrations to the Bible, published in the form of wood engravings as *Die Bibel in Bildern* (1852–60) and in an English edition as *Schnorr's Bible Pictures* (1855–60).

Schönfeld, Johann Heinrich (1609–82/3). German painter and etcher. From about 1633 to 1651 he lived in Italy (mainly Rome and Naples). His career there is rather obscure and it is only after he settled in Augsburg in 1652 that his development can be traced through a succession of dated works. He was versatile and prolific, painting historical and *genre subjects as well as many altarpieces for churches in southern Germany. His style was lively and *eclectic, drawing on various Italian influences, and in his delicate colouring and lightness of touch he anticipates elements of German *Rococo art.

Schongauer, Martin (d. 1491). German engraver and painter, active in Colmar,

Alsace, the best-known member of a family of artists (his father and two of his brothers were goldsmiths; two other brothers were painters and engravers). In his day Martin was probably the most famous artist in Germany; the young *Dürer hoped to study in his workshop, but when he arrived in Colmar in 1492 the master had recently died. Although he was renowned as a painter, few surviving pictures can be confidently attributed to him; the most important, and the only dated example, is the Madonna in the Rose Garden (1473, Dominican church, Colmar). However, about 115 of his engravings are known (all bearing his initials) and these show that he was the greatest master of the technique before Dürer. His work was strongly influenced by Netherlandish art, above all by Rogier van der *Weyden, but Schongauer had a powerful imagination of his own. Most of his prints are on religious themes, but there are also various secular subjects. In them he brought a new richness and maturity to engraving, expanding the range of tones and textures, so that an art that had previously been the domain of the goldsmith took on a more painterly quality. The gracefulness of his work became legendary, giving rise to the nicknames 'Hübsch ("charming") Martin' and 'Schön ("beautiful") Martin'.

School of London. An expression coined by R. B. *Kitaj in 1976 and given wide currency when it was used as the title of a British Council exhibition that toured Europe in 1987—'A School of London: Six Figurative Painters' (the six were Michael *Andrews, Frank *Auerbach, Francis *Bacon, Lucian *Freud, Kitaj himself, and Leon *Kossoff). In 1989 the term was used as the title of a book by Alistair Hicks—The School of London: The Resurgence of Contemporary Painting. The book covers other artists apart from the original six, including Howard *Hodgkin. It is not clear what the label is meant to mean and some critics have denied that any such thing as a School of London exists.

School of Paris. See ÉCOLE DE PARIS.

Schooten, Joris van. See REMBRANDT.

Schwind, Moritz von (1804–71). Austrian painter and illustrator, active mainly in south Germany. He was born in Vienna and trained at the Academy there and then under *Cornelius at the Munich Academy (where Schwind himself became a professor in 1846). His work represents the tail end of Germanic *Romanticism, characteristically depicting an idealized fairy-tale Middle Ages, with knights in armour, damsels in distress, enchanted woods and castles, and much loving depiction of costume, architecture, etc. He painted several murals, but he was at his best working on a small scale, as in his numerous book illustrations and his woodcuts for Fliegende Blätter, a humorous Munich periodical. In his young days Schwind, who was an accomplished violinist, had been friendly with Franz Schubert and late in life he depicted Schubert's Vienna circle in a number of drawings.

Schwitters, Kurt (1887–1948). German painter, sculptor, maker of constructions, writer, and typographer, a leading figure of the *Dada movement who is best known for his invention of 'Merz'. Schwitters first applied this word to collages made from refuse, but he came to use it of all his activities, including poetry. He used the word as a verb as well as a noun: a fellow artist was once nonplussed when Schwitters asked him to merz with him. In his early work Schwitters was influenced by *Expressionism and *Cubism, but after the First World War (in which he served for a time as a draughtsman) he became the chief (indeed, virtually only) representative of Dada in Hanover. In 1918 he began making collages from refuse such as bus tickets, cigarette wrappers, and string, and in 1919 he invented Merz. The name was reached by chance: whilst he was fitting the word Commerzbank (from a business letterhead) into a collage, Schwitters cut off some letters and used what was left. He called the collages Merzbilden (Merz pictures) and in about 1923 began to make a sculptural or architectural variant—the Merzbau (Merz building)—in his house in Hanover (it was destroyed by bombing in 1943). From 1923 to 1932 he published a magazine called Merz and in this period he was much occupied with typography. In 1937 his work was declared *degenerate by the Nazis and in the same year he fled to Norway, where at Lysaker he began a second Merzbau (destroyed by fire in 1951). When the Germans invaded Norway in 1940, he moved to England, where he lived for the rest of his life—in London (after release from an internment camp) from 1941 to 1945, and then at Ambleside in the Lake District. Here, in an old barn in Langdale, he began work on his third and final *Merzbau*, with financial aid from the Museum of Modern Art, New York. It was unfinished at his death and is now in the Hatton Gallery, Newcastle upon Tyne. The day before he died Schwitters received British citizenship.

Scipione (Gino Bonichi) (1904–33). Italian painter. He was the son of a soldier and adopted his pseudonym (in 1927) in homage to Scipio Africanus, the Roman general who defeated Hannibal. He studied briefly (1924–5) at the Academy in Rome before being expelled with his friend Mario Mafai (1902–65), with whom he introduced a romantic *Expressionist vein into Italian painting in opposition to the pomposity of much of the art that was favoured under Mussolini's Fascist government. His subjects were mainly scenes of modern Rome, painted with violent brushwork and a feeling of visionary intensity. His career was very short, virtually ending in 1931 because of the tuberculosis that killed him, but he was highly influential, becoming a symbol of heroic individuality to Italian artists after the Second World War.

Scopas of Paros. One of the most celebrated Greek sculptors, active in the mid-4th century BC. He is recorded as working on the Mausoleum of Halicarnassus, the temple of Artemis at Ephesus, and the temple of Athena Alea at Tegea, of which *Pausanias says he was the architect. Sculptural remains from all three buildings have survived, and although none of them can be certainly associated with Scopas, it is likely that he or his workshop was responsible for certain pieces that show a distinctive style and are of a quality consonant with his elevated reputation. Among them are three slabs from the Mausoleum (BM, London) showing the Battle of Greeks and Amazons, which display the intensity of expression and the characteristically deep-set eyes that are considered typical of his work. Several other pieces have been associated with him on stylistic grounds. In spite of the lack of solid evidence, Scopas is presumed to have ranked with *Praxiteles and *Lysippus as the leading Greek sculptor of the mid- to late 4th century BC, his work

heralding the emotionalism of *Hellenistic sculpture.

Scorel, Jan van (1495–1562). Netherlandish painter, the first artist to bring the ideals of the Italian *Renaissance to the area we today call Holland. He was born in Schoorl near Alkmaar, and his training is said to have included a period in Utrecht with *Gossaert, who probably encouraged him to visit Italy. Scorel set out in about 1518 and according to van *Mander's account he visited various German cities on his way south, including Nuremberg, where he met *Dürer. When he reached Venice, he joined a group of pilgrims going to the Holy Land and visited Crete and Cyprus as well as Bethlehem and Jerusalem. After returning to Venice he made his way to Rome, where Pope Adrian VI, a native of Utrecht, appointed him curator of the papal collection of antiquities. Adrian died in 1523, however, and the following year Scorel returned to Utrecht, where he spent most of the rest of his life. He was the illegitimate son of a priest and Scorel himself took holy orders (this did not stop him fathering six children). He soon became the dominant artist in the northern Netherlands and his reputation spread to other countries (Francis I is said to have tried to engage him to work in France). Most of his work was religious, but he was also an outstanding portraitist. His paintings show how closely he had studied *classical sculpture and the works of *Raphael and *Michelangelo while he lived in Rome. He was also influenced by the sensuous beauty of Venetian painting, as is seen particularly clearly in his *Death of Cleopatra* (c.1523, Rijksmuseum, Amsterdam), a reclining nude in the *Giorgione tradition. Unlike the works of many other Netherlandish masters, however, Scorel's pictures are no mere jumble of Renaissance motifs. His *Presentation in the Temple* (c.1535, KH Mus., Vienna), for example, is set in a convincingly *Bramantesque building and the dignified figures are well integrated in their spatial setting. On the other hand, his interest in atmospheric effects is part of his northern heritage. Scorel was highly influential in the Netherlands, and his pupils included some of the leading artists of the next generation, notably *Heemskerck and *Mor.

Scott, Kathleen (1878–1947). British portrait sculptor, born Kathleen Bruce. She studied at the *Slade School and in Paris under *Rodin. In 1908 she married Captain Robert Falcon Scott (Scott of the Antarctic), who died on his return from the South Pole in 1912. Her most famous work is the statue commemorating him (unveiled 1915) in Waterloo Place, London. She did portrait busts of many other distinguished contemporaries. After her husband's death she was granted the rank of a widow of a Knight Commander of the Order of the Bath and was known as Lady Scott. In 1922 she married Lieutenant-Commander Edward Hilton-Young, who in 1935 became Baron Kennet; some reference books list her as Lady Kennet. Her son, **Sir Peter Scott** (1909–89), was a distinguished ornithologist and conservationist and also a noted painter and illustrator of wildfowl.

Scott, Samuel (1702?–72). English marine and topographical painter. He began as a marine painter in the tradition of the van de *Veldes, but in the 1740s he turned to topographical views (usually of the London riverside) in the manner of *Canaletto, who was then enjoying great success in England. He was not simply a mechanical imitator, however, and had a feeling for the English atmosphere that is lacking in Canaletto, who brought the Venetian light with him to England. Scott also could achieve a distinctive grandeur of design, as in *An Arch of Westminster Bridge* (c.1750, Tate, London), which is often considered his masterpiece. He left London in 1765 and settled in Bath for reasons of health (he suffered from gout), evidently painting little in his later years.

Scott, Tim. *See* NEW GENERATION.

Scott, William (1913–89). British painter of still life (usually involving kitchen objects) and abstracts. In 1937–9 he lived in France, and he said: 'I picked up from the tradition of painting in France that I felt most kinship with—the still life tradition of *Chardin and *Braque, leading to a certain kind of abstraction which comes directly from that tradition.' His work continued to be based on still life, but for a time in the 1950s he painted pure abstracts. They featured forms such as circles and squares, but they were not geometrically exact and were bounded by sensitive painterly lines. In the late 1960s and 1970s his style became more austere. Although his work was restricted in range and undemonstrative in character, Scott came to be regarded as one of the leading British artists of his generation.

Scott, William Bell (1811–90). Scottish painter and poet. He was head of the Government School of Design in Newcastle upon Tyne, 1843–64, and his best-known works are near Newcastle, at Wallington Hall, Northumberland: a series (1857–61) representing Northumbrian history and including the well-known *Iron and Coal*, one of the earliest representations in art of heavy industry. Bell was a close friend of *Rossetti, and his work has affinities with *Pre-Raphaelitism in its Romanticism and love of historical detail. His literary output included much poetry and several books on art, among them a memoir (1850) of his brother **David Scott** (1806–49), a history painter and book illustrator. Their father, **Robert Scott** (1771–1841), was an engraver.

Scottish Colourists. A term applied to four Scottish painters who in the period c.1900–14 each spent some time in France and were strongly influenced by the rich colours and bold handling of recent French painting, notably *Fauvism: they are F. C. B. Cadell (1883–1937), J. D. *Fergusson, Leslie Hunter (1879–1931), and S. J. Peploe (1869–1933). The term was popularized by a book by T. J. Honeyman dealing with Cadell, Hunter, and Peploe (*Three Scottish Colourists*, 1950), but it is now usual to add Fergusson to their number, even though he stands apart from the rest in that he returned to live in France after the First World War, whereas the other three remained in Scotland. All four painters knew each other, and they exhibited together as 'Les Peintres de L'Écosse Moderne', at the Galerie Barbazanges, Paris, in 1924, but they did not function as a group. They have been described as the first 'modern' Scottish artists; certainly they were the main channel through which *Post-Impressionism reached their country. None of them was represented in Roger *Fry's Post-Impressionist exhibitions of 1910 and 1912, but this reflects insular English attitudes towards Scottish art rather than the quality of their work.

screenprinting. A printing technique based on *stencilling, originally used for commercial work but now popular with artists for creative printmaking. The essence of the technique is that a fine mesh screen, stretched tightly over a wooden frame, is placed above a sheet of paper and colour is forced through the mesh with a rubber blade called a squeegee. Usually the screen is made of silk—hence the terms silkscreen printing, which is preferred in the USA, and serigraphy (from Lat., *sericum*: 'silk'); however the screen can also be made of cotton, nylon, or metal, so the more inclusive term is useful. There are various ways of applying the design to the screen. The earliest and most basic was to attach a cut-out stencil to it. A refinement of this method is to paint the design directly on the screen with a varnish-like substance that blocks the holes in the mesh. The blocked-out areas form the negative part of the design, the colour being squeezed through the untouched parts of the screen. However, more sophisticated methods enable the artist to create a positive design directly on the screen with a waxy or waterproof medium that is eventually dissolved to allow the ink through only in the parts that have been so treated. Photographic images can be used in the design by shining a light through a transparency onto a chemically treated mesh. Screenprints are almost invariably coloured, a different screen generally being used successively for each colour. The origins of the technique are murky, but it seems to have come to Europe from Japan in the late 19th century. It was not until the early 1960s, however, that it made an important impact in the art world. It was especially favoured by *Pop artists, whose bold images were well served by its capacity for strong, flat colour and its relative crudeness of detail (subtle handling is discouraged because of the texture of the mesh). The artist who more than any other put it on the map was Andy *Warhol.

Scrotes, Guillim (William Stretes) (active 1537–53). Netherlandish portrait painter. He is first heard of in 1537, when he became court painter to Mary of Hungary (*see* HABSBURG), regent of the Netherlands, and by 1545 he was working in England for Henry VIII, who paid him a very high salary (about twice what his predecessor *Holbein had earned). His appointment continued under Edward VI. Only a handful of paintings, all

done in England, can be confidently attributed to him, among them a full-length portrait of Edward VI in the Royal Collection (several other versions exist). They show Scrotes to have been a highly accomplished practitioner in the international *Mannerist court style and he was an important figure in introducing the full-length portrait to England. He is last heard of in 1553 and may have left England after Edward's death in that year.

scumble. A layer of opaque colour brushed lightly over a previous layer of another colour in such a way that the lower layer is only partly obliterated and shows through irregularly. Together with *glazing, scumbling allows a range of textural and colouristic effects that ensured *oil painting's dominance over other media. Similar effects can now be obtained with *acrylic.

Sebastiano del Piombo (Sebastiano Luciani) (*c*.1485–1547). Venetian painter, active mainly in Rome. According to *Vasari, he trained with Giovanni *Bellini, but his early work was most strongly influenced by *Giorgione, whose *Three Philosophers* (KH Mus., Vienna) Sebastiano is said to have completed after the master's death in 1510. Their styles, indeed, can be so close as to cause paintings to be disputed between them, most notably the unfinished *Judgement of Solomon* (Kingston Lacy, Dorset, NT). This large and impressive work was attributed to Giorgione by *Ridolfi, but scholarly opinion now increasingly gives it to Sebastiano. The half-length *Salome* (or *Judith*?) (1510, NG, London) shows the magnificent painterly skills of an undoubted work of Sebastiano at this date; it has a sensuous beauty reminiscent of Giorgione, but also a statuesque grandeur that is Sebastiano's own. In 1511 he moved to Rome at the invitation of the banker and patron Agostino *Chigi, and he remained there for the rest of his life apart from a visit to Venice in 1528–9 after the Sack of Rome. For Chigi he painted mythological frescos at the Villa Farnesina, where *Raphael also worked. It was with *Michelangelo rather than Raphael, however, that Sebastiano formed a friendship and a professional relationship. Michelangelo not only recommended him to people of influence, but also made drawings for him to work from, as with the *Raising of Lazarus* (1517–19, NG, London). This was commissioned by Cardinal Giulio de' *Medici (later Pope Clement VII) for the cathedral in Narbonne (of which he was archbishop); it was painted in rivalry with Raphael's *Transfiguration* (Pinacoteca, Vatican), intended for the same church, and Vasari suggests that Michelangelo helped Sebastiano in order to discredit the Raphael faction, who had denigrated his powers as a colourist. Under Michelangelo's guidance Sebastiano's work became grander in form whilst losing much of its beauty of handling, the lack of sensuous appeal being accentuated when he began experimenting with painting on slate. Some of the finest works of Sebastiano's Roman years are his portraits, and after Raphael's death (1520) he had no rival in the city in this field, his work attaining a distinctive sombre dignity. Clement VII, the subject of one of Sebastiano's finest portraits (1526, Mus. di Capodimonte, Naples), appointed him to the lucrative post of keeper of the papal seals in 1531 and after this he was less active as a painter. The seals were made of lead, *piombo* in Italian, hence Sebastiano's nickname.

secco (It.: 'dry'). Term applied to a technique of mural painting in which the colours are applied to dry plaster, rather than wet plaster as in *fresco. The colours were usually *tempera or *pigments ground in lime water; if lime water was used, the plaster had to be damped before painting, a method described by *Theophilus and popular in northern Europe and in Spain. In Italian *Renaissance art the finishing touches to a true fresco would often be painted *a secco*, as it is easier to add details in this way; because the secco technique is much less permanent, such passages have a tendency to flake off with time. Thus in *Giotto's *Betrayal* in the Arena Chapel, Padua, the details of many of the soldiers' weapons are now missing.

Section d'Or. Group of French painters who worked in loose association between 1912 and 1914, when the First World War brought an end to their activities. The name, which was also the title of a short-lived magazine published by the group, was suggested by Jacques *Villon in reference to the mathematical ratio known as the *golden section, reflecting the interest of the artists involved in questions of pro-

portion and pictorial discipline. Other members of the group (who held one exhibition, in 1912) included *Delaunay, *Duchamp, *Duchamp-Villon, *Gleizes, *Gris, *Léger, *Metzinger, and *Picabia. The common stylistic feature of their work was a debt to *Cubism and several of them worked in the *Orphist style.

Segal, George (1924–2000). American sculptor. His career was slow to mature. He studied at various art colleges and took a degree in art education at New York University in 1950, but until 1958 he worked mainly as a chicken farmer, painting *Expressionist nudes in his spare time. In 1958 he made his first sculpture and in 1960 he began producing the kind of work for which he became famous—life-size unpainted plaster figures, usually combined with real objects to create strange ghostly tableaux (*The Gas Station*, 1963, NG, Ottawa). The figures were made from casts taken from the human body; he used his family and friends as models. In the 1970s he began to incorporate sound and lighting effects in his work. Segal has been classified with *Pop art and *Environment art, but his work is highly distinctive, his figures and groups dwelling in a lonely limbo in a way that captures a disquieting sense of spiritual isolation.

Segantini, Giovanni (1858–99). Italian painter, mainly of figure compositions in landscape settings, active for most of his career in the Swiss Alps. His early work was naturalistic, but from the later 1880s he developed a *divisionist technique and a liking for *Symbolist subjects (*The Punishment of Luxury*, 1891, Walker AG, Liverpool). He exhibited widely and was one of the few Italian artists of his time with an international reputation. There is a Segantini museum at St Moritz.

Segers, Hercules (c.1589/90–1633/8). Dutch painter and etcher of landscapes, one of the most original and most enigmatic figures in the history of Dutch art. His name is now often spelled 'Seghers', but 'Segers' was the form used by himself and his contemporaries. Few details of his life are known. He was born in Haarlem, studied with Gillis van *Coninxloo in Amsterdam, and worked also in Utrecht and The Hague, where he is last mentioned in 1633. The woman who was evidently his second wife is described as a widow in 1638. Hardly more than a dozen surviving paintings can be securely attributed to him, although contemporary documents show he certainly painted more. None of the paintings are dated and his chronology is difficult to reconstruct. He specialized in mountainous scenes, fantastic or visionary in conception but advanced in the naturalistic treatment of light and atmosphere. They are usually fairly small, but they suggest vast distances, and with their jagged rocks, shattered tree trunks, and menacing skies convey a sense of almost tragic desolation. Only *Rembrandt and *Ruisdael among Dutch artists attained a similar degree of emotional intensity in landscape painting, and Segers certainly influenced Rembrandt, who owned no fewer than eight of his paintings. One of these, *Mountain Landscape* (c.1630, Uffizi, Florence), now Segers's most famous picture, was attributed to Rembrandt until 1871 and he may have touched it up when it was in his collection. Segers's etchings are also rare (the latest catalogue lists 54, with 183 known impressions) and are perhaps even more original than his paintings. He experimented with coloured inks and dyed papers, so that extraordinarily different impressions could be made from the same plate, a dark paper printed with pale ink transforming a daylight scene into a haunting nocturnal view. Sometimes he printed on linen, which emphasized the vigorous and grainy quality of his work. Every print was an individual work rather than an item in a standardized commercial edition: *Hoogstraten said that he 'printed paintings'. These works are unique in European art of the time, and it is often pointed out that some of them have a strange spiritual kinship with Chinese art. The best collection is in the print room of the Rijksmuseum, Amsterdam. In 1678 Hoogstraten published a highly coloured account of Segers's unhappy career, his desperate experiments with etchings, and his eventual poverty and drunkenness (he says that he was killed by falling downstairs when intoxicated). Although the account may be exaggerated, Segers certainly had financial problems (he was forced to sell his house in Amsterdam in 1631), and it seems likely that he was little appreciated in his day.

Seghers, Daniel (1590–1661). The leading Flemish flower painter of his generation. He was born in Antwerp, where he was a pupil of Jan *Brueghel and became a member of the painters' guild in 1611. In 1614 he became a Jesuit lay brother and in 1625 was ordained a priest. After spending two years at Jesuit headquarters in Rome he returned to Antwerp in 1627 and lived there for the rest of his life, working at his monastery; the words 'Society of Jesus' usually follow his signature on his paintings. He enjoyed considerable fame and his distinguished visitors included the future Charles II of England. Most of his works were not sold, but were presented by the Jesuits to dignitaries as tokens of esteem or honour; the recipients in return sent treasures including holy relics and a gold palette and brushes. Seghers's work consists mainly of garlands of flowers painted around a religious image (typically a Madonna and Child or a *Pietà) by another artist. He collaborated with his friend *Rubens in this way. Much rarer are his bouquets of flowers in a glass vase, where brilliant colours stand out against a dark background (*A Vase with Flowers*, 1643, Gemäldegalerie, Dresden). Their comparative simplicity makes it easier to appreciate his lovely creamy touch (his brushwork was broader than Brueghel's but unerringly sure) and they rank among the most beautiful flower pieces ever painted.

Seghers, Gerard (1591–1651). Flemish painter of religious subjects, active mainly in his native Antwerp, where he is said to have been taught by *Janssen. He probably spent most of the second decade of the 17th century in Italy (he evidently also visited Spain during this time) and he became one of the very few noteworthy Flemish *Caravaggesque artists. By the late 1620s, however, he had fallen under the all-pervasive influence of *Rubens (*Assumption of the Virgin*, 1629, Mus. de Peinture et de Sculpture, Grenoble). Seghers enjoyed a successful career supplying altarpieces for churches in Antwerp and other Flemish cities, and he was also an international art dealer.

Seghers, Hercules. See SEGERS.

seicento (It.: '17th century'). See QUATTROCENTO.

Seilern, Count Antoine. See COURTAULD.

Seisenegger, Jakob (*c*.1504/5–67). Austrian painter, chiefly a portraitist. In 1531 he became court painter to the emperor Ferdinard I at Augsburg and he also worked for other members of the *Habsburg family. He was a painter of modest talent, but has some importance in the development of the full-length court painter to the emperor portrait; his best-known work is the full-length of Charles V (1532, KH Mus., Vienna), which served as a model for the more famous one by *Titian (Prado, Madrid). Seisenegger travelled widely, working in Italy, the Netherlands, and Spain, as well as in various cities in central Europe—Innsbruck, Prague, Vienna.

Seligmann, Kurt (1900–62). Swiss-born painter, printmaker, designer, and writer who became an American citizen. From 1929 to 1938 he lived in Paris, where he became involved with the *Surrealist movement. His paintings of this time had a magical and apocalyptic character, with hazy shapes and swirling draperies fading into a landscape. In 1939 he emigrated to the USA and settled in New York. His work in his new country included sets for ballet and modern dance and a series of pictures called 'Cyclonic Forms' in which he purported to express his reactions to the American landscape. He made a serious study of the occult and wrote a book called *The Mirror of Magic* (1948).

Senefelder, Aloys (1771–1834). German writer who in 1798 invented *lithography as a cheap means of reproducing his plays. He soon realized the artistic possibilities of his invention, which he publicized in two books (1809 and 1818). The second was translated into English as *A Complete Course of Lithography* (1819).

sepia. A brown pigment made from the ink of cuttlefish and other marine creatures. It is mentioned by Roman writers and was perhaps used in the ancient world for writing, but it was evidently not until the late 18th century that it was much used in art—for ink drawings and, because of its semi-transparent quality, in *washes. When first applied to paper, sepia is a warm black, but it gradually turns reddish brown. It is more opaque than *bistre, which it tended to replace in the 19th century, but it can be difficult to tell them apart (and to distinguish them from other brown pigments, especially as different types of ink

were sometimes mixed). The terms tend to be used fairly loosely.

Sequeira, Domingos António de (1768–1836). The leading Portuguese painter of his period, the only one with an international reputation. He studied in Rome 1788–95, and in 1802 he was appointed first court painter in Lisbon. In 1810 he was imprisoned for collaborating with the French invaders during the Peninsular War, but he successfully protested his innocence and after his release in 1811 he designed the celebrated silver table service (1813–16) presented by Portugal to the Duke of Wellington for his part in defeating the French (it is now in the Wellington Museum, London). He continued working in Lisbon until 1823, when he went into exile because of an illiberal new regime and he spent the rest of his life in Paris and (from 1826) Rome. Sequeira was a prolific and versatile painter, mainly of religious subjects and portraits. His early work was *Neoclassical in style, but some of his later work is tinged with *Romantic feeling and is sketchy in handling. Although a much lesser artist, he is a kind of Portuguese equivalent of *Goya.

Séraphine (or **Séraphine de Senlis**) (Séraphine Louis) (1864–1942). French *naive painter. After being orphaned very young, she spent her youth as a farm-hand and later entered domestic service in Senlis. She began painting when she was about 40 and was 'discovered' by Wilhelm *Uhde in 1912. Her pictures are mainly fantastic, minutely detailed compositions of fruit, leaves, and flowers. She was intensely devout and painted in a trance-like state of religious ecstasy, regarding her works as offerings to the Virgin Mary. In the late 1920s her reason began to fail and she became obsessed with visions of the end of the world. She died in a home for the aged at Clermont.

Sergel, Johan Tobias (1740–1814). Swedish sculptor and draughtsman of German parentage, active mainly in his native Stockholm. His early works are in a French *Rococo style, but he abandoned this during an eleven-year stay in Rome (1767–78) and became the leading Swedish exponent of *Neoclassicism. He was a much livelier artist than many Neoclassical sculptors, however, and although his mature work has impressive clarity of form, it also possesses warmth and vitality. In Rome he was best known for his spirited sketches in clay and terracotta, but after his return to Sweden he was mainly a portraitist. He was court sculptor to Gustavus III and his most important work is a bronze statue of the king (1790–1808) in front of the Royal Palace in Stockholm. Sergel was a prolific draughtsman, many of his drawings being *Romantic in spirit, in a style similar to those of *Fuseli, who was a friend during his period in Rome. He became a professor at the Stockholm Academy in 1780 and was appointed director in 1810.

Serial art. A term that from the 1960s, especially in the USA, has been applied to two types of avant-garde art (although the two types may overlap and have in common the fact that they are usually produced by mathematically minded artists). First, it has been used to describe a kind of *Minimal art in which simple, uniform, interchangeable elements (often commercially available objects such as bricks) are assembled in a regular, easily apprehended arrangement. Carl *Andre is a noted exponent of this kind of work. Secondly, more broadly, the term has been applied to works of art that are conceived in series or as part of a larger group; often the individual work is regarded as incomplete in itself, needing to be seen within the context of the whole.

serigraphy. *See* SCREENPRINTING.

Serov, Valentin (1865–1911). Russian painter and graphic artist, son of the composer Alexander Serov. He studied privately under *Repin from an early age and then in 1880–5 at the Academy in St Petersburg, where he became a friend of *Vrubel. His work includes landscapes, genre pictures, and historical scenes, as well as book illustrations, but he is best known as a portraitist. In this field he was the greatest Russian painter of his time and a match for any artist in the world. Like *Sargent, he was a cosmopolitan figure, used to moving in high society, and he brought to his work something of the same quality of aristocratic authority and poise associated with the American's portraits. Like Sargent, too, he painted with superb technical freedom and finesse, and he was just as good with informal por-

traits as with grand showpieces. His two most famous paintings (both in the Tretyakov Gal., Moscow) are intimate early works, the breathtakingly beautiful *Girl with Peaches* (1887) and the almost equally lovely *Girl in the Sunshine* (1888); later, as his fame grew, he painted many of the leading Russian celebrities of his time, particularly artists, musicians, and writers. Serov was a member of the *World of Art group and some of his later work shows a tendency towards flat *Art Nouveau stylization. The most remarkable example is a nude, almost monochromatic portrait of the dancer Ida Rubinstein (Russian Mus., St Petersburg), painted in Paris in 1910. Serov had a difficult personality (he could be gloomy and rude), but he was greatly admired for the integrity and sincerity of his work. *See also* ABRAMTSEVO COLONY.

Serpotta, Giacomo (1656–1732). Sicilian sculptor in *stucco. He was the greatest of all virtuosi in his medium and with the exception of *Antonello da Messina the most distinguished artist to come from Sicily. Unlike Antonello, he spent almost all his life on the island and his work is mainly found in the churches of his native Palermo. His icing-sugar-white figures—elegant, delicate, charming, and joyous in spirit—are amongst the finest expressions of the *Rococo in Italian art. He is particularly well known for his playful *putti, but his finest single figure is generally acknowledged to be the enchantingly coquettish *Fortitude* (1714–17) in the Oratoria del Rosario di S. Domenico, Palermo. His father **Gaspare** (1634–70), his brother **Giuseppe** (1653–1719), and his son **Procopio** (1679–1755) were also sculptors, mainly in stucco.

Sérusier, Paul (1864–1927). French painter and art theorist. In 1888 he met *Bernard and *Gauguin at Pont-Aven. He was converted to their *Symbolist views and soon afterwards was one of the founders of the *Nabis, a group inspired by Gauguin's expressive use of colour and rhythmic pattern. After visiting the school of religious painting at the Benedictine monastery at Beuron in Germany in 1897 and 1903 his ideas became permeated with concepts of religious symbolism. His early paintings had typically featured Breton peasants, but from about 1900 he concentrated on religious subjects. However, his paintings are generally considered of less interest than his ideas on art, which he set out in his book *ABC de la peinture* (1921), dealing with colour relationships and systems of proportion.

settecento (It.: '18th century'). *See* QUAT-TROCENTO.

Seuphor, Michel (1901–99). Belgian-born painter, printmaker, writer, and editor who became a French citizen in 1954. In 1925 he settled in Paris, where he was one of the founders of the *Cercle et Carré association of abstract artists in 1929 and editor of its journal. His artistic work is in a geometrical abstract style, but he is better known for his writings. They include dictionaries of abstract painting (1957) and modern sculpture (1959), both of which have been translated into English.

Seurat, Georges (1859–91). French painter and draughtsman, the founder and greatest exponent of *Neo-Impressionism. Seurat was the son of comfortably-off parents and his career took an unusual course: he never had to worry about earning a living and pursued his artistic researches with single-minded dedication. In 1878 he entered the École des *Beaux-Arts in Paris, but his studies were interrupted by military service in 1879. He returned to Paris in 1880 and for the next two years devoted himself to drawing (he was one of the subtlest and most original draughtsmen of the 19th century, typically working with very broad, velvety areas of tone, using a *conté crayon on textured paper). In spite of this mastery of black and white, as a painter he turned for inspiration to artists in the colourist tradition—notably *Delacroix and the *Impressionists. In addition to studying the work of such painters, Seurat read aesthetic and scientific treatises, and he made it his aim to establish a rational system for achieving the kind of vibrant colour effects that the Impressionists in particular had arrived at instinctively. The method he evolved was to place small touches of unmixed colour side by side on the canvas, producing an effect of greater luminosity by this 'optical mixture' than if the colours had been physically mixed together on the palette. In his first major painting, *Bathers at Asnières* (1883–4, reworked 1887, NG, London), Seurat was still experimenting with his technique, but

his next large work, *Sunday Afternoon on the Island of La Grande Jatte* (1884–6, Art Inst. of Chicago), is a completely mature statement of his ideals. *La Grande Jatte* was shown at the final Impressionist exhibition in 1886 and led to the recognition of Seurat as a leader of the avant-garde. The critic Félix Fénéon coined the term *pointillism in reference to this painting to describe the technique of using myriad dots of colour, but Seurat himself preferred the term *divisionism.

From 1887 Seurat began to turn his attention to the significance of line in painting, believing that certain directions of lines could express specific emotions: horizontal lines represented calmness, for example, while upward- and downward-sloping lines represented happiness and sadness respectively. He embodied his beliefs in paintings such as *Le Chahut* (1890, Rijksmuseum Kröller-Müller, Otterlo), in which the raised legs of the dancers performing 'Le Chahut' (a sort of cancan) express 'happiness'. Seurat died very suddenly at the age of 31, evidently from meningitis, although his friend *Signac said that he 'killed himself by overwork'. He was so dedicated to his work and kept himself to himself to such an extent that until his death few people knew he had a mistress and son. His mistress, Madeleine Knobloch, is represented in *Woman Powdering Herself* (1890, Courtauld Gal., London). Seurat's work was highly influential, but his disciples rarely approached his skill, and even less his level of inspiration, in applying his theories; their paintings often look mechanical and lack his gently satirical humour. In power of composition he stands above not only his followers, but also virtually all other painters of his period. He planned his pictures with extraordinary care, and they have nothing of the sense of the passing moment associated with Impressionism. Rather, they have a highly formalized quality and a conscious grandeur that has caused Seurat to be compared with such revered masters as *Piero della Francesca and *Poussin.

Severe style. A term applied to the style characteristic of much Greek sculpture in the period *c*.480 BC–*c*.450 BC, transitional between the *Archaic and *Classical periods. Winckelmann had applied the word 'severe' to works of the time before

*Phidias, but the term 'Severe style' did not acquire a specific meaning until the 20th century, particularly with the publication of the book *Der strenge Stil* (1937) by the Danish scholar Vagn Poulsen. Typical features of the Severe style include simplicity and severity of form, grandeur and elevation of spirit, and an increase in characterization compared with the Archaic period. *Myron is the best-known sculptor of the period, but his work is sometimes described as early Classical rather than Severe.

Severini, Gino (1883–1966). Italian painter, designer, and writer on art, active mainly in Paris. He first settled there in 1906, and he played an important role in transmitting the ideas of French avant-garde art to the *Futurists, both of whose manifestos of painting he signed in 1910. His work was strongly influenced by *Cubism (he knew *Braque and *Picasso) and he concerned himself with the problem of conveying a sense of movement and action by breaking up his picture space into contrasting and interacting rhythms (*Suburban Train Arriving in Paris*, 1915, Tate, London). He was influenced by theories of mathematical proportion and in 1921 published a book on the subject, *Du Cubisme au classicisme*. In the 1920s his style became more traditional and he carried out several decorative commissions, including murals for churches in Switzerland. He also worked as a theatrical designer. Severini returned to Italy in 1935, but in 1946 he settled permanently in Paris. In the later 1940s his style once again became semi-abstract.

Sezession. Name adopted by several groups of painters in Germany and Austria who in the 1890s broke away ('seceded') from the official academies, which they regarded as too conservative, and organized their own, more avant-garde exhibitions. The first of these groups was formed in Munich in 1892, its leading members being Franz von *Stuck and Wilhelm Trübner (1851–1917), and there were Sezessionen also in Vienna (1897), with Gustav *Klimt as first president, and Berlin (1899), with Max *Liebermann as first president. When in 1910 a number of young painters were rejected by the Berlin Sezession— among them members of Die *Brücke— they started the Neue Sezession, with Max *Pechstein a prominent figure.

Sezessionstil. *See* ART NOUVEAU.

Sforza. Italian family who ruled Milan for most of the period from 1450 to 1535 (there were interruptions in 1499–1512 and 1515–21). The most famous member of the family was **Ludovico** (1452–1508), who was effectively ruler of the city from 1480 to 1499, when he was driven out by the invading French; he was known as 'Il Moro' (the Moor) because of his dark complexion. His court was one of the most splendid in Europe and the greatest artists to work for him were *Bramante and *Leonardo da Vinci.

sfumato (It., 'faded away', from *fumo*: 'smoke'). Term used to describe the blending of tones or colours so subtly that they melt into one another without perceptible transitions—in *Leonardo's words, 'without lines or borders, in the manner of smoke'. Leonardo was a supreme exponent of sfumato and *Vasari regarded his ability to mellow the precise outlines characteristic of the earlier *quattrocento as one of the distinguishing marks of 'modern' painting.

Shahn, Ben (1898–1969). American painter, illustrator, photographer, designer, teacher, and writer, born at Kovno, Lithuania, then part of Russia. His family emigrated to the USA in 1906 and settled in New York. Shahn's background (his father had been sent to Siberia for revolutionary activities) and early life (he grew up in a Brooklyn slum) gave him a hatred of cruelty and social injustice, which he expressed powerfully in his work. He first made a name with a series of pictures (1931–2) on the Sacco and Vanzetti case (these two Italian immigrants had been executed for murder in 1927 on very dubious evidence, and many liberals believed that they had really been condemned for their anarchist political views). The paintings are in a deliberately awkward, caricature-like style that vividly expresses his anger and compassion. In 1933 he was assistant to Diego *Rivera on the latter's murals for the Rockefeller Center, New York, and subsequently he painted a number of murals himself, notably for the Bronx Post Office, New York (1938–9), and the Social Security Building, Washington (1940–1). From 1935 to 1938 he worked as an artist and photographer for the Farm Security Administration, a government agency that documented rural poverty. During the Second World War his work included designing posters for the Office of War Information. After the war he returned to easel painting and was also active as a book and magazine illustrator and as a designer of mosaics and stained glass. His later work tended to be more fanciful and reflective and less concerned with social issues. From the 1950s he gave more time to teaching and lecturing and in 1956–7 he was Charles Eliot Norton Professor of Poetry at Harvard University. His lectures there were published as *The Shape of Content* (1957), in which he summarized his humanistic, anti-abstract artistic philosophy.

Shannon, Charles. *See* RICKETTS.

shaped canvas. A term that began to be used in the 1960s for paintings on *supports that departed from the traditional rectangular format. Non-rectangular pictures were of course not new at this time: *Gothic and *Renaissance altarpieces often had pointed or rounded tops, the oval was particularly popular in the *Baroque and *Rococo periods, and so on. The phrase 'shaped canvas', however, usually alludes particularly to a type of abstract painting that emphasizes the 'objecthood' of the work, proclaiming it as something that exists entirely in its own right and not as a reference to, or reproduction of, something else. Various artists have been claimed as the 'inventor' of the shaped canvas in this sense, but its most prominent exponent has undoubtedly been Frank *Stella, who has used such shapes as Vs, lozenges, and fragments of circles. The leading British exponent has been Richard Smith (1931–), who has sometimes used a kite-shaped format in which the canvas is stretched on rods that are part of the visual structure of the picture. He was one of the artists represented in an exhibition entitled 'The Shaped Canvas', organized by Lawrence *Alloway at the Guggenheim Museum, New York, in 1974. The shaped canvas has also occasionally been used by modern figurative painters, notably Anthony *Green.

Shchukin, Sergei. *See* HERMITAGE.

Shee, Sir Martin Archer (1769–1850). Irish portrait painter and writer on art, active from 1788 in London. There he became second only to *Lawrence as the leading society portraitist, and in 1830 he succeeded him as president of the *Royal Academy, which he guided through a difficult period when it was under attack from *Haydon and other disaffected artists. Examples of his work—which in style lies between the bravura of Lawrence and the precision of *West—are in the National Portrait Gallery, London. He wrote *Rhymes on Art* (1805), in which he urged national patronage of artists, and *Elements of Art* (1809), a poem in six cantos.

Sheeler, Charles (1883–1965). American painter and photographer, the best-known exponent of *Precisionism. Between 1904 and 1909 he made several trips to Europe, and he gradually abandoned the bravura handling of *Chase (his teacher at the Pennsylvania Academy of the Fine Arts) for a manner influenced by European modernism—the paintings he exhibited at the *Armory Show of 1913, for example, were much indebted to *Cézanne. In 1912 Sheeler took up commercial photography for a living while continuing to paint. He worked for a while in fashion photography, but his shy personality was not suited to this world, and he concentrated more on very mundane subjects such as plumbing fixtures. The clarity needed in such work helped to transform his style of painting to a meticulous smooth-surfaced manner that was the antithesis of his early approach. He began to paint urban subjects in about 1920 and over the next decade shifted from simplified compositions influenced by *Cubism (on 'the borderline of abstraction' in his own words) to highly detailed photographic-like images. In 1927 he was commissioned to take a series of photographs of the Ford Motor Company's plant at River Rouge, Michigan. His powerful images, presenting a pristine view of American industry, were widely reproduced and brought him international acclaim. Increasingly, also, he was recognized as the finest painter in the Precisionist style, his work standing out as much for its formal strength as for its technical polish. Sheeler's paintings continued in this realistic vein in the 1930s, but in the mid-1940s his style changed dramatically; he began using multiple viewpoints and bold unnaturalistic colours, although his brushwork remained immaculately smooth. In 1959 he suffered a stroke and had to abandon painting and photography.

Shinn, Everett (1876–1953). American painter and graphic artist. He began his career as a reporter-illustrator on the *Philadelphia Press*. His colleagues on the newspaper included *Glackens, *Luks, and *Sloan, who like Shinn became members of The *Eight and the *Ashcan School in New York (where he moved in 1896). Shinn differed from his associates in his choice of subject, preferring scenes from the theatre and music hall to low-life imagery. However, in 1911 he painted murals on local industrial subjects for Trenton City Hall, New Jersey, and these have been described as the earliest instance of *Social Realist themes in public mural decoration. He also did decorations for the interior of the Belasco Theatre, New York. In addition Shinn painted fashionable portraits, illustrated numerous books, wrote plays, and worked as an art director for motion pictures.

Siberechts, Jan (1627–c.1703). Flemish landscape painter who settled in England in the early 1670s. He is best known as the first professional painter of 'portraits' of English country houses; two views of Longleat, Wiltshire (1675 and 1676), are still preserved in the house. He also painted topographical views that stand at the beginning of the English landscape tradition (*Henley from the Wargrave Road*, 1698, River and Rowing Mus., Henley-on-Thames).

siccative. A substance mixed with oil paint to make it dry more quickly. Siccatives are dangerous aids, as they may cause cracking or darken a picture.

Sickert, Walter Richard (1860–1942). British painter, printmaker, teacher, and critic, one of the most important figures of his time in British art. He was born in Munich of a Danish-German father and an Anglo-Irish mother and his outlook was appropriately cosmopolitan. The family settled in London in 1868. Both his father and his grandfather were painters, but Sickert—after a good classical education—initially trained for a career on the stage, 1877–81. He toured with Sir Henry Irving's company but never progressed beyond small parts and in 1881 he abandoned acting and became a student at the *Slade School. In the following year he became a pupil of *Whistler, and in 1883 he worked in Paris with *Degas. Between 1885 and 1905 he spent much of his time in Dieppe, living there 1899–1905, and also visited Venice several times. From 1905, when he returned to England, he became the main channel for influence from avant-garde French painting in British art—inspiring a host of younger artists with the force of his personality as well as the quality of his work. The *Allied Artists' Association (1908), the *Camden Town Group (1911), and the *London Group (1913) were all formed largely by artists in his circle. In 1918–22 he again lived in or near Dieppe, then settled permanently in England, living in London and Brighton before moving to Broadstairs, Kent (1934), and finally to Bathampton, near Bath (1938).

Sickert took the elements of his style from various sources but moulded them into a highly distinctive manner. From Whistler he derived his subtle modulations of tone, although his harmonies were more sombre and his touch rougher, using thick crusty paint. To Degas he was indebted particularly for his method of painting from photographs and for the informality of composition this encouraged. His favourite subjects were urban scenes and figure compositions, particularly pictures of the theatre and music hall and drab domestic interiors. Sickert himself wrote in 1910 that 'The more our art is serious, the more will it tend to avoid the drawing-room and stick to the kitchen.' This attitude permeates his most famous painting, *Ennui*, a compelling image of a stagnant marriage, of which he painted several versions, that in the Tate, London (c.1914), being the largest and most highly finished. From the 1920s Sickert received many honours. His later works—often based on press photographs or Victorian illustrations—are very broadly handled, with the canvas often showing through the paint in places. The colour is generally much higher keyed than in his earlier work and sometimes almost *Expressionist in its boldness. The prevailing critical opinion for many years was that these late works marked a significant decline, but major claims have recently been made for them, particularly following the 1981 *Arts Council exhibition 'Late Sickert: Painting 1927 to 1942'.

As well as painting, Sickert was an outstanding etcher (he learnt the technique from Whistler) and a great teacher (he opened seven private art schools, each of brief duration, and also taught part-time at Westminster School of Art, 1908–12 and 1915–18). He was celebrated for his wit and charm and was a stimulating talker and an articulate writer on art; Osbert Sitwell edited a posthumous collection of his writings entitled *A Free House!* (1947). Sickert was married three times; his third wife (from 1926) was the painter Thérèse Lessore (1884–1945). His brother **Bernard Sickert** (1862/3–1932) was a landscape painter and etcher. He was a member of the *New English Art Club.

Since the 1970s there have been several misguided attempts (in books and television programmes) to implicate Sickert in the gruesome, unsolved Jack the Ripper murders that brought terror to the Whitechapel district of London in autumn 1888: apart from other considerations, there is evidence that Sickert was in France when most of the crimes were committed.

Siegen, Ludwig von (1609–*c*.1680). German soldier and amateur artist who invented the technique of *mezzotint. The earliest of his few surviving prints, a portrait of the Landgravine Amelia Elizabeth of Bohemia, dated 1642, was sent by Siegen to the Landgrave with a letter stating that the invention was his. Prince *Rupert, whom he probably met in Brussels in 1654, perhaps learnt the technique from him.

Signac, Paul (1863–1935). French painter, printmaker, and writer. He began in the *Impressionist manner, but met *Seurat in 1884 and became an ardent disciple of his views and technical method. After Seurat's death in 1891 he was the acknowledged leader of the *Neo-Impressionist group, and in 1899 he published *D'Eugène Delacroix au néo-impressionnisme*, which was long regarded as the authoritative work on the subject. The book was, however, more in the nature of a manifesto in defence of the movement than an objective history. It reflected Signac's use of more brilliant colour from about 1890, as he moved away from the scientific precision advocated by Seurat to a freer and more spontaneous manner. His work had a great influence on *Matisse, who visited him at St Tropez in 1904 (a keen yachtsman, Signac spent a good deal of time on the Mediterranean and French Atlantic coasts; harbour scenes were his favourite subjects).

significant form. *See* BELL, CLIVE.

Signorelli, Luca (*c*.1440/50–1523). Italian painter from Cortona, active in various cities of central Italy, notably Arezzo, Florence, Orvieto, Perugia, and Rome. According to *Vasari (who was related to him and 'as a child of 8' met 'this good old man'), Signorelli was a pupil of *Piero della Francesca, and this seems highly probable on stylistic grounds, for his solid figures and sensitive handling of light echo the work of the master. Signorelli differed from Piero, however, in his interest in the representation of action, which put him in line with contemporary Florentine artists such as the *Pollaiuolo brothers. He must have had a considerable reputation by about 1483, when he was engaged to complete the cycle of frescos on the walls of the Sistine Chapel in Rome, left unfinished by *Botticelli, *Ghirlandaio, *Perugino, and *Rosselli. (It is not known why these four artists abandoned the work in 1482, but it has been suggested that they simply downed tools because of slow payment.) Signorelli completed the scheme with distinction, but his finest works are in Orvieto Cathedral, where he painted a magnificent series of frescos illustrating the end of the world and the Last Judgement (1499–1504). In these grand and dramatic scenes he displayed a mastery of the nude in a wide variety of poses surpassed at that time only by *Michelangelo. Vasari says that 'Luca's works were always highly praised by Michelangelo' and several instances of close similarity between the work of the two men can be cited; perhaps most interesting is the enigmatic seated nude youth in Signorelli's *Last Acts and Death of Moses* in the Sistine Chapel, which is remarkably close to some of the *Ignudi* painted by Michelangelo on the ceiling of the chapel a quarter of a century later. By the end of his career, however, Luca had become a conservative artist, working in provincial Cortona, where his large workshop produced numerous altarpieces. Several examples of his work are in the National Gallery, London.

Signorini, Telemaco. *See* MACCHIAIOLI.

silhouette. An outline image in a single flat colour against a plain background, giving the appearance of a shadow cast by a solid figure. The term is applied particularly to profile portraits in black against white (or vice versa), either painted or cut from paper, which were extremely popular from about 1750 to about 1850, when photography virtually killed the art. The word silhouette derives from Étienne de Silhouette (1706–67), French finance minister under Louis XV, who was notorious for his parsimony and—according to some accounts—cut shadow portraits as a hobby; hence the phrase 'à la silhouette' came to mean 'on the cheap'. In Britain silhouette portraits were generally called 'shades' or 'profiles' up to the end of the 18th century.

silkscreen printing. *See* SCREENPRINTING.

Siloé, Diego de (*c*.1495–1563). Spanish architect and sculptor, one of the leading figures in the transition from *Gothic to *Renaissance in Spanish art. He was the son of **Gil de Siloé** (d. *c*.1501), who is of uncertain origins (contemporary references suggest both Orleans and Antwerp as his native city) but who settled in Burgos and is regarded as the outstanding Spanish sculptor of the 15th century and the country's last great exponent of the Gothic tradition. Gil's extant work includes two royal tombs (1489–93) in the monastery of Miraflores, Burgos: the first is of John II of Castile and his wife Isabella of Portugal, the second of their son Prince Alfonso. Diego formed his style in Italy, where he collaborated with Bartolomé *Ordóñez. By 1519 he had returned to Burgos, where he carried out several important commissions in the cathedral. They include the tomb of Bishop Luis de Acuña (1519) in the Chapel of St Anne and the altarpiece for the same chapel (1522), but his greatest work there is the *Escalera dorada* (Golden Stairway) of 1519–23, and it was as an architect rather than as a sculptor that he emerged as one of the great figures of Spanish art. His masterpiece is Granada Cathedral, where he took over as architect in 1528.

silverpoint. *See* METALPOINT.

Silvestre, Israël (1621–91). French etcher, the best-known member of a family of artists. He worked much for Louis XIII and was drawing master to the young Louis XIV.

His output was large and varied, forming an invaluable source of historical information.

singerie. A depiction of monkeys (Fr., *singes*) engaged in playful activities, often dressed in human clothes and acting out human roles. The conceit of monkeys involved in human occupations goes back to medieval manuscripts, but the term *singerie* is most commonly applied to a type of decorative painting associated with the French *Rococo. Claude *Audran and his one-time assistant *Watteau were noted exponents.

sinopia. Term applied to a reddish-brown chalk used for the underdrawing of a *fresco and also to the drawing itself. *Sinopie* have sometimes been uncovered during restoration work when a fresco is detached from the wall, revealing the lower layer of plaster (*see*, for example, TRAINI).

Siqueiros, David Alfaro (1896–1974). Mexican painter, one of the trio of muralists (with *Orozco and *Rivera) who dominated 20th-century Mexican art. He was a political activist from his youth and in 1914 abandoned his studies at the Academy of San Carlos in Mexico City to join the revolutionary army fighting against President Huerta. His services were appreciated by the victorious General Carranza, who in 1919 sponsored him to continue his studies in Europe, where he was friendly with Rivera (later they became rivals). On returning to Mexico in 1922 he took a leading part in the artistic revival fostered by President Alvaro Obregón. Siqueiros was active in organizing the Syndicate of Technical Workers, Painters, and Sculptors and was partly responsible for drafting its manifesto, which set forth the idealistic aims of the revolutionary artists: 'our own aesthetic aim is to socialize artistic expression, to destroy bourgeois individualism ... We proclaim that this being the moment of social transition from a decrepit to a new order, the makers of beauty must invest their greatest efforts in the aim of materializing an art valuable to the people, and our supreme object in art, which today is an expression for individual pleasure, is to create beauty for all, beauty that enlightens and stirs to struggle.'

Siqueiros's political activities led to his imprisonment or self-imposed exile several times; from 1925 to 1930 he completely abandoned painting for political activity and he later fought in the Spanish Civil War. It was not until 1939 that he eventually completed a mural in Mexico—*Portrait of the Bourgeoisie* for the headquarters of the Union of Electricians in Mexico City (his slow start had prompted Rivera to retort in answer to criticism from him: 'Siqueiros talks: Rivera paints!'). Thereafter, however, Siqueiros's output was prodigious. He painted many easel pictures as well as murals, and though he insisted they were subordinate to his wall paintings, they were important in helping to establish his international reputation. His murals are generally more spectacular even than those of Orozco and Rivera—bold in composition, striking in colour, freely mixing realism with fantasy, and expressing a raw emotional power. In contrast with the sense of disillusionment and foreboding sometimes seen in Orozco's work, Siqueiros always expressed the dynamic urge to struggle; his work can be vulgar and bombastic, but its sheer energy is astonishing. He often experimented technically—working on curved surfaces and using airbrushes and synthetic pigments—and his last major work, the Polyforum Siqueiros in Mexico City (completed 1971), is a huge auditorium integrating architecture, sculpture, and painting. In his late years Siqueiros was showered with honours from his own country and elsewhere; he received the Lenin Peace Prize in 1967, for example, and in the following year became the first president of the newly founded Mexican Academy of Arts.

Sisley, Alfred (1839–99). Anglo-French *Impressionist painter; although he is generally regarded as French, his parents were English and he was a British citizen throughout his life (he twice unsuccessfully tried to become a naturalized Frenchman). His father was a businessman who spent much of his life in Paris, and Sisley was destined for a commercial career before he turned to painting. In 1862 he entered the studio of *Gleyre and there met *Renoir, *Monet, and *Bazille, with whom he formed the early nucleus of the Impressionist group. Like Monet, Sisley devoted himself almost exclusively to landscape, but his work was much less varied. He made several visits to England, but otherwise rarely travelled, and most of his pictures are of scenes

in and around Paris. The best are among the most lyrical and gently harmonious works of Impressionism, delicate in touch and with a beautiful feeling for tone. Sisley was given a generous allowance by his wealthy father and his early life was happy: Renoir described him as 'a delightful human being' and said he 'could never resist a petticoat', However, after the family business failed in 1871 because of the Franco-Prussian War, his father was unable to support him and thereafter he spent much of his life in poverty, never winning the success or renown of his former colleagues. He still remains something of a Cinderella among the Impressionists, claimed as their own by neither the French nor the English.

Sixtus IV, Pope. *See* ROVERE.

size. Glue made from animal products (such as skin or bone), or, more loosely, any fairly weak glue. It is used in art mainly for filling the porous surface of wooden *panels or *canvases to provide a suitable foundation for the *priming (*see* GROUND). Size is also used as a *medium—paint mixed with it is called *distemper.

Skeaping, John. *See* HEPWORTH.

sketch. 'A rough drawing or delineation of something, giving the outlines or prominent features without the detail, especially one intended to serve as the basis of a more finished picture, or to be used in its composition' (*OED*). This was the original meaning of the word, and it was not until the latter part of the 18th century that it acquired the additional sense of 'a drawing or painting of a slight or unpretentious nature'. A sketch should be distinguished from a 'study', which is a representation of a detail to be used in a large composition and may be highly finished. *See also* BOZZETTO and MODELLO.

Slade, Felix (1790–1868). English art collector and philanthropist. He left a great part of his collection, notable particularly for glass, to the *British Museum and in his will he endowed chairs of fine art at the universities of London (University College), Oxford, and Cambridge. The professorships at Oxford and Cambridge involve only the giving of lectures, intended for a general audience, but in London the Slade School of Fine Art, opened in 1871, is an institution giving practical instruction. The first professor was Sir Edward *Poynter, who founded the Slade tradition of emphasis on drawing from the nude. Rapidly overtaking the *Royal Academy (where the teaching methods were considered arid and academic) as the most important art school in the country, the Slade had its heyday in the period from about 1895 to the First World War. Its students then included some of the most illustrious names in 20th-century British art—Augustus and Gwen *John, Wyndham *Lewis, Paul *Nash, Ben *Nicholson, Stanley *Spencer, and so on. Poynter's successors in London have included *Legros, Frederick Brown (1851–1941), who was professor from 1892 to 1917, presiding over the School's golden age, *Tonks, *Coldstream, and *Gowing. The first Slade professors at Oxford and Cambridge respectively were *Ruskin and the architect Matthew Digby Wyatt. Their successors have included many eminent art historians.

Sleigh, Sylvia. *See* ALLOWAY and FEMINIST ART.

Slevogt, Max (1868–1932). German painter and illustrator, with *Corinth and *Liebermann one of his country's leading exponents of *Impressionism. He was born in Bavaria and studied in Munich, then at the *Académie Julian, Paris, 1889–90. In 1901 he settled in Berlin, where he taught at the Academy from 1917. Slevogt's early work was sombre, but from about 1900 his style became lighter, looser, and more colourful. His subjects included landscapes, portraits, and scenes from contemporary life; he loved the theatre and his best-known works include a number of portrayals of the Portuguese baritone Francesco d'Andrade in his most celebrated role as Mozart's Don Giovanni. Although his vigorous brushwork, bold effects of light, and energetic sense of movement give his work great dash, he never adopted the fragmentation of colours typical of the Impressionists and always retained something of the Bavarian *Baroque tradition. He also differed from the Impressionists in that he devoted a good deal of his time to large decorative schemes; these include a fresco of *Golgotha* in the Friedenskirche at Ludwigshafen (1932), often considered his masterpiece. He was a prolific illustrator for books and journals.

Sloan, John (1871–1951). American painter and graphic artist. During the 1890s he worked as a newspaper illustrator in Philadelphia, and he started painting seriously in 1896, influenced by Robert *Henri. In 1904 he settled permanently in New York, where he and Henri were among the members of The *Eight. Sloan was the most political member of the group and as well as taking his most characteristic subjects from everyday lower-class New York life, he did illustrations for socialist periodicals, including *The Masses*, of which he was art editor from 1912 to 1916. However, he was not interested in using his art for what he called 'socialist propaganda' and he resigned from the magazine after a dispute over policy. His paintings of the pre-First World War period are generally solid, broadly brushed, and low-keyed in colour, typically featuring street scenes or domestic interiors; however, he could also be sharply satirical and occasionally he expressed himself in a totally different vein, as in *Wake of the Ferry* (1907, Phillips Coll., Washington), a hauntingly melancholic marine picture. After the *Armory Show he broadened the scope of his work to include landscapes and nudes and his style became harder and brighter. He also made etchings throughout his career. Sloan was a popular teacher at the *Art Students League and other schools. In 1939 he published an autobiographical-critical book, *Gist of Art*.

Slodtz. Family of French artists. The head of the family was **Sébastien** (1655–1726), a sculptor and designer, who was Flemish by birth. He had three sculptor sons: **Sébastien-Antoine** (1695–1754), **Paul-Ambroise** (1702–58), and **René-Michel** called Michel-Ange (1705–64). All four of them worked for the Menus Plaisirs (the office that designed costumes, festivities, etc. for the court), as did another son of Sébastien, the painter **Dominique Slodtz** (1711–64); a fifth brother, **Jean-Baptiste** (1699–1759), was also a painter. Michel-Ange was the only member of the family to attain great distinction. From 1728 to 1747 he lived in Rome, where his admiration for *Michelangelo won him his nickname. His best-known work is the marble *St Bruno* (1744, St Peter's, Rome), which shows the nervous sensitivity of his style. In France he made several major tombs, notably that of

Languet de Gergy (completed 1753, St Sulpice, Paris), which shows the influence of
*Bernini in its *Baroque rhetoric and use
of different coloured marbles. *Houdon
was Slodtz's most important pupil.

Sluter, Claus (d. 1405/6). Netherlandish
stone sculptor, active mainly in Dijon. He
was the greatest sculptor of his time in
northern Europe and a figure of enormous
importance in the transition from *International Gothic to a more weighty and naturalistic style. Sluter is first mentioned in
Brussels (c.1379) in a document that says
he came from Haarlem. In 1385 he entered
the service of Philip the Bold, Duke of Burgundy, in his capital Dijon. All of Sluter's
surviving work was done for Philip, and
almost all of it remains in Dijon. For the
Chartreuse de Champmol, a monastery
founded by Philip, he carved figures for the
portal of the chapel in the early 1390s, and
made a fountain group, the only part of
which to survive intact is the base, known
as the *Well of Moses* (1395–1403). The monastery was destroyed during the French Revolution, and the portal and the *Well of Moses*
are now part of the psychiatric hospital that
occupies its site. The Well features six full-
length figures of prophets of monumental
dignity; they convey an intense sense of
physical presence, and as character studies
rival the prophets of *Donatello, which
they preceded by about twenty years. Originally Sluter's figures were painted (by
*Malouel) and the figure of Jeremiah is
known to have worn copper spectacles, the
record of payment for which still survives.
Of the Calvary group that surmounted the
Well (symbolizing the 'Fountain of Life')
only fragments survive in the Archaeological Museum in Dijon; they include the
head and torso of the figure of Christ—one
of Sluter's noblest works, in which the expression of suffering stoically endured is
deeply moving. Sluter's last work was the
tomb of Philip the Bold, begun in 1404 and
unfinished at the sculptor's death (Mus.
B.-A., Dijon). Most of the work on it was
carried out by Sluter's nephew and assistant
Claus de Werve (d. 1439), but the figures of
pleurants (weepers or mourners) that form a
frieze around the sarcophagus are from the
master's own hand, and although they are
only about 40 cm (15 in.) high they possess
massive solemnity. They show Sluter's

extraordinary ability to use the heavy folds
of drapery for expressive effect; indeed
some of the mourners are so completely
enveloped in their voluminous cowls that
they are in effect nothing else but drapery.
Sluter's influence was enormous—on
painters as well as sculptors. The emphatic
plasticity of the *Master of Flémalle's figures, for example, has Sluter as its source,
and in his *Entombment* (Courtauld Gal.,
London, c.1410/20), which stands at the
head of the Early Netherlandish tradition
of painting, the angel who wipes away a
tear with the back of his hand is a quotation
from the *Well of Moses*.

Sluyters, Jan (1881–1957). Dutch painter,
active mainly in Amsterdam. He was one of
the best-known artists in the Netherlands in
the interwar period and the one in whom
French modernism is most variously reflected. His early works show the influence
of his countrymen van *Gogh and *Breitner, and of *Fauvism. He also experimented
with *Cubism before finally developing a
lively personal style of colourful *Expressionism that is best seen in his nudes—he
had a predilection for painting nude children.

Smart, John (c.1742–1811). One of the
leading British *miniaturists of his period.
His style was meticulous, bright, and pretty.
He worked mainly in London but was in
India 1785–95.

Smet, Gustave de (1877–1943). One of
the leading Belgian *Expressionist painters.
His early work was *Impressionist in style,
but he was influenced towards Expressionism by Jan *Sluyters and Henri *Le Fauconnier, whom he met in Holland when he took
refuge there during the First World War.
Typically de Smet painted scenes of rural
and village life in which forms are treated
in a schematic way owing something to
*Cubism; there is often an air of unreality
reminiscent of that in *Chagall's work (*Village Fair*, c.1930, Mus. voor Schone Kunsten,
Ghent). His brother **Léon de Smet** (1881–
1966) was also a painter.

Smibert, John (1688–1751). Scottish-born
portrait painter who emigrated to America
in 1728 and settled in Boston in 1730. Previously he had travelled in Italy and practised
successfully in London in an uninspired
style derived from *Kneller. After he settled

in America his work became somewhat more vigorous. He brought with him a small collection of copies, casts, and prints, and he opened a shop in Boston where he sold artists' materials and engravings of the works of well-known artists. His collection was displayed above the shop, forming in effect America's first art gallery, and together with his own paintings it became the cornerstone of the New England Colonial portrait style. *Copley and *Trumbull were among the artists familiar with the collection.

Smith, David (1906–65). The most original and influential American sculptor of his generation. He began to study art at Ohio University in 1924 but soon dropped out of the course, and in the summer of 1925 he worked at the Studebaker motor plant at South Bend, Indiana, where he acquired the skills in metalwork that stood him in good stead later in his career. From 1926 to 1930 he studied painting at the *Art Students League of New York, while supporting himself by a variety of jobs. Among his friends at this time were Arshile *Gorky and Willem *de Kooning. He turned to sculpture in the early 1930s, making his first welded iron pieces (probably the first by an American artist) in 1933. These were inspired by Julio *González, to whom Smith said he owed his 'technical liberation', but he always maintained that there was no essential difference between painting and sculpture and his aesthetic outlook was more influenced by *Kandinsky, *Mondrian, and *Cubism. By the time of his first one-man exhibition in 1938 he was producing sculpture of considerable originality, constructing compositions from steel and 'found' scrap, parts of agricultural machinery, etc. He had a love of technology, and wrote: 'The equipment I use, my supply of material, comes from factory study, and duplicates as nearly as possible the production equipment used in making a locomotive ... What associations the metal possesses are those of this century: power, structure, movement, progress, suspension, destruction, brutality.'

Smith settled at Bolton Landing in upstate New York in 1940. In the same year he exhibited a set of fifteen bronze *relief plaques entitled *Medals for Dishonor* stigmatizing violence and greed. He was employed as a welder on defence work 1942–4, then returned to sculpture, and from this time began to build an international reputation. During the 1940s and 1950s his sculpture was predominantly open and linear, like three-dimensional metal calligraphy (*Hudson River Landscape*, 1951, Whitney Mus., New York). From the end of the 1950s, however, his style became more monumental and geometrical, with boxes and cylinders of polished metal joined at odd angles. Although the forms are often massive, the effect they create is not one of heaviness but of unstable dynamism, the exhilarating sense of freedom being enhanced by the reflection of sunlight from the bright surfaces (they are generally intended for outdoor settings). These works were often created in series, such as *Zig*, *Cubi*, and *Voltri*. They initiated a new era in American sculpture, and gave Smith a place as the peer of the great *Abstract Expressionist painters who were his contemporaries. Like the most famous of the Abstract Expressionists, Jackson *Pollock, Smith died in an automobile accident.

Smith, Jack. *See* KITCHEN SINK SCHOOL.

Smith, John. *See* VERMEER.

Smith, John Raphael. *See* DE WINT.

Smith, Joseph. *See* CANALETTO.

Smith, Joshua. *See* DOBELL.

Smith, Sir Matthew (1879–1959). British painter. He studied at the *Slade School, 1905–7, and for a short time in Paris (1911) under *Matisse. Thereafter he identified strongly with French art and during the interwar years he spent much of his time in France, mainly in Aix-en-Provence and Paris. He was delicate in health and of a nervous disposition, but this is hardly apparent from his work, which uses colour in a bold, unnaturalistic manner echoing the *Fauves. His lush brushwork, too, has great vigour, and he was one of the few British painters to excel in painting the nude, his dark saturated colours and opulent fluency of line creating images of great sensuousness. He also painted landscapes (most notably a series done in Cornwall in 1920) and still lifes. Frank *Auerbach and Francis *Bacon are among the many artists who have admired Smith's painterliness; Bacon said he was 'one of the very few English painters since *Constable and *Turner to be concerned with painting—that is, with attempting to make idea and technique inseparable'. His work is in many public galleries, the best collection being in the Guildhall Art Gallery, London.

Smith, Richard. *See* SHAPED CANVAS.

Smith, Tony (1912–80). American sculptor, painter, and architect. He served an apprenticeship in architecture as clerk of works to Frank Lloyd Wright and practised as an architect from 1940 to 1960, during which time he also painted. He began to take an interest in sculpture around 1940, but although he taught at various colleges in the 1940s and 1950s (in addition to his architectural career) and was closely associated with leading avant-garde figures such as *Newman, *Pollock, *Rothko, and *Still, he did not exhibit sculpture publicly until 1964. From that time he quickly emerged as one of the leading exponents of *Minimal art. His work was sometimes very large in scale, composed of bold geometrical shapes (often repeated modular units) that he had industrially manufactured in steel. Many of his works were placed outdoors, helping to bring to American sculpture a new interest in the environment. A well-known example is *Gracehoper* (1972, Detroit Inst. of Arts), which one can walk through. His daughter **Kiki Smith** (1954–) is a sculptor and *Body artist.

Smithson, Robert (1938–73). American sculptor and experimental artist. In the 1960s his work belonged mainly to the category of *Minimal art; he was interested in mathematical impersonality and as well as making block-like steel sculptures he experimented with reflections and mirror images. From the late 1960s he turned to *Conceptual art; he expressed his ideas mainly through *Land art and became the best-known artist working in this field. In 1968 he began a series of 'Sites' and 'Non-Sites'. The latter consisted of photographs and plans of locations he had visited (particularly derelict urban or industrial sites) displayed with specimens of rock or geological refuse he had gathered there, arranged into random heaps or in metal or wood bins: 'Instead of putting a work of art on some land, some land is put into the work of art.' Smithson then moved on to

large-scale earthworks, the best known of which is the enormous *Spiral Jetty* (1970), a spiral road running out into Great Salt Lake, Utah (it has periodically become submerged and then reappeared with changing water levels). He was killed in a plane crash when he was surveying a work in progress, *Amarillo Ramp* in Texas. Smithson wrote many articles expounding his views on art: *The Writings of Robert Smithson*, edited by Nancy Holt (his widow), was published in 1979.

Smithsonian Institution. A research institution and educational centre founded by the bequest of the English scientist James Smithson (1765–1829) 'for the increase and diffusion of knowledge' and established by congressional act in Washington DC in 1846. Smithson was an illegitimate son of Hugh Smithson Percy, Duke of Northumberland, and it is thought to have been resentment over the circumstances of his birth that caused him to make the bequest to the USA rather than his native country: 'My name shall live . . . when the titles of the Northumberlands . . . are extinct and forgotten.' The Smithsonian administers many prestigious cultural organizations in Washington, including the National Gallery of Art, the National Portrait Gallery, and the Joseph H. Hirshhorn Museum and Sculpture Garden.

Snyders, Frans (1579–1657). Flemish painter of animals, hunting scenes, and still life, active mainly in his native Antwerp. He was a pupil of Pieter *Brueghel the Younger and travelled in Italy 1608–9. Back in Antwerp, he became a close friend of *Rubens, also recently returned from Italy (he was eventually executor of Rubens's will). Snyders often collaborated with Rubens; he painted animals, fruits, and flowers in Rubens's pictures, and Rubens painted figures in his. He later had the same kind of reciprocal arrangement with *Jordaens, and also collaborated with van *Dyck, *Janssen, and Cornelis de *Vos (his brother-in-law). Snyders's independent works show he was the finest animal painter of his time; the best are his scenes of fighting wild animals and hunts, which have a tremendous sense of *Baroque vitality.

Socialist Realism. The name of the officially approved type of art in Soviet Russia and other Communist countries, involving in theory a faithful and objective reflection of real life to educate and inspire the masses, and in practice the compulsory and uncritical glorification of the State. Socialist Realism was an aspect of the dictatorship of Stalin, who was leader of the Soviet Union from the death of Lenin in 1924 until his own death in 1953. Alan Bird (*A History of Russian Painting*, 1987) writes that 'He saw all aspects of avant-garde culture, including painting, as subversive infiltrations of the purity of Soviet life' and that his minister Andrei Zhdanov 'made himself responsible for imposing an iron control on artistic expression'. The principles of Socialist Realism began to take shape in the late 1920s and were proclaimed in the 1932 decree 'On the Reconstruction of Literary and Art Organizations' (before this, the term 'Heroic Realism' had often been used, but 'Socialist Realism' now became the official label). It was never defined specifically in terms of style and in its early days it saw expression in some outstanding works, notably the paintings of Alexander Deineka (1899–1969); however, it became increasingly associated with stereotyped images painted in a conventional academic manner. In the 1930s there were four main types of Socialist Realist paintings: domestic scenes, portraits, industrial and urban landscapes, and scenes on collective farms. During the Second World War, patriotic scenes from Russian history were added to the list. After the death of Stalin there was some relaxation of strictures, but the system still remained stifling to creativity, and any form of experiment remained extremely difficult. In the West, Socialist Realism remained synonymous with repression, and its products were generally regarded as morally tragic and aesthetically comic, although the merits of painters such as Arkady Plastov (1893–1972), a specialist in farm scenes, are now being recognized.

Social Realism. A very broad term for painting (or literature or other art) that comments on contemporary social, political, or economic conditions, usually from a left-wing viewpoint, in a realistic manner. Often the term carries with it the suggestion of protest or propaganda in the interest of social reform. However, it does not imply any particular style; Ben *Shahn's caricature-like scenes on injustice and social hyp-

ocrisy in the USA, the dour working-class interiors of the *Kitchen Sink School in Britain, and the declamatory political statements of *Guttoso in Italy are all embraced by the term. *See also* REALISM.

Société Anonyme, Inc. (or a Museum of Modern Art). An association founded in 1920 by Katherine *Dreier, Marcel *Duchamp, and *Man Ray for the promotion of contemporary art in America by lectures, publications, travelling exhibitions, and the formation of a permanent collection. In French the term *société anonyme* means 'limited company', so the name—suggested by Man Ray—was intended as a tautological *Dada jest; as Miss Dreier loved to explain, it meant 'incorporated corporation'. However, the work of the society was serious and trailblazing. Its museum, which opened at 19 East 47th Street, New York, in 1920, was the first in the USA, and one of the earliest anywhere, to be devoted entirely to modern art (although as it was concerned mainly with temporary exhibitions, the *Phillips Collection has the distinction of being the first permanent American museum in the field). Between 1920 and 1940 the Société organized 84 exhibitions, through which such artists as *Klee, *Malevich, *Miró, and *Schwitters were first exhibited in America. To some extent, therefore, the Société carried on the tradition that had been started by the 291 Gallery of *Stieglitz in the years before the *Armory Show, and to some extent also it prepared the way for the *Museum of Modern Art, which was founded in 1929. The Museum of Modern Art soon eclipsed the Société Anonyme and Miss Dreier's finances were in any case badly hit by the Depression, but she continued to serve as president (as Duchamp did as secretary) until the Société officially closed in 1950. Nine years earlier, in 1941, they had presented the superb permanent collection that the Société had built up (over 600 works) to Yale University Art Gallery.

Society of Artists. An association of artists founded in London in 1760 and incorporated by Royal Charter in 1765 (after which it was known as the Incorporated Society of Artists). It held annual exhibitions and was the main forerunner of the *Royal Academy. *Hayman and *Lambert were leading figures of the society in its early years; it was soon overshadowed by the Academy, but it remained active until 1791.

Society of Independent Artists. A society formed in New York in December 1916 as a successor to the Association of American Painters and Sculptors, which had been dissolved—its task accomplished—after mounting the *Armory Show in 1913. The Society's aim was to give progressive artists an opportunity to show their work by holding annual exhibitions in rivalry with the conservative *National Academy of Design. These shows were organized on the model of the French *Salon des Indépendants, without jury or prizes, giving anyone the right to exhibit on payment of a modest fee. The first show, in April 1917, featured about 2,500 works by about 1,200 artists and was probably the largest art exhibition ever held in the USA. However, it is remembered mainly because of a work that was not shown, for Marcel *Duchamp (one of the Society's officials) resigned after his *ready-made in the form of a urinal was rejected. Although much recondite aesthetic theory has been read into this gesture, it is likely that the main purpose was to demonstrate the incongruity of a society with the professed purpose of allowing anyone to exhibit anything. The first president of the Society was William *Glackens; he was followed by John *Sloan, who held the post from 1918 until his death in 1951. Annual exhibitions continued to be held until 1944, but they soon declined in terms of quantity and quality.

Sodoma, Il (Giovanni Antonio Bazzi) (1477–1549). Italian painter, born at Vercelli and active chiefly in and around Siena, where he settled in about 1500, but also in Rome. *Vasari, who disliked him, explains the origin of his nickname 'the sodomite' in this fashion: 'His manner of life was licentious and dishonourable, and as he always had boys and beardless youths about him of whom he was inordinately fond, this earned him the nickname of Sodoma; but instead of feeling shame, he gloried in it, writing stanzas and verses on it, and singing them to the accompaniment of the lute.' Sodoma (who was married and had children) himself used the name in his signature, and Vasari's explanation of it has been questioned. Vasari also tells us that Sodoma kept a men-

agerie of strange animals 'so that his home resembled a veritable Noah's ark'. He was a prolific painter of frescos and easel pictures, and he drew on a variety of sources that were not always fully digested; consequently his work often has incongruous juxtapositions and a general air of uncoordination, but it also possesses charm and a flair for decoration. His fresco of the *Marriage of Alexander and Roxane* (c.1516), painted for the banker Agostino *Chigi in his villa (now the Villa Farnesina) in Rome, is often cited as his finest work. In his time Sodoma was considered the leading artist in Siena, but later critics have come to rank *Beccafumi above him.

Soft art. Term applied to sculpture using non-rigid materials, a vogue of the 1960s and 1970s. The materials employed have been very diverse: rope, cloth, rubber, leather, paper, canvas, vinyl—anything in fact that offers a certain persistence of form but lacks permanent shape or rigidity. The earliest example of Soft art was perhaps the typewriter cover that Marcel *Duchamp mounted on a stand and exhibited in 1916. However, this belongs rather to the category of *ready-mades, and Soft art as a movement is generally traced to Claes *Oldenburg's giant replicas of foodstuffs (ice-cream sundaes, hamburgers, pieces of cake, etc.) made from stuffed vinyl and canvas. Other artists who have experimented with soft materials have been many and diverse, representing a variety of movements, including *Arte Povera, *Pop art, and *Surrealism.

soft-ground etching. A method of *etching that produces prints characterized by softness of line or a grainy texture. The waxy *ground used to coat the plate is softer and stickier than in normal etching, so that it adheres to anything pressed into it. Over this ground is laid a sheet of paper on which the artist draws with a pencil. Under the pressure of the pencil strokes the ground sticks to the back of the paper, so that when it is lifted the wax immediately underneath the lines comes away with it, while the rest remains in place. The plate is then immersed in acid, and printed in the normal way. Depending on the texture of the paper used for the drawing, the printed lines are granular, coarse, or fine: thus if the paper is smooth, the lines resemble pencil, but if rough, they are more like chalk. Soft-ground etchings bear a strong likeness to prints in the *crayon manner, but are generally a little softer and less regular. The technique was invented in the mid-18th century and flourished until about 1830, when it was generally superseded by *lithography. Although it was chiefly used for reproductive prints, a number of excellent original soft-ground etchings were produced by *Gainsborough, *Cotman, and *Girtin. Interest in the technique has revived among some modern artists.

Soft Style. *See* MASTER THEODORIC.

Solimena, Francesco (1657–1747). The leading Neapolitan painter of the first half of the 18th century. In a long and extremely productive career he painted frescos in many of the greatest churches in Naples and came to dominate the artistic life of the city. His vigorous style, often marked by dramatic lighting, owed much to the example of such *Baroque artists as *Giordano (his outstanding predecessor in Naples), *Lanfranco, and *Preti, but it also has a firmness of structure and a clarity of draughtsmanship that show his allegiance to the *classical tradition of *Raphael and Annibale *Carracci. Although chiefly a religious painter, he was also a good portraitist. Solimena's paintings were in demand all over Europe and he became one of the wealthiest and most famous artists of the time. His influence was spread also by his celebrity as a teacher. *Ramsay was among his pupils and *Fragonard copied his work when he visited Naples in 1761.

Solomon, Simeon (1840–1905). British painter and illustrator, a member of a well-known family of artists. He was part of *Rossetti's circle and a friend of *Burne-Jones, and his work shows strong *Pre-Raphaelite influence. In the 1860s he built up a reputation as an illustrator as well as a painter, but then sank into a life of idleness and dissipation (in 1873 he was convicted of homosexual offences and although he was let off lightly his career was ruined by the incident). His later years were spent in a pathetically bohemian existence, and he died of alcoholism. His sister **Rebecca** (1832–86), who painted portraits and anecdotal historical scenes, also died an alcoholic. Their brother **Abraham** (1823–62) painted

scenes from literature and contemporary life, some of which attained great popularity and were much reproduced as prints.

Somer, Paul van (*c*.1577–1621/2). Flemish portrait painter who settled in England in 1616 and became—with Cornelius *Johnson and Daniel *Mytens—the leading portraitist working at the court of James I. His finest work is *Queen Anne of Denmark* (1617, Royal Coll.), an imposing full-length, but more archaic in style than similar portraits by Mytens.

Sorolla y Bastida, Joaquín (1863–1923). Spanish painter and illustrator, active mainly in his native Valencia and in Madrid. He was a prolific and popular artist, working on a wide variety of subjects—*genre, portraits, landscapes, historical scenes—and producing many book illustrations. His pleasant and undemanding style was marked by brilliant high-keyed colour and vigorous brushwork, representing a kind of conservative version of *Impressionism. He was well known outside Spain, and in 1910–20 he painted a series of fourteen mural panels for the Hispanic Society of America in New York (*see* HUNTINGTON), representing scenes typical of the various provinces of Spain. His former home in Madrid is now a museum dedicated to his work.

Sotheby's. The oldest and largest firm of auctioneers in the world. It was founded by the London bookseller Samuel Baker, whose first recorded auction was in 1744. On his death in 1778, his estate was divided between his partner George Leigh and his nephew John Sotheby. The last of the Sotheby family to be involved in the firm died in 1861. Although Sotheby's extended its range to take in prints, coins, medals, and antiquities of various kinds, books long remained the primary concern of the company, and it was not until after the First World War that paintings and other works of art became a major part of its business (before this time most important picture sales were held by *Christie's). In 1964 Sotheby's bought Parke-Bernet, America's largest fine art auctioneers, and it now has major salerooms in London, New York, Geneva, and Monaco, with numerous branches throughout the world.

sotto in sù, di (It.: 'from below upwards'). Term applied to an extreme form of *illusionistic foreshortening in which figures or objects painted on a ceiling appear to be floating or suspended in space above the viewer. *Mantegna's Camera degli Sposi in the Ducal Palace in Mantua is the first major example, and *Correggio was a noted exponent, but the device is associated particularly with *Baroque decoration.

Soutine, Chaïm (1893–1943). Lithuanian-born painter who settled in France in 1913 and became one of the leading *Expressionists of the *École de Paris. His friends in the circle of expatriate artists there included *Chagall and also *Modigliani, who painted a memorable portrait of him (1917, NG, Washington). Soutine suffered from depression and lack of confidence in his work (he was reluctant to exhibit and sometimes destroyed his own pictures), and he endured years of desperate poverty until the American collector Dr Albert C. *Barnes bought a number of his paintings in 1923. Thereafter he was free from need, although he continued to suffer from ill health and a disposition towards self-torment. Soutine's work included landscapes, portraits, and figure studies of characters such as choirboys and pageboys. His style is characterized by thick, convulsive brushwork, through which he could express tenderness as well as turbulent psychological states. There is something of an affinity with van *Gogh, although Soutine professed to dislike his work and felt more kinship with the Old Masters whose work he studied in the Louvre; his pictures of animal carcasses, for example, are inspired by *Rembrandt's *Flayed Ox*. However, the gruesome intensity of works such as *Side of Beef* (1925, Albright-Knox AG, Buffalo) was not gained simply through study of similar pictures, for Soutine visited abattoirs and even brought a carcass into the studio. His neighbours complained of the smell of the rotting meat and called the police, whom Soutine harangued on the subject of how much more important art was than sanitation. The filthy state in which he lived during his years of poverty was notorious: the poet André Salmon recalled that Soutine once consulted a specialist about earache and that 'In the canal of the painter's ear the doctor discovered, not an abscess, but a nest of bed bugs.'

Soyer, Moses (1899–1974) and **Raphael** (1899–1987). Russian-born painters, twins,

who emigrated to America in 1912 and became US citizens in 1925. They are best known for their *Social Realist subjects, particularly those of the Depression years of the 1930s, in which they depicted the lives of working people with sympathy and at times a touching air of melancholy, as in Raphael's well-known *Office Girls* (1936, Whitney Mus., New York). Both brothers also did many self-portraits and wrote on art. Moses wrote articles defending Social Realism and attacking *Regionalism; Raphael published several autobiographical volumes and a book on Thomas *Eakins (1966). Another brother, **Isaac** (1907–81), who moved to America in 1914, was also a painter.

spalliera. An Italian term originally used to describe a painting set into the wall panelling of a room in the *Renaissance period and now by extension applied to any similar painted piece of furniture of the time, such as the headboard or footboard of a bed or the backboard of a *cassone. No *spalliere* survive in situ as wall panelling, but detached examples are in numerous museums; they are often difficult to distinguish from detached cassone panels, as they tend to be similar in size and shape.

Spare, Austin. *See* AUTOMATISM.

Spatialism (or **Spazialismo**). A movement founded by Lucio *Fontana in Milan in 1947 in which he grandiosely intended to synthesize colour, sound, space, movement, and time into a new type of art. The main ideas of the movement were anticipated in his *Manifesto blanco* (White Manifesto) published in Buenos Aires in 1946. In it he spoke of a new 'spatial' art in keeping with the spirit of the post-war age. On the negative side it repudiated the illusory or 'virtual' space of traditional easel painting; on the positive side it was to unite art and science to project colour and form into real space by the use of up-to-date techniques such as neon lighting and television. Five more manifestos followed; they were more specific in their negative than their positive aspects, and carried the concept of Spatialism little further than the statement that its essence consisted in 'plastic emotions and emotions of colour projected upon space'. In 1947 Fontana created a 'Black Spatial Environment', a room painted black, which was considered to have fore-shadowed *Environment art. His holed and slashed canvases (beginning in 1949 and 1959 respectively) are also considered to embody Spatialism. An example of the slashed type (the slash made with a razor blade) is *Spatial Concept Waiting* (1960, Tate, London). Although Fontana's ideas were vague, his outlook was influential, for he was one of the first to promote the idea of art as gesture or performance, rather than as the creation of an enduring physical work.

Spencer, Sir Stanley (1891–1959). English painter, one of the most original figures in 20th-century British art. He was born in Cookham in Berkshire and lived for most of his life in the village, which played a large part in the imagery of his paintings. His education was fairly elementary, but he grew up in a family in which literature, music, and religion were dominant concerns and his imaginative life was extremely rich. He said he wanted 'to take the inmost of one's wishes, the most varied religious feelings…and to make it an ordinary fact of the street', and he is best known for pictures in which he set biblical events in his own village; his visionary attitude has been compared to that of William *Blake. Spencer was a prize-winning student at the *Slade School (1908–12) and served in the army from 1915 to 1918, first at the Beaufort War Hospital in Bristol, then in Macedonia. He was appointed an *Official War Artist in 1918, but his experiences during the war found their most memorable expression a decade later when he painted a series of murals for the Sandham Memorial Chapel at Burghclere in Hampshire (1927–32), built to commemorate a soldier who had died from an illness contracted in Macedonia. The arrangement of the murals consciously recalls *Giotto's Arena Chapel in Padua, but Spencer painted in oil, not fresco, and he concentrated not on great events, but on the life of the common soldier, which he depicted with deep human feeling. There is no violence, and Spencer said that the idea for one of the scenes—*The Dug-Out*—occurred to him 'in thinking how marvellous it would be if one morning, when we came out of our dug-outs, we found that somehow everything was peace and the war was no more'.

By this time Spencer was a celebrated figure, his greatest public success having been *The Resurrection: Cookham* (1924–6, Tate, London), which when exhibited in 1927 was hailed by the critic of *The Times* as 'the most important picture painted by any English artist in the present century'. He continued: 'What makes it so astonishing is the combination in it of careful detail with modern freedom of form. It is as if a *Pre-Raphaelite had shaken hands with a *Cubist.'

Spencer was again an Official War Artist during the Second World War, when he painted a series of large canvases showing shipbuilding on the Clyde (Imperial War Mus., London) that memorably capture the heroic teamwork that went into the war effort. His career culminated in a knighthood in the year of his death, but his life was not a smooth success story, and in the 1930s he somewhat alienated his public with the expressive distortions and erotic content of his work. In 1935 he resigned as an Associate of the *Royal Academy when two of his pictures, considered caricature-like and poorly drawn, were rejected for the annual summer exhibition, but he rejoined the Academy in 1950. In 1937 he divorced his first wife, the painter Hilda Carline (1889–1950), and married Patricia Preece (1900–71), also a painter, but Hilda continued to play a large part in his life: he painted pictures in memory of her and even wrote letters to her after her death. Some of his nude paintings of Patricia vividly express not only the sexual tensions of his life, but also his belief in the sanctity of human love; the best known is the double nude portrait of himself and Patricia known as *The Leg of Mutton Nude* (1936, Tate). In his later years Spencer acquired a reputation as a landscapist as well as a figure painter. He also occasionally did portraits. There is a gallery devoted to Spencer at Cookham, containing not only paintings, but also memorabilia such as the pram that this eccentric figure used for pushing his painting equipment around the village. His younger brother **Gilbert Spencer** (1892–1979) was also a painter of imaginative subjects and landscapes, working in a style close to that of Stanley.

Spinario (from Lat., *spina*: 'thorn'). Ancient bronze statue of a seated boy extracting a thorn from his left foot (Capitoline Museum, Rome). It is recorded in Rome as early as the 12th century and during the *Renaissance it was one of the most influential and copied of ancient sculptures. Its fame endured and it was one of the ancient works taken by Napoleon to Paris, where it remained from 1798 to 1815. Various stories grew up from the Renaissance onwards to explain the subject, the most popular being that the statue commemorates a shepherd boy called Gnaeus Martius who delivered an important message to the Roman Senate and only when his task was accomplished stopped to remove a thorn from his foot. It is now generally thought that the *Spinario* is a Roman *pastiche of about the 1st century BC, combining a *Hellenistic body with a head of earlier date (the way in which the hair falls suggests that the head was meant to be in an upright position rather than looking down as it is now).

Spinello Aretino (*c.*1350–1410). Italian painter, first securely documented in 1373. He came from Arezzo (hence the name Aretino) and probably trained in Florence, perhaps under Agnolo *Gaddi. He was the most prolific muralist of his time and undertook large fresco cycles all over Tuscany. The last of these was devoted to the Sienese pope Alexander III in the Palazzo Pubblico in Siena (1408–10); he was the first non-Sienese painter to work in the building. He also painted altarpieces. Spinello borrowed ideas freely from other painters, notably *Giotto, but his style was sturdy and vigorous. Several fresco fragments by him are in the National Gallery, London. His son **Parri Spinelli** (1387–1453) was also a painter.

Spitzweg, Carl (1808–85). German painter and illustrator, active in his native Munich. He began his career as a pharmacist, but he gave this up for art in 1833 when a legacy made him financially independent; he had been interested in art from childhood but had no professional training. Although he travelled widely (England, France, Italy, and elsewhere), he was provincial in his choice of subjects and is an outstanding representative of the *Biedermeier style. His pictures are generally small, humorous in content, and full of lovingly depicted anecdotal detail (*The Poor Poet*, 1839, Neue Pin., Munich, and other ver-sions). He also painted excellent landscapes that show a debt to the *Barbizon School.

Spranger, Bartholomeus (1546–1611). Netherlandish painter and designer who had an international career and played an important part in the spread of *Mannerism in northern Europe. He trained in his native Antwerp, where he came under the influence of Frans *Floris, then travelled via France to Italy, where he spent a decade (1565–75), mainly in Rome. After five years in Vienna, he finally settled in Prague, where he was appointed court painter by the emperor Rudolf II (*see* HABSBURG) in 1581. His paintings are often of mythological or allegorical subjects and are highly polished and sophisticated—close in style to those of his fellow court painter Hans von *Aachen. Spranger had met van *Mander in Rome and through drawings that he gave him his style was carried to Haarlem. *Goltzius and other engravers made many prints of his designs (Spranger also made a few etchings himself) and his work was widely influential in the years around 1600.

Squarcione, Francesco (*c.*1395–*c.*1468). Italian painter, active in Padua. He is an enigmatic figure, who is important in terms of the pupils he trained, rather than for his own work. In a history of Padua published in 1560 he is patriotically described as a famous and benevolent master, with many pupils and a large collection of *antique sculpture gathered on youthful journeys through Greece and Italy. Modern research, however, shows that for many years he was discreditably involved in a series of lawsuits with pupils who, resentful of his exploitation of their talents, had broken their apprenticeships with him (*Mantegna was the most famous litigant). No traces of his collection remain, but it is likely that something of the antiquarian erudition of the university town of Padua rubbed off on the young men who spent time in his workshop. It is impossible to assess any stylistic debt to Squarcione himself, however, as so little is known about his work, and his traditional role as the founder of a distinctive 'Paduan style' is highly questionable.

Staël, Nicolas de (1914–55). Russian-French painter, born in St Petersburg, son of Baron Vladimir Ivanovich de Staël-

Holstein. In 1919 his family was forced to leave Russia (he would later become incensed if anyone suggested they had 'fled') and moved to Poland. Both parents had died by 1922 and Nicolas and his two sisters were adopted by a family of rich Russian expatriates in Brussels, where he studied at the École des Beaux-Arts, 1932-6. In the next two years he travelled widely (France, Italy, Spain, North Africa), then in 1938 settled in Paris, where he studied briefly with *Léger. On the outbreak of war in 1939 he joined the Foreign Legion and was sent to Tunisia. He was demobilized in 1941 and moved to Nice, where he turned from figurative to abstract art, although the forms he used were usually suggested by real objects. In 1943 he returned to Paris and after the war he quickly gained a reputation as one of the leading abstract painters of the *École de Paris, his work showing a sensuous delight in handling paint that was unrivalled at the time. Typically his works feature luscious blocks or patches of thick paint (often applied with a knife), subtly varied in colour and texture. In 1951 he began to reintroduce figurative elements into his work, his subjects including landscapes and still life. From 1952 he spent much of his time working in the bright light of the south of France, and his late works are often very intense in colour. In spite of critical and financial success, de Staël felt that he had failed to reach a satisfactory compromise between abstraction and figuration, and he committed suicide.

staffage. Term applied to small figures and animals in a painting that are not essential to the subject but are used to animate the composition. Landscape painters, notably in 17th-century Flanders and Holland, often employed other artists to paint the staffage in their work (*see*, for example, POE-LENBURGH).

stained glass. Glass that has been given translucent colour in any of various ways, used particularly for creating pictorial designs in church windows. In its most characteristic development and its highest achievements it is essentially an art of Western Christendom, practised most splendidly in the west and north of Europe as an adjunct to *Gothic architecture. Its early history is obscure, and the first surviving complete windows—in Augsburg Cathedral

and datable *c.*1050-1150—show an art already nearly perfect in technique. Medieval windows are generally made up of hundreds of small pieces of glass of varied colours and shapes held together by strips of lead—somewhat like a jigsaw puzzle with dark outlines around the pieces. Windows of any size were made up of several panels so treated, and these were set in a framework of iron ('armature') that served not only as a support against wind pressure, but also to accentuate the main lines of the design of the window. The period from roughly 1150 to 1250 was the greatest age of stained glass: colours were strong and simple; designs were bold and fresh; and the feelings conveyed were lofty and awe-inspiring. From the 15th century, stained glass tended towards a greater pictorialism, imitating the effects of oil painting, and this trend reached its height in the 18th century, when some artists painted on glass more or less as they would on canvas. With the Gothic Revival in the 19th century there came a return to medieval principles, and William *Morris and his associates (notably *Burne-Jones) were among the foremost designers in this spirit. In the 20th century many noteworthy artists have designed stained-glass windows, in both figurative and abstract veins—among them *Chagall, *Matisse, and *Piper.

Stanfield, Clarkson (1793-1867). English painter, best known for his marine subjects. From 1808 to 1816 he was a sailor, mainly in the merchant service, although he was in the Royal Navy for a time after being press-ganged. He began his artistic career as a theatrical scene painter and creator of *dioramas, sometimes working in collaboration with his friend David *Roberts, but from the 1830s he concentrated on easel paintings. With these he gained the reputation of being 'England's van de *Velde', and apart from *Turner he was indeed the best British marine painter of his period. His work is represented in numerous British collections, including the National Maritime Museum, London, and the art gallery of his native Sunderland.

Stantons of Holborn. A family of English mason-sculptors with a large workshop at Holborn in London managed successively by **Thomas** (1610-74), his nephew **William** (1639-1705), and the latter's son

Edward (1681–1734). They were much patronized by the lesser aristocracy and the professional classes, and their monuments are found in many parts of England. Their designs are usually conservative, but William was one of the best English sculptors of his generation.

Stanzione, Massimo (1585?–1656?). Neapolitan painter. Like so many artists in his city at this time, he was strongly influenced by *Caravaggism, but his style has a distinctive refinement and grace that has earned him the nickname 'the Neapolitan Guido *Reni'. He was head of the busiest studio in Naples, and many of his works are still in the churches of the city, his masterpiece being the eloquent *Lamentation* (1638) in the Certosa di S. Martino. His most important pupil was *Cavallino. Stanzione probably died in the terrible plague that struck Naples in 1656.

state. Term applied to any of the identifiable stages through which a *print has passed as an artist creates or alters the design. The first state is represented by the initial proof taken from the plate. If no alterations are made, this will also be the 'only state'. Often, however, particularly in *etching, the artist will alter the design several times before reaching the final state; several impressions may be taken from the printing surface each time it is altered, but sometimes only a unique impression may exist. Differences in states may be so subtle that experts can disagree as to whether they are in fact intentional or are simply the result of chance or wearing of the plate. Some of *Rembrandt's etchings, however, exist in radically different states involving a major rethinking of the design.

Stedelijk Museum, Amsterdam. *See* RIJKSMUSEUM.

Steen, Jan (1625/6–79). Dutch painter. He is best known for his humorous *genre scenes, warm-hearted and animated works in which he treats life as a vast comedy of manners. In Holland he ranks next to *Rembrandt, *Vermeer, and *Hals in popularity and the expression a 'Jan Steen household' has become part of the Dutch language to describe the kind of lively, untidy home depicted in so many of his paintings. According to *Houbraken, Steen's 'paintings are like his way of life and his way of

life like his paintings', and in his biography he concentrates on the 'buffoonery' of his work. This, however, gives a misleadingly one-sided view of Steen, for he has many other facets. He painted portraits, historical, mythological, and religious subjects (he was a Catholic), and the animals, birds, and still lifes in his pictures rival those by any of his specialist contemporaries. As a painter of children he was unsurpassed. Moreover, even his most comic paintings often have a serious underlying theme, as he points out human folly or frailty—his favourite topics include various forms of immoderation, such as excessive drinking, squandering money, or giving way to lust or anger (in many of his pictures he includes inscriptions that explain or underline the meaning).

Steen was born and died in Leiden, but he moved around a good deal and spent much of his career in The Hague and Haarlem. He is said to have studied successively with the history painter Nicolaus Knüpfer (1603–55) in Utrecht, with Adriaen van *Ostade in Haarlem, and with Jan van *Goyen (whose daughter he married) in The Hague. Although he was highly prolific (about 800 paintings are attributed to him), he often had difficulty earning a living and at his death his widow (his second wife) was left with a large family and heavy debts. His financial problems were caused partly by a series of wars against England (and later France), 1652–78, which had a ruinous effect on the Dutch economy in general and the art market in particular. In 1654 his father, a brewer, set him up in a brewery in Delft, but the venture was unsuccessful, and in 1672 he opened a tavern in Leiden, although he continued to paint. Because of these beery connections, Steen is seen in the popular imagination as a drunken profligate, but there is nothing in the known facts of his life to justify this reputation; many of his pictures are indeed set in taverns, but he also painted scenes of impeccable genteelness, and he must have been a dedicated worker to produce his large output in a fairly short career. His work is uneven, but at its best is remarkable for sheer beauty of technique, as well as for richness of characterization and inventiveness in composition. *Reynolds praised his 'strong and manly' brushwork, and his deftness of touch is sometimes reminiscent of

Hals, although Steen's handling is more detailed. As a colourist he was one of the subtlest artists of his time, his use of salmon-red, rose, pale yellow, dove grey, and blue-green being highly distinctive. He had no recorded pupils, but his work was much imitated.

Steenwyck, Hendrick van the Elder (d. 1603) and **Hendrick van the Younger** (d. 1649). Flemish painters, father and son, specialists in architectural views. Little is known of the career of either man, but the father, who was probably a pupil of *Vredeman de Vries, is regarded as the creator of the church interior as a special branch of painting. Both father and son painted small pictures of real and imaginary *Gothic churches, sometimes as eerie nocturnal scenes. There are several examples of the work of Hendrick the Younger in the National Gallery, London; in two of them the figures are credited to Jan *Brueghel.

Steer, Philip Wilson (1860–1942). English painter, son of a portrait painter **Philip Steer** (1810–71). With *Sickert (his friend and exact contemporary), Steer was the leader among the progressive British artists of his generation who looked to France for inspiration. He trained in Paris 1882–4 (revisiting France four times between 1887 and 1891), and was a founder member of the *New English Art Club in 1886. In 1892 the Anglo-Irish novelist George Moore wrote, 'it is admitted that Mr Steer takes a foremost place in what is known as the modern movement' and around this time Steer was indeed at his peak, producing the beach scenes and seascapes that are regarded not only as his finest works but also as the best *Impressionist pictures painted by an Englishman. They are remarkable for their great freshness and their subtle handling of light, and unlike Sickert's paintings they are devoid of any social or literary content. Among them are several depicting the seaside resort of Walberswick in Suffolk, where he had friends and often stayed at this period. After about 1895 his work became more conventional and more closely linked to the English tradition of *Gainsborough (especially in his portraits), *Turner, and *Constable. In the 1920s he turned increasingly to watercolour. He taught at the *Slade School from 1893 to

1930 and in 1931 was awarded the Order of Merit. His sight began to fail in 1935 and he had stopped painting by 1940.

Stein, Gertrude (1874–1946). American writer, collector, hostess, eccentric, and self-styled genius. She settled in Paris in 1903 and her home at 27 rue de Fleurus became famous as a literary and artistic salon; many distinguished American visitors to Paris found it their introduction to modern French painting. With her brother, the art critic **Leo Stein** (1872–1947), who lived with her from 1903 to 1912, she was one of the first collectors of the work of *Braque, *Matisse, and *Picasso (who painted a well-known portrait of Gertrude, 1905–6, Met. Mus., New York); another brother, Michael, and his wife Sarah, were also collectors. Gertrude's writings, which she claimed to be a literary counterpart to *Cubism, are often opaque in style, concerned with the rhythm and sound of words rather than their meaning. The best-known and most approachable of her many books is *The Autobiography of Alice B. Toklas* (1933), which in fact is her own autobiography, composed as though by Miss Toklas (1877–1967), her secretary and companion from 1907. Alfred H. *Barr, Jr, writes that Leo Stein was 'the critic who first felt that Matisse *and* Picasso were the two important artists of his time', but Stein later turned his back on their work, describing Cubism as 'godalmighty rubbish'. Clive *Bell maintained that 'Neither Gertrude or Leo had a genuine feeling for visual art ... Pictures were pegs on which to hang hypotheses.'

Stella, Frank (1936–). American painter, a leading figure of *Post-Painterly Abstraction. In his early work he was influenced by *Abstract Expressionism, but after settling in New York in 1958 he was impressed by the flag and target paintings of Jasper *Johns and the direction of his art changed completely. He began to emphasize the idea that a painting is a physical object rather than a metaphor for something else, saying that he wanted to 'eliminate illusionistic space' and that a picture was 'a flat surface with paint on it—nothing more'. These aims were first given expression in a series of black 'pinstripe' paintings in which regular black stripes were separated by very thin lines. They made a big impact when four of them were shown at the Museum of Modern

Art's '16 Americans' exhibition in 1959, inspiring a mixture of praise and revulsion. To identify the patterning more completely with the shape of the picture as a whole he began—from the beginning of the 1960s— to use notched and *shaped canvases, often painting in flat bands of bright colour. In the 1970s he began to experiment with paintings that included cut-out shapes in relief and he abandoned his impersonal handling for a spontaneous, almost graffiti-like manner (*Guadalupe Island, Caracara*, 1979, Tate, London). He has been an influential figure, not only in painting but also on the development of *Minimal sculpture (his friends have included Carl *Andre and Donald *Judd).

Stella, Joseph (1877–1946). Italian-born American painter. He emigrated to the USA in 1896, but from 1909 to 1912 he lived in Italy and France, where he had his first significant contacts with modern art. He was particularly influenced by *Futurism and he became the leading American exponent of the style. His first and most famous Futurist painting was *Battle of Lights, Coney Island, Mardi Gras* (1913–14, Yale Univ. AG), a densely fragmented portrayal of a crowded amusement park at night. In works such as this Stella gave a romanticized image of the industrialized townscape of New York. In particular he was obsessed with Brooklyn Bridge, which he described as 'a shrine containing all the efforts of the new civilization of America' (*Brooklyn Bridge*, 1917–18, Yale Univ. AG). He soon abandoned the Futurist idiom, but industrial and urban themes continued to inspire him. Stella was active in the administration of two leading avant-garde associations— the *Society of Independent Artists and the *Société Anonyme—and in the early 1920s he experimented with various styles, including *Precisionism. In the 1920s and 1930s he spent much of his time in Italy and France (he lived in Paris 1930–4). From the mid-1920s his work grew more conservative and included mystical and sacred subjects.

stencil. A thin sheet of metal, paper, or other suitable material perforated with a design (or often lettering) that is reproduced on paper, fabric, or other surface when the sheet is laid on them and colour is brushed, rubbed, or sprayed through the openings. A 'negative stencil' is one in which an object is placed on a surface and colour is deposited around it. Stencilling was probably the earliest method to be devised of duplicating a design and it has a long history in fabric printing, for example. Prints made entirely by stencilling are uncommon, but the method was often used to add colour to cheap popular *woodcuts. In France, where it is called *pochoir*, stencilling has been much employed in book illustration. The more sophisticated technique of *screenprinting is based on stencilling.

Stepanova, Varvara. See RODCHENKO.

Stern, Irma (1894–1966). South African painter. From 1913 to 1920 she studied in Germany, mainly Berlin. She was influenced particularly by *Expressionism and was the most important figure in introducing European modernism to South Africa, where her work (mainly figure subjects) initially caused outrage. Her home in Cape Town is now a museum dedicated to her.

Stevens, Alfred (1817–75). English sculptor, painter, and designer, born at Blandford Forum in Dorset, the son of a housepainter. With the assistance of the local rector, who recognized his talent, Stevens was sent to study in Italy in 1833, at the age of 15, and remained there until 1842. He worked with *Thorvalden in Rome, and laid the foundations of his style in the study of the *Renaissance masters, above all *Raphael. After his return to England he taught at the Government School of Design (later the *Royal College of Art), 1845–7, and in 1850–7 he was chief designer to a Sheffield firm of bronze- and metal-workers. In 1856 he entered the competition for the Wellington Monument to be erected in St Paul's Cathedral, and although his design was placed sixth, he was eventually awarded the commission. It occupied him for the rest of his life and was plagued with bureaucratic problems. It was not finally completed until 1912, when the equestrian group at the top was cast from Stevens's model. Nevertheless, it is not only Stevens's masterpiece (indeed, the only one of his large schemes to come to fruition and survive), but also the greatest piece of sculpture produced in England in the 19th century. The architectural elements form a splendid, bold composition, and the two bronze groups *Valour and Cowardice* and *Truth and Falsehood* have an almost *Michelangelesque grandeur and vigour.

Apart from the Wellington Monument, Stevens's finest work was the decoration for the dining room at Dorchester House, London (c.1856), a sumptuous residence built for the millionaire R. S. Holford. It was demolished in 1929 (the Dorchester Hotel now occupies the site), but a fireplace is in the Victoria and Albert Museum, London, and many of the fittings are in the Walker Art Gallery, Liverpool, which has an outstanding Stevens collection. He was a masterful craftsman in numerous media—marble, bronze, silver, porcelain—and was also a painter, although he destroyed much of his work because it did not satisfy him. His unexecuted designs included schemes for the decoration of the interior of the dome of St Paul's Cathedral and the Reading Room at the British Museum, recorded in his superb drawings, which are particularly well represented in Cambridge (Fitzwilliam Mus.), Liverpool (Walker AG), London (Tate Britain), Oxford (Ashmolean Mus.), and Sheffield (Mappin AG). These drawings are very much in the High Renaissance tradition, and it is to this era that Stevens belonged in spirit.

Stevens, Alfred-Émile (1823–1906). Belgian painter, active mainly in Paris, where he settled in 1852. From about 1860 he achieved immense success with his pictures of young ladies in elegant interiors dressed in the height of fashion. His skill in rendering fine materials earned him the title 'the *Terborch of France'. He was a friend and supporter of *Manet and influenced *Whistler, with whom he was one of the first enthusiasts for Japanese art. Stevens also painted coastal and marine scenes in a rather freer, more *Impressionistic style, similar to that of *Boudin or *Jongkind. His brother **Joseph** (1819–92) was also a painter, mainly of animals, and in his day was almost as famous and successful as Alfred (both brothers were made members of the Legion of Honour). Another brother, **Arthur** (1825–99), was an art critic and dealer, and Alfred's son, **Léopold** (1866–1935), was a painter.

Stieglitz, Alfred (1864–1946). American photographer, editor, and art dealer who during the first two decades of the 20th century did more than anyone else to bring European avant-garde art before the American public. The son of a German immigrant, he spent most of the 1880s in Berlin and returned to the USA in 1890 with an international reputation as a photographer. His 291 Gallery (at 291 Fifth Avenue, New York), which he opened in 1905, presented the first American exhibitions of *Matisse (1908), *Toulouse-Lautrec (1909), Henri *Rousseau (1910), *Picabia (1913), and *Severini (1917), and the first one-man exhibition of *Brancusi anywhere (1914). It also gave the first exhibition of children's art and the first major exhibition of African art in America. Stieglitz also championed American artists, among them Georgia *O'Keeffe, whom he married in 1924. From 1903 to 1917 he edited the journal *Camera Work*, which he published from the 291 Gallery. At first devoted to photography, it was later extended to cover all the visual arts and opened its pages to avant-garde American writers. The 291 Gallery was closed in 1917 when the building was pulled down, but Stieglitz continued his work with the Intimate Gallery (1925–9) and An American Place (1929–46). In his own medium of photography, Stieglitz was a brilliant innovative artist. Learning from the avant-garde paintings that he exhibited, he experimented with various modes of abstraction and his work went a long way to revolutionize the concept of the photographic image and to establish photography as an independent art form. He formed an impressive collection of art, much of which was donated to the Art Institute of Chicago.

Stifter, Adalbert (1805–68). Austrian writer and painter. Up to about 1840 painting took priority in his artistic output, but thereafter he dedicated himself more to writing. He is now regarded as one of the outstanding Austrian novelists of the 19th century, but he enjoyed little success in his lifetime, and full recognition of his stature came only after the First World War. For much of his career he worked as a tutor, then an educational administrator. His later years were clouded by the suicide of an adopted daughter in 1859 and he took his own life, cutting his throat with his razor, whilst suffering agonizing pain from what was thought to be cancer. As a painter he was self-taught, and as in his writing eschewed heroic events in favour of simple, everyday happenings. His sensitive perception of nature comes out in his remarkably fresh landscapes. There is a museum devoted to his work in Vienna.

Stijl, De (Dutch: 'The Style'). The name of a group of mainly Dutch artists founded in Leiden in 1917 and of the journal they published to set forth their ideas. It was a very loose association, held together mainly by Theo van *Doesburg. The other members were, like him, mainly painters (*Mondrian was the most important), but they also included the sculptor Georges *Vantongerloo and the architect and designer Gerald Rietveld (1888–1964). Their common aim was to find laws of equilibrium and harmony that would be applicable to life and society as well as art, and their style was one of austere abstract clarity (see NEO-PLASTICISM). The journal was founded by van Doesburg and Mondrian in 1917 and van Doesburg continued to edit it until 1928 (it appeared roughly monthly, but irregularly; the place of publication—befitting van Doesburg's peripatetic career—also varied). A final issue (number 90) was published in 1932 by Mme van Doesburg in memory of her husband, after whose death in 1931 the group disbanded. At first the journal was devoted exclusively to Neo-Plasticism, but a *Dadaist element crept in. Mondrian ceased to contribute to *De Stijl* after 1924 and in 1926 van Doesburg published the manifesto of a splinter movement that he called *Elementarism. Despite this lack of cohesion, *De Stijl* was probably the most influential of the many avant-garde publications in Europe between the two wars. It was, however, in architecture and the applied arts (including furniture design and typography), rather than painting and sculpture, that it had its greatest influence —notably at the *Bauhaus and in the clean-lined architectural style known as 'International Modern', of which Rietveld's Schröder House in Utrecht (1924) is an early and famous example.

Still, Clyfford (1904–80). American painter, one of the major figures of *Abstract Expressionism but the one least associated with the New York art scene. In the 1930s he taught at Washington State College, Pullman, and after working in war industries in California, 1941–3, he taught for two years at the Richmond Professional Institute, Richmond, Virginia. He then lived

briefly in New York (1945–6), where he had a one-man exhibition at Peggy *Guggenheim's Art of This Century gallery in 1946. Although he stood somewhat apart from the other Abstract Expressionists, he was friendly with Mark *Rothko (they had met in 1943), the two men sharing a sense of almost mystical fervour about their work. In 1946–50 he taught at the California School of Fine Arts in San Francisco, then lived in New York, 1950–61. By the time he returned to New York, Still had created his mature style and had a rapidly growing reputation. He was one of the pioneers of the very large, virtually monochromatic painting. But unlike *Newman and Rothko, who used fairly flat, unmodulated pigment, Still used heavily loaded, expressively modulated impasto in jagged forms. His work can have a raw aggressive power, but in the 1960s it became more lyrical. In 1961 Still moved to Maryland to work in tranquillity away from the art world. Scorning galleries, dealers, and critics, and rarely exhibiting, he considered himself something of a visionary who needed solitude to give expression to his high spiritual purpose, and he gained a reputation for cantankerousness and pretentiousness—his comment on his painting *1953* (1953, Tate, London) is typical of his high-flown prose: 'there was a conscious intention to emphasize the quiescent depths of the blue by the broken red at its lower edge while expanding its inherent dynamic beyond the geometries of the constricting frame …In addition, the yellow wedge at the top is a re-assertion of the human context—a gesture of rejection of any authoritarian rationale or system of politico-dialectical dogma.' Still presented large groups of his paintings to the Albright-Knox Art Gallery, Buffalo, the Metropolitan Museum, New York, and the San Francisco Museum of Art, and his work is represented in many other major collections.

Stimmer, Tobias (1539–84). Swiss painter, draughtsman, and woodcut designer, active mainly in his native Schaffhausen and in Strasbourg, where he died. He was a versatile artist, whose work included façade decorations (notably that of the Haus zum Ritter, 1568–70, now in the Museum zu Allerheiligen, Schaffhausen), portraits in a *Holbeinesque style, and a large output of prints. He also decorated the astronomical clock in Strasbourg Cathedral (1571–4). His reputation in his lifetime stood very high. Several other members of his family were artists, notably his brother **Abel** (1542–1606), a painter and etcher.

stipple engraving. A printmaking technique in which the design is made up of countless small dots or flecks, producing softly graded tones. It was a popular reproductive technique in the late 18th and early 19th centuries, when it was often used in conjunction with the *crayon manner, from which it derived. Both were rendered obsolete by *lithography. Stipple engraving was almost entirely confined to England, where Francesco *Bartolozzi was an outstanding exponent.

Stokes, Adrian (1902–72). British writer and painter. An intensely subjective writer with an interest in psychoanalysis, Stokes responded passionately, even ecstatically, to art, believing its task was to show the 'utmost drama of the soul as laid-out things'. Many admirers regard him as the most eloquent and poetic English art critic since *Ruskin, although others find his prose hard going. His best-known books are *The Quattro Cento* (1932) and *The Stones of Rimini* (1934); *The Critical Writings of Adrian Stokes*, edited by Lawrence *Gowing, appeared in three volumes in 1978. Stokes began to paint in 1936 and became a student at the *Euston Road School in 1937. From 1939 to 1946 he lived near St Ives, Cornwall, with its flourishing group of painters (*see* ST IVES SCHOOL).

Stom, Matthias (c.1600–c.1650). Dutch painter, active mainly in Italy. In art-historical literature he is often called Matthias Stomer, but 'Stom' is the form that occurs in contemporary documents and on his only signed and dated picture, *St Isidore Agricola* (1641, Chiesa degli Agostiniani, Caccamo, Sicily). The details of his life are obscure, but he was one of the most prolific and committed of *Caravaggesque artists, working in the master's idiom long after it had gone out of fashion in most places. He evidently came from Amersfoort, near Utrecht, and is first documented in 1630, in Rome. A few years later he moved to Naples, and from about 1640 he lived in Sicily. There are about 200 surviving pictures by him, mainly religious works but also including mythological and *genre scenes. They are remarkable for their psychological intensity and their distinctive clay-like treatment of flesh.

Stone, Nicholas (c.1587–1647). English sculptor, mason, and architect. The son of a Devonshire quarryman, he trained in London, where he met Hendrik de *Keyser, who visited the city in 1606–7. Stone went to Amsterdam with de Keyser and worked for him until 1613, when he married his daughter and returned to England. He quickly established himself as the outstanding tomb sculptor in the country, surpassing his contemporaries in technical skill as a marble cutter and outdoing them in introducing new ideas: the monument to Francis Holles (d. 1622; Westminster Abbey), for example, has the first English example of a figure in Roman armour. In 1619 Stone became master mason for Inigo *Jones's Banqueting House in Whitehall, and in 1632 master mason to the crown. His contact with the court gave him a knowledge of the *antique sculpture in Charles I's collection and his work after c.1630 shows a change in style, marked by an attempt to imitate antique drapery, as in the monument to John and Thomas Lyttelton (1634, Magdalen College, Oxford). His large workshop produced monuments of many types, and we are unusually well informed about its activities, as an office notebook covering the period 1614–41 and an account book for the period 1631–42 still survive (Soane Mus., London). Much less of his work as an architect is extant (and it is sometimes not clear whether he was the designer as well as the mason of the buildings on which he worked), but he is recognized as the creator of 'a vernacular classical architecture of considerable charm and accomplishment' (Howard Colvin, *A Biographical Dictionary of British Architects 1600–1840*, 1978). The outbreak of civil war in 1642 seems to have brought his career to an end. After his death the youngest of his three sons, **John Stone** (1620–67), ran the family practice, even though he does not appear to have been a sculptor himself.

Stone, Reynolds (1909–79). British engraver, letter-cutter, designer, and painter. After working for the Cambridge University Press and a commercial printer, he set up on his own as a wood engraver in 1934 and from 1939 also practised (self-taught) as a letter-cutter in stone. His highly varied output included book illustrations (his speciality was quiet rural scenes), memorial tablets (including that to Sir Winston Churchill in Westminster Abbey, 1965) and the design of £5 and £10 notes for the Bank of England (1963–4).

stopping-out varnish. An acid-resisting varnish used in *etching and similar print-making processes.

Stoskopff, Sébastien (1597–1657). French still-life painter, active in Paris, where he lived 1621–40 (in this period he also made a visit to Venice, in 1629), and thereafter in his native Strasbourg. He painted in a spare, stiff, almost archaic style that has appealed greatly to modern taste—most of his paintings have come to light since the 1930s. The best collection is in the Musée de l'Œuvre de Notre-Dame, Strasbourg.

Stoss, Veit (c.1450–1533). German sculptor, with *Riemenschneider the greatest woodcarver of his age (he also worked in stone). He is first recorded in 1477, when he moved from Nuremberg to Cracow in Poland. There he carved his largest work, the huge altarpiece for St Mary's church (1477–89), and also made the red marble tomb of King Casimir IV in the cathedral (1492). In 1496 he returned to Nuremberg, where he continued to prosper. However, in 1503 his career was blighted when he forged a document in an attempt to recoup some money he regarded as having been misappropriated in an investment—an offence for which he was tried, convicted, and branded through both cheeks. He was also confined to the city limits of Nuremberg (he fled but returned), and although he was to some extent rehabilitated, he never regained his former position. He died a wealthy man, but his old age was embittered by disputes with the city authorities.

A good many documented and signed works by Stoss survive and his style is distinctive—bold and powerfully characterized, with exaggerated gestures and expressions and draperies rendered in an ornate, almost calligraphic manner. Indeed, Stoss's work is so individual that the famous figure of St Roch in SS. Annunziata, Florence, is almost universally accepted as his, even though it is undocumented and was attributed by *Vasari to 'Janni Francese' (Janni the Frenchman). Vasari wrote eloquently of the virtuosity of the carving, describing the draperies as 'cut almost to the thinness of paper, and with a beautiful flow in the arrangement of the folds, so that nothing more wonderful is to be seen'. Stoss sometimes, as here, left his figures unpainted, but otherwise his work is entirely in the late *Gothic spirit. He is recorded as being a painter and engraver as well as a sculptor and he also declared himself competent as a civil engineer.

Stothard, Thomas (1755–1834). English painter, book illustrator, and designer. He was a prolific and versatile artist, admired for his work in various fields. His paintings were mainly small-scale historical pieces in a charmingly sentimental manner, but he also did occasional more ambitious works, for example the decoration of the staircase at Burghley House (1799–1803) and of the dome of the Advocates' Library, Edinburgh (1822). His book illustrations were mainly for English novels and poetry. As a designer he ranged from monuments to jewellery. His son **Charles Alfred Stothard** (1786–1821) was a draughtsman and antiquarian.

Stradano or **Stradanus, Giovanni.** *See* STRAET.

Straet, Jan van der (1523–1605). Netherlandish painter and designer, active for almost all his career in Italy, where he was known as Giovanni Stradano (or Stradanus or della Strada). He was born in Bruges, had his main training in Antwerp with *Aertsen, and moved to Italy in about 1545. A protégé of *Vasari, he worked in various Italian cities, but mainly in Florence, where he was much employed by the *Medici family. He assisted Vasari with frescos in the Palazzo Vecchio, for example, but his main work for the Medici was as a tapestry designer. His *Mannerist style was influenced by Vasari, but it always retained a Netherlandish accent and he was admired for his skill in *genre painting, a northern speciality. Several of his designs were published in engravings.

Streeter, Robert (1621–79). English painter, appointed serjeant-painter to

Charles II in 1660. In the words of Sir Ellis *Waterhouse, 'he left no branch of painting untried and would have been a universal genius had he been endowed with the requisite talent'. The most important of his few surviving works is the allegorical ceiling painting of *Truth Inspiring the Arts and Sciences* (1668–9) in the Sheldonian Theatre, Oxford. This is a heavy-handed work, but noteworthy as the most ambitious attempt at a piece of *Baroque decoration by any Englishman before *Thornhill (Streeter had travelled in Italy during the Commonwealth). His reputation was evidently high in his day, for Samuel Pepys in his celebrated *Diary* calls him a 'famous history-painter' who 'lives very handsomely', and Robert Whitehall, whose ability as a poet happily matched that of Streeter as a painter, eulogized the Sheldonian ceiling in the immortal lines '... future ages must confess they owe | To Streeter more than Michael Angelo' (*Urania, or a Description of the Painting of the Top of the Theatre at Oxford*, 1669). Streeter's son **Robert** (d. 1711) succeeded him as serjeant-painter.

Streeton, Sir Arthur (1867–1943). Australian painter, active mainly in Melbourne. He was a prolific landscape painter, working in an *Impressionist style similar to that of his friend Tom *Roberts. Between 1898 and 1924 he spent most of his time abroad (in 1918 he was an *Official War Artist with the Australian forces in France). His work became stereotyped, but he was enormously popular in his own country, regarded as the foremost portrayer of the remote and awesome Australian landscape. By the end of his life he had long enjoyed the status of a national institution.

stretcher. The wooden framework on which a *canvas is stretched and fixed. Wedges in the inner corners enable the canvas to be tightened if it slackens.

Strigel, Bernhard (1460–1528). German painter, born and mainly active in Memmingen, near Ulm, where he was a leading figure in the period of transition from late *Gothic to *Renaissance. Most of his paintings are on religious subjects, but in his later years he turned more to portraiture, notably in the service of the emperor Maximilian I (*see* HABSBURG). In 1515 he was summoned to Vienna by the emperor and

there painted the *Family of Maximilian I* (KH Mus., Vienna), one of the earliest group portraits in German art.

Strong, Sir Roy. *See* VICTORIA AND ALBERT MUSEUM.

Strozzi, Bernardo (1581–1644). The leading Genoese painter of his period. He became a Capuchin monk in 1598, hence his nicknames, Il Prete Genovese ('the Genoese priest') and Il Cappuccino ('the Capuchin'). In 1610 he was allowed to leave his monastery to support his sick and widowed mother and his unmarried sister. By 1630 his mother was dead and his sister had married, and Strozzi is said to have been pressurized to return, this accounting for his move in 1630/1 to Venice (where he spent the rest of his life). Strozzi was successful and prolific in both Genoa and Venice, painting portraits and allegorical and *genre scenes (often of musicians) as well as religious works. The sensuous richness of his style was influenced by *Rubens (who worked in Genoa), but his paintings are highly distinctive, with an air of refinement and tenderness that recalls van *Dyck (who also worked in Genoa). During Strozzi's time in Venice there was a dearth of native talent in the city, and with two other 'foreigners', *Feti and *Liss, he kept alive the painterly tradition of the 16th century.

Stuart, Gilbert (1755–1828). American portrait painter. With *Copley he was the outstanding American portraitist of his period and he is regarded as the creator of a distinctively American style of portraiture. Much of his early career was spent in Scotland (*c.*1771–2), England (1775–87), and Ireland (1787–92). After he settled permanently in America in 1793, he worked briefly in New York City, then moved to Philadelphia (1794/5), Washington (1803), and finally Boston, where he settled in 1805. He quickly established himself as the outstanding portraitist in the country and painted many of the notables of the new republic. His portraits of George Washington are his most famous works—he created three types, all of which were endlessly copied: the 'Vaughan' type (1795, NG, Washington), the 'Lansdowne' type (1796, Pennsylvania Academy of the Fine Arts, Philadelphia), and the 'Athenaeum' type

(1796, MFA, Boston), which is one of the most famous images in American art, being used on the country's one-dollar bill. Stuart's style is notable for its strength of characterization (Benjamin *West said he 'nails the face to the canvas') and its fluent brushwork. His work had great influence on the next generation of American painters.

Stubbs, George (1724–1806). English animal painter and engraver, celebrated as the greatest of all horse painters. He was born in Liverpool, the son of a leatherworker, and his life up to his mid-thirties (which is poorly documented) was spent mainly in the north of England. Although he worked briefly with the painter Hamlet Winstanley (1694–1756), he was virtually self-taught as an artist. Early in his career he seems to have earned his living chiefly as a portraitist, and he also made the illustrations (based on his own dissections) for Dr John Burton's treatise on midwifery (1751); Stubbs had studied anatomy at the County Hospital in York, where Burton was a doctor. In 1754 he visited Rome, then spent eighteen months working in isolation in Lincolnshire, dissecting and drawing horses in preparation for a book on equine anatomy. He moved to London in about 1758 and, unable to find an engraver to do the work, he made the plates himself, and in 1766 published his famous book *The Anatomy of the Horse*. It was a great success, prized for its beauty as well as its scientific accuracy and Stubbs was soon in demand as a painter, not only for his 'portraits' of horses with their owners or grooms, but also for his conversation pieces in which the sitters were grouped in and around a carriage. His command of anatomy was matched by his ability to depict the beauty and grace of his equine subjects without sentimentalizing them and his range of feeling was wide, extending from the lyrical calm of *Mares and Foals in a River Landscape* (c.1763–8, Tate, London) to the full-blooded *Romanticism of his series of pictures on the theme of a horse attacked by a lion (the largest—c.1762—is in the Yale Center for British Art, New Haven). He is said to have derived his fascination for the subject from having witnessed a lion attacking a horse in Morocco on his way back from Italy, but he may also have been familiar with a much copied *antique statue on the theme.

Stubbs painted many other animals apart from horses—among them a moose, a rhinoceros, a zebra, and numerous dogs. At his death he was working on *A Comparative Anatomical Exposition of the Structure of the Human Body with that of a Tiger and a Common Fowl*, the drawings for which are in the Yale Center for British Art. His scientific curiosity extended to the materials he used and he experimented with painting in *enamel on earthenware panels manufactured for him by the great potter Josiah Wedgwood. Such projects took up much time but did not make him money and in his final years he was in financial difficulties. He kept his great powers until the end, however, and one of his finest works, painted when he was 75, is the enormous *Hambletonian, Rubbing Down* (1799, Mount Stewart House, County Down, NT), showing the champion horse looking strained and exhausted after winning a race in which it was 'much cut with the whip' and 'shockingly goaded' with the spur. It is a magnificent, heroic, almost tragic image. Stubbs was for long classified as merely a superior sporting painter, but his reputation now stands very high; indeed he is placed alongside *Gainsborough and *Reynolds in the front rank of English painters of his age.

stucco. A light, malleable plaster-like substance made from dehydrated lime (calcium carbonate) mixed with powdered *marble and glue and sometimes reinforced with hair. It is used for sculpture and architectural decoration, both external and internal. In a looser sense, the term is applied to a plaster coating applied to the exterior of buildings, and the words plaster and stucco are often used more or less interchangeably; in strict usage of the terms, however, plaster can be differentiated by the fact that it is made from calcium sulphate. Stucco has been known to virtually every civilization, and in Europe it was exploited most fully from the 16th century to the 18th century, notable exponents being the artists of the School of *Fontainebleau and Giacomo *Serpotta. By adding large quantities of glue and colour to the stucco mixture, *stuccatori* were able to produce a material that could take a high polish and assume the appearance of marble. Indeed, sometimes it is difficult to distinguish from real marble without touching it (marble feels colder).

Stuck, Franz von (1863–1928). German painter, sculptor, and graphic artist, active mainly in Munich, where he was a founding member of the *Sezession in 1893. In 1895 he became a professor at the Munich Academy, where *Kandinsky and *Klee were among his pupils. His favourite subjects were mythological and allegorical scenes, often treated in a morbidly erotic *Symbolist style: he did at least eighteen pictures of a naked woman entwined with an enormous snake under such titles as *Sensuality*, *Sin*, and *Vice*. He had an extraordinarily high reputation in his day (now badly faded) and enjoyed a princely lifestyle. The house in which he lived in Munich is now a museum dedicated to him. He designed and decorated it, attempting to create the ideal of the *Gesamtkunstwerk* ('total work of art').

Sturm, Der (The Storm). Name of a magazine and an art gallery in Berlin, both of which were founded and owned by Herwarth Walden (1878–1941?), a writer and composer whose aim was to promote avant-garde art in Germany. The magazine ran from 1910 to 1932 and the gallery from 1912 to 1932. They became the focus of modern art in Berlin, introducing the work of the *Cubists and *Futurists to Germany, for example, and publicizing the *Expressionism of the *Blaue Reiter group. Walden left Germany in 1932 because of the economic depression and the rise of Nazism and moved to the Soviet Union, where he is said to have died as a political prisoner in 1941.

Subleyras, Pierre (1699–1749). French painter who settled permanently in Rome in 1728 after winning the *Prix de Rome the previous year. He painted a variety of subjects, including portraits and still lifes, but he is most highly regarded for his religious pictures, which are much more serious in spirit than most French works of the *Rococo period. His most famous work is the *Mass of St Basil*, painted for St Peter's, but now in S. Maria degli Angeli. This huge picture was highly acclaimed when it was unveiled in 1748, but Subleyras died before he could follow up his success. He has subsequently been something of an underrated figure, but a major exhibition of his work in Paris and Rome in 1987 did much to establish his reputation as one of the outstanding French painters of his period.

Sublime. An aesthetic concept that originated in ancient Greece and played a particularly important part in 18th-century writings about art. It denoted a category of aesthetic experience, associated with ideas of awe and vastness, that was held to be distinct from (although often discussed in conjunction with) the 'Beautiful' and the *Picturesque. The outstanding work on the concept of the Sublime in English is Edmund Burke's *A Philosophical Enquiry into the Origin of our Ideas of the Sublime and Beautiful* (1757). This book was one of the first to realize (in contrast with the emphasis on clarity and precision during the Age of Enlightenment) the power of suggestiveness to stimulate the imagination. Speaking of painting, Burke says that 'a judicious obscurity in some things contributes to the effect of the picture', because in art as in nature 'dark, confused, uncertain images have a greater power on the fancy to form the grander passions than those which are more clear and determinate'. The cult of the Sublime had varied expressions in the visual arts, notably the taste for the 'savage' landscapes of Salvator *Rosa and the popularity among painters of subjects from Homer, Milton, and Ossian (the legendary Gaelic warrior and bard, whose verses—actually fabrications—were published in the 1760s to great acclaim). In literature, the 'Gothic novel', in which mystery and horror were the essential ingredients, appealed to the same sentiments. The first Gothic novel was Horace *Walpole's *The Castle of Otranto* (1764), and when crossing the Alps in 1739 Walpole expressed the essence of the imaginative appeal of the Sublime in his memorable exclamation: 'Precipices, mountains, torrents, wolves, rumblings—Salvator Rosa.' The vogue for the Sublime, with that for the Picturesque, helped shape the attitudes that led to *Romanticism.

Suger, Abbot (*c*.1081–1151). French churchman and statesman, one of the greatest patrons of the Middle Ages. He was adviser to Louis VI and Louis VII, acting as regent in 1147–9 during the latter's absence on the Second Crusade, but he is remembered mainly for the rebuilding of the abbey of Saint-Denis, near Paris, of which he was abbot from 1122 until his death. Suger's reconstruction and redecoration of the abbey was the most important landmark in the emergence of the *Gothic style in architecture and sculpture. In the 1140s he wrote an autobiographical account of the work—a unique document of the time. It was edited and translated (1946) by Erwin *Panofsky, who wrote that Suger was 'frankly in love with splendour and beauty in every conceivable form: it might be said that his reponse to ecclesiastical ceremonial was largely aesthetic'. He thought that through the splendour and brilliance of material treasure, men were led to an appreciation of spiritual glories. Suger commissioned several items of furnishing and sacred vessels for the abbey, some of which survive, notably an antique porphyry vase that he had converted into the shape of an eagle (Louvre, Paris).

Suisse, Académie. *See* ACADÉMIE.

Sully, Thomas (1783–1872). The pre-eminent American portrait painter of his period, active mainly in Philadelphia. He was born in England, but moved to America as a child. Subsequently he made two visits to England—in 1809–10, when he received advice from *West, and in 1837–8, to paint Queen Victoria for the Society of the Sons of St George of Philadelphia (a preliminary version is in the Wallace Coll., London). His style, distinguished by fluid, glossy brushwork and romantic warmth and dash, reveals his great admiration for *Lawrence. In his later work, however, he tended towards a genteel sentimentality. Sully was highly successful and extremely productive. He is said to have painted some 2,000 portraits (he also made *miniatures), but his best-known work is probably one of his (also very numerous) history paintings—*Washington Crossing the Delaware* (1819, MFA, Boston).

Superrealism. Style of painting (and to a lesser extent sculpture), popular from the late 1960s, particularly in the USA and Britain, in which subjects are depicted with a minute and impersonal exactitude of detail. Hyperrealism and Photographic Realism (or Photorealism) are alternative names, and some artists who practise the style do indeed work from photographs (sometimes using colour slides projected on the canvas); sharpness of detail is evenly distributed over the whole picture (except where out-of-focus effects in the photograph are faithfully recorded), but the scale is sometimes greatly enlarged. (Some critics prefer to use the terms 'Photographic Realism' or 'Photorealism' only when a picture has been painted direct from a photograph, but most are not so restrictive.) The immediate progenitor of Superrealism was *Pop art; banal subject matter from the consumer society was common to both, and certain artists, such as Malcolm *Morley and Mel *Ramos, overlap both fields. The kind of humour found in Pop is very rare in Superrealism, however, which tends to be cool and impersonal, with subjects often chosen because they are technically challenging (involving multiple reflections, for example). Like Pop, Superrealism was a hit commercially, but it was less well received critically. Some critics, indeed, regard it as involving a great deal of painstaking work but very little else; others think that its exponents can achieve a strange kind of intensity, the effect of the indiscriminate attention to detail being—somewhat paradoxically—to create a strong feeling of unreality.

The leading American Superrealist painters include: Chuck *Close, whose speciality is giant portrait heads; Don Eddy (1944–), notable for scenes involving reflections in shop windows; Richard Estes (1936–), most of whose work is devoted to the urban landscape; and Audrey Flack (1931–), who is unusual in that she aims for emotional effect in her still lifes of religious symbols and images of vanity and death. Philip *Pearlstein is sometimes labelled a Superrealist but stands somewhat apart. British Superrealist painters include Graham Dean (1951–), Michael English (1943–), and Michael Leonard (1933–), whose work includes highly detailed portrait drawings in a style mimicking the Old Masters. The leading Superrealist sculptors have been the Americans John *De Andrea and Duane *Hanson.

support. The material—*canvas, wooden *panel, *paper, or other substance—on which a painting or drawing is executed; usually a support is prepared with a *ground before paint is applied.

Suprematism. Russian abstract art movement, created by and chiefly associated with *Malevich. He claimed that he began producing Suprematist pictures in 1913, but he coined the name and officially launched the movement in 1915. His Suprematist paintings were the most radically pure abstract works created up to that date, for he limited himself to basic geometric shapes—the square, rectangle, circle, cross, and triangle—and a narrow range of colours, reaching the ultimate distillation of his ideas in a series of paintings of a white square on a white ground (*c.*1918), after which he announced the end of Suprematism. The spiritual ideas that he attempted to embody in Suprematism are difficult to summarize, for his writing is often vague and mystical; he thought that 'The Suprematists have deliberately given up the objective representation of their surroundings in order to reach the summit of the "unmasked" art and from this vantage point to view life through the prism of pure artistic feeling.' In spite of his wish to create a pure abstract art, some artists applied Suprematist designs to functional objects such as pottery and textiles, and Malevich's work was influential for a time even on scientifically minded artists such as *Rodchenko. Suprematism, indeed, made a powerful impact on the avant-garde in Russia until the Soviet regime demanded work that was socially useful (*see* CONSTRUCTIVISM) and it later had great influence on the development of art and design in the West.

Surikov, Vasily. *See* WANDERERS.

Surrealism. Movement in art and literature flourishing in the 1920s and 1930s, characterized by a fascination with the bizarre, the incongruous, and the irrational. It was closely related to *Dada, its principal source; several artists figured successively in both movements, each of which was conceived as a revolutionary mode of thought and action—a way of life rather than a set of stylistic attitudes. Both were strongly antirationalist and much concerned with creating effects that were disturbing or shocking, but whereas Dada was essentially nihilist, Surrealism was positive in spirit. The movement originated in France. Its founder and chief spokesman was the writer André *Breton, who officially launched it with his first *Manifeste du surréalisme*, published in 1924; however, it had been taking shape for a few years before this and the term 'surréalisme' had been coined by *Apollinaire in 1917. The central idea of the move-

ment was to release the creative powers of the unconscious mind, or as Breton put it, 'to resolve the previously contradictory conditions of dream and reality into an absolute reality, a super-reality'. Essentially it aimed at breaching the dominance of reason and conscious control by releasing primitive urges and imagery, and Breton and other members of the movement drew liberally on Freud's theories concerning the unconscious and its relation to dreams. The way in which they set about exploration of submerged impulses and imagery varied greatly (in spite of Breton's demands there was little doctrinal unity, and defections, expulsions, and personal attacks are a feature of the history of the movement). Some artists, for example *Ernst and *Masson, cultivated various spontaneous techniques such as *frottage in an effort to eliminate conscious control (*see* AUTOMATISM). At the other extreme, *Dalí, *Magritte, and others painted in a scrupulously detailed style to give a hallucinatory sense of reality to scenes that make no rational sense.

Paris remained the centre of Surrealism until the Second World War, when the emigration of many European artists to the USA made New York the new hub of its activity. It had an impact in many other places and indeed became the most widely disseminated and controversial aesthetic movement of the 1920s and 1930s, spread partly by a series of major international exhibitions. Two of the most important took place in 1936: the International Surrealist Exhibition at the New Burlington Galleries in London, and 'Fantastic Art, Dada, Surrealism' at the Museum of Modern Art, New York. Surrealism did not take root in Germany (Ernst, the major German Surrealist, lived mostly in France and the USA), but it flourished vigorously in Belgium—in the work particularly of Magritte, the most inspired of all Surrealist painters, and *Delvaux, the most long-lived upholder of the tradition. Many artists who were not in sympathy with the political aims of Surrealism (for a time it was associated with the French Communist Party), and who were never formal members of the movement, nevertheless found its ideas stimulating and were influenced by its imagery. In Britain, Henry *Moore and Paul *Nash were among the major artists who went through a Surrealist phase. The English Surrealist Group was founded in 1936, but it was social rather than revolutionary in its aims.

Although it broke up as an organized movement during the war and by this time had spent its main force, the spirit of Surrealism lived on. With its stress on the marvellous and the poetic, it offered an alternative approach to the formalism of *Cubism and various types of abstract art, and its methods and techniques continued to influence artists in many countries. It was, for example, a fundamental source for *Abstract Expressionism. Among the artists who most unwaveringly kept the Surrealist spirit alive was the British painter Conroy Maddox (1912–2005), who in 1978 said, 'No other movement has had more to say about the human condition, or has so determinedly put liberty, both poetic and political, above all else.'

Sutherland, Graham (1903–80). British painter, printmaker, and designer. He abandoned an apprenticeship as a railway engineer to study engraving and etching, 1921–6, and up to 1930 worked exclusively as a printmaker. His etchings of this period are in the *Romantic and visionary tradition of Samuel *Palmer. In the early 1930s he began experimenting with oils (following a decline in the market for prints), and by 1935 he had turned mainly to painting. His paintings of the 1930s show a highly subjective response to nature, inspired mainly by visits to Pembrokeshire. He had a vivid gift of visual metaphor and his landscapes are not topographical, but semi-abstract patterns of haunting and monstrous shapes rendered in his distinctively acidic colouring (*Entrance to a Lane*, 1939, Tate, London). From 1940 to 1945 he was employed as an *Official War Artist, mainly recording the effects of bombing; his poignant pictures of shattered buildings are among the most famous images of the home front. Soon after the war he took up religious painting, with a *Crucifixion* (1946) for St Matthew's, Northampton (he received the commission at the dedication of Henry *Moore's *Madonna and Child* in this church), and also portraiture, with *Somerset Maugham* (1949, Tate). It was in these two fields that he chiefly made his mark in his later career. The Maugham portrait has an almost *caricature quality (Maugham's friend Sir Gerald *Kelly said it made him look 'like an old

Chinese madam in a brothel in Shanghai'), and his most famous portrait, that of Winston Churchill (1954), was so hated by the sitter (who thought it made him look 'half-witted') that Lady Churchill destroyed it. Sutherland's most celebrated work, however, has become widely popular—it is the immense tapestry of *Christ in Glory* (completed 1962) in Coventry Cathedral. In addition to such figure subjects, Sutherland continued to paint landscapes—many of them inspired by the French Riviera, where he lived for part of every year from 1947—and late in his career he returned to printmaking, producing coloured lithographs. Apart from paintings and prints, his work included ceramics and designing posters and stage costumes and decor. He was one of the most famous British artists of the 20th century and received many honours, notably the Order of Merit in 1960. His reputation was high abroad; indeed in his later career he was probably more admired by foreign than by British critics, who tended to find his work old-fashioned. *See also* NEO ROMANTICISM

Swanenburgh, Jacob van. *See* REMBRANDT.

Swart van Groningen, Jan (*c.*1500–*c.*1560). Netherlandish painter, book illustrator, and designer of stained glass. He came from Groningen, worked in Antwerp and Gouda, and also travelled to Italy early in his career. His pictures show that he was familiar with the work of *Dürer, *Holbein, *Scorel, and other northern artists who were impressed by Italian *Renaissance art, but in spite of this his style has a certain archaic charm. He had a predilection for showing people wearing high hats, turbans, and other odd headgear.

Sweerts, Michiel (1618–64). Flemish painter, an enigmatic and exceedingly attractive artist. Nothing is known of his training or early career. From about 1646 to about 1656 he lived in Rome, where he came into contact with the 'Bamboccianti' (*see* LAER). He painted *genre scenes in their manner, but his work is in a class apart because of the quiet, melancholy dignity of his figures and his exquisite tonality. His other pictures in Rome included views of artists' studios (an example dated 1652 is in the Detroit Institute of Arts). By 1656

Sweerts had returned to his native Brussels; he set up a life drawing class in that year and in 1659 became a member of the painters' guild. By 1661 he was in Amsterdam, where he joined a missionary group (he was almost fanatically devout and zealous—giving his possessions to the poor, sleeping on a hard floor, and so on). In 1662 he sailed from Marseilles to the Orient, but his fellow missionaries found him quarrelsome and unstable, and he was dismissed at Isfahan in Persia; he made his own way to Goa in India, where he died in a Portuguese mission station. Towards the end of his career, Sweerts seemed to have worked mainly as a portraitist. Like his genre scenes, his portraits are distinguished by delicate and subdued colour harmonies and great sensitivity of expression and handling. They have often been compared with the work of *Vermeer, to whom Sweerts's *Portrait of a Girl* (Leicestershire Mus. and AG, Leicester) was once attributed.

Sylvester, David. *See* KITCHEN SINK SCHOOL.

Symbolism. A loosely organized movement in literature and the visual arts, flourishing *c*.1885–*c*.1910, characterized by a rejection of direct, literal representation in favour of evocation and suggestion. It was part of a broad anti-materialist and anti-rationalist trend in ideas and art towards the end of the 19th century and specifically marked a reaction against the naturalistic aims of *Impressionism. Symbolist painters tried to give visual expression to emotional experiences, or as the poet Jean Moréas put it in a Symbolist Manifesto published in *Le Figaro* on 18 September 1886, 'to clothe the idea in sensuous form'. Just as Symbolist poets thought there was a close correspondence between the sound and rhythm of words and their meaning, so Symbolist painters thought that colour and line in themselves could express ideas or feelings. Symbolist critics were much given to drawing parallels between the arts, and *Redon's paintings, for example, were compared with the poetry of Baudelaire and Edgar Allan Poe and with the music of Claude Debussy. Many painters were inspired by the same kind of imagery as Symbolist writers (the femme fatale is a common theme), but *Gauguin and his followers (*see* SYNTHETISM) chose much less flamboyant subjects,

often peasant scenes. Religious feeling of an intense, mystical kind was a feature of the movement, but so was an interest in the erotic and the perverse—death, disease, and sin were favourite subjects. Stylistically, Symbolist artists varied greatly, from a love of exotic detail to an almost primitive simplicity in the conception of the subject, and from firm outlines to misty softness in the delineation of form. A general tendency, however, was towards flattened forms and broad areas of colour—in tune with *Post-Impressionism in general. By freeing painting from what Gauguin called 'the shackles of probability' the movement helped to create the aesthetic premisses of much 20th-century art. Although chiefly associated with France, Symbolism had international currency, and such diverse artists as *Burne-Jones, *Hodler, and *Munch are regarded as part of the movement in its broadest sense. Symbolist sculptors include the Norwegian Gustav *Vigeland and the Belgian Georg Minne (1866–1941).

Synchromism. An abstract or semi-abstract movement in painting founded in 1912 by Stanton *Macdonald-Wright and Morgan *Russell, two American artists living in Paris (they met there in 1911). The term 'synchromism' means literally 'colours together'; it was coined by Russell and both he and Macdonald-Wright were much concerned with the purely abstract use of colour (in 1912 Russell said that he wished to do 'a piece of expression solely by means of colour and the way it is put down, in showers and broad patches, distinctly separated from each other, or blended... but with force and clearness and large geometric patterns'). In the period 1911–14 the Synchromists were working in a similar direction to the *Orphists but more or less independently and the two Americans were appalled when they were dismissed by some critics as followers of their European counterparts. Although Synchromism petered out with the First World War (during which Macdonald-Wright and Russell were separated), it influenced several American artists over the next few years (notably *Benton), and its founders hold distinguished places in the vanguard of abstract art.

Synthetism. Term applied to a manner of painting associated with *Bernard,

*Gauguin, and their associates at Pont-Aven in Brittany. It involved the simplification of forms into large-scale patterns and the expressive purification of colours. Bernard believed that form and colour must be simplified for the sake of more forceful expression, and Gauguin spoke much of 'synthesis', by which he meant a blending of abstract ideas of rhythm and colour with visual impressions of nature. He advised his disciples to 'paint by heart' because in memory coloured by emotion natural forms become more integrated and meaningful. Bernard and Gauguin each claimed credit for developing Synthetism and they probably acted as mutual catalysts. Synthetism was at its most vital between about 1888 and 1894, but some artists working at Pont-Aven continued the style well into the 20th century. It was influential on the *Nabis and has affinities with the more literary *Symbolism. *See also* CLOISONNISM.

Systemic art. Term coined by Lawrence *Alloway in 1966 to describe a type of abstract art characterized by the use of very simple standardized forms, usually geometric in character, either in a single concentrated image or repeated in a system arranged according to a clearly visible principle of organization. The chevron paintings of *Noland are examples of Systemic art. It has been described as a branch of *Minimal art, but Alloway extended the term to cover *Colour Field Painting.

T

Tacca, Pietro (1577–1640). Florentine sculptor, mainly in bronze, the chief pupil and follower of *Giambologna. After his master's death in 1608, Tacca completed a number of his works and succeeded him as sculptor to the *Medici Grand Dukes of Tuscany. Tacca's works for them include his masterpieces, the four *Slaves* (c.1615–24) at the foot of *Bandinelli's statue of Ferdinand I de' Medici in Leghorn. His last work is an equestrian statue (1634–40) of Philip IV of Spain (*see* HABSBURG) in the Plaza de Oriente, Madrid, in which the king is shown on a rearing horse. This *Baroque pose was imposed on Tacca, having been already used in pictures of Philip by *Rubens and *Velázquez (a copy of a painting by one or the other of these artists was sent to Florence to act as a model). The smooth, generalized treatment of the work shows, however, that Tacca remained essentially a *Mannerist sculptor. Tacca's son **Ferdinando** (1619–86) was also a sculptor; his best works are his graceful bronze statuettes.

Tachisme (from Fr., *tache*: 'spot' or 'blotch'). A type of abstract painting popular in the late 1940s and 1950s characterized by the use of irregular dabs or splotches of colour. The term was first used in this sense in about 1951 and was given wide currency by the French critic Michel Tapié in his book *Un art autre* (1952). In its intuitive, spontaneous approach, Tachisme had affinities with *Abstract Expressionism (although it initially developed independently of it), and the term is often used as a generic label for any European painting of the time that parallels the American movement. However, Tachisme was primarily a French phenomenon (Jean *Fautrier, Georges *Mathieu, and the German-born but Paris-based *Wols were among the leading exponents), and Tachiste paintings are characteristically more suave, sensual, and concerned with beautiful handling (*belle facture*) than the work of the Abstract Expressionists, which can be aggressively raw in comparison. The terms *abstraction lyrique* (*lyrical abstraction), *Art Autre (other art), and *Art Informel (art

without form) are sometimes used synonymously with Tachisme, although certain critics use them to convey different nuances, sometimes corresponding with niceties of theory rather than with observable differences in practice. It seems reasonable, however, to regard Tachisme as one aspect of the broader notion of Art Informel. To add to the confusion of terminology, the word *tachisme* was used differently in the 19th century, being applied pejoratively to the *Impressionists and the *Macchiaioli.

tactile values. Term introduced into art criticism by Bernard *Berenson in his *Florentine Painters of the Renaissance* (1896) to describe those qualities in a painting that he regarded as stimulating the sense of touch. He thought that *Giotto was the first master since classical antiquity whose painting demonstrated these qualities, which he considered to be a distinctive feature of Florentine painting and held to be 'life enhancing'. His theories were not very cogent, and the term is now little used.

Taddeo di Bartolo (c.1362–c.1422). Sienese painter. He was the leading painter in Siena in the first two decades of the 15th century and also worked in and for other cities. His style was conservative, but his frescos of Roman heroes (1413–14) in the Palazzo Pubblico in Siena are forward-looking in subject—early examples of the type of Famous Men cycle that became popular in the *Renaissance.

Taeuber-Arp, Sophie (*née* Taeuber) (1889–1943). Swiss artist, the wife and frequent collaborator of Jean *Arp. She met Arp in Zurich in 1915 and married him in 1922. Her prolific output included *collages, embroideries, paintings, puppets, sculpture, and stage designs, much of her work being in an abstract style distinguished by its rhythmic vitality. She died from an accident with a leaking gas stove.

Taft, Lorado (1860–1936). American sculptor, writer, and teacher. He studied at the École des *Beaux-Arts in Paris, 1880–6, and taught sculpture at the Art Institute of Chicago, 1886–1929. In his day Taft was well known for portraits and allegorical public sculpture, particularly fountains such as The Fountain of Time (1922, Washington Park, Chicago), but he is now remembered mainly for his books *The History of American Sculpture* (1903), the first comprehensive work on the subject, and *Modern Tendencies in Sculpture* (1921), in which he defended the academic tradition and attacked abstraction. In addition to writing and teaching, Taft spread his ideas as a public lecturer, touring clubs and schools in Illinois. His studio in Chicago has been preserved as a national monument.

Takis (Panayotis Vassilakis) (1925–). Greek experimental artist, active mainly in Paris, best known for his highly original work in *Kinetic sculpture. His creations often employ magnetic fields in which various metal objects produce changing patterns—the magnet's 'live force and vibration gives life to what has seemed to be dead material'. In 1960 he suspended the poet Sinclair Beiles on a metal frame between two powerful magnets at the Galerie Iris Clert in Paris. Sometimes he combines light effects and music with movement.

Tamayo, Rufino (1899–1991). Mexican painter, printmaker, sculptor, and collector, born in Oaxaca, the son of Zapotec Indians. Apart from the trio of great muralists—*Orozco, *Rivera, and *Siqueiros—he was probably the most celebrated Mexican artist of the 20th century, but his work was very different from theirs, for he was concerned with pictorial values rather than with the political messages they held so dear. From 1921 to 1926 he worked at the National Archaeological Museum in Mexico City, and native folk art traditions helped to shape his eclectic but distinctive style; *Surrealism was another strong influence. From 1936 to 1950 he lived in New York, although he returned regularly to Mexico, and from 1957 to 1964 he lived in Paris, then settled permanently in Mexico. By this time he was internationally famous, with a list of major exhibitions and distinctions to his credit, including the Grand Prize for Painting at the 1953 São Paolo *Bienale. His work was varied in subject, including still lifes, portraits (notably many of his pianist wife, Olga), nudes, animals, and scenes of the culture and myths of the Mexican Indians. He

did several murals in Mexico, but usually worked on canvas affixed to the wall rather than in fresco. His work also included a large number of prints in various techniques and sculpture in bronze and iron. Some of his late sculptures were very large (*Conquest of Space*, 1983, San Francisco International Airport). Throughout his life Tamayo was an ardent collector. He donated his collections to the city of Oaxaca to form museums of Pre-Columbian art (1974) and contemporary art (1981).

Tanguy, Yves (1900–55). French-born painter who became an American citizen in 1948. Whilst working at various odd jobs in Paris he began sketching café scenes that were praised by *Vlaminck, and in 1923 he decided to take up art seriously after being greatly impressed by the work of de *Chirico; he had no formal artistic training. In 1925 he met André *Breton and joined the *Surrealist group. His work developed quickly and by the time of his first one-man exhibition, at the Galerie Surréaliste in 1927, he had already created a distinctive style. Characteristically he painted in a scrupulous technique reminiscent of that of *Dalí, but his imagery is highly distinctive, featuring marine- or lunar-like landscapes whose ghostly plains are scattered with structures that suggest giant weathered bones arranged into fantastic pylons. In 1939 he met the American Surrealist painter Kay *Sage in Paris; he followed her to the USA and they married in 1940. After the Second World War he built up an international reputation.

Tanning, Dorothea. *See* ERNST.

Tàpies, Antoni (1923–). The leading Spanish painter to emerge in the period since the Second World War, active mainly in his native Barcelona. He studied law at Barcelona University from 1943 to 1946 and was largely self-taught as an artist. His early works were in a *Surrealist vein influenced by *Klee and *Miró, but in about 1953, after turning to abstraction, he began working in mixed media, in which he has made his most original contribution to art. He incorporated clay and marble dust in his paint and used discarded materials such as paper, string, and rags, and then (from about 1970) more substantial objects such as parts of furniture. He explained his belief in the validity of commonplace materials in his essay *Nothing is Mean* (1970). Tàpies has travelled extensively and his ideas have had worldwide influence. Apart from paintings he has also made etchings and lithographs.

Target Exhibition. Exhibition organized in Moscow by *Larionov, *Goncharova, and *Malevich in March 1913, at which *Rayonism was launched. Malevich also showed works in his 'Cubo-Futurist' style.

Tassi, Agostino (Agostino Buonamici) (*c*.1580–1644). Italian painter, active mainly in Rome. He was one of the outstanding *quadratura* specialists of the period, his most famous work being the illusionistic architectural setting for *Guercino's celebrated *Aurora* fresco (1621–3) in the Casino of the Villa Ludovisi, Rome. Tassi also painted small landscapes in the manner of *Bril and *Elsheimer, and for centuries he was remembered mainly because he taught *Claude, his significance as a decorative painter being forgotten. His other claim to fame is that in 1612 he stood trial for allegedly raping Artemisia *Gentileschi. The verdict of the court is unknown; Tassi is said to have spent some time in prison, but he was at liberty by 1613. However, it is certain that he was an unsavoury character (he was even suspected of murdering his wife).

Tate, Sir Henry (1819–99). British sugar tycoon and art collector. In 1890 he offered the nation his collection, consisting mainly of the work of Victorian contemporaries, on condition that the Government found a suitable site for a gallery. Following great controversy over where it should be located, the Tate Gallery opened at Millbank, overlooking the Thames, in 1897, on a site previously occupied by part of Millbank Prison. The building is an undistinguished classical structure designed by Sidney R. J. Smith, an architect who is otherwise virtually unknown. At the time of its opening, the Tate was not the independent gallery that had been envisaged by its founder. It was subordinate to the *National Gallery and was intended only for recent British art (its official title was the National Gallery of British Art, although it was referred to as the Tate Gallery from the beginning and this name was formalized in 1932). It began to be established as a historical collection of British art in 1910 when a group of works by Alfred

*Stevens was added and a wing was opened to accommodate most of the paintings left in *Turner's studio at his death, which had previously been housed (but in the main unexhibited) at the National Gallery. In 1916 the Tate was given the additional responsibility of forming the national collection of modern art. It was not until 1954, however, that it became completely independent of the National Gallery (although transfers are still made between the two institutions). There have been several extensions to the building (some of them paid for by Sir Joseph and Lord *Duveen), and in 1987 a new gallery—the Clore Gallery (named after Sir Charles Clore (1904–79), a businessman and philanthropist who was one of the Tate's greatest benefactors)—was opened to house works by Turner, including not only the oil paintings already at the Tate, but also watercolours and drawings previously in the *British Museum. In 1988 a new branch of the Tate Gallery was opened in Liverpool and in 1993 another one in *St Ives. The creation of these two outstations reflected not only a desire to share the Tate's collections with regional audiences, but also the fact that the gallery had outgrown its site in London. In 1994 the Tate Trustees announced a decision to create a new museum to house the gallery's modern collections in the decommissioned Bankside Power Station, a huge, starkly magnificent building occupying a prime site on the Thames opposite St Paul's Cathedral. It was designed by Sir Giles Gilbert Scott and built in 1947–63; the remodelling into a gallery was carried out by the Swiss architects Jacques Herzog and Pierre de Meuron. This new gallery opened to the public in 2000 under the name Tate Modern. The original Tate Gallery at Millbank then became known as Tate Britain.

Tatlin, Vladimir (1885–1953). Russian painter, designer, and maker of abstract constructions, the founder of *Constructivism. He ran away to sea at the age of 18 and until 1914 combined painting with the life of a merchant seaman; many of his earlier pictures are of maritime subjects, notably *The Sailor* (1911–12, Russian Mus., St Petersburg), a self-portrait. From 1910 he showed work at several avant-garde exhibitions in Russia and worked in close association with *Goncharova and *Larionov, who had known him as a boy. In 1914 Tatlin visited Berlin and Paris. He haunted *Picasso's studio and on his return to Russia began making a series of abstract *Painted Reliefs*, *Relief Constructions*, and *Corner Reliefs* inspired by Picasso's sculptural experiments. Very few of these revolutionary works survive, most being known only from photographs; it appears that they were made of a variety of materials—tin, glass, wood, plaster, etc. After the October Revolution of 1917, Tatlin's constructions made from 'real materials in real space' were felt to be in accordance with the new 'culture of materials' and he threw himself wholeheartedly into the demand for socially oriented art, declaring: 'The events of 1917 in the social field were already brought about in our art in 1914, when material, volume and construction were laid as its basis.' In 1919 he was commissioned to design the Monument to the Third International (the organization set up by the Bolsheviks to coordinate the activities of Communist movements throughout the world). The huge monument—in the form of a leaning, openwork, spiral tower in iron and glass—was intended for a position in the centre of Moscow. It was to be both functional and symbolic, housing various offices of the revolutionary government and including such features as an immense projector for throwing propaganda images onto clouds. Tatlin described it as 'A union of purely plastic forms (painting, sculpture and architecture) for a utilitarian purpose'. A model was exhibited in December 1920 at the exhibition of the VIIIth Congress of the Soviets. *Gabo condemned the design as impracticable and it was never executed (it was intended to be much bigger than the Eiffel Tower), but it is recognized as the outstanding symbol of Soviet Constructivism. (The original model has been destroyed, but there is a reconstruction in the Moderna Museet, Stockholm.) The Monument was the culmination of Tatlin's artistic career, and the rest of it is something of an anticlimax. He was active in teaching and administration, and his own work was mainly in the field of *applied art, designing furniture, workers' clothes, etc. In the late 1920s and early 1930s he devoted his energies to designing a glider, which he called *Letatlin* (a compound of his name and the Russian word for 'to fly'). From the 1930s his main

activity was theatre design, and his later years were spent in lonely obscurity. In 1948 the Communist Party declared him an 'enemy of the people'.

Tchelitchew, Pavel (1898–1957). Russian-born American painter and stage designer. In 1918 he fled Moscow because of the Revolution and in 1923 settled in Paris, where he made a reputation as a stage designer and also became one of the leading exponents of *Neo-Romanticism in painting. His subjects included landscapes, portraits, and figure compositions (among them circus scenes recalling *Picasso's work in his Blue Period). Some of his paintings were fairly naturalistic, but others used multiple images and violent distortions of perspective. He moved to the USA in 1934 and became an American citizen in 1952. In America he was again in demand as a stage designer, but he grew tired of this kind of work and gave it up in 1942 to concentrate on painting. The best-known picture of his American period is probably *Hide and Seek* (1942, MoMA, New York), a *Surrealist-like work in which strangely coloured children's heads weirdly metamorphose into vegetable forms (such subjects reflect something of his belief in the occult—he thought he possessed magical powers). From 1949 he lived mainly in Italy.

Teerlinc, Levina. *See* BENING.

tempera. A term originally applied to any paint in which the pigment is dissolved in water and mixed (tempered) with an organic gum or glue, but now generally confined to the most common form of the medium—egg tempera. Usually only the yolk of the egg is used, but the white by itself or both yolk and white together have also been used. Egg tempera was the most important technique for panel painting in Europe from the beginning of the 13th century until the end of the 15th century, when it began to be overtaken by *oil. After being neglected for about 400 years, tempera painting had a limited revival in the 20th century, the Americans *Cadmus, *Tooker, and *Wyeth being noted exponents.

Ten, The (more formally, Ten American Painters). A group of well-established American painters from Boston and New York who exhibited together from 1898 to 1919 after resigning from the Society of

American Artists, whose exhibitions they considered too conservative and too large. Most of the members of the group had studied in Paris in the 1880s and the common factor in their work was an interest in *Impressionism. Childe *Hassam and W. M. *Chase were the best-known members. The Ten was also the name of a group of American *Expressionist painters who exhibited together from 1935 to 1940. *Gottlieb and *Rothko were among the members.

tenebrism (from It., *tenebroso*: 'obscure'). Term describing predominantly dark tonality in a painting. It is applied mainly to the 17th-century followers of *Caravaggio in Italy and elsewhere.

Teniers, David the Younger (1610–90). Flemish painter, the most important member of a family of Antwerp artists. His output was huge and varied (about 2,000 pictures have been attributed to him), but he is best known for his peasant scenes—similar to those of *Brouwer, although less hearty. In 1651 he was appointed court painter in Brussels to Archduke Leopold Wilhelm of Austria (*see* HABSBURG), governor of the Spanish Netherlands, and he was also made custodian of the archduke's art collection. He compiled a catalogue of part of it, published in 1660 as *Theatrum Pictorium*, and made small copies of them to assist the engravers who produced the illustrations (his copies are now widely dispersed; examples are in the Courtauld Gallery and Wallace Collection, London). Teniers also painted several larger pictures showing the archduke with his paintings in a fictionalized gallery setting (an example, dated 1651, is in Petworth House, Sussex, NT). His other distinguished patrons included Queen Christina of Sweden, Philip IV of Spain, and various nobles, and his success brought him considerable wealth. His father, **David the Elder** (1582–1649), was primarily a painter of religious scenes. Few pictures are known that are certainly by him, and many formerly attributed to him are now given to his son, with whom he may have collaborated. David the Younger's son, **David III** (1638–85), was one of the many artists who imitated his father's work. Several other family members were painters.

Tenniel, Sir John (1820–1914). English illustrator. He is remembered chiefly for his brilliant illustrations to Lewis Carroll's *Alice's Adventures in Wonderland* (1865) and its sequel *Through the Looking-Glass* (1871), which now seem inseparable from the text, and for his long association with *Punch*; he worked for the periodical from 1850 to 1901, succeeding *Leech as chief cartoonist in 1864.

Terborch (or **Ter Borch**), **Gerard the Younger** (1617–81). Dutch painter and draughtsman of interiors and small portraits. A highly precocious artist—his earliest dated drawing (in the Rijksmuseum, Amsterdam) is from 1625—Terborch studied with his father, **Gerard the Elder** (1584–1662), in his native Zwolle, and with Pieter de *Molyn in Haarlem. Unlike most of the Dutch artists of his time, he travelled extensively. In 1635 he visited London, and according to *Houbraken he travelled in France, Italy, and Spain. From about 1645 to 1648 he was in Germany, where he painted the *Swearing of the Oath of Ratification of the Treaty of Münster* (1648, NG, London), a group portrait of the signatories to the treaty that gave the Dutch independence from Spain. In 1654 he finally settled in Deventer, where he won both professional and social success. After beginning his career with guardroom scenes, he turned to pictures of elegant society, to which his gifts for delicate characterization and exquisite depiction of fine materials were ideally suited. His best-known work, the subject of a charming passage by *Goethe, is the so-called *Parental Admonition* (*c*.1655, versions in the Rijksmuseum, Amsterdam, and the Gemäldegalerie, Berlin). It is symptomatic of Terborch's unvaryingly tasteful decorum that the true theme of this picture is a man making a proposition to a courtesan (the coin that he proffers to his 'daughter' has been partially erased in the Berlin version and it is omitted in the engraving Goethe knew). Terborch taught Caspar *Netscher and influenced other artists, including Eglon van der *Neer.

Terbrugghen, Hendrick (1588?–1629). Dutch painter, one of the earliest and finest exponents of *Caravaggism in northern Europe. Born into a Catholic family, he grew up in Utrecht, studied there with *Bloemaert, then spent several years in Rome (*c*.1605–14). On his return to the Netherlands he became with *Honthorst the leader of the Caravaggism associated with the Utrecht School. A second journey to Italy, *c.*1620, has been postulated, as his later works are generally more thoroughly Caravaggesque than his earlier ones. Terbrugghen was chiefly a religious painter, but he also produced some remarkable *genre works, notably a pair of paintings of *Flute Players* (1621, Staatliche Kunstsammlungen, Kassel), which in their subtle tonality—with dark figures placed against a light background—anticipated by a generation the achievement of painters of the Delft School such as *Fabritius and *Vermeer. Although he was praised by *Rubens, who visited Utrecht in 1627, Terbrugghen was neglected by 18th- and 19th-century collectors and historians. The rediscovery of his sensitive and poetic paintings was part of the reappraisal of Caravaggesque art during the 20th century.

terracotta (It.: 'baked earth'). Clay baked to become hard and compact. Since very early times it has been used to make figures and architectural ornaments, and it is to these, rather than pottery vessels, that the word 'terracotta' usually refers. Clay is found all over the world in many different colours and qualities. Coloured clay is commoner than white. The presence of certain chemicals, such as iron oxide, affects the colour of the baked product, so terracotta works are not necessarily of the reddish-brown colour that is normally associated with the word. Firing may produce a wide range of colour from light buff to deep red or black. The hardness and strength of the baked clay vary according to the temperature at which it has been fired. During the firing the clay shrinks by about one-tenth of its volume, sometimes more, sometimes less, according to its quality and the amount of moisture.

Tessin, Count Carl Gustav. *See* TIEPOLO.

Testa, Pietro (1612–50). Italian draughtsman, printmaker, and painter, born in Lucca (hence his nickname 'Il Lucchesino') and active mainly in Rome. He trained with *Domenichino and was employed by Nicolas *Poussin's patron Cassiano dal Pozzo to make antiquarian drawings, but his bizarre imagination brings him closer in spirit to his contemporaries of romantic temperament such as *Castiglione and *Rosa. Al-

though he had little success as a painter and spent much of his career in poverty, he was recognized as an outstanding draughtsman and etcher. He died by drowning, and it was rumoured that he had killed himself.

Theed, William (1804–91). English sculptor. He was the son of a painter and sculptor of the same name (1764–1817), best known for his pediment group *Hercules Taming the Thracian Horses* (Royal Mews, London, *c.*1816), one of the earliest works to show the influence of the *Elgin Marbles. Theed the Younger trained with his father, under E. H. *Baily, and at the *Royal Academy Schools. In 1826 he moved to Rome and worked under *Thorvaldsen and John *Gibson. He returned to London in 1848 and became one of the most distinguished and prolific Victorian sculptors. His work includes numerous busts and statues and the colossal group of *Africa* (1864–9) for the Albert Memorial in Kensington Gardens.

Theophanes the Greek (Rus., 'Feofan Grek', *c.*1330–*c.*1410). Painter from Constantinople, active mainly in Russia. Several fresco cycles by him are recorded in early sources, but only part of one survives, in the church of the Transfiguration at Novgorod (1378). Although fragmentary, this is one of the outstanding monuments of Russian medieval art, showing the highly personal version of the *Byzantine style that Theophanes brought to Russia; his figures are vigorous and strongly characterized, and his brushwork has an almost impressionistic freedom and dash. The other main works associated with him are a series of nine large *icons (*c.*1405) in the Cathedral of the Annunciation, Moscow. According to a contemporary source Theophanes was also famous as a manuscript *illuminator. No signed or documented work in this field is known by him, but several examples have been attributed to him on stylistic grounds. He made a great impression on painting in Novgorod and Moscow in the 15th century, notably on *Rublev.

Theophilus. The pseudonym adopted by the author of a medieval treatise on arts and crafts entitled *De diversis artibus* (The Various Arts). It has been variously dated from the 9th to the 13th century. C. R. Dodwell, who produced the standard edition of the text, with English translation (1961), assigns it to a date between 1110 and 1140. It is the most important source of information on medieval artistic techniques and is unusual for its time in its references to the artist's attitude to his work. Various early manuscripts are extant, but the treatise did not become generally known until the late 18th century. G. E. *Lessing produced the first printed edition, posthumously published in 1781, and an English edition, made from another manuscript, appeared in the same year. Little or nothing is known with certainty about the writer, but internal evidence suggests that he was a German Benedictine monk and also a practising craftsman whose primary interest lay in metalwork. He has been plausibly identified with Roger of Helmarshausen, a goldsmith and monk at the abbey of Helmarshausen, near Kassel, who is documented as the maker of a portable altar (1100, Paderborn Cathedral Treasury) for Bishop Henry of Werl. Other works have been attributed to him.

Thoma, Hans (1839–1924). German painter. Early in his career he specialized in landscapes—mainly scenes from his native Black Forest—and these are now considered his best works. Later he turned to figurative subjects, including Wagnerian themes; these won him an immense reputation in his day, but are now considered rather ponderous. The largest collection of his works is in the Kunsthalle in Karlsruhe, of which he was director from 1899.

Thomson, Tom (1877–1917). Canadian landscape painter, one of the main creators of an indigenous Canadian school of painting. Most of his career was spent as a commercial artist in Toronto, and it was only in 1914 that he was able to take up painting full time. Much of his painting was done out of doors, notably a series of fluently spontaneous oil sketches he produced in Algonquin Park, a huge nature reserve north-west of Toronto. Among his more formal paintings, the most famous is the bold and brilliantly coloured *Jack Pine* (1917, NG, Ottawa), which has become virtually a national symbol of Canada. Thomson's career ended tragically when he was mysteriously drowned in Algonquin Park, but his ideals were continued by the artists who formed the *Group of Seven, to whom

he was an inspiration. His death was probably an accident, but the uncertainty surrounding it helped to establish him as a legendary figure in Canadian art.

Thoré, Théophile (1807–69). French writer on art. He ranks alongside *Baudelaire as the most perceptive French art critic of his time (he was among the first to acclaim *Courbet, *Daumier, *Manet, *Monet, and *Renoir and to see the weakness of *Meissonier), and he also made memorable contributions to the study of earlier art. Above all, he is remembered for virtually rediscovering *Vermeer, a brilliant feat of connoisseurship and historical detective work. He was originally a political journalist and he published much of his work under the pseudonym W. Bürger when he was living in exile.

Thornhill, Sir James (1675–1734). English decorative painter. He was the only native painter to challenge the foreign decorative artists who worked in England during the period in the late 17th and early 18th century when there was a vogue for wall and ceiling paintings in the *Baroque manner. His two finest works are the ceiling of the Painted Hall (1707–14) at Greenwich Hospital (now Royal Naval College), London, the main scene of which shows William and Mary enthroned, and the *grisaille paintings on the life of St Paul (1716–19) in the dome of St Paul's Cathedral, London (he beat *Pellegrini and Sebastiano *Ricci in the competition for the commission). Thornhill was highly regarded by his contemporaries and won numerous distinctions. He was appointed history painter to George I in 1718, and in 1720 he was knighted and made serjeant-painter; in 1722 he became Member of Parliament for a seat in his home county of Dorset. In addition to his decorative paintings, he also produced portraits, book illustrations, and architectural designs. *Hogarth was his pupil and son-in-law.

Thorn-Prikker, Johan (1868–1932). Dutch painter and designer. Early in his career he passed through phases of *Impressionism and *Post-Impressionism, then changed to an elaborate linear style with which he became a leading exponent of *Symbolism and *Art Nouveau, as in his most famous painting—the mystical, erotic *The Bride* (1893, Rijksmuseum Kröller-Müller, Otterlo). From 1893 he concentrated on the design of mosaics, murals, and stained glass, mainly for churches, continuing in this vein after he settled in Germany in 1904. He taught at several art schools in Germany and was a major figure in the development of modern religious art. His masterpiece is perhaps the cycle of windows in the Romanesque church of St George in Cologne, completed in 1930.

Thornycroft, Sir Hamo (1850–1925). British sculptor, one of the leading exponents of the *New Sculpture. Early in his career he concentrated on idealized figures in which he expressed a 'poetic mood' praised by the critic Edmund Gosse; the best-known example is probably *The Mower* (1884, Walker AG, Liverpool; there are also several smaller versions). From the 1890s, however, he was increasingly preoccupied with portrait sculpture and above all public monuments, becoming perhaps the most distinguished British practitioner in this field in the early 20th century. His statues, dignified and thoughtful in tone, include those of Oliver Cromwell outside the Houses of Parliament, London (unveiled 1899), Alfred the Great in Winchester (1901), Gladstone in the Strand, London (1905), Lord Armstrong in Newcastle upon Tyne (1906), Lord Curzon in Calcutta (1912), and Edward VII in Karachi (1915). These are all in bronze, but he also worked in stone.

Both his father, **Thomas Thornycroft** (1815–85), and his mother, **Mary Thornycroft** (1814–95), were sculptors. They were primarily portraitists, but Thomas is now chiefly remembered for his dramatic Boadicea monument at Westminster Bridge, London, showing the fearsome warrior queen in her chariot. He began work on the group in 1856 and was encouraged by Prince Albert, who lent him horses as models. The plaster model was complete at Thornycroft's death, but it was not cast in bronze until 1897, after his son had presented it to the nation, and it was finally erected in 1902.

Thorvaldsen (or **Thorwaldsen**), **Bertel** (1770?–1844). Danish sculptor, active mainly in Rome, next to *Canova the most celebrated sculptor of the *Neoclassical movement. He studied at the Academy in his native Copenhagen, where he won a scholarship to Italy. In 1797 he reached Rome and henceforth regarded the day of his arrival (8 March) as his 'Roman birthday'. He made his name with the statue *Jason* (1802–3, Thorvaldsens Mus., Copenhagen), which was based on the *Doryphoros* of *Polyclitus, and his growing reputation resulted in so many commissions that by 1820 he had 40 assistants in his Roman workshop. In that year, on a visit to Copenhagen, he began planning the sculptural decoration of the newly built church of Our Lady, including marble statues of Christ and the Twelve Apostles, and this project occupied him intermittently until 1842. His other major works include the tomb of Pius VII in St Peter's, Rome (1824–31), and a monument to Lord Byron (1829–35, Trinity College, Cambridge). He also produced numerous portrait busts. In 1838 he returned finally to Denmark, a celebrity whose authority in the arts was sovereign. A museum was built in his honour in Copenhagen (1839–48), itself a remarkable piece of neo-antique architecture; his tomb is in the courtyard. In addition to his own sculptures, the museum contains works he collected, including pictures by contemporary painters (notably the *Nazarenes) as well as antiquities. Thorvaldsen aimed at reviving the sublimity of Greek sculpture, but he never went to Greece and (in common with other artists of his time) based his knowledge mainly on late *Hellenistic or Roman copies. He did, however, gain close familiarity with Greek sculpture from the restorations he made to the recently excavated sculptures from the Temple of Aphaia in Aegina, which in 1816 passed through Rome on their way to Munich (they are now in the Glyptothek there). Compared with Canova he is cool and calculating; his sculptures are more logically worked out and have great precision and clarity, but they lack Canova's sensitive surfaces. According to the taste of the time, his work has been praised for its nobility and classical calm or dismissed as frigid and empty.

Thulden, Theodoor van (1606–69). Flemish painter and engraver, the son-in-law of Hendrick van *Balen. He was born and died in 's Hertogenbosch, but he spent much of his career in Antwerp. Like most contemporary painters of historical and religious subjects, he was strongly influenced by *Rubens (with whom he collaborated in the 1630s), but his work has a distinctive and appealingly sweet charm. He had numerous commissions both inside and outside Flanders, and he also worked in The Hague and Paris.

Tibaldi, Pellegrino (1527–96). Italian *Mannerist painter and architect. He was born in Lombardy and brought up in Bologna. From about 1547 to 1553 he worked in Rome, and his style in painting, distinguished by grand, if sometimes rather ponderous, figures, was based mainly on the work of *Michelangelo, for whom he had a lifelong admiration. His finest paintings are frescos illustrating the story of Ulysses (c.1555) in the Palazzo Poggi (now University), Bologna. From the mid-1560s Tibaldi worked a good deal as an architect, chiefly in and around Milan, where he was much employed by the archbishop, Charles Borromeo; he was appointed chief architect to the cathedral in 1567. In 1587 he moved to Spain to work on the decoration of the *Escorial, for which he produced a large amount of decorative painting. His work there was influential in the development of Spanish Mannerism. He returned to Milan, ennobled by Philip II (see HABSBURG), in the year of his death.

Tiepolo, Giambattista (1696–1770). Venetian painter, draughtsman, and etcher. He was the greatest Italian (and arguably the greatest European) painter of the 18th century, his work bringing to a glorious conclusion the Italian tradition of fresco decoration begun by *Giotto 400 years earlier. His output was prodigious (his career is essentially a story of ceaseless work) and his services were sought from Spain to Sweden. He trained with the history painter Gregorio Lazzarini (1655–1730), but according to Lazzarini's biographer, Vincenzo da Canal (1732), Tiepolo soon departed from his master's 'diligent manner, and, being all fire and spirit, adopted one that was rapid and free'. Initially he was influenced by the sombre and dramatic style of *Piazzetta and worked mainly in oils. However, from the mid-1720s he turned increasingly to fresco and his palette lightened, with *Veronese becoming an important influence on his style. He was described by his contemporaries as 'Veronese reborn' and he shared with his great predecessor a love of pageantry and sparkling colour (and he often used

16th-century costume in his paintings). However, whereas Veronese's work always has a *Renaissance solidity, Tiepolo created exhilarating effects of airy space, particularly in his ceiling frescos, in which the central area often depicts open sky. For all its lightness, however, Tiepolo's work was always underpinned by superb draughtsmanship; it was this that allowed him to depict figures soaring overhead so fluently and convincingly.

In 1726–8 Tiepolo carried out his first major work outside Venice, the fresco decoration of the Archbishop's Palace in Udine, and this led to a string of commissions for various places in north Italy. By 1736 his fame was such that he was invited to Stockholm to decorate the Royal Palace—an invitation he declined because the fee offered was too small. Count Carl Gustav Tessin (1695–1770), the Swedish diplomat and art collector who tried to secure his services, was impressed by his 'spirited and obliging' character as well as by his 'amazing speed. He paints a picture in less time than it takes another to grind his colours.' Up to this time, Tiepolo's work had been predominantly secular, but from the late 1730s to the late 1740s he also produced a series of major religious paintings for Venetian churches, including a series of three huge canvases depicting scenes from Christ's Passion (c.1740) for S. Alvise (still in situ). These three pictures make 'a tremendous emotional assault on the spectator' (Michael Levey, *Tiepolo*, 1986) and are much closer in style to *Tintoretto than to Veronese. After this period, secular decorative commissions once again dominated Tiepolo's output, although he continued to produce altarpieces throughout his career; he also occasionally ventured into other areas, as with the ravishing *Young Woman with a Parrot* (c.1760, Ashmolean Mus., Oxford). His most important secular work of the 1740s and perhaps the greatest of all his works in Venice was the decoration of the Palazzo Labia (c.1745), which includes celebrated frescos of the *Meeting of Antony and Cleopatra* and the *Banquet of Antony and Cleopatra* (their story was one to which he returned several times). Here, as in other commissions, he was assisted by his expert in *quadratura, Gerolamo Mengozzi Colonna.

In 1750 Tiepolo left Italy for the first time, to carry out a very lucrative and prestigious commission to decorate the Rezidenz (palace) of the prince-bishop of Würzburg in Germany. The building was designed by Balthasar Neumann, the greatest architect of the age in central Europe, and it forms a worthy setting for Tiepolo's most glorious works. Like *Rubens, he could make even the most ponderous allegory come alive, and here the unpromising task of paying tribute to the lacklustre prince-bishop brought forth resplendent visions full of light and colour. Tiepolo first decorated the Kaisersaal (used as a state dining room) and then the ceiling of the grandiose Treppenhaus (stairwell), completing the work in 1753, when he returned to Venice. In 1757 another peak of his career came with the decoration of a series of rooms in the Villa Valmarana, near Vicenza, with scenes from Homer, Virgil, Ariosto, and Tasso. Here the scale is more intimate and the mood more tender, most of the subjects being concerned with the theme of love.

Tiepolo's last large-scale work in Italy was the enormous ceiling of the ballroom in the Villa Pisani at Strà, near Padua, which he began in 1760. Whilst working on it he was summoned to Madrid by Charles III—'I am bound to respond to His Majesty's urging'—and spent the remaining eight years of his life there. He was 66 when he arrived in Madrid in 1762 but he still had formidable energy and by 1766 he had completed three ceilings in the royal palace, including that of the huge throne room, on which he depicted the *Apotheosis of Spain*. His last major commission was a series of seven altarpieces for the church of S. Pascual in Aranjuez, near Madrid, works with a solemnity and inwardness that were new to his art. They were completed in 1769 and installed in 1770, soon after Tiepolo's death. Within a few years they had been replaced with pictures by *Mengs and other artists—a sign of the growing taste for *Neoclassicism. (There is no firm evidence of personal animosity between the two painters, but according to a colourful legend Mengs was so jealous of Tiepolo that he hired thugs to beat him up; he hid in a tree to watch the attack but fell and injured himself, whereupon his rival—with characteristic nobility—did what he could to help him.) Tiepolo's Aranjuez altarpieces are now dispersed and partly lost; the five surviving *modelli* for them are in the Courtauld Gal-

lery, London, and show that he kept his masterly fluency with the brush until the end of his life. He was as prolific a draughtsman as he was a painter (an outstanding collection of his drawings is in the Victoria and Albert Museum, London) and was also one of the finest etchers of his period, although his output in this field was small; *Goya was especially indebted to his graphic work.

Tiepolo was married to Cecilia Guardi, the sister of the *Guardi brothers, and he had two painter sons, **Giandomenico** (1727-1804), usually known as Domenico, and **Lorenzo** (1736-1776). They were their father's chief assistants on several of his major projects; both of them accompanied him to Spain and Lorenzo remained there for the rest of his life. He produced some attractive etchings and pastel portraits, but has much less independent substance as an artist than Domenico, who was a painter and etcher of some distinction. Although he imitated his father's manner closely when he assisted him, in his own work he has a distinct style—much more down-to-earth, with lively observation of everyday life. The contrast with his father can best be seen at the Villa Valmarana, where Domenico decorated the guesthouse at the same time that Giambattista was engaged on the main building; the subjects include scenes of peasant life. As an etcher he is best known for his set of 24 prints on the theme of the Flight into Egypt (1749).

Tiffany, Louis Comfort (1848-1933). American designer, interior decorator, and architect, his country's most famous exponent of the *Art Nouveau style. He was born in New York, the son of a prosperous jeweller, and spent virtually all his career there. His initial training was as a painter, but in the 1870s he turned more to the decorative arts and founded an interior decorating business in 1879. Tiffany became famous above all for his highly distinctive glass vases and lamps, but until about 1900 his firm was better known for stained glass and mosaic work (it did interiors for many socially prominent New Yorkers as well as for clubs). Most of his architectural work has perished, including his own mansion on Long Island, Laurelton Hall (1903-5), which was regarded as his masterpiece; however, the main entrance of this building survived the fire that destroyed the building in 1957 and is now in the Metropolitan Museum, New York. Tiffany was also an art patron and established a foundation that provided study and travel grants for students.

Tillmans, Wolfgang. *See* TURNER PRIZE.

Tinguely, Jean (1925–91). Swiss sculptor and experimental artist. He had an international career, working in Paris, New York, and elsewhere. His work was concerned mainly with movement and the machine, satirizing technological civilization. His boisterous humour was most fully demonstrated in his auto-destructive works, which turned *Kinetic art into *Performance art. The most famous was *Homage to New York*, presented at the Museum of Modern Art, New York, on 17 March 1960. The object on which the work was based was constructed of an old piano and other junk; it failed to destroy itself as programmed and caused a fire. Tinguely was also an innovator in promoting the idea of spectator participation, as in his *Rotozazas*, in which the spectator plays ball with a machine. His most famous work is somewhat more traditional—the exuberant Beaubourg Fountain (1980) outside the *Pompidou Centre, Paris, done in collaboration with Niki de *Saint Phalle; it features fantastic mechanical birds and beasts that spout water in all directions.

Tino di Camaino (*c*.1280–1337). Sienese sculptor, chiefly of tombs, active in Pisa, Florence, and Naples, as well as his native city. He was the most important follower of Giovanni *Pisano, whom he probably assisted for a time, but Tino's style was more calm and reserved, with an imposing block-like massiveness. His early career was spent mainly in Siena and Pisa, but his chief works are in Florence (where he worked intermittently from 1318 to 1323) and Naples (where he lived from about 1324 until his death). In Florence he produced, most notably, the tomb of Bishop Antonio d'Orso (1321) in the cathedral, which features possibly the earliest example of a seated effigy. In Naples his work included tabernacled tombs for the Angevin court, notably that of Queen Mary of Hungary (*c*.1325) in S. Maria Donnaregina. They show a move away from the sober grandeur of his earlier work to a more elegant, osten-tatious, *Gothic style. Tino also worked as an architect.

Tintoretto (Jacopo Robusti) (1518?–94). Venetian painter. His nickname derives from his father's profession of cloth dyer (*tintore*). He ranks second only to *Titian among the Venetian painters of his time and had a prolific and successful career. Whereas most of Titian's later paintings were done for foreign patrons, Tintoretto worked mainly for Venetian clients and in particular was the dominant figure in supplying religious pictures for the city's churches and charitable institutions; he is only once recorded outside Venice (when he visited Mantua in 1580 in connection with a commission from the *Gonzaga family) and the bulk of his work remains in the buildings for which it was painted. Little is known about his character or personal life, and his career up to the time he was about 30 is poorly documented. His biographer *Ridolfi says that he began an apprenticeship with Titian but was quickly dismissed because the master was jealous of his draughtsmanship. On stylistic evidence, it has been suggested that he may also have studied with *Bonifazio Veronese, Paris *Bordone, or *Schiavone. He is first documented in 1539, by which time he was working independently, but the first work in which he announced a distinctive voice is *St Mark Rescuing the Slave* (1548, Accademia, Venice), in which many of the qualities of his maturity, particularly his love of foreshortening, begin to appear. To help him with the complex poses he favoured, Tintoretto used to make 'little models of wax and clay' (Ridolfi), which he arranged on something like a miniature stage set, enabling him to use artificial illumination to experiment with lighting (*Poussin later used a similar method). He sometimes suspended the models from strings, which must have helped with poses of aerial figures. This method of composing explains the frequent repetition in Tintoretto's works of the same figures seen from different angles. He was a formidable draughtsman and Ridolfi says that he had inscribed on his studio wall the motto 'The drawing of *Michelangelo and the colour of Titian'. However, although he clearly admired these two great elder contemporaries, he was very different in spirit from either of them—more emotive, using violent movement and vivid exaggerations of light. His drawings, unlike Michelangelo's detailed life studies, are brilliant, rapid notations, bristling with energy, and his colour is generally more sombre and mystical than Titian's. It is in freedom of brushwork that he most resembles Titian, although his touch is rougher, and the qualities he shares with Michelangelo are an epic imagination and almost superhuman vigour.

St Mark Rescuing the Slave was at first rejected by the Scuola di S. Marco, which had commissioned it (presumably expecting something more traditional), and the resulting publicity helped establish Tintoretto as the most exciting young painter in Venice. From this point his career was essentially the story of a succession of major religious commissions (including further ones from the Scuola di S. Marco after it had overcome its resistance to the controversial picture). His greatest works are the vast series of paintings he produced between 1564 and 1587 for the Scuola di S. Rocco, the wealthiest of the Venetian *scuole* (literally schools)—charitable institutions that performed such functions as caring for orphans and the sick. Tintoretto began his long association with S. Rocco with the most famous episode in his career, when in 1564 he won the competition for the initial commission—a ceiling painting of *St Roch in Glory*—by somehow managing to install a full-sized picture whilst his rivals merely produced the specified sketches (he was renowned for the speed at which he worked). This clever ruse was regarded by some as underhand tactics and Tintoretto was evidently willing to undercut competitors' prices and even to work without pay if it helped to gain him the commissions he wanted. Unlike the notoriously avaricious Titian, he seems to have been unconcerned with money as an end in itself, and his religious paintings are the expression of a deeply devout nature. In S. Rocco he created one of the greatest of all interpretations of the Christian story. The work was carried out in three phases: first he decorated the *albergo* (committee room) with scenes of Christ's Passion (1565–7); this was followed by the great hall (1575–81), which has Old Testament scenes on the ceiling and New Testament scenes on the wall; and finally came the lower hall (1583–7), which has

scenes of the life of the Virgin Mary and the Nativity of Christ. There is an extraordinary range and depth of feeling in these paintings, from the cosmic drama of the *Crucifixion* (1565) to the tender intimacy of the *Nativity* scenes. Henry James wrote that 'We shall scarcely find four walls elsewhere that enclose within a like area an equal quantity of genius', and said of the stupendous *Crucifixion*: 'Surely no single picture in the world contains more of human life; there is everything in it, including the most exquisite beauty.'

In addition to his religious works, Tintoretto painted portraits and occasional mythological scenes (*Origin of the Milky Way*, *c*.1575–80, NG, London). Although portraiture was never central to his activity, he was the best Venetian portraitist of his time apart from Titian and was particularly good at depicting old men, showing the dignity and weariness of age (a self-portrait of *c*.1590 is in the Louvre). In his later work particularly he must have used a good deal of studio help; his son **Domenico** (*c*.1560–1635) became his foreman, and another son, **Marco** (1561–1637), and a daughter, **Marietta** (*c*.1554–90), were among his other assistants. However, he showed no diminution of powers in old age, and his career ended with one of his greatest masterpieces, the *Last Supper* (1592–4, S. Giorgio Maggiore, Venice), a scene of incandescent spirituality.

Tintoretto had considerable influence, most notably on El *Greco, who absorbed the visionary energy and intensity of his work. He continued to be a respected figure in Venice throughout the 17th century, but his reputation was lower elsewhere, and in the rational climate of the 18th century his work tended to be dismissed for an alleged lack of intellectual control (even in his lifetime *Vasari had admired his powerful imagination but lamented his 'haphazard' design and indifference to traditional ideals of finish). In the age of *Romanticism, however, his intense individuality brought him back into favour. No one played a more important role in his rehabilitation than *Ruskin, whose first encounter with the Scuola di S. Rocco in 1843 left him 'perfectly prostrated'. *See also* VERONESE.

Tischbein. Dynasty of German painters. The best-known of them, **Johann**

Heinrich Wilhelm Tischbein (1751–1829), was a friend of *Goethe and is now remembered almost solely for his famous portrait *Goethe in the Roman Campagna* (1786–7, Städelsches Kunstinstitut, Frankfurt). He is often called 'Goethe' Tischbein, and the two other leading members of the family, his uncle and cousin, were nicknamed after their main place of work: **Johann Heinrich the Elder**, 'Kassel' Tischbein (1722–89), and **Johann Friedrich**, 'Leipzig' Tischbein (1750–1812). They were principally portraitists. Other members of the family were active until the late 19th century.

Tissot, James (1836–1902). French painter, illustrator, and printmaker. Early in his career he painted historical costume pieces, but in about 1864 he turned with great success to scenes of contemporary life, usually involving stylish women. Following his alleged involvement in the turbulent events of the Paris Commune (1871) he moved to London, where he lived from 1871 to 1882. He was just as successful there as he had been in Paris and lived in some style in fashionable St John's Wood; in 1874 Edmond de *Goncourt wrote sarcastically that he had 'a studio with a waiting room where, at all times, there is iced champagne at the disposal of visitors, and around the studio, a garden where, all day long, one can see a footman in silk stockings brushing and shining the shrubbery leaves'. His pictures are distinguished most obviously by his love of painting women's costumes: indeed, his work—which has a fashion-plate elegance and a chocolate-box charm —has probably been more often reproduced in works on the history of costume than on the history of painting. He also, however, had a gift for wittily observing nuances of social behaviour. In 1882, following the death of his mistress Kathleen Newton (the archetypal Tissot model— beautiful but rather vacant), he returned to France, and in 1885 he underwent a religious conversion when he went into a church to 'catch the atmosphere for a picture'. Thereafter he devoted himself to religious subjects; he visited the Holy Land in 1886–7 and 1889, and his illustrations to the Bible were enormously popular, both in book form and when the original drawings were exhibited. For many years after his death Tissot was generally dismissed as vulgar and superficial, but since the 1970s there has been an upsurge of interest in him, expressed in saleroom prices for his work as well as in numerous books and exhibitions devoted to him.

Titian (Tiziano Vecellio) (c.1485–1576). The greatest painter of the Venetian School and one of the supreme figures of world art. In the course of a very long and highly prolific career he dominated Venice's art during its golden age and also worked for many illustrious patrons outside the city; his paintings have had a profound and enduring influence on European art. Most of his career is well documented, but his early years are somewhat obscure and his date of birth has long been a subject of scholarly debate, for the evidence concerning it is contradictory; certainly he was very old when he died, although probably not quite as old as some accounts suggest (traditionally he lived to be 99). He was probably a pupil of Giovanni *Bellini, and in his early work he came under the spell of *Giorgione, with whom he had a close relationship. In 1508 (the first secure point in his career) they collaborated on the external fresco decoration (destroyed) of the Fondaco dei Tedeschi (German warehouse) in Venice, and after Giorgione's early death in 1510 Titian is said to have completed a number of paintings that his friend left unfinished. The authorship of certain works (some of them famous) is still disputed between them. Titian's first surviving works that can be precisely dated are three frescos on the life of St Antony of Padua in the Scuola del Santo, Padua (1511), noble and dignified paintings with an almost central Italian firmness and monumentality. Although they show impressive skill in handling fresco, he hardly ever used the medium again, working almost exclusively in oils. In the same year that these murals were painted, *Sebastiano del Piombo left Venice for Rome, and with him gone and Giorgione dead, only the aged Bellini stood between Titian and supremacy. After Bellini died in 1516, he was virtually unchallenged as the leading painter in Venice until his own death 60 years later, although in his final decades he worked mainly for foreign patrons, allowing younger artists such as *Tintoretto and *Veronese to flourish in the domestic arena.

In the second decade of the century Titian moved away from Giorgione's dreamily romantic style and developed a much more robust manner of his own. There is still a good deal of Giorgione's enigmatic poetry in the allegorical *Sacred and Profane Love* (*c*.1514, Borghese Gal., Rome), but it is tempered by worldliness, and Titian's style soon became much more dynamic. This is seen particularly clearly in the work that more than any other stamped his authority in Venice—the huge altarpiece of the *Assumption of the Virgin* (1516–18, S. Maria dei Frari, Venice). It is one of the largest pictures he ever painted and one of the greatest, matching the achievements of his most illustrious contemporaries in Rome in grandeur of form and surpassing them in splendour of colour. The soaring movement of the Virgin, rising from the closely packed group of Apostles towards the hovering figure of God the Father, looks forward to the *Baroque. Similar qualities are seen in Titian's two most famous altarpieces of the 1520s: the *Virgin and Child with Saints and Members of the Pesaro Family* (the Pesaro Altarpiece) (1519–26, S. Maria dei Frari), a bold diagonal composition of great magnificence, and the *Death of St Peter Martyr* (completed 1530), which he painted for the church of SS. Giovanni e Paolo, Venice, having defeated *Palma Vecchio and *Pordenone in competition for the commission. The painting was destroyed by fire in 1867, but it is known through copies and engravings; trees and figures together form a violent centrifugal composition appropriate to the action, and *Vasari described it as 'the most celebrated, the greatest work ... that Titian has ever done'. The young Titian had important secular as well as ecclesiastical commissions, notably a set of three mythological pictures (1518–23) for Alfonso d'*Este, his first princely patron—the *Worship of Venus*, the *Bacchanal* (both in the Prado, Madrid), and *Bacchus and Ariadne* (NG, London). He was also busy as a portraitist. Many of his early portraits are of unknown sitters, as with the exquisite *Man with a Glove* (*c*.1520, Louvre, Paris), but later he painted some of the most famous personalities of the day.

Titian's success brought him a substantial income and from 1531 he lived in a palatial house in Venice, with gardens overlooking the lagoon. In 1533 the emperor Charles V (*see* HABSBURG) appointed him court painter and elevated him to the rank of count palatine and Knight of the Golden Spur. This was an unprecedented honour for a painter, and *Ridolfi tells a revealing anecdote concerning the respect Titian was accorded even by the emperor himself: Titian dropped a brush and when Charles picked it up for him he protested 'Sire, I am not worthy of such a servant', to which the emperor replied 'Titian is worthy to be served by Caesar.' Although he had probably had a fairly basic education (he knew no Latin), he does indeed seem to have been at ease in the elevated society of his patrons; contemporary accounts say he was well-mannered and a good conversationalist, and his best friend was the celebrated poet Pietro Aretino. Titian had first met the emperor in 1530, when he was crowned in Bologna. Although he made several short visits such as this to towns in northern Italy, he was reluctant to journey far from Venice and he turned down Charles's invitation to go to Spain to paint portraits of the royal family. In the 1540s, however, he overcame his resistance to travelling long distances, visiting Rome in 1545–6 at the invitation of Pope Paul III (Alessandro *Farnese) and then Augsburg in Germany in 1548 to work at Charles's court. He returned to Augsburg in 1550–1. His work in Rome included a celebrated portrait of the pope with his grandsons, Cardinal Alessandro and Ottavio Farnese (Mus. di Capodimonte, Naples), and he brought with him a painting of *Danaë* (*c*.1544–5, Mus. di Capodimonte), previously commissioned by the cardinal. It is one of his most gloriously sensuous treatments of the female nude, and a papal legate writing to the cardinal in 1544 stressed its overtly erotic character by comparing it with Titian's own slightly earlier *Venus of Urbino* (1538, Uffizi, Florence): 'the nude that Your Reverence saw ... in the apartment of the Duke of Urbino [Guidobaldo della *Rovere] looks like a nun compared with this one.' According to Vasari, *Michelangelo praised the colouring of *Danaë* but found fault with the drawing. Titian's work in Augsburg included *Charles V on Horseback* (1548, Prado, Madrid), the largest and grandest of all his portraits.

The greatest patron of Titian's later career was Charles's son, Philip II of Spain, whom he first met in 1549 in Milan. Initially Philip was unimpressed with Titian's work, finding his brushwork too broad, but he came to admire him above all other painters, and eventually—rather than commissioning specific works from him—he was content to accept whatever the master cared to send him. Like his father, Philip was intensely devout, and Titian's work for him included religious pictures as well as portraits. However, the most famous works he painted for him were a series of seven erotic mythological subjects (c.1550–c.1562) based (sometimes loosely) on Ovid's *Metamorphoses*: *Danaë* (a variant of the earlier picture for Cardinal Farnese) and *Venus and Adonis* (Prado), *Perseus and Andromeda* (Wallace Coll., London), the *Rape of Europa* (Gardner Mus., Boston), *Diana and Actaeon* and *Diana and Calisto* (Ellesmere Coll., on loan to NG of Scotland), and the *Death of Actaeon* (NG, London). Titian referred to these pictures as *poesie* (poems), and they are indeed highly poetic visions of distant worlds, quite different from the sensual realities of his earlier mythological paintings. By this time his style had changed greatly from that of his youth, with an emphasis on inner feeling rather than external drama, his colours mellow and glowing rather than rich and resonant, and his brushwork loose and almost impressionistic. It has been argued that the extreme freedom of handling in some of his final works is a result of their being unfinished and perhaps partly a consequence of failing eyesight. The situation is complicated by the fact that in his later career Titian is known to have made extensive use of assistants, among them his brother **Francesco Vecellio** (c.1490–1559/60) and his son **Orazio Vecellio** (1525–76). Nevertheless, there can be no doubt that Titian's final works include some of his most sublime creations, and his career ends with the awe-inspiring *Pietà* (c.1575–6, Accademia, Venice), which is said to have been intended for his own tomb and was evidently finished after his death by *Palma Giovane.

Titian was recognized as a towering genius in his own time (*Lomazzo described him as 'the sun amidst small stars not only among the Italians but all the painters of the world') and his reputation as one of the giants of art has never been seriously questioned (it has been commonplace for centuries to describe him as the greatest of all

colourists). He was supreme in every major branch of painting practised in his time and his achievements were so varied—ranging from the joyous evocation of pagan antiquity in his early mythologies to the depths of tragedy in his late religious paintings—that he has been an inspiration to artists of very different character. Van *Dyck, *Poussin, *Rubens, and *Velázquez are among the painters who have particularly revered him. In many subjects he set patterns that were followed by generations of artists, particularly in portraiture; more than anyone else he was responsible for widening the scope of portraiture beyond the head-and-shoulders type that prevailed in the 15th century, not only by popularizing the half-length and the full-length, but also by varying his poses and introducing accessories such as a dog, a book, or a classical column. In technique he was just as influential, for he was the first to show the limitless expressive potential of oil paint, creating a vibrant pictorial surface in which the artist's personal 'handwriting' is evident in every touch of the brush. According to Palma Giovane, 'in the final stages he worked more with his fingers than with his brush', and Vasari wrote that his late works 'are executed with bold, sweeping strokes, and in patches of colour, with the result that they cannot be viewed from near by, but appear perfect at a distance ... The method he used is judicious, beautiful, and astonishing, for it makes pictures appear alive and painted with great art, but it conceals the labour that has gone into them.'

Titian's greatness as an artist, it appears, was not matched by his character, for he was notoriously avaricious. In spite of his wealth and status, he claimed he was impoverished, and Erwin *Panofsky comments that 'his tax declaration of 1566 ... would land him in jail today'. Titian, however, was lavish in his hospitality towards his friends, notably Pietro Aretino and the sculptor and architect Jacopo *Sansovino. These three were so close that they were known in Venice as the triumvirate, and they used their influence with their respective patrons to further each other's careers.

Tobey, Mark (1890–1976). American painter. In 1918 he became a convert to the Baha'i faith and much of his subsequent work was inspired by an interest in Oriental art and thought. He lived mainly in Seattle, but travelled widely and from 1931 to 1938 was artist-in-residence at Dartington Hall, a progressive school in Devon, England. Following a visit to the Far East in 1934–5, he developed a distinctive style of painting that he called 'white writing', characterized by calligraphic white patterns overlying dimly discerned suggestions of colour beneath. Although he painted representational pictures in this style, he turned increasingly to abstractions. Their *all-over manner anticipated and perhaps influenced Jackson *Pollock, but unlike *Action Painters, Tobey believed that 'painting should come through the avenues of meditation rather than the canals of action'. Unusually for an American painter, he was more highly esteemed abroad than in his own country, and he was influential on French *Tachisme in the 1950s. In 1960 he moved to Switzerland and settled in Basle.

Toft, Albert. *See* NEW SCULPTURE.

Tomaso da Modena (*c*.1325–*c*.1379). Italian painter, one of the leading artists of his day in northern Italy. His earthy, humane, and naturalistic style is well seen in his series of frescos of famous Dominicans (signed and dated 1352) in the chapter house of S. Niccolò in Treviso. The saintly figures are shown meditating, writing, and reading (the first dated example of spectacles being worn appears here) and Tomaso shows a remarkable ability to depict intellectual activity. His reputation was such that work was commissioned from him by the emperor Charles IV in Bohemia, and two panels by Tomaso are still in Karlstein Castle, near Prague. It is unlikely that he visited Bohemia, but there is some kinship between his work and that of his leading Bohemian contemporary, *Master Theoderic.

tondo (It.: 'round'). A painting or *relief sculpture of circular shape.

Tonks, Henry (1862–1937). British painter, draughtsman, and teacher. He was interested in art from childhood, and in 1893 he abandoned his successful medical career to become a teacher at the *Slade School. (However, he worked in plastic surgery during the First World War.) Tonks re-

mained at the Slade until 1930 (as professor from 1918), and became the most renowned and formidable teacher of his generation— 'in appearance tall, gaunt, and severe' (*DNB*). Under him the Slade maintained its position as the dominant art school in Britain (although it was now challenged by the *Royal College of Art), and he was a major influence as an upholder of traditional values and an opponent of modern ideas: 'I don't believe I really like any modern development.' He set high standards for his pupils, particularly in draughtsmanship (his own forte) and he got on well with them, in spite of being notorious for his sarcasm and abruptness. Because of his refusal to move with the times he was increasingly looked on as a back number by more progressive artists and students, but he remained a dominant presence in the art world. Tonks's own paintings are mainly figure subjects, often consciously (or self-consciously) poetic in spirit: Sir John *Rothenstein refers to 'the sheer prettiness of much of his art', but his pictures often look rather laborious, partly because of his technique of 'Tonking', which involved using an absorbent material to soak excess oil from the canvas after each day's work and so produce a dry surface for the next session. His best-known work is probably *Saturday Night in The Vale* (1928–9, Tate, London), which shows the novelist and critic George Moore reading aloud to a gathering at Tonks's studio in The Vale, Chelsea. Moore complained that he had been made to look like a 'flabby old cook', whereas Tonks had depicted himself as a young and elegant 'demi-god'.

Tooker, George (1920–). American painter. He studied at the *Art Students League of New York, 1943–4. His teachers there included Reginald *Marsh, and it was from him and Paul *Cadmus (with whom he studied privately) that he acquired his preference for painting in egg *tempera. His technique is scrupulously detailed in the manner of the Old Masters, but his subjects express the spiritual desolation and debilitating uniformity of modern life. The figures in his paintings all look more or less like one another and go through life as if on a conveyer belt, tense and drained of energy. They are physically close to one another, but emotionally distant. *Subway*

(1950, Whitney Mus., New York) is perhaps his most famous work—a terrifying vision of Kafkaesque isolation.

Toorop, Jan (1858–1928). Dutch painter, graphic artist, and designer. He was born in Java (at this time a Dutch colony) and moved to the Netherlands with his family when he was 13. Toorop's work reflected many of the main stylistic currents of his time and he was a leading figure in the *Symbolist and *Art Nouveau movements. His most characteristic paintings are literary subjects depicted with flowing lines, as in his masterpiece, *The Three Brides* (1893, Rijksmuseum Kröller-Müller, Otterlo), a ghostly scene with an exotic feeling that recalls his origins in Java. In 1905 he was converted to Catholicism and thereafter concentrated mainly on religious works. Toorop's prolific output included book illustrations, designs for stained glass, and posters. His daughter **Charley Toorop** (1891–1955) trained as a musician but began to paint in about 1914. Her early work was influenced by her father's Symbolism, but later her style became more solid and naturalistic.

Topolski, Feliks (1907–89). Polish-born painter and draughtsman who settled in England in 1935 and became a British subject in 1947. A versatile and prolific artist, he is perhaps best known for his large murals, notably the *Coronation of Elizabeth II* (30×1.2 m (100×4 ft)) in Buckingham Palace (1958–60). He was an *Official War Artist 1940–5, and his other work includes portraits and book illustrations. His style is characterized by the use of vigorous swirling line.

Torres-García, Joaquín (1874–1949). Uruguayan painter and art theorist, active mainly in Europe. In 1891 his family moved to Spain and he grew up in Barcelona, where he was part of an avant-garde circle that included the young *Picasso. After a visit to New York (1920–2), he settled in France (1924–32), where he developed a severely geometrical, two-dimensional *Constructivist style, and in 1929 founded the review *Cercle et Carré* with Michel *Seuphor. In 1934 he returned to Uruguay, where he opened an art school. He wrote various works on art theory and by his example and teaching did much to promote Con-

structivist and *Kinetic art in South America. There is a museum of his work in his native Montevideo.

Torrigiano (or **Torrigiani**), **Pietro** (1472–1528). Florentine sculptor. He was trained under *Bertoldo di Giovanni in the *Medici 'academy' and in a quarrel broke the nose of his fellow student *Michelangelo, permanently disfiguring him. This assault on his favourite so angered Lorenzo de' Medici that Torrigiani fled Florence and in the 1490s he seems to have worked mainly in Rome; he is also said to have spent some time as a soldier. In 1504 he is documented in Avignon, and in 1509–10 he worked in the Netherlands for Margaret of Austria (*see* HABSBURG). By 1511 he had moved to England, where he executed his most important works, chief among them the tomb of Henry VII and his wife Elizabeth of York (1512–18) in Westminster Abbey. The two sensitive bronze effigies, made with the aid of death masks, have a *Gothic elegance, but the figures of angels at the corners of the tomb and the exquisite decorative work introduced a pure *Renaissance style into England. It had little immediate influence, however. In about 1522 Torrigiano left England for Spain, abandoning a projected tomb for Henry VIII. According to *Vasari, he was imprisoned by the Inquisition on a charge of sacrilege and starved himself to death.

Torriti, Jacopo (active 1290s). Italian mosaicist and painter. Nothing is known of his life, but he signed mosaics commissioned by Pope Nicholas IV for the apses of two churches in Rome, St John Lateran (c.1291), and S. Maria Maggiore (c.1295), and he must have been one of the leading contemporaries of *Cavallini. The mosaic in St John Lateran appears to have been a reworking of an earlier design and was reconstructed in the 19th century, so Torriti's style can best be assessed from the less restored mosaic in S. Maria Maggiore. Here, in the main scene of the *Coronation of the Virgin* and subsidiary scenes from the life of the Virgin, Torriti recaptures something of the vitality of late *antique mosaics; he was clearly influenced in his choice of colour by the pale delicate harmonies and silvery lights of the 5th-century mosaic on the triumphal arch of the same church. A number of frescos in the Upper Church of

S. Francesco, Assisi, have been attributed to Torriti because of their stylistic similarity to the S. Maria Maggiore mosaic.

Toulouse-Lautrec, Henri de (1864–1901). French painter, printmaker, and draughtsman, one of the most colourful figures in 19th-century art. The son of an outrageously eccentric nobleman, he grew up with a love of horses and sport, but as a result of inherited illness and two falls when he was in his early teens the bones in his legs atrophied and he became permanently stunted. (Accounts of his height vary, but he was certainly not the midget of popular imagination. He was about 5 ft (1.5 m) tall—above the minimum height for military service—but his head looked disproportionately large and he walked with difficulty. Lautrec was stoical about his condition, never mentioning it except in jest; his deformity did not prevent him from attracting women as beautiful as Suzanne *Valadon, and his courage in coming to terms with it helped to give him a hatred of any kind of pretence—a quality that emerges in the frankness of his art.) He showed an early talent for drawing (his father and one of his uncles were amateur artists) and in 1882 he began to study with *Bonnat. The following year he became a pupil of *Cormon, and in January 1884, aged 19, he was given an allowance and set up in a studio of his own in the Montmartre district of Paris, an area notorious for bohemianism and seedily glamorous nightlife. Almost all his work is taken from this world and his scenes of cafés, brothels, and nightclubs (notably the Moulin Rouge) have helped to create the popular image of fin-de-siècle Paris. He led a notoriously dissipated life, but he was always a dedicated professional artist, and it was a matter of pride that he kept his earnings in a separate bank account from his parental allowance (his work sold well, but he was constantly short of money because he was so extravagant). Even after a hard night's drinking he would arrive early at the printing workshop to supervise the production of his lithographs, and his output was very large considering his brief life.

Lautrec received a solid, traditional training with Bonnat and Cormon (two of the most renowned teachers of the day), and although his work often gives a wonderful feeling of spontaneity, it was in fact based on constant application as a draughtsman. In this he resembles *Degas, who was the *Impressionist he admired most. It was partly from him and partly from Japanese prints (see UKIYO-E) that Lautrec derived his striking use of oblique compositions, in which a scene is vividly observed as if in a sideways glance. Again like Degas, Lautrec was unconventional technically; he often painted on cardboard with very thin oil paint and he sometimes mixed normally separate media such as oil and pastel. However, whereas Degas had a reputation for aloofness, Lautrec was warm-hearted and his work is full of human sympathy. There is sometimes humour, but more often there are feelings of melancholy, disillusionment, or despair, especially in his brothel scenes. Prostitutes proved to be ideal models for him, as they were so unselfconscious in moving around naked or semi-naked, and he represented their lives with no attempt to glamorize, moralize, or sentimentalize. Lautrec sometimes lodged in brothels for weeks at a time and the prostitutes came to regard him as a friend. He concentrated on the tedious routine of their profession—waiting for clients, undergoing compulsory medical examinations, and so on—and he was particularly sensitive in depicting the lesbian relationships that often developed between them. A more extrovert side to his talents is seen in his celebrated poster designs, with which he achieved his greatest public success. Although he produced only about 30 posters (the first in 1891), he created such masterfully bold and arresting designs that he is almost universally regarded as the greatest of all artists in this field.

Suffering from alcoholism and syphilis, Lautrec became seriously ill in 1899 and he died two years later, aged 36. In 1922 his mother presented a large collection of his work to the museum in his native city of Albi, which was renamed the Musée Toulouse-Lautrec. The museum houses memorabilia as well as works of art, including Lautrec's walking stick, which ingeniously opens up to reveal a tiny glass and flask of brandy.

Tournier, Nicolas (1590–1638/9). French painter. Very little is known of his life and most of the attributions to him are speculative, but he seems to have been—with the exception of Georges de *La Tour—the most individual and sensitive of French *Caravaggesque painters. He was in Rome c.1619-26, then is recorded in Carcassonne in 1627 and in Toulouse from 1632. The works attributed to him in his Roman period are *genre scenes of music making, dice-playing, etc. (A Musical Party, City Art Mus., St Louis), but after he returned to France he concentrated on religious pictures. There are examples in the Louvre, Paris, and in the Musée des Augustins, Toulouse, including a huge, badly damaged Battle of Constantine influenced by *Piero della Francesca's treatment of the subject at Arezzo—this at a time when Piero was virtually forgotten. More typical of Tournier's paintings in the museum at Toulouse are the Lamentation and the Entombment, which show the grace and refinement of his style.

Towne, Francis (1739/40–1816). English landscape painter, primarily in watercolour. He spent most of his life in Exeter, where he earned a good living as a teacher, and his work was little known outside his locality, but he is now regarded as one of the most individual watercolourists of his day. His method of painting in flat *washes over a brown pen-and-ink outline was employed with a severe economy of means and he had an eye for geometrical structure that gives his pictures an affinity with those of certain 20th-century artists such as John *Nash. His best works include some done when he passed through Switzerland in 1781 returning from a visit to Italy. He also visited Wales and the Lake District.

Traini, Francesco (documented 1321–63?). Pisan painter. Only one work is certainly known to be by him—the signed *polyptych of St Dominic and Scenes from his Life (1345, Mus. Naz., Pisa). The most important works attributed to him are frescos in the Campo Santo in Pisa—the celebrated Triumph of Death, with accompanying scenes of the Last Judgement, Hell, and Legends of the Hermits. These, among the outstanding Italian paintings of the 14th century, were badly damaged by bombs in the Second World War, but this brought to light, by way of partial compensation, the beautiful *sinopie, which are now shown in the Museo delle Sinopie, Pisa. The frescos include many telling details of death's victims and have been seen as a reflection of the horrors of the Black Death of 1348, but some authorities consider them earlier and perhaps the work of the mysterious *Buffalmacco.

trecento (It.: '14th century'). See QUATTRO-CENTO.

Tretchikoff, Vladimir (1913–). Russian-born painter who settled in South Africa in 1946 and became a citizen of the country, one of the most financially successful but also one of the most critically reviled artists of the 20th century. Typically his pictures depict Oriental beauties (notably The Chinese Girl, 1952), African tribesmen and tribeswomen portrayed as the noble savage, or flowers—often he shows a single bloom, accompanied by tear-like drops of water and with titles such as The Weeping Rose. His enormous popular success has depended not only on his choice and treatment of subject, but also on his skilful marketing. As well as showing extensively in South Africa, he organized several tours of his work in Britain, Canada, and the USA between 1953 and 1973 (the peak period of his fame), exhibiting in major department stores rather than galleries. The paintings themselves were generally not for sale, but reproductions of them sold in vast quantities. Tretchikoff has been the subject of several books and documentary films, including one for the BBC. To most critics, however, his work is excruciatingly vulgar, and he has been dubbed the 'King of Kitsch'.

Tretyakov, Pavel (1832–98). Russian businessman and art collector. He made a fortune in the textile industry and devoted much of it to his passion for art. Initially he bought Western works, but he soon came to specialize in Russian art and by 1860 he had conceived the idea of a national museum; in that year he wrote, 'Being a true and ardent lover of painting, I could not think of anything better than to set up a repository of works of art that would benefit many, please everyone, and be accessible to all.' He wanted the collection to be representative, so he bought all kinds of pictures, not merely ones that appealed to him personally; he also commissioned many contemporary artists to produce work (he gave much encouragement and assistance to the *Wanderers). In 1874 his collection was opened to the public in a specially built gallery next to his Moscow mansion. After the death of his younger brother **Sergei** (1834–92), also an art lover, Tretyakov decided to present their combined collections to the city of Moscow; the reformed gallery opened in 1893 as the Pavel and Sergei Tretyakov Moscow City Art Gallery. After Tretyakov's death, his mansion was incorporated in the gallery, the structures being unified by a new façade (1902) designed by Viktor *Vasnetsov in a picturesque 'old Russian' style. Following the 1917 revolution, the gallery was declared national property and renamed the State Tretyakov Gallery in 1918. Up to this time there had been a few foreign works in the collection, but these were now dispersed and it became devoted exclusively to Russian art. With the addition of works confiscated after the revolution, the collection grew to enormous size. A new wing was added in the 1930s, and in 1985–95 a huge new museum was built, incorporating the much-loved Vasnetsov façade into the structure. Modern works (from the time of the 1917 revolution) have been transferred to the New Tretyakov Gallery, specially built for this purpose in Gorky Park. Between them, the two galleries contain more than 100,000 works, mainly paintings and graphic art, although there is also, for example, a good collection of jewellery.

Trevisani, Francesco (1656–1746). Italian painter, trained in Venice and active in Rome from about 1678. After the death of *Maratta in 1713, he succeeded him as 'the most famous, prosperous and prolific painter in Rome, with connections all over Europe' (Ellis *Waterhouse). His output included frescos, altarpieces, devotional works, mythological scenes, and portraits, including several of British visitors. His style was similar to Maratta's, but sweeter and more colourful.

triptych. A picture or carving consisting of three parts, usually a central panel flanked by wings (or folding shutters). As with the *diptych, the folding triptych lent itself to the making of portable altarpieces; the delicate inner surfaces were protected by the outer leaves, although these might be painted or carved on their outer as well as their inner surfaces. Some triptychs, however, are very large, for example the two

by *Rubens in Antwerp Cathedral. *See also* POLYPTYCH.

Tristán, Luis (*c*.1585–1624). Spanish painter, active mainly in Toledo, where he was a pupil of El *Greco *c*.1603–6. After spending some time in Italy he was back in Toledo by 1613, and the death of El Greco the following year left him the leading painter in the city. His style (notably his characteristically elongated proportions) owes much to the master, but Tristán is more sober, marking the transition from *Mannerism to a more naturalistic approach (*Adoration of the Shepherds*, 1620, Fitzwilliam Mus., Cambridge).

trompe-l'œil (Fr.: 'deceives the eye'). Term applied to a painting (or a detail of one) that is intended to deceive the spectator (if only briefly) into thinking that it is a real object rather than a two-dimensional representation of it. Such virtuoso displays of skill often have a humorous intent, and anecdotes of almost miraculous feats of trompe-l'œil are typical of periods in which *naturalism has been cultivated, such as the *Classical age in Greece (*see* PARRHASIUS) and the Italian *Renaissance. *Vasari, for example, records that the young *Giotto tricked his master *Cimabue by painting on the nose of a figure on which he was engaged 'a fly so lifelike that when Cimabue returned to carry on with his work he tried several times to brush it off with his hand, under the impression that it was real, before he realized his mistake'. Petrus *Christus's *Portrait of a Carthusian* (*c*.1446, Met. Mus., New York) is an example of a painting with such a trompe-l'œil fly, here on a painted ledge at the bottom of the picture, rather than on the sitter's nose. Sometimes the term 'trompe-l'œil' is used loosely to refer to any type of pictorial illusionism (for example *quadratura), but such usage deprives a useful term of its precision.

Troost, Cornelis (1696–1750). Dutch painter, printmaker, and draughtsman, active mainly in his native Amsterdam, the outstanding Dutch artist of the 18th century. He made his name with a lively group portrait of the *Amsterdam Inspectors of the Collegium Medicum* (1724, Rijksmuseum, Amsterdam) and continued to enjoy success as a formal portraitist and painter of *conversation pieces. However, he painted numerous other types of picture, including theatrical subjects (he had close connections with the theatre and acted professionally in his youth). His most famous work—made in his favourite technique of pastel and water-colour—is a series of five pictures entitled *NELRI* (1740, Mauritshuis, The Hague); the name is derived from the first letters of the Latin inscriptions that accompany the five views of the activities of a group of men during the night of a reunion. Troost has been described as 'the Dutch *Hogarth', but unlike his great English contemporary, he is a humorist without an ulterior motive; he never attempted to teach or preach.

Troy, Jean-François de (1679–1752). French painter and tapestry designer. His successful career was based initially on large historical and allegorical compositions (*Time Unveiling Truth*, 1733, NG, London), but he is now most highly regarded for his smaller and more spirited scenes of elegant social life. They are among the best of those that rode on the wave of *Watteau's success—indeed *The Alarm* (1723, V&A, London) was attributed to Watteau in the 19th century. In 1738 de Troy was appointed director of the French Academy in Rome, and he spent the rest of his life there. He was one of a family of painters, his father and teacher, **François de Troy** (1645–1730), being a successful painter of fashionable portraits and director of the Académie Royale from 1708 to 1711.

Troyon, Constant (1810–65). French painter. He was born in Sèvres and began his career as a porcelain decorator (the family trade) at the famous factory there. In the 1830s, however, he took up landscape painting, and became one of the leading figures of the *Barbizon School. He visited Holland in 1847, and the influence of *Cuyp and *Potter is seen in his fondness for including cows in his pictures. Late in his career he turned to seascapes, the freshness and freedom of his work influencing *Boudin and *Monet in this genre. Troyon was a prolific and internationally successful painter, and his work is in many public collections in France and elsewhere.

Trübner, Wilhelm. *See* SEZESSION.

Trumbull, John (1756–1843). American painter. Trumbull fought in the American War of Independence (for a time he was aide-de-camp to George Washington) and his career was devoted mainly to depicting the outstanding events and personalities of the Revolution. He was strongly influenced by Benjamin *West, with whom he studied in London (he made several visits there, and during the first of them, 1780–3, was imprisoned in reprisal for the hanging of a British agent in America). In 1817 he became president of the American Academy of Fine Arts in New York, but his tyrannical attitude, especially towards young painters, led to many members leaving to set up the *National Academy of Design in 1825. His pictures did not sell well, so in 1831 he gave those in his studio to Yale University Art Gallery in exchange for an annuity. The most famous of his works there, and one of the most reproduced images in American art, is *The Declaration of Independence* (1786–97), in which most of the portraits were painted from life. His larger works are usually fairly stodgy, but his smaller pictures and sketches can be much livelier. Trumbull, who died an embittered old man, published an autobiography in 1841.

truth to material(s). A belief that the form of a work of art should be inseparably related to the material in which it is made. The phrase was much used in aesthetic discussions in the 1930s and is particularly associated with Henry *Moore, who in *Unit One* (1934) wrote that 'Each material has its own individual qualities ... Stone, for example, is hard and concentrated and should not be falsified to look like soft flesh ... It should keep its hard tense stoniness.' Moore later admitted that the idea of truth to materials had become a fetish and in 1951 he conceded that it should not be made into a criterion of value, 'otherwise a snowman made by a child would have to be praised at the expense of a *Rodin or a *Bernini' (commenting on the elaborate curls in the wig of his bust of Louis XIV, Bernini—according to a contemporary report—said that it was 'no easy thing to attain that lightness in the hair to which he aspired, for he had to struggle against the contrary nature of the material').

Tucker, William (1935–). British-born abstract sculptor, writer on art, and teacher who settled in the USA in 1976 and later became an American citizen. In 1965 he was among the artists included in the *New Generation exhibition at the Whitechapel Art Gallery, London, which marked the emergence of a new British sculptural avant-garde inspired by his teacher Anthony *Caro. His work is in various materials and often makes striking use of colour. In 1974 he published *The Language of Sculpture* and in 1975 he organized a major Arts Council exhibition at the Hayward Gallery, London, entitled 'The Condition of Sculpture'.

Tuke, Henry Scott (1858–1929). British painter. He studied at the *Slade School, 1875–80, then in Italy and Paris, where he was strongly influenced by contemporary French *plein-air painting. Tuke had known and loved Cornwall since childhood and after he returned to England in 1883 he settled there, living first at *Newlyn and then from 1885 in a cottage near Falmouth. His favourite subject—which he made his own—was nude boys in a sunlit atmosphere against a background of sea or shore. At first the freshness of these works—so different to the frigid studio nudes to which the public was accustomed—caused prudish objections (Tuke was a founder member of the *New English Art Club in 1886 and the sight of one of his paintings caused the dealer Martin Colnaghi to withdraw his financial backing for the group's first exhibition). However, they soon became favourites with the public and are now regarded as being among the finest and most individual works of English *Impressionism. Tuke also painted portraits throughout his life.

Tura, Cosimo (or **Cosmè**) (c.1430–95). Italian painter, the first major artist of the Ferrarese School. Almost all his career was spent in Ferrara, where he worked for the *Este family from 1452 and was appointed court painter in 1458. His sculptural figure style was influenced by *Mantegna and also by *Piero della Francesca (who worked in Ferrara in the 1440s), but its feverish, metallic quality is highly distinctive. Most of his surviving work is religious, including two huge shutters (1469) for the organ of Ferrara Cathedral, now in the Cathedral Museum: they represent the Annunciation and 'St George and the Princess'. Good examples of his work on a smaller scale are in the National Gallery, London. Tura was an important influence on the other two major painters of the 15th-century Ferrarese School—*Cossa and *Roberti. The latter replaced him as court painter in 1486 and Tura died poor.

Turnbull, William (1922–). British sculptor and painter. After serving as an RAF pilot in the Second World War he studied at the *Slade School, 1946–8, then in 1948–50 lived in Paris, where he saw a good deal of his fellow Scot and Slade student *Paolozzi and met such illustrious figures as *Brancusi and *Giacometti. As a sculptor Turnbull moved from *Surrealistic and primitivist works to painted steel geometrical constructions in the manner of *Caro. As a painter he was one of the first British artists to work in a style similar to that of the American *Colour Field Painters.

Turner, John Doman. *See* CAMDEN TOWN GROUP.

Turner, J. M. W. (Joseph Mallord William) (1775–1851). English painter, one of the greatest figures in the history of landscape painting. His family called him Bill or William, but he is now invariably known as J. M. W. Turner (which is how he usually signed his pictures). Precociously gifted, he became a student at the *Royal Academy Schools in 1789 and first exhibited a watercolour at the Academy in 1790, when he was only 15. He studied regularly at the Academy until 1793, and during this time also had lessons from Thomas Malton (1748–1804), a topographical watercolourist who specialized in neat and detailed town views. From 1791 he began making regular sketching tours in various parts of Britain, producing many drawings of *Picturesque views and architectural subjects that he later used as the basis of watercolours or sold to engravers. At this time his work was more polished but less poetic than that of his friend *Girtin. Initially he painted only in watercolour, but in 1796 he first exhibited an oil at the Academy, *Fishermen at Sea* (Tate, London). Only three years later, in 1799, he was elected an Associate of the Royal Academy and in 1802, two months before his twenty-seventh birthday, he became the second-youngest person ever elected a full Academician (only *Lawrence had achieved the distinction at a younger age). His career also flourished financially, for he was hardworking, a good businessman, and frugal by nature (he lived rather squalidly, but he was not miserly or ungenerous, as is sometimes maintained).

From early in his career Turner was aware of his place in the tradition of landscape painting and he often produced works in homage to (or rivalry with) his great predecessors such as *Claude (whom he particularly revered) and Willem van de *Velde the Younger. However, he soon began to paint more original pictures in which he depicted the violence of nature in powerful *Romantic fashion. *The Shipwreck* (1805, Tate) was one of his first works in this vein, and one of the most celebrated is *Snow Storm: Hannibal and his Army Crossing the Alps* (1812, Tate), of which a contemporary newspaper (the *Examiner*) wrote: 'This is a performance that classes Mr Turner in the highest rank of landscape painters...the moral and physical elements are here in powerful unison blended by a most masterly hand, awakening emotions of awe and grandeur.' During these years, however, he continued exhibiting more conventional pictures and still earned a good deal of his large income through work for engravers. His most ambitious engraving project was his *Liber Studiorum* (Book of Studies), conceived in emulation of Claude's *Liber Veritatis* and intended to show the range of his own work; between 1807 and 1819 he issued 71 of a projected 100 plates.

Turner made his first journey to the Continent in 1802, during a temporary peace in the war with France, visiting Paris like so many other artists to see pictures looted by Napoleon, which were then on exhibition. From Paris he travelled on to Switzerland. The resumption of war made Continental travel impossible for more than a decade, and Turner did not go abroad again until 1817, when he visited Belgium, Holland, and the Rhine. He first visited Italy two years later, and from then until 1845 made fairly regular journeys abroad (including three more to Italy, the last in 1840). Unlike his contemporary *Constable, who concentrated on painting the places he knew best, Turner was inspired to a great extent by what he saw on his travels (he lived in London all his life, but the city appears fairly infrequently in his paintings). The mountains and lakes of Switzerland and the haunting beauty of Venice, in particular, provided him with an enduring fund of sub-jects. He was inspired by history (especially ancient history) and literature as well as nature. Many of the paintings he exhibited at the Royal Academy were accompanied by verses printed in the catalogue, and from 1800 he added lines of poetry he had composed himself.

From the 1830s Turner's painting became increasingly personal and free, with detail subordinated to general effects of colour and light. To many critics it was incomprehensible, and one of his most celebrated pictures—*Snow Storm: Steam-Boat off a Harbour's Mouth* (1842, Tate)—is said to have been dismissed as 'soapsuds and whitewash'. Turner's wealth and status allowed him to remain indifferent to such attacks, and he continued to have many admirers, including some who regarded him as the outstanding genius of the day. His most important patron was the 3rd Earl of Egremont (1751–1837), who was unusual among collectors of the time in buying contemporary British art (sculpture as well as painting) on a large scale. Turner had a studio at Petworth, Egremont's country house in Sussex, and several of his paintings are still to be seen there (although their ownership was transferred to the Tate Gallery in 1984). Turner's other great champion was the young *Ruskin, who first met him in 1840 and wrote eloquently of him in the first volume of *Modern Painters*, published in 1843. By this time some of Turner's compositions were almost abstract, the forms dissolved in a haze of light and colour, the paint so delicate it appears almost to have been floated onto the canvas: 'He seems to paint with tinted steam, so evanescent and so airy', wrote Constable. Turner's originality lay not only in such handling of colour and light, but also in his use of the power, beauty, and mystery of nature to express deep human concerns. For example, *The Fighting Temeraire* (1839, NG, London), showing a ship that had fought at Trafalgar being towed to the breaker's yard, is not just a beautiful marine scene, but also a poignant elegy for a passing era.

For many years Turner was a prominent figure at the Royal Academy (he was professor of perspective 1807–38 and in 1845–6 he took over the president's duties when Sir Martin Archer *Shee was ill). However, he always carefully guarded his private life and in his later years he became more and more of a recluse, sometimes calling himself Mr Booth (assuming the name of his mistress Sophia Booth; he never married but had two long-term relationships, both with widows, and is rumoured to have fathered several children). After his death, Ruskin (his executor) destroyed many erotic drawings that he found among his works, thinking that they tainted his hero's memory. In his will Turner left plans for disposing of his fortune (he wanted to found an almshouse for 'poor and decayed male artists') and for the creation of a special gallery at the National Gallery to display certain of his paintings (he had a huge stock of his work, including not only pictures that had never been sold, but also favourite paintings that he had bought back at auction). However, the will was contested by longforgotten cousins (one of whom had a lawyer son with the splendidly Dickensian name of Jabez Tepper), and they won Turner's money in 1856; at the same time the Court of Chancery awarded all the works remaining in his possession at his death to the National Gallery—about 300 oils and 19,000 drawings and watercolours. Most of these are now in the Clore Gallery at Tate Britain, but a few of Turner's most famous oils remain in the National Gallery.

Turner Prize. An annual prize of £25,000 for British achievement in the visual arts, named after J. M. W. *Turner. It was established in 1984 by the Patrons of New Art, a body founded two years earlier (as part of the Friends of the Tate Gallery) to encourage the collection of contemporary art. The regulations have changed somewhat since the prize was inaugurated. Originally it was awarded for 'the greatest contribution to art in Britain in the previous twelve months' and was open to critics and administrators (who were shortlisted but never won) as well as artists; since 1991 those eligible are British artists under the age of 50 who have had 'an outstanding exhibition or other presentation of their work' in the previous twelve months. The original sponsors, Drexel Burnham Lambert, suffered a financial collapse in 1990 and the prize was suspended that year; since then it has been sponsored by Channel 4 Television, which broadcasts the award ceremony live from

Tate Britain. The director of the Tate is on the jury that makes the award. Like the Booker Prize in literature, the Turner Prize attracts a great deal of publicity, but much of this attention has been expressed as damning criticism, as it is regarded by many as showcasing all that is most pretentious and self-regarding in contemporary art. The winners of the prize have been: 1984, Malcolm *Morley; 1985, Howard *Hodgkin; 1986, *Gilbert & George; 1987, Richard Deacon (1949–); 1988, Tony Cragg (1949–); 1989, Richard *Long; 1990, prize suspended; 1991, Anish *Kapoor; 1992, Grenville Davey (1961–); 1993, Rachel *Whiteread; 1994, Antony *Gormley; 1995, Damien *Hirst; 1996, Douglas Gordon (1967–); 1997, Gillian Wearing (1963–); 1998, Chris Ofili (1968–); 1999, Steve McQueen (1969–); 2000, Wolfgang Tillmans (1968–); 2001, Martin Creed (1968–); 2002, Keith Tyson (1969–); 2003, Grayson Perry (1960–); 2004, Jeremy Deller (1966–).

turpentine. A *resinous liquid exuded from various species of pine tree, which in its distilled form ('spirits of turpentine') has been used since the 15th century as a *diluent, or thinner, for *oil paint.

Turrell, James. *See* LAND ART.

Twombly, Cy (1928–). American abstract painter and draughtsman. His distinctive style is characterized by apparently random scrawls and scribbles on white or black grounds. In his rejection of traditional ideas of composition he shows an affinity with the *all-over style initiated by Jackson *Pollock, though Twombly's work is looser than that of Pollock. In 1957 he settled in Rome.

typology. In Christian *iconography a system whereby figures and scenes from the Old Testament were thought of as prefiguring those of the New Testament. It became the custom in biblical illustration for Old Testament 'types' to be juxtaposed with or subordinated to New Testament 'antitypes', to demonstrate visually that the promise of the Old Testament was fulfilled in the New. Thus Abraham's willingness to sacrifice his son Isaac was seen as foreshadowing God's sacrifice of Christ, and David was seen as a 'type' of Christ, his fight with Goliath prefiguring Christ's struggle with Satan. Occasionally classical myths or other secular sources were also accepted as types. Typological illustration is found in virtually every field of visual art throughout the Middle Ages (the earliest examples date from the 3rd cen- tury), and occasionally occurs afterwards. It reached a wide popular audience in *block books.

Tyson, Keith. *See* TURNER PRIZE.

Tzara, Tristan. *See* DADA.

Uccello, Paolo (Paolo di Dono) (c.1397–1475). Florentine painter, one of the most distinctive artists of the early *Renaissance. *Vasari says he was called 'Uccello' (which means 'bird') because he loved animals, and birds in particular, and he seems to have been regarded as something of an eccentric. He is first documented c.1412 as one of *Ghiberti's apprentices, but he is not known to have worked as a sculptor. From 1425 to 1427 he is recorded in Venice, where he worked as a mosaicist at St Mark's, but nothing survives there that can be certainly associated with him. By 1431 he was back in Florence, where he spent most of the rest of his life (he worked in Padua, 1444–5, and in Urbino, 1465–8). In 1436 he painted his first dated surviving work—a huge fresco in Florence Cathedral depicting an equestrian statue, a monument to the English condottiere Sir John Hawkwood (d. 1394). It demonstrated the fascination with *perspective that was central to his style. His two other surviving large-scale works are a series of poorly preserved frescos on Old Testament themes (probably 1430s and 1440s) in the 'Green Cloister' of S. Maria Novella, Florence, and the *Battle of San Romano* (c.1455), a series of three panels depicting a minor Florentine victory against the Sienese in 1432. The panels formed part of a decorative scheme in the Palazzo *Medici but they are now separated, with one each in the National Gallery, London; the Louvre, Paris; and the Uffizi, Florence. Uccello's other works include the decoration of the clock-face and designs for stained-glass windows in Florence Cathedral, and two enchanting paintings that are generally considered to date from late in his career—*St George and the Dragon* (NG, London), one of the earliest known Italian paintings on canvas, and *The Hunt in the Forest* (Ashmolean Mus., Oxford). In spite of his major commissions in Florence Cathedral, his career was not particularly successful in worldly terms: Vasari says that 'he came to live a hermit's life', and in his tax return of 1469 Uccello described himself as 'old without means of livelihood ...and unable to work'.

Uccello was long regarded more as a curiosity than a serious artist (in 1896 *Berenson dismissed him as a mathematician rather than a painter and said that artistically he 'accomplished nothing'); however, he is now one of the best-loved painters of his time, admired for the power and vigour of his forms, the beauty of his colouring, and his lively and witty imagination. His work presents a striking—and often captivating—combination of two seemingly opposing stylistic currents: the decorative tradition of *International Gothic and the scientific involvement with perspective of the early Renaissance. Vasari maintained that Uccello wasted his time 'on the finer points of perspective' and presents him as an amiable fanatic who worked into the night and when told to come to bed by his wife would reply: 'What a sweet mistress is this perspective!' He undoubtedly took his enthusiasm to extraordinary lengths (in the *Battle of San Romano* the broken weapons and even the corpses recede neatly in accordance with the perspective scheme), but his effects were appropriate to his subjects and to the decorative charm of his pictures rather than mere technical exercises. In *The Hunt in the Forest*, for example, he creates not only an atmosphere of fairy-tale romance, but also, through the way in which the horses and dogs move swiftly back into space, an exhilarating sense of darting energy. Uccello's name became so identified with the subject of perspective that he was often said to have invented it: *Ruskin, for example, wrote in a letter to Kate *Greenaway, 'I believe the perfection of perspective is only recent. It was first applied in Italian art by Paul Uccello. He went off his head with love of perspective.'

Uden, Lucas van (1595–1672). Flemish landscape painter and engraver, active mainly in his native Antwerp. The longstanding tradition that he worked in *Rubens's studio and painted landscape backgrounds for him is now discredited, but he was certainly strongly influenced by the master. His pictures are often large and have something of Rubens's sweep and richness. The figures were often added by other artists.

Udine, Giovanni da (1487–1561/4). Italian painter, stuccoist, and architect, born at Udine near Venice. He was one of *Raphael's leading assistants in Rome and is chiefly important for his role in reviving antique techniques of *stucco and the ancient taste for *grotesques, inspired by archaeological discoveries. His light and graceful style, seen best in the Vatican Loggie (1517–19), was imitated all over Europe, particularly by *Neoclassical designers. In 1522 he returned to Udine; he spent most of the rest of his life there, but he had further sojourns in Rome (where he died) and also worked in Florence and Venice.

Uffizi, Florence. The chief public gallery of Florence. The nucleus of the collection derives from the collections of the *Medici family, and the Uffizi Palace was begun by *Vasari in 1560 for Cosimo I de' Medici, Grand Duke of Tuscany. It originally housed government offices (Italian *uffizi*), hence the building's name. In 1565 Vasari built a corridor over the Ponte Vecchio connecting the Uffizi with the *Pitti Palace. The Uffizi was completed in about 1580 and soon afterwards Francesco I de' Medici (Cosimo's son) had part of it remodelled as gallery space in which to display the family collections. Subsequently the building has been much altered, enlarged, and restored (it was damaged in the Second World War, by flooding in 1966, and by a terrorist bomb in 1993), but it remains the best testimony to Vasari's skill as an architect. The last of the Medici line, Anna Maria Luisa, presented the collections to the city of Florence in 1737, and the transformation of the Uffizi into a public gallery was largely the work of Grand Duke Pietro Leopoldo (later the emperor Leopold II; *see* HABSBURG), who reigned 1765–90. He reorganized the collections to make them more coherent, appointed scholarly staff (including *Lanzi) to care for them, and allowed public visiting free of charge. In the 19th century the Uffizi was again radically reorganized. Much archaeological material was placed in the Museo Archeologico, while the medieval and *Renaissance sculpture and the rich collection of *applied art were transferred to the *Bargello. The Uffizi picture collection on the other hand was enriched by early Italian works gained from suppressions of churches and monasteries and confiscations of religious property. Although it is primarily famous for its incomparable representation of Florentine Renaissance painting, the Uffizi also has outstanding works from other Italian and non-Italian schools (for example, Hugo van der *Goes's Portinari Altarpiece) and important examples of *antique sculpture. The collection of prints and drawings in the Gabinetto dei Disegni e Stampe is one of the finest in the world, and the gallery of artists' self-portraits, begun by Cardinal Leopoldo de' Medici in the 17th century, is unrivalled.

Ugo da Carpi (d. 1532). Italian printmaker, a pioneer of the *chiaroscuro woodcut. He was born at Carpi in Emilia and worked in Venice, Rome, and elsewhere. In 1516 he requested from the Venetian senate a patent for his method 'of making from woodcuts prints that seem as though painted', and although there are German examples earlier than any known by Ugo, he may have discovered the technique independently. Certainly his prints achieve their pictorial effect better than those of the Germans. They are often based on designs by *Raphael and *Parmigianino.

Ugolino di Nerio (active 1317–27). Sienese painter, a close follower of *Duccio. His only certain work is a large *polyptych painted for the high altar of S. Croce, Florence; it formerly bore the signature 'Ugolino da Siena', but this has disappeared. The altarpiece was dismantled in the 16th century and is now widely dispersed; several panels are in the National Gallery, London. *Vasari says Ugolino painted 'many pictures and chapels in all parts of Italy' and several paintings are attributed to him on stylistic grounds. His style was charming, but must have been something of an anachronism in the Florence of *Giotto's day. In the first edition of the *Lives* Vasari says he died in 1339; in the second edition he gives the date as 1349.

Uhde, Wilhelm (1874–1947). German collector, dealer, and writer on art, active mainly in France. After studying in Munich and Florence, he settled in Paris in 1904 and by the following year he was buying pictures by *Picasso and *Braque at a time when these artists were practically unknown. Uhde was also one of the first to discover Henri *Rousseau; he published the first monograph on him in 1910 and in 1912 organized the first retrospective exhibition of his work. Subsequently he was best known for discovering and encouraging other *naive artists, such as *Bombois and *Séraphine.

Ukiyo-e (Jap.: 'pictures of the floating world'). Term applied to the dominant movement in Japanese art of the 17th to the 19th century. It refers to the subjects from everyday life, with its ever-shifting fashions, favoured by printmakers in this period. Typical subjects were theatre scenes, actors in well-known roles, and prostitutes and bathhouse girls. Japanese prints began arriving in European ports in the 1850s (*Monet bought one in Le Havre in 1856) and greatly influenced avant-garde French artists, to whom their flat decorative colour and expressive pattern came as a revelation.

Underwood, Leon (1890–1975). British sculptor, painter, printmaker, teacher, and writer. A versatile and original figure, Underwood was out of sympathy with the main trends of modernism, describing abstraction as 'artfully making emptiness less conspicuous'. Nevertheless, from the 1960s critics began to speak of him as the 'father of modern sculpture in Britain', in view of the streamlined stylized forms of his stone carvings and bronzes in the 1920s and 1930s and the influence of his teaching. He taught at the *Royal College of Art (where Henry *Moore was among his pupils) from 1920 to 1923, resigning after an argument with William *Rothenstein, and at his own Brook Green School in Hammersmith, which he opened in 1921 and ran intermittently until 1938. Underwood travelled widely and wrote several books, notably on African art. He illustrated his books (and a few by other authors) with etchings and woodcuts. His painting, which was sometimes influenced by primitive art, was generally less interesting than his sculpture.

Unit One. A group of avant-garde British artists formed in 1933, its members including Barbara *Hepworth, Henry *Moore, Paul *Nash, and Ben *Nicholson. The group held one exhibition, in London in 1933 (it toured to six provincial venues in 1934–5), and published a book, *Unit One: The Modern Movement*

in English Architecture, Painting and Sculpture, edited by Herbert *Read, in 1934. In the introduction to this volume (which was originally intended as the first of a series), Read explained that the name was chosen because 'though as persons, each artist is a *unit*, in the social structure they must, to the extent of their common interests be *one*'. The group had no common doctrine or programme and was breaking up by 1935. Despite its short life, however, it made a considerable impact on British art of the 1930s, helping to promote abstraction and *Surrealism.

Urban VIII, Pope. *See* BARBERINI.

Utrillo, Maurice (1883–1955). French painter. The illegitimate son of Suzanne *Valadon, he took his surname from the Spanish painter Miguel Utrillo (1862–1934), who legally recognized him as his son in order to help him (his real father—according to some sources—was *Puvis de Chavannes, who was 40 years older than Valadon). He began to paint in 1902 at the urging of his mother, who hoped that it would remedy the alcoholism to which he had been a victim since his boyhood. Valadon gave him his first lessons, but he was largely self-taught. He had a successful joint exhibition with his mother in 1923, and subsequently he became prosperous and critically acclaimed. However, he continued to be an alcoholic (in 1934 the Tate Gallery wrongly said that he had died of drink that year, thus bringing on the Trustees' heads a libel suit, settled out of court). In his later years he devoted as much time to religious devotions as to painting. Utrillo was highly prolific, painting mainly street scenes in Montmartre. The period from about 1910 to 1916 is known as his 'white period' because of the predominance of milky or chalky tones in his pictures, and it is generally agreed that he did his best paintings during this time. They subtly convey solitude and emotional emptiness and have a delicate feeling for tone and atmosphere, even though he often worked from postcards. His later work is livelier but less touching. Utrillo's work is in many museums and (no doubt because of the deceptive simplicity of his paintings) he is among the most forged of modern artists.

Uytewael, Joachim. *See* WTEWAEL.

V

Valadon, Suzanne (1865–1938). French painter. As a girl she worked as a circus acrobat, but had to abandon this after a fall and then became an artists' model and the reigning beauty of Montmartre. The artists she posed for included *Renoir, *Puvis de Chavannes, and *Toulouse-Lautrec (each of whom numbered among her lovers). Lautrec brought her drawings to the attention of *Degas, who encouraged her to develop her artistic talent and she became a full-time painter in 1896. Valadon owed little to formal training or to the influence of the artists with whom she associated and her painting has a fresh and personal vision. Her subjects included portraits and still lifes, but she was at her best in figure paintings, which often have a splendid earthy vigour and a striking use of bold contour and flat colour. After the First World War she achieved critical and financial success, but in her final years her health was undermined by the excesses of her life. Maurice *Utrillo was her son.

Valckenborch. Family of Netherlandish landscape and *genre painters, the most important members of which were the brothers **Lucas I** (c.1535–97) and **Marten I** (1534–1612). Both of them began their careers in Malines and ended them in Frankfurt, where they ran a flourishing workshop together (in between their paths diverged as their lives were disrupted by war and religious persecution). They worked in the tradition of Pieter *Bruegel, characteristic subjects including winter landscapes and the Tower of Babel.

Valdés Leal, Juan de (1622–90). Spanish painter and etcher, born and mainly active in Seville. He settled there permanently in 1656 after spending part of his early career in Cordova, and following *Murillo's death in 1682 he was the leading artist in the city. Like Murillo, he was primarily a religious painter, but he was very different in style and approach. He had a penchant for macabre or grotesque subject matter, and his style is characterized by feverish excitability, with a vivid sense of movement, brilliant colouring, and dramatic lighting. His most celebrated works are two powerful allegories of Death (1670–2) in the Hospital de la Caridad, Seville: In ictu oculi (In the Twinkling of an Eye), showing a skeleton snuffing out the flame of life and trampling on the attributes of earthly achievement; and Finis gloriae mundi (The End of Worldly Glory), depicting rotting corpses in a crypt. He also *polychromed *Roldán's sculpture on the high altar in the Caridad. Several other members of his family were artists.

Valenciennes, Pierre-Henri de (1750–1819). French landscape painter. Between 1769 and 1785 he spent several years in Italy, and his style was influenced most notably by Nicolas *Poussin. He became a leading upholder of the classical tradition in landscape painting and he argued that landscape should be considered equal in status to *history painting. However, although his finished pictures were in a grand, highly composed style, he was also a leading exponent of the oil sketch; he thought that direct study from nature was a prerequisite for his formal works. His ideas were promoted not only through his paintings, but also through his book Élémens de perspective pratique (1800) and through his teaching at the École des *Beaux-Arts in Paris, where he became a professor in 1812.

Valentin, Moïse (also called **Le Valentin** and **Valentin de Boulogne**) (c.1591–1632). French *Caravaggesque painter active in Rome for all his known career (he is first securely documented there in 1620 but probably arrived appreciably earlier). His life is obscure; the name 'Moïse' (the French form of Moses) by which he was called was not his Christian name (which is unknown) but a corruption of the Italian form of 'monsieur'. He did, however, have one major public commission—the Martyrdom of St Processus and St Martinian (1629–30, Pinacoteca, Vatican), painted for St Peter's as a pendant to *Poussin's Martyrdom of St Erasmus. About eighty works are attributed to him. They vary in subject—religious, mythological, and *genre scenes and portraits—but the same models often seem to reappear in them, and all his work is marked by an impressively solemn, at times melancholic, dignity. He was one of the best of Caravaggio's followers and one of the most dedicated, still painting in his style when it had gone out of fashion. *Baglione says that he died after taking a cold bath in a fountain following a drinking bout; his death was much lamented in Rome's artistic community.

Valentiner, William (1880–1958). German-American art historian, one of the foremost connoisseurs of Dutch painting, on which he published numerous books. From 1906 to 1908 he worked at the Kaiser-Friedrich Museum, Berlin, under *Bode, then moved to the *Metropolitan Museum in New York, where one of his innovations was to ban the attendants from smoking cigars while they were on duty. He stayed there until 1914, then served in the German army in the First World War. At this time he knew various German *Expressionist artists, notably *Schmidt-Rottluff, and helped to promote their work in the USA. In 1921 Valentiner began working at the Detroit Institute of Arts, of which he was director from 1924 to 1945 and where he commissioned murals from Diego *Rivera. He was then director of the County Museum of Art in Los Angeles (1946–54) and the first director of the North Carolina Museum at Raleigh (1955–8). Valentiner also founded the *Art Quarterly* (1938), a leading scholarly journal.

Valette, Adolphe. *See* LOWRY.

Vallotton, Félix (1865–1925). Swiss-born painter, printmaker, illustrator, sculptor, and writer who settled in Paris in 1882 and became a French citizen in 1900. In the 1890s he worked a good deal in woodcut, and apart from *Gauguin he was the most important French pioneer of the revival of this medium. During the same period he exhibited with the *Nabis (he was a friend of *Bonnard and *Vuillard). After the turn of the century he concentrated on painting; in his canvases he took over something of the simplifications of form and sharp contrasts between blocks of light and shadow that characterize his woodcuts. His subjects included landscapes, portraits, nudes, and interiors. He wrote art criticism and also the novel *La Vie meurtrière* (posthumously published, 1930), which is illustrated by himself.

Vanderbank, John (1694–1739). English painter and book illustrator of Dutch extraction. He had a considerable practice as a portraitist in the years immediately succeeding the death of *Kneller, and *Vertue says he started the fashion for depicting ladies in *Rubens costume. His best work is vigorous, but often marred by sloppy handling. He was one of the founders of the *St Martin's Lane Academy in 1720.

Vanderlyn, John (1775–1852). American painter, active mainly in or near New York. Between 1796 and 1815 he lived in Europe (apart from brief visits to America) and his style was closer to mainstream *Neoclassicism and *Romanticism than that of almost any other American painter of his generation. He was the first American painter to study in Paris and also worked in Rome. His best-known painting is *Ariadne Asleep on Naxos* (1812–14, Pennsylvania Academy of the Fine Arts, Philadelphia), a reclining figure in the tradition of the Venuses of *Giorgione and *Titian that is regarded as the finest American nude before *Eakins. Although such works won him considerable renown in France, he was much less successful in America, where he worked mainly as a portraitist, and he died poor and embittered.

vanitas (Lat.: 'vanity' or 'emptiness'). A type of still-life picture depicting an object or collection of objects symbolizing the brevity of life and the transience of all earthly pleasures and achievements. Typical motifs are a skull, an hourglass, a watch, a smoking candle, and a flower losing its petals. Such paintings were especially popular in Dutch and Spanish art of the 17th century. At this time vanitas elements were often found in portraits and figure paintings as well as in pure still lifes.

Vanloo, Carle. *See* LOO.

Vantongerloo, Georges (1886–1965). Belgian sculptor, painter, architect, and writer on art, active mainly in France, one of the pioneers of a mathematical approach to abstract art. In 1917 he joined the De *Stijl group and turned from the conventionally naturalistic style he had previously practised to abstract sculptures in which he applied the principles of *Neo-Plasticism to three dimensions (*Interrelation of Volumes*, 1919, Tate, London). From 1919 to 1927 he lived in the French Riviera resort of Menton and then for the rest of his life in Paris, where he was a member of *Cercle et Carré and one of the founders of *Abstraction-Création. From 1928 he began to design ambitious (and unrealized) architectural projects, including a 'Skyscraper City' (1930), whose cubiform structure resembles that of his sculptures. In the 1940s his sculpture became more varied as he began using wire and perspex, exploring effects of reflection and refraction. His paintings were based on horizontal and vertical lines until 1937, when he introduced rhythmic curving lines, rejecting his friend *Mondrian's idea that only constructions based on the right angle reflect the harmony of the universe.

Varley, Frederick. See GROUP OF SEVEN.

Varley, John (1778–1842). English landscape painter in watercolour, a protégé of Dr *Monro. Varley represents the transition between tinted topographical drawing and the bolder, more fully developed manner of watercolour painting characteristic of the 19th century. As well as being a leading painter, he was the most popular and enthusiastic teacher of his day; his pupils included *Cox, *De Wint, *Linnell, *Mulready (his brother-in-law), and Samuel *Palmer, and he published various instructional works. He also wrote a treatise on astrology (1828), a subject in which he had an obsessive interest. His eccentricities helped endear him to William *Blake, who was a close friend. In spite of his success, Varley constantly had money problems (he had a large family and an improvident wife) and he was imprisoned for debt on several occasions. His brothers **Cornelius** (1781–1873) and **William** (1785–1856) and his sister **Elizabeth** (1783–1864) were also watercolourists, and several descendants carried on the family tradition.

varnish. Solution, usually of *resin in oil or a synthetic equivalent, used as a protective coating on the surface of a painting. Ideally varnish should be colourless and transparent, but most have darkened with age. Some artists have used varnish as a paint *medium.

Vasarely, Victor (1908–97). Hungarian-born painter who became a French citizen in 1959, the main originator and one of the leading practitioners of *Op art. He settled in Paris in 1930, and for the next decade worked mainly as a commercial artist, particularly on the designing of posters, showing a keen interest in visual tricks such as *trompe-l'œil effects. From 1943 he turned to painting and about four years later he adopted the method of geometrical abstraction for which he was best known. Typically he created a hallucinatory impression of movement through visual ambiguity, using alternating positive–negative shapes interrupted in such a way as to suggest underlying secondary shapes. His fascination with the idea of movement led him to experiment with *Kinetic art and he also collaborated with architects in such works as his relief in aluminium for Caracas University (1954) and the French Pavilion at 'Expo' 67' in Montreal, hoping to create a kind of urban folk art. From the mid-1950s he wrote a number of manifestos, which, together with his paintings, were a major influence on younger artists working in the same fields. Among them is his son, **Jean-Pierre** (1934–), who works under the name Yvaral.

Vasari, Giorgio (1511–74). Italian painter, architect, and writer, born in Arezzo and active mainly in Florence and Rome. In his day he was a leading painter, architect, and artistic impresario, but his activities in these fields have been completely overshadowed by his role as the most important of all artistic biographers. His great book, generally referred to as *Lives of the Artists*, has earned him the title of the father of art history; it is not only the fundamental source of information on Italian *Renaissance art, but also a key document in shaping attitudes about the period for centuries afterwards. (The book was first published in Florence in 1550 as *Le vite de' più eccellenti architetti, pittori, et scultori italiani* (The Lives of the Most Eminent Italian Architects, Painters, and Sculptors); in 1568 there was a second, much enlarged edition, in which the title is slightly changed, the painters being mentioned first.) Vasari wrote from a particular aesthetic viewpoint, and his book is not only a collection of biographies but also a critical history of style. He believed that art is in the first instance imitation of nature and that progress in painting consists in the perfecting of the means of representation. He thought that such representational skills had been taken to high levels in *classical antiquity, that art had then passed through a long period of decline in the Middle Ages, and that it had begun to revive in the 14th century in Tuscany (he was heavily biased in favour of his own region). The main theme of the *Lives* was to set forth this revival—its initiation by *Cimabue and *Giotto, its steady advance at the hands of such artists as *Brunelleschi, *Donatello, and *Masaccio, and its culmination with *Leonardo, *Raphael, and above all *Michelangelo, whom Vasari idolized and whose biography was the only one of a living artist to appear in the first edition of his book (the second edition adds accounts of several artists then living, including Vasari's autobiography). The idea of artistic 'progress' that he promoted subsequently coloured most writing on the period. Given the wide scope and vast size of the book (the second edition has roughly the same wordage as the Bible), it is not surprising that it contains many errors and contentious points (see, for example, *Andrea del Castagno and *Andrea del Sarto). However, by the standards of the time Vasari was a diligent researcher and he gathered together an enormous amount of invaluable information, which he presented in a lively style, full of memorable anecdotes. Moreover, his qualitative judgements have generally stood the test of time well: the artists and works he most admired are by and large still the ones we most admire today. His book became the model for artistic biographers in other countries, such as van *Mander in the Netherlands, *Sandrart in Germany, and *Palomino in Spain.

As a painter, Vasari was one of the most prolific decorators of his period, but he is not now highly regarded, his work representing the most inbred and affected kind of *Mannerism. His best-known achievement in this field is probably the decoration (1546) of the grand salon in the Palazzo della Cancelleria, Rome, with scenes celebrating the life of Pope Paul III, commissioned by his grandson, Cardinal Alessandro *Farnese. Pressed for quick results by the cardinal, Vasari enlisted a team of assistants and finished the work within a hundred days, earning the room its nickname of the Sala dei Cento Giorni. When Michelangelo was told of the remarkable speed with which the work had

been accomplished, he is said to have made the withering response 'E si vede' (So it appears). As an architect Vasari has a higher reputation; his most important building is the *Uffizi in Florence, and he designed and decorated his own house in Arezzo, now a museum dedicated to him. Vasari was the first important collector of drawings, using them partly as research material for his biographies, for the insight they gave into the creative process, and he also played the leading role in establishing Florence's Accademia del Disegno (see ACADEMY).

Vasnetsov, Viktor (1848–1926). Russian painter, illustrator, designer, and architect, active mainly in Moscow. His early paintings were chiefly of contemporary subjects, sometimes involving the urban poor, but from about 1880 he specialized in scenes from Russian history and legend, combining carefully researched details with a feeling for the romance of myth. He is probably best known for the huge, stirring *Bogatyrs* (1881–98, Tretyakov Gal., Moscow), showing three mighty folk heroes keeping watch on the Russian frontier, but his range extended to lyrical scenes from fairy tales. Vasnetsov also worked as a portraitist, book illustrator, stage designer, and occasional architect. He designed his own house in Moscow (1894), now a museum dedicated to him, and most memorably the façade of the *Tretyakov Gallery (1902). *See also* ABRAMTSEVO COLONY and WANDERERS.

Vatican Museums. Institutions housing the enormous collections of antiquities and works of art accumulated by the papacy since the beginning of the 15th century. As the leaders of the Christian Church the popes have always commanded the services of the best artists of the day, and they have also been continually showered with gifts. The Vatican collections are consequently among the largest and most important in the world, housed in a complex of buildings in the papal palace and elsewhere in the Vatican. There are several separate museums and the visitor to them is also admitted to the exhibition rooms of the Vatican Library and to various suites of *Renaissance painting, of which the most important are the Sistine Chapel, decorated by *Michelangelo and others, and the Stanze, decorated by *Raphael and others. The museums had their origin with Julius II

(Giuliano della *Rovere, ruled 1503–13), who placed some of the most famous works of *antique sculpture in the Cortile del Belvedere (Belvedere Court), accessible to artists, connoisseurs, and scholars. However, it was not until the 18th century that further development took place. Small museums of sacred and pagan art were created in 1756 and 1767 respectively, but the decisive impetus was provided by Popes Clement XIV (1769–74) and Pius VI (1775–99). They built an extension to the Vatican palace to house classical statuary, and this—named after them as the Museo Pio-Clementino—still forms the heart of the Vatican Museums. It is in a handsome *Neoclassical style that was highly influential on museum architecture elsewhere. The Vatican Museums are still primarily famous for their classical statues, including the *Apollo Belvedere*, the *Belvedere Torso*, and the *Laocoön*, but they also contain great riches in, for example, Egyptian art, jewellery, and vestments. The Pinacoteca (picture gallery) was founded in 1909 and the present building was opened in 1932. It has an impressive if somewhat haphazard collection, devoted mainly to Italian painting of the 13th century to the 17th century. There is also a collection of modern religious art (opened 1973), much of it merely of curiosity value.

Vaughan, Keith (1912–77). British painter, draughtsman, designer, and writer. In the 1940s, with his friend John *Minton, he was one of the leading exponents of *Neo-Romanticism, characteristic works of this time being coloured drawings of moonlit houses. His later work, in which he concentrated on his favourite theme of the male nude in a landscape setting, became grander and more simplified, moving towards abstraction (*Leaping Figure*, 1951, Tate, London). Vaughan also designed textiles and book-jackets, and he taught part-time at several art schools in London, notably the *Slade. His varied activities brought him critical and financial success, but he felt deep insecurity about his work and his role in life, as is revealed in his book *Journal and Drawings* (1966), extracts from a diary he had begun in 1939 (a new edition appeared in 1989). As well as containing many perceptive comments about art, it gives a remarkably frank (and often amusing) account of his homosexual and masturbatory activities and of the struggle with cancer that led to his suicide.

Vauxcelles, Louis. *See* FAUVISM.

Vecchietta (Lorenzo di Pietro) (1410–80). One of the outstanding Sienese artists of the 15th century, a painter, sculptor, goldsmith, architect, and military engineer. His nickname, meaning 'little old one', first appears in 1442 and repeatedly thereafter in documents relating to him, but its origin is unknown. On stylistic grounds he is assumed to have been a pupil of *Sassetta, but he also came under the influence of Florentine art and his large-scale paintings have a monumentality rare in Siena in the *quattrocento. As a sculptor he worked in wood and marble and late in his career in bronze, this change in medium probably reflecting the influence of *Donatello, who was in Siena 1457–9. *The Risen Christ* (1476, S. Maria della Scala, Siena) has something of Donatello's sinewy expressiveness. Donatello's influence may also account for the strength and plasticity of Vecchietta's later paintings, such as the fresco of *St Catherine* (1461) in the Palazzo Pubblico in Siena (1461) and the triptych of the *Assumption of the Virgin* (c.1462) in Pienza Cathedral. Several of the leading Sienese artists of the next generation were taught by him, notably *Francesco di Giorgio and *Neroccio dei Landi.

Vecellio, Francesco and **Orazio.** *See* TITIAN.

veduta (It.: 'view'). Term applied to a representation of a town or landscape that is essentially topographical, specifically one that is faithful enough to allow the location to be identified (an imaginary but realistic-looking view can be called a *veduta ideata*). Painters of *vedute* (for example *Canaletto and *Guardi) are called *vedutisti*.

Veen, Otto van (c.1556–1629). Flemish painter. From c.1575 to c.1580 he was in Italy, where he is said to have been a pupil of Federico *Zuccaro, and after working in various places in Germany and Flanders he settled in Antwerp in about 1592. He was an uninspired *Mannerist painter, but he became busy and successful, his work including portraits, illustrations for *emblem books, and altarpieces inspired by Italian masters such as *Correggio and *Parmigianino (*Mystic Marriage of St Catherine*, 1589, Mus.

Royaux, Brussels). His love of Italian art and his scholarly inclinations (he often Latinized his name to Octavius Vaenius) must have been appreciated by *Rubens, who completed his training in van Veen's studio. After Rubens returned from Italy in 1608, van Veen's work looked old-fashioned and his career petered out.

vehicle. The liquid in which *pigment is suspended to form paint—the 'carrier'. The word can be applied to either the *medium or the *diluent, or to a mixture of both; thus the vehicle of *oil painting might be either *linseed oil, or *turpentine, or both together.

Velázquez (or **Velasquez**), **Diego** (1599–1660). The greatest painter of the Spanish School, chiefly celebrated as one of the supreme portraitists in world art. He was born in Seville, where in 1610/11 he was apprenticed to *Pacheco (possibly following a brief period of study with *Herrera the Elder). In 1617 he qualified as a master painter and in the following year he married Pacheco's daughter. Velázquez was exceptionally precocious and while he was still in his teens he painted pictures that display commanding presence and complete technical mastery. Pacheco's style in religious paintings was 'dry and insipid' (*Palomino); Velázquez revitalized it by following his master's advice to 'go to nature for everything', and in works such as the *Immaculate Conception* (c.1618, NG, London) and the *Adoration of the Magi* (1619, Prado, Madrid) he developed a more lifelike approach to religious art, in which the figures are treated like portraits rather than *ideal types (his young wife may be the model for the Virgin in both these pictures). The light, too, is realistically observed, even though it has a mysterious, spiritual quality. In their strong *chiaroscuro as well as their naturalism such pictures show an affinity with the work of *Caravaggio and his followers, but the supple, clotted brushwork is already entirely Velázquez's own. In addition to religious pictures, his early work included several *bodegones, a type of *genre scene to which he brought a new seriousness and dignity; the best known among them is *The Waterseller of Seville* (c.1620, Wellington Mus., London), in which the water dripping down the jug shows his remarkable ability to create a sense of almost palpable reality.

In 1622 Velázquez paid a short visit to Madrid, during which he painted a portrait of the poet Luis de Góngora (MFA, Boston). In the following year he was recalled to the capital by Philip IV's (*see* HABSBURG) chief minister, the Count-Duke Olivares, and painted a portrait of the king (now lost) which pleased Philip so much that he appointed Velázquez one of his court painters and declared that now only he should paint his portrait. Thus, at the age of 24, he suddenly became the country's most prestigious painter, and he kept his position as the king's favourite unchallenged for the rest of his life. With his appointment as court painter, the direction of Velázquez's work changed. He entirely abandoned *bodegones*, and although he painted historical, mythological, and religious pictures intermittently throughout his career, he was from now on primarily a portraitist. Technically, too, his work changed as a result of his move to Madrid, his palette lightening and his brushwork becoming broader and more fluid under the influence particularly of the *Titians in the royal collection. Although his portraits of the king and his courtiers are grand and dignified, he humanized the formal tradition of court portraiture derived from *Mor and *Sánchez Coello, setting his models in more natural poses and giving them greater life and character. The king (who was six years younger than Velázquez) had an extremely high opinion of the artist's personal qualities as well as his artistic skills, and the warmth with which he treated him was considered astonishing, given the stiff etiquette for which the Spanish court was renowned. In 1627 Philip made Velázquez 'usher of the chamber', the first of a series of appointments that brought him great prestige but took up much of his time in trivial bureaucratic matters, thus partly accounting for his fairly small output as a painter. He was conscientious in his duties, however, and evidently well suited to them temperamentally: the Italian painter Marco Boschini (1605–81) described him as 'a courtly gentleman of such great dignity as distinguishes any person of authority'.

In 1628–9 *Rubens visited Spain on a diplomatic mission and he and Velázquez became friends. Palomino records that the contact with Rubens 'revived the desire Velázquez had always had to go to Italy', and the king duly gave him permission to travel there. He was in Italy from 1629 to 1631, visiting Genoa, Venice, and Naples, but spending most of his time in Rome. Two major paintings date from this period—*Joseph's Coat* (Escorial, Madrid) and *The Forge of Vulcan* (Prado), works that show how his brushwork loosened still further under the influence of the great Venetian masters and how his mastery of figure composition matured. The 1630s and 1640s (before he again left for Italy) were the most productive period of Velázquez's career. His series of royal and court portraits continued and he expanded his range in a series of glorious equestrian portraits (Prado). In these he showed an unprecedented ability to attain complete atmospheric unity between foreground and background in the landscape. Their rhetorical poses are in the *Baroque tradition, but they are without bombast or allegorical embellishments and as portraits are characteristically direct. The same ability to look beyond external trappings to the human mystery beneath is seen in his incomparable series of portraits of the pitiful court fools (Prado)—dwarfs and idiots whom Philip, like other monarchs, kept for his amusement. Velázquez presents them without any suggestion of caricature, but with pathos and human understanding, as if they too are worthy of his respect. During the 1630s and 1640s he occasionally painted religious and mythological works, but they are all eclipsed by his great masterpiece of contemporary history painting, the *Surrender of Breda* (1634–5, Prado), one of a series of twelve paintings by various court artists glorifying the military triumphs of Philip's reign that were executed for the new Buen Retiro Palace in Madrid. The composition is highly organized, but Velázquez creates a remarkable sense of actuality and no earlier picture of a contemporary historical event had seemed so convincing. Characteristically, he concentrates on the human drama of the situation, as Ambrogio Spínola, the chivalrous Spanish commander, receives the key of the town from Justin of Nassau, his vanquished Dutch counterpart, with a superb gesture of magnanimity.

Between 1648 and 1651 Velázquez paid another visit to Italy to purchase paintings and antiquities for the royal collection (he may have been there briefly in 1636 but the

evidence is inconclusive). Again, he spent most of the time in Rome, where he painted several portraits, including two of his most celebrated works—*Juan de Pareja* (1650, Met. Mus., New York) and *Pope Innocent X* (1650, Gal. Doria Pamphili, Rome). Juan de Pareja (*c*.1610–*c*.1670), who was himself a painter, was Velázquez's mulatto slave (his master granted him his freedom while they were in Rome), and Velázquez painted this portrait because he felt he needed some practice before tackling that of the pope. The *Innocent X* is by common consent one of the world's supreme masterpieces of portraiture, unsurpassed in its breathtaking handling of paint and so incisive in characterization that the pope himself said the picture was 'troppo vero' (too truthful). While in Rome Velázquez fathered an illegitimate son, Antonio, by a widow named Martha, but nothing is known of what became of mother or child. They may have been on Velázquez's mind when he applied for (and was refused) permission to return to Italy in 1657, but his life and work continued to unfold with the same sober dignity and the skeleton in his cupboard remained hidden until 1983, when the documentation was first published.

In his final years in Madrid, Velázquez continued to acquire new honours (the greatest was being made a knight of the Order of Santiago in 1659) and to reach new heights as a painter. His last portraits are mainly of the new young queen, Mariana of Austria (Philip's second wife, whom he married in 1649), and of the royal children. In these works his brushwork has become increasingly sparkling and free, and the gorgeous clothes the sitters wore (such a change from the sombre costumes of the king and male courtiers) allowed him to show his prowess as a colourist (several examples are in the Kunsthistorisches Museum, Vienna). Velázquez never ceased to base his work on scrutiny of nature, but his means grew increasingly subtle, so that detail is entirely subordinated to overall effect. Thus in his late works space and atmosphere are depicted with unprecedented vividness, but when the pictures are looked at closely the forms dissolve into what Kenneth *Clark called 'a fricassee of beautiful brushstrokes'. As Palomino put it, 'one cannot understand it if standing too close, but from a distance it is a miracle.'

The culmination of Velázquez's career is *Las Meninas* (The Maids of Honour) (*c*.1656, Prado). It shows him at his easel, with various members of the royal family and their attendants in his studio, but it is not clear whether he has shown himself at work on a portrait of the king and queen (who are reflected in a mirror) when interrupted by the Infanta Margarita and her maids of honour or vice versa. Velázquez's prominence in the picture seems to assert his own importance and his pride in his art, but in the background he has included two pictures by Rubens showing the downfall of mortals who challenge the gods in the arts. Apparently spontaneous but in the highest degree worked out, it is both Velázquez's most complex essay in portraiture and an expression of the high claims he made for the dignity of his art. Luca *Giordano called it 'the Theology of Painting' because 'just as theology is superior to all other branches of knowledge, so is this the greatest example of painting'. Posterity has endorsed his verdict, for in a poll of artists and critics in the *Illustrated London News* in August 1985, *Las Meninas* was voted—by some margin—'the world's greatest painting'.

The number of good contemporary copies of Velázquez's work indicates that he ran a busy studio, but of his pupils only his son-in-law *Mazo achieved any kind of distinction. As with most Spanish painters, Velázquez remained little known outside his own country until the Napoleonic Wars brought Spain into the mainstream of European affairs. The opening of the *Prado in 1819, with 44 of his paintings on display, made his work much more accessible than it had ever been before, and from the mid-19th century his technical freedom was an inspiration to many progressive artists, above all *Manet, who regarded him as the greatest of all painters. The bulk of Velázquez's work is still in Spain, and his genius can be fully appreciated only in the Prado, which has most of his key masterpieces. Outside Spain, he is best represented in London—in the National Gallery, which has his only surviving female nude, the *Rokeby Venus* (*c*.1648), in the Wellington Museum, and in the Wallace Collection.

Velde, Esaias van de (1587–1630). Dutch painter, one of the most important figures in the development of his country's tradition

of naturalistic landscape. He was born in Amsterdam, where he was perhaps the pupil of Gillis van *Coninxloo, and worked in Haarlem (*c*.1610–18) and The Hague (1618 onwards). His earliest works are in the *Mannerist tradition, but by 1615 he had already moved away from the panoramic effect and high viewpoint of his predecessors. His fresh brushwork and directness of vision herald the subsequent accomplishment of his pupil Jan van *Goyen and of Salomon van *Ruysdael. In addition to pure landscapes, Esaias painted various figure subjects in landscape settings; he was also a prolific etcher and draughtsman. There were other artists in his family, notably his cousin **Jan van de Velde II** (*c*.1593–1641), but he was not related to Willem van de *Velde.

Velde, Willem van de the Elder (1611–93). Dutch marine painter. He came from a naval family and devoted himself to the drawing and painting of ships. His pictures, which are frequently *grisailles, contain faithful and detailed portraits of vessels (of much value to naval historians) and for a time he was an official artist for the Dutch fleet. In the winter of 1672–3, when the Netherlands were at war with England, he moved to London and entered the service of Charles II; why he left his country at a critical moment in its fortunes remains unclear. **Willem the Younger** (1633–1707), his son, is one of the most illustrious of all marine painters. He was the pupil of his father and of Simon de *Vlieger. Like his father, he gave very accurate portrayals of ships, but he is distinguished from him by his feeling for atmosphere and his majestic sense of composition. He left Amsterdam for England with his father in 1672–3 and in 1674 Charles II gave them a yearly retaining fee of £100 each; the father received his 'for taking and making draughts of sea fights' and the son 'for putting the said draughts into colours for our particular use'. They did not switch their allegiance to England completely: both subsequently painted pictures of naval battles for the Dutch as well as the English market. Willem the Younger's influence, however, was particularly great in England, where the whole tradition of marine painting stemmed from him. His younger brother, **Adriaen** (1636–72), was a versatile and prolific artist in spite of his short life. He is said to have been a pupil of his father and of Jan *Wijnants. His output included various types of landscapes (most notably some fresh and atmospheric beach scenes) and also religious and mythological works, portraits, and animal pictures. He also made etchings and often painted the figures into the landscapes of other artists, notably *Hobbema and *Ruisdael.

vellum. See PARCHMENT.

Venus de Milo. A marble statue of Aphrodite (Venus), the best known of all ancient statues, found on the small Greek island of Melos (or Milos) in 1820 and now in the Louvre, Paris. A plinth (now lost) found with the statue was signed '... andros [Alexandros or Agasandros] of Antioch on the Maeander', but nothing is known of this sculptor. Originally the statue was thought to date from the *Classical age of Greek sculpture, but it is now put appreciably later—*c.*100 BC—and is thought to be a sophisticated combination of older styles—the goddess's head derives from the later 5th century BC, her nudity from the 4th century, and her spiral, omnifacial posture from the *Hellenistic age. The *Venus de Milo* arrived in the Louvre (1821) soon after the *Medici Venus* had been returned to Italy (1815), and its enormous fame stemmed from French determination to persuade the world that they had gained a greater treasure than they had lost: Martin Robertson (*A History of Greek Art*, 1975) writes that its 'extraordinary reputation, which started by propaganda, has become perpetuated by habit'. Many 19th-century critics went into raptures about the figure, which was thought to represent the apogee of female beauty, perfectly combining grandeur with gracefulness, but *Renoir described it as a 'big gendarme'. The statue's arms are missing and many conjectures have been made as to what the goddess might have been holding: it has been suggested for example that she is intended as Venus Victrix, and so would have been shown with the golden apple presented to her by Paris when he adjudged her more beautiful than her rivals Juno and Minerva.

Verhaecht (or **van Haecht**), **Tobias** (1561–1631). Flemish painter, now remembered almost solely because he was *Ru-

bens's first teacher. Apart from a sojourn in Italy as a young man, Verhaecht spent his career in his native Antwerp. He was a landscape specialist, working in a style similar to Paul *Bril's, and had no detectable influence on his great pupil. His son, **Willem van Haecht** (1593–1637), was a painter, best known for pictures of art collections (*The Picture Gallery of Cornelis van der Geest*, 1628, Rubenshuis, Antwerp).

Verhulst, Mayken. See BRUEGEL and COECKE VAN AELST.

Verhulst, Rombout (1624–98). Flemish sculptor active mainly in Holland. In the 1650s he was the most important assistant to Artus *Quellin I in the sculptural decoration of the town hall in Amsterdam. By 1663 he had settled in The Hague, where he became a leading sculptor of busts and tombs. The noble and sensitively cut monument to Admiral Michiel de Ruyter (1681) in the Nieuwe Kerk in Amsterdam is perhaps his masterpiece.

verism. An extreme form of *realism, in which the artist makes it his aim to reproduce with rigid truthfulness the exact appearance of his subject, repudiating all imaginative interpretation. The term has been applied, for example, to certain Roman portrait sculptures. In a different sense, the term 'Veristic *Surrealism' is sometimes applied to pictures that claim to reproduce hallucination in exact and unselective detail; *Dalí is the best-known exponent of works of this type.

Vermeer, Jan (1632–75). Dutch painter. Among the great Dutch artists of the 17th century, he is now second in renown only to *Rembrandt, but he made little mark during his lifetime and then long languished in obscurity. Almost all of the contemporary references to him are in colourless official documents and his career is in many ways enigmatic. As far as is known, he lived all his life in his native Delft and rarely made even local journeys outside it. He became a member of the painters' guild there in 1653 and was twice elected *hooftman* (headman), but it is not known who taught him. His name is often linked with that of Carel *Fabritius, but it is doubtful if he can have been Vermeer's teacher in the formal sense; this distinction may belong to Leonaert *Bramer, although there is no similarity between their work. Only about 35 to 40 paintings by Vermeer are known, and although some early works may have been destroyed in the disastrous Delft gunpowder explosion of 1654, it is unlikely that the figure was ever much larger; this is because most of the Vermeers mentioned in early sources can be identified with surviving pictures, whilst only a few pictures now attributed to him are not mentioned in these sources—thus there are few loose ends. This small output may be at least partially explained by the fact that he almost certainly earned most of his living by means other than painting. His father kept an inn and was a picture-dealer and Vermeer very likely inherited both businesses. In spite of this he had grave financial troubles (he had a large family to support—his wife bore him fifteen children, eleven of whom survived him). His money problems increased after the French invasion of 1672, which devastated the Dutch economy, and his widow was declared insolvent the year after his death.

Only three of Vermeer's paintings are dated—*The Procuress* (1656, Gemäldegalerie, Dresden), *The Astronomer* (1668, Louvre, Paris), and its companion *The Geographer* (1669, Städelsches Kunstinstitut, Frankfurt). (Another signed and dated work, *St Praxedis Mopping up the Blood of the Martyrs* of 1655, appeared in the 1960s, but its authenticity has been questioned. It is in a private collection.) It is difficult to fit his other paintings into a convincing chronology, but his work nevertheless divides into three fairly clear phases. The first is represented by only two works—*Christ in the House of Mary and Martha* (NG, Edinburgh) and *Diana and her Companions* (Mauritshuis, The Hague)—both probably dating from a year or two before *The Procuress*. They are so different from Vermeer's other works—in their comparatively large scale, their subject matter, and their handling of paint—that *Diana and her Companions* was for a time attributed to an obscure namesake, Jan Vermeer of Utrecht (*c.*1630–after 1692). *The Procuress* marks the transition to the middle phase of Vermeer's career, for although it is fairly large and warm in tonality—like the two history paintings—it is a contemporary life scene, as were virtually all Vermeer's pictures from now on. In the central part of his career (into which most of his work falls)

Vermeer painted those serene and harmonious images of domestic life that for their beauty of composition, brushwork, and treatment of light raise him into a different class from any other Dutch genre painter. The majority show one or two figures in a room lit from the onlooker's left, engaged in domestic or recreational tasks. The predominant colours are yellow, blue, and grey, arranged in flawlessly cool harmonies, and the compositions have a purity and dignity that confer on them an impact out of relation to their small size. In reproduction his pictures can look quite smooth and detailed, but Vermeer often applies the paint broadly, with variations in texture suggesting the play of light with exquisite vibrancy—the Dutch artist and critic Jan Veth (1864–1925) aptly described his paint surface as looking like 'crushed pearls melted together'. From this period of Vermeer's greatest achievement also date his only landscape—the incomparable *View of Delft* (Mauritshuis), in which he surpassed even the greatest of his specialist contemporaries in lucidity and truth of atmosphere—and his much-loved *Little Street* (Rijksmuseum, Amsterdam). Another painting of this period is somewhat larger in size and unusual in subject for him—*The Artist's Studio* (KH Mus., Vienna), in which Vermeer shows a back view of a painter, perhaps a suitably enigmatic self-portrait. In the third and final phase of his career Vermeer's work lost some of its magic as it became somewhat harder. There are still wonderful passages of paint in all his late works, but the utter naturalness of his finest works is gone. The only one of his paintings that might be considered a failure, the *Allegory of Faith* (Met. Mus., New York), belongs to this period. His wife was a Catholic and he may well have been converted to her religion, but this rather lumbering figure shows he was not at ease with the trappings of *Baroque allegory. There are symbolic references in other paintings by him, but they all—except for this one—make sense on a straightforward naturalistic level.

No drawings by Vermeer are known and knowledge of his working methods has largely to be deduced from close examination of his paintings. It is virtually certain, however, that he sometimes made use of a *camera obscura; the exaggerated perspective in some of his pictures (in which foreground figures or objects loom unexpectedly large) and the way in which sparkling highlights appear slightly out of focus are effects duplicated by unsophisticated lenses. The scientist Antony van Leeuwenhoek (1632–1723), celebrated for his work with microscopes, became the executor of Vermeer's estate and it may well have been an interest in optics that brought them together. Vermeer's paintings were admired in his lifetime, but after his death his name quickly passed into obscurity. During the 18th century his pictures were sometimes attributed to other artists who were better known at the time, such as Frans van *Mieris, and in 1833 the British picture dealer John Smith (1781–1855), a pioneer in the scholarly study of Dutch art, wrote of Vermeer: 'This painter is so little known, by reason of the scarcity of his works, that it is quite inexplicable how he attained the excellence many of them exhibit.' The key figure in rediscovering Vermeer was *Thoré, who published a series of articles on him in the *Gazette des Beaux-Arts* in 1866 and memorably dubbed him 'the Sphinx of Delft'.

Vernet. Family of French painters, three members of which attained distinction. **Claude-Joseph Vernet** (1714–89) was one of the leading French landscape painters of his period. From 1734 to 1753 he worked in Rome, where he was influenced by the light and atmosphere of *Claude and also by the more wild and dramatic art of Salvator *Rosa. With Hubert *Robert, he became a leading exponent of a type of idealized and somewhat sentimental landscape that had a great vogue at this time. Vernet was particularly celebrated for his paintings of the seashore and seaports, and on returning to Paris in 1753 he was commissioned by Louis XV to paint a series of the seaports of France. He produced fifteen (more were planned but not executed), now divided between the Louvre and the Musée Maritime, Paris. His son **Antoine-Charles-Horace**, known as 'Carle' (1758–1836), painted large battle pictures for Napoleon, notably the *Battle of Marengo* (1806, Versailles), and after the restoration of the monarchy he became official painter to Louis XVIII, for whom he did racing and hunting scenes. **Émile-Jean-Horace Vernet** (1789–1863), known as Horace Vernet, son of Carle, was one of the most prolific of French military painters, specializing in scenes of the Napoleonic era. A portrait of Napoleon and four battle pieces by him are in the National Gallery, London. He also did animal and Oriental subjects. From 1828 to 1834 he was director of the French Academy in Rome.

Veronese, Paolo (Paolo Caliari) (*c*.1528–88). Italian painter, born in Verona (from which his nickname derives). He trained there with the undistinguished Antonio Badile (*c*.1518–60), whose daughter he later married, but from about 1553 he was based in Venice and he is considered a member of the Venetian School. With *Tintoretto he became the dominant figure in Venetian painting in the generation after *Titian and he had many major commissions. Although he was sometimes in direct competition with Tintoretto, generally they worked for rather different markets and they seem to have been on good terms personally. Both of them were at their best on a large scale, but whereas Tintoretto concentrated on religious pictures, Veronese also did numerous secular commissions. Some of his finest work was produced outside Venice and in fresco, whereas Tintoretto worked almost exclusively in the city itself and in oils. Stylistically they had little in common: Tintoretto's most characteristic paintings are intensely emotional, with the drama played out in a dark, brooding atmosphere; Veronese preferred the clear light of day and subjects that made their impact through pomp rather than passion.

Veronese established a distinctive style early in his career and thereafter developed relatively little. Few of his paintings are dated or can be reliably dated, so his chronology is difficult to construct. Similarly, because he had such a highly organized studio and his output was so large, there can be problems in distinguishing the work of his own hand. Nevertheless, his status and achievement are clear. He was one of the greatest of all decorative artists, delighting in painting enormous pageant-like scenes that bear witness to the material splendour of Venice in its Golden Age. Marble columns and costumes of velvet and satin abound in his work, and he used a sumptuous but delicate palette in which pale blue, orange, silvery white, and lemon yellow predominate. In his religious works his penchant was for feast scenes from the Bible. His love of richness and ornament got him into trouble with the Inquisition in a famous incident in 1573 when he was interrogated about a painting of the *Last Supper* that he had crowded with such irrelevant and irreverent figures as 'a buffoon with a parrot on his wrist...a servant whose nose was bleeding...dwarfs and similar vulgarities'. Veronese staunchly defended his right to artistic licence: 'I received the commission to decorate the picture as I saw fit. It is large and, it seemed to me, it could hold many figures.' He was instructed to make changes, but the matter was resolved by simply changing the title of the picture so that it represented a less solemn meal from the Bible, the *Feast in the House of Levi*. It was painted for the refectory of the monastery of SS. Giovanni e Paolo, Venice, and is now in the Accademia.

Veronese's secular works include the delightfully light-hearted frescos (including *illusionistic architecture and enchanting landscapes) decorating the Villa Barbaro at Maser, near Treviso (c.1561), a series of four canvases, *Allegory of Love* (c.1575, NG, London), probably painted for the emperor Rudolf II (see HABSBURG), and the resplendent *Triumph of Venice* (c.1585) on the ceiling of the Hall of the Great Council in the Doges' Palace, Venice. He also painted portraits. His studio was carried on after his death by his brother **Benedetto Caliari** (1538-98) and his sons **Carlo** (c.1567-92/6) and **Gabriele** (1568-1631). He had no significant pupils, but his influence on Venetian painting was important, particularly in the 18th century, when he was an inspiration to the masters of the second great flowering of decorative painting in the city, above all *Tiepolo.

Verrio, Antonio (c.1639-1707). Italian decorative painter who settled in England in 1671/2 and enjoyed an enormously successful and well-remunerated career. He was much employed at royal buildings—Whitehall Palace, Windsor Castle, and Hampton Court—and also worked at great aristocratic houses such as Burghley and Chatsworth. His success was based on his self-assertiveness and the lack of native talent in his field rather than on his skills as an artist, for his work is at best mediocre (and often dismal) judged by European

standards. *Laguerre, his one-time assistant, was a better painter but had less worldly success.

Verrocchio, Andrea del (Andrea di Cioni) (c.1435-88). Florentine sculptor, painter, and metalworker, one of the outstanding Italian artists of his period. His nickname Verrocchio ('true eye') was given to him not because of his sharpness of vision, but evidently because early in his career he worked for a family of that name. He is said to have studied in *Donatello's workshop, but his main training was as a goldsmith, and delicacy of craftsmanship is one of the salient features of his work. Only one work in precious metal by him survives, however—a silver *relief of the *Beheading of John the Baptist* (1477-80), done for the Baptistery in Florence and now in the Cathedral Museum. His major activity was as a sculptor, principally in bronze, but also in marble and terracotta, and his two most famous works rank with the statues of Donatello that inspired them among the great masterpieces of Italian sculpture, whilst also showing the great differences in approach between the two artists. Verrocchio's *David* (c.1475, Bargello, Florence) is more refined, and less broodingly intense than Donatello's *David* in the same museum, and Verrocchio's masterpiece, the equestrian statue of the condottiere Bartolommeo Colleoni in Venice (begun 1481, cast after Verrocchio's death, and unveiled in 1496), has a magnificent sense of movement and swagger, but less of the heroic dignity of Donatello's *Gattamelata* statue in Padua. It is much harder to assess Verrocchio's stature as a painter, as very few works exist that can be convincingly assigned to his own hand. Nevertheless numerous paintings came from his workshop, which was the largest in Florence at this time, and he trained distinguished painters, most notably *Leonardo da Vinci, who assisted his master with the *Baptism of Christ* (c.1470, Uffizi, Florence), one of the few paintings indisputably by Verrocchio. Leonardo took his superb craftsmanship from Verrocchio and also shared his fascination with two contrasting types—the tough old warrior (as in the *Colleoni* monument) and the epicene youth (as in the *David*). Leonardo's enormous fame has tended to cast a shadow over Verrocchio, but nevertheless he is generally regarded as the greatest Italian sculptor between Donatello and *Michelangelo.

Vertue, George (1684–1756). English engraver and antiquarian. He was a prolific engraver of portraits and antiquarian subjects (he was appointed official engraver to the Society of Antiquaries in 1717), but he is important chiefly for the voluminous notes he collected relating to the history of art in England (now in the BL, London). After his death they were bought by Horace *Walpole, who used them as a basis for his *Anecdotes of Painting in England* (1762–71), and the notebooks themselves—an invaluable storehouse of information—were published in six volumes, plus an index, in 1930–50.

Veth, Jan. *See* VERMEER.

Victoria and Albert Museum (V&A), London. Museum housing the world's greatest collection of *applied art as well as a large and varied collection of *fine art. It was the brainchild of Prince Albert and grew out of the Great Exhibition (1851), the profits from which were used to buy a site in South Kensington for a cultural centre of museums and colleges. Whilst the site was being developed, the nucleus of the collection, consisting of objects of applied art bought from the Great Exhibition, was temporarily displayed at Marlborough House and named the Museum of Manufactures. This opened in 1852 and the following year it was renamed the Museum of Ornamental Art. At this time the Central School of Practical Art (which became the *Royal College of Art) was also based in Marlborough House. In 1857 both institutions moved to South Kensington, where the museum collections soon expanded greatly in range and size. A new building on the same site was begun in 1899, designed by Sir Aston Webb, and at the ceremony of laying the foundation stone by Queen Victoria, the name of the museum was changed to 'The Victoria and Albert Museum'. The building was opened by King Edward VII in 1909; at this time the scientific collections were moved to the nearby Science Museum. Prince Albert's ideal when he conceived the museum was to improve the standard of design in Britain by making the finest models available for study, and the first dir-

ector, Sir Henry Cole (1808–82), echoed this when he declared his policy was 'to assemble a splendid collection of objects representing the application of fine arts to manufacture'. However, the collections have—through a flood of acquisitions—become extraordinarily diverse, and a later director, Sir Roy Strong (1935–), has written that 'Any visitor to the Victoria and Albert Museum today is likely to be bemused as to what exactly is the central thread that animates these discrepant if marvellous collections. The answer is that there is none. For over a century the Museum has proved an extremely capacious handbag.' It incorporates, for example, the national collections of post-*classical sculpture (excluding modern, the province of the *Tate), of British *miniatures, of *watercolours, and English silversmiths' work. The National Art Library is also part of the museum. There are great collections of ceramics, furniture, and musical instruments, and Oriental art is strongly represented. The celebrated highlights include *Raphael's tapestry *cartoons (on loan from the Royal Collection), which form the most important ensemble of High *Renaissance art outside Italy, and the collection of *Constable's work—the largest anywhere (the bulk of it was presented by his daughter).

Victory of Samothrace. Celebrated larger-than-life Greek marble statue (Louvre, Paris) showing winged Victory (Nike) alighting on the bows of a galley. The figure, discovered on the Greek island of Samothrace in 1863, is lithely outstretched and draped with magnificent swirls. It was erected around 200 BC above a rocky pool, presumably to celebrate a victory in a sea battle; it showed its best view obliquely and from below, and now is appropriately and dramatically placed at the top of the main staircase in the Louvre.

Video art. A broad term applied to works created by visual artists in which video and television equipment and technology are used in any of various ways. The German artist Wolf Vostell (1932–98) incorporated working television sets in *assemblages in 1959, but the creator of video art as a genre is usually regarded as Nam June Paik (1932–), a Korean musician, *Performance artist, and sculptor, who settled in New

York in 1964 and acquired a portable Sony video recorder in 1965 as soon as this new equipment was available there. He is said to have made his first recording on the day he bought the recorder and to have showed the tape the same evening at an artists' club, the Café-a-Go-Go. Paik had trained as a pianist, and after he turned to video he often collaborated with the cellist Charlotte Moorman (1940–94), notably in *Bra for Living Sculpture* (1969), in which she played her instrument whilst wearing a bra incorporating two miniature television screens (predictably dubbed 'boob tubes'). (Moorman was arrested for indecent exposure whilst performing in another Paik work.) Whereas Paik sees himself as an entertainer (he has often appeared on television chat shows), another well-known specialist in video art, the American Bill Viola (1951–), is more serious—his detractors might say portentous—in tone. A representative work is *To Pray Without Ceasing* (1992), which Viola describes as 'a contemporary "book of hours" and image vigil to the infinite day, functioning as an unfolding sequence of prayers for the city'. It consists of a twelve-hour cycle of images accompanied by a recording of a voice reciting poetry by Walt Whitman. 'The images are projected continuously, 24 hours a day, seven days a week', comments Viola. 'During the day, sunlight washes out the image and only the voice is present. The video playback is synchronized to the time of day by computer.' Rapid advances in computer and video technology have encouraged many artists to work in the field, which became highly fashionable in the 1990s: the *Turner Prize was won by video artists in 1996, 1997, and 1999.

Vien, Joseph-Marie (1716–1809). French painter. He won the *Prix de Rome in 1743 and was in Rome from 1744 to 1750. At this time, excavations at Herculaneum and Pompeii were causing great excitement in the art world, and Vien's interest in the ancient Roman paintings that were unearthed helped him to gain a reputation (partly self-promoted) as a pioneer of the *Neoclassical style. He was enthusiastic for the ideas of *Winckelmann, but his *classicism was of a very superficial kind; his most characteristic works are sentimental genre or allegorical pictures with pseudo-antique trappings (*The Cupid Seller*, 1763, Château

de Fontainebleau). Nevertheless, he gauged the taste of the time well and had a career of exemplary success, becoming director of the French Academy in Rome (1775–81) and first painter to the king (1789). In spite of this royal appointment, he survived the Revolution and was ennobled by Napoleon in 1808. He had many pupils, of whom the most important was J.-L. *David. His son, **Joseph-Marie the Younger** (1762–1848), was also a painter, mainly of portraits.

Vigée-Lebrun, Élisabeth (1755–1842). French portrait painter, daughter of the pastellist **Louis Vigée** (1715–67), from whom she received her first lessons. Renowned for her beauty, wit, and charm as well as for her talent, she had a highly successful career, with many eminent sitters, notably Queen Marie Antoinette; she portrayed the queen numerous times (initially in 1778, KH Mus., Vienna) and they became friends. On the outbreak of the Revolution in 1789 she left France with her daughter, leaving behind her husband, the picture dealer Jean-Baptiste Lebrun, to whom she was unhappily married. She worked in Italy (1789–93), Vienna (1793–4), and St Petersburg (1795–1801), before returning to Paris in 1802. Disliking the Napoleonic regime, she worked in England in 1803–5, but then settled permanently in France, thereafter making only short visits abroad. She received distinguished patronage wherever she went and was admitted to several *academies. Her work is graceful, charming, pleasingly sentimental, and delicately executed. Her memoirs (3 vols., 1835–7) give a lively picture of the Europe of her day as well as an account of her own works, and vividly demonstrate what a redoubtable woman she was: 'on the day that my daughter was born I never left my studio and I went on working…in the intervals between labour pains.'

Vigeland, Gustav (1869–1943). The most famous of Norwegian sculptors. He studied in Oslo and Copenhagen and then (1892–5) in Paris and Italy, spending a few months with *Rodin. At this time he worked in a painstakingly naturalistic style, but in 1900 he began studying medieval sculpture in preparation for restoration work on Trondheim Cathedral and this led to his work becoming expressively stylized. In the same year he made his first sketches for the massive project that occupied much of his energies for the rest of his life (it was completed the year after his death)—a series of allegorical groups at Frogner Park, Oslo. Originally only a fountain was planned, but with the help of assistants he went on to create numerous other groups, including a column 17 m (55 ft) high composed of intertwining bodies. The symbolism of the scheme is not clear, but essentially it represents 'a statement of the doubt, disillusion, and physical decline that beset humanity in its passage through this world' (George Heard Hamilton, *Painting and Sculpture in Europe: 1880–1940*, 1967). Reactions to the whole megalomaniac conception, involving scores of bronze and granite figures, have been mixed, some critics finding it stupendous, others tasteless and monotonous.

Vignon, Claude (1593–1670). French painter, born in Tours and active mainly in Paris. His highly eclectic style was formed mainly in Italy, where he worked *c*.1616–*c*.1622, and his openness to very diverse influences was later fuelled by his activities as a picture dealer. Paradoxically, in view of his varied sources of inspiration, his style is the most distinctive of any French painter of his generation—highly coloured and often bizarrely expressive. *Elsheimer and the *Caravaggisti were strong influences on his handling of light, and his richly encrusted brushwork has striking affinities with *Rembrandt, whose work Vignon is known to have sold. There are examples of his paintings in the Louvre; he also produced etchings and book illustrations. Vignon is said to have fathered 34 children by his two wives; his sons **Claude the Younger** (1633–1703) and **Philippe** (1638–1701) and his daughter **Charlotte** (1639–?) were also painters.

Villon, Jacques (1875–1963). French painter and graphic artist, the elder brother of Marcel *Duchamp and Raymond *Duchamp-Villon. His original name was Gaston Duchamp, but he changed it in 1895 because of his admiration for the 15th-century poet François Villon. In 1894 he began studying law in Paris, but he soon abandoned it for art, initially earning his living mainly as a newspaper illustrator. In 1911 he began experimenting with *Cubism, and the following year he was one of the founders of the *Section d'Or group. After the First World War he began painting geometrical abstracts, but in the 1920s he earned his living mainly as a printmaker (he was an expert etcher). In 1921 he had a one-man exhibition at the *Société Anonyme, New York, and for most of the interwar period he was probably better known in the USA than in Europe. During this time he alternated between abstraction and a highly schematized type of figuration. After the Second World War he enjoyed substantially greater recognition than in the earlier part of his career, winning the Grand Prize for Painting at the Venice *Biennale in 1958, when he was in his eighties.

Vinckboons, David (1576–1630/3). Dutch painter and printmaker of Flemish birth, the best-known member of a family of artists. His father, the painter **Philip Vinckboons** (1545–1601), left Antwerp because of religious intolerance (he was a Protestant) and David spent most of his life in Amsterdam. He specialized in genre scenes in landscape settings and is a transitional figure between the decorative *Mannerist tradition and the more naturalistic style associated with 17th-century Dutch painting. His scenes depicting village festivals show the influence of Pieter *Bruegel, and Vinckboons is credited with introducing some of his motifs into Holland. It is sometimes claimed that Vinckboons's works can always be identified by the presence of a finch (*vinck*) in a tree (*boom*), but the painstaking student usually finds that the bird has flown. His son **Philips Vingboons** (1607/8–78) was a leading architect in Amsterdam.

Vingt, Les (Les XX). Group of progressive Belgian painters and sculptors (originally twenty in number, hence the name) who exhibited together from 1884 to 1893. The members included James *Ensor and Jan *Toorop. They showed not only their own work, but also paintings by non-Belgian artists such as *Cézanne, van *Gogh, and *Seurat. The group was influential in spreading the ideas of *Neo-Impressionism and *Post-Impressionism and became the main Belgian forum for *Symbolism and *Art Nouveau. Although the group dissolved in 1893, its work was carried on by an association called La Libre Esthétique, which ran from 1894 to 1914. Most of the leading Belgian avant-garde artists of the period were members.

Viola, Bill. *See* VIDEO ART.

Vischer. Family of German sculptors active in Nuremberg. **Hermann the Elder** (d. 1488) established the family bronze-foundry, and the business was inherited by his son **Peter the Elder** (c.1460–1529), the best known of the Vischers. He was assisted by five sons: **Hermann the Younger** (c.1486–1517), **Peter the Younger** (1487–1528), **Hans** (c.1489–1550), **Jacob**, and **Paulus**. The masterpiece of the Vischer workshop is the spectacular bronze shrine over the sarcophagus of St Sebald in the church dedicated to him in Nuremberg. The first design—a drawing (by Peter the Elder?) in the Academy, Vienna—dates from 1488, but work began only in 1508 and continued until 1519. Through journeys of the younger generation the workshop had by that time gained a good deal of knowledge of Italian bronzes and in particular the work of north Italian sculptors. Thus the Sebald tomb became a fascinating mixture of *Gothic and *Renaissance styles. The canopy remains Gothic, as also the main figures of the Apostles standing before the supports; but the base of the tomb is inhabited by biblical, mythological, and decorative figures conceived in a genuine Renaissance spirit. Peter the Elder included a celebrated self-portrait (complete with tools and leather apron) among these figures. He also made two splendid free-standing figures (1512–13) of Theodoric and King Arthur for the tomb of the emperor Maximilian I (*see* HABSBURG) in the Hofkirche, Innsbruck. **Georg** (c.1522–92), a son of Hans, was the last artist member of the Vischer family; he seems to have specialized in small decorative bronzes such as inkwells.

Vittoria, Alessandro (1525?–1608). Italian sculptor, born at Trent and active mainly in Venice, where he settled in 1543. He trained under Jacopo *Sansovino and succeeded him as the leading sculptor in the city, dominating the art in a way somewhat comparable to his contemporary *Giambologna in Florence. His output was large and varied, including tombs, altars, statues, portraits, and architectural ornament, notably the vault over the ceremonial entrance to the Doges' Palace, the Scala d'Oro (1557–9). This is in gilded *stucco, and he also worked in bronze, marble, and terracotta. Temperamentally he was a modeller rather than a carver, and his marbles tend to be lacking in warmth compared with his work in other media. His formidably characterized portrait busts are now perhaps his most admired works; his sitters included some of the leading Venetian personalities of the time.

Vivarini. Family of Venetian painters. **Antonio** (c.1420–76/84) seldom worked independently. He collaborated first with his brother-in-law, the German-born Giovanni d'Alemagna (active 1441–50), and then from the 1450s with his own younger brother, **Bartolomeo** (c.1432–c.1499). The pictures produced by these partnerships are usually large *polyptychs with stiff, archaic-looking figures and very elaborate carved and gilded frames in the *Gothic tradition. Bartolomeo's independent works date from the 1460s onwards. He continued to paint polyptychs, but he modernized his style somewhat by imitating *Mantegna. **Alvise** (c.1445–1503/5), son of Antonio, is the best-known member of the family. He presumably trained in the family workshop, but his work was more modern in style than that of his father or uncle, influenced particularly by Giovanni *Bellini. None of the Vivarini had much originality. There are examples of the work of all three in the National Gallery, London.

Vivin, Louis (1861–1936). French *naive painter. He had a passion for painting from childhood, but could not devote himself to it regularly until he retired from the Post Office in 1922. In 1925 he was 'discovered' by Wilhelm *Uhde and subsequently won wide recognition. His work included *genre scenes, flower pieces, hunting scenes, and views of Paris, notable for their charmingly wobbly perspective effects.

Vlaminck, Maurice de (1876–1958). French painter, printmaker, and writer. A colourful and many-sided character, as a young man he earned his living mainly as a racing cyclist and orchestral violinist, painting in his spare time virtually without instruction. Indeed, he delighted to inveigh against all forms of academic training and boasted that he had never set foot inside the

*Louvre: 'I try to paint with my heart and my loins, not bothering with style.' In 1901 an exhibition of van *Gogh's work in Paris overwhelmed him, intensifying his love of pure colour, and with *Matisse and *Derain he became a leading exponent of *Fauvism, often using paint straight from the tube in exuberant compositions—mainly landscapes. From 1908, however, his palette darkened and his work became more solidly constructed, under the influence of *Cézanne. In 1910–14 he was also mildly influenced by *Cubist stylization, although he came to dislike *Picasso and regard him as a charlatan. After the First World War he moved from Paris and in 1925 he settled in a farmhouse in Eure-et-Loir. His later work became rather slick and mannered, but he built up an international reputation. In addition to painting he wrote novels and several volumes of memoirs.

Vlieger, Simon de (c.1601–53). Dutch painter, mainly of marine subjects, active in his native Rotterdam, Delft, and Amsterdam. One of the outstanding marine painters of his period, he moved from stormy subjects in the manner of *Porcellis to serene and majestic images that influenced van de *Cappelle (who owned a large collection of his work) and Willem van de *Velde the Younger (whom he taught). De Vlieger also painted landscapes; he was a prolific draughtsman, made etchings, and designed stained-glass windows for the Niewe Kerk in Amsterdam.

Vollard, Ambroise (1866–1939). French dealer, connoisseur, publisher, and writer, one of the most important champions of avant-garde art in the early 20th century. In 1893 he opened a gallery in Paris and in 1895 he gave the first important exhibition of *Cézanne. Other landmark events included the first one-man exhibitions of *Picasso (1901) and *Matisse (1904). His clientele included some of the leading collectors of the day, among them Albert C. *Barnes and Gertrude and Leo *Stein. In addition to buying and selling paintings, Vollard played an important role as a publisher by encouraging his artists to work as printmakers. He commissioned them to illustrate books (literary classics as well as contemporary works) and also issued independent portfolios of prints, most notably Picasso's *Vollard Suite*, consisting of 100 etchings on various themes made

between 1930 and 1937. His portrait was painted many times, among others by *Bonnard, Cézanne, Picasso, *Renoir, and *Rouault. Vollard's writings included books on Cézanne and *Degas and the autobiographical *Recollections of a Picture Dealer* (1936).

Vorticism. An avant-garde British art movement launched in 1914; it was related to *Cubism and *Futurism and was mainly concerned with the visual arts, but it also embraced literature (its name was suggested by the American poet Ezra Pound, to whom the vortex represented 'the point of maximum energy', an expression of the dynamism of modern life). Vorticism was highly aggressive in tone, celebrating movement and the machine, and attacking what was considered the complacency and sentimentality of contemporary British culture. It was short-lived, its vigour being dissipated by the First World War, but it had a powerful, revitalizing impact on British art. The central figure of the movement, as a theorist as well as an artist, was Wyndham *Lewis, who edited its journal *Blast* (only two numbers appeared, in 1914 and 1915). He later claimed that 'Vorticism…was what I, personally, did, and said, at a certain period', but there was clearly a close similarity of style between his harsh, angular, mechanistic paintings and the work of several of his associates, including Henri *Gaudier-Brzeska, William *Roberts, and Edward *Wadsworth, each of whom signed the Vorticist manifesto that appeared in the first number of *Blast*. The Vorticists held only one exhibition, at the Doré Gallery, London, in June 1915. Apart from the formal members, the artists taking part included David *Bomberg and C. R. W. *Nevinson. Jacob *Epstein was not included, but his work was reproduced in *Blast* and he is generally considered part of the movement. Several of the artists represented in the exhibition were now producing pure abstracts, and the show was far too advanced for the critics, who treated it as an incomprehensible joke. By this time the war was scattering the Vorticists (Gaudier-Breszka had already been killed in action), and Lewis's attempts to revive the movement after the war were unsuccessful.

Vos, Cornelis de (1584?–1651). Flemish painter, active in Antwerp. He painted historical, allegorical, mythological, and religious works, but excelled chiefly as a portraitist. His finest paintings are his portraits of children, which have great sensitivity and charm without lapsing into sentimentality. A splendid self-portrait of *The Artist with his Family* (1621, Mus. Royaux, Brussels) shows him looking happy and proud with his own children. In style he was close to *Rubens and van *Dyck but more down to earth (his sitters were typically solid members of the bourgeoisie rather than aristocrats or intellectuals). His brother **Paul de Vos** (1595?–1678) painted hunting scenes and still lifes in the style of Frans *Snyders, who was the brother-in-law of the de Vos brothers. In 1637 all three helped Rubens execute pictures for the Torre de la Parada, Philip IV of Spain's (*see* HABSBURG) hunting-lodge near Madrid.

Vos, Maerten de (1532–1603). Netherlandish painter, active mainly in his native Antwerp. In about 1552 he went to Italy (perhaps in company with *Bruegel) and worked in *Tintoretto's studio in Venice; he also visited Rome and probably Florence. By 1558 he was back in Antwerp, and after the death of Frans *Floris in 1570 he became one of the leading artists in the city. The altarpieces that make up the bulk of his output show the influence of Italian *Mannerism in their slender elegance, but his warmth of colour looks forward to *Rubens and the Flemish *Baroque. His rare portraits are notably direct and in the Netherlandish rather than the Italian tradition (*Antoine Anselme and his Family*, 1577, Mus. Royaux, Brussels). He was a prolific draughtsman and many prints were made of his compositions.

Vostell, Wolf. *See* FLUXUS and VIDEO ART.

Vouet, Simon (1590–1649). The leading French painter of the first half of the 17th century. His early years are obscure, but according to *Félibien he was precocious and worked as a portraitist in England when he was only 14. He certainly made a visit to Constantinople in 1611–12 before moving to Italy, where he lived from 1613 to 1627, mainly in Rome. During this period he achieved a considerable reputation and became president of the Accademia di S. Luca (*see* ACADEMY) in 1624. His early work in Italy was much influenced by *Caravaggio, but he later developed an *eclectic style in which *Baroque tendencies were tempered by the *classicism of Guido *Reni and *Domenichino. In 1627 Louis XIII recalled Vouet to Paris and made him his court painter, launching him on an extremely busy and prosperous career. His compromise style proved exactly to the taste of his French clients; he offered them something more lively and modern than the prevailing tired *Mannerism but less extreme than the dramatic naturalism of the Caravaggesque or the full emotionalism of the Baroque. Only when *Poussin returned from Rome to Paris in 1640–2 was Vouet's dominance threatened. He painted religious and allegorical works and portraits and was employed on several major decorative schemes, sometimes in conjunction with Jacques *Sarrazin. Little of his best decorative work survives, however. Vouet was a versatile and hardworking artist rather than a great one and his success and influence depended on his having hit upon a style that suited the taste of the day at a time when French painting was at a low ebb. He introduced new life and a tradition of solid competence and many of the leading members of the next generation of painters passed through his studio, including *Le Brun, Hubert *Le Sueur, and *Mignard. Examples of Vouet's work are in many French museums.

Vredeman de Vries, Hans (c.1527–c.1606). Netherlandish painter, architect, engineer, and designer, active in Germany and Prague, as well as in Amsterdam, Antwerp, and The Hague. He was famous in his lifetime for his skill in *illusionistic architectural decoration, but much of his work was of a temporary nature (triumphal arches for festivities and so on) and few paintings are known by him (one of them is *Christ in the House of Mary and Martha* in the Royal Collection, which is set in an extremely elaborate interior). He is now remembered primarily for his many books and prints containing *perspective studies of fanciful palaces, courts, gardens, furniture, and decorative work. They had wide circulation in northern Europe and had great influence on architecture and decoration.

Vrel, Jacobus (active 1654–62). Dutch painter, an enigmatic figure who has only recently gained recognition as one of the most charmingly idiosyncratic masters of his time. Nothing at all is recorded of his life, his name surviving solely through the signatures on some of his paintings. About 40 pictures by him are known—either sparse interiors or quiet street scenes. They show a remarkably fresh, almost *naive vision and have a sense of tranquil poetry that has led them to be compared to the work of *Vermeer. Several of his paintings have, indeed, formerly gone under Vermeer's name, for example *Street Scene* in the Getty Museum, Los Angeles. Because of the similarity of spirit, it has been surmised that Vrel, too, worked in Delft, but some authorities consider it likely that he lived in a provincial town rather than a major art centre.

Vries, Adriaen de (c.1545–1626). Netherlandish sculptor active mainly in central Europe, notably for the emperor Rudolf II (*see* HABSBURG) in Prague. He spent most of the 1580s in Italy, where he assisted *Giambologna in Florence and Pompeo *Leoni in Milan. His first independent documented work is *Mercury and Psyche* (1593, Louvre, Paris), made for Rudolf II. This, like most of his sculpture is in bronze, a material in which he imitated Giambologna's sleek and elegant *Mannerist style with great accomplishment; he played a leading role in spreading this style to northern Europe. His major works included two fountains in Augsburg (1599, 1602) and another made for Fredericksberg Castle, Copenhagen (1615–17). The figures from the Copenhagen fountain were taken by the Swedes as war booty in 1659 and are now in the Palace of Drottningholm near Stockholm. None of de Vries's commissions came from the Low Countries.

Vrubel, Mikhail (1856–1910). Russian painter and designer, the outstanding exponent of *Symbolism in his country. His first important work was the restoration of murals in the 12th-century church of St Cyril, Kiev, and in his subsequent career he showed an affinity with the spirituality of medieval religious art. In 1889 he moved from Kiev to Moscow and there was taken up by the wealthy art patron Savva Mamon-

tov (*see* ABRAMTSEVO COLONY); a portrait (1897) of him by Vrubel is in the Tretyakov Gallery, Moscow. In 1890 he began to produce interpretations of Mikhail Lermontov's poem *The Demon* and the theme became central to his work. In treating it he passed from fairly naturalistic depictions to highly idiosyncratic anguish-ridden images rendered in brilliant fragmented brushwork that recalls the effects of medieval mosaics. The obsessive treatment of the theme reflected his own emotional instability; in 1902 the first symptoms of approaching insanity became apparent, in 1906 he went blind, and he died in a lunatic asylum. Although he was little appreciated for most of his career, he had become well known by the time of his death and had great influence on Russian painting in the early 20th century.

Vuillard, Édouard (1868–1940). French painter, draughtsman, designer, and lithographer. In the 1890s he was a member of the *Nabis and at this time painted intimate interiors and scenes from Montmartre, his sensitive patterning of flattish colours owing something to *Gauguin and something to *Puvis de Chavannes, but creating a distinctive manner of his own. He also designed posters and theatrical sets. From about 1900 he turned to a more naturalistic style and with *Bonnard became the main practitioner of *Intimisme, making use of the camera to capture fleeting, informal groupings of his friends and relatives in their homes and gardens. He had several close female friends and preferred painting women and children to men. His work also included landscapes and portraits. Although he was financially successful, he lived modestly, sharing an apartment with his widowed mother until her death in 1928; she often features in his paintings. He was reserved and quiet in personality, although affectionate and much liked. For many years he kept a detailed journal in which he revealed his thoughtful attitude towards art and life.

Waagen, Gustav Friedrich (1794–1868). German art historian. In 1822 he published a book on the van *Eycks that made his reputation and led to his appointment as director of the recently founded Gemäldegalerie in Berlin in 1832. In 1844 he became the first holder of a university chair in art history when he was appointed professor at Berlin University. A frequent traveller, with a great reputation as a connoisseur, Waagen is best remembered for his notes on works of art in public and private collections in various countries, which are a mine of information. Outstanding among them is *Treasures of Art in Great Britain* (3 vols., 1854), translated into English by Lady *Eastlake; a supplementary volume entitled *Galleries and Cabinets of Art in Great Britain* was published in 1857.

Wadsworth, Edward (1889–1949). British painter, printmaker, draughtsman, and designer. A friend of Wyndham *Lewis, he was a member of the *Vorticist group (1914–15); his work of this time included completely abstract pictures such as the stridently geometrical *Abstract Composition* (1915, Tate, London). In the First World War he worked on designing dazzle camouflage for ships, turning his harsh Vorticist style to practical use. This experience provided the subject for one of his best-known paintings, the huge *Dazzle-Ships in Drydock at Liverpool* (1919, NG, Ottawa). The lucidity and precision seen here were enhanced when Wadsworth switched from oil painting to tempera in about 1922. At the same time his style changed, as he abandoned *Cubist leanings for a more naturalistic idiom. He had a passion for the sea and often painted maritime subjects, developing a distinctive type of highly composed marine still life, typically with a *Surrealistic flavour brought about by oddities of scale and juxtaposition and the hypnotic clarity of the lighting (*Satellitium*, 1932, Castle Mus., Nottingham). In the 1920s and 1930s he was among the most European in spirit of British artists. He travelled widely on the Continent and in 1933 contributed to the Paris journal *Abstraction-Création*. In the same year he was a founder member of *Unit One. Around this time he again painted abstracts (influenced by *Arp), but he reverted to his more naturalistic style in 1934. During the 1930s he had several commissions for murals, notably two panels for the liner *Queen Mary* in 1938. As a graphic artist he is best known for his vigorous, angular woodcuts of ships and machinery, which played a part in the revival of the technique after the First World War. For an artist, Wadsworth was 'unusually business-like, answering letters by return of post and punctiliously fulfilling his commissions' (*DNB*), but he has been aptly described by Sir John *Rothenstein as 'a true poet of the age of machines'.

Waldmüller, Ferdinand Georg (1793–1865). One of the leading Austrian painters of the *Biedermeier period. He painted portraits, *genre subjects, and still life, but is perhaps best known for his landscapes, which in their loving attention to detail illustrate his belief that the close study of nature should be the basis of painting. In 1829 he became professor of painting at the Vienna Academy, but he had a stormy relationship with it because his views were at odds with its traditional teaching methods; he wrote several treatises urging academic reform.

Walker, Dame Ethel (1861–1951). British painter and occasional sculptor. In 1900 she became the first woman member of the *New English Art Club and it was there that she mainly exhibited, building a reputation as one of the outstanding British women artists of her period. She painted portraits, flower pieces, interiors, and seascapes in an attractive *Impressionist style, but her most individual works are large decorative compositions inspired by her vision of a Golden Age. They show the influence of French *Symbolist painting as well as her interest in philosophy and religion (*The Zone of Hate*, 1914–15, and *The Zone of Love*, c.1930–2; both Tate, London).

Walker, Robert (*c*.1600/10–1658). English portrait painter. He has a certain niche in history as he was the portraitist most favoured by Oliver Cromwell and the Parliamentarians during the Interregnum (1649–60), but his work is generally dull and derivative (mainly of van *Dyck). A few of his pictures, however, are more personal (*Self-portrait*, Ashmolean Mus., Oxford).

Wallace Collection, London. National museum consisting of the collection built up in the 18th and 19th centuries by the Seymour-Conway family, Earls and later Marquesses of Hertford; it was bequeathed to the nation in 1897 by Lady Wallace, widow of Sir Richard Wallace, the illegitimate son of the 4th Marquess of Hertford, and opened to the public in 1900. It is located in Hertford House, the former London residence of the family. The collection, the largest of its date to be preserved intact, reflects the tastes of various members of the family, but particularly of the 4th Marquess (Richard Seymour-Conway, 1800–70) and his son Sir Richard Wallace (1819–90), who spent much of their lives in Paris. The Marquess bought most of the superb representation of 18th-century French art (furniture as well as paintings) that is the collection's chief glory; Sir Richard added much *Renaissance decorative art and the magnificent collection of armour, rivalled in Britain only by that in the Royal Armouries. Other areas in which the Wallace Collection is particularly rich are 17th-century Dutch and Flemish painting (its most famous exhibit is Frans *Hals's *The Laughing Cavalier*); 18th-century English portraits; and the works of *Bonington (the best representation anywhere). In 2000, marking the Wallace Collection's centenary, an extension to the building was opened, created partly by glazing over what had been the central courtyard.

Wallis, Alfred (1855–1942). British *naive painter of sailing ships and landscapes. He went to sea as a cabin boy and cook at the age of 9, and from about 1880 worked as a fisherman in Cornwall. In 1890 he opened a rag-and-bone store in St Ives and after retiring from this did odd jobs, including selling ice cream. He began to paint in 1925 to ease the loneliness he felt after his wife's death and was discovered by Ben *Nicholson and Christopher *Wood in 1928, the unselfconscious vigour of his work making a powerful impression on them. Wallis painted from memory and imagination, usually working with ship's paint on scraps of cardboard or wood. Although he rapidly became the best known of British naive artists, he died in a workhouse.

walnut oil. *Drying oil obtained from the common walnut. It was one of the earliest oils used in painting, and perhaps the commonest *medium in the early days of *oil painting, but it is little used today. It dries more slowly than *linseed oil but has less tendency to turn yellow.

Walpole, Horace (1717–97). English collector, connoisseur, man of letters, and amateur architect. He was the fourth son of Sir Robert Walpole, Britain's first prime minister, and in 1791 he became 4th Earl of Orford. In 1739–41 he made the *Grand Tour, travelling in France and Italy with the poet Thomas Gray. His literary fame rests on his voluminous correspondence and on *The Castle of Otranto* (1764), the first 'Gothic novel'. In the history of taste he is primarily important for his house at Twickenham, Strawberry Hill, which he bought in 1747 and extended into a showpiece of the Gothic Revival, employing professional architects to work from his sketches. He filled the building with his collections and it became such a tourist attraction that he took to issuing admission tickets. In 1757 he established a printing press at Strawberry Hill, from which he issued his *Anecdotes of Painting in England* (4 vols., 1762–71), based on *Vertue's notebooks.

Wals, Goffredo. *See* CLAUDE.

Wanderers (or **Itinerants**) (Russ., 'Peredvizhniki'). Association of Russian painters active from 1870 to 1923. The formal name of the organization was 'Association of Travelling [or Wandering] Art Exhibitions', the word 'travelling' referring to the fact that its exhibitions were shown successively in various Russian towns (including Astrakhan, Kharkov, Kiev, Kursk, Odessa, and Saratov), not just in the country's two elite art centres, Moscow and St Petersburg. This desire to reach a wide public was inspired by democratic social ideals; like other members of the Russian intelligentsia at this time, the Wanderers wanted to bring culture to the common people, to help educate and inspire them. The nucleus of the association was formed by a number of art students—led by *Kramskoi—who had left the St Petersburg Academy in 1863 because of its rigid traditionalism. They had refused to accept 'The Feast of the Gods in Valhalla' as a competition subject because it was so irrelevant to contemporary social needs. In contrast to such rarefied subjects, the Wanderers not only wanted to depict ordinary people, but also to show such people a vision of moral worth and hope in the future. Consequently their paintings were realistic and easily intelligible. Sometimes they were overtly political, dealing with issues such as rural poverty or corruption in the Church, but many pictures shown in the exhibitions were unpolemical; there were, for example, numerous landscapes and portraits. The first Wanderers' exhibition was held in 1871; it was highly successful and 47 more followed, held virtually every year until 1923. Many of the outstanding Russian painters of the late 19th century were members. Among them were Nikolai Ghe (1831–94), whose work included some starkly powerful scenes of Christ's Passion; Isaak Levitan (1860–1900), one of the leading Russian landscapists of the time; Vasily Perov (1834–82), whose scenes of rural and urban poverty perhaps best illustrate the social conscience of the Wanderers in their early days; Ilya *Repin; Vasily Surikov (1848–1916), best known for depicting events from his country's history; and Viktor *Vasnetsov. By the turn of the century the association had passed its peak as a major force in the country's cultural life and in its later years it was regarded as upholding conservative rather than radical values. In 1923 it merged with the Association of Artists of Revolutionary Russia, which had been founded the previous year. After the imposition of *Socialist Realism in the 1930s, the Wanderers were extolled as its precursors.

Wappers, Gustaf (1803–74). Belgian painter, active mainly in Antwerp, where he became a professor at the Academy in 1833. He was an enormous success in his day with his elaborate historical costume pieces, catching the public imagination with patriotic themes that appealed to the Belgian people, who had just won their independence (*Episode from the Belgian Revolution of 1830*, 1834, Mus. Royaux, Brussels).

Such works have dated badly, however. In 1845 he was created a baron, and in 1853 he settled in Paris.

War Artists' Advisory Committee. *See* OFFICIAL WAR ART.

Warburg, Aby (1866–1929). German art historian. His main field of study was the art of the Florentine *quattrocento, which he tried to understand as part of the intellectual history of the time. In particular he was impressed by the hold that religious loyalties and astrological superstition retained on the minds of Renaissance merchants and princes, indicating that the subject matter of the paintings they commissioned was no mere pretext for the display of artistic fancies. Warburg published little, but his ideas had great influence. The superb library that he built up in his home in Hamburg developed into a research institute, which was transferred to London in 1933 to escape the Nazi regime and in 1944 was incorporated in the University of London as the Warburg Institute. Its field of study is now officially defined as 'the history of the *classical tradition' ('das Nachleben der Antike'), but its intellectual range encompasses, in *Panofsky's words, 'the history of art, the history of religion and superstition, the history of science, the history of cultic practices (including pageantry) and the history of literature'. Ernst *Gombrich, who wrote a biography of Warburg (1970; rev. edn. 1986), is one of the many distinguished scholars associated with the Institute.

Ward, James (1769–1859). English painter and printmaker. He was trained as a mezzotint engraver by his brother **William** (1766–1826) and by John Raphael Smith (*see* DE WINT) and began painting in about 1790. Until about the end of the century he painted mainly anecdotal *genre scenes in the manner of his brother-in-law George *Morland, but he then turned to the paintings of animals in landscape settings for which he is chiefly remembered. They are often dramatic and *Romantic in character and their rich colouring was influenced by *Rubens (*Bulls Fighting*, 1803, V&A, London). His taste for natural grandeur and the *Sublime is most memorably expressed in the enormous *Gordale Scar* (1812–14, Tate, London). Ward had many admirers, including

*Delacroix and *Géricault, but he became disillusioned with the art world and lived in retirement in Hertfordshire from 1830. He continued to exhibit, but he became something of a religious obsessive and died in poverty aged 90.

Ward, John Quincy Adams (1830–1910). American sculptor, active mainly in New York. He was the most prolific sculptor of public monuments of his period, working until the end of his long life. His portrait statues, equestrian figures, allegorical groups, war memorials, and architectural decorations have solid dignity but none of the genius of his contemporary *Saint-Gaudens.

Warhol, Andy (1928–87). American painter, printmaker, sculptor, draughtsman, film-maker, and writer, one of the most famous and controversial artists of the 20th century. During the 1950s he was enormously successful as a commercial artist in New York (specializing in shoe advertisements). In 1960 he began making pictures based on mass-produced images such as newspaper advertisements and comic strips, then in 1962 of Campbell's soup cans. They were exhibited in that year with sensational success and Warhol soon became the best-known figure in American *Pop art. In the same vein as his soup cans he did pictures of Coca-Cola bottles and made equally banal sculptures of Brillo soap-pad boxes and similar cartons. He also embarked on a lengthy series of pictures of Marilyn Monroe, Elvis Presley, Elizabeth Taylor, and other celebrities. Similar in method but different in effect were his pictures of disasters such as car crashes and views of the electric chair. Whatever the subject in his pictures, he often made use of rows of repeated images. The *screenprinting process that he favoured allowed infinite replication, and he was opposed to the idea of a work of art as a piece of craftsmanship, handmade and expressing the personality of the artist: 'I want everybody to think alike. I think everybody should be a machine.' In keeping with this outlook he used clippings of 'dehumanized' illustrations from the mass media as his sources, turned out his works like a manufacturer, and called his studio 'The Factory'. There he was surrounded by a crowd of helpers and hangers-on, described by Robert *Hughes as 'cultural space-debris, drifting fragments from a variety of sixties subcultures'. Warhol liked to give the idea that he took a paternal interest in his followers, but Eric Shanes (*Warhol*, 1991) writes that 'Just how cynical he could be in his dealings with his entourage is demonstrated by an incident that occurred in October 1964 when one of his hangers-on, Freddie Herko, committed suicide by jumping from a fifth-floor window in Greenwich Village while high on LSD: Warhol was heard to complain repeatedly that Herko should have forewarned him so that he could have filmed his death.'

In 1965 Warhol announced his retirement as an artist to devote himself to films and to managing the rock group the Velvet Underground, but in fact he never gave up painting and in the 1970s he made an enormous amount of money churning out commissioned portraits of wealthy patrons. In the 1980s he sometimes collaborated with other painters, including the *Graffiti artist Jean-Michel Basquiat. As a film-maker, Warhol became perhaps the only 'underground' director to be well known to the general public. His first films were silent and virtually completely static: *Sleep* (1963)—a man sleeping for six hours; and *Empire* (1964)—the Empire State Building seen from one viewpoint for eight hours—'I like boring things.' Later films, such as the two-screen *Chelsea Girls* (1966), gained widespread attention because of their voyeuristic concentration on sex. In 1968 Warhol was shot and severely wounded by a bit-part player in one of his films, a member of SCUM (The Society for Cutting Up Men), an incident that added to his legendary status. By this time he was perhaps already more famous for his celebrity-courting lifestyle and deliberately bland persona than for his art; indeed, it could be argued that his advertising skills were nowhere more brilliantly deployed than in promoting himself. In purely financial terms his success in promoting himself was prodigious. At his death (following a routine gall bladder operation) he left a fortune estimated at $100,000,000, most of which went to create an arts charity, the Andy Warhol Foundation. His status as an artist, however, is controversial. Even his most fervent admirers tend to admit that he added little to his achievement as a painter after the mid-

1960s, but large claims are sometimes made for his earlier works. Warhol published a celebrity magazine called *Interview*, and several books appeared under his name, some genuinely written by him, others put together from tapes. *The Diaries of Andy Warhol* appeared posthumously in 1989. In 1994 a museum dedicated to his work opened in his home town of Pittsburgh.

wash. A thin, transparent layer of *watercolour or diluted *ink spread evenly over a fairly broad area of paper and showing no brush marks.

Washington Color Painters. *See* NOLAND.

watercolour. Term that can, in its broadest sense, be applied to any paint bound with a *medium (generally *gum arabic) soluble in water. In normal parlance, however, the term 'watercolour' usually refers specifically to a type of painting in which the lighter tones are not obtained by mixing white pigment with the colours but by diluting them with water so that the light is given by the paper or other support showing more strongly through the thinner layers of paint. It can thus be distinguished from other kinds of painting, such as *gouache, that use water as a medium but are opaque. Although there are isolated earlier examples of leading artists making memorable use of watercolour (*Dürer and van *Dyck, for example), it was not until the 18th century, in England, that it became a major medium, particularly for landscape painting, in which it lent itself to rendering subtle atmospheric effects. In the wake of *Impressionism, the capacity of watercolour to achieve spontaneous expression was more widely appreciated and it ceased to be so much of an English speciality. Among the modern artists who have been great exponents of the technique (in their very different ways) are *Cézanne, *Dufy, *Grosz, *Klee, *Nolde, and *Sargent.

water-glass painting (also called mineral painting and stereochromy). A method of mural painting, intended to prove resistant to the effects of damp and pollution, that had a brief vogue in the 19th century. It is essentially a variation of *fresco; after the paint has been applied to the plaster, it is coated with a solution of water glass (potassium silicate or sodium silicate), which provides a protective film when it dries. As water glass is strongly alkaline it can be used only with certain pigments. Some of the mural paintings in the House of Lords (*see* MACLISE) were executed in the medium, because it was thought that they would be proof against the damp and dirty atmosphere of London, but they deteriorated within ten years. Later the process was improved, but because of its complexity and limitations it never became popular.

Waterhouse, Sir Ellis (1905–85). British art historian. In a highly distinguished career he was director of the National Galleries of Scotland (1949–52), director of the Barber Institute of Fine Arts, Birmingham (1952–70), and the holder of many other prestigious posts in Britain and the USA. His publications were centred on two main areas, British painting of the 18th century and Italian *Baroque painting, his chief books being *Baroque Painting in Rome* (1937; rev. edn. 1976), *Painting in Britain 1530–1790* (1953 and several rev. edns.), *Italian Baroque Painting* (1962), a monograph on *Gainsborough (1958) and two on *Reynolds (1941 and 1973), *The Dictionary of British 18th-Century Painters* (1981), and *The Dictionary of British 16th- and 17th-Century Painters* (published posthumously 1988). He wore his great erudition lightly and few other art historians wrote so entertainingly.

Waterhouse, John William (1849–1917). English painter. Early in his career he concentrated on scenes from the Greek and Roman world in a manner similar to that of *Alma-Tadema, but in the 1880s he turned to literary themes, painted in a distinctive, dreamily romantic style. In approach he was influenced by the *Pre-Raphaelites, but his handling of paint is quite different from theirs—rich and sensuous. His work includes such classic Victorian anthology pieces as *The Lady of Shalott* (1888, Tate, London) and *Hylas and the Nymphs* (1896, Manchester AG).

Watt, Alison. *See* GLASGOW SCHOOL OF ART.

Watteau, Jean-Antoine (1684–1721). The greatest French painter of his period and one of the key figures of *Rococo art. He was born at Valenciennes, which had passed to France from the Spanish Netherlands only six years before his birth, and he was regarded by contemporaries as a

Flemish painter. There are indeed strong links with Flanders in his art, but it also has a sophistication that is quintessentially French. He moved to Paris in about 1702 and c.1704–8 he was a pupil and assistant of *Gillot, who stimulated his interest in scenes from the theatre and daily life. After leaving Gillot he worked for a year or two for Claude *Audran, who as well as being a leading decorative painter was curator of the Luxembourg Palace; Watteau thus had access to *Rubens's *Marie de Médicis* paintings, which were of enormous influence on him, even though Rubens's robustness was far removed from the exquisite sensitivity that characterized his own art. Rubens was one of the prime inspirations for the type of picture with which Watteau is most associated—the fête galante (*see* FÊTE CHAMPÊTRE)—in which beautifully dressed young people idle away their time in a dreamy, romantic, pastoral setting. The tradition of lovers in a parkland setting goes back via *Giorgione to the medieval type known as the 'Garden of Love', but Watteau was the first painter to make the theme his own, and his individuality in this respect was recognized by his contemporaries. In 1717 he submitted a characteristic work, *The Pilgrimage to the Island of Cythera* (Louvre, Paris; a slightly later variant is in Schloss Charlottenburg, Berlin), as his reception piece to the Academy, and owing to the difficulty of fitting him into recognized categories he was received as a 'peintre de fêtes galantes', a title created expressly for him. He was, indeed, a highly independent artist, who did not readily submit to the will of patrons or officialdom, and the novelty and freshness of his work liberated French painting from the yoke of Italian influence, creating a truly 'Parisian' outlook that endured until the *Neoclassicism of J.-L. *David. Watteau's world is a highly artificial one (apart from scenes of love he took his themes mainly from the theatre), but underlying the frivolity is a feeling of melancholy, reflecting the certain knowledge that all the pleasures of the flesh are transient. This poetic gravity distinguishes him from his imitators, and parallels are often drawn between Watteau's own life and character and the content of his paintings. He was notorious for his irritable and restless temperament and died young of tuberculosis, and it has been sug-

gested that the pervasive melancholic mood of his pictures was related to the constant reminders of his own mortality that his illness entailed. In 1719–20 he visited London to consult the celebrated physician Dr Richard Mead (who was also an art collector), but the hard English winter worsened his condition. His early death came when he may have been making a new departure in his art, for his last important work combines something of the straightforward naturalism of his early pictures in the Flemish tradition with the elegant sophistication of his fêtes galantes: it was painted as a shop sign for the picture dealer Edmé Gersaint and is known as *L'Enseigne de Gersaint* (1721, Gemäldegalerie, Berlin).

Watteau was slipshod in matters of material technique (another aspect of his listless temperament) and many of his paintings are in consequence in a poor state of preservation. A complete picture of his genius depends all the more, then, on his numerous superb drawings, many of them scintillating studies from the life. He collected his drawings into large bound volumes and used these books as a reference source for his paintings (the same figure often appears in more than one picture). In spite of his difficult character, Watteau had many loyal friends and supporters who recognized his genius, and although his reputation suffered with the Revolution and the growth of Neoclassicism, he always had distinguished admirers. It is perhaps as a colourist that he has had the most profound influence. His method of juxtaposing flecks of colour on the canvas was carried further by *Delacroix and later reduced to a science by *Seurat and the *Neo-Impressionists. Among his immediate followers, the principal figures were *Lancret and J.-B. *Pater. He also had a nephew and a great-nephew (father and son) who worked more or less in his manner. They are both known as 'Watteau de Lille' after their main place of work—**Louis Watteau** (1731–98) and **François Watteau** (1758–1823).

Watts, G. F. (George Frederic) (1817–1904). English painter and sculptor. In 1843 he won a prize in the competition for the decoration of the Houses of Parliament; no commission resulted from this, but he used the prize money to visit Italy, where the great *Renaissance masters helped shape his high-minded attitudes towards art. After returning to England in 1847, he established a solid reputation in intellectual circles, but popular fame did not come until the early 1880s, following exhibitions of his work in Manchester (1880) and London (1881). In old age he was the most revered figure in British art, and in 1902 he was the only artist among the twelve original holders of the newly instituted Order of Merit. His style was early influenced by *Etty, but the *Elgin Marbles, *Michelangelo, and the great Venetian painters (notably *Titian) were his avowed exemplars in his desire 'to affect the mind seriously by nobility of line and colour'. He aimed to invest his work with moral purpose and his most characteristic paintings are abstruse allegories that were once enormously popular but now seem vague and ponderous (*Hope*, 1886, Tate, London, and other versions). His portraits of great contemporaries (*Gladstone*, *Tennyson*, *J. S. Mill*, etc., NPG, London) have generally worn much better. As a sculptor, he is remembered chiefly for his equestrian piece *Physical Energy* (1904). A cast of it forms the central feature of the Cecil Rhodes Memorial, Cape Town, and another is in Kensington Gardens, London. Watts was twice married, his first wife being the celebrated actress Ellen Terry. Only 16 at the time of the wedding in 1864, she was 30 years his junior and they separated the following year. His former house at Compton, near Guildford, Surrey, is now the Watts Gallery, devoted to his work. Wilfrid *Blunt was curator 1959–85.

Wearing, Gillian. *See* TURNER PRIZE.

Weber, Max (1881–1961). Russian-born American painter, sculptor, printmaker, and writer, whose work more than that of any other American artist synthesized the latest European developments at the beginning of the 20th century. He emigrated to New York with his parents when he was 10. From 1905 to 1908 he travelled in Europe, studying in Paris at the *Académie Julian and with *Matisse, admiring early *Cubism and becoming a friend of Henri *Rousseau. After his return to New York in 1909 he rapidly became a controversial figure—no other American avant-garde artist of the time exhibited more widely or was more harshly attacked. His work was influenced by *Fauvism and *primitive art (he was one of the first American artists to show interest in it), but most importantly by Cubism (in sculpture as well as painting). After about 1917, however, Weber's work became more naturalistic. During the 1930s his subjects often expressed his social concern and in the 1940s his work included scenes with rabbis and Jewish scholars—mystical recollections of his Russian childhood. He published several books, including *Cubist Poems* and the autobiographical *Max Weber* (1945).

Weenix, Jan Baptist (1621?–1660/1?). Dutch painter. From 1642/3 to 1646/7 he was in Italy, and on his return to his native Amsterdam he painted Italianate landscapes close in style to those of *Berchem, who is said to have been his cousin. Later he turned mainly to pictures of still life with dead game; he also painted portraits. His son, **Jan Weenix** (1642?–1719), specialized in hunting trophy subjects similar to those of his father; indeed, it is often difficult to tell their work apart. Most of his career was spent in Amsterdam, but from 1702 to 1712 he worked at Düsseldorf for the Elector Palatine. Both artists were prolific (Jan told *Houbraken that his father could paint three half-length life-size portraits in a day) and are represented in many public collections.

Weight, Carel (1908–97). British painter. In the Second World War he served with the Royal Engineers and Army Education Corps and was appointed an *Official War Artist in 1945, working in Austria, Greece, and Italy. He began teaching at the *Royal College of Art in 1947 and was professor of painting there from 1967 until his retirement in 1973. Weight was something of a maverick figure ('I don't like the art world very much. I don't like the dealers and I don't like the critics') and his work is highly individual. His best-known paintings are imaginative figure compositions, set in suburban surroundings. They are superficially realistic, but feature idiosyncratic perspective effects and strange human dramas, producing a feeling that is sometimes humorous and sometimes menacing: 'My art is concerned with such things as anger, love, fear, hate and loneliness, emphasized by the ordinary landscape in which the dramatic scene is set.' Weight also painted portraits and landscapes.

Weissenbruch, Jan Hendrik (1824–1903). Dutch landscape and marine painter, one of the outstanding artists of the *Hague School. His work is distinguished by its subtle handling of tone and feeling for atmosphere. His cousin **Johannes** (or **Jan) Weissenbruch** (1822–80), a painter and lithographer, specialized in town views in the detailed manner of 17th-century artists such as Jan van der *Heyden.

Wentworth, Richard. *See* NEW BRITISH SCULPTURE.

Werefkin, Marianne von. *See* NEUE KÜNSTLERVEREINIGUNG.

Werenskiold, Erik (1855–1938). Norwegian painter, printmaker, and illustrator. He was one of the leading personalities in Norwegian art, the friend of numerous writers and intellectuals and a symbol of national culture. His work included landscapes, in which he showed an affectionate yet unsentimental approach to his native land, portraits of many of the leading Norwegians of his day (*Henrik Ibsen*, 1895, NG, Oslo), lithographs, etchings, and book illustrations. After the turn of the century he was influenced by *Cézanne.

Werff, Adriaen van der (1659–1722). Dutch painter of religious and mythological scenes and portraits, active mainly in Rotterdam. He combined the precise finish of the Leiden tradition (learned from his master Eglon van der *Neer) with the classical standards of the French Académie Royale and became the most famous Dutch painter of his day, winning international success and earning an enormous fortune. *Houbraken, writing in 1718, considered him the greatest of all Dutch painters and this was the prevailing critical opinion throughout the 18th century. His reputation crumbled in the 19th century, when he was thought to have betrayed the Dutch naturalistic tradition, and he is now considered an extremely accomplished but rather sentimental and repetitive minor master. Van der Werff also worked as an architect in Rotterdam, designing elegant house façades. His brother, **Pieter van der Werff** (1661–1722), was his principal pupil and assistant, imitating his style closely and making many copies of his work.

Wesselmann, Tom (1931–). American painter, one of the best-known exponents of *Pop art. He often incorporates elements of *collage or *assemblage in his work, using household objects such as television sets and sometimes including sound effects. Typically his subjects are aggressively sexual and he is best known for his continuing series *Great American Nude* (began 1961), in which the nude becomes a depersonalized sex symbol set in a realistically depicted commonplace environment. He emphasizes the woman's nipples, mouth, and genitals, with the rest of the body depicted in flat, unmodulated colour. In other works he isolates parts of the body still further, as in his *Smoker* series, in which the mouth—often depicted on a huge scale—becomes a provocatively erotic symbol. In the 1980s he began making massive 'drawings' cut from sheets of aluminium or steel. He has also made prints in a variety of techniques.

West, Benjamin (1738–1820). American history and portrait painter who spent almost all his career in England. After early success as a portraitist in New York, he studied for three years in Italy (1760–3), chiefly in Rome, then settled in London. There he soon repeated the professional and social success he had enjoyed in Italy, in part because of the novelty value of his being an American. Initially West had set up as a portraitist in London, but it was as a *history painter that he made his mark. In Rome he had been in contact with the circle of Gavin *Hamilton and *Mengs, and his early work is in a determined but rather flimsy *Neoclassical style (*Agrippina Landing at Brundisium with the Ashes of Germanicus*, 1768, Yale Univ. AG). With his famous *Death of Wolfe* (1770, NG, Ottawa), however, he broke new ground. This was not, as is sometimes asserted, the first history painting to feature contemporary costume (Edward Penny (1714–91), for example, had painted the same subject in modern dress in 1764 (Ashmolean Mus., Oxford)); however, it was the first picture in such vein to become a popular and critical success in Britain. It was exhibited in 1771 at the *Royal Academy (of which West had been a foundation member in 1768) and was so admired that West had to make several replicas. George III admitted he had been wrong to think it 'very ridiculous to exhibit heroes in coats, breeches, and cocked hats' and he appointed West his official history painter the following year. West's innovation was soon adopted by other artists, most notably his countryman *Copley, and it marks an important turning point in taste. In 1792 West succeeded *Reynolds as president of the Royal Academy; he resigned in 1805 following internal squabbles, but he resumed the post the following year and held it until his death. In his later works, his style grew away from Neoclassicism; he was in the vanguard of the *Romantic movement with paintings such as the melodramatic *Saul and the Witch of Endor* (1777, Wadsworth Atheneum, Hartford), and his *Death on a Pale Horse* (1817, Philadelphia Mus. of Art) has been hailed as a forerunner of *Delacroix. West's historical importance far outweighs the quality of his work, which (in spite of its modernity in ideas) is generally pedestrian. He was the first American painter to achieve an international reputation and was an inspiration to many of his countrymen. Many young Americans who followed him to London benefited from his generosity in advice and practical help, including *Allston, Copley, and *Morse, so he well deserves his title of 'the father of American painting'.

Westall, Richard (1765–1836). English painter and illustrator. He painted a few pictures for *Boydell's Shakespeare Gallery, but he made his name chiefly in book illustration, in which field he was one of the most prolific artists of the day. As a watercolourist he was noted for his unusually rich colour effects.

Westmacott, Sir Richard (1775–1856). English *Neoclassical sculptor. The son of a sculptor also called **Richard** (1747–1808), he trained first under his father and then from 1793 to 1796 in Rome, where he worked in *Canova's studio. After his return to London, he soon had a very large practice, second only to *Chantrey. His best-known work is the huge *Achilles* statue (unveiled 1822) in Hyde Park; it honours the Duke of Wellington and is made of bronze from French cannon captured during his campaigns. At the time the figure's conspicuous nudity was considered shocking or amusing, especially considering it had been paid for by a group of lady subscribers. His last major work was the group of the *Progress of Civilization* on the pediment of the British Museum (installed 1851). His work is dignified but often rather pedestrian in handling. He was professor of sculpture at the *Royal Academy from 1827 to 1854. Two of his brothers, **George** (active 1799–1827) and **Henry** (1784–1861), were sculptors, as was his son, another **Richard Westmacott** (1799–1872). *See also* MARCUS AURELIUS.

Weyden, Rogier van der (c.1399–1464). The outstanding Netherlandish painter of the mid-15th century. He was one of the greatest and most influential European artists of his time, but there is little secure knowledge about his career. None of the surviving paintings associated with him are signed, dated, or verified by indisputable contemporary documentation, but several can be identified from early sources, and the style these show is so distinctive that a coherent oeuvre has been built up around them. His early career, however, is still a particularly problematic area, as the sparse evidence relating to it is teasingly equivocal. In 1427 a certain 'Rogelet [little Roger] de la Pasture' began an apprenticeship with Robert Campin in Tournai, and in 1432 he became a master in the city's painters' guild. It is generally accepted that these two documentary records refer to Rogier van der Weyden (the French and Flemish forms of the name both meaning 'Rogier of the Meadow'), although it is uncertain why he should have started his apprenticeship so late. There are no documented pictures surviving from Campin's hand, but he is generally agreed to be identical with the *Master of Flémalle, so the whole question of Rogier's relationship with his master is based on stylistic analysis. Some scholars have argued that the Master of Flémalle should be identified with the young Rogier rather than with Campin, but the prevailing opinion is now that Rogier's work shows a development from the powerfully naturalistic and expressive style of his master towards greater refinement and spirituality. Rogier's celebrated *Descent from the Cross* (c.1440, Prado, Madrid), for example, is close to the Master of Flémalle's *Crucified Thief* fragment (Städelsches Kunstinstitut, Frankfurt) in its dramatic force and use of a plain gold background, but it has a new poignancy and exaltedness.

By 1435 Rogier had moved to Brussels and in 1436 he was appointed official painter to the city. There is evidence that he made a pilgrimage to Rome in 1450, but otherwise nothing to indicate that he ever left Brussels again. His work there included four large panels on the theme of justice for the courtroom of the town hall (these were his most famous pictures until they were destroyed during the French bombardment of the city in 1695), but all his surviving paintings are either religious pictures or portraits. The portraits are all of fairly similar type, showing the sitter, whether male or female, bust-length and in three-quarter view, with aristocratic bearing and a pious expression. They are among the finest of their time, but Rogier's reputation rests mainly on his religious works, which are remarkable for their magisterial power of design and their emotional intensity and sensitivity. The contrast with the cool objectivity of his great precursor Jan van *Eyck was well summed up by Erwin *Panofsky: 'Roger's world is at once physically barer and spiritually richer than Jan van Eyck's. Where Jan observed things that no painter had ever observed, Roger felt and expressed emotions and sensations—mostly of a bitter or bittersweet nature—that no painter had ever recaptured.' Unlike Jan, Rogier seems to have had numerous assistants and pupils, for the number of good contemporary copies and versions of his paintings indicates that he ran a busy workshop. His pictures were exported to France, Germany, Spain, and Italy (where he was one of the few northern artists of the time to be highly regarded), and many of the types and motifs he invented or popularized became part of the common currency of artistic ideas until well into the 16th century. However, although his work was revered, knowledge of the man himself quickly faded, so much so that in van *Mander's biographies he is inadvertently split into two artists—Rogier van der Weyden and Rogier of Bruges. After the destruction of his most conspicuous works in Brussels in 1695, he was virtually forgotten. Interest in him revived in the mid-19th century, but it was not until the 20th century that he took his place among the greatest European painters.

Wheatley, Francis (1747–1801). English painter. His early works were mainly small full-length portraits and *conversation pieces in the manner of *Zoffany. In 1779 he moved to Dublin to escape creditors, and after his return to London in 1783 his work broadened in scope. It included landscapes, history paintings, and life-size portraits, but he is best known for works produced to be engraved for the print market. He is particularly remembered for his enormously popular *Cries of London* (14 paintings, 1792–5; prints published 1793–7), showing street-vendors, milkmaids, and so on. The paintings are now dispersed; examples are at Upton House, Warwickshire (NT).

Whistler, James McNeill (1834–1903). American painter, printmaker, and designer, active mainly in England. He spent part of his childhood in Russia (where his father had gone to work as a civil engineer) and was an inveterate traveller. His training as an artist began indirectly when, after his discharge from West Point Military Academy for 'deficiency in chemistry', he learnt etching as a US navy cartographer. In 1855 he moved to Paris, where he studied intermittently under *Gleyre, made copies in the Louvre, acquired a lasting admiration for *Velázquez, and became a devotee of the cult of the Japanese print (see UKIYO-E) and oriental art and decoration in general. The circles in which he moved can be gauged from his friend *Fantin-Latour's *Homage to *Delacroix*, in which Whistler is portrayed alongside *Baudelaire, *Manet, and others. He settled in London in 1859, but often returned to France. His first major oil painting, *At the Piano* (1858–9, Taft Mus., Cincinnati), was well received at the *Royal Academy exhibition in 1860 and he soon made a name for himself, not just because of his talent, but also on account of his flamboyant personality. He was famous for his wit and dandyism, and loved controversy. His lifestyle was lavish and he was often in debt. Dante Gabriel *Rossetti and Oscar Wilde were among his famous friends.

Whistler's art is in many respects the opposite to his ostentatious personality, being discreet and subtle, but the creed that lay behind it was radical. He believed that painting should exist for its own sake, not to convey literary or moral ideas, and he often gave his pictures musical titles to suggest an analogy with the abstract art of music: 'Art should be independent of all claptrap—should stand alone, and appeal to the artistic sense of eye or ear, without confounding this with emotions entirely foreign to it, as devotion, pity, love, patriotism, and the like. All these have no kind of concern with it, and that is why I insist on calling my works "arrangements" and "harmonies".' He was a laborious and self-critical worker, but this is belied by the flawless harmonies of tone and colour he created in his paintings, which are mainly portraits and landscapes, particularly scenes of the Thames. No less original was his work as a decorative artist, notably in the Peacock Room (1876–7) for the London home of the Liverpool shipping magnate Frederick Leyland (now reconstructed in the Freer Gallery, Washington), where the graceful, stylized patterning anticipated much in the *Art Nouveau style of the 1890s (Aubrey *Beardsley saw the room in about 1891 and was greatly impressed by it).

In 1877 Whistler showed his *Nocturne in Black and Gold: The Falling Rocket* (1875, Detroit Inst. of Arts) at the opening exhibition of the *Grosvenor Gallery. *Ruskin attacked it in print, accusing him of 'flinging a pot of paint in the public's face', and Whistler sued him for libel. He won the action, but the awarding of only a farthing's damages with no costs was in effect a justification for Ruskin, and the expense of the trial led to Whistler's bankruptcy in 1879—a tribulation he endured with dignity. His house was sold and he spent a year in Venice (1879–80), concentrating on the etchings that helped to restore his fortunes when he returned to London. He was one of the greatest of all etchers (some critics rank him second only to *Rembrandt) and also made lithographs. In his fifties he began to achieve honours and substantial success (he also made a happy marriage, in 1888, to Beatrix Godwin, widow of the architect E. W. Godwin, with whom he had collaborated, but she died only eight years later). In 1891 his portrait of Thomas Carlyle (1872–3) was bought by the Corporation of Glasgow, becoming the first of his oils to enter a public collection in Britain, and in the same year his most famous work, *Arrangement in Grey and Black: Portrait of the Painter's Mother* (1871), was bought by the French state (it is now in the Musée d'Orsay, Paris).

Whistler's paintings are related to *Impressionism (although he was more inter-

ested in evoking a mood than in accurately depicting the effects of light), to *Symbolism, and to *Aestheticism, and he played a major role in introducing modern ideas to British art. Those who were most immediately influenced by him included his pupils Walter Greaves (1849–1930), Gwen *John, the Australian-born Mortimer Menpes (1860–1938), and Walter *Sickert. His aesthetic creed was explained in his *Ten O'Clock Lecture* (1885) and this, and much else on art and society, was republished in *The Gentle Art of Making Enemies* (1890).

Whistler, Rex (1905–44). British painter, graphic artist, and stage designer. He is best known for his decorations in a light and fanciful style evocative of the 18th century, notably the series of murals *In Pursuit of Rare Meats* (1926–7) in the restaurant of the Tate Gallery (now Tate Britain). He also did numerous book illustrations and much work for the stage, including ballet and opera. He was killed in action in the Second World War. His brother **Sir Laurence Whistler** (1912–2000), a writer and glass engraver, published several books on him.

Whiteread, Rachel (1963–). British sculptor. In 1988 she began making a novel type of sculpture consisting of casts of domestic features or the spaces around them (such as the space under a bed). These pieces, carrying 'the residue of years and years of use' culminated in *Untitled (House)* (1993), a concrete cast of an entire house in Grove Road in the East End of London. The house itself was demolished once the cast was made, leaving Whiteread's ghostly replica on the site. It helped win her the *Turner Prize in 1993 and attracted so much attention that it made her probably the most famous artist in Britain apart from Damien *Hirst (although, unlike Hirst, she does not court publicity). The Turner jury praised the work for 'its combination of austere monumentality and immediacy of reference to the everyday world', its 'haunting qualities' and its 'poetic strangeness'. Many people, however, regarded it as an ugly lump of concrete, and in spite of a vigorous campaign to save it, the work was demolished in 1994. Following her success as the first woman to win the Turner Prize, in 1997 Whiteread became the first woman to represent Britain with a solo show at the Venice *Biennale (Barbara *Hepworth in 1950 and

Bridget *Riley in 1968 had shared the British Pavilion). In 2000 her memorial to Austrian Jews killed by the Nazis was installed in the Judenplatz, Vienna.

Whitney, Gertrude Vanderbilt (1875–1942). American sculptor, patron, and collector, the founder of the Whitney Museum of American Art, New York. She was the daughter of Cornelius II Vanderbilt, an immensely wealthy railroad magnate, and turned seriously to art after her marriage in 1896 to Harry Payne Whitney, a financier and world-class polo player. Her training as a sculptor included periods at the *Art Students League and in Paris, where she knew *Rodin. She won several major commissions, notably for monuments commemorating the First World War, including the Washington Heights War Memorial, New York (1921). Her style was traditional, but she was sympathetic towards progressive art and is much more important as a patron than as an artist. In 1907 she opened her New York studio as an exhibition space for young artists, and in 1914 she put her patronage on a more formal basis when she bought the house adjoining her studio, converted it into galleries, and opened it as the Whitney Studio; later she founded a series of organizations in New York with the same aim of helping young artists—the Friends of Young Artists (1915), the Whitney Studio Club (1918), and the Whitney Studio Galleries (1928). In 1929 she offered to donate her own collection of about 500 American paintings, sculptures, and drawings to the *Metropolitan Museum, New York, but the gift was turned down. Consequently in 1930 she announced the founding of the Whitney Museum of American Art and it opened the following year at 10 West 8th Street in a group of converted brownstone buildings. In 1954 the museum moved to a new building at 22 West 54th Street on land provided by the *Museum of Modern Art, and in 1966 to its present home—a spectacular building designed for it by Marcel Breuer at 945 Madison Avenue. The museum now has the largest and finest collection of 20th-century American art in the world, as well as a good representation from earlier periods. Every other year it holds the Whitney Biennial, a major showcase for work by living artists. Mrs Whitney donated funds to many other good causes, artistic and otherwise,

but she was 'a woman of modest disposition who carried out her public activities quietly' (*Dictionary of American Biography*).

Wiener Werkstätte (Ger.: 'Viennese Workshop'). Arts and Crafts cooperative studio established in Vienna in 1903 by members of the *Sezession. The workshop produced everything from jewellery to complete room decorations, including mosaics (*see* KLIMT). Its designers and craftsmen aimed, like William *Morris, to combine usefulness with aesthetic quality. Again like Morris, they found that their necessarily high prices prevented them from reaching the wide public they hoped for. Ultimately the venture was an economic failure and it closed in 1932.

Wiertz, Antoine (1806–65). Belgian painter, one of the great eccentrics in the history of art. In 1832 he won the Belgian *Prix de Rome and when he visited Italy in 1834 he was overwhelmed by *Michelangelo. His other great artistic hero was *Rubens and he tried to follow in their footsteps with enormous and high-flown religious, historical, and allegorical canvases. The results now seem almost dementedly bombastic and melodramatic, but he had many admirers among his countrymen. The Belgian government was keen to promote a national school of painting and in 1850–1 built him a special studio in Brussels (now the Musée Wiertz). He worked there in isolation for the rest of his life, seeing himself as an artist-philosopher and totally convinced of his own genius. Some of his work is erotic or macabre in character and anticipates Belgian *Symbolism.

Wijnants, Jan (d. 1684). Dutch landscape painter, active first in Haarlem, then from about 1660 in Amsterdam, where he also ran an inn. He specialized in landscapes with dunes and sandy roads, inspired by the countryside around Haarlem—unpretentious, naturalistic views that were favourites with collectors in the 18th century. The figures in his paintings were evidently always painted by other artists, including *Wouwerman. He, too, was an excellent painter of dunescapes and it is uncertain if one influenced the other. Wijnants was prolific and his work is in many public collections. Adriaen van de *Velde is said (by *Houbraken) to have been his pupil and *Gainsborough was among the artists he influenced.

Wilde, Johannes (1891–1970). Hungarian-born art historian who became an Austrian citizen in 1928 and a British citizen in 1947. From 1923 to 1938 he was on the staff of the *Kunsthistorisches Museum in Vienna and he gained an international reputation with his work on the Italian (particularly the Venetian) paintings there. He made many contributions to the attribution and dating of pictures, and one of his most important achievements was the systematic use of X-rays, not only as a tool for discovering the physical condition of a painting but also as a guide to the individual artist's creative process. Following the annexation of Austria by Nazi Germany in 1938, Wilde resigned from the Kunsthistorisches Museum and moved to England. From 1948 to 1958 he taught at the *Courtauld Institute, where he was an inspirational figure—Kenneth *Clark described him as 'the most beloved and influential teacher of art history of his time'. Wilde published comparatively little, and, as Anthony *Blunt wrote, 'his wisdom was mainly dispensed in lectures, supervisions and private conversation'. During his lifetime only two of his major contributions appeared in book form in English, both on *Michelangelo's drawings—in the catalogue of the 15th- and 16th-century drawings at Windsor Castle (1949, with A. E. Popham) and in his catalogue of Michelangelo's drawings in the British Museum (1953). In these two works, which demonstrate his keen sensibility as well as his great learning, Wilde effectively reversed the 'revisionist' tendency whereby many genuine drawings by Michelangelo had been rejected. After his death, two collections of lectures were published: *Venetian Art from Bellini to Titian* (1974) and *Michelangelo* (1978).

Wildens, Jan (*c.*1586–1653). Flemish landscape painter, active in his native Antwerp, where he became a master in the painters' guild in 1604. He is best known for painting landscape backgrounds for other artists, particularly his friend *Rubens, but his finest independent work—*Winter Landscape with a Hunter* (1624, Gemäldegalerie, Dresden)—shows he was an accomplished master in his own right.

Wilding, Alison. *See* NEW BRITISH SCULPTURE.

Wiligelmo (active *c.*1100). Italian sculptor. His name is known only from an inscription on the façade of Modena Cathedral—'Among sculptors, your work shines forth, Wiligelmo. How greatly you are worthy of honours.' He must have been the main sculptor of the *reliefs on the façade (scenes from Genesis together with figures of prophets), which date from soon after 1099, when the cathedral was begun. In these works he created a distinctive style (his figures are squat and full of earthy vigour) that was the fountainhead of *Romanesque sculpture in northern Italy.

Wilkie, Sir David (1785–1841). Scottish painter. He trained in Edinburgh and then in 1805 moved to London, where he studied briefly at the *Royal Academy Schools. His *Village Politicians* (priv. coll.) was the hit of the RA exhibition of 1806 and he established himself as the most popular *genre painter of the day. He was strongly influenced in technique and subject matter by 17th-century Netherlandish artists such as *Ostade and *Teniers, and the public loved the wealth of lively and often humorous incident in his paintings. His *Chelsea Pensioners Reading the Gazette of the Battle of Waterloo* (1822, Wellington Mus., London), commissioned by the Duke of Wellington, was so popular when shown at the Royal Academy that a rail had to be erected in front of it to protect it from the crowds. In 1825–8 Wilkie travelled abroad for reasons of health and his style changed radically under the influence particularly of Spanish painting, becoming grander in subject matter and broader in touch. The change was regretted by many of his contemporaries. In 1840 he went to the Holy Land to research material for his biblical paintings and on the return journey died at sea; his friend *Turner commemorated him in *Peace: Burial at Sea* (1842, Tate, London). Wilkie's success did much to establish the popularity of anecdotal painting in England and many Victorian artists were influenced by him.

Williams, Fred (1927–82). Australian painter and printmaker, regarded as the most original portrayer of his country's landscape. He studied in his native Melbourne, 1944–9, then in London, 1951–6.

His earliest etchings, often with music-hall subjects, were produced at about this time. He returned to Australia in 1957, and from the late 1950s began to paint landscapes revealing a distinctly personal vision of the country's landscape, such as *Charcoal Burner* (1959, NG of Victoria, Melbourne). Unlike other modern Australian artists who had memorably portrayed aspects of their country's landscape (notably Arthur *Boyd, Russell *Drysdale, and Sidney *Nolan), Williams rarely featured the human figure in his paintings and his work conveys a sense of primeval mystery and remoteness. In the 1970s he broadened his range to include marine subjects and murals.

Willing, Victor. *See* REGO.

Willumsen, Jens Ferdinand (1863–1958). Danish painter, sculptor, architect, engraver, potter, and collector. In 1888–9 he visited Paris, and he lived in France from 1890 to 1894, abandoning his early naturalistic style under the impact of *Gauguin (whom he met in Brittany) and *Symbolism. His work became highly individual, notable for its obscure and disturbing subject matter and glaringly bright colours (*After the Tempest*, 1905, NG, Oslo). His sculpture is often *polychromatic, using mixed media, showing the influence of *Klinger. Willumsen was also influenced by El *Greco, on whom he wrote a long book (2 vols., 1927). He was one of the leading personalities of his time in Danish art, idolized as a genius by his admirers, but decried by others. There is a museum devoted to him at Frederikssund, near Copenhagen.

Wilson, Richard (1713/14–82). British painter, born in rural north Wales, the son of a well-connected clergyman who encouraged his interest in art as well as giving him a good classical education. Wilson became the leading British landscape painter of his generation, but initially he seems to have worked mainly as a portraitist. He began his training in London in 1729 and was working independently by 1735, but the decisive change in his career did not come until his visit to Italy in 1750–7, when he decided to devote himself exclusively to landscape. He is said to have done this at the urging of Francesco *Zuccarelli, whom he met in Venice and whose portrait (1751, Tate, London) he painted, but he was more obviously influenced by the painting of *Claude and by the natural surroundings of Rome where Claude had worked.

Back in London Wilson became successful with his Italian landscapes and applied the same classical compositional principles to English and Welsh views, as in his celebrated *Snowdon from Llyn Nantlle* (c.1765, versions in Walker AG, Liverpool, and Castle Mus., Nottingham). He also painted large historical landscapes more or less in the manner of *Dughet or Salvator *Rosa (*Destruction of the Children of Niobe*, 1760, Yale Center for British Art, New Haven, and other versions), and these too sold well. Wilson, however, had a prickly nature and a problem with drink, and in the early 1770s his career went into a sharp decline. The *Royal Academy (of which he had been a founder member in 1768) helped him out by appointing him librarian, but in 1781 his family took him (now a pitiable figure) back to Wales. His work is of great importance in the history of British art, for he transformed landscape from an art that was essentially topographical to one that could be a vehicle for ideas and emotions, often by evoking nostalgia for the past. He had several pupils, notably Thomas *Jones, as well as numerous imitators, and he was admired by such later artists as *Cotman, *Crome, *Constable, and *Turner.

Wilson, Richard (1953–). *See* INSTALLATION.

Wilson, Scottie (Robert) (1891–1972). British self-taught painter of imaginative subjects, born in Glasgow of working-class parents. A colourful character, he ran away from home at the age of 16, did military service in India and South Africa, and lived in Canada from about 1930 to 1945. He started to draw in the 1930s. After the Second World War he settled in London and became something of a character in the art world (he was barely literate and fond of the bottle), although he became reclusive in old age. He made a good living selling his work to dealers but lived in very modest circumstances. Unlike the work of most *naive artists (with whom he is sometimes grouped), his pictures (often in coloured inks) were not 'realistic' renderings of scenes from the daily life with which he was familiar, but decorative fantasies incorporating stylized birds, fishes, butterflies, swans, flowers, self-portraits, and totem-pole heads. The last of these, no doubt reminiscences of Canada, were rather fancifully thought by some commentators to represent the powers of evil in contrast to the powers of good symbolized in the images taken from nature. All his work, however, was decorative rather than symbolic.

Wilton, Joseph (1722–1803). English sculptor. He trained in Flanders and with *Pigalle in Paris, then was in Italy from 1747 until 1755. On his return to London he rapidly became successful, his patrons including George III, for whom he did carving on a new state coach (1762, Royal Coll.), still in use today. He was a close friend of the architect Sir William Chambers, with whom he often collaborated (notably on the decorative carving of Chambers's masterpiece, Somerset House), and he was one of the original members of the *Royal Academy. His portraits are generally regarded as his best works, his monuments showing him hesitating between various styles. Much of his work was executed by assistants. His talents were considerable, but he was more interested in social life than his work; in 1768 he inherited a fortune from his father (a manufacturer of ornamental plaster) but dissipated it and became bankrupt in 1793. Considering the quality of his training and his friendship with key figures in the art world, his career is a story of wasted opportunity.

Wilton Diptych. *See* INTERNATIONAL GOTHIC.

Winckelmann, Johann Joachim (1717–68). German art historian and archaeologist, a key figure in the *Neoclassical movement and in the development of art history as an intellectual discipline. He was the son of a poor cobbler, but through hard work he gained a good education, studying at the universities of Halle and Jena. For several years he was a schoolteacher, before obtaining the post of librarian to Count Heinrich von Bünau at Nöthnitz, near Dresden, in 1748. This gave him the opportunity to absorb himself in the study of classical antiquity, and in 1755 he managed to reach his goal of Rome. The previous year he had converted to Catholicism to enhance his chances of obtaining a scholarly appointment in Rome, and this did indeed help

him to become librarian to Cardinal Alberigo Archinto, whom he had met in Germany. On Archinto's death in 1758 he became librarian to Cardinal Alessandro *Albani, a leading collector of antiquities, and this allowed him to lead a life of scholarly research through which he established a European reputation as a writer. In 1768, on the way back to Rome from a visit to Germany and Austria, he was murdered in Trieste; ostensibly he was killed for the sake of some gold and silver medallions he was carrying (gifts from the empress Maria Theresa; *see* HABSBURG), but it has been suggested that he had formed a homosexual relationship with his murderer (who was executed).

Winckelmann's two most important books are *Gedanken über die Nachahmung der griechischen Werke in der Malerei und Bildhauerkunst*, published in 1755, shortly before he left for Rome (*Fuseli published an English translation in 1765 under the title *Reflections on the Painting and Sculpture of the Greeks*), and *Geschichte der Kunst des Altertums* (History of Ancient Art), published in 1764 (this is the first occurrence of the phrase 'history of art' in the title of a book). In these immensely influential works he proclaimed the superiority of Greek art and culture, combining rapturous descriptions of individual works (above all the *Apollo Belvedere*) with historical analysis. He never went to Greece and unwittingly based most of his observations on Roman copies, but his account of the stylistic development of Greek sculpture was a milestone in archaeological writing, and he is regarded as having laid the foundations of modern methods of art history. His analysis of ancient Greek culture as a unity, and his interpretation of art as an index of the spirit of the time were novel (he thought that when social conditions in general were good, then art was good, and when one declined the other did also); these ideas were subsequently developed into an entire philosophy of culture by 19th-century German writers. He refined the notions of how a work may be dated or its place of origin located and explained the character of works of art by reference to such factors as climate, religious customs, and social conditions. His interpretation of classical antiquity influenced many contemporaries—notably *Mengs—and it helped to determine aspects of German education into the 20th century.

Winstanley, Hamlet. *See* STUBBS.

Winterhalter, Franz Xaver (1805–73). German painter. Early in his career he worked mainly as a lithographer, but he became famous as the leading court portrait painter of his time. From 1834 he was based mainly in Paris, but he travelled widely and painted royals from several European countries. He was a particular favourite of Queen Victoria, who called him 'excellent, delightful Winterhalter' (the Royal Collection has more than a hundred of his paintings), and he was also much employed by Napoleon III of France and his wife the empress Eugénie. His style was romantic, glossy, and superficial and his portraits have until recently generally been valued more as historical records than as works of art. However, a major exhibition devoted to him at the National Portrait Gallery, London, and the Petit Palais, Paris, in 1987 brought renewed appreciation of his work. His brother **Hermann** (1808–91) was his assistant. A watercolour by Hermann, *A Girl of Frascati* (signed but until recently given to his brother), is in the Wallace Collection, London.

Wiszniewski, Adrian. *See* GLASGOW SCHOOL.

Wit, Jacob de (1695–1754). The outstanding Dutch decorative painter of the 18th century, active mainly in his native Amsterdam. He had his principal training in Antwerp and learned much from *Rubens's ceiling paintings in the Jesuit church there (his drawings became valuable records after the paintings were destroyed by fire in 1718). De Wit's style, however, was much lighter than Rubens's, with a *Rococo delicacy and charm. He was a Catholic and was the first Dutch artist since the 16th century to carry out a good deal of decorative work for Catholic churches, but he was at his best in domestic ceiling decorations (*Bacchus and Ceres in the Clouds*, 1751, Huis Boschbeek, Heemstede). His name has entered the Dutch language to describe a kind of *trompe-l'œil imitation of marble *reliefs for which he was renowned; such pictures, usually set over a chimney piece or door, are called *witjes* (Dutch, *wit*: 'white'). De Wit was also an etcher and a noted collector of Old Master drawings.

Witt, Sir Robert. *See* COURTAULD.

Witte, Emanuel de (c.1616–91/2). Dutch painter, born at Alkmaar and active there, then in Rotterdam (by 1639), Delft (by 1641), and Amsterdam (by 1652). His range was wide, including history paintings, *genre scenes (notably of markets), and portraits, but after he settled in Amsterdam he concentrated on architectural paintings (primarily church interiors—both real and imaginary). *Houbraken wrote that 'in the painting of churches, no one was his equal with regard to orderly architecture, innovative use of light and well-formed figures', and this verdict has been endorsed by posterity, for his paintings are very different in spirit from the sober views of most Dutch architectural specialists, making powerful use of the dramatic play of light and shadow in the lofty interiors. His life was unhappy (he was constantly in debt) and when his body was found in an Amsterdam canal it was suspected that he had committed suicide.

Wittkower, Rudolf (1901–71). Anglo-German art historian. He was born and brought up in Germany, but held British citizenship through his father, who had been born in England. After studying at the universities of Munich and Berlin, he worked at the Biblioteca Hertziana in Rome from 1923 to 1933. From 1934 to 1956 he was on the staff of the *Warburg Institute in London and from 1949 to 1956 was also professor of history of art at University College London. In 1956 he moved to Columbia University, New York, as head of the Department of Fine Arts and Archaeology, which under his direction became one of the leading centres of art-historical scholarship in the USA. After he retired in 1969 he was *Kress professor at the National Gallery in Washington and *Slade professor at Cambridge. Wittkower's many books and articles were devoted mainly to Italian art and architecture of the 16th and 17th centuries, and his writings form one of the cornerstones in the study of the Italian *Baroque. His major books, several of which have appeared in revised editions, include: *Architectural Principles in the Age of Humanism* (1949), *Gian Lorenzo Bernini* (1955), *Art and Architecture in Italy: 1600–1750* (1958), *Sculpture* (1977), and (with his wife **Margot Wittkower**) *Born under Saturn: The Character and Conduct of Artists* (1963).

Witz, Konrad (*c*.1400–44/6). German-born painter from Rottweil in Swabia, active in Switzerland and generally considered a member of the Swiss School. He became a member of the painters' guild in Basle in 1434 and evidently spent the rest of his career there and in Geneva. Little else is known of him and few paintings by him survive. These few, however, show that he was remarkably advanced in his *naturalism, suggesting a knowledge of the work of his contemporaries Jan van *Eyck and the *Master of Flémalle. In place of the soft lines and lyrical qualities of *International Gothic, Witz's paintings are characterized by heavy, almost stumpy, figures, whose ample draperies emphasize their solidity. His most famous works are the four surviving panels (forming two wings) from the altarpiece of St Peter that he painted for the cathedral in Geneva. These are now in the Musée d'Art et d'Histoire there; the central panel is lost. One of the panels, the *Miraculous Draught of Fishes*, is Witz's masterpiece and his only signed and dated work (1444). The landscape setting depicts part of Lake Geneva (one of the earliest recognizable landscapes in art) and Witz's naturalism is even more remarkable in his observation of reflection and refraction in the water.

Wölfflin, Heinrich (1864–1945). Swiss art historian, professor at the universities of Basle (1893–1901), Berlin (1901–12), Munich (1912–24), and Zurich (1924–34). He was one of the most influential art historians of his period, and several of his books are still widely read. They include *Die klassische Kunst* (Classic Art, 1899), on the art of the High *Renaissance; *Kunstgeschichtliche Grundbegriffe* (Principles of Art History, 1915); and a monograph on *Dürer (1905). His work concentrated on stylistic analysis, and he attempted to show that style—in painting, sculpture, and architecture—follows evolutionary principles. *Principles of Art History* presents his ideas in the most highly developed form, discussing the transformation from *Renaissance to *Baroque in terms of contrasting visual schemes—for example the development from linear to painterly (*malerisch*). Wölfflin's view that style was a force in its own right rather than an intellectual abstraction and his lack of interest in *iconography are out of tune with much modern thinking on art history, and his approach is often over-rigid; however, he was a figure of great importance in establishing his subject as an intellectually demanding discipline. Herbert *Read wrote: 'it could be said of him that he found art criticism a subjective chaos and left it a science.'

Wolgemut, Michael (*c*.1434–1519). German painter and woodcut designer, active in his native Nuremberg. In 1472 he married the widow of Hans *Pleydenwurff and took over his workshop, the most prosperous in the city. It produced numerous large altarpieces in which there is little sign of a distinctive individual personality, and Wolgemut is more important for his book illustrations. Amongst many other books he illustrated was Hartmann Schedel's *Weltchronik* (1493), the most enterprising attempt of its time at combining letterpress with woodcut illustration. Hitherto illustrations in printed books had often been embellished by *illumination, but Wolgemut tried to refine the technique of woodcut so that it could achieve its own distinctive effects without hand painting. He is now best remembered as the teacher of *Dürer.

Wols (Alfred Otto Wolfgang Schulze) (1913–51). German-born painter active mainly in France; he adopted the pseudonym Wols in 1937 from fragments of his name on a torn telegram. In 1932 he studied briefly at the *Bauhaus, then moved to Paris, where he worked as a photographer. He lived in Spain 1933–5, but after being imprisoned for political activities he returned to Paris. As a German citizen he was interned at the outbreak of war, but he was liberated in 1940 and lived in poverty in the south of France. At the end of the war he returned to Paris and was befriended by the writers Jean-Paul Sartre and Simone de Beauvoir, for whose books he did illustrations. In the late 1940s he began to make a name for himself as a painter, but his irregular life, poverty, and excessive drinking undermined his health and he died aged only 38. His posthumous fame far outstripped his reputation during his lifetime and he came to be regarded as the 'primitive' of *Art Informel and one of the most original masters of expressive abstraction.

Wood, Christopher (1901–30). British painter, mainly of landscapes, harbour scenes, and figure compositions. In 1921 he studied at the *Académie Julian in Paris and subsequently travelled widely on the Continent. To influences from modern French art (*Picasso and *Diaghilev were among his friends), he added an entirely personal lyrical freshness and intensity of vision, touched with what Gwen *Raverat felicitously described as 'fashionable clumsiness'. In a remarkably short time he achieved a position of high regard in the art worlds of London and Paris, but he was emotionally unstable and his early death was probably suicide (he was killed by a train). After this he became something of a legend as a youthful genius cut off before his prime. Much of Wood's best work was done in Cornwall, where he and his friend Ben *Nicholson discovered the *naive painter Alfred *Wallis in 1928.

Wood, Derwent. *See* NEW SCULPTURE.

Wood, Grant (1892–1942). American painter, active mainly in Iowa, his native state. Early in his career he was an artistic jack-of-all-trades. The turning point in his life came when he obtained a commission to make stained-glass windows for the Cedar Rapids Veteran Memorial Building in 1927 and went to Munich to supervise their manufacture the following year. Influenced by the Early Netherlandish paintings he saw there in the Alte Pinakothek, he abandoned his earlier *Impressionist style and began to paint in the meticulous, sharply detailed manner that characterized his mature work (he has been called 'the *Memling of the Midwest'). His subjects were taken mainly from the ordinary people and everyday life of Iowa and he became recognized as one of the leading exponents of *Regionalism. He first came to national attention in 1930 when his painting *American Gothic* won a bronze medal at an exhibition of the Art Institute of Chicago, which now owns the painting. Although at the time it aroused violent controversy and was deplored as an insulting caricature of plain country people, the painting later gained great popularity and is now one of the most familiar and best-loved images in American art. In 1931 Wood introduced an element of humorous fantasy in *The Midnight Ride of Paul Revere* (Met. Mus., New York) and in 1932 he painted his famous satirical picture *Daughters of the Revolution* (Cincinnati Art Mus.), described as 'three sour-visaged and repulsive-looking females, represented as disgustingly smug and smirking because of their ancestral claim to be heroes of the American Revolution'. His other work includes some vigorous stylized landscapes, and during the 1930s he supervised several Iowa projects of the *Federal Art Project. In 1934 he became assistant professor of fine arts at the University of Iowa.

woodcut. Term applied to the technique of making a print from a block of wood sawn along the grain and also to the print so made. Although the term is often loosely used for any type of print made from wood, it refers specifically to those made from blocks in which the grain runs lengthways across the surface (as in a plank of wood). It can thus be distinguished from *wood engraving, in which the print is made from wood sawn across the grain, which produces a surface capable of taking finer detail. Woodcut is the oldest technique for making prints and its principles are very simple. The design is drawn on a smooth block of wood (almost any wood of medium softness can be used—beech, pear, sycamore for example) and the parts that are to be white in the print are cut away with knives and gouges, leaving the design standing up in relief. This is then inked and pressed against a sheet of paper. The origins of the technique are obscure (the principle was employed in fabric printing in China at least as early as the 3rd century AD). There is evidence that woodcuts as we know them were being produced in Europe in the 14th century, but the earliest surviving reliably dated example is perhaps the *St Christopher* (1423) by an unknown artist in the John Rylands Library, Manchester. Many of the earliest woodcuts were crude popular religious images designed to be sold at fairs and pilgrim shrines (*see also* BLOCK BOOK), but in skilled hands the technique could produce much more sophisticated results. It was at its peak in the first thirty years of the 16th century, in both individual prints and book illustrations, with *Dürer being the supreme master. Thereafter it lost ground to *line engraving, which could produce subtler effects. In the late 19th and early 20th centuries, however, there was a major revival of interest in the woodcut as a medium of original artistic expression. *Gauguin and *Munch were the great pioneers in the 1890s, using the grain of the wood to create bold and vigorous textural effects, and they were followed by the German *Expressionists (notably the members of Die *Brücke). The coloured woodcut, using different blocks for each colour, was particularly popular in Japan (*see* UKIYO-E). *See also* CHIAROSCURO WOODCUT.

wood engraving. Term applied to the technique of making a print from a block of hardwood (usually boxwood) sawn across the grain and to the print so made. The technique derives from the *woodcut, but because of the harder and smoother surface and the use of the *burin and other tools associated with the copperplate engraver, the effect is generally finer and more detailed (although there is a middle ground where the two techniques produce very similar results). Wood engraving developed in the 18th century and its first great exponent was Thomas *Bewick (his contemporary William *Blake also made some superb wood engravings, but these were little known at the time). Bewick ushered in the technique's heyday, which coincided with a great expansion in journalism and book publishing from about 1830. From then until about 1890, when it was superseded by photomechanical processes, it was the most popular medium for illustration. The *Dalziel brothers in England and Gustave *Doré in France were among the most prolific exponents during this period. Although it was no longer commercially viable for everyday printing, wood engraving continued to be used in the 20th century for original prints and the illustration of expensive books. It was a favourite technique of Eric *Ravilious, for example.

Woodrow, Bill. *See* NEW BRITISH SCULPTURE.

Woolner, Thomas (1825–92). English sculptor. He was a founder of the *Pre-Raphaelite Brotherhood in 1848, the only sculptor among the members. His early career was unsuccessful, so he decided to try his hand at gold-prospecting in Australia; his departure in 1852 inspired Ford Madox *Brown's picture *The Last of England* (1852–5, City AG, Birmingham). Woolner

found little gold in Australia, but he began to prosper as a portrait sculptor, and after returning to England in 1854 he made a name for himself with his marble bust of his friend Alfred Tennyson of 1857 (Trinity College, Cambridge, and several replicas). His work was praised for its lifelikeness and he produced portraits of many other distinguished sitters. Woolner also did a few figure subjects, occasionally painted, and wrote poetry.

Wootton, John (*c.*1682–1764). English landscape and sporting painter. He is best known for pictures involving horses, with which he made a handsome living, but his main contribution to British painting was the introduction of the *ideal landscape—Horace *Walpole said his works in this vein 'approached towards Gaspar Poussin [i.e. *Dughet], and sometimes imitated happily the glow of *Claude Lorrain'. His landscape manner was continued by George *Lambert.

World of Art (Russ., 'Mir Iskusstva'). The name of an informal association of Russian artists formed in St Petersburg in 1898 and of the journal they published from 1899 to 1904; the association lasted, with interruptions, until 1924, but its heyday was over long before this. *Diaghilev was the journal's editor, and his contributors and collaborators included Léon *Bakst and Alexandre *Benois. The group encouraged interchange with Western art (many articles published in the journal had previously appeared in European magazines) and became the focus for avant-garde developments in Russia. In particular it promoted the *Art Nouveau style. Some of the artists involved in the group (notably Nikolai *Roerich) were also interested in evoking the spirit of ancient Russia, and this synthesis of old and new was best expressed in their decor for Diaghilev's ballet company, which revolutionized European stage design when he brought it to Paris in 1909.

Worpswede. A north German village near Bremen that in the last decade of the 19th century became the centre of a colony of artists, following the example of the *Barbizon School in France. The most famous artist to work there was Paula *Modersohn-Becker, and the 'Worpswede School' is sometimes regarded as one of the roots of German *Expressionism.

Wotruba, Fritz (1907–75). The leading Austrian sculptor of the 20th century. His masterly craftsmanship won him acclaim from early in his career, as when his work was shown in an exhibition of Austrian art in Paris in 1929; Aristide *Maillol is said to have refused to believe that such sculpture could have been done by a 22-year-old. In his most characteristic works he carved directly in stone, preferring a hard stone with a coarse texture. His early pieces were in a naturalistic style reminiscent of Maillol, but he moved towards abstraction by reducing his figures to bare essentials. His approach was similar to *Brancusi's, but in contrast to Brancusi's smooth, subtle abstractions, Wotruba's figures are solid, block-like structures. They were left in a rough state, creating a feeling of primitive power. Wotruba also worked in bronze, and near the end of his life he branched out into architecture, designing the church of the Holy Trinity on the outskirts of Vienna (constructed 1974–6). After the Second World War he taught at the Vienna Academy and his work was admired and imitated by many younger Austrian artists, bringing about a revival of sculpture in his country.

Wouters, Rik (1882–1916). Belgian painter, sculptor, and printmaker. He is regarded as his country's leading exponent of *Fauvism, but his career was cut tragically short when he died following operations for cancer of the eye. His work is less violent in colour than that of the French Fauvists and often has a quality of serene intimacy, notably in portraits of his wife Nel, who was his favourite model (*The Artist's Wife*, 1912, Pompidou Centre, Paris).

Wouwerman (or **Wouwermans**), **Philips** (1619–68). The most celebrated member of a family of Dutch painters from Haarlem, where he worked virtually all his life. He became a member of the painters' guild in 1640 and is said by a contemporary source to have been a pupil of Frans *Hals. The only thing he has in common with Hals, however, is his nimble brushwork, for he specialized in landscapes of hilly country with horses—cavalry skirmishes, camps, hunts, travellers halting outside an inn, and so on. In this genre he was immensely prolific and also immensely successful—*Houbraken says he left his daughter a dowry of 20,000 guilders. He had many imitators, including his brother **Peter** (1623–82), and his great popularity continued throughout the 18th century, when he was a favourite with princely collectors and engravings after his work had wide circulation. Subsequently he has perhaps been underrated, for although his work generally follows a successful formula, he maintained high standards; his draughtsmanship is elegant, his composition sure, his colouring delicate, and his touch lively.

Wright, John Michael (1617–94). English portrait painter. He was apprenticed to George *Jamesone in Edinburgh, 1636–41, then spent a long period abroad, chiefly in Rome, where in 1648 he became a member of the Accademia di S. Luca (see ACADEMY), the only British painter of the 17th century to have this distinction. On his return to England in 1656 he won many patrons among his fellow Catholics and became *Lely's chief rival, although he never had his great worldly success and died in modest circumstances. His style was less glossy than Lely's but more penetrating and individual in characterization, his sitters tending to look thoughtful rather than merely glamorous (*Magdalen Aston*, Castle Mus., Nottingham). Wright's most unusual work is an allegorical ceiling painting (Castle Mus.) done for Charles II's bedroom at Whitehall Palace; it cannot be considered a success, but it is interesting as an attempt at *Baroque decoration by someone who was familiar with the works of Pietro da *Cortona (whom he described as 'the greatest master of his time'). Wright was a collector, antiquarian, and scholar, a man of considerable culture; in 1685–7 he accompanied an embassy from James II to Pope Innocent XI and wrote an account of it in Italian, published in 1687 (Eng. trans., 1688).

Wright, Joseph (1734–97). English painter, born and principally active in Derby and generally known as 'Wright of Derby'. He was one of the most original, versatile, and accomplished British artists of the 18th century and the first major English painter whose career was based outside London. In 1751–3 and again in 1756–7 he trained under *Hudson in London, and after returning to Derby he made a name as a portraitist in the Midlands, his works displaying fluent composition and a firm grasp of character. In the 1760s he began to paint candlelit scenes of various types, showing the fascination with unusual lighting effects that was to run throughout his career. He was influenced in some of these by Dutch painting, but in his depictions of the contemporary scientific world he broke new ground—his most famous work, *An Experiment on a Bird in the Air Pump* (1768, NG, London), has been described by Sir Ellis *Waterhouse as 'one of the wholly original masterpieces of British art'. Such works won him a considerable reputation, and in 1772 James *Northcote called him 'the most famous painter now living for candlelights'. In 1768-71 Wright worked in Liverpool, and in 1773-5 visited Italy, where he assiduously studied the *antique but was even more impressed by the eruption of Vesuvius he witnessed and by a kind of man-made equivalent—the great fireworks display held annually at the Castel S. Angelo in Rome (he painted several pictures of both subjects). On his return to England in 1775 he moved to Bath, hoping to fill the gap left by *Gainsborough's departure for London, but his more forthright style did not please sophisticated society there and in 1777 he returned to Derby. He remained there for the rest of his life apart from short journeys when he made tours of the Lake District in 1793 and 1794 (landscape became increasingly important towards the end of his career). Appropriately, Derby Art Gallery has far and away the finest collection of his work.

Wright, Willard Huntington. *See* MAC-DONALD-WRIGHT.

Wtewael (or **Uytewael**), **Joachim** (1566–1638). Dutch painter, mainly of religious and mythological subjects. After travelling in Italy and France *c.*1588–92, he settled in his native Utrecht, where he became one of the leading Dutch exponents of *Mannerism. His highly distinctive, charmingly artificial style, which remained untouched by the naturalistic developments happening around him, was characterized by acidic colours and elegant figures in wilfully distorted poses. The best collection of his work, including a self-portrait (1601), is in the Centraal Museum, Utrecht.

Wyeth, Andrew (1917–). American painter, son and pupil of a well-known muralist and illustrator of children's books, **Newell Convers Wyeth** (1882–1944). Wyeth's work consists almost entirely of depictions of the people and places of the two areas he knows best—the Brandywine Valley around his native Chadds Ford, Pennsylvania, and the area near Cushing, Maine, where he has his summer home. He usually paints in watercolour or *tempera with a precise and detailed technique, and often he conveys a sense of loneliness or nostalgia (trappings of the modern world, such as motor cars, rarely appear in his work). He became famous with *Christina's World* (1948), which was bought by the Museum of Modern Art, New York, in 1949 and has became one of the best-known images in American art. It depicts a friend of the artist, Christina Olson, who had been so badly crippled by polio that she moved by dragging herself with her arms. She is shown in a field on her farm in Maine, 'pulling herself slowly back towards the house'. Building on the picture's fame, Wyeth has gone on to have an enormously successful career. However, critical opinion on him is widely divided: J. Carter Brown, director of the National Gallery in Washington, called him 'a great master', whereas Professor Sam Hunter, one of the leading authorities on 20th-century American art, has written: 'What most appeals to the public, one must conclude, apart from Wyeth's conspicuous virtuosity, is the artist's banality of imagination and lack of pictorial ambition. He comfortably fits the commonsense ethos and non-heroic mood of today's popular culture, despite his occasional lapses into gloomy introspection.'

Yáñez, Fernando (active 1506–31). Spanish painter. He is first certainly documented in 1506 in Valencia, where he collaborated with Fernando Llanos (active 1506–16) in painting twelve large panels of the *Life of the Virgin* for the main altarpiece of the cathedral (1507–10). From the style of these paintings it is overwhelmingly likely that the 'Ferrando Spagnuolo' who in 1505 is recorded assisting *Leonardo da Vinci on the *Battle of Anghiari* was either Yáñez or Llanos. They were 'the first non-Italian painters to assimilate the style of the High *Renaissance and practice it in a foreign land' (Jonathan Brown, *Painting in Spain: 1500–1700*, 1998). Their respective shares in the altarpiece are a matter of debate, although there is a tendency now to see Yáñez as the more gifted. Various other paintings are attributed to each of them working independently, but their careers are ill-defined.

YBAs. *See* YOUNG BRITISH ARTISTS.

Yeames, William Frederick (1835–1918). British painter. He specialized in scenes from British history, particularly of the Tudor and Stuart periods, treated in an anecdotal and often melodramatic way that looks forward to Hollywood 'costume' movies. Most of his work has been forgotten, but one of his pictures has achieved enduring fame as an archetypal image of Victorian sentimentality, the Cromwellian tear-jerker *'And When Did You Last See Your Father?'* (1878, Walker AG, Liverpool).

Yeats, Jack Butler (1871–1957). The best-known Irish painter of the 20th century, son of **John Butler Yeats** (1839–1922), a barrister who became a successful portrait painter, and brother of the poet William Butler Yeats. Initially he worked mainly as an illustrator and did not regularly paint in oils until about 1905. His subjects included Celtic myth and everyday Irish life, through which he contributed to the upsurge of nationalist feeling in the arts that accompanied the movement for Irish independence. His early paintings were influenced by French *Impressionism, but he then developed a more personal *Expressionistic style characterized by vivid colour and extremely loose brushwork (there is some similarity to the work of *Kokoschka, who became a great friend in the last decade of Yeats's life). Although he has many admirers, some critics think that his late paintings often degenerate into a muddy mess. Yeats was a writer as well as a painter—the author of several plays, novels, and volumes of poetry, as well as *Life in the West of Ireland* (1912) and *Sligo* (1930).

Young British Artists (YBAs). An imprecise term applied to a number of highly publicized British avant-garde artists active from the 1980s, several of whom are well known for their grubbily glamorous lifestyles as well as for what they create; they do not form an organized group and their work is diverse, but there are ties of friendship linking many of them and they have been supported chiefly by Charles *Saatchi. Their work has been showcased in several exhibitions, most notably 'Sensation' at the Royal Academy, London, in 1997, which generated a great deal of controversy, including various forms of protest against it. The two best-known artists who featured in 'Sensation' are Damien *Hirst and Rachel *Whiteread. Among the others are the brothers Dinos (1962–) and Jake (1966–) Chapman, whose work includes figures modelled on bland shop-window dummies but with horrible mutilations or freakish mutations; Tracey Emin (1963–), whose work is largely autobiographical and includes *My Bed* (1999, Saatchi Gal., London), featuring her own unmade bed accompanied by assorted debris from her life; Gary Hume (1962–), who paints large figurative pictures characterized by flat, reductive forms; Sarah Lucas (1962–), whose work often has sexual themes, for example *Two Fried Eggs and a Kebab* (1992, Saatchi Gal.), in which the foods, arranged on a table, mimic breasts and female genitals; Chris Ofili (1968–), whose trademark is incorporating elephant dung in his paintings (he hit on the idea whilst in Zimbabwe on a travelling scholarship in 1992); Marc Quinn (1964–), best known for *Self* (1991, Saatchi Gal.), a three-dimensional self-portrait head made of his own frozen blood (it is displayed in a refrigerated cabinet); and Jenny Saville (1970–), who paints huge pictures of mountainously obese nude women.

Young Contemporaries. Exhibition of works by British art students held in London since 1949 on a roughly annual basis (lack of funds or organization—they are generally arranged by the students themselves—has sometimes prevented the shows taking place). The first Young Contemporaries exhibition was held at the Royal Society of British Artists (RBA Galleries). Other venues have included the *Institute of Contemporary Arts, and some of the exhibitions have toured the provinces. The most famous Young Contemporaries show was that of 1961, when British *Pop art first appeared in force in the work of Derek *Boshier, David *Hockney, Allen *Jones, R. B. *Kitaj, and Peter *Phillips, all of them students or former students at the *Royal College of Art.

In 1974 the name was changed to 'New Contemporaries'.

Ysenbrandt (or **Isenbrandt**), **Adriaen** (d. before 1551). Netherlandish painter. He became a master in the Bruges painters' guild in 1510 and is said by an early source to have been a pupil of Gerard *David. Otherwise, virtually nothing is recorded of him and there are no signed or documented works. However, in 1902 the Belgian art historian Georges Hulin de Loo proposed Ysenbrandt as the author of a large group of paintings deriving from David, and the identification has generally been accepted. Previously the paintings had been attributed to Jan *Mostaert and the anonymous Master of the Seven Sorrows of the Virgin, named after a *diptych of the subject divided between the church of Notre-Dame in Bruges and the Musées Royaux in Brussels. Because of the uncertainty, some authorities prefer to use the name Ysenbrandt in inverted commas.

Yvaral. *See* VASARELY.

Z

Zadkine, Ossip (1890–1967). Russian-born sculptor who worked mainly in Paris and became a French citizen in 1921. He moved to Paris in 1909 after spending four years in Britain (sent there by his father—a professor of classics—to learn 'English and good manners'). By 1912 he was friendly with many leading figures in avant-garde art, among them *Apollinaire, *Archipenko, *Brancusi, *Lipchitz, and *Picasso. He deeply admired *Rodin, but *Cubism had a greater impact on his work. His experiments with Cubism, however, had none of the quality of intellectual rigour and restraint associated with Picasso and *Braque, for Zadkine's primary concern was with dramatically expressive forms. The distinctive style he evolved made great use of hollows and concave inflections, his figures often having openings pierced through them. In 1915 he joined the French army but was invalided out after being gassed. He worked in Paris through the 1920s and 1930s, and spent the Second World War in New York (where he taught at the *Art Students League), returning to Paris in 1944. Often Zadkine's work can seem merely melodramatic, but for his greatest commission—the huge bronze *To a Destroyed City* (completed 1953) standing at the entry to the port of Rotterdam—he created an extremely powerful figure that is widely regarded as one of the masterpieces of 20th-century sculpture. With its jagged, torn shapes forming an impassioned gesture mixing defence and supplication, it vividly proclaims anger and frustration at the city's destruction and the courage that made possible its rebuilding. This work gave Zadkine an international reputation and many other major commissions followed it. The house in which he lived in Paris is now a museum dedicated to his work.

Zeuxis (active latter 5th century BC). Greek painter from Heraclea (probably meaning the town of that name in southern Italy, rather than the one on the Black Sea). None of his works survive, but ancient writers describe him as one of the greatest of Greek painters and he was renowned for his remarkable powers of verisimilitude, as is indicated by a famous anecdote concerning a competition with a rival (*see* PARRHASIUS). Another story tells how when called upon to paint a picture of Helen of Troy for a temple at Croton he assembled the five most beautiful maidens of the city and combined the best features of each into one figure of *ideal beauty—an early example of an idea that later became commonplace in aesthetic theory. He is said to have specialized in panels rather than murals. According to legend, Zeuxis died laughing while painting a picture of a funny-looking old woman, and the story has occasionally formed the basis for later artists' self-portraits. Aert de *Gelder painted himself as Zeuxis (1685, Städelsches Kunstinstitut, Frankfurt) and *Rembrandt's 'Laughing' *Self-Portrait* (c.1665, Wallraf-Richartz-Mus., Cologne) has also been interpreted in this way.

Zoffany, Johann (1733–1810). German-born painter who settled in England in 1760 after working in Rome. He was patronized by the famous actor David Garrick and made his name with paintings representing scenes from plays, usually depicting Garrick in one of his favourite parts. They show how quickly he adapted to English taste, and he also painted *conversation pieces of much the same small scale and in the same relaxed vein. No doubt because of his German background, he was taken up by George III and Queen Charlotte and he painted numerous works for the royal family. The two most important (still in the Royal Collection) are *The Academicians of the Royal Academy* (1772) and *The Tribuna of the Uffizi* (1772–8). For the latter he made a long visit to Florence (1772–9) and when he returned to England he found that the vogue for conversation pieces had passed its peak. Because of the slump in his market he moved to India in 1783 and made a fortune painting Indian princes and expatriate Britons before returning to England in 1789. As a wealthy man he now had no need to earn a living from his work and he seems to have stopped painting in about 1800. At the time of his death he was regarded as a curiosity from another age and for many years his paintings were valued chiefly as historical records (they are sharp and clear in detail and contain a wealth of information about costume, etc.); however, he is now also appreciated for his charm and recognized as an artist who brought new life to the conversation piece.

Zorach, William (1889–1966). Lithuanian-born American sculptor. Initially Zorach worked as a painter in a vivid *Fauvist style, but he took up sculpture in 1917 and abandoned painting (apart from watercolours) about five years later. His sculpture is figurative and its salient characteristics are firm contours, block-like bulk, and suppression of details: 'I owe most', he said, 'to the great periods of primitive carving in the past—not to the modern or the classical Greeks, but to the Africans, the Persians, the Mesopotamians, the archaic Greeks and of course to the Egyptians.' He was a pioneer in America of the revival of *direct carving in stone and wood and in this as well as in his formal austerity he exercised a powerful influence on modern American sculpture. He had numerous major commissions, including relief carvings for the Municipal Court Building, New York (1958). His most famous work is not a carving, however, but the aluminium *Spirit of the Dance* (1932) for Radio City Music Hall, New York—a heroic female figure that was banished for a time because of its nudity but reinstated by public pressure. Zorach taught at the *Art Students League from 1929 to 1966. His wife, **Marguerite Thompson Zorach** (1887–1968), was one of America's leading modernist painters in the years immediately before and immediately after the *Armory Show (1913), in which both she and her husband exhibited. At this time she painted in a style influenced by Fauvism and *Expressionism. In her later career, however, much of her time was spent selflessly helping her husband with his sculptural commissions, producing many of the preliminary drawings for his work.

Zorn, Anders (1860–1920). Swedish painter and etcher. After leaving the Stockholm Academy in 1881 because of its restrictive and outdated ideas, he travelled widely, becoming the most cosmopolitan Scandinavian artist of his time and an international success. He was based in London (1882–5), then Paris (1888–96), and visited Spain, Italy, the Balkans, North Africa, and (on several occasions) the USA, where he painted three presidents. Originally he worked almost exclusively in watercolour, but in 1887–90 he abandoned the medium for oils. In 1896 he settled permanently at Mora in Sweden, building his own house, which is now a museum dedicated to him. He painted three main types of pictures: portraits, *genre scenes (often depicting the life and customs of the area in which he lived), and female nudes. It is for his nudes—unashamedly healthy and voluptuous works—that he is now best known. He often painted them in landscape settings and delighted in vibrant effects of light on the human body, depicted through lush brushwork that recalls the handling of his friend Max *Liebermann. Zorn also gained a great reputation for his etchings and he occasionally made sculpture.

Zuccarelli, Francesco (1702–88). Italian painter of landscapes, often featuring mythological subjects. He was born near Florence and studied in Rome, but he is associated chiefly with Venice, where he settled in about 1730 and worked in the vein of pastoral landscape popularized by Marco *Ricci. Like *Canaletto, Zuccarelli was patronized by the English entrepreneur Joseph Smith and his work found a ready market in England. When Richard *Wilson (still primarily a portrait painter) visited Venice in 1751 he painted Zuccarelli's portrait and it is said to have been Zuccarelli's encouragement that induced him to concentrate on landscape. In 1752–62 and again in 1765–71 Zuccarelli worked in England, where his delicate *Rococo style gained him great success (he was one of the founder members of the *Royal Academy in 1768). In 1772 he was elected president of the Venetian Academy, but soon afterwards he retired to Florence.

Zuccaro, Taddeo (1529–66) and **Federico** (c.1540–1609). Italian *Mannerist painters, brothers, from the neighbourhood of Urbino. Taddeo worked mainly in Rome and although he was only 37 when he died he had made a great name for himself as a fresco decorator, working most notably for the

*Farnese family in their palace at Caprarola. His style was based on *Michelangelo and *Raphael and tended to be rather dry and wooden. Federico took over his brother's flourishing studio, continuing the work at Caprarola and also the decoration of the Sala Regia in the Vatican (begun by Taddeo in 1561). His talent was no more exceptional than Taddeo's, but he became even more successful and won himself a European reputation—indeed for a time he was probably the most famous living painter. In 1574 he travelled via Lorraine and the Netherlands to England, where he is said to have painted many court portraits, although the only works dating from this visit that can be safely attributed to him are two drawings in the British Museum portraying Elizabeth I and Robert Dudley, Earl of Leicester. (Many anonymous portraits of the period are improbably attributed to him.) After working in Florence, Rome, and Venice, he spent three years in Spain (1585–8), painting altarpieces and frescos for the *Escorial. However, his visit was not a success, partly because his arrogance offended his Spanish colleagues. Back in Rome he was elected the first president of the new Accademia di S. Luca, founded in 1593 (see ACADEMY). Like many of his contemporaries he believed that correct theory would produce good works of art and he wrote several treatises, of which the most important is L'idea de' pittori, scultori, et architetti (1607). Zuccaro also worked as an architect, designing a doorway in the form of a grotesque face (one enters through the open mouth) for his house in Rome, the Palazzo Zuccaro, which he bequeathed to the Accademia to use as its headquarters (it is now the Biblioteca Hertziana). The two flanking windows are treated in similar bizarre fashion.

Zucchi, Antonio. *See* KAUFFMANN.

Zuloaga, Ignacio (1870–1945). Spanish painter. He came from a long line of craftsmen (his father was a metalworker) and was mainly self-taught as an artist. Much of his career was spent in Paris, where he was on friendly terms with *Rodin, *Gauguin, and *Degas, but his art is strongly national in style and subject matter. Bullfighters, gypsies, and brigands were among his subjects, and he also painted religious scenes and society portraits (these were one of the main sources of the considerable fortune

he earned). His inspiration came from the great Spanish masters of the past, notably *Velázquez and *Goya, and he is credited with being one of the first to 'rediscover' El *Greco. He had a great reputation in his lifetime (unusually for a Spanish artist, his standing was higher abroad than at home), but his work now often looks rather stagy. There are museums devoted to him in Segovia and the Basque fishing port of Zumaya, two of his principal places of work in Spain.

Zurbarán, Francisco de (1598–1664). Spanish painter, born in the village of Fuente de Cantos in Extremadura and active mainly in Seville, which lies about 100 km (60 miles) to the south. He trained in Seville, 1614–17, then spent the next decade working at Llerana, near his birthplace. In 1627 he made his name with a powerful *Christ on the Cross* (Art Inst. of Chicago), painted for the Dominican monastery of S. Pablo in Seville, and its success led him to settle in the city in 1629. In 1634–5 he visited Madrid, where he worked for Philip IV (see HABSBURG), painting for the Buen Retiro Palace a series of ten pictures on the Labours of Hercules and a large historical scene, *The Defence of Cadiz* (all now in the Prado, Madrid); apart from these pictures, a few portraits, and some masterly still lifes, he devoted himself almost entirely to religious images. His most characteristic works are single figures of monks and saints in meditation or prayer (for example, two paintings of St Francis in the National Gallery, London, one of them dated 1639). The figures are usually depicted against a plain background, standing out with massive physical presence. In such compositionally simple and emotionally direct altarpieces, Zurbarán showed himself to be an ideal interpreter of Counter-Reformation ideals, combining austere *naturalism with mystical intensity. Many of his pictures were painted in series, notably a set of eight pictures of Hieronymite saints for the Order's monastery at Guadalupe (1639–40); these remain in situ and 'constitute the best surviving example of a series of monastic history painted in the seventeenth century' (Jonathan Brown, *Painting in Spain: 1500–1700*, 1998).

The 1630s marked the peak of Zurbarán's career, and after 1640 his stream of major commissions dried up. Subsequently he produced most of his work for the South American market, much of it being done by assistants. In the later 1640s *Murillo began to overtake him as the most popular painter in Seville, and Zurbarán's work lost something of its power and simplicity as he tried to come to terms with the softer, sweeter, lighter style of his rival. By the later 1650s he was experiencing financial problems, partly caused by the loss in warfare of ships bringing payments from his South American clients. In 1658 he moved to Madrid, where he spent his final years, but he failed to revive his career there. His son **Juan** (1620–49), who died young of the plague, is known from a few impressive still-life paintings.

Oxford Paperback Reference

The Concise Oxford Dictionary of Art & Artists
Ian Chilvers

Based on the highly praised *Oxford Dictionary of Art*, over 2,500 up-to-date entries on painting, sculpture, and the graphic arts.

'the best and most inclusive single volume available, immensely useful and very well written'

Marina Vaizey, *Sunday Times*

The Concise Oxford Dictionary of Art Terms
Michael Clarke

Written by the Director of the National Gallery of Scotland, over 1,800 entries cover periods, styles, materials, techniques, and foreign terms.

A Dictionary of Architecture
James Stevens Curl

Over 5,000 entries and 250 illustrations cover all periods of Western architectural history.

'splendid ... you can't have a more concise, entertaining, and informative guide to the words of architecture'

Architectural Review

'excellent, and amazing value for money ... by far the best thing of its kind'

Professor David Walker

More Art Reference from Oxford

The Grove Dictionary of Art

The 34 volumes of *The Grove Dictionary of Art* provide unrivalled coverage of the visual arts from Asia, Africa, the Americas, Europe, and the Pacific, from prehistory to the present day.

'succeeds in performing the most difficult of balancing acts, satisfying specialists while ... remaining accessible to the general reader'

The Times

The Grove Dictionary of Art – Online
www.groveart.com

This immense cultural resource is now available online. Updated regularly, it includes recent developments in the art world as well as the latest art scholarship.

'a mammoth one-stop site for art-related information'

Antiques Magazine

The Oxford History of Western Art
Edited by Martin Kemp

From Classical Greece to postmodernism, *The Oxford History of Western Art* is an authoritative and stimulating overview of the development of visual culture in the West over the last 2,700 years.

'here is a work that will permanently alter the face of art history ... a hugely ambitious project successfully achieved'

The Times

The Oxford Dictionary of Art
Edited by Ian Chilvers

The Oxford Dictionary of Art is an authoritative guide to the art of the western world, ranging across painting, sculpture, drawing, and the applied arts.

'the best and most inclusive single-volume available'

Marina Vaizey, *Sunday Times*

Oxford Paperback Reference

The Concise Oxford Companion to English Literature
Margaret Drabble and Jenny Stringer

Based on the best-selling *Oxford Companion to English Literature*, this is an indispensable guide to all aspects of English literature.

Review of the parent volume
'a magisterial and monumental achievement'

Literary Review

The Concise Oxford Companion to Irish Literature
Robert Welch

From the ogam alphabet developed in the 4th century to Roddy Doyle, this is a comprehensive guide to writers, works, topics, folklore, and historical and cultural events.

Review of the parent volume
'Heroic volume ... It surpasses previous exercises of similar nature in the richness of its detail and the ecumenism of its approach.'

Times Literary Supplement

A Dictionary of Shakespeare
Stanley Wells

Compiled by one of the best-known international authorities on the playwright's works, this dictionary offers up-to-date information on all aspects of Shakespeare, both in his own time and in later ages.

OXFORD

Oxford Paperback Reference

The Oxford Dictionary of Dance
Debra Craine and Judith Mackrell

Over 2,500 entries on everything from hip-hop to classical ballet, covering dancers, dance styles, choreographers and composers, techniques, companies, and productions.

'A must-have volume ... impressively thorough'

Margaret Reynolds, *The Times*

Who's Who in Opera
Joyce Bourne

Covering operas, operettas, roles, perfomances, and well-known personalities.

'a generally scrupulous and scholarly book'

Opera

The Concise Oxford Dictionary of Music
Michael Kennedy

The most comprehensive, authoritative, and up-to-date dictionary of music available in paperback.

'clearly the best around ... the dictionary that everyone should have'

Literary Review

Oxford Paperback Reference

The Kings of Queens of Britain
John Cannon and Anne Hargreaves

A detailed, fully-illustrated history ranging from mythical and pre-conquest rulers to the present House of Windsor, featuring regional maps and genealogies.

A Dictionary of Dates
Cyril Leslie Beeching

Births and deaths of the famous, significant and unusual dates in history – this is an entertaining guide to each day of the year.

'a dipper's blissful paradise ... Every single day of the year, plus an index of birthdays and chronologies of scientific developments and world events.'

Observer

A Dictionary of British History
Edited by John Cannon

An invaluable source of information covering the history of Britain over the past two millennia. Over 3,600 entries written by more than 100 specialist contributors.

Review of the parent volume
'the range is impressive ... truly (almost) all of human life is here'
Kenneth Morgan, *Observer*

OXFORD

Oxford Paperback Reference

The Concise Oxford Dictionary of World Religions
Edited by John Bowker

Over 8,200 entries containing unrivalled coverage of all the major world religions, past and present.

'covers a vast range of topics ... is both comprehensive and reliable'

The Times

The Oxford Dictionary of Saints
David Farmer

From the famous to the obscure, over 1,400 saints are covered in this acclaimed dictionary.

'an essential reference work'   *Daily Telegraph*

The Concise Oxford Dictionary of the Christian Church
E. A. Livingstone

This indispensable guide contains over 5,000 entries and provides full coverage of theology, denominations, the church calendar, and the Bible.

'opens up the whole of Christian history, now with a wider vision than ever'

Robert Runcie, former Archbishop of Canterbury

Oxford Paperback Reference

The Concise Oxford Dictionary of Quotations
Edited by Elizabeth Knowles

Based on the highly acclaimed *Oxford Dictionary of Quotations*, this paperback edition maintains its extensive coverage of literary and historical quotations, and contains completely up-to-date material. A fascinating read and an essential reference tool.

The Oxford Dictionary of Humorous Quotations
Edited by Ned Sherrin

From the sharply witty to the downright hilarious, this sparkling collection will appeal to all senses of humour.

Quotations by Subject
Edited by Susan Ratcliffe

A collection of over 7,000 quotations, arranged thematically for easy look-up. Covers an enormous range of nearly 600 themes from 'The Internet' to 'Parliament'.

The Concise Oxford Dictionary of Phrase and Fable
Edited by Elizabeth Knowles

Provides a wealth of fascinating and informative detail for over 10,000 phrases and allusions used in English today. Find out about anything from the 'Trojan horse' to 'ground zero'.

Oxford Paperback Reference

The Concise Oxford Dictionary of English Etymology
T. F. Hoad

A wealth of information about our language and its history, this reference source provides over 17,000 entries on word origins.

'A model of its kind'

Daily Telegraph

A Dictionary of Euphemisms
R. W. Holder

This hugely entertaining collection draws together euphemisms from all aspects of life: work, sexuality, age, money, and politics.

Review of the previous edition
'This ingenious collection is not only very funny but extremely instructive too'

Iris Murdoch

The Oxford Dictionary of Slang
John Ayto

Containing over 10,000 words and phrases, this is the ideal reference for those interested in the more quirky and unofficial words used in the English language.

'hours of happy browsing for language lovers'

Observer

Oxford Companions

'Opening such books is like sitting down with a knowledgeable friend. Not a bore or a know-all, but a genuinely well-informed chum ... So far so splendid.'

Sunday Times [of *The Oxford Companion to Shakespeare*]

For well over 60 years Oxford University Press has been publishing Companions that are of lasting value and interest, each one not only a comprehensive source of reference, but also a stimulating guide, mentor, and friend. There are between 40 and 60 Oxford Companions available at any one time, ranging from music, art, and literature to history, warfare, religion, and wine.

Titles include:

The Oxford Companion to English Literature
Edited by Margaret Drabble
'No guide could come more classic.'

Malcolm Bradbury, *The Times*

The Oxford Companion to Music
Edited by Alison Latham
'probably the best one-volume music reference book going'

Times Educational Supplement

The Oxford Companion to Western Art
Edited by Hugh Brigstocke
'more than meets the high standard set by the growing number of Oxford Companions'

Contemporary Review

The Oxford Companion to Food
Alan Davidson
'the best food reference work ever to appear in the English language'

New Statesman

The Oxford Companion to Wine
Edited by Jancis Robinson
'the greatest wine book ever published'

Washington Post

OXFORD